LOGISTICAL MANAGEMENT

THE INTEGRATED SUPPLY CHAIN PROCESS

McGraw-Hill Series in Marketing

Anderson, Hair, and Bush: Professional Sales Management
Bennett: Marketing
Bovée, Houston, and Thill: Marketing
Bovée, Thill, Dovel, and Wood: Advertising Excellence
Bowersox and Closs: Logistical Management: The Integrated Supply Chain Process
Bowersox and Cooper: Strategic Marketing Channel Management
Buskirk and Buskirk: Selling: Principles and Practices
Dobler, Burt, and Lee: Purchasing and Materials Management: Text and Cases
Douglas and Craig: Global Marketing Strategy
Guiltinan and Paul: Cases in Marketing Management
Guiltinan and Paul: Marketing Management: Strategies and Programs
Johnson, Kurtz, and Scheuing: Sales Management: Concepts, Practices, and Cases
Kinnear and Taylor: Marketing Research: An Applied Approach
Loudon and Della Bitta: Consumer Behavior: Concepts and Applications
Lovelock and Weinberg: Marketing Challenges: Cases and Exercises
Monroe: Pricing
Moore and Pessemier: Product Planning and Management: Designing and Delivering Value
Rossiter and Percy: Advertising and Promotion Management
Stanton, Etzel, and Walker: Fundamentals of Marketing
Ulrich and Eppinger: Product Design and Development
Zeithaml and Bitner: Services Marketing

LOGISTICAL MANAGEMENT

THE INTEGRATED SUPPLY CHAIN PROCESS

Donald J. Bowersox
The John H. McConnell University Professor of Business Administration
Michigan State University

David J. Closs
Professor of Marketing and Logistics
Michigan State University

THE McGRAW-HILL COMPANIES, INC.

New York St. Louis San Francisco Auckland Bogotá
Caracas Lisbon London Madrid Mexico City Milan Montreal
New Delhi San Juan Singapore Sydney Tokyo Toronto

Authors must have
understanding families or the
preparation of a manuscript
would be impossible during
the demanding years devoted
to the work. For their patience
and support, this book is
dedicated to our families.

McGraw-Hill

A Division of The McGraw·Hill Companies

This book was set in Times Roman by Ruttle, Shaw & Wetherill, Inc.
The editor was Karen Westover;
the production supervisor was Leroy A. Young.
The cover was designed by Joan Greenfield.
Quebecor Printing/Fairfield was printer and binder.

LOGISTICAL MANAGEMENT:
THE INTEGRATED SUPPLY CHAIN PROCESS

This book is printed on acid-free paper.

1 2 3 4 5 6 7 8 9 0   FGR   FGR   9 0 9 8 7 6 5

ISBN 0-07-006883-6

Library of Congress Cataloging-in-Publication Data

Bowersox, Donald J.
   Logistical management : the integrated supply chain proces /
Donald J. Bowersox, David J. Closs. — 1st ed.
     p.   cm — (McGraw-Hill series in marketing)
   Updated ed. of : Logistical management. 3rd ed. c1986.
   Includes bibliographical references and index.
   ISBN 0-07-006883-6
   1. Physical distribution of goods—Management.   2. Materials
management.   I. Closs, David J.   II. Title.   III. Series.
HF5415.7.B66   1996
658.7—dc20   95-42252

ABOUT
THE AUTHORS

DONALD J. BOWERSOX is John H. McConnell Professor of Business Administration at Michigan State University. He received his Ph.D. in marketing at Michigan State and has worked with industry throughout his career. He is the author of many publications in journals and proceedings, including *Harvard Business Review* and *Journal of Marketing.* Besides *Logistical Management,* Dr. Bowersox's most recent books include *Marketing Channels* and *Logistical Excellence: It's Not Business as Usual.* Dr. Bowersox has led a number of industry-supported research studies, the most recent of which was supported by the United Parcel Service Foundation and investigated the best practices of logistics managers around the world. The results are published in *World Class Logistics: The Challenge of Managing Continuous Change.*

DAVID J. CLOSS is Professor of Marketing and Logistics at Michigan State University. He received his Ph.D. in marketing and logistics from Michigan State. Dr. Closs is the author or coauthor of many publications in journals and proceedings, Systems Editor of the *Journal of Business Logistics,* and coauthor of *Simulated Product Sales Forecasting.* He has taught logistics management to executives in North America, western and central Europe, and Australia. Dr. Closs has been involved in a number of industry-supported research projects focusing on sales forecasting, information technology applications, and best practices in logistics.

v

CONTENTS

PREFACE   xvii

PART 1   INTEGRATED LOGISTICS   1

1   Logistics   3

ABOUT LOGISTICAL COMPETENCY   6
THE LOGISTICAL MISSION   8
     Service • Total Cost • Conclusion
THE LOGISTICAL RENAISSANCE   13
     Regulatory Change • Microprocessor Commercialization •
     The Information Revolution • Quality Initiatives • Alliances
DEVELOPMENT PROFILE   20
QUESTIONS   22

2   Logistical Operations Integration   24

THE WORK OF LOGISTICS   25
     Network Design • Information • Transportation • Inventory •
     Warehousing, Material Handling, and Packaging • Conclusion
INTEGRATED LOGISTICS   33
     Inventory Flow • Information Flow
OPERATING OBJECTIVES   41
     Rapid Response • Minimum Variance • Minimum Inventory •
     Movement Consolidation • Quality • Life-Cycle Support
BARRIERS TO INTERNAL INTEGRATION   45
     Organization Structure • Measurement Systems • Inventory
     Ownership • Information Technology • Knowledge Transfer Capability
LOGISTICAL PERFORMANCE CYCLES   46
     Physical Distribution Performance Cycles • Manufacturing Support
     Performance Cycles • Procurement Performance Cycles
MANAGING OPERATIONAL UNCERTAINTY   54
SUMMARY   55
QUESTIONS   56

3 Customer Service 57

CUSTOMER-FOCUSED MARKETING 58
    The Marketing Concept • Logistics as a Core Strategic
    Competency • Life-Cycle Planning Framework
CUSTOMER SERVICE DEFINED 66
BASIC SERVICE CAPABILITY 67
    Availability • Operational Performance • Reliability • Conclusion
INCREASING CUSTOMER EXPECTATIONS 75
THE PERFECT ORDER 76
VALUE-ADDED SERVICES 78
    Customer-Focused Services • Promotion-Focused
    Services • Manufacturing-Focused Services • Time-Focused
    Services • Basic Service • Conclusion
CUSTOMER SATISFACTION AND SUCCESS: 83
  THE BERGEN BRUNSWIG EXAMPLE
    Cost-Effectiveness • Market Access • Market Extension •
    Market Creation
SUMMARY 86
QUESTIONS 87

4 Supply Chain Relationships 88

CHANNEL STRUCTURE 90
THE ECONOMICS OF DISTRIBUTION 93
    Traditional Functions • Specialization • Assortment
CHANNEL RELATIONSHIPS 100
    Supply Chain Competitiveness • Risk, Power, and
    Leadership • Elements of Success
LOGISTICAL SERVICE ALLIANCES 108
    Factors Stimulating Service-Based Alliances • Increasing Service
    Provider Efficiency • Integrated Logistics Service Providers
SUMMARY 113
QUESTIONS 114

Appendix to Chapter 4: Marketing Channel Structure 114

DESCRIPTIVE INSTITUTIONAL APPROACH 115
    Merchant Middlemen • Functional Middlemen
THE GRAPHIC APPROACH 118
COMMODITY GROUPINGS 119
FUNCTIONAL TREATMENTS 119
CHANNEL ARRANGEMENT CLASSIFICATION 119
    Single Transaction Channels • Conventional Channels •
    Voluntary Arrangements (VAs)
CONCLUSION 124

5   Global Logistics   **126**

LOGISTICS IN A GLOBAL ECONOMY   127
    Forces Driving the Borderless World • Barriers to Global Logistics •
    The Global Challenge
VIEWS OF GLOBAL LOGISTICS   140
    Importing and Exporting: A National Perspective • The Stateless
    Enterprise • Conclusion
GLOBAL OPERATING LEVELS   144
    Arm's-Length Relationship • Internal Export • Internal
    Operations • Insider Business Practices • Denationalized
    Operations • Conclusion
THE INTERLINKED GLOBAL ECONOMY   147
    Stages of Regional Integration • Integration Status
THE GLOBAL SUPPLY CHAIN   158
    Performance-Cycle Length • Operations • Systems
    Integration • Alliances • Conclusion
SUMMARY   166
QUESTIONS   168

Case A: Integrated Logistics   **169**

QUESTIONS   172

Case B: Whitmore Products: Time-Based Logistics at Work   **172**

CURRENT OPERATIONS   175
TIME-BASED LOGISTICS   175
THE PROPOSAL   176
QUESTIONS   177

Case C: Zwick Electrical: Developing a Global Logistics Strategy **177**

ABB ASEA BROWN BOVERI LTD.   179
    History • Organization
SIEMENS AG   180
    History • Organization
QUESTIONS   182

PART 2   LOGISTICAL RESOURCES   **183**

6   Information   **185**

INFORMATION FUNCTIONALITY AND PRINCIPLES   186
    Information Functionality • Principles of Logistics
    Information • Conclusion

INFORMATION ARCHITECTURE   194
     Planning/Coordination • Operations • Inventory Deployment and
     Management • Logistics Information System Flow • Conclusion
APPLICATIONS OF NEW INFORMATION TECHNOLOGIES   204
     Electronic Data Interchange • Personal Computers • Artificial
     Intelligence/Expert Systems • Communications • Bar Coding and
     Scanning • Conclusion
ELECTRONIC DATA INTERCHANGE STANDARDS   215
     Communication Standards • Information Standards •
     Future Directions
SUMMARY   220
QUESTIONS   221

7   Forecasting   222

GENERAL FORECAST CONSIDERATIONS   223
     The Nature of Demand • Forecast Components •
     Forecast Approaches
THE FORECAST PROCESS   227
     Forecast Technique • Forecast Support System •
     Forecast Administration • Conclusion
FORECAST TECHNIQUES   232
     Technique Categories • Forecast Error
SUMMARY   240
QUESTIONS   240

    Problem Set A: Information-Forecasting   241

8   Inventory Strategy   243

INVENTORY FUNCTIONALITY AND PRINCIPLES   244
     Inventory Types and Characteristics • Inventory Functionality •
     Inventory-Related Definitions • Cost of Carrying Inventory
PLANNING THE INVENTORY RESOURCE   258
     Determining Order Point (When to Order?) • Determining Lot Size
     (How Much?)
ACCOMMODATING UNCERTAINTY   266
     Accommodating Demand Uncertainty • Performance-Cycle
     Uncertainty • Determining Order Point with
     Uncertainty • Replenishment Ordering
SUMMARY   279
QUESTIONS   280

9   Inventory Management   281

INVENTORY MANAGEMENT POLICIES   282
     Inventory Control • Reactive Methods • Planning
     Methods • Adaptive Logic

MANAGEMENT PROCESSES   298
   Strategy Development Process • Methods for Improved Inventory
   Management
SUMMARY   306
QUESTIONS   307

Problem Set B: Inventory   308

10 Transportation Infrastructure   311

TRANSPORT FUNCTIONALITY AND PRINCIPLES   312
   Transport Functionality • Principles • Participants in Transportation
   Decisions
TRANSPORT INFRASTRUCTURE   316
   Modal Characteristics • Modal Classification • Transportation
   Formats • Conclusion
SUPPLIERS OF TRANSPORTATION SERVICES   330
   Single-Mode Operators • Specialized Carriers • Intermodal
   Operators • Nonoperating Intermediaries • Conclusion
SUMMARY   338
QUESTIONS   339

11 Transportation Regulation   340

TYPES OF REGULATION   341
   Economic Regulation • Safety and Social Regulation
HISTORY OF TRANSPORTATION REGULATION   343
   Pre-1920 • 1920 to 1940 • 1940 to 1976 • 1976 to the Present
INTERSTATE DEREGULATION   350
   Motor Carrier • Air Transport • Rail Transport • Other Carriers •
   The Future of Federal Economic Regulation
INTRASTATE REGULATION   356
CURRENT REGULATORY ISSUES   358
   Collective Rate Making and Antitrust Immunity • Contract
   Definition • The Future Status of the ICC • Hidden
   Discounts • Undercharges • Hazardous Materials
SUMMARY   363
QUESTIONS   363

12 Transportation Management   364

BASIC TRANSPORT ECONOMICS AND PRICING   364
   Economic Factors • Cost Structures • Pricing Strategies • Rating
TRANSPORT DECISION MAKING   378
   Transport Documentation • Traffic Department Responsibilities
SUMMARY   385
QUESTIONS   385

Problem Set C: Transportation   387

13 Warehouse Management   389

STORAGE FUNCTIONALITY AND PRINCIPLES   390
The Concept of Strategic Storage • Warehouse
Functionality • Warehouse Operating Principles
DEVELOPING THE WAREHOUSE RESOURCE   399
Warehousing Alternatives • Warehousing Strategy • Planning
the Distribution Warehouse • Initiating Warehouse Operations
SUMMARY   416
QUESTIONS   417

14 Material Handling   418

MANAGING THE WAREHOUSE RESOURCE   419
Handling Requirements • Storage Requirements
MATERIAL HANDLING   421
Basic Handling Considerations • Mechanized
Systems • Semiautomated Handling • Automated
Handling • Information-Directed Systems • Special Handling
Considerations • Conclusion
SUMMARY   434
QUESTIONS   434

15 Packaging   435

PERSPECTIVES   436
Consumer Packaging (Marketing Emphasis) • Industrial Packaging
(Logistics Emphasis)
DAMAGE PROTECTION   439
Physical Environment • Outside Elements
MATERIAL-HANDLING EFFICIENCY/UTILITY   441
Product Characteristics • Unitization • Communication
CHANNEL INTEGRATION   445
ALTERNATIVE MATERIALS   446
Traditional Materials • Emerging Trends
SUMMARY   451
QUESTIONS   451

Problem Set D: Warehousing-Handling   452

PART 3 LOGISTICS SYSTEM DESIGN   455

16 Logistics Positioning   457

LOGISTICS REENGINEERING   458
Systems Integration • Benchmarking • Activity-Based
Costing • Quality Initiatives

REENGINEERING PROCEDURE   462

LOGISTICS ENVIRONMENTAL ASSESSMENT   463

    Industry-Competitive Assessment • Geomarket
Differentials • Technology Assessment • Material-Energy
Assessment • Channel Structure • Economic-Social
Projections • Service Industry Trends • Regulatory
Posture • Conclusion

TIME-BASED LOGISTICS   470

    Postponement • Consolidation • Operating Arrangements:
Anticipatory versus Response-Based • Conclusion

ALTERNATIVE LOGISTICS STRATEGIES   479

    Structural Separation • Logistical Operating Arrangements

STRATEGIC INTEGRATION   488

LOGISTICS TIME-BASED CONTROL TECHNIQUES   489

    Supply-Driven Techniques • Demand-Driven Techniques

SUMMARY   494

QUESTIONS   494

17 Integration Theory   **495**

LOGISTICS LOCATION STRUCTURE   496

    Spectrum of Location Decisions • Local Presence Paradigm

WAREHOUSE LOCATION PATTERNS   499

    Market-Positioned Warehouses • Manufacturing-Positioned
Warehouses • Intermediately Positioned Warehouses

TRANSPORTATION ECONOMIES   501

    Cost-Based Warehouse Justification • Transportation Cost
Minimization

INVENTORY ECONOMIES   503

    Service-Based Warehouse Justification • Inventory Cost Minimization

LEAST-TOTAL-COST DESIGN   509

    Trade-off Relationships • Critical Assumptions and Limitations

FORMULATING LOGISTICAL STRATEGY   512

    The Least-Total-Cost System Design • Threshold Service •
Service Sensitivity Analysis • Finalizing Logistical Strategy

SUMMARY   521

QUESTIONS   522

18 Planning and Design Methodology   **523**

METHODOLOGY   524

PHASE I: PROBLEM DEFINITION AND PLANNING   524

    Feasibility Assessment • Project Planning

PHASE II: DATA COLLECTION AND ANALYSIS   534

    Assumptions and Data Collection • Analysis

PHASE III: RECOMMENDATIONS AND IMPLEMENTATION   540

    Recommendations • Implementation • Conclusion

DECISION SUPPORT SYSTEMS 545
Define Functional Requirements • Define Relative
Importance • Identify Alternatives • Rate Each Alternative •
Select Package and Negotiate with Supplier
SUMMARY 548
QUESTIONS 548

19 Planning and Design Techniques 550

LOGISTICS AD HOC ANALYSIS 551
Freight Lane Analysis • Inventory Analysis • Segment Profitability
LOCATION APPLICATIONS 554
Location Decisions • Location Analysis Techniques • Location
Analysis Data Requirements
INVENTORY APPLICATIONS 570
Inventory Analysis Decisions • Inventory Analysis Techniques
TRANSPORTATION APPLICATIONS 573
Transportation Analysis Decisions • Transportation Analysis
Techniques • Transportation Analysis Data
Requirements • Conclusion
ENTERPRISE MODELING 578
SUMMARY 580
QUESTIONS 580

Case D: Westminster Company: A System Design Assessment 581

COMPANY PROFILE 581
WESTMINSTER TODAY 581
WESTMINSTER'S DISTRIBUTION NETWORK 582
QUESTIONS 584

Case E: Alternative Distribution Strategies 585

RETAIL INTEREST 586
OPERATING PROCEDURES 586
SUMMARY 587
QUESTIONS 587

Case F: Michigan Liquor Control Commission 587

HISTORY OF MICHIGAN LIQUOR DISTRIBUTION SYSTEM 588
THE LIQUOR DISTRIBUTION PROCESS 588
CURRENT ISSUES 590
CHALLENGES OF SYSTEM REDESIGN 591
QUESTIONS 591

PART 4   **LOGISTICS ADMINISTRATION**   593

20   Organization   595

LOGISTICAL ORGANIZATIONAL DEVELOPMENT   597
STAGES OF FUNCTIONAL AGGREGATION   599
     Stage 1 Organization • Stage 2 Organization • Stage 3
     Organization • Empirical Confirmation: Stages 1 to 3
STAGE 4: A SHIFT IN EMPHASIS FROM FUNCTION TO PROCESS   606
STAGE 5: BEYOND STRUCTURE: VIRTUALITY AND ORGANIZATIONAL
   TRANSPARENCY   608
ISSUES AND CHALLENGES   611
     Concepts Having Logistical Significance • Careers and
     Loyalty • Managing Change
THE MANAGEMENT OF ALLIANCES   626
     Initiating an Alliance • Implementing an Alliance • Maintaining
     Alliance Vitality
SUMMARY   630
QUESTIONS   630

21   Planning, Costing, and Pricing   632

OPERATIONS PLANNING   633
     The Nature of Logistical Plans • The Final Operating
     Plan • Operating Plan Modification
LOGISTICAL DESIGN METRICS   642
     Total-Cost Analysis • Outsource Considerations •
     Cost-Revenue Analysis
PRICING   658
     Price Fundamentals • Various Pricing Issues
SUMMARY   666
QUESTIONS   667

22   Performance Measurement and Reporting   668

LOGISTICAL MEASUREMENT   669
     Dimensions of Performance Measurement • Internal Performance
     Measurement • External Performance Measurement •
     Comprehensive Supply Chain Measurement
CHARACTERISTICS OF AN IDEAL MEASUREMENT SYSTEM   682
     Cost/Service Reconciliation • Dynamic Knowledge-Based
     Reporting • Exception-Based Reporting
LEVELS OF MEASUREMENT AND INFORMATION FLOW   683
     Direction • Variation • Decision • Policy
REPORT STRUCTURES   686
     Status Reports • Trend Reports • Ad Hoc Reports
SUMMARY   690
QUESTIONS   691

23 Dimensions of Change: A Seminar Focus 692

A VIEW TOWARD THE NEW MILLENNIUM 693
A SEMINAR FOCUS 695
SEMINAR TOPIC 1: HOW ADEQUATE IS THE GLOBAL
  LOGISTICS INFRASTRUCTURE? 696
    Issues and Questions
SEMINAR TOPIC 2: ASSESSMENT AND CONTROL TO IMPROVE
  LOGISTICS PERFORMANCE 698
    Issues and Questions
SEMINAR TOPIC 3: ORGANIZATIONAL EVALUATION 700
    The Case for Functional Specialization • The Case for Functional
    Decentralization • The Case for Horizontal Expansion • Issues and
    Questions
SEMINAR TOPIC 4: FULL-SERVICE DISTRIBUTION COMPANIES 702
    Forces Stimulating FSDC Development • Service Risk •
    Issues and Questions
SEMINAR TOPIC 5: INFORMATION TECHNOLOGY 703
    The Evolution of Application Development • End-User
    Computing • Who Should Do What? • Issues and Questions
SEMINAR TOPIC 6: GLOBAL LOGISTICS 706
    The Prerequisites for Global Success • Issues and Questions
EPILOGUE 708

Case G: Woodson Chemical Company 711

COMPANY BACKGROUND 711
INDUSTRY BACKGROUND 712
WCC'S NORTH AMERICAN DISTRIBUTION NETWORK 713
QUESTIONS 714

Case H: Performance Control 715

COMPANY BACKGROUND 715
PERFORMANCE STATISTICS 715
CONCLUSION 716
QUESTIONS 716

Case I: Managing Change in Wholesaling: The Case of Wilmont 717
  Drug Company

COMPANY BACKGROUND 717
WHOLESALING 717
REVITALIZATION PLAN/CHANGE MANAGEMENT MODEL 718
CONCLUSION 719
QUESTIONS 719

AUTHOR INDEX 720
SUBJECT INDEX 723

PREFACE

Over the last four decades, the discipline of business logistics has advanced from the warehouse and transportation dock to the boardroom of leading global enterprises. We have had the opportunity to be actively involved in this evolution through research, education, and advising. This first edition of *Logistical Management: The Integrated Supply Chain Process* reviews the development and fundamentals of the discipline. It also presents our vision of the future of business logistics and its role in enterprise competitiveness.

The history of the *Logistical Management* manuscript began in 1958. As some readers are aware, early contributions were presented in two editions of *Physical Distribution Management.* The first, a collaboration with two other authors published in 1961, represented the initial attempt to integrate physical distribution activities into a single book. In 1968, the second edition of *Physical Distribution Management,* again a collaboration, was substantially rewritten as a new book because of developments in the field during the intervening seven years. An early version of *Logistical Management,* published in 1974, contained material from the two previous works. However, after 1974, the ever-expanding subject content once again required a new and broader approach to logistics. The view of total logistics was further developed and refined in another edition of *Logistical Management,* published in 1978. A 1986 edition, with new coauthors, offered a refinement of selected materials and extended the breadth and scope of logistical responsibilities.

To recognize the significance of change in both the discipline and the text, this 1996 edition is given an extended title and designated a first edition. Now under the authorship of Bowersox and Closs, and published by McGraw-Hill, *Logistical Management* once again expands the material and perspective to reflect the increasing role of logistics in global competitive strategy.

Business logistics includes all the activities to move product and information to, from, and between members of a supply chain. The supply chain provides the framework for businesses and their suppliers who join to bring goods, services, and information efficiently to ultimate consumers. *Logistical Management: The Integrated Supply Chain Process* presents the mission, business processes, and strategies needed to achieve integrated supply chain management. We hope the text achieves three fundamental objectives: (1) presenting a comprehensive description of existing logistical practices within the private and public sectors of society; (2) describing ways and means to apply logistics principles to achieve competitive advantage; and (3) providing a conceptual approach for integrating logistics as a core competency in enterprise strategy.

It would be impossible to list all the individuals who have made significant contributions to the contents of the book. Special thanks are due to James B. Henry, Dean of the Eli Broad College of Business and the Eli Broad Graduate School of Management at Michigan State University, and to Robert W. Nason, Chairperson of the Department of Marketing and Logistics at Michigan State University, for maintaining a collegial environment that fosters creativity and application of integrated logistics concepts. We also express our gratitude to Professor Emeritus Donald A. Taylor of Michigan State University, who has been a guiding force throughout our careers. In addition, for their specific aid with the manuscript, our appreciation goes to Mark L. Bennion, Bowling Green State University; M. Bixby Cooper and O. Keith Helferich, Michigan State University; Patricia J. Daugherty, University of Georgia; Martin Dresner, University of Maryland, College Park; John Grabner, Ohio State University; James Kenderdine, University of Oklahoma; Bernard J. LaLonde, Ohio State University; Bill Moser, Ball State University; Jay U. Sterling, University of Alabama; and Katherine Straughn, Auburn University; all of whom provided detailed reviews of the manuscript and offered numerous suggestions for improving the presentation.

As active members of the Council of Logistics Management, formerly the National Council of Physical Distribution Management, we have been the fortunate recipients of contributions by many council members to the development of this manuscript. In particular, we wish to acknowledge the continued assistance of George Gecowets and his staff, who maintain an open door to the academic community.

Over the past twenty-nine years, business executives who have attended the annual Michigan State University Logistics Management Executive Development Seminar have been exposed to the basic concepts developed in the text and have given freely of their time and experience. Special appreciation goes to the United Parcel Service Foundation for a grant assisting in the development of this manuscript and for a generous funding of the World Class Logistics Research initiative, which has added substantially to the relevancy of the text. We also acknowledge long-standing support to Michigan State logistics, through the funding of an endowed chair, provided by John H. McConnell, founder and chairperson of Worthington Industries.

The number of individuals involved in teaching logistics around the world expands daily. To this group in general, and in particular to our colleagues at Michigan State University, whose advice and assistance made it possible to complete this text, we express our sincere appreciation.

Teachers receive continuous inspiration from students over the years and, in many ways, the final day of judgment in a professional career comes in the seminar or classroom. We have been fortunate to have the counsel of many outstanding young scholars who currently are making their marks on the academic and business worlds. In particular, we appreciate the input of students who have used this text in manuscript form and made suggestions for improvement. We also acknowledge the contributions of current and former doctoral students, particularly Drs. David

J. Frayer, Robb Frankel, and Judith W. Schmitz, and of Steven R. Clinton, who participated extensively in case development and editorial support. Doctoral student Thomas J. Goldsby provided valuable assistance throughout manuscript preparation, managed the complex process of obtaining publication permissions, and guided development of the teaching support manual.

We wish to acknowledge the contributions of Felicia Kramer and Pamela Kingsbury, for manuscript preparation on several earlier versions of the text. Cheryl Lundeen, who prepared many drafts of the manuscript, provided outstanding support for this edition, and Stacy Kannawin added further support as the text was refined for publication. Without Felicia, Pam, Cheryl, and Stacy, this long published text, in its many revisions, would not be a reality.

With so much able assistance, it is difficult to offer excuses for any shortcomings that might appear. The faults are solely our responsibility.

Donald J. Bowersox

David J. Closs

LOGISTICAL MANAGEMENT

THE INTEGRATED
SUPPLY CHAIN PROCESS

PART ONE

INTEGRATED LOGISTICS

Chapter 1   Logistics
Chapter 2   Logistical Operations Integration
Chapter 3   Customer Service
Chapter 4   Supply Chain Relationships
  Appendix   Marketing Channel Structure
Chapter 5   Global Logistics
   Case A   Integrated Logistics
   Case B   Whitmore Products: Time-Based Logistics
             at Work
   Case C   Zwick Electrical: Developing a Global Logistics
             Strategy

LOGISTICS

ABOUT LOGISTICAL COMPETENCY
THE LOGISTICAL MISSION
   Service
   Total Cost
   Conclusion
THE LOGISTICAL RENAISSANCE
   Regulatory Change
   Microprocessor Commercialization
   The Information Revolution
   Quality Initiatives
   Alliances
DEVELOPMENT PROFILE
QUESTIONS

Logistics is unique: it never stops! Logistics is happening around the globe, twenty-four hours of every day, seven days a week during fifty-two weeks a year. Few areas of business operations involve the complexity or span the geography typical of logistics. Logistics is concerned with getting products and services where they are needed when they are desired. Most consumers in highly developed industrial nations take a high level of logistical competency for granted. When they go to the store, they expect products to be available and fresh. It is difficult to visualize accomplishing any marketing or manufacturing without logistical support.

Modern logistics is also a paradox. Logistics has been performed since the beginning of civilization: it's hardly new. However, implementing best practice of logistics has become one of the most exciting and challenging operational areas of business and public sector management.[1]

Logistics involves the integration of information, transportation, inventory, warehousing, material handling, and packaging. All of these areas of work provide a variety of stimulating jobs. These jobs combine to make overall logistics management a challenging and rewarding career. Because of the strategic importance of logistical performance, an increasing number of successful logistics executives are being promoted to senior management.

The excitement and newness of logistics stem from a combination of traditional work areas into an integrated strategic initiative. The successful senior logistics executive serves as a cross-functional orchestrator of work both within and beyond his/her firm. Within the firm the challenge is to coordinate individual job expertise into an integrated competency focused on servicing customers. In most situations the desired scope of such coordination transcends the individual enterprise, reaching out to include customers as well as material and service suppliers. In a strategic sense, the senior logistics officer leads a boundary-spanning initiative to facilitate effective supply chain relationships. The excitement of contemporary logistics is found in making the combined results of internal and external integration one of the core competencies of an enterprise.

The operating responsibility of logistics is the geographical positioning of raw materials, work-in-process, and finished inventories where required at the *lowest cost possible*. It is through the logistical process that materials flow into the vast manufacturing capacity of an industrial nation and products are distributed through marketing channels to consumers. The complexity of logistics is awesome. In the United States alone, the structure of marketing involves approximately 1.5 million retailers and over 460,000 wholesalers.[2] To move products and materials to and from these businesses, 14.9 million commercial trucks were registered in 1992.[3] To support logistics, total manufacturing, wholesale, and retail, inventory investment in 1994 exceeded $893 billion.[4]

---

[1]The term *logistics* is not specific to the business or public sector. The basic concepts of logistical management are applicable throughout private and public enterprise activities. Over the years, common titles used to describe all or parts of the material discussed in this text have been *business logistics, physical distribution, materials logistics management, materials management, physical supply, logistics of distribution, marketing logistics, inbound logistics,* and *total distribution.* In 1991, the Council of Logistics Management modified its 1976 definition of physical distribution management by first changing the term to *logistics* and then changing the definition as follows: "Logistics is the process of planning, implementing and controlling the efficient, effective flow and storage of goods, services and related information from the point of origin to the point of consumption for the purpose of conforming to customer requirements." Although this definition does not incorporate all specific terms used in this text, it does reflect the need for total movement management from point of material procurement to location of finished product distribution.

[2]"County Business Patterns—1989," United States Department of Commerce, Bureau of the Census, issued August 1991.

[3]This figure was provided by the Department of Statistical Services of the American Trucking Associations, Inc.

[4]Robert V. Delaney, Sixth Annual "State of Logistics Report," presented to the National Press Club, Washington, D.C., June 5, 1995. See footnote 5 for a detailed explanation of physical distribution versus logistics supply chain inventory.

Logistics adds value when inventory is correctly positioned to facilitate sales. Creating logistics value is costly. Although it is difficult to measure, most experts agree that the annual expenditure to perform logistics in the United States was just under 10 percent of the 1994 gross national product (GNP).[5] Put in another perspective, for every trillion dollars spent on GNP, the associated logistical cost was over 100 billion dollars. Expenditure for transportation in 1994 was $425 billion, which represented 6.3 percent of GNP. The logistics of our economy is truly big business! Trends in the aggregate cost of logistics over the past two decades are summarized in Table 1-1.

For individual firms, logistics expenditures typically range from 5 to 35 percent of sales depending on the type of business, geographical area of operation, and weight/value ratio of products and materials. Logistics typically accounts for one of the highest costs of doing business, second only to materials in manufacturing or cost of goods sold in wholesaling or retailing. It is clear that logistics, while vital to business success, is expensive.

Despite these impressive cost comparisons, the true excitement of logistics is not cost containment or reduction. The excitement comes from understanding how select firms position their logistical competency to gain competitive advantage. Firms that enjoy world-class logistical competency can gain competitive advantage by providing customers with superior service. While perfect orders are difficult to achieve, logistically sophisticated firms seek such lofty performance and are committed to continuous improvement. Leading firms typically have information systems capable of monitoring logistical performance on a real-time basis, giving them the capability to identify potential operational breakdowns and take corrective action prior to customer service failure. In situations where timely corrective action is not possible, customers can be notified in advance and offered alternatives, thereby taking the surprise out of forthcoming service failures. By performing above industry average in terms of inventory availability as well as speed and consistency of delivery, logistically sophisticated firms are attractive suppliers and ideal business partners.

This book is concerned with how managers plan, implement, and sustain their firm's logistical operations. *Logistical management includes the design and administration of systems to control the flow of material, work-in-process, and finished inventory to support business unit strategy.*

---

[5]Robert V. Delaney of Cass Logistics, Inc., estimates two series of data: physical distribution system and logistics supply chain. The physical distribution system series includes manufacturing, wholesale and trade inventory, and cost of transportation and administration, and is displayed in relation to the gross national product (GNP). In 1992, Delaney began reporting logistics supply chain series data, which added the cost of all business inventory, including agriculture, mining, construction, and services. This new series data are reported in relation to gross domestic product (GDP). GDP, as of December 1991, is the preferred measure of economic performance for the United States Commerce Department, and while both GNP and GDP measure total goods and services produced, GNP covers output by United States residents regardless of location and GDP covers workers and capital within United States borders (*New York Times National Edition*, Dec. 4, 1991, p. C1). Delaney estimates the annual physical distribution system at 9.8 percent GNP in 1994 with transportation at 6.3 percent GNP. The total cost of logistics in 1994 was $660 billion under the physical distribution system or $730 billion for the logistics supply chain system. The difference is based on increased inventory carrying costs. GNP in 1994 was $6.73 trillion as compared to GDP at $6.74 trillion.

TABLE 1-1 UNITED STATES LOGISTICS COSTS*

Year	Inventory carrying cost	Transportation cost	Administrative cost	Total cost
1974	119	116	9	244
1975	110	116	9	235
1976	116	133	10	259
1977	126	150	11	287
1978	155	175	13	343
1979	200	193	16	409
1980	243	205	18	466
1981	283	236	21	540
1982	255	240	20	515
1983	228	244	19	491
1984	257	250	20	527
1985	240	265	20	525
1986	233	271	20	524
1987	243	288	21	552
1988	266	313	23	602
1989	311	331	26	668
1990	298	352	26	678
1991	270	360	25	655
1992	243	379	25	647
1993	250	394	26	670
1994	277	425	28	730

*All costs are in billions of dollars.
Source: Robert V. Delaney, Sixth Annual "State of Logistics Report," presented to the National Press Club, Washington, D.C., June 5, 1995.

The overall goal of logistics is to achieve a targeted level of customer service at the lowest possible total cost. Logistics involves detailed and complex work. Logistics managers are responsible for planning and administrating this work.

This chapter introduces logistical management, starting with a description of how logistical competency fits into a firm's overall strategic positioning. It is fundamentally important to view logistics in the context of how it can be exploited as a core competency. Next, the logistical mission of a typical enterprise is reviewed in terms of service, cost, and operating objectives. This generic mission statement explores the operational dynamics of logistics. The third section reviews recent developments that have converged to attract widespread attention to logistical competency. A final section provides an overview of topics developed in subsequent chapters.

ABOUT LOGISTICAL COMPETENCY

A useful way to view logistical competency is to develop an integrated framework that defines and relates key concepts. Such an integrative framework serves to relate the most finite aspects of logistics to overall enterprise strategy. It is important that persons involved in day-to-day logistics work have a basic understanding of how their specific job fits into the big picture. It is equally important for managers involved in logistics to envision how outstanding or competitively superior logistical performance can become the cornerstone of overall enterprise strategy. An integrating framework is provided in Table 1-2. The following discussion relates logistics activity from basic work to business strategy.

Basic work consists of specific jobs that are essential to logistical performance. These jobs run the gamut from order picking to truck driving to the chief logistics officer (CLO). Because of the nature of logistics, basic work involves many people. The geographical scope of logistical operations means that the vast majority of essential work is performed outside the vision of direct supervision. Within the broad assortment of different logistics jobs, countless specialized tasks are required. Each of these specific tasks is a potential target for work standardization, simplification, or potential elimination during logistics reengineering.

In Chapters 6 through 15, traditional *functional areas* of logistics are developed and discussed. Logistical functions have typically served as the organizational focus to perform and administer logistics work. For example, transportation procurement, performance, and administration were typically performed by a traffic department. The net result was that specific activities, such as transportation, were often managed as end objectives in and of themselves, rather than as parts contributing to achieving overall logistical performance goals. The essence of integration is to position functional excellence so that it can make maximum contribution to overall logistical process competency. In this sense, the challenge for logistical managers is to avoid a "silo mentality," or tunnel vision, that is often inherent in a functional orientation. The role of logistical senior management is cross-functional coordination. As such, the functional areas of logistics are appropriately viewed as resources to be integrated. The performance cycle provides the operational structure for logistical integration.

TABLE 1-2   LOGISTICAL INTEGRATION HIERARCHY

- *Strategic positioning and universal process.* Focus regarding how a firm selects to compete involves four processes essential to success: creation of customer value, planning, control, and succession generation. All firms must perform all universal processes for long-term survival and growth.

- *Competencies.* Performance areas essential to achieving universal processes. A wide variety of competencies are required for long-term survival. A firm typically excels in a few, which are referred to as core competencies.

- *Performance cycle.* Operational structure for logistics execution. Structure that integrates temporal and spatial aspects of logistical operations linking procurement, manufacturing, support, and physical distribution.

- *Function.* Traditional areas of logistics specialization essential for operational excellence. Must be viewed as integral parts of overall logistical competency, not as unique performance areas.

- *Basic work.* Specific jobs that must be performed within functions to satisfy logistical requirements.

Performance cycle structure links functions and basic work necessary to complete order-to-delivery operations. As will be detailed in Chapter 2, different operating requirements and performance expectations are typical in procurement, manufacturing support, and physical distribution operations of a firm. These performance cycles are often multiecheloned in structure and are deployed in a flexible manner to achieve operational goals. The configuration of performance cycles creates an operational network for achieving customer service goals. This network of performance cycles is the essence of integrated logistical system design. It is important to keep in mind that logistical integration of business operations occurs both in time and across geography. This is typically referred to as logistical *temporal/spatial integration.*

Logistical competency is a relative assessment of a firm's capability to provide competitively superior customer service at the lowest possible total cost. When a firm decides to differentiate itself on the basis of logistical competency, it seeks to outperform competitors in all facets of operations. This typically means that logistical performance is dedicated to supporting any or all marketing and manufacturing requirements in a manner that exploits delivery capability. In short, the strategy is to provide superior service at a total cost below industry average. The service platform of superior logistic achievers is typically characterized by alternative logistical capabilities, emphasizing flexibility, time-based performance, operational control, postponement capabilities, and most of all a commitment to perfect service performance.

Expectations concerning logistical competency directly depend on a firm's *strategic positioning.* All enterprises must perform logistics to achieve their basic business goals. How important logistics is in a strategic sense depends on the emphasis placed on proactively using such competency to gain competitive advantage. One *universal process* that all firms must successfully complete is the creation of *customer value.* Such value is essential to gaining and retaining a loyal customer base. One of several competencies required to create customer value is logistics. The typical enterprise finds distinctive competitive advantage by virtue of focusing to excel in one or a limited number of competencies. This strategic positioning becomes, in the eyes of customers, what the firm's excellence is all about—*its core competency.* A world-class firm will typically perform all required competencies above industry average, but will build excellence around a few managerially selected core competencies. Lesser resources and managerial attention is directed to noncore competencies. When logistics becomes a cornerstone of basic business strategy, it must be managed as a core competency. On the basis of this discussion of how logistics fits into overall business strategy, it is now possible to examine the typical mission in greater detail.

THE LOGISTICAL MISSION

Thus far it has been established that the logistics of an enterprise is an integrated effort aimed at helping create customer value at the lowest total cost. Logistics exists to satisfy customer requirements by facilitating relevant manufacturing and marketing operations. At a strategic level, logistics managers seek to achieve a previously agreed upon quality of customer service through state-of-the-art operating competency. The challenge is to balance service expectations and cost expenditures in a manner that achieves business objectives.

Service

Almost any level of logistical service can be achieved if a firm is willing to commit the necessary resources. In today's operating environment, the limiting factor is economics, not technology. For example, a dedicated inventory can be maintained in close geographical proximity to a major customer. A fleet of trucks can be held in a constant state of delivery readiness. To facilitate order entry, dedicated communications can be maintained on a real-time basis between the customer's business and a supplier's logistical operation. Given this high state of logistical readiness, a product or component could be delivered within minutes of identifying a customer requirement. The availability of inventory could be even faster if a supplier agrees to consign inventory to a customer. Such consignment would eliminate the need to perform logistics in response to a customer's requirements. While such extreme service commitment might constitute a sales manager's dream, it would be costly and typically is not necessary to support most marketing and manufacturing operations.

In final analysis, logistical service is a balance of service priority and cost. If a specific material is not available when required for manufacturing, it may force a plant shutdown, causing significant cost penalty and potential loss of sales and even the loss of a good customer. The profit impact of such failure could be significant. In contrast, the profit impact of an unexpected two-day delay in delivering products to replenish a warehouse could be minimal or even insignificant in terms of impact on overall operational performance. In most situations, the cost-benefit impact of logistical failure is directly related to the importance of service performance to the customer involved. The more significant the service failure impact upon the customer, the greater the priority placed on logistical performance.

Basic logistical service is measured in terms of (1) availability, (2) operational performance, and (3) service reliability. *Availability* means having inventory to consistently meet customer material or product requirements. According to the traditional paradigm, higher inventory availability required greater inventory investment. Technology is providing new ways to achieve high inventory availability without associated high capital investments. Developments in inventory availability are critical because of its fundamental importance.

Operational performance deals with the elapsed time from order receipt to delivery. Operational performance involves delivery *speed* and *consistency*. Naturally, most customers want fast delivery. However, fast delivery is of limited value if it is erratic. A customer gains little benefit when a supplier promises next-day delivery but, more often than not, is late. To achieve smooth operations, firms typically seek first to achieve consistency of service and then to improve delivery speed. Other aspects of operational performance are also important. A firm's operational performance can be viewed in terms of how *flexible* it is in accommodating unusual and unexpected customer requests. Another aspect of operational performance is *malfunction and recovery.* Few firms can promise and perform perfectly in every situation all of the time. It is important to gauge the likelihood of something going wrong. Malfunction refers to the probability of logistical performance involving failures, such as damaged products, incorrect assortments, or inaccurate documentation. When such malfunctions occur, a firm's performance can be measured in terms of *required time to recover.* Operational performance is concerned with how a firm handles all aspects of customer requirements, including service failure, on a day in and day out basis.

Service reliability involves the quality attributes of logistics. The key to quality is accurate measurement of availability and operational performance. Only through comprehensive performance measurement is it possible to determine if overall logistical operations are achieving desired service goals. To achieve service reliability, it is essential to identify measures to assess inventory availability and operational performance. For logistics performance to continuously meet customer expectations, it is essential that management be committed to continuous improvement. Logistical quality does not come easy: it's the product of careful planning supported by training, comprehensive measurement, and continuous improvement. To improve service performance, goals need to be established on a selective basis. Some products are more critical than others because of their importance to the customer and their relative profit contribution. The level of basic logistical service should be realistic in terms of customer expectations and requirements. In most cases, firms confront marketing situations wherein customers have different sales potential and some may require unique services. Thus, managers must realize that customers are different and that services must be matched to accommodate unique preferences and purchase potential. In general, firms tend to be overly optimistic when committing to average or basic customer service performance. Inability to consistently meet an unrealistically high basic service target might result in more operating and customer problems than if less ambitious goals had been made at the outset. Unrealistic across-the-board service commitments can also dilute a firm's capability to satisfy special requirements of high-potential customers.

Total Cost

In 1956, a monograph discussing air freight economics provided a new perspective on logistical cost.[6] In an effort to explain conditions under which high-cost air transport could be justified, Lewis, Culliton, and Steele conceptualized the total cost of logistics. Total cost was positioned to include *all* expenditures necessary to perform logistical requirements. The authors illustrated an electronic parts distribution strategy wherein the high variable cost of direct factory to customer air transport was more than offset by reductions in inventory and field warehouse costs. They concluded that the *least total cost* logistical way to provide desired customer service was to centralize inventory in one warehouse and make deliveries

---

[6]Howard T. Lewis, James W. Culliton, and Jack D. Steele, *The Role of Air Freight in Physical Distribution,* Boston: Division of Research, Graduate School of Business Administration, Harvard University, 1956.

TOTAL COST PROVIDES FRESHNESS

Brooklyn Brewery currently distributes Brooklyn Lager and Brown Ale in the United States. Brooklyn Brewery has been in operation for three years, and while it has not yet established a national presence in the United States, it is creating a niche for itself in the $20 billion per year Japanese market.

Brooklyn Brewery had no immediate plans to export its beer to Japan until Keiji Miyamoto of Taiyo Resources Limited, an international subsidiary of Taiyo Oil Company, visited the brewery. Miyamoto believed that Japanese consumers would like the beer and convinced Brooklyn Brewery to meet with Hiroyo Trading Company to discuss marketing to Japan. Hiroyo Trading suggested that Brooklyn Brewery ship the beer by air to Japan and advertise its unique freshness for an import beer.

Not only is this an interesting marketing strategy, but it is also a unique logistical operation as no other breweries currently export beer by air to Japan because of the high costs. Brooklyn Brewery shipped its first case of Brooklyn Lager to Japan in December 1989 and used a variety of air carriers over the first few months. Eventually, Emery Worldwide-Japan was selected as the sole air carrier for Brooklyn Brewery. Emery was chosen because of the value-added services it offered to Brooklyn Brewery. Emery takes delivery of the beer at its terminal at J.F.K. International Airport and arranges for transport on a commercial flight headed for Tokyo. Emery includes custom clearance through its Japanese custom brokers. These services help maintain the integrity of the product's freshness claim.

The freshness claim is achieved since the beer arrives direct to the customer from the brewery within the week it is manufactured. The average order cycle for beer shipped overseas is forty days. The freshness of the beer allows it to be priced at a premium, five times higher than beer shipped by sea. While Brooklyn Lager is an average-priced beer in the United States, in Japan it is a premium product and receives significantly higher margins.

The high price of the Lager has not hindered sales of the beer in Japan. In 1988, its first year in Japan, Brooklyn Brewery achieved a half million dollars in sales. Sales increased to $1 million in 1989 and $1.3 million in 1990. The total export business accounts for 10 percent of Brooklyn Brewery's total sales.

In the future, Brooklyn Brewery will change the packaging by shipping kegs instead of bottles to reduce air freight costs. The keg weight is equivalent to bottled beer but will reduce the chance of damage due to broken glass. Kegs may require less protective packaging as well, which further reduces the cost of shipment. Exporting to other foreign countries is next on the horizon for Brooklyn Brewery.

Based on Deborah Castalano Ruriani, "Casebook: Brooklyn Brewery," *Distribution,* January 1991, pp. 55–56.

using air transportation. The total-cost perspective remains viable today as illustrated by the sidebar on Brooklyn Brewery.

This concept of total cost, although basic, had not previously been applied to logistical analysis.[7] Probably because of the economic climate of the times and the radical departure in suggested practice, the total-cost proposition generated a great deal of attention. The prevailing managerial practice, reinforced by accounting and financial control, was to focus attention on achieving the lowest possible cost for each function of logistics with little or no attention to total costs. Managers typically focused on minimizing functional cost, such as transportation, with the expectation that such effort would achieve the lowest combined cost. The total-cost concept

---

[7]The total-cost concept, developed in greater detail in Chapter 17, is a specialized form of break-even analysis. For early foundations, see J. Brooks Heckert and Robert B. Milner, *Distribution Costs,* New York: The Ronald Press Company, 1940, chap. 15; and Donald R. Longman and Michael Schiff, *Practical Distribution Cost Analysis,* Homewood, Ill.: Richard D. Irwin, Inc., 1955, pp. 35–37.

opened the door to examining how functional costs interrelate. Subsequent refinements provided a more comprehensive understanding of logistical cost components and identified the critical need for developing functional cost analysis and activity-based costing capabilities.[8] However, the implementation of effective logistical process costing remains a challenge in the 1990s. Many long-standing practices of accounting continue to serve as barriers to fully implementing total-cost logistical solutions.

The appropriate level of logistics cost expenditure must be related to desired service performance. The simultaneous attainment of high availability, operational performance, and reliability is expensive. A significant managerial challenge stems from the fact that logistical cost and increased performance have a nonproportional relationship. A firm that supports customer commitments of high inventory availability delivered on a reliable overnight basis may experience double the logistical cost in comparison to a less ambitious commitment. The same firm, committed to overnight service at 100 percent consistency, could easily dissipate profits by attempting to provide service that customers may not need, expect, or even want. The key to achieving logistical leadership is to master the art of matching competency with key customer expectations and requirements. This customer commitment is the core of formulating logistics strategy.

Conclusion

The typical enterprise seeks to develop and implement an overall logistical competency that satisfies key customer expectations at a realistic total-cost expenditure. Very seldom will either the lowest possible total cost or the highest attainable customer service constitute the desirable logistics strategy. A well-designed logistical effort must have high customer response capability while controlling operational variance and minimizing inventory commitment.

Significant advances have been made in the development of tools to aid management in the measurement of cost/service trade-offs. Formulation of a sound strategy requires a capability to estimate cost required to achieve alternative service levels. Likewise, alternative levels of system performance are meaningless unless viewed in terms of overall business unit marketing and manufacturing strategies.

Leading-edge firms realize that a well-designed and operated logistical system can help achieve competitive advantage. The melding of human and physical assets required to create a cost-effective logistical system is difficult for a competitor to duplicate. The design and implementation of such a system cannot be developed and put into place without considerable managerial and financial commitment to training and development over an extended period of time. *As a general rule, firms*

---

[8]For a classic foundation in transactional cost analysis, see Oliver E. Williamson, *Markets and Hierarchies: Analysis and Antitrust Implications,* New York: The Free Press, 1975. For more current information on activity-based costing and direct product profitability, see Robin Cooper and Robert S. Kaplan, ''Profit Priorities from Activity-Based Costing,'' *Harvard Business Review,* **69:**3, May–June 1991, pp. 130–135; Robin Cooper and Robert S. Kaplan, ''Measure Costs Right: Make the Right Decision,'' *Harvard Business Review,* **66:**5, September–October 1988, pp. 96–103; and *Direct Product Profit Manual,* Food Marketing Institute, 1986. This topic is developed in Chapter 21.

that obtain a strategic advantage based on logistical competency establish the nature of their industry's competition.

Given this brief overview, one can appreciate why well-managed firms devote great attention to developing and continuously improving their logistical competency. Such has not always been the case. To complete the foundation for the study of logistics management, it is useful to gain some understanding of how and why logistics has gained boardroom attention.

THE LOGISTICAL RENAISSANCE

Prior to the 1950s, the typical enterprise performed the work of logistics purely on a functional basis. No formal concept or theory of integrated logistics existed.[9]

The neglect of logistics during this evolution of marketing can be attributed to three important factors. First of all, before computers and quantitative techniques were widely available, there was no reason to believe that logistical functions could be integrated or that such cross-functional integration would improve overall performance. In the decades that followed, changes in logistical management practices began to evolve. Emerging information technology was not to be denied the fertile arena of logistics. Early computer applications and quantitative techniques focused on improving performance of specific logistical functions such as order processing, forecasting, inventory control, transportation, and so forth. The potential for achieving significant improvement sparked interest in cross-functional integration.

A second major factor contributing to a change in overall management attitude was the volatile economic climate. The continuous pressure for profit improvement that began in the early 1950s along with erratic market conditions has continued into the 1990s. To date, this profit pressure focuses managerial attention on cost containment, avoidance, and reduction. Logistics to this day remains a relatively untapped arena for productivity improvement.

Thus, technology and economic necessity combined in the 1950s to spark change in logistical practice that continues today. However, attempts to develop integrated logistics management faced significant opposition in many firms. Managers who had traditionally been responsible for specific functions, such as transportation or purchasing, were often suspicious of organizational changes that were considered essential to the implementation of the broader processes of logistics. The basic idea that overall total cost might be reduced by increased spending in a specific

---

[9]Numerous early references to logistics can be located in business literature. Arch W. Shaw, *An Approach to Business Problems,* Cambridge, Mass.: Harvard University Press, 1916, pp. 101–110, discussed the strategic aspects of physical distribution. Other early references are found in Fred E. Clark, *Principles of Marketing,* New York: Macmillan Publishing Co., Inc., 1922; Theodore N. Beckman, *Wholesaling,* New York: The Ronald Press Company, 1926; Percival White, *Scientific Marketing Management,* New York: Harper and Row, 1927; Ralph Borsodi, *The Distribution Age,* New York: Appleton-Century-Crofts, 1929; and Richard Webster, "Careless Physical Distribution: A Monkey-Wrench in Sales Management Machinery," *Sales Management,* **19,** July 6, 1929, p. 21. For a comprehensive review of early literature, see Bernard J. LaLonde and Leslie M. Dawson, "Early Development of Physical Distribution Thought," in *Reading in Physical Distribution Management,* New York: Macmillan Publishing Co., Inc., 1969, pp. 9–18. The historical review presented in this introduction is updated from an article originally published in 1969; see Donald J. Bowersox, "Physical Distribution Development, Current Status and Potential," *Journal of Marketing,* **33,** January 1969, pp. 63–70.

functional area was difficult to defend, given traditional accounting and performance measurement practice. For example, traffic managers had traditionally been measured by transportation expenditure expressed as a percentage of sales. Given traditional accounting, spending more on transportation to achieve superior customer service performance or in an effort to lower total cost could be viewed as deterioration of transport management. It is understandable why all managers did not embrace integrated logistics with equal enthusiasm.

A third deterrent to widespread adoption of integrated logistics was the difficulty in quantifying the hard core return on investment that could be achieved. In part, quantification problems resulted from a general managerial failure to develop a clear understanding of the true cost of inventory. Given general accounting procedures, it was difficult to place a specific financial return on reducing inventory investment or to quantify the value of superior customer service performance. In short, many logisticians had serious difficulty in selling logistical integration to senior executives schooled in functional management and traditional accounting procedures.

These basic factors, coupled with natural resistance to change, meant that not all initial efforts to implement logistical principles were successful. Several attempts to implement new concepts failed. The would-be logistician was often viewed as an empire builder out for personal gain. Such natural suspicion, along with a ''Don't fix it if it ain't broke'' mentality, combined to stifle many early attempts to introduce logistical process management. However, because of a few outstanding success stories, the fundamental concept of integrated logistics survived.

During the 1980s and early 1990s logistics practice underwent a renaissance that involved more change than in all decades combined since the industrial revolution.[10] The most significant drivers of this change were (1) significant regulatory change, (2) microprocessor commercialization, (3) the information revolution, (4) widespread adoption of quality initiatives, and (5) the growth of partnerships and strategic alliances. A brief discussion of the impact of each is essential to understanding where best practice logistics currently stands and where it appears to be headed.

Regulatory Change

Within a few months in the summer and fall of 1980, the economic and political infrastructure of transportation in the United States was cast on a radical course of reform as a result of the passage of the Motor Carrier Regulatory Reform and

---

[10]For materials that elaborate on the strategic potential of logistical management, see Roy D. Shapiro, ''Get Leverage from Logistics,'' *Harvard Business Review,* **62:**3, May–June 1984, pp. 119–126; and Graham Sharman, ''The Rediscovery of Logistics,'' *Harvard Business Review,* **62:**5, September–October 1984, pp. 71–79. Also see Ronald H. Ballou, *Business Logistics Management,* 3d ed., Englewood Cliffs, N.J.: Prentice-Hall, Inc., 1992; Roy W. Shapiro and James L. Heskett, *Logistics Strategy: Cases and Concepts,* St. Paul, Minn.: West Publishing Company, 1985; and George Stalk, Philip Evans, and Lawrence E. Shulman, ''Competing on Capabilities: The New Rules of Corporate Strategy,'' *Harvard Business Review,* **70:**2, March–April 1992, pp. 57–69.

Modernization Act (MCA-80) and the Staggers Rail Act.[11] While the basic intent underlying each act was significantly different, in combination they created an environment for transportation innovation. The years following legislative enactment were characterized by a wide range of administrative and judicial actions that further relaxed restraints concerning services, prices, and commitments provided by common and contract carriers. Similar deregulatory efforts occurred in various nations throughout the world. Regulatory modification also changed the range of permissible private transportation. From 1980 forward, the transportation structure of the United States has radically changed. The 1993 passage of the Negotiated Rates Act followed by the August 8, 1994, signing of the Airport and Airway Improvement Act, which preempted intrastate trucking regulation, and the August 26, 1994, Trucking Industry Regulatory Reform Act (TIRRA), which further reduced federal regulation, all combined to push transportation closer to a free market system.

Chapter 11 offers comprehensive coverage of significant changes in transportation regulation and the resultant impact on logistical performance. While the economic impact on shipper and carrier operations has been significant, one collateral benefit of transportation deregulation is often overlooked. As a result of the widespread general publicity that deregulation continues to receive, senior management attention is increasingly attracted to rethinking traditional practice. The boardroom became more receptive to hearing about logistical solutions for productivity improvement.

Microprocessor Commercialization

Many experts predicted that the commercialization of microprocessor technology and distributed data processing during the early 1980s would ultimately eliminate mainframe transaction computing. This prediction began to move closer to reality in the early 1990s. The logistical sector was a willing recipient of this new distributed, high-powered computing technology. Low-cost data processing was particularly significant to logistics operations, which remain among the biggest users of a firm's computer resources.

Microcomputers are now abundant in most logistical organizations. Low-cost hardware combined with advanced software provides the computing power to complete most transaction, performance control, and decision support information processing at the user level. Software that permits microprocessors to participate interactively in distributed processing with mainframe resident database management systems has been available since the mid-1980s.

The impact of the microprocessor on integrated logistics has been far-reaching. Computing resources are available to manage overall logistics as an integrated process from procurement through manufacturing to finished goods distribution. The capability to engage in logistical resource planning of these interrelated areas using a relational database offers an information foundation for achieving unprec-

---

[11]Public Laws 96-296 and 96-488, respectively. These laws, as well as others briefly noted here, are discussed in greater detail in Chapter 11.

edented levels of logistical performance.[12] The fact is that new generations of more powerful and less expensive hardware scheduled to be available in the 1990s, combined with open systems architecture, will continue to stimulate information-driven logistical innovation.

The Information Revolution

The impact of new communication technology upon logistical performance paralleled development of the microprocessor. For example, during the 1980s managers began to experiment with how to utilize bar code technology to improve logistical performance. They also began to use electronic data interchange (EDI) to facilitate data transfer between businesses. The immediate impact of all types of electronic scanning and transfer was an increase in the availability of timely information regarding nearly every aspect of logistical performance. Many firms began to experiment with computer-to-computer linkages with customers and suppliers to facilitate timely and accurate information transfer and database access.

By the early 1990s it was clear that even more powerful communication technologies were on the verge of commercialization. The capability to transmit sight, sound, and written messages is predicted to become increasingly available and economical. Many firms began to experiment with voice-activated technologies to facilitate accuracy and ease of access. The facsimile (fax) became a widespread mode of communication offering an easy-to-use and low-cost method of exchanging hard-copy documents. The ability to track information on a real-time basis via satellite communications introduced a Star Wars aura to logistical operations. The result of fast, accurate, and comprehensive information technology introduced the era of time-based logistics. Operational arrangements based on quick and reliable information exchange provided the basis for new strategies to achieve excellent logistical performance. Examples include just-in-time (JIT), quick-response (QR), continuous replenishment (CR), and automatic replenishment (AR) strategies. These techniques, discussed in detail in Chapter 16, offer a way to elevate logistical performance while simultaneously reducing inventory exposure to a minimum.

For the foreseeable future, the impact of communication technology on logistical practice will offer continued opportunity to improve process integration. For over a decade the one aspect of logistics that continues to reduce in effective cost is information.[13] In contrast, most other components of logistical cost have increased equal to or greater than the prevailing inflation rate.

Quality Initiatives

One of the most important drivers of logistical change was the widespread adoption of total quality management (TQM) throughout industry. At some time during the

---

[12]The overall area of how computers and information technology affect logistics and how they are used is the focus of Chapter 6.

[13]For thoughts throughout time regarding the cost and impact of information technology on logistical performance, see Andrew Kerr, "Information Technology: Creating Strategic Opportunities for Logistics," *International Journal of Physical Distribution and Materials Management,* **19:**5, 1989, pp. 15–17; and Alan J. Stenger, "Information Systems in Logistics Management: Past, Present, and Future," *Transportation Journal,* **26:**1, 1986, pp. 65–82.

growth and prosperity of the post-World War II years, many industrialized nations forgot the basic message of "doing things right the first time." Led by the challenges of serious global competition, industrialized nations of the world were forced to take the benefits of quality seriously. The idea of zero defects in products and services quickly expanded to logistical operations. Firms began to realize that an otherwise excellent product delivered late or damaged was not acceptable. Poor logistical performance served to eradicate product quality initiatives. While quality pioneers like W. Edwards Deming and Joseph M. Juran helped managers worldwide understand the "quest for quality," little direction was given on how to achieve quality in the logistical process.[14] The magic pipeline of an industrialized nation never rests. Maintaining quality in a process that takes place across a global playing field and occurs 168 hours each and every week is a monumental challenge. The sidebar on quality in the automotive industry illustrates the challenges and rewards.

Widespread senior management commitment to quality initiatives became a serious force demanding increased logistical performance. It became clear that a "plain vanilla" or "one size fits all" approach to logistics would not meet quality requirements. Firms were forced to reengineer their logistics systems to satisfy a variety of different customer expectations. For example, a manufacturer with twenty key customers who, in combination, make up over 80 percent of all sales must understand that the same level of logistical performance will not fully satisfy the requirements of all accounts. Leading-edge firms typically implement a portfolio of unique logistical solutions to accommodate the quality-driven expectations of each key customer. Thus, quality concerns served to drive best logistical thinking from a pure efficiency focus toward becoming a strategic resource.

Alliances

The decade of the 1980s marked a period when the idea of developing partnerships and alliances became basic to best logistics practice. After decades during which business relationships were characterized by power-based adversarial negotiations, managers began to appreciate the potential of cooperation. The most basic form of cooperation is developing efficient interorganizational working arrangements. Firms went even further and began to think of both customers and suppliers as business partners. The idea was to reduce duplication and waste by concentrating on ways of doing business that facilitated joint success.[15]

The development of alliances transcends a wide variety of different research and operational areas within and between business and government organizations. The general notion of developing cooperative working arrangements was institu-

[14]For an in-depth examination of the philosophies of Deming and Juran, see Mary Walton, *Deming Management at Work,* New York: Putnam, 1990; and Joseph M. Juran, *Juran on Leadership for Quality,* New York: The Free Press, 1989.

[15]For a broad discussion of alliances, see Donald J. Bowersox, "The Strategic Benefits of Logistics Alliances," *Harvard Business Review,* **68:**4, July–August 1990, pp. 36–45; Russell Johnston and Paul R. Lawrence, "Beyond Vertical Integration: The Rise of the Value-Adding Partnership," *Harvard Business Review,* **66:**4, July–August 1988, pp. 94–101; Kenichi Ohmae, "The Global Logic of Strategic Alliances," *Harvard Business Review,* **67:**2, March–April 1989, pp. 143–154; and Rosabeth Moss Kanter, "Collaborative Advantage: The Art of Alliances," *Harvard Business Review,* **72:**4, July–August 1994, pp. 96–108.

Get lost. That's essentially what Buick Motor Division told Michael A. Plumley in 1983. Citing poor-quality parts, the General Motors Corp. unit dropped Plumley Co., which since 1967 had been a supplier of hoses and other rubber gear. But instead of quitting, Plumley fought back. It stepped up worker training and started a quality drive that has taken it to the front ranks of America's auto-parts industry. Today, the $80 million company holds quality awards from GM, Chrysler, and Nissan, and is one of 16 suppliers in the world to have earned Ford's Total Quality Excellence (TQE) award.

Pushed by their customers, a handful of small U.S. parts makers have remade themselves into industry pacesetters. They have retrained their employees, upgraded equipment, and worked to make their own suppliers comply with ever more demanding standards. They didn't have the resources of such corporate giants as Xerox Corp. or Motorola Inc., so they compensated. "It's a little bit of smarts, a lot of hard work, and constancy of purpose," says Plumley, chairman and CEO of Plumley Co.

To identify these top-drawer outfits, *Business Week* asked consultant ELM International Inc. in East Lansing, Michigan, to search its data base for auto suppliers that had won quality awards from at least two of Detroit's Big Three and also from one Japanese transplant. More than half of these 48 suppliers were the U.S. units of such Japanese heavy-weights as Nippondenso Co., the world's largest independent auto-parts maker. Most of the rest were major players or their divisions: Good-

year, Michelin, the Spicer Universal Joint Division of Dana Corp. But a handful of them were small companies.

At first glance, three of the group have little in common. At the Springfield (Tennessee) plant of Perstorp Components Inc., chemicals and recycled plastics are mixed in large vats, poured out like cookie dough, then cut and baked into noise-deafening floor insulation for Ford Rangers and Jeep Grand Cherokees. Manchester Stamping Corp. in Manchester, Michigan, cranks out brackets, door latches and other steel parts—most no larger than your hand—from a row of metal presses. At Plumley's Paris (Tennessee) factories, some workers carefully glue oil retaining rubber seals to engine parts, while others make, bend and trim rubber engine hoses into pretzel-like shapes.

BACK TO SCHOOL

All three share one distinction, however: an unwavering focus on excellence. "Customer satisfaction is as good a definition of quality as there is," says Art Mulwitz, Perstorp's vice-president for operations. "The key to pleasing your customers is not shipping mistakes." Sounds simple, but some of these manufacturers weren't even sure how many mistakes were getting out the door when they began to look inward.

In the early 1980s, Ford Motor Co. insisted that parts makers jump into statistical process-control classes to learn how to limit variations in production. Number-

tionalized in 1984 by the enactment of the National Cooperative Research and Development Act and the Production Amendments of 1993.[16] This national legislation and its subsequent modification signaled fundamental change in traditional antitrust enforcement of the Justice Department. Firms were quick to respond with a wide variety of new and innovative arrangements. The practice of outsourcing selected logistical activities to specialists grew rapidly in the 1980s. Logistics-based alliances became one of the most visible examples of cooperative arrange-

[16]On October 11, 1984, President Reagan signed into law the National Cooperative Research Act of 1984 (Public Law 98-462) in an effort "to promote research and development, encourage innovation, stimulate trade, and make necessary and appropriate modifications in the operation of the antitrust laws." This law enables research and development activities to be jointly performed up to the point where prototypes are developed. The law further determined that antitrust litigation would be based on rule of reason, taking into account all factors affecting competition. An extension to this act was signed into law by President Clinton on June 10, 1993. The extension, National Cooperative Production Amendments of 1993 (Public Law 103-42), allows joint ventures to go beyond just research to include the production and testing of a product, process, or service. This creates a new act called the National Cooperative Research and Production Act of 1993 to replace the 1984 act. Furthermore, this new act establishes a procedure for business to notify the Department of Justice and the Federal Trade Commission of their cooperative arrangement in order to qualify for "single-damages limitation on civil antitrust liability."

crunching wasn't all they learned. Plumley, for example, found that an inspector responsible for measuring hoses couldn't read a ruler. In mid-1984, the company began remedial classes for workers. Since then, more than 65 have earned a high-school general equivalency degree.

Now, new hires get 14 hours of training: 10 in statistics, 4 in problem-solving techniques. Manchester Stamping pays tuition and book fees for employees who manage at least a "C" average at any school—technical, junior college, or the University of Michigan. At any given time, 10 of the company's 80 employees are enrolled somewhere. "I'd like to see 50% of our people doing it," says President and CEO Wayne T. Hamilton. As Plumley's employees got better at monitoring quality, they grew dissatisfied with their machinery, which couldn't produce parts at tight enough tolerances. So the company spent $28 million to upgrade. The other two companies have followed suit. For instance, Perstorp's investments included a $20,000 shop-floor computer that automatically plots quality charts showing how many pieces of insulation are outside the acceptable thickness limits of 2.912 mm to 2.988 mm.

Relieving workers of drawing such graphs saved the company more than $40,000 in the first year, says Mulwitz. Meanwhile, Manchester replaced virtually all of its presses—a four-year, $4 million expenditure.

Just as the auto makers had, parts makers came down hard on their suppliers. Manchester had more than 30 steel suppliers in 1985; today, it has five. And now that it's writing bigger orders, it can demand faster service

on, say, a new alloy for a special part. Plumley tracks its suppliers' performance and invites the best to an annual ceremony and golf match.

THE PAYOFF

All this pays tangible dividends. At Perstrop, waste is down to 0.7% of sales from 2.5% a few years ago, and the company has become a model of quality control for its parent, Perstorp AB, a Swedish chemical company. Plumley's TQE status allows it to look at—and prepare bids on—future Ford projects ahead of its competitors. Manchester's Hamilton says its award from Honda Motor Corp.'s Marysville (Ohio) plant has opened the door for work with other Japanese carmakers.

Still, the task never ends. In mid-November, Plumley learned that it won't get its sixth straight Quality Master Award this year from Nissan. Likewise, Manchester may not get a repeat nod from Honda. It shipped a single bad part this year out of some 2 million, the result of a plating mistake that a subcontractor made after Manchester had stamped the part. "We didn't do it, but we're still responsible for it," says Hamilton. He laughingly recalls being proud in 1989, when 99.9996% of the parts Manchester shipped were defect-free. Now that perfection is within reach, such performance just isn't good enough.

From James B. Treece, "Quality," *Business Week,* Nov. 30, 1992, pp. 70–71. Reprinted with permission from McGraw-Hill, Inc.

ments.[17] Many logistical alliances were built around the competencies of specialized service firms that offered efficient operating systems to link buyers and sellers. Chapter 4, dealing with supply chain relationships, provides a more in-depth look at the role of alliances in logistics. Aspects related to managing alliances are discussed in Chapter 20. The sidebar illustrates how Sun Microsystems Inc. has utilized cooperative arrangements to gain efficiency.

In summary, the fifteen-year period from 1980 to 1995 represented a logistical renaissance. Landmark changes in regulatory infrastructure, the availability of low-cost computing, the revolution in information technology, widespread quality initiatives, and the universal acceptance of alliances all combined to create renewed thinking regarding almost every facet of logistics. It became increasingly clear that some managers learned and benefited far better than others from the lessons of these developmental years. Those who learned best were able to reengineer their firm's logistical competencies to the point that operational excellence became a

[17]Donald J. Bowersox, "The Strategic Benefits of Logistics Alliances," *Harvard Business Review,* **68**:4, July–August 1990, pp. 36–45.

fundamental part of their basic business strategy. This book seeks to capture the lessons learned from their experience.

DEVELOPMENT PROFILE

Overall logistical management is concerned with operations and coordination. Operations deal with strategic movement and storage. To complete the total operations mission, attention must be directed to integrating physical distribution, manufacturing support, and procurement into a single logistical process. These three areas, functioning as an integrated and coordinated process, can best provide operational management of materials, semifinished components, and finished products moving between locations, supply sources, and customers of an enterprise.

The mission of the logistical system is measured in terms of total cost and performance. Performance measurement is concerned with the availability of inventory, operational capability, and quality of effort. Logistical costs are directly related to desired level of performance. As a general rule, the greater the desired performance, the higher the total logistics cost. The key to effective logistical performance is to develop a balanced effort of service performance and total-cost expenditure.

This first chapter introduced and traced the development of key concepts and served to link superior logistical performance to enterprise strategy. The overall text is divided into four parts. The objective of Part One is to introduce and discuss integrated logistics. This initial chapter, plus the remaining chapters of Part One, provide a strategic orientation to logistical operations and control. Chapter 2 provides a detailed treatment of interfaces and requirements that drive internal logistical integration. In Chapter 3, the nature of customer service and the relationship of logistics to marketing strategy are discussed. Supply chain relationships, including the role of logistics services suppliers, are discussed in Chapter 4. Chapter 5 provides an overview of global logistics. All indicators suggest that the years ahead will require increased globalization of logistical systems.

The subject matter of Part Two is presented in ten chapters that cover the functional areas of a logistical system. Chapter 6, on information technology, develops logistical information requirements, including order management. Chapter 7 deals with forecasting. Inventory is covered in Chapters 8 and 9. Transportation infrastructure, regulation, and management are presented in Chapters 10, 11, and 12, respectively. Chapter 13 covers warehousing. Material handling is treated in Chapter 14. Packaging is the subject of Chapter 15. The chapters in Part Two are supported by short problems to highlight typical logistics decisions in each area.

Part Three is concerned with logistical system design. Chapter 16 is devoted to the formulation of logistics strategy. Chapter 17 presents the foundations of logistical integration theory. Chapter 18 develops system planning and design methodology. Chapter 19 is devoted to design techniques.

In Part Four, emphasis shifts to administration. Chapter 20 is devoted to organization. Chapter 21 covers planning, costing, and pricing. Chapter 22 discusses performance measurement and reporting. Chapter 23 offers concluding commentaries concerning future logistics challenges.

SUN IS SHINING—WITH A LOT OF HELP FROM ITS FRIENDS

For years, Sun Microsystems Inc. had big problems shipping its workstations on time. Customers could wait weeks for orders. Things got so bad finally that Sun just gave up. It shut down its 18 distribution centers around the world and turned the work over to Federal Express Corp. and others. "A few people thought we were insane," admits Robert J. Graham, vice-president for worldwide operations. But Sun subsequently set shipment records.

Even as the company, based in Mountain View, California, has blossomed into a $3.6 billion operation, its management has heeded a simple corporate commandment: Thou shalt not do thyself what others can do better.

RELYING ON OTHERS

By hiring others to do everything from circuit-board assembly to customer support, Sun can focus on the things it does best: designing microprocessors, writing software, and marketing workstations. And to help keep those core functions efficient, Sun has split them among several independent subsidiaries, each chartered to make a profit. "That's the only way to run the computer business," says Chief Executive Scott G. McNealy. Indeed, it seems rivals such as IBM and Digital Equipment Corp. are beginning to agree.

Perhaps the best symbol of Sun's approach is how it handles its crown jewel, the Sparc microprocessor. When Sun created Sparc in 1987, it couldn't afford a chip factory, so it licensed Texas Instruments, Fujitsu, Cypress Semiconductor, and others to make them in competition with each other. Today, Sun could afford to make its own chips, but it still doesn't. Why? Because the $500 million that it would require buys lots of engineering and marketing. Likewise, Sun avoids spending millions building and staffing factories by contracting work out to manufacturers such as Solectron Corp. While doubling shipments since 1990, Sun has cut its manufacturing work force by 10%, to just 2,000 people. And it has Eastman Kodak Co., Bell Atlantic Business Systems Inc., and others do the repairs on its machines in the field.

DIFFERENT LEAGUE

The results are dazzling. Sun's 12,800 employees generate $280,000 each in annual sales, topping all but Silicon Graphics Inc. in the workstation market and putting Sun in a different league from, say, IBM, which gets $188,000 per employee. Marvels Goldman, Sachs & Co. analyst John C. Levinson: "They blow everybody away on almost every measure."

Sun's don't-do-it-yourself approach has drawbacks. The SuperSparc microprocessor it developed with Texas Instruments Inc. was a year late, depressing profits. But later, it convened a task force of engineers, purchasing people, and others from Sun and TI to speed things up and get the new MicroSparc chip ready months ahead of schedule.

Still, it's unclear how far Sun can take its lean-and-mean model, especially as it moves into more complex computers. Recently, for example, Sun brought some circuit-board assembly in-house because outside contractors couldn't do it the way Sun needed. Sure, it cost more to do in-house. But, McNealy says, it had to be done to get a new model out faster. Even in a deconstructed computer business, sometimes another rule applies: If you want something done right, do it yourself.

From Robert D. Hof, "Deconstructing the Computer Industry," *Business Week*, Nov. 23, 1992, pp. 92–93. Reprinted with permission from McGraw-Hill, Inc.

Thus, the subject matter development begins with a comprehensive discussion of integrated logistical management (Part One), followed by a detailed treatment of the functional areas that combine to form the logistical system of an enterprise (Part Two). At the conclusion of the first two parts, the stage will be set for in-depth treatment of the two fundamental responsibilities of a logistical manager: system design (Part Three) and administration (Part Four). Short cases are presented following Parts One, Three, and Four to facilitate discussion of key concepts. Selected chapters in Part Two are followed by problems relating to the developed material.

The decision to focus coverage on the individual enterprise made it necessary to select subjects of most concern to overall logistical management and omit others from explicit coverage. Three omissions are noteworthy.

First, all logistical managers have a specific stake in the maintenance of a viable national transportation system. The determination of national policy and the encouragement of sound public investment in the transportation infrastructure require active involvement of logistical professionals at all levels of government. Issues of macrotransportation are not specifically discussed. Chapters 10 and 11 present the background of regulation and review the transportation infrastructure within which logistical systems must be designed. This material introduces the reader to major issues of national policy concern.

Second, the text does not extensively discuss the important subject of logistical ecology. Various aspects of logistical systems, particularly transportation and packaging, are potential causes of environmental pollution. On the positive side, the logistical delivery system is one of the nation's most available resources to help reduce or eliminate ecological problems. For example, solid waste disposal and package-material recycling depend on effective reverse logistical movement for successful transfer of society's waste to processing points. The prime reason for not discussing logistical ecology as a separate topic is an inability to separate practices and responsibilities from overall logistics topical development. Environmental and ecological topics are treated as appropriate throughout the text.

A final note concerns subject matter development and the format used to integrate locational analysis and theory. The network of facilities used in a logistical system provides and limits the potential for operating effectiveness and efficiency. To a large degree, facility location influences all components of the logistical system. To stress these interrelationships when most relevant, locational considerations are discussed at several points throughout the text rather than in one explicit area. In Chapter 2, the network concept of fixed facilities and order cycles is introduced in the structure for logistical functional integration. Location is also an integral part of inventory management discussed in Chapter 9 and transportation infrastructure treated in Chapter 10. The location-related considerations of warehousing are presented in Chapter 13. The integration of spatial and temporal considerations in the formulation of logistical strategy and integration policy is developed in-depth in Chapters 16 and 17. Techniques to assist managers in selecting specific locations are covered in Chapter 19. Although this format has the disadvantage of spreading the treatment of location throughout the text, it has the advantage of developing the salient aspects of location as an integral part of each affected subject area.

QUESTIONS

1 Develop a statement regarding why no formal or integrated concept of logistics prevailed prior to 1950.
2 What is the fundamental logic that supports total-cost analysis?
3 Develop an example to illustrate a trade-off between cost and service.
4 What is strategic positioning? How does logistics relate to the universal processes that all organizations must achieve?

5   Define the meaning of *core competency*. What is required to position a specific activity as a core competency?

6   Discuss how functional integration can benefit logistics and the firm as a whole.

7   Discuss the three measures of logistical service and the importance of each.

8   Why is accurate measurement of inventory availability and operational performance important? Discuss.

9   Describe how consistency and speed affect transportation cost and service.

10   What major factors contributed to what is referred to as the logistical renaissance? Do you agree with the authors' assessment that a renaissance began in the 1980s? Be specific concerning the basis of your agreement or disagreement.

CHAPTER 2

LOGISTICAL OPERATIONS INTEGRATION

THE WORK OF LOGISTICS
  Network Design
  Information
  Transportation
  Inventory
  Warehousing, Material Handling,
    and Packaging
  Conclusion
INTEGRATED LOGISTICS
  Inventory Flow
  Information Flow
OPERATING OBJECTIVES
  Rapid Response
  Minimum Variance
  Minimum Inventory
  Movement Consolidation
  Quality
  Life-Cycle Support

BARRIERS TO INTERNAL INTEGRATION
  Organization Structure
  Measurement Systems
  Inventory Ownership
  Information Technology
  Knowledge Transfer Capability
LOGISTICAL PERFORMANCE CYCLES
  Physical Distribution Performance Cycles
  Manufacturing Support Performance Cycles
  Procurement Performance Cycles
MANAGING OPERATIONAL UNCERTAINTY
SUMMARY
QUESTIONS

In Chapter 1, logistics was positioned within an enterprise as one of the competencies that contributes to the universal process of creating customer value. When logistical operations are highly integrated and positioned as a core competency, they can serve as the cornerstone for strategic advantage. The belief that integrated performance will produce superior results over loosely managed individual functions is the fundamental paradigm of logistics.

Chapter 2 identifies key concepts that are fundamental to planning and achieving logistical integration. The initial section of the chapter reviews the basic work that must be performed to fulfill logistical requirements. The successful execution and coordination of specific jobs that must be performed within the areas of physical distribution, manufacturing support, and procurement are essential to achieving the logistical mission. The second section discusses the framework for operational integration. Activities related to inventory and information flow are discussed in terms of integrating physical distribution, manufacturing support, and procurement. The third section reviews operating objectives that firms seek to achieve through integrated logistics. Next, performance-cycle structure is introduced as the basic unit of analysis to achieve integration. It is through a series of performance cycles that the logistics of an enterprise is operationally linked, both internally and externally, with customers and suppliers to create a supply chain. The basic proposition is that regardless of size and complexity, logistical systems can best be understood and designed in terms of performance-cycle structure and dynamics. The final topic is day-to-day performance-cycle operational variance. Variance in operational performance is the primary source of uncertainty that must be accommodated in logistical systems design and administration.

Some qualifications are in order regarding the formal organization of human resources devoted to logistics. Managers are acutely interested in organizational structure because it directly reflects responsibility, title, compensation, and power. Many managers have the perception that grouping responsibility for all logistical activity into a single organizational unit will automatically stimulate effective integration. This perception is wrong because it emphasizes structure over managerial practice. Formal organization structure alone is not sufficient to guarantee integrated logistical performance. Some of the most highly integrated logistical operations exist without organizational accountability to a single executive. Other enterprises that have highly formalized logistics reporting arrangements also achieve superior results. Generalization regarding how logistics organizations should ideally be structured is premature at this point of subject development. Logistical organization structures vary significantly depending on specific mission, type of business, and available human resources. The goal in creating logistical sensitivity is to stimulate all managers within an enterprise to think and act in terms of *integrated capabilities and economies.* Generalized guidelines regarding logistical organizations are reserved for discussion in Chapter 20, once the foundations of integration are firmly established.

THE WORK OF LOGISTICS

Logistical competency is achieved by coordinating (1) network design, (2) information, (3) transportation, (4) inventory, and (5) warehousing, material handling, and packaging. Work related to these functional areas is combined to create the capabilities needed to achieve logistical requirements. Attention is directed to an introductory discussion of each facet of logistical work and how they interact in a typical business.

Two qualifications are important when discussing logistical work from the vantage point of a single enterprise. First, all firms require the support and cooperation of many other businesses to complete their overall logistical process. Such cooperation unites the firms in terms of common goals, policies, and programs. From the perspective of the total supply chain, efficiency is improved by eliminating duplication and waste. However, cross-organizational coordination requires joint planning and relationship management. The process of developing and managing supply chain relationships is discussed in Chapters 4 and 20.

Second, there are service firms that perform logistical work on behalf of their customers such as transportation carriers or warehouse firms. Such specialists are supplemental to or may be substitutes for a customer's employees performing the involved work. When outside specialists are used in a logistical system, they must be willing to accept reasonable managerial direction and control from their customers. Therefore, while the performance of a specific task may be outsourced to specialists, the contracting firm's management remains responsible for successful performance of the required work.

Network Design

Classical economics neglected the importance of facility location and overall network design. When economists originally discussed supply-and-demand relationships, facility location and transportation cost differentials were assumed to be either nonexistent or equal among competitors. However, the number, size, and geographical relationship of facilities used to perform logistical operations directly affect customer service capabilities and cost. Network design is a primary responsibility of logistical management since a firm's facility structure is used to provide products and materials to customers. Typical logistics facilities are manufacturing plants, warehouses, cross-dock operations, and retail stores. Determining how many of each type of facility are needed, their geographic locations, and the work to be performed at each is a significant part of network design. In specific situations, facility operation may be outsourced to service specialists. Regardless of who does the actual work, all facilities must be managed as an integral part of a firm's logistical network.

The network design requirement is to determine the number and location of all types of facilities required to perform logistics work. It is also necessary to determine what inventory and how much to stock at each facility and where to assign customer orders for shipment. The network of facilities forms a structure from which logistical operations are performed. Thus the network incorporates information and transportation capabilities. Specific work tasks related to processing customer orders, maintaining inventory, and material handling are all performed within the network design framework.

The design of a network must consider geographical variations. The fact that a great deal of difference exists between geographical markets is easy to illustrate. The fifty largest United States metropolitan markets in terms of population account for over 55 percent of all product sales.[1] Therefore an enterprise, marketing on a

---

[1]"Metropolitan Statistical Areas Ranked by Volume of Sales: 1987," United States Department of Commerce, Bureau of the Census, Retail Trade-Geographic Area Series.

national scale, must establish logistical capabilities to service these prime markets. A similar geographic disparity exists in typical material and component part source locations. When a firm is involved in global logistics, issues related to network design become increasingly more complex. The sidebar discussion of Laura Ashley's network design highlights such complexity.

LOCATION REDESIGN

Laura Ashley, based in the United Kingdom, produces women's and children's fashions, curtain and upholstery fabric, wallpaper, linens, and decorating accessories in trademark floral patterns. While it had always maintained excellence in product design and development, Laura Ashley suffered sinking profits because of its complex, costly, and inefficient logistics system. Laura Ashley found that too many carriers and too many systems were resulting in an overall loss of managerial control. To regain control, Laura Ashley had to reorganize its logistical operations. Implementation of Laura Ashley's new logistics structure began with the transfer of all in-house logistics operations to Business Logistics, a division of Federal Express. Business Logistics' task was to restructure, improve, and manage every aspect of the flow of goods and information within the Laura Ashley supply chain.

Prior to reorganization, Laura Ashley had five major warehouses, eight principal carriers, and ten unconnected management systems. The result was extremely long lead times for customers, huge inventories, and too many stockouts. A customer looking for a fast-selling item from a warehouse in Germany would be told that the item was out of stock and that new supplies would not arrive for several months. At the same time, the item could be overstocked in a warehouse in Wales. On average, 16 percent of all product lines were out of stock at the retail stores.

Laura Ashley realized that it needed to reanalyze the location of its current facilities. The recommendation was to close all warehouses except one in the United Kingdom, which would be converted from serving local customers only to serving global customers. The single location, at Newtown, allows close proximity to the manufacturing sites in the United Kingdom. The Newtown facility is a world "processing center," acting as a logistics clearinghouse for Laura Ashley products. While the single hub concept would probably require higher transportation costs, Laura Ashley felt that the cost would be offset by increased efficiency. In the past, the problem of unpredictable demand resulted in higher inventory to cover up uncertainty and maintain customer service.

Laura Ashley knew that it would have more predictable flow with a single service location as opposed to a number of small locations. Random demand could now be pooled over the entire market area, allowing spikes in one area to level out low demand in another. Transportation costs were offset by turn rate in inventory. In fact, Laura Ashley discovered that the single hub system actually decreased transportation costs by reducing the amount of cross shipping. By shipping direct to the retail store from the United Kingdom warehouse, the lead time from order to shipment was about the same but the product was shipped only once instead of being shipped and handled at many different locations.

Laura Ashley has taken its reorganization beyond just cost reduction. The firm now sees the opportunity to increase service and flexibility, and it plans to resupply shops anywhere in the world within twenty-four to forty-eight hours. Advanced systems and communications will be used to monitor and control world inventory. Federal Express's global carrier networks will ensure that goods arrive at their destination in time. Laura Ashley also plans to launch a mail-order business that will feature forty-eight hour delivery to the end consumer's door anywhere in the world. Its current $10 million mail-order business has been growing strong, but until now the company had to limit growth because it could not keep up with expanding orders. The new superior location network will make this growth possible and profitable.

Based on information provided by Larry Stevens, "Back from the Brink," *Inbound Logistics,* September 1992, pp. 20–23; and company-specific information printed by Federal Express Business Logistics Europe.

The importance of continuously modifying the facility network to accommodate change in demand-and-supply infrastructures cannot be overemphasized. Product assortments, customers' supplies, and manufacturing requirements are constantly changing in a dynamic, competitive environment. Although relocation of all logistics facilities being used at one time is inconceivable, considerable latitude exists in relocation or redesign of specific facilities. Over time all facilities should be evaluated to determine if their location is desirable. The selection of a superior locational network can provide the first step toward competitive advantage. Logistical efficiency is directly dependent on and limited by the network structure. Specifics to guide location decisions are treated throughout the text when appropriate to provide comprehensive coverage.

Information

The importance of information to logistical performance has historically not been highlighted. This neglect resulted from the lack of suitable technology to generate desired information. Management also lacked full appreciation and in-depth understanding of how fast and accurate communication could improve logistical performance. Both of these historical deficiencies have been eliminated. Current technology is capable of handling the most demanding information requirements. If desired, information can be obtained on a real-time basis. Managers are learning how to use such information technology to devise new and unique logistical solutions.

However, the technology is only as good as the quality of information. Deficiencies in the quality of information can create countless operational problems. Typical deficiencies fall into two broad categories. First of all, information received may be incorrect with respect to trends and events. Because a great deal of logistics takes place in anticipation of future requirements, an inaccurate appraisal or forecast can cause inventory shortage or overcommitment. Overly optimistic forecasts may result in improper inventory positioning. Second, information related to order processing may be inaccurate with respect to a specific customer's requirements. The processing of an incorrect order creates all the cost of logistics but typically does not result in a sale. Indeed, logistics costs are often increased by the expense of inventory return and, if the sales opportunity still exists, the cost of once again trying to provide the desired service. Each error in the composition of information requirements creates potential disturbance for the total supply chain.

The benefit of fast information flow is directly related to the balance of work procedures. It makes little sense for a firm to accumulate orders at a local sales office for a week, mail them to a regional office, process the orders on a batch basis, assign them to a distribution warehouse, and then ship them via air to achieve fast delivery. Electronic data interchange (EDI) from the customer's office with slower surface transportation may have achieved even faster overall delivery at a lower total cost. The key objective is to balance components of the logistical system.

Forecasting and order management are two areas of logistical work that depend on information. The logistics forecast is an effort to estimate future requirements.

The forecast is used to guide the positioning of inventory to satisfy anticipated customer requirements. Logistics managers' track record in forecasting is not impressive. Therefore, one of the main reasons managers use information to achieve positive control of logistical operations is their desire to replace forecasting inaccuracy with faster response to customer requirements. Control concepts such as just-in-time (JIT), quick response (QR), and continuous replenishment (CR) represent approaches to positive logistical control made possible by the application of recently developed information technology.[2] One of the main jobs of logistics managers is to plan and implement their firm's strategy regarding the desired combination of forecasting and operational control.

Order management concerns the work involved in handling specific customer requirements. The customer order is the main transaction in logistics. Logistics services both external and internal customers. External customers are those that consume the product or service and any trading partners that purchase products or services for resale. Internal customers are organizational units within a firm that require logistical support to perform their designated work. The process of order management involves all aspects of managing customer requirements from initial order receipt to delivery, invoicing, and often collection. The logistics capabilities of a firm can be only as good as its order management competency.

The more efficient the design of a firm's logistical system, the more sensitive it is to information accuracy. Finely tuned time-based logistical systems have no excess inventory to accommodate operational errors because safety stocks are held to a minimum. Incorrect information and delays in order processing can cripple logistics performance. Information flow renders a logistical system dynamic. Thus, quality and timeliness of information are key factors in logistical operations. Chapter 6 provides an in-depth discussion of information technology and logistical requirements, including specific treatment of forecasting and order management.

Transportation

Given a facility network and information capability, transportation is the operational area of logistics that geographically positions inventory. Because of its fundamental importance and visible cost, transportation has received considerable managerial attention over the years. Almost all enterprises, big and small, have managers responsible for transportation.

Transportation requirements can be accomplished in three basic ways. First of all, a private fleet of equipment may be operated. Second, contracts may be arranged with transport specialists. Third, an enterprise may engage the services of a wide variety of carriers that provide different transportation services on an individual shipment basis. These three forms of transport are typically referred to as *private, contract,* and *common carriage.* From the logistical system viewpoint, three factors are fundamental to transportation performance: cost, speed, and consistency.

The *cost* of transport is the payment for movement between two geographical locations and expenses related to administration and maintaining in-transit inven-

---

[2]These concepts are developed in detail in Chapter 16, which focuses on logistical strategy.

tory. Logistical systems should be designed to utilize transportation that minimizes total system cost. This means that the least expensive transportation does not always result in the lowest total cost of movement.

Speed of transportation is the time required to complete a specific movement. Speed and cost of transportation are related in two ways. First, transport firms, capable of providing faster service, typically charge higher rates. Second, the faster the transportation service, the shorter the time interval during which inventory is in transit and unavailable. Thus, a critical aspect of selecting the most desirable method of transportation is to balance speed and cost of service.

Consistency of transportation refers to variations in time required to perform a specific movement over a number of shipments. Consistency is a reflection of the dependability of transportation. For years, transportation managers have considered consistency the most important characteristic of quality transportation. If a given movement takes two days one time and six days the next, the unexpected variance can create serious logistical operational problems. If transportation lacks consistency, inventory safety stocks will be required to protect against unpredictable service breakdowns. Transportation consistency affects both the seller's and the buyer's overall inventory commitment and related risk. With the advent of new information technology to control and report shipment status, logistics managers have begun to seek faster service while maintaining consistency. The value of time is important and will be discussed repeatedly. It is also important to understand that the quality of transportation performance is critical to time-sensitive operations. Speed and consistency combine to create the quality aspect of transportation.

In the design of a logistical system, a delicate balance must be maintained between transportation cost and quality of service. In some circumstances low-cost, slow transportation will be satisfactory. In other situations, faster service may be essential to achieve operating goals. Finding and managing the desired transportation mix is a primary responsibility of logistics.

There are three aspects of transportation that managers should keep in mind concerning the logistical network. First, facility selection establishes a network structure that creates the framework of transportation requirements and simultaneously limits alternatives. Second, the total cost of transportation involves more than the freight bill. Third, the entire effort to integrate transport capability into a logistical system may be defeated if delivery service is sporadic and inconsistent. Chapters 10 to 12 develop the role of transportation in the logistics value chain.

Inventory

The inventory requirements of a firm depend on the network structure and the desired level of customer service. Theoretically, a firm could stock every item sold in a facility dedicated to service each customer. Few business operations could afford such a luxurious inventory commitment because the risk and total cost would be prohibitive. The objective is to achieve the desired customer service with the minimum inventory commitment, consistent with lowest total cost. Excessive inventories may compensate for deficiencies in basic design of a logistics network and to some degree inferior management. However, excessive inventory used as a crutch will ultimately result in higher than necessary total logistics cost.

Logistical strategies are designed to maintain the lowest possible financial assets in inventory. The basic goal of inventory management is to achieve maximum turnover while satisfying customer commitments. A sound inventory management policy is based on five aspects of selective deployment: customer segmentation, product requirements, transport integration, time-based requirements, and competitive performance. Each aspect of selectivity is briefly discussed.

Every enterprise that sells products to a variety of customers confronts a range of transaction profitability. Some customers are highly profitable and have growth potential, while others do not. The profitability of a customer's business depends on the products purchased, sales volumes, price, value-added services required, and supplemental activities necessary to develop and maintain an ongoing relationship. Highly profitable customers constitute the core market for an enterprise. Inventory strategies need to be focused on meeting requirements of such core customers. The key to effective segmented logistics rests in the inventory priorities designed to support core customers.

Most enterprises experience a substantial variance in volume and profitability across product lines. If no restrictions are applied, a firm may find that less than 20 percent of all products marketed account for more than 80 percent of total profit. While the so-called 80/20 rule or Pareto principle is common, management can avoid excessive cost by implementing inventory strategies that consider fine-line product classification. A realistic assessment of which low-profit or low-volume products should be carried is the key to avoiding excessive cost. For obvious reasons, an enterprise wants to offer high availability and consistent delivery on more profitable products. High-level support of less profitable items, however, may be necessary to provide full-line service to core customers. The trap to avoid is high service performance on less profitable items purchased by fringe or noncore customers. Therefore, product line profitability must be considered when developing a selective inventory policy. Many enterprises find it desirable to hold slow-moving or low-profit items at a central distribution warehouse. The actual delivery performance can be matched to customer importance when orders are received. Core customers may be serviced by fast, reliable air service, while other orders to fringe customers are delivered by less expensive ground transportation.

Selection of the product assortment to be stocked at a specific facility has a direct impact on transportation performance. Most transportation rates are based on the volume and size of specific shipments. Thus, it may be sound strategy to stock sufficient products at a warehouse to be able to arrange consolidated shipments to a customer or geographic area. The corresponding savings in transportation may more than offset the increased cost of holding the inventory.

Commitments to deliver products rapidly to fulfill customer requirements are important drivers of logistics. Such time-based arrangements seek to reduce overall inventories by developing the capability to respond rapidly to exact requirements of manufacturing or retail customers. If products and materials can be delivered quickly, it may not be necessary to maintain inventories at manufacturing plants. Likewise, if retail stores can be replenished rapidly, less safety stock must be maintained forward in the supply chain. The alternative to stockpiling and holding safety stock is to receive the exact quantity of inventory at the time required. While such time-based programs reduce customer inventory to absolute minimums, the savings must be balanced against other costs incurred in the time-sensitive logistical process. For example, time-based programs tend to reduce shipment sizes, which increases the number, frequency, and cost of shipments. This, in turn, can result in higher transportation costs. For a logistical arrangement to be effective and efficient it must achieve trade-offs that result in the desired customer service at the lowest total cost.

Finally, inventory strategies cannot be created in a competitive vacuum. A firm is typically more desirable to do business with if it can promise and perform rapid and consistent delivery. Therefore, it may be necessary to position inventory in a specific warehouse to provide logistical service even if such commitment increases total cost. Sound inventory policies are essential to gain a customer service advantage or to neutralize a strength that a competitor currently enjoys. Material and component inventories exist in a logistical system for different reasons than finished product inventory. Each type of inventory and the level of commitment must be viewed from a total-cost perspective. Understanding the interrelationship between facility, network, transportation, and inventory decisions is fundamental to integrated logistics. The specifics that lead to a fine-tuned inventory strategy are developed in Chapters 8 and 9.

Warehousing, Material Handling, and Packaging

Four of the functional areas of logistics—network design, information, transportation, and inventory—can be engineered into a variety of different operational arrangements. Each arrangement will have the potential to achieve a level of customer service at an associated total cost. In essence, these four functions combine to create a system solution for integrated logistics. The final functions of logistics—warehousing, material handling, and packaging—also represent an integral part of an operating solution. However, these functions do not have the independent status of the four previously discussed. Warehousing, material handling, and packaging are an integral part of other logistics areas. For example, merchandise typically needs to be warehoused at selected times during the logistics process. Transportation vehicles require material handling for efficient loading and unloading. Finally, the individual products are most efficiently handled when packaged together into shipping cartons or other types of containers.

When warehouses are required in a logistical system, a firm can choose between obtaining the services of a specialist or operating its own facility. The decision is broader than simply selecting a facility to store inventory, since many activities essential to the overall logistical process are typically performed while products are warehoused. Examples of such activities are sorting, sequencing, order selection, transportation consolidation, and, in some cases, product modification and assembly.

Within the warehouse, material handling is an important activity. Products must be received, moved, sorted, and assembled to meet customer order requirements. The direct labor and capital invested in material-handling equipment are a major part of total logistics cost. When performed in an inferior manner, material handling can result in substantial product damage. It stands to reason that the fewer times a product is handled, the less potential exists for product damage, and the overall efficiency of the warehouse is increased. A variety of mechanized and automated devices exist to assist in material handling. In essence, each warehouse and its material-handling capability represent a minisystem within the overall logistical process.

To facilitate handling efficiency, products in the form of cans, bottles, or boxes are typically combined into larger units. The initial unit, the *master carton,* provides two important features. First of all, it serves to protect the product during the logistical process. Second, the master carton facilitates ease of handling by creating one large package rather than a multitude of small, individual products. For efficient handling and transport, master cartons are typically consolidated into larger units. The most common units for master carton consolidation are pallets, slip sheets, and various types of containers.

When effectively integrated into an enterprise's logistical operations, warehousing, material handling, and packaging facilitate the speed and overall ease of product flow throughout the logistical system. In fact, several firms have engineered devices to move broad product assortments from manufacturing plants directly to retail stores without intermediate handling. Details related to warehousing, material handling, and packaging are discussed in Chapters 13, 14, and 15.

Conclusion

In the context of overall business performance, logistics exists to allow inventory to achieve desired time, place, and possession benefits at the lowest total cost. Inventory has little value until it is positioned at the right time and location to support ownership transfer or value-added creation. If a firm does not consistently satisfy time and place requirements, it has nothing to sell. To achieve the maximum strategic benefits of logistics, the full range of functional work must be performed on an integrated basis. Excellence in each aspect of functional work is relevant only when viewed in terms of improving the overall efficiency and effectiveness of integrated logistics. This requires that the functional work of logistics be integrated to achieve business unit goals.

INTEGRATED LOGISTICS

The conceptualization of integrated logistics is illustrated in the shaded area of Figure 2-1. Logistics is viewed as the competency that links an enterprise with its customers and suppliers. Information from and about customers flows through the enterprise in the form of sales activity, forecasts, and orders. The information is refined into specific manufacturing and purchasing plans. As products and materials are procured, a value-added inventory flow is initiated that ultimately results in ownership transfer of finished products to customers. Thus, the process is viewed in terms of two interrelated efforts, inventory flow and information flow. Prior to discussing each flow in greater detail, two observations are in order.

First, viewing internal operations (the shaded area of Figure 2-1) in isolation is useful to elaborate the fundamental importance of integrating all functions and

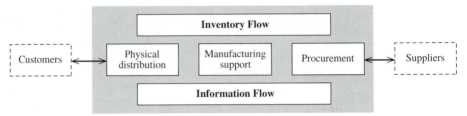

FIGURE 2-1 Logistical integration.

work involved in logistics. While such integration is prerequisite to success, it is not sufficient to guarantee that a firm will achieve its performance goals. To be fully effective in today's competitive environment, firms must expand their integrated behavior to incorporate customers and suppliers. This extension, through external integration, is referred to as *supply chain management* and is covered in Chapter 4.

Second, the basic process illustrated in Figure 2-1 is not restricted to for-profit business, nor is it unique to manufacturing firms. The need to integrate requirements and operations occurs in all businesses as well as within public sector organizations. For example, retailing or wholesaling firms typically link physical distribution and purchasing, since traditional manufacturing is not required. Nevertheless, retailers and wholesalers must complete the logistics value-added process. The same is true of all public sector organizations that manufacture products or provide other services.

Inventory Flow

The operational management of logistics is concerned with movement and storage of materials and finished products. Logistical operations start with the initial shipment of a material or component part from a supplier and are finalized when a manufactured or processed product is delivered to a customer.

From the initial purchase of a material or component, the logistical process adds value by moving inventory when and where needed. Providing all goes well, a material gains value at each step of its transformation into finished inventory. In other words, an individual part has greater value after it is incorporated into a machine. Likewise, the machine has greater value once it is delivered to a buyer.

To support manufacturing, work-in-process inventory must be moved to support final assembly. The cost of each component and its movement becomes part of the value-added process. The final or meaningful value that is added occurs only with final ownership transfer of products to customers when and where specified.

For a large manufacturer, logistical operations may consist of thousands of movements, which ultimately culminate in the delivery of products to an industrial user, retailer, wholesaler, dealer, or other customer. For a large retailer, logistical operations may commence with the procurement of products for resale and may terminate with consumer pickup or delivery. For a hospital, logistics starts with procurement and ends with full support of patient surgery and recovery. The significant point is that regardless of the size and type of enterprise, logistics is essential and requires continuous management attention. For better understanding it is useful to divide logistical operations into three areas: physical distribution, manufacturing support, and procurement. These components are illustrated in the center of Figure 2-1 as the combined logistics operational units of an enterprise.

Physical Distribution The area of *physical distribution* concerns movement of a finished product to customers. In physical distribution, the customer is the final destination of a marketing channel. The availability of the product is a vital part of each channel participant's marketing effort. Even a manufacturer's agent, which typically does not own inventory, must depend on inventory availability to perform expected marketing responsibilities. Unless a proper assortment of products is efficiently delivered when and where needed, a great deal of the overall marketing effort can be jeopardized. It is through the physical distribution process that the time and space of customer service become an integral part of marketing. Thus physical distribution links a marketing channel with its customers. To support the wide variety of marketing systems that exist in a highly commercialized nation, many different physical distribution systems are utilized. All physical distribution systems have one common feature: they link manufacturers, wholesalers, and retailers into marketing channels that provide product availability as an integral aspect of the overall marketing process.

Manufacturing Support The area of *manufacturing support* concentrates on managing work-in-process inventory as it flows between stages of manufacturing. The primary logistical responsibility in manufacturing is to participate in formulating a master production schedule and to arrange for timely availability of materials, component parts, and work-in-process inventory. Thus, the overall concern of manufacturing support is not *how* production occurs but rather *what, when,* and *where* products will be manufactured. Manufacturing support has one significant difference when compared with physical distribution. Physical distribution attempts to service the desires of customers and therefore must accommodate the uncertainty of consumer and industrial demand. Manufacturing support involves movement requirements that are under the control of the manufacturing enterprise. The uncertainties introduced by random customer ordering and erratic demand accommodated by physical distribution are not present in most manufacturing operations. From the viewpoint of overall planning, the separation of manufacturing support from outbound (physical distribution) and inbound (procurement) activities provides opportunities for specialization and improved efficiency.

Procurement *Procurement* is concerned with purchasing and arranging inbound movement of materials, parts, and/or finished inventory from suppliers to manufacturing or assembly plants, warehouses, or retail stores. Depending on the situation, the acquisition process is commonly identified by different names. In manufacturing, the process of acquisition is typically called *purchasing.* In government circles, acquisition has traditionally been referred to as *procurement.* In retailing and wholesaling, *buying* is the most widely used term. In many circles, the process is referred to as inbound logistics. Although differences do exist concerning acquisition situations, the term *procurement* is used here to include all types of purchasing. The term *material* is used to identify inventory moving inbound to an enterprise, regardless of its degree of readiness for resale. The term *product* is used to identify inventory that is available for consumer purchase. In other words, materials are involved in the process of adding value through manufacturing, whereas products are ready for consumption. The fundamental distinction is that products result from the value added to material during manufacturing, sorting, or assembly.

Procurement is concerned with availability of the desired material assortments where and when needed. Whereas physical distribution is concerned with outbound product shipments, purchasing is concerned with inbound materials, sorting, or assembly. Under most marketing situations involving consumer products, such as a grocery manufacturer that ships to a retail food chain, the manufacturer's physical distribution is the same process as a retailer's procurement operations. Although similar or even identical transportation requirements may be involved, the degree of managerial control and risk related to performance failure varies substantially between physical distribution and procurement.

Within a typical enterprise, the three areas of logistics overlap. Viewing each as an integral part of the overall value-adding process creates an opportunity to capitalize on the unique attributes of each while facilitating the overall process. The prime concern of an integrated logistical process is to coordinate overall value-added inventory movement. The three areas combine to provide integrated management of materials, semifinished components, and products moving between locations, supply sources, and customers of the enterprise. In this sense, logistics is concerned with strategic management of total movement and storage. Table 2-1 provides a more exacting definition of the day-to-day work involved in each subprocess of logistics.

Information Flow

Information flow identifies specific locations within a logistical system that have requirements. Information also integrates the three operating areas. The primary objective of developing and specifying requirements is to plan and execute integrated logistical operations. Within individual logistics areas, different movement requirements exist with respect to size of order, availability of inventory, and urgency of movement. The primary objective of information sharing is to reconcile these differentials. In the discussion that follows it is important to stress that information requirements parallel the actual work performed in physical distribution, manufacturing support, and procurement. Whereas these areas contain the actual logistics work, information facilitates coordination of planning and control of day-to-day operations. Without accurate information the effort involved in the logistical system can be wasted.

Logistical information involves two major types of flows: coordination flows and operational flows. The overall relationship between the two logistical infor-

TABLE 2-1 SPECIFIC OPERATING CONCERNS OF PHYSICAL DISTRIBUTION, MANUFACTURING SUPPORT, AND PROCUREMENT IN OVERALL LOGISTICS

Physical distribution
Activities related to providing customer service. Requires performing order receipt and processing, deploying inventories, storage and handling, and outbound transportation within a channel of distribution. Includes the responsibility to coordinate with marketing planning in such areas as pricing, promotional support, customer service levels, delivery standards, handling return merchandise, and life-cycle support. The primary physical distribution objective is to assist in revenue generation by providing strategically desired customer service levels at the lowest total cost.

Manufacturing support
Activities related to planning, scheduling, and supporting manufacturing operations. Requires master schedule planning and performing work-in-process storage, handling, transportation, and time phasing of components. Includes the responsibility for storage of inventory at manufacturing sites and maximum flexibility in the coordination of geographic and final assemblies postponement between manufacturing and physical distribution operations.

Procurement
Activities related to obtaining products and materials from outside suppliers. Requires performing resource planning, supply sourcing, negotiation, order placement, inbound transportation, receiving and inspection, storage and handling, and quality assurance. Includes the responsibility to coordinate with suppliers in such areas as scheduling, supply continuity, hedging, and speculation, as well as research leading to new sources or programs. The primary procurement objective is to support manufacturing or resale organizations by providing timely purchasing at the lowest total cost.

mation flows is illustrated in Figure 2-2. In-depth treatment of information is reserved for Chapter 6, at which time the architecture of logistical information systems is explained in greater detail. The objective at this point is to provide an introductory overview of the information requirements necessary to drive an integrated logistics system.

Planning and Coordination Flows Coordination is the backbone of overall information system architecture among value chain participants. Coordination results in plans specifying (1) strategic objectives, (2) capacity constraints, (3) logistical requirements, (4) inventory deployment, (5) manufacturing requirements, (6) procurement requirements, and (7) forecasting.

The primary drivers of the overall value chain are the *strategic objectives* that result from marketing and financial goals. Strategic objectives detail the nature and location of customers, which are matched to the required products and services to be performed. The financial aspects of strategic plans detail resources required to support inventory, receivables, facilities, equipment, and capacity.

Capacity constraints coordinate internal and external manufacturing requirements. For nonmanufacturing participants in the value chain, this form of capacity planning is not required. Given strategic objectives, capacity constraints identify

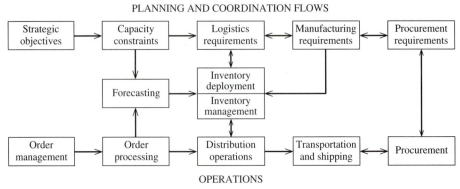

FIGURE 2-2   Logistics information requirements.

limitations, barriers, or bottlenecks within basic manufacturing capabilities and determine appropriate outsource requirements. To illustrate, whereas Kellogg owns the brand and distributes *Cracklin Oat Bran,* all manufacturing is performed by a third party on a contract basis. The result of capacity constraints is a plan that places strategic objectives in a time-phased schedule that details facility utilization, financial resources, and human requirements.

Logistics requirements specify the work that distribution facilities, equipment, and labor must perform to implement the capacity plan. Using inputs from forecasting, promotional scheduling, customer orders, and inventory status, logistics requirements specify value chain performance.

Inventory deployments are the interfaces between planning/coordination and operations that detail the timing and composition of where inventory will be positioned. A major concern of deployment is to balance timing and consolidation to create efficiency as inventory flows through the value chain. Inventory is unique in that it is an integral part of both the planning/coordination and operational flows involved in logistics. From an information perspective, deployment specifies the *what, where,* and *when* of the overall logistics processes. From an operational viewpoint, inventory management is performed as a day-to-day event. Because of this duality, inventory deployment and management are illustrated in Figure 2-2 between the planning/coordination and operational information flows.

In production situations, *manufacturing* plans are derived from logistical requirements and typically result in inventory deployment. The primary deliverable is a statement of time-phased inventory requirements that drives master production scheduling (MPS) and manufacturing requirements planning (MRP). The deliverable from manufacturing requirements is a day-to-day production schedule that can be used to specify material and component requirements.

Procurement requirements schedule material and components for inbound shipment to support manufacturing requirements. In retailing and wholesaling situations, procurement involves maintaining product supplies. In manufacturing situations, purchasing must facilitate inbound materials and component parts from suppliers. Regardless of the situation, purchasing coordinates decisions concerning supplier qualifications, degree of desired speculation, third-party arrangements, and feasibility of long-term contracting.

Forecasting utilizes historical data, current activity levels, and planning assumptions to predict future activity levels. Logistical forecasting is generally concerned with relatively short-term predictions (i.e., less than ninety days). The forecasts predict periodic (usually monthly or weekly) sales levels for each product, forming the basis of logistics requirement and operating plans.

The overall purpose of information planning/coordination flow is to integrate specific activities within a firm and to facilitate overall integrated performance. Unless a high level of coordination is achieved, the potential exists for operating inefficiencies and excessive inventory. Planning/coordination is illustrated in the health care business by the sidebar discussing how hospitals use information to improve efficiency and customer service.

Operational Requirements   The second aspect of information requirements is concerned with directing operations to receive, process, and ship inventory as required to support customer and purchase orders. Operational information requirements deal with (1) order management, (2) order processing, (3) distribution operations, (4) inventory management, (5) transportation and shipping, and (6) procurement.

Order management refers to the transmission of requirements information between value chain members involved in finished product distribution. The primary activity of order management is accurate entry and qualification of customer orders. This transfer of requirements between value chain participants is typically achieved by phone, mail, facsimile (fax), or electronic data interchange. The impact of

---

HOSPITAL'S CURE FOR INEFFICIENCY

Dr. James J. Cimino had a problem. To find out if his patient's confusion was a sign of neurological disease, Cimino needed to test the man's spinal fluid. But scheduling a visit to Columbia Presbyterian Hospital's busy neurology unit was difficult. So he made a note in his computer: Order a spinal tap the next time the patient's chronic heart condition brought him to the New York city hospital's emergency room. Two weeks later, the patient was there. And yes, having read Cimino's note—which was stored with the patient's records in the hospital's computer system—doctors did the spinal tap.

The case exemplifies how reengineering hospitals with sophisticated computer networks can help cure one of medicine's worst ills—inefficiency. "Up to 40% of all hospital costs are related to the generation and stor-

age of information, so it makes sense that information technology can improve efficiency," says Dr. William M. Tierney of Wishard Memorial Hospital in Indianapolis.

Wishard now requires doctors to order all drugs and treatments for patients via computer. The system then automatically warns of potential problems, such as allergic reactions or duplicated tests. Doctors tend to make fewer mistakes and order fewer tests. The result: costs per patient are $900 less. "To stay competitive," concludes Tierney, "doctors really have to get into the electronic medium."

From John Carey, "The Technology Payoff," *Business Week,* June 14, 1993, p. 60. Published with permission from McGraw-Hill, Inc.

information technology on order management is extensive.[3] The availability of low-cost information transfer has revolutionized the order management process.

Order processing allocates inventory and assigns responsibility to satisfy customer requirements. The traditional approach has been to assign available inventory or planned manufacturing to customers according to predetermined priorities. In technology-rich order processing systems, two-way communication linkage can be maintained with customers to generate a negotiated order that satisfies customers within the constraints of planned logistical operations.

Distribution operations involve information flows required to facilitate and coordinate performance within logistics facilities. The primary purpose of a logistical facility is to provide material or product assortments to satisfy order requirements. Emphasis is placed on scheduled availability of the desired assortment with minimal duplication and redundant work effort. The key to distribution operations is to store and handle specific inventory as little as possible while still meeting customer order requirements.

Inventory management is concerned with using information to implement the logistics plan as specified. Using a combination of human resources and information technology, inventory is deployed and then managed to satisfy planned requirements. The work of inventory management is to make sure that the overall logistical system has appropriate resources to perform as planned.

Transportation and shipping information directs the movement of inventory. To achieve efficiency, it is important to consolidate orders so as to fully utilize transportation capacity. It is also necessary to ensure that the required transportation equipment is available when needed. Finally, because ownership transfer often results from transportation, supporting documentation is required.

Procurement is concerned with the information necessary to complete purchase order preparation, modification, and release while ensuring overall supplier compliance. In many ways information related to procurement is similar to that involved in order processing. Both forms of information exchange serve to facilitate operations that link a firm with its customers and suppliers. The primary difference between procurement and order processing is the type of operation that results from requirements transfer.

The overall purpose of operational information is to provide the detailed data required for integrated performance of physical distribution, manufacturing support, and procurement operations. Whereas planning/coordination flows provide information concerning planned activities, operational requirements are needed to direct the day-to-day logistics work. Within the context of information and inventory flows, the managers within an enterprise must achieve some specific objectives to fully exploit logistical competency. The operating objectives of integrated logistics are reviewed next.

---

[3]For more detail, see James R. Stock, ''Managing Computer, Communication and Information Technology Strategically: Opportunities and Challenges for Warehousing,'' *The Logistics and Transportation Review*, **26**:2, June 1990, pp. 132–148; and Lucas D. Introna, ''The Impact of Information Technology on Logistics,'' *International Journal of Physical Distribution and Logistics Management*, **21**:5, 1991, pp. 32–37.

OPERATING OBJECTIVES

In terms of logistical system design and administration, each firm must simultaneously achieve at least six different operational objectives. These operational objectives, which are the primary determinants of logistical performance, include rapid response, minimum variance, minimum inventory, movement consolidation, quality, and life-cycle support. Each objective is briefly discussed.

Rapid Response

Rapid response is concerned with a firm's ability to satisfy customer service requirements in a timely manner. Information technology has increased the capability to postpone logistical operations to the latest possible time and then accomplish rapid delivery of required inventory. The result is elimination of excessive inventories traditionally stocked in anticipation of customer requirements. Rapid response capability shifts operational emphasis from an anticipatory posture based on forecasting and inventory stocking to responding to customer requirements on a shipment-to-shipment basis. Because inventory is typically not moved in a time-based system until customer requirements are known and performance is committed, little tolerance exists for operational deficiencies.

Minimum Variance

Variance is any unexpected event that disrupts system performance. Variance may result from any aspect of logistical operations. Delays in expected time of customer order receipt, an unexpected disruption in manufacturing, goods arriving damaged at a customer's location, or delivery to an incorrect location—all result in a time disruption in operations that must be resolved. Potential reduction of variance relates to both internal and external operations. All operating areas of a logistical system are subject to potential variance. The traditional solution to accommodating variance was to establish safety stock inventory or use high-cost premium transportation. Such practices, given their expense and associated risk, have been replaced by using information technology to achieve positive logistics control. To the extent that variances are minimized, logistical productivity improves as a result of economical operations. Thus, a basic objective of overall logistical performance is to *minimize variance*.

Minimum Inventory

The objective of *minimum inventory* involves asset commitment and relative turn velocity. Total commitment is the financial value of inventory deployed throughout the logistical system. Turn velocity involves the rate of inventory usage over time. High turn rates, coupled with inventory availability, mean that assets devoted to inventory are being effectively utilized. The objective is to reduce inventory deployment to the lowest level consistent with customer service goals to achieve the lowest overall total logistics cost. Concepts like *zero inventory* have become increasingly popular as managers seek to reduce inventory deployment.[4] The reality of reengineering a system is that operational defects do not become apparent until inventories are reduced to their lowest possible level. While the goal of eliminating all inventory is attractive, it is important to remember that inventory can and does facilitate some important benefits in a logistical system. Inventories can provide improved return on investment when they result in economies of scale in manufacturing or procurement. The objective is to reduce and manage inventory to the lowest possible level while simultaneously achieving desired operating objectives. To achieve the objective of *minimum inventory,* the logistical system design must control commitment and turn velocity for the entire firm, not merely for each business location.

Movement Consolidation

One of the most significant logistical costs is transportation. Transportation cost is directly related to the type of product, size of shipment, and distance. Many logistical systems that feature premium service depend on high-speed, small-shipment transportation. Premium transportation is typically high-cost. To reduce transportation cost, it is desirable to achieve *movement consolidation.* As a general rule, the larger the overall shipment and the longer the distance it is transported, the lower the transportation cost per unit. This requires innovative programs to group small shipments for consolidated movement. Such programs must be facilitated by working arrangements that transcend the overall supply chain. Alternative ways to achieve effective consolidation are detailed in Chapter 12.

Quality

A fifth logistical objective is to seek continuous *quality* improvement. Total quality management (TQM) has become a major commitment throughout all facets of industry. As noted in Chapter 1, overall commitment to TQM is one of the major forces contributing to the logistical renaissance. If a product becomes defective or if service promises are not kept, little, if any, value is added by the logistics. Logistical costs, once expended, cannot be reversed. In fact, when quality fails, the logistical performance typically needs to be reversed and then repeated. Logistics itself must perform to demanding quality standards. The management challenge of achieving zero defect logistical performance is magnified by the fact that logistical operations typically must be performed across a vast geographical area at all times of the day and night. The quality challenge is magnified by the fact that most logistical work is performed out of a supervisor's vision. Reworking a customer's order as a result of incorrect shipment or in-transit damage is far more costly than performing it right the first time. Logistics is a prime part of developing and maintaining continuous TQM improvement.

---

[4]For more information, see Robert W. Hall, *Zero Inventories,* Homewood, Ill.: Dow Jones-Irwin, 1983; and K. A. Wantuck, *Just-in-Time for America: A Common Sense Production Strategy,* Milwaukee, Wis.: The Forum, 1989.

Life-Cycle Support

The final logistical design objective is *life-cycle support.* Few items are sold without some guarantee that the product will perform as advertised over a specified period. In some situations, the normal value-added inventory flow toward customers must be reversed. Product recall is a critical competency resulting from increasingly rigid quality standards, product expiration dating, and responsibility for hazardous consequences. Return logistics requirements also result from the increasing number of laws prohibiting disposal and encouraging recycling of beverage containers and packaging materials. The most significant aspect of reverse logistical operations is the need for maximum control when a potential health liability exists (i.e., a contaminated product). In this sense, a recall program is similar to a strategy of maximum customer service that must be executed regardless of cost. Johnson & Johnson's classical response to the Tylenol crisis is an example of turning adversity into advantage. The operational requirements of reverse logistics range from lowest total cost, such as returning bottles for recycling, to maximum performance solutions for critical recalls. The important point is that sound logistical strategy cannot be formulated without careful review of reverse logistical requirements.[5]

Some products, such as copying equipment, derive their primary profit from selling supplies and providing aftermarket service. The importance of service support logistics varies directly with the product and buyer. For firms marketing consumer durables or industrial equipment, the commitment to life-cycle support constitutes a versatile and demanding operational requirement as well as one of the largest costs of logistical operations. The life-cycle support capabilities of a logistical system must be carefully designed. As noted earlier, reverse logistical competency, as a result of worldwide attention to environmental concerns, requires the capacity to recycle ingredients and packaging materials. Life-cycle support, in modern terms, means *cradle-to-cradle* logistical support.[6]

---

[5]James R. Stock, *Reverse Logistics,* Oak Brook, Ill.: The Council of Logistics Management, 1992.

[6]Cradle-to-cradle logistical support means going beyond reverse logistics and recycling to include the possibility of aftermarket service, product recall, and product disposal. All the possible occurrences must be considered early in the design stages of the product to ensure effective life-cycle support. This kind of design process looks at the ways to take back products or processing aids to reuse and recycle them. Some examples include BMW, which is designing cars that can be dismantled easily allowing parts to be recycled. In this way, instead of buying an entirely new car, the customer may just buy parts of a new car and recycle the old parts such as body panels. Dow Chemical is looking at ways to take back solvents used in fertilizers as well as make more soluble products. For information on these examples, see "Growth vs. Environment," *Business Week,* May 11, 1992, pp. 66–75. Another interesting example is found at Levi Strauss & Co., which is using denim scraps to make paper and corrugated boxes in an effort to ensure life-cycle support. This example was discussed in "We Knew There Was a Reason to Save Our Tattered Dungarees," *The Wall Street Journal,* November 30, 1992, p. B1. Currently, this cradle-to-cradle support system is becoming the focus of government directives in an attempt to force companies to operate under a new mind-set. The European Community (EC) is demanding that manufacturers and distributors "take back 60 to 70 percent of all packaging and containers by 1995" as discussed in Andersen Consulting and Cranfield School of Management's *Reconfiguring European Logistics Systems,* Oak Brook, Ill.: The Council of Logistics Management, 1993, p. 241. This means that firms must think not only in terms of how their product is designed, used, and discarded, but also about how the package encasement is handled. Firms now must consider how to initially make a product and its package (cradle) and then how to remake or reuse both (to cradle). In other words, the product and package life cycle must now continuously rejuvenate themselves.

WHY TYLENOL REMAINS NUMBER ONE

Johnson & Johnson's McNeil Consumer Products Division was hit with a major crisis in September 1982. Their top-selling product line, Tylenol, was linked to seven deaths in the Chicago area. At the time of the incident, Tylenol enjoyed 35 percent of the $1 billion analgesic market, but by the end of September, this market share had dropped 80 percent.* Currently, Tylenol is again the top-selling brand with approximately 30 percent of the now $2.7 billion analgesic market.† How was Johnson & Johnson (J&J) able to regain market share and a leading image after such a damaging tragedy? Its recovery was successful because of reverse logistics capability coupled with a marketing strategy that focused on protecting the consumer and going above and beyond what was necessary to instill trust and an image of security. This recovery plan is a positive prototype for other corporations to follow, which, in effect, may increase the potential for voluntary product recalls across a variety of industries.

When the first news reports hit about cyanide-tainted Extra-Strength Tylenol Capsules, J&J was unsure whether the tampering occurred in its manufacturing operations or at the retail level. As such, its first efforts were directed at pinning down the problem. As soon as the lot numbers were identified from the first few deaths, J&J stopped production in the plant responsible. At the same time, it halted all Tylenol commercials nationwide and began recalls that eventually involved 31 million bottles of product, which had a retail value of $100 million.*

Another strategy that J&J took was to work openly and closely with the media. J&J has traditionally maintained a distance from the press, but in this case it felt that openness and honesty would help reduce consumer panic and provide a vehicle for disseminating critical information. A crisis team was put together that included J&J as well as McNeil executives and top managers. This team was quite sure that the tampering had occurred at the retail level since the incident was isolated to Chicago's West Side and other samples from the same lot were normal. Regardless, they began the recall with the remaining 93,000 bottles from this lot. The expenses of this first phase of the recall included $1 million just for phone calls and telegrams to doctors, hospitals, and distributors.*

The sixth poisoning ensured that the tampering was at the retail level since the bottle came from a lot manufactured at its second plant. Since the cause was now isolated, J&J could concentrate on containment. The first step was to advocate a total recall. While this step was in some ways unnecessary, J&J felt it was a key step to ensure consumer confidence. At first, the FBI and FDA advised against a total recall because of the potential psychological response of the person who tampered with the product and the response of consumers in general. However, after a copycat strychnine poisoning in California, all parties agreed that complete removal was the best solution.

This total recall entailed the following: (1) advertisements stating that NcNeil would exchange tablets for capsules, (2) thousands of letters to the trade to explain the incident and recall procedures, (3) media statements, (4) a sales force of over 2,000 employees to contact doctors and pharmacists to regain trust and restore their recommendations that had traditionally served as the main promotional avenue for Tylenol products, (5) an extensive reverse logistics system that included buying products back from retailers and consumers and shipping returns to disposal centers, and (6) creating a tamperproof package. It is estimated that recall costs were at least $100 million, most of which involved the reverse logistics operations.†

By January 1983, the new tamperproof bottles of Tylenol were on the retail shelf. Consumer confidence was obviously regained as a result of the extensive voluntary recall program, effective public relations, and sales programs and repack operations. This confidence was shown by the fact that at the end of the year, Tylenol had regained almost 30 percent of the market.‡ Although market share has remained at about 30 percent, sales dollars have more than doubled, since the total industry sales were about $1 billion in the early 1980s but are now $2.7 billion.

---

*Thomas Moore, "The Fight to Save Tylenol," *Fortune,* **106:**11, Nov. 29, 1982, pp. 44–49.

†"Johnson & Johnson Sets Nighttime Tylenol," *Advertising Age,* Feb. 18, 1992, p. 1.

‡Marc G. Weinberger and Jean B. Romeo, "The Impact of Negative Product News," *Business Horizons,* **32:**1, January–February 1989, pp. 44–50.

BARRIERS TO INTERNAL INTEGRATION

Organizations do not implement internal logistics integration in a vacuum. It is important to recognize obstacles, or barriers, that often serve to inhibit internal process integration. Integration barriers originate in traditional practices related to organization structure, measurement systems, inventory ownership, information technology, and knowledge transfer capability. Each potential barrier is discussed below.

Organization Structure

The traditional organization structure for conducting business prevents any cross-functional process from being implemented. Most traditional organizations are structured to divide authority and responsibility according to functional work. In essence, both structure and budget closely follow the work to be performed. The traditional practice is to assemble all persons related to performing specific work into a functional department such as inventory control, warehousing operations, or transportation. Each of these organizations becomes concerned with achieving its own functional excellence. Since the goal of integration is cooperation among functional areas, the formal organizational structure can hinder success. Popular terms to describe traditional functions are the *sandbox* or *silo mentality*. In part, this managerial preoccupation with function is caused by the fact that most managers are rewarded for achieving functional excellence. The general belief that prevailed was that functions, excellently executed, would combine to create overall superior performance. Successful integration of a process such as logistics requires managers to look beyond their organizational structure and facilitate cross-functional coordination. This may or may not be best accomplished by creating a new organization structure. However, regardless of whether the organization structure is realigned, significant modification of how an organization deals with cross-functional matters is essential for successful process integration.

Measurement Systems

Traditional measurement systems have also made cross-functional coordination difficult. Most measurement systems mirror organization structure. To successfully facilitate integration of logistics functions, a new scorecard must be developed. Managers must be encouraged to view their specific functions as part of a process rather than as stand-alone activities. Managers may, at times, have to assume increased costs within their functional area for the sake of lower costs *throughout* the process. Unless a measurement system is created that does not penalize managers, logistical integration will be more theory than practice.

Inventory Ownership

It is a fact that inventory can help a specific function achieve its mission. The traditional approach to inventory ownership is to maintain adequate supply to gain comfort and protect against demand and operational uncertainty. The availability of inventory, for example, can support long manufacturer runs resulting in maximum economy of scale. Forward commitment of inventory to local markets can also serve to facilitate sales. While such practices create benefits, they have a related cost. The critical issue is the cost-benefit relationship and the risks related to incorrectly located or obsolete inventory.

Information Technology

Information technology is the key resource to achieve integration. However, similar to performance measurement, information system applications tend to be designed along organization lines. Many databases are limited to specific functions and are not easily accessed on a cross-functional basis. The need to share information has resulted in the development of data warehouses that exist for the sole purpose of sharing information between systems. Until schemes are developed to transfer information, the existing applications can serve as a barrier to process integration because critical data cannot be readily shared.

Knowledge Transfer Capability

Knowledge is power in most business situations. An additional barrier to integration is limitation in the ability to share experience. Failure to transfer information or knowledge containment tends to foster the functional orientation by developing a workforce composed of specialists. The failure to transfer knowledge can also create a barrier to continued integration when an experienced employee retires or for some other reason leaves the firm. In many cases, replacement personnel are not available to ''learn'' from the experienced worker. The more serious situation is a failure of many firms to develop procedures and systems for transferring cross-functional knowledge. Process work often involves many employees and is not limited to any specific functional area. Transfer of this type of knowledge and experience is difficult to standardize.

LOGISTICAL PERFORMANCE CYCLES

The primary unit of analysis for integrated logistics is the performance cycle. Viewing logistical integration in terms of performance cycles provides a basic perspective of the dynamics, interfaces, and decisions that must link to create an operating system. At a basic level, suppliers, the firm, and its customers are linked together by communications and transportation. The facility locations that performance cycles *link* together are referred to as *nodes.*

In addition to nodes and links, a logistical performance cycle requires inventory. Inventory is measured in terms of *asset level* deployed to support operations. Inventory committed to a system consists of base stock and safety stock positioned to protect against variance. It is at the facility nodes that work related to logistics occurs. Within nodes, inventory is stocked or flows through the node, necessitating a variety of different types of material handling and at least limited storage. While a degree of handling and in-transit storage takes place within transportation, such activity is minor in comparison to that typically performed within a logistical facility, such as a warehouse.

Performance cycles become dynamic as they accommodate *input/output* requirements. The *input* to a performance cycle is an order that specifies requirements for a product or material. A high-volume system will typically require a variety of different performance-cycle arrangements to satisfy overall order requirements. When requirements are highly predictable or relatively low, the performance cycles required to provide logistical support can be simplified. For example, the overall performance-cycle structure required to support a large retail enterprise like Target or Wal-Mart is far more complex than the operating structure requirements of a direct mail-order company.

System *output* is the level of performance expected from the logistical operation. To the extent that operational requirements are satisfied, the performance-cycle structure is *effective* in accomplishing its mission. *Efficiency* is related to resource expenditure necessary to achieve logistical effectiveness. The effectiveness and efficiency of performance cycles are key concerns in logistical management.

Depending on the operational mission of a particular performance cycle, required activities may be under the complete control of a single firm or may involve multiple firms. For example, manufacturing support cycles are typically under complete control of a single enterprise. In contrast, performance cycles related to physical distribution and procurement normally involve customer or supplier participation. Performance cycles span the overall supply chain and link participating firms.

It is important to realize that transaction frequency varies between performance cycles. Some performance cycles are established to facilitate a one-time purchase or sale. In such a case the cycle is designed, implemented, and then abolished, once the transaction is complete. Other performance cycles represent long-term arrangements. A complicating fact is that any operation or facility in one logistical arrangement may also be a participant in a vast number of different performance cycles. For example, the warehouse facility of a hardware wholesaler might receive merchandise from several hundred manufacturers on a regular basis. Likewise, a for-hire transportation carrier typically participates in numerous different performance cycles, spanning a wide variety of industries.

When one considers an enterprise of national or multinational scope involved in marketing a broad product line to numerous customers—engaging in basic manufacturing and assembly, and procuring materials and components on a global basis—the notion of individual performance cycles linking all operations is difficult to comprehend. It is almost mind-boggling to estimate how many performance cycles exist in the logistical systems of General Motors or IBM.

Regardless of the number and different types of performance cycles a firm uses to satisfy its logistical requirements, *each* must be individually designed and operationally managed. The fundamental importance of performance-cycle design and operation cannot be overemphasized. The performance cycle is the basic unit of design and operational control. A performance-cycle perspective is important to satisfy logistical requirements. *In essence, the performance-cycle structure is the framework for implementation of integrated logistics.* Figure 2-3 illustrates the performance-cycle structure of the three basic logistical operating areas. Figure 2-4 illustrates a complex network of performance cycles arranged in a multi-echeloned structure.

Three points are significant to understanding the architecture of integrated logistical systems. First of all, the performance cycle is the fundamental unit for integrated analysis of logistical functions. Second, the performance-cycle structure in terms of link and node arrangement is basically the same whether one is concerned with physical distribution, manufacturing support, or procurement. However, considerable differences exist in the *control* that a firm enjoys over a specific type of performance cycle. Third, regardless of how vast and complex the overall logistical system structure is, essential interfaces and control processes must be identified and evaluated in terms of individual performance-cycle arrangements when seeking process integration.

To better understand this important concept, the similarities and differences in the nature of physical distribution, manufacturing support, and procurement performance cycles are discussed and illustrated in greater detail.

Physical Distribution Performance Cycles

Physical distribution operations involve processing and delivering customer orders. Physical distribution is integral to marketing and sales performance because it provides timely and economical product availability. The overall process of gaining and maintaining customers can be broadly divided into transaction-creating and

FIGURE 2-3   Logistical performance cycles.

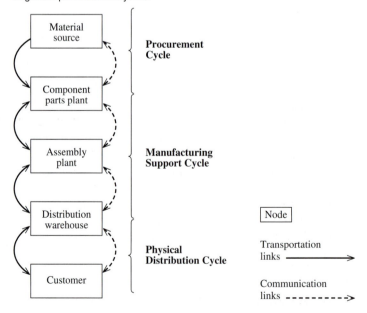

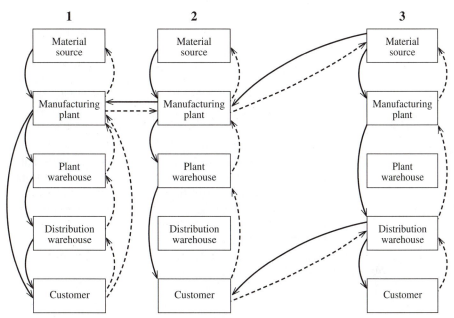

FIGURE 2-4   Structure of a multiecheloned flexible logistical network.

physical-fulfillment activities. The transaction-creating activities are advertising and selling. Physical distribution performs the physical-fulfillment activities. The typical physical distribution performance cycle involves five related activities. They are order transmission, order processing, order selection, order transportation, and customer delivery. The basic physical distribution performance cycle is illustrated in Figure 2-5.

From a logistical perspective, physical distribution links a firm with its customers. Physical distribution resolves marketing and manufacturing initiatives into an integrated effort. The interface between marketing and manufacturing can be conflictive. On the one hand, marketing is dedicated to delighting customers. In most firms, minimal limits are imposed by marketing and sales when it comes to accommodating customers. Often, this means that marketing and sales would like to maintain a broad product line with high inventory regardless of each product's actual profit potential. In this way, any customer's requirement, no matter how small or large, would be satisfied. The expectation is that zero defect service will be achieved and customer-focused marketing efforts will be supported.

The traditional mind-set in manufacturing is to control cost, which typically is achieved by long, stable production runs. Continuous manufacturing processes maintain economy of scale and generate lowest per unit cost. Under this type of process, a narrow line of products is mass-produced. Inventory has traditionally served to resolve the inherent conflict in these two philosophies. The use of inventory to reconcile operations typically means forward deployment throughout the logistical system in *anticipation* of future sale. Products are shipped to warehouses

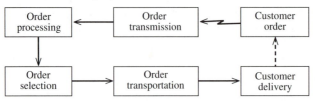

FIGURE 2-5   Basic physical distribution performance-cycle activities.

on the basis of forecasted requirements, acknowledging that they might be moved to the wrong market and at the wrong time. The end result of such risky decisions is that critical inventory can be improperly deployed in an attempt to efficiently support customer service requirements. At this point, the important concept to keep in mind is that the physical distribution performance cycle operates downstream from manufacturing toward the customer. Inventories committed to physical distribution, if correctly positioned, represent the maximum potential value that can be achieved by the logistical process.

The very fact that physical distribution deals with customer requirements means that related operations will be more erratic than characteristic of manufacturing support and procurement performance cycles. Attention to *how* customers order products is essential to reduce physical distribution operational variance and simplify transactions. First, every effort should be made to improve forecast accuracy. Second, a program of order management coordination with customers should be initiated to reduce uncertainty as much as possible. Third, and finally, physical distribution performance cycles should be designed to be as flexible and responsive as possible.

The key to understanding physical distribution performance-cycle dynamics is to keep in mind that customers initiate the process by ordering. The logistical response capability of the selling enterprise constitutes one of the most significant competencies in overall marketing strategy.

Manufacturing Support Performance Cycles

The manufacturing support performance cycle provides production logistics. Manufacturing can be viewed as being positioned between the physical distribution and procurement operations of a firm. Manufacturing logistical support has the primary objective of establishing and maintaining an orderly and economic flow of materials and work-in-process inventory to support production schedules. Specialization desired in physical distribution and procurement can create a gray area concerning responsibility for positioning and timing of inventory within the manufacturing enterprise. The movement and storage of product, materials, and semifinished parts and components between enterprise facilities represent the operational responsibility of manufacturing support logistics. Similar activity takes place in retail and wholesale firms that must select assortments of inventory to move to the next level in the value-added chain. Because manufacturing logistics represents the most complex internal support operations, it is presented here for discussion.

The isolation of manufacturing support as a distinct operating area is a relatively new concept in logistical management. The justification for focusing on performance cycles to support manufacturing is found in the unique requirements and operational constraints of modern production strategies. To provide maximum flexibility, traditional paradigms concerning economy of scale are being reevaluated to accommodate quick manufacturing switchover and shorter production runs. Exacting logistical support is required to perfect these strategies. It is important to once again stress that the mission of logistical manufacturing support is to facilitate the what, where, and when of production, *not* the how. The goal is to support all manufacturing requirements in the most efficient manner.

Manufacturing support is significantly different when compared with either physical distribution or procurement. Manufacturing support logistics is typically captive to a firm, whereas the other two performance areas must deal with the behavioral uncertainty of external customers and suppliers. Even in situations when contract manufacturing is used to augment internal capacity, overall control is greater than in the other two operating areas. Maximum exploitation of this control is the prime justification for treating manufacturing support as a separate logistical operating area.

Within a typical manufacturing organization, procurement provides materials and externally manufactured components when and where needed. Once a firm's manufacturing operation is initiated, subsequent requirements for interplant movement of materials or semifinished products are classified as manufacturing support. Logistical operations are restricted to dock-to-dock movement within the firm and any intermediate storage required. When production is completed, finished inventory is allocated and deployed either directly to customers or to distribution warehouses for subsequent customer shipment. At the time of this movement, physical distribution operations are initiated.

When a firm has multiple plants that specialize in specific production activities, the manufacturing support system may require a vast network of performance cycles. To the extent that specialized plants perform unique stages of production and fabrication prior to final assembly, numerous handlings and transfers are typically required to complete the manufacturing process. It is the job of manufacturing logistics to facilitate this process. In select situations, the complexity of manufacturing support may exceed that of physical distribution or procurement.

Manufacturing support operations, as contrasted to either physical distribution or procurement, are limited to movement under internal management control. Therefore, in conducting manufacturing support logistics, the variance introduced by random-order entry and erratic supplier performance can be controlled, thereby permitting more timely and continuous operations resulting in less overall safety stock.

Procurement Performance Cycles

Several activities or tasks are required to facilitate an orderly flow of materials, parts, or finished inventory into a manufacturing or distribution complex. They are (1) sourcing, (2) order placement and expediting, (3) transportation, and (4) receiving. These activities, as illustrated in Figure 2-6, are required to complete the procurement process. Once materials, parts, or resale products that were procured are received, the subsequent storage, handling, and transportation requirements to facilitate either manufacturing or redistribution are appropriately provided by other performance cycles. Because of the limited scope of procurement operations, it is currently being widely identified as *inbound logistics.* The sidebar about Lands' End illustrates how inbound logistics can create successful overall performance.

With three important differences, the procurement cycle is similar to the customer order processing cycle. First of all, delivery time, size of shipment, method of transport, and value of products involved are substantially different in procurement. Procurement often requires very large shipments, which may use barge, deep-water vessels, unit trains, and multiple truckloads to transport. While exceptions do exist, the typical goal in procurement is to perform inbound logistics at the lowest cost. The lower value of materials and parts in contrast to finished products means that a greater potential trade-off exists between cost of maintaining inventory in transit and time required to use low-cost modes of transport. Since the cost of maintaining materials and most component parts in the supply pipeline is less per day than the cost of maintaining finished inventory, there is normally no benefit for paying premium rates for faster inbound transport. Therefore, performance cycles in purchasing are typically longer than those associated with customer order processing.

Of course, for every rule there are exceptions. When high-value components are employed in manufacturing, emphasis typically shifts to smaller purchases of exact requirements that need positive logistical control. In such situations, the value of the material or component might justify the use of premium high-speed and reliable delivery services.

For example, a plant that manufactures cake mix uses a large amount of flour in its production process. Since flour in bulk quantities is relatively inexpensive, it makes sense for the firm to purchase flour in extremely large quantities that are shipped by rail. It would not make a lot of sense to purchase small quantities, losing the price discount for ordering bulk and paying to ship flour in smaller, high-cost transportation movements. For example, an automotive customizer buying a component part such as an electronic sunroof could purchase on a requirement basis. Sunroof packages are significantly different for every car, and each package is relatively expensive. As such, the customizer is more likely to order small amounts, maybe one at a time, to avoid holding inventory and may be willing to pay premium transportation for fast delivery.

FIGURE 2-6   Procurement-cycle activities.

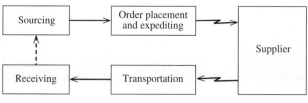

LANDS' END INBOUND OPERATIONS

Lands' End is one of the best-known mail-order companies because of its focus on high-quality merchandise, excellent product guarantees, and quick service. Serving a customer base of 6 million out of a 500,000-square-foot distribution center in Dodgeville, Wisconsin, is not an easy task. Lands' End manages the extensive operation with two phone centers and 900 order operators. Much of its success is attributed to the company's inbound logistics system.

Lands' End works with some 250 suppliers that manufacture and merchandise products to meet specific, high-quality specifications. Furthermore, Lands' End has developed partnerships with inbound carriers as well. Lands' End produces thirteen catalogs every year, which equates to one each month plus a special Christmas issue. Each catalog is filled with new products, seasonal items, and a variety of choices in clothing, luggage, bedding, and bath products.

To make this selection available, Lands' End sets strict operating goals for its procurement performance cycle. The main goal is to ensure that all merchandise offered in an upcoming catalog is available at the Dodgeville distribution center before final mailing of the catalog. This enables Lands' End to deliver customer orders within twenty-four hours even on the first day the catalog arrives at the customer's home.

In order to achieve this goal, Lands' End concentrates on quality with its suppliers and carriers. In terms of supplier relations, Lands' End performs extensive quality inspection upon material receipt as well as sending teams to suppliers' facilities to assess their operations and offer suggestions for improvements. Furthermore, all suppliers are given a manual that explains Lands' End requirements and specifications for quality merchandise.

In terms of carriers, Lands' End controls all inbound transportation movements. This control allows it to develop partnership arrangements with key carriers to reduce costs by consolidating volumes and distances. In addition, Lands' End shares information by allowing electronic linkage between specific carriers and its Dodgeville distribution center.

Lands' End feels that its outbound success, achieved through a superior physical distribution system, is directly related to its successful inbound system. The efficient and cost-effective procurement process is maintained by concentrating on quality and partnerships with the inbound value chain.

Based on Deborah Catalano Ruriani, "Where Perfection Begins," *Inbound Logistics,* November 1992, pp. 20–23.

A second unique feature of purchasing is that the number of suppliers a firm uses is typically less than the customer base it services. This difference is illustrated in the sidebar on Lands' End. This company has a customer base of over 6 million, but only deals with about 250 suppliers. In physical distribution operations, each firm is only one of many participants in an overall supply chain. In contrast, the procurement performance cycle is usually more direct. Materials and parts are often purchased directly from either the original manufacturer or a specialized industrial wholesaler. The utilization of direct channels is an important factor in the design of a logistical system for procurement.

Finally, since the customer order processing cycle handles orders in response to customers' requirements, random ordering must be accommodated by the physical distribution system. In contrast, the procurement system *initiates* orders. The ability to determine when and where products are purchased serves to substantially reduce operational variance.

The three major differences in procurement, as contrasted to the physical distribution order cycle, permit more orderly programming of logistical activities. The major uncertainty in procurement is the potential of price changes or supply discontinuity. A final feature of performance-cycle structure that is critical to all facets of logistics is operational uncertainty.

MANAGING OPERATIONAL UNCERTAINTY

A major objective of logistical management is to reduce performance-cycle uncertainty. The dilemma is that the structure of the performance cycle itself, operating conditions, and the quality of logistical operations combine randomly to create variance.

Figure 2-7 illustrates the magnitude of variance that can result in performance-cycle operations. The performance cycle illustrated pertains to finished goods inventory delivery. The time distributions, provided in the figure, reflect the statistical history related to performance of each work task. The diagram illustrates the minimum to maximum time required for each task and the resulting time distribution for the overall performance cycle. The vertical dashed line reflects the average or expected time for overall performance of each required task.

In terms of specific tasks, the variance results from the nature of the work involved. Order transmission is highly reliable when electronic transfer (EDI) is used and very erratic when handled through normal mail. Regardless of the level of technology deployed, operational variance will occur as a result of daily changes in workload and resolution of unexpected events.

Time and variance related to order processing are a function of workload, degree of automation, and policies related to credit approval. Order selection, speed, and associated delay are directly related to capacity, material-handling sophistication, and human resource availability. When a product is out of stock, the time to perform order selection must include manufacturing replenishment to return the product to stock. The transportation time requirements are a function of distance, shipment size, type or mode of transport, and operating conditions. Final delivery to customers can vary depending on authorized receiving times, delivery appointments, workforce availability, and specialized unloading and equipment requirements.

In Figure 2-7 the total order delivery cycle ranges from five to forty days. The five-day cycle reflects the unlikely event that each task is performed in the fastest possible time. The forty-day cycle represents the equally unlikely opposite extreme wherein each task consumes the maximum time. The expected order cycle performance time, assuming immediate product availability, is ten days. The task of performance-cycle management is to do whatever is required to control combined variance so that actual operations require ten days as often as possible. Whenever actual performance is more or less than ten days, action may be required to satisfy customer requirements. Such expediting and deexpediting require extra resources and reduce overall logistical efficiency.

The goal of performance-cycle management is to conform to expected or standard time. Delayed performance results in potential disruption of operations. If such delays occur on a regular basis, it becomes necessary to establish inventory safety stocks to cover variances. When performance occurs faster than expected, adjustments must be made to handle and store inventory that arrives before it is required. Given the inconvenience and expense of either early or late delivery, it is no wonder that logistics managers place a premium on operational consistency. Once consistent operations are achieved, every effort should be made to reduce the planned performance-cycle duration to a minimum. While consistency is the primary goal, faster order cycles reduce inventory risk and improve turn performance.

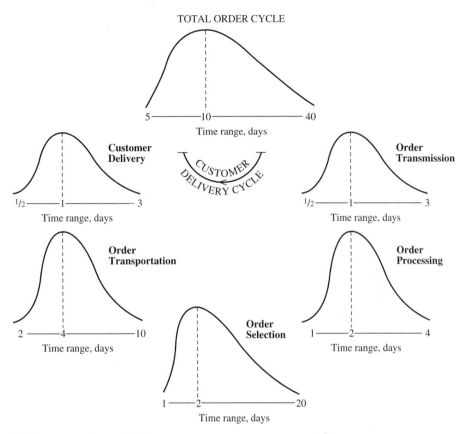

FIGURE 2-7   Performance-cycle uncertainty.

SUMMARY

The actual work of logistics is functional in nature. Facility locations must be established, information formulated and shared, transportation arranged, inventory deployed, and (to the extent required) warehousing, material-handling, and packaging activities performed. The traditional orientation was to perform each functional task as well as possible with limited consideration given to how one work area affects another. Because the work of logistics is extremely detailed and complex, there is a natural tendency to become functionally focused. Functional excellence is important but not to the detriment of the overall logistical integration.

The functions of logistics are combined into three primary operational areas: physical distribution, manufacturing support, and procurement. To achieve internal integration, the inventory and information flows between these areas must be coordinated. The three operating areas must be synchronized toward the simultaneous attainment of (1) rapid response, (2) minimum variance, (3) minimum inventory, (4) movement consolidation, (5) quality, and (6) life-cycle support.

In logistics system design, the unit of analysis is the performance cycle. The performance-cycle structure provides a logic for combining the *nodes, levels, links,* and *activities* essential to physical distribution, manufacturing support, and procurement operations. Many similarities exist among performance cycles dedicated to these vital logistics areas. It is also important to understand that a number of critical differences exist between the nature and the degree of managerial control possible with physical distribution, manufacturing support, and procurement operations. Fully understanding these similarities and differences is critical to planning and controlling overall logistical integration. The proposition presented is that regardless of size and complexity, logistical systems are best understood and evaluated in terms of performance-cycle structure.

The final section of the chapter introduced the realities of performance-cycle variance and the challenges of managing operational uncertainty. The nature of the task involved in managing and implementing performance-cycle work is prone to considerable variance. Unexpected delays as well as unexpected successes can combine to increase or decrease the elapsed time required to complete a performance cycle. Both early and late delivery are undesirable and may be unacceptable from an operational perspective. The goal is to achieve consistency. The challenge is to design a network of performance cycles capable of doing the required logistical work as rapidly but, even more important, as consistently as possible.

Chapter 2 has developed some important foundations of the logistical discipline. These insights regarding the nature of logistics work, the importance of achieving internal operational integration, the resolution of conflicting operating objectives, the performance-cycle structure as the unit of analysis, and the management of operational uncertainty combine to form a logically consistent set of concepts regarding what is essential to logistical excellence. These fundamental concepts become the foundations for further development throughout the chapters that follow. Chapter 3 focuses on customer requirements that drive logistical performance.

QUESTIONS

1 Describe the concept of value-added inventory flow. How are the costs of logistics related to the value-added flow?
2 Illustrate a common trade-off that occurs between basic work areas of logistics.
3 Illustrate from your experience an example where failure to perform on an integrated basis has resulted in service failure.
4 Discuss and elaborate on the following statement: "The selection of a superior location network can create substantial competitive advantage."
5 How does the "quest for quality" affect logistical operations? Do concepts such as "total quality" have relevancy when applied to logistics?
6 Describe the fundamental similarities and differences between procurement, manufacturing support, and physical distribution performance cycles as they relate to logistical control.
7 Discuss uncertainty as it relates to the overall logistical performance cycle. How can order cycle variance be controlled?
8 The chapter provides six operational objectives that are the primary determinants of logistical performance. Select one of the six objectives, and provide an example of how a firm would satisfy that objective if logistics was positioned as a core competency.
9 Compare and contrast a performance-cycle node and a link. Give an example of each.
10 Why are physical distribution operations described as more erratic than manufacturing and procurement operations?

CUSTOMER SERVICE

CUSTOMER-FOCUSED MARKETING
The Marketing Concept
Logistics as a Core Strategic Competency
Life-Cycle Planning Framework
CUSTOMER SERVICE DEFINED
BASIC SERVICE CAPABILITY
Availability
Operational Performance
Reliability
Conclusion
INCREASING CUSTOMER EXPECTATIONS
THE PERFECT ORDER
VALUE-ADDED SERVICES
Customer-Focused Services

Promotion-Focused Services
Manufacturing-Focused Services
Time-Focused Services
Basic Service
Conclusion
CUSTOMER SATISFACTION AND
SUCCESS: THE BERGEN BRUNSWIG
EXAMPLE
Cost-Effectiveness
Market Access
Market Extension
Market Creation
SUMMARY
QUESTIONS

Logistics contributes to an organization's success by providing customers with timely and accurate product delivery. The key question is, Who is the customer? For logistics, the customer is any delivery destination. Typical destinations range from consumers' homes to retail and wholesale businesses to the receiving docks of a firm's manufacturing plants and warehouses. In some cases the customer is a different organization or individual who is taking ownership of the product or service being delivered. In many other situations the customer is a different facility of the same firm or a business partner at some other location in the supply chain. Regardless of the motivation and delivery purpose, the customer being serviced is the focal point and driving force in establishing logistical performance requirements. It is important to fully understand customer service deliverables when establishing logistical strategy. This chapter details the nature of customer service and the development of facilitating strategies.

The first section of the chapter presents the fundamental concepts that underlie customer-focused marketing, with discussion of how logistics fits into a firm's overall marketing strategy. The notion of differentiation or segmentation of logistics performance to satisfy unique customer requirements is becoming increasingly popular. Most industries now have one or more competitors that position logistical competency as their main strategic resource. The initial section concludes with a discussion of logistical support requirements across the product life cycle. The primary purpose of the initial section is to establish a marketing context as a background for defining and subsequently discussing customer service.

The second section provides a working definition of customer service. The definition becomes a framework for the next section, which reviews the range of factors involved in basic customer service competency. Basic customer service is defined in terms of availability, performance, and reliability.

The sections that follow expand on the pressures impacting a firm's continued commitment to high-quality basic customer service. They highlight the reality that customer expectations are always changing: in fact, across the board, customers are becoming more demanding. As such, the concept of a shrinking service window is presented. This notion that precise operational performance is becoming the prevailing expectation is further highlighted in a discussion of the perfect order.

Finally, the chapter moves beyond basic service and introduces the concept of matching value-added services to unique customer requirements. The text discusses the selective deployment of value-added services and makes the fundamental point that outsourcing, the performance of such services by highly specialized firms, is becoming popular. The final section illustrates the dynamics involved in moving a business relationship from customer service to satisfaction and beyond.

Chapter 3 is critical for a full understanding of forces that shape logistical strategy. Little else is significant if the customer's expectations are not fully met.

CUSTOMER-FOCUSED MARKETING

The logical starting point is to understand how logistical competency contributes to marketing performance. Firms, guided by market opportunity, view satisfying customer requirements as the motivation behind all activities. The objective of marketing initiatives is to penetrate specific markets and generate profitable transactions. This posture, often referred to as the marketing concept, emerged as part of the post-World War II shift from seller- to buyer-dominated markets. In this section attention is directed to three fundamental concepts. First, the essence of a marketing orientation to business planning is developed. Next, the increased attention to developing logistics as a core competency is discussed. This notion of treating logistical competency as a strategic resource is critical to customer service planning. Finally, the changing nature of most desired logistics practice is examined in terms of product life-cycle requirements. It is important to understand that logistical performance should be modified over time to accommodate changing marketing requirements. The sidebar on 7-Eleven Japan illustrates an application of customer-focused marketing.

The Marketing Concept

The marketing concept advocates the identification of specific customer needs and then responds to those needs by focusing available resources to uniquely satisfy those customer requirements. The fundamental idea is that the greatest success will result when all work-related activities contribute to meeting customer expectations. The marketing concept builds on three fundamental ideas: customer needs are more basic than products or services, products and services become meaningful only when available and positioned from the customer's perspective, and volume is secondary to profit. Logistical competency fits into the marketing success equation because of the way it affects each of these fundamental ideas.

The belief that customer requirements are more basic than products or services places a priority on fully understanding what drives market opportunities. The key

---

PHILOSOPHY OF MANAGEMENT—JAPANESE STYLE

In May 1974, Ito-Yokado Company opened its first 7-Eleven store in Japan after having bought franchise rights from the Southland Corporation. Ito-Yokado is Japan's most profitable retailer and has managed to hold that title in part due to the unique customer service philosophy maintained at 7-Eleven. In fact, as the success of 7-Eleven grew and it became Japan's largest convenience store chain, Ito-Yokado paid $430 million for 70 percent of the United States company in 1990.

The philosophy of management rests on one simple idea: President Toshifumi Suzuki will not "sell what he wouldn't eat." Consequently, three times each week, Suzuki and other top managers meet for a lunch consisting of the products potentially carried at 7-Eleven. These products range from instant noodles to prepackaged sandwiches to boiled octopus. Any products that are stale or lack good taste are not carried. Suzuki doesn't stop here. Random spot-checks for product freshness are conducted in the stores as well by a team of 200 full-time testers.

This customer-oriented philosophy is backed up by logistical capability. Japan's 7-Eleven has one of the most sophisticated product tracking systems in the world. The $200 million system regulates inventory levels and also tracks customer preference. The clerks

help in this process by keying in customer attributes such as sex and approximate age for every purchase. These orders are transmitted instantaneously to distribution centers and manufacturers to monitor buying trends constantly. Manufacturers use point-of-sale data not only to schedule their own production facilities but also to drive new product innovations. Inventory is held to a minimum and any slow-moving items are discontinued. Shelf space is closely monitored and allocated to meet local preferences.

Suzuki's ideas are paying off. 7-Eleven Japan is able to capture a 42 percent operating margin and is estimated to have pretax profits of $680 million on sales of $1.44 billion this year. With its 1990 purchase, 7-Eleven Japan is making a move to test its state-of-the-art technology and customer focus in the United States as well. Test stores are currently being pursued in Austin, Detroit, and Reno. This test includes the logistical challenge of daily delivery of fresh goods. Preliminary results show a 10 percent increase in sales.

Based on information provided by Karen Lowry Miller, "Listening to Shoppers' Voices," *Business Week*, 1992 Special Issue—Reinventing America, p. 69.

is to understand and develop the combination of products and services that will satisfy customers. For example, if customers will be satisfied given three choices of different colored appliances, it makes little sense to offer six colors. It also makes little sense to try to market only white appliances if color selection is important from a customer's perspective. The basic idea is to develop sufficient insight into basic needs so that products and services can be matched to these opportunities. Successful marketing begins with an in-depth study of customers to identify product and service opportunities. If these opportunities can be economically satisfied, then the potential exists to develop a business relationship: customer needs are more basic than products.

For marketing to be successful, products and services must be available to customers. In other words, customers must be readily able to obtain the products they desire. To facilitate purchase action, a selling firm's resources need to be focused on customers and product positioning. Four economic utilities add product or service value to customers: form, possession, time, and place. The product's *form* is, for the most part, generated during the manufacturing process. For example, form utility results from the assembly of parts and components for an automobile. In the case of services, the composite of activities required to create and deliver a satisfactory customer package constitutes form utility. In the case of a haircut, form utility is achieved when activities—such as shampoo, cut, and styling—are completed. Marketing creates *possession* by informing potential customers of product/service availability and by enabling ownership exchange. Thus, marketing serves to identify and convey the physical and behavioral attributes of a product or service and to develop mechanisms for buyer-seller transaction. Logistics is expected to provide the balance of the value equation—*time* and *place* requirements. Essentially, this means that logistics must ensure the product or service is available *when* and *where* desired by customers. In the case of products, the achievement of time and place requires significant effort and is expensive. In a service transaction, the desired benefits are typically consumed while the service is being performed. However, products are often required to perform the service. During completion of a haircut, shampoo and conditioner are consumed. Businesses—such as travel agencies, dry cleaners, and even churches—require and consume products while performing their respective services. Profitable transactions will materialize only if all four essential utilities are combined in a timely manner, relevant to customers.

The third fundamental aspect of marketing as a business philosophy is the importance of stressing profitability as contrasted to sales volume. An important dimension of success is the degree of profitability resulting from accumulated transactions, not the volume of units sold. Therefore, variations in all four basic utilities—form, possession, time, and place—are justified if a particular customer or segment of customers value and are willing to pay for the modification. Going back to the appliance example, suppose cream, ivory, and tan are the color options available, but a customer requests a yellow refrigerator. If the customer is willing to pay extra for the unique color option, then the request can and should be accommodated, providing a positive contribution margin can be achieved. Since markets typically consist of many different segments, each of which has a unique set of requirements, the challenge is to match product/service offering to the unique needs of specific segments. Such segmental marketing should be driven by profit opportunity, not sales volume. The final refinement of marketing strategy is based on an acknowledgment that all specific aspects of a product/service offering are subject to modification when justified on the basis of profitability.[1]

Logistics as a Core Strategic Competency

A basic but useful way to view integrated marketing is by taking a marketing mix perspective. A marketing mix is a compilation of activities designed to attract customers while simultaneously achieving business objectives. The so-called four p's—product/service, promotion, price, and place—constitute a generic marketing mix. The key to formulating an effective mix strategy is to integrate resources committed to these activities into an effort that maximizes customer impact. As noted earlier, logistics is the process that satisfies the broad requirements of time and place utility. In short, logistics ensures that customer requirements involved in timing and location of inventory and other related services are satisfactorily performed. Thus, the output of logistical performance is customer service.

The impact of logistics on customers need not be passive. Alternative methods of delivery are available to achieve significantly different levels of inventory availability and lead times as desired throughout the supply chain. Logistical competency is a tangible way to attract customers that place a premium on time- and place-related performance. For other customers, the critical dimensions of an overall marketing effort could be promotion or price. Regardless of the marketing mix emphasis, logistical performance is an integral part of all strategies because no ownership transfer can occur without fulfilling time and place requirements. However, selected situations exist where logistics can form a core competency that is difficult to duplicate.

Perhaps the leading example of how two firms joined forces to exploit logistics as a business strategy is the Procter & Gamble/Wal-Mart success story. Senior management at both firms was able to envision a new way of conducting business that has served as the impetus for rewriting the "best practice" handbooks. While the results of their cooperative alliance are truly impressive, the fact remains that both firms separately developed extraordinary individual commitments to logistical competency prior to striking their joint partnership. The following quotes offer a glimpse of how the firms' senior management independently viewed logistical competency:

> Distribution and transportation have been so successful at Wal-Mart because senior management views this part of the company as a competitive advantage, not as some afterthought or necessary evil. And they support it with capital investment. A lot of companies don't want to spend any money on distribution unless they have to. Ours

---

[1]The classic article on this point is Wendell R. Smith, "Product Differentiation and Market Segmentation as Alternative Marketing Strategies," *Journal of Marketing,* **20,** July 1956, pp. 3–8. Also, see Theodore Levitt, "Marketing Myopia," *Harvard Business Review,* **38:**4, July–August 1960, pp. 45–56; R. C. Blattberg and S. K. Sen, "Market Segmentation Using Models of Multidimensional Purchasing Behavior," *Journal of Marketing,* **38,** October 1974, pp. 17–28; and J. T. Plummer, "The Concept and Application of Life Cycle Segmentation," *Journal of Marketing,* **38,** January 1974, pp. 33–37.

spends because we continually demonstrate that it lowers our costs. This is a very important strategic point in understanding Wal-Mart.[2]

I have the growing conviction that the product supply conception is perhaps the single most important thing that can influence our profit performance over the next several years.[3]

Whereas logistics is not the only capability that contributes to overall success, it is fundamental to servicing customers. Aspects of logistical strategic positioning are discussed in greater detail in Chapter 16. At this point it is important to understand that how logistics competency plays out in a competitive situation depends on its fit to the marketing initiatives of a firm. These initiatives illustrate the dimensions of customer service requirements. In a typical marketing situation, the desired customer service performance changes over time. To plan marketing strategy in a dynamic context, managers often use life-cycle modeling. A brief review of product life-cycle dynamics will serve to illustrate how logistical customer service requirements related to a specific product/segment situation will change over time. The product life-cycle structure offers a useful framework for viewing the dynamics associated with customer service requirements planning.

Life-Cycle Planning Framework

From the discussion thus far, it should be clear that logistics can be positioned to provide far more than passive support for marketing. The inventory availability and customer response time of a firm's service program should vary, depending on the market opportunity and competitive situation confronted. The need for viewing logistical requirements across time can be illustrated using the product life-cycle framework.[4] The product life-cycle framework illustrates the competitive conditions a firm typically experiences during the market life of a product.[5]

Figure 3-1 illustrates four stages of the product life cycle: introduction, growth, saturation-maturity, and obsolescence-decline. Detailed discussion of all marketing-related issues confronted in each life-cycle stage is beyond the scope of this book. However, this section will show how the firm's marketing mix should be modified to accommodate the customer requirements at each stage. Emphasis will be placed on the changing nature of logistical requirements across the life cycle.

---

[2]Joe Hardin, executive vice president of logistics and personnel, Wal-Mart, in Sam Walton with John Huey, *Sam Walton, Made in America: My Story,* New York: Doubleday, 1992, p. 206.

[3]John Smale, retired chairman of Procter & Gamble, in Brian Dumaine, "P & G Rewrites the Marketing Rules," *Fortune,* November 6, 1989, p. 46.

[4]The product life cycle is a special application of the broader concept of time accommodation presented in the discussion of logistics integration objectives in Chapter 2.

[5]For an early work concerning overall marketing strategy during the product life cycle, see Theodore Levitt, "Exploit the Product Life Cycle," *Harvard Business Review,* **43:**6, November–December 1965, pp. 81–94; and Peter F. Kaminski and David R. Rink, "PLC: The Missing Link between Physical Distribution and Marketing Planning," *International Journal of Physical Distribution and Materials Management,* **14:**6, 1984, pp. 77–92; Joseph Cavinato, "Product Life Cycle: Logistics Rides the Roller Coaster," *Distribution,* **86:**9, September 1987, pp. 12–20; and Milind Lele, "Matching Your Channels to Your Products' Life Cycle," *Business Marketing,* **71:**12, December 1986, pp. 60–69.

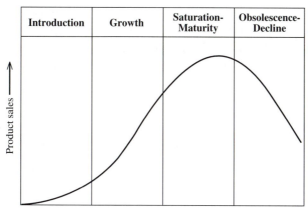

| Introduction | Growth | Saturation-Maturity | Obsolescence-Decline |

FIGURE 3-1   Product life-cycle concept.

Introduction   During the *introduction* stage of a new product, high product availability and logistical flexibility are required. Since the primary objective of introduction is to gain a market foothold, having inventory available to customers is critical. The planning of logistical support for new products must also enable a firm to provide rapid and consistent replenishment. The fact that no reliable movement history is available and that forecasts are, at best, projections means that replenishment plans need to be contingency-based. Typically a high degree of advertising and promotion is required during the introductory stage as potential customers are informed of a product's attributes and persuaded to make initial purchases. For example, a retail chain may agree to stock a new product on a trial basis but only if it is accompanied by a trade promotional discount or slotting allowance. If the product gains customer acceptance, rapid inventory replenishment will be required. Inventory shortages or erratic delivery during this critical time could dilute the marketing strategy. If the product fails to gain customer acceptance, there is a high probability that this will occur during product introduction. Thus, logistics plays a prominent role in the integrated marketing effort. Since market position is not secure, shipment sizes tend to be small and order frequency erratic as firms and their customers hedge against the possibility of ending up with potentially unsalable merchandise. As a result of these characteristics the logistical costs typical of introductory service are high.

In the past, most growth came from line expansion of existing products or acquisition of brands from other firms. In contrast, future growth is projected to be highly dependent on new-product development. This changing emphasis toward new products is important to logistics for three reasons.

First, greater emphasis on new-product development means that future logistical systems must be designed to accommodate a wider variation in product lines and associated stocking units. Special handling, transportation, and packaging requirements will increase as the product line expands, requiring greater system flexibility. Should the expanded product line require special equipment, such as refrigerated trucks or rail tank cars, the task of logistics becomes even more complex.

A second consideration is an increased need to service many different markets through multiple channels. As markets expand, products typically become more specialized and are sold to a smaller group of customers. To reach these specialized markets, it typically means that customers must be serviced through multiple marketing channels. The result may be fragmentation of product volume across these expanded channels, resulting in less opportunity to consolidate logistical volume for cost control.[6]

A final implication of increased new-product introduction is the fact that marketing is far from an exact science. As noted earlier, development requires an interpretation of customer needs. In addition, the potential product must be developed and associated attributes communicated into an end-use context to inform and persuade potential buyers. More than half of all new products introduced do not enjoy sufficient longevity in the marketplace to recover their development costs.[7] From a logistical viewpoint, it is difficult to project which products will be winners and which will lose. Extreme care must be taken not to increase risk and influence product failure by being unable to logistically support the product during introduction. On the other hand, inventory stockpiling and logistics in anticipation of sales that never materialize can be extremely expensive. As such, new-product logistics is a balancing act between providing sufficient logistics and avoiding too much support or commitment during new-product introduction.

Growth   At the *growth* stage of the life cycle, the product achieves a degree of market acceptance and sales become somewhat more predictable. Logistical emphasis typically shifts from a need to service at *any cost* to a more balanced service/cost performance. Customer service commitments are typically planned to achieve profit projections. The key is to achieve break-even volume as soon as possible and then expand market coverage. Since products are gaining increased customer acceptance, the potential exists to achieve a high level of profitable transactions during the growth stage. Market penetration is expanding at an increasing rate. Terms and conditions of sale are typically adjusted to reflect volume discounts and promotional commitments made to encourage maximum efficiency. During the growth stage, the marketing challenge is to sell into growing demand. An enterprise at this stage of the growth cycle has maximum opportunity to design logistical operations to help leverage profits. The marketing situation is one that requires few, if any, special logistics services. Channels for successful marketing are relatively simple and clearly defined. For example, the product is typically sold only through limited and traditional distributors. These conventional outlets sell the product at an increasing volume offering maximum opportunity for achieving logistical economies of scale.

The appropriate level of customer service to logistically support market growth is a complex question. Operating capacity to provide high levels of product availability along with rapid and consistent response to customer orders is costly. The

---

[6]Varied aspects of channel structure and associated logistical accommodation are covered in Chapter 4.

[7]Many authors use different numeric values to discuss product failure rates and the potential for recovering development costs. For example, Christopher Power et al., ''FLOPS: Too Many New Products Fail,'' *Business Week,* August 16, 1993, pp. 76–82, discussed a study by Kuczmarski & Associates, who found that only 56 percent of new products are still on the market five years after introduction.

following section on basic customer service will provide evidence that the *cost* of escalating the customer service level increases at a far faster rate than the level of actual performance achieved. Therefore, enterprises offering very high levels of customer service can expect to confront high total logistics costs.

Failure on the part of managers to appreciate the relationship of service commitment and its cost-revenue impact can result in creating unrealistic customer expectations. Given current logistics technology, almost any level of service is possible if a firm is willing to pay the price. In fact, many firms make a service commitment that exceeds requirements for successful marketing. The key is to make such commitments by strategic design—not by accident. The basic customer service commitment or platform is discussed in subsequent sections of this chapter. At this point it is important to stress that a firm's basic customer service commitment to support a product is formulated during the relative business prosperity of the growth stage of the product life cycle.

Saturation-Maturity   The *saturation-maturity* stage is characterized by intense competition. A successful product typically generates competition from a variety of substitutes. In response, price and service adjustments become a standard strategic accommodation. Logistical performance during the saturation stage typically becomes highly selective. Competitors adjust their basic service commitment and offer unique value-added service in an effort to create loyalty among major customers. Increased expenditures may be allocated to logistical performance to ensure exceptional service to key customers.

In mature marketing situations traditional channels become blurred and complex. For example, retailers sell wholesale, wholesalers sell retail, hardware stores sell clothing, department stores sell food, food stores sell appliances, and discount and warehouse clubs sell everything. The resultant structure of marketing arrangements is often referred to as *scrambled merchandising*.

Scrambled merchandising repositions business relationships. Finished goods often move to a retailer through multiple logistics arrangements provided by wholesalers, distributors, jobbers, assemblers, and even direct from manufacturers. In some cases, goods bypass conventional retailers altogether and move directly to consumer homes. These changing patterns of shipment require substantial accommodation by logistical support systems.

To accommodate multiple-channel logistics during life-cycle maturity, many manufacturers and retailers establish distribution warehouses. The purpose of establishing a warehouse network is to be able to satisfy the service requirements of many different channels. The simple task of delivering manufacturing output directly to a few customer destinations is replaced by a variety of alternative distribution capabilities matched to specific customer requirements. Under multichannel logistics, less volume is delivered to any one location, and special services are performed for specific customers. The typical result is higher per-unit logistics costs. The competitive conditions of maturity increase the complexity of logistics and reinforce the need for operational flexibility.

Obsolescence-Decline   The great prosperity of growth and saturation-maturity ends when a product enters the *obsolescence-decline* stage. When a product is dying, management is balancing the alternatives of product closeout or restricted continued distribution. Logistical performance must be positioned to support ongoing business without taking excessive risk in the event that a product must be eliminated. Thus, minimum risk becomes a more important goal than achieving the lowest per-unit cost of logistics.

The product life cycle, while somewhat abstract and oversimplified, illustrates the typical range of basic logistical strategies needed to accommodate service requirements over time. No ''must do'' rules exist. Logistical performance, like all other elements of the marketing mix, needs to be strategically adjusted to the market and competitive situation. The level and nature of logistical support change across the life cycle. In general, new-product introductions require high levels of logistical performance and flexibility to accommodate rapid changes in volume projections. This emphasis typically shifts toward service/cost rationalization during the growth and saturation-maturity stages of the life cycle. At the obsolescence-decline stage a firm needs to position logistics to minimize risk. In addition, a logistical system must be designed to maintain flexibility and be capable of adjusting to counter a competitive activity at any specific point in time. This requires a clear perspective of just what customer service is and how it should be deployed.

CUSTOMER SERVICE DEFINED

Marketing identifies the appropriate logistical performance. The critical strategic issue is to determine the combination of services and their desired format that will support and stimulate profitable transactions.

Although most senior managers agree that customer service is important, they find it difficult to explain exactly what it is and does. Two interpretations commonly expressed are *easy to do business with* and *sensitive to customer needs*. While such generalizations have appeal from a qualitative perspective, it is difficult to interpret what ''easy to do business with'' means for firms that deal with numerous customers on a daily basis. To develop a customer service strategy, it is necessary to develop a working definition of customer service.

LaLonde and Zinszer have researched various ways that customer service can be viewed: (1) as an activity, (2) in terms of performance levels, and (3) as a philosophy of management.[8] Viewing customer service as an *activity* suggests that it is capable of being managed. Thinking of customer service in terms of *performance levels* has relevancy providing it can be accurately measured. The notion of customer service as a *philosophy of management* exemplifies the importance of customer-focused marketing. All three dimensions are important to understand what is involved in successful customer service.

A broad definition of customer service should embody elements from all three perspectives. LaLonde and his associates offer the following definition:

> Customer service is a process for providing significant value-added benefits to the supply chain in a cost-effective way. This definition illustrates the trend to think of customer

---

[8]See Bernard J. LaLonde and Paul H. Zinszer, *Customer Service: Meaning and Measurements,* Chicago, Ill.: The Council of Logistics Management, 1976.

service as a process-focused orientation that includes supply chain management concepts.[9]

It is clear that excellent customer service performance seems to add value for all members of the supply chain. Thus, a customer service program must identify and prioritize all activities important to accomplish operating objectives. A customer service program also needs to incorporate measures for evaluating performance. Performance needs to be measured in terms of goal attainment and relevancy. The critical question in planning a customer service strategy remains, Does the cost associated with achieving the specified service goals represent a sound investment and, if so, for what customers? Finally, it is possible to offer key customers something more than high-level basic service. Extra service beyond the basics is typically referred to as *value-added.* Value-added services, by definition, are unique to specific customers and represent extensions over and above a firm's basic service program.

BASIC SERVICE CAPABILITY

In Chapter 1, three fundamental dimensions of customer service were identified: availability, performance, and reliability. These attributes are now discussed in greater detail. Numerous research studies have examined the relative importance of the three service attributes in different business situations. The general conclusion is that all three aspects of service are important. However, a given service attribute may be more or less important depending on the specific marketing situation.

Availability

Availability is the capacity to have inventory when it is desired by a customer. Availability can be achieved in a variety of ways. The most common practice is to stock inventory in anticipation of customer orders. The appropriate number, location, and stocking policy of warehouses is one of the basic issues in logistical system design.[10] Typically an inventory stocking plan is based on forecasted requirements and may incorporate differential stocking strategies for specific items as a result of sales popularity, importance of the specific item to the overall product line, profitability, and the value of the merchandise. Inventory can be classified into two groups: base stock determined by forecasted requirements and held to support basic availability, and safety stock to cover demand that exceeds forecasted volumes and to accommodate unexpected operational variances.

The warehousing network deployed by specific firms selling to the same types of customers can vary extensively. Johnson & Johnson subsidiaries have traditionally favored a limited network of three or four facilities to service the United States. Nabisco Foods uses in excess of ten facilities to support customer logistical require-

[9]Bernard J. LaLonde, Martha C. Cooper, and Thomas G. Noordewier, *Customer Service: A Management Perspective,* Oak Brook, Ill.: The Council of Logistics Management, 1988.
[10]See Chapter 17.

ments across the same geographical area. As a general rule, the larger the number of warehouse facilities in a system, the greater the average inventory required to support a given level of inventory availability.

An important aspect of availability is a firm's safety stock policy. Safety stock exists to accommodate forecast error and cushion delivery delays during base stock replenishment. As a general rule, the greater the desire to protect against out-of-stocks, the larger the safety stock required. Thus, high safety stock commitment typically means larger average inventory. In high-variance situations, safety stock can constitute greater than half of a firm's average inventory.

Many firms develop alternative logistics arrangements to supplement their ability to meet customer inventory requirements. A firm may operate two warehouses with one designated as a primary service location and the other as a secondary or backup supply source. Suppose the primary warehouse is a large automated distribution center in Chicago and the secondary facility is a small, less efficient operation in St. Louis. The primary warehouse is the location the firm would like to ship the most product from in order to take advantage of the automated equipment, efficiency, and location. However, the secondary or backup warehouse is available in the event a stockout condition develops at the primary distribution warehouse. To the maximum extent possible, firms using a secondary or backup warehouse seek to do so in a manner transparent to their customers. Occasionally, the primary location will have only a portion of an order while the secondary location will be able to satisfy remaining requirements. In such cases, unless the two parts of the order can be combined prior to delivery, the customer will be inconvenienced by a split delivery. The fact that the selling firm makes extraordinary efforts to have inventory available rather than back-ordering part of a shipment can be turned into a positive indication of dedication and commitment to satisfying customer requirements. Such instances of meeting customer requirements when operational problems occur have been referred to as *immaculate recovery*.[11] They are discussed in more detail later in this chapter when the concept of the perfect order is developed.

It should be clear that achieving high levels of consistent inventory availability requires a great deal more planning than allocating inventory to warehouses on the basis of sales forecasts. In fact, the key is to achieve high levels of inventory availability for selected or core customers while holding overall investment in stock and facilities at a minimum. Such exacting performance requires total integration of all logistical resources and clear goals regarding availability commitments to specific customers. Exacting programs of inventory availability are not conceived or managed on "the average." Therefore, availability is based on the following three performance measures: stockout frequency, fill rate, and orders shipped complete. These three measures determine a firm's ability to meet specific customer inventory requirements.

Stockout Frequency   Stockout frequency is the probability that a stockout will occur. In other words, this measure indicates if a product is available to ship to

---

[11]James L. Heskett, W. Earl Sasser, Jr., and Christopher W. L. Hart, *Service Breakthroughs: Changing the Rules of the Game*, New York: The Free Press, 1990.

customers. A stockout occurs when demand exceeds product availability. The stockout frequency is a measure of how many times demand for a specific product exceeds availability. The aggregation of all stockouts across all products is an indication of how well a firm is positioned to provide basic service commitments. This measures does not consider the fact that some products may be more critical in terms of availability than others. However, stockout frequency is a starting point in measuring inventory availability.

Fill Rate   Fill rate measures the *magnitude or impact* of stockouts over time. Just because a product is out of stock does not necessarily mean that a customer requirement is going unsatisfied. Before a stockout affects service performance, it is necessary to confront a customer requirement. Then it becomes important to identify that the product is not available and to determine how many units the customer wanted. Fill rate performance is typically specified in customer service objectives. By measuring the magnitude of stockouts, a firm's track record in meeting customer requirements can be determined. For example, if a customer orders 50 units and only 47 units are available, the order fill rate is 94 percent (47/50). To effectively measure fill rate, the typical procedure is to evaluate performance over a specified time that includes multiple customer orders. Thus, fill rate performance can be calculated for a specific customer or for any combination of customers or business segment desired.

Fill rate can also be used to differentiate the level of service to be offered on specific products. In the earlier example, if all 50 products were critical, an order fill rate of 94 percent could result in a stockout in the customer's operation and create considerable dissatisfaction. However, if most of the 50 products were relatively slow movers, a fill rate of 94 percent could be satisfactory. The customer may accept a back-order or even be willing to reorder the short items. A firm can identify products that are critical and should have higher fill rates on the basis of customer requirements. Fill rate strategies can then be developed to meet customer expectations.

Stockout frequency and fill rate both depend on customer order practices. For example, if a firm places frequent replenishment orders for small quantities, the probability of stockout frequency will increase as a result of shipment variability. In other words, each replenishment order represents an equal chance for a delivery delay. Thus, as the number of orders that impact safety stock increases, more stockouts will occur. On the other hand, if a firm places fewer large replenishment orders, the potential stockout frequency will be less and the expected fill rate will be higher. Stockout frequency and fill rate are inversely related through order quantity. These relationships will be more fully developed in Chapters 8 and 9.

Orders Shipped Complete   Orders shipped complete is a measure of the times that a firm has all the inventory ordered by a customer. It is the strictest measure since it views full availability as the standard of acceptable performance. Orders shipped complete establishes the potential times that customers will receive perfect orders, providing all other aspects of performance have zero defects.

These three availability measures combine to identify the extent to which a firm's inventory strategy is meeting customer expectations. They also form the basis to evaluate the appropriate level of availability to incorporate in a firm's basic service platform.

Operational Performance

The fundamental perspective of viewing logistical competency in terms of performance cycles was established in Chapter 2. The performance cycle was positioned as the operational structure of logistics. At that point performance cycles were differentiated by mission, type of customer being serviced, and the degree of operational variance experienced over time. Operational measures specify the expected performance cycle in terms of (1) speed, (2) consistency, (3) flexibility, and (4) malfunction/recovery. Operational performance involves logistical commitment to expected performance time and acceptable variance.

Speed Performance-cycle speed is the elapsed time from when an order is placed until shipment arrival. Such commitment must be viewed from a customer's perspective. The time required for performance-cycle completion can be very different depending on logistical system design. Given today's high level of communication and transportation technology, order cycles can be as short as a few hours or as long as several weeks.

Of course, the highest commitment to both inventory availability and operational speed is customer inventory consignment. In consignment arrangements, the product is inventoried at a customer's business establishment in anticipation of need. While consignment may be ideal from a customer's perspective, it can be an expensive way for a supplier to do business. Consignment arrangements are typically limited to critical items that can result in significant loss in efficiency or effectiveness if they are not available exactly when required, such as machine parts and emergency medical supplies. Typical consignment situations are found in business-to-business marketing and the health care industry. The decision for a supplier to consign as contrasted to a customer holding safety stock is often a reflection of the relative power in a business relationship.

The more typical business arrangement is for a supplier's delivery commitment to be based on customers' expectations in terms of performance-cycle speed. In critical situations, service can be performed in a few hours by special delivery from a local warehouse or on an overnight basis using highly reliable transportation services. Usually, the business relationship is formed around performance-cycle expectations that facilitate efficient logistical operations while meeting customer requirements. In order words, not all customers need or want maximum speed if it results in an increase in price or effective logistics cost.

Performance-cycle timing has a direct relationship to inventory requirements. Typically, the faster the planned performance, the lower the level of inventory investment required by customers. This relationship between performance time and customer inventory investment is at the heart of time-based logistics arrangements.[12]

---

[12]See Chapter 16.

Consistency While speed of service is critical, most logistical managers place greater emphasis on consistency. Consistency refers to a firm's ability to perform at the expected delivery time over a large number of performance cycles. Failure to be consistent translates directly into customers needing to carry extra safety stock to protect against possible late delivery. Whereas availability is concerned with the ability to ship products when required and performance-cycle speed is concerned with the commitment to complete all work requirements necessary to deliver specific orders at a prescribed time, consistency deals with compliance to delivery commitments over time. The issue of consistency is fundamental to logistical operations.

Flexibility Operational flexibility refers to a firm's ability to handle extraordinary customer service requests. A firm's logistical competency is directly related to how well unexpected circumstances are handled. Typical events requiring flexible operations are (1) modifications in basic service arrangements such as one-time changes in ship-to destinations, (2) support of unique sales and marketing programs, (3) new-product introductions, (4) product phaseout, (5) disruption in supply, (6) product recall, (7) customization of service levels for specific markets or customers, and (8) product modification or customization performed while in the logistics system, such as pricing, mixing, or packaging.[13] In many ways the essence of logistical excellence rests in the ability to be flexible. As a general rule, a firm's overall logistical competency depends on the capability to ''go the extra yard'' when appropriate to satisfy a key customer requirement. Picker International illustrates logistical flexibility in the sidebar provided.

Mulfunction/Recovery Regardless of how fine-tuned a firm's logistical operation is, malfunctions will occur. The continuous performance of service requirements under all types of operational situations is a difficult task. Sometimes, programs can be established to prevent or accommodate special situations, thereby preventing malfunction. As will be discussed later, such extraordinary commitments must be reserved for justifiable situations. In terms of the basic service program, the key is to anticipate that mulfunctions or service breakdowns will occur and to have in place contingency plans to accomplish recovery. Thus, the basic service program guarantees a high level of service with the realization that no program is fail-safe. When service failures occur, the customer service program should have contingency plans that identify expected recovery and measure compliance.

Reliability

Logistics quality is all about reliability. A fundamental quality issue in logistics is the ability to comply to levels of planned inventory availability and operational performance. Beyond service standards, quality compliance involves a capability

---

[13]Donald J. Bowersox, Patricia J. Daugherty, Cornelia L. Dröge, Dale S. Rogers, and Daniel L. Wardlow, *Leading Edge Logistics: Competitive Positioning for the 1990's,* Oak Brook, Ill.: The Council of Logistics Management, 1989, p. 198.

FLEXIBILITY FOR LIFE

Picker International manufactures magnetic resonance imaging (MRI) equipment, CAT scanners, X-ray equipment, and nuclear medical systems. The distribution of such equipment requires that Picker maintain high flexibility and speed in delivery, especially in emergency shipments. Picker sees its most critical type of shipment occurring when a machine is out of service, a patient is waiting, and a hospital is unable to perform the necessary diagnostic evaluations. Picker's logistics team has developed a three-pronged approach to the problem depending on the urgency of the situation. In other words, the method used depends on whether the hospital has an alternative means to perform diagnosis.

If the situation is extremely critical, the parts or equipment can be driven to the hospital within one to two hours from one of Picker's sixteen third-party support banks located throughout the country. If slightly more time is available, Picker can have the necessary equipment delivered to the hospital within four or five hours by having a courier take the needed parts or equipment to the airport and fly it next-flight-out for delivery to the site. Finally, if the hospital can wait a day, Picker can deliver the parts overnight via its air carrier partners.

Picker's logistics team has realized that if their products do not reach the customer in time, it could mean loss of life. By maintaining logistical flexibility, Picker not only is able to provide a high level of service to its customer, the hospital, but also is able to serve the needs of the hospital's customers, the patient.

Based on Perry A. Trunick, Helen L. Richardson, and Thomas Andel, ''Logistics Excellence Is Its Own Reward,'' *Transportation and Distribution,* **33:**9, September 1992, p. 52.

and willingness to rapidly provide accurate customer information regarding logistical operations and order status. Research indicates that the ability of a firm to provide accurate information is one of the most significant measures of customer service competency. Increasingly, customers indicate that advanced information concerning the contents and timing of an order is more critical than complete order fulfillment. Customers detest surprises! More often than not, customers can adjust to a stockout or late delivery situation if they receive advanced notification.

In addition to service reliance, a major part of service quality is continuous improvement. Logistical managers, similar to other managers within the firm, are concerned with meeting operational objectives with as few malfunctions as possible. One way to achieve these objectives is to learn from malfunctions and improve the operating system to prevent reoccurrence.

The key to achieving logistical quality is measurement. Inventory availability and operational performance are critical in the eyes of customers. However, high-level performance can be maintained only by exacting measurement of achievements and failures. Three aspects of measuring service quality are important: variables, units, and base.

Measurement Variables   The performance activities that are specified in the basic service program represent the items to be measured for reliance assessment. Table 3-1 presents a list of variables typically used to measure service. The table also identifies if the variable is measurable at a specific point in time or over time. Variables measured at a point in time are typically referred to as *static variables.* Static variables are useful for assessing a logistics system's current state of readiness. For example, a review of existing back-orders, the number of stockouts, or the level of in-transit inventory provides early warning status of potential future

TABLE 3-1   SERVICE MEASUREMENT VARIABLES

Variables	Measurement period
Sales	Over time
Orders	Over time
Returns	Over time
Back-orders	Over time/point in time
Stockouts	Over time/point in time
Canceled orders	Over time
Canceled lines	Over time
Back-order recovery	Over time
Back-order age	Over time/point in time
Short shipments	Over time
Damage claims	Over time
Number of expedites	Over time

customer service problems. Variables measured over time, called *flow variables,* track system performance across time such as over a week, month, or quarter. Regardless of the specific variables used to calibrate customer service performance, the associated measures must be appropriately monitored. For example, it does not make sense to measure canceled orders at a specific point in time.

Measurement Units   A second aspect of reliability measurement is the selection of unit measures. Table 3-2 lists some physical unit measures that can be tracked. For example, it is possible to track and report stockouts in both units and sales or inventory dollars. Although both measures are generated from the same activity, they do not provide the same managerial information. When stockouts are measured in terms of units, the performance measurement across the range of product values from high to low is treated on an equal basis. On the other hand, the reporting of stockout performance in terms of sales dollars places emphasis on stockouts of higher value inventory. As a general rule, senior management is usually more concerned when the stockouts relate to high-margin, fast-moving, or critical products. The selection of measurement units can have a significant impact on reliability assessment.

Measurement Base   A final consideration in reliability measurement is the selected measurement base. The measurement base defines how performance reporting is aggregated. Table 3-3 lists some alternative levels of measurement aggregation. The measures are listed from total system aggregation to specific product performance. Grouping the overall logistical system into one measure summarizes

TABLE 3-2   MEASUREMENT UNITS

1	Cases	5	Dollars
2	Units	6	Dozens
3	Lines	7	Broken cases
4	Weight	8	Gallons

TABLE 3-3   SERVICE MEASUREMENT BASE

1	Overall system level	5	Order level
2	Sales area level	6	Customer level
3	Product group level	7	Broken cases
4	Brand level	8	Gallons

customer service performance on a grand system scale. Such aggregated perform-ance is relatively easy to measure since it requires the maintenance of a limited performance database. However, such aggregated measurement may camouflage potential problems by averaging performance. On the other hand, when perform-ance is measured at a specific product or customer level, it is difficult to generalize overall status and detect potential systemwide problems. Athough it is difficult to capture and maintain data at the customer or product detail level, such reporting does pinpoint specific problems.

Management must evaluate the trade-offs when selecting the most appropriate combination of measures, units, and aggregation base to assess reliability. While measurement detail facilitates the timely identification of specific problems, the resources required to collect, maintain, and analyze the information are substantial. However, such specific measurement is essential to support segmented service strategies: no customer is average. Fortunately, significant advancements in infor-mation technology for data collection, maintenance, and analysis, coupled with declining cost, have made specific customer service performance evaluation more of an everyday reality.

Conclusion

To implement a basic service platform, it is necessary to specify the level of basic service commitment to customers. In other words, what will be the basic service provided in terms of availability, operational performance, and reliability for *all* customers?

The fundamental question—how much basic service should a logistical system provide?—is not easy to answer.[14] At the highest level of policy formulation, the answer depends on a firm's overall marketing strategy and relative emphasis placed on specific elements of the marketing mix. If a firm seeks to differentiate on the basis of logistical competency, then high levels of basic service are essential. If the main competitive feature is price, then it is highly unlikely that a firm will be able or will desire to implement high-level logistical performance because of the need for cost control. Once again, the level of basic service to provide is a question of essential trade-offs and determination of the available competencies that will be most apt to influence customer behavior. Evidence suggests that logistical perform-ance is increasingly becoming a critical competency.

In terms of overall logistical performance, the basic customer service platform or program should be the level of support provided to *all* customers. It is important to stress that a firm should not deliberately violate its basic service program by offering or limiting it only to selected customers. Basic service is just what the name implies—*a minimum level of support provided to all customers*. The choice is not to provide lower basic service to marginally profitable customers. The critical decision is whether or not to do business with such customers. Once a customer's order is accepted, a firm is obligated to service the business in accordance with its

---

[14]This determination of service level is a critical aspect of strategic positioning. Approaches to establish-ing a basic service plan that nets a least-total-cost design are discussed in Chapter 17.

basic service commitment. Anything less is clear discrimination. On the other hand, performance at a level above basic service and the provision of value-added services represent extra commitment justified by the unique business situation. This form of providing extra service is similar to adding options that are over and above the features of a base model automobile, such as a sunroof or leather interior. The expectation is that customers will pay for the extras. In the case of logistics, over-and-above service can be compensated by service upcharges or the awarding of more business. The extreme level of service-based competency is when a supplier becomes a sole source provider of a product or service.

INCREASING CUSTOMER EXPECTATIONS

An important consideration in determining a firm's basic service program rests on understanding customer expectations. In almost every industry one or more firms use logistics as a core strategy to gain customer loyalty. These firms commit resources to achieve high levels of basic service competency that are difficult for competitors to duplicate. The result is a form of competition that is forged in a ''catch me if you can'' approach to logistical operations that tends to increase overall customer expectations.

The phenomenon of escalating customer expectations is illustrated by what is often referred to as the *shrinking service window.* Most industries have traditionally had an explicit or implied service level that was generally accepted as satisfactory or adequate. If a firm wanted to be a serious competitor in an industry, it was expected that it would achieve the minimum industry service expectations. For example, in the 1970s a performance cycle of seven to ten days with an inventory fill rate of 92 percent was generally acceptable performance for grocery manufacturers. By the early 1980s expectations escalated to order delivery within a five- to seven-day window with acceptable minimum fill rate increasing to 95 percent. Today's minimal service expectations are closer to a three- to five-day delivery and fill rates approaching 98 percent. As illustrated in Figure 3-2 the shrinking service window identifies a clear trend toward performance at a higher level and at a faster pace.

FIGURE 3-2   Shrinking service window.

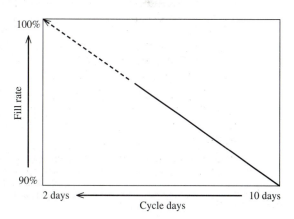

In actual practices, when a firm places a purchase order that specifies an exact delivery requirement or appointment in terms of time and location, it is clear that the traditional concept of an acceptable service window is instantaneously transformed to a *point in time*. If the customer's expectation is that suppliers will provide 100 percent inventory availability in a timely, error-free manner, then the service commitment is for *perfect order* performance.

THE PERFECT ORDER

The ultimate in logistics quality is to do everything right and do it right the first time. The notion of the perfect order is that desired customer service capability, in terms of availability and operational performance, should be synchronized to achieve target service goals each and every time. The order should also be complete in terms of all aspects of service from order receipt to delivery coupled with error-free invoicing. In other words, the total order cycle performance must be orchestrated with zero defects. This means that availability and operational performance must be perfectly executed and that all support activities, such as invoice accuracy and appropriate product presentation, must be completed exactly as promised to the customer. In many ways the concept of a perfect order is the logical extension of quality. Such service performance is possible given today's technology—but it is expensive. Therefore, few firms commit to zero defects as a basic service strategy offered across the board to all customers. The point is that such high-level performance is a strategic option and it can be committed to on a selective basis.

In terms of resources committed, zero defect performance typically cannot be supported solely by virtue of inventory commitment and positioning. Extremely high fill rates typically require high inventory commitments to cover all potential order requirements and operational variations. One service location may not have sufficient inventory to meet all customer availability requirements. To facilitate timely shipments from secondary locations, it is desirable to have predetermined procedures to accommodate service requirements in a timely manner.

The typical perfect order program involves activities that exceed the basic service program. The commitment to perfect order performance is usually based on agreements that develop from close working relationships between a supplier and selected customers. The general topic of alliances and relational marketing is discussed in Chapter 4. At this point, it is sufficient to underline the fact that perfect order commitments are usually implemented in highly structured working arrangements. These arrangements develop over time and often are supported by significant amounts of information exchange between involved businesses to facilitate and maintain an in-depth understanding of requirements. Perfect order expectations are not typically dropped on suppliers without advanced warning.

The industrial tape business at 3M acknowledges the loyalty of its top-volume or most select customers by identifying them as members of the ''Platinum Club.'' Among other things, being a platinum customer means that 3M commits to providing the exact quantity of every product ordered within the predetermined service time, each and every time. To achieve such perfect order performance, 3M has implemented a variety of contingency procedures for obtaining inventory required

ZERO DEFECT SERVICE FROM A CARRIER

As a general trend, shippers are using fewer and fewer carriers in an attempt to increase quality, reduce costs, and develop closer working relations. Most shippers establish a core group of carriers that can meet strict quality standards as defined by the shipper's organization. By providing zero defect service, Schneider National, Inc. (SNI), the nation's largest truckload and specialized carrier group, is able to meet a wide range of quality standards. As such, SNI is considered by many shippers as a key candidate for participation in customized partnership arrangements.

SNI's corporate vision supports zero defect service by including commitment to the never-ending improvement of quality. SNI strives to surpass customer expectations and become the carrier of choice in its industry. One way SNI provides zero defect service is by utilizing a satellite tracking system. SNI has invested millions of dollars into this technology to align itself more closely with the customer as well as provide employees more time to work on continuous improvement. SNI uses the Qualcomm Star Serv system, a network that provides real-time, two-way communications between SNI and its drivers. One benefit of this system is that it allows vehicles to be tracked within a quarter mile of their current location every two hours.

The Star Serv network creates benefits for both the customer and SNI. Since data are more accurate and quickly received, shippers are now better able to manage in-transit inventories and make changes in service requirements. Furthermore, diversion strategies are simplified, allowing shippers to quickly change the destination of a shipment in transit. Access to real-time pickup and delivery confirmation has improved forecasting. Furthermore, potential problems are recognized faster, making immaculate recovery a possibility.

SNI's benefits include a reduction in voice communication costs and greater scheduling efficiency. Managers' time is now more flexible since dispatching drivers is no longer their main concern. Managers can concentrate on improving operations and communicating with customers rather than scheduling drivers. In addition, equipment is better utilized to increase productivity. Perhaps most important, zero defect service has positioned SNI as a leader among carriers, as a result of its reliable customer service and accurate delivery and information exchange. This has enabled SNI to create a core competency that is difficult to match.

Based on Agis Saplukis, "Computers Give Truckers an Edge," *New York Times National Edition,* May 25, 1992, p. 17; and Schneider National, Inc., Sales Publications.

to fill a platinum customer order when it is not available at the primary service location. These methods range from transferring inventory from secondary locations to searching worldwide for products at other 3M facilities and, when appropriate, arranging for direct delivery using premium transportation service. In select situations inventory previously sold to other "platinum club members" is "borrowed" to meet a new-order requirement. The goal is never to back-order an item, thereby making it abundantly clear that 3M is committed to do whatever it takes to make perfect service a reality for a platinum club member. The objective of the perfect order strategy is to build customer loyalty for 3M and slam the door of opportunity on competitors.

In the hospital service industry, Johnson & Johnson follows a practice for selected customers wherein all back-orders are automatically assigned for shipment from a secondary supply point using premium overnight transportation service. In some situations, the back-ordered product filled from a secondary supply point actually arrives at a customer's business before the main order arrives from the primary service location.

The force behind a commitment to zero defect performance is an understanding that the customers receiving the service will respond by granting preferred supplier status for the products involved. Colonial Hospital Supplies' extensive commitment to service selected hospitals within twelve hours means that product requirements must be defined and satisfied to the individual nurse station or surgical unit level. The expectation is that fast, reliable service will result in a near exclusive buyer-supplier relationship. For a perfect order program to be legal from an antitrust viewpoint, any customer must be eligible to participate in the upgraded service provided the customer is willing and able to commit and satisfy expectations related to purchase volume, exclusivity, or other requirements. It is important to keep in mind that perfect order performance commitment is over and above a firm's basic service program. The basic service commitment is offered without discrimination to all customers. Those customers that participate in zero defect programs must be willing to develop alliance relationships and commit significant future business.

The managerial and operational effort required for perfect order performance is expensive to implement and requires outstanding information support. Such superior service performance must be focused on customers that require, appreciate, and are willing to respond to such exceptional performance with increased purchase loyalty. If a firm desires to deploy a perfect order strategy, it is essential that it fully understand the risk and potential downside. Zero defect commitment has no room for error. The customer expectation is that the promised performance will, in fact, be there each and every time. Only if the commitment is real, believable, and consistently achieved will such logistical performance translate into efficiencies for the customer. No room exists for lip service: the proof of the perfect order is zero defect performance each and every time.

VALUE-ADDED SERVICES

The notion of value-added service is significantly different from the logistical performance involved in basic customer service capability and perfect order accommodation. Value-added services refer to unique or specific activities that firms can jointly work out to increase their effectiveness and efficiency. Value-added services solidify business arrangements. Value-added services are easy to illustrate but difficult to generalize because they are customer-specific.

A clear distinction exists between basic service, zero defect, and value-added services. Basic service is the customer service program upon which a firm builds its fundamental business relationships. All customers are treated equally at a specified level to build and maintain overall customer loyalty. Zero defect leading to perfect order performance is the maximum level of logistical availability, operational performance, and reliance. Perfect order commitments can be offered to select customers as a way to gain and maintain preferred supplier status. Value-added services represent alternatives to a zero defect commitment as a way to build customer solidarity.

Table 3-4 provides a list of value-added services that are observable in the relationships between grocery manufacturers and retailers or wholesalers. A common characteristic among firms that exploit value-added services is their high

TABLE 3-4   TYPICAL VALUE-ADDED SERVICES PROVIDED BY GROCERY MANUFACTURERS

Price marking	**Cross-dock facilitator**
	Advanced shipment notification
Packaging	Mixed store-ready pallets
Special packs	Precise delivery times
Inner packs	**Special shipment**
Special marking	Drop shipment
Point-of-sale presentations	Direct store delivery
Vendor-managed inventory	Quick and continuous replenishment

degree of unyielding commitment to basic service performance.[15] When a firm is committed to developing unique value-added solutions for major customers, it rapidly becomes involved in customized or tailored logistics. In effect it is doing unique things to help specific customers achieve their expectations. Motorola's ability to produce a customer-unique pager or Toyota's capability to build a car to customer specification and deliver it within a week are prime examples of how value can be added to an otherwise basic product. In a value-added context, firms can provide unique product packages, create customized labels, create special bulk packaging, offer information services to facilitate purchasing, place prices on products, build point-of-sale displays, and so forth, to stimulate business. In a purely logistical context, value-added services may require direct store delivery or be facilitated by a cross-dock arrangement or any other service that creates continuous value for key customers. Value-added services are most typically observed in well-established channel relationships.

In a logistical context, a great number of the day-to-day value-added options that buyers and sellers agree to are performed by service specialists such as carriers, warehousing firms, and companies that specialize in such operations. For example, in the case of a trucking company, value-added service goes beyond the provision of basic transportation and may incorporate additional services such as sorting and sequencing to meet unique requirements of specific shippers. The following example illustrates the extent of one value-added service performed by a warehouse specialist:

> The warehouse operator agreed to repackage bubble gum and soccer balls into a combined promotional package. On the surface the task sounds simple. However, consider the steps involved: (1) weigh and package three pounds of bubble gum from a bulk carton container; (2) inflate the soccer ball; (3) place the bubble gum bag into the soccer ball box; (4) place the soccer ball on top of the box; (5) shrink wrap ball and box; and (6) place six completed units into a master carton, label and seal.[16]

The end product of the illustrated value-added service was the unique creation of a customized point-of-sale promotional package to support the customer's product

---

[15]Joseph B. Fuller, James O'Conor, and Richard Rawlinson, ''Tailored Logistics: The Next Advantage,'' *Harvard Business Review,* **71:**3, May–June 1993, pp. 87–98.

[16]Donald J. Bowersox, Patricia J. Daugherty, Cornelia L. Dröge, Dale S. Rogers, and Daniel L. Wardlow, *Leading Edge Logistics: Competitive Positioning for the 1990's,* Oak Brook, Ill.: The Council of Logistics Management, 1989.

marketing strategy. The warehouse service firm was able to provide the value-added activities at a lower cost than either of the firms supplying the primary ingredients. This ability to specialize in unique solutions is a fundamental reason for a growing trend toward using specialized service providers to perform value-added operations. Such providers can achieve economy of scale and retain essential flexibility while allowing the marketing companies involved to focus on their core business requirements.

The range of value-added services spans a broad number of business-stimulating activities. Research of firms that specialize in performing value-added services identified five primary performance areas: customer-focused services, promotion-focused services, manufacturing-focused services, time-focused services, and basic service.

Customer-Focused Services

Customer-focused value-added services offer buyers and sellers alternative ways to distribute products using third-party specialists. For example, UPS developed a unique system to deliver Nabisco's Planters-Life Savers snack products to outlets not traditionally serviced by candy and tobacco distributors. A division of Exel Distribution established a creative order entry service and arranged for home delivery of Procter & Gamble disposable diapers for premature babies. It is also common for warehouses to provide pick-price-repack services to facilitate distribution of standard manufacturer products in unique configurations as required by warehouse, club, and convenience stores. A final example of customer-focused value-added services is fulfillment. Fulfillment consists of processing customer orders for manufacturers, delivering directly to stores or homes, and providing such follow through as detailing required to maintain retail store shelf stocking. Such specialized value-added service can be effectively used to support new-product introduction as well as seasonal distribution on a local market basis.

Promotion-Focused Services

Promotion-focused value-added services involve the assembly of unique point-of-sale display modules coupled with a wide variety of other related services aimed at stimulating sales. Point-of-sale displays can contain multiple products from different suppliers mixed in a multitiered display unit designed to fit a special retail store. In select situations, promotion-focused value-added services may involve special presentations for in-store product sampling and even direct-mail promotion. Many promotion-focused value-added services include logistical support of point-of-sale advertising and promotion materials. In numerous situations gifts and premium merchandise included in a promotional effort are handled and shipped by service specialists.

Manufacturing-Focused Services

As the name implies, manufacturing-focused value-added services involve unique product assortment and delivery to support manufacturing. Since every customer's physical facilities and manufacturing assembly are unique, it follows that the delivery and presentation of inbound materials and components should ideally be customized. One warehouse firm repackages a popular consumer dishwashing soap in as many as six different carton configurations to support alternative promotion and class of trade requirements. In another situation, surgical kits are assembled to satisfy the unique requirements of specific physicians. Still another example is a warehouse that cuts and installs various lengths and sizes of hose to fit pumps to individual customer specification. These are a few selected examples of value-added services being performed in the logistical channel by specialists. These specialists are able to reduce risk by postponing product finalization until customized orders are received. The sidebar on sequencing provides an example of value-added services in a manufacturing situation. While hiring specialists to perform value-added services may mean that cost per unit is higher than if the activity was incorporated as part of high-speed manufacturing, the reduction in anticipatory risk related to producing incorrect products is a significant benefit. Rather than produce unique products based on forecast requirements, basic products can be modified to accommodate specific customer requirements. The result is improved customer service.

Time-Focused Services

Time-focused value-added services involve using specialists to sort, mix, and sequence inventory prior to delivery. A popular form of time-based value-added service is the just-in-time (JIT) feeder warehouse. Under this concept suppliers make daily deliveries to a JIT facility located adjacent to an assembly plant. The feeder warehouse sorts multiple vendor components into exact quantities that are sequenced for delivery to the assembly line when and where required. The objective

---

SEQUENCING TO INCREASE EFFICIENCY

When an automotive manufacturer was getting ready to build a new car in an existing manufacturing plant, it looked for ways to increase efficiency and reduce inventory commitment. One area examined for improvement was its subassembly. This subassembly took the headliner (carpet for the roof) and assembled the console unit and overhead lights prior to assembling the entire component in the car. The headliner came in six different colors to match the interior, seats, and carpet. Also, there was an upper- and lower-level console and two different styles of lights. Altogether that equates to twenty-four different options.

With this many options, the subassembly area took up a lot of space that was needed to build the new car. As such, the manufacturing plant looked at moving this subassembly operation to a customizer that would per-

form the actual assembly operations. Also, the customizer would handle dispersement.

Dispersement to the plant would have to involve sequencing the headliner components so that when the parts arrived at the plant, they were in the exact order in terms of color and options as were required. For example, if a blue interior car with upper-level console and lighting options was first, followed by a gray interior lower-level option car, then a blue headliner component needed to be first, followed by the gray component, with both having the correct options.

This is a fictitious example using authors' experiences with customization and sequencing operations for option-oriented subassembly processes.

is to reduce assembly plant handling and inspection to an absolute minimum. This type of JIT service is the primary method used to support assembly at Honda in Marysville, Ohio. While somewhat different conceptually, Exel Distribution mixes food manufacturer products to exact assortments required by specific Shaw's retail food stores. This customer mixing service eliminates or avoids warehousing on the part of both manufacturers and Shaw's. The key feature of time-focused services is that they eliminate unnecessary work and facilitate maximum speed of service. Logistics time-based strategies, a primary form of competitive superiority, are discussed in Chapter 16.

Basic Service

In addition to the unique or tailored forms of value-added services, specialists can be used to provide day-to-day execution of all or part of a firm's basic customer service program. A wide range of services are available from specialists to support any or all logistical requirements. While a large number of companies perform transportation and warehousing services, the list of additional innovative and unique services such as inventory management, order processing, invoicing, and return merchandise handling covers the gamut of supply chain logistics. Many firms offer comprehensive logistical service packages that provide shippers with what amounts to turnkey services. For example, Roadway Logistics Services functions as a third-party transportation service provider for Libbey-Owens-Ford Glass (LOF). Not only does Roadway perform transportation services, but it also arranges for other carriers to handle segments of LOF's freight and facilitates necessary administration and carrier payment using still another specialized service provider, Cass Logistics, Inc. By using this form of outside specialist to help perform basic logistics services, LOF has reduced the number of total carriers involved in its business. At one point, LOF dealt with over 530 carriers, but now that operation is managed through a much narrower base.[17]

Conclusion

Value-added services are both easy to illustrate and difficult to generalize. Because such services are typically designed to satisfy the requirements of specific customers, the arrangements are unique. Value-added services can be performed directly by participants in a business relationship or by service specialists. During the past decade, buyers and sellers have increasingly turned to specialists because of their flexibility and capability to concentrate on providing the required service. This outsourcing of the responsibility to perform value-added services, combined with a trend toward offering more such enhancements, has been a primary stimulant behind the growth in the logistics service industry. Nevertheless, regardless of how the specific service arrangement is organized and implemented, it is clear that logistics-based, value-added services are a growing dimension of overall customer service performance.

[17]Ed Root, Presentation at the Logistics Management Executive Development Seminar, East Lansing, Mich., May 10–15, 1993.

CUSTOMER SATISFACTION AND SUCCESS: THE BERGEN BRUNSWIG EXAMPLE

The strategy of using logistics competency to gain competitive advantage is based on a broad commitment to customer-focused marketing. The fundamental idea is that a firm's long-term ability to expand market share faster than overall industry growth depends on attracting and holding an industry's most successful customers. The notion of customer-focused marketing is to concentrate resources on selected key accounts that place a high priority on a supplier's logistical competency. The ideal arrangement would involve predetermined agreement to achieve profitable growth of a customer's business. The idea is basic: as customers succeed, so will their preferred suppliers. The potential benefit of close working relationships is best understood by contrasting basic customer service with the highly popularized concept of customer satisfaction and with the more advanced notion of customer success.

In terms of customer impact, the fundamental concept is basic service. As noted earlier, basic service is typically viewed in terms of availability, operational performance, and reliability. The traditional wisdom behind providing these basic service attributes has been that suppliers should try to be good—but not too good. In other words, the long-standing paradigm has been that extremely high levels of service are prohibitively expensive to offer across the board to all customers. Most recently the paradigm has somewhat shifted among progressive firms. The more current belief is that providing availability and timely delivery of products to customers is not an extraordinary commitment. Therefore, the basic level of overall service has escalated to higher levels of day in and day out performance. However, the typical commitment still falls short of the perfect order.

The notion of customer satisfaction propels commitment beyond basic service. It involves a combination of highly selective value-added service arrangements and, as appropriate, the commitment of perfect order performance. Customer satisfaction is a total enterprise commitment that has recently been popularized by authors such as Peters and Austin, Zemke and Schaaf, and Schlesinger and Heskett, who emphasize the importance of delighting selected customers by providing whatever services are necessary and expanding extraordinary effort to ensure fail-safe performance.[18] The so-called immaculate recovery involves actions discussed earlier that require extraordinary efforts—such as flying products from around the globe—to be sure that key customers' requirements are satisfied. The idea of exceeding expectations or delighting customers has intrinsic appeal. However, most proponents agree that such extra performance must be strategically focused on customers that have high profit potential if associated cost is to be justified.

The most demanding service commitment is to focus on facilitating customer success. By definition, a success program and its related commitments focus on long-term business relationships that have growth potential and offer high probability of achieving the desired results. To ensure that a customer is successful may

---

[18]Tom Peters and Nancy Austin, *A Passion for Excellence,* New York: Random House, Inc., 1985; Ron Zemke and Dick Schaaf, *The Service Edge,* New York: New American Library, 1989; and Leonard A. Schlesinger and James L. Heskett, ''The Service-Driven Service Company,'' *Harvard Business Review,* **69**:5, September–October 1991, pp. 71–81.

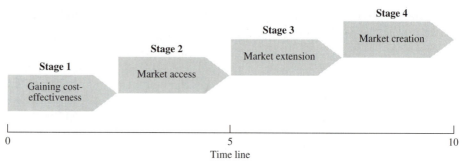

FIGURE 3-3   Development of business success based on logistical competency.

require a supplier to help reinvent the way a product is sold or distributed. A classical example is the transformation of IKEA from a relatively small Swedish mail-order furniture operation to a global retailer of home furnishings. The fundamental transformation required a deep commitment to meeting customer requirements in a creative manner and was achieved only by exacting support of suppliers.[19]

A similar approach to working with customers to achieve success is used by Baxter Healthcare Corporation to support hospitals.[20] The creation of such long-term success programs requires careful planning and can involve several steps to ultimately create new joint market opportunities.

The following discussion of Bergen Brunswig's model of how to stimulate change is a comprehensive example of how a firm can focus on customer success. Bergen Brunswig used a four-stage process to enhance the business success of its retail drugstore customers: cost-effectiveness, market access, market extension, and market creation. The long-term process is illustrated in Figure 3-3. The Bergen Brunswig model illustrates the fusion of information technology required to develop cross-organizational success.

Bergen Brunswig developed a creative logistics-based program to exchange information and become operationally involved with drug retailers. Retailer alliances initiated by Bergen Brunswig and other selected drug wholesalers have revolutionized the independent pharmacy segment of the retail drug industry. Whereas ten years ago drugstores were serviced by well over 200 wholesalers, today 5 wholesale firms dominate total industry sales. The wholesale sector has emerged from the brink of collapse to logistically support approximately 70 percent of all retail drugstore distribution.[21] Industry efficiency improvements have been significant. Tailoring services to specific customers has served to establish incentives for maintaining long-term alliances. The nature of Bergen Brunswig's cus-

---

[19]Richard Normann and Rafael Ramirez, ''From Value Chain to Value Constellation: Designing Interactive Strategy,'' *Harvard Business Review,* **71:**4, July–August 1993, pp. 65–77.

[20]Betty Conway, ''Improving Customer Profitability: The Ultimate Customer Satisfaction,'' *Annual Proceedings of the Council of Logistics Management,* **1,** 1991, pp. 307–313.

[21]*1992 Drug Store Market Guide,* Mohegan Lake, N.Y.: Melnor Publishing, Inc., p. XV.

tomer service initiative is reviewed to illustrate how logistical competency can be used to gain competitive superiority.

Cost-Effectiveness

The first and most fundamental step was to gain cost-effectiveness. It was essential that the process and necessary related controls be in place to ensure that basic services could be provided at a consistently high level of performance and in a cost-effective manner. From a managerial perspective, it is prerequisite that a firm be able to efficiently perform the basic logistic services required by customers. Most firms that are serious about quality agree there is little room for basic operational error. Unless a firm is able to deliver quality service at reasonable cost, there is no reason for customers to commit additional business and there is limited possibility of moving forward toward a more exacting relationship.

Market Access

The market access stage consisted of higher-level commitments to customers that expressed a willingness to cooperate in efforts to achieve joint objectives. In other words, market access consists of buyers and sellers working together and sharing basic information to facilitate smooth joint operations. It is important to stress that no real level of customer selectivity was involved in market access. For example, Bergen Brunswig needed to establish a basic service commitment to all druggists who were willing to utilize them as a wholesale supplier. The only differential in the timing or level of service during the access stage was determined by the customer's purchase quantity. Once Bergen Brunswig offered retailers a specific service program, it became a principle of fundamental business fairness and legality that each druggist who purchased required volumes would receive equal basic services. For Bergen Brunswig, this commitment meant daily replenishment of exact inventory requirements within a consistent delivery schedule.

Market Extension

Market extension intensifies a business arrangement. Extension is based on moving toward zero defects and introducing value-added services in an effort to solidify and expand the business relationship. At this point the relationship became highly selective since the number of customers that were willing or able to participate was limited. In Bergen Brunswig's strategy, such value-added alliances consisted of a variety of programs to improve the competitiveness of selected customers that were willing to commit to Bergen Brunswig as almost a sole-source supplier. Typical of such value-added innovations were sophisticated bar coding, computer terminals for pharmacy checkout counters, point-of-sale encoding, shelf plan-o-gramming, immediate price change administration, profitability, and inventory turn reports. These innovations were designed to increase operating efficiency and extend overall competitiveness. Such value-added services were offered only to customers that committed to an extended business relationship.

Market Creation

The final stage, market creation, requires full commitment to a customer's success. While all previous stages contribute to competence, the final stage represents above-and-beyond initiatives to enhance success. In the case of Bergen Brunswig, one form of market creation consisted of researching and developing new and innovative ways to make relatively small druggists increasingly competitive with larger vertically integrated chains. For example, Bergen Brunswig pioneered and cooperatively tested such revenue-generating devices as selling cut flowers and carryout food. Creative arrangements also extended to the implementation of joint systems that electronically linked Bergen Brunswig to its retail customers for purposes of providing a full range of process control services.

The full impact of logistics is felt at every stage of the process. It is important to gain control and become cost-effective. High-level basic service is the key to market access. During market extension, the commitment to perfect performance and value-added services solidifies the basic business arrangement. The relationship matures into a long-term situation wherein future growth is attained by helping the customer achieve the most successful business possible. The development of a business relationship built on advanced customer service performance takes time—as much as ten years or more. The trust aspects of joint operations and free information exchange that are fundamental to such collaborations cannot be engineered and implemented in an untested, unseasoned business arrangement.

SUMMARY

Logistics exists for the sole purpose of providing external and internal customers with timely and accurate product delivery. Therefore, customer service is the key element in developing a logistics strategy.

The notion of customer-focused marketing finds its roots in the marketing concept. The fundamental ideals of the marketing concept are that (1) customer needs are more basic than products or services, (2) products and services become meaningful only when viewed and positioned in a customer context, and (3) volume is secondary to profit.

To implement a marketing strategy it is essential to view all activities related to the process of gaining and maintaining customers. Logistics is one of these key competencies that can be developed as a core strategy. To the extent that a firm builds its competitive advantage on logistical competency, it will enjoy a uniqueness that is difficult to duplicate. However, no competitive situation is static. Therefore, logistical performance must be viewed in a life-cycle context in which customer requirements are constantly changing.

Customer service itself is aimed at providing significant value-added benefits for the entire supply chain. To be superior, a firm needs a basic service capability that balances availability, operational performance, and reliability. Since there are no substitutes for performance, a firm needs to develop and implement a basic service program for all of its customers. How much to offer as part of the basic customer service platform requires careful cost-benefit analysis. This is a strategic decision because, generally speaking, customers' expectations are increasing. More and more, business situations call for exacting customer service commitments.

The strategy of perfect order service is to enhance performance by doing whatever it takes to satisfy important key customers. This requires significant human and financial resources so that the payoff in terms of customer purchase loyalty will result. To the extent that customers are cooperative, higher-level performance can be developed in the form of value-added services. Whereas zero defect refers to higher basic service performance, value-added service refers to doing new and unique things to help key customers become successful. Because no two value-added commitments are necessarily the same, many firms have turned to outside specialists to perform service requirements.

Going beyond basic service to create customer satisfaction and facilitate long-term success requires significant overall commitment. The profile of Bergen Brunswig illustrated how a long-term arrangement can build on logistical competency. In Chapter 4 attention is directed to the supply chain relationships that constitute the playing field for logistical competency.

QUESTIONS

1 What considerations should be employed to identify the appropriate customer service measures? Then, define quantitative measures for ongoing evaluation.

2 Explain the fundamental trade-off between customer service costs and benefits. How are trade-offs justified?

3 Define availability, and discuss ways to measure and track it.

4 Compare and contrast speed and flexibility as operational performance activities. In some situations, is one activity more critical than the other? Why or why not?

5 Identify ways a firm can develop malfunction/recovery contingency plans to proactively manage crisis situations.

6 What are the important logistical concerns during the introduction stage of a product's life cycle? During growth? During saturation-maturity stage? During obsolescence-decline stage?

7 Define basic service, zero defect or perfect order service, and value-added service. Provide two examples of each.

8 Explain this sentence: ''The phenomenon of increasing customer expectations is clearly observed in what logisticians refer to as the *shrinking service window*.'' Why is this important? What are the implications for logistics?

9 How do the five categories of value-added services differ? How are these five categories similar?

10 Discuss how an existing firm could use or has used Bergen Brunswig's four-stage process of cost-effectiveness, market access, market extension, and market creation to gain competitive superiority.

CHAPTER 4

SUPPLY CHAIN RELATIONSHIPS

CHANNEL STRUCTURE

THE ECONOMICS OF DISTRIBUTION
  Traditional Functions
  Specialization
  Assortment

CHANNEL RELATIONSHIPS
  Supply Chain Competitiveness
  Risk, Power, and Leadership
  Elements of Success

LOGISTICAL SERVICE ALLIANCES
  Factors Stimulating Service-Based Alliances
  Increasing Service Provider Efficiency
  Integrated Logistics Service Providers

SUMMARY

QUESTIONS

Appendix: Marketing Channel Structure

DESCRIPTIVE INSTITUTIONAL APPROACH
  Merchant Middlemen
  Functional Middlemen

GRAPHIC APPROACH

COMMODITY GROUPINGS

FUNCTIONAL TREATMENTS

CHANNEL ARRANGEMENT
  CLASSIFICATION
  Single Transaction Channels
  Conventional Channels
  Voluntary Arrangements (VAs)

CONCLUSION

Almost from the start, Henry Ford envisioned a totally self-sufficient industrial empire. In River Rouge, just southwest of Detroit, Ford developed a huge manufacturing complex that included an inland port and an intricate network of rail and road transportation. Ford's objective was *control.* To achieve this goal, he set out to develop the world's first complex vertically integrated firm.[1]

[1]Carol Gelderman, *Henry Ford: The Wayward Capitalist,* New York: St. Martin's Press, 1981, pp. 226–270.

To ensure a reliable supply of materials Ford invested in coal mines, iron-ore deposits, timberlands, glass factories, and even land to grow soybeans used to manufacture paint. Ford's commitment to self-sufficiency extended to buying 2.5 million acres in Brazil to develop a rubber plantation he called Fordlandia.

Ford's desire for control went beyond material and components. To transport materials to River Rouge and finished product to dealers he invested in railroads, trucks, and both Great Lakes and ocean vessels. The idea was to control all aspects of inventory moving from a network of over forty manufacturing, service, and assembly plants throughout the United States, Canada, Australia, New Zealand, the United Kingdom, and South Africa to dealers throughout the globe.

This was clearly one of the most ambitious vertical integration schemes, and Ford found he needed help. At the peak of Ford's vertical extension the firm faced economic, regulatory, and labor union barriers that eventually required products and services to be provided by a network of independent suppliers.[2] The key to effective marketing was finally found by developing a strong network of independent dealers. As time passed, Ford discovered that specialized firms could perform most essential work as well as or better than his own bureaucracy. In fact, these specialists often outperformed Ford's own units with respect to quality and cost. Entrepreneurial firms soon became contributors to Ford's network. Over time, the Ford strategy shifted from ownership-based control to one of orchestrating channel relationships. The financial resources at Ford were shifted to developing and maintaining core manufacturing competencies. Ford found out that in the final analysis, *no firm can be self-sufficient.*

This chapter treats the complex topic of how firms develop and manage logistical supply chain relationships. In the aggregate, over 5 million firms are engaged in the process of manufacturing and distributing products in the United States. Over 2 million of these firms provide essential services required to position materials and products when and where required.

The first section of this chapter deals with overall channel structure in highly developed industrial economies. The sophisticated structure includes elements much broader than logistical operations. In this initial section the overall scope of channels is examined because it is important that logistics professionals fully understand broad-based channel dynamics. The channel should be viewed as the logistical playing field. The next section presents the economics of distribution that underlie and influence specific channel arrangements. The key to developing successful relationships is to understand specialization and assortment. The following section discusses the nature of logistical relationships. Attention is directed to supply chain competitiveness; the relationship of risk, power, and leadership; and the characteristics of successful supply chain management. The final section discusses logistical service alliances. The objective of the chapter is to develop an understanding of the importance of supply chain relationships. An appendix is provided to offer extended discussion of the full range of structure alternatives available in overall channel design.

---

[2]For discussion on these barriers, see Booton Herndon, *Ford,* New York: Weybright and Talley, 1969, pp. 171–175; and Carol Gelderman, *Henry Ford: The Wayward Capitalist,* New York: St. Martin's Press, 1981, pp. 270–275.

CHANNEL STRUCTURE

Among the least understood areas of business is the complex grouping of institutions referred to as the distribution or marketing channel. The channel is the arena within which a free market system performs ownership exchange of products and services. It is the battlefield of business where a firm's ultimate success or failure is determined. The diversity and complexity of channel arrangements make it difficult to describe and generalize the challenges managers confront when developing a comprehensive channel strategy. Business managers need to understand channel economics and relationship management in order to plan and implement satisfactory business arrangements. In actual practice considerable planning and negotiation precede establishment of a channel structure. Once a strategy is implemented, it is common for managers to constantly change or modify one or more facets of their channel arrangement. Thus, channel arrangements are dynamic as firms constantly seek to improve their relative position. A superior channel structure can lead to competitive advantage.

A working definition is a useful way to understand the broad scope of channel considerations. The American Marketing Association defines a distribution channel as *the structure of intracompany organizational units and extracompany agents and dealers, wholesale and retail, through which a commodity, product, or service is marketed.*[3] In a technical sense, a channel is a group of businesses that take ownership title to products or facilitate exchange during the marketing process from original owner to final buyer.

Figure 4-1 illustrates an overall generic channel structure required to complete the marketing process. One advantage of graphing channel arrangements in a flow diagram format is the ability to show, in a logical sequence, the variety and positioning of institutions that participate in ownership transfer. Of particular interest in Figure 4-1 is the range of institutions that products may pass through and

---

[3]American Marketing Association definition as shown in Michael J. Baker, *Dictionary of Marketing and Advertising,* 2d ed., New York: Nichols Publishing, 1990, p. 47.

FIGURE 4-1   Generic channels of distribution.

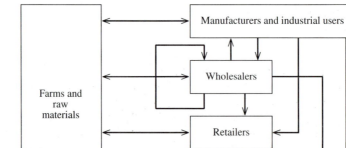

the alternative paths they can physically follow as they flow from original owner to final buyer. For example, retail stores may purchase from all levels of supply ranging from farmers to wholesalers. Despite the attractive simplicity of descriptive flowchart structures such as Figure 4-1, they provide only minimal assistance to managers concerned with developing and implementing a channel strategy.

Figure 4-2 illustrates the range of channel participants involved in food distribution in the United States. Figure 4-3 provides a mapping of alternative arrangements and the resultant channel structure that J. R. Simplot utilizes to distribute a

FIGURE 4-2   Food channel participants in the United States. *(Adapted from Thomas R. Pierson, Food Industry Institute, Michigan State University, unpublished. Reproduced with permission.)*

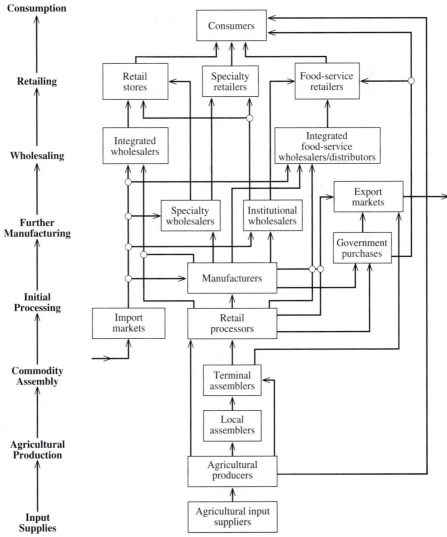

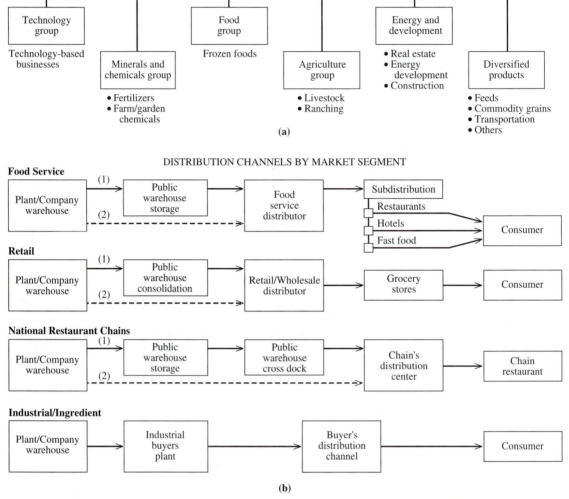

FIGURE 4-3   Channel alignment of one manufacturer. *(J. R. Simplot Company, Logistics Group. Reproduced with permission.)*

broad product assortment to different market segments. These figures clearly illustrate distribution complexity in terms of the channel relationships that must be negotiated, implemented, and managed. A way to give meaning to channel descriptions is to focus on the relationship required to make channels function. Thus, channels are properly viewed as *systems of relationships among businesses that participate in the process of buying and selling products and services.*[4]

[4]Donald J. Bowersox and M. Bixby Cooper, *Strategic Marketing Channel Management,* New York: McGraw-Hill, Inc., 1992, p. 4.

Relationship management is a relatively new label applied to an old and fundamental area of business. Since the beginning of commercial activity, managers have been concerned with developing and positioning customer and supplier relationships. The new thrust behind the popularity of relationship management is based on the belief that successful business arrangements are most likely to result when participating firms cooperate in planning and executing performance. The emphasis on *cooperation* represents a shift from managing relationships on the basis of power-driven *adversarial* approaches. The underlying paradigm is that all parties to the arrangement will be better off if emphasis is focused on joint problem solving to improve overall efficiency and effectiveness. The basic premise of relationship management is that cooperation between all participants in a channel system ultimately will result in synergism leading to the highest level of joint achievement. This shift in priority toward building relationships is extremely important for logistics. As noted in Chapter 1, the widespread advent of logistical-based alliances is one of the main forces behind the logistical renaissance. Later in this chapter, attention will focus on the development of supply chain management and the role that logistics alliances can play in such relationships.

As a basis to understanding channel relationships it is important to stress that not all channel members have an equal stake in the success of each arrangement. To visualize this variance in commitment, it is useful to group channel participants as primary or specialized. A *primary channel participant* is a business that is willing to participate in the inventory ownership responsibility or assume other significant aspects of financial risk. A *specialized channel participant* is a business that participates in channel relationships by performing essential services for primary participants for a fee. To illustrate, a retailer is a primary channel member that typically has a majority of business assets committed to inventory and accepts the associated risk. In contrast, a trucking firm's involvement in a channel may be limited to moving products between two geographical locations for a specified fee. Because the carrier's involvement and associated risk are limited to performing the specific transportation service, the carrier is referred to as a specialist.

Table 4-1 provides a range of businesses that are typically considered primary and specialized channel participants. While gauging relative risk between primary and specialized channel members is important, the fundamental focus when developing channel relationships is to determine how the capabilities of all potential participants can be orchestrated into a relational network capable of satisfying end customer expectations.

THE ECONOMICS OF DISTRIBUTION

The foundation for developing a successful channel arrangement rests in fully understanding the underlying economics of distribution. The economic aspects of channel relationships extend beyond issues of logistical operations.

Several distinct functions must be completed to achieve effective distribution. As a general rule, specialists can perform these functions in a manner superior to firms that have other core competencies. For example, a package distribution specialist like United Parcel Service can perform transportation in a manner typi-

TABLE 4-1   TYPICAL PRIMARY AND SPECIALIZED CHANNEL PARTICIPANTS

Primary participants	
Manufacturers (industrial, consumer) Agriculture Mining	Wholesalers (merchant wholesalers, agents) Retailers

Specialized participants	
Functional specialists	Support specialists
Transportation Warehousing Assembly Fulfillment Sequencing Merchandising	Financial Informational Advertising Insurance Advisory/research Arrangers

cally superior to a privately operated delivery service. In a channel situation, the combined capabilities of primary and specialized participants should achieve a basic requirement called *assortment.* Assortment consists of sorting and configuring a variety of products and commodities to satisfy the exact buyer requirements. The primary objective of a distribution channel is to create value by generating acceptable form, possession, time, and place. Assortment is the channel process that results in the above attributes. In order to design an effective channel, it is essential that the requirements related to each attribute be specified. Attention in this section is focused on those attributes that are basically achieved through logistical operations. Logistical operations are the primary source of achieving time and place in a channel arrangement. Through the provision of value-added services, logistics can also make significant contributions to facilitating the correct form and conditions that most satisfy possession. Thus, logistical operations are a prime contributor to overall channel success.

This section examines the above concepts in depth. Initially the functional requirements of overall distribution are examined. Next, the concept of specialization is reviewed. This sets the framework for description and illustration of the assortment process.

Traditional Functions

A functional approach to what a channel does provides a logical explanation of the overall distribution process. Figure 4-4 illustrates the most commonly agreed upon list of traditional functions. A *function,* from a channel perspective, represents work considered to be universal to marketing and logistics of all products and services. In the typical channel arrangement, a specific function may be alternatively performed by different channel members. However, it must be performed for the channel to be successful. It also may be performed or duplicated numerous times. For example, storage may be performed by a manufacturer, wholesaler,

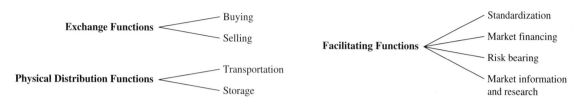

FIGURE 4-4   Marketing functions.

retailer, and even the final buyer. On the other hand, market financing might be performed by only one institution for the overall distribution channel. The lesson learned from Henry Ford stressed that no firm can be totally self-sufficient. Successful distribution involves precise cooperation among many participants and requires aggregate performance of essential functional work.

Early scholars grouped functional requirements for effective distribution under three headings: exchange, physical distribution, and facilitating.[5] The *exchange functions* involved broad activities related to buying and selling. As such, exchange concerns activities required to transfer ownership. The *physical distribution function* is the origin of what is referred to in this book as logistics. The essential activity consists of getting the right products to the right place at the right time. In contemporary logistics the scope of operational concern is significantly broader than transportation and storage, transcending broad supply chain arrangements. Logistics is viewed as encompassing all work related to inventory positioning, which can also involve aspects of satisfying form and possession requirements. The traditional *facilitating functions* include standardization, market financing, risk bearing, and market information and research activities.

Two basic concepts—specialization and assortment—provide valuable insight into how the work related to achieving these universal functional requirements gets done. These concepts are discussed next.

Specialization

Specialization is a fundamental driver of distribution efficiency. In actual practice some types of businesses can introduce economies to the logistical process because they are capable of performing essential functions better than others. While functions, as defined above, are essential to the distribution process, it is not necessary for any channel participants to be held responsible for performance of any specific activity. In fact, the economic justification for specialized channel participants is their ability to superiorly perform a specific function. Thus, while a given business may be expendable in a specific distribution network, the basic functions must be performed. For example, a privately owned transportation carrier can be sold and replaced by a public contract carrier, but the *function* of delivery must still occur.

Specialization is fundamental to efficient business. When one considers the sheer

[5]For a discussion of traditional functional classification, see Rayburn D. Tousley, Eugene Clark, and Fred E. Clark, *Principles of Marketing,* New York: Macmillan, 1962, pp. 14–20.

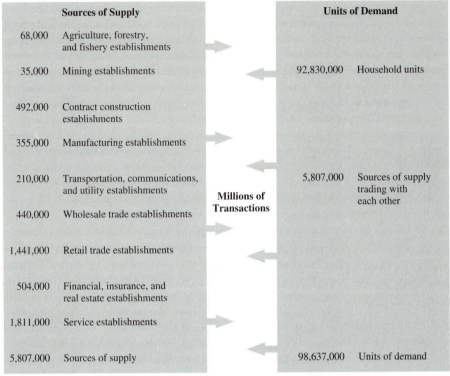

FIGURE 4-5   Exchange: matching demand and supply in the United States. (1992 Statistical Abstract of the United States, *U.S. Department of Commerce, p. 526.*)

magnitude of logistical requirements that must be satisfied in a highly developed economy, the reasons for underlying specialization become obvious. Figure 4-5 provides a statistical profile of exchange requirements in the United States economy.

The logic of specialization is based on economies of scale and scope. The general notion has long standing in the business literature.[6] When a firm specializes in performance of a specific function, it develops the scale and scope to achieve operational economies. These economic benefits, coupled with associated expertise, represent the core competency of the specialized business.

The logistics service provider market includes many different types of specialized firms. The most notable in terms of the sheer number of firms are for-hire transportation and warehouse service companies. Additional special service providers include material handlers, custom brokers, pallet providers, and packaging designers. In recent years, the growth of a new specialized industry consisting of facilitators has mushroomed. Facilitators are firms that specialize in providing

---

[6]George E. Stigler, ''The Division of Labor Is Limited by the Extent of the Market,'' *Journal of Political Economy,* **59:**3, June 1951, pp. 185–193.

customized packaging, insertion of marketing incentives, coupon redemption for mechandise, and other essential value-added services. The economic justification for facilitators is their expertise in providing desired services more efficiently than their primary channel counterparts.

The justification for outsourcing all or part of the logistical requirements to business specialists is found in economies of scale and expertise. Specialization is the underlying construct of product assortment. Assortment is most efficiently achieved through specialization.

Assortment

Channel arrangements typically involve cooperative performance by a number of independent businesses that orchestrate their activities to deliver products and material assortments to the right location at the desired time. As noted earlier, to satisfy assortment requirements, a number of essential functions must be performed by channel participants. From an efficiency viewpoint, the essential functions should ideally be performed with minimum duplication. The management of supply chain relationships involves working out logistical solutions that introduce simplification and standardization to reduce duplication and associated waste. The goal is to achieve as much synergism as possible during product assortment. To fully appreciate the importance of developing logistical relationships, it is essential to understand how assortment is accomplished in a channel arrangement.

Assortment has received considerable attention in business literature.[7] It is the process of creating and positioning a mix of products desired by a customer. At strategically positioned locations in a distribution channel, products must be concentrated, sorted, and dispersed to the next location in the supply chain. Assortment accomplishes this task. The assortment process has three basic steps: concentration, customization, and dispersion.

Concentration   Concentration refers to the collection of large quantities of a single product or several different products so that they can ultimately be sold as a group. A manufacturer's consolidation warehouse is a prime example. Large shipments of products produced at various factories are transferred to the consolidation warehouse. When a customer order is received, each item or product demanded is collected into a unique assortment. The use of a consolidated channel structure reduces overall transactions since the customer can place a single order to the consolidation warehouse rather than placing separate orders to each manufacturing facility for the specific items produced there.

An alternative arrangement is to use the services of an industrial distributor or wholesaler. The use of such specialists allows manufacturers and retailers to achieve the benefits of concentration without directly performing the associated work. The basic principle of concentration is referred to as minimum total transaction. The principle illustrates that the total transactions required to complete assortment can be reduced by introducing specialists. In essence, this highlights

[7]Wroe Alderson, *Marketing Behavior and Executive Action,* Homewood, Ill.: Irwin, 1957, chap. 7.

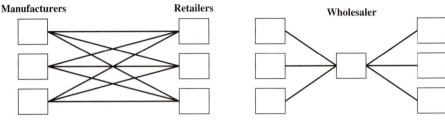

FIGURE 4-6   Principle of minimum total transactions.

the power of specialization. Figure 4-6 shows how inclusion of a wholesaler or distributor in a channel structure significantly reduces the total number of transactions required to provide product assortments.

Customization   The process of sorting and grouping products into unique combinations is referred to as customization. Customization results in products and quantities that uniquely satisfy a specific customer's requirements. Manufacturers may offer customers mixed or combination truckloads of products. Such mixed shipments allow customers to maintain minimum inventory for that supplier while realizing the benefits of lower transportation cost as a result of volume shipment.

The capability of a firm to achieve effective customization is at the heart of developing a supply chain arrangement. For a firm to sell all products and deliver in a single shipment with one invoice, it is usually necessary to make substantial changes in conventional business practice. The Procter & Gamble Company sidebar illustrates the massive change required to effectively position the firm to logistically perform customization requirements.

The customization trend in contemporary business is far broader than simply sorting products into standard combinations. Customization often involves special packaging to create unique products for sale through exclusive channel arrangements. For example, warehouse stores, such as SAM'S, have thrived on the presentation of unique product packs. This trend is even more pronounced with the advent of special bulk-size combinations in almost all retail formats. Customization also involves the value-added assembly of unique promotional displays. Such displays may contain seasonal promotions such as holiday wrapping or packaging, new-product promotions, trial samples, point-of-sale displays, or a host of other creative marketing tactics. The overall process of customization is a critical part of the value-added channel process.

Dispersion   Dispersion consists of shipping unique assortments to customers when and where specified. Dispersion is the final assortment step.

Firms that position logistics as a core competency build competitive advantage around their expertise in performing all or part of the essential assortment process. The primary business of wholesalers is performing assortment in a manner that reduces cost and risk for other channel members. Over the past several years,

RETAILERS OF P&G TO GET NEW PLAN ON BILLS, SHIPMENTS

Procter & Gamble Co. is telling retailers today it will standardize and streamline the way they pay for and receive shipments of its products.

It wasn't clear precisely how much the changes will save the Cincinnati-based consumer-products company, though Edwin L. Artzt, P&G's chairman, has complained publicly about the extra costs created by the company's convoluted invoice and order systems.

"We see some saving in the long," said a P&G spokeswoman. She added that P&G has invested more than $250 million during the past three to four years in a broad-based effort to simplify its wholesale and retail distribution systems. "We see this as an opportunity to take costs out of the system and ultimately lower the cost of our brands to consumers," the spokeswoman said.

Currently, retailers ordering P&G health and beauty aids such as Pert shampoo and Oil of Olay lotions qualify for 2% cash discounts when they pay the company within 30 days. Retailers that order P&G soaps, such as Ivory or Zest, and food and beverage brands such as Duncan Hines cake mix or Hawaiian Punch have only 10 days to qualify for the 2% discount. They have 15 days to pay for paper goods such as Puffs facial tissues to receive the 2% discount.

Under the new system, there won't be any distinction among these categories. Whether they're ordering Crisco shortening, Crest toothpaste, or Charmin toilet tissue, retailers will have 19 days to qualify for the 2% discount. The changes don't affect P&G's cosmetics and fragrance brands, however.

Additionally, under the new plan, the payment clock will start ticking when the retailer receives the merchandise. Currently, it starts when the products leave P&G warehouses. This will give retailers across the board a few more days in which to pay the company. However, stores that buy more health and beauty aids than food products will, on average, have slightly less time to qualify for the discount. In contrast, supermarkets will have a few more days.

P&G also will move to a shipping system designed to encourage retailers to order full truckloads of its products, a plan that has been under consideration since last fall.

Currently, retailers can order partial or full truckloads, depending on their needs. Moreover, they can order from only one product category. For example, a retailer ordering Tide laundry detergent can't combine that order with Folgers coffee. As a result, stores often end up with far more of one category than they need.

Under the new system, retailers will be allowed to order truckloads containing a variety of P&G brands from different categories. "Customers who choose to combine orders can better manage inventories because they receive only the quantity of products they need, when they need them," P&G said. "Customers will place fewer orders and will be out of stock less often."

Retailers still will be able to order single-category truckloads under the new system. Small retailers that don't want to order by the truckload will be able to share loads with other small retailers, but will have to pay a premium.

P&G is telling retailers that, while some of them will have to pay sooner to qualify for discounts, everyone will benefit because there will be fewer invoices and less inventory piling up in their warehouses.

By changing payment and shipping terms, P&G will decrease the number of invoices retailers handle by 25% to 75%, according to the company. For retailers, the cost of handling each P&G invoice is between $35 and $75, P&G said.

P&G estimates that its own savings will be substantial in the long run. The company says that as many as 25% of orders, or 27,000 a month, require manual corrections by P&G employees.

Source: Gabriella Stern, *The Wall Street Journal,* June 22, 1994, p. A12.

merchant wholesalers have increased in importance at the very time when vertical integration by large retailers and manufacturers was projected to eliminate their economic justification. In some industries such as pharmaceuticals, experts thought that traditional wholesalers would become extinct, as their customers implemented direct buy programs.[8] The fact of the matter is that the wholesale structure of these industries is currently flourishing. It appears that many potential economies of vertical integration were not sufficient to offset the loss of innovative specialization and risk sharing. The strategically located wholesaler or distributor is positioned to perform the assortment process for a number of different retailers and manufacturers, thereby reducing risk, duplication of effort, and the number of transactions required to satisfy logistical requirements.

CHANNEL RELATIONSHIPS

Since a variety of different types of work must be accomplished to satisfy logistical requirements, it is not surprising that numerous firms typically combine competencies to create a channel arrangement. Only through channelwide cooperation can marketing and logistical requirements for successful distribution be fully satisfied.[9] Each potential channel participant is viewed by others as having core competency in performing unique services. Since, over the long run, each participant enjoys rewards or suffers losses as a result of total channel success, there is growing recognition of the benefits of cooperating with customers and suppliers in the development of supply chain arrangements.

[8]The years 1984 to 1988 were seen as having significant impact on the American wholesale industry as "wholesalers and distributors began to strategically reprogram their operations . . . in the face of mounting competitive pressure . . . and the growing importance of direct buying programs in institutional, industrial and retail markets," according to Robert D. Lusch, Deborah S. Coykendall, and James M. Kenderdine, *Wholesaling in Transition: An Executive Chart Book,* 1990, University of Oklahoma, Norman, Okla.: Distribution Research Program, p. 8.

[9]For a sample of recent contributions in a number of different areas of interorganizational collaboration, see Robert M. Morgan and Shelby D. Hunt, "The Commitment-Trust Theory of Relationship Marketing," *Journal of Marketing,* **58,** July 1994, pp. 20–38; Jan B. Heide, "Interorganizational Governance in Marketing Channels," *Journal of Marketing,* **58:**1, January 1994, pp. 71–85; Robert A. Robicheaux and James E. Coleman, "The Structure of Marketing Channel Relationships," *Academy of Marketing Science,* **22:**1, 1994, pp. 38–51; Louis P. Bucklin and Sanjit Sengupta, "Organizing Successful Co-Marketing Alliances," *Journal of Marketing,* **57:**2, April 1993, pp. 32–46; David N. Burt and Michael F. Doyle, *The American Keiretsu: Strategic Weapon for Global Competitiveness,* Homewood, Ill.: Business One Irwin, 1993; Martha C. Cooper and Lisa M. Ellram, "Characteristics of Supply Chain Management and Implications for Purchasing and Logistics Strategy," *The International Journal of Logistics Management,* **4:**1, 1993, pp. 13–24; Lisa M. Ellram and Martha C. Cooper, "The Relationship between Supply Chain Management and Keiretsu," *The International Journal of Logistics Management,* **4:**1, 1993, pp. 1–12; Thomas Hendrick and Lisa Ellram, *Strategic Supplier Partnering: An International Study,* Tempe, Ariz.: Center for Advanced Purchasing Studies, 1993; Peter Hines, "Integrated Materials Management: The Value Chain Redefined," *The International Journal of Logistics Management,* **4:**1, 1993, pp. 13–22; Andrea Larson, "Network Dyads in Entrepreneurial Settings: A Study of the Governance of Exchange Relationships," *Administrative Science Quarterly,* **37,** 1993, pp. 76–104; Frank K. Sonnenberg, "Partnering: Entering the Age of Cooperation," *Journal of Business Strategy,* **13:**3, May–June 1992, pp. 49–52; James C. Anderson and James A. Narus, "A Model of Distributor Firm and Manufacturing Firm Working Partnerships," *Journal of Marketing,* **54:**1, January 1990, pp. 42–58; Jan B. Heide and George John, "Alliances in Industrial Purchasing: The Determinants of Joint Action in Buyer-Seller Relationships," *Journal of Marketing Research,* **XXVII,** February 1990, pp. 24–36; and Robert E. Spekman and Kirti Sawhney, "Toward a Conceptual Understanding of the Antecedents of Strategic Alliances," Report No. 90-114, *Marketing Science Institute,* August 1990.

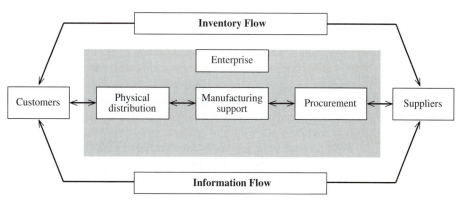

FIGURE 4-7   Supply chain integration.

The basic notion of supply chain management is grounded on the belief that efficiency can be improved by sharing information and by joint planning. The enactment of the Cooperative Research and Development Act of 1994, as amended in 1993, signaled a significant shift in the federal government's antitrust position to encourage firms to work cooperatively to foster increased competitiveness.[10] Widespread realization that cooperation is both permissible and encouraged has stimulated interest in the formation of supply chain relationships.

Figure 2-1 can now be modified to illustrate extension of logistical integration from the internal coordination of procurement, manufacturing support, and physical distribution to include customers and suppliers. Figure 4-7 illustrates an overall supply chain focusing on integrated management of all logistical operations from original supplier procurement to final consumer acceptance.

The supply chain perspective shifts the channel arrangement from a loosely linked group of independent businesses to a coordinated effort focused on efficiency improvement and increased competitiveness. In essence, overall orientation is shifted from inventory management by each individual participant to a pipeline perspective.

While not all collaborative arrangements involve logistics, the number that do is surprising. The following discussion of logistical relationships will develop three dimensions of such arrangements: supply chain competitiveness; relative risk, power, and leadership; and elements of successful supply chain management.

Supply Chain Competitiveness

The motive behind the formation of supply chain arrangements is to increase channel competitiveness. The basic idea is derived from two paradigms.

First, the fundamental belief is that cooperative behavior will reduce risk and greatly improve the efficiency of the overall logistical process. To achieve a high degree of cooperation, it is necessary for key supply chain participants to share

---

[10]For details, see footnote 16, Chapter 1.

information. Such information sharing should not be limited to transaction data. Equally or more important is a willingness to share strategic information so that firms can jointly plan the best ways and means to satisfy requirements. This cooperative paradigm is based on the belief that information collaboration is essential to allow participating firms to do the right things faster and more efficiently.

The second paradigm is elimination of waste and duplicate effort. At the root of this paradigm is the fundamental belief that substantial amounts of inventory deployed in a traditional channel constitute a risky commitment. Sharing information and joint planning can eliminate or reduce risk associated with much of this inventory speculation. In fact, if information is shared and used properly, much of the inventory positioned between the end of a production line and the customer checkout can be eliminated from the channel. One industry study concluded that the average dry grocery product requires 104 days to reach the supermarket checkout counter from the time it comes off the supplier's line.[11] The same study reported a total of 66 weeks for the apparel supply chain to move raw material through the production process to the retailer. The average inventory of sutures in the health care industry ranges from 12 to 18 months' supply.[12] The central notion behind supply chain rationalization is *not that inventory is bad* and should be totally eliminated. Rather, inventory deployment should result from economic and service necessities and not from tradition and anticipatory practices. The key to improved performance is to do the right things more often and do them faster. As one observer stated, ''The goal of the enlightened firm is to do more and more with less and less until it does everything with nothing.''[13]

The strategic implications for logistics contained in these basic paradigms are developed in depth in Chapter 16. The main idea is to think in terms of logistical system reengineering in the context of manufacturers, wholesalers, retailers, and service specialists working together.

In the mass merchandise industries, retailers like Wal-Mart, Kmart, JC Penney, Target, and Walgreens have formed supply chain arrangements aimed at improved competitiveness. Using a combination of internal resources and cooperation with their suppliers, these firms have positioned their logistical competency as a core business strategy.[14] Their record in terms of retail growth and profitability speaks for itself.

Several manufacturers have arranged supply chains in such diverse industries as chemicals, textiles, building supplies, and household tools. Firms like Dupont, Levi Strauss and Company, Owens-Corning Fiberglas, and Black & Decker have

---

[11]*Efficient Consumer Response: Enhancing Consumer Value in the Grocery Industry,* Kurt Salmon Associates, Inc., January 1993, p. 26.

[12]Presentation by William C. Copacino, Andersen Consulting, before the Health and Personal Care Distribution Conference, Longboat Key, Fla.: October 21, 1992.

[13]Dr. Robert F. Lusch in a speech entitled ''Strategic Pathways for Wholesalers/Distributors: Winning in the 1990s'' at The Grainger Seminar on Supply-Chain Management and the Strategic Roles of Channel Members on July 28, 1992, at the University of Wisconsin-Madison.

[14]For an insightful discussion of the development of collaborative arrangements between retailers and manufacturers, see Andre J. Martin, *Infopartnering,* Essex Junction, Vt.: Oliver Wright Publications, Inc., 1994.

pioneered revolutionary new ways to improve the value processes of their specific supply chains.

At the wholesale level, drug suppliers such as McKesson, Bergen Brunswig, FoxMeyer, and Colonial Hospital Supply have moved from near extinction to become dominant suppliers in their industry.[15] Food wholesalers and cooperatives such as Sysco, Spartan Stores, Fleming, and SuperValu have revolutionized traditional logistics practices. Similar developments can be observed in the paper and supplies industry by firms such as Zellerbach, Unisource [formerly Paper Corporation of America (PCA)], and Resource Net International (formerly International Paper). Likewise, Ace in the hardware business and W. W. Grainger in industrial supplies have revolutionized conventional logistics practice in their respective fields.

These examples of revolutionary change are not limited to specific firms, their trading partners, and service suppliers. In the case of the food industry two major trade associations, the Grocery Manufacturers of America (GMA) and the Food Marketing Institute (FMI), as well as other interested groups have joined forces to provide a leadership structure for conventional food companies to compete with alternative formats such as warehouse club stores, convenience stores, and mass merchandisers. The initiative, known as *efficient consumer response* (ECR), is a blueprint for building an industrywide solution to counteract competitive deterioration.[16] The Coca-Cola Retailing Research Council sponsored a study designed to facilitate improved logistics replenishment in the food industry. The research, completed by Mercer Management Consulting, was entitled *New Ways to Take Costs out of the Retail Food Pipeline.*[17]

All of these diverse examples have common grounds with respect to fundamental features. First, the new practices of logistics are technology-driven. Effective time-based logistics management is a proven strategy to increase competitiveness. Second, logistical solutions that result in lasting distinctiveness combine the experience and talents of key supply chain participants from trading partners to service providers. At the heart of several of the examples highlighted is a solid commitment to create a supply chain culture. The mechanism by which the supply chain is effectively integrated and competitive superiority achieved can best be accomplished through voluntary arrangements.

Risk, Power, and Leadership

Acknowledged dependency is a prime force in the development of supply chain solidarity. To the degree that managers acknowledge their joint dependency, the potential exists to develop cooperative relationships. This dependency is what

---

[15]In 1991, McKesson had roughly 23 percent of drug industry market share, followed by Bergen Brunswig with 13.8 percent and FoxMeyer with 9.4 percent. In total, these three companies had over 46 percent of the market. It is obvious that they hold a dominant position.

[16]*Efficient Consumer Response: Enhancing Consumer Value in the Grocery Industry,* Kurt Salmon Associates, Inc., January 1993.

[17]*New Ways to Take Costs out of the Retail Food Pipeline: Making Replenishment Logistics Happen,* prepared by Mercer Management Consulting for the Coca-Cola Retailing Research Council, 1992.

motivates their willingness to negotiate functional transfer, share key information, and participate in joint operational planning. Three concepts—risk, power, and leadership—are essential to understanding how supply chain arrangements work.

Risk Enterprises that participate in supply chain arrangements each acknowledge a specific performance role. They also share a joint belief that they will be better off in the long run as a result of the collaboration. Each enterprise specializes in an area or function that coincides with its unique core competency. By cooperating, each specialized function becomes integrated in the supply chain.

As a general rule, a channel member whose competency is highly specialized assumes less risk with respect to overall performance. Since its function is unique, it is possible that other supply chains will also require its services, thus minimizing the risk associated with any one arrangement. A retailer or a wholesaler incurs risk as a result of stocking products for a specific manufacturer. The traditional practice is to hedge risk by offering customers an assortment of many different manufacturers' products, thereby reducing reliance on any supplier.

In contrast, a processor or manufacturer with a limited product line may be totally captive to the capabilities of a limited number of supply chain arrangements. In essence, the manufacturer may be "betting the business" that the arrangement will be successful. For manufacturers, channel selection is risky business. The disproportionate risk among channel members is of central importance in determining how logistical relationships develop and are managed. Some channel members have a deeper dependence on channel success than others. Therefore, members with the most at stake can be expected to assume more active roles and shoulder greater responsibility for facilitating channel cooperation.

Power In a practical sense, the prerogative and even the obligation to spearhead cooperation rest with the supply chain participant that enjoys the greatest relative power.[18] Over the last decade significant power has shifted from manufacturers to retailers because of consumer patronage.

While not universal to all aspects of business, the general shift of power to retailers has resulted from four somewhat unique events. First, the general trend has been toward ownership consolidation within specific retail areas, meaning that channels are dominated by fewer firms having more extensive coverage of consumer trading areas. Second, retailers have access to vital information concerning what is happening in the marketplace. The combination of point-of-sale data and near real-time communication capability means that consumer trends can be identified and accommodated as soon as they begin to materialize. Walgreens maintains in-store computers and continuous satellite transmission to keep merchandise buyers posted on developing market trends. A third factor that has favored retailers is the increasing difficulty and high cost that manufacturers confront in developing new brand franchises. The fact of the matter is that many premium private-label

---

[18]Peter F. Drucker, "The Economy's Power Shift," *The Wall Street Journal,* September 24, 1992, p. A-16.

items have greater category penetration than so-called national brands. For example, the Gap and The Limited almost exclusively distribute their private branded merchandise. Finally, the whole process of logistical replenishment has shifted from a push to a pull posture. The exact timing and sophisticated orchestration of a high-velocity market-paced logistics system are ideally determined from the point of consumer purchase. When consumers purchase products, the final or ultimate potential value achieved by the supply chain has become a reality.

While the above noted forces are a modern reality, not all contemporary factors favor a shift of power forward in the supply chain. One major countervailing force has been the rapid deterioration of traditional channel structures. In the not so distant past, marketing channels were clearly defined by product line. As noted earlier in Chapter 3, because of today's scrambled merchandising environments, products are often cross-channel distributed to accommodate specific markets. New retail formats in almost all consumer-based industries have begun to blur traditional channel arrangements. The result is that manufacturers are finding new channel options to distribute their products.

As a substitute for full reliance on traditional brand franchises, manufacturers have been reengineering their operations to become the dominant supplier or trade franchise for selected consumer products or categories. The movement toward achieving a trade franchise positions manufacturers to offer greater value to their prospective channel partners. In addition to offering superior brands at competitive prices, a dominant trade franchise involves several key operational attributes that increase a firm's attractiveness as a supply chain participant.

To create a dominant trade franchise involves the following attributes: (1) willingness to develop cooperative arrangements, (2) manufacturing and logistical flexibility to accommodate supply chain partner requirements, (3) rationalization of supply base to ensure ability to accommodate frequent schedule changes without becoming an impediment to flexibility, (4) tailored marketing and merchandise programs, (5) availability of information linkages to accommodate cross-organizational operations, and (6) short, responsive, flexible, and reliable order cycles to facilitate rapid replenishment of customer requirements. Of course it goes without saying that the ideal supplier will perform at or below average industry logistics cost.

Because both manufacturers and distributors have repositioned traditional operations, the potential exists to create improved working relationships. *As a general rule, powerful firms tend to link together in the development of supply chain arrangements.* For the arrangement to be successful the dominant parties to the cooperative arrangement need to be receptive to change.

Leadership   Just as individual organizations need leaders, so do supply chains. At present, no definitive generalization can be made concerning which firm should ideally assume leadership responsibility. In many situations, specific firms are thrust into a leadership position purely as a result of their size, economic power, customer patronage, or comprehensive trade franchise. In some successful arrangements there is a clear presence of superior power on the part of one participating enterprise that is acknowledged in the form of mutual dependency and respect on the part of

TABLE 4-2   SUPPLY CHAIN LEADERSHIP VISIONS

- *A medical products manufacturer.* Maximize customer satisfaction and profitability through world-class supply chain arrangements. These promote operational excellence and utilize information technology, allowing management of the channel relationship and the physical flow of products worldwide.
- *An appliance manufacturer.* Commitment to the mutual sharing of information and technology to reduce total supply chain cycle time with associated costs tailored to meet the unique requirements of specific customers.
- *Computer manufacturer.* A flawless, fast, and simple delivery of value perceived by our customers such that the firm becomes the benchmark toward which others strive.
- *Major food retailer.* A willingness to share information to achieve short, reliable delivery and ensured product availability. The firm is committed to developing long-term relationships with suppliers that are willing to jointly plan merchandising and logistical operations.
- *Mass merchant.* It is essential that all waste and duplication be eliminated between operations of preferred suppliers and those of the firm's logistics and merchandising groups. Information will be fully shared and operations modified as necessary to enable improved competitiveness. The firm is committed to sharing benefits with high-performance preferred vendors.

all supply chain members. In other situations leadership appears to gravitate to the firm that initiates the relationship.

Substantial research confirms the fact that success of a supply chain arrangement is directly correlated to the presence of constructive leadership capable of stimulating cooperative behavior between participating firms.[19] The essence of channel leadership is to ensure that functions essential to logistical integration are performed by the appropriate firm. Maintaining a total supply chain perspective is particularly important to logistical relationships. The leadership role involves creating function spin-off and absorption agreements between businesses participating in the arrangement.[20]

Table 4-2 provides a summary of statements that specific firms used to communicate their supply chain vision to potential participants. One critical role of leadership is to create a mutually acceptable set of expectations concerning the potential benefits that will result from involvement in the relationship. What appears to be evolving is a style of channel leadership that encourages informal communication and a high degree of commitment to experimentation.

Elements of Success

A question still remains concerning what factors will result in successful supply chain relationships. It is also important to identify obstacles that must be overcome to achieve success. The sidebar summarizes the findings of comprehensive research

[19]Judith M. Schmitz, Robb Frankel, and David J. Frayer, "Vertical Integration without Ownership: The Alliance Alternative," *Association of Marketing Theory and Practice Annual Conference Proceedings,* Spring 1994, pp. 391–396.

[20]For the original discussion, see Bruce Mallen, "Functional Spin-off: A Key to Anticipating Change in Distribution Structure," *Journal of Marketing,* **37:**3, July 1973, pp. 18–25.

EIGHT I's THAT CREATE SUCCESSFUL WE's

The characteristics of effective intercompany relationships challenge many decades of Western economic and managerial assumptions. For example, most Westerners assume that modern industrial companies are run best by professional managers operating within limited, contractual Western obligations. And most Westerners assume that any person with the requisite knowledge, skills and talents can be a manager in the modern corporation. Although smaller companies, family businesses and companies that are operating in developing countries have retained ''premodern'' characteristics, the ''rational'' model has been considered the ideal to which all organizations would eventually conform.

Intercompany relationships are different. They seem to work best when they are more family-like and less rational. Obligations are more diffuse, the scope for collaboration is more open, understanding grows between specific individuals, communication is frequent and intensive, and the interpersonal context is rich. The best intercompany relationships are frequently messy and emotional, involving feelings like chemistry or trust. And they should not be entered into lightly. Only relationships with full commitment on all sides endure long enough to create value for the partners.

Indeed, the best organizational relationships, like the best marriages, are true partnerships that tend to meet certain criteria:

INDIVIDUAL EXCELLENCE

Both partners are strong and have something of value to contribute to the relationship. Their motives for entering into the relationship are positive (to pursue future opportunities), not negative (to mask weaknesses or escape a difficult situation).

IMPORTANCE

The relationship fits major strategic objectives of the partners, so they want to make it work. Partners have long-term goals in which the relationship plays a key role.

INTERDEPENDENCE

The partners need each other. They have complementary assets and skills. Neither can accomplish alone what both can together.

INVESTMENT

The partners invest in each other (for example, through equity swaps, cross-ownership, or mutual board service) to demonstrate their respective stakes in the relationship and each other. They show tangible signs of long-term commitment by devoting financial and other resources to the relationship.

INFORMATION

Communication is reasonably open. Partners share information required to make the relationship work, including their objectives and goals, technical data, and knowledge of conflicts, trouble spots or changing situations.

INTEGRATION

The partners develop linkages and shared ways of operating so they can work together smoothly. They build broad connections between many people at many organizational levels. Partners become both teachers and learners.

INSTITUTIONALIZATION

The relationship is given a formal status, with clear responsibilities and decision processes. It extends beyond the particular people who formed it, and it cannot be broken on a whim.

INTEGRITY

The partners behave toward each other in honorable ways that justify and enhance mutual trust. They do not abuse the information they gain, nor do they undermine each other.

From Rosabeth Moss Kanter, ''Collaborative Advantage: The Art of Alliances,'' *Harvard Business Review,* **72:**4, July–August 1994, p. 100. Reprinted by permission.

completed by Rosabeth Moss Kanter. Her study involved more than 500 interviews with managers in 37 firms from 11 different areas of the world that participated in collaborative arrangements. Tables 4-3 and 4-4 summarize success factors and common obstacles directly related to supply chain relationships. The summary factors are drawn from research completed by Andersen Consulting. These findings indicate the attributes of retailers and wholesalers that have enjoyed successful supply chain arrangements.

Prospects for the continued development of strategic arrangements appear bright. The president of the Grocery Manufacturers of America recently predicted that such arrangements "will explode over the next five years and become the prevailing way of doing business."[21] However, a note of caution should be interjected concerning the ideal duration of a successful arrangement. Ample evidence suggests that managers must plan for the ultimate dismantling or renovation of a supply chain arrangement. While some arrangements may encounter a natural death as a result of losing momentum, others may persevere to the point that they no longer embody leading-edge practice.[22]

This section has provided an overview of how the primary participants in a supply chain relationship link together. As noted earlier, a common logistics practice is for individual firms in a supply chain to create alliances with specific service suppliers. The next section discusses logistics service alliances, which are an important part of supply chain management.

LOGISTICAL SERVICE ALLIANCES

Webster defines the noun *alliance* as "being allied; a bond or connection . . . an association to further the common interests of the members."[23] All of the above descriptions fit the wide range of new logistics service relationships being developed throughout the globe. As shippers and service firms explore and experiment with building alliances, they are typically "managing in uncharted areas." This section highlights factors that stimulate logistics service alliances. It concludes with a broad review of the range of typical alliances involving service providers. The rapid growth of the integrated logistics service industry is also examined. Beyond a doubt, this industry has mushroomed over the past five years in direct response to perceived market potential. Finally, the generally recognized "do's and don'ts" of alliancing are reviewed.

Factors Stimulating Service-Based Alliances

The appeal of logistical service alliances is fueled by several macrotrends in overall business philosophy. Such service alliances are a direct reflection of senior management's desire to concentrate basic business resources on core competency. The

---

[21]Quote from C. Manly Molpus, president and CEO, Grocery Manufacturers of America, Inc., in Stephen Dowdell, "The Ties That Bond," *Supermarket News,* June 13, 1994, p. 19.
[22]Gary Hamel and C. K. Prahalad, "Competing for the Future," *Harvard Business Review,* **72:**4, July–August 1994, pp. 122–128.
[23]*Webster's Ninth New Collegiate Dictionary,* Springfield, Mass.: Merriam-Webster, Inc., 1988.

TABLE 4-3   FACTORS INCREASING LIKELIHOOD OF SUPPLY CHAIN RELATIONSHIP SUCCESS

Retailers	Manufacturers
• High level of cooperation	• Information sharing
• Similarity of goals/objectives	• Recognition of mutual benefits
• Clear communications	• Controlled implementation
• Senior management support	• Joint task force
• Control of inventory	• Commitment/resource dedication
	• Benefits realization

Source: Reprinted by permission of Andersen Consulting.

TABLE 4-4   COMMON OBSTACLES CONFRONTED WHEN CREATING SUPPLY CHAIN RELATIONSHIPS

Retailers	Manufacturers
• Low-volume stockkeeping units (SKUs)	• Lack of communication
• Resistance of manufacturers to change	• Trust level
• Information systems	• Noncompatible systems
• Noncompatible data formats	• Understanding of technical issues
	• Resistance of customers to change
	• Readiness of retailers

Source: Reprinted by permission of Andersen Consulting.

idea of outsourcing support activities to specialists results from the desire to "right-size" organizations and to focus activities on "what they know how to do best." Logistics activities are prime candidates for outsourcing. Four attributes of logistical operations are essential to build strong working relationships: mutual dependency, core specialization, power clarity, and emphasis on cooperation. Each is discussed.

Mutual Dependency   A relationship that is built around the performance of logistical service must acknowledge a great deal of dependency. The performance of a service either happens as planned or does not: there are no gray areas. Therefore, service providers involved in an alliance *must* acknowledge dependency. Information technology increasingly makes real-time performance measurement of logistical operations affordable. Several carriers such as Schneider National, Roadway, Federal Express, and United Parcel Service offer positive tracking of shipments to ensure that all customers remain fully informed of expected and actual delivery performance. As such, mutual dependency exists on both sides of the relationship.

Core Specialization   A second characteristic of logistical service alliances is the high degree of core specialization involved in day-to-day operational performance. The simple fact of the matter is that most logistical services benefit from economy of scale and are highly vulnerable to diseconomy of scale. Therefore, an enterprise whose core competency involves performing an essential service has intrinsic appeal for firms that require the service. The logistical specialist is better positioned to perform essential service day in and day out than a firm with primary competency in making or selling products. Therefore, the appeal of the logistics specialist is a logical extension of the basic doctrines of scale and scope economies.

Power Clarity   A third characteristic of a logistical relationship is how it plays out in the typical power/conflict dynamics of an interorganizational arrangement. As noted earlier, the real power in supply chain arrangements typically belongs to manufacturers or distributors. The demand for logistics is derived from market acceptance of basic manufacturing, wholesaling, and retail business strategies. In other words, nothing moves on a continuous basis unless it sells on a continuous basis. Suppliers of logistical services inherently acknowledge that primary firms are dominant in determining the managerial direction of an overall supply chain arrangement. Whereas significant power struggles may occur between dominant institutions in a channel, few if any of these confrontations and the associated conflict directly impact service providers. This clarity of power focuses the attention of suppliers on providing their designated services.

Cooperation Emphasis   Finally, since specialized role performance and legitimate power to orchestrate the channel process are not in question, the service provider is ideally positioned to cooperate. In fact, zero defect execution of specified tasks and ''being easy to do business with'' are the primary appealing attributes of preferred service specialists. Thus, the marketing strategy of a highly successful service provider builds on a platform of cooperation. The slogan ''Whatever it takes, wherever it is'' captures the typical service provider's dual commitment to excellence and cooperation.

Increasing Service Provider Efficiency

Just as primary firms have undertaken initiatives to improve their supply chain posture, service firms themselves also use alliances to improve their competitiveness. The formation of alliances between service suppliers to increase their operating capabilities and efficiencies is widespread.

Highly visible alliances have focused on bringing together the inherent advantages of firms that specialize in the performance of specific services. A few transportation firms have vertically integrated by virtue of ownership, such as Union Pacific's purchase of Overnite Transportation Company. However, such multimodal acquisitions remain rare. The more common solution for creating strong intermodal fusion has been the strategic alliance.

Several large truckload carriers have created alliances for intermodal, trailer-on-flatcar, and double-stack container service. In essence, motor carriers perform the pickup and delivery and limited line-haul freight to facilitate subsequent rail movement. The railroads, in turn, provide long-haul freight movement. Regularly scheduled intermodal train service provides the economies of rail. The motor carrier pickup and delivery service provides the inherent benefits of truck flexibility. A leader in the development of these coordinated services is J. B. Hunt Transport Services, Inc., which has established alliances with Burlington Northern, the Southern Pacific, and Santa Fe Railway companies. It would appear that the possibilities for creative alliances are limited only by the participants' imagination. In the case of the J. B. Hunt/Santa Fe alliance, Ralston Purina and United Parcel Service (UPS) are important participants. Ralston is a frequent trailer-on-flatcar shipper, and UPS is the largest purchaser of such services to support its extensive package distribution business. The four companies working together are able to trade off and accommodate each other's requirements. For example, if Ralston Purina needs extra capacity at late notice, UPS may be able to make some of its leased capacity available. Thus, payoffs from an alliance can benefit a wide range of participating firms.

While transportation firms have traditionally joined forces through regulated working agreements, the strategic alliances of the 1990s break with tradition. Many regional less-than-truckload (LTL) carriers are forming horizontal alliances with other LTL carriers so that they can effectively compete with large nationwide carriers such as Roadway, Consolidated Freightways, and Yellow Transport. What the regional carriers are doing is sharing customers through an alliance that allows them to offer one-stop nationwide shopping, as discussed in the sidebar. Some regional LTL firms have gone as far as linking up with national truckload haulers to provide line-haul service. For example, Southeastern Freight and Viking Freight have such arrangements with J. B. Hunt and Schneider National.

REGIONAL ALLIANCES CREATE TRANSCONTINENTAL MOVES

Shippers, requiring shorter lead times and better service, have created a new level of competition between regional and national carriers. Regional carriers have responded to this new competition by forming strategic alliances to bridge regional service areas enabling transcontinental movements.

Southeastern Freight Lines of Columbia, South Carolina, was one of the pioneers in forming regional carrier alliances. Its alliance is with Central Freight Lines (of Waco, Texas) and Viking Freight System (of San Jose, California).

Under the arrangement, Southeastern picks up freight in its region and transports it to a consolidation center in Atlanta. Depending on the customer's location, the freight is picked up by Viking for delivery to Los Angeles or by a carrier hired by Central for delivery to Dallas. Central hires national long-haul carriers such as J. B. Hunt or Schneider National to transport material from Atlanta to Dallas. Once in Dallas, though, Central handles delivery to the final customer.

When the freight arrives at either Central's dock in Dallas or Viking's dock in Los Angeles, the consolidated load is broken down into smaller regional and local deliveries. These regional and local deliveries are handled by Central and Viking as required. This alliance has allowed regional carriers operating in an integrated fashion to deliver product one to two days faster than transcontinental carriers. The delivery is faster because transcontinental carriers often hold freight to consolidate loads and may handle product more often by reconsolidating at major hub locations.

Excellent service is also achieved under this alliance. Southeastern takes responsibility and risk by retaining full ownership of material in transit until final delivery. Furthermore, Southeastern tracks all shipments through its information system. Another benefit is that customers receive only one bill of lading regardless of how many carriers actually handle the freight. Southeastern then handles payment to each carrier.

Based on Lisa H. Harrington, "Strategic Alliances: Road to the Future," *Inbound Logistics,* **12**:8, August 1992, pp. 20–23.

Regional warehouse firms have created similar alliances for integrated marketing and service. Associated Warehouses, Inc., is an example. Similar working alliances exist among pool distributors, freight forwarders, and facilitation companies.

Many service providers have extended their basic competitiveness by adding new and unique value-added services. Many service suppliers have become experts in performing tasks that are generally perceived as inconvenient or a burden for their customers to perform. The result is creativity and expertise that benefit their customers. The range of documented value-added services includes such activities as assembly, sortation, sequencing, basic and promotional packaging, repacking, pricing, and labeling. For an extensive period, Schneider National provided basic data processing support for 3-M transportation. The range of such services clearly is limited only by the customer's need and the resources of the service supplier.

As a result of this massive change, a new format of logistical services, called the *integrated service provider,* has emerged to accommodate the growing requirements of its customer base. Because this aspect of the service industry has experienced such explosive growth, it is discussed next.

Integrated Logistics Service Providers

In less than a five-year period, over 100 new firms were established with the expressed objective of providing integrated logistical services to shipper customers.[24] The vision of these firms was to offer a service sufficiently comprehensive to provide all or a significant part of a shipper's total logistical requirements. To date, no standard terminology exists to describe this explosive industry. Some names that have been used are *third-party logistics, contract logistics,* and *logistical utilities.* The title used here is *integrated logistics service providers,* because almost all industry participants provide a service that is broader than a single function. In other words, the industry participants offer potential customers the ability to purchase two or more aspects of their overall logistical requirements from one supplier. These services were traditionally sold by separate providers. One example is warehousing and transportation, where the integrated service provider receives customer orders, picks and packs the merchandise, and then completes delivery. The typical approach is for the integrated firm to perform the specified services under single ownership. However, many have created alliances to extend their ability to market single-source logistics service.

The integrated logistics service market has been estimated to range in size from $6 billion to $9 billion per year with a projected potential to reach $60 billion by the year 2000.[25] Few argue that the provision of integrated services represents a significant business opportunity. Participants in the industry are generally recognized as having originated from five basic businesses: carrier-based, warehouse-based, forwarder/broker-based, information-based, and customer-based.

---

[24]For a comprehensive list of firms that are active suppliers of integrated logistics services, see *Traffic Management,* July 1994, pp. 145–170.

[25]Projections include $42 billion with the following source: Pat Byrne of A. T. Kearney, Inc., in Mark Voorhees, ''Sorting Out the Third Party Circus,'' *American Shipping,* **34:**10, October 1992, p. 62; and $60 billion with the following source: Robert Delaney of Cass Logistics, Inc., in E. J. Muller, ''Third Party Catches On,'' *Distribution,* July 1992, p. 60.

The carrier- and warehouse-based firms are essentially integrating into each other's basic business via acquisition. The provision of transportation and storage in combination with a broad range of basic and value-added services offers shippers the potential single-source purchase of an integrated service package. Most firms offer information management services to facilitate physical performance. The vast majority of integrated service firms have their origin in what are commonly called *asset businesses.* In the eyes of some of their competitors this prior investment in assests introduces a potential marketing bias. The concern is that the logistics service firm will force business toward its parent company. While undoubtedly some such practice occurs, most of these firms go out of their way to guarantee the best solution to meet a shipper's requirement. To illustrate, Roadway Logistics provides single-source transportation management for Libbey-Owens-Ford. To perform the service, it facilitates the purchase of selected transportation services from a variety of competitors.[26]

The forwarder/broker-based, information-based, and customer-based firms each offer a unique justification for their service orientation. The forwarder/broker firms stress their ability to link operational assets across providers of whatever service is required to satisfy their customer logistics requirements. As would be expected, the information-based services stress the use of technology to orchestrate operating arrangements.

The customer-based integrated service firms are an extension of a firm's basic business capabilities. Their original strategy was to sell experience and capacity in a specific industry. Over time, all integrated service companies can be expected to offer whatever service shippers are willing to purchase. These service-driven solutions are typically operationalized in the form of comprehensive alliances.

SUMMARY

Supply chain relationships are among the most complex and least understood areas of logistics operations. In this chapter, the distribution channel was positioned as the battlefield of business. It is within the channel that the ultimate success or failure of a business is determined. The success or failure is clearly related to competition. It is also related to a firm's ability to establish effective supply chain relationships.

Relationship management is a relatively new name applied to old and important areas of business. It involves development and management of supply chain arrangements. A typical supply chain relationship involves primary trading partners and service providers. The difference between these ''participants'' is the nature of the activities performed and the risk they are willing to assume.

Some fundamental economies of distribution determine channel arrangements. Several indispensable functions must be completed to achieve satisfactory performance. The capabilities of some firms to perform selected activities better than others result from specialization. Some firms make provision of selected services their core competency. The overall supply chain must complete the assortment of merchandise that results in the right products being at the right place at the right time.

---

[26]Ed Root, presentation at the Logistics Management Executive Development Seminar, East Lansing, Mich.: May 10–15, 1993.

Henry Ford found out that no firm can be self-sufficient in performing all aspects of assortment.

The development and maintenance of effective relationships require significant change in traditional managerial practice. Executives must learn how to manage by persuasion and cooperation as opposed to coercion. To develop effective supply chain arrangements, executives must learn the ins and outs of managing across boundaries. A growing body of knowledge is being accumulated to assist managers in developing successful cooperative arrangements.

The establishment and maintenance of logistical service alliances were referred to as ''managing in uncharted areas.'' Many macrotrends in business are causing managers to explore these new options for purchasing key services. In practice, logistical service alliances tend to focus on achieving supply chain competitiveness or making service providers more efficient. While the ''art of alliancing'' is a growing body of knowledge, the experience gained by early pioneers offers useful guidelines.

The appendix to this chapter offers a detailed discussion of the full range of channel relations. This appendix should provide useful background to determine where supply chain arrangements and alliances fit into the overall range of channel alternatives. It also serves as background for readers who have not previously studied the supply channel area.

Chapter 5 shifts to the global arena. Whereas the dimensions of domestic logistics are broad-based, global horizons introduce significantly more complex and demanding requirements.

QUESTIONS

1 Define the term *distribution channel.* Discuss the differences between primary and secondary channel participants. Provide an example of each.
2 Discuss the following statement about distribution channels: ''It's the battlefield of business wherein a firm's ultimate success or failure is determined.''
3 Why is specialization a fundamental factor in distribution efficiency?
4 Discuss the steps of assortment.
5 Why is leadership important in supply chain arrangements?
6 Discuss the impact of power on supply chain management.
7 What factors appear to be important determinants of supply chain success?
8 How do supply chain arrangements increase competition?
9 Describe some of the ways in which service providers have increased efficiency by improving their supply chain posture.
10 Describe and provide examples of value-added services.

APPENDIX: Marketing Channel Structure

Unlike those concerned with logistics, marketing managers have traditionally acknowledged that distribution channels consist of a fantastically complex network of organizations grouped in a variety of combinations. Each organization linked in a distribution channel exists for a reason and performs services in anticipation of a return on investment and effort. The marketing task is never considered complete until the final owner has been satisfied with respect to pretransaction anticipations. In fact, a considerable degree of marketing effort centers around measurement of pretransaction anticipation and posttransaction satisfaction. Thus, marketing horizons are not limited by the operating boundaries of the enterprise. The basic acknowledgment of a wider spectrum of planning and the realistic approach to interorganizational relationships render a channel approach superior to that of a single firm. The marketing approach eliminates the limitations of dealing only with vertically controlled systems.

Five general approaches are used by marketing writers to study and describe channels: descriptive institutional approach, graphic approach, commodity groupings, functional treatments, and channel arrangement classification.

DESCRIPTIVE INSTITUTIONAL APPROACH

The institutional approach to channel analysis focuses on the identification, description, and classification of middlemen institutions. Such institutions are grouped with respect to the marketing services they perform. Figure 4A-1 typifies the analytical framework. At the first level, the distinction is made between merchant and functional middlemen. Merchant middlemen take title to the goods with all ownership risks. Functional middlemen escape the risks of ownership but provide some necessary service to both client and customer.

At the second level, the distinction between range and type of wholesale services is made. Full-function middlemen typically buy in large quantities, break bulk, assemble, assort, sell, and deliver. In performing these activities, the full-function middleman maintains a

warehouse, employs a sales force that calls on the trade regularly, provides for physical distribution, extends trade credit, manages the collection of accounts, and serves in an advisory capacity or as an informational link to both suppliers and customers. The limited-function wholesaler is so designated because the range of services offered falls short of that provided by a full-function middleman. On the other hand, the split-function middleman usually operates as both a retailer and a wholesaler.

The third level of Figure 4A-1 represents descriptive criteria commonly applied to the various categories of wholesalers specified by the first two levels. Every student of business administration should have a working understanding of marketing institutions, because they serve as the basis for all other methods of studying channel structures.

Merchant Middlemen

Included in this section are those wholesalers that buy and sell of their own initiative, thereby dealing with the risks of ownership.

Regular Wholesalers   The service, or regular, wholesaler operates a full-function enterprise. Usually the firm is independently owned and handles consumer goods. The regular wholesale firm purchases in large volume from producers and manufacturers, accepts delivery at one or more of its warehouses, breaks down and stores its purchases, sends out its sales force to canvass the trade, assembles orders in relatively small quantities, delivers orders to its customers, extends credit, assumes the risks of inventory and receivables,

FIGURE 4A-1   An analytical framework of middlemen in the structure of distribution.

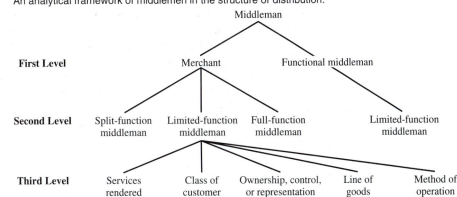

offers advisory service to its customers, and supplies marketing information to both customers and suppliers. The regular wholesale firm is the dominant retail source of supply in many mass-distributed consumer-goods lines.

Industrial Distributors   The industrial distributor is also classified as a regular or full-function wholesaler. As such, these distributors provide essentially the same services enumerated above. The industrial distributor is differentiated from other full-function wholesalers by customers serviced and by the nature of inventory sold. Customers purchase goods for consumption, for use within their enterprise, or as an unfinished item subject to further processing. Although retailers are not technically excluded as a class of customer, in practice they are a minimal source for the distributor. Most of the distributor's trade comes from manufacturing firms, public utilities, railroads, mines, and service establishments (e.g., doctors, hairstylists, hotels, and restaurants). The industrial distributor often specializes in servicing one industry segment, such as automotive or mining.

Drop Shippers   Drop shippers are limited-function wholesalers in that they seldom take physical possession of the goods. Commodities such as coal, lumber, construction materials, agricultural products, and heavy machinery are bulky and require the economies of shipment by carload lots. The drop shipper purchases the carload from the supplier in anticipation of a future order. Once a buyer is found, the drop shipper assumes the responsibility and ownership until the shipment is accepted by the customer. Because no warehouse facilities are maintained, the drop shipper's risk of title bearing varies with the time lag between purchase and sale of the carload. Apart from this risk, the drop shipper also incurs the risks and costs of credit extension and receivables collection. The distinction between the practice of drop shipping and the drop shipper is important. Drop shipping is the practice of shipping an order direct from the suppliers to the customer, although a middleman might be involved in the transaction. For example, central purchasing might order a large quantity of bulk merchandise. Instead of direct shipment to the firm's distribution warehouse, the company might allocate portions of the shipment directly to its retail store. This practice is termed *drop shipping*. The *drop shipper,* on the other hand, is a distinct middleman that arranges for shipment, takes title, assumes responsibil-

ity for shipment, and functions as a merchant middleman in the overall distribution channel.

Cash-and-Carry   Wholesalers   Cash-and-carry wholesalers are limited-function middlemen that operate on a cash basis with no merchandise delivery. Chiefly found in the grocery trade, they were established to serve the small retailer whose order size was not large enough to justify delivery. By stocking staple merchandise, employing no salespeople, and eliminating delivery services and credit, such middlemen can economically serve the smaller retailer. To take advantage of such services, the retailer must travel to the warehouse, find and assemble an order, carry it to a central checkout location, pay cash, load it on a truck, and transport the order to the retail location.

Wagon Distributors (Jobbers)   Utilized mainly by the grocery trade, the wagon distributor is a limited-function wholesaler that specializes in high-margin specialty items or quick-turnover perishables. These intermediaries purchase from producers, may or may not maintain a warehouse, and employ one or more drivers to call on the trade regularly. Sales and delivery are performed simultaneously. The customer selects merchandise from the truck's limited assortment and closes the transaction with a cash payment.

Rack Jobbers   Rack jobbers, or service merchandisers, are classified as full-function intermediaries in that they perform all the regular wholesaling functions plus some retailing functions. Dealing in extensive lines of nonfood merchandise, driver-salespeople regularly service grocer accounts. Typically, a sales representative on call performs a stock control function to ensure that display racks are adequately stocked, properly price-marked, and arranged in an attractive manner. Generally, a rack jobber will be responsible for stock rotation. The retailer is usually billed on a consignment basis, paying only for merchandise sold since the jobber's last visit.

Assembling Wholesalers   Primarily dealing in agricultural products, the assembling wholesaler reverses the common procedure in terms of order size. This category of wholesaler buys the output of many small farmers, assembles and grades the product, ships in economical quantities to central markets, and sells in larger quantities than those purchased.

Semijobbers Semijobbers are considered to be split-function middlemen because they operate at both the wholesale and the retail level of the distribution channel. Usually semijobbers are limited- or full-function wholesalers that participate in some retail sales; however, some are retailers that find it advantageous to be classified as wholesalers for at least a small portion of their operation. Automotive suppliers are an example of the first case. The second case is not typical of any particular retailing segment but is a strategy aimed at gaining lower prices or developing business in two separate market segments.

Functional Middlemen

Wholesalers in the functional category do not take title; nevertheless, they perform many wholesale functions. All middlemen included in this classification are, by definition, limited-function wholesalers because they do not assume the risks of inventory ownership.

Selling Agents Selling agents serve their clients in lieu of a sales organization. They are contracted to sell output of one or more manufacturers as long as the lines handled are supplementary and do not compete directly. Because their principals, or clients, are generally small firms, as illustrated by the textile industry, they are often called upon for financial assistance in terms of loans, carrying credit for the client or collecting receivables. Furthermore, agents serve as collectors, analysts, and dispensers of marketing data. For these services, selling agents are remunerated on a commission basis.

Manufacturers' Agents Manufacturers' agents are similar to selling agents in that they act as substitutes for a direct sales organization, are hired on a continuing contractual basis, represent relatively small enterprises, provide market intelligence, and are reimbursed by commissions. They differ from selling agents inasmuch as they do not sell the entire output of their clients, are limited to a specific geographic territory, and have little control over prices, discounts, and credit terms. A manufacturer's agent or representative usually represents a number of manufacturers that produce noncompetitive but related lines.

Commission Merchants Unlike agents, commission merchants are rarely used on a regular contractual basis. Instead, they are engaged for a single transaction or, more commonly, to facilitate the disposal of a particular lot of goods. Once contracted, the commission merchant takes possession, but not title, of the goods, provides warehousing facilities, and displays either a sample or the entire lot to prospective purchasers. Once negotiations begin, the commission merchant is usually empowered to accept the best offer as long as it exceeds a previously stipulated minimum price. To facilitate negotiations and speed the closing of transactions, the commission merchant may choose to extend credit at risk. In practice, commission merchants commonly extend credit, bill the customer, collect the account, provide a final accounting, and remit the proceeds less commission to the client. Such a wholesaling operation is of vital importance to the marketing of livestock, grain, and other agricultural products.

Brokers Brokers serve as catalysts for classes of buyers and sellers that would normally have considerable difficulty in meeting for purposes of negotiation. A broker's entire function is to stimulate and arrange contacts between the two groups. It is understood that brokers do not permanently represent either the buyer or the seller. Furthermore, they do not handle the goods, they rarely take physical possession, and they do not provide financial assistance to clients. The brokerage fee is paid by the client, whether it is the buyer or the seller. In no case can a broker legally receive a fee from both parties to a transaction. Brokers are widely used in foreign trade by small manufacturers of convenience goods and by wholesale grocers.

Auction Companies Auction companies are widely used in marketing fruit, tobacco, and livestock. They provide a physical setting conducive to marketing specific lots of commodities. Facilities are usually available to all those offering commodities and to all those bidding for them. The auction company is paid by the seller and usually receives a flat fee per transaction or a percentage of the sale.

Petroleum Bulk Stations Stations provide the storage and wholesale distribution for the petroleum industry. Such establishments may be owned by refining companies and operated on a basis similar to that of manufacturers' sales branches. Alternatively, they may be owned and operated independently.

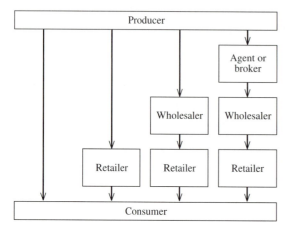

FIGURE 4A-2   Typical channel structure alternatives in consumer-goods distribution.

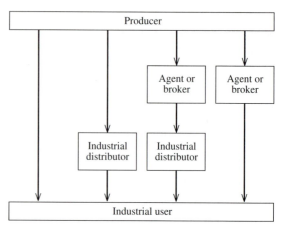

FIGURE 4A-3   Typical channel structure alternatives in industrial-goods distribution.

THE GRAPHIC APPROACH

Flow graphs are a useful technique to identify the flow of ownership title of raw materials and finished products. These graphs illustrate the range of alternatives in institutional selection at all levels of the marketing process.

The graphic approach to describing a structure of distribution is shown in Figures 4A-2 and 4A-3. In Figure 4A-2 the most common variations in consumer-goods channels are illustrated. Of the four channels shown, the most typical for the consumer is the whole-sale-retail-consumer structure. Most mass-produced consumer goods reach the market through a wholesaler and retailer. The channel selected by the manufacturer depends on the characteristics of the product, the buying habits of the consumer, and the overall marketing strategy of the firm. For example, a large personal sales force is required for successful marketing of a product nationwide directly to the consumer. Such companies as Avon Products and Fuller have selected this method of distribution. On the other hand, a manufacturer with limited capital resources and a limited product line might elect to hire a broker or an agent to sell products in consumer channels.

In Figure 4A-3 a description of alternative channels for industrial-goods distribution is presented. Most high-volume items in industrial markets move directly from producer to consumer. Industrial distributors often handle supplies, replacement parts, and small orders of bulk items. In this sense the industrial middleman performs much the same function as the wholesaler in consumer channels. One major difference between con-

sumer and industrial channels is that the incidence of functional middlemen such as selling agents, brokers, and manufacturers' agents is much greater in industrial channels than in consumer channels.

The structures described in Figures 4A-2 and 4A-3 should be regarded as general patterns. There are a great number of possible variations in channel structure in addition to those shown in these charts depending on the product, the customer, and the entrepreneurial vision of the channel members. The neat graphs of distribution channels have been confused by the expanded tendency toward *scrambled merchandising*.[1] An organization once considered only a wholesaler may now function within the channel as a retailer too. Retailers and manufacturers, in turn, have assumed many traditional duties of wholesalers. This extension of activities has been referred to as *integrated wholesaling*. Under integrated wholesaling, the retail operation performs the functions traditionally assumed by the wholesale intermediary.

The main advantage of a graphic approach is that it illustrates the many links in modern marketing. With graphs, the multiplicity of institutions is presented in a logical sequence. However, the simplicity of flow diagrams tends to understate some complexities of designing the proper channel structure for an individual firm.

---

[1]*Scrambled merchandising* refers to the identical product being offered for sale in several different types of retail outlets, for example, garden rakes sold at gasoline service stations as well as in hardware, garden, discount, and department stores. It is also referred to as *channel jumping* and *conglomerate marketing*.

COMMODITY GROUPINGS

In an effort to limit the range of considerations in channel planning, several studies have been completed with the objective of defining channel structure in detail for specific commodities. Generally empirical in nature, commodities studies combine a description of institutions with a graphic illustration of primary ownership flows. Although they are very useful in some situations, such commodity-channel treatments are too specific for general planning.

FUNCTIONAL TREATMENTS

The functional approach to channel structure developed as a result of attempts to provide a logical explanation of the overall marketing process. The functional approach to viewing channels was covered in Chapter 4.

CHANNEL ARRANGEMENT CLASSIFICATION

Acknowledged dependency is the prime indication of channel solidarity. As such, dependency provides a useful way to classify observable relationships. Three channel classifications are identified ranging from least to most open expression of dependence: single transaction channels, conventional channels, and voluntary arrangements (VAs). Each form of channel involvement reflects a different degree of logistical performance commitment. Figure 4A-4 provides a graphic illustration of channel arrangements based on acknowledged dependence. This classification also provides a distinction between transaction and relational structures. In transaction arrangements little or no dependency exists. Participants feel no responsibility to each other. The laws and obligations that govern buying and selling operate as the sole foundation for ownership transfer. While all types of channels have logistical requirements, those classified as relational offer the greatest opportunity for developing interorganizational arrangements.

Single Transaction Channels

A great many business transactions are negotiated with the expectation that the relationship will be a one-time event. Examples of single transaction channels are real estate sales, stock and bond ownership transfer, and the purchase of durable equipment such as processing plants and heavy machinery.

From a logistical viewpoint, firms that are involved in single transaction channels need to work out one-time arrangements to complete required logistical commitments. Once all specifications are agreed to by the parties and the transaction is completed, no further logistics-related obligation exists.

While single transaction channel engagements are not important in terms of relationship management, they are significant to the businesses involved. Requirements to complete promised delivery are often technical and difficult to accomplish. The movement of oversized equipment, such as a printing press, typically requires special permits and is often restricted to specific times of the day or year. In some situations, special transportation and material-handling equipment are required to accommodate size and weight of the products involved. If a firm deals primarily with single transactions, logistics performance is critical and typically represents a significant cost of overall operations. Failure to develop repetitive patterns of business with repeat buyers makes each logistical assignment a unique event. Even if the logistical activity proceeds without a glitch and all parties are highly satisfied, the likelihood of a repetitive transaction is minimal.

Conventional Channels

Firms involved in conventional channels do not perceive or acknowledge extensive dependence. The conventional channel is best viewed as a loose arrangement or affiliation of firms that buy and sell products on an as needed basis. Firms in conventional channels link up to buy and sell products on the basis of immediate

FIGURE 4A-4   Classification of channel relationships based on acknowledged dependency.

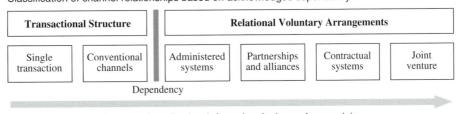

requirements without concern for future or repeat business. The prime determinant of the timing and extent of transactions is selling price.

Firms involved in conventional channels frequently seek benefits of joint specialization. Participating firms typically establish a business niche, which allows them to offer unique products or services. The extensive practice of ''forward buy'' diversions in the food industry, as discussed in the sidebar, is a prime example of a transaction-dominated channel. The buy and sell process is guided by the ''diversion hot wire,'' which contains information concerning what is available and the current price. Each diversion is a unique transaction.

Firms involved in a conventional channel develop operational capabilities to provide services necessary to fulfill their basic business mission. From the viewpoint of doing business with other members of the channel, the expectation is that commercial activity will continue as long as all involved are satisfied. If dissatisfaction develops, parties seek new solutions. Conventional channel members have little or no loyalty to each other. Little or no attempt is made to cooperatively improve the efficiency of the supply chain. The reason for the lack of emphasis on buyer-seller cooperation is directly related to failure of the participants to perceive joint dependency. The duration of a conventional channel ranges from one order to years of continued business involvement.

Activity in a conventional channel is conducted on a transaction-to-transaction basis. The typical transaction is adversarial in that the negotiation is price-dominated, creating an us-against-them posture. In other words, the involved firms fail to work out a formalized long-term relationship. This means that either party is free to exit the relationship whenever it wishes. Involvement occurs until a better deal comes along. Little or no concern exists for the welfare of the other parties.

The term *conventional* reflects the widespread existence of this common type of business relationship. Most channels have some operations that follow this format. The primary element here is transaction price. The channel arrangement can be terminated simply by a member refusing to buy or sell a product at a specific time. It is not uncommon for firms to start and stop doing business with each other several times within a single year.

The logistics of conventional channels requires that each firm develop and maintain an autonomous operational capability. Emphasis is on internal efficiency. While some routinization of operations does result from

repetitive transactions, such patterns are subject to terminate at any time. Specialists that provide services to firms involved in conventional channels typically work for a single enterprise and are loyal to that firm. In other words, specialists are loyal to the primary channel member that arranges their services. This specific relationship between the service provider and customer ranges from adversarial to highly relational. In some situations, a degree of continuity develops between the primary firm and the service specialists, in which case the relationship can become long-term and highly dependent. The key point is that such relationships do not involve channel trading partners. Each is a unique arrangement between a buyer and a seller of services.

Two points are significant concerning conventional channels. First, they are an important part of the overall business structure because of their sheer transaction volume. The relationship described as conventional is by far the most common channel arrangement in free market economies. Second, because firms do not develop synergisms with trading partners, opportunities to gain efficiency by virtue of cooperation are sacrificed in favor of maintaining autonomy.

Voluntary Arrangements (VAs)

The distinctive feature of voluntary arrangements is that participating firms acknowledge dependency and develop joint benefits by cooperating. Thus, the various forms of VAs represent relationship management practice within logistical channels. In order to participate in a behavioral channel system, each channel member must be willing to perform specific duties. The joint belief is that coordination among channel members will result in performance that is superior to what would occur with independent action. An important additional belief is that all parties participating in the VA will benefit from the cooperative arrangement. On the basis of this assumption, the relative competitive unit is the channel system.

The overall relationship of a VA is typically orchestrated by a firm that is acknowledged as the leader. The leader is most often the dominant firm in the channel in terms of market share, size, or technical skills. The firm that provides leadership typically has the greatest relative power in the channel system.

While acknowledged dependency is the cohesive force in VA arrangements, it also creates conflict. Managers may feel that their firm is not getting a fair share of benefits or that they are being placed in an unnec-

FORWARD BUY: PROFIT FROM PROMOTIONS

Manufacturers have traditionally offered two types of promotional discounts to increase product sales. One type is directed at end consumers in the form of coupons and rebates. The other is directed at retailers to encourage them to stock their shelves with the manufacturer's brands. This second form is often referred to as a trade promotion or discount. The intent of both forms of discount is that the end consumer will benefit. In other words, a consumer who mails in a rebate or uses a coupon sees a direct cash benefit. If the retailer buys a product on a discount and prices the product in its store accordingly, the consumer also directly benefits from the sale price.

However, this benefit depends on the retailer's willingness to reduce the price for the consumer. Unfortunately, many retailers, hurt by economic and competitive pressures, are not passing these savings on but are keeping some portion of the discount themselves to improve their own financial performance.

Retailers "forward buy" from manufacturers. This practice entails buying more merchandise than required because it is offered at a special wholesale price. The retailer sells a portion of the order at a promotional price. Later, the remaining product is sold at the original price such that the retailer receives a higher margin. Under this scenario, the consumer directly benefits from the manufacturer's wholesale deal only on a portion of the product sold.

Often, the retailer is unable to sell all the product bought on the special deal. In this case, the retailer "diverts" the product by selling it to another retailer outside the area where the manufacturer's deal was offered or to a "diverter" whose sole job involves buying product on sale and reselling it at a higher price. Both the retailer and the diverter can make a profit on the product. Again, the consumer is shorted on the discount.

An illustration of the steps involved in the forward buy/diversion process is as follows:

1   A manufacturer offers a one-week special on paper towels to stores in California. The special gives 20 percent off the regular list price.

2   A retailer in California buys 10,000 cases, and the manufacturer expects the 20 percent savings to be passed directly to the consumer.

3   The retailer advertises a sale on paper towels and sells 5,000 cases at a discounted price. This price may be anything up to or equal to 20 percent off.

4   The retailer ends the promotion and sells another 3,000 cases at the higher regular price.

5   The retailer wants to sell the remaining 2,000 cases and is in a hurry to make space in its warehouse. The retailer sells the 2,000 cases to a diverter at 18 percent off the manufacturer's original list price. The diverter sells the 2,000 cases to a retailer in Nevada at 15 percent off the manufacturer's list price. The retailer in Nevada thinks this is a good price since the 20 percent off deal was never offered outside California.

All the firms involved in the five steps discussed above operate in a conventional channel. In other words, these firms do business with each other on the basis of their immediate requirements. Future business, for example between the retailer in California and the diverter, may never occur. It occurred in step 5 because the timing and extent of the transaction were right, based on the 18 percent off price.

Adapted from Bachary Schiller, "Not Everybody Loves a Supermarket Special," *Business Week,* February 17, 1992, p. 64.

essarily risky position. When potential or real conflict develops, it is essential that it be resolved in order to maintain channel solidarity. For a VA to have stability the leader must resolve conflict situations in terms of the long-term interests of the overall channel. Finally, since VAs are expected to exist for a substantial time period, it is important that the leader provide a vision of the future, facilitate joint planning, and institute change management as necessary to maintain competitive superiority.

In a broad sense, all channel systems that involve two independent firms have a degree of relationship structure. When relationships are managed to achieve joint goals and participating firms feel obligated to each other, the relationship becomes a VA. In terms of logistical channels and associated performance requirements, four forms of VA are common: administered systems, partnerships and alliances, contractual systems, and joint ventures. As one would expect, the formalization of member dependency increases as the arrangement moves from administered system to joint venture.

Administered Systems   The least formal VA is the administered system. The interesting feature of an administered arrangement is that typically no formal or stated dependency is acknowledged on the part of participants. Usually, a dominant firm assumes leadership responsibility and seeks cooperation of trading partners and service suppliers. While bordering on a conventional channel arrangement, an administered system seems to be guided by a mutual understanding that all independent companies will be better off if they work together and ''follow the leader.''

On the part of the leader, it is essential that decisions be made in a manner that takes each channel participant's welfare into consideration. All channel members must view the relationship as fair and equitable. Operational stability is dependent on the leader sharing rewards as opposed to purely adversarial give-and-take negotiation that typifies a conventional channel. With enlightened leadership, an administered voluntary arrangement can be maintained over an extended period of time. The dominant firm providing leadership can operate at any channel level; however, most examples of administered systems are led by dominant retailers.

As suggested above, a thin line of demarcation separates an administered marketing system from a conventional channel. While no formal agreements exist, discussion with executives who function in such chan-

nels reveals that firms clearly feel dependent and seek to perform in a way consistent with directions provided by the acknowledged leader. Many of the new competitive strategies, seeking to explore technology to reduce time and performance risk, function in an administered channel structure. Perhaps the best perspective is to view the administered system as a benevolent dictatorship. For a potential participant, the decision is whether or not to accept the general guidelines for performance as outlined by the channel leader. Participants trust that the leader will perform in a consistent manner for the total supply chain.

Many firms perceive the benefits possible from working together in the channel but are not comfortable with the lack of formalization that is characteristic of the administered arrangement. In some situations, two or more relatively powerful firms such as Wal-Mart and Procter & Gamble may desire to work closer but feel the need to develop a more structured relationship. When such formalization takes place, the dependency of the relationship becomes widely acknowledged and the participating firms form partnerships and alliances.

Partnerships and Alliances   As firms require greater clarity and longer-term commitment than typically provided in an administered system, they seek to formalize their relationships with other businesses. The typical extension of dependency is to form a partnership and over time extend the relationship toward an alliance. In these voluntary arrangements two or more firms give up some of their operational autonomy in an effort to jointly pursue specific goals. Needless to say, the expectation is that the arrangement will prevail for a substantial period of time. Because of the importance of the partnership/alliance format, the next section of this appendix is devoted exclusively to the managerial challenges involved in establishing and maintaining such relationships. At this point, it is sufficient to describe the difference between a partnership and an alliance and to position each type of cooperation in the overall framework of VAs.

A great many business arrangements are referred to by the participating managers as partnerships. Along with administered systems, the partnership working relationship is at the lower end of the dependency scale. While firms clearly acknowledge dependence on each other, their tolerance to be led is minimal. In other words, the acknowledgment of a level of loyalty tends to solidify repetitive business transactions as long as everything else is satisfactory. The commitment to the joint business arrangement typically falls short of a willingness to modify fundamental business methods and procedures to accommodate partners' requests. Nevertheless, a true partnership reflects a dependency commitment far greater than an administered arrangement. At the very least, such partnerships build on the expressed desire to work together that typically involves an attitude of "working out differences" and, most of all, a level of information sharing. The weak link of many fledgling partnerships is the ability to resolve truly disruptive differences of opinion. A typical example of such conflict often involves price increases. If a firm's response to a supplier's requested price increase is to open the "business to bid," then the quality of the partnership arrangement is doubtful. Conversely, the same is true if the supplier announces a price increase without partnership consultation. A true partnership arrangement must approach such routine adjustments in a problem-solving format. If such interorganizational compatibility exists, the partnership is moving toward an alliance.

The essential feature of an alliance is a willingness of participants to modify basic business practices.[2] If managers feel that the overall business arrangement can benefit from best practice modification and they are willing to change, then the relationship is a true alliance. The motivation behind alliances is more fundamental than simply "locking in the business." While repetitive business is important, emphasis on best practice is aimed at reducing duplication and waste and facilitating joint efficiencies. *In essence, the alliance goal is to cooperatively build on the combined resources of participating firms to improve the performance, quality, and competitiveness of the channel.* Such cooperation requires a commitment to information sharing and problem solving. The expected result is a "win-win" for all participants—especially the consumer or final buyer.

While partnerships are relatively easy to find, true alliances are more difficult to identify. Several high-profile alliances in the drug, garment, building supply, mass merchandise, and food industries have recently gained national publicity. Developing alliances has appeal because they can magnify the economic and market leverage of individual firms without financial investment. What results is the power of cooperation. The human and financial resources of alliance members are pooled to improve the overall competitiveness of the channel arrangement. The challenges of developing and managing alliances are sufficiently important to warrant additional discussion in the final section of this appendix.

Contractual Systems   As the name implies, many firms desire to conduct business within the confines of a formal contract. The most common forms of contractual agreements in logistical relationships are franchises, dealerships, and agreements between service specialists and their customers. The commitment to a contract takes the relationship out of the *pure* voluntary framework that is characteristic of an alliance. In place of pure cooperation, the contractual arrangement establishes a set of legal obligations.

Many firms desire contracts because of the stability gained by formalizing commitment. In the case of a franchise or dealership, the formal agreement serves as a guarantee concerning a firm's rights and obligations related to representing a service or product in a specific geographical area. The granting firm is ensured that conformance to specified ways of conducting business will occur and that a required minimum purchase will be made. Franchises and dealerships are most common in the marketing structure of automotive and fast-food industries. In logistical service industries, several warehouses and equipment leasing firms are franchised by national networks. One of the most visible franchise arrangements is Hertz Truck Leasing. However, a vast number of logistical business relationships involve contracts between service providers and their customers.

One of the most common forms of VA contracting involves for-hire transportation. Prior to transportation deregulation in the early 1980s, the rules that governed a transportation contract were specific and enforced by the Interstate Commerce Commission. In more recent years, contracting rules have been liberalized resulting in a proliferation of unique arrangements. The most common contract between a shipper and carrier specifies the expected level of performance and establishes the fee or rate to be paid for the service. A typical example would be a carrier's agreement to regularly provide a predetermined amount of a specific type of equipment to a shipper (e.g., two temperature-controlled trailers a week). The shipper, in turn, may agree to load and position the equipment for efficient line-

---

[2]Based on information from two studies: *New Ways to Take Costs out of the Retail Food Pipeline: Making Replenishment Logistics Happen,* prepared by Mercer Management Consulting for the Coca-Cola Retailing Research Council, 1992; and *Efficient Consumer Response: Enhancing Consumer Value in the Grocery Industry,* Kurt Salmon Associates, Inc., 1993.

haul pickup by the carrier. The contract specifies the obligation of participating parties and the negotiated price.

Contracts are also widely used in the warehouse services industry. Both the provider and the buyer of specialized services may benefit from longer-term agreements that specify obligations of each party under different operating situations. A form of contract that is gaining popularity is the ''upside/downside agreement.'' The basic provision here is that the warehouse operator shares productivity benefits with the customer during periods of high utilization when maximum benefits of scale economies are experienced. When business is at a low point, the customer's responsibility may include making extra payments to help cover the warehouse operator's fixed cost. The idea is as simple as sharing benefits and spreading risk.

Many logistical contracts involve the use of specialized transportation, computer and material-handling equipment, dedicated buildings and work crews, information software, and unique processing or packaging equipment. In situations where the customer requires exclusive use of specialized products or services, a formal contract provides the guarantees necessary for the provider to assume the associated risks. The contract may serve as collateral for financing equipment and buildings. While seldom noted as the primary reason for contracting, such formal agreements typically specify dissolution terms. In this sense, a contract is similar to a prenuptial agreement in that it specifies termination rights and obligations.

The contract is a vital part of many logistical arrangements. Because many logistics relationships require extensive capital investment, participating company shareholders and financial providers desire contractual agreements to specify risk. Therefore, some degree of contracting is common throughout the range of voluntary relational arrangements.

Joint Ventures   Some logistical arrangements are simply too capital intense for development by a single service provider. Therefore, two or more firms may select to jointly invest in an arrangement. The strictest joint venture involves two or more firms joined economically to create a new business entity. While such start-ups from scratch are not common in logistics, opportunities exist for future development.

The more likely joint venture scenario occurs when a shipper decides to fully outsource all of its logistics requirements—including facilities, equipment, and day-to-day operations—to a third-party or contract service provider. A logical way to arrange this outsourcing is to establish a partnership between the shipper and service firm. The establishment of a business relationship where all management groups participate serves to reduce the risk, especially when broad-based exclusive arrangements are required.

The shipper–service firm relationship has been used to establish new formats for service companies. Several logistics service companies have been spun off from shipper organizations. The idea is to leverage the operational expertise, information systems, facilities, and equipment of the shipper firm by offering services to other shipper organizations. Essentially, the shipper firm expands to offer logistical services as a common or contract carrier. To enter the service industry in this fashion typically involves establishing a stand-alone subsidiary that is at least partially owned by its active management. Service firms that have followed this spin-off strategy with varied degrees of success are AMR Distribution Services, Caterpillar Logistics Services, Inc., Grace Logistics Services, KLS Logistics Services (Kaiser Aluminum), Logi Corporation (Rockwell International), Sears Logistics, and Tower Group International (McGraw-Hill, Inc.). Whereas most multifunctional logistics service companies are spun off or established as subsidiaries of a parent service company, the specific firms listed originated as proprietary, privately owned logistical organizations that expanded to become public service providers.

CONCLUSION

The logistics channel is complex. In addition to the relationships that exist between organizations that sell and buy products, numerous business transactions take place between service providers and their customers. The structures of the resulting business relationships span the range of channel classifications. Single transaction channels occur frequently in the arrangement of one-time moves of equipment and commodity purchases. The famous Russian wheat deals of the 1970s represent one of the most highly publicized single transactions.

The majority of transportation services are purchased on the spot market, which falls into a conventional-type channel structure. Even when transportation service purchases are repetitive, they often are based on price. As such, relationships will quickly shift if the buyer can find a better deal.

The area classified as voluntary arrangements (VAs) has gained considerable attention from senior corporate logistics executives and their service company counterparts. The trade press abounds with examples of all four of the classifications discussed. The alliance format appears to have great appeal to both shippers and service providers. Several alternative alliance formats have emerged that unite different combinations of shippers and service providers. In addition, several industry trade associations have facilitated member involvement in alliances by sponsoring research and training initiatives. The dynamics of developing and managing alliances justifies a deeper investigation into this growing cooperative phenomenon.

GLOBAL LOGISTICS

LOGISTICS IN A GLOBAL ECONOMY
    Forces Driving the Borderless World
    Barriers to Global Logistics
    The Global Challenge
VIEWS OF GLOBAL LOGISTICS
    Importing and Exporting: A National
      Perspective
    The Stateless Enterprise
    Conclusion
GLOBAL OPERATING LEVELS
    Arm's-Length Relationship
    Internal Export
    Internal Operations
    Insider Business Practices
    Denationalized Operations
    Conclusion

THE INTERLINKED GLOBAL ECONOMY
    Stages of Regional Integration
    Integration Status
THE GLOBAL SUPPLY CHAIN
    Performance-Cycle Length
    Operations
    Systems Integration
    Alliances
    Conclusion
SUMMARY
QUESTIONS

Whereas an effective logistics system is important for domestic operations, it is absolutely *critical* for global manufacturing and marketing. Domestic logistics focuses on performing value-added services in a relatively controlled environment. Global logistics operations must accommodate all domestic requirements and also deal with increased uncertainties associated with distance, demand, diversity, and documentation.

The operating challenges faced by global logistics systems vary significantly within operating regions. The North American logistics vision is one of open geography with extensive demand for land-based transportation and relatively limited need for cross-border documentation. The European logistician, on the other hand, views operations from a perspective characterized by relatively compact geography involving numerous political, cultural, regulatory, and language barriers. The Pacific Rim logistician has an island perspective that requires extensive water or air shipment to transcend vast distances. These different perspectives require logistics managers who operate globally to develop a wide variety of capabilities and expertise.

In the past, an enterprise could survive with a unique North American, European, or Pacific Rim logistics perspective. Specifically, an enterprise could achieve substantial success through regional logistics capability. While this is still true for some firms, those that desire to grow and prosper are finding a regional business strategy is no longer adequate. In order to allow manufacturing and marketing scale economies to support market growth, enterprises are developing global logistics expertise. The extended global capabilities must include international transportation, cultural diversity, multilanguage capability, and extended supply chain operations.

Chapter 5 discusses the rationale for global operations and elaborates on the requirements that make them unique in comparison to domestic logistics. The overall purpose of the chapter is to compare global and domestic logistical operations. The initial sections focus on forces, barriers, and challenges involved in global logistics. Five major forces that are influencing global logistics are initially reviewed. Attention is then directed to a discussion of perceptions and practices that are barriers to global expansion. This initial section concludes with an overview of the global logistics challenge. Next, a comparison is made between nationalistic and stateless perspectives of global logistics. The discussion reviews the management and logistics implications of each perspective. The following section outlines five stages of typical global operations and stresses how major business initiatives change as a firm progressively becomes more globalized. The next section discusses the development status in each major trading region of the world. Attention is also directed to selected developing regions that are positioned to become major future trading areas. The final section summarizes the major differences in global logistics operations including performance-cycle length, supply chain operations, the role of alliances, and systems integration.

LOGISTICS IN A GLOBAL ECONOMY

Global operations increase logistics cost and complexity. In regards to cost, estimated 1991 logistics expense for industrialized nations exceeds $2 trillion, or 11.7 percent of combined gross domestic product (GDP). Table 5-1 lists GDP and estimated logistics cost by country.

In terms of complexity, global operations increase uncertainty and decrease capability to control. Uncertainty results from greater distances, longer lead times, and decreased market knowledge. Control problems result from the extensive use of intermediaries coupled with government intervention in such areas as customs requirements and trade restrictions.

TABLE 5-1   ESTIMATED NATIONAL LOGISTICS COST (1991)

Country	Gross domestic product (billion $)	Estimated total logistics bill (billion $)	Logistics as % of GDP
Asian region			
Australia	483	54	11.2
China*	345	50	14.5
Hong Kong*	63	10	15.9
Indonesia*	94	12	12.8
Japan	3,363	340	10.1
Korea	283	35	12.4
Philippines	45	6	13.3
Singapore	40	8	20.0
Taiwan*	148	20	13.5
Asian total	4,864	535	11.0
European region			
Austria	164	20	12.2
Belgium	193	25	13.0
Denmark	125	16	12.8
Finland	130	15	11.5
France	1,200	140	11.7
Germany	1,566	185	11.8
Greece	57	8	14.0
Iceland	6	1	16.7
Ireland	42	6	14.3
Italy	1,151	145	12.6
Netherlands	286	35	12.2
Norway	106	14	13.2
Portugal	59	8	13.6
Spain	527	64	12.1
Sweden	237	30	12.7
Switzerland	228	30	13.2
United Kingdom	1,015	124	12.2
European total	7,092	866	12.2
North American region			
Canada	593	70	11.8
Mexico	208	30	14.4
United States	5,673	658	11.6
North American total	6,474	758	11.7
Industrial total	18,430	2,159	11.7

*1990 data used for countries not having 1991 data.
Source: Adapted from International Financial Statistics, Washington, D.C., International Monetary Fund.

These unique challenges complicate development of an efficient and effective global logistics system. However, in today's economy, globalization cannot be avoided. As such, logistics must resolve these concerns and complications. Fortunately, there are forces that both motivate and facilitate globalization and necessitate borderless logistics operations. This first section examines the forces motivating globalization, identifies major barriers to borderless logistics operations, and summarizes the resulting logistics challenge.

Forces Driving the Borderless World

There are many forces driving firms to enter the international arena. These forces serve as both motivators and facilitators. Enterprises are motivated to expand global operations to grow and survive. Global operations are also facilitated through developing technologies and capabilities. The five forces driving global operations are economic growth, supply chain perspective, regionalization, technology, and deregulation. The role of each force is discussed and illustrated. These forces and their interaction are depicted in Figure 5-1.

Economic Growth   Since World War II, firms in many industrialized economies have enjoyed annual double-digit percentage increases in revenue and profit. This growth trend resulted from a combination of improved market penetration, product-line expansion, domestic geographic expansion, more efficient operations, and increased market size resulting from high birthrates. Since the population of major industrial countries has stabilized or even declined, most of these traditional strategies no longer support sustained revenue and earnings growth.

The decline in economic growth in industrialized countries occurred at about the same time manufacturing and logistics productivity began to increase as a result of new technology deployment. The result was excess capacity. Given this environment, the most direct means for an enterprise to increase revenue and profit is through global expansion into other developed regions and into developing nations. Such expansion requires the integration of global manufacturing with marketing capabilities and the initiation of logistics support for new business locations. Thus, the search for growth and profit is a fundamental force driving enterprises to serve global markets.

FIGURE 5-1   Forces driving globalization.

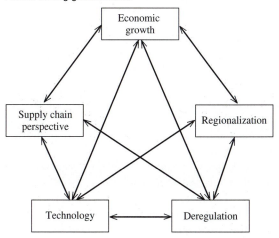

Supply Chain Perspectives   The second force driving global logistics is widespread adoption of a total supply chain perspective by manufacturers and large-scale distributors. Historically, managers have focused on reducing procurement cost and manufacturing expense within their own enterprise. Expenses incurred by other channel members typically were not viewed as important when making logistics or product sourcing decisions. The widespread reversal of this trend toward relationship development was discussed in Chapter 4.

Firms traditionally sought logistical control by performing as many essential activities as possible internally. Internal performance typically resulted in private warehouses, transportation, and information processing.

While such privatization maximized control, it also increased the assets required to support logistics operations. Commitment of assets to logistics is not critical from the viewpoint of profitability. However, in terms of ''return on assets'' (ROA), it is desirable to reduce the capital deployed to support any business activity. Logistics managers found that they could reduce capital deployed by outsourcing the performance of a wide range of logistics activities. As a result, the use of service specialists became common practice during the 1980s.

This experience with outsourcing proved critical in terms of financial global expansion. While attempting to develop cost-effective operations to support global expansion, firms capitalized on their earlier learning experience. They were willing to develop alliances with global suppliers that could provide expertise and quality logistics service at a reasonable cost for activities such as international freight consolidating and forwarding, international transportation, documentation, and facility operations.

Regionalization   As indicated above, the need to develop new markets to sustain growth was a primary force that encouraged firms to seek customers outside their ''home'' country. The typical initial choices of expansion-minded firms were countries in nearby geographic regions. To promote regional trade and protect trading partners from outside competition, countries began to formalize partnerships through treaties. Examples of such agreements are the European Community (EC 92) and the North American Free Trade Agreement (NAFTA). The Dean Foods sidebar illustrates such a regional strategy. Ohmae's triad view suggests that the world is evolving into three major trading regions: Europe, North America, and the Pacific Rim.[1] While each region does not restrict trade with other regions, the agreement strongly promotes and facilitates intraregional trade.

Such regionalization is resulting in an industrialized triad with each part having relatively equal population and economic strength. Table 5-2 compares the demographics of major global regions and summarizes current trade levels. Intraregional trading is facilitated by reducing tariffs, minimizing customs requirements, developing common shipping documentation, and supporting common transportation and handling systems. The ultimate goal is to treat intraregional movements as if they had the same country origin and destination.

---

[1]Kenichi Ohmae, ''The Triad World View,'' *Journal of Business Strategy,* 1986, pp. 8–19.

DEAN FOODS POSITIONING FOR NORTH AMERICAN MARKET

Howard M. Dean, the chief executive of Dean Foods Company, is developing a plan to market dairy products and frozen vegetables in Mexico. This is a dramatic move for this $2.3 billion Chicago-based company whose sales have been solely in the United States. With the opening of the Mexican market allowed by the North American Free Trade Act, Dean Foods is taking the opportunity to introduce 90 million new customers to its products.

Milk is a particularly attractive opportunity since half the Mexican population is under eighteen years of age (prime milk drinkers) and the country has a shortage of fresh milk since wholesalers and retailers have little incentive to push the product because of government price ceilings.

Prior to entering this venture, Dean assigned two managers to research Mexican marketing and logistics requirements. Dean also sought out the expertise of Tetra Pak, one of its packaging suppliers that operates a large Mexican facility.

Dean first targeted the Mexican dairy market by establishing a joint venture. The joint venture builds on the experience of a distributor that handled Dean's milk and dairy shipments to border towns. Mexico now consumes one-third of Dean's El Paso Dairy output.

Dean Foods' joint venture still requires solutions for several problems. The first problem is one of refrigeration. Most product is sold in small ''mom and pop'' stores that have little refrigeration. Because of the reduced space and shelf life at these small stores, Dean changed from gallon jugs to small cartons. A second problem concerns supermarkets, which often shut off electricity overnight causing ice-cream products to repeatedly melt and refreeze, thus hurting product quality. One solution Dean is considering is the purchase of its own refrigerated cases and compensating the stores for maintaining 24-hour electricity. A third problem is the shortage of Mexican dairy farms. This shortage is forcing Dean to consider developing relationships with raw milk producers without actually running the farms. A fourth problem is low-quality milk since there are fewer Mexican quality control regulations. Forty percent of all milk sold is unpasteurized and goes straight from the cow to the consumer.

While there are many potential difficulties, Dean's management views the situation as an opportunity to obtain a large share of a big market. But Mr. Dean says, ''We've got to move quickly. The opportunity is now.''

Based on Lois Therrien and Stephen Baker, ''Market Share Con Leche,'' *Business Week,* Special Edition: Reinventing America, 1992, p. 122.

Country political borders have traditionally served as a barrier to trade. For example, a United States transport movement of 750 miles requires less than two days. In pre-EC 92 Western Europe, a similarly distant move that crossed national borders typically exceeded four days. The extra time required to accommodate political requirements adds to logistics cost while not adding value to the ultimate consumer. Although regionalization efforts are designed to facilitate trade, government restrictions and requirements continue to cause logistical bottlenecks. However, the net efforts of regionalization have been toward facilitation of global logistics.

Technology Communication and information technology represent a fourth force stimulating international operations. Mass market communications exposed international consumers to foreign products, thus stimulating a convergence of global needs and preferences. ''Whatever their nationality, consumers in the Triad increasingly are exposed to similar motivations, seek the same kinds of life-styles,

TABLE 5-2   REGIONAL DEMOGRAPHIC AND MERCHANDISE TRADE*

	Population		Exports		Imports (FOB)		1989 GDP
	Million 1990	% Change 1980–90	Value 1990	% Change 1980–90	Value 1990	% Change 1980–90	Value
North America	275	1.0	525	6.0	641	7.0	6,474
Latin America	451	2.0	148	3.0	133	0.5	950
Western Europe	438	0.5	1,613	7.0	1,685	6.0	7,092
Central/Eastern Europe and U.S.S.R.	407	1.0	182	0.0	187	0.0	161
Africa	645	3.0	94	2.5	93	0.0	368
Middle East	126	3.0	132	5.0	103	0.0	185
Asia	2,903	1.5	791	9.5	765	8.0	4,864
Total	5,245	1.5	3,485	5.5	3,607	5.5	20,094

*In billions of dollars.
Source: Adapted from OECD Economic Surveys (country), *Paris: Organization for Economic Cooperation and Development,* Annual; *World Trade Annual;* and United Nations Statistical Office Annual.

and desire similar products. They all desire the best products available, at the lowest price possible."[2] The demand for blue jeans in Asian and Eastern European countries, and athletic shoes throughout the world, has increased as a result of widespread media exposure. Cable News Network (CNN), USA Today, and other satellite communications promote a variety of products and stimulate demand on a global basis.

A second expansion force resulting from technological development is an increased capability to exchange information facilitated by widespread availability of computers and communication networks. Historically, international commercial documentation such as orders, delivery requirements, and customs forms were typically hard-copy paper that required extensive time to transfer and often contained many errors. Prior to advanced communication technologies, the performance cycle from order commitment to order receipt was nine months to replenish Adidas shoes in the United States from the Orient. The total performance cycle has been reduced to three months through the use of enhanced information technology that speeds order requirements communication, production scheduling, shipment scheduling, and customs clearance.

As the world becomes more real-time oriented, demand for world-class products and services will increase. Although politicians regularly stress the importance of "homegrown" products, the average consumer neither knows nor cares where the product is actually produced as long as it offers the best perceived value. For example, while the Honda Accord is typically viewed as a foreign automobile by United States consumers, it has one of the highest percentages of domestic content of any car assembled or sold in this country. Honda has been among the top five selling automobiles in the United States over the past five years. The preferences

[2]Kenichi Ohmae, "The Global Logic of Strategic Alliances," *Harvard Business Review,* **67**:2, March–April 1989, pp. 143–154.

of well-traveled and knowledgeable citizens are influencing governments to rethink import restrictions and the consequences of political border barriers.

Deregulation   Deregulation of a number of key industries is a fifth driving force toward a borderless world. The two primary deregulated industries are finance and transportation.

Financial Deregulation   Global finance and foreign exchange are facilitated through a number of changes in regulations and procedures. Government, in the form of institutions such as the United States Export-Import Bank, and multigovernment-sponsored credit institutions, such as the International Monetary Market, serve to extend and guarantee long-term export and import credits above and beyond individual bank capabilities. This not only increases the availability of funds but reduces individual bank risk and increases trade potential.

The International Monetary Market (IMM) also provides the mechanism to exchange currencies and trade futures at market rates. Although the IMM originated in 1972, its impact increased significantly in 1987 with the establishment of a global electronic automated transaction system.[3] Global financial information standards are a key factor in the international trade increase.

Another factor is the elimination of the gold standard as support for individual currencies. The United States dropped the gold standard in the early 1970s, which allowed other major currencies to float against the dollar through the IMM agreement. Fixed monetary rates had previously restricted trade by setting artificially high levels for major currencies of industrialized nations. High exchange rates made international trade expensive because of the artificially high cost of goods. Floating rates facilitate free currency movement and tend to synchronize global booms and recessions. In addition, interest rates, capital markets, and the overall investment climate are more interlinked and interdependent given global monetary systems.

The free flow of currency exchange is particularly evident in contemporary financial markets. The United States dollar, for example, facilitates the global flow of goods while being only minimally affected by differences in individual country wage rates. In fact, these markets support an annual volume of foreign currency exchange in equity and capital transactions that is 300 times larger than the annual goods exchange between triad members.[4] The difference in magnitude between currency and goods exchange explains why directional shifts in goods exchange have only a minor impact on exchange rates.

Transportation Deregulation   The United States initiative to deregulate transportation during the early 1980s has gradually spread throughout the globe. Despite the fact that overall global deregulation has advanced at a slower rate than in the United States, three global changes concerning intermodal ownership and operation, privatization, and cabotage and bilateral agreements have occurred. The global trade impact of each is discussed.

---

[3]Leo Melamed, ''Evolution of the International Monetary Market,'' *Cato Journal,* **8:**2, Fall 1988, pp. 393–404.
[4]Kenichi Ohmae, *The Borderless World,* New York: HarperCollins Publishers, 1991, p. 157.

Historically, there have been regulatory restrictions concerning international transportation ownership and operating rights. Carriers have traditionally been limited to operating within a single transportation mode with few joint pricing and operating agreements. Specifically, steamship lines could not own or manage land-based operations such as motor or rail carriers. Without joint ownership, operations, and pricing agreements, international shipping was complicated as a result of the number of parties involved. International shipments typically required multiple carriers to perform and manage the freight flow. In addition, carrier operations were typically limited. For example, foreign-owned carriers could not operate in many nations located between domestic origins and destinations. There were also limitations for carriers when they made pickups or deliveries in foreign countries. Specifically, government rather than market forces determined the extent of services foreign-owned carriers could perform. Although some ownership and operating restrictions remain, marketing and alliance arrangements among countries have substantially improved transportation flexibility. The removal of multimodal ownership restrictions in the United States occurred with the combined enactment of the deregulatory acts noted in Chapter 1. Similar restrictions were removed in most other industrialized nations. An example of the increased flexibility is United Parcel Service's (UPS) current capability to serve over 190 countries in a seamless manner via ownership, joint marketing, and operating agreements. Internally, UPS may provide service by carrying a package with a combination of rail, motor, air, and water transportation. Such agreements facilitate international shipment efficiency and trade, as well as increase the possibility of one-stop logistics services.

A second transportation stimulant to globalization has been increased carrier privatization. Historically, many international carriers were owned and operated by "home country" governments to promote trade and provide strategic reserves in case of war. One such example is Air France. Government-owned carriers would sometimes subsidize operations for their home country enterprises while placing surcharges on "foreign" enterprises. Artificially high pricing and poor service often made it costly and unreliable to ship via government carriers. Inefficiencies also resulted from strong unionization and work rule restrictions. The combination of high cost and operating inefficiencies caused many government carriers to operate at a loss.

In an effort to improve service, many governments have privatized major carriers, while others are considering it. For example, the United Kingdom and Canada are in the process of privatizing air, motor, and rail carriers. The European Community is completing other large-scale privatization and infrastructure projects to meet increased business demands resulting from EC 92 initiatives.[5] Forced to operate in the competitive marketplace, privatized carriers must improve service and be more consistent and competitively priced. The result is facilitated international trade.

Changes in cabotage and bilateral service agreements are the third regulatory factor influencing international trade. Cabotage laws require passengers or goods moving between two domestic ports to utilize only domestic carriers. For example,

---

[5]"EC Infrastructure Projects and Privatization Expand the Export Market for U.S. Companies," *Business America,* **112**:13, July 1, 1991, p. 10.

water shipments from Los Angeles to New York must use a United States carrier. The same cabotage laws restrict a Canadian driver from transporting a back-haul load to Detroit once a shipment originating in Canada is unloaded in Texas. Cabotage laws protect domestic transportation industries, even though they reduce overall transportation equipment utilization.

The European Community is relaxing cabotage restrictions to increase trade efficiency. It is projected that reduced cabotage restrictions will save United States corporations 10 to 15 percent in intra-European shipping costs.[6] European Transport Ministers have reached agreement to open Europe as a single transport market by 1998.[7] Several prominent United States trucking companies, such as Yellow Freight and Carolina Freight, have opened offices and entered into operating agreements with European carriers. Although NAFTA does not allow motor carrier cabotage, American trucking firms will be able to carry international cargo into Mexican border states by the end of 1995 and throughout Mexico by the end of 1999. Mexican trucking firms will be allowed reciprocal treatment in the United States on the same timetable.

Bilateral service agreements require that a balanced number of carriers registered in each country be authorized to operate between origin and destination points. Such agreements serve to limit the total number of international carriers that serve key specific gateways. In addition, bilateral agreements may result in duplicate service and excess capacity in low-volume gateways. The consensus is that traditional bilateral agreements are shifting toward multilateral arrangements with separate considerations for passenger and freight transport.[8] This intergovernmental arrangement and cooperation will yield improved transport service while simultaneously reducing transportation rates. The net result should favor international trade.

Barriers to Global Logistics

While many forces facilitate borderless operations, some significant barriers continue to impede global logistics. Three barriers are significant: markets and competition, financial barriers, and distribution channels. Figure 5-2 illustrates this perspective. Global logistics management must balance the cost of overcoming these barriers with the potential benefits of international trade to achieve the actual benefits of successful international operations. Each barrier is described.

Markets and Competition   Perceived and real market and competitive barriers include entry restrictions, information availability, pricing, and competition. Entry restrictions limit market access by placing legal or physical barriers on importing. An example of a physical barrier is the European practice of local presence, which requires that market-based manufacturing or distribution facilities be established prior to market access. An example of a legal entry barrier is the Japanese practice

---

[6]Karen E. Thuermer, ''Will the Barriers Come Tumbling Down?'' *Global Trade,* August 1992, pp. 10–15.

[7]John G. Parker, ''Europe's Motor Carrier Act of 1993,'' *Transport Topics,* **3025,** July 26, 1993, pp. 3, 24.

[8]Bruce Vail, ''Move to Multilateral Air Deals,'' *American Shipper,* August 1993, p. 10

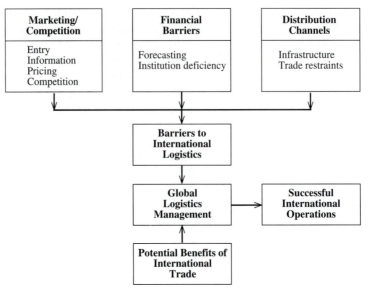

FIGURE 5-2   Barriers to international logistics.

of allowing local retailers to ''vote'' on acceptance of new retailers, particularly foreign ones, into the market.

Poor information availability is another global logistics barrier. In addition to limited information availability regarding market size, demographics, and competition, little coordinated information is available defining import and documentation requirements. Typical requirements differ by government and even by specific case. Most governments require that documentation be completed and processed prior to shipment. In many cases, if the documentation is not flawless, the shipment is delayed or impounded. While correct documentation is important for all shipments, it is critical for international transportation.

Pricing and the related topic of tariffs are other marketing-related barriers. International pricing is strongly influenced by exchange rates. The situation confronted by United States distributors of German automotive parts illustrates how exchange rates affect logistical requirements. The common practice is to delay ordering replenishment parts until as late as possible to reduce risk and investment. However, when the German mark rises compared to the United States dollar, as it did in the early 1990s, a more cost-effective strategy may be to stock up on parts and take advantage of the favorable exchange rate.

Tariffs represent another traditional barrier. Tariffs were originally designed to protect domestic industries by increasing prices on imported goods. Tables 5-3 and 5-4 illustrate tariff levels between the United States and Canada and between the United States and Mexico prior to free trade agreements between the countries. Tariffs complicate international trade in two ways. First, tariffs are an additional cost element that must be considered when evaluating foreign sources of supply. Second, tariffs are political, subject to quick change as government policy alters.

TABLE 5-3   AVERAGE UNITED STATES AND CANADIAN TARIFFS BY COUNTRY
AS A PERCENTAGE OF SALE PRICE (1988)

	United States tarriffs on imports from:		Canadian tariffs on imports from:	
	Canada	Other	United States	Other
Agriculture	1.6	1.8	2.2	1.8
Food	3.8	4.8	15.5	13.6
Textiles	7.2	9.1	16.9	16.4
Clothing	18.4	21.4	23.7	22.1
Leather products	2.5	3.8	4.0	8.7
Footwear	9.0	8.9	21.5	21.9
Wood products	0.2	3.8	2.5	4.9
Furniture and fixtures	4.6	2.9	14.3	14.1
Paper products	0.0	1.3	6.6	6.5
Printing and publishing	0.3	0.7	1.1	1.0
Chemicals	0.6	3.5	7.9	7.0
Petroleum products	0.0	0.1	0.4	0.1
Rubber products	3.2	2.0	7.8	6.5
Nonmetal mineral products	0.3	7.2	4.4	8.5
Glass products	5.7	5.8	6.9	7.9
Iron and steel	2.7	3.9	3.1	4.5
Nonferrous metals	0.5	0.8	3.3	2.7
Metal products	4.0	4.4	8.6	8.9
Nonelectric machinery	2.2	3.2	4.6	4.8
Transportation equipment	4.5	4.1	7.5	7.1
Misc. manufactures	0.0	2.5	0.0	2.5
Average	0.9	2.0	5.0	5.3

Source: Drusilla K. Brown and Robert M. Stern, "A Modeling Perspective," in *Perspectives on United States–Canadian Free Trade Agreement,* eds. Robert M. Stern, Philip H. Trezise, and John Whalley, Washington, D.C.: The Brookings Institute, 1987.

TABLE 5-4   UNITED STATES AND MEXICAN TARIFFS ON IMPORTS FROM EACH OTHER
AS A PERCENTAGE OF PRODUCT SALE PRICE

Description	Mexican tariffs on imports from U.S. (percent)	U.S. tariff on imports from Mexico* (percent)
Food preparations	20.0	10.0
Soups without meat	N.A.	7.0
Toothpaste	N.A.	4.9
Women's blouses	20.0	16.4
Women's dresses	20.0	17.7
Finished metal products	20.0	N.A.
Appliances/refrigerators	20.0	10.0
Automotive components	20.0	2.2
Floor polishers	20.0	N.A.
Lab instruments	10.0	N.A.

*May be tariff-free if GATT-eligible (country holds most-favored nation status).
Source: United States Customs Service, Telephone Interview with Import Specialist, October 1990; and United States Department of Commerce, Mexican Tariff Schedules, 1990.

Tariffs serve as a barrier to logistics planning since trade flow direction and volume can change overnight. While the NAFTA and EC 92 eliminate many tariffs within North America and Europe, substantial tariffs remain between regions.

GATT (General Agreement on Tariffs and Trade) is a multilateral trade mechanism for improving trade relations among signatory trading partners. It is designed to increase trade consistency, improve trade relations, and reduce bilateral agreements. A fundamental GATT principle requires that tariff reductions negotiated between any two members be extended to all members. Since GATT was founded in 1948, there have been eight ''rounds'' of negotiations resulting in an increase in tariff consistency. However, despite this effort, tariff differentials still exist and remain effective barriers for international logistics.

While most international firms have experience in highly competitive environments, different rules concerning competitive governance also serve as global logistics barriers. For example, the United States government fosters private enterprise, and, as such, it maintains an arm's-length relationship with business and prohibits price collusion. However, these economic policies are not a global standard. Global competitors, such as United States–based Boeing, must contend with firms such as Airbus Industries that have a home field advantage in Europe because of the French government's majority ownership. The competitive barrier is a combination of a lack of awareness regarding global rules and the necessity to conform to the norms of particular geographic regions.

Financial Barriers   The financial barriers to global logistics result from forecasting and the institutional infrastructures. While it is not easy to forecast in any situation, it is particularly difficult in global environments. The domestic forecasting challenge is to predict unit or dollar sales based on customer trends, competitive actions, and seasonality. In a global environment, these challenges are compounded by exchange rates, customs actions, and government policy complexities.

Institutional infrastructure barriers result from major differences in how facilitating intermediaries such as banks, insurance firms, legal counselors, and transportation carriers operate. Services and capabilities that are taken for granted in the United States are often not available or are administered differently in foreign countries. The banking, insurance, and legal systems as well as the omnipresent transportation systems common in the United States are in their infancy in most less developed countries. To illustrate this point, interviews with managers in Eastern Europe indicate that payment receipt and processing can take two or three weeks, even within a single city! These long processing times often occur in economies where *monthly* inflation exceeds 5 percent. Such delays significantly complicate order processing and increase financial and inventory risk.

The combination of financial and institutional uncertainty makes it difficult to plan product and financial requirements. As a result, logistics managers must allow for additional inventory, transportation lead time, and financial resources to operate globally.

Distribution Channels   Distribution channel differences such as infrastructure standardization and trade agreements are a third barrier confronting logistics managers. Infrastructure standardization refers to differences in transportation and material-handling equipment, warehouse and port facilities, and communication systems. While there have been recent efforts to improve standardization with respect to containerization, there are still major differences in global transportation equipment such as vehicle dimensions, capacity, weight, and rail gauge. It is not even necessary to go beyond United States boundaries to find differences in permissible transportation equipment length and weight restrictions on a state-by-state basis.

When infrastructure is not standardized, it is necessary for products to be unloaded and reloaded into different vehicles or containers as they cross national boundaries, resulting in increased cost and time. Infrastructure problems are common within the United States when ocean carriers require ocean containers to be unloaded prior to domestic shipment.

Trade restriction barriers can influence channel decisions, such as the rules that restrict the volume of imports or increase duties once a specified volume has been reached. There are, for example, trade agreements for all tuna imports from American Samoa into the United States. The agreement levies a 15 percent tariff when total annual imports exceed a specified level. When the specified level is reached, tuna importers build inventories in bonded warehouses for shipment release following the beginning of the next year. The use of bonded warehouses on the United States mainland means that the tariffs are not assessed until the product is shipped to local warehouses. While the tactic of using bonded warehouses reduces tariff expense, it increases logistics complexity and cost, since it requires inventory buildup and temporary warehousing. Not only is this a problem when individual enterprises use this tactic, but it is further compounded since competitors also vie to get their product imported under the same import restrictions while minimizing their duty and storage expense. This example illustrates how trade agreements that limit quantities or require special conditions increase international logistics complexity.

The Global Challenge

Firms desiring to expand globally need to assess the balance of forces that encourage such activity and the barriers they must overcome. Increasing international trade requires logistics managers to develop both a global awareness and a global perspective. Managers must be aware of the aforementioned logistics barriers, consider alternative solutions, and have the insight to apply them in nontraditional environments.

While logistics principles are the same domestically and globally, operating environments are more complex and costly. Cost and complexity are represented by the four D's—distance, documents, diversity in culture, and demands of customers.[9] Distances are longer. Documentation is more extensive. Customers demand variation in products and services to satisfy cultural differences, within both countries and regions. Developing strategies and tactics to respond to the ''four D'' environment is the global challenge for logistics management.

[9] Donald J. Bowersox, ''Framing Global Logistics Requirements,'' *Proceedings of the Annual Conference of the Council of Logistics Management,* Oak Brook, Ill.: Council of Logistics Management, pp. 267–278.

Global logistics development requires creation of an international operating philosophy and vision. The vision must result in operating strategies, performance expectations, measurement, and decision alternatives. The following section contrasts two perspectives of international trade.

VIEWS OF GLOBAL LOGISTICS

The continuum of global trade perspectives ranges from an importing and exporting orientation to the concept of a stateless enterprise. While there are certainly intermediate positions, the different perspectives are highlighted by reviewing extremes. The following section compares conceptual and managerial implications of enterprise focus, process orientation, and structural relationships associated with each extreme perspective. The section concludes with an examination of the logistical differences between national and stateless enterprise perspectives.[10]

Importing and Exporting: A National Perspective

The national perspective considers all international activity as importing and exporting. The enterprise's organization within each country is focused on internal operations and views each transaction from a national perspective of what it will do for the local operation. Typically, when firms are guided by this philosophy, their operation in each country is managed as an autonomous unit with performance measurement focused on its own profit and loss statement, including self-generation of assets.

A national perspective influences logistical decisions in three ways. First, sourcing and resource choices are based on artificial constraints. The constraints may be in the form of use restrictions or price surcharges. A *use restriction* is a limitation, usually government-imposed, that restricts import sales or use. For example, the enterprise may require that internal divisions be used for material sources even though prices or quality are not competitive. *Price surcharges* are artificial price increases on foreign-sourced products imposed by governments or home country operations to maintain the viability of local suppliers. In combination, use restrictions and pricing surcharges limit management's ability to select what otherwise would be the preferred supplier.

Second, confronting logistics with a nation-by-nation perspective increases planning complexity. A fundamental logistics objective is smooth product flow in a manner that facilitates efficient capacity utilization. Barriers resulting from government intervention make it difficult to achieve this objective. The tuna example, cited earlier, demonstrates how government policies cause artificial diversions of product flow.

Third, a national perspective attempts to extend domestic logistics systems and operating practices around the globe. While this philosophy simplifies matters at a policy level, it increases operational complexity since exceptions are typically

---

[10]This discussion builds on the work of Kenichi Ohmae as presented in *The Borderless World,* New York: HarperCollins Publishers, 1991.

numerous. Local managers must handle such exceptions while remaining within corporate policies and procedures. As a result, local logistics management must accommodate cultural, language, employment, and political environments without full support and understanding of corporate headquarters.

The national perspective both decreases and increases decision complexity for logistics managers. Decision complexity is decreased since the enterprise limits alternatives under consideration by eliminating global sourcing and dictating suppliers. On the other hand, logistics decision complexity is increased by the addition of noneconomic constraints such as political policy or subsidiary ownership that can change overnight. This combination often results in less-than-competitive product quality and price.

Perhaps the most visible example of a national perspective, both politically and socially, is found in Japan's distribution system. Japan has more than 1.5 million small (less than 3,200 square feet of floor space) neighborhood shops that account for more than 50 percent of retail sales—compared with 3 percent in the United States and 5 percent in Europe.[11] Since World War II, one of Japan's top economic priorities has been to maintain this network of small shops for cultural reasons. A vast, multitiered network of wholesalers evolved to supply the shops, often providing daily delivery on cash-and-carry service. These wholesalers are linked to manufacturers and/or to Japan's huge trading companies via another tier of large distributors. As a result, 20 percent of all Japanese workers are employed in distribution.[12]

Protection of this distribution system takes many forms. In particular, distribution legislation, such as the 1974 Large Retail Stores Law, regulates the opening of new stores larger than 5,400 square feet. The approval involves an extended negotiation that often exceeds eight or more years with local officials and retailers. As one might expect, the law has severely limited the entry of western-style retailing in Japan. Sociocultural forces also contribute to distribution inefficiencies. Traditional Japanese society involves a rigid code of interpersonal obligations that serve to maintain social harmony, group welfare, and hierarchical relationships. These societal characteristics promote close ties between wholesalers, as well as between wholesalers and retailers. Foreign manufacturers, especially American, find it difficult to penetrate these complex social-business linkages. American manufacturers have attempted several strategies to improve access to Japanese markets. One approach involved building brand awareness in the highly brand-conscious Japanese consumer and relying on a "pull" method of acquiring distribution. While this strategy has worked for some highly visible global brands, manufacturers with weaker brand identities are forced to rely on the huge Japanese trading companies for market access. In recent years, most, if not all, firms emphasized quality as the key determinant of consumer product offerings. Another strategy, utilized by large firms such as Toys "R" Us, attempted to establish direct distribution and bypass the numerous tiers of wholesalers between typical United States manufacturers and Japanese consumers. Except for firms with the ability to utilize direct distribution, most foreign companies have found little or limited success penetrating the Japanese distribution system.

---

[11]"You Can't Remove Cultural Barriers," *Transportation & Distribution,* **32:**6, June 1991, pp. 43–45.
[12]"Revolution in Japanese Retailing," *Fortune,* February 7, 1994, pp. 143–146.

Today, however, the traditional Japanese distribution system is beginning to break down because of a variety of internal and external economic pressures.[13] First, the consumer has become increasingly price-conscious as a result of a three-year recession. The drop in value of the dollar against the yen, to record post–World War II levels, has lowered the effective price of imports. In fact, a recent poll in Japan discovered that price, not quality, now determines most purchases.[14] Second, brand loyalty is eroding as giant retailers offer more low-priced private house brands of diverse products such as televisions and soft drinks. Third, innovative small firms are avoiding traditional supply and distribution channels and are selling goods at cut-rate prices. Finally, foreign retailers such as Toys "R" Us have brought mass merchandising practices to Japan—and have benefited from relaxations in the Large Store Retail Law that increase store hours and the number of allowable business days per week. These changes in the structure of Japanese distribution suggest that over time, global economic conditions have the potential to drastically alter a traditional, national trading perspective.

The Stateless Enterprise

The *stateless enterprise* perspective, which is also known as "companyism," contrasts sharply to operations under a national perspective. The stateless concept was popularized in a *Business Week* article describing enterprises that are effectively making decisions with little regard to national boundaries.[15] These enterprises have the capacity to juggle multiple identities and loyalties and resemble insiders in whatever area they operate. For example, even though the stateless enterprise may have its historical foundations in Germany, Japan, or the United States, a high percentage of its sales, ownership, and assets are outside the country of origin. The stateless enterprise is also likely to have senior management and boards of directors representing a broad range of nationalities and global experiences. Examples of firms that fit these specifications are ABB (Switzerland), Dow Chemical (United States), ICI (Britain), Hoechst (Germany), Nestlé (Switzerland), and Philips (Netherlands).[16]

Examples of global firms operating as stateless enterprises can be seen in China. Although China is estimated to be the world's third largest economy, it very much remains a third-world country in many respects—particularly concerning logistics and channel infrastructure. China has poor communications, no intermodal systems or boxcar availability or container tracer capability, no cargo airlines, and virtually nonexistent roads outside major cities. Firms preparing to invest in Vietnam face similar conditions. For these reasons, several of the largest United States firms currently operating in China are relying heavily on local managers to run logistics operations. Both AT&T and Procter & Gamble believe that their Chinese operations cannot be run by managers from the United States because of such underdeveloped business systems, the rapid rate of change, and exploding trade volume. Questions

---

[13]"A Bargain Basement Called Japan," *Business Week,* June 27, 1994, pp. 42–43.
[14]"Revolution in Japanese Retailing," *Fortune,* February 7, 1994, pp. 143–146.
[15]"The Stateless Corporation," *Business Week,* May 14, 1990, p. 98.
[16]Ibid., p. 103.

of supply chain distribution for Procter & Gamble are handled by its general manager in Guangzhou. In fact, the general manager has almost complete freedom regarding product-line sourcing, regardless of the country of origin. Similarly, AT&T's logistics person in Shanghai determines operating policy for the company's network systems division. This division has responsibility for providing the foundation for a modern phone system in China. A recent informal survey of logistics managers indicates that business in China has never been better but that the country is one of the most challenging experiences in business today.[17] Given these conditions, the logistics of operating in China and other developing regions of the world are indeed quite challenging.

What are the logistics implications of a stateless enterprise? The first implication is that managers are able to identify and evaluate alternative strategies and have the authority for implementation. In the case of logistics management, this requires investments of time and effort to identify and evaluate alternatives for materials, logistics service suppliers, manufacturing and warehousing locations, and customer alliances. These requirements particularly affect the stateless enterprise because of the geographic scope and cost of its operations, as well as the attendant risk involved in decisions of such magnitude and complexity.

A second logistics implication is the need to develop and implement flexible systems and procedures. While basic logistic principles suggest that substantial scale economies are preferable to support global development and implementation, the stateless enterprise is sensitive to local market requirements. For example, business elements other than a country's language must be adapted in order to support the concept of global localization or customization. The system must also adapt to differences in documentation, packaging, pricing, and operations. To provide this flexibility, firms are adopting a data warehousing concept.[18] The data warehouse is a database general enough to accommodate the information needs of the global enterprise with a flexible user interface that can be customized to individual market needs and procedural differences. Each market receives its own door to the warehouse so that each country can meet its specific needs.

The experience of Dow Chemical illustrates typical problems associated with poorly integrated global systems. In the past, Dow systems and procedures differed by business unit and global location. The lack of integration increased operating complexity while it decreased capability to respond to customers on a global basis. To resolve this problem, Dow management has initiated a long-range plan to implement an integrated system capable of providing customers with whatever information they may want about a product they have ordered or consider ordering, regardless of their global location. This localized integration requires sensitivity to local market needs while providing information structures to support a common knowledge base.[19]

---

[17]"China Logistics: Remote Control Won't Work," *American Shipper,* July 1994, pp. 47–54.

[18]International Business Machines, *Computer Integrated Logistics CIL Architecture in the Extended Enterprise,* Document Number SC67-0216-0, March 27, 1991.

[19]Marilyn J. Cohodes, "Finding the Right Distribution Software," *Datamation,* **37:**14, July 15, 1991, pp. 61–62.

Conclusion

The enterprise's global perspective determines how logistics management treats international operations. The historical perspective usually positioned international logistics as an exception. This implies a home country focus, exporting of home country processes, and limited consideration of alternative sources and suppliers. While this was the historical norm, such a perspective is no longer acceptable to firms with ownership status, customer base, and asset base located throughout the globe or to firms that are driven to competitiveness and sustained growth. As enterprises face more demands from global customers, governments, and suppliers, an increasing number have begun to adopt a stateless perspective. The philosophical shift requires logistics managers to refine their procedures, practices, and capabilities.

GLOBAL OPERATING LEVELS

The previous discussion contrasted two extreme perspectives of globalization. This section traces the levels of enterprise evolution from domestic logistics operations to becoming a global competitor. The duration of each level is a reflection of managerial philosophy rather than elapsed time. The five levels are arm's-length relationship, internal export, internal operations, insider business, and denationalized operations. Figure 5-3 illustrates the risk and return associated with each global operating stage.

Arm's-Length Relationship

Level 1 is characterized by an arm's-length relationship between an enterprise and an international distributor that serves a country or region. The enterprise, which probably has limited international experience, either sells or consigns its goods to

FIGURE 5-3 Risk-return trade-off for global operations.

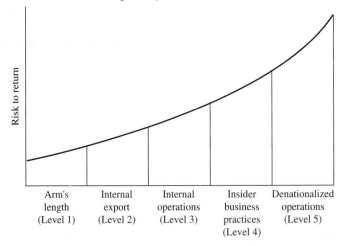

the international specialist, which accepts responsibility for ordering, providing international transportation, completing documentation, as well as coordinating marketing, inventory management, invoicing, and product support. On the positive side, the arm's-length relationship significantly lowers the enterprise's risk by providing staff and expertise to establish and manage necessary relationships and operations. On the negative side, the arm's-length relationship reduces the firm's contribution margin and decreases product and logistical control.

Internal Export

Level 2 enterprises develop the expertise to coordinate and manage international transportation and documentation. However, the local agent or distributor is retained to provide marketing, inventory management, invoicing, and product support. Thus, the enterprise might increase its contribution margin by internalizing some of the export activities but still uses specialized assistance for marketing, sales, and customer service activities once the product is exported. The risk also exists that internalizing selected logistics activities may increase cost as a result of less expertise. Lack of internal sales, marketing, and distribution support for the international market also reduces the enterprise's sensitivity to local requirements.

Internal Operations

Level 3 is characterized by development of operations in the local or foreign country. Internal operations include combinations of marketing, sales, production, and distribution. Establishment of local facilities and operations increases market awareness and sensitivity. This is typically referred to as *local market presence.* However, the internal operations stage often uses parent company practices, management, and personnel, rather than employing locals. The rationale for home country staffing is that headquarters can rely on international operations to better execute policy if proven company managers are in charge. Since managers are assigned from the home country, this first foothold of internal operations strongly reflects home country operations. The internal operations stage increases enterprise control and sensitivity in comparison to the initial two stages but still relies heavily on home country values, procedures, and operations.

Insider Business Practices

The fourth level further internalizes international operations and institutes local business practices. This level of sophistication typically involves hiring host country management, marketing, and sales organizations and may include the use of local business systems. This stage requires that headquarters management support local management decisions regarding practices and procedures. As insider operations develop, a separate host country philosophy emerges. However, the home country philosophy is clearly dominant. Individual international operations are still measured against home country expectations and standards.

Minnesota Mining and Manufacturing (3M) illustrates a successful global perspective as it is one of the world's 100 largest enterprises with 1992 global revenues of $6.8 billion. 3M has been operating internationally for nearly half of its 90 years.

Approximately 50 percent of its revenue is derived from outside the United States. 3M operates 23 major businesses and manufactures over 60,000 products that require more than 100 basic technologies. There are 89,000 3M employees in fifty-five countries.

3M's product success is the result of research spending. In 1991 and 1992, research constituted 6.6 percent of total sales, which is double the U.S. manufacturing average. Research and development is carried out in twenty-one countries, and manufacturing and converting operations occur in forty-one countries. 3M has committed to locating laboratory sites wherever the driving forces of products or technologies exist.

3M management believes in formulating different global strategies for its products across international markets. For example, as countries in Europe move toward a more unified internal market, 3M is creating three business centers (utility tapes, disposable products, and automotive and aerospace products) that will oversee R&D, manufacturing, sales, marketing, and distribution throughout the continent. European operations are assisted by fifty cross-functional European Management Action Teams (EMATs) that attempt to balance the needs of local subsidiaries with the corporation's need for global direction.

In the Asia-Pacific area, the approach is primarily one of support operations, although the 3M research center in Japan is becoming increasingly important. In Latin America, national issues predominate; therefore, most business is conducted on a national rather than regional basis. In North America, 3M is reordering business strategy in light of the U.S.–Canada Free Trade Agreement and NAFTA.

Although 3M utilizes various global strategies, the basic strategy rests on the following core principles: (1) get in ahead of the competition; (2) hire qualified local people (fewer than 200 of 3M's 39,000 international employees are Americans), and give them a great deal of autonomy; (3) start small with a modest investment and gradually build a local presence; and (4) maintain flexibility through a shared management structure incorporating responsibility and communication to provide immediate responsiveness to new opportunities.

In recent years, 3M and other world-class manufacturers have shortened production runs, reorganized plant layout by product rather than by process technology, allotted greater local control on the shop floor, and utilized JIT inventory methods to increase manufacturing productivity and flexibility. These changes provide increased responsiveness to customer demands. In order to obtain the benefits of these changes, global manufacturing strategy must also be integrated with marketing and logistics.

The firm's extensive geographic scope of manufacturing and research presents a complex logistics support task. 3M's logistics vision for the 1990s is to be the best service company in warehousing, packaging, data processing, customer service, and transportation. A major goal of this vision is to eliminate redundant logistics costs. For example, in Western Europe, 3M has invested significant resources to improve order processing through EDI, which means rethinking the role of subsidiary location, since customers can now deal directly with the manufacturing location. The company has also improved distribution through building larger, more efficient warehouses to replace numerous minidistribution centers.

Global manufacturing requires logistics networks that affect the environments of many countries. 3M is considered one of the premier corporate global citizens regarding environmental issues. 3M's environmental policy emphasizes developing manufacturing processes to achieve "zero waste." The company stresses that "total quality equals no loss" (i.e., total quality means no waste). 3M's 3P program (pollution prevention pays) was initiated in 1975 and is now a subset of its group environmental policy. The 3P program is probably the best known and most successful antipollution program ever launched by a company. In fact, 3M claims to have benefited on the bottom line from its environmental policy. Less waste means more efficient manufacturing, fewer logistical movements of hazardous materials, reduced potential liabilities, and less nonproductive reverse logistics costs. 3M's commitment to quality is further supported by an extensive and effective customer satisfaction measurement system that is considered one of the very best in American business.

Based on information in "Can American Manufacturers Compete outside the U.S.?" *Financial Executive,* September–October 1990, pp. 24–31; "3M Run Scared? Forget about It," *Business Week,* September 16, 1991, p. 59; and "Good to Be Green," *Management Today,* February 1989, pp. 46–52.

Denationalized Operations

The denationalized operations level maintains foreign country operations and develops a regionalized headquarters to oversee the coordination of operations in the area. At this point, the enterprise is stateless in the sense that no specific home or parent country dominates policy. Senior management likely represents a combination of nationalities. Denationalized operations function on the basis of local marketing and sales organizations and are typically supported by world-class manufacturing and logistics operations. Product sourcing and marketing decisions can be made across a wide range of global alternatives. Systems and procedures are designed to meet individual country requirements and are aggregated as necessary to share knowledge and for financial reporting. The sidebar discussion of the 3M Company describes many characteristics of a firm with denationalized operations.

Conclusion

While most enterprises engaged in global logistics are operating at levels 2, 3, and 4, a truly international firm must focus on denationalizing operations. Enterprises in any of the other stages will retain a home country perspective with its implicit pecking order. However, denationalized operations require a significant level of management trust across countries and cultures. Such trust can grow only as managers increasingly live and work in other cultures. While this cross-culturalization is beginning to occur, it will be some time before it transcends a broad range of logistics managers.

THE INTERLINKED GLOBAL ECONOMY

As discussed throughout this chapter, global economies are increasingly interlinked by material suppliers, logistical systems, manufacturing capacity, and markets. It is natural that this interconnectedness take the form of regional alliances that leverage geographic proximity and scale economies. The major triad regions developing are North America, Europe, and the Pacific Rim. It is likely that Eastern Europe will join with the Western European countries and that South America will ultimately link up with North America. Although there is considerable speculation, the ultimate resolution involving the former Soviet Union states and African countries is not clear. As regional alliances emerge, they evolve through four stages of integration. This section introduces these stages and reviews each region's development status.

Stages of Regional Integration

The four stages of economic integration are free trade agreement, customs union, common market, and economic union.

The first stage, a *free trade agreement,* eliminates tariffs on trade between countries in a region. Specifically, a free trade agreement is defined when:

Each participant in the free-trade area expects to gain by specializing in the production of goods and services in which it possesses comparative advantages and by importing from other countries in the group products and services in which it faces comparative disadvantages. Thus, trade should be created among member countries, giving them less-expensive access to more goods.[20]

A free trade agreement may either stimulate or reduce interregional trade. Such agreements can also reduce access of the firms to more efficient producers or markets outside their region.

The second stage, a *customs union,* eliminates tariffs between member countries and establishes a common external tariff structure toward other regions and non-member countries. Under this and the remaining two stages, member countries are required to give some control over economic policies to the group. The advantage of a customs union is that none of the member nations in the union can position themselves to gain a tariff advantage at the expense of other countries.

The third integration stage, a *common market,* is characterized by the same tariff policy as the customs union. In addition, a common market allows factors of production such as labor and capital, as well as goods and people, to move freely between member countries as dictated by market conditions.

The *economic union* is the fourth and most advanced stage of development because it implies harmonization of economic policies beyond a common market. Economic union standardizes monetary and fiscal policy among member countries. While not absolutely required, an economic union likely includes common currency and harmonized tax structures. The economic union implies that all goods and production factors can move freely according to market conditions and that no major fluctuations in monetary exchange and interest rates will occur.

Integration Status

This section reviews the current status of each major global region, including a summary of current and proposed trade acts. It also discusses the logistics implications of each trade act and the strategies reported by enterprises to accommodate and take advantage of regional changes.

North America   North America took the first step toward economic integration when the Canada–United States Free Trade Agreement (FTA) was implemented on January 1, 1989. This act has produced promising trends in trade, investment, and commercial cooperation. Both countries have realized significant expansion of exports. The most important provision of the agreement is the elimination of all tariffs on goods traded between the United States and Canada by 1998, particularly since Canadian tariffs were among the highest in the industrialized world.

The FTA greatly expands the potential for United States and Canadian businesses to sell their products to each other's federal government, especially for smaller contract awards. The FTA also reinforces relatively liberal service industry

[20]Robert Grosse and Duane Kujawa, *International Business: Theory and Managerial Applications,* 2d ed., Homewood, Ill.: Irwin, 1992, p. 273.

and investment regulations between the two countries: potentially, over 150 service industries across many sectors are affected by the agreement regulations. Finally, both nations must make publicly available all proposed laws and regulations that relate to any service trade issue, in order to allow participation by affected parties in the regulatory process.

The second step in economic integration, the North American Free Trade Agreement (NAFTA), was concluded in August 1992 between the United States, Canada, and Mexico. The NAFTA agreement, which took effect January 1, 1994, eliminates all tariffs among the three countries over a fifteen-year period and creates a free trade zone that extends from the Yukon to the Yucatán.

The goals of both agreements, particularly NAFTA, are to enhance North American competitiveness relative to Europe and Asia by (1) improving the climate for cross-border investment and trade, and (2) reducing administrative costs and delays associated with trade. The drive to accomplish these goals is generating new transportation routes and strategic alternatives and is forging many new partnerships to facilitate cargo movement.

The NAFTA impact on logistics integration efforts will be different in Canada than in Mexico. In the past, United States manufacturers established local operations in Canada primarily to maintain a marketing presence. However, logistics support of manufacturing operations was constrained because of four conditions: Canada's manufacturing base is centered almost entirely in Ontario and Quebec, Canadian manufacturing labor costs are generally higher than those in the United States, the Canadian warehousing industry lags behind United States efficiency and technology, and East-West transportation movement across Canada's vast hinterland markets is expensive. For these reasons, NAFTA-stimulated trade and transportation in Canada are projected to develop in a North-South direction. It is anticipated that this North-South development will allow more markets to be effectively serviced by fewer distribution facilities, which will provide increased scale economies.

Although the logic of North-South movement increases access to populous markets on both sides of the Canada–United States border, most Canadian restructuring has been targeted toward manufacturing efficiencies rather than improved logistics operations.[21] While sufficient time has not transpired since the NAFTA agreement to make generalizations regarding enterprise logistics strategy, initial research indicates that some changes have occurred in strategies of production and distribution service areas.[22] Increased competition resulting from NAFTA will pressure Canadian firms to innovate and adopt best United States logistics practice and should steadily improve United States–Canadian integration.

Several Canadian carriers have anticipated an increasingly competitive market and have made strategic efforts to shift away from traditional East-West movements to a more North-South orientation.[23] The Canadian National Railway has integrated its three United States subsidiaries to create a significant marketing and operational

---

[21]"Logistics Strategies for the North American Market," *Distribution*, April 1992, p. 32.

[22]John C. Taylor and David J. Closs, "Logistics Implications of an Integrated U.S.–Canada Market," *International Journal of Physical Distribution & Logistics Management*, **23**:1, 1993, pp. 3–13.

[23]"Canadian Railways," *Distribution*, March 1992, pp. 38–43.

presence in the Midwest and eastern United States. It has also created strategic alliances with Burlington Northern and Norfolk Southern railroads. Canadian Pacific Ltd.'s CP Rail System has also expanded by purchasing several United States railroads. Canadian Pacific is now the seventh largest North American railroad, operating from coast to coast in Canada and offering a major United States presence. Contract agreements between several United States and Canadian carriers have also been established to provide wider geographic motor carrier service throughout Canada. The small package segment will become more competitive with expanded Canadian coverage by United Parcel Service and Roadway Package System.

Currently, United States companies are establishing Mexican operations to take advantage of low-cost labor and to gain access to a major consumer market in which half of the population will be under the age of twenty. Although most manufacturing in Mexico is located near the United States–Mexico border, most of the buying power is concentrated in the central portion of the country. Therefore, the majority of retail growth as well as distribution and warehousing development will occur in this central region. Current Mexican transportation infrastructure is incapable of supporting major cross trade between the United States and central Mexico.

For the foreseeable future, these restrictions will force most Canadian and United States enterprises that set up manufacturing plants in Mexico to accommodate a particular supply-chain management design. Specifically, parts vendors are and will be primarily located in the United States, with maquiladora assembly plants located along the United States–Mexico border. Final distribution will be handled through facilities in the southwestern and midwestern United States. A *maquiladora* is a facility that manufactures, assembles, or produces raw materials and components that have been temporarily imported to Mexico. Products are then shipped back to the originating country or to a third country for final assembly and distribution. No duties are charged by the Mexican government on the imported inventory and equipment moving into the maquiladoras. Duties are paid only on the value added in Mexico when the finished goods are reexported to the country of origin.[24]

United States motor carriers are now permitted to transport international cargo into Mexican border states and will be permitted to carry shipments throughout Mexico by 1999.[25] Mexican motor carriers will receive reciprocal treatment. The pact also phases out barriers to bus service and cross-border investment in transportation companies and expands opportunities for United States railroads in Mexico.

There has been a tremendous amount of carrier preparation with respect to increased trade between the United States and Mexico. Improved rail services include (1) an increased number of stack trains between the midwestern United

---

[24]James E. Groff and John P. McCray, ''Maquiladoras: The Mexico Option Can Reduce Your Manufacturing Cost,'' *Management Accounting,* January 1991, pp. 43–46.

[25]Kenneth H. Bacon, ''Trade Pact Is Likely to Step Up Business Even before Approval,'' *Wall Street Journal,* August 13, 1992, p. A10.

States and Mexico, (2) nonstop integrated rail-barge connections, and (3) either rail or motor shipment options to the Mexican border from the United States. Trucking improvements include (1) door-to-door service movement on a single freight bill, (2) expedited and more frequent less-than-truckload service, (3) improved tracing, and (4) wider geographic service. Streamlined brokerage services and procedures are now available through several specialized service providers. Major distribution facilities are being constructed in Mexico.

With the passage of the FTA and the approval of NAFTA, North American governments have established the entire continent as a relevant logistic landscape. While it is clear that the logistics infrastructure could not support such continental operations in the past, the necessary partnerships are developing through alliances. With the expanded possibilities resulting from free trade agreements, North American logistics managers must particularly refine their strategies regarding material sources, manufacturing locations, distribution sites, and service providers.

Europe   European economic integration discussions began shortly after World War II and eventually culminated with the formation of the European Economic Community (EEC) in 1957. The original members (Belgium, France, Germany, Italy, Luxembourg, and the Netherlands) were joined by Denmark, Ireland, and the United Kingdom (1973); Greece (1981); and Portugal and Spain (1985). The EEC established a plan to eliminate intercountry tariffs, create common external tariffs, and guide economic policy regarding tax structures, exchange rates and controls, immigration among member countries, and agricultural support programs.

A second trade association, the European Free Trade Association (EFTA), was formed in 1960 and included Liechtenstein, Switzerland, Sweden, Finland, Norway, Iceland, and Austria. EFTA signed trade pacts with Czechoslovakia, Poland, Hungary, Turkey, and Israel in 1991 and 1992. The European Community, or EC (formerly the EEC), eliminated trade barriers with EFTA in late 1991.

In 1985, the EC Commission outlined the necessary steps to achieve a single common market allowing free movement of labor, capital, and goods by the end of 1992. This process was termed EC 92 (European Community Integration by 1992). Formal implementation efforts have been in process since 1987.

Another aspect of European integration is monetary union. The Maastricht Treaty, which requires legislative approval by all twelve EC states, mandates a central European bank and currency by 1999. The treaty met with some resistance in several EC countries in 1992. Although single-market integration will not fail without monetary union, it is considered a critical business and political signal to the rest of the world.

EC administrative reforms are already providing benefits to European transportation and trade. Shipment spot checks within nations have replaced systematic customs formalities, thus speeding traffic flows and preventing long border delays. Transportation and trade are also facilitated by development of a single administrative document (SAD). The SAD eliminates duplicate customs documents for goods shipped between countries and replaces approximately twelve forms for each participating country. The SAD also facilitates EDI transmission and statistical information collection at border crossings. The SAD itself was eliminated in 1993 since border checks occur only to monitor criminal activities and to report value and origin of cargo at the point of destination. Except for trade with countries outside the EC, all customs documentation has vanished.[26] EC efforts to standardize customs procedures and clearance through introduction of EDI are also in progress.

EC 92 significantly affects enterprises that view their European operations as international. For large multinational companies, the creation of a single market permits production and distribution system rationalization, or streamlining, as barriers to cross-national shipments are eliminated. EC 92 improvements in intra-European distribution, warehousing, and infrastructure can save companies millions of dollars. Many firms are consolidating extensive European facility networks to become pan-European both strategically and operationally.

A report of the Council of Logistics Management has summarized the perceptions and strategies of enterprises as they reconfigure European logistics systems.[27] The key findings of the study are summarized in five major categories: business and logistics environment in Europe today, European logistics strategy responses, critical management issues, achieving and sustaining logistics excellence, and European logistics: future challenges. Table 5-5 summarizes conclusions within each category.

A specific consideration in reconfiguring European logistics is transportation strategy, which is significantly influenced by demographics and geography. The European population density is three times that of the United States, making business centers more easily serviced by motor carriage. Over-the-road hauling provides 70 percent of all EC freight movements and is projected to increase by 60 percent before the year 2000.[28]

As remaining cabotage restrictions are eliminated, national carriers that service the entire region will be allowed to pick up and back haul cargo throughout the EC. Reduced cabotage restrictions are a key requirement for resolving European road congestion and environmental issues. However, new entrants face stiff opposition from many of the small ''family-size'' trucking companies that constitute a significant proportion of European operators. European road infrastructure is also a considerable problem. A recent EC Commission proposal suggested a $450 billion plan for comprehensive European transportation improvements over the next decade.[29]

Rail offers a viable solution to numerous European transportation problems, although it faces several formidable hurdles. First, national protectionist politics have contributed to the financial, technical, and physical barriers of European rail integration. For example, high-speed rail systems have been independently developed in France, Germany, Italy, and Spain but have many operational incompatibilities. Second, many countries on the periphery of Europe simply do not have a

---

[26]Hans van der Hoop, ''It's 1993: No More Bars to Being Single (Part 1 of 2),'' *Distribution,* **92:**2, February 1993, p. 26.
   [27]Kevin A. O'Laughlin, James Cooper, and Eric Cabocel, *Reconfiguring European Logistics Systems,* Oak Brook, Ill.: The Council of Logistics Management, 1993, pp. 7–18.
   [28]''Will the Barriers Come Tumbling Down?'' *Global Trade,* August 1992, pp. 10–15.
   [29]Ibid.

TABLE 5-5   KEY FINDINGS OF RECONFIGURING EUROPEAN LOGISTICS SYSTEM STUDY

1 *The business and logistics environment in Europe today*
   a Europe is a dynamic, rapidly changing marketplace.
   b European transportation infrastructure congestion will negatively influence service reliability.
   c Environmental regulation—particularly with regard to recycling, refurbishment, and disposal of products, packaging materials, and pallets—will have a major impact on logistics practices.
   d Shippers expect transport prices to rise over the next decade as a result of increased taxes and fees even though prices are expected to fall in the short term because of competition and deregulation.

2 *European logistics strategy responses*
   a Integration (i.e., connecting dispersed operations and regions through a common logistics system) and rationalization (i.e., streamlining of logistics systems to achieve better results with fewer resources) are appropriate logistics responses in Europe.
   b Logistics integration will occur with or without the Maastricht Treaty.
   c Integration increases choices regarding logistics strategy, which also increases management complexity.
   d Logistics integration and rationalization have resulted in significant logistics cost reductions.
   e High interest rates in Europe are contributing to logistics integration by encouraging firms to focus on supply-chain management initiatives leading to inventory reduction.

3 *Critical management issues*
   a Logistics is becoming a board-level position in many firms.
   b Many firms report early successes, but few have long-range logistics vision.
   c Reconfiguring logistics systems requires a total supply chain approach.
   d Corporate organizations must be realigned by process to promote integrated logistics management.
   e Planning and control systems are critical to the success of integrated logistics strategies.
   f Firms must acquire the inventory and transportation analysis tools necessary to develop effective logistics strategies.

4 *Achieving and sustaining logistics excellence*
   a European third-party logistics services must be more proactive in meeting shippers' new requirements.
   b Flexibility to react to changing market demands, transport economics, and the competitive environment is the watchword for European logistics system design.

5 *European logistics: Future challenges*
   a Develop a vision of the future of the European marketplace to exploit change rather than be overwhelmed by it.
   b Exploit change in new Europe by considering trends toward higher-value product, increased cross-border trade, better information and communications technology, increased environmental considerations, and Eastern European involvement.

Source: Kevin A. O'Laughlin, James Cooper, and Eric Cabocel, *Reconfiguring European Logistics Systems,* Oak Brook, Ill.: The Council of Logistics Management, 1993, pp. 7–15.

viable rail infrastructure. Finally, many European railroads are state-owned, inefficient, and expensive to operate. They are designed for passenger travel and have access to limited right-of-way and terminal space.[30]

Intermodalism is an undeveloped option in European transportation because of a lack of standardized containers, piggyback trailers (which are referred to as *swap*

[30]Ibid.

bodies), and operational systems. Acceptable trucking connections and short travel distances between European countries remain barriers to intermodal arrangements.

In summary, EC logistics managers are facing dramatic changes in their operating environment as a result of EC 92 initiatives and the opening of Eastern and Central European markets. EC logistics managers are responding to EC 92 initiatives in two ways. First, manufacturing and logistics networks are being integrated and rationalized to take advantage of reduced government restrictions. These changes allow an enterprise to benefit from manufacturing and distribution scale economies by maintaining fewer large facilities and shipping products greater distances. Second, with less transport regulation, many European and global carriers are building alliances to facilitate pan-European transportation and storage services. These integrated carriers frequently offer more complete services at lower prices. EC logistics managers must review these offerings and form alliances with providers that can effectively service their enterprise. The sidebar on Unisys illustrates the application of selected initiatives and results gained for integrated European logistics.

The Asia-Pacific Region   In the Asia-Pacific region, Japan and the "four dragons"—South Korea, Hong Kong, Taiwan, and Singapore—have risen to industrial prominence primarily by exporting to the United States and selected European and South American countries. In recent years, the booming export-oriented economies of Malaysia, the Philippines, Thailand, and Indonesia must be added as members of the group. The latter four countries have capitalized on a huge supply of cheap and relatively well-educated labor to establish significant trade with Japan, South Korea, and Taiwan.

The Asia-Pacific region is generally considered a growing economic force in the world today, and the region is projected to continuously expand. Interport Asian trade between nations in Asia is the fastest growing segment of ocean liner traffic. The region is also the United States' largest trading partner. United States exports to the Asia-Pacific market grew 5 and 7 percent in 1989 and 1990, respectively.[31]

The ASEAN Free Trade Area (AFTA) was created in 1992 by six countries (Brunei, Indonesia, Malaysia, the Philippines, Singapore, and Thailand). The goal is to reduce tariffs from current levels to under 5 percent and eventually attain duty-free access over a fifteen-year period beginning January 1993. Although agreement details are not finalized, the plan has enormous potential since the region contains approximately 310 million people.[32]

Significant logistics infrastructure development is occurring there as well. The extensive distances between countries within the region are motivating development of air, sea, and intermodal options. Singapore—which has developed comprehensive government sales, distribution, and administration operations—is rapidly being positioned as the economic hub of the Malay Peninsula and ultimately

---

[31]Helen L. Richardson, "Exports to PacRim Grow," *Transportation & Distribution,* April 1991, pp. 61–62.

[32]"Asia: Integration of the World's Most Dynamic Economics," *TOKYO Business Today,* June 1992, pp. 26–29.

UNISYS DESIGNS FOR A NEW EUROPE

Unisys Corporation, the $8.7 billion computer giant formed from the merger of Burroughs and Sperry, has focused considerable effort on redefining its European logistics systems over the last five years.

Unisys produces and markets computer equipment ranging from personal computers to large networks. Although some products are manufactured in Europe, Unisys imports about 70 percent of the equipment sold in Europe from the United States, Canada, Brazil, and the Far East. The process began in 1987, one year after European Community leaders agreed to create a unified market.

The first step was a comprehensive review of its European operations with an eye toward enhancing competitiveness in a single unified market. This review found that Unisys was unable to comprehensively track and monitor its shipments to customers. There was no process to control shipments except through each subsidiary.

The review identified four initiatives that would help Unisys adapt to the integrated environment. The first is an integrated information system to manage the delivery process. The delivery management system facilitates total shipment control using extensive electronic data interchange (EDI) for scheduling, releasing, tracking, notification, and invoicing. Although the system was primarily designed to track freight movements, it also helps Unisys meet new reporting requirements necessary for value-added tax (VAT) collection in each country.

The second initiative was the development of a computerized production-forecasting system nicknamed UMPS for Unisys manufacturing planning system. UMPS, an MRP system, predicts future demand and allows coordination of component sourcing, produc-

tion, and inbound shipments for all European operations. UMPS controls European inbound product flow and has reduced finished product inventory.

With the computer systems in place to control inbound and outbound product flow, Unisys' third initiative was to centralize its European inventory by reducing the number of warehouses. The original 1988 European operations audit identified five main distribution centers and fourteen subsidiary warehouses. Unisys initially closed all the subsidiary warehouses and then phased out four of the distribution centers.

The single remaining facility is located in Seneffe, Belgium. The consolidation resulted in a 72 percent reduction in space and a 76 percent reduction in inventory.

The final initiative focused on the number of intra-European carriers. The number of carriers was reduced to four from the pre-1988 level of seventy. Carrier negotiations were also centralized at the Seneffe logistics center. The carrier consolidation became possible only when the European Community finally relaxed restrictions on the number of permits granted to truckers to engage in cross-border hauling.

Warehouse and carrier consolidation along with the information management systems has positioned Unisys to compete in a borderless Europe. Bob Marshall, Unisys' European director of operations, described the situation: "The development in Europe in 1992 can only be equaled by 1776. It's exciting and challenging to be a part of it."

Based on information in James Aaron Cooke, "How Unisys Got Ready for a Unified Europe," *Traffic Management,* **31**:9, September 1992, pp. 45–48.

---

may emerge as the center point for the entire Asia-Pacific region. Singapore offers one of the three premier sea-air port facilities in the world. Malaysia is also becoming a distribution hub and an important global trade center.

Strong growth in the air cargo market is projected in the region. In East Asia, air cargo growth is forecasted to increase 6 to 8 percent annually through the year 2000. By the year 2010, two-thirds of the world's air cargo traffic will be derived from East Asia and the Pacific Rim countries.[33]

[33]Marcia Jedd, "Integrators Race for Globalism," *Global Trade,* July 1992, pp. 25–27.

Integrated trade and requisite transportation will also increase between the Asia-Pacific region and North America, particularly Mexico. Many Asia-Pacific firms that are experts in offshore development utilizing low-cost labor are moving operations to Mexico and planning additional investments to capitalize on the North American Free Trade Agreement.

There are several important, unknown factors regarding future development of the Asia-Pacific region. For example, continued market growth based on the United States demand for exports is critical to continued Asia-Pacific success. Political stability in mainland China, Eastern Russia, North Korea, Hong Kong, and the Philippines is an additional uncertainty.

Efforts to reshape and improve logistics in the region appear to spring from essentially similar perceptions and strategies as those in Western Europe. However, analysis of specific attitudes and perspectives is at best speculative at this point in time. Relatively little research has been conducted in the region regarding logistics strategy, particularly compared to the extensive research under way in Europe.

Developing Nations   While the triad regions account for the majority of industrial activity in the world, there are tremendous growth opportunities in the lesser developed areas. However, it is necessary to design and implement significant logistics infrastructure to take advantage of these opportunities. The developing regions often have limited distribution channels and poor transportation. The status and opportunities of the developing regions of Eastern Europe and Central and South America are discussed because of their potential to emerge and affect the triad areas.

Eastern Europe   Eastern Europe consists of Bosnia, Bulgaria, the Commonwealth of Independent States (formerly the Soviet Union), Croatia, Czech and Slovak Federal Republics, Hungary, Poland, Romania, and Serbia. Each country faces the formidable challenge of transforming its industry, infrastructure, and facilities from state-directed to competition-driven market economies. Complicating the transformation are the distinctly different cultures, histories, and political environments of each country despite the fact that they were once members of a single Communist bloc.

Nearly all Eastern European industry was previously owned by the state in the form of very large companies. Transformation into smaller private companies, whether of domestic or foreign ownership, is a difficult social, political, and economic task. The size and nature of the resulting companies profoundly affect the structure and capability of the manufacturing base and distribution process in each country. Under guidance of state-owned economies, three separate logistics and distribution systems existed—one each for domestic, Eastern Europe, and foreign markets.[34] This unwieldy and inefficient structure is changing as each country's economy slowly transforms itself into a single, self-directed market.

Distribution system changes will occur very slowly in Eastern Europe because of equipment limitations, worker resistance to change, and poor transportation

---

[34]Hugh Guigley, "Eastern Europe Waits for Logistics," *Transportation & Distribution,* February 1991, pp. 50–54.

infrastructures that result from many years of neglect and failure to invest by previous governments. Roads, railways, and especially communication facilities are underdeveloped, resulting in high logistics and transaction costs. Enormous infrastructure investment is necessary to achieve basic operational capability in the near future.

In spite of these problems, many Western European third-party logistics operators are planning to expand beyond EC boundaries into Eastern Europe either on their own or through joint ventures or strategic alliances. Growth opportunities are visualized to be particularly attractive in the Czech Republic, Germany, Hungary, Poland, and the Slovak Republic.

Central and South America Latin America has traditionally been an area of highly protected markets and economies. In order to emulate the success of Korea, Taiwan, and other Asian countries and to achieve global competitiveness, Latin America must invest in its people, particularly with regard to education and health services. Historically, business in this region has relied on natural resources and land rather than people to create wealth. Continuation of that perspective will not permit Latin American markets to integrate with the rest of the world.

International trade with Latin America is dominated by ocean transport. As United States exports have increased to this area, more shipping lines have initiated service to Latin America and have included more frequent sailings and more competitive pricing. However, integrated logistics within Latin America has been difficult to achieve because of protectionist import duties, inland shipping tariffs, and lack of competition.

The Caribbean island of Curaçao, off the coast of Venezuela, is a prime example of how global logistics integrates the world. Curaçao is developing into the key distribution link between European markets and those in the Caribbean and Latin America. The island has a highly educated, multilingual, and productive workforce; a stable government with a currency tied to the United States dollar; and associate membership in the European Community (EC) because it is a member of the Netherlands Kingdom. The port of Curaçao has a container tracking system and modern cargo facilities, handles sea-air freight, and is developing a telecommunications network to provide ship and airplane tracking that will eventually tie into the European port of Rotterdam (in the Netherlands) and achieve a truly global information network.

Other Latin American countries—particularly Argentina, Brazil, and Chile—are stabilizing their economies and seeking stronger relationships with North America. The free market revolution sweeping from Mexico to Chile is causing the emergence of regional trade pacts and the decline of tariff barriers, thus opening up a potential bonanza for other global operations. United States exports to Central and South America have more than doubled to $60 billion in the last five years.[35] Population estimates project that Latin America will represent a market of more than 500 million people by the year 2005.[36] Latin American socialism is declining

---

[35]Joseph V. Barks, "Penetrating Latin America," *International Business,* **7**:2, February 1994, p. 78.
[36]Jeffrey R. Sharlach, "A New Era in Latin America," *Public Relations Journal,* **49**:9, September 1993, p. 26.

while foreign direct investment and operating investments are increasing. Latin governments are deregulating and signing regional free trade pacts.

They are also trying to raise the living standards and give hope to the poor, accounting for as much as 40 percent of their people.[37] Multinationals are rapidly reshaping their Latin American operations. These once sheltered subsidiaries are being groomed for global competition as trade barriers fall. Business units are modernizing, cutting costs, and increasing product quality by linking operations and taking advantage of alliances. While the concept of such operational integration is easy, it has proved difficult in practice. Latin American logisticians must use transport modes that charge steep prices for abominable service. Another problem is the impact of widely fluctuating inflation rates when consolidating operations and inventory across borders.[38] While the opportunities are significant, the logistics challenges are substantial as well.

Although government policies have historically restricted trade and development in Eastern European and Latin American economies, those conditions are changing rapidly. Countries are opening up to the outside world for goods, services, and financial resources. Unfortunately, now that governments are interested in stimulating and promoting trade, the existing infrastructures are ofen unable to support the desired trade level because logistic and transportation facilities have been neglected. Since governments do not have the resources to develop the necessary infrastructure, it is likely that considerable development will need to be privately financed. While infrastructure development will be very expensive, potential market opportunities are substantial. As noted earlier, many international logistics service providers are developing their own infrastructures. This creates opportunities for global logistics managers, but will necessitate careful monitoring of the infrastructure changes as they occur.

THE GLOBAL SUPPLY CHAIN

The previous section reviewed the development status of each global region and discussed logistics challenges facing enterprises operating within and between these regions. To meet those challenges, logistics management must evaluate the complexity of global supply chains and focus on the major differences between domestic and international operations. This section discusses major differences including (1) performance-cycle length, (2) operations, (3) systems integration, and (4) alliances. Each difference is discussed, and the logistics implications are reviewed.

Performance-Cycle Length

The performance-cycle length is the major difference between domestic and global operations. Instead of three- to five-day transit times and four- to ten-day total

---

[37]"Latin America: The Big Move to Free Markets," *Business Week,* June 15, 1992, pp. 50–53.

[38]"Multinationals Step Lively to the Free-Trade Bossa Nova," *Business Week,* June 15, 1992, pp. 56–60.

performance cycles, global operations often require performance cycles measured in terms of weeks or months. For example, it is common for automotive parts from Pacific Rim suppliers to take sixty to ninety days from replenishment order release until order receipt at a United States manufacturing facility.

The reasons for a longer performance cycle are communication delays, financing requirements, special packaging requirements, ocean freight scheduling, long transportation times, and customs clearance. Communication is delayed by time zone and language differences. Financing causes delays since most international trade requires letters of credit. Special packaging requirements are necessary to protect products from handling and water damage since containers often incur high humidity levels from temperature and weather conditions. Once a product is containerized, it must be scheduled on a ship with the correct loading and unloading equipment for the destination port. This process alone can require up to thirty days if the origin and destination ports are not located on high-volume traffic lanes or if the ships moving to the desired port lack the necessary equipment. Transit time, once the ship is en route, ranges from ten to twenty-one days. Customs clearance adds a minimum of one day, and usually more, to the extended performance cycle. Although it is increasingly common to utilize EDI to preclear product shipments through customs prior to arrival at international ports, the elapsed performance-cycle time is still lengthy.

The combination and complexity of these activities cause international performance cycles to be longer, less consistent, and less flexible than those for typical domestic operations. The reduced consistency, in particular, increases logistics planning difficulty. The longer performance cycle also results in higher inventory requirements because significant product is in transit at any point in time. This requires continuous evaluation of inventory and space requirements while awaiting arrival and clearance of international shipments.

Operations

There are a number of major differences that must be considered when operating in a global environment. First, international operations require multiple languages for both product and documentation. A technical product such as a computer or a calculator must have local characteristics such as keyboard characters and language on both the product itself and the manual. From a logistics perspective, language differences dramatically increase complexity since a product is limited to a specific country once it has been customized with respect to language. For example, even though Western Europe is much smaller than the United States in a geographic sense, it requires relatively more inventory to support marketing efforts since separate inventories are required to accommodate each language. Although product proliferation due to language requirements has been reduced through multilingual packaging, this is not always an acceptable strategy. In addition to product language implications, international operations require multilingual documentation for each country that the shipment passes through. Although English is the general language of commerce, some countries require that transportation and customs documentation be provided in the local language. This increases the time and effort for international operations since complex documents must be translated prior to shipment. These communication and documentation difficulties can be overcome through standardized EDI transactions.

The second operating difference is the increased number of products necessary to support global operations. This is partially due to the language differences discussed above. However, there may also be differences intrinsic to the product itself such as performance features, power supply characteristics, and safety requirements. While they may not be substantial, the small differences between country requirements may significantly increase required stockkeeping units (SKUs) and subsequent inventory levels.

The third operating difference is the sheer amount of documentation required for international operations. While domestic operations can generally be completed using only an invoice and bill of lading, international operations require substantial documentation regarding order contents, transportation, financing, and government control. Table 5-6 lists and describes common forms of international documentation. Figure 5-4, parts *a* through *c*, illustrates sample financing and transportation documentation.

The bill of lading master (Figure 5-4*a*) describes the consignor or exporter and consignee or customer, forwarding agent, routing instructions (which are ports of loading and unloading), transportation mode, and shipment contents. The customs invoice (Figure 5-4*b*) describes the vendor, consignee and appropriate delivery address, conditions of sale and terms of payment, shipment contents, purchase order number(s), pricing information, weight, and invoice number. The exporter's certificate of origin (Figure 5-4*c*) describes the consignor and consignee, the vendor, origin criteria, shipment contents, tariff classification, weight or quantity, and invoice number(s) and date(s).

TABLE 5-6   COMMON FORMS OF INTERNATIONAL LOGISTICS DOCUMENTATION

- *Export irrevocable commercial letter of credit.* A contract between an importer and a bank that transfers liability for paying the exporter from the importer to the (supposedly more creditworthy) importer's bank.

- *Bank draft (or bill of exchange).* A means of payment for an import-export transaction. Two types exist: transaction payable on sight with proper documents *(sight draft),* and transaction payable at some fixed time after acceptance of proper documents *(time draft).* Either type of draft accompanied by instructions and other documents *(but no letter of credit)* is a *documentary draft.*

- *Bill of lading.* Issued by the shipping company or its agent as evidence of a contract for shipping the merchandise and as a claim to ownership of the goods.

- *Combined transport document.* May replace the bill of lading if goods are shipped by air *(airway bill)* or by more than one mode of transportation.

- *Commercial invoice.* A document written by the exporter to precisely describe the goods and the terms of sale (similar to a shipping invoice used in domestic shipments).

- *Insurance certificate.* Explains what type of coverage is utilized (fire, theft, water), the name of the insurer, and the exporter whose property is being insured.

- *Certificate of origin.* Denotes the country in which the goods were produced in order to assess tariffs and other government-imposed restrictions on trade.

BILL OF LADING MASTER

2. EXPORTER (Principal or seller-licensee and address including ZIP Code)		5. DOCUMENT NUMBER	5a. B/L or AWB NUMBER
SAMPLE CORPORATION SPECIAL PARTS DIVISION 5151 HIGHWAY 97 EDEN PRAIRIE MN US		345ADM38	
	ZIP CODE 55344	6. EXPORT REFERENCES DJB-BILL2 PO 234	

3. CONSIGNED TO	7. FORWARDING AGENT (Name and address - references)
JAPAN CONSIGNEE FUKIDE BUILDING NO. 2 4-1-21 TORANOMON, MINATO-KU TOKYO 105 JAPAN	FORWARDER NAME FORWARDER ADDRESS LINE NR 1 FORWARDER CITY NY 001254545
	8. POINT (STATE) OF ORIGIN OR FTZ NUMBER MN

4. NOTIFY PARTY/INTERMEDIATE CONSIGNEE (Name and address)	9. DOMESTIC ROUTING/EXPORT INSTRUCTIONS
JAPAN DISTRIBUTORS FUKIDE BUILDING NO. 2 4-1-21 TORANOMON, MINATO-KU TOKYO JAPAN 105	

12. PRE-CARRIAGE BY	13. PLACE OF RECEIPT BY PRE-CARRIER MINNEAPOLIS

14. EXPORTING CARRIER ATL CONVEYOR V.38A	15. PORT OF LOADING/EXPORT LONG BEACH	10. LOADING PIER/TERMINAL LONG BEACH TERMINAL 5

16. FOREIGN PORT OF UNLOADING (Vessel and air only) TOKYO, JAPAN	17. PLACE OF DELIVERY BY ON-CARRIER TOKYO JAPAN	11. TYPE OF MOVE OCN	11a. CONTAINERIZED (Vessel only) [X] Yes [ ] No

MARKS AND NUMBERS (18)	NUMBER OF PACKAGES (19)	DESCRIPTION OF COMMODITIES in Schedule B detail (20)	GROSS WEIGHT (Kilos) (21)	MEASUREMENT (22)
JAPAN CONSIGNEE PO 234 L/C312567				
ACLU 123456 P213456 P213457	2	COMPUTER PARTS & ACCESS.	585 KILO	214.39 CF

FIGURE 5-4   *(a)* Sample international transportation documentation. *(Vocam Systems, Bloomington, Minn.)*

CANADA CUSTOMS INVOICE
FACTURE DES DOUANES CANADIENNES

1. Vendor (Name and Address) / Vendeur (Nom et adresse)

SAMPLE CORPORATION
SPECIAL PARTS DIVISION
5151 HIGHWAY 97
EDEN PRAIRIE, MN 55344

2. Date of Direct Shipment to Canada / Date d'expédition directe vers le Canada

3. Other References (Include Purchaser's Order No.)
Autres références (inclure le n° de commande de l'acheteur)

PO 76   See below for PO Nrs

4. Consignee (Name and Address) / Destinataire (nom et adresse)

CANADA CONSIGNEE
1234 FRANCE AVE
SUITE 1234
B.C. BRITISH COLUMBIA
VANCOUVER B31Y2
CA CANADA

5. Purchaser's Name and Address (if other than Consignee)
Nom et adresse de l'acheteur (S'il diffère du destinataire)

CANADIAN PURCHASER
123 PROVINCE ST.
VANCOUVER 123H3C
CA CANADA

6. Country of Transhipment / Pays de transbordement

7. Country of Origin of Goods / Pays d'origine des marchandises

UNITED STATES

IF SHIPMENT INCLUDES GOODS OF DIFFERENT ORIGINS ENTER ORIGINS AGAINST ITEMS IN 12
SI L'EXPÉDITION COMPREND DES MARCHANDISES D'ORIGINES DIFFÉRENTES, PRÉCISER LEUR PROVENANCE EN 12

8. Transportation: Give Mode and Place of Direct Shipment to Canada
Transport: Préciser mode et point d'expédition directe vers le Canada

VANCOUVER
B.C. BRITISH COLUMBIA

9. Conditions of Sale and Terms of Payment (i.e. Sale, Consignment Shipment, Leased Goods, etc.)
Conditions de vente et modalités de paiement (p. ex. vente, expédition en consignation, location de marchandises, etc.)

OPEN ACCOUNT
TOTAL FOB MINNEAPOLIS

10. Currency of Settlement / Devises du paiement

USD

11. No. of Pkgs N° de colis	12. Specification of Commodities (Kind of Packages, Marks and Numbers, General Description and Characteristics, i.e. Grade, Quality) Désignation des articles (Nature des colis, marques et numéros, description générale et caractéristiques, p. ex. classe, qualité)		13. Quantity (State Unit) Quantité (Préciser l'unité)	14. Unit Price Prix unitaire	15. Total
TOTAL PIECES:	7				
	51109169-018 GROUND CABLE	TW	2	10.0000	20.00
	PO: 34567 REF:		EACH		
	51109818-100 FD PWR SUPPLY 5.25 FD	US	15	119.0000	1785.00
	PO: 34567 REF:		EACH		
	51109909-100 SURGE SUPPR. (A/A)	US	5	149.0000	745.00
	PO: 34567 REF:		EACH		
	51201274-100 SUPPORT PLATE	KR	18	115.0000	2070.00
	PO: 34567 REF:		EACH		
	51303409-305 FLOPPY KEYBOARD CABLE	US	18	15.0000	270.00
	PO: 34567 REF:		EACH		
	51303508-200 220V RATE POWER CORD 230V	US	4	155.0000	620.00
	PO: 34567 REF:		EACH		

18. If any of fields 1 to 17 are included on an attached commercial invoice, check this box ☐
Si les renseignements des zones 1 à 17 figurent sur la facture commerciale, cocher cette boîte

Commercial Invoice No. / N° de la facture commerciale   DJB-CABILL

16. KILO Total Weight / Poids Total KILO

Net	Gross / Brut
1558.15	1871.24

17. Invoice Total Total de la facture

5510.00

19. Exporter's Name and Address (if other than Vendor)
Nom et adresse de l'exportateur (S'il diffère du vendeur)

20. Originator (Name and Address) / Expéditeur d'origine (Nom et adresse)

SAMPLE CORPORATION
SPECIAL PARTS DIVISION
EDEN PRAIRIE, MN 55344
ATTN: BRIAN BROWN

21. Departmental Ruling (If applicable) / Décision du Ministère (S'il y a lieu)

22. If fields 23 to 25 are not applicable, check this box ☒
Si les zones 23 à 25 sont sans objet, cocher cette boîte

23. If included in field 17 indicate amount:
Si compris dans le total à la zone 17, préciser:

(i) Transportation charges, expenses and insurance to the place of direct shipment to Canada
Les frais de transport, dépenses et assurances à partir du point d'expédition directe vers le Canada
$

(ii) Cost for construction, erection and assembly incurred after importation into Canada
Les coûts de construction, d'érection et d'assemblage après importation au Canada
$

(iii) Export packing
Le coût de l'emballage d'exportation
$

24. If not included in field 17 indicate amount:
Si non compris dans le total à la zone 17, préciser:

(i) Transportation charges, expenses and insurance to the place of direct shipment to Canada
Les frais de transport, dépenses et assurances jusqu'au point d'expédition directe vers le Canada
$

(ii) Amounts for commissions other than buying commissions
Les commissions autres que celles versées pour l'achat
$

(iii) Export packing
Le coût de l'emballage d'exportation
$

25. Check (If applicable):
Cocher (S'il y a lieu)

(i) Royalty payments or subsequent proceeds are paid or payable by the purchaser
Des redevances ou produits ont été ou seront versés par l'acheteur ☐

(ii) The purchaser has supplied goods or services for use in the production of these goods
L'acheteur a fourni des marchandises ou des services pour la production des marchandises ☐

DEPARTMENT OF NATIONAL REVENUE - CUSTOMS AND EXCISE   MINISTÈRE DU REVENU NATIONAL - DOUANES ET ACCISE

FIGURE 5-4 (cont.) *(b)* Sample international transportation documentation. *(Vocam Systems, Bloomington, Minn.)*

DEPARTMENT OF THE TREASURY
UNITED STATES CUSTOMS SERVICE

APPROVED THROUGH 4/30/89
OMB No. 1515-0164

U.S.-CANADA FREE TRADE AGREEMENT

EXPORTER'S CERTIFICATE OF ORIGIN

19 CFR 10.307(d)

PAGE: 1

1. GOODS CONSIGNED FROM (Exporter's business name, address, country, tax identification number)	2. IF BLANK CERTIFICATION
SAMPLE CORPORATION SPECIAL PARTS DIVISION EDEN PRAIRIE, MN 55344 US UNITED STATES	EFFECTIVE DATE .... EXPIRATION DATE ....
3. GOODS CONSIGNED TO (Consignee's name, address, country) CANADA CONSIGNEE 1234 FRANCE AVE VANCOUVER B31Y2 CA CANADA	4. PRODUCER'S NAME, ADDRESS, COUNTRY, TAX IDENTIFICATION NUMBER (If different from exporter)

5. ORIGIN CRITERIA FOR GOODS COVERED BY THIS CERTIFICATE:

A. Wholly produced or obtained in Canada or the United States; or
B. The goods have been transformed in the United States or Canada so as to be subject:
  1) to a change in tariff classification as described in the Rules of Annex 301.2; or
  2) to a change in tariff classification as described in the Rules of Annex 301.2 and the value of originating materials plus the direct cost of processing in Canada or the United States is not less than 50 percent or, as required by Section VI Rule 15 of Annex 301.2, 70 percent of the value of exported goods; or
  3) to Rule 5 section XII of Annex 301.2; or

C. No change in tariff classification because goods and parts are provided for in the same tariff subheading or goods were imported in unassembled or disassembled form and were classified pursuant to General Rule of Interpretation 2a) of the Harmonized System, and the value of originating materials plus the direct cost of assembly in Canada or the United States is not less than 50 percent of the value of exported goods.

6. SPECIAL DECLARATION FOR TEXTILE PRODUCTS SUBJECT TO TARIFF RATE QUOTA:

A. Apparel goods cut and sewn in Canada or the United States from fabric produced or obtained in a third country.
B. Non-wool fabric and non-wool made-up textile articles, woven or knitted in Canada from yarn produced or obained in a third country.

7. Origin Criterion (See Fields 5 or 6)	8. Description of Goods	Tariff Classification (To Six Digits)	9. Gross Weight or Other Quantity	10. Invoice Number(s) & Date(s)
5B2	GROUND CABLE	8473.30	2 EACH	DJB-CABILL 02/27/92
5A	FD PWR SUPPLY 5.25 FD	8473.30	15 EACH	DJB-CABILL 02/27/92
5A	SURGE SUPPR. (A/A)	8473.30	5 EACH	DJB-CABILL 02/27/92
5B1	SUPPORT PLATE	8473.30	18 EACH	DJB-CABILL 02/27/92
5A	FLOPPY KEYBOARD CABLE	8473.30	18 EACH	DJB-CABILL 02/27/92
5A	220V RATE POWER CORD 230V	8473.30	4 EACH	DJB-CABILL 02/27/92

11. CERTIFICATION OF ORIGIN

I certify that the information and statements herein are correct, that all the goods were produced in Canada or the United States, that they comply with the origin requirements specified for those goods in the United States-Canada Free Trade Agreement, and that further processing or assembly in a third country has not occured subsequent to processing or assembly in Canada or the United States.
I agree to maintain, and present upon request, the documentation to support this certification and, if this is a blanket certification, to inform the importer or other appropriate party of any change that would affect the validity of this certification.

This certificate consists of_____ pages.

PLACE AND DATE	AUTHORIZED SIGNATURE	TITLE
EDEN PRAIRIE 02/27/92	BRIAN BROWN	EXPORT COORDINATOR

Customs Form 353 (120188)

FIGURE 5-4 (cont.) *(c)* Sample international transportation documentation. *(Vocam Systems, Bloomington, Minn.)*

The fourth operating difference is that effective global inventory management cannot be preoccupied with inventory ownership and physical location. Current practice in many firms places inventory management responsibility in numerous locations with each attempting to justify its inventory level by providing exemplary service. This individualistic perspective results in substantially more inventory than is necessary to meet total supply chain demand. For example, one medical products firm required three separate inventories—plant, European gateway, and individual country—to serve Europe from the United States. The result was substantially more inventory than necessary.

The fifth operating difference is the complexity of international transportation. The services and capabilities taken for granted in a domestic market such as the United States are often unavailable internationally. This is particularly true in underdeveloped countries. While it is common to form a contract with a single or limited number of carriers in a domestic market, international best practice suggests the use of multiple vendors with segmentation by transportation mode. In the international transportation market contracting a single carrier to effectively manage the services of other carriers is not a viable option for a shipper. At this point in time, there are no carriers with the global reach and strength to effectively accomplish this role, although United Parcel Service and TNT are emerging as likely possibilities.

The complexity of global logistics is particularly evident with regard to conditions in the maritime or ocean shipping industry. Ocean shipments play a critical role in meeting today's competitive requirements of providing time-sensitive delivery to manufacturing plants and showrooms, as well as addressing the seasonal variations in product and merchandising campaigns. Most global logistics movements utilize water transportation. Improved reliability due to EDI capability and intermodal arrangements has made ocean shipment an increasingly attractive option for service and timeliness as well as cost considerations. There are, however, a number of issues regarding the maritime industry that have specific implications for contemporary and future global logistics.

First, today's notion of efficient supply chain logistics typically means selecting a few key supply chain partners and negotiating close alliances with them. In the maritime industry, this is nearly impossible if the desirable ocean liner partners happen to belong to one or more liner conferences, as do most reputable carriers. A conference is a group of ocean carriers that agree to set common rates and abide by those rates in order to stabilize volume and other factors. There are a number of international ocean liner conferences in existence. Conferences will often allow a shipper to discuss service contract terms with a preferred carrier and to designate which conference member or members it prefers to carry its cargo. But no specific carrier's name will appear on an agreement since the shipper contracts with the conference, not a specific carrier. With the increased attention to logistics in today's business climate, many shippers' councils or industry groups believe that conferences are preventing their members from moving forward into crucially important partnerships. In effect, the shippers argue that without the ability to choose a transport partner, a shipper cannot implement an effective logistics solution. The conference system also makes it difficult for shippers to arrange global contracts.

Second, liner freight rates have been depressed by overcapacity and slow replacement of aging vessels. The overcapacity problem is similar to conditions in the less-than-truckload motor carrier industry immediately following deregulation. Although liner conferences have attempted to set rates at levels sufficiently high to ensure profitability, independent liners are undercutting conference rates to attract volume and remain in business. Therefore, most major liners are under financial pressure. In addition, as liner conference members add new vessels with greater capacity in an effort to reduce cost and invest in more sophisticated technological capability, they create additional overcapacity unless the older vessels are retired rather than sold to independent liners.

Third, the maritime industry continues to struggle with the global East-West imbalance of trade. As long as Pacific Rim economies continue to grow and export far more goods than they import, temporary container shortages and shipping supply-demand imbalances will complicate logistical planning efforts for ocean carriers and their intermodal partners.

Fourth, the growth in containerized freight has reduced the flexibility of many liners to handle freight with unusual characteristics, such as heavy machinery or automobile chassis. In effect, efforts to increase handling speed and reduce damage via containerization are somewhat offset by the inability to move a wider variety of freight. These circumstances may create equipment shortages at particular times and places.

Finally, a common dilemma encountered by transportation buyers in both North America and Asia involves equipment shortages to handle the growing volume of intermodal goods resulting from continued expansion of trade in the Pacific Rim. Although the recession of the past several years in Japan has slowed the country's infrastructure improvements, development throughout other key countries in Asia is progressing. For example, Korea's rail expansion program, the introduction of double-stack trains in India, and China's growing attention to inland infrastructure all assist in spreading intermodalism across Asia. Addressing the dilemma should allow the maritime industry to become a more efficient and effective part of the global logistics strategic effort.

Systems Integration

Historically, international information systems in multinational enterprises have shown little commonality. This was acceptable since each country's operation was viewed as a separate and autonomous legal entity. While this strategy provides local responsiveness and flexibility, the subsequent cost of poor intercountry coordination may be prohibitive in competitive terms. Therefore, the third global supply chain operating difference is the requirement for increased operational coordination through systems integration. This includes the ability to route orders and manage inventory requirements using EDI from any place in the world. Since new hardware and software represent substantial capital investment, this is not a short-term change. Few enterprises have integrated global logistics information systems.

Alliances

The fourth difference in international operations is the role of alliances. While alliances with carriers and specialized service suppliers are important for domestic operations, they become even more important internationally. Without alliances, it would be necessary for an enterprise operating internationally to maintain contacts with retailers, wholesalers, manufacturers, suppliers, and service providers throughout the world. The simple maintenance of these relationships alone would be time-consuming. International alliances can provide market access and expertise as well as reduce the inherent risk in global operations.

Conclusion

The differences cited above suggest that global logistics is significantly more complex than its domestic counterpart. Transit times are longer and less consistent, the number of products and inventory levels are greater, and the relationships are more complex. Nevertheless, enterprise growth requires that international markets be successfully tapped.

SUMMARY

Global operations are an evolving frontier that is increasing demand on logistics management. Chapter 5 reviewed the forces behind the concept of the borderless world. Enterprises are driven toward global operations to achieve market growth and to obtain access to low-cost and/or high-quality labor, material, and production capacity. As international trade increases, logistical demands increase correspondingly because of longer supply chains, less certainty, and more documentation. While the forces of change push toward borderless operations, logistical management still confronts market, financial, and channel barriers. The barriers are exemplified by the four D's of distance, demand, diversity, and documentation. The logistics challenge is to allow the enterprise to take advantage of the benefits of global marketing and manufacturing while maintaining both cost and service effectiveness.

The enterprise view of global operations can range from internally focused nationalism to globally focused ''companyism.'' Nationalistic firms view international operations as merely importing and exporting between autonomous organizations, even though they may have common ownership. The nationalistic perspective focuses on manufacturing and logistics decisions that are optimal for a country but suboptimal for the global enterprise. Logistics managers in a firm with a nationalistic perspective will face decisions restricted to local supply sources, carriers, and alliances. The companyism perspective, on the other hand, focuses the enterprise on providing unique cost-effective, value-added offerings to consumers in each global market. Firms reflecting the companyism perspective consider global sources for all materials and services. The sourcing decision is based on the best value for the customer. As such, the companyism perspective increases demands on logistical management since it requires consideration of a broad range of alternatives and more decentralized decision making. The trend to globalize is shifting more firms toward a stateless perspective. Logistical management must adapt to the challenges of this opportunity.

As an enterprise expands its global operation, it may evolve through a series of five stages. The initial stages of arm's-length relationships and internal exports use third parties to perform international activities. The enterprise's risk and potential gain are minimized during these stages. In the internal operations and insider business stages, the enterprise begins to develop localized operations in international markets. In the final stage of denationalized operations, enterprise managers operate regionalized headquarters that simultaneously are responsive to individual markets and make materials management and logistics decisions that optimize enterprise performance.

Three regional trading alliances are evolving as the focus of the global economy. The alliances—which are structured around EC 92, NAFTA, and AFTA—are designed to increase regional trade and enhance each region's global competitiveness. Europe's EC 92 initiative is the furthest advancement in an effort to create monetary unity. Although they do not have a common market background, Asia and North America are advancing quickly into free trade agreements. It is likely that the lesser developed countries in Eastern Europe and South America will join the EC and NAFTA alliances, respectively.

While global logistics principles are similar to those in domestic supply chains, global logistics presents some unique challenges. First, global performance cycles are generally much longer because of greater distances, more intermediaries, and significant use of slow ocean travel. Second, global logistics operations are more complex as a result of the increased number of stockkeeping units (SKUs), more extensive documentation, a greater number of inventory stocking locations, and less developed service suppliers such as carriers and warehouse operators. Third, demands on information systems are increased because of requirements for extended communication, alternative languages, and process flexibility. The fourth challenge is the effort to develop and maintain global manufacturing, logistics, and marketing alliances.

While alliances offer local expertise and provide effective operating economies, the effort to identify and manage multiple global alliances is substantial. Global alliances will be facilitated by the development of integrated distribution and transportation networks. These challenges increase demands on logistical management by requiring greater market sensitivity and evaluation of more complex alternatives.

An enterprise can achieve future growth, increase economies of scale, and improve profitability through global marketing and operations. Global operations increase logistics importance and place more demands on logistics management. Logistics must respond to these challenges through increased awareness of the available alternatives and improved decision-making capability.

QUESTIONS

1   Explain the concept of *regionalization* of world trade, and describe how it affects logistical challenges and performance.

2   Discuss the major changes in the transportation deregulation environment that facilitate international transportation and increase international trade.

3   What is transportation infrastructure capability, and how is it a barrier to international logistics performance?

4   How does a national perspective of global logistics restrict logistical policy and decision making?

5   Compare and contrast a national perspective and a stateless enterprise perspective regarding customer value-added offerings.

6   How do geographic and demographic differences between Europe and North America affect logistics strategies in EC 92 and NAFTA markets?

7   What are the differences in performance-cycle length between domestic and global operations, and how do they affect logistical planning?

8   Discuss the role that language plays in complicating logistical operations.

9   Explain why a facility network structure requires greater flexibility for global operations compared to domestic operations.

10   What are the major pitfalls in coordinating finished inventory requirements for servicing global markets? How can these pitfalls be ovecome?

CASES

CASE A: Integrated Logistics

Tom Lippet, sales representative for DuPont Engineering Polymers (DEP), felt uneasy as he drove to his appointment at Grad Automotive Manufacturing (GARD). In the past, sales deals with GARD had proceeded smoothly. Oftentimes competitors were not even invited to bid on the GARD business. Mike O'Leary, purchasing agent at GARD, claimed that was because no competitor could match DEP's product quality.

But this contract negotiation was different. Several weeks before the contract renewal talks began, O'Leary had announced his plan to retire in six months. GARD management quickly promoted Richard Binish as O'Leary's successor. Although Binish had been relatively quiet at the previous two meetings, Lippet sensed that it would not be "business as usual" with Binish. While the contract decision ultimately depended on O'Leary's recommendation, Lippet felt that Binish might pose a problem.

Binish, thirty-five, had worked for a Fortune 500 firm following completion of his undergraduate degree in operations management. While with the Fortune 500 firm Binish had become extensively involved with JIT and quality programs. He had returned to school and earned an M.B.A. with a concentration in purchasing and logistics. Eager to make his mark, Binish had rejected offers to return to large corporations and instead accepted GARD's offer in inventory management.

GARD, an original equipment manufacturer (OEM) for United States auto producers and aftermarket retailers, makes a wide variety of plastic products for automobiles and light trucks. Examples of GARD products are dashboards, door and window handles, and assorted control knobs. When Binish began working with GARD's inventory management, he applied the 80/20 rule, illustrating to management that 80 percent of GARD's business was related to 20 percent of its

product line. Over the next three years, as contracts expired with customers and suppliers, Binish trimmed GARD's product line. GARD management was impressed with the positive impact on GARD's profits as unprofitable contracts and products were discarded. A trimmer product line composed primarily of faster-moving products also resulted in higher inventory velocity.

Thus, when O'Leary announced his retirement plans, management immediately offered Binish the position. After taking a few days to review GARD's purchasing practices Binish felt that he could make an impact. He accepted management's offer. As he learned his way around the purchasing department, Binish tried to stay in the background. But he found himself soon questioning many of O'Leary's practices. He particularly disdained O'Leary's frequent "business lunches" with long-time associates from GARD suppliers. Despite these feelings, Binish made an effort not to be openly critical of O'Leary. Such efforts did not, however, prevent him from asking more and more questions about GARD's purchasing process.

O'Leary, for his part, felt that his style had served GARD well. Prices were kept low, and quality was generally within established parameters. Although O'Leary typically maintained a wide network of suppliers, critical materials were sourced from a limited number of them. In those cases contract bids were a ritual, with the winner known well in advance.

DEP was one such winner. Its polymers were a critical feedstock material in GARD's manufacturing process. When O'Leary began sourcing from DEP nearly fifteen years ago, there was no question that DEP polymers were the best on the market. GARD's production managers rarely complained about problems caused by substandard polymers. O'Leary reasoned that the fewer complaints from manufacturing, the better.

"Hi, Tom! Come on in! Good to see you. You remember Richard Binish, don't you?" Lippet's spirits were buoyed by O'Leary's cheery greeting.

Steve Clinton prepared this case for class discussion. Actual facts have been altered to maintain confidentiality and to provide an enhanced business situation.

"Absolutely! How are you, Richard? Coming out from the old horse's shadow a bit now?"

Binish politely smiled and nodded affirmatively. Light banter continued as the three moved down the hallway to a small conference room.

"Well, great news, Tom! DEP has the contract again!" O'Leary paused and then continued. "But there's going to be a slight modification. Instead of the traditional two-year contract we're only going to offer a one-year deal. Nothing personal, just that management feels it's only fair to Richard that these last contracts I negotiate be limited to a year. That way he doesn't get locked into any deals that might make him look bad!" O'Leary roared with laughter at his last comment.

"It is certainly no reflection on DEP," Richard interjected. "It simply gives me a chance to evaluate suppliers in the coming year without being locked into a long-term contract. If my evaluation concurs with what Mr. O'Leary has told me about DEP, I see no reason that our successful relationship won't continue."

"Entirely understandable," replied Tom as his mind pondered the meaning of Binish's *evaluation.* "I'm confident you'll find DEP's service and product every bit as good as Mike has told you."

Following the meeting O'Leary invited Lippet to join him for a cup of coffee in GARD's lunchroom. Binish excused himself, saying that he had other matters to attend to.

As they enjoyed their coffee, O'Leary sighed. "You'll be seeing some changes coming, Tom. The best I could do was get you a year."

"I'm not sure I understand. As far as I know, GARD's never had a major problem with DEP's products."

"We haven't," O'Leary replied. "At least not under the guidelines I hammered out with management. But there will be some changes by next year."

"Such as?"

"Well, you remember when I started buying from DEP? You were the leaders, no question about it. Now I knew some other suppliers had moved up since then, but I figured, hey, if it ain't broke, don't fix it! As long as DEP's price was in line, I knew I wouldn't have any troubles with manufacturing. Less headaches for me. Now it turns out that Binish has some other ideas about purchasing. I can tell you for a fact that he's sampled several lots of DEP feedstock. He's also invited other potential suppliers to submit samples. The long and short of it is that there's not much difference between DEP and the competition in terms of product."

"I still don't clearly understand the problem, Mike."

"In Binish's terms, product merely becomes a 'qualifying criteria.' If everyone's product is comparable, especially in something such as polymer feedstock, how do you distinguish yourself? Binish claims that companies will need to demonstrate something called 'order winning criteria' to get our business in the future."

"I still don't see a problem. We have our reviews with GARD every year. Our service performance has always been found to be acceptable."

"True. But acceptable according to my guidelines. Let me throw a number at you. On average GARD schedules delivery ten days from date of order. I count on-time delivery as plus or minus two days from scheduled delivery date. That's a five-day service window. GARD's minimum service threshold within this five-day window is 95 percent. DEP had a 96.2 percent record last year using my window. Do you know what Binish is talking?"

"Probably three?"

"Exactly. And do you know what DEP's performance is if we use a three-day service window?"

"No, Mike, I really don't."

"Well, Tom. Sorry to tell you but it's 89.7 percent. Worse yet, with Binish, not only will the window decline but the threshold level will be bumped up to 96 percent. And that's only going to be for the first three years after I retire. After that Binish is shooting for same-day delivery with only 96.5 percent service capability. Right now using same-day delivery DEP has only 80 percent flat. You aren't even close to being in the game."

"So we've got a one-year contract essentially to demonstrate that we can deliver service as well as product?"

"You understand the problem now."

Polymer feedback production requires a mixture of chemical compounds. DEP's manufacturing process relies heavily on six principal compounds (A–F). DEP's current procurement policy is to source each of these compounds from three suppliers determined through an annual bidding process. Typically the firm with the lowest price is considered the best bid. The top bid receives 60 percent of DEP's business, while the other two firms receive 25 and 15 percent, respectively. Management feels that this policy protects DEP from material shortages and unreasonable price increases. Table 1 indicates the current compound suppliers and their performance statistics (percentage of business/delivery time from order date/fill rate).

TABLE 1

Supplier	Chemical compounds					
	"A"	"B"	"C"	"D"	"E"	"F"
Company 1	60% 3–8 days 93%	60% 2–9 days 94.5%			15% 5–8 days 92%	15% 6–9 days 94%
Company 2	25% 4–6 days 95%	25% 3–4 days 96%	15% 2–4 days 98%	15% 2–4 days 98.7%		
Company 3	15% 2–5 days 95.5%	15% 2–4 days 98%			25% 5–9 days 97.5%	25% 4–6 days 98.7%
Company 4			60% 4–9 days 96.5%	60% 2–9 days 97%		
Company 5					60% 4–7 days 98.3%	60% 4–6 days 97%
Company 6			25% 3–6 days 98.4%	25% 3–5 days 96%		

DEP currently uses the following performance criteria:

1 *Delivery of "A."* On-time considered 4 days from date of order ± 2 days.
2 *Delivery of "B."* On-time considered 4 days from date of order ± 2 days.
3 *Delivery of "C."* On-time considered 4 days from date of order ± 2 days.
4 *Delivery of "D."* On-time considered 5 days from date of order ± 2 days.
5 *Delivery of "E."* On-time considered 6 days from date of order ± 2 days.
6 *Delivery of "F."* On-time considered 6 days from date of order ± 2 days.
7 Minimum acceptable fill rate on all compounds is 92 percent.

The manufacture of polymer feedstock is highly standardized. DEP has continually invested in technologically advanced manufacturing equipment. As a result, DEP can quickly change processes to manufacture different polymers.

In order to avoid material shortages and thereby maximize production, DEP normally maintains a seven-day supply of each compound. An earlier attempt at JIT manufacturing was abandoned after DEP experienced material shortages and production shutdowns. As a result, the manufacturing department is opposed to any reimplementation of JIT-type concepts.

The manufacturing department is electronically linked to the procurement and marketing/sales departments. Marketing/sales receives customer orders by phone or facsimile. The orders are then entered into the information system. This allows manufacturing to monitor incoming materials shipments as well as schedule production runs. Under this system most customer orders are produced within six to eight days of order.

Following production, orders are immediately sent to a warehouse a short distance from DEP. At the warehouse shipping personnel verify manufacturing tickets, match the manufacturing ticket with the purchase order, and prepare shipping documents. Once the shipping documents are completed, the order is prepared for shipment (e.g., palletized, shrink-wrapped, etc.) and labeled. Once a shipment is labeled, delivery is scheduled. Three to six days normally elapse from the time an order leaves manufacturing until it is shipped from the warehouse.

Physical distribution is divided between the private DEP truck fleet and common carriers. The majority of DEP's customers are within a 200-mile radius. DEP trucks service these customers via twice-a-week delivery routes. Customers beyond this delivery zone are serviced through common carriers; delivery time fluctuates according to location and distance but rarely exceeds six days from time of shipment.

QUESTIONS

1   Diagram the DEP-GARD supply chain. What stages are adding value? What stages are not?
2   Using the primary DEP suppliers (60 percent of business) what is the minimum performance cycle for the supply chain diagrammed above? What is the maximum?

3   Can the performance cycle be improved through use of the 25 and 15 percent suppliers? What trade-offs must be made to use these suppliers?
4   If you were Tom Lippet, what changes would you make in DEP's operations? Why? What problems do you foresee as you try to implement these changes?
5   Assuming you can make the changes mentioned in question 4, how would you "sell" Richard Binish on DEP's next bid? What will likely be "qualifying criteria" and "order winning criteria"? Will these change over time? What does this suggest about supply chain management?

CASE B: Whitmore Products: Time-Based Logistics at Work

John Smith had just returned from what may prove to be one of his most important sales calls. John, a sales representative for a top furniture manufacturer, had been meeting with a representative from HomeHelp, a major home decorating retailer. It seems the buyer, Nan Peterson, and the product team she heads had just returned from the annual Council of Logistics Management Conference. At the conference, Nan's team had attended several sessions on time-based logistics strategies. Even though Nan and her team had just been exposed to the new strategies, they felt it had the potential for significant competitive advantage in their industry.

At the meeting with John, Nan explained that HomeHelp is an entrepreneurial company that encourages product teams to try new products and channel relations. The few rules a team has to follow are simple: (1) deal only with manufacturers (no independent distributors are contacted), and (2) keep costs low and service high. The second rule highlights HomeHelp's basic business philosophy. HomeHelp is a design and home decorating retail chain that follows the warehouse club format. As such, a premium is placed on maintaining low overhead to support an "every day low price" (EDLP) strategy. Service is also a premium since HomeHelp targets two distinct customer segments: do-it-yourself consumers, who need special in-store guid-

ance, and interior decorators, who need speedy checkouts and convenient delivery or pickup.

Nan explained that the team has been considering applying time-based logistics strategies to furniture. Such an arrangement had the potential to improve product availability for in-store customers while reducing overall inventory. HomeHelp's close relationship with professional decorators required continued attention to improve its profitability and to ensure long-term growth. Interior decorators need convenient and exacting service, and HomeHelp feels that time-based logistics applied to furniture could be an important step to improving profitability.

HomeHelp's main concern is that the furniture industry as a whole appears to be trailing other industries in terms of sophisticated logistics operations. For example, the furniture industry has invested little in information technology and maintains high inventories throughout the channel, including at the retail level. The results other firms reported for their innovative logistics applications gave HomeHelp a new insight into how an alliance with a furniture manufacturer might create a best practice distribution system with lower costs and less inventory.

Nan told John that his company, Whitmore, had the potential to achieve an exclusive distribution arrangement with HomeHelp if the two companies could create time-based logistical capability. Whitmore was chosen since the business press had recently featured articles on its new organization plan that focused on channels of distribution and leading-edge logistics strategies. In

Judith M. Schmitz prepared this case for discussion. Actual facts have been altered to maintain confidentiality and to provide an enhanced business situation.

addition, Whitmore was beginning to invest in information technology. She felt that both companies should be able to reduce overall channel costs and offer customers superior product availability. Her specific request was for John to formulate a tentative proposal within three weeks in order to "strike while the iron was hot." Nan knew that the timing and unexpected opportunity created a great challenge for Whitmore, but she explained that HomeHelp strives to maintain a leading edge. Furthermore, HomeHelp wants to increase annual growth to 20 percent and feels that furniture offers the best opportunities. As such, top management attention is on this potential business arrangement.

As John walked to his regional sales manager's office, it was hard to conceal his excitement. The potential HomeHelp offered was enormous. However, the effort required to get all groups at Whitmore involved would be great. The first step was to convince top management of the unique opportunity so that a team could be formed to create the proposal HomeHelp was expecting.

John's boss, Frank Harrison, was on the phone as John walked in. John carefully planned his words while Frank finished his conversation. As Frank hung up the phone, John blurted out, "We've got the potential for an exclusive with HomeHelp, but they want a customized delivery system. The proposal's due in three weeks. I think we need the top brass in on this one. It's big."

Frank's reply was typical, "It's not April 1 again already, is it John? What's the problem with our current system? Three weeks! It will never happen." After John explained the meeting with Nan, Frank got on the phone to arrange a senior management review. Surprisingly, a business planning meeting was scheduled for the coming Friday. Frank and John could get on the agenda under new business. What a break! It was Wednesday, and John began to reorganize his calendar to concentrate on the Friday meeting.

The first item John focused on was researching HomeHelp. He discovered that HomeHelp operated over 200 warehouse-style stores in eighteen states with the average store covering over 100,000 square feet and offering 25,000 different products. Typical sales breakdown is 50 percent wallpaper and draperies, 25 percent accessory pieces, 20 percent lighting and electrical fixtures, and 5 percent furniture. The potential for growth in furniture was clear. Furniture included fabric-covered items such as sofas, loveseats, and reclining chairs, as well as wooden products such as tables, dinettes, and end pieces. HomeHelp was the industry leader with 10 percent of the $80 billion home decorating retail market. Forecasts indicate that the market will reach $100 billion by 1998. Industry observers predict that HomeHelp is positioned to enjoy up to 20 percent of total industry sales.

HomeHelp is dedicated to service. In-store classes illustrate design techniques, repair, and installation procedures on wallpaper, drapes, and lighting and electrical fixtures. The classes are taught by HomeHelp's employees, most of whom are retired or part-time professional decorators and contractors. HomeHelp provides installation service in a majority of its stores as well as professional decorating services. Both services are offered on a fee basis.

Forty percent of HomeHelp's sales involve professional decorators. The remaining 60 percent come from do-it-yourself consumers. The professional segment is quite large, and HomeHelp works closely with this group to meet service requirements. Affiliated professionals, called Propartners, have separate checkout lanes, a commercial credit program, and delivery services. Currently, Propartners customers purchase only 10 percent of HomeHelp's home furniture. Nan feels that this low sales level results from two factors. First, the delivery service offered by HomeHelp is contracted out to local moving companies with the cost to HomeHelp passed on to the customer. Delivery for a piece of furniture typically adds 8 percent to the price HomeHelp charges for the product. This increase makes the overall price of purchase within $10 to $30 of the price charged by the competition, which offers free delivery. The close price range, accompanied by the psychological effect of free delivery, prompts many Propartners customers to purchase furniture elsewhere. While not a major concern, the use of moving companies sometimes creates delays and fails to meet delivery promises.

Second, each HomeHelp store's inventory is restricted to display items plus a limited stock of fast-moving products. Typically, only 7 percent of all customer orders can be filled from store inventory. As such, if a store does not have a specific piece of furniture, an order for the item is forwarded to a regional warehouse where the item is taken from inventory and sent to the store the following day. Furniture is available for delivery, or customers can pick it up, two days after original order, assuming the regional warehouse has stock. If the regional warehouse is out of stock, the piece is typically not available for shipment or pickup for five to seven days, because an interfacility transfer or manufacturer shipment is required.

Since many Propartners are working on remodeling/redecorating projects, unexpected problems and delays can easily cause schedule changes. On a day-in and day-out basis, the exact time of furniture delivery and installation is difficult to accurately gauge. Propartners would like to be able to place an order forty-eight hours (or less) before the expected completion to reduce cost of rescheduling. Working on shorter timetables would improve their efficiency and cash flow and is perceived by Propartners as a major benefit. Currently, Propartners buy mostly from independent distributors that have more flexible delivery programs.

Friday's meeting was long. Frank and John weren't scheduled to present their ideas until near the end, and they hoped it wouldn't run overtime, forcing them to be rescheduled. Finally, it was their turn. Frank started the presentation and discussed how long and hard a struggle it had been to develop a relationship with HomeHelp. Then John spoke of the benefits. He built on the need to develop new business relationships because Whitmore was involved in an alliance with a retailer in financial trouble. This retailer, Happy Home & Living, had historically accounted for 25 percent of Whitmore's sales, but this figure was dropping dramatically. Happy Home & Living's erratic purchases were creating undercapacity in Whitmore's manufacturing facilities.

Furthermore, HomeHelp had a relationship with decorators, a customer group that Whitmore had been targeting under its reorganization plan. Whitmore's image was that of a value leader—good quality furniture at a low price. Attracting professional decorators to its products would definitely enhance Whitmore's image. Furthermore, Whitmore hoped to have some direct contact with professional decorators to get firsthand information on upcoming fashion trends.

Finally, an exclusive arrangement with HomeHelp appeared critical for the future. Home furniture manufacturing is heavily consolidated among a few key players, meaning stiff competition. While the home decorating industry remains heavily fragmented, HomeHelp is a leader and appears positioned to grow faster than competitors. Even though HomeHelp currently has only 10 percent of the market share, it has unlimited growth potential and is often referred to as the Wal-Mart of the home decorating industry.

Reaction from senior management was mixed. While many were excited about the potential, they were also cautious. The long-term relationship with Happy Home & Living that had prospered for fifty years was clearly becoming a potential problem for Whitmore. Relying on Happy Home & Living had created a false sense of security, and when Happy Home & Living suffered financially during the recessions of the eighties, Whitmore also suffered. Furthermore, Happy Home & Living's reputation as a quality retailer was beginning to decline. In fact, it was getting the reputation for providing low-quality, outdated products. Top management was afraid to launch another close relationship that tied Whitmore's success to another company. Frank responded that HomeHelp had achieved at least 10 percent growth each year for the last fifteen years, even through the recessions. The main reason for this growth was its advertising strategy, which convinced consumers who couldn't afford a new home that they could afford to remodel/redesign their current one.

Another concern was the shift in traditional operations necessary to support a customized delivery system. While no concrete evidence was available on the exact requirements of customized delivery, it was still apparent that the service being requested was unique and nontraditional, and might require major reorganization and financial investment. Also, several board members wondered how traditional customers, not interested in time-based logistics, would benefit. Their specific concern was that the commitment to HomeHelp would increase the overall cost of doing business with all customers. In short, some customers would be overserviced at a cost penalty. John agreed that these were serious concerns, but he reminded the group of the potential benefits that could result from a successful shift to time-based logistics. Not only was the exclusive agreement with HomeHelp important, but this "test case" with a major retailer could forge a leading-edge path for Whitmore, resulting in difficult-to-duplicate competitive advantage. Furthermore, John was convinced that HomeHelp would make a move to time-based logistics in the furniture segment with or without Whitmore. After extended discussion, the group decided to assign a task team, with John as the leader, to take the steps necessary to determine if an arrangement with HomeHelp was in Whitmore's best interest and, if so, to develop the requested business proposal. The proposal would need approval before the presentation to HomeHelp. A special review meeting was scheduled in two weeks.

First, John felt that the team had to detail Whitmore's current operations. Then, an appropriate time-based system would need to be defined and compared to current operations to isolate changes necessary to offer excellent service support. A modified system would also need to be outlined and the cost and benefits determined. The issue of coexistence of current and time-based response capabilities was also a concern.

CURRENT OPERATIONS

Whitmore currently has two manufacturing facilities and six regional distribution centers. One manufacturing facility is located in Grand Rapids, Michigan, while the other is in Holland, Michigan. The Grand Rapids facility produces fabric-covered items, such as sofas, cushioned chairs, and recliners. The plant in Holland produces wooden items such as tables and end pieces. The six distribution centers are located throughout the United States with one adjacent to each manufacturing facility. Orders are received from customers electronically as well as by phone through sales representatives. Only 40 percent of Whitmore's customers are electronically linked to the ordering system.

Whitmore's manufacturing facilities forecast sales to create the production schedule. Forecasts are locked in six weeks prior to assembly. Three of the distribution centers carry a full line of product inventory and seek to maintain a minimum on-hand quantity for each product. When inventory hits the predetermined minimum, a restock order is sent to the appropriate manufacturing facility. The other distribution centers stock only the fast-moving products. When a customer order is received, it is assigned to the distribution center closest to the customer. If the product ordered is not available, the required item is transferred from the closest distribution center that has the required stock. If multiple products are ordered, the original order is held until the out-of-stock item is available to ship, so that customers receive all requirements in one delivery. No shipments are sent directly from the manufacturing plant to the customer; all orders are processed through a distribution center.

Whitmore's customers are dealers at the retail level that maintain their own inventory of Whitmore's products. When customers' inventory is low, they place replenishment orders. These orders are transmitted to Whitmore's designated distribution center. Distribution centers review their orders nightly in an effort to consolidate truckloads and schedule efficient delivery routes. When a full load is available, orders are assembled and loaded to facilitate sequenced delivery. Typi-

cal order cycle time is three to six days when inventory is available at the initially assigned distribution center. Interfacility inventory transfers typically add two to three days to the order cycle. When an item is back-ordered to a manufacturing plant, eight to twelve more days are added to the order cycle. When factory back-orders are required, a partial order may be sent to the dealer or retailer. However, no firm policy exists concerning when to ship and when to hold partial orders. Currently Whitmore uses a national for-hire carrier to handle all its outbound deliveries to customers and interfacility movements between distribution centers. This carrier is already working with food and clothing customers that operate on a time-based logistics system.

TIME-BASED LOGISTICS

John felt that it was important for the task team to talk with a representative from another company concerning its experience with time-based logistics. John contacted an old college roommate working at JeanJean, a clothing manufacturer, to see if he could help. John's old roommate, Phil Williams, arranged for John's team to visit JeanJean to discuss QuickJeans, its proprietary time-based system.

In JeanJean's system, retailers play a major role. When a product sells in a retail store, the bar code on that product is scanned, and this information is transmitted electronically to JeanJean. This is called point-of-sale (POS) data. POS data detail the size, color, and style of product sold and are transmitted directly to JeanJean's manufacturing facilities where they are used to derive production schedules in response to consumer sales. Rapid movement of information replaces the need to forecast. To the Whitmore team, it looked as though information was being traded for inventory. Product replenishment was exact and done within days of the sale depending on each retail store's volume. For example, high-volume stores receive daily replenishment shipments, whereas lower-volume retail outlets are served less frequently. The time-based system was flexible and able to accommodate a variety of different replenishment styles on the basis of individual retail customer requirements.

This type of system reduces response order cycle time and inventory. Since delivery is tied to actual sales, consumer trends are responded to quickly, reducing obsolescence. Furthermore, daily or weekly replenishment cycles allow the retail outlet to carry significantly less inventory while improving stockout performance.

JeanJean was also able to reduce inventory by 20 percent by timing production to POS data. This reduction was even more impressive when JeanJean explained that its sales increased by 25 percent. Even though transportation cost doubled, it was more than justified by the savings in inventory and the benefits of knowing for sure that product was needed to service customers.

The QuickJeans solution was technology-driven. Electronic data interchange (EDI), used to transmit POS data, and bar codes were essential to making the system work. EDI was also utilized for invoicing and payments, advanced shipment notification, and delivery verification. This reduction in paperwork and clerical tasks benefited both JeanJean and its customers.

To implement QuickJeans, JeanJean had to change its fundamental business processes not just with its customers but also within its manufacturing plants. Flexible manufacturing required quick product changeovers to be fully responsive to the POS data. Furthermore, the ability to produce small runs of necessary product was a key requirement.

The management at JeanJean pointed out that one of the most difficult parts of implementing time-based logistics was the sales decline that resulted from ''deloading the channel.'' This ''sales hit'' was created by the false sense of expected sales and anticipatory inventory that resulted from manufacturing according to forecast, not to actual need. JeanJean had to wait until inventory at the retail stores, retail warehouses, Jean-Jean warehouses, and manufacturing facilities moved through the channel system before QuickJeans began to work and show the expected benefits. This created tension among JeanJean's top management because it was a cost not originally expected when they bought into the QuickJeans program.

The main cost to implement QuickJeans was the investment in technology. For example, JeanJean invested over $1 million in scanners, lasers to make distribution operations fast and efficient, and ticket printers to label products with retailers' unique bar codes. Key retailers spent close to the same amount to purchase new equipment to scan the bar codes. This investment was not a one-time deal either. The need to reinvest to upgrade technology has remained constant from the start. Some retailers, especially locally owned stores, didn't want to participate in QuickJeans because of the initial investment. However, the retailers that participated were so pleased that most have placed JeanJean on their preferred supplier list.

JeanJean provided John's team with a flowchart of

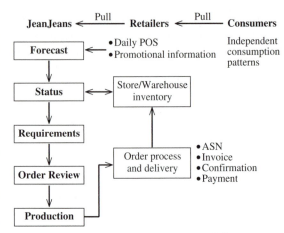

FIGURE 1   QuickJeans: A time-based logistics system.

its QuickJeans operation as shown in Figure 1. The chart shows that daily transmission of POS data, as well as information on promotional specials, is provided by the retailer. This information is used to calculate an initial production schedule. Inventory already on hand in JeanJean's warehouse as well as in its retail customers' storage areas is subtracted from the schedule, creating production requirements for all JeanJean's products. These requirements are reviewed by an order specialist, who creates a final production schedule that is transmitted to the appropriate manufacturing plant. This order specialist also manages orders from retailers that are not involved in QuickJeans. All products are bar coded after manufacturing as required. Delivery is initiated by an electronic advanced shipping notification (ASN) to tell the retailer what products are on the way. Delivery is direct to the retail store unless an alternative site is specified. On receiving the order at the designated location, the bar code is scanned and compared to the ASN and invoice. If the information matches, the retailer pays the invoice electronically.

THE PROPOSAL

John's team was finally ready to present its time-based delivery system to top management, and they hoped the proposal would be accepted. The presentation to HomeHelp was scheduled in three days. The Whitmore task team had worked hard and was confident its proposal had strong selling features for both Whitmore and HomeHelp. The special meeting with top management was called to order.

The task team called the project "Customized Distribution: Creating Time-Based Customer Response" and began discussing how the proposal was developed, including the meeting with JeanJean. The team felt that Whitmore could benefit greatly from accepting the HomeHelp challenge.

Each HomeHelp store will transmit POS data on furniture sales at the close of each day. HomeHelp will not carry any Whitmore inventory in its regional warehouses and will carry only a limited amount of furniture and display items in each store. The POS transmission will include furniture items actually sold from inventory at the store and the furniture ordered, but not in stock. The POS transmission will be sent to a central information service. The information service will sort the POS data and compare them to inventory on hand at each Whitmore distribution center. Furniture in stock will be consolidated, while those items that are not in stock will be added to the production schedule and manufactured the next day. After manufacturing, the products will be delivered to the distribution center, where initial consolidation of in-stock items occurs and the entire order is shipped out to the customer. After shipment, the on-hand quantities at the distribution centers will be examined to determine if a replenishment needs to occur. If the on-hand quantity is too low, a replenishment order will be sent to the appropriate manufacturing plant.

QUESTIONS

1 What are the major business propositions for Whitmore and HomeHelp to consider in evaluating this proposal? Is time-based logistics the right strategy for each company?

2 What are the benefits and barriers (short- and long-term) to this proposal for both Whitmore and HomeHelp? What other factors need to be considered?

3 If you were Whitmore's top management, what suggestions would you make to improve the current proposal for long-run viability?

4 If you were HomeHelp, would you accept or reject the proposal? Why?

CASE C: Zwick Electrical: Developing a Global Logistics Strategy

"Did the consultants come up with anything?" asked Wilton Zwick.

His brother, Carlton, nodded affirmatively. "There are several possible alternatives. In terms of alliances it looks like they have identified two potential partners. Here, take a look for yourself."

Wilton quickly scanned the report's front page. "Hmm, Asea Brown Boveri and Siemens?"

Carlton and Wilton Zwick are, respectively, president and vice president of Zwick Electrical Incorporated (ZEI), a privately held company. Carlton joined ZEI in 1973 after earning a marketing degree. After receiving an engineering degree in 1975 Wilton spent four years with an electrical-products division of a major firm in Pittsburgh. He then joined ZEI in late 1979.

ZEI began operations in 1952 when Gunther Zwick, Carlton and Wilton's father, opened for business in Cleveland, Ohio. In the early years ZEI's product line was limited to electric motors and parts. The company gradually expanded its product line to include power transformers, high-voltage switchgear, and metering devices. By the mid-1960s ZEI had added production facilities in Cincinnati, Ohio, and Louisville, Kentucky.

In 1968 gaps in ZEI's product line prompted the elder Zwick to purchase EL Transmission and Power (ELTP), a Memphis-based power transmission equipment company. Although ELTP's Memphis headquarters was closed, ZEI retained the Memphis distribution center and engineering department. ELTP's manufacturing plants in Chattanooga (Tennessee), Springfield (Missouri), and Shreveport (Louisiana) continued operations under ZEI.

During the 1970s no further acquisitions were made. The plants in Cincinnati and Chattanooga were significantly expanded to handle ZEI's increasing business. Minor renovations were made in the Cleveland and Springfield facilities.

Athough business took a sharp downturn in the early 1980s, ZEI management remained optimistic about the future. At Wilton's urging, the engineering staffs were increased and plans were made to build a modern facility in the Southeast. In 1984 ZEI opened a new plant

Steve Clinton prepared this case for class discussion. Actual facts have been altered to maintain confidentiality and to provide an enhanced business situation.

and distribution center in Greenville, South Carolina. This plant specializes in power transformers and high-voltage switchgear.

In 1987 Gunther retired from ZEI. At that time he appointed Carlton as president and Wilton as executive vice president. In reality Carlton is in charge of everything except product design. Wilton oversees product design and consequently works closely with the engineering and production departments.

Following the downturn of the early 1980s ZEI enjoyed modest growth until 1988. At that time it became apparent that the American power business, plagued by overcapacity, had stagnated. It became obvious that ZEI's Cleveland, Louisville, and Shreveport plants were seriously outdated. A decision was made in 1990 to renovate Shreveport and close production facilities in Cleveland and Louisville.

This decision was particularly difficult for Carlton to accept. Carlton believed that ZEI could not expect loyalty from its workers unless it demonstrated concern for their welfare in difficult times. Wilton, although sympathetic to the plight of the workers, had been watching European and Japanese firms erode America's market share in the power business. He felt that ZEI must remain competitive. If that meant closing noncompetitive facilities, so be it.

At this time the Zwick brothers also decided that ZEI needed to aggressively pursue international markets. ZEI had sporadically exported in the past—but only if a foreign customer initiated the contact. Electing for a more proactive posture, ZEI entered into an agreement with an export management company, Overseas Venture Management (OVM).

OVM acts primarily as a manufacturer's representative for ZEI in Western Europe. OVM receives a commission on each sale of ZEI product plus a fixed rate for representing ZEI at European trade fairs. In 1989, the first year of the agreement, OVM sales represented less than one-half of 1 percent of total ZEI sales. That figure improved to slightly more than 1 percent in 1990.

The Zwick brothers were generally pleased with OVM's performance. Although OVM sales in 1991 and 1992 represented less than 3 percent of total ZEI sales, trade fair appearances had generated considerable interest in ZEI's line of power semiconductors (electronic switching devices for high-voltage transmission). In fact, power semiconductors represented 70 percent of ZEI's European sales in 1991 and 1992. In particular, the rebuilding of Eastern Europe offered a potentially lucrative power semiconductor market. OVM sales were expected to increase modestly in 1993.

Future growth in Europe was threatened, however, by stagnant economies and the fear of "Fortress Europe." In 1987 European leaders agreed, through the Single European Act, to create a single, integrated market. This borderless Europe opened protected markets, creating a large regional trading bloc. Some business analysts predicted that this trading bloc will erect trade barriers designed to protect European-domiciled companies, thus leading to a "fortress" mentality.

Troubled by such predictions abroad and eroding market share at home, ZEI sought the advice of an international consulting firm. In initial discussions with the consultants the Zwick brothers had underscored three primary objectives:

1 Maintain ZEI's access to international markets as regional trading blocs develop. The Zwick brothers believe that several of their products could attain substantial success abroad.

2 Increase international sales of ZEI products at a greater pace than OVM had attained. ZEI would like international sales to be 15 to 20 percent of company sales by the year 2000. The Zwick brothers doubt a manufacturer's representative will be able to produce that level of sales.

3 Find complementary product lines from overseas suppliers to add to ZEI's United States product line. Product development costs hamper ZEI's efforts to develop complete product lines in-house. Evidence suggests that ZEI is losing business to domestic and foreign competitors that offer more complete product lines. Many of those competitors enjoy substantially lower product development and production costs by developing and sourcing products from lower-cost countries.

As the dialogue with ZEI continued, the consultants identified several areas of concern. First, despite ZEI's nearly five-year relationship with OVM, the level of international business "savvy" with ZEI was quite low. Second, neither Zwick brother indicated any desire to relocate outside the United States. Third, the Zwick brothers were so accustomed to making their own decisions that consultants wondered how effectively they would work with an outside organization. Of course, the consultants also realized that foreign competition and sliding profits had convinced many American companies to reexamine the way they did business.

With that in mind, the consulting firm has suggested that ZEI consider, as one alternative, entering into a business relationship with either ABB Asea Brown Boveri (ABB) or Siemens AG.

ABB ASEA BROWN BOVERI LTD.

I'd rather be roughly right and fast than exactly right and slow. The cost of delay is greater than the cost of an occasional mistake. [Percy Barnevik, president and chief executive, ABB Asea Brown Boveri Ltd.]

Guided by that kind of thinking, Percy Barnevik, in 1987, fashioned a merger between two prominent European firms: Asea AB (Sweden) and BBC Brown Boveri Ltd. (Switzerland). In typical Barnevik style the merger was quietly initiated and quickly concluded, deftly avoiding possible delays from government, union, or shareholder opposition. The result of this Swedish-Swiss merger, ABB, found itself with 180,000 employees and annual sales of about $18 billion (Figure 1).

Effective October 1, 1993, ABB reorganized into four business segments (power plants, power transmission and distribution, industrial and building systems, and transportation) and three economic regions (Europe, the Americas, and Asia Pacific). Prior to the reorganization ABB had six business segments: power plants, power transmission, power distribution, industry, transportation, and various activities.

Each business segment is composed of distinct business areas (BAs). Under the new alignment ABB has fifty BAs. The bulk of its revenues is still generated by the power-related business segments (Figure 2). Chief competitors—GE (U.S.), Siemens (Germany), Hitachi and Mitsubishi (Japan)—have all diversified away from the power industry.

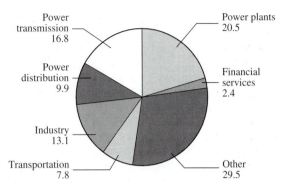

FIGURE 2 ABB annual sales percentage by segment (1991).

History

Prior to the merger, Asea AB and BBC Brown Boveri Ltd. were widely regarded as national industrial treasures in their respective countries. Each firm had earned that respect by developing and supplying products for nearly a century.

Brown Boveri, primarily a manufacturer of heavy-duty transformers and generators, had large customer bases in Germany and the United States. But the engineer-led firm had been experiencing declining profits since the late 1970s. An analyst's report identified "empire-building" subsidiaries as a major problem. Lacking a clear corporate strategy, many Brown Boveri subsidiaries independently engaged in R&D, marketing, and production. Such duplicative costs contributed to "dividend-free" years in 1986 and 1987.

In the late 1970s Asea AB was slowly growing, a dominant force in the Swedish electrical engineering and power plant market. That changed in 1980. Barnevik took over the firm and began to behave in a very un-Swedish manner. First order of business? Slash overhead at Asea headquarters. In the first 100 days Barnevik reduced Asea's main office staff from 1,700 to 200. (This was to become a Barnevik trademark. In subsequent acquisitions the first order of business was always the severe reduction of headquarters personnel.) Responsibility was shifted downward as numerous profit centers, with specific target goals, were established. Throughout the 1980s other Scandinavian firms were acquired (Stromberg-Finland, Flotech-Denmark, Elektrisk Bureau-Norway) in an effort to widen Asea's electromechanical product line as well as its distribution channels. Further expansion took Asea beyond Europe to Asia and North America. In eight years Barnevik tripled Asea's sales and increased earnings fivefold.

FIGURE 1 ABB annual sales percentage by segment (1987).

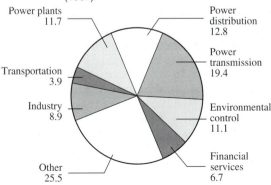

While on this acquisition/growth binge Barnevik was contemplating the future European landscape. A borderless Europe would open protected markets. For Asea that meant an opportunity to wrest part of the power plant market away from domestic firms. This realization eventually led Barnevik to approach Brown Boveri. The Asea/Brown Boveri merger, domiciled in Zurich, Switzerland, became official January 5, 1988.

After the merger Barnevik rationalized, or streamlined, the ABB workforce and then launched a series of acquisitions. In 1989 ABB entered a joint venture with Italy's state-owned Finmeccanica and completed a buyout of Westinghouse Electric Corporation's United States power transmission and distribution business. The following year saw ABB (1) assume control of Combustion Engineering, an American boiler and nuclear plant builder; (2) move into Eastern Europe with a majority position in Zamech, a Polish turbine maker; and (3) establish links with an East German electrical-equipment supplier, Bergmann-Borsig. In 1991 ABB acquired Bergmann-Borsig and continued its aggressive investment in Central and Eastern Europe by entering into approximately thirty joint ventures. By 1992 ABB held roughly 1,300 subsidiaries spread across Europe, Asia, North America, Latin America, Africa, Australia, and New Zealand. In 1993 it was reported that ABB would expand further into Asia and Eastern Europe.

Organization

In order to control this far-flung network ABB employs a matrix organization, divided by products and geography.

The four major product lines are subdivided into BAs. Each BA manager is responsible for setting global strategy for that product line. That responsibility includes setting and monitoring factory cost and quality standards, allocating export markets among the BA factories, and personnel management and development.

Within each of the three primary geographical regions ABB is divided by country. Country managers deal with national and local governments, unions, laws, and regulations. They operate traditional national companies. But the country managers also work across BAs by coordinating all operations within their assigned country. It is this latter role that links business segments and attempts to create an efficient distribution and service network across product lines.

At a still lower level is the company manager. This person is responsible for a single facility and its products. The company manager reports to two bosses: the BA manager and the country manager.

This matrix organization creates what Barnevik prefers to call a "multidomestic" rather than a multinational company. It is, in Barnevik's opinion, the multidomestic firm that can truly "think global, act local." Company managers are usually nationals of the country in which they are employed. Naturally they are familiar with local customs and marketplace. But they are also forced to think globally because of the BA manager's global strategy (i.e., export markets) for the domestically produced goods. As a consequence, ABB plants typically produce a variety of products for the local market and a narrower line for export. The narrower line reflects the particular specialty or core product of that plant. Barnevik notes that this strategy forces a plant to be flexible to meet specific local needs while still producing internationally competitive products for export.

In order for the matrix system to work Barnevik tries to "overinform." Information is continually disseminated in face-to-face meetings between executive committee members and business area, country, and company managers. But it is Abacus, ABB's management information system, that ties the highly decentralized company together. Abacus provides centralized reporting to ABB's 1,300 subsidiaries and 5,000-plus profit centers.

In addition to traditional financial performance measures Barnevik reviews aggregated and disaggregated results by business segments, country, and companies. It is within this latter information that Barnevik discerns trends and problems. With little fanfare, the situation is discussed with appropriate ABB personnel. A course of action is quickly planned and implemented.

SIEMENS AG

Siemens, a German company, has fifteen business segments: power generation, power transmission and distribution, industrial and building systems, drives and standard products, automation, private communication systems, public communication networks, defense electronics, automotive systems, semiconductors, medical engineering, passive components and electron tubes, transportation systems, audio and video systems, and electromechanical components. In addition, a 1990 merger with Nixdorf resulted in the formation of Sie-

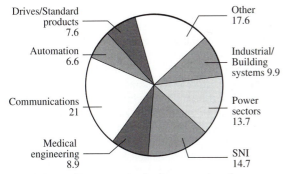

Drives/Standard products 7.6
Automation 6.6
Communications 21
Medical engineering 8.9
Other 17.6
Industrial/Building systems 9.9
Power sectors 13.7
SNI 14.7

FIGURE 3 Siemens annual sales percentage by segment (1992).

mens Nixdorf Informationssysteme AG (SNI). SNI, second largest computer company in Europe after IBM, is a separate legal entity. Figure 3 indicates the relative importance of the various business segments.

History

In 1847 Werner Siemens and J. G. Halske formed Siemens & Halske (S&H) to manufacture and install telegraphic systems. The company was successful and within ten years found itself constructing an extensive telegraph system in Russia as well as developing the first successful deep-sea telegraphic cable.

Spurred by such accomplishments S&H diversified into other products. By the late 1800s S&H had become involved in telephones, electrical lighting, X-ray tubes, and power-generating equipment.

Growth continued into the 1900s until the outbreak of World War I. With civilian demand dampened, S&H sought military contracts. During the war the company supplied the German military with communication devices, explosives, rifle components, and aircraft engines.

Defeat of the German state carried a penalty for S&H. Its assets in England and Russia were seized by the respective governments. Despite such losses S&H continued operations, concentrating on electrical manufacturing. In 1923 S&H began producing radio receivers. Soon thereafter the firm once again moved into international markets, setting up an electrical subsidiary in Japan and developing hydro projects in Ireland and the Soviet Union.

War again interrupted S&H's business. During World War II S&H devoted the majority of its manufacturing capacity to military orders. The company's

electrical skills were utilized in the development of an automatic-pilot system for airplanes and the German V-2 rocket. As a result, S&H factories were frequently targeted for Allied bombing raids. After the Soviet army gained control of Berlin in 1945, S&H's corporate headquarters was destroyed.

Following World War II S&H relocated to Munich. By the early 1950s S&H was again producing a variety of products for consumer electronics, railroad, medical, telephone, and power-generating equipment markets. S&H established an American subsidiary in 1954. By the end of the 1950s S&H had broadened into data processing and nuclear power.

In 1966 S&H underwent a major reorganization. All subsidiaries were brought under the direct control of the parent company. In turn, the parent company reincorporated and emerged with a new name, Siemens AG.

By the 1970s Siemens had once again become a respected international competitor in electrical manufacturing. Siemens displaced Westinghouse as the world's number two electrical manufacturer. This pitted Siemens against number one General Electric in numerous markets in the 1970s and 1980s.

Despite a series of acquisitions and mergers in the 1980s Siemens remained a Euro-centered organization for the next decade. Sales in 1992 show that 75 percent of Siemens' sales occur in Europe, with 46 percent of that amount in Germany alone (Figure 4).

Organization

From 1847 until 1981 a Siemens family member controlled the day-to-day operations. That changed with the retirement of Peter von Siemens in 1981. Since that

FIGURE 4 Siemens sales percentage by region.

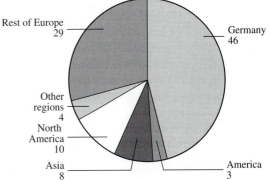

Rest of Europe 29
Germany 46
Other regions 4
North America 10
Asia 8
America 3

time the company has been directed by non-Siemens family members.

Siemens corporate structure is based on the concept of decentralized responsibility. This philosophy is supported by a flat hierarchy and, consequently, short decision-making paths. Management believes that decentralized organization guarantees maximum market responsiveness in today's competitive environment.

The corporate structure is characterized by three primary divisions: groups, regional units, and corporate divisions and centralized services. The groups are the previously mentioned fifteen business segments as well as several legally independent business entities (e.g., SNI). Headed by a group president, the group has worldwide responsibility for its business activity. The groups are intended to act as ''stand-alone'' businesses, resembling an independent company.

The role of the regional units is to implement the business goals of the groups. The regional units must encourage maximum local entrepreneurial responsibility while ensuring that local units understand each group's overall strategy. In most cases the regional unit deals directly with local subsidiaries.

The utilization of corporate divisions and centralized services is intended to separate staff functions from service units. Within the corporate divisions there are five main corporate departments: finance, research and development, human resources, production and logis-

tics, and planning and development. These departments provide general guidelines and serve as a coordinating function in their particular area. This coordinating function supports each group's business while keeping Siemens' overall strategic goals in mind.

Having finished the consultants' report Wilton Zwick leaned back in his chair and wondered about ZEI's future. He realized that ZEI's decision would, in large measure, determine the company's future. A misstep at this juncture might be disastrous. A correct decision, however, could launch a new era of growth and prosperity.

QUESTIONS

1 At what stage of global operations are ZEI, ABB, and Siemens? Justify your answer.

2 Beyond a simple sales perspective, why might ZEI want to consider greater international activity?

3 From a ZEI perspective, what advantages and disadvantages do ABB and Siemens offer?

4 Alliances with ABB and Siemens are only one alternative contained in the consultants' report. What other alternatives do you think the report might contain?

5 What course of action do you think ZEI should pursue? Why?

PART TWO

TWO

LOGISTICAL RESOURCES

Chapter 6   Information

Chapter 7   Forecasting

Problem Set A   Information-Forecasting

Chapter 8   Inventory Strategy

Chapter 9   Inventory Management

Problem Set B   Inventory

Chapter 10   Transportation Infrastructure

Chapter 11   Transportation Regulation

Chapter 12   Transportation Management

Problem Set C   Transportation

Chapter 13   Warehouse Management

Chapter 14   Material Handling

Chapter 15   Packaging

Problem Set D   Warehousing-Handling

CHAPTER 6

INFORMATION

INFORMATION FUNCTIONALITY AND
   PRINCIPLES
   Information Functionality
   Principles of Logistics Information
   Conclusion
INFORMATION ARCHITECTURE
   Planning/Coordination
   Operations
   Inventory Deployment and Management
   Logistics Information System Flow
   Conclusion
APPLICATIONS OF NEW INFORMATION
   TECHNOLOGIES
   Electronic Data Interchange

Personal Computers
Artificial Intelligence/Expert Systems
Communications
Bar Coding and Scanning
Conclusion
ELECTRONIC DATA INTERCHANGE
   STANDARDS
   Communication Standards
   Information Standards
   Future Directions
SUMMARY
QUESTIONS

As discussed in Chapter 2, information flow is a key element of logistics operations. Common forms of logistics information include customer and replenishment orders, inventory requirements, warehouse work orders, transportation documentation, and invoices. In the past, information flow was largely paper-based and resulted in slow, unreliable, and error-prone information transfer. Paper-based information flow both increases operating cost and decreases customer satisfaction. Since technology costs are declining and usage is easier, applications offer logistics managers the capability to more efficiently, effectively, and rapidly move and manage information electronically. Electronic information movement and management provide the opportunity to reduce logistics expense through increased coordination and to enhance service by offering better information to customers.

Chapter 6 discusses the role, design, and application of logistics information management. Following this introduction, the first section describes information functionality and principles from a logistics perspective. The functionality discussion contrasts logistics transaction systems, management control, decision analysis, and strategic planning applications. The discussion includes a description of each application type, example decisions, objectives, and cost-benefit characteristics. The first section also provides guidelines for logistics information system (LIS) development.

The next section describes the logistics information infrastructure including both coordination and operational requirements. Coordination requirements include strategic objectives, capacity constraints, logistics requirements, manufacturing requirements, and procurement requirements. Operational requirements include order management, order processing, distribution operations, transportation and shipping, and procurement. Inventory deployment and management provide the interface between coordination and operational requirements. The section describes component objectives, functions, and interfaces.

Information technology is advancing at a phenomenal rate in terms of speed and storage capability with simultaneous dramatic reductions in cost and size. While the current state of information technology is continuously evolving, several advances significantly influence logistics operations. The last sections identify and describe key technologies and logistics applications. The specific technologies include electronic data interchange (EDI), personal computers, artificial intelligence/expert systems, wireless communications, and bar coding and scanning.

INFORMATION FUNCTIONALITY AND PRINCIPLES

From its inception, logistics focused on efficient flow of goods through the distribution channel. Information flow was often overlooked because it was not viewed as being important to customers. In addition, the speed of information exchange/transfer was limited to the speed of paper. Timely and accurate information is now more critical for effective logistics systems design for three reasons. First, customers perceive that information about order status, product availability, delivery schedule, and invoices is a necessary element of total customer service. Second, with the goal of reducing total supply chain inventory, managers realize that information can effectively reduce inventory and human resource requirements. In particular, requirements planning using the most current information can reduce inventory by minimizing demand uncertainty. Third, information increases flexibility with regard to how, when, and where resources may be utilized for strategic advantage. The Council of Logistics Management recognized this change in 1988 when it incorporated ''material, in-process, finished goods and *information*'' into its definition of logistics.

This section describes logistics information systems (LIS) from two perspectives. First, LIS functions are discussed in terms of justifications and benefits. Second, the characteristics of the best LIS are described and illustrated.

Information Functionality

Logistics information systems are the threads that link logistics activities into an integrated process. The integration builds on four levels of functionality: transaction, management control, decision analysis, and strategic planning systems.

Figure 6-1 illustrates logistics activities and decisions at each level of information functionality. As the pyramid shape suggests, LIS management control, decision analysis, and strategic planning enhancements require a strong transaction system foundation.

The most basic level, the transaction system, initiates and records individual logistics activities. Transaction activities include order entry, inventory assignment, order selection, shipping, pricing, invoicing, and customer inquiry. For example, customer order receipt initiates a transaction as the order is entered into the information system. The order entry transaction initiates a second transaction as inventory is assigned to the order. A third transaction is then generated to direct the material handlers to select the order. A fourth transaction directs the movement, loading, and delivery of the order. The final transaction prints or transmits the invoice for payment. Throughout the process, order status information must be available when customers desire such information. Thus, the customer order performance cycle is completed through a series of information system transactions. The transaction system is characterized by formalized rules, interfunctional communications, a large volume of transactions, and an operational day-to-day focus.

FIGURE 6-1   Information functionality.

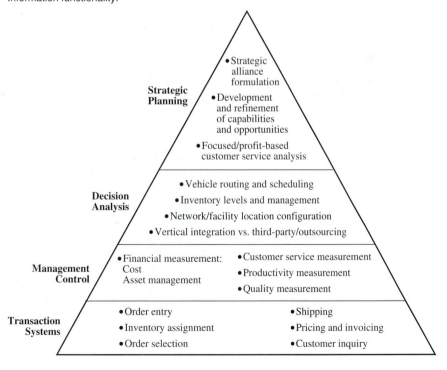

Strategic Planning
- Strategic alliance formulation
- Development and refinement of capabilities and opportunities
- Focused/profit-based customer service analysis

Decision Analysis
- Vehicle routing and scheduling
- Inventory levels and management
- Network/facility location configuration
- Vertical integration vs. third-party/outsourcing

Management Control
- Financial measurement: Cost Asset management
- Customer service measurement
- Productivity measurement
- Quality measurement

Transaction Systems
- Order entry
- Inventory assignment
- Order selection
- Shipping
- Pricing and invoicing
- Customer inquiry

The combination of structured processes and large transaction volume places a major emphasis on information system *efficiency.*

The second level, management control, focuses on performance measurement and reporting. Performance measurement is necessary to provide management feedback regarding service level and resource utilization. Thus, management control is characterized by an evaluative, tactical, intermediate-term focus that evaluates past performance and identifies alternatives. Common performance measures include financial, customer service, productivity, and quality indicators. As an example, specific performance measures include transportation and warehousing cost per pound (cost measure), inventory turnover (asset measure), case fill rate (customer service measure), cases per labor hour (productivity measure), and customer perception (quality measure). Chapter 22 defines these measures in detail and illustrates additional ones.

While it is necessary that LIS report past logistic system performance, it is also important that LIS be able to identify exceptions as they are being processed. Management control exception information is useful to identify potential customer or order problems. For example, proactive LIS should be capable of predicting future inventory shortages on the basis of forecasted requirements and anticipated receipts.

While some management control measures, such as cost, are very well defined, other measures such as customer service are less specific. For example, customer service can be measured internally (from the enterprise's perspective) or externally (from the customer's perspective). While internal measures are relatively easy to track, external measures are more difficult to obtain since they require monitoring performance on an individual customer basis.

The third level, decision analysis, focuses on decision applications to assist managers in identifying, evaluating, and comparing logistics strategic and tactical alternatives. Typical analyses include vehicle routing and scheduling, inventory management, facility location, and cost-benefit analysis of operational trade-offs and arrangements. Chapters 18 and 19 discuss some of these alternatives and "what if" questions in detail. Decision analysis LIS must include database maintenance, modeling and analysis, and reporting components for a wide range of potential alternatives. Similar to the management control level, decision analysis is characterized by a tactical, evaluative focus. Unlike management control, decision analysis focuses on evaluating future tactical alternatives, and it needs to be relatively unstructured and flexible to allow consideration of a wide range of options. Therefore, users require more expertise and training to benefit from its capability. Since there are typically fewer decision analysis applications than transactions, decision analysis LIS emphasis shifts more to *effectiveness* (identifying profitable versus unprofitable accounts) rather than *efficiency* (faster processing or increased transaction volume while utilizing fewer staff resources).

The final level, strategic planning, focuses on information support to *develop* and *refine* logistics strategy. These decisions are often extensions of the decision analysis level but are typically more abstract, less structured, and long-term in focus. Examples of strategic planning decisions include synergies made possible through strategic alliances, development and refinement of firm capabilities and market opportunities, as well as customer responsiveness to improved service. The

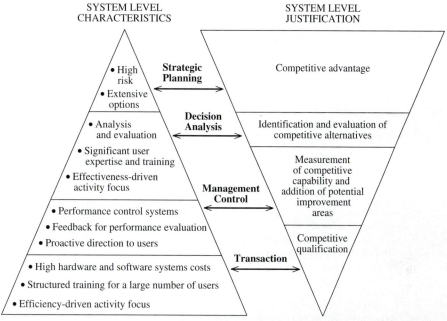

SYSTEM LEVEL
CHARACTERISTICS

SYSTEM LEVEL
JUSTIFICATION

- High risk
- Extensive options

Strategic Planning

Competitive advantage

- Analysis and evaluation

Decision Analysis

Identification and evaluation of competitive alternatives

- Significant user expertise and training
- Effectiveness-driven activity focus

Management Control

Measurement of competitive capability and addition of potential improvement areas

- Performance control systems
- Feedback for performance evaluation
- Proactive direction to users

Competitive qualification

- High hardware and software systems costs
- Structured training for a large number of users
- Efficiency-driven activity focus

Transaction

FIGURE 6-2 LIS usage, decision characteristics, and justification.

LIS strategic planning level must incorporate lower-level data collection into a wide range of business planning and decision-making models that assist in evaluating the probabilities and payoffs of various strategies.

Figure 6-2 presents system usage and decision characteristics along with justification for each level of LIS functionality. Historically, LIS development focused on improving transaction system efficiencies as a basis of competitive advantage. The primary justification was to reduce transaction cost to allow lower prices. However, as LIS expenditures have increased without always providing corresponding reductions in cost, justifying enhanced or additional LIS applications has become increasingly difficult.

The relative shape of Figure 6-2 illustrates LIS development and benefit-cost characteristics. The left side illustrates the development and maintenance characteristics, while the right side shows the benefits. Development and maintenance costs include hardware, software, communications, training, and personnel. In general, a solid base requires greater LIS investments for transaction systems and corresponding reductions in investment for higher system levels. Transaction system costs are high because of the large number of system users, heavy communication demands, high transaction volume, and significant software complexity. Transaction system costs are also relatively well defined and exhibit more certainty with respect to benefits or returns. Users of higher-level systems must invest more in time, training, and strategic decision making, and correspondingly incur more uncertainty and risk with regard to system benefits.

Figure 6-2 also illustrates relative benefits of each LIS level. As noted previously, transactions system benefits of efficiency involve faster processing and fewer staff resources. However, communication and processing speed have increased to the point where these characteristics are a competitive qualifier rather than a competitive advantage. Effective management control and decision analysis provide benefits of strategic insight into competitive capability and alternative strategy formulation. For example, management control systems may demonstrate a firm's ability to leverage price, or external customer service audits may identify opportunities for selective, customer-focused programs. Finally, strategic planning ability to assess customer/product profitability, segment contribution, or alliance synergies can have a major impact on enterprise profitability and competitiveness.

In the past, most expenditures focused on improving transaction system efficiency. While these investments offered returns in terms of speed and somewhat lower operating costs, expected benefits in terms of cost reductions have not always materialized. However, recent LIS applications focus on management control, decision analysis, and strategic planning components. For example, warehouse and transportation transaction systems are incorporating significant management controls to measure labor and facilitate productivity. The productivity measures are used to reward good performance and improve poor performance. For decision analysis, many LIS incorporate quantitative models to assist in evaluating distribution facility location, inventory levels, and transportation routes. Newer LIS applications are also being developed in conjunction with reengineered processes. Instead of simply automating logistics flow, enterprises are reengineering their logistics procedures to reduce the number of cycles and sequential activities.

Principles of Logistics Information

Logistics information systems must incorporate six principles to meet management information needs and adequately support enterprise planning and operations. The following discussion reviews important principles for designing or evaluating LIS applications.

Availability   First, logistics information must be readily and consistently available. Examples of information required include order and inventory status. While enterprises may have substantial data regarding logistics activities, these data are often paper-based or very difficult to retrieve from computer systems.

Rapid availability is necessary to respond to customers and improve management decisions. This is critical since customers frequently need quick access to inventory and order status information. Another aspect of availability is the ability to access required information, such as order status, regardless of managerial, customer, or product order location. The decentralized nature of logistics operations requires that information be capable of being accessed and updated from anywhere in the country or even the world. In this way, information availability can reduce operating and planning uncertainty.

Accuracy   Second, logistics information must accurately reflect both current status and periodic activity for measures such as customer orders and inventory levels. Accuracy is defined as the degree to which LIS reports match actual physical counts or status. For example, smooth logistics operations require actual inventory to match LIS reported inventory at better than 99 percent accuracy. When there is low consistency between physical and information system inventory levels, buffer or safety inventory is necessary to accommodate the uncertainty. Just as in the case of information availability, increased information accuracy decreases uncertainty and reduces inventory requirements.

Timeliness   Third, logistics information must be timely to provide quick management feedback. Timeliness refers to the delay between when an activity occurs and when the activity is visible in the information system. For example, in some situations, it takes hours or days for the system to recognize a new order as actual demand, since the order is not always directly entered into an active demand database. As a result, there is a delay in recognizing actual demand, which reduces planning effectiveness and increases inventory.

Another example of timeliness concerns inventory updates when product is moved from ''work in process'' to ''finished goods'' status. Although a continuous physical product flow may exist, information system inventory status may be updated on an hourly, shift, or daily basis. Obviously, real-time or immediate updates are more timely, but they also result in increased record-keeping efforts. Bar coding, scanning, and EDI facilitate timely and effective recording.

Information system timeliness refers to system status, such as inventory levels, as well as management controls, such as daily or weekly performance reports. Timely management controls provide information when there is still time to take corrective action or to minimize the loss. In summary, timely information reduces uncertainty and identifies problems, thus reducing inventory requirements and increasing decision accuracy.

Exception-Based LIS   Fourth, LIS must be exception-based to highlight problems and opportunities. Logistics operations typically contend with a large number of customers, products, suppliers, and service companies. For example, the inventory status for each product-location combination must be reviewed regularly to schedule replenishment orders. Another repetitive activity is the status review of outstanding replenishment orders. In both cases, a large number of products or replenishment orders typically require review. Oftentimes, the review process requires asking two questions. The first question concerns whether any action should be taken for product or replenishment orders. If the first answer is yes, the second question concerns the type of action that should be taken. Many LIS require that reviews be completed manually, although they are increasingly being automated. The rationale for still using manual procedures is that many of the decisions are unstructured and require judgment on the part of the user. State-of-the-art LIS incorporate decision rules to identify these ''exception'' situations that require management attention and/or decision making. Planners or managers are then able to focus their efforts on situations that require the most attention or offer the best opportunity to improve service or reduce cost. Table 6-1 illustrates an exception-based inventory management report. The sample report, which provides detailed

TABLE 6-1   EXCEPTION-BASED INVENTORY MANAGEMENT REPORT

Product	Time	Level	Action	Order	Dates
A	Immediate	Out of stock	———	No open PO*	———
B	Immediate	Out of stock	Expedite	Firm PO for 100	Past due
C	Within LT	Out of stock	Expedite	Plan MO† for 100	Due 6/29 to 7/01
D	Immediate	Using safety	Expedite	Firm MO for 200	Past due
E	Within LT	———	Release	System order for 200	On 6/08
F	Beyond LT	Out of stock	Expedite	Firm PO for 100	Due 6/29 to 7/05
G	Within LT	Excess stock	Cancel	Plan PO for 150	Due 10/01
H	Within LT	Excess stock	Defer	Firm MO for 100	Due 10/01 to 12/01

*PO: purchase order.
†MO: manufacturing order.

recommendations for multiple items, suggests replenishment ordering, expediting, and rescheduling actions that should be taken for effective inventory management. For each item, the listing identifies the stock level and time for action and suggests the date and form of future actions. This type of exception report allows planners to use their time refining suggestions rather than wasting time identifying products that require decisions.

Additional examples of exception situations that LIS should highlight include very large orders, products with little or no inventory, delayed shipments, or declining operating productivity. In summary, state-of-the-art LIS should be strongly exception-oriented and should utilize the system to identify decisions that require management attention.

Flexibility   Fifth, logistics information systems must contain the capability to be flexible in order to meet the needs of both system users and customers. Information systems must be able to provide data tailored to specific customer requirements. For example, some customers may want order invoices aggregated across certain geographic or divisional boundaries. Specifically, Retailer A may want individual invoices for each store, while Retailer B may desire an aggregated invoice that totals all stores. A flexible LIS must be able to accommodate both types of requirements. Internally, information systems must be upgradable to meet future enterprise needs without incurring debilitating costs in terms of financial investment and/or programming time.

Appropriate Format   Finally, logistics reports and screens should be appropriately formatted, meaning that they contain the right information in the right structure and sequence. For example, LIS often include a distribution center inventory status screen, with one product and distribution center listed per screen. This format requires that a customer service representative check inventory status at each distribution center when attempting to locate inventory to satisfy a specific customer order. In other words, if there are five distribution centers, it requires a review and comparison of five computer screens. Appropriate format would provide a single screen with the inventory status for all five distribution centers. The

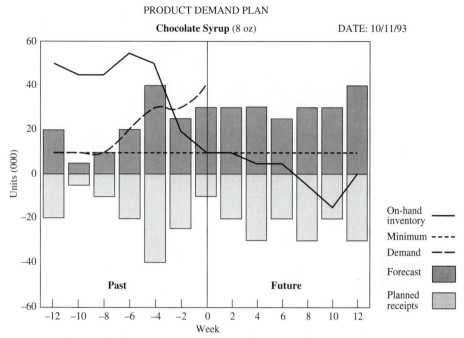

PRODUCT DEMAND PLAN

Chocolate Syrup (8 oz)   DATE: 10/11/93

FIGURE 6-3 Appropriate format screen.

combined screen makes it much easier for a customer representative to identify the best source for the product.

Another example of an appropriate format is a screen or report that contains and effectively presents all relevant information for a decision maker. Figure 6-3 illustrates such a screen for inventory planners. The screen integrates past and future information regarding on-hand inventory, minimum inventory, demand forecast, and planned receipts for a single item at a distribution center. The graphical presentation, which integrates inventory flows and level, facilitates inventory planning and ordering by focusing the planner on the weeks when projected on-hand inventory may drop below minimum levels. For example, a planner reviewing the screen in Figure 6-3 can easily see that current (week 0) on-hand inventory is right at the minimum and that there will be a stockout during week 7 if no action is taken.

Conclusion

Information is viewed as one of the keys to logistics competitive advantage for the future. However, simple existence of a logistics information system is not adequate to achieve this goal. Competitive LIS must build on a transaction system foundation to include management control, decision analysis, and strategic planning modules. As the modules are developed or refined, state-of-the-art LIS must incorporate the characteristics of information availability, accuracy, timeliness, exceptionality, flexibility, and appropriate formatting.

INFORMATION ARCHITECTURE

Logistics information systems combine hardware and software to manage, control, and measure the logistics activities discussed in the previous section. Hardware includes computers, input/output devices, and storage media. Software includes system and application programs used for processing transactions, management control, decision analysis, and strategic planning. Figure 6-4 and Table 6-2 build on Figure 2-2 and illustrate the typical logistics information system architecture. The architecture includes both the information base to maintain the data warehouse and the execution components. The information base contains purchase orders, inventory status, and customer orders. The data warehouse contains information describing the past activity levels and the current status, and is the basis for planning future requirements.

The execution components initiate, monitor, and measure the activities required to fulfill customer and replenishment orders. These activities take two forms. The first are the planning and coordination activities to produce and deploy inventory. The second are the operating activities to receive, process, ship, and invoice customer orders.

Planning and coordination include the activities necessary to schedule procurement, production, and logistics resource allocation throughout the enterprise. Specific components include definition of strategic objectives, rationalization of capacity constraints, and determination of logistics, manufacturing, and procurement requirements.

Operations include the transaction activities necessary to manage and process orders, operate distribution facilities, schedule transportation, and integrate procurement resources. This process is completed for both customer and enterprise replenishment orders. Customer orders reflect demands placed by enterprise customers. Replenishment orders control finished good movement between manufacturing and distribution facilities.

Inventory deployment and management is the interface between planning/coordination and operations. Inventory deployment and management monitors and controls the buffer stock whenever a ''make to order'' strategy is not possible.

FIGURE 6-4   Logistics information system architecture.

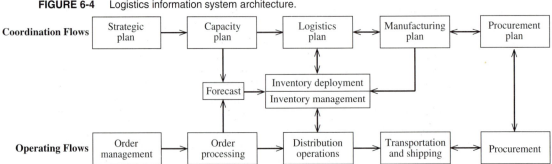

TABLE 6-2   LOGISTICS INFORMATION SYSTEM FUNCTIONALITY

Order management	Order processing	Inventory management	Distribution operations	Transportation and shipping	Procurement
• Order entry (manual, electronic, blanket)	• Create blanket order	• Forecast analysis and modeling	• Assign and track storage locations	• Carrier selection	• Match and pay
• Credit check	• Generate invoice	• Forecast data maintenance and updates	• Inventory control	• Carrier scheduling	• Open order review
• Inventory availability	• Generate order selection documents	• Forecast parameter selection	• Labor scheduling	• Dispatching	• Purchase order entry
• Order acknowledgment	• Inventory reservation	• Forecast technique selection	• Lot control	• Document preparation	• Purchase order maintenance
• Order modification	• Process blanket order	• Inventory parameter selection	• Order selection location replenishment	• Freight payment	• Purchase order receipt
• Order pricing	• Reassign order source	• Inventory simulation	• Receiving and put away	• Performance measurement	• Purchase order status
• Order status inquiry	• Release reserved inventory	• Inventory requirements planning	• Storage	• Shipment consolidation and routing	• Quote request
• Price and discount extensions	• Release blanket order	• Promotion data integration	• Performance measurement	• Shipment rating	• Requirements communication
• Promotion check	• Verify shipment	• Replenishment order build, release, and scheduling		• Shipment scheduling	• Schedule receipt appointment
• Reassign order source		• Service objective definition		• Shipment tracing and expediting	• Supplier history
• Returns processing				• Vehicle loading	
• Service management					

Individual planning/coordination and operations modules and their functions are discussed, including a review of the processes and linkages for each stage.

Planning/Coordination

Logistics system planning/coordination components form the information system backbone for manufacturers and merchandisers. These components define core activities that guide enterprise resource allocation and performance from procurement to product delivery.

As illustrated in Figure 6-4, planning/coordination includes material planning activities both within the enterprise and between distribution channel members. The specific components are (1) strategic objectives, (2) capacity constraints, (3) logistics requirements, (4) manufacturing requirements, and (5) procurement requirements. Each planning/coordination component is discussed.

Strategic Objectives Primary information drivers for many enterprises are strategic objectives that define marketing and financial goals. These strategic objectives are typically developed for a multiyear planning horizon that often includes quarterly updates. Marketing's strategic objectives define target markets, products, marketing mix plans, and the role of logistics value-added activities such as service levels or capabilities. The objectives include customer base, breadth of products and services, planned promotions, and desired performance levels. Marketing goals are the customer service policies and objectives that define logistics activity and performance targets. The performance targets include service availability, capability, and the quality elements discussed under customer service. Financial strategic objectives define revenue, sales and production levels, and corresponding expense, as well as capital and human resource constraints.

The combination of marketing and financial objectives defines the markets, products, services, and activity levels that logistics managers must accommodate during the planning horizon. Specific goals include projected annual or quarterly activity levels such as shipments, dollar volume, and total cases. Specific events that must be considered include product promotions, new-product introductions, market rollouts, and acquisitions. Ideally, the marketing and financial plans should be integrated and consistent. Inconsistencies will result in poor service, excess inventory, or failure to meet financial goals.

The combination of marketing and financial strategic objectives provides direction for other enterprise plans. While the process of establishing strategic objectives is, by nature, unstructured and wide ranging, it must develop and communicate a plan detailed enough to be operationalized.

Capacity Constraints Capacity constraints and logistics, manufacturing, and procurement requirements evolve from the strategic objectives. Capacity constraints are determined by internal and external manufacturing, warehousing, and transportation resources. Using activity levels defined by the strategic objectives, capacity constraints identify material bottlenecks and effectively manage resources to meet market demands. For each product, capacity constraints determine the "where," "when," and "how much" for production, storage, and movement. The constraints consider aggregate production and throughput limitations such as annual or monthly capacity.

Capacity problems can be resolved by resource acquisition, speculation, or postponement of production or delivery. Capacity adjustments can be made by acquisition or alliances such as contract manufacturing or facility leasing. Speculation reduces bottlenecks by anticipating production capacity requirements through prior scheduling or contract manufacturing. Postponement delays production and shipment until specific requirements are known and capacity can be allocated. It may be necessary to offer customer incentives such as discounts or allowances in order to postpone delivery. The capacity constraints introduce the time dimension into the enterprise's strategic objectives by considering facility, financial, and human resource limitations. These constraints have a major influence on logistics, manufacturing, and procurement schedules.

Capacity constraints link the enterprise's aggregate operating plan to weekly or daily logistics requirements. These constraints are a major influence on monthly or weekly production for each manufacturing location. Capacity flexibility depends on the nature of the product and lead time. For the long term, there is usually substantial flexibility, since a full range of postponement, speculation, and acquisition strategies may be used. However, in the short term, such as within the current week, there is limited flexibility, since resources are generally committed. Capacity constraint integration with the remaining enterprise requirement systems varies across organizations. The best enterprises typically demonstrate a high level of integration across all planning/coordination components.

Logistics Requirements   Logistics requirements coordinate the facility, equipment, labor, and inventory resources necessary to accomplish the logistics mission. For example, the logistics requirement component schedules shipments of finished product from manufacturing plants to distribution centers and retailers. The shipment quantity is calculated as the difference between customer requirements and inventory level. Logistics requirements are often implemented using distribution requirements planning (DRP) as an inventory management and process control tool. DRP is further discussed in Chapter 9. Future requirements are based on forecasts, customer orders, and promotions. Forecasts are based on sales and marketing input in conjunction with historical activity levels. Customer orders include current orders, future committed orders, and contracts. Promotional activity is particularly important when planning logistics requirements, since it often represents a large percentage of total volume and has a large impact on capacity. Current inventory status is product available to ship. Table 6-3 illustrates the computation for determining logistics requirements.

Specifically, for each planning period (e.g., weekly or monthly), the sum of forecast plus future customer orders plus promotional volume represents period demand. It is not easy to determine the percentage of the forecasted volume that is accounted for by the known customer orders, so some judgment must be made. Typically, period demand is actually a combination of the three, since current forecasts may incorporate some future orders and promotional volume. When determining period demand, it is important that the overlap between forecast, future customer orders, and promotions be considered. Period logistics requirements then equal period demand less inventory-on-hand less planned receipts. Using this form, each period would ideally end with zero inventory available so that planned receipts would exactly equal period demand. While perfect coordination of demand and

TABLE 6-3   LOGISTICS REQUIREMENTS

+	Forecasts (sales, marketing, input, histories, accounts)
+	Customer orders (current orders, future committed orders, contracts)
+	Promotions (promotion, advertising plans)
=	Period demand
−	Inventory-on-hand
−	Planned receipts

Period logistics requirements

supply is ideal from an inventory management perspective, it may not be the best strategy for the firm.

Logistics requirements must be integrated with both capacity constraints (upstream) and manufacturing requirements (downstream) to obtain optimal system performance. Poorly integrated logistics and manufacturing components typically result in finished goods inventory at the end of the production line that is not visible when logistics requirements are determined.

Manufacturing Requirements   Manufacturing requirements schedule production resources and attempt to resolve day-to-day capacity bottlenecks within the materials management system. Primary bottlenecks result from raw material shortages or daily capacity limitations. Manufacturing requirements determine the master production schedule (MPS) and manufacturing requirements plan (MRP). The MPS defines weekly or daily production and machine schedules. Given the MPS, the MRP coordinates the purchase and arrival of materials and components to support the desired manufacturing plan. Although this discussion presents logistics requirements and manufacturing requirements serially, they actually must operate in parallel. This is particularly true for enterprises utilizing demand flow or market-paced manufacturing strategies. These strategies coordinate production schedules directly with market demands or orders and reduce the need to forecast or plan. In a sense, demand flow or market-paced manufacturing strategies design all production as ''make to order'' and thus totally integrate logistics and manufacturing requirements.

Procurement Requirements   Procurement requirements schedule material releases, shipments, and receipts. Procurement requirements build on capacity constraints, logistics requirements, and manufacturing requirements to demonstrate long-term material requirements and release schedules. The requirement and release schedule is then used for purchasing negotiation and contracting.

Conclusion   While each planning/coordination component can operate (and in the past frequently has operated) independently, such independence often leads to inconsistencies that create excess manufacturing and logistics inventory as well as decreased operating efficiencies. Inconsistency often results when each component uses a different forecast. Historically, it was not uncommon for enterprises to have different forecasts for each component since each was controlled by different organizational units. For example, the strategic objectives may justify high forecasts to motivate the sales force, while logistics may plan on more conservative forecasts. Similarly, inconsistencies between logistics, manufacturing, and procurement requirements cause facility and processing inefficiencies that result in unnecessary safety stocks to buffer independent operations.

Today many enterprises are increasing coordination to reduce forecast inconsistency, resulting in lower inventories. Increased coordination can be achieved through the use of common databases and forecasts and with more frequent information exchange. Best practice logistics enterprises use planning/coordination integration as a major source of improved effectiveness.

Operations

Operations include the information activities required to receive, process, and ship customer orders and to coordinate the receipt of purchase orders. Operations components are (1) order management, (2) order processing, (3) distribution operations, (4) transportation and shipping, and (5) procurement. Each component is described below including a review of key functions and interfaces.

Order Management   Order management is the entry point for customer orders and inquiries. It allows entry and maintenance of customer orders using communication technologies such as mail, phone, fax, or EDI. As orders or inquiries are received, order management enters and retrieves required information, edits for appropriate values, and then retains acceptable orders for processing. Order management can also offer information regarding inventory availability and delivery dates to establish and confirm customer expectations. Order management, in conjunction with customer service representatives, forms the primary interface between the customer and the enterprise LIS.

Table 6-2 lists primary order management functionality. It includes entry for blanket, electronic, and manual orders. Blanket orders are large orders that reflect demand for a merchandiser over an extended time period such as a quarter or a year. Future shipments against blanket orders are triggered by individual order releases. Order management creates and maintains the customer and replenishment order base that affects the remaining operations components.

Order Processing   Order processing assigns or allocates available inventory to open customer and replenishment orders. Allocation may take place on a real-time (i.e., immediate) basis as orders are received or in a *batch* mode. Batch mode means that orders are grouped for periodic processing, such as by day or shift. While real-time allocation is more responsive, a batch process provides the firm with more control over situations when inventory is low. For example, in a batch process, order processing can be designed to assign stock from current inventory only, or from scheduled production capacity. An LIS is more responsive if it allows inventory assignment from scheduled production capacity. However, there is a trade-off since assigning scheduled production capacity reduces the firm's ability to reschedule production. The "best" order processing applications operate interactively in conjunction with order management to generate an order solution that satisfies both customer requirements and enterprise resource constraints. In this type of operational environment, the customer service representative and the customer interact to determine the combination of products, quantities, and performance-cycle length that is acceptable to both parties. When there is conflict in order processing, possible solutions include delivery date adjustments, product substitutions, or shipment from an alternative source.

Table 6-2 lists typical order processing functionality, which includes inventory assignment, back-order creation and processing, order selection document generation, and order verification. Order selection documents, in paper or electronic form, direct distribution operations to select an order from the distribution center or warehouse and pack it for shipment. The customer or replenishment order, with its allocated inventory and corresponding order selection material, links order processing with distribution center physical operations.

Distribution Operations Distribution operations incorporate LIS functions to guide distribution center physical activities including product receipt, material movement, and storage and order selection. Distribution operations are often termed *inventory control* or *warehousing* systems. Distribution operations direct all activities within distribution centers using a combination of batch and real-time assignments. In a batch environment, the LIS develops a list of instructions or tasks to guide each material handler in the warehouse. Material handlers are the individuals who operate material-handling equipment such as fork trucks and pallet jacks (material-handling technology is discussed in detail in Chapter 14). In a sense, this list is the handler's ''to do'' list for the hour or shift. In a real-time environment, information-directed technologies such as bar coding, radio frequency communication, and automated handling equipment operate interactively with LIS to reduce the elapsed time between decision and action. The real-time information-directed technologies, discussed in detail later in the chapter, provide more operation flexibility and reduce internal performance-cycle time requirements.

Table 6-2 lists typical distribution operations functionality. Historically, distribution operations have focused on directing warehouse operations and activities including guiding product movement and storage. A state-of-the-art distribution operations LIS must also plan operating requirements and measure performance. Operations planning includes personnel and resource scheduling. Performance measurement includes developing personnel and equipment productivity reports.

Transportation and Shipping Transportation and shipping includes LIS functions to plan, execute, and manage transport and movement activities. These activities include shipment planning and scheduling, shipment consolidation, shipment notification, transport documentation generation, and carrier management. These activities guarantee efficient transport resource utilization as well as effective carrier management.

A unique characteristic of transportation and shipping LIS is that it often involves three parties—shipper, carrier, and consignee (recipient). To effectively manage the process, a basic level of information integration must exist in order for information to be shared. Information sharing requires standardized data formats for transport documents. Current data coordination efforts focus on integrating transport documents with other commercial documents such as orders, invoices, and shipment notification.

Table 6-2 lists transportation and shipping functionality. Transportation and shipping generates the documentation to release the order for shipment and measures the enterprise's ability to deliver the order satisfactorily. Historically, transportation and shipping emphasized document generation and rate determination. Transport documents include manifests and bills of lading and are specifically discussed in Chapter 12. Rates are the carrier charges incurred for product movement. The large number of shipments made by most enterprises requires automated and exception-based LIS that can reduce errors and identify cost savings. With the increased opportunity to reduce cost through better transport management, contemporary LIS transportation and shipping functionality emphasizes performance monitoring, rate auditing, routing and scheduling, invoicing, reporting, and decision analyses. A state-of-the-art transportation and shipping LIS incorporates increased planning and performance measurement capability.

Procurement   Procurement manages purchase order preparation, modification, and release, in addition to tracking vendor performance and compliance. Although procurement systems have not traditionally been considered part of LIS, the importance of integrating procurement is obvious when managing the entire supply chain. Integration of procurement and logistics schedules and activities allows coordination of material receipt, facility capacity, and transportation back-haul.

For integrated logistics, procurement LIS must track and coordinate receiving and shipping activities to optimize scheduling of facility, transport, and personnel resources. For example, since loading and unloading docks are often a critical facility resource, effective procurement LIS should coordinate the use of the same carrier for both deliveries and shipments. This capability requires LIS to have both receipt and shipment visibility. Logistic system integration can be further enhanced through electronic integration with suppliers. Table 6-2 lists procurement functionality. A state-of-the-art procurement LIS provides plans, directs activities, and measures performance, coordinating inbound and outbound activity movement.

Conclusion   Coordinated, integrated operations LIS is the minimum standard for logistics competitiveness today. Coordination and integration allow smooth and consistent customer and replenishment order information throughout the enterprise and offer current order status visibility. Also, integrated information sharing reduces delays, errors, and personal requirements. While operations LIS is typically well integrated, it is necessary to continuously review the system to ensure that no bottlenecks develop and customer flexibility is maintained. Best practice firms are improving operational performance by integrating operations LIS across firm boundaries with suppliers and customers.

Inventory Deployment and Management

Inventory deployment and management is the primary interface between planning/coordination and operations. Its role is to plan requirements and manage finished inventory from production until customer shipment. Decisions include "where, when, and how much." Specifically, where should finished inventory be placed in the channel? When should replenishment orders be placed? How much should be ordered? Firms with "make to order" materials systems have essentially integrated their planning/coordination and operations so that there is minimal need for inventory deployment and management. The first component of the inventory deployment and management system is the forecast module. The forecast module predicts product requirements by customer for each distribution center to support enterprise planning. The forecast process is discussed in detail later in this chapter.

The other components of inventory deployment and management are deployment decision aids ranging from simple reactive models to complex planning tools. The decision aids are necessary to guide inventory planners in deciding when and how much to order. Reactive models respond to current demands and inventory environment on the basis of reorder point and order quantity parameters. In other words, they make replenishment decisions by reacting to current inventory levels. Planning tools anticipate future requirements according to forecasts and cycle time projections. The planning tools allow managers to identify potential problems while they can still be resolved.

Inventory deployment and management systems also differ in the amount of human interaction required. Some applications need inventory planners to manually place or approve all replenishment orders. Such systems do not illustrate the exception-based criteria discussed earlier, since all replenishment orders require explicit planner approval. More sophisticated applications automatically place replenishment orders and monitor their progress through the replenishment cycle. The sophisticated applications illustrate a more exception-based philosophy, since planners are required to intervene only for "exceptional" replenishment orders.

Primary factors of inventory deployment and management are the customer service objectives established by management. Service objectives define target fill rates for customers and products. The combination of service objectives, demand characteristics, replenishment characteristics, and operating policies determines the "where, when, and how" identified above. Effective inventory deployment and management can significantly reduce the level of inventory assets required to meet specific service objectives. Chapter 9 offers additional details.

Besides initiating basic inventory decisions, inventory deployment and management must measure inventory performance by monitoring inventory level, turns, and productivity. Table 6-2 lists inventory deployment and management functionality for a relatively sophisticated logistics application. Note that the functionality includes a number of forecast-related activities. Inventory deployment and management requires estimates of future demands in the form of implicit or explicit forecasts. Implicit, or "default," forecasts assume that next month's sales will be the same as last month's. Explicit forecasts are developed more scientifically using information about the enterprise, customer, and competitor actions. The basic proposition is that more integrated forecast information facilitates inventory deployment and management and results in lower inventory requirements.

Logistics Information System Flow

While Figure 6-5 illustrates the conceptual structure of the logistics information system, it also graphs the flow from more of a process perspective. The schematic contains the major system elements including (1) modules, (2) data files, (3) management and data entry activities, (4) reports, and (5) communication links. Modules are the actual routines that process data or information, such as entering orders or assigning inventory. Data files are the information structures that store task-specific data such as orders or inventory records. The data files replace the file cabinets of the past. Management and data entry activities represent the interfaces

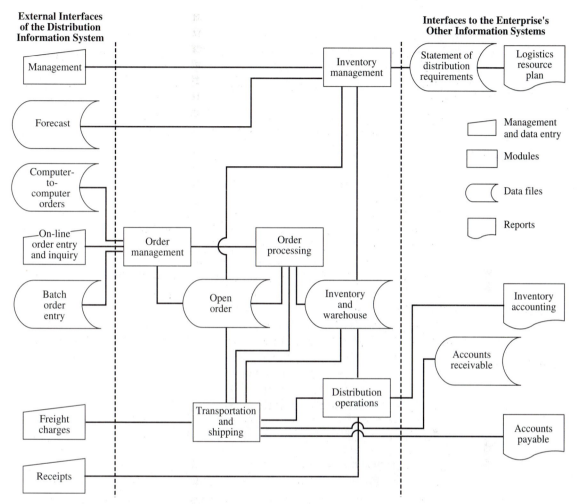

FIGURE 6-5   Logistical information system flow.

where the LIS must obtain input from an external environment such as a decision maker or another firm. Reports provide information regarding logistics activity and performance links. Communication links are the internal and external interfaces between LIS components and the outside environment.

The logistics information system flow should incorporate the following five modules: order entry, order processing, transportation and shipping, distribution operations, and inventory management. The files contain the data and information base to support the communications activities. The major database structures that are required for supporting distribution communications are (1) order file, (2) inventory and warehouse files, (3) accounts receivable file, and (4) distribution requirements file.

The management and data entry activities occur when data must be entered into the system or when management must enter a decision. The general instances for this intervention include (1) order entry, (2) order inquiry, (3) forecast development and reconciliation, (4) freight rating, and (5) warehouse receipts and adjustments. The reports consist of numerous summary, detail, and exception listings to provide hard-copy information documenting system activities and performance. The links identify the information flow between the subsystems, files, entry activities, and reports.

Conclusion

LIS is the backbone of modern logistics operations. In the past, this infrastructure has focused on initiating and controlling activities required to take, process, and ship customer orders. For today's enterprises to remain competitive, the role of information infrastructure must be extended to include requirements planning, management control, decision analysis, and integration with other members of the channel. This section has identified major components of the logistics information infrastructure, reviewed individual roles, and discussed the importance of integration and flexibility. Many firms are reviewing both inter- and intraenterprise information flow to incorporate more integration and flexibility while minimizing cost.

Since information technology is evolving much faster than most other logistics capabilities such as transportation and material handling, new technologies must be constantly reviewed to determine potential logistics applications. It is impossible for a textbook to offer timely information regarding the status of all information technologies. However, there are several technologies that have demonstrated widespread logistics applications. The following section discusses these.

APPLICATIONS OF NEW INFORMATION TECHNOLOGIES

Logistics managers see information technology as a major source of improved productivity and competitiveness. Unlike most other resources, information technology is increasing in both speed and capacity while declining in cost. While new capabilities are identified daily, five specific technologies have demonstrated widespread logistics applications. These include electronic data interchange (EDI), personal computers, artificial intelligence/expert systems, communications, and bar coding and scanning. The following section discusses these technologies and applications.

Electronic Data Interchange

EDI is identified as intercompany computer-to-computer exchange of business documents in standard formats. EDI describes both the capability and practice of communicating information between two organizations electronically instead of via the traditional forms of mail, courier, or even fax. The capability refers to the ability of computer systems to communicate effectively. The practice refers to the ability of the two organizations to effectively utilize the information exchanged.

Logistics information consists of real-time data on company operations—inbound material flows, production status, product inventories, customer shipments and incoming orders, among others. . . . From an external perspective, companies need to communicate order shipment and billing information with vendors or suppliers, financial institutions, transportation carriers and customers. Internal functions exchange information on production schedule and control data.[1]

Direct EDI benefits include (1) increased internal productivity, (2) improved channel relationships, (3) increased external productivity, (4) increased ability to compete internationally, and (5) decreased operating cost.[2] EDI improves productivity through faster information transmission as well as reduced information entry redundancy. Accuracy is improved by reducing the number of times and individuals involved in data entry. EDI impacts logistics operating cost through (1) reduced labor and material cost associated with printing, mailing, and handling paper-based transactions; (2) reduced telephone, fax, and telex communication; and (3) reduced clerical cost. JC Penney found that switching from paper to electronic media reduced its cost per invoice from \$0.29 to \$0.05.[3] In another example, Texas Instruments reports that EDI has reduced shipping errors by 95 percent, field inquiries by 60 percent, data entry resource requirements by 70 percent, and global procurement cycle time by 57 percent.[4]

Personal Computers

The personal computer (PC) has become almost ubiquitous in today's logistics environment. Reduced hardware size and increased capability have extended information technology applications from the desks of managers and customer service representatives to the field. PCs are influencing logistics management in three ways. First, low cost and high portability bring accurate and timely information to the decision maker whether in the office, at the warehouse, or on the road. In the past, individuals had to make decisions with information that was hours or even days old. Now the decision, whether it is strategic (such as which markets to service) or operational (such as which product to pick next in the warehouse), can be made with the most current information. There are numerous logistics examples where timely information increases the added value provided by chain members such as warehouse operators and carriers. For example, transport vehicle–based computers improve driver reporting and decision ability by recording delivery information, reporting vehicle location, and identifying lowest-cost fuel stops.[5] The AmeriCares sidebar illustrates how information technology can support global operations of a not-for-profit enterprise.

Second, responsiveness and flexibility offered by decentralized PCs enable more focused service and capability. The use of large mainframe computers implies

[1]*The Business Revolution,* prepared by Temple, Barker & Sloane, Inc., for the DECWorld Corporate Leaders Forum, 1987.

[2]Margaret Emmelhainz, *EDI: A Total Management Guide,* New York: Van Nostrand Reinhold, 1990.

[3]Gary Robins, "Cutting Down the Freight Weight," *STORES,* February 1993, p. 29.

[4]Clay Youngblood, "EDI Trial and Error," *Transportation and Distribution,* **34:**4, April 1993, p. 46.

[5]Stan Graff, "Computers Can Help Drivers Add Value to Your Service," *Transport Topics,* **3015,** May 17, 1993, pp. 16–17.

AMERICARES DELIVERS

AmeriCares, based in Connecticut, is a nonprofit international humanitarian organization that supports long-term health programs and provides immediate response to emergency needs. The organization was founded in 1982 by Robert Macauley, the chief executive officer of Virginia Fibre Corporation. AmeriCares solicits tax-deductible donations of medical supplies and other relief materials from individuals, American corporations, and foundations. AmeriCares yearly distributes more than 7 million pounds of supplies by land, sea, and air to over eighty countries around the world.

By developing close relationships with more than 1,000 major pharmaceutical manufacturers and health care companies, AmeriCares has received more than $6 billion in donated medical supplies over the past ten years. In its first year of operation, AmeriCares delivered $3.2 million in supplies. By 1992, this figure had grown to $150 million. The target for 1995 is $1 billion. Relief provided is primarily prescription medications, but also includes over-the-counter products, diagnostic products and equipment, medical instruments, hospital supplies, food, and nutritional supplements.

To expedite donations from companies, AmeriCares has developed a network with donor company personnel in the areas of finance, corporate affairs, taxes, quality assurance, inventory control, environment, customer service, operations, traffic, and international business.

The relationship with drug manufacturers has been aided by a provision in the 1986 Tax Act allowing up to 200 percent deductions for inventory donated to help infants, the needy, or the sick. In addition to the tax breaks, pharmaceutical donations save manufacturers by reducing excess product destruction, returns processing, and paperwork.

Most companies ship products directly to an AmeriCares warehouse. AmeriCares utilizes a computerized product donation system that documents all pertinent information about donations and relays details about product assessment, distribution, and shipping destination back to the donor company. As a result of receiving all its supplies through donations and because its CEO and Advisory Board receive no compensation or perks, AmeriCares is able to maintain an astonishingly low overhead of less than 1.5 percent. In addition, AmeriCares maintains a staff of only seventeen full-time workers, with forty domestic volunteers and thousands of volunteers in other countries.

AmeriCares maintains dating and handling records for all donations to ensure efficient movement of products. Stockpiling of medicines in warehouses is avoided through the use of a state-of-the-art inventory system. Once need is established, supplies are moved quickly, usually within thirty to sixty days of receipt. The only exception is nondated disaster supplies that are kept in the Stamford, Connecticut, warehouse. These supplies are ready to be moved to any disaster area within twenty-four hours. While AmeriCares airlifts supplies to disaster areas such as Bosnia, the former Soviet Union, and Ethiopia, the majority of disaster relief is delivered to its destination by land or sea. AmeriCares privately arranges for all transportation. All products are distributed free of charge.

AmeriCares' emergency response program allows the organization to offer immediate action-oriented relief. Upon notification of a disaster, AmeriCares activates a network of communication sources, gathers information regarding the nature and scope of the disaster, and begins working on the logistics of sending shipments to the disaster area. Often within hours of a disaster, AmeriCares dispatches teams to the location to receive and distribute all materials. The team also develops a product needs list that is used to determine the type and amount of health care products most needed, and how much follow-up support will be necessary.

AmeriCares sees no psychological or physical barriers to providing relief. AmeriCares is always on the way to a disaster, rushing emergency medicine, food, surgical teams, and other support that has led AmeriCares to become known as "the humanitarian arm of corporate America."

From AmeriCares' Annual Report 1991 and 1992; AmeriCares' Questions and Answers; AmeriCares' Emergency Response; AmeriCares' Ongoing Relief Programs; and James R. Norman, "I'm Nothing but a Beggar," *Forbes,* March 29, 1993, p. 90.

relatively inflexible operations in conjunction with unreliable connections to the field. Rather than risk shutting down a plant or warehouse because of data communications failure, logistics managers often prefer manual procedures. PCs make it cost-effective to have decentralized, flexible, and even redundant processing for even the smallest site or function. The use of local area networks (LANs), wide area networks (WANs), and client/server architecture offers the benefits of decentralization, responsiveness, flexibility, and redundancy while providing data integration throughout the enterprise. A LAN is a network of PCs that use phone lines or cable to communicate and share resources such as storage and printers. A LAN is restricted to a relatively small geographical location such as an office or warehouse, while a WAN can operate across a wide geography. Client/server architecture uses the decentralized processing power of PCs to provide LIS operating flexibility. The "server" is a large computer (usually mainframe or minicomputer) that allows common data to be shared by a number of users. The "client" is the network of PCs that access the data and manipulate them in different ways to provide extensive flexibility. A partnership between American Airlines and CSX has developed a client/server-based network, known as Encompass, that can globally track inventory in motion.[6] The network includes PCs located at key sites around the globe as well as in transport vehicles. A railroad consortium employs a similar technology to offer multiple communication paths so that customers can obtain shipment information when desired.[7] A survey of top United States executives suggests that LANs and client/server applications will significantly advance information technology applications over the next decade.[8]

Third, interactive PCs with graphics capabilities facilitate development of generic decision support applications such as facility location, inventory analysis, and routing and scheduling. The number and capability of such applications has grown significantly since the introduction of PCs. PCs have promoted such applications by (1) offering a standardized development platform, (2) facilitating use through interactive graphics, and (3) providing analytical methods to efficiently evaluate logistics alternatives. The annual Andersen Distribution Software Review is a timely source regarding software availability and capability.[9]

Artificial Intelligence/Expert Systems

Artificial intelligence (AI) and expert systems are another information-based technology contributing to logistics management. AI is an umbrella term describing a group of technologies aimed at making computers imitate human reasoning. AI is concerned with symbolic reasoning rather than numeric processing. AI includes

---

[6]Garry Ray, "Encompass Keeps on Globally Tracking," *Computerworld,* **26:**50, December 14, 1994, p. 89.

[7]"Rebuilding America's Railroads: The Information Evolution," *Railway Age,* **194:**2, February 1993, p. 85.

[8]Peter Lewis, "Top Executives Seeking More from Technology," *New York Times,* April 25, 1993, p. 10F.

[9]Andersen Consulting, *Logistics Software,* Oak Brook, Ill.: The Council of Logistics Management, 1995.

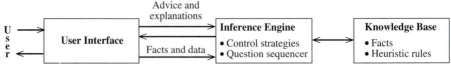

FIGURE 6-6   Basic structure of an expert system.

technologies such as expert systems, natural language translators, neural networks, robotics, speech recognition, and 3D vision.

Expert systems are one category of AI that has experienced successful logistics applications.

> Expert systems offer an economical and practical way to capture, refine and proliferate management skills. These systems provide a framework in which to document the questions and answers that experts use to solve analytical and operational problems. With expert systems, the know-how of one "expert" can be put in the hands of many workers to improve consistency, accuracy and productivity throughout the network. These systems allow more effective management of the organization's most critical resource—"knowledge."
>
> An expert system program captures and stores logistics knowledge as rules (heuristics), policies, checklists and logic, in a "knowledge base" in much the same way a conventional computer program stores numeric information in a database. As a result, expert system programs tend to be much easier to modify, update, and enlarge than conventional computer programs.[10]

Logistics expert systems are applied where expertise can increase the firm's return on assets. Applications include carrier selection, international marketing and logistics, inventory management, and information system design.

As Figure 6-6 illustrates, expert systems include three components: knowledge base, inference engine, and user interface. The knowledge base contains the expertise in the form of a series of "if . . . then" conditions. It is typically developed by interviewing a series of "experts" regarding the data and logic used to make decisions. For example, an experienced transportation manager develops key data items and guidelines to use when selecting a carrier for a specific shipment. An experienced forecaster would have a knowledge base regarding the best forecast technique to use. The integration and coordination of this decision logic across a number of experts develop a substantial knowledge base that allows less experienced personnel to make more effective decisions.

The inference engine searches the knowledge base to identify the rules that are relevant for a specific decision. For example, the traffic manager attempting to make a decision about a motor carrier does not want to use the rules developed for rail transportation. The inference engine determines the relevant rules and the sequence in which they should be evaluated. The user interface facilitates the interaction between the decision maker and the expert system. The interface formats the key questions to the user in natural language and then interprets the responses.

---

[10]Mary Kay Allen and Omar K. Helferich, *Putting Expert Systems to Work in Logistics,* Oak Brook, Ill.: The Council of Logistics Management, 1990.

TABLE 6-4   EXPERT SYSTEMS APPLICATION POTENTIAL IN LOGISTICS

		Decision Level		
		Operational	Tactical	Strategic
	Analyze	Hazardous chemical adviser	Determine sales/market share impact	Predict profit impact for foreign plant alternatives
	Plan	Job shop scheduler	Vehicle dispatch adviser	International logistics business planner
Problem Type	Operate	Suggest retail inventory actions	Assist in requisition and decision making	Monitor and improve logistics performance
	Train	Instruct inventory managers	Train manufacturing staff	Instruct buyers on controls
	Control	Warehouse pick operation	Flexible manufacturing	Maximize worldwide sourcing

Source: Mary Kay Allen and Omar K. Helferich, *Putting Expert Systems to Work in Logistics,* Oak Brook, Ill.: The Council of Logistics Management, 1990, p. xvii.

A good interface allows the user to refine the knowledge base as additional information or expertise is obtained.

Expert systems have demonstrated their ability to improve logistics productivity and quality. Table 6-4 summarizes a variety of logistics expert systems applications. ''The ability to transform data and information into usable knowledge, to extract and share rare expertise, and to manage knowledge as a vital competitive resource are the concerns of expert systems and artificial intelligence.''[11] While there are limited logistics applications of AI and expert systems, many prototypes have demonstrated significant returns. It is likely that there will be substantial future dividends from knowlege acquisition and structuring.

Communications

Information technology also significantly enhances logistics performance through faster and widespread communication. Historically, logistics activities had a distinct communications disadvantage since they involved movement in either a transport or a material-handling vehicle or were very decentralized. As a result, information and directions were often removed in terms of both time and location from the

[11]Ibid.

actual activity. Application of radio frequency (RF), satellite communications, and image processing technologies has overcome these problems caused by product movement and geographic decentralization.

Radio frequency technology is used within relatively small areas, such as distribution centers, to facilitate two-way information exchange. A major application is real-time communication with material handlers such as forklift drivers and order selectors. RF allows forklift drivers to have instructions and priorities updated on a real-time basis rather than using a hard copy of instructions printed hours earlier. Real-time communication offers more flexibility and responsiveness and often provides improved service with less resources. Logistics RF applications include two-way communication of warehouse selection instructions, warehouse cycle count verification, and label printing. United Parcel Service uses speech-based RF to read ZIP codes from incoming packages and print routing tickets to guide package movement through its Grand Rapids, Michigan, sort facility.[12]

Satellite technology allows communication across a wide geographic area such as a region or even the world. The technology is similar to microwave ''dishes'' used for home television in areas outside the reach of cable. Figure 6-7 illustrates two-way communication between corporate headquarters and both vehicles and remote locations such as stores.

Satellite communication provides a fast and high-volume channel for information movement around the globe. Schneider National, a nationwide truckload carrier, uses communication dishes on the top of its trucks to allow communication between drivers and dispatchers. The real-time interaction provides up-to-date information regarding location and delivery and allows dispatchers to redirect trucks in response to need or traffic congestion. Retail chains also use satellite communication to quickly transmit daily sales back to headquarters. Wal-Mart uses satellites to transmit daily sales figures to activate store replenishment and to provide input to marketing regarding local sales patterns.[13]

Image processing applications rely upon facsimile (fax) and optical scanning technology to transmit and store freight bill information, as well as other supporting documents such as proof of delivery receipts or bills of lading. The rationale for this new service is that timely shipment information is almost as important to the customer as delivering the goods on time.[14] As freight is delivered to customers, support documentation is sent to image processing locations, electronically scanned, and logged into the system.

Electronic images of the documents are then transmitted to a main data center where they are stored on optical laser disks. By the next day, customers can access the documents through computer linkages or a phone call to their service representative. Customer requests for a hard copy of a document can be filled within minutes by a fax transmission. Customer benefits include more accurate billing, faster response from carrier personnel, and easy access to documentation. The carrier

---

[12]A detailed discussion of RF can be found in Bruce Richmond, *Radio Frequency Date Communication for Warehousing and Distribution,* Chicago, Ill.: Warehouse Education and Research Council, 1993.

[13]George Stalk, Philip Evans, and Lawrence E. Shulman, ''Competing on Capabilities: The New Rules of Corporate Strategy,'' *Harvard Business Review,* March–April 1992, pp. 57–69.

[14]''Burlington Air to Improve Image Processing,'' *Journal of Commerce,* March 29, 1993, p. 3B.

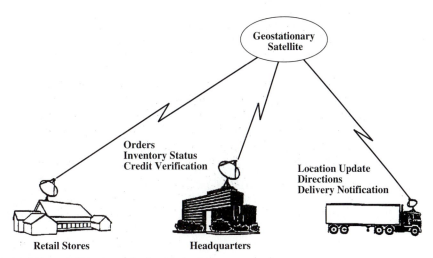

FIGURE 6-7   Logistics satellite communication applications.

also benefits because the system eliminates filing paper documents, reduces the chance that important information will be lost or misplaced, and provides improved credibility with customers.

RF technology, satellite communication capability, and image processing require substantial capital investment prior to obtaining any returns. However, the primary benefit of these communication technologies is not lower cost but improved customer service. Improved service is provided in the form of more timely definition of tasks, quicker shipment tracing, and faster transfer of sales and inventory information. There will be increased demand for these communication technology applications as customers observe the competitive benefits of real-time information transfer.

Bar Coding and Scanning

Information collection and exchange are critical for logistics information management and control. Typical applications include tracking receipts at the warehouse and sales at the grocery store. In the past, collection and exchange were done manually with error-prone and time-consuming paper-based procedures. Bar coding and electronic scanning are identification technologies that facilitate logistics information collection and exchange. Although these auto identification (ID) systems require significant capital investment for users, increased domestic and international competition is encouraging shippers, carriers, warehouses, wholesalers, and retailers to develop and utilize auto ID capability in order to compete in today's marketplace. Auto ID allows channel members to quickly track and communicate movement details with a low probability of error.

Bar coding refers to the placement of computer readable codes on items, cartons, containers, and even railcars. Most consumers are aware of the universal product code (UPC) that is present on virtually all consumer products. UPC bar codes, used first in 1972, assign a unique five-digit number to each manufacturer and product. Standardized bar codes reduce errors when receiving, handling, or shipping product. For example, a bar code distinguishes package size and flavor.

While UPC is used extensively in the consumer goods industry for retail check-outs, other channel members desire more detailed information. While retailers are concerned with individual items, shippers and carriers are interested in the contents of pallets or containers. Therefore, a need exists for bar codes to identify cartons, pallets, or containers of products. Although it is possible to have a document listing pallet contents, the paperwork may be lost or damaged while in transit. To provide encoded information that can be attached to the in-transit shipment, a computer readable code is necessary that contains information regarding shipper, receiver, carton contents, and any special instructions. However, incorporating this amount of information into a bar code overwhelms the capability of a ten-digit UPC. The basic problem is that marketers do not want bar codes to take up valuable space on packages because it reduces product information and advertising design space. On the other hand, including more information within existing space would make the codes too small and increase scanning errors.

In order to resolve these problems, bar code research and development have proceeded in a number of directions. Two of the most significant logistics developments are multidimensional codes and container codes. Newer multidimensional codes such as stacked Code 49 and Code 16K and the highly advanced PDF 417 offer the potential for including more encoded information within existing package space. For example, older one-dimensional linear bar codes are able to encode approximately fifteen to eighteen characters per inch. Multidimensional codes such as Code 49 and Code 16K are able to dramatically increase information transfer capability because their design allows them to "stack" one bar code on top of another. Figure 6-8 presents a representative sampling of bar codes. The more advanced codes such as PDF (portable data file) 417 utilize a stacked matrix design that can store 1,800 characters per inch.

Bar code development is proceeding quickly in a number of directions as the

FIGURE 6-8   Bar code examples. (*Symbol Technologies, Inc.*)

PDF 417

Code 1

Code 49

Code 16K

Codablock

Datacode

Softstrip

Vericode

alternatives in Figure 6-8 illustrate. The industry objective is to be able to include as much information as possible in the smallest area. The limitation is that smaller and more compact codes increase the potential for scanning errors. Newer codes incorporate error detection and correction capabilities. Table 6-5 presents an overview of common bar codes.

TABLE 6-5   COMPARISON OF COMMON BAR CODES

Background	Strengths	Weaknesses
Datamatrix (Datacode)		
• Developed for small-item marking	• Readable with relatively low contrast • Density for small numbers of characters	• Limited error correction capability • Proprietary code • Not laser readable • Only readable with expensive area scanner
Codablock 39/128		
• Developed in Europe	• Straightforward decoding based on one-dimensional symbology • Public domain	• No error correction • Low density • Does not support full ASCII
Code 1		
• Most recent matrix code	• Best error correction capability of matrix codes • Public domain	• Limited industry exposure • Not laser readable • Only readable with expensive area scanner
Code 49		
• Developed for small-item marking	• Readable with current laser scanners • Public domain	• No error correction • Low capacity
Code 16K		
• Developed for small-item marking	• Readable with current laser scanners • Public domain	• No error correction • Low capacity
PDF 417		
• Developed to represent large amounts of data in small physical areas • Reduce reliance on EDI (knowledge travels with the label)	• Dramatically increased capacity • Error correction capability • Reads information vertically and horizontally • Public domain	• Requires technological development to reduce scanning cost • Testing required for highly advanced applications

Definitions: *Capacity* refers to the number of characters that can be coded within a specific area. *Public domain* means that the code can be used freely without paying royalties. *Error correction* means that coding errors can be identified and corrected.

TABLE 6-6   BENEFITS OF AUTOMATIC IDENTIFICATION TECHNOLOGIES

- *Shippers.* Improve order preparation and processing; eliminate shipping errors; reduce labor time; improve record keeping; reduce physical inventory time
- *Carriers.* Freight bill information integrity; customer access to real-time information; improved record keeping of customer shipment activity; shipment traceability; simplified container processing; monitor incompatible products in vehicles; reduced information transfer time
- *Warehousing.* Improved order preparation, processing, and shipment; provide accurate inventory control; customer access to real-time information; access considerations of information security; reduced labor costs; receiving accuracy
- *Wholesalers/retailers.* Unit inventory precision; price accuracy at point of sale; improved register checkout productivity; reduce physical inventory time; increased system flexibility

The UCC 128 Serial Shipping Container Code, which is gaining wide acceptance as the international standard, uniquely identifies each container in a shipment and improves routing and traceability. UCC 128 allows manufacturers and distributors to provide container identification from production to point of sale. UCC 128 is used in conjunction with an EDI advance ship notice (ASN), which precisely identifies carton contents. By 1997, it is projected that over 90 percent of all shipments in the medical, retail, apparel, and wholesale drug industry will use UCC 128 symbology.[15] Primary users of UCC 128 are expected to be general merchandise retailers, along with grocery and pharmaceutical industries that will utilize the information for tracking expiration dates, lot numbers, and production dates.

Bar code development and applications are increasing at a very rapid rate. Table 6-6 summarizes the benefits and opportunities available through auto ID technologies. While the benefits are obvious, it is not clear which symbologies will be adopted as industry standards. Standardization and flexibility are desirable to accommodate the needs of a wide range of industries. However, standardization and flexibility also increase cost, making it more difficult for small- and medium-sized shippers, carriers, and receivers to implement standardized technologies. While continued convergence to common standards is likely, surveys indicate that select industries and major shippers will continue to use proprietary codes to maximize their competitive position.

Another key component of auto ID technology is the scanning process, which is the "eye" of a bar code system. A scanner optically collects bar code data and converts them to usable information. There are two types of scanners: handheld and fixed-position. Each type can utilize contact or noncontact technology. Handheld scanners are either laser guns (noncontact) or wands (contact). Fixed-position scanners are either automatic scanners (noncontact) or card readers (contact). Contact technologies require the reading device to actually touch the bar code. This reduces scanning errors but decreases flexibility. Laser gun technology is currently the most popular (65 percent), outpacing wands.[16]

---

[15]"An Innovator Looks to the Future," *Modern Materials Handling,* **47:**2, February 1992, p. 5.
[16]"Bar Coding Continues Gains," *Chain Store Age Executives,* May 1991, p. 162.

Scanner technology has two major applications in logistics. The first is point of sale (POS) in retail stores. In addition to ringing up receipts for consumers, retail POS applications provide accurate inventory control at the store level. POS allows precise tracking of each stockkeeping unit (SKU) sold and facilitates replenishment since actual unit sales can be quickly communicated to the supplier. Tracking of actual sales reduces uncertainty and allows buffer inventories to be removed. In addition to providing accurate resupply and marketing research data, POS can provide more timely strategic benefits to all channel members.

The second logistics scanner application is for material handling and tracking. Through the use of scanner guns, material handlers can track product movement, storage location, shipments, and receipts. While this information can be tracked manually, it is very time-consuming and subject to error. Wider usage of scanners in logistical applications will increase productivity and reduce errors. For example, Walgreens reported that scanning technology automated store replenishment, improved marketing efforts, and decreased total inventories by 8 percent.[17]

Conclusion

The above discussion reviews information technologies that are influencing logistics capabilities and performance. The technical capabilities are increasing so fast that substantial expertise is required to remain knowledgeable. The influx and widespread application of information technology require that logistics managers develop or have access to this expertise. The Frank's Nursery and United Parcel Service sidebars illustrate recent dramatic logistics information technology applications. It is necessary to integrate logistics requirements with current information technology capabilities to maintain a competitive edge in today's business environment.

ELECTRONIC DATA INTERCHANGE STANDARDS

Communication and information standards are essential for electronic data interchange (EDI). Communication standards define the technical characteristics so that the computer hardware can correctly interpret the interchange. Communication standards determine the character sets, transmission priority, and speed. Information standards dictate the structure and content of the document being transmitted. They specifically define the types of documents and the sequence of data when a document is transmitted. Industry organizations have developed and refined two general standards as well as numerous industry-specific standards in an effort to standardize both communication and information interchange.

Although the following review is not intended as a technical reference manual, it is designed to provide some background regarding the standards used in logistics. The specific topics include the communication standards and the information standards, which are also called transaction sets.

---

[17]Faye Brookman, "Innovative Chain Ranks No. 1," *STORES*, April 1993, p. 22.

FRANK'S NURSERY & CRAFTS

Recognition of information technology's benefits has reached into areas of retailing that once seemed unlikely. Frank's Nursery & Crafts—a retail chain of 290 home, gardening, and crafts stores, based in Detroit, Michigan—has become a powerful advocate for high-technology retailing. Over the past three years, Frank's has invested $25 million in technology application, a significant commitment for a company with 1992 sales of $557 million.

The company has recently implemented bar coded merchandise and two communication technologies: a satellite network and wireless RF (radio frequency) scanning. Larry Buresh, vice president of information systems and distribution, says, "We invest to improve customer service."

Nearly 95 percent of Frank's merchandise is now bar coded. An increasing percentage of house plant and nursery vendors now supply bar coded merchandise. Frank's produces internally generated bar code labels for the balance of the inventory, including tie-on tags for plants.

A $4 million satellite network connecting Frank's stores directly to VisaUSA, Inc., has solved a long-standing problem of long checkout lines. The direct linkup has cut credit card authorization time from up to forty-five seconds via phone to just seven seconds. A further benefit is that eliminating the middleman's fees from the previous phone-based procedure has paid for the satellite system. The new system also allows company headquarters to control advertising messages piped in over store speakers, select background music, and control the volume at each location.

By July 1992, all Frank's stores were fully installed with a wireless RF network that utilizes a spread spectrum broadcasting technique. The RF network enabled Frank's to develop two valuable in-store applications for handheld wireless scanners. Both applications, price verification and order entry, were previously paper-based procedures that relied extensively on store personnel labor hours.

Price verification, which is the procedure of matching prices on labels against a price lookup file, was previously done by referencing a master price listing. Many employees preferred to cart the products up to the POS registers and scan the price there rather than use the listing. This process was inefficient and reduced the frequency of price checks. Now, employees need only scan an item's bar code with a handheld wireless scanner and compare the price on the screen to the price on the label. The new process saves time, improves price accuracy, and redirects employee labor hours toward customer service rather than cumbersome administrative tasks.

The order entry application was also developed with the objective of providing more time for store personnel to focus on customer service. Each of Frank's stores is responsible for replenishment of basic in-stock items. Additional quantities for advertised products are the responsibility of corporate merchandisers. In the past, employees would spend hours each day recording the inventory status of thousands of craft and plant products. Now, employees walk up and down the store aisles and scan product bar codes with the handheld wireless scanner. Store personnel compare the scanned on-hand quantity to a computer-generated shelf label containing a target on-hand quantity and then simply enter the necessary replenishment quantity in the scanner. The order is processed in real time by the in-store processor and later sent on to company headquarters for further processing. Frank's estimates that the wireless reorder application has cut total labor hours required for store replenishment by 75 percent. The chain's in-stock position has also significantly improved.

Frank's envisions numerous other future applications for the RF network. Handheld wireless scanners are being phased in for use in physical inventories. Scanner usage is also planned for the company's three distribution centers for (1) receiving applications based on UCC 128 shipping container codes with EDI-based advance shipment notices; (2) item status applications to provide merchandise managers with critical on-order quantity, rate of sale, cost, retail, and other information during store visits; and (3) wireless POS applications on portable cash registers to handle sidewalk and tent sales.

By utilizing information technology, Frank's Nursery & Crafts is "growing" its business in a big way, and in more than just the traditional sense of the words.

From "The Technology Payoff: High Tech Keeps a Retailer from Wilting," *Business Week*, June 14, 1993; and "Frank's Upgrades Technology to Improve Customer Service," *STORES*, June 1993.

TECHNOLOGY AT UPS

United Parcel Service (UPS) is the largest distribution company in the world. In 1992, UPS' revenues were approximately $16 billion and its package and document volume approached 2.9 billion pieces—more than 11 million packages a day for over 1 million regular customers. The company provides manufacturers, wholesalers, retailers, and service companies with a wide variety of ground-based and air package and document service offerings, as well as numerous value-added services.

Prior to 1986, UPS did not rely on information technology to drive its distribution business. At that time, Ken C. "Oz" Nelson, a senior vice president and now chairman and CEO, was selected to head up a Technology Task Force with the strategic objective of fundamentally overhauling company technology and transforming the functional, operations-oriented company into a proficient user of modern technology. The Task Force began with a five-year plan and a $1.5 billion budget. The plan was completed on schedule; however, UPS spent the allotted money well before the five years were up and acknowledges that the effort cost "multibillions." By 1991, UPS' communication network linked 6 mainframes, 250 minicomputers, 40,000 personal computers, and approximately 75,000 handheld units between 1,300 distribution sites around the world.

The company's assessment of necessary strategic information technology applications was based on a highly accurate vision of future markets and customer requirements. Throughout the 1980s, UPS had dominated the surface/ground-based parcel market with its fleet of big brown trucks and timely delivery. However, by the late 1980s company revenues had begun to flatten out as rivals chipped away at UPS' market by utilizing differentiated pricing tactics and innovative technologies for tracing and billing. Surface carriers increasingly compete with air carriers in order to provide reliable, time-definite scheduled delivery service. In the air express segment, time-based management strategies focusing on both time and cost reduction have increased deferred shipment.

UPS is committed to information technology advancement and utilization, with services beyond overnight shipment. This trend is expected to continue into the foreseeable future. Many large shippers desire single-source provision of a complete range of distribution services. As competition heightens, service requirements have become more stringent. Customers are looking to control costs and increase efficiency through greater information. Dick Green, vice president of marketing for UPS, believes that providing information services is now a critical competitive element in the package delivery business. Green says, "We're building toward offering the across-the-board information service that customers are looking for."

UPS has enhanced its service offering through broad applications of three information-based technologies. First, bar coding and scanning allow UPS to selectively track and report on shipment status twenty-four hours a day, seven days per week, simply by calling a toll-free number. This value-added service (MaxiTrac) is available for GroundTrac and air delivery.

Second, UPS delivery drivers now carry computer clipboards that utilize digital pen–based technology to sequence routes and collect delivery information. The clipboard allows the driver to digitally record the shipment recipient's signature to provide receipt verification. The computerized clipboard coordinates driver information, reduces errors, and speeds up delivery.

Third, UPS' most advanced information technology application is the 1993 creation of a national wireless communication network utilizing fifty-five cellular phone carriers. The cellular phone technology allows drivers to transmit real-time tracking information from their trucks to central UPS computers. Wireless mobile technology and system support from UPS' $100 million data center in Mahwah, New Jersey, enable the company to provide electronic data storage and retrieval to track the company's millions of daily deliveries around the globe. To support the company's increased European operations, UPS has also installed a satellite earth station at the Mahwah facility to provide a direct link between the United States and Germany.

UPS is committed to information technology advancement and utilization. The company is prepared to invest an additional $3 billion toward system expansion to meet its future objective: making real-time package tracing a reality by the year 1997.

Sources: "Buyers Take All in Package Slugfest," *Purchasing,* October 22, 1992; "UPS Delivers More to Its Customers," *Sales & Marketing Management,* September 1992; "After a U-Turn, UPS Really Delivers," *Business Week,* May 31, 1993; "Technology Briefs," *Global Trade and Transportation,* June 1993; and "UPS Head Lauded for IS Use," *ComputerWorld,* March 1, 1993.

TABLE 6-7 COMPARISON OF COMMUNICATION TRANSACTION FORMATS

Quantity	Unit	Paper format No.	Description	Price	ANS X.12 format
3	Cse	6900	Cellulose sponges	12.75	IT13 • CA • 127500 • VC • 6900 N/L
12	Ea	P450	Plastic pails	.475	IT1 • 12 • EA • 4750 • VC • P450 N/L
4	Ea	1640Y	Yellow dish drainer	.94	IT1 • 4 • EA • 9400 • VC • 1640Y N/L
1	Dz	1507	6" plastic flower pots	3.40	IT1 • 1 • DZ • 34000 • VC • 1507 N/L

Source: Mercer Management, Inc., reprinted with permission.

Communication Standards

The most generally accepted communication standards are ASC X.12 (American Standards Committee X.12) and UN/EDIFACT (United Nations/Electronic Data Interchange for Administration, Commerce and Transport). X.12 is promoted as the United States' standard, while EDIFACT is used by the United Nations as more of a global standard. Each organization has defined a structure for exchanging common data types between supply chain partners. Experts indicate that the most likely migration path is to EDIFACT standards.[18] Table 6-7 illustrates the difference between communications using paper and electronic format.

Information Standards

Information standards are implemented via transaction sets. A transaction set is a set of codes that describe related electronic documents. Table 6-8 lists the common logistics-related industry-specific standards. For each industry, the transaction set defines the document types that can be transmitted. Documents are related in that they are used for a common logistics activity such as ordering, warehouse operations, and transportation. Table 6-9 lists commonly used logistics transaction sets.

The transaction code indicates whether the electronic communication is a warehouse shipping order (Code 940) or a warehouse inventory status report (Code 941). In addition to the transaction code, a warehouse transaction contains warehouse number, item number, and quantity.

Future Directions

While applications are migrating toward common standards, there is still conflict regarding the ultimate goal. While a single common standard facilitates information interchange between partners in any industry and country, many firms believe that strategic advantage can be achieved only with proprietary EDI capabilities. Proprietary capabilities allow the firm to offer customized transactions that efficiently meet information requirements. While the basic advantage of standard EDI transaction sets is low cost and high flexibility, there are two major disadvantages.

[18]Gregory B. Harter, "What Can We Expect," *Transportation and Distribution,* **34:**4, April 1993, p. 42.

TABLE 6-8   PRIMARY LOGISTICS INDUSTRY EDI STANDARDS

- UCS (Uniform Communication Standards): grocery
- VICS (Voluntary Inter-Industry Communication Standards Committee): mass merchandisers
- WINS (Warehouse Information Network Standards): warehouse operators
- TDCC (Transportation Data Coordinating Committee): transportation operators
- AIAG (Automotive Industry Action Group): automotive industry

First, a standard transaction set must accommodate the needs of all types of users, thus making it more complex. The complexity results because different users require transactions with different characteristics, and a standard transaction set must accommodate them all. For example, the grocery industry requires a five-digit UPC, while the electrical supply industry requires a twenty-digit item code. Standardized logistics EDI transactions must accommodate both. Second, standard EDI transactions do not provide competitive advantage since they can be readily duplicated by competitors.

Many firms resolve this dilemma through the use of value-added networks (VANs). A VAN, illustrated in Figure 6-9, is a common interface between sending and receiving systems. The VAN adds "value" by managing transactions, translating communication standards, and reducing the number of communication linkages. Transaction management includes broadcasting of messages to subsets of

TABLE 6-9   COMMONLY UTILIZED EDI TRANSACTION SETS

Document transaction	UCS number	VICS number
Purchase order	875	850
Purchase order change	876	860
Manufacturer price change to customer	879	in process
Invoice	880	810
Item maintenance	888	N/A
Price sales catalog	N/A	832
Promotion announcement	889	N/A

Document transaction	WINS number
Warehouse shipping order	940
Warehouse inventory status report	941
Warehouse stock transfer shipment advice	943
Warehouse stock transfer receipt advice	944
Warehouse shipping advice (verification)	945
Warehouse inventory adjustment advice	947

Document transaction	TDCC number
Motor carrier shipping information	204
Motor carrier freight details and invoice	210
Motor carrier shipment status inquiry	213
Motor carrier shipment status message	214

Source: Uniform Code Council, Inc., 1992.

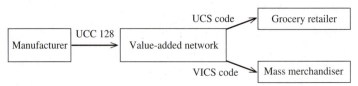

The value-added network collects transaction messages and information from a manufacturer and then translates those messages and information into appropriate industry-specific communication standards.

FIGURE 6-9 Value-added networks (VANs).

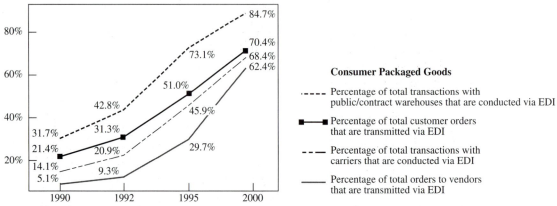

FIGURE 6-10 Growth in EDI usage. (*Bernard J. Lalonde,* Career Patterns in Logistics, *Columbus: Ohio State University, 1992.*)

suppliers, carriers, or customers and receipt of messages from customers using different communication standards.

As Figure 6-10 illustrates, EDI use has demonstrated significant growth in the past, and further growth is expected for the future. While there will be a significant migration to a common standard in EDIFACT, evidence indicates that a number of influential firms will continue to use proprietary standards to create a competitive advantage.

SUMMARY

Information is a major factor for enhancing logistics competitiveness. Information is one of the few resources whose capabilities are increasing while cost is declining. These characteristics uniquely position information as the key technology to enhance logistics planning, operations, and measurement.

Chapter 6 discussed logistics information system functionality and contrasted the differences between transaction systems, management control systems, decision analysis systems, and strategic planning systems. The comparison included the relative applications, cost, benefit, focus, and development strategies for each system level. While the historical logistics focus has been on transaction systems, sophisticated transaction systems alone are not adequate to achieve a competitive advantage.

An important part of Chapter 6 was the discussion of a conceptual logistics information system. The design included planning and coordination to integrate strategic objectives, capacity constraints, logistics requirements, manufacturing requirements, and procurement requirements. Planning and coordination also control product manufacturing and allocation activities. The design included operations flow, which controls order receipt and fulfillment activities. Operations involve order management, order processing, distribution, transportation and shipping, and procurement. Inventory deployment and management is the interface that controls the inventory necessary to maintain optimal production and order fulfillment efficiencies. This conceptual design elaborated the information model first introduced in Chapter 2.

The next section reviewed major information technologies affecting logistics operations. The technologies include EDI, personal computers, artificial intelligence/expert systems, communications, and bar coding and scanning. Each technology was described, with a discussion of logistics applications and benefits.

Improved information technology lowers processing cost for orders, reduces planning and operating uncertainty, and assists an enterprise in meeting strategic objectives. Best practice logistics firms find that it is less expensive to manipulate information than to move inventory. However, information can provide a competitive advantage only when it can support transaction, management control, decision analysis, and strategic planning capabilities. Chapter 7 discusses forecasting, an integral part of developing logistical information requirements.

QUESTIONS

1 Compare and contrast the primary focus of the different levels of LIS functionality.
2 Explain the notion of *exception-based* LIS capability. Why is it critical to corporate planning and operations?
3 How and why does inventory deployment and management act as the primary interface between planning/coordination and operations in the logistics information flow?
4 How has development of the personal computer influenced logistics management?
5 How do communication technology applications assist logistics in providing improved customer service?
6 How do bar coding and scanning technologies facilitate information collection and exchange throughout the supply chain?
7 Discuss and illustrate the concept of substituting information for inventory.
8 What is the difference between a communication standard and an information standard for EDI transactions?
9 What is a VAN (value-added network), and how does it resolve the disadvantages of different EDI transaction sets?
10 How does information technology facilitate formalization of operating processes?

FORECASTING

GENERAL FORECAST CONSIDERATIONS
    The Nature of Demand
    Forecast Components
    Forecast Approaches
THE FORECAST PROCESS
    Forecast Technique
    Forecast Support System
    Forecast Administration
    Conclusion

FORECAST TECHNIQUES
    Technique Categories
    Forecast Error
SUMMARY
QUESTIONS

Forecasts drive logistics information system planning and coordination. A forecast is a projection or prediction of the volume or number of units that will likely be produced, shipped, or sold. The forecast may be specified in unit or dollar terms and may be for an individual item, for a customer, or aggregated across a number of items and customers. A typical logistics forecast is a prediction for weekly or monthly shipments from a distribution center for an individual item. Forecasts may be aggregated across time periods for analysis and reporting.

Production and facility capacity planning and coordination require accurate forecasts. These forecasts and the resulting planning effectiveness allow logistics managers to proactively allocate resources rather than reacting to needs with expensive changes in capacity or inventory. Accurate forecasts allow managers to smooth resource demands to minimize expensive spikes in both capacity and inventory. Forecasting increases logistics effectiveness by enabling exchange and coordination of information rather than inventory. The advanced communications technologies discussed earlier offer many opportunities to share forecasts with customers and with a number of forecast users within an enterprise. Projected cash flow and business activity are based on the strategic objectives forecast. Production and facility capacity demands are based on the capacity constraints forecast. Logistical requirements forecasts determine product allocation to distribution centers, wholesalers, and, to a growing extent, retailers. Manufacturing requirements forecasts influence production schedules, which, in turn, determine procurement requirements. In order to achieve supply chain integration, it is obvious that a common forecast should drive all activities. For example, logistics requirements should consider major marketing promotions so that logistics can operate within capacity constraints. In the past, it was typical for each activity to develop its own forecast, because it was difficult to communicate and develop a common one. However, demands for reduced inventories and information technology advances have brought about increased forecast integration efforts across the firm and throughout the supply chain. Thus, it is necessary to develop a forecast procedure integrating financial, marketing, sales, production, and logistics perspectives. The following section reviews general forecast considerations and then describes a conceptual structure for an integrated forecast process.

Chapter 7 focuses on how to integrate forecasting into logistical information requirements. The first section develops general forecast considerations. It starts with a review of the typical nature of demand, which is then related to forecast components and alternative approaches.

The next section presents a process to guide the development of an effective forecast. It discusses generalized aspects of selecting and supporting a forecast technique. A major aspect of effective forecasting is the administration of the overall forecast process.

The last section focuses on the more technical aspects of forecasting. Specific techniques are introduced and discussed. The section concludes with a discussion of calibration and measurement of forecast error. In total, Chapter 7 positions the role of forecasting as an integral part of meeting logistical information requirements.

GENERAL FORECAST CONSIDERATIONS

Forecasting is the prediction of demands by location, stockkeeping unit (SKU), and time period for the purpose of planning logistics operations. To develop an integrated forecast process, logistics management must consider all possible sources of information and the likely system users. Prior to determining a forecast process, it is important to understand the nature of demand and the major forecast components. Each is discussed.

The Nature of Demand

Forecasted demand can be classified as either dependent or independent. Dependent demand is exemplified by the vertical sequence characteristic of purchasing and manufacturing situations. One example of vertical dependence would be component parts, such as tires, that are assembled to form finished goods, such as automobiles.

In this dependent demand situation, tire requirements *depend* on the automotive assembly schedule. Vertical dependence may extend through several channel levels such as raw material suppliers, component manufacturers, assembly operations, and distributors. Horizontal dependent demand is a special situation where an attachment, promotion item, or operator's manual is included with each item shipped. One example of horizontally dependent demand would be the forecast for tennis balls for a promotion that provides free tennis balls with the purchase of a tennis racket. In this case, the ball forecast *depends* on the tennis racket forecast. In horizontal demand situations, the item demanded is not required to complete the manufacturing process but may be needed to complete the marketing process.

The important point is that estimated demand for a base item is initially determined using forecast, inventory status, and requirements planning. However, once the purchasing or manufacturing plan is defined, component-parts requirements or insertions (e.g., the tires and tennis balls in the prior examples) can be calculated directly and do not need to be forecasted separately. Thus, component item forecast can be derived directly from the forecast of the base item. If there are substantial changes in base item requirements, it may be necessary to modify the component requirements. However, the dependent demand relationship does not change. It is not usually necessary to forecast a dependent demand item since its activity level can be better determined using the base item.

Demand for a given item is independent when it is not related to the demand for another item. For example, demand for a refrigerator is probably not related to the demand for milk. So, forecasting milk will not contribute significantly to improved refrigerator forecasts. Independent demand items, which include most end-use consumer and industrial goods, must be forecasted individually.

Forecasting is both time- and data-intensive. However, when dependent demand exists, the forecaster should take advantage of the situation and forecast only base item requirements. As a rule, dependent relationships should be used whenever possible.

Forecast Components

Logistics requires a forecasted quantity for planning and coordination. The forecast is generally a monthly or weekly figure for each SKU and distribution location. While the forecasted quantity is generally a single figure, the value is actually made up of six components. These components are base demand, seasonal factors, trends, cyclic factors, promotions, and irregular quantities. Assuming that the base demand is the ''average'' sales level, the other components are indexes or factors that are multiplied by the base level to make a positive or negative adjustment.

The resulting forecast model is

$$F_t = (B_t \times S_t \times T \times C_t \times P_t) + I$$

where F_t = forecast quantity for period t

B_t = base level demand for period t

S_t = seasonality factor for period t

T = trend component: quantity increase or decrease per time period
C_t = cyclic factor for period t
P_t = promotional factor for period t
I = irregular or random quantity

While some forecasts may not include all components, it is useful to understand the behavior of each so that it can be tracked and incorporated appropriately. The characteristics of each component are briefly reviewed.

The *base* demand is the quantity that is left after the remaining components have been removed. A good estimate of base demand is the average over an extended time. The base demand is the appropriate forecast for items that have no seasonality, trend, cyclic, or promotional components.

The *seasonal* component is a generally recurring upward and downward movement in the demand pattern, usually on an annual basis. An example is the annual demand for toys, with high demand just prior to Christmas and then low demand during the first three quarters of the year. It can be said that the demand pattern of toys exhibits low seasonality during the first three quarters with peak seasonality for the last quarter. It should be noted that the seasonality discussed above refers to the consumer retail level. Seasonality at the wholesale level precedes consumer demand by approximately one quarter. The seasonality factor or index has an average value of 1.0 for all periods (e.g., months), but individual monthly seasonality factors can range from 0 to 12. An individual seasonality factor of 1.2 indicates that sales are projected at 20 percent above an average period.

The *trend* component is defined as the long-range general movement in periodic sales over an extended period of time. This trend may be positive, negative, or neutral in direction. A positive trend means that sales are increasing across time. For example, the trend for personal computer sales during the decade of the 1990s is increasing. Over the product life cycle, the trend direction may change a number of times. For example, because of a change in people's drinking habits, beer consumption changed from an increasing trend to a neutral trend during the early 1980s. Increases or decreases in trend are dependent on changes in overall population or consumption patterns. A knowledge of which factor impacts sales is significant when making such projections. For example, a reduction in the birthrate implies that a reduction in the demand for disposable diapers will follow. However, a trend toward usage of disposable as contrasted to cloth diapers may cause an increased demand for a specific product category, even though overall market size is decreasing. These are obvious examples of forecast trend. While the impact of trend on short-range logistical forecasts is subtle, it must still be considered when developing the forecast. Unlike the other forecast components, the trend component influences base demand in the succeeding time periods. The specific relationship is

$$B_{t+1} = B_t \times T$$

where B_{t+1} = base demand in period $t + 1$
B_t = base demand in period t
T = periodic trend index

The trend index with a value greater than 1.0 indicates that periodic demand is increasing, while a value less than 1.0 indicates a declining trend.

The *cyclic* component is characterized by swings in the demand pattern lasting more than a year. These cycles may be either upward or downward. An example is the business cycle in which the economy has traditionally swung from recession to expansion every three to five years. The demand for housing is typically tied to this business cycle as well as the resulting demand for major appliances.

The *promotional* component characterizes demand swings initiated by the firm's marketing activities, such as advertising, deals, or promotions. These swings can often be characterized by sales increases during the promotion followed by sales declines as customers work off inventory purchased to take advantage of the promotion. Promotions can be deals offered to the consumer or deals offered only to the trade (wholesalers and retailers). The promotion can be regular and thus take place at the same time each year. From a forecasting perspective, a regular promotion component resembles a seasonal component. An irregular promotion component does not necessarily occur during the same time period, so it must be tracked and incorporated separately. The promotional component is particularly important to track, especially for consumer industries, since it has a major influence on sales. In some industries, promotional sales account for 50 to 80 percent of annual volume. This does not suggest that sales would be only 20 percent of current levels if there were no promotions. It does imply that promotions result in demand that is more ''lumpy'' than would otherwise be the case. The promotional component is different from the other forecasting components in that its timing and magnitude are controlled, to a large extent, by the firm.

The *irregular* component includes the random or unpredictable quantities that do not fit within the other categories. Because of its random nature, this component is impossible to predict. When developing a forecast process, the objective is to minimize the magnitude of the random component by tracking and predicting the other components.

It is beyond the scope of this text to provide a detailed discussion of how to calculate each forecast component. Several texts provide such detailed calculations.[1] The important point is that the forecaster must recognize the potential impact of different components and treat them appropriately. For example, the treatment of a seasonal component as a trend component reduces forecast accuracy over time. The components that are significant to a particular item situation must be identified, analyzed, and incorporated with appropriate forecast techniques.

Forecast Approaches

Forecasts can be developed from two perspectives, the top-down approach and the bottom-up approach.

---

[1]Many of the texts used for business statistics provide detailed discussions of the methodology. A particularly good treatment is provided by Lawrence L. Lapin, *Statistics for Modern Business Decisions*, Fort Worth, Tex.: Dryden Press, 1993, pp. 339–436.

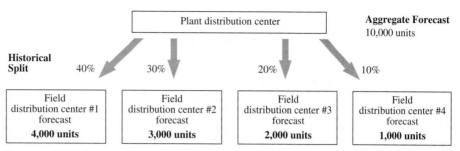

FIGURE 7-1 Top-down forecast example.

Top-Down Approach The top-down or decomposition approach, as illustrated in Figure 7-1, develops a national level SKU forecast and then spreads the volume across locations on the basis of historical sales patterns. As an example, suppose the aggregate monthly forecast for the entire country is 10,000 units. Assume that the firm uses four distribution centers to service the demand with a historical split of 40, 30, 20, and 10 percent, respectively. In this situation, forecasts for individual distribution centers are projected to be 4,000, 3,000, 2,000, and 1,000, respectively.

Forecast management must select the best approach for each particular situation. The top-down approach is centralized and appropriate for stable demand situations or when the demand levels are changing uniformly throughout the market. For example, when demand levels are increasing 10 percent uniformly across all markets, the use of the top-down approach facilitates development of new detailed forecasts, since all changes are relative.

Bottom-Up Approach On the other hand, the bottom-up approach is decentralized since each distribution center forecast is developed independently. As a result, each forecast can more accurately track and consider demand fluctuations within specific markets. However, the bottom-up approach requires more detailed record keeping and makes it more difficult to incorporate systematic demand factors such as the impact of a major promotion.

While forecast management does not have to accept one alternative at the expense of the other, an acceptable combination must be selected. The correct combination must trade off the detail tracking of the bottom-up approach with the data manipulation ease of the top-down approach.

THE FORECAST PROCESS

Logistics planning and coordination require the best possible estimate of SKU-location demand. Although forecasting is far from an exact science, a growing number of enterprises are implementing integrated forecasting processes that incorporate data from multiple sources, sophisticated mathematical and statistical

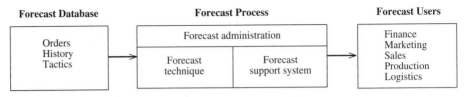

FIGURE 7-2   Effective forecast process.

techniques, elaborate decision support capability, and trained and motivated personnel.

The time horizon for logistics operational forecasts is normally one year or less. Depending on the plan's intended use, forecasts may be required on a daily, weekly, monthly, quarterly, semiannual, or annual basis. The most common forecast period is one month. The important requirement is that the basic planning horizon be selected to accommodate logistical operations.

An effective forecasting process requires a number of key components. Figure 7-2 illustrates the components and their interrelationships. First, the foundation of the forecasting process is the forecast database, which includes information such as orders, order history, and the tactics that were used to obtain those orders such as promotions, special deals, or strikes. Other environmental data, such as the state of the economy and competitive actions, should also be included. In order to support effective forecasting, this database must contain timely historical and planning information in a manner facilitating its manipulation, summarization, analysis, and reporting. The specific database requirements include flexibility, accuracy, maintainability, and timeliness.

Second, an effective forecasting process must develop an integrated, consistent forecast that supports the needs of users (i.e., finance, marketing, sales, production, and logistics). In particular, users require accurate, consistent, detailed, and timely output.

Finally, the development of an effective forecast requires a procedure that integrates three components: forecast technique, forecast support system, and forecast administration. Each component is described.

Forecast Technique

The forecast technique is the mathematical or statistical computation used to translate numerical parameters, including history, into a forecast quantity. Techniques include time-series modeling, in which sales history is a major factor, and correlation modeling, in which relationships with other independent variables are the major factor. Selected forecast techniques are discussed in detail in the next section. Techniques alone cannot deal with the complexities that are experienced in modern business forecasting. As a result, it is increasingly apparent that accurate forecasting requires integration of the forecast techniques with appropriate support and administrative systems.

Forecast Support System

The forecast support system includes the data manipulation capability to gather and analyze data, develop the forecast, and communicate the forecast to relevant personnel and planning systems. This component supports the maintenance and manipulation of the data and allows consideration of external forecast factors such as the impact of promotions, strikes, price changes, product-line changes, competitive activity, and economic conditions. The system must be designed not only to allow these changes but actually to encourage them. For example, the marketing manager may know that the promotion scheduled for next month is likely to increase sales by 15 percent. However, if it is difficult to change the forecast figures for next month, the adjustment may not be done. Similarly, when a package size change is announced, it is obvious that the future forecast history should be changed to reflect the new package size. If this is difficult to accomplish within the constraints of the system, the individual completing the forecast will probably not make the adjustments. It is thus very important that an effective forecasting process include a support system to facilitate the maintenance, update, and manipulation of the historical database and the forecast. While it is not difficult to understand why this ability to make adjustments is necessary, it is often difficult to operationalize for thousands of SKUs at multiple locations. This combination of SKUs and locations means that many thousands of data points must be maintained on a regular basis. In order to complete this maintenance effectively, the forecast support system must include significant automation and exception procedures.

Forecast Administration

Forecast administration includes the organizational, procedural, motivational, and personnel aspects of the forecast function and their integration into the other firm functions. The organizational aspect concerns individual roles and responsibilities. Specific questions include: (1) Who is responsible for developing the forecast? (2) How is forecast accuracy and performance measured? and (3) How does forecast performance affect job performance evaluation and rewards? Procedural aspects concern individual understanding of the relative impact of forecasting activities, information systems, and techniques. Specific questions include: (1) Do forecast analysts understand how their actions influence logistics coordination requirements? (2) Are forecast analysts knowledgeable regarding the capabilities of the forecast system, and are these capabilities used effectively? and (3) Are forecast analysts knowledgeable about technique differences?

It is important that these questions be answered in detail when defining the forecast administration function. If these questions are not addressed, forecasting responsibility and measurement often obtain a ''loose'' definition that results in a lack of accountability. For example, if marketing, sales, production, and logistics each develop a forecast independently, there is no integrated forecast and no overall accountability. If an integrated forecast is desirable, it is necessary to specifically define each group's forecast responsibility and then hold them accountable with

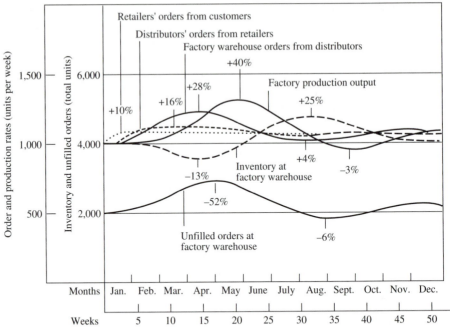

FIGURE 7-3 Response of a simulated production-distribution system to a sudden 10 percent increase in sales at the retail level. (*Jay W. Forrester,* Industrial Dynamics, *Cambridge, Mass.: The MIT Press, 1961; and "Industrial Dynamics,"* Harvard Business Review, **36,** *July–August 1958, p. 43.*)

specific measurements. Effective forecast administration requires that organizational and procedural considerations be well defined. Without them, even though the forecast technique and the forecast support systems are adequate, the overall forecasting process will yield less than optimal performance.

Dynamic modeling illustrates what can happen when there is a lack of forecast coordination across multiple members of the supply chain. From initial stimulant to feedback, the cost of direct communication of sales or forecasts is overshadowed by the cost of a faulty message. Since a great deal of logistical action is initiated in anticipation of future transactions, communications containing overly optimistic predictions or projections may stimulate a fever of ultimately useless work. Analysis of communications between channel members suggests that anticipation has a tendency to amplify as it proceeds between participants in a logistical network. Each error in the interpretation of transaction requirements creates a disturbance for the total logistical channel. In his classic work, Forrester simulated channel interrelationships to demonstrate how the total channel may enter into an oscillating corrective pattern, resulting in a series of over-and-under adjustments to real market requirements.[2] Figure 7-3 illustrates the channel inventory oscillations that were simulated when the retailer increased demand by 10 percent.

---

[2]Jay W. Forrester, *Industrial Dynamics,* Cambridge, Mass.: The MIT Press, 1961; and "Industrial Dynamics," *Harvard Business Review,* **36,** July–August 1958, p. 43.

TABLE 7-1   FORECAST IMPROVEMENTS NEEDED

Area needing improvement	System component	Percentage of companies
Systems to analyze forecast errors	Support system	36
Systems to revise forecasts	Support system	34
Sophistication of forecast techniques	Techniques	32
Documentation of forecast procedures and assumptions	Administration	30
Management control in forecasting	Support system	25
Data processing resources	Support system	24
Management education in using forecasts	Administration	22
Management performance changes	Support system	21
Specialized staff	Support system	16

Adapted from D. H. Drury, "Issues in Forecasting Management," *Management International Review,* **30:**4, 1990, p. 324.

By the very nature of its mission, a distribution channel must be sensitive to transaction requirements. The system stands ready to initiate the logistical process upon receipt of a message. Extreme care must be taken to structure the communication function with a high degree of reliability while retaining the flexibility required for change and adaptation.

Conclusion

As Figure 7-2 previously illustrated, it is important to realize that an optimum design requires an integrated and consistent combination of components. Historically, it was thought that intensive effort in one of the individual components such as technique could overcome problems in the other components. The design process must adequately consider the strengths and weaknesses of each individual component and design for the optimal performance of the integrated system. To illustrate this point, many logistics managers are reviewing current forecasting processes. A survey of 234 Canadian companies identified improvement initiatives and the percentage of companies undertaking them. Table 7-1 summarizes the results. They indicate many forecast problems concerning support systems and administration and fewer problems with forecast technique. These results are supported by the number of companies reporting initiatives in forecast systems development, documentation, and control. Failure to improve these forecast areas constrains the firm's ability to improve forecast accuracy. Examples of the design and implementation of an integrated forecast process are provided by G. E. Silicones and Nabisco Foods.[3]

Even though the forecast technique is only one component of the overall forecast process, it is useful to understand the breadth of techniques available and the measures to evaluate them. The following section presents a sample.

[3]Robert M. Duncan, "Quality Forecasting Drives Quality Inventory at G. E. Silicones," *Industrial Engineering,* **24:**1, January 1992, pp. 18–21; and David J. Closs, Susan L. Oaks, and Joseph P. Wisdo, "Design Requirements to Develop Integrated Inventory Management and Forecasting Systems," *Annual Proceedings of the Council of Logistics Management,* **II,** 1989, pp. 233–259.

FORECAST TECHNIQUES

Logistical forecasting requires the selection of appropriate mathematical or statistical techniques to generate periodic forecasts. The effective use of a technique requires matching the characteristics of the situation with the abilities of the technique. In their classical article, Makridakis and Wheelwright suggest the following criteria for evaluating the applicability of a technique: (1) accuracy, (2) the forecast time horizon, (3) the value of forecasting, (4) the availability of data, (5) the type of data pattern, and (6) the experience of the forecaster.[4] Each alternative forecast technique must be evaluated both qualitatively and quantitatively with respect to these criteria.

There are literally hundreds of articles describing approaches and effectiveness of forecasting alternatives. During the last four decades, forecasting techniques have become increasingly complex because of the addition of advanced statistical and analytical capabilities. The general development assumes that greater complexity and sophistication result in improved forecast accuracy. While this is often true, considerable research has indicated that simpler is sometimes better. The more sophisticated techniques do not always provide significantly better results, particularly when one considers the resource requirements, in terms of both information and expertise.[5]

While it would be advantageous to be able to identify a specific forecast technique (simple or complex) that is appropriate for each application, the development and evaluation of forecast techniques are not that exact. The selection of the appropriate technique is much more of an art than a science. Simply stated, logistical management should choose the technique or techniques that provide the best results. The concept of focus forecasting illustrates one approach that is based on results.[6] Focus forecasting incorporates a number of techniques ranging from very simple to reasonably complex. For each time period, multiple forecasts are generated for each SKU. Focus forecasting then applies the forecast using the technique that would have been the most accurate if it was used for the most recent historical time period. For example, suppose that it was necessary to create a forecast for June. At the end of May, focus forecasting would create a forecast for May with all the data available from the end of April, applying a number of techniques. The May forecast for each technique is compared with May's actual sales to determine which technique *would* have been the most accurate for May. The assumption is that the best technique for June is the one that would have been best for May.

Technique Categories

There are three categories of forecast techniques: qualitative, time series, and causal. The qualitative techniques use data such as expert opinion and special

---

[4]Spyros Makridakis and Steven C. Wheelwright, ''Forecasting: Issues and Challenges for Marketing Management,'' *Journal of Marketing,* **55,** October 1977, pp. 24–37.

[5]For a detailed analysis of the results, see J. Scott Armstrong, ''Forecasting by Extrapolation: Conclusions from 25 Years of Research,'' *Interfaces,* **14:**6, November–December 1984, pp. 52–66.

[6]Bernard T. Smith and Oliver W. Wight, *Focus Forecasting: Computer Techniques for Inventory Control,* New York: Van Nostrand Reinhold, 1978.

information to forecast the future. A qualitative technique may or may not consider the past. Time-series techniques focus entirely on historical patterns and pattern changes to generate forecasts. Causal techniques, such as regression, use refined and specific information regarding variables to develop a relationship between a lead event and forecasted activity.

Qualitative Techniques   Qualitative techniques rely heavily on expertise and are quite costly and time-consuming. They are ideal for situations where little historical data and much managerial judgment are required. Using input from the sales force as the basis to forecast for a new region or a new product is an example. However, qualitative methods are generally not appropriate for logistics because of the time required. Qualitative forecasts are developed using surveys, panels, and consensus meetings. The next sections provide a detailed discussion of time-series and causal techniques.

Time-Series Techniques   Time-series techniques are statistical methods using historical sales data that contain relatively clear and stable relationships and trends. Time-series analysis is used to identify (1) systematic variations in the data resulting from seasonality, (2) cyclic patterns, (3) trends, and (4) the growth rates of these trends. Once individual forecast components are identified, time-series techniques assume that the future will be similar to the past. This implies that existing demand patterns will continue into the future. The assumption is often reasonably correct in the short term. Thus, these techniques are most appropriate for short-range forecasting. However, unless the demand patterns are reasonably stable, techniques do not always produce accurate forecasts.

When the rate of growth or the trend changes significantly, the demand pattern experiences a turning point. Since time-series techniques use historical demand patterns and weighted averages of data points, they are typically not sensitive to turning points. As a result, other approaches must be integrated to determine when turning points will likely occur.

Time-series techniques include a variety of methods that analyze the pattern and movement of historical data. On the basis of specific recurring characteristics, techniques of varying sophistication can be used. Four time-series techniques are discussed in order of increasing complexity. They are moving average, exponential smoothing, extended smoothing, and adaptive smoothing.

Moving Average   Moving average forecasting uses an average of the most recent period's sales. The average may contain any number of previous time periods, although one-, three-, four-, and twelve-period averages are common. A one-period moving average results in next period's forecast being projected by last period's sales. A twelve-period moving average, such as monthly, uses the average of the last twelve periods. Each time a new period of actual data becomes available, it replaces the oldest time period's data. Thus the number of time periods included in the average is held constant.

Although moving averages are easy to calculate, there are several limitations. Most significantly, they are unresponsive or sluggish to change, and a great amount of historical data must be maintained and updated to calculate forecasts. If the historical sales variations are large, average or mean value cannot be relied on to render useful forecasts. Other than the base component, moving averages do not consider the forecast components discussed earlier.

To partially overcome these deficiencies, weighted moving averages have been introduced as refinements. The weight places more emphasis on recent observations. Exponential smoothing represents a form of weighted moving average.

Mathematically, moving average is expressed as

$$F_t = \sum_{i=1}^{n} \frac{S_{i-1}}{n}$$

where F_t = moving average forecast for period t
$\quad S_{i-1}$ = sales for time period $i - 1$
$\quad\quad n$ = total number of time periods

For example, an April moving forecast based on sales of 120, 150, and 90 for the previous three months is calculated as follows:

$$F_{\text{April}} = \frac{120 + 150 + 90}{3} = 120$$

Exponential Smoothing   Exponential smoothing bases the estimate of future sales on the weighted average of the previous demand and forecast levels. The new forecast is a function of the old forecast incremented by some fraction of the differential between the old forecast and actual sales realized. The increment of adjustment is called the *alpha factor.* The basic format of the model is

$$F_t = D_{t-1} + (1 - \alpha) F_{t-1}$$

where F_t = forecasted sales for a time period t
$\quad F_{t-1}$ = forecast for time period $t - 1$
$\quad D_{t-1}$ = actual demand for time period $t - 1$
$\quad\quad \alpha$ = alpha factor or smoothing constant ($0 \leq \alpha \leq 1.0$)

To illustrate, assume that the forecast for the most recent time period was 100 and actual sales experience was 110 units. Furthermore, assume that the alpha factor is 0.2. Then, substituting,

$$F_t = \alpha D_{t-1} + (1 - \alpha) F_{t-1}$$

$$= (0.2)(110) + (1 - 0.2)(100)$$

$$= 22 + 80 = 102$$

Thus, the new forecast is for product sales of 102 units.

The prime advantage of exponential smoothing is that it permits a rapid calculation of a new forecast without substantial historical records and updating. Thus, exponential smoothing is highly adaptable to computerized forecasting. Depending on the value of the smoothing constant, it is also possible to monitor and change technique sensitivity.

The major decision when using exponential smoothing is selecting the alpha factor. If a factor of 1 is employed, the net effect is to use the most recent period's sales as forecast for the next period. A very low value, such as 0.01, has the net effect of reducing the forecast to almost a simple moving average. Large alpha factors make the forecast very sensitive to change and therefore highly reactive. Low alpha factors tend to react slowly to change and therefore minimize response to random fluctuations. However, the technique cannot tell the difference between seasonality and random fluctuation. Thus, exponential smoothing does not eliminate the need for judgmental decisions. In selecting the value of the alpha factor, the forecaster is faced with a trade-off between eliminating random fluctuations and having the forecast fully respond to demand changes.

Extended Smoothing The basic model can be extended to include trend and seasonality considerations. These techniques are known as *exponential smoothing with trend* and *exponential smoothing with seasonality,* respectively.

Extended exponential smoothing incorporates the influence of trend and seasonality when specific values for these components can be identified. The extended smoothing calculation is similar to that of the basic smoothing model, except that there are three components and three smoothing constants to represent the base, trend, and seasonal components.

Similar to basic exponential smoothing, extended smoothing allows rapid calculation of new forecasts with minimal record keeping. The technique's ability to respond depends on the smoothing constant values. Higher values provide rapid responses but may lead to overreaction. The major characteristic of extended techniques is that they directly consider trend and seasonal components. While this is definitely an advantage, it is also a weakness. Extended techniques are often considered to be overly sensitive because of the inability to correctly segment the individual forecast components. This oversensitivity may lead to forecast accuracy problems.

Adaptive Smoothing Adaptive smoothing provides a regular review of alpha factor validity. The alpha value can be reviewed at the conclusion of each forecast period to determine the exact value that would have resulted in a perfect forecast. Once determined, the alpha factor used to generate the subsequent forecast is adjusted to a value that would have produced a perfect forecast. Thus, managerial judgment is partially replaced by a systematic and consistent method of updating alpha.

More sophisticated forms of adaptive smoothing include an automatic tracking signal to monitor error. When the signal is tripped as a result of excessive error, the constant is automatically increased to make the forecast more responsive to smoothing recent periods. If the recent period sales demonstrate substantial change, increase responsiveness should decrease forecast error. As the forecast error is reduced, the tracking signal automatically returns the smoothing constant to its original value.

TABLE 7-2   FOOTBALL COFFEE CONSUMPTION AND TEMPERATURE

Date	Temperature (°F)	Coffee consumption (000 cups)
9/10	65	21
9/24	42	32
10/1	58	19
10/15	32	29
10/29	28	40
11/12	20	43
9/16	72	18
9/30	62	24
10/14	40	33
10/21	56	24
11/11	25	36
11/18	30	38

$$y = 49.775 - 0.45\,x \qquad r^2 = 0.88$$

where y = coffee consumption
x = temperature

Adaptive smoothing techniques adjust their sensitivity to the current situation. While adaptive techniques are designed to systematically adjust for error, their weakness is that they sometimes overreact by interpreting random error as a trend or seasonal. This misinterpretation leads to increased errors in the future.

Causal Techniques   Forecasting by regression estimates sales for an SKU on the basis of other independent factors. For example, coffee sales at a football game are usually a function of temperature. Lower temperatures result in increased sales. Table 7-2 lists temperature and coffee consumption for the home games over the last two seasons. Using linear regression with temperature as the causal or independent variable, the quantitative relationship is illustrated at the bottom of Table 7-2.[7] The regression equation ($y = 49.775 - 0.45x$) demonstrates that for each degree of temperature increase (x value increases by 1), the coffee consumed declines by 450 cups ($0.450 \times 1°F \times 1,000$ cups). The correlation coefficient, commonly included with regression analysis, defines the proportion of variance in the dependent variable (i.e., coffee consumption) by the independent variable (i.e., temperature). The correlation coefficient can range from 0 to 1 with a value of 1 indicating that the independent and dependent variables perfectly correspond. In this example, change in temperature explains 88 percent of the change in coffee consumption.

If a good relationship can be identified (such as between temperature and coffee consumption), the information can be used to effectively predict requirements. In

[7]The calculations for linear regression can be done on all computer spreadsheets and on most calculators. The formulas and assumptions for regression analysis can be found in basic business statistics texts.

this example, the anticipated requirements for coffee, cups, sugar, and cream can be determined in advance using the weather forecast. Causal or regression forecasting works well when a leading variable such as temperature can be identified. However, such situations are not particularly common for logistics applications. If the SKU forecast is based on a single factor, it is referred to as simple regression analysis. The use of more than one forecast is known as *multiple regression.*

Regression forecasts use the correlation between a leading or predictable event and the dependent SKU's sales. No cause-effect relationship need exist between the product's sale and the independent event if a high degree of correlation is consistently present. A correlation assumes that the forecasted sales are preceded by some leading independent factor such as the sale of a related product. However, the most reliable use of regression forecasting of sales is based on a cause-effect relationship. Since regression can effectively consider external factors and events, causal techniques are more appropriate for long-term or aggregate forecasting. For example, they are commonly used to generate annual or national sales forecasts.

Forecast Error

Forecast accuracy refers to the difference between corresponding forecasts and actual sales. Forecast accuracy improvement requires error measurement and analysis. There are three steps for reducing forecast error. First, appropriate measures must be defined. Second, measurement level must be identified. Finally, feedback loops must be established to improve forecast efforts. Each step is discussed.

Error Measurement   Forecast error can be measured on either an absolute or a relative basis using a number of methods. While forecast error can be defined generally as the difference between actual demand and forecast, a more precise definition is needed for calculation and comparison. Table 7-3 provides monthly unit demand and forecast for a specific personal computer model at a regional distribution center. This example illustrates alternative forecast error measures.

One approach for error measurement is to add the errors over time, such as illustrated in column (4). With this approach, errors are summed over the year and a simple average is calculated. As shown, the average is very near zero even though there are some months with significant error. The concern with this approach is that the positive errors cancel negative errors, masking a significant forecasting problem. In order to avoid this, an alternative approach is to ignore the ''sign'' and evaluate absolute error.

Column (5) illustrates the computation of the absolute error and the resulting mean absolute deviation (MAD). While the MAD approach is often used to measure forecast error, MAD places equal weight on small and large deviations. Another alternative is to square the error and then use the mean squared error for comparing forecast alternatives. Column (6) illustrates the squared error approach. The advantage of squared error is that it penalizes larger errors more than smaller ones. For example, the MAD approach penalizes a forecast deviation of 2 only twice as much as a deviation of 1. The squared error approach penalizes a forecast meas-

TABLE 7-3   MONTHLY PERSONAL COMPUTER DEMAND AND FORECAST

(1) Month	(2) Demand	(3) Forecast	(4) Error	(5) Absolute error	(6) Squared error
January	100	110	−10	10	100
February	110	90	20	20	400
March	90	90	0	0	0
April	130	120	10	10	100
May	70	90	−20	20	400
June	110	120	−10	10	100
July	120	120	0	0	0
August	90	110	−20	20	400
September	120	70	50	50	2500
October	90	130	−40	40	1600
November	80	90	−10	10	100
December	90	100	−10	10	100
Sum	1200	1240	−40	200	5800
Mean	100	103.3	−3.3	16.7[a]	483.3[b]
Percent (error/mean)		3.3%[c]		16.7%[d]	22.0%[e]

a = mean absolute deviation (MAD)
b = mean squared error
c = mean error/mean demand

d = absolute value of mean forecast error/mean demand
e = square root of sum of errors squared/mean demand

urement deviation of 2 four times more than a forecast deviation of 1. The use of the squared error approach penalizes a system more for a few large errors than for a large number of small errors.

Although the mean, absolute, and squared errors are good measures for evaluating individual SKUs and locations, they are not good measures when evaluating aggregate forecast performance. For example, the measures treat a mean error of 40 the same, whether the SKU's monthly demand is 40 or 4,000. The first case illustrates a 100 percent error, which indicates relatively poor forecasting. For the second case, however, the forecast error is 1 percent, which demonstrates very accurate forecasting. To compare forecasts across SKUs and locations with different mean demands, error percentages are usually calculated by dividing a mean error measure by mean demand. The mean error measure can be the absolute measure illustrated in column (4) of Table 7-3 or the squared error measure illustrated in column (6). Table 7-3 shows the two measures and their relative magnitude. The relative measure of squared error (22.0 percent) is much larger than the relative mean forecast error (3.3 percent) because the squared measure penalizes large errors significantly more than small ones. While either relative error measure is appropriate for comparison purposes, the relative forecast using squared error facilitates identification of "problem" SKUs.

Measurement Level   The second step considers measurement level or aggregation. Assuming that individual SKU detail is recorded, forecast error can be

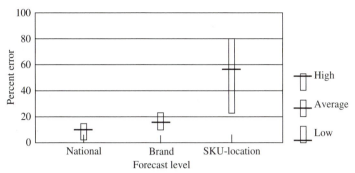

FIGURE 7-4 Range of comparative forecast errors.

calculated for individual SKU-location combinations, for groups of SKUs or locations, and nationally. Generally, more aggregation results in lower relative forecast errors. For example, Figure 7-4 illustrates comparative forecast errors at the national, brand (groups of SKUs), and SKU-location level. Here, relative forecast is calculated using the squared errors. The figure depicts the minimum, maximum, and mean relative forecast error for a sample of firms marketing consumer products. As Figure 7-4 illustrates, while a relative error of 40 percent is average for an SKU-location level of aggregation, it would reflect very poor forecasting if measured at the national level.

There are two considerations when determining level of forecast aggregation. First, less aggregation facilitates problem identification and focuses efforts to improve forecast performance. Second, less aggregation (i.e., more detailed error analysis) requires more computation and storage resources because of the number of SKU-location combinations for the typical firm. However, this is a minor consideration with the availability of low-cost computing and exception-based processing.

As noted in the discussion of current forecast techniques, a major concern is identification and tracking of forecast error. To provide long-term consistency, it is necessary that measurement level(s) be defined and that error be tracked regularly. As Figure 7-4 illustrates, relative forecast error for both individual items and aggregates can be plotted over time to record changes in forecast effectiveness.

Feedback The third step is to establish appropriate forecast feedback loops so that the process can be improved. Forecast improvement results when individuals are motivated to identify problems and improvement opportunities and are recognized with bonuses or competitive rewards. With appropriate motivation, forecasters can identify major sources of error and develop techniques and information to reduce them. In some cases, more sophisticated forecasting techniques, such as focus forecasting, have led to dramatic improvements. In other cases, it is possible to significantly reduce forecast error through improved communication regarding marketing activities such as price changes, promotions, or package changes. When evaluating forecast performance, it is important to recognize that a perfect forecast is not likely and thus expectations should not be set too high.

SUMMARY

Through the forecast, the enterprise establishes common volume goals to guide the entire logistics system. These goals identify the "what, where, and when" of product sales. The objective is to assimilate as much information as possible, analyze it, and develop a forecast with the desired accuracy in a timely manner. With the advent of high-speed communication and information processing at relatively low cost, it becomes imperative that management assess its forecasting ability. Forecast improvements—through either information sharing, thorough analysis, or increased expertise—result in significant inventory reductions.

Chapter 7 positioned forecasting in the overall process of satisfying logistical information requirements. The technology aspects of forecasting may not be as challenging as the integration of the results into logistical operational planning. Attention in Chapters 8 and 9 is directed to inventory management, which represents one of the primary users of forecast results.

QUESTIONS

1   What are the three components of an integrated forecast process, and how are they related?

2   How does the nature of demand affect forecast accuracy?

3   Compare and contrast the role of the forecast support system with forecast administration.

4   What factors are relevant to determine the level of sophistication required for a forecast technique?

5   Other than the starting point, what are the primary differences between top-down and bottom-up forecasting procedures?

6   Why is accountability a major factor in successful forecasting?

7   One company may have several different forecasts to accommodate a single business requirement. Why do you think the multiple forecast practice develops?

8   Compare and contrast the basic logic behind time-series and causal forecast techniques. Under what conditions would each logic be applicable?

9   What is the fundamental difference in logic between moving average and exponential smoothing?

10   If forecast errors are so large, why do businesses place so much emphasis on developing and improving forecasting?

PROBLEM SET A: INFORMATION-FORECASTING

1 Mike McNeely, logistics manager for the Illumi-nation Light Company, has considered replacing the firm's manual customer order management system with electronic ordering, an EDI application. He estimates that the current system, including labor, costs $2.50/order for transmission and processing when annual order volume is under 25,000. Should the order volume equal or exceed 25,000 in any given year, Mr. McNeely will have to hire an ad-ditional customer service representative to assist with order reception in the manual process. This would raise the variable cost to $3.00/order. He has also estimated the rate of errors in order placement and transfer to be 12 per 1,000 orders.

EDI would cost $100,000 up front to implement, and variable costs are determined to be $0.50/order regardless of volume. EDI could acquire and main-tain order information with an error rate of 3 per 1,000 orders. An EDI specialist would be required to maintain the system at all times as well. Her salary would be $38,000 in the first year and would increase 3 percent each year thereafter.

Order errors cost $5.00 per occurrence on aver-age to correct in the manual system. EDI errors cost $8.00 on average to correct, since the specialist in-spects the system for flaws on most occasions.

a If the firm expects order volume over the next five years to be 20,000, 22,000, 25,000, 30,000, and 36,000 annually, would EDI pay for itself within the first five years?

b What effects aside from cost might Mr. Mc-Neely consider when implementing EDI?

2 Mr. McNeely currently batches orders for process-ing under the manual order management system. The orders are batched for daily processing. If Mr. McNeely opts to implement EDI, might this affect his current means of order processing? If so, how?

3 Quality Marketing Technologies, Inc., has hired you as a sales representative. You have been asked to call on Quikee Stop, a small convenience store chain with five locations in your region. What ben-efits of UPC and bar coding applications might you illustrate to encourage Quikee Stop to utilize these technologies to track sales at its retail outlets?

4 Comfortwear Hosiery, Inc., produces men's socks

at its manufacturing facility in Topeka, Kansas. The socks are stored in a warehouse near the factory prior to delivery to distribution centers located in Los Angeles, Memphis, and Dayton. The ware-house uses a top-down forecasting approach when determining the expected quantities demanded at each distribution center.

The aggregate monthly forecast for June is 12,000 pairs of socks. Historically, the Los Angeles distribution center has demanded 25 percent of the warehouse's stock. Memphis and Dayton have de-manded 30 and 35 percent, respectively. The re-maining 10 percent is shipped directly from the warehouse.

a On the basis of the aggregate forecast, how many pairs of socks should you expect each distribution center to demand in June?

b Suppose the aggregate forecast for July results in a 6 percent increase over June's forecast. How many pairs of socks would each distribu-tion center anticipate in July?

5 Ms. Kathleen Boyd, director of logistics for the Scenic Calendar Company, wishes to evaluate two methods of time-series forecasting. She has col-lected quarterly calendar sales data for the years 1993 and 1994.

1993		1994	
Qtr.	Actual sales	Qtr.	Actual sales
1	1,200	1	1,300
2	800	2	800
3	200	3	250
4	1,000	4	1,200

a Use the moving averages technique to find fore-casted sales for the third quarter of 1994 on the basis of actual sales from the previous three quarters.

b Use simple exponential smoothing to forecast each quarter's sales in 1994 given that Ms. Boyd qualitatively forecasted 900 calendars for quar-ter 4, 1993. Ms. Boyd has assigned an alpha factor of 0.1 for time-series sensitivity.

c Repeat the simple exponential smoothing problem above with Ms. Boyd employing an alpha factor of 0.2.

d How well do the moving averages and simple exponential smoothing techniques seem to work in Ms. Boyd's situation? In what ways do the techniques appear to fail?

6 Michael Gregory, logistics manager of Muscle Man Fitness Equipment, has determined that his current forecast system for national sales has historically shown a 20 percent error rate. Because of this level of error, Muscle Man's distribution center managers maintain inventory at their locations costing the company, on average, $3,000 per month.

By improving his forecast methodology and shortening forecast horizons, Mr. Gregory anticipates cutting the error level down to 12 percent. With improved forecasting, Muscle Man's distribution center managers have indicated that they feel comfortable with lower inventory levels. Mr. Gregory anticipates monthly inventory carrying cost reductions of 40 percent.

a If the forecast system improvement will cost $1,000 more per month than the old system, should Mr. Gregory implement the change?

b Why might Muscle Man's customers encourage the firm to improve its forecasting capabilities?

CHAPTER 8

INVENTORY STRATEGY

INVENTORY FUNCTIONALITY AND
   PRINCIPLES
   Inventory Types and Characteristics
   Inventory Functionality
   Inventory-Related Definitions
   Cost of Carrying Inventory
PLANNING THE INVENTORY RESOURCE
   Determining Order Point (When to Order?)
   Determining Lot Size (How Much?)

ACCOMMODATING UNCERTAINTY
   Accommodating Demand Uncertainty
   Performance-Cycle Uncertainty
   Determining Order Point with Uncertainty
   Replenishment Ordering
SUMMARY
QUESTIONS

Inventory decisions are high-risk and high-impact from the perspective of logistics operations. Commitment to a particular inventory assortment and subsequent shipment to a market or region in anticipation of future sales determine a number of logistics activities. Without the proper inventory assortment, marketing may find that sales are lost and customer satisfaction will decline. Likewise, inventory planning is critical to manufacturing. Raw material shortages can shut down a manufacturing line or modify a production schedule, which, in turn, introduces added expense and potential for finished goods shortages. Just as shortages can disrupt planned marketing and manufacturing operations, overstocked inventories also create problems. Overstocks increase cost and reduce profitability through added warehousing, working capital requirements, deterioration, insurance, taxes, and obsolescence.

   Chapter 8 introduces inventory from three perspectives. The first section reviews inventory functionality and principles to establish a common foundation regarding inventory basics. The review describes various inventory types and characteristics including manufacturing, wholesale, and retail. Inventory functionality is then described and illustrated. Next, the section establishes definitions for common inventory terms. Finally, the first section describes inventory carrying cost and its primary components.

The next section discusses basic inventory decision rules. The decisions include inventory tracking, determining when to replenish inventory, and determining the amount to replenish. For each inventory decision, major considerations are reviewed and guidelines are developed. The inclusion of provisions to accommodate freight rates and discounts allows lot sizing to take advantage of operational realities.

The final section extends the discussion of inventory management decision rules to incorporate uncertainty. The introduction of uncertainty makes the decision rules more realistic with respect to the challenges faced in day-to-day inventory management.

INVENTORY FUNCTIONALITY AND PRINCIPLES

Formulating inventory policy requires an understanding of inventory's role in a manufacturing/marketing enterprise. In order to grasp the importance of the inventory, one must envision the magnitude of assets committed in a typical enterprise. Table 8-1 presents sales, net profit, and inventory investment for selected consumer and industrial goods manufacturers and merchandisers. As the table indicates, a significant percentage of assets for many firms are inventory-related. As new products are added, inventory investment increases, resulting in even higher inventory deployment. The magnitude of committed assets and the relative percentage of total resources involved imply that inventory represents a significant cost center. The reduction of a firm's inventory commitment by a few percentage points can provide dramatic profit improvement.

TABLE 8-1   SELECTED DATA FOR CONSUMER AND INDUSTRIAL GOODS MANUFACTURERS AND MERCHANDISERS*

Company	Sales	Net income	Total assets	Inventory investment	Inventories as a % of assets
Johnson & Johnson	13,753	1,030	11,884	1,742	14.70
RJR-Nabisco	15,734	319	32,041	2,776	8.70
Dow Chemical	18,971	276	25,360	2,692	10.60
Bergen Brunswig	5,048	61	1,412	548	38.80
Fleming Companies	12,938	113	3,118	959	30.80
Ace Hardware	1,871	61	595	213	35.80
Kmart	37,724	941	18,931	8,752	46.20
JC Penney	18,009	777	13,563	3,258	24.00
Dillards	4,714	236	4,107	1,106	26.90

*$ millions.
Source: 1992 Annual Reports.

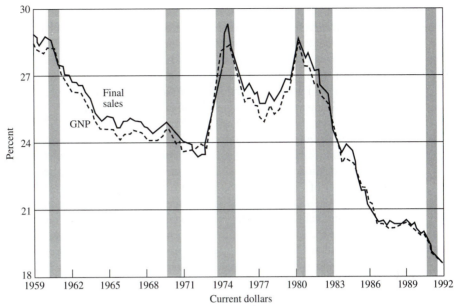

FIGURE 8-1   Inventories as a percentage of both final sales and GNP. (*Robert V. Delaney,* CLI's "State of Logistics" Annual Report, *Cass Logistics, Inc., 1992.*)

Although inventory assets remain substantial, effective inventory management has decreased the amount required to support current sales and GNP (gross national product), as Figure 8-1 illustrates. Even as the number of SKUs has increased through product proliferation, logistics managers have been able to reduce operating inventories. The improvement is due to management focus and implementation of just-in-time and other time-based strategies.

Nevertheless, there is still substantial opportunity for improving inventory productivity. The opportunity arises from the integrated supply chain's ability to use information exchange and management focus to reduce uncertainty and resultant inventories. Reengineering supply chain processes to reduce inventories requires a thorough understanding of inventory elements and dynamics. Each is discussed.

Inventory Types and Characteristics

The holding of inventory is risky because of the capital investment and the potential for obsolescence. First, investments for inventory cannot be used to obtain other goods or assets that could improve enterprise performance. Alternatively, funds supporting inventory investment must be borrowed, increasing the firm's interest expense. A second form of risk is the possibility that the product will be pilfered or become obsolete. These factors and the relative magnitude of assets that are inventory-related contribute substantially to the riskiness of most enterprises. It is important to understand that the nature and extent of risk vary depending on an enterprise's position in the distribution channel.

Manufacturing   For the manufacturer, inventory risk has a long-term dimension. The manufacturer's inventory commitment starts with raw material and component parts, includes work-in-process, and ends with finished goods. In addition, prior to sale, finished goods must often be transferred to warehouses in close proximity to wholesalers and retailers. Although a manufacturer may have a narrower product line than retailers or wholesalers, the manufacturer's inventory commitment is relatively deep and of long duration.

Wholesale   Wholesaler risk exposure is narrower but deeper and of longer duration than that of retailers. The merchant wholesaler purchases large quantities from manufacturers and sells small quantities to retailers. The economic justification of the merchant wholesaler is the capability to provide retail customers with assorted merchandise from different manufacturers in smaller quantities. When products are seasonal, the wholesaler is also forced to take an inventory position far in advance of selling, thus increasing depth and duration of risk.

One of the greatest hazards of wholesaling is product-line expansion to the point where the width of inventory risk approaches that of the retailer, while depth and duration of risk remain characteristic of traditional wholesaling. For example, traditional full-line hardware and food wholesalers have faced a difficult situation during the past decade. Expansion of product lines has increased the width of inventory risk. In addition, their retail clientele has forced a substantial increase in depth and duration by shifting inventory responsibility back to wholesalers. The pressure of product-line proliferation, more than any other single factor, has forced the number of general wholesalers to decline, with specialized operations taking their place.

Retail   For a retailer, inventory management is fundamentally a matter of buying and selling. The retailer purchases a wide variety of products and assumes a substantial risk in the marketing process. Retailer inventory risk can be viewed as wide but not deep. Because of high rents, retailers place prime emphasis on inventory turnover and direct product profitability. Turnover measures inventory velocity and is calculated as the ratio of annual sales divided by average inventory.

Although retailers assume a position of risk on a variety of products, their position on any one product is not deep. Risk is spread across more than 10,000 SKUs in a typical supermarket. A discount store offering general merchandise and food often exceeds 25,000 SKUs. A full-line department store may have as many as 50,000 SKUs. Faced with this width of inventory, retailers attempt to reduce risk by pressing manufacturers and wholesalers to assume greater and greater inventory responsibility. Pushing inventory ''back up'' the marketing channel has resulted in retailer demand for fast delivery of mixed-product shipments from wholesalers and manufacturers. Specialty retailers, in contrast to mass merchandisers, normally experience less width of inventory risk because the lines they handle are narrower. However, specialty retailers must assume greater risk with respect to depth and duration.

If an individual enterprise plans to operate at more than one level of the distribution channel, it must be prepared to assume additional inventory risk. For example, the food chain that operates a regional warehouse assumes risk related to the wholesaler operation over and above the normal retail operations. To the extent that an enterprise becomes vertically integrated, inventory must be managed at all levels of the marketing channel.

Inventory Functionality

The ideal inventory process consists of manufacturing a product to a customer's specifications once an order is placed. This is called a *make-to-order* operation and is characteristic of customized equipment. Such a system does not require stockpiles of materials or finished goods in anticipation of future sales. While a zero-inventory manufacturing/distribution system is not always practical, it is important to remember that each dollar invested in inventory must be traded off against other logistics resources and must demonstrate an effective total cost return.

Inventory is a major area of asset deployment that should provide a minimum return for the capital invested. Accounting experts have long recognized that a measurement problem exists since the typical corporate profit and loss statement does not adequately display the true cost or benefits of inventory investments.[1] Lack of measurement sophistication makes it difficult to evaluate the trade-offs among service levels, operating efficiencies, and inventory levels. Most enterprises carry an average inventory that exceeds their basic requirements. This generalization can be understood better through a careful examination of the four prime functions underlying inventory commitments.

Geographical Specialization   One function of inventory is to allow *geographical specialization* for individual operating units. Because of the requirements for factors of production such as power, materials, water, and labor, the economical location for manufacturing is often a considerable distance from major markets. For example, tires, batteries, transmissions, and springs are significant components in automobile assembly. The technology and expertise to produce each of these components are traditionally located in proximity to material sources in order to minimize transportation. This strategy leads to geographical separation of production so that each automobile component can be produced economically. However, geographical separation requires internal inventory transfer to completely integrate components into final assembly.

Geographical separation also requires inventories to create market assortments. Manufactured goods from various locations are collected at a single warehouse and then combined as a mixed-product shipment. For example, Procter & Gamble uses distribution centers to combine products from its laundry, food, and health care divisions to offer the customer a single integrated shipment. Such warehouses are examples of geographical separation and integrated distribution made possible by inventory.

Geographical separation permits economic specialization between the manufac-

---

[1]Douglas M. Lambert, *The Development of an Inventory Costing Methodology,* Chicago, Ill.: National Council of Physical Distribution Management, 1976, p. 3; and *Inventory of Carrying Cost, Memorandum 611,* Chicago, Ill.: Drake Sheahan/Stewart Dougall, Inc., 1974.

turing and distribution units of an enterprise. When geographical specialization is utilized, inventory in the form of materials, semifinished goods or components, and finished goods is introduced to the logistical system. Each location requires a basic inventory. In addition, in-transit inventories are necessary to link manufacturing and distribution. Although difficult to measure, the economies gained through geographical specialization are expected to more than offset increased inventory and transportation cost.

Decoupling   A second inventory function, *decoupling,* provides maximum operating efficiency within a single manufacturing facility by stockpiling work-in-process between production operations. Decoupling processes permit each product to be manufactured and distributed in economical lot sizes that are greater than market demands. Warehouse inventory produced in advance of need permits distribution to customers in large quantity shipments with minimum freight cost. In terms of marketing, decoupling permits products manufactured over time to be sold as an assortment. Thus decoupling tends to ''buffer,'' or cushion, the operations of the enterprise from uncertainty. Decoupling differs from geographical specialization: the former enables increased operating efficiency at a single location, while the latter includes multiple locations. To a significant degree, modern concepts of time-based competition discussed in Chapter 16 have reduced, but not eliminated, the economic benefits of decoupling.

Balancing Supply and Demand   A third inventory function, *balancing,* is concerned with elapsed time between consumption and manufacturing. Balancing inventory reconciles supply availability with demand. The most notable examples of balancing are seasonal production and year-round consumption. Orange juice is one such product. Another example of year-round production with seasonal consumption is antifreeze. Balancing inventories link the economies of manufacturing with variations of consumption.

The managerial reconciliation of time lags in manufacturing and demand involves a difficult planning problem. When demand is concentrated in a very short selling season, manufacturers, wholesalers, and retailers are forced to take an inventory position far in advance of the peak selling period. For example, in lawn furniture manufacturing, production must be in high gear by early fall for units that will not be sold until the following spring or summer. In early January and February manufacturers' inventories peak and start to decline as orders for furniture begin to flow through the marketing channel on their way to wholesalers and retailers. Retail sales begin in early spring and hit a peak between Memorial Day and Labor Day. However, after July 4 retailing shifts from a seller's market to a buyer's market. Price competition dominates as retailers attempt to reduce inventory and eliminate seasonal carryover. Thus, from a retailer's viewpoint, an inventory position for the entire selling system must be planned six months prior to the peak selling season. Any attempt to supplement inventories after Memorial Day is risky.

Although lawn furniture is an extreme example, almost all products have some seasonal variation. Inventory stockpiling allows mass consumption or mass manufacturing of products regardless of seasonality. The balancing function of inventory requires investment in seasonal stocks that are expected to be fully liquidated within the season.[2] The critical planning problem is how much inventory to stockpile to enjoy maximum sales while minimizing the risk of carryover into the next selling season.

Buffer Uncertainties   The *safety stock* or *buffer stock* function concerns short-range variation in either demand or replenishment. Considerable inventory planning is devoted to determining the size of safety stocks. In fact, most overstocks are the result of improper planning.

The safety stock requirement results from uncertainty concerning future sales and inventory replenishment. If uncertainty exists, it is necessary to protect inventory position. In a sense, safety stock planning is similar to purchasing insurance.

Safety stock protects against two types of uncertainty. The first type concerns demand in excess of forecast during the performance cycle. The second type of uncertainty involves delays in the performance-cycle length itself. An example of demand uncertainty is a customer request of more or less units than planned. Performance-cycle length uncertainty results from a delay in order receipt, order processing, or transportation.

Statistical and mathematical techniques for aiding managers in planning safety stock are developed in Chapter 9. At this point, it is important to realize that the probability and magnitude of each type of uncertainty can be estimated. The function of safety stock inventory is to provide a specified degree of protection against both types of uncertainty.

Conclusion   The four functions of inventory are geographical specialization, decoupling, balancing supply and demand, and buffering uncertainties with safety stock. These functions define the inventory investment necessary for a specific system to execute management's objectives. Given a specific manufacturing/marketing strategy, inventories planned and committed to operations can be reduced only to a level consistent with performing the four inventory functions. All inventories exceeding the minimum level represent excessive commitments.

At the minimum level, inventory invested to achieve geographical specialization and decoupling can be modified only by changes in facility location and operational processes of the enterprise. The minimum level of inventory required to balance supply and demand depends on the difficult task of estimating seasonal requirements. With accumulated experience, the inventory required to achieve marginal sales during periods of high demand can be projected fairly well. A seasonal inventory plan can be formulated based on this experience.

Inventories committed to safety stocks represent the greatest potential for improved performance. These commitments are operational in nature and can be adjusted rapidly in the event of an error or a change in policy. A variety of techniques are available to assist management in planning safety stock commitments. Given these conditions, this chapter focuses on a thorough analysis of safety

---

[2]This type of buying is often referred to as *promotional buying*.

stock relationships and policy formulation. To the extent that an enterprise becomes vertically integrated, inventory must be managed at multiple levels of distribution. The management of staged inventories characteristic of vertically integrated firms is complex because of a need for multilevel policy formulation and control. Regardless of whether the inventory requirement is at the manufacturing, wholesaling, or retailing level, or whether it is single-level or echeloned, the same basic techniques and principles of inventory management apply.

Inventory-Related Definitions

This section reviews definitions related to an inventory management policy. It begins by defining specific terms and relationships that are fundamental to inventory dynamics. The second part discusses the sawtooth relationship between the performance cycle and average inventory.

Inventory Policy   *Inventory policy* consists of guidelines concerning what to purchase or manufacture, when to take action, and in what quantity. It also includes decisions regarding inventory positioning and placement at plants and distribution centers. For example, some firms may decide to postpone inventory positioning by maintaining stock at the plant. Other firms may use a more speculative policy by electing to place more product in local distribution centers to have it closer to the market. The development of sound inventory policy is the most difficult issue within overall inventory management.

The second inventory policy element concerns inventory management strategy. One approach is to manage inventory at each distribution center independently. The other extreme considers inventory interdependence across distribution sites by managing inventory centrally. Centralized inventory management requires more coordination and communication.

Service Level   The *service level* is a target specified by management. It defines the performance objectives that the inventory function must be capable of achieving. The service level can be defined in terms of an order cycle time, case fill rate, line fill rate, order fill rate, or any combination of the above. The performance cycle is the elapsed time between the release of a purchase order by a customer and the receipt of the corresponding shipment. A case fill rate defines the percentage of cases or units ordered that can be shipped as requested. For example, a 95 percent case fill rate indicates that, on average, 95 cases out of 100 could be filled from available stock. The remaining 5 cases would be back-ordered or deleted. The line fill rate is the percentage of order lines that could be filled completely. Each line on an order is a request for an individual product, so an order may have multiple lines. For example, when a customer order is received requesting 80 units of product A and 20 units of product B, the order contains 100 cases and two lines. If there are only 75 units of product A available and all 20 of product B, the case fill would be 95 percent $[(75+20)/(80+20)]$ and the line fill would be 50 percent $(^1\!/_2)$. Order fill is the percentage of customer orders that could be filled completely. In the example above, the order could not be completely filled, so the resulting order fill would be zero.

The inventory function is a major element of the logistics process that must be integrated to meet service objectives. While a traditional approach to achieving a higher service level is to increase inventory, other approaches include use of faster transportation modes, better information management to reduce uncertainty, or alternative sources of supply. While it is the task of overall logistics management to meet the prescribed service objectives, inventory management plays a particular key role.

Average Inventory   *Average inventory* consists of the materials, components, work-in-process, and finished products typically stocked in logistical facilities. From a policy viewpoint, the appropriate level of inventory must be determined for each facility. Average inventories include cycle, safety stock, and transit inventory components. Each is discussed below.

Cycle Inventory   *Cycle inventory,* or *base stock,* is the portion of average inventory that results from the replenishment process. At the beginning of a performance cycle, stock is at a maximum level. Daily customer demands "draw off" inventory until the stock level reaches zero. Prior to this, a replenishment order is initiated so that stock will arrive before a stockout occurs. The replenishment order must be initiated when the available inventory is greater than or equal to the customer demand during the performance-cycle time. The amount ordered for replenishment is called the *order quantity*. The average inventory held as a result of the order process is referred to as *base stock.* Another commonly used term to identify this aspect of inventory is *lot size stock.*[3] Considering only the order quantity, average cycle inventory or base stock equals one-half of the order quantity.

Safety Stock Inventory   The second part of average inventory is the stock held to protect against the impact of uncertainty on each facility. This portion of inventory, as noted earlier, is called *safety stock.* Safety stock inventory is used only at the end of replenishment cycles when uncertainty has caused higher than expected demand or longer than expected performance-cycle times. The basic premise of safety stock is that a portion of average inventory should be devoted to cover short-range variation in demand and replenishment. Given safety stock, average inventory equals one-half of the order quantity plus the safety stock.

Transit Inventory   A subject of special interest is transit inventory, which represents stock that is either moving or awaiting movement in transportation vehicles. This portion of total inventory is referred to as *transit* or *pipeline inventory.* Transit inventory is necessary to achieve order replenishment. From a logistics management perspective, transit inventory introduces two sources of complexity into the supply chain. First, transit inventory represents real assets and must be paid for, even though it is not accessible or usable. Second, there has typically been a high degree of uncertainty associated with transit inventory because shippers were unable to determine where a transport vehicle was located or when it was likely to arrive. While satellite communications have somewhat reduced this un-

---

[3]These terms are used interchangeably.

certainty, shippers still have limited accessibility to such information. Increased focus on smaller order amounts, more frequent order cycles, and just-in-time strategies have resulted in transit inventory becoming a larger percentage of total inventory assets. As a result, greater attention is being directed toward reducing the amount of transit inventory and its associated uncertainty.

A specific enterprise may or may not have legal ownership of transit inventory depending on terms of purchase. If ownership is transferred at shipment destination, inventory in transit is not owned by the consignee. The opposite is true when merchandise ownership is transferred at origin. Under conditions of origin transfer, transit inventory should be treated as part of average inventory.

Example of Average Inventory over Performance Cycles   In initial policy formulation, it is necessary to determine how much inventory to order at a specified time. For purposes of illustration, assume the following conditions. First, let the replenishment performance cycle be a constant 20 days. Second, let the daily sales rate during the replenishment performance cycle be 10 units per day. Third, assume that the ordering enterprise takes ownership of the inventory upon delivery. Fourth, assume that the replenishment order quantity is 200 units. Although such assumptions regarding certainty remove realistic inventory policy formulation complexity, they serve to illustrate basic policy principles.

Figure 8-2 illustrates these relationships. This type of chart is referred to as a *sawtooth diagram* because of the series of right triangles. Since complete certainty exists with respect to replenishment and usage, orders are scheduled to arrive just as the last unit is sold. Thus, no inventory beyond average base stock is held. Since the rate of sale in the example is 10 units per day and it takes 20 days to complete inventory replenishment, a sound reorder policy would be to order 200 units every 20 days. Given these conditions, terminology related to policy formulation can be identified.

First, the reorder point is specified as 200 units on hand. The reorder point defines when a replenishment order is initiated. In this example, whenever the quantity on hand plus the replenishment order from the supplier drops below 200, an additional order for 200 units is placed. Since the reorder point equals the

FIGURE 8-2   Inventory relationship: constant sales and performance cycle.

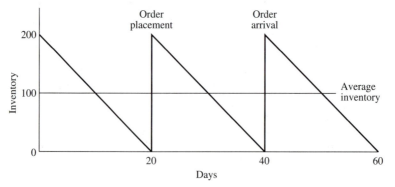

reorder quantity, the daily inventory level ranges from a maximum of 200 (the reorder quantity) to a minimum of zero over the performance cycle. Different approaches to determine reorder quantity are discussed later. Note that it is not particularly common that the reorder point equals the performance-cycle demand.

Second, average inventory is 100 units, since stock on hand exceeds 100 units one-half of the time (10 days) and is less than 100 units one-half of the time. In fact, average inventory is equal to one-half the 200 unit order quantity. Note that this does not consider the transit inventory.

Third, assuming a work year of 240 days, 12 purchases will be required during the year. Therefore, over a period of one year, 200 units will be purchased 12 times (2,400 total units). Sales are expected to equal 10 units per day over 240 days (2,400 total units). As discussed above, average inventory is 100 units. Thus inventory turns will be 24 (2,400 total sales/100 units of average inventory).

In time, the sheer boredom of such routine operations would lead management to ask some questions concerning the arrangement. What would happen if orders were placed more frequently than once every 20 days? Why not order 100 units every 10 days? Why order as frequently as every 20 days? Why not reorder 600 units once every 60 days? Assuming that the inventory performance cycle remains a constant 20 days, what would be the impact of each of these alternative ordering policies on reorder point, average base inventory, and inventory turnover?

The policy of ordering a smaller volume of 100 units every 10 days means that two orders will always be outstanding. Thus the reorder point would remain 200 committed units on hand or on order to service average daily sales of 10 units over the 20-day inventory cycle. However, average inventory on hand would drop to 50 units, and inventory turnover would increase to 48 times per year. The policy of ordering 600 units every 60 days would result in an average base inventory of 300 units and a turnover of approximately 8 times per year. These alternative ordering policies are illustrated in Figure 8-3.

The figure demonstrates that average inventory is a function of the reorder quantity and that lower quantities result in lower average inventory. While the prior example suggests that smaller reorder quantities result in lower inventory

FIGURE 8-3   Alternative order quantity and average inventory.

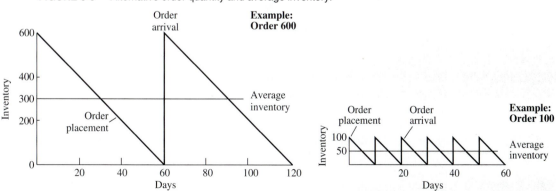

levels, there are other factors such as performance-cycle uncertainties, purchasing discounts, and transportation economies that should be considered when determining the most desirable inventory policy.

An exact policy concerning order quantity can be calculated by balancing the cost of ordering and the cost of maintaining average inventory. The economic order quantity (EOQ) model provides a specific answer to the balancing of these two critical cost components. By determining the EOQ and dividing it into forecasted annual demand, the frequency and size of order that minimize the total cost of inventory are identified. Prior to reviewing EOQ, it is necessary to identify costs typically associated with ordering and maintaining inventory.

Cost of Carrying Inventory

Inventory carrying or maintenance cost is the cost associated with holding inventory. It is a major component of logistical operating cost. As discussed in Chapter 1, the carrying cost accounts for approximately 37 percent of total logistics cost for the average manufacturing enterprise. Inventory carrying cost is generally computed by multiplying the carrying cost percentage by the average inventory value. Since inventory amounts to a larger relative percentage of assets for wholesalers, distributors, and retailers, the carrying cost is a relatively higher percentage of total logistics cost for them compared to manufacturers.

This section discusses inventory carrying cost from three perspectives. First, the development of an appropriate carrying cost percentage is described and illustrated. Second, the carrying cost impact on enterprise finances is discussed. Third, the influence that the carrying cost percentage can have on logistics decisions and strategies is reviewed.

Determining Inventory Carrying Cost Percentage Inventory carrying cost is the financial charge that results from assessing the carrying cost percentage against the average value of inventory. For example, assuming carrying cost of 20 percent, the annual inventory cost for an enterprise with $1 million in average inventory is $200,000 (20 percent $\times$ $1,000,000). While the calculation of carrying cost is obvious, determining the appropriate carrying cost percentage is not straightforward.

Finding the cost of maintaining inventory requires management judgment, estimation of average inventory levels, assignment of inventory-related costs, and a degree of direct measurement. The accounts traditionally included in the cost of maintaining inventory are capital, insurance, obsolescence, storage, and taxes. The final figure should be expressed as an annual percentage value applied to average inventory. Determination of the cost of maintaining inventory across a broad group of products or raw materials requires substantial analysis. While cost of capital can be applied to average inventory holdings, expenses associated with insurance, obsolescence, storage, and taxes may vary depending on the specific attributes of each product. Once agreement has been reached on the appropriate figure for computing inventory carrying cost, that figure should be held constant during logistical system analysis.

TABLE 8-2 INVENTORY CARRYING COST COMPONENTS

Element	Average	Ranges
Capital cost	15.00%	8–40%
Taxes	1.00	0.5–2
Insurance	0.05	0–2
Obsolescence	1.20	0.5–2
Storage	2.00	0–4
Totals	19.25%	9–50%

Capital Cost   The most controversial aspect of maintenance cost is the appropriate charge to place on invested capital. Experience with a variety of enterprises indicates that figures range from the prevailing prime interest rate to 25 percent.[4] The logic for using the prime interest rate or a specified rate pegged to the prime rate is that cash to replace capital invested in inventory can be purchased in the money markets at that rate. Higher managerially specified rates are based on an expected target return on investment for all funds available to the enterprise. This target rate is often called a "hurdle" rate. Any funds invested in inventory lose their earning power, restrict capital availability, and limit other investment.

Confusion may result from the fact that top management frequently does not establish a clear-cut capital cost policy to be applied uniformly in decision making. For logistical planning, the cost of capital must be thought out clearly since the final rate of assessment will have a profound impact on system design. Table 8-2 illustrates the mean and range of capital cost percentages for a number of manufacturing firms.

Taxes   Some locations tax inventory as property while it is held in distribution facilities. The tax rate and means of assessment usually differ by location. Typically, the tax cost is a direct levy based on the inventory level on a specific day of the year or average inventory level over a period of time. Some locations do not assess any inventory tax. Table 8-2 reviews typical tax assessments as a percentage of inventory value.

Insurance   Insurance cost is a direct levy normally based on estimated risk or exposure over time. Risk and exposure depend on the nature of both the product and the storage facility. For example, high-value products that are easily stolen and hazardous products that are combustible result in relatively higher insurance cost. Insurance cost is also influenced by facility preventative characteristics such as security cameras and sprinkler systems. The mean and range for insurance cost percentages are presented in Table 8-2.

Obsolescence   Obsolescence is the deterioration of product in storage and is not covered by insurance. The cost calculations are based on past experience in terms of the amount of product that must be marked down, given away, or destroyed. Obsolescence also can be expanded to include marketing loss when a

---

[4]For a list of thirteen different approaches to arrive at this figure, see Douglas M. Lambert, *The Development of an Inventory Costing Methodology,* Chicago, Ill.: National Council of Physical Distribution Management, 1976, pp. 24–25.

product becomes obsolete in terms of model design. The assignment or obsolescence cost should be approached with caution and should be limited to direct loss related to inventory storage. Charges related to obsolescence should be expressed as a percentage of average inventory, as Table 8-2 illustrates.

Storage   Storage cost covers facility expenses related to product holding rather than product handling. The cost must be allocated to specific products since it is not related directly to inventory value. Depending on the type of warehouse facility used (e.g., public or private), total storage charges may be direct or may require allocation. With privately owned facilities, the total annual depreciated expense of the warehouse must be calculated in terms of a standard measure such as cost per day per square or cubic foot. The cost of total annual occupancy for a given product can then be assigned by multiplying the daily occupied physical space by the standard cost factor for the year. This figure can then be divided by the total number of units of merchandise processed through the facility to determine average storage cost per merchandise unit. For public warehouses, charges typically include a storage component that is assessed on inventory at the end of each month. From a public warehouse operations perspective, monthly storage charges are based on space utilization in order to cover fixed costs of the storage facility. Table 8-2 illustrates typical inventory storage assessments.

Conclusion   As Table 8-2 illustrates, a typical annual inventory carrying cost is near 20 percent, but it may range from 9 to 50 percent depending on enterprise policies. The carrying cost percentage is assessed against the average inventory value for each SKU and distribution location. The resulting inventory carrying cost can then be traded off against other logistics cost components to finalize logistical management policies.

Impact on Financial Records   Unlike the other logistics cost elements such as transportation or warehousing that are usually included in an enterprise's profit and loss statement, inventory carrying cost is not as apparent. Table 8-3 illustrates the profit and loss statement and balance sheet for a typical manufacturer or merchandiser. While the inventory itself turns up as an asset on the balance sheet, there is usually no corresponding entry for inventory carrying cost.

The major element of inventory carrying cost results from the capital invested in inventory. For example, having a $105,000 inventory implies that there is $105,000 less in capital available for other uses. Specifically, the $105,000 must be borrowed as working capital to pay for the inventory, otherwise retained earnings must be reduced by $105,000 to pay for it. In the first case, the enterprise must pay interest on the borrowed funds. In the second case, the firm cannot invest the retained earnings for other capital projects.

While inventory carrying cost is not a direct entry on the profit and loss statement, it should be clear from the previous discussion that carrying costs do make a significant impact on the enterprise's financial activities. Although the presence of carrying cost on the financial statements is not as obvious as other logistics cost elements such as transportation, it is still very significant and real.

Impact on Decisions and Strategy   As discussed above, there is some discretion with respect to determining an enterprise's carrying cost percentage. Some

TABLE 8-3   TYPICAL MANUFACTURER'S PROFIT AND LOSS STATEMENT AND BALANCE SHEET

Income Statement

Sales		$4,000,000
Cost of goods sold:		
Beginning finished goods inventory	$ 500,000	
Cost of goods manufactured	2,400,000	
Goods available for sale	$2,900,000	
Ending finished goods inventory	(300,000)	2,600,000
Gross margin		$1,400,000
Operating expenses:		
Selling expenses	$ 600,000	
Administrative expenses	300,000	(900,000)
		$ 500,000

Balance Sheet

Current assets:		
Cash	$ 120,000	
Accounts receivable	300,000	
Raw materials inventory	50,000	
Finished goods inventory	55,000	
Total current assets		$ 525,000
Fixed assets:		
Land	$2,500,000	
Building and equipment	9,000,000	
Accumulated depreciation	(4,500,000)	
Total fixed assets		7,000,000
Total assets		$7,525,000
Current liabilities:		
Accounts payable		$ 100,000
Owner's equity:		
Common stock	$ 600,000	
Retained earnings	6,825,000	
Total owner's equity		7,425,000
Total liabilities and equity		$7,525,000

firms use low carrying cost percentages such as 12 percent, with the argument that the appropriate capital cost is their internal cost of funds. Other enterprises apply higher percentages such as 40 percent, using the argument that capital invested in inventory should be assessed the same charge as capital invested for other uses. The impact of each approach is discussed next.

A relatively low carrying cost percentage reduces inventory influence on total cost decisions and makes transportation cost relatively more important. As a result, logistics total cost decisions and strategies would attempt to minimize transportation expenses by using more distribution centers, which maintains product closer to markets. Additional distribution centers typically require additional inventory since more sites require additional safety stock. Thus, lower carrying cost percentages result in strategies that replace expensive transportation with relatively cheaper inventory. Conversely, relatively high carrying cost percentages divert logistics strategies in the opposite direction and thus result in efforts to centralize inventory in a small number of locations and allow for longer (and therefore more expensive) transportation movements.

In conclusion, although enterprises use wide discretion when determining the appropriate carrying cost percentage, the decision must accurately reflect the capital cost component since the percentage and resulting relative magnitude of inventory carrying cost will significantly influence optimum logistics strategy.

PLANNING THE INVENTORY RESOURCE

The previous sections reviewed inventory's role in the value-added process and documented the cost of holding or maintaining inventory. This section describes the key parameters and procedures for planning inventory. The discussion focuses on three issues: when to order, how much to order, and inventory control procedures. The descriptions of procedures and parameter development pertain to an individual distribution center. While centers for a particular enterprise may use the same procedures, there will likely be different parameters since the demand and replenishment environment are different for each facility.

Determining Order Point (When to Order?)

As discussed earlier, the reorder point determines when a resupply shipment should be initiated. The reorder point, which is defined by item and distribution center, can be specified in terms of units or days of supply.

This discussion focuses on determining reorder points under conditions of demand and performance-cycle certainty. The certainty conditions imply that future demands and performance-cycle lengths are known.

The basic reorder point formula is

$$R = D \times T$$

where R = reorder point in units
D = average daily demand
T = average performance-cycle length

To illustrate this calculation, assume demand of 10 units/day and a 20-day performance cycle. In this case,

$$R = D \times T$$
$$= 10 \text{ units/day} \times 20 \text{ days} = 200 \text{ units}$$

The use of the reorder point formulations discussed above implies that the resupply shipment will arrive just as the last unit is shipped to a customer. This approach is satisfactory as long as both demand and performance cycle are certain. When there is uncertainty in either demand or performance-cycle length, an inventory buffer is necessary to compensate for the uncertainty. The buffer, which is usually called *safety stock,* handles customer demands during longer than expected performance cycles or above average daily demand. When this buffer stock is necessary for conditions of uncertainty, the reorder point formula is

$$R = D \times T + \text{SS}$$

where R = reorder point in units
      D = average daily demand
      T = average performance-cycle length
    SS = safety or buffer stock in units

Computation of safety stock requirements under conditions of uncertainty is discussed later in the chapter.

Determining Lot Size (How Much?)

The lot sizing concept balances the cost of maintaining inventories against the cost of ordering. The key to understanding the relationship is to remember that average inventory is equal to one-half the order quantity. Therefore, the larger the order quantity, the larger the average inventory and, consequently, the greater the maintenance cost per year. However, the larger the order quantity, the fewer orders required per planning period and, consequently, the lower the total ordering cost. Lot quantity formulations identify the precise quantities at which the annual combined total cost of ordering and maintenance is lowest for a given sales volume. Figure 8-4 illustrates the basic relationships. The point at which the sum of ordering cost and maintenance cost is minimized represents the lowest total cost. The above discussion presents the basic lot sizing concepts and identifies the fundamental objectives. Simply stated, the objectives are to identify the ordering quantity or period that minimizes the total cost of inventory maintenance and ordering.

FIGURE 8-4   Economic order quantity.

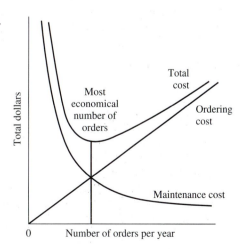

Economic Order Quantity   The economic order quantity (EOQ) is the replenishment order quantity that minimizes the combined cost of inventory maintenance and ordering. Identification of such a quantity assumes that demand and costs are relatively stable throughout the year. Since an EOQ is calculated on an individual product basis, the basic formulation does not consider the impact of joint ordering of products. EOQ extensions are discussed later in this chapter.

The most efficient method for calculating economic order quantity is mathematical. Earlier in this chapter a policy dilemma regarding whether to order 100, 200, or 600 units was discussed. The answer can be found by calculating the applicable EOQ for the situation. Table 8-4 contains the necessary information.

To make the appropriate calculations, the standard formulation for EOQ is

$$EOQ = \sqrt{\frac{2C_o D}{C_i U}}$$

where EOQ = economic order quantity (EOQ)

C_o = cost per order

C_i = annual inventory carrying cost

D = annual sales volume, units

U = cost per unit

Substituting from Table 8-4,

$$EOQ = \sqrt{\frac{2 \times 19 \times 2400}{0.20 \times 5.00}}$$

$$= 91,200 = 302 \text{ (rounded to 300)}$$

Total ordering cost would amount to $152 (2400/300 × $19.00) and maintenance cost $150 [300/2 × (5 × 0.20)]. Thus, after rounding to allow ordering in multiples of 100 units, annual reordering and maintenance costs have been equated.

To benefit from the most economical purchase arrangement, orders should be placed in the quantity of 300 units rather than 100, 200, or 600. Thus, over the year, eight orders would be placed, and average base inventory would be 150 units. An EOQ of 300 implies that additional inventory in the form of base stock has been introduced into the system. Average inventory has been increased from 100 to 150 units on hand.

While the EOQ model determines the optimal replenishment quantity, it does require some rather stringent assumptions that constrain its direct application. The

TABLE 8-4   FACTORS FOR DETERMINING EOQ

Annual demand volume	2,400 units
Unit value at cost	$5.00
Inventory carrying cost percentage	20% annually
Ordering cost	$19.00 per order

major assumptions of the simple EOQ model are (1) satisfaction of all demand; (2) continuous, constant, and known rate of demand; (3) constant and known replenishment performance-cycle time; (4) constant price of product that is independent of order quantity or time (i.e., no purchase quantity or transportation price discounts are available); (5) infinite planning horizon; (6) no interaction between multiple items of inventory; (7) no inventory in transit; and (8) no limit on capital availability. The constraints imposed by some of these assumptions can be overcome through computational extensions, as discussed next. However, the EOQ concept illustrates the importance of the trade-offs associated with holding and acquisition cost.

Relationships involving the inventory performance cycle, inventory cost, and economic order formulations are useful for guiding inventory planning. First, the EOQ is found at the point where annualized order cost and maintenance cost are equal. Second, average base inventory equals one-half order quantity. Third, the value of the inventory unit, all other things being equal, will have a direct relationship on the duration of the performance cycle: in effect, the higher the value, the more frequently orders will be placed.

EOQ Extensions   While the EOQ formulation is relatively straightforward, there are some other factors that must be considered in actual application. The most persistent problems are those related to various adjustments necessary to take advantage of special purchase situations and unitization characteristics. Three typical adjustments are volume transportation rates, quantity discounts, and other adjustments. Each category is discussed.

Volume Transportation Rates   In the EOQ formulation discussed previously, no consideration was given to the impact of transportation cost on order quantity. When products are purchased on a delivered basis and the seller pays transportation cost from origin to the inventory destination, such neglect may be justified. The seller is responsible for the shipment until it arrives at the customer's place of business. However, when product ownership is transferred at origin, the impact of transportation rates on total cost must be considered when determining order quantity.

As a general rule, the greater the weight of an order, the lower the cost per pound of transportation from any origin to destination. A freight-rate discount for larger-size shipments is common for both truck and rail and is found in most transportation rate structures. Thus, all other things being equal, an enterprise naturally wants to purchase in quantities that maximize transportation economies. Such quantities may be larger than the purchase quantity determined using the EOQ method. Increasing order size has a twofold impact on inventory cost. Assume for purposes of illustration that the most desirable transportation rate is obtained when a quantity of 480 is ordered as compared to the EOQ-recommended order of 300 calculated earlier.[5] The first impact of the larger order is to increase the average base inventory from 150 to 240 units. Thus ordering in larger quantities increases inventory carrying cost.

---

[5]To determine transportation rates, the unit quantity must be converted to weight.

TABLE 8-5   EOQ DATA REQUIREMENTS FOR CONSIDERATION OF
TRANSPORTATION ECONOMIES

Annual demand volume	2,400 units
Unit value at cost	$5.00
Inventory carrying cost percentage	20% annually
Ordering cost	$19.00 per order
Small shipment rate	$1.00 per unit
Large shipment rate	$0.75 per unit

The second impact is a decrease in the number of orders required. The decreased number of orders increases the shipment size, which provides better transportation economies.

To complete the analysis, it is necessary to formulate the total cost with and without transportation savings. While this calculation can be directly made by modification of the EOQ formulation, comparison provides a more insightful answer. The only additional data required are the applicable freight rates for ordering in quantities of 300 and 480. Table 8-5 provides the data necessary to complete the analysis.

Table 8-6 provides the analysis of total cost. Taking into consideration the potential transportation savings by purchasing in larger lot sizes, total annual cost by purchasing 480 units five times per year rather than the EOQ solution of 300 units eight times per year results in approximately a $570 savings.

The impact of volume transportation rates on total cost of procurement cannot be neglected. In the example above, the equivalent rate per unit dropped from $1 to $0.75, or by 25 percent. The cost-per-hundredweight range from minimum weight LTL to carload minimum weight may significantly exceed this 25 percent figure. Thus any EOQ must be tested for transportation cost sensitivity across a range of weight breaks if transportation expenses are the buyer's responsibility.

A second point illustrated in the data of Table 8-6 is the fact that rather substantial changes in the size of an order and the number of orders placed per year resulted in only a modest change in the total cost of maintenance and ordering. The EOQ quantity of 300 had a total annual cost of $302, whereas the revised order quantity had a comparative cost of $335. EOQ formulations are much more sensitive to significant changes in order cycle or frequency. Likewise, substantial changes in cost factors are necessary to significantly affect the economic order quantity.

TABLE 8-6   VOLUME TRANSPORTATION RATE MODIFIED EOQ

	Alternative 1: $q_e = 300$	Alternative 2: $q_e = 480$
Inventory carrying cost	$ 150	$ 240
Ordering cost	152	95
Transportation cost	2,400	1,800
Total cost	$2,702	$2,135

TABLE 8-7   QUANTITY DISCOUNTS

Cost	Quantity purchased
$5.00	1–99
4.50	100–200
4.00	201–300
3.50	301–400
3.00	401–500

Finally, two factors regarding inventory cost under conditions of origin purchase are noteworthy. (Origin purchase means that the buyer is responsible for freight cost and product risk when the product is in transit.) First, the buyer assumes full risk on inventory at time of shipment. Depending on time of required payment, this could mean that transit inventory is part of the enterprise's average inventory and therefore subjected to an appropriate charge.[6] It follows that any change in weight break leading to a shipment method with a different in-transit time should be assessed the added cost or savings as appropriate in a total-cost analysis.

Second, the transportation cost must be added to the purchase price to obtain an accurate assessment of the value of goods tied up in inventory. Once the inventory has been received, the amount invested in the product must be increased by the transportation expenses. Inventory carrying cost should then be assessed on the combined cost of the item plus transportation.

Quantity Discounts   Purchase quantity discounts represent an EOQ extension analogous to volume transportation rates. Table 8-7 illustrates a sample schedule of discounts. Quantity discounts can be handled directly with the basic EOQ formulation by calculating total cost at any given volume-related purchase price to determine associated EOQs. If the discount at any associated quantity is sufficient to offset the added cost of maintenance less the reduced cost of ordering, then the quantity discount offers a viable alternative. It should be noted that quantity discounts and volume transportation rates each affect larger purchase quantities. This does not necessarily mean that the lowest total-cost purchase will always be a larger quantity than would otherwise be the case under basic EOQ.

Other EOQ Adjustments   A variety of special situations may occur that will require adjustments to the basic EOQ. Examples are (1) production lot size, (2) multiple-item purchase, (3) limited capital, and (4) private trucking. Production lot size refers to the most economical quantities from a manufacturing perspective. Multiple-item purchase describes situations when more than one product is bought concurrently, so that quantity and transportation discounts must consider the impact of product combinations. Limited capital refers to situations with budget limitations for total inventory investment. Since the product line must be satisfied within the budget limitations, order quantities must recognize the need to allocate the inventory investment across the product line. Private trucking influences order quantity

---

[6]In such situations, the cost of inventory investment should be appropriately charged, provided that it is paid for at origin.

since it represents a fixed cost once the decision is made to replenish product. If it is decided to use a private fleet to transport replenishment product, the enterprise should fill the truck regardless of the EOQ. It does not make sense to transport a half-empty truck simply so that the order quantity represents the EOQ.

Another consideration when establishing the order quantity is the unitization characteristic. Many products are stored and moved in standard units such as cases or pallets. Since these standardized units are designed to fit transportation or handling vehicles, there may be significant diseconomies when the EOQ is not a unit multiple. As an example, suppose that a pallet can hold 200 units of a specified product. Using an EOQ of 300 units would imply shipments of 1.5 pallets. From a handling or transportation utilization perspective, it is probably more effective to order one or two pallets either alternatively or permanently. Standard unit multiples should be considered when determining EOQ. Chapter 15 presents a more comprehensive discussion of unitization characteristics and their strategic impact.

While standard unit EOQ consolidations are important, their significance is declining as shippers' ability and willingness to provide mixed units or mixed pallets increase. Mixed units or pallets contain product combinations and are designed to provide a product assortment while maintaining transportation and handling economies.

Discrete Lot Sizing Not all resupply situations operate with uniform usage rates like those in the previous EOQ computations. In many manufacturing situations, the demand for a specific component tends to occur at irregular intervals and for varied quantities. The irregular nature of usage requirements is a consequence of demand being dependent upon the production schedule. That is, the required assembly parts must be available at the time manufacture occurs. Between requirement times, no need exists to maintain component inventory in stock if it can be obtained when needed. Inventory servicing of *dependent demand* requires a modified approach to the determination of order quantities, referred to as *discrete lot sizing*. Identification of the technique as ''discrete'' means that the procurement objective is to obtain a component quantity equal to the net requirements at a specific point in time. Because component requirements fluctuate, purchase quantities using discrete lot sizing will vary between orders. A variety of lot sizing techniques are available. The options of (1) lot-for-lot sizing, (2) period order quantity, and (3) time-series lot sizing are discussed next.

Lot-for-Lot Sizing The most basic form of discrete ordering is to plan purchases to cover net requirements over a specified period. No consideration is given to the cost of ordering under *lot-for-lot sizing*. In one sense, the lot-for-lot technique is pure dependent-demand-oriented, since no ordering economies are considered. The order quantity exactly matches manufacturing or demand quantity. The basic technique is often used when the item being purchased is inexpensive and the requirements are relatively small and irregular. Lot-for-lot sizing often uses electronic order transfer and premium transportation to minimize processing and delivery time.

Period Order Quantity The *period order quantity* (POQ) technique builds on the EOQ logic. Here, three steps are performed to accomplish component procurement. First, the standard EOQ is calculated. Second, the EOQ quantity is divided into forecasted annual usage to determine order frequency. Third, the number of orders is divided into the relevant time period (e.g., fifty-two for weeks or twelve for months) to express the order quantity in time periods.

To illustrate, let's work with an EOQ of 300 and a forecast of 2,400. To adjust to a twelve-period year, the POQ technique would be as follows:

$$EOQ = 300$$

$$Forecast = 2,400$$

$$Orders\ per\ year = \frac{2,400}{300} = 8.00$$

$$Order\ interval = \frac{12}{8.00} = 1.5\ months$$

Under the POQ application, orders are planned approximately every six weeks. The typical order is 300 units unless usage deviates from planned quantity and requires a "catch-up" or "light" resupply order.

The main advantage of the POQ approach is that it considers inventory carrying cost and thereby minimizes inventory carryover. The disadvantage is that similar to the basic EOQ, POQ also requires stable demand to realize its full potential.

Time-Series Lot Sizing The fundamental objective of time-series lot sizing is to combine requirements over several periods to arrive at a procurement logic. The time-series approach is dynamic because the order quantity is adjusted to meet current requirement estimates. This is in contrast to basic EOQ, which is static in the sense that once the order quantity is computed, it continues unchanged for the demand planning horizon.

The key to dynamic lot sizing is that requirements are expressed in varying quantities across time rather than in usage rates per day or week, as is typical of the basic EOQ. Given substantial usage fluctuation, fixed order quantities are replaced by a lot sizing system that can calculate an economical order given changing and intermittent usage. Three such techniques are widely discussed in the literature and are briefly reviewed here: least unit cost, least total cost, and part-period balancing.

Least unit cost seeks to identify a combination of requirements over a number of periods resulting in the lowest cost per SKU. Starting with initial period net requirements, each future period's per unit requirements are evaluated to determine a combined quantity for a given number of periods in which the unit cost is minimized. The least-unit-cost approach essentially evaluates purchasing requirements in incremental number of weeks of supply into the future. The first week considers one week of supply. The analysis then considers adding a second week. Unit cost—including quantity discounts, ordering cost, inventory carrying cost, and transportation cost—is evaluated for each option. While the discount, ordering, and transportation costs will cause average unit cost to decline as more periods are added, inventory carrying cost will increase as more time periods are added because of the additional inventory. Thus, order quantities and order frequency will vary substantially under the least-unit-cost technique. While this approach does provide a way to overcome the static features of EOQ and POQ, the technique may cause unit costs to vary widely between time periods.

The *least-total-cost approach* seeks the quantity that minimizes total cost for successive periods. In this sense, least total cost, which is the balancing of ordering and carrying, is similar to EOQ in objective. The fundamental difference is that order interval is varied to seek the least total cost. The calculation is based on a ratio of ordering to carrying cost (C_o/C_i), called the *economic part-period*. The economic part-period defines the quantity of a specific component that, if carried in inventory for one period, would result in a carrying cost equal to the cost of ordering. The least-total-cost technique selects order sizes and intervals that most nearly approximate the economic part-period calculation. Thus, order sizes remain fairly uniform; however, substantial differences do occur in elapsed time between order placement. The least-total-cost technique overcomes the failure of the least unit cost to consider trade-offs across the overall planning period.

Part-period balancing is a modified form of the least-total-cost technique that incorporates a special adjustment routine called *look-ahead/look-back*. The main benefit of this feature is that it extends the planning horizon across more than one ordering point to accommodate usage peaks and valleys when calculating order quantities. Adjustments are made in order time or quantity when a forward or backward review of more than one order requirement indicates that modifications to the economic part-period may be beneficial. The typical procedure is to first test the look-ahead feature to determine if more time results in approximation of the economic part-period quantity. Look-back is typically utilized if look-ahead leaves the lot size unchanged. In this sense, look-back means that a future order, which under the economic part-period rule would normally be scheduled for delivery during the fourth period, should be advanced if earlier delivery would reduce total cost. The net result of incorporating the look-ahead/look-back feature is that it turns the application of the economic part-period concept into a simultaneous review of multiple periods.

Conclusion   The varied approaches to discrete lot sizing all seek to overcome assumptions regarding the uniform usage characteristic of basic EOQ calculations. Whereas EOQ results in a uniform quantity that may be ordered in a fixed or variable time interval, discrete-lot-sizing techniques seek greater flexibility to accommodate irregular usage. The approaches reviewed here have had varying degrees of success.

ACCOMMODATING UNCERTAINTY

Although it is useful to review basic inventory relationships under conditions of certainty, formulation of inventory policy must realistically consider uncertainty. One of the main functions of inventory management is to protect against occurrence of out-of-stocks.

As noted earlier in the chapter, two types of uncertainty have a direct impact on inventory policy. Demand uncertainty concerns the fluctuation in the rate of sales during the inventory performance cycle. Performance-cycle uncertainty involves inventory replenishment cycle variations. First, the role of demand uncertainty in computing safety stock levels is discussed under the condition of constant replenishment. In the next section both types of uncertainty are handled on a simultaneous basis.

Accommodating Demand Uncertainty

Sales forecasting projects unit demand during the inventory performance cycle. Even with good forecasting, demand during the replenishment cycle often exceeds or falls short of what is anticipated. To provide protection against a stockout when demand exceeds forecast, safety stock is added to base inventory. Under conditions of demand uncertainty, average inventory is defined as one-half of the order quantity plus safety stock. Figure 8-5 illustrates the inventory performance cycle under conditions of demand uncertainty. The dashed line reflects the forecast. Under conditions of demand certainty, replenishment is designed to arrive just as the last unit of inventory is shipped to customers. The solid line illustrates inventory on hand from one performance cycle to the next when there is demand uncertainty. The task of planning safety stock consists of three steps. First, the likelihood of stockout must be gauged. Second, demand potential during periods of stockout must be estimated. Finally, a policy decision is required concerning the degree of stockout protection to introduce into the system.

Assume for purposes of illustration that the inventory performance cycle is 10 days. Historical experience indicates that daily sales range from 0 to 10 units with average daily sales of 5 units. The economic order is assumed to be 50, the reorder point is 50, the planned average inventory is 25, and sales during the performance cycle are expected to be 50 units.

Figure 8-5 provides a recap of actual sales history over three consecutive inven-

FIGURE 8-5 Inventory relationship with demand uncertainty and constant performance cycle.

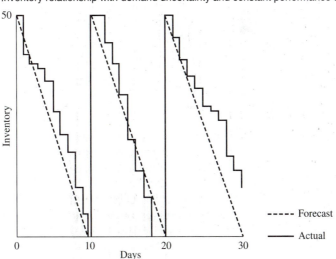

TABLE 8-8   TYPICAL DEMAND EXPERIENCE DURING THREE REPLENISHMENT CYCLES

	Forecast cycle 1			Stockout cycle 2			Overstock cycle 3	
Day	Demand	Accumulated	Day	Demand	Accumulated	Day	Demand	Accumulated
1	9	9	11	0	0	21	5	5
2	2	11	12	6	6	22	5	10
3	1	12	13	5	11	23	4	14
4	3	15	14	7	18	24	3	17
5	7	22	15	10	28	25	4	21
6	5	27	16	7	35	26	1	22
7	4	31	17	6	41	27	2	24
8	8	39	18	9	50	28	8	32
9	6	45	19	Stockout	50	29	3	35
10	5	50	20	Stockout	50	30	4	39

tory performance cycles. During the first cycle, although daily demand experienced variation, the average of 5 units per day was maintained. Total demand during cycle 1 was 50 units, as expected. During cycle 2, demand totaled 50 units in the first 8 days, resulting in a stockout. Thus no sales were possible on days 9 and 10. During cycle 3, demand reached a total of 39 units. The third performance cycle ended with 11 units remaining in stock. Over the 30-day period total sales were 139 units, for average daily sales of 4.6 units.

From the history recorded in Table 8-8 management can observe that stockouts occurred on 2 of 30 total days. Since sales never exceeded 10 units per day, no possibility of stockout exists on the first 5 days of the performance cycle. Stockouts could occur on days 6 through 10 based on the remote possibility that demand during the first 5 days of the cycle averaged 10 units per day and no inventory was carried over from the previous period. Since over the three performance cycles 10 units were sold on only one occasion, it is apparent that the real risk of stockout occurs only during the last few days of the performance cycle, and then only when sales exceed the average by a substantial margin.[7]

Some approximation is also possible concerning the level of sales that could have occurred had stock been available on days 9 and 10 of cycle 2. A maximum of 20 units could have been sold if inventory had been available. On the other hand, it is remotely possible that even if stock had been available, no demand would have occurred on days 9 and 10. On the basis of an average demand of 4 to 5 units per day, a reasonable appraisal of lost sales is 8 to 10 units.

It should be apparent that the risk of stockouts created by variations in sales is limited to a short time and includes a small percentage of total sales. However, management should take some protective action to realize available sales and avoid the risk of possible deterioration in customer relations. Although the sales analysis

---

[7]In this example, daily statistics are used. An alternative, which is technically more correct from a statistical viewpoint, is to utilize demand over performance cycles. The major limitation of order cycles is the length of time and difficulty required to collect the necessary data.

TABLE 8-9   FREQUENCY OF DEMAND

Demand/day	Frequency (days)	Demand/day	Frequency (days)
Stockout	2	Five units	5
Zero	1	Six units	3
One unit	2	Seven units	3
Two units	2	Eight units	2
Three units	3	Nine units	2
Four units	4	Ten units	1

presented in Table 8-8 helps achieve an understanding of the problem, the appropriate course of action is still not clear. Statistical probability can be used to assist management in determining safety stock requirements under these conditions of uncertainty.

In order to provide a basis for understanding this analysis, the following discussion applies statistical techniques to the demand uncertainty problem.

The sales history over the 30-day period has been arranged in Table 8-9 in terms of a frequency distribution. The main purpose of frequency distribution is to make an appraisal of variations around the average daily demand.

Given an expected average of 5 units per day, demand exceeded average on 11 days and was less than average on 12 days. An alternative way of illustrating a frequency distribution is with a bar chart, as in Figure 8-6.

Given the historical frequency of demand, it is possible to determine an exact calculation of how much safety stock would be necessary to provide a specified degree of protection. Probability theory is based on the random chance of a given occurrence out of a large number of occurrences. In the situation illustrated, the frequency of occurrences is 28 days. Although in actual practice more than 28 events would be desirable, a limited sample illustrates the application of probability theory to setting safety stocks.

The probability of occurrences assumes a pattern around a measure of central tendency, which is the average value of all occurrences. While a number of frequency distributions are utilized in inventory control, the most basic is the *normal distribution.*

A normal distribution is characterized by a symmetrical bell-shaped curve, illustrated in Figure 8-7. The essential characteristic of a normal distribution is that the three measures of central tendency are identical. The mean (average) value, the median (middle) observation, and the mode (most frequently observed) value are all the same number. To the extent that these three measures are the same or nearly identical, a frequency distribution is classified as normal.

The basis for prediction using a normal distribution is the standard deviation of observations around the measures of central tendency. The *standard deviation* is a measure of dispersion of events within specified areas under the normal curve. For the inventory management case, the event is unit sales per day, and the dispersion is the variation in daily sales levels. Within ± 1 standard deviation, 68.27 percent of all events occur. This means that 68.27 percent of the days will have daily sales

FIGURE 8-6   Historical analysis of demand history.

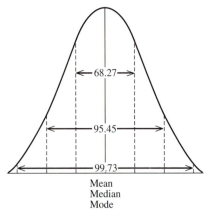

FIGURE 8-7   Normal distribution.

within ± 1 standard deviation of the average daily sales. Within ± 2 standard deviations, 95.45 percent of all events occur. At ± 3 standard deviations, 99.73 percent of all events are included. In terms of inventory policy, the standard deviation provides a means of estimating the safety stock required to obtain a specified degree of protection above the average demand.

The first step in setting safety stocks is to calculate the standard deviation. The formula for standard deviation is

$$\sigma = \sqrt{\frac{\Sigma F_i D_i^2}{n}}$$

where σ = standard deviation
$\quad\quad F_i$ = frequency of event i
$\quad\quad D_i$ = deviation of event from mean for event i
$\quad\quad n$ = total observations available

The necessary data to determine standard deviation are contained in Table 8-10. Substituting from Table 8-10,

$$\sigma = \sqrt{\frac{181}{28}} = \sqrt{6.46} = 2.54$$

Owing to the inability to add stock except in complete units, the standard deviation of the data in Table 8-10 is rounded to 3 units. In setting safety stocks, 2 standard deviations of protection, or 6 units, would guard against 95.45 percent of all events included in the frequency distribution. However, the only situations of concern are the probabilities of events that exceed the mean value. No problem exists concerning inventory to satisfy demand equal to or below the average. Thus,

TABLE 8-10 CALCULATION OF STANDARD DEVIATION OF DAILY DEMAND

Units	Frequency (F_i)	Deviation from mean (D_i)	Deviation squared (D_i^2)	$F_iD_i^2$
0	1	-5	25	25
1	2	-4	16	32
2	2	-3	9	18
3	3	-2	4	12
4	4	-1	1	4
5	5	0	0	0
6	3	$+1$	1	3
7	3	$+2$	4	12
8	2	$+3$	9	18
9	2	$+4$	16	32
10	1	$+5$	25	25
$n = 28$	$\bar{s} = 5$			$\Sigma F_iD_i^2 = 181$

on 50 percent of the days, no safety stock is required. Safety stock protection at the 95 percent level will, in fact, protect against 97.72 percent of all possible events. This added benefit results from what is typically called a one-tail statistical application.

The above example illustrates how statistical probability can assist with the quantification of demand uncertainty. However, demand conditions are not the only source of uncertainty. Therefore, attention is now directed to the treatment of performance-cycle uncertainty.

Performance-Cycle Uncertainty

Performance-cycle uncertainty means that inventory policy cannot assume consistent delivery. The planner should expect that the performance-cycle length will have a high frequency around the average and be skewed in excess of the planned duration.

From a planning viewpoint, it would be possible to establish the safety stock policy around the minimum possible days, the average expected days, or the maximum possible days of the inventory performance cycle.

Using the minimum or maximum limits, the resultant safety stock would be substantially different. Remember that safety stocks exist to protect against demand uncertainty during replenishment. Consequently, policies centered around minimum performance value would provide inadequate protection, and those formulated around maximum value would result in excessive safety stocks.

If the impact of performance-cycle uncertainty is not evaluated statistically, the most common practice is to formulate safety stock policy on the planned or average experiences of replenishment days. However, if there is substantial variation in the performance cycle, formal evaluation is necessary. In manufacturing planning sit-

TABLE 8-11   CALCULATION OF STANDARD DEVIATION OF REPLENISHMENT CYCLE DURATION

Performance cycle (days)	Frequency (F_i)	Deviation from mean (D_i)	Deviation squared (D_i^2)	$F_i D_i^2$
6	2	−4	16	32
7	4	−3	9	36
8	6	−2	4	24
9	8	−1	1	8
10	10	0	0	0
11	8	+1	1	8
12	6	+2	4	24
13	4	+3	9	36
14	2	+4	16	32
				$\Sigma F_i D_i^2 = 200$

$$N = 50 \qquad t = 10$$

$$\sigma = \sqrt{\frac{F_i D_i^2}{N}} = \sqrt{\frac{200}{50}} = \sqrt{4} = 2 \text{ days}$$

uations that deal with derived demand, the major form of uncertainty is the performance cycle.

Table 8-11 represents a sample frequency distribution of performance cycles. Although 10 days is the most frequently occurring experience, replenishment ranges from 6 to 14 days. If the performance cycle is assumed to follow a normal bell-shaped distribution, an individual performance cycle would be expected to fall between 8 and 12 days 68.27 percent of the time.

From a practical viewpoint, when cycle days drop below 10, no immediate problem exists with safety stock. If the actual performance cycle was consistently below the planned performance cycle over a period of time, then adjustment of expected duration would be in order. The situation of most immediate concern occurs when the time duration of the performance cycle exceeds the expected value of 10 days.

From the viewpoint of the probability of exceeding 10 days, the frequency of such occurrences from the data in Table 8-11 can be restated in terms of performance cycles greater than 10 days and equal to or less than 10 days. In the example data, the standard deviation would not change because the distribution is normal. However, if the actual experience had been skewed in excess of the expected cycle duration, then a Poisson distribution may have been the most appropriate.[8] In Poisson frequency distributions, the standard deviation is equal to the square root of the mean, and as a general rule, the smaller the mean, the greater the degree of skewness.

[8]Rein Peterson and Edward A. Silver, *Decision Systems for Inventory Management and Production Planning,* 2d ed., New York: John Wiley & Sons, 1985.

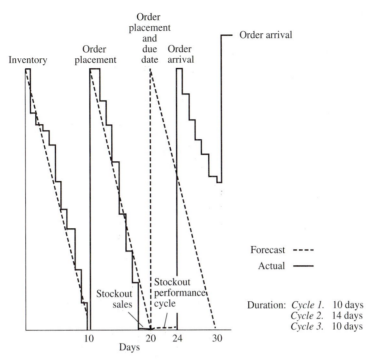

FIGURE 8-8   Combined demand and performance-cycle uncertainty.

Determining Order Point with Uncertainty

The inventory performance cycle has been identified as the combination of order communication, processing, and transportation times. These elements create an information and physical product flow between two locations. The integrated performance cycle forms the central context for planning inventory policy. Up to this point, all discussions related to safety stock have assumed a constant time value for the duration of the performance cycle. For example, in the illustration concerning the establishment of safety stocks to cover sales uncertainty, the duration of the cycle was assumed as a 10-day constant. The more typical situation confronting the inventory planner is illustrated in Figure 8-8, where both demand and inventory performance-cycle uncertainties exist. In this section the nature of uncertainty concerning the performance cycle is reviewed, and methods are introduced for estimating combined probabilities of both types of uncertainty.

Treating demand uncertainty and performance-cycle uncertainty consists of combining two independent variables. The duration of the cycle is, at least in the short run, independent of the daily demand. However, in setting safety stocks, the joint impact of the probability of both demand and performance-cycle variation must be determined.

TABLE 8-12 FREQUENCY DISTRIBUTION: DEMAND AND REPLENISHMENT UNCERTAINTY

Demand distribution		Replenishment cycle distribution	
Daily sales	Frequency	Days	Frequency
0	1	6	2
1	2	7	4
2	2	8	6
3	3	9	8
4	4	10	10
5	5	11	8
6	3	12	6
7	3	13	4
8	2	14	2
9	2		
10	1		
	$n = 28$	$n = 50$	
	$T = 5$	$T = 10$	
	$S_s = 2.54$	$S_t = 2$	

Table 8-12 presents a summary of sales and replenishment cycle performance. The key to understanding the potential relationships of the data in Table 8-12 is the 10-day performance cycle. Total demand during the 10 days could range from 0 to 100 units. On each day of the cycle, the demand probability is independent of the previous day for the entire 10-day duration. Assuming the full range of potential situations illustrated in Table 8-12, total sales during replenishment could range from 0 to 140 units. With this basic relationship between the two types of uncertainty in mind, safety stock requirements can be determined by either numerical or simulated procedures.

Numerical Compounding: Demand and Replenishment Uncertainty   The exact compounding of two independent variables involves multinominal expansion. While this type of procedure requires extensive calculations when demand and performance-cycle distributions follow the shape of those illustrated in Table 8-12, the solution provides a direct approach to determine the average and standard deviation of demand during the performance cycle.

A direct method to combine the standard deviations of the demand and performance-cycle frequency distributions to approximate the combined standard deviation is provided by the convolution formula:

$$\sigma_c = \sqrt{TS_s^2 + D^2 S_t^2}$$

where σ_c = standard deviation of combined probabilities
$\quad\quad T$ = average performance-cycle time
$\quad\quad S_t$ = standard deviation of the performance cycle
$\quad\quad D$ = average daily sales
$\quad\quad S_s$ = standard deviation of daily sales

Substituting from Table 8-12,

$$\sigma_c = \sqrt{10.00(2.54)^2 + (5.00)^2(2)^2}$$

$$= \sqrt{64.52 + 100} = \sqrt{164.52}$$

$$= 12.83 \text{ (rounded to 13)}$$

This formulation provides the convoluted or combined standard deviation of T days with an average demand of D per day when the individual standard deviations are S_t and S_s, respectively. The average for the combined distribution is simply the product of T and D, or 50.00 (10.00 $\times$ 5.00).

Thus given a frequency distribution of daily sales from 0 to 10 units per day and a range in replenishment cycle duration of 6 to 14 days, 13 units (1 standard deviation multiplied by 13 units) of safety stock are required to protect 68.27 percent of all performance cycles. To protect at the 97.72 percent level, it is necessary to plan a 26-unit safety stock.

It is important to note that the specific event being protected against is a stockout during the replenishment order cycle. The 68.27 and 97.72 percent levels are *not* product availability levels. These percentages reflect the probability of a stockout during a given order cycle. For example, with a 13-unit safety stock, stockouts would be expected to occur during 31.73 (100 − 68.27) percent of the performance cycles. This implies that, over time, if a distribution center initiates 100 replenishment orders while maintaining a 13-unit safety stock, the center would expect to deplete the stock while awaiting receipt of 32 percent of the replenishment orders.

Although this percentage provides the probability of a stockout, it does not indicate the relative magnitude of the stockout. The relative magnitude of a stockout indicates the percentage of units stocked out relative to the total amount demanded. In addition to being affected by the probability of a stockout, the relative magnitude is influenced by the replenishment order size. This concept is further detailed next.

Average inventory requirements would be 25 units if no safety stock was desired. The average inventory with 2 standard deviations of safety stock is 51 units [25 + (2 $\times$ 13)]. This inventory level would protect against stockouts during 97.72 percent of the performance cycles. Table 8-13 summarizes the alternatives confronting the planner in terms of assumptions and corresponding impact on average inventory.

Estimating Fill Rate The fill rate represents the magnitude of a stockout rather than the probability. Fill rate is the desired customer service objective. The case

TABLE 8-13   SUMMARY OF ALTERNATIVE ASSUMPTIONS CONCERNING UNCERTAINTY
AND IMPACT ON AVERAGE INVENTORY

	Order quantity	Safety stock	Average inventory
Assume constant S sales and constant T performance cycle	50	0	25
Assumes demand protection $+2\sigma$ and constant T perform-ance cycle	50	6	31
Assume constant S demand and $+2\sigma$ performance-cycle protection	50	20	45
Assume joint $+2\sigma$ for demand and performance-cycle	50	26	51

fill rate is the percentage of units that can be filled when requested from available inventory. Figure 8-9 graphically illustrates the difference between stockout probability and stockout magnitude. Both illustrations in Figure 8-9 have a safety stock of 1 standard deviation, or 13 units. For both situations, given any performance cycle, the probability of a stockout is 31.73 percent. However, during a 20-day period, the example at the left illustrates two instances where the stock may be depleted. These instances are at the ''ends'' of the cycle (as noted by the circles). In the example at the right, where the order quantity has been doubled, the system has the possibility of stocking out only once during the 20-day cycle. So, while both situations face the same demand patterns, the first one has more stockout opportunities and potential. In general, for a given safety stock level, increasing the order quantity decreases the relative magnitude of potential stockout and, conversely, increases customer service availability.

The mathematical formulation of the relationship is

$$\text{SL} = 1 - \frac{f(k)\sigma_c}{Q}$$

FIGURE 8-9   Impact of order quantity on stockout magnitude.

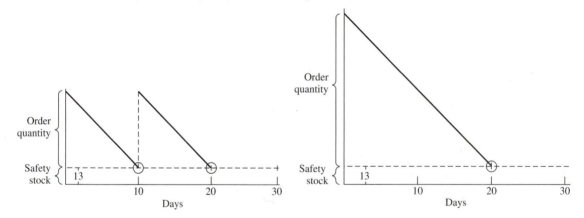

TABLE 8-14   INFORMATION FOR DETERMINING
              REQUIRED SAFETY STOCK

Desired service level	99 percent
σ_c	13
Q	300

where SL = the stockout magnitude (the product availability level)
    $f(k)$ = a function of the normal loss curve, which provides the area
        in a right tail of a normal distribution
    σ_c = the combined standard deviation considering both demand
        and replenishment cycle uncertainty
    Q = the replenishment order quantity

To complete the example, suppose a firm desired 99 percent product availability. Assume the Q was calculated to be 300 units. Table 8-14 summarizes the required information.

Since $f(k)$ is the item used to calculate safety stock requirements, the above equation must be solved for $f(k)$ using algebraic manipulation. The result is

$$f(k) = (1 - \text{SL}) \times (Q/\sigma_c)$$

Substituting from Table 8-14,

$$f(k) = (1 - 0.99) \times (300/13)$$

$$= 0.01 \times 23.08 = 0.2308$$

The calculated value of $f(k)$ is then compared against the values in Table 8-15 to find the one that most closely approximates the calculated value. For this example, the value of K that most closely meets this condition is 0.4. The required safety stock level is

$$\text{SS} = K \times \sigma_c$$

where SS = safety stock in units
    K = the K factor that corresponds with $f(k)$
    σ_c = the combined standard deviation

So, substituting in the example

$$\text{SS} = K \times \sigma_c$$

$$= 0.4 \times 13 = 5.2 \text{ units}$$

TABLE 8-15   TABLE OF LOSS INTEGRAL FOR STANDARDIZED NORMAL DISTRIBUTION

K	f(k)	K	f(k)	K	f(k)	K	f(k)
0.0	0.3989	0.8	0.1202	1.6	0.0232	2.4	0.0027
0.1	0.3509	0.9	0.1004	1.7	0.0142	2.5	0.0020
0.2	0.3068	1.0	0.0833	1.8	0.0110	2.6	0.0014
0.3	0.2667	1.1	0.0686	1.9	0.0084	2.7	0.0010
0.4	0.2304	1.2	0.0561	2.0	0.0074	2.8	0.0007
0.5	0.1977	1.3	0.0455	2.1	0.0064	2.9	0.0005
0.6	0.1686	1.4	0.0366	2.2	0.0048	3.0	0.0003
0.7	0.1428	1.5	0.0293	2.3	0.0036		

The safety stock level required to provide a 99 percent product fill rate when the order quantity is 300 units is approximately 5 units. Table 8-16 shows how the calculated safety stock levels vary for other order quantities. An increased order size can be used to compensate for decreasing the safety stock levels, or vice versa. The existence of such a trade-off implies that there is an optimum combination of replenishment order quantities that will result in the desired customer service level at the minimum cost.

Replenishment Ordering

When reviewing the strategy of the customer service availability level, clarification regarding safety stocks in dependent situations is required. The critical aspect of managing dependent demand is understanding that inventory requirements are a function of known events and are generally not random. Therefore dependent demand does not require forecasting since uncertainty is eliminated. It follows that no specific safety stock is necessary to support a time-phased procurement program such as MRP. The basic notion of time phasing is that parts and subassemblies need not be carried in inventory as long as they are available when needed.

The case for carrying no safety stocks under conditions of dependent demand rests on two assumptions: that procurement replenishment is predictable and constant, and that vendors and suppliers maintain adequate inventories to satisfy 100 percent of purchase requirements. The second assumption may be operationally attained by use of volume-oriented purchase contracts that ensure vendors and suppliers of eventual purchase.[9] In such cases the safety stock requirement still

[9]The practice became more common as a result of emphasis placed on just-in-time procurement strategies.

TABLE 8-16   IMPACT OF ORDER QUANTITY ON SAFETY STOCK

Order quantity (Q)	K	Safety stock
300	0.4	5.2
200	0.65	8.4
100	1.05	13.6

exists for the overall channel, although the primary responsibility has been shifted to the supplier.

The assumption of performance-cycle certainty is more difficult to achieve. Even in situations where private transportation is used, an element of uncertainty is always present. The practical result is that safety stocks do exist in most dependent demand situations.

Three basic approaches have been used to introduce safety stocks into a system coping with dependent demand. First, a common practice is to put *safety time* into the requirements plan. Thus a component is ordered one week earlier than needed to ensure timely arrival. A second approach is to increase the requisition by a quantity specified by some estimate of expected forecast error. For example, it may be assumed that forecast error will not exceed 5 percent. This procedure is referred to as overforecasting top-level demand. The net result is to increase procurement of all components in a ratio to their expected usage plus a "cushion" to cover forecast error. Components common to different end products or subassemblies covered by the overforecasting technique will naturally experience greater quantity buildups than single-purpose components and parts. To accommodate the unlikely event that all common assemblies will simultaneously require safety stock protection, a widely used procedure is to set a total safety stock for an item at a level less than the sum of 5 percent protection for each potential usage. The third method is to utilize the previously discussed statistical techniques for setting safety stocks directly to the component rather than to the item of top-level demand.

SUMMARY

In summary, this chapter positioned the importance of inventory in logistical operations. The risks associated with holding inventory at each level of the distribution channel were assessed, along with potential internal and external conflicts for the enterprise. The basic inventory functions of geographical specialization, decoupling, balancing supply and demand, and safety stock protection against uncertainty were identified. While there is substantial focus on reducing channel inventories, some level of inventory is typically necessary to accomplish the above functions, resulting in a lower total system cost.

The chapter reviewed the basic elements of planning inventory policy. It provided inventory definitions and relationships. The relationship between the performance cycle, order quantity, and average inventory was discussed and illustrated. The cost of inventory was described in terms of maintenance and ordering. Tradeoffs between key cost elements were explored. The difference between independent and dependent demand was developed as a planning focus.

In the third section attention was directed to issues that managers should consider when planning inventory strategy. The concept of economic order quantity was developed and described as the traditional approach to determine how much product to order. Several special adjustments to the basic EOQ were noted, with emphasis placed on volume transportation rates and quantity discounts. In addition, a discussion was devoted to discrete lot sizing techniques commonly used in manufacturing procurement situations. The perpetual and periodic inventory review procedures were described and illustrated.

A critical aspect in formulating inventory policy is the identification of the inventory management goals of customer service, profitable inventory allocation, prediction and control of inventory requirements, and total-cost integration. In the final section, a thorough review of demand and replenishment uncertainty was presented, followed by a discussion of methods for determining safety stock requirements on the basis of desired service and uncertainty level.

QUESTIONS

1 How does inventory functionality, related to uncertainty, differ from geographic specialization, decoupling, and supply-and-demand balancing?
2 What impact does the cost of carrying inventory show on the traditional profit and loss statement of the enterprise?
3 Describe the differences between demand and replenishment cycle uncertainty, and identify the activities that can be performed to reduce the uncertainty.
4 Discuss the relationship between service level, uncertainty, safety stock, and order quantity. How can trade-offs between these elements be made?
5 Discuss the disproportionate risk of holding inventory by retailers, wholesalers, and manufacturers. Why has there been a trend to push inventory back up the channel of distribution?
6 Compare and contrast economic and discrete lot sizing. Be specific concerning the benefits that each offers. Under what operating conditions would each of them be appropriate?
7 What is the difference between the probability of a stockout and the magnitude of a stockout?
8 Discuss the major inventory management goals. Why should management consider profitable allocation as a goal?
9 What logic supports the following statement: ''In terms of day-to-day inventory performance, lead time uncertainty has a greater impact than demand uncertainty.''
10 Discuss the difference between discrete and EOQ lot sizing.

INVENTORY MANAGEMENT

INVENTORY MANAGEMENT POLICIES
  Inventory Control
  Reactive Methods
  Planning Methods
  Adaptive Logic
MANAGEMENT PROCESSES
  Strategy Development Process
  Methods for Improved Inventory Management
SUMMARY
QUESTIONS

Managers must establish and implement inventory policies on the basis of strategic considerations. This requires the development of a managerial process. Chapter 9 is devoted to inventory management and addresses issues of policy development and implementation.

First, the chapter describes overall inventory management policies. While Chapter 8 focused on inventory decisions for a single item at a single location, Chapter 9 discusses inventory management for a range of stockkeeping units (SKUs) and at multiple locations. (An SKU is a specific item purchased by the customer including color and size uniqueness.) The chapter describes reactive methods, which respond to product demand at individual locations, and planning methods, which facilitate product allocation across a number of location and channel levels. Then it compares and contrasts reactive and planning inventory methods and offers guidelines for their application.

Next, the chapter discusses advanced inventory management practices that include fine-line classification to focus management efforts, systematic inventory management guidelines, and measurement and suggestions for improving inventory performance. These practices provide the foundation for focusing the inventory resource on key areas of business opportunity.

INVENTORY MANAGEMENT POLICIES

Inventory management is the integrated process that operationalizes the firm's and the value chain's inventory policy. The reactive or pull inventory approach uses customer demand to pull product through the distribution channel. An alternative philosophy is a planning approach that proactively schedules product movement and allocation through the channel according to forecasted demand and product availability. A third, or hybrid, logic uses a combination of the first two approaches resulting in an inventory management philosophy that responds to product and market environments. Each approach is reviewed, and application guidelines are presented.[1]

Inventory Control

Inventory control is a mechanical procedure for implementing an inventory policy. The accountability aspect of control measures units on hand at a specific location and tracks additions and deletions to the base quantity. Accountability and tracking can be performed by manual or computerized techniques. The primary differentials are speed, accuracy, and cost.

In order to implement the desired inventory management policies, control procedures must be devised. These define how often inventory levels are reviewed and compared against the inventory parameters defining when to order and how much to order. The following discussion reviews these control alternatives and outlines the implications for each. Inventory control procedures can be characterized as either perpetual or periodic. A modified approach is also presented.

Perpetual Review   A perpetual inventory control process reviews inventory status daily to determine replenishment needs. To utilize this type of control system, accurate accountability is necessary for all stockkeeping units. Computer assistance is needed to implement the perpetual concept effectively.

A perpetual review process is implemented through a reorder point and order quantity. As discussed earlier,

$$\text{ROP} = D \times T + \text{SS}$$

where ROP = reorder point in units
      D = average daily demand in units
      T = average performance-cycle length in days
    SS = safety or buffer stock in units

---

[1]This discussion is adopted from David J. Closs, ''An Adaptive Inventory System as a Tool for Strategic Inventory Management,'' *Proceedings of the 1981 Annual Conference of the National Council of Physical Distribution Management,* 1981, pp. 659–678.

TABLE 9-1   SAMPLE DEMAND, PERFORMANCE
                CYCLE, AND ORDER QUANTITY

Average daily demand	20 units
Performance cycle	10 days
Order quantity	200 units

The order quantity is determined using EOQ, EOQ extensions, or another approach as discussed earlier.

For purposes of illustration, let us assume that there is no uncertainty, so no safety stock is necessary. Table 9-1 summarizes demand, performance cycle, and order quantity characteristics. For this example,

$$\text{ROP} = D \times T + \text{SS}$$

$$= 20 \text{ units/day} \times 10 \text{ days} + 0 = 200 \text{ units}$$

The perpetual review compares the sum of on-hand and on-order inventory to the item's reorder point. On-hand inventory represents the quantity that physically resides in the particular distribution facility. On-order inventory represents quantities that have been ordered from suppliers. If the on-hand plus on-order quantity is less than the established reorder point, the inventory control process will initiate another replenishment order. Mathematically, this can be stated as

$$\text{If } I + Q_o \leq \text{ROP then order } Q$$

where I = inventory on hand
Q_o = inventory on order from suppliers
ROP = reorder point units
Q = order quantity units

For the previous example, a replenishment order of 200 is placed whenever the sum of on-hand and on-order inventory is less than or equal to 200 units. Since the reorder point equals the order quantity, the previous replenishment shipment would arrive just as the next replenishment is initiated.

The average inventory level for a perpetual review system can be calculated as

$$\bar{I} = Q/2 + \text{SS}$$

where $\bar{I}$ = average inventory in units
Q = order quantity units
SS = safety stock units

Average inventory for the previous example is calculated as

$$\bar{I} = Q/2 + \text{SS}$$

$$= 200/2 + 0 = 100 \text{ units}$$

Most illustrations throughout this text are based on a perpetual review system with a fixed reorder point. The reorder formulation is derived from two assumptions: purchase orders for the item under control will be placed when the reorder point is reached, and the method of control provides a continuous monitoring of inventory status. If these two assumptions are not satisfied, the control parameters (ROP and Q) determining the perpetual review must be refined.

Periodic Review   Periodic inventory control reviews the inventory status of an item at regular time intervals such as weekly or monthly. For periodic review, the basic reorder point must be adjusted to consider the extended intervals between reviews. The formula for calculating the periodic review reorder point is

$$ROP = D(T + P/2) + SS$$

where ROP $=$ reorder point
$D =$ average daily demand
$T =$ average performance-cycle length
$P =$ review period in days
SS $=$ safety stock

Since inventory status counts are completed only at a specific time, any item could fall below the desired reorder point prior to the review period. Therefore, the assumption is made that the inventory will fall below ideal reorder status prior to the periodic count approximately one-half of the review times. Assuming a review period of 7 days and using conditions similar to those of the perpetual example, the ROP then would be as follows:

$$ROP = D(T + P/2) + SS$$
$$= 20(10 + 7/2) + 0 = 20(10 + 3.5) = 270 \text{ units}$$

The average inventory formulation for periodic review is

$$\bar{I} = Q/2 + (P \times D)/2 + SS$$

where $\bar{I} =$ average inventory in units
$Q =$ order quantity units
$P =$ review period in days
$D =$ average daily demand
SS $=$ safety stock

For the preceding example, the average inventory is calculated as

$$\bar{I} = Q/2 + (P \times D)/2 + SS$$
$$= 200/2 + (7 \times 20)/2 + 0 = 100 + 70 = 170 \text{ units}$$

Because of the time interval introduced by periodic review, periodic control systems generally require larger average inventories than perpetual systems.

Modified Control Systems To accommodate specific situations, variations and combinations of the basic periodic and perpetual control systems have been developed. Most common are the replenishment level system and the optional replenishment system. Each is briefly noted to illustrate the range of modified systems available for control purposes.

The target level *replenishment system* is a fixed-order-interval system that provides for short-interval periodic review. With complete status on inventory similar to the perpetual concept, the system establishes an upper limit or replenishment level for reordering. The review period is added to the lead time, and the target replenishment level (TGT) is defined as

$$TGT = SS + D(T + P)$$

where TGT $=$ replenishment level
 SS $=$ safety stock
 D $=$ average daily demand
 T $=$ average performance-cycle length
 P $=$ review period in days

The general reordering rules become

$$Q = TGT - I - Q_o$$

where Q $=$ order quantity
 TGT $=$ replenishment level
 I $=$ inventory status at review time
 Q_o $=$ quantity on order

Assuming a review period of 5 days, average expected sales of 20 units/day, zero safety stock, and a replenishment cycle of 10 days,

$$TGT = D(T + P) + SS$$
$$= 20(10 + 5) + 0 = 300 \text{ units}$$

Since the replenishment cycle is longer than the review period, it is necessary to consider outstanding orders. Assume there is one outstanding order for 100 units at the time of the review and the current inventory is 50 units. Then

$$Q = TGT - I - Q_o$$
$$= 300 - 50 - 100 = 150 \text{ units}$$

Under the target replenishment system, the size of order is determined without reference to lot sizing. Emphasis is placed on maintaining inventory levels below a maximum, which is the target or order-up-to level. The maximum is protected as an upper level since inventory will never exceed the replenishment level and can reach the replenishment level only if no unit sales are experienced between the replenishment initiation order and the following review period. Under these conditions the average inventory is

$$\bar{I} = (DP)/2 + SS$$

where $\bar{I}$ = average inventory
 D = average daily demand
 P = review period in days
 SS = safety stock

A variation of the target replenishment system is the *optional replenishment system,* which is sometimes referred to as the (s,S) or min-max system. Similar to the target level replenishment system, the optional system substitutes a variable order quantity for a specific lot size. However, the optional replenishment system introduces a modification to limit the lower size of the variable order quantity. As a result, the inventory level is perpetually maintained between an upper and lower bound. The upper bound exists to establish a maximum inventory level, and the lower bound guarantees that replenishment orders will at least be equal to the difference between the maximum (S) and the minimum (s) level. The basic replenishment rule is

$$\text{If } I + Q_o < s \text{ then } Q = S - I - Q_o$$

where I = inventory status at review time
 Q_o = quantity on order
 s = minimum stock level
 Q = order quantity
 S = maximum stock level

The minimum or (s) level is determined similarly to ROP. When there is no uncertainty,

$$s = D \times T$$

where s = minimum stock level
 D = average daily demand
 T = average performance-cycle length

When demand and performance-cycle uncertainty exist, the minimum stock level (s) must be incremented by an allowance for safety stock.

The min-max system can be implemented in terms of absolute units of product, days' supply, or a combination of both. In the case of absolute units, both the minimum and the maximum are defined in terms of a specific number of units. For example, suppose the minimum and maximum are defined to be 100 and 400 units, respectively. The resulting replenishment rule is

$$\text{If } I + Q_o < 100 \text{ then } Q = 400 - I - Q_o$$

where the terms are the same as defined above. If the inventory and quantity currently on order are 75 and 0, respectively, the resulting quantity to order is 325 ($Q = 400 - 75$). The min-max policy can also be implemented using ''days' supply'' parameters. For example, the minimum can be defined as 10 days' supply. For each replenishment review, the days' supply is converted to a specific number of units by multiplying it by the current forecast. The days' supply approach has the advantage of being dependent on the forecast, so it responds to changes in demand.

Reactive Methods

The reactive inventory system, as the name implies, responds to a channel member's inventory needs by drawing the product through the distribution channel. Replenishment shipments are initiated when available warehouse stock levels fall below a predetermined minimum or order point. The amount ordered is usually based on some lot sizing formulation, although it may be some variable quantity that is a function of current stock levels and a predetermined maximum level. In summary, a reactive inventory system waits for customer demand to pull the product through the system. For example, each retailer independently makes a choice regarding when and how much to order from the wholesaler or distribution center. In turn, each wholesaler or distribution center orders independently from its suppliers. The series of independent actions results in uncertainty at each reorder point throughout the distribution channel. Multiple levels of uncertainty require significant safety stock to provide adequate performance.

The basic perpetual or periodic review control process discussed earlier exemplifies a typical reactive system. Figure 9-1 illustrates a reactive inventory environment for a distribution center and the two wholesalers that it serves. The figure shows the current inventory (I), reorder point (ROP), order quantity (Q), and average daily demand (D) for each wholesaler. A review of the wholesaler inventory indicates that a resupply order for 200 units should be placed by Wholesaler A from the distribution center. Since current inventory is above ROP for Wholesaler B, no resupply action is necessary at this time. However, more thorough analysis illustrates that the independent actions by Wholesaler A will likely cause a stockout at Wholesaler B within a few days. Wholesaler B will likely stock out because its inventory level is close to the reorder point and the supplying distribution center will not have enough inventory to fill Wholesaler B's replenishment request.

In order to provide a more detailed understanding of a reactive inventory control system, the following discussion reviews its assumptions and implications. First, the system is founded on the basic assumption that all customers, market areas, and products contribute equally to profits. ABC or fine-line classification may be

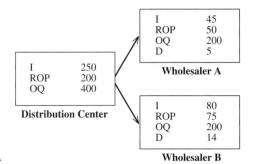

FIGURE 9-1   A reactive inventory environment.

used to strategically establish desired inventory to meet those customer, market, and product levels. However, a pure reactive system minimizes anticipatory inventory movements and thus eliminates the logic that makes these movements for high-volume products.

Second, the reactive system assumes infinite availability at the source (i.e., no significant manufacturing or storage capacity constraints exist). This assumption, which significantly limits the system, implies that product can be produced as desired and stored at the production facility until required by the distribution center.

Third, reactive inventory logic assumes infinite inventory availability at the supply location. In other words, there are no constraints of facility capacity or inventory availability. The combination of assumptions two and three implies relative resupply time certainty. The reactive inventory logic provides for no backorders or stockouts when processing replenishment orders.

Fourth, reactive decision rules assume that performance-cycle time can be predicted and that cycle lengths are independent. This means that each performance cycle is a random event and that extended cycles don't generally occur for subsequent replenishment orders. Although reactive logics assume no control over cycle times, many managers are, in fact, able to influence performance-cycle length through expediting and alternative sourcing strategies.

Fifth, reactive inventory logic operates best when customer demand patterns are relatively stable and consistent. Ideally, demand patterns should be stable over the relevant planning cycle for statistical reactive logic to operate correctly. Most reactive system decision rules assume demand patterns based on standard normal, gamma, or Poisson distribution functions. When the actual demand function does not resemble one of the above, the statistical inventory decision rules based on these assumptions will not operate correctly. For example, if the actual sales pattern is ''lumpy'' because of several large accounts, actual safety stock requirements would be higher than predicted using the standard normal distribution. Lumpy demand, as opposed to smooth demand, is characterized by periodic large orders that stress inventory capabilities. Lumpy demand requires additional safety stock to meet desired service objectives. Since demand patterns for most products are constantly changing as a result of various trends, marketing programs, and competitive actions, it can be difficult to identify what the appropriate stable demand pattern is or should be.

Sixth, reactive inventory systems determine each distribution center's timing and quantity of replenishment orders independently of all other sites, including the supply source. Thus, there is little potential to effectively coordinate inventory requirements across multiple distribution centers. The ability to take advantage of inventory information is not utilized—a serious defect when information and its communication are among the few resources that are decreasing in cost in the distribution channel.

The final assumption characteristic of reactive inventory systems is that performance-cycle length should not be correlated with demand. The assumption is necessary to develop an accurate approximation of the variance of the demand over the performance cycle. For many situations, however, higher demand levels often create longer performance cycles since they also increase the demands on inventory and transportation resources. This implies that periods of high demand should not necessarily correspond to extended performance cycles caused by stockouts or limited product availability.

The above discussion outlines many of the assumptions and resulting problems in classical reactive inventory logic. The problems include overly simplified demand patterns, ''infinite'' availability and capacity, no segmented profitability consideration, and failure to coordinate information regarding requirements across multiple facilities. Operationally, most inventory managers overcome the limitations through the skillful use of manual overrides. However, these overrides often lead to suboptimal inventory decision making since the resulting combination of decisions uses neither consistent decision rules nor consistent inventory management criteria.

Planning Methods

Inventory planning methods use a common information base to coordinate inventory requirements across multiple locations or stages in the value-added chain. Planning activities may occur at the plant warehouse level to coordinate inventory allocation and delivery to multiple distribution centers. Planning may also occur to coordinate inventory requirements across multiple channel partners such as manufacturers and retailers.

Two inventory planning methods are fair share allocation and distribution requirements planning (DRP). Each is described and illustrated.

Fair Share Allocation   Fair share allocation is a simplified inventory management planning method that provides each distribution facility with an equitable or ''fair share'' of available inventory from a common source such as a plant warehouse. Figure 9-2 illustrates the network structure, current inventory level, and daily requirements for three distribution centers served by a common plant warehouse.

Using fair share allocation rules, the inventory planner determines the amount of inventory that can be allocated to each distribution center from the available inventory at the plant warehouse. For this example, assume that it is desirable to

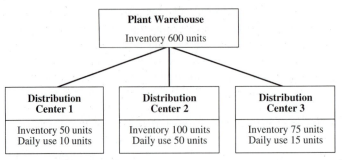

FIGURE 9-2   Fair share allocation example.

retain 100 units at the plant warehouse; therefore, 500 units are available for allocation. The calculation to determine the common days' supply is

$$DS = \frac{A_j + \sum\limits_{j=1}^{n} I_j}{\sum\limits_{j=1}^{n} D_j}$$

where DS = common days' supply for distribution center inventories
$\quad A_j$ = inventory units to be allocated from plant warehouse
$\quad I_j$ = inventory in units for distribution center j
$\quad D_j$ = daily demand for distribution center j

In this example,

$$DS = \frac{500 + (50 + 100 + 75)}{10 + 50 + 15}$$

$$= \frac{500 + 225}{75} = 9.67 \text{ days}$$

So, the fair share allocation dictates that each distribution center should be brought up to 9.67 days of stock. The amount to be allocated to each distribution center is determined by

$$A_j = (DS - I_j/D_j) \times D_j$$

where A_j = amount allocated to distribution center j
$\quad$ DS = days' supply that each distribution center is brought up to
$\quad I_j$ = inventory in units for distribution center j
$\quad D_j$ = daily demand for distribution center j

The amount allocated to distribution center 1 for this example is

$$A_1 = (9.67 - 50/10) \times 10$$

$$= (9.67 - 5) \times 10$$

$$= 4.67 \times 10 = 46.7 \text{ (rounded to 47 units)}$$

The allocations for distribution centers 2 and 3 can be determined similarly and are 383 and 70 units, respectively.

While fair share allocation coordinates inventory levels across multiple sites, it does not consider site-specific factors such as differences in performance-cycle time, economic order quantity, or safety stock requirements. Fair share allocation methods are therefore limited in their ability to manage multistage inventories.

Distribution Requirements Planning (DRP)   DRP is a more sophisticated planning approach that considers multiple distribution stages and the characteristics of each stage. DRP is the logical extension of manufacturing requirements planning (MRP), although there is one fundamental difference between the two techniques. MRP is determined by a production schedule that is defined and controlled by the enterprise. On the other hand, DRP is guided by customer demand, which is not controllable by the enterprise. So, while MRP generally operates in a dependent demand situation, DRP operates in an independent environment where uncertain customer demand determines inventory requirements. The manufacturing requirements planning component coordinates the scheduling and integration of materials into finished goods. MRP controls inventory until manufacturing or assembly is completed. DRP then takes coordination responsibility once finished goods are received in the plant warehouse.

DRP Process   Figure 9-3 illustrates the conceptual design of a combined DRP/ MRP system that integrates finished goods, work-in-process, and materials planning. DRP coordinates inventory levels, plans inventory movement, and (if necessary) reschedules inventory between levels.

The fundamental DRP planning tool is the schedule, which coordinates requirements across the planning horizon. There is a schedule for each SKU and each distribution facility. Schedules for the same SKU are integrated to determine the overall requirements for replenishment facilities such as a plant warehouse.

Figure 9-4 illustrates DRP schedules for three distribution centers and a central supply facility. The schedules are developed using weekly time increments known as *buckets*. Each bucket projects one period of activity. Although weekly increments are the most common, daily or monthly periods are used as well. For each site and SKU, the schedule reports current on-hand balance, safety stock, performance-cycle length, and order quantity. In addition, for each planning period, the schedule reports gross requirements, scheduled receipts, and projected on-hand inventory and planned orders. Gross requirements reflect demands from customers and other distribution facilities supplied by the site under review. Scheduled receipts are the replenishment shipments planned for arrival at the distribution center. Projected on-hand inventory refers to the anticipated week-ending level. It is equal

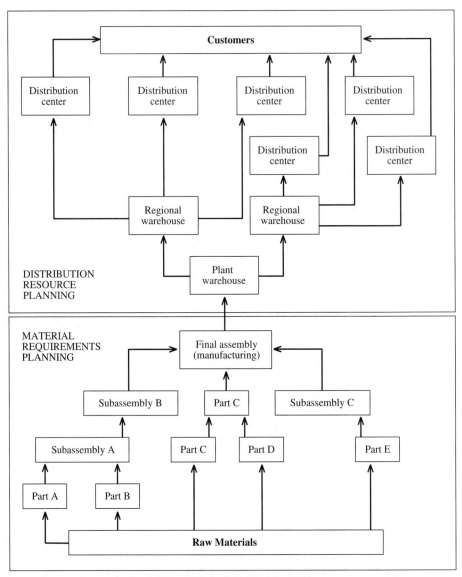

FIGURE 9-3   Conceptual design of integrated DRP/MRP system. *("How DRP Helps Warehouses Smooth Distri-bution,"* Modern Materials Handling, ***39:6,*** *April 1984, p. 53.)*

to the prior week's on-hand inventory less the current week's gross requirements plus any scheduled receipts.

Planned orders are the suggested replenishment demands to be placed on the source. DRP applications use the planning reports or screens illustrated in Figure 9-4 to project future inventory requirements for each level of the supply chain, whether it is under the control of single or multiple firms. The sidebar discusses the interpretation and dynamics of these DRP screens or reports.

DRP Benefits and Constraints   An integrated inventory planning system such as DRP offers a number of benefits for management. Major organizational beneficiaries include marketing and logistics. The major marketing benefits are:

1   Improved service levels that increase on-time deliveries and decrease customer complaints

2   Improved and more effective promotional and new-product introduction plans

3   Improved ability to anticipate shortages so that marketing efforts are not expended on products with low stock

4   Improved inventory coordination with other enterprise functions, since DRP facilitates a common set of planning numbers

5   Enhanced ability to offer customers a coordinated inventory management service

The major logistics benefits are:

1   Reduced distribution center freight costs resulting from coordinated shipments

2   Reduced inventory levels, since DRP can accurately determine what product is needed and when

3   Decreased warehouse space requirements because of inventory reductions

4   Reduced customer freight cost as a result of fewer back-orders

5   Improved inventory visibility and coordination between logistics and manufacturing

6   Enhanced budgeting capability, since DRP can effectively simulate inventory and transportation requirements under multiple planning scenarios

While planning approaches to inventory management offer significant benefits, there are some constraints to their effectiveness.

First, inventory planning systems require accurate and coordinated forecasts for each distribution center. The forecast is necessary to direct the flow of goods through the distribution channel. Ideally, the system does not maintain excess inventory at any location, so little room for error exists in a lean inventory planning system. To the extent that this level of forecast accuracy is possible, inventory planning systems operate well. However, this requires forecasts for each distribution center and SKU as well as adequate lead time to allow product movement. With such requirements, three potential sources for error exist. The forecast itself may be wrong, it may have predicted demand at the wrong location, or it may have predicted demand at the wrong time. In any event, forecast error can be a significant concern when forecasts are used to guide inventory planning systems.

Second, inventory planning requires consistent and reliable performance cycles for movement between distribution facilities. While variable performance cycles can be accommodated through safety lead times, performance-cycle uncertainty reduces planning system effectiveness.

Third, integrated planning is subject to system nervousness, or frequent rescheduling, because of production breakdowns or delivery delays. System nervousness leads to fluctuation in capacity utilization, rescheduling cost, and confusion

Boston Distribution Center

On-hand balance: 352   Lead time: 2 weeks
Safety stock: 55   Order quantity: 500

	Past due	Week							
		1	2	3	4	5	6	7	8
Gross requirements		50	50	60	70	80	70	60	50
Scheduled receipts						500			
Projected on-hand	352	302	252	192	122	542	472	412	362
Planned orders				500					

Chicago Distribution Center

On-hand balance: 220   Lead time: 2 weeks
Safety stock: 115   Order quantity: 800

	Past due	Week							
		1	2	3	4	5	6	7	8
Gross requirements		115	115	120	120	125	125	125	120
Scheduled receipts		800							
Projected on-hand	220	905	790	670	550	425	300	175	855
Planned orders							800		

San Diego Distribution Center

On-hand balance: 140   Lead time: 2 weeks
Safety time: 2 weeks   Order quantity: 150

	Past due	Week							
		1	2	3	4	5	6	7	8
Gross requirements		20	25	15	20	30	25	15	30
Scheduled receipts						150			
Projected on-hand	140	120	95	80	60	180	155	145	110
Planned orders				150					

Central Supply Facility

On-hand balance: 1,250
Safety stock: 287
Lead time: 3 weeks
Order quantity: 2,200

	Past due	Week							
		1	2	3	4	5	6	7	8
Gross requirements	0	0	0	650	0	0	800	0	0
Scheduled receipts									
Projected on-hand	1250	1250	1250	600	600	600	2000	2000	2000
Master sched.-rcpt.							2200		
Master sched.-start				2200					

└──────→ To Material Requirements Planning Schedule ──────→

FIGURE 9-4   DRP planning process. *("How DRP Helps Warehouses Smooth Distribution,"* Modern Materials Handling, ***39:6****, April 1984, p. 57.)*

in deliveries. This is intensified by the volatile operating environment characteristic of distribution. Uncertainties such as supply transportation performance cycles and vendor delivery reliability can cause an extremely nervous DRP system. Logistics planners are better prepared to cope with frequent scheduling changes by utilizing uncertainty buffering methods, such as safety stock, when they understand the potential causes of the problem. While DRP is not the universal solution for inventory management, many firms such as Dow Chemical and Eastman Kodak have reported substantial performance improvements with its use.

Adaptive Logic

A combined inventory management system may be used to overcome some of the problems inherent in either a reactive or a planning method. The factors that might make a reactive system better in one situation may change over the course of time to favor an inventory planning system. Thus, the ideal approach is a method that incorporates elements of both types of logic and allows different strategies to be used with specific customer or product segments.

Description   An adaptive inventory management system is one that combines reactive and inventory planning logics. The rationale for an adaptive system is that

DRP: A SAMPLE APPLICATION

MMH, Inc. has three distribution centers (DCs) located across the United States, and a central supply facility at its manufacturing plant in Quebec, Canada. Here's how their distribution resource planning (DRP[II]) system works over an eight-week period:

The Boston DC has a safety stock level set at 55 units of widgets. When stock goes below that level, the DC sends out an order for 500 more widgets. The lead time for shipment from the central facility to the Boston DC is two weeks.

The DRP display for the Boston DC shows the demand forecast, called *gross requirements,* for eight weeks. Starting with an on-hand balance of 352 widgets, the DC forecasts that it will have only 42 widgets during week five (the 122 widgets on hand minus the 80 in gross requirements).

This is below the safety stock level, so DRP initiates a planned order of 500 widgets during week three (week five minus the lead time). Stock comes, as forecasted, and the DC is back to safe operating levels.

Widgets are a high-volume seller in Chicago, so the Chicago DC has a higher gross requirement than the Boston DC. It also orders more widgets at a time.

The DRP display for the Chicago DC shows that 800 widgets are already in transit (scheduled receipts) and due to arrive in week one. They do, and the next order, for 800 widgets, is placed in week six to satisfy the upcoming below-safety stock condition in week eight.

Through experience, the San Diego DC expresses their safety stock as safety time (two weeks).

Examining the DRP display, the DC realizes that without replenishment, 30 widgets (60 minus 30) would be remaining in week five, five widgets (30 minus 25) in week six, and a negative on-hand balance of ten (5 minus 15) in week seven. So, the DC initiates a planned order for 150 widgets in week three—week seven minus the safety time minus the lead time (four weeks total).

The DRP display for the central supply facility is similar to that for the DCs; however, it displays recommendations for the master schedule in terms of the start and receipt of manufacturing orders.

The gross requirements in the facility are caused by the DCs; the Boston and San Diego DCs produced demands for a total of 650 widgets in week three, while Chicago DC produced demands for 800 widgets in week six. The facility finds it will have a negative on-hand balance in week six. Therefore it initiates a master schedule order in week three of 2,200 widgets to cover the shortage.

From "How DRP Helps Warehouses Smooth Distribution," *Modern Materials Handling,* **39**:6, April 1984, p. 57. *Modern Materials Handling,* copyright 1984 by Cahners Publishing Company, Division of Reed Holdings, Inc.

---

customer demand must usually be treated as independent; however, there are some channel situations when demand can be treated as dependent. Thus, at some locations and times within the distribution channel, an interface must exist between independent and dependent demand. The uniqueness of an adaptive inventory management logic is that it changes as environmental conditions change. For example, during some parts of the year it may be most efficient to push products to field warehouses, while at other times the best alternative may be to hold the stock at the manufacturing location and wait for customers to pull it through the distribution channel.

Another example of different inventory management requirements is illustrated in the relationship between manufacturers and retailers. Usually, retailers generate replenishment orders as required, and manufacturers react to them. However, in some situations such as the relationship between Kmart and the Johnson & Johnson Customer Support Center, the manufacturer (Johnson & Johnson) has assumed the responsibility of managing retailer distribution center inventory. As a result, the manufacturer has visibility of two (or more) levels of channel member demand, which results in less uncertainty and reduces safety stock requirements. While this arrangement is appropriate for some relationships, it is not appropriate for all customers or products because it is information-intensive.

An adaptive inventory management system must adjust itself in terms of location and time. In other words, the appropriate systems may change for different locations and also for different times of the year. This adjustment capability requires that the information base for such a system be totally integrated. With today's data management techniques, it is possible to maintain the necessary level of information. The primary difficulty in implementing such a system is determining the decision rules that should be used for making adjustments. The following discussion reviews both the factors that should be considered when selecting the appropriate logic and the adjustment categories. It then utilizes these factors to determine heuristic decision rules.

Adaptive Decision Factors   Inventory management should consider the relative contribution or profitability of individual market segments. For segments or products that are highly profitable and generate consistent sales, the appropriate decision rule is to push inventory to the market since there is little risk of poor allocation. This rule overcomes two limitations of the reactive system while eliminating the risk of a pure inventory planning method. First, inventories can be moved from upstream facilities, which may be above capacity at volumes that provide transport scale economies. Second, an adaptive and selective logic does not push slow or inconsistent movers. Thus, markets and products that are selected to utilize the inventory planning logic must be reviewed periodically to assess profitability, volume, and consistency characteristics.

The difference between independent and dependent demand is the second factor that influences the selection of an appropriate inventory management logic. Since the adaptive system recognizes the two different types of demand, it attempts to utilize the logic that best fits the situation. The basic decision rule is to use planning methods or logic whenever possible to minimize costs, but to avoid overcommitting stock where a high degree of uncertainty exists. The key issue concerns whether demand can be best treated as independent or dependent.

Many forms of uncertainty exist at each interface in the channel. The three broad types of uncertainty are supply, demand, and performance cycle. The inventory management logic must be designed to treat all three forms of uncertainty at different points in time. Reactive inventory systems consider performance-cycle and demand uncertainty but fail to allow for supply or availability uncertainty. Inventory planning systems allow for supply uncertainty but have limited consideration of performance-cycle and demand uncertainty. The ideal inventory logic should be able to treat all three sources of uncertainty.

Just as in the case of economies of scale, the uncertainty factor must be addressed for each interface (i.e., relationship between supplier and customer) in the distribution channel. As a general rule, however, once the decision is made to utilize a planning system at one echelon in the channel, inventory planning must be used at all echelons. To determine which type of system is appropriate, the combination of the three uncertainties must be investigated for each echelon or location. The following heuristic decision rules should be used in selecting the appropriate type of system for each stage.

For situations where there are supply uncertainties or allocation restrictions, a planning-based system is the most appropriate to efficiently allocate available inventory. An inventory planning system facilitates the supply of the product to markets, where it can be sold the most profitably or with the greatest degree of certainty. The planning approach can also be used to manage shipments to markets or customers that can most easily survive without them. For example, replenishment requests from customers that can survive with existing inventories may be delayed so that product can be shipped to customers that are actually out of stock.

Performance-cycle time uncertainty should be treated with a reactive inventory system. Reactive logic will create smaller shipment quantities and less risk of having a large shipment delayed in transit or incorrect allocation of a large amount of inventory. The use of a planning system in this situation might cause a large shipment to be delayed or to arrive early. Demand uncertainty at individual distribution centers is another consideration for determining the appropriate inventory management system. For situations where demand is relatively stable or predictable, the planning logic is the most efficient since it can take advantage of the transport economies discussed previously. For situations were demand is not consistent or predictable, the reactive logic is the most appropriate because stock commitment to lower echelons is postponed until there is some evidence of need.

The final factor for deciding the most appropriate inventory management system is the capacity of the channel interface. This refers to either the production capacity of the manufacturing facilities or the storage capacity of the various distribution centers and warehouses. A reactive logic assumes that there are no capacity limitations at any distribution facilities, so use of such logic may cause problems when restrictions do exist. Thus, when there are capacity limitations at the plant or storage facility level, the inventory planning logic moves product from an overcapacity location more effectively.

The above heuristic decision rules indicate the general logic requirements for various channel situations. Table 9-2 summarizes how a management logic situation may consist of a combination of factors.

Up to this point, the discussion has described an adaptive inventory system and identified when the adjustments might be appropriate. The following section outlines the dimensions for adjustment.

The three inventory management adjustment categories are temporal, spatial, and product. First, the system must have the ability to adapt over time. The factors discussed above certainly change over time. For example, agricultural food products such as beans and peas are widely available in the late summer and early autumn, so processing for the entire year must be done at that time. For many firms, this means that manufacturing locations may be overstocked, and thus a planning approach is appropriate. However, when supplies are decreasing in the spring and summer, switching over to a reactive system to avoid product overcommitment might be a better approach.

Second, the system should have the ability to adapt by location and echelon.

TABLE 9-2   SUGGESTED INVENTORY MANAGEMENT LOGIC

Use proactive logic under conditions of:	Use reactive logic under conditions of:
Highly profitable segments	Cycle time uncertainty
Dependent demand	Demand uncertainty
Economies of scale	Destination capacity limitations
Supply uncertainty	
Source capacity limitations	
Seasonal supply buildup	

This modification process is called *spatial adjustment.* For each channel stage, the factors discussed must be investigated to determine which inventory logic would be the most appropriate. In general, the echelons closer to the manufacturer would tend to use a planning logic, while those closest to the market would tend toward a reactive logic. However, the point or stage at which the logic switches from inventory planning to reactive may shift over time. In the above food example, during the packing season it is appropriate to push the product all the way through the channel to the final customer. On the other hand, during the spring and summer when manufacturing location supplies are low, a reactive system is more appropriate for the majority of channel stages. The switch from a planning to a reactive system for the processed food example would likely take place in the early spring.

The final adjustment that an adaptive system must make is product-based. As product availability or demand changes, the system should be able to switch from one approach to the other in order to provide the most efficient means for distribution. In some situations this capability may call for the operation of dual systems (e.g., one for proactive products and one for reactive products). In other words, high-volume products would be managed with planning systems, while low-volume products would be better served by a reactive method.

MANAGEMENT PROCESSES

An integrated inventory management strategy defines the policies and process used to determine where to place inventory, when to initiate replenishment shipments, and how much to allocate.

This section discusses the strategy development process and describes methods used by firms to improve inventory management effectiveness.

Strategy Development Process

The strategy development process employs three steps to classify products and markets, define segment strategies, and operationalize policies and parameters. Each step is described and illustrated.

Product/Market Classification   The objective of product/market classification is to focus and refine inventory management efforts. Product/market classification, which is also called fine-line or ABC classification, groups products or markets with similar characteristics to facilitate inventory management. The classification process recognizes that not all products and markets have the same degree of importance. Sound inventory management requires that classification be consistent with enterprise strategy and service objectives.

Classification can be based on a variety of measures. The most common are sales, profit contribution, inventory value, usage rate, and nature of the item. The typical classification process sequences products or markets so that entries with similar characteristics are grouped together. Table 9-3 illustrates product classification using sales. The products are classified (listed) in descending order by sales volume, so the fast movers (high-volume products) are listed first followed by slower-moving items.

Classification by sales volume is one of the oldest methods used to establish selective policies or strategies. For most marketing or logistics applications, a small percentage of the entities (e.g., products, markets, orders, or suppliers) account for a large percentage of the volume (such as sales). This operationalization is often called the *80/20 rule,* or *Pareto's law.* The 80/20 rule, which is based on extensive observations in industry, states that for a typical enterprise 80 percent of the sales volume are typically accounted for by 20 percent of the products. A corollary to the rule is that 80 percent of enterprise sales are accounted for by 20 percent of the customers. The reverse perspective of the rule would state that the remaining

TABLE 9-3   PRODUCT MARKET CLASSIFICATION (SALES)

Product identification	Annual sales (in 000s)	Percentage total sales	Accumulated Sales (%)	Accumulated Products (%)	Classification category
1	$ 45,000	30.0	30.0	5	A
2	35,000	23.3	53.3	10	A
3	25,000	16.7	70.0	15	A
4	15,000	10.0	80.0	20	A
5	8,000	5.3	85.3	25	B
6	5,000	3.3	88.6	30	B
7	4,000	2.7	91.3	35	B
8	3,000	2.0	93.3	40	B
9	2,000	1.3	94.6	45	B
10	1,000	0.7	95.3	50	B
11	1,000	0.7	96.0	55	C
12	1,000	0.7	96.7	60	C
13	1,000	0.7	97.4	65	C
14	750	0.5	97.9	70	C
15	750	0.5	98.4	75	C
16	750	0.5	98.9	80	C
17	500	0.3	99.2	85	C
18	500	0.3	99.5	90	C
19	500	0.3	99.8	95	C
20	250	0.2	100.0	100	C
	$150,000				

20 percent of sales are obtained from 80 percent of the products, customers, etc. In general terms, the 80/20 rule implies that a majority of sales volume (or any other classification factor) results from relatively few products or customers.

Once items are classified or grouped, it is common to label each category with a character or description. High-volume, fast-moving products are often described as ''A'' items. The moderate-volume products are called the ''B'' items, and the low-volume or slow movers are known as the ''C's.'' These character labels indicate why this process is often referred to as *ABC analysis.* While fine-line classification often uses three categories, some firms use four or five to further refine classifications. Grouping of similar products facilitates management efforts to establish focused inventory strategies for each product segment. For example, high-volume or fast-moving products are typically targeted for higher service levels. This often implies that fast-moving items will be provided with relatively more safety stock. Conversely, slower-moving items may be allowed relatively less safety stock, which results in lower service levels.

In special situations, classification systems may be based on multiple factors. For example, item gross margin and importance to customers (e.g., criticality such as that for medical products) could be weighted to develop a combined index instead of simply using sales volume. The weighted rank array would then group items that have similar profitability and importance. The inventory policy (including safety stock levels) is then established using the weighted rank. The following considerations are important when designing classification systems.

When classifying on the basis of unit volume, it is important to realize that a differential will exist in a product line between total dollar sales and unit volume. Often, low-value items that generate high unit sales during a performance cycle account for only a small percentage of total dollar sales.

When classifying by unit value, it is important to consider that high-value items are more expensive to protect than items with lower value. However, the high-value items may also be more profitable. Recall that (according to the EOQ rules) higher unit value and higher unit volume result in smaller economic order quantities and more frequent replenishment orders. The ideal inventory performance cycle would thus be short for items having high value and high usage.

The classification array defines the product or market groups that will be assigned similar inventory strategies. The use of item groups facilitates the identification and specification of inventory strategies since it considers the common characteristics of each group without requiring tedious specification of individual items. It is much easier to track and manage three to ten groups instead of hundreds of individual items.

Segment Strategy Definition The second step in the development process defines the integrated inventory strategy for each product/market group or segment. The integrated strategy includes specification for all aspects of the inventory management process including service objectives, forecasting method, management technique, and review cycle.

The key to establishing selective management strategies is the realization that product segments have different degrees of importance with respect to achieving the enterprise mission. Desired differences in inventory responsiveness should be designed into the policies and procedures used for inventory management.

Table 9-4 illustrates a sample integrated strategy for four item categories. In this case, the products are grouped by sales volume ("A," "B," or "C") and according to whether they are promotional or basic stock items. Promotional items are those that are commonly sold via consumer or trade promotion and therefore encounter considerable demand lumpiness. Lumpy demand patterns are characteristic of promotional periods with high volume followed by postpromotion periods with relatively low demand.

Table 9-4 depicts a management segmentation scheme based on service objectives, forecasting procedure, review period, inventory management approach, and replenishment monitoring frequency. Additional or fewer characteristics of the inventory management process may be appropriate for some enterprises. Although this table should not be interpreted as an absolute inventory standard, it does suggest some characteristics of the best processes. The rationale behind each element is presented.

The first characteristic concerns the service objective for the inventory management process. The "A" items are assigned a high service objective since there are typically few items (as per the 80/20 rule), and they significantly affect overall customer service performance because of their high volume. Conversely, a lower service objective is appropriate for slow-moving items because they involve low-volume products and thus have relatively small impact on customer service performance.

The second characteristic has to do with forecast procedure. Since promotional item sales are influenced by the promotional calendar, their forecast should be developed using a top-down explosion of the total promotion volume. The demand for the remaining product categories (i.e., "A" regular, "B," and "C" items) is less lumpy, so forecasts should be developed using sales history, time-series methods, and bottom-up forecasting.

The third characteristic involves the replenishment review period. While minimizing the number of inventory reviews may not be as important as it was in the past because of today's advanced information capabilities, it is still vital for manual elements of the review process. For example, when replenishment or purchase orders must be generated manually, personnel time constraints may limit the inventory management process to weekly reviews. However, fast-moving items may

TABLE 9-4 INTEGRATED STRATEGY

Fine-line classification	Service objective	Forecasting procedure	Review period	Inventory management	Replenishment monitoring
A—promotional	99%	Aggregate schedule	Perpetual	Planning—DRP	Daily
A—regular	98	Sales history	Perpetual	Planning—DRP	Daily
B	95	Sales history	Weekly	Planning—DRP	Weekly
C	90	Sales history	Biweekly	Reorder point	Biweekly

require more frequent reviews to avoid stockouts. Assuming that different review periods are appropriate, high-volume items should use perpetual review while the "B" and "C" items should be reviewed on a periodic basis such as weekly or biweekly, respectively.

The fourth characteristic concerns the specific inventory management logic for each group. The continuum of options ranges from a pure reactive system to a planning method as discussed earlier. It is likely that higher-volume products can be forecasted with relatively greater accuracy because demand is more stable or because additional effort is possible to develop better forecasts since there are fewer "A" items.

Low-volume items are usually more difficult to forecast because they typically have relatively greater demand uncertainty. Assuming that better forecasts are possible for "A" items and that substantial scale benefits exist for planned product movements to distribution facilities and customers, a planning or distribution requirements planning (DRP) approach should be used for high-volume products. Conversely, reactive inventory management is more appropriate for low-volume items so that speculative movement downstream in the channel can be minimized. The reactive logic also minimizes the data collection and manipulation required to support inventory planning system application for the large number of low-volume items.

The final characteristic involves the replenishment monitoring frequency. This refers to the review and expediting efforts to ensure that replenishment orders arrive on time. The monitoring process may include inquiries to the supplier and the carrier to identify shipment status and determine its arrival time. If the monitoring determines that the replenishment order will not arrive on time, replenishment should be expedited or an alternative source identified. Table 9-4 suggests daily monitoring for high-volume items and weekly monitoring of low-volume items. Daily monitoring is appropriate for high-volume products because even a one- or two-day stockout would negatively affect service. On the other hand, low-volume items can be monitored weekly since the inventory position does not change as rapidly and stockouts will not affect service performance as significantly.

Integrating the above characteristics defines a process that focuses management efforts on providing high service performance for the bulk of the sales or unit volume ("A" items) and establishing low inventory and personnel requirements for a large percentage of products ("B" and "C" items). While an initial strategy may be designed for three or four groups, experience and the desire to refine service performance and reduce inventory motivate additional strategies. These can be implemented by increasing the number of groups and refining the policies and procedures for each.

Operationalized Policies and Parameters   The final step implements the focused inventory management strategy by defining detailed procedures and parameters. The procedures define data requirements, software applications, performance objectives, and decision guidelines. The parameters delineate the actual numeric values such as review period length, service objectives, inventory carrying cost percentage, order quantities, and reorder points. The combination of parameters either determines or can be used to calculate the precise quantities necessary to make inventory management decisions.

Once the procedures and parameters have been implemented, the environment and performance characteristics must be monitored on a regular basis. Ongoing monitoring is necessary to ensure that the inventory management system is meeting desired objectives and that the customer and product environment does not change substantially. For example, as demand increases for a specific product, inventory process monitoring should recognize the need and perhaps suggest a shift from a reactive to an inventory planning system.

Methods for Improved Inventory Management

The previous discussion describes the overall inventory management process. Once it is in place and operating smoothly, some firms use additional initiatives to improve inventory effectiveness. The initiatives include (1) policy definition and refinement, (2) information integration, and (3) expert systems application. An example of each follows.

Policy Definition and Refinement   Inventory management incorporates a number of policies and procedures that guide inventory-related decisions. These involve performance measures and training. The role of each is discussed.

Performance Measures   Clear and consistent performance measures for inventory planners are key ingredients in the inventory management process. These measures must reflect the trade-off between service and inventory level. For example, if planner performance measures focus solely on inventory level, the planner's tendency is to minimize inventory levels with a potential negative impact on service. Conversely, a singular focus on service will lead the planner to disregard inventory level. Inventory management performance measures must clearly reflect the trade-offs desired by the enterprise, and the reward structure for individuals who maintain the system must be defined to reflect requirements. The specification must provide a clear and consistent definition of the goals and an understanding of how goal achievement affects personnel performance evaluations.

Training   Inventory management is a very complex discipline because of the number of factors involved in the process as well as its impact on other enterprise functions such as production and procurement. It is also important to understand the nature and dynamics of the interfaces between enterprise inventory management and other entities within the value chain. In response to these factors, many firms are increasing both the amount and the sophistication of training to improve inventory management decision making.

Two types of training are appropriate. First, planners should understand how inventory parameters such as service objectives, review periods, order quantity, safety stock, and inventory management logic influence inventory operations and performance. For example, the planner should understand how review periods, order quantities, and safety stock can be traded off to meet service objectives.

Second, planners should understand how their inventory management decisions affect other members of the value chain. For example, when inventory management

HOW DRP DRIVES DISTRIBUTION IMPROVEMENT

In the mid-to-late 1980s, many large manufacturers began to recognize that existing, internally developed inventory forecasting and planning systems were no longer adequately meeting the demands of their domestic and international distribution networks. These systems were generally characterized as highly reactive, with very limited capability to provide visibility toward future logistics situations.

Typically, manufacturers wanted to create an integrated logistics system bringing together all planning and control information so that management could view and analyze total material flows. Such integration could achieve efficiencies in corporatewide logistics activities as well as provide improved customer service. Additionally, manufacturers wanted to reduce inventories—in particular, by replacing safety stocks with more precise information regarding *what* the product-specific material requirements were and *when* they were needed.

In 1985, Dow Chemical U.S.A. initiated the first stages of a combined MRP/DRP program to reduce utilization of inventory to buffer demand and manufacturing uncertainty. The program was first tested at the individual business unit level and subsequently implemented for management of finished goods inventory throughout its network of distribution centers. Prior to the development of the program, Dow was using a variety of manual and automated systems along separate functional lines, rather than on an integrated basis. Edward H. Huller of Dow's chemical and metals product department noted that "by implementing a comprehensive software system we knew we could integrate the databases and all the different functional areas. That would give each area a better idea about how their decisions impact the division's total business." Dow determined that the company needed a system that would accomplish everything from sales forecasting and production scheduling to inventory management and distribution planning, in addition to providing the capability to network its systems.

In the past eight years, Dow has become extremely satisfied with its DRP system and its ability to be flexible and adaptable as the company grows. Specifically, Dow has identified six principal benefits of the system. First, and most important, there has been a dramatic improvement in internal communication capability. Kenneth E. Steele, project manager in business operations planning, comments that "for the first time, everyone can work with the same set of numbers. This improves the quality of communications because people don't have to spend time figuring out where and how

another person got his number." Second, the system has helped Dow reduce inventories where possible, better identify areas where inventory is necessary, and increase stock levels in areas in order to meet different degrees of service commitment. Third, the system's analysis and modeling function enables manufacturing to optimize production costs in terms of production run length. Fourth, production quality control has also improved because better production planning allows uninterrupted production runs. Fifth, transportation costs have declined because of a reduction in premium transportation usage. Savings are directly attributable to the increased ability to plan rather than react to transportation situations and requirements. Finally, the system has allowed Dow to more effectively manage product profitability on an individual product level and to better handle the company's working capital.

In the late 1980s, the Eastman Kodak Company faced similar problems with respect to its international finished goods distribution network. Kodak had information spread across two or three separate systems, with no open sharing of information among the involved personnel. The result was inaccurate forecasting and excessive inventories, scrap charges, and transportation expedites. Kodak's goals were to achieve significant reductions in each of these problem areas.

Kodak's implementation of DRP also extended over several years. Kodak spokespersons emphasize that DRP is much more than just a new piece of software that duplicates previous historical processes. According to Kodak system analysts, significant effort is involved to prepare and train system users to accept new business methods and philosophies with regard to *both* software and the planning function. Kodak has found that DRP can provide an integrated system in which planners get a full, clear picture of what is happening at all points in their distribution network. Forecast quality has improved, as has control and monitoring capability.

Dow Chemical and Eastman Kodak are examples of how DRP can create powerful, responsive systems that assist firms in controlling inventories and distribution—the critical job of getting product to the right place at the right time and in the right quantities.

Sources: "Eastman Kodak Streamlines Its Product Distribution," *Industrial Engineering,* **22**:9, September 1990, pp. 42–44; and "MRP/DRP Aids Dow Chemical," *Production & Inventory Management Review & APICS News,* **8**:11, November 1988, pp. 33–34.

elects to build up finished goods inventory to support a customer promotion, the planner should understand how that decision will influence production and procurement. If the buildup is substantial, production or procurement may not have the ability and capacity to fulfill the demand. Similarly, inventory planners must also consider the impact of demand declines and surges on the resources of other value chain partners.

EXPERT INVENTORY MANAGEMENT

Inventory management effectiveness can have a major influence on enterprise profitability. Inventory management capability directly determines the inventory levels required to achieve desired service levels. More effective inventory management can also result in increased sales revenue. For many firms, inventory represents their largest single asset, so improved inventory performance can result in significant cash flow and profitability improvements. To attain improved performance, inventory managers must make more accurate and timely decisions regarding when and how much to order.

To determine an appropriate reorder quantity, inventory managers must make decisions that involve a number of interrelated considerations including sales volume, transportation rates, inventory carrying cost, discounts, and lot sizing. Given the number of interrelated considerations, even experienced inventory managers would find it difficult to determine optimal replenishment order quantities and time. Expert systems technology has been applied to assist inventory managers in determining order quantities, timing of order placement, and handling of special problems requiring expertise. The expert systems are designed to guide managers through the evaluation process so that all relevant considerations are addressed.

Air Force inventory management employs two expert systems to enhance inventory performance. The Inventory Management Assistant (IMA) was designed for the U.S. Air Force Logistics Command, which currently supports 19,000 aircraft worldwide with an inventory of 916,000 types of spare parts. IMA was developed to assist inexperienced inventory managers in the verification of input data used to determine repairable parts inventory replenishment requirements. Specifically, all replenishment data are verified and vali-

dated to ensure that replenishment requests are accurate. Inaccurate replenishment requests result in the wrong product being ordered and a required item being out of stock. IMA has allowed inventory managers to improve their effectiveness by 8 to 10 percent for normal problem situations and by 15 to 18 percent for complex situations. As an extra bonus, the expert system caught a $600,000 error in the stocking of one item during the test phase.

IVAN (an expert system for inventory planning) helps inventory managers plan safety stock requirements for parts used in microprocessor-based product manufacturing. The system objective is to minimize inventory holding costs by reducing the amount of time parts spend in the logistics pipeline between vendor and production workstations and by reducing safety stocks where possible. Specifically, for each item, the system makes recommendations regarding part delivery frequency, manufacturing routing, and safety stock requirements, considering factors such as part value, carrying cost, production schedule, and projected lead time. Decreasing time spent in the pipeline results in improved customer service, reduced response time, and reduced inventory carrying cost.

Other examples of expert systems applied to inventory management include (1) a critical item system for the U.S. Navy Retail Centers, (2) a system to assist in requisition/inventory decisions interfaced to materials requirements planning for Federal-Mogul, and (3) the Infoscan system for collecting and scanning retail data for errors.

Source: M. K. Allen and O. K. Helferich, *Putting Expert Systems to Work in Logistics* (Oak Brook, Ill.: Council of Logistics Management, 1990), pp. 58–62.

Information Integration   Inventory effectiveness and performance can be substantially increased and uncertainty decreased by integrating requirements information (forecasts, orders, marketing plans, inventory status, and shipment status) across the enterprise and among channel partners. As discussed in Chapter 6, current technology facilitates information exchange using global networks, electronic data interchange, and satellite communications. For example, common forecasts and a consistent measure of inventory availability reduce the uncertainty between enterprise systems and result in less need for buffer inventory. The sidebar on Dow Chemical and Eastman Kodak illustrates how improved information integration both within the enterprise and across the supply chain results in greater inventory effectiveness.

Expert Systems Application   Expert systems represent another initiative that firms utilize to enhance inventory performance. As described in Chapter 6, these systems use a computerized knowledge base to share inventory management expertise across the enterprise. This shared expertise can supplement the training and awareness discussed above. Expert systems may provide insight into the review period, inventory management logic, and strategies to employ with each product/market group. Results indicate that expert systems can provide substantial improvements in productivity and inventory performance.[2]

SUMMARY

The initial section reviewed the inventory management alternatives of reactive, inventory planning, and adaptive logic. The reactive logic was considered the most appropriate for items with low volume, high demand, and high performance-cycle uncertainty because it postpones the risk of inventory speculation. Inventory planning logic is more appropriate for high-volume items with relatively stable demand. Inventory planning methods offer the potential for more effective inventory management because they take advantage of improved information and economies of scale. Adaptive logic adjusts between the two alternatives, depending on product and market conditions.

The final section discussed processes for implementing overall system inventory management strategy. The basic position was that inventory-related cost allocations must be evaluated in terms of potential revenue. The section reviewed the concept of ABC or fine-line classification analysis as a means of segmenting products and markets with similar inventory management requirements. The discussion then suggested that unique inventory strategies should be considered for each classification group. Such unique strategies might differentiate on service objectives, forecast procedure, review period, inventory management logic, or replenishment monitoring. Once the integrated strategy is specified, inventory performance can be further enhanced through definition and refinement of inventory management policies, information integration, and application of expert systems technology.

[2]Mary Kay Allen and Omar Keith Helferich, *Putting Expert Systems to Work in Logistics,* Oak Brook, Ill.: Council of Logistics Management, 1990, pp. 60–64.

QUESTIONS

1 Data suggest that while overall average inventory levels are declining, the relative percentage being held by manufacturers is increasing. Explain why you think this observation is either true or false. Describe how such a shift could benefit the operations of the entire channel and how manufacturers could take advantage of the shift.

2 Discuss the differences between reactive inventory logics and inventory planning logics. What are the advantages of each? What are the major implications of each?

3 Compare and contrast the use of perpetual and periodic review inventory control systems. Describe how the two techniques could be integrated into a combined inventory control system.

4 Illustrate how fine-line inventory classification can be used with product and market segments. What are the benefits and considerations when classifying inventory by product, market, and product/market?

5 What advantage does DRP have over a fair share method of inventory deployment?

6 In developing an integrated inventory management logic, what factors should be considered in identifying the appropriate methods to use for each product category?

7 Customer-based inventory management strategies allow the use of different service levels (availability) by the customer. Discuss the rationale for such an approach. Are such strategies discriminatory? Justify your position.

8 How can inventory management capabilities take advantage of the potential of expert systems?

9 What procedure and strategies can be used to reduce safety stock requirements for a fixed distribution system design? What are the trade-offs?

10 When all is said and done, how important is inventory in the logistics total-cost equation?

PROBLEM SET B: INVENTORY

1 Mr. Stan Busfield, distribution center manager for Hogan Kitchenwares, must determine when to resupply his stock of spatulas. The distribution center experiences a daily demand of 400 spatulas. The average length of the performance cycle for spatulas is 14 days. Mr. Busfield requires that 500 spatulas be retained as safety stock to deal with demand uncertainty.

    a Use simple reorder point logic to determine the order quantity for spatulas.

    b On the basis of your answer to part (a), find Mr. Busfield's average inventory level of spatulas.

2 Mr. Busfield recently completed a course in logistics management and now realizes that there are significant costs associated with ordering and maintaining inventory at his distribution center. Mr. Busfield has learned that the economic order quantity (EOQ) is the replenishment logic that minimizes these costs. In an effort to find the EOQ for measuring cups, Mr. Busfield has gathered relevant data. He expects to sell 44,000 measuring cups this year. Hogan Kitchenwares acquires the measuring cups for $0.75 each from Shatter Industries. Shatter charges $8.00 for processing each order. In addition, Mr. Busfield estimates his company's inventory carrying cost to be 12 percent annually.

    a Find Mr. Busfield's EOQ for measuring cups. Assume that Mr. Busfield accepts ownership of products upon arrival at his distribution center.

    b Now assume that Mr. Busfield must arrange for inbound transportation of the measuring cups since Hogan accepts ownership of products at the supplier's shipping point. Quantities of fewer than 4,000 measuring cups cost $0.05 per unit to ship. Quantities of 4,000 or more cost $0.04 per unit to ship. Determine the difference in annual total costs associated with an EOQ of 4,000 units and the EOQ level found in part (a)

above when transportation costs must be considered.

    c Given the information above and the low-cost EOQ alternative determined in part (b), use period order quantity (POQ) logic to determine the number of orders Hogan would place each year for measuring cups and the time interval between orders.

3 Mr. Dave Jones manages the warehouse inventory for Athleticks, a distributor of sports watches. From his experience, Mr. Jones knows that the PR-5 jogging watch has an average daily demand of 100 units and a performance cycle of 8 days. Mr. Jones requires no buffer stock at this time. Assume an order quantity of 1,200 units.

    a Assume that Mr. Jones perpetually reviews inventory levels. Find the reorder point for the PR-5 jogging watch.

    b Find the average inventory level of the PR-5 watch.

    c How might the reorder point change if Mr. Jones reviews inventory once each week? Find the reorder point under these conditions.

    d Find the average inventory level of the PR-5 watch under this periodic review.

4 Mr. John Estes oversees the distribution of Tastee Snacks products from the plant warehouse to its two distribution centers in the United States. The plant warehouse currently has 42,000 units of the company's most popular product, Chocolate Chewies. Mr. Estes retains 7,000 units of the product at the warehouse as a buffer. The Cincinnati distribution center has an inventory of 12,500 units and daily requirements of 2,500 units. The Phoenix distribution center has an inventory of 6,000 units and daily requirements of 2,000 units.

    a Determine the common days' supply of Chocolate Chewies at each distribution center.

Dallas Distribution Center

On-hand balance: 220   Performance cycle: 1 week
Safety stock: 80   Order quantity: 200

	Past due	Week					
		1	**2**	**3**	**4**	**5**	**6**
Gross requirements		60	70	80	85	90	80
Scheduled receipts							
Projected on-hand							
Planned orders							

DC1

Lexington Distribution Center

On-hand balance: 420   Performance cycle: 2 weeks
Safety stock: 100   Order quantity: 400

	Past due	Week					
		1	**2**	**3**	**4**	**5**	**6**
Gross requirements		100	115	120	125	140	125
Scheduled receipts							
Projected on-hand							
Planned orders							

DC2

Evansville Warehouse

On-hand balance: 900   Lead time: 2 weeks
Safety stock: 250   Order quantity: 650

	Past due	Week					
		1	**2**	**3**	**4**	**5**	**6**
Gross requirements	0						
Scheduled receipts							
Projected on-hand							
Master sched.-rcpt.							
Master sched.-start							

b Given the above information and your answer to part (a), use fair share allocation logic to determine the number of Chocolate Chewies to be allocated to each distribution center.

5 Stay Safe International manufactures industrial safety equipment at its plant in Evansville, Indiana. The company has initiated distribution requirements planning (DRP) to coordinate finished goods distribution from the plant to distribution centers in Dallas, Texas, and Lexington, Virginia.

    a Given the accompanying information regarding hardhats, complete the DRP schedule for the warehouse and each distribution center in the tables.

    b Suppose that, without warning, no more than 500 units can be distributed from the warehouse to the distribution centers on a given week because of a manufacturing breakdown. Hardhats sell for $12 each out of the Dallas distribution center and $14 from Lexington. Discuss whether the warehouse should delay shipments until both distribution center requirements can be satisfied or allocate on the basis of need.

6 Scorekeeper, Inc., manufactures stadium scoreboards. The table below illustrates the demand for Scorekeeper's scoreboards over the past 25 days. The mean of daily demand is 6 units.

Day	Demand	Day	Demand	Day	Demand
1	4	10	10	18	6
2	3	11	8	19	7
3	4	12	7	20	6
4	6	13	5	21	6
5	7	14	6	22	5
6	8	15	4	23	7
7	6	16	2	24	8
8	5	17	5	25	9
9	6				

a   Is the demand distribution normal? How do you know?

b   Calculate the standard deviation for daily demand. Assume in this case that the performance cycle is constant.

The table below summarizes Scorekeeper's performance cycles over the past 40 replenishments. The expected cycle duration is 12 days.

Performance cycle (in days)	Frequency (f)
10	4
11	8
12	16
13	8
14	4

c   Is the performance-cycle distribution normal? How do you know?

d   Calculate the standard deviation for the performance cycle.

e   Given your answers to parts (b) and (d), find the safety stock required at one combined standard deviation under conditions of demand and performance-cycle uncertainties. Round the safety stock quantity to the nearest whole unit.

f   If the typical order quantity is 72 units, find the average inventory at 3 standard deviations under demand and performance-cycle uncertainty.

g   Scorekeeper is striving for a 99 percent product availability level. Given that the replenishment order quantity is 72 units, as well as your answer to part (e), find the function value of the normal loss curve $f(k)$.

h   Use Table 8-15 to find the value for K, given your answer to part (g), and calculate the required safety stock for the desired 99 percent availability level.

i   What would be the required safety stock for 99 percent availability should the order quantity change to 60 units? What would be the resulting average inventory?

CHAPTER 10

TRANSPORTATION INFRASTRUCTURE

TRANSPORT FUNCTIONALITY
AND PRINCIPLES
  Transport Functionality
  Principles
  Participants in Transportation Decisions
TRANSPORT INFRASTRUCTURE
  Modal Characteristics
  Modal Classification
  Transportation Formats
  Conclusion

SUPPLIERS OF TRANSPORTATION
  SERVICES
  Single-Mode Operators
  Specialized Carriers
  Intermodal Operators
  Nonoperating Intermediaries
  Conclusion
SUMMARY
QUESTIONS

The logistician's view of transportation services has changed dramatically during the last fifteen years. Prior to federal deregulation in the late 1970s and early 1980s, transportation service offerings were restricted and rates were relatively fixed. In this environment, the logistician's role could be likened to a purchaser of any other commodity such as coal or grain. There was very little differentiation among suppliers of transportation in terms of either quality or price.

Deregulation allowed more pricing flexibility for carriers and also significantly reduced restrictions on transportation services and relationships. Increased pricing freedom and availability of new services and relationships require today's logistician to be more proactive in identifying the most desirable combination of carrier services and pricing structures to meet the firm's objectives.

A wider range of transportation alternatives exists today for product or raw material movement than ever before. For example, a firm may consider for-hire transportation, private transportation, or a variety of contractual arrangements with different transport specialists. Service options include changes in billing, information availability, product liability, and pickup and delivery practices. Carriers and shippers now have the flexibility to negotiate responsibility for all transportation-related activities.

Chapter 10 is the first of three chapters devoted to examining the role of transportation in light of this dramatically different operating environment. It starts by reviewing transportation functionality and principles. This initial section presents an overview of the functionality provided by carriers, develops underlying operating principles, and examines the range of transportation decision makers. Next, the chapter details the transport infrastructure, identifying transport modes and their operating characteristics as well as traditional classification of the various formats for selling transportation services. Finally, the chapter outlines the range of transportation provider businesses and services that are available to support logistical operations.

TRANSPORT FUNCTIONALITY AND PRINCIPLES

Transportation is one of the most visible elements of logistics operations. As consumers, we are accustomed to seeing trucks and trains moving product or parked at a distribution facility. While this experience provides a good visual understanding of transportation elements, it does not allow the necessary depth of knowledge to understand transportation's role in logistics operations. This section establishes that foundation by reviewing functionality provided by transportation and the underlying principles of transport operation.

Transport Functionality

Transportation functionality provides two major functions: product movement and product storage. Each is briefly described.

Product Movement   Whether the product is in the form of materials, components, assemblies, work-in-process, or finished goods, transportation is necessary to move it to the next stage of the manufacturing process or physically closer to the ultimate customer. A primary transportation function is product movement up and down the value chain. Since transportation utilizes temporal, financial, and environmental resources, it is important that items be moved only when it truly enhances product value.

Transportation involves the use of temporal resources because product is inaccessible during the transportation process. Such product, commonly referred to as *in-transit* inventory, is becoming a significant consideration as a variety of supply chain strategies such as just-in-time and quick-response practices reduce manufacturing and distribution center inventories.

Transportation uses financial resources because internal expenditures are necessary for private fleets or external expenditures are required for commercial or public transportation. Expenses result from driver labor, vehicle operating cost, and some allocation for general and administrative costs. In addition, consideration of other expenses resulting from product loss or damage must be made.

Transportation uses environmental resources both directly and indirectly. In direct terms, it is one of the largest consumers of energy (i.e., fuel and oil) in the domestic United States economy. In fact, it accounts for close to 67 percent of all domestic oil use.[1] Although this level of consumption has decreased over time because of more fuel-efficient vehicles and operating practices, it is likely to remain steady in the future as a result of increased global operations, which require relatively greater transportation distances. Indirectly, transportation creates environmental expense through congestion, air pollution, and noise pollution. Although it is increasingly popular to allocate "real dollars" for these environmental costs, the charges do not cover all environmentally related expenses.

The major objective of transportation is to move product from an origin location to a prescribed destination while minimizing temporal, financial, and environmental resource costs. Loss and damage expenses must also be minimized. At the same time, the movement must take place in a manner that meets customer demands regarding delivery performance and shipment information availability.

Product Storage   A less common transportation function is temporary storage. Vehicles make rather expensive storage facilities. However, if the in-transit product requires storage but will be moved again shortly (e.g., in a few days), the cost of unloading and reloading the product in a warehouse may exceed the per diem (daily) charge of storage in the transportation vehicle.

In circumstances where warehouse space is limited, utilizing transportation vehicles may be a viable option. One method involves loading product on the vehicle and then having it take a circuitous or indirect route to its destination. With a circuitous route, transit time is greater than with a more direct route. This is desirable when the origin or destination warehouse has limited storage capacity. In essence, the transportation vehicle is being used as a temporary storage option but is moving rather than sitting idle.

A second method to achieve temporary product storage is diversion. This occurs when an original shipment destination is changed while the delivery is in transit. For example, suppose a product is initially scheduled to be shipped from Chicago to Los Angeles. However, if during the delivery process it is determined that San Francisco is in greater need of the product or has available storage capacity, the product could be diverted to the alternative destination of San Francisco. Traditionally, the telephone was used to direct diversion strategies. Today, satellite communication between enterprise headquarters and vehicles more efficiently handles the task.

In summary, although product storage in transportation vehicles can be costly, it may be justified from a total-cost or performance perspective when loading or unloading costs, capacity constraints, or the ability to extend lead times are considered.

---

[1] Holly Idelson, "After Two-Year Odyssey, Energy Strategy Clears," *Congressional Quarterly,* October 10, 1992, p. 3146.

Principles

There are two fundamental principles guiding transportation management and operations. They are *economy of scale* and *economy of distance*. Economy of scale refers to the characteristic that transportation cost per unit of weight decreases when the size of the shipment increases. For example, truckload (TL) shipments (i.e., shipments that utilize the entire vehicle's capacity) cost less per pound than less-than-truckload (LTL) shipments (i.e., shipments that utilize a portion of vehicle capacity). It is also generally true that larger capacity transportation vehicles such as rail or water are less expensive per unit of weight than smaller capacity vehicles such as motor or air. Transportation economies of scale exist because fixed expenses associated with moving a load can be spread over the load's weight. As such, a heavier load allows costs to be ''spread out,'' thereby decreasing costs per unit of weight. The fixed expenses include administrative costs of taking the transportation order, time to position the vehicle for loading or unloading, invoicing, and equipment cost. These costs are considered fixed because they do not vary with shipment volume. In other words, it costs as much to administer a shipment of 1 pound as it does to administer a 1,000-pound shipment. To illustrate, suppose the cost to administer a shipment is $10.00. Then the 1-pound shipment has a per unit of weight cost of $10.00, while the 1,000-pound shipment has a per unit of weight cost of $0.01. Thus, it can be said that an economy of scale exists for the 1,000-pound shipment.

Economy of distance refers to the characteristic that transportation cost per unit of distance decreases as distance increases. For example, a shipment of 800 miles will cost less than two shipments (of the same combined weight) of 400 miles. Transportation economy of distance is also referred to as the *tapering* principle since rates or charges taper with distance. The rationale for distance economies is similar to that for economies of scale. Specifically, the relatively fixed expense incurred to load and unload the vehicle must be spread over the variable expense per unit of distance. Longer distances allow the fixed expense to be spread over more miles, resulting in lower overall per mile charges.

These principles are important considerations when evaluating alternative transportation strategies or operating practices. The objective is to maximize the size of the load and the distance that it is shipped while still meeting customer service expectations.

Participants in Transportation Decisions

In order to understand transportation decision making, it is necessary to first understand the transportation environment, which is unique compared to many commercial enterprises. Buyers and sellers (e.g., a household consumer and a retail store) are the major, if not the only, participants in most commercial transactions. Buyers and sellers alone negotiate the terms and conditions and then consummate the sale. While government involvement is necessary for some commercial transactions, it is not customary for most.

However, unlike most commercial buying and selling, transportation transactions are often influenced by five parties: the shipper (originating party), the con-

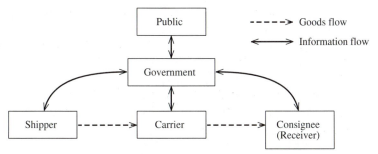

FIGURE 10-1   Relationship between the shipper, the consignee, and the public.

signee (destination party or receiver), the carrier, the government, and the public. Figure 10-1 illustrates the relationship between these parties. They may be related by ownership in some situations, such as when company-owned vehicles are used to transport goods between two company locations. In many cases, however, the parties are independently owned and operated. In order to understand the complexity of the transportation environment, it is necessary to review the role and perspective of each party.

Shippers and Consignees   The shipper and consignee have the common objective of moving goods from origin to destination within a prescribed time at the lowest cost. Services include specified pickup and delivery times, predictable transit time, zero loss and damage, as well as accurate and timely exchange of information and invoicing.

Carriers   The carrier, as the intermediary, takes a somewhat different perspective. Carriers desire to maximize their revenue associated with the transaction while minimizing the costs necessary to complete the transaction. The perspective suggests that a carrier wants to charge the highest rate that the shipper (or consignee) will accept and minimize the labor, fuel, and vehicle costs required to move the goods. To achieve this objective, the carrier desires flexibility in pickup and delivery times to allow individual loads to be consolidated into economic moves.

Government   The government maintains a high interest level in the transaction because of transportation's impact on the economy. Government desires a stable and efficient transportation environment to sustain economic growth. Transportation enables the efficient movement of products to markets throughout the country and thus promotes product availability at a reasonable cost. The situation in the Soviet Union prior to its breakup demonstrates the impact of an inadequate transportation system. Although not the only reason, the transportation system was a contributing factor in the Soviet economy's inability to supply food to the market even though adequate production existed.[2]

[2]Hugh Quigley, ''Eastern Europe Waits for Logistics,'' *Transportation and Distribution*, **32:**2, February 1991, pp. 50–54.

A stable and efficient commercial economy requires that carriers offer competitive services while operating profitably. Many governments are more involved with carrier activities and practices than with other commercial enterprises. Involvement may take the form of regulation, promotion, or ownership. Governments regulate carriers by restricting the markets they can service or by setting the prices they can charge. Governments promote carriers by supporting research and development or by providing rights-of-way such as roadways or air traffic control systems. In countries like the United Kingdom or Germany, some carriers are owned by the government, which maintains absolute control over markets, services, and rates. Such control allows government to have a major influence on the economic success of regions, industries, or firms.

The Public   The final participant, the public, is concerned with transportation accessibility, expense, and effectiveness, as well as environmental and safety standards. The public ultimately determines the need for transportation by demanding goods from around the world at reasonable prices. While minimizing transportation cost is important to consumers, trade-offs associated with environmental and safety standards also require consideration. The effects of air pollution and oil spills remain a significant transportation issue even though there have been tremendous strides in pollution reduction and consumer safety during the past two decades. The cost of reducing the risk of environmental or vehicle accidents is passed on to consumers, who must collectively judge how much safety is necessary.

The transportation relationship is complex because of the interaction between the parties. This leads to frequent conflicts between parties with a microinterest—shippers, consignees, and carriers—as well as parties with a macrointerest—government and the public. These conflicts have led to duplication, regulation, and restrictions of transportation services.

TRANSPORT INFRASTRUCTURE

Transportation infrastructure consists of the rights-of-way, vehicles, and carrier organizations that offer transportation services on a for-hire or internal basis. The nature of the infrastructure also determines a variety of economic and legal characteristics for each mode or multimodal system. A mode identifies the basic transportation method or form.

Modal Characteristics

The five basic transportation modes are rail, highway, water, pipeline, and air. The relative importance of each mode can be measured in terms of system mileage, traffic volume, revenue, and the nature of traffic composition. Each mode is discussed with respect to these measures.[3]

[3]For a more detailed discussion, see Charles A. Taff, *Management of Physical Distribution and Transportation,* 7th ed., Homewood, Ill.: Richard D. Irwin, Inc., 1984; Roy J. Sampson, Martin T. Farris, and David L. Shrock, *Domestic Transportation: Practice, Theory, Policy,* 6th ed., Boston, Mass.: Houghton Mifflin Company, 1990; John J. Coyle, Edward J. Bardi, and Joseph L. Cavinato, *Transportation,* 3d ed., St. Paul, Minn.: West Publishing Company, 1990; and *National Transportation Statistics Annual Report,* 1992, Washington, D.C.: U.S. Department of Transportation, U.S. Government Printing Office, August 1993.

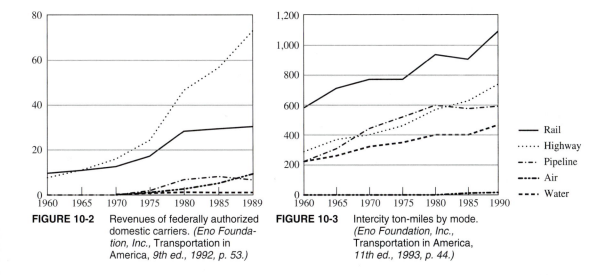

FIGURE 10-2 Revenues of federally authorized domestic carriers. *(Eno Foundation, Inc.,* Transportation in America, *9th ed., 1992, p. 53.)*

FIGURE 10-3 Intercity ton-miles by mode. *(Eno Foundation, Inc.,* Transportation in America, *11th ed., 1993, p. 44.)*

To understand the impact of each mode, it is necessary to consider their relative revenues and volumes. Figures 10-2 and 10-3 illustrate total modal revenue and ton-miles for intercity for-hire freight. Ton-mile is a standard measure of freight activity that considers both the amount (tons) and the distance (miles) moved. It is calculated by multiplying the number of tons by the number of miles for each shipment. The figures illustrate the overall growth of each mode and the relative increase of air and highway modes in revenue per ton-mile.

Rail Network   Historically, railroads have handled the largest number of ton-miles within the continental United States. As a result of the early establishment of a comprehensive rail network connecting almost all cities and towns, railroads dominated intercity freight tonnage until after World War II. This early superiority resulted from the capability to transport large shipments economically and to offer frequent service, which gave railroads a somewhat monopolistic position. However, with the advent of serious motor carrier competition following World War II, the railroads' share of revenues and ton-miles started to decline.

In 1990, railroads transported 37.4 percent of total intercity ton-miles: projections to the year 2000 indicate that rail market share will stabilize at approximtely this level.[4] Stabilization of rail market share represents a major accomplishment compared to the period 1947–1970 when railroads experienced a serious decline. In terms of total percentage of intercity transportation ton-miles, railroads transported 54.0 percent in 1947, 39.2 percent in 1958, 36.4 percent in 1980, and 37.0 percent in 1992. The decline in revenue was even more significant, dropping from almost 40 percent in 1950 to 20.9 percent in 1982.[5]

Railroads once ranked first among all modes in terms of the number of miles in service. The extensive development of roads and highways to support the growth

[4]Eno Transportation Foundation, Inc., *Transportation in America,* 9th ed., 1991, p. 64.
[5]Ibid.

of automobiles and trucks after World War II altered this ranking. In 1982 there were 165,000 miles of track in the United States. By 1989, track mileage had declined to 148,000 miles as a result of the liberalized abandonment provisions in the Staggers Rail Act.[6]

The capability to efficiently transport large tonnage over long distances is the main reason railroads continue to handle significant intercity tonnage and revenue. Railroad operations incur high fixed costs because of expensive equipment, right-of-way (railroads must maintain their own track), switching yards, and terminals. However, rail experiences relatively low variable operating costs. The replacement of steam by diesel power reduced the railroads' variable cost per ton-mile, and electrification offers potential for more reductions. New labor agreements have reduced workforce requirements, further decreasing variable costs.

Recently, rail traffic has shifted from transporting a broad range of commodities to a focus on specific products. The greatest source of railroad tonnage comes from raw material extractive industries located a considerable distance from improved waterways. Despite historical service problems, the rail fixed-variable cost structure is still superior for long-haul moves. Since the 1950s, railroads have segmented the transportation market by focusing on carload and container traffic. Marketing emphasis has further increased since passage of the Staggers Rail Act. Railroads are becoming more responsive to specific customer needs, emphasizing bulk industries and heavy manufacturing, rather than simply offering standardized rail service. Railroads have expanded their intermodal operations through alliances and motor carrier ownership. For example, United Parcel Service, primarily a motor carrier, is the largest consumer of rail service in the United States through alliances with railroads. Railroads are also increasing intermodal services by taking ownership of motor carriers, such as Union Pacific's acquisition of Overnight Express, and acquisition of barge lines.

To provide improved service to major rail users, progressive railroads have concentrated on the development of specialized equipment, such as the enclosed trilevel automobile car, cushioned appliance cars, unit trains, articulated cars, and double-stack containers. Unit trains are an entire train carrying a single product. Typically, the product is a bulk commodity such as coal or grain. Unit trains have also been used to support assembly operations for the automobile industry. The unit train is faster and less expensive to operate than traditional trains since it can bypass railyards and go direct to the product's destination. Articulated cars have an extended rail chassis that can haul up to ten containers on a single flexible unit. The unit reduces weight and time required for interchanging railcars. Double-stack railcars, as the name implies, have two levels of containers thereby doubling the capacity of each car. Containers are essentially truck bodies without wheels. Double stacks also significantly reduce damage as a result of their design. These technologies are being applied by the railroads to reduce weight, increase carrying capacity, and facilitate interchange.

The prior examples are by no means a comprehensive review of recent railroad innovations. They are characteristic of the attempts being made to retain and

---

[6]Ibid.

REBIRTH OF THE UNION PACIFIC

United States railroads have lost business to trucks, barges, and other freight haulers for the better part of the last fifty years. To counter this trend, railroads such as the Union Pacific (UP) have begun initiatives to streamline management structure, refine procedures, embrace quality initiatives, and reduce crew costs. UP, the nation's second largest railroad, began its restructuring in 1987 by developing and implementing a comprehensive quality program focused on customer satisfaction, efficient resource utilization, and managed growth and profitability.

One major force driving UP's business success is innovative technology adoptions. One example is consolidation of 160 regional customer service offices into a national Customer Service Center in St. Louis. The center handles 20,000 calls daily with issues ranging from order placement to shipment tracing.* The center enhances service by providing customers with a single contact point.

A second example is UP's new centralized state-of-the-art dispatch facility in Omaha. The high-tech Harriman Dispatching Center, which was built within the shell of a 100-year-old freight-handling facility, consolidates the operations of ten regional dispatching centers. Each side of the dispatch center is one football field in length and contains a series of video panels displaying all rail activity within the dispatcher's zone. The brightly colored screens identify train and track status, train contents, and maintenance team location. Communication between the Dispatching Center and trains is possible using both computer and voice connections with UP locomotive cabs. The conductor is in direct communication with the Dispatching Center al-lowing frequent updates of assignments and task completions. Since the Dispatching Center automatically updates shipment status, the Customer Service Center can provide customers with immediate status and delivery information.† Prior to the computerized communication, railcars often sat idle for an extra day at a "lost" opportunity cost of $14.40 per day because of poor coordination of shipment status and railcar availability. The opportunity cost is enormous with 180,000 cars on the UP system.‡

The real-time information and operating integration have dramatically improved both operational efficiency and customer satisfaction. Additional service improvements are envisioned through railcar and container radio tracking systems.

Increased service, new freight cars, and car refurbishing programs have enabled UP to take volume and market share from motor carriers. There is increasing shipper acknowledgment of UP's improved delivery performance and pricing programs. UP has also initiated partnerships with major truckload carriers such as J. B. Hunt and Schneider National to offer integrated intermodal services that are profitable to both parties. Leading-edge technology coupled with UP's diverse traffic mix and efficient route system indicates a promising future for the Union Pacific Railroad.

*Armand V. Feigenbaum, "The Making of a World Class 1 Railroad," *Railway Age,* February 1992, pp. 20–21, 86.

†Joseph Weber, "Big Rail Is Finally Rounding the Bend," *Business Week,* November 11, 1991, pp. 128–129.

‡Daniel Machalba, "Union Pacific's High-Tech Style Generates Business," *The Wall Street Journal,* June 8, 1992, p. B5.

improve railroads' share of the overall transportation market. It is clear that significant changes are occurring in traditional concepts of railroading. The 1970s issues of survival and potential nationalization gave way in the 1980s to the revitalization of a rail network. Evidence suggests that railroads will become the transportation and intermodal leaders of the 1990s.

Motor Carriers Highway transportation has expanded rapidly since the end of World War II. To a significant degree the rapid growth of the motor carrier industry results from door-to-door operating flexibility and speed of intercity movement.

TABLE 10-1   EXPENSE COMPONENTS FOR OVER-THE-ROAD MOTOR CARRIERS: TL AND LTL COST (1988 CENTS/MILE)

	GVW (lb)	Drivers	Vehicle	Fuel	Tires	Repair	Overhead	Total
			Truckload (TL) vans					
5-axle 48′	52,500	30.0	20.0	19.1	3.0	8.5	22.0	102.6
5-axle twin 28′	59,800	30.7	20.8	21.0	3.0	9.8	22.0	107.3
7-axle triple 28′	83,400	31.9	24.8	25.5	4.3	12.7	27.3	126.6
			Less-than-truckload (LTL) carriers					
5-axle 48′	55,400	38.9	16.0	19.4	3.0	8.7	138.0	224.0
5-axle twin 28′	63,200	39.7	16.6	21.3	3.0	10.1	149.3	240.1
7-axle triple 28′	88,500	41.2	19.8	26.1	4.3	13.2	186.9	291.5

Source: Jack Faucett Associates, *The Effect of Size and Weight Limits on Truck Costs,* a working paper prepared for U.S. Department of Transportation, Federal Highway Administration, Washington, D.C., October 1991.

Motor carriers have flexibility because they are able to operate on all types of roadways. In 1989, over 3.8 million miles of highway were available to motor carriers, which is more mileage available than all other modes combined.[7] The total interstate system represents approximately 43,000 miles, while total federal aided primary roads exceed 344,000 highway miles.[8]

In comparison to railroads, motor carriers have relatively small fixed investments in terminal facilities and operate on publicly maintained highways. Although the cost of license fees, user fees, and tolls is considerable, these expenses are directly related to the number of over-the-road units and miles operated. The variable cost per mile for motor carriers is high because a separate power unit and driver are required for each trailer or combination of tandem trailers. Labor requirements are also high because of driver safety restrictions and the need for substantial dock labor. Table 10-1 illustrates the expense components for over-the-road truckload motor carriers. Segmenting these into fixed costs (which include overhead and vehicle) and variable costs (which include such items as driver, fuel, tires, and repair) results in a structure of low fixed and high variable costs. In comparison to railroads, motor carriers are best suited to handle small shipments moving short distances.

The characteristics of motor carriers favor manufacturing and distributive trades, short distances, and high-value products. Motor carriers have made significant inroads into rail traffic for medium and light manufacturing. Because of delivery flexibility, they have captured almost all freight moving from wholesalers or warehouses to retail stores. The prospect for maintaining stable market share in highway transport remains bright. In 1990, with the exception of small package goods moving in premium service, almost all less-than-15,000-pound intercity shipments (LTL) were transported by motor carriers. The motor carrier industry is not without problems. The primary difficulties relate to increasing cost to replace equipment,

[7]*National Transportation Strategic Planning Study,* United States Department of Transportation, March 1990, p. 5-2.
[8]Eno Transportation Foundation, Inc., *Transportation in America,* 9th ed., 1991, p. 64.

maintenance, driver wages, and platform and dock wages. Although accelerating labor rates influence all modes of transport, motor carriers are more labor-intensive, which causes higher wages to be a major concern. To counteract this trend, carriers have placed considerable attention on improved line-haul scheduling that bypasses terminals, computerized billing systems, mechanized terminals, tandem operations that pull two or three trailers by a single power unit, and utilization of coordinated intermodal systems. These enhancements reduce labor intensity and, thus, cost.

One threat to the for-hire motor carrier industry is over-the-road transportation by shipper-owned trucks or by specialized carriers under contract to perform transport services for shippers. In 1980, over 50 percent of all intercity truck tonnage was hauled by private fleet operations. Following deregulation, this proportion increased to 66 percent by 1987.[9] The proportion declined to 56 percent by 1991 as shippers realized the numerous complexities and problems of operating a private fleet.[10] Major private fleet issues include justifying return on investment, compliance with government regulations, customer service quality, and lack of state tax uniformity. The relative private fleet share is expected to continue to decline through the year 2000.

Since 1980, deregulation has dramatically changed the nature of the motor carrier industry. The industry segments, which have become more definitive since deregulation, include truckload (TL), less-than-truckload (LTL), and specialty carriers.

The TL segment includes loads over 15,000 pounds that generally do not require intermediate stops for consolidation. Although large firms such as Schneider National and J. B. Hunt provide nationwide TL service, the industry is characterized by a large number of relatively small carriers and is generally very price competitive. The TL industry is the mode that is closest to the economist's model of pure competition.

The LTL segment of the industry includes loads less than 15,000 pounds that generally require stops at intermediate terminals for consolidation. Because of terminal costs and relatively higher marketing expenses, LTL experiences a higher percentage of fixed costs than TL. These characteristics have caused extensive industry consolidation, since deregulation resulted in a small number of relatively large carriers. The major nationwide LTL carriers include Yellow Freight, Consolidated Freightways, Roadway, and TNT Freightways.

Specialty carriers include package haulers such as Federal Express and United Parcel Service. These firms focus on specific requirements of a market or product. Despite the aforementioned problems, it is quite apparent that highway transportation will continue to function as the backbone of logistical operations for the foreseeable future.

Water Transport   Water is the oldest mode of transportation. The original sailing vessels were replaced by steamboats in the early 1800s and by diesel power

---

[9]Bernard Campbell, ''Strategy: Economic Forecast: Good News, Bad News for Trucking,'' *Fleet Owner,* **84:**1, January 1989, p. 103.

[10]Gene S. Bergoffen, ''Private Fleets Position for the Future,'' *Transportation and Distribution Industry Week,* April 1992, p. T-2.

in the 1920s. A distinction is generally made between deep-water and navigable inland water transport.

Domestic water transportation—which involves the Great Lakes, canals, and navigable rivers—has maintained a relatively constant annual ton-mile share of 15 to 16 percent over the past four decades.[11] While the share has remained relatively constant, the mix has changed dramatically. The percentage of river and canal ton-miles has increased from 4.9 to 13.2 percent since the 1950s, while the Great Lakes ton-miles have decreased from 10.5 to 2.8 percent. These figures illustrate a shift of bulk product transportation from rail and highway to lower-cost water movements on rivers and canals.

In 1989, 25,777 miles of inland waterways were available, not including the Great Lakes or coastal shipping.[12] Fewer system miles exist for inland water than for any other transportation mode.

The main advantage of water transportation is the capacity to move extremely large shipments. Water transport employs two types of vessels. Deep-water vessels, which are generally designed for ocean and Great Lakes use, are restricted to deep-water ports for access. In contrast, diesel-towed barges, which generally operate on rivers and canals, have considerably more flexibility.

Water transport ranks between rail and motor carrier in respect to fixed cost. Although water carriers must develop and operate their own terminals, the right-of-way is developed and maintained by the government and results in moderate fixed costs compared to rail and highway. The main disadvantages of water transport are the limited range of operation and speed. Unless the origin and destination of the movement are adjacent to a waterway, supplemental haul by rail or truck is required. The capability of water to carry large tonnage at low variable cost places this mode of transport in demand when low freight rates are desired and speed of transit is a secondary consideration.

Typical inland water freight includes mining and basic bulk commodities such as chemicals, cement, and selected agricultural products. In addition to the restrictions of navigable waterways, terminal facilities for bulk and dry cargo storage and load-unload devices limit the flexibility of water transport. Labor restrictions on loading and unloading at docks create operational problems and tend to reduce the potential range of available traffic. Finally, a highly competitive situation has developed between railroads and inland water carriers in areas where parallel routes exist.

Great Lakes transportation is also oriented toward bulk products such as coal, grain, and ore. While deep-water vessels transport a significant proportion of bulk products, an increasing volume of ocean movements utilizes containers for nonbulk items. Containerized cargo facilitates vessel loading and unloading and enhances intermodal capability by increasing the efficiency of cargo transfer between highway, rail, and water.

Inland and Great Lakes water transport will continue to be a viable option in future logistical systems. The slow passage of inland river transport can provide a

[11]Eno Transportation Foundation, Inc., *Transportation in America,* 9th ed., 1991, p. 44.
[12]Ibid., p. 64.

form of warehousing in transit if fully integrated into overall system design. Improvements in ice-breaking equipment appear to be on the verge of eliminating the seasonal limitations. In addition, the North American Free Trade Agreement will be a catalyst for increased utilization of the St. Lawrence Seaway to link new producer and consumer markets in Mexico, the Midwest, and the Canadian cities of Toronto and Montreal.

Pipelines   Pipelines are a significant part of the United States transportation system. In 1989, they accounted for over 53 percent of all crude and petroleum ton-mile movements.[13] The 585 billion tons of product transported by petroleum pipelines in 1990 represent 20.4 percent of all intercity ton-miles in the United States, which is a decline from a 1975 peak of 24.5 percent.

In 1960, 190,944 miles of pipeline were operational in the United States. By 1970, that figure had jumped to 218,671 miles. By 1989, the operational mileage had declined slightly to 214,599 miles.[14]

In addition to petroleum, the other important product transported by pipeline is natural gas. Similar to petroleum, natural gas pipelines in the United States are privately owned and operated, and many gas companies act as both gas distribution and contract transportation providers. Pipelines are also utilized for transport of manufacturing chemicals, pulverized dry bulk materials such as cement and flour via hydraulic suspension, and sewage and water within cities and municipalities.[15]

The basic nature of a pipeline is unique in comparison to all other modes of transport. Pipelines operate on a twenty-four-hour basis, seven days per week, and are limited only by commodity changeover and maintenance. Unlike other modes, there is no empty "container" or "vehicle" that must be returned. Pipelines have the highest fixed cost and lowest variable cost among transport modes. High fixed costs result from the right-of-way, construction and requirements for control stations, and pumping capacity. Since pipelines are not labor-intensive, the variable operating cost is extremely low once the pipeline has been constructed. An obvious disadvantage is that pipelines are not flexible and are limited with respect to commodities that can be transported: only products in the form of gas, liquid, or slurry can be handled.

Experiments regarding potential movement of solid products in the form of slurry or hydraulic suspension continue to be conducted. Coal slurry pipelines have proved to be an efficient and economical mode of transporting coal over long distances. Coal slurry lines require massive quantities of water, which is a significant concern of environmentalists, particularly in selected areas where water is scarce and large coal reserves are located. Currently, only one coal slurry line is operational in the United States (the Black Mesa in the Southwest). Noncoal slurry pipelines are common in many foreign countries.

---

[13]"Pipelines Handle Most U.S. Oil Shipments," *Oil and Gas Journal*, October 7, 1991, p. 111.

[14]Eno Transportation Foundation, Inc., *Transportation in America*, 9th ed., 1991, p. 64.

[15]Donald F. Wood and James C. Johnson, *Contemporary Transportation*, 4th ed., New York: Macmillan Publishing Company, 1993, pp. 159–160.

Air Transport   The newest but least utilized mode of transport is air freight. Its significant advantage lies in the speed with which a shipment can be transported. A coast-to-coast shipment via air requires only a few hours contrasted to days with other modes of transportation. One prohibitive aspect of air transport is the high cost. However, this can be traded off for high speed, which allows other elements of logistical design, such as warehousing or inventory, to be reduced or eliminated. Air transport still remains more of a potential opportunity than a reality. Although the mileage is almost unlimited, air freight accounts for significantly less than 1 percent of all intercity ton-miles. Air transport capability is limited by lift capacity (i.e., load size constraints) and aircraft availability. Traditionally, most intercity air freight utilized scheduled passenger flights. While this practice was economical, it resulted in a reduction of both capacity and flexibility. The high cost of jet aircraft, coupled with the erratic nature of freight demand, has limited the assignment of dedicated planes to all-freight operations. However, premium air carriers such as Federal Express and United Parcel Service Overnight provide dedicated global freight operation. While this premium service was originally targeted at documents, it has expanded to include larger parcels. For example, both United Parcel and Federal Express have extended their air freight service to include overnight delivery from a centralized distribution center located at their air hub. This is an ideal service for firms with a large number of high-value products and time-sensitive service requirements.

The fixed cost of air transport is low compared to rail, water, and pipeline. In fact, air transport ranks second only to highway with respect to low fixed cost. Airways and airports are generally developed and maintained with public funds. Likewise, terminals are normally maintained by local communities. The fixed costs of air freight are associated with aircraft purchase and the requirement for specialized handling systems and cargo containers. On the other hand, air freight variable cost is extremely high as a result of fuel, maintenance, and the labor intensity of both inflight and ground crews.

Since they require wide open space, airports are generally not integrated with other modes of transportation, with the exception of highways. However, there is greater interest in further integrating air transport with other modes and developing ''all freight'' airports to reduce conflict with passenger operations. For example, Alliance Airport (located outside of Dallas) was designed to bring together industry, major transportation modes, and government to facilitate production, international trade, and distribution from a single location.

No particular commodity dominates the traffic carried by air freight operations. Perhaps the best distinction is that most air freight is handled on an emergency rather than a routine basis. Firms typically utilize scheduled or nonscheduled air cargo movements when the situation justifies the high cost. Products with the greatest potential for regular air movement are those having high value or extreme perishability. When the marketing period for a product is extremely limited—such as for Christmas items, high-fashion clothing, or fresh fish—air transport may be the only practical method for logistical operations. Routine logistics products such as parts or consumer catalog items are also candidates for air freight.

Modal Classification

The basic modes of transportation were reviewed in terms of historical development and share of intercity ton-miles and freight revenue. The essential operating characteristics of each mode were noted, including the relationship between fixed and variable costs. Table 10-2 compares modes in terms of market share, revenue, cost, and traffic composition. Table 10-3 summarizes the fixed-variable cost structure of each mode. Table 10-4 ranks modal operating characteristics with respect to speed, availability, dependability, capability, and frequency. These characteristics will be discussed.

Speed refers to elapsed movement time. Air freight is the fastest of all modes. Availability is the ability of a mode to service any given pair of locations. Highway carriers have the greatest availability since they can drive directly to origin and destination points. Dependability is the potential variance from expected or published delivery schedules. Pipelines, because of their continuous service and limited interference from the weather and congestion, rank highest in dependability. Capability is the ability of a mode to handle any transport requirement, such as load size. Water transport is the most capable. The final classification is frequency, which relates to the quantity of scheduled movements. Pipelines, again because of their continuous service between two points, lead all modes in frequency.

As Table 10-4 shows, the appeal of highway transport is in part explained by its high ranking across all five characteristics. Operating on a world-class highway system, motor carriers rank first or second in all categories except capability.

TABLE 10-2   MODAL COMPARISON VITAL STATISTICS AND DOMINANT TRAFFIC COMPOSITION

Mode	Market share percentage*		Revenue[†]		Nature of traffic composition
	1980	1990	1980	1990	
Rail	37.5	37.4	2.87	2.66	Extracting industries Heavy manufacturing Agricultural commodities
Highway	22.3	25.7	18.00	24.38	Medium and light manufacturing Distribution between wholesalers and retailers
Water	16.4	16.1	0.77	0.754	Mining and basic bulk commodities Chemicals Cement Some agricultural products
Pipeline	23.6	20.4	1.325	1.441	Petroleum Coal slurry
Air	0.2	0.4	46.31	139.50[‡]	No particular commodity Emergency rather than regular basis

*(In intercity ton-miles.) Eno Transportation Foundation, Inc., *Transportation in America,* December 1991, p. 10.
[†](In cents per ton-mile.) Ibid., p. 12.
[‡]Includes domestic scheduled air carriers plus Federal Express (domestic operations).

TABLE 10-3   COST STRUCTURE FOR EACH MODE

- *Rail.* High fixed cost in equipment, terminals, tracks, etc. Low variable cost.
- *Highway.* Low fixed cost (highways in place and provided by public support). Medium variable cost (fuel, maintenance, etc.).
- *Water.* Medium fixed cost (ships and equipment). Low variable cost (capability to transport large amount of tonnage).
- *Pipeline.* Highest fixed cost (rights-of-way, construction, requirements for control stations, and pumping capacity). Lowest variable cost (no labor cost of any significance).
- *Air.* Low fixed cost (aircraft and handling and cargo systems). High variable cost (fuel, labor, maintenance, etc.).

TABLE 10-4   RELATIVE OPERATING CHARACTERISTICS BY TRANSPORTATION MODES*

Operating characteristics	Rail	Truck	Water	Pipeline	Air
Speed	3	2	4	5	1
Availability	2	1	4	5	3
Dependability	3	2	4	1	5
Capability	2	3	1	5	4
Frequency	4	2	5	1	3
Composite score	14	10	18	17	16

*Lowest rank is best.

Although substantial improvements in motor capability resulted from relaxed size and weight limitations on interstate highways and approval to use tandem trailers, it is not realistic to assume that motor transport will surpass rail or water capability.

Transportation Formats

In addition to classifying transportation by mode, another common grouping is the legal status, or format of carrier operating authority. Unlike most free enterprise operations, governments may restrict carriers to specific markets and services to maintain carrier and market stability. The restrictions limit competition in individual markets, so carriers are able to operate in a stable pricing and competitive environment. Individual carrier restrictions, called *operating authority,* form the legal authorization to transport goods and commodities between two points.

A frequent method of grouping transportation alternatives is by the class of operating authority. A carrier must comply with specific Federal and Interstate Commerce Commission (ICC) rules and restrictions to transport goods and commodities for each operating authority classification. Over the past decade, the ICC's operating policies have shifted to reflect a commitment to simplify the carrier licensing process and improve highway safety. The elimination of unnecessary barriers to entry, careful monitoring of carrier safety records, and encouraging new and expanded carrier operations have increased the quality and quantity of the service provided.

From an operating authority perspective there are four carrier classes: common, contract, private, exempt. Each carrier class may exist within any transportation mode. Prior to deregulation in the early 1980s, distinct differences existed between the classes, and carrier ownership was limited to a single legal class and mode. For example, a rail carrier could not own a motor carrier. Since deregulation, many firms have been granted dual operating authorities in two or more classes or modes. For example, some private carriers have been granted common and contract carrier rights. In addition, government has encouraged intermodalism whereby two different modes have joint operating agreements or common ownership.

Even though the legal classifications are not as restrictive today, they still influence some carrier practices. The following section discusses the characteristics of each legal classification.

Common Carriers   The basic foundation of the public transportation system is the common carrier. Common carriers have the responsibility to offer service at nondiscriminatory prices to the public. The operating authority received by a common carrier may include the right to transport all commodities, or it may limit transport to specialized commodities such as steel, household goods, or computers. In addition, the operating authority specifies the geographical area the carrier may service and indicates if such service is to be on a scheduled or unscheduled basis.

Historically, a common carrier could be granted operating authority only after demonstrating a public need for its services. This placed the burden of proof on the carrier and gave potential competitors the opportunity to oppose the need for new entrants. Since deregulation, carriers desiring certification are only required to demonstrate the ability to serve without necessarily establishing market need. Currently, the ICC will grant operating authority to a carrier if it determines that the carrier's proposed operations will (1) serve a useful purpose and (2) respond to a demand or need, without conflicting with public convenience and necessity.

A common carrier is required to publish the rates it charges for transport service, supply adequate facilities, provide service to all points prescribed in its certificate of authority (unless withdrawal is authorized by the appropriate regulatory agency), deliver the goods within a reasonable time, charge reasonable rates, and refrain from discrimination against customers. In many cases, these rates are published in computerized format to facilitate reference and maintenance. In addition to base rates, most carriers offer discounts for key customers.

The Motor-Carrier Regulatory Reform and Modernization Act of 1980 (MCA-80) provided common carriers with greater flexibility regarding market entry, routing of service, and rate making. This flexibility, combined with simplified and expedited licensing procedures, has dramatically altered the transportation industry. Increased consolidation and concentration in many transportation modes as a result of deregulation have provoked some concern with advocates of competition, who point out that one of the intended effects of deregulation was to increase competition, not reduce it.

A historical problem for common carriers has been that the number of customers (and thus the volume of freight) is difficult to forecast. Increased legal flexibility for common carriers has encouraged the formation of strategic alliances and formal long-term relationships in an attempt to remedy the uncertainty of freight volume by providing financial and planning stability for both common carriers and shippers.

Contract Carriers   Contract carriers provide transport services for select customers. Although contract carriers must receive authorization, requirements are normally less restricted than common carrier operating authority. The basis for the contract is an agreement between a carrier and a shipper for a specified transportation service at a previously agreed cost. For example, the agreement may be a contract to move a single load or a number of loads over time. The business agreement becomes the basis for the contract carrier to receive a permit to transport the specified commodities.

Prior to deregulation, contract carriers were limited to eight active contracts at any point in time. This restricted the number of customers for contract carriers and limited their ability to compete directly with common carriers. Deregulation relaxed and eventually removed this restriction, thus expanding the contract carrier market. Currently, contract carriers can transport for numerous shippers and are not required to charge the same amount to each shipper. A May 1992 ruling by the ICC abolished contract carrier regulations of property. The result is that many long-standing and cumbersome requirements for freight contracts no longer exist. "The commission made its decision based on its conclusion that contract regulations are not required by law, have outlived their usefulness and in general cause more harm than good. The commission further concluded that its contract requirements sometimes contradict the deregulatory goals of the Motor-Carrier Act of 1980."[16]

A special legal class of contract transportation is the owner-operator or independent trucker. The owner-operator typically owns a tractor and may own a trailer. Using this equipment, an owner-operator provides line-haul service on a regular or trip-by-trip basis for other legal forms of transportation such as contract carriers. Recent rulings authorize owner-operators to make business arrangements with common, contract, exempt, and private carriers. Prior to the 1980s owner-operators were limited to providing service to common and contract carriers only.

Private Carriers   A private carrier consists of a firm providing its own transportation. Private carriers are not for hire and are not subject to economic regulation, although they must comply with regulations concerning hazardous goods movement, employee safety, vehicle safety, and other social regulations established by government agencies such as the Department of Transportation (DOT).[17]

The firm must own or lease the transport equipment and provide managerial direction regarding transportation operations. The primary distinction between private and for-hire carriage is that the transportation activity must be incidental to the primary business of the firm to qualify as private carriage. For example, Frito Lay owns the trucks that deliver its snack products to retail stores. Frito Lay's

---

[16]"Contract Freight Regulations Go the Way of the Dinosaurs," *Traffic Management,* **31:**7, July 1992, pp. 16–17.

[17]John E. Tyworth, Joseph L. Cavinato, and C. John Langley, Jr., *Traffic Management: Planning, Operations and Control,* Prospect Heights, Ill.: Waveland Press, Inc., 1991, p. 30.

primary business is snack food, not transportation. Prior to deregulation, the private carrier was required to own the products it transported; that is no longer the case. Now, a private carrier such as Frito Lay can transport goods for another company to reduce ''empty miles.''

Private trucking significantly increased throughout the early 1980s. Many firms took advantage of regulatory changes to increase direct control over their operations and to reduce costs of ''empty miles'' through back-hauls. (A back-haul is the return trip to the distribution center once the product has been delivered to the market.)

However, the cost/service gap between private fleets and other carriers has narrowed because of deregulation. As a result, many firms have reduced their private carrier operations in order to refocus managerial skills and resources on the core operations of their basic business. Competitive conditions in many industries have encouraged firms to seek the talents and leverage of for-hire carriers that specialize in transportation planning and operations.

Exempt Carriers   Exempt carriers, as their name implies, are not constrained by economic regulation. The traditional exemption was for specific commodities hauled or markets served. Typical exempt commodities include unprocessed agricultural products and extracted raw materials. Typical exempt markets include the zones around airports or metropolitan areas. Exempt carriers, however, must comply with the licensing and safety laws of the states in which they operate. If the exempt carrier is engaged in interstate movement, rates must be published.

The general scope of exemption has expanded since 1980. Several provisions of the 1980 deregulatory acts increased exempt privileges. Exemptions for motor and water carriers originated from the need for farmers to transport seasonal and unprocessed agricultural products to manufacturing centers. Today, exempt carriers operate across a broad range of commercial activity. The ICC has also relaxed regulation on rail traffic and services, allowing perishable traffic, piggyback service, and some boxcar movements to achieve exempt status.

Conclusion   From the perspective of logistical system design, the distinctions between transportation formats are slight. The main considerations are operating restrictions, financial commitment, and operating flexibility.

Since deregulation, operating restrictions limiting practices and services have been greatly relaxed. However, some restrictive laws and regulations still exist regarding each form of cartage and for many intrastate and international moves. These restrictions—concerning the service regions, commodities, and pricing— must be considered in logistical system design.

Commitment refers to the degree of financial involvement or obligation the shipper offers the carrier. The least amount of commitment applies to common carriers, since each party's obligation is limited to a single shipment. Contract operations demonstrate greater commitment since typical agreements between carriers and shippers extend for six months to one year. It is important to understand that the financial relationship for both common and contract carriers varies directly with the tonnage transported. In private transport, the commitment is longer and involves both fixed costs of equipment and variable operating costs. This obligation can be reduced by equipment leasing or utilizing owner-operators. The commitment associated with exempt cartage is difficult to generalize, since it can range from very little to extensive.

The greatest latitude in terms of operating flexibility is naturally associated with private transport. However, it should be noted that failure to schedule private transport effectively can lead to costly operations. Exempt and contract cartage rank second to private carriage in terms of operating flexibility. Since the contract operator is retained by the shipper, considerable scheduling discretion can be exercised concerning routes, stops, and times. The number of common carriers implies that service availability is great. However, the shipper does not legally have a great deal of direct control over common carrier operation. While the common carrier must service all shippers on a relatively equal basis, good management dictates that the common carrier will tailor service around the requirements of large and frequent shippers.

Conclusion

The transportation infrastructure available in the United States is superior to that of any other nation in the world. Although problems do exist within and between modes, shippers have many choices for transport between two locations. Within the five basic modes, several legal forms exist. In addition, intermodal arrangements, specialized carriers, and auxiliary transportation add to the alternatives. The task in logistical system design is to select the transport mix that best satisfies overall transportation requirements.

Ultimately, selection of a transportation mix should be fully integrated into the overall logistical effort. In evaluating potential modes and carriers, the value or service rendered by a specific combination or mix must be measured in terms of corresponding cost. The vitality of a sound national transportation system rests with common carriers; they are the backbone of the transport network. Most enterprises utilizing private, exempt, and contract carriers also offer frequent shipments to common carriers. In fact, the largest users of private trucking are usually the largest users of common carrier transport. The general belief among professional traffic managers is that every effort should be made to support a sound common carrier network capacity.

SUPPLIERS OF TRANSPORTATION SERVICES

Transportation services are offered by a combination of suppliers. Historically, government policy limited providers to single-mode operation. This restriction was designed to promote competition between modes and thus limit the potential for monopoly practices experienced in the early railroad era. The limitations were lifted following deregulation so that carriers could develop integrated intermodal services to more efficiently and effectively meet the needs of customers. The following sections review the services that are offered by different carrier types. The description also includes examples of carriers that are representative of each category.

Single-Mode Operators

The most basic carrier type is a single-mode operator that offers service utilizing only one transport mode. This degree of focus allows a carrier to become highly specialized, competent, and efficient.

However, the approach creates significant difficulties for intermodal transport because it requires negotiation and a transaction with each individual carrier. Airlines are an example of a single-mode carrier for both freight and passenger service since they only offer service from airport to airport. The shipper or passenger is responsible for movement to and from the airport. A series of single-mode operations require more management effort and, thus, increase cost.

Specialized Carriers

Over the past several decades a serious problem existed in small-shipment transportation. It was difficult for a common carrier to provide a reasonably priced small-shipment service because of significant overhead cost associated with terminal and line-haul service. This overhead forced motor carriers to assign a minimum charge for handling any shipment. The minimum was generally in the range of $100, regardless of shipment size or distance. Railroads do not offer small-shipment service. As a result of the minimum charge and the lack of low-cost rail alternatives, an opportunity existed for companies offering specialized service to enter the small-shipment or package-service market.

Package services represent an important part of transportation infrastructure, and the influence of carriers in this segment is increasing because of their size and intermodal capabilities. However, the variety of services offered do not fall neatly into the traditional modal classification scheme since packages travel by rail, motor, and air. Package-service classification provides both regular and premium transportation, further blurring modal distinction. The characteristics of each are discussed and illustrated below.

Basic Package Services   Numerous carriers offer package delivery services within commercial zones of metropolitan areas. As noted earlier, this type of service is classified as exempt common carriage. Other carriers offer package delivery service on an intrastate and interstate basis. The most recognizable carriers are United Parcel Service (UPS), the U.S. Postal Service, and Roadway Package System (RPS).

The original service offered by UPS was contract delivery of local shipments for department stores. Over the past two decades, UPS has made substantial inroads into more diverse intercity package movements. In fact, UPS has expanded its scope of overall operating authority by shipping packages that conform to specified size and weight restrictions nationwide and globally for consumers and business enterprises. By specializing in small packages, UPS has been able to provide cost-effective overnight service between most cities within 300 miles. For shippers located at key commercial centers, UPS two-day service covers approximately 55 percent of the continental United States population.

UPS has various capabilities and offers many postal carrier services including

TABLE 10-5   EXAMPLE OF INTEGRATED PARCEL CARRIER SERVICES

Freight services

- *Next-day air.* Guaranteed overnight air delivery for letters and packages
- *Second-day air.* Air delivery at substantial savings compared to overnight
- *Ground delivery service.* Routine two-day delivery within 800 miles from origin
- *Hundredweight service.* Contract service for multipackage shipments over 200 pounds sent to single consignee at one location on a single day
- *Ground saver.* High-volume business-to-business package delivery between designated metropolitan areas
- *International air.* Automatic daily pickup and expedited delivery to more than 180 countries
- *Air cargo service.* Oversized/heavy domestic and international freight
- *Service to Canada.* Ground and air delivery with computer linkup between both countries' customs offices
- *Worldwide expedited package service.* Multipackage alternative to air freight
- *Worldwide document service.* Document delivery requiring minimal customs clearance
- *Truck leasing.* Full-service vehicle leasing and rental

Value-added services

- *Electronic tracking.* Monitors shipments from pickup to delivery
- *Advanced label imaging system (ALIS).* Bar code package tracking labels for customer inquiry
- *Delivery confirmation service.* Automatic proof of delivery via bar coding
- *Customs clearance service.* Expedited service for UPS International Air
- *MaxiShip package processing system.* Software program to assist customer management of shipping operations
- *MaxiTrac customer access software.* Direct customer linkup to the UPS tracking and tracing systems for on-line delivery information
- *Consignee billing.* Management and direct payment of inbound customer transportation charges
- *Inventory express.* Logistical support (inventory control, distribution, and reporting) for time-sensitive products requiring fast, reliable distribution
- *On-call air pickup.* Same-day pickup for all UPS air services via customer phone call
- *UPS properties.* Facility development for site leasing close to UPS operations

---

Source: United Parcel Service promotional materials.

ground and premium air. Table 10-5 summarizes the integrated services offered by package carriers such as UPS. It is interesting to note that ground service frequently involves intermodal movement by using a combination of truck and rail carriers.

The U.S. Postal Service operates ground and air parcel service. Charges for parcel post are based on weight and distance. Generally, parcels must be delivered to a post office for shipment. However, in the case of large users and when it is convenient for the Postal Service, pickup may be provided at the shipper's location. Intercity transport is accomplished using air, highway, rail, and even water; and the legal forms of transport utilized in parcel post include common and contract cartage. Delivery is provided to the destination by the Postal Service.

RPS has developed as a niche carrier by focusing on business-to-business parcel transportation. In many cases, all three of these regular package carriers are expanding to include services traditionally provided by air and LTL motor carriers. These service extensions broaden their market and facilitate single-carrier operation.

The importance of basic parcel service cannot be overemphasized. One of the fastest-growing forms of marketing in the United States is nonstore retailing, in which catalog orders are placed by telephone or mail for subsequent home delivery. Figure 10-4 illustrates this growth in terms of value. The bulk of nonstore retailing for home delivery is transported via UPS and the U.S. Postal Service.

Premium Package Services   Several carriers—such as Federal Express (Fed Ex), Roadway, Emery Worldwide, and DHL—have entered the package or premium transportation market over the past two decades. Most organizations that provide routine package service also offer premium service. UPS, for example, offers next-day and second-day delivery, while the U.S. Postal Service provides priority delivery.

The first widely recognized premium package service was provided by Federal Express in 1973. Fed Ex offers nationwide overnight service utilizing a fleet of dedicated cargo aircraft. The original Fed Ex service attracted attention because of the innovative line-haul plan in which all packages were flown nightly to a terminal hub located in Memphis, Tennessee, for sorting and redistribution. Fed Ex's original service offering has been considerably expanded by reducing package size and weight restrictions and by adding global destinations.

The potential for rapid growth in parcel service has attracted many competitors into overnight premium package service. In addition to specialized firms like Fed Ex, UPS, Airborne Freight, Emery Worldwide, and Purolator Courier, major motor carriers and airlines have begun to offer competitive service. Many of these carriers have also adopted the hub-and-spoke operating environment. These services appeal to commercial business because they fill a need for rapid delivery in emergency situations. They also appeal to infrequent business and personal shippers.

FIGURE 10-4   Charting U.S. mail-order sales growth. *("Mail Order Top 250+," Direct Marketing, July 1992, p. 20.)*

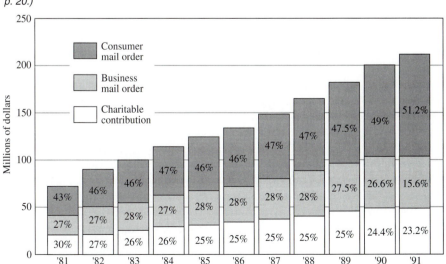

Intermodal Operators

Intermodal operators use multiple modes of transportation to take advantage of the inherent economies of each and thus provide integrated service at the lowest total cost. Many efforts have been made over the years to integrate the different transport modes into ''one-stop'' movement from the shipper's perspective. Initial attempts at modal coordination trace back to the early 1920s, but cooperation was constrained by regulatory restrictions designed to limit monopoly practices. Intermodal offerings became common during the 1950s with the advent of integrated rail and motor transport (commonly called *piggyback* service). The popularity of such offerings has increased significantly as a means to provide more efficient and effective transportation.

Technically, coordinated or intermodal transportation could be arranged among all basic modes. Descriptive terms—piggyback, fishyback, trainship, and airtruck—have become standard transportation jargon. For each intermodal combination, the objective is to integrate the most advantageous characteristics of each mode to achieve optimal performance. For example, a common intermodal combination is motor-rail, which integrates the flexibility of motor for short distances with the low line-haul cost associated with rail for longer distances. The following sections describe intermodal services and illustrate applications of each type.

Piggyback/TOFC/COFC/Roadrailer   The best known and most widely used intermodal system is the trailer or container on a flatcar (TOFC or COFC). Containers are the ''boxes'' utilized for intermodal product storage and movement between motor freight, railroads, or water transportation. They are typically 8 feet wide, 8 feet high, and 20 to 40 feet long, and do not have highway wheels. Trailers, on the other hand, are of similar width and height but can be as long as 53 feet and have highway wheels. As the name implies, a trailer or container is placed on a railroad flatcar for some portion of the intercity line haul and pulled by a truck for the remaining travel. Line-haul costs are the expenses of moving railcars or trucks between cities. For railroads, line-haul costs also include the expense of maintaining the right-of-way and track on main lines. Since the development of the original TOFC, the various combinations of trailer or container on flatcar (double-stacked, for instance) have increased significantly.

A variety of TOFC piggyback service plans are available. Each plan defines the responsible party (i.e., railroad or motor carrier) for each segment of the move as well as billing and payment arrangements. Table 10-6 illustrates the variety of TOFC operating plans. They differ by responsibility for equipment, pickup, delivery, and invoicing.

While the TOFC concept facilitates direct transfer between rail and motor carriage, it also presents several technical limitations. The placement of a trailer with highway wheels on a railcar can lead to wind resistance, damage, and weight problems. On the other hand, these containers can be transferred to water carriers, allowing access to multiple modes.

Roadrailer, another technology that facilitates shifts between rail and highway carriage, is a trucktrailer chassis that can be fitted with either rubber wheels or steel rail trucks. With the rubber wheels, the vehicle is a highway trailer. With steel rail

TABLE 10-6 SUMMARY OF TOFC PLANS

- *Plan I.* Railroad movement of common motor carrier trailers, with the shipment moving on one bill of lading with billing done by the trucker. Traffic moves under rates in regular motor carrier tariffs. Motor carrier handles ramp-to-door termed service at origin and destination.
- *Plan II.* Railroad does line haul and performs terminal service, moving rail-owned trailers or containers on flatcars under one bill of lading.
- *Plan II $1/4$.* Railroad provides trailer, flatcar, and line haul and performs either origin or destination terminal service.
- *Plan II $1/2$.* Railroad furnishes the trailer, flatcar, and line haul, but the shipper performs the origin and destination terminal service.
- *Plan III.* Railroad provides line haul, while shipper and/or consignee provides trailers and performs terminal service. Typical rates are based on a flat charge per trailer.
- *Plan IV.* Shipper or forwarder furnishes a trailer-loaded flatcar, either owned or leased. The railroad makes a flat charge for loaded or empty-car movements, furnishing only line haul.
- *Plan V.* Traffic moves generally under joint rate. Either mode may solicit and bill for traffic.

trucks, the vehicle is a short railcar. The Roadrailer line-haul cost is reported to be 50 percent less than comparable over-the-road motor transport.[18] The Roadrailer concept facilitates modal interchange without requiring extensive material-handling equipment.

Containerships Fishyback, trainship, and containerships are examples of the oldest form of intermodal transport. They utilize waterways, which are one of the least expensive modes for line-haul movement. The fishyback, trainship, and containership concept loads a truck trailer, railcar, or container onto a barge or ship for the line-haul move. Such services are provided in coastal waters between Atlantic and Gulf ports, from the Great Lakes to coastal points, and along inland navigable waterways.

A variant of this intermodal option is the "land bridge" concept, which moves containers by a combination of sea and rail. It is commonly used for cargo bound for Europe from the Pacific Rim. Rather than incur the time and expense of an all-water move, containers are shipped to the west coast of North America from the Pacific Rim, loaded on railcars for movement to the east coast, and then reloaded onto ships for transport to Europe. The land bridge concept is based on the benefit of ocean and rail combinations that utilize a single tariff, which is lower than the total cost of the separate rates.

Two other international intermodal options are miniland bridge (minibridge) and microbridge. Minibridge is a variant of land bridge in which freight movement originates or terminates at a point within the United States. Microbridge refers to door-to-door service available along the west coast of the United States rather than traditional port-to-port services. Door-to-door service places the responsibility of shipment movement and/or delivery on the transportation carrier. Port-to-port ser-

---

[18]"Is Roadrailer the Answer for Europe?" *Railway Age,* **193**:2, February 1992, p. 15.

vice places the responsibility of movement to the origin port and from the destination port to the final destination on the shipper or consignee.

Coordinated Air and Truck Another form of intermodal transport is the combination of air and truck. Local cartage is a vital part of every air movement because air freight must eventually be transported from the airport to the final delivery destination. Air-truck movements usually provide service and flexibility comparable to straight motor freight.

Air-truck is a common combination for premium package services, such as those provided by UPS and Federal Express, but it can also be used for more standard freight applications for several reasons. First, there is a lack of air freight transport to smaller cities in the United States. These cities are often served by narrow-body aircraft and commuter planes that are ill-equipped to handle standard freight. Thus, motor carriage into small cities from metropolitan airports provides a needed service at a competitive cost. Second, package carriers, while well suited to serve small cities, are not as able to handle heavy freight. They focus on envelope and small parcel packages, since these segments are more profitable. Also, package carriers' internal handling systems operate with conveyors that have difficulty processing heavier freight. As a result, many air carriers have extended their motor freight range to provide service to expanded areas.

Conclusion The concept of intermodalism is appealing to both shippers and carriers because of the economic potential of linking two modes. In fact, several authorities have suggested that the only way to maintain a strong national transportation network is to encourage and foster increased intermodalism. These efforts are of prime interest to logistical planners because such development increases the options available in system design. The deregulatory trend of the 1980s substantially relaxed barriers to multimodal ownership. Figure 10-5 illustrates the dramatic growth over the past decade, with millions of loadings, trailers, and containers. Logistics managers credit this growth to lower cost and improved service provided by intermodal operations. The next decade should witness continued expansion. It should be noted, however, that intermodal growth results primarily from increased container use rather than truck trailers. Containers offer more flexibility because they can be readily interchanged between multiple modes. In 1992, for the first time, more than half of intermodal shipments used containers rather than trailers.

Nonoperating Intermediaries

Other transportation service providers are nonoperating intermediaries that typically do not own or operate equipment but broker the services of other firms. Their function is somewhat analogous to that of wholesalers in marketing channels. A typical nonoperating intermediary might begin by aggregating a quantity of small shipments from various shippers and then purchasing intercity transportation on a volume-rate basis. The intermediary typically offers shippers a rate lower than the corresponding common carrier rate for the shipment size. The profit margin of the intermediary is the differential between the rate charged the shipper and the cost

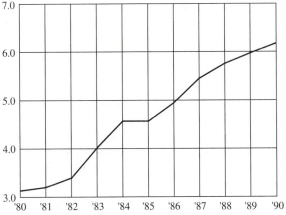

FIGURE 10-5   Growth of intermodal rail loadings (millions of loadings, trailers, and containers). *(Association of American Railroads.)*

of transport service purchased from the carrier. Nonoperating intermediaries often purchase a major share of their intercity or line-haul service from legal forms of transport, although they may also operate their own over-the-road equipment. Nonoperating intermediaries are often exempt carriers that perform pickup and delivery services within municipal commercial zones.

The intermediaries economically justify their function by offering shippers lower rates for movement between two locations than would otherwise be possible by direct shipment via common carriers. Because of peculiarities in the common carrier rate structure such as minimum freight charges, surcharges, and less-than-volume rates, conditions exist whereby nonoperating intermediaries can provide savings to shippers. These specific enabling conditions are detailed in Chapter 12. Interestingly, there are cases when intermediaries charge higher rates than shippers could obtain from other legal carriers: the justification for the higher charges is faster delivery and/or more complete service. The primary intermediaries are freight forwarders, shippers' associations, and brokers.

Freight Forwarders   Freight forwarders are for-profit businesses that consolidate small shipments from various customers into a bulk load and then utilize a common carrier (surface or air) for transport. At the destination, the freight forwarder splits the bulk load into the original smaller shipments. Local delivery may or may not be included in the forwarder's service. The main advantage of the forwarder is a lower rate because of the bulk load and, in most cases, faster transport of small shipments than would be experienced if the individual customer dealt directly with the common carrier. Freight forwarders accept full responsibility for shipment performance.

Shippers' Associations/Cooperatives and Agents   Shippers' associations are operationally similar to freight forwarders in that they consolidate individual small loads into bulk shipments to gain cost economies. However, shippers' associations are voluntary nonprofit entities where members, operating in a specific industry, join to manage small-shipment purchases. Typically, members purchase products from common sources, or the sources of supply are located in one area. Usually, purchase orders occur frequently, but in small lot sizes. Department stores, for example, often participate in shippers' associations since a large number of different products may be purchased at one location, such as the garment district in New York City.

The association is implemented when a group of shippers establish an administrative office at a point of frequent merchandise purchase (e.g., New York City). The office arranges for individual purchase orders to be delivered to a local facility. When sufficient volume is accumulated, a consolidated shipment is sent to each member's facility. As indicated earlier, some associations operate their own intercity transportation, with the legal status of an exempt carrier. Each member is billed for its portion of the shipment plus a prorated share of the association's fixed costs.

Brokers   Brokers are intermediaries that coordinate transportation arrangements for shippers, consignees, and carriers. They also locate shipments for exempt carriers and owner-operators. Brokers, who must obtain a license from the ICC, typically operate on a commission basis. Prior to deregulation, they played a minor role because of restrictions on their operations. Now, brokers provide more extensive services such as shipment matching, rate negotiation, billing, and tracing.

Conclusion

Traditionally, the transportation supply market included a large number of relatively segmented carriers. Segmentation was based on multimode operation and service restriction, which reduced the alternatives offered to shippers as well as carrier competitiveness and responsiveness. While this made shipper decisions easier, it also resulted in transportation system inefficiencies and higher cost.

As discussed above, deregulation has significantly increased carrier flexibility. It is now common for them to use the most efficient combination of multimodal transport and to offer the ancillary services demanded by each customer.

SUMMARY

Transportation is a key activity in the logistics value chain as it moves product through the various stages of production and ultimately to the consumer. Chapter 10 reviewed transportation's role, infrastructure, suppliers, economics, and decision making. The objective was to provide an overview of transportation resources and an understanding of the factors influencing transportation management.

Following the introduction, the chapter first reviewed transportation functionality and principles. The primary functions included product movement, product storage, and integration of international production and distribution operations. The major transportation principles involving economies of scale and economies of distance were discussed and illustrated. The perspectives and considerations of each party involved in the transportation process were also reviewed.

Next, the chapter provided an overview of the transportation infrastructure. It compared and contrasted the operating, service, and economic characteristics of the major transport modes including rail, motor, water, pipeline, and air. Transportation legal formats—such as common, contract, private, and exempt carriers—were reviewed and illustrated. Finally, the chapter described suppliers of transportation services, which included single-mode operators, specialized carriers, intermodal operators, and nonoperating intermediaries.

QUESTIONS

1 Describe the five modes of transportation, identifying the most significant characteristics of each. What is the basic concept behind intermodal movement?

2 Why have the railroad miles declined during a period of national growth?

3 Railroads have the largest percentage of intercity freight ton-miles, but motor carriers have the largest revenue. How do you justify this relationship?

4 Why is motor carrier freight transportation the most preferred method of product shipment?

5 In today's world, are there any essential differences between transportation formats?

6 Are independent or owner-operator truckers a legal form of transportation given the current regulatory provisions? Support your answer.

7 Among the TOFC plans, which is most popular and why?

8 How can the recent rapid growth of premium package services such as Federal Express be justified on an economic basis?

9 What is the concept of ''one-stop'' transportation buying? What factors support the logic of integrated transportation services?

10 What is the role of a freight broker? Do you feel that this service will grow or decline in the future?

11

TRANSPORTATION REGULATION

TYPES OF REGULATION
   Economic Regulation
   Safety and Social Regulation
HISTORY OF TRANSPORTATION
REGULATION
   Pre-1920
   1920 to 1940
   1940 to 1976
   1976 to the Present
INTERSTATE DEREGULATION
   Motor Carrier
   Air Transport
   Rail Transport
   Other Carriers
   The Future of Federal Economic Regulation

INTRASTATE REGULATION
CURRENT REGULATORY ISSUES
   Collective Rate Making and Antitrust
     Immunity
   Contract Definition
   The Future Status of the ICC
   Hidden Discounts
   Undercharges
   Hazardous Materials
SUMMARY
QUESTIONS

Changes in government regulation have significantly influenced transport availability and operation. Logistical managers need to have some understanding of this regulatory background to fully understand the logic underlying today's transportation system. The rationale, background, history, and current status of regulation are reviewed in Chapter 11.

    Since transportation has a major impact on both domestic and international commerce, government has often taken special interest in both controlling and promoting transportation activities. Control may take the form of both federal and state government regulation, as well as a wide range of administrative and judicial decisions. With the passage of the Act to Regulate Interstate Commerce on February 4, 1887, the federal government began an active role in protecting the public interest with respect to performance and provision of transportation services.

Chapter 11 discusses the past and present role of government in regulating transportation. It first classifies the types of transportation regulation. Transportation regulatory history is briefly reviewed to provide a foundation for current issues. Interstate deregulation and intrastate regulation are then discussed. Finally, the chapter reviews the current status of regulatory issues that influence logistics management.

TYPES OF REGULATION

Government transportation regulation can be classified into the categories of (1) economic regulation of business practices, and (2) safety and social regulation. It is important to differentiate between these categories because deregulatory efforts have focused on economic aspects, while more stringent regulatory efforts have been directed toward safety and social issues. Each is briefly described below.

Economic Regulation

The control of business practices is one of the oldest forms of government regulation. To provide dependable transportation service and to foster economic development, both federal and state governments have actively utilized economic regulation. In the United States, government involvement has spanned over 100 years in an effort to make transportation equally available to all users without discrimination. Basic regulatory policy has attempted to foster competition among privately owned transportation companies. To encourage economical and widespread transportation supply, the government invested in public infrastructure such as highways, airports, waterways, and deep-water ports. However, to actually provide transportation service, the government supported and regulated a system of privately owned for-hire carriers.

Because of transportation's importance to economic growth, the government believed that carriers required special protection to ensure service availability and stability. Availability means that appropriate carrier services will be accessible to any enterprise requiring them. Stability means that carriers will be guaranteed sufficient profits to ensure viable long-term operation. Economic regulation is generally implemented by controlling entry, rates, and services.

Entry Regulation   Entry regulation controls carrier entry and exit as well as the markets served. In order to ensure stability, historical entry regulation constrained the number of carriers in larger markets and supported the number of carriers in smaller markets. Entry restrictions dictate the regions and origin-destination combinations that can be serviced by each carrier. The restrictions sought to reduce the cutthroat competitive characteristics in larger markets while ensuring viable service levels for smaller markets. The counterparts to entry restrictions are exit limitations. In order to ensure appropriate service levels, economic regulation limits a carrier's ability to leave a market if it would result in a substantial reduction in service. Carriers sometimes argued that exit constraints forced them to serve unprofitable markets.

Rates   The second aspect of economic regulation focuses on rate-related practices. Specific considerations include rate making, rate changes, rate subsidies, and actual rates. Rate making refers to the practice of setting rates. Single-line rates are the rates between origin and destination offered by a single carrier. A joint rate is a single rate between origin and destination offered by multiple carriers that cooperate to provide product shipment. While joint price setting is considered collusion in most industries, collective rate making has been allowed in the transportation industry to facilitate development of joint rates. When the transportation industry was strictly regulated prior to 1980, collective rate making was allowed for both joint and single-line rates. In the joint rate situation, each carrier must determine its cost, overhead allocation, and profit for activities involved in handling the shipment; then a joint rate is presented to the customer. Since deregulation, collective rate making is not allowed for interstate shipments.

Rate changes are the practices required to increase or decrease rates. In most industries, firms are allowed to change prices at will, although competitive practices sometimes limit this flexibility. Prior to deregulation, carriers were not allowed to change rates unless they could justify the necessity to do so before the Interstate Commerce Commission. The need for an increase (or decrease) would require demonstrating that costs are increasing or decreasing. Temporary rate changes, such as those resulting from increases in fuel prices, were implemented via rate surcharges. Since deregulation, carriers have been given flexibility to change rates up to a certain amount (generally 7 to 15 percent) each year without justification. Currently, rate change restrictions have been removed for interstate carriers.

Rate subsidies refer to the practice of assisting, or subsidizing, one segment of carrier operation by allowing higher rates on a different segment. It has been argued that the high cost of providing service in small markets has been subsidized by the rates charged in the relatively lower cost major markets. Similarly, it has been argued that relatively protected common carrier rates subsidize more competitive contract carrier rates for those operating in both market segments. Subsidies have been allowed historically when governments desired to promote or develop a market segment. Rate subsidies are also provided by the government in the form of support of rights-of-way. This argument has been a source of contention by railroads for the last fifty years. Specifically, rail carriers point out that the government subsidizes motor carriers since it builds and maintains the highway system, while railroads are required to build, maintain, and pay taxes on their rights-of-way. It is also argued that the airways and waterways are subsidized as well by government development programs and user fees.

Actual rates refer to the charges that are incurred by the shipper or consignee for shipment. Prior to deregulation, actual rates had to be filed with the Interstate Commerce Commission, and only the filed rate could be charged. In addition, no discounts or rebates could be given. Since deregulation, carriers have been allowed to discount filed rates.

Services The third aspect of regulation concerns the services provided by the carrier. Prior to deregulation, service offerings were relatively consistent across carriers and included product transport, loading and unloading, loss and damage liability, and limited information about shipment status and invoicing. In general, there was a wide breadth of services but very limited service quality. After deregulation, shippers and consignees sought carriers that could provide more quality services while possibly negotiating to restructure other responsibilities like liability and loading. Practices such as *release value rates* and *shipper load and count* have resulted from such negotiations.

Conclusion As previously discussed, the prime focus of business regulation was to control entry, rates, and service level provided by for-hire carriers. In addition, traditional regulatory practice treated each mode independently. This approach limited carrier ability to develop intermodal relationships and offerings. By 1970 federal economic regulation had reached the point where it affected 100 percent of rail and air ton-miles, 80 percent of pipeline, 43.1 percent of trucking, and 6.7 percent of domestic water carriers.[1] As discussed in subsequent sections of this chapter, the degree of direct government economic regulation began to change during the 1970s and took a dramatic turn in 1980 with the passage of major deregulatory legislation. The contemporary regulatory environment continues to be dominated by a trend toward free market competition, although there are some calls for reregulation to maintain carrier stability, particularly in airline and LTL motor carrier markets.

Safety and Social Regulation

In direct contrast to relaxed economic transportation regulation, the 1970s and 1980s saw more demanding safety and social regulation. Since its inception in 1966, the Department of Transportation (DOT) has taken an active role regarding transport and handling of hazardous material, rules related to maximum work hours, and vehicle safety. The scope of this activity was further institutionalized by the passage of the Transportation Safety Act of 1974. Additional legislation affecting logistical performance has been passed over the ensuing twenty years. Table 11-1 presents major laws that significantly affect logistical planning and performance. Additional emphasis on transportation safety has increased because of environmental and related liability lawsuits.

HISTORY OF TRANSPORTATION REGULATION

This section offers an overview of the transition from regulated to strategic transportation. First, it provides a brief synopsis of events from 1887 to 1975. This

---

[1]Derived from the *1972 National Transportation Report,* Washington, D.C.: Department of Transportation, U.S. Government Printing Office, November 1972, pp. 2–44.

TABLE 11-1   MAJOR FEDERAL ENVIRONMENTAL LAWS AFFECTING LOGISTICS

Name and citation of law	General description	Impact on logistics
1 The Clean Air Act (CAA) 42 U.S.C. 7401-7642 as recently amended by P.L. 101-549, November 1990	Regulates emissions into the air by all stationary and mobile sources. The major emphasis is on coal-powered utilities, toxic plant emissions, and vehicle emissions, especially in urban areas where air quality is below national standards.	More stringent vehicle emission standards will raise operating costs of fleets and rates for trucking. Transportation, distribution, and even commuting activity in the largest cities in the country will become increasingly regulated by individual state and municipal governments.
2 The Clean Water Act (CWA) 33.U.S.C. 1251-1387 The National Pollutant Discharge Elimination System	Regulates discharge of any pollutants into the "waters" of the United States, which is broadly interpreted. Requires permit applications for storm water runoff from 100,000 business sites including transportation and distribution facilities.	Application for permits for storm water runoff were due to be filed in November 1991. Water quality standards will be forthcoming from the EPA, and treatment of storm water runoff will likely be required.
Wetlands Regulation Section 404 of CWA	Regulates dredging and discharge of fill into the "waters" of the United States.	Port dredging and construction are severely limited. Current regulations define "waters" to include vast areas of perfectly dry land that is characterized by certain soils and vegetation, so building of distribution facilities on or near such property is also severely limited. Wetland studies of any suspect property should be done before it is acquired.
3 The Resource Conservation and Recovery Act (RCRA) 42 U.S.C. 6901-6991(i)	Establishes a comprehensive cradle-to-grave regulatory scheme governing storage, disposal, and transportation of solid and hazardous wastes. Up for reauthorization, and more restrictions are expected on interstate movement of waste.	Extreme pressure on companies to reduce the amount of toxic and waste materials moving through the logistics stream. Stringent requirements for manifesting, labeling, and monitoring of hazardous waste movements.
Underground Storage Tanks (USTs) 42 U.S.C. 6991, et seq.	Establishes standards, notification requirements, and financial responsibility for underground storage tanks.	Mandates replacement of most old tanks and remediation of sites with average cost per tank around $100,000. Higher environmental standards and liability for new USTs such that many companies will choose not to have them.
4 The Comprehensive Environmental Response Compensation and Liability Act (CERCLA) 42 U.S.C. 9601, et seq., which includes Superfund Amendments and Reauthorization Act of 1986 (SARA or Superfund)	Imposes broad—and virtually unlimited—liability for cleanup of sites contaminated by hazardous substances.	Creates an absolute mandate to find alternatives to disposal of even mildly hazardous substances. Environmental inspection vital before buying, leasing, or using distribution sites.

Sources: The 1993 Information Please® Environmental Almanac compiled by World Resources Institute, Houghton Mifflin Co., Boston & New York, 1993. Mackenzie L. Davis and David A. Cornwell, *Introduction to Environmental Engineering,* 2d ed., McGraw-Hill, Inc., New York, 1991. Thomas A. Foster, "The Gospel of Green," *Distribution,* **91:**1, January 1992, pp. 27–28. Stanley Hoffman, "HAZMAT: The New Facts of Life," *Distribution,* **92:**1, January 1993, pp. 40–44.

Name and citation of law	General description	Impact on logistics
5 DOT Docket HM-181; HM-126F	Requires all hazardous material employers to train and test all employees involved with hazardous materials handling, storage, and movement at least once every two years. Applies to nearly all hazardous materials transportation (except bulk shipments by water carrier), regardless of package or shipment size, frequency of shipment, degree of hazard of products shipped, size of the hazardous material firm, or the number of employees.	Significant training, inspection, and examination costs—particularly regarding vehicle inspection, segregation of incompatible materials, and securing freight.
6 Intermodal Surface Transportation Efficiency Act of 1991 (ISTEA), P.L. 102-240	Six-year, $151 billion plan for highway and mass transit to develop an "economically efficient, environmentally sound foundation for the United States to compete in the global economy and move people and goods in an energy-efficient manner."	Created an Office of Intermodalism within the Department of Transportation; creates a new national highway system; dedicates significant funds for long-term infrastructure needs; freezes the use of long combination vehicles (LCVs) to the twenty states that currently permit them; extends 2.5 cents of 1991 Gasoline Fuel Tax through 1999.
7 Hazardous Materials Transportation Act 49 CFR 171-179	Regulates the transportation by air, highway, or water of off-site hazardous waste within the United States. Closes the critical linkage between the generator (manufacturer) of hazardous waste and the ultimate off-site treatment, storage, or disposal of such waste. Also gives officials special authority to deal with transportation accidents.	Significantly increases transportation firm responsibility for storage, movement, and handling of hazardous materials moving through the logistics stream.

historical review establishes the foundation for the economic deregulation of the 1980s. Next, the section outlines regulatory activities since 1980 with an emphasis on subsequent legislative, administrative, and judicial actions. Finally, the section reviews current transportation policy and discusses the future federal administrative outlook.

Pre-1920

The purpose of interstate regulation is to scrutinize the activities of for-hire carriers in the public interest. Since railroads dominated early overland transportation, they initially enjoyed the position of a near monopoly. Individual states maintained the legal right to regulate discriminatory practices within their borders, but no federal regulation existed to provide consistent interstate controls. In 1887, the Act to

Regulate Commerce was passed by Congress and became the foundation of United States transportation regulation.[2] The act also created the Interstate Commerce Commission (ICC).

The gradual refinement of federal regulatory power over carrier pricing evolved from legislation and judicial decisions from 1900 through 1920. At the turn of the century, destructive competitive practices resulted from independent rate making among carriers. Although the ICC had the authority to review groups of rates with respect to their just and reasonable nature once the rates were placed into effect by individual carriers, no regulation existed over proposed rate making. Attempts at joint rate making by railroads had been declared illegal. In 1903 the railroads supported the passage of the Elkins Act. This legislation reduced under-the-table rebates and special concessions and increased the penalty for departures from published rates. It did not, however, eliminate the cause of discriminatory practices—independent and nonregulated rate making.

The passage of the Hepburn Act in 1906 began to establish federal regulatory power over rate making. The just-and-reasonable-review authorization of the 1887 act was expanded to include examination of maximum rates. However, the regulatory posture remained ex-post (after the fact) until passage of the Mann-Elkins Act in 1910. This act permitted the ICC to rule on the reasonableness of proposed rates prior to their effective date and to suspend rates when they appeared discriminatory.

The posture of modern rate regulation was completed with the passage of the Transportation Act of 1920. The review power of the ICC was expanded to prescribe reasonableness of minimum as well as maximum rates. The ICC was instructed to assume a more aggressive nature concerning proposed rates. The original Act to Regulate Commerce was modified to instruct the commission to initiate, modify, and adjust rates as necessary in the public interest. The 1920 act also changed the name of the 1887 act to the Interstate Commerce Act.

1920 to 1940

Several additional transportation laws were enacted during this period. With some exceptions, their primary objective was to clarify issues related to the basic acts of 1887 and 1920. In 1935 the Emergency Transportation Act further instructed the ICC to set standards with respect to reasonable rate levels. By the 1930s motor carriers had become an important transportation factor. In 1935 the Motor-Carrier Act placed the regulation of common carrier highway transportation under the jurisdiction of the ICC. This act, which became part II of the Interstate Commerce Act, defined the basic nature of the legal forms of common, contract, and exempt motor carriers.

In 1938 the Civil Aeronautics Act established the Civil Aeronautics Authority (CAA) as the ICC's counterpart for regulating air transport. The powers and charges of the CAA were somewhat different from those of the ICC, in that the act specified

---

[2]For an early history of legislative attempts prior to 1887, see L. H. Hanley, *A Congressional History of Railroads in the United States, 1850–1887*, Bulletin 342, Madison: University of Wisconsin, 1910.

that the CAA would promote and actively develop the growth and safety of the airline industry. In 1940 the functions of the original CAA were reorganized into the Civil Aeronautics Board (CAB) and the Civil Aeronautics Administration, now known as the Federal Aeronautics Administration (FAA). In addition, the National Advisory Committee on Aeronautics was formed in the mid-1930s and in 1951 became known as the National Aeronautics and Space Administration (NASA). Through the 1960s NASA concentrated attention on aerospace. However, NASA is specifically charged with the responsibility for increasing aviation safety, utility, and basic knowledge through the use of science and technology. Thus, in the structure that resulted, the CAB regulated rate making; the FAA administered the airway system; and NASA was concerned with scientific development of aerospace, commercial, and civil (private) aviation.

The regulation of pipelines has not been as clear-cut as that of railroads, motor carriers, and air transport. In 1906 the Hepburn Act declared that selected pipelines, primarily oil, were in fact common carriers. The need for regulation developed from the early market dominance that the Standard Oil Company gained by developing crude oil pipelines to compete with rail transport. In 1912 the ICC took action that was upheld by the Supreme Court to convert private pipelines into common carriers. While there are substantial differences between pipeline and other forms of regulation, for all effective purposes the ICC fully regulated pipeline traffic. Interestingly, a significant difference regarding pipeline regulation is that this type of common carrier was allowed to transport goods owned by the carrier.

1940 to 1976

Regulation of water transport prior to 1940 was extremely fragmented. Some standards existed under both the ICC and the United States Maritime Commission. In addition, a series of acts placed regulation of various aspects of the domestic water transport network under specific agencies. For example, the Transportation Act of 1940 put domestic water transport under ICC jurisdiction and gave the Federal Maritime Commission authority over water transport in foreign commerce and between Alaska and Hawaii and other United States ports.

It is important to understand that the ICC did not set or establish rates for carriers under its regulatory jurisdiction. Rather, it reviewed and either approved or disapproved rates. Carriers under federal regulation were exempt from the antitrust provisions of the Sherman, Clayton, and Robinson-Patman Acts with respect to collaboration in rate making. Such exemption was provided by the Reed-Bulwinkle Act of 1948, which permitted carriers to participate in rate-making bureaus. Cooperative rate making was a common feature among for-hire carriers. In particular, for-hire transportation carriers in motor and rail organized freight bureaus that standardized cooperative pricing and published price tariffs for specific geographical areas. The action of the bureaus was subject to ICC sanction.

From 1970 until 1973 several acts were passed to aid the rapidly deteriorating rail situation in the United States. In 1970 the Rail Passenger Service Act established the National Railroad Passenger Corporation (AMTRAK). The Regional Rail Reorganization Act of 1973 (3-R) was passed to aid seven major northeastern railroads that were facing bankruptcy. As a result of 3-R Act provisions, the Consolidated Rail Corporation (CONRAIL) began to operate portions of the seven lines on April 1, 1976.

The establishment of AMTRAK and CONRAIL represented the first modern attempt of the federal government to own and operate transportation services. While the subsequent passage of the Railroad Revitalization and Regulatory Reform Act of 1976 (4-R) and the Rail Transportation Improvement Act of 1976 provided financial support for AMTRAK and CONRAIL, these acts also began to reverse the trend of regulatory expansion that had prevailed for nine decades.

1976 to the Present

In the early 1970s a concentrated attempt was gaining momentum to review and modify existing economic regulation to accommodate the demands and requirements of contemporary society. As early as 1955 a Presidential Advisory Committee recommended increased transportation competition. Its recommendations were published in a 1960 report issued by the Commerce Department.[3] A Senate Committee in 1961 drafted a recommended National Transportation Policy. Among other recommendations the 1961 report advocated formation of a Department of Transportation (DOT).[4] After its formation in 1966, the Department of Transportation became the dominant force seeking regulatory modification. From 1972 to 1980 the DOT introduced or significantly influenced legislation at two-year intervals to modify the regulatory scope of for-hire carriers.[5]

The initial direct effort aimed at regulatory reform was administrative in nature. From 1977 to 1978 CAB Chairman Alfred Kahn forced de facto deregulation of the Civil Aeronautics Board by virtue of administrative rulings that encouraged air carriers to actively compete in free market discounting and by easing new carrier entry. In 1977 the Federal Aviation Act was amended to deregulate domestic air cargo carriers, freight forwarders, and shippers' associations with respect to pricing and entry. The standard for entry into the air cargo industry was modified to require

[3]Department of Commerce, *Federal Transportation Policy and Program,* Washington, D.C.: U.S. Government Printing Office, 1960.

[4]Senate Committee on Commerce, *National Transportation Policy,* 87th Congress, Washington, D.C.: U.S. Government Printing Office, 1961. The Department of Transportation was established by Public Law 86-670 in 1966 and initiated operation on April 1, 1967.

[5]For varied opinions regarding the desire for and preferred nature of regulatory revamping, see *Analysis and Criticism of the Department of Transportation Motor Carrier Reform Act,* Washington, D.C.: American Trucking Association, 1976; Rupert L. Murphy, "Private or For-Hire?" *Distribution Worldwide,* September 1975, pp. 39–41; Stephen Tinghitella, "The Day the ICC Died," *Traffic Management,* December 1975, p. 14; and Jim Dixon, "The Spectre of Distribution," *Distribution Worldwide,* September 1975, pp. 29–30. Harry J. Newman, "The Key to Reform Is Gradualism"; W. Doyle Beatenbough, "There Is Room for Improvement"; Lee Cisneros, "Regulation Is Simply the Balance Wheel"; J. B. Speed, "There Has to Be a Cross-Subsidization of Freight Rates"; B. A. Franzblau, "There Must Be a More Rational Approach"; Tom Cornelius, "Deregulation Would Cause a Chaotic Situation"; W. Stanhaus, "Our System Can Be Improved"; and E. Grosvenor Plowman, "The Need Is for Rational Regulatory Improvement," all in "Deregulation, Reregulation or Status Quo?" *Distribution Worldwide,* September 1975, pp. 31–38. W. K. Smith, "Shipper/Common Carrier Relationship"; and Wayne M. Hoffman, "Regulation of Transportation: How Much Is Enough?" both in *Transportation at a Turning Point,* Syracuse, N.Y.: Syracuse University Printing Service, 1981.

that a new competitor be judged fit, willing, and able to carry out the proposed service. The traditional regulatory criteria of judging entry applications on the basis of public convenience and necessity were eliminated. The change meant that a potential carrier no longer had to prove a need for the proposed service. On October 24, 1978, the Airline Deregulation Act was passed, extending free market competition to all forms of passenger air transport. A significant provision of the Airline Deregulation Act was a mandate to the executive branch to close down the Civil Aeronautics Board on or before January 1, 1985.[6]

A further significant step toward deregulation was taken with the passage of the Railroad Revitalization and Regulatory Reform Act of 1976 (4-R). The 4-R Act introduced a wide range of guidelines for the regulation of railroad marketing. An important provision was the introduction of a zone of reasonableness or zone of rate flexibility (ZORF) in pricing. This permitted carriers considerable latitude in pricing policy and became a common feature of subsequent legislation. ZORF permitted rail carriers to increase or decrease prices by 7 percent annually. While many advocates of deregulation were critical of the 4-R Act because it "didn't go far enough," the legislation did introduce several significant new standards and practices in rate making.

In 1976, the drive toward a careful review of existing regulatory policy and practice intensified as Congress established a nineteen-member National Transportation Policy Study Commission (NTPSC). The commission's charter was mandated by Public Law 94-280 (May 5, 1976). The broad-based mission of this commission reflected the regulatory climate of the times. The law required "a full and complete investigation and study of the transportation needs and of the resources, requirements and policies of the United States to meet such expected needs." Furthermore, the NTPSC was to "take into consideration all reports on National Transportation Policy which have been submitted to Congress." It should "evaluate the relative merits of all modes of transportation in meeting our transportation needs" and "recommend those policies which are most likely to insure that adequate transportation systems are in place which will meet the needs for safe and efficient movements of goods and people."[7]

The commission's 527-page final report was issued in June 1979. It contained 16 chapters, 5 appendixes, 74 figures, and 211 tables. As noted later in this section, the scope and magnitude of the NTPSC report were necessary to help integrate the fragmented National Transportation Policy. However, the study's thirty-seven-month time frame was too long to contain the momentum for regulatory change.

Upon assuming office as chairman of the Interstate Commerce Commission in 1977, A. Daniel O'Neil appointed a special task force to recommend ways in which the ICC could internally improve the regulation of motor carriers. The report—commissioned on June 2, 1977—was completed in thirty-four days and offered thirty-nine reform proposals. To a significant degree, Chairman O'Neil's approach

---

[6]The CAB was officially closed December 31, 1984.

[7]National Transportation Policy Study Commission, *National Transportation Policy through the Year 2000,* Washington, D.C.: U.S. Government Printing Office, 1979. For a discussion of specific policy issues, see Gayton E. Germane, *Transportation Policy for the 1980s,* Reading, Mass.: Addison-Wesley Publishing Company, 1983.

was similar to that of Chairman Alfred Kahn at the CAB. The task force report was important because it represented the first major effort on the part of the ICC to internally respond to DOT's pressure for regulatory reform.

The struggle for regulatory change in railroads and trucking was accomplished in 1980 with the passage of the Motor-Carrier Act and the Staggers Rail Act. Significant aspects of each piece of legislation are highlighted.

INTERSTATE DEREGULATION

This section reviews the interstate regulation status of each major mode of transport.

Motor Carrier

Since enactment of the Motor-Carrier Act of 1935, the landmark piece of motor carrier legislation was the passage of Public Law 96-296, which was signed into law by President Carter on July 1, 1980. The swift resolution of differences between existing House and Senate bills under committee consideration and the subsequent rapid approval by the House, Senate, and the President still stand as monuments to the speed of the democratic process when it is politically advantageous. Even the most dedicated proponents for change were shocked by the rapid compromise and approval. After more than eighteen months of study and review the controversial bill was resolved into an acceptable form within days and signed into law within hours.

The important point concerning the rapid approval process is that most contemporary observers agree that the Motor-Carrier Act of 1980 (MC-80) fell far short of providing a sound motor carrier deregulatory platform. A later review of the significant legislative, administrative, and judicial change that has followed passage of MC-80 will testify to the deficiencies in the initial law. For those who were proponents of deregulation, the law was a long-awaited first step forward. To opponents, MC-80 represented the end of stability and the start of turbulent, if not chaotic, competition. The underlying philosophy of MC-80 and highlights of its basic features are reviewed.

MC-80 was designed to encourage competition and efficiency within the for-hire motor carrier industry. The act's basic premise was that carrier authorization had been too restrictive over the years and subsequently resulted in an operating environment with an insufficient number of carriers to provide effective competition. The traditional practice required the ICC to authorize operating rights in the form of a Certificate of Convenience and Necessity. As the name implies, the approval of a new certificate was granted only when it could be proved that the proposed service was necessary and in the public interest. Until passage of MC-80 it was the responsibility of the carrier that was seeking new or expanded operating rights to prove necessity under potential protest by interested parties such as competitors. MC-80 reversed the burden of proof by requiring the protesting party to prove that granting operating rights would be inconsistent with public convenience and necessity. The basis for review of new applicants was a "fit, willing, and able" test similar to the one introduced previously in air regulation.

In addition to relaxed entry, MC-80 expanded the number of industry competitors by changing regulations regarding existing carriers. A controversial provision of the law authorized private carriers to perform compensated intercorporate hauling. The so-called back-haul provision authorized pickup allowances to encourage effective utilization of private trucks in the food industry. Traditionally, products had been sold on a uniform zone delivered basis. However, the new provision allowed shippers to pick up back-hauls of raw material or finished goods after deliveries had been made. Under this arrangement, the market is divided into geographic zones with a delivered price established for each zone. Regulations concerning contract carriers and independent owner-operators were relaxed as well to permit a broader range of participation in for-hire transportation. Finally, exemption status was expanded with respect to agricultural carriers and small shipments incidental to air transport. Agricultural cooperatives were authorized to haul up to 25 percent of their total interstate tonnage in the form of nonfarm, nonmember goods.

Several provisions of MC-80 relaxed industry pricing practices. The zone of rate flexibility (ZORF) originally tested in the 4-R Act was introduced in the motor carrier industry. A zone of 10 percent annual rate increase or decrease was established within which the ICC could not investigate, suspend, revise, or revoke any rate on the basis of reasonableness. In addition, the ICC was authorized to expand the ZORF by 5 percent if justified by competitive conditions. This expansion was authorized in 1984. Under provisions of MC-80, the ZORF is adjusted to accommodate changes in the producer price index, an indicator of cost-of-living or cost-of-business conditions in the general economy. The introduction of ZORF did not eliminate ICC involvement in motor carrier pricing. The ICC retained the authority to protect against discriminatory practices and predatory pricing. Carriers were also given more freedom regarding the nature of released value rates without ICC approval. Finally, the act seriously challenged the industry's collective rate-making practices. As noted earlier, carriers were permitted to collectively set rates through the use of rate bureaus. MC-80 limited the scope of collective rate making by prohibiting discussion of single-line rate proposals after January 1, 1984. In general, MC-80 challenged the status and practice of rate bureaus by requiring a review by a Motor Carrier Rate-Making Commission.

Other significant provisions of MC-80 dealt with rule changes designed to increase industry efficiency. Not only were carriers given a more liberal hand in expanding services, but they were also authorized to modify existing service if they could increase efficiency. In the traditional process of granting operating rights, many carriers were restricted to specific routes or were required to pass through specified gateways during line-haul movements. MC-80 encouraged carriers to eliminate gateways and circuitous routes. Carriers were also permitted to apply for relaxation of commodity requirements and the need to service specified cities if operating efficiency could be improved.

The structural impact of MC-80 on the for-hire motor carrier industry has been dramatic. It is clear that the number of authorized motor carriers has increased significantly. In 1980, there were 17,000 ICC-regulated motor carriers. In 1981, the first year following the passage of MC-80, approximately 3,500 new operating authorities were granted.[8] By 1990, the number of authorized carriers was greater than 40,000.[9] Without question, many of the new entrants have participated only in small contracts or on irregular routes. In fact, approximately two out of every three first-time applications for new operating authority were for contract carriage.[10] Prior to passage of MC-80, no single general commodity common carrier was authorized to service all locations within the continental United States. Since 1980, the ICC has granted nationwide operating authority to over 5,000 carriers. Numerous new route applications have also been submitted.

An important and well-publicized concern is the high degree of failure among carriers that existed prior to the passage of MC-80. For example, of the top twenty LTL carriers in operation in 1979, thirteen had disappeared through either mergers (three) or bankruptcy (ten) by 1988.[11] Most industry observers believe that the "shakeout" of the long-haul LTL market is about complete; in fact, it is now dominated by a number of large carriers such as Yellow Freight, Consolidated Freightways, Roadway Express, and TNT. These successful carriers have the financial, technological, and managerial resources necessary to operate an extensive system of terminals, trucks, and personnel. The shakeout of regional LTL markets and carriers is still in process.

Several other aspects of MC-80 have significantly altered the for-hire motor carrier industry. As the number of operating authorities expanded throughout the 1980s, competition for freight became increasingly fierce. The shift in channel power from manufacturer to retailers allowed large retailers to leverage shipment volume in order to gain reduced rates from motor carriers. As a result, freight rates have been decreasing for both TL (since 1981) and LTL (since 1984) carriers. Further exacerbating the situation is the common practice of severe rate discounting (often 50 to 55 percent) from published tariff rates in order to attract other carriers' volume or, at minimum, maintain a carrier's individual freight volume. Such rate discounting has significantly cut into motor carrier revenues. Despite the considerable number of motor carrier bankruptcies caused by these events, many observers believe that overcapacity still exists in the motor carrier industry.

Another result of MC-80 lies in the changing composition of the motor carrier industry labor force. With the advent of deregulation, the level of unionized labor has dropped from 60 percent in the late 1970s to 28 percent in 1985. In the opinion of some observers, this development has severely reduced the impact of organized labor on industry operations.

Finally, as financial conditions have worsened, many marginally performing carriers have kept operating because they did not have the reserves of capital to cover pension debts. Federal retirement laws, especially MPPAA (Multi-Employer Pension Plan Amendments Act), protect the pension plans of retired employees at the expense of owners. If a company with a large pension liability liquidates, the

[8]*Investor News,* November 1982.
[9]Thomas Gale Moore, "Unfinished Business in Motor Carrier Deregulation," *Regulation,* Summer 1991, p. 52.
[10]Ibid.
[11]James Aaron Cooke, "The Shakeout Intensifies," *Traffic Management,* **29:**5, May 1990, pp. 39–43.

Pension Benefit Guarantee Corporation can claim the owner's equity to cover pension obligations.

Without question, considerable industry turmoil has resulted from the pricing latitude provided by MC-80. Some carriers have carefully tied the quality of their services to rates. However, as noted above, others have engaged in massive discounting without appropriate cost reductions in operating practices. The carriers, new or old, that have prospered since MC-80 are those that improved efficiency by eliminating undesirable activities, increased equipment utilization, and decreased operational variance. This form of quality performance became possible and was rewarded within the provisions of MC-80.

As a result of the Trucking Industry Regulatory Reform Act of 1994 (TIRRA), the Interstate Commerce Commission is changing its policies to "lessen or remove, where appropriate, regulatory burdens and curtail or eliminate ICC activities that do not serve statutory goals."[12] New policy interpretations ease motor carrier entry, eliminate tariff filing requirements, and extend the use of exemption authority for motor carrier transportation. Congress eliminated, as a licensing standard, the public convenience and necessity test for common carriers and the public interest test for contract carriers. Effective January 1, 1995, the entry standard for common and contract carriers focuses primarily on safety and insurance requirements. TIRRA's most significant change is the elimination of the filed rate doctrine. This means that carriers are no longer required to file rates with the ICC, which should considerably reduce the fear of potential undercharge disputes. The commission determined that rates established by independent carrier actions, even if the carrier is a member of a rate bureau or the rate is dependent on a mileage guide tariff, are not subject to the filed rate doctrine. TIRRA also grants the ICC authority to exempt motor carriers (except household goods carriers) from certain regulations, as the ICC has done for the railroads since 1976. Under TIRRA, the only areas in which exemption authority could not be applied are cargo loss and damage, insurance, safety fitness, antitrust immunity, and further changes in tariff filing requirements.

Air Transport

The goal of airline deregulation was to increase competition and provide customers with better service at relatively lower cost. Each airline evolved toward a hub-and-spoke route system following deregulation as a means to efficiently provide service to a broad number of markets. "Hubs" are large airports where passenger traffic "spokes," from smaller satellite airports, are consolidated for subsequent outbound flights to other destinations within the hub's service area or to other distant hubs.

Initially, deregulation increased the number of competitors in the airline industry. However, many of these carriers have merged or gone out of business in the ensuing shakeout. The result is a high degree of industry concentration, particularly at major hub airports. Single carrier hubs such as Atlanta, Dallas–Ft.

---

[12]*Interstate Commerce Commission News,* **94:**251, Washington, D.C., October 24, 1994.

Worth, and Minneapolis report that more than 60 percent of their passengers use the "hub" airline.[13]

Mergers have left the airline industry with eight major carriers and several smaller ones. While airline rates have generally declined, there is evidence of higher rates at highly concentrated hubs. As a result of deregulation in the United States and privatization of other international carriers, additional airline alliances, partnerships, and mergers are likely on a global scale. Such airline integration is projected to bring the high service capabilities and performance that have been developed in the United States to a global market. While there have been a number of complaints from consumers and transportation analysts regarding airline service and prices, the effectiveness of a competitive environment in the United States airline industry is arguably superior to more regulated environments common throughout other parts of the world.

Rail Transport

On October 14, 1980, President Carter deregulated the railroad industry by signing the Staggers Rail Act (Public Law 96-488). This act was a continuation of a trend initiated in the 3-R and 4-R Acts and supplemented by passage of the Rail Transportation Improvement Act in 1976. The prevailing regulatory policy was to be proactive toward rebuilding a strong rail system. The Staggers Rail Act continued this trend.

The dominant philosophy of the Staggers Act was to provide railroad management with the freedom necessary to revitalize the industry. As such, the most significant provisions of the Staggers Act extended the freedom in rate making initiated by the 4-R Act. The concept of ZORF pricing expanded to permit adjustment of any rate on the basis of a percentage increase in the railroad cost recovery index. The important feature of this provision is that railroads were now authorized to lower rates to meet competition and also to raise rates to cover operating cost increases. Carriers were also given increased flexibility with respect to surcharges and cancellations, rules regarding burden of proof in judgments of market dominance, minimum rates, and general rate increases. Contract rate agreements between individual shippers and carriers were specifically legalized.

In addition to price flexibility, railroad management was given liberalized authority to proceed with abandonment of poorly performing existing rail line service. This authority was supported by a streamlined approval process. The act also provided the framework for a liberalized attitude toward mergers and increased the ability of railroads to be involved in motor carrier service.

Similar to MC-80, the Staggers Act raised serious questions concerning the future role of rate bureaus. The act prohibited the discussion of, or voting on, single-line rates and significantly altered existing practice on joint-line rates.

The impact of the Staggers Rail Act has resulted in important changes in the

---

[13]For a more detailed discussion, see Andrew N. Kleit, "Competition with Apology: Market Power and Entry in the Deregulated Airline Industry," *Regulation,* Summer 1991, pp. 68–75; and Elizabeth E. Bailey, "Airline Deregulation: Confronting the Paradoxes," *Regulation,* Summer 1992, pp. 18–25.

structure and vitality of the rail industry. Prior to deregulation, one leading railroad executive referred to the industry as offering plain vanilla service with plain vanilla equipment.[14] Little differentiation existed between railroads. Rates were set by consensus, followed specific industry structures such as grain or steel, and were insensitive to marketplace requirements. Deregulation has created the opportunity to quickly adjust prices and equipment allocation to specific markets, to tailor rates and services, to develop contract and incentive rates, to eliminate unprofitable routes, and to manage a railroad on an innovative basis. As a result of this freedom, active rail mileage has decreased from 179,000 in 1980 to 148,069 in 1989.[15] The number of class I or major railroads has also declined from 45 in 1979[16] to 13 in 1991[17] as a result of consolidation. Conversely, many more short-line railroads, typically nonunion and with less restrictive operating rules, have been created or have taken over route operations shed by the major railroads.

Similar to motor carriers' response to MC-80, not all railroads have reacted in a positive manner to the Staggers Rail Act. Their behavior has ranged from excessive and ruinous rate cutting to far-ranging innovation based on satisfying market needs. After the initial five years of operation under the Staggers Act, the industry began to show increased stability and financial revitalization. Today the railroads are seeking prosperity by responding to customer needs and have clearly overcome the famous Levitt criticism of being market myopic.[18] Current railroad growth reflects a strong trend toward intermodal operations as advances are made in merging, starting, or acquiring motor carrier operations. For example, on July 24, 1984, the ICC voted unanimously to approve the merger of the CSX Corporation and American Commercial Lines, Inc. This joined what was at that time the nation's second largest railroad holding company and one of the largest barge operations, and was an unprecedented step toward intermodal ownership. Intermodalism is also evidenced in the 1992 CSX Corporation Annual Report, which lists subsidiaries in rail, truck, container shipping, barge, and customized transportation.[19] Similar trends have occurred with other major railroads, including Burlington Northern, Norfolk-Southern, and Union Pacific.

Other Carriers

The 1984 Shipping Act partially deregulated the ocean transport industry. This legislation allowed carriers greater scheduling, pricing, and contractual flexibility in order to improve service and competition. Today, shippers are increasingly demanding the freedom to negotiate shipping contracts with ocean carriers independently and privately rather than through shipping conferences.

Finally, the Bus Regulatory Act of 1982, the Surface Freight Forwarder Dereg-

---

[14]Based on unpublished remarks by James A. Hagen, "Sales and Services in a Deregulated Environment," presented at Northwestern University Transportation Center, Evanston, Ill., January 25, 1984.

[15]Eno Transportation Foundation, Inc., *Transportation in America,* 9th ed., 1991, p. 64.

[16]*Moody's Transportation Manual,* New York: Moody's Investors Service, 1980.

[17]Ibid., 1992.

[18]Theodore Levitt, "Marketing Myopia," *Harvard Business Review,* **38,** July–August 1960, pp. 45–56.

[19]CSX Corporation Annual Report, Richmond, Va., 1992.

ulation Act of 1984, and the Customs Brokers Act of 1984 completed the major undertaking of modal economic deregulation.

The Future of Federal Economic Regulation

Ex Parte 522, issued October 1994, examined the need for federal economic regulation of interstate surface transportation. The recommendations, included in the Trucking Industry Regulatory Reform Act of 1994,[20] describe and evaluate the primary responsibilities of the Interstate Commerce Commission and propose continuation, modification, or elimination of the ICC role. The act removes ICC economic control over motor, water, and intermodal surface transportation, but retains some degree of regulation for pipelines and rail because of the monopolistic characteristics resulting from their high fixed charges. Futhermore, under provisions of the act, federal regulatory functions are to be assigned to an independent federal agency, while licensing roles will be assigned to the Department of Transportation.

Given the ICC's substantially weakened role following passage of the Trucking Industry Regulatory Reform Act of 1994, the commission has reinterpreted or clarified its role as less of a rate authority and more of a mediator regarding carrier-shipper disputes. The ICC still maintains as well as monitors carrier insurance and financial and safety fitness.

INTRASTATE REGULATION

This section provides a brief overview of the nature of intrastate regulation and its impact on transportation performance. While domestic transportation regulation has primarily focused on interstate movements, most states have similarly regulated intrastate transport. These regulations, which only cover shipments within a single state, limit vehicle size, market entry, rates, and routes. Specifically, forty-two states regulate intrastate transportation, and eight states do not. Delaware and New Jersey have never regulated common or contract freight. Several states (Alaska, Arizona, Florida, Maine, Vermont, and Wisconsin) have followed the lead of the federal government and deregulated transportation in the early 1980s.[21] Because of the confusion of having some intrastate movements regulated while interstate movements were not, there was significant (albeit not universal) pressure on Congress to deregulate all transportation. In general, unions and carriers with intrastate authority wanted to maintain the status quo. However, in 1994, Congress passed and the President signed a bill preempting state control over rates, routes, and services. States will continue to regulate safety, truck size and weight, routing of hazardous materials, and all carrier financial responsibility. Carriers can still be involved in rate bureaus if they desire.[22]

---

[20]Trucking Industry Regulatory Reform Act of 1994, S.B. 2275.

[21]Cassandra Chrones Moore, "Intrastate Trucking: Stronghold of the Regulators," *Policy Analysis,* **204,** February 16, 1994, p. 6.

[22]Thomas A. Strah, "Congress Passes Intrastate Deregulations," *Transport Topics,* August 15, 1994, p. 1.

The costs of intrastate regulations and the difficulties involved in repealing such legislation are considerable. In particular, the express package industry has sought to reduce the operating restrictions of intrastate regulation. In response to the efforts of Federal Express and UPS, several states have taken steps to strengthen their position.

An example of intrastate regulatory efforts was the 1991 attempt by several states to regulate Federal Express' intrastate truck movement. However, a 1992 ruling by the United States Supreme Court stated that California could not regulate trucking operations of a federally certified airline.[23] Other states and cities have attempted to limit carrier access at certain times or with certain hazardous materials. These attempts were constrained by a 1991 federal court decision limiting state or local control and barring:

> New York City from enforcing its own equipment and design standards on vehicles carrying hazardous materials into the city. It backed the statutory preemption provisions of the Hazardous Materials Transportation Uniform Safety Act of 1990, which gave the federal government control over equipment design as well as hazardous materials classification, packaging and handling.[24]

The counterargument to federal regulation of transportation is "states' rights," which claims that intrastate commerce is within the control of individual states and that such regulation is necessary to guarantee service availability and stability (particularly to small communities) and to ensure safe trucking operations. Considerable research, however, fails to support these arguments.[25]

In an effort to increase intrastate regulatory consistency across states, the ICC attempted to expand the scope of interstate transportation. Interstate commerce traditionally describes product moved across state lines. In a 1993 statement (Motor Carrier Interstate Transportation from Out-of-State through Warehouses in Points in Same State), the ICC ruled that shipments from warehouses to markets in the same state could be deemed interstate movements if the commodity had originally been shipped from out of state.[26] The ICC argued that such shipments are part of a "continuing movement" and that interstate rates should apply. In an effort to gain more direct control over intrastate regulation, the Federal Aviation Administration Authorization Act[27] essentially preempted economic regulation of intrastate transportation. The preemption was placed in the act because Congress found that the states' regulation of intrastate transport has (1) imposed an unreasonable burden on interstate commerce; (2) impeded the free flow of trade, traffic, and transportation of interstate commerce; and (3) placed an unreasonable cost on American

---

[23]Thomas M. Strah, "Deregulation: A States' Rights Issue," *Transport Topics,* March 30, 1992, p. 34.

[24]Roger Gilroy, "Court Strikes NYC Hazmat Rules," *Transport Topics,* October 28, 1991, p. 1.

[25]Cassandra Chrones Moore, "Intrastate Trucking: Stronghold of the Regulators," *Policy Analysis,* **204,** February 16, 1994, pp. 27–37.

[26]For further discussion of continuing movement rates, see David M. Cawthorne, "ICC's New Intrastate Rules," *Traffic World,* No. 6, Vol. 230, No. 4436, May 11, 1992, p. 11; and Robert P. James, "ICC Pledges More Vigorous Fight against Intrastate Truck Regulators," *Traffic World,* No. 6, Vol. 230, No. 4436, pp. 11–12.

[27]Federal Aviation Administration Authorization Act of 1994, H.R. 103-2739.

consumers. The provision preempts state regulation of prices, routes, and services for direct air carriers and related motor carriers. The purpose is to level the playing field as completely as possible between air carriers on the one hand and motor carriers on the other, with respect to intrastate economic trucking regulation. The net effect was to remove regulation of intrastate transportation.

CURRENT REGULATORY ISSUES

A number of economic issues have developed as a result of the quick passage of carrier deregulation. In the normal course of legislation, there is adequate time for all parties to review a bill from a variety of perspectives to identify potential concerns. MC-80 passed so quickly that several problems were not identified. The specific issues involved collective rate making and antitrust immunity, contract definition, future status of the ICC, hidden discounts, undercharges, and hazardous materials. Each issue is described, and its status is discussed.

Collective Rate Making and Antitrust Immunity

Prior to deregulation, motor carriers met in committees, or *rate bureaus,* to collectively determine and publish the rates they would charge. The process was slow and inflexible. Following deregulation, motor carriers and railroads were given greater freedom to set and adjust prices, and thus the price parity of regulated transportation no longer exists.

Rate bureaus received antitrust immunity from Congress in 1948. They typically operate on a regional basis and earn their income through dues paid by motor carrier members. There are still currently more than eighty rate bureaus operating throughout the United States, although the seven largest are the most influential. Historically, rate bureaus have enjoyed enormous influence in the trucking industry, but over the past few years their power has dramatically declined as major LTL carriers have withdrawn from the bureaus and now independently publish rates and negotiate shipper contracts.

Since many carriers no longer recognize a need for traditional rate bureau services, the bureaus' future existence is uncertain. In response to this trend, many bureaus are adjusting their strategic focus in order to serve a different customer base. An increasing proportion of their revenues are now generated by small and medium-sized carriers that rely on them to provide services such as statistical data and rate analysis, which would not be cost-effective for the carriers to do on their own. Some bureaus are also branching out into non-traditional areas like market and financial analysis to secure a viable operating position for the future. Even with these expanded services, it is not likely that rate bureaus will survive.[28]

---

[28]Mitchell E. MacDonald, ''Rate Bureaus: Is Time Passing Them By?'' *Traffic Management,* **31**:8, August 1992, pp. 46–48.

Contract Definition

Deregulation relaxed the requirements for creating a contract between a shipper and a carrier. Under regulation, the scope and number of contracts for a carrier were limited to ensure the viability of TL common carriage. As noted earlier, each carrier was allowed a maximum of eight active contracts at any point in time. Deregulation increased contracting flexibility and now allows virtually all TL volume to move under contract rates. However, logistics managers must continuously monitor the definition of contract carriage to ensure that their transportation operation is within legal guidelines. This is particularly relevant for intrastate and international operations, which continue to refine the definition of a contract.

As an example, Michigan's deregulation legislation requires three criteria for a legal transportation contract. First, the agreement must be for a minimum of one year. Second, the vehicle must be used exclusively by a single shipper, meaning that two shippers cannot each contract for half a load. Finally, a common carrier must not have provided comparable service during the previous year.[29] It is obvious that satisfying all three conditions simultaneously is not simple. While contract transportation is more common today than in the past, it is still more restrictive than contracting for other goods and services. It is likely that TL contracts will continue their trend toward increased competition, while a variety of constraints will remain on LTL contracting in order to maintain common carrier viability.

The Future Status of the ICC

The ICC's viability and importance as a regulatory body have been challenged in recent years. Since deregulation, changes in motor carrier entry requirements and rate-setting regulations have significantly reduced the agency's role. Those parties who believe the ICC has outlived its usefulness suggest that transferring the agency's remaining functions to the Department of Transportation or merging it with the Federal Maritime Commission would increase the efficiency of the federal government and simplify transportation of goods. Opponents of such efforts argue that the ICC serves a valuable function as an independent, bipartisan agency and is relatively unaffected by more politically controlled government offices such as the Department of Transportation. The status of the ICC is dependent on the funding of the United States Congress, and while it appears that the agency will continue to operate for the immediate future, it will do so in an increasingly reduced role because of diminished budget allocations. Legislative attempts to close down the ICC will become more likely in future congressional sessions.

Hidden Discounts

The Elkins Act of 1903 restricted carriers from providing discounts or rebates to shippers. Carriers were required to specifically charge the filed rate. Deregulation authorized discounts from the published rates. Discounting practices have become

---

[29]"Michigan Reform Bill Heads for Governor's Desk," *Transport Topics,* December 20, 1993, p. 7.

common, ranging from 30 to 50 percent. While discounting is an acceptable and perfectly legal practice, hidden discounts cause concern since they potentially reduce the credibility of the shipper.

As an example, there is the potential for a hidden discount when the freight terms are "prepay and add" by the shipper. This means that the shipper pays the freight bill and adds the amount to the customer's invoice. If the carrier provides a discount to the shipper, the shipper should acknowledge the discount by reducing the amount of the freight bill on the customer's invoice. The hidden discount becomes an issue when the customer receives a freight bill for $100, but the actual amount charged to the shipper is $75 ($100 freight bill minus a 25 percent discount).

Discounts and rebates are common for large shippers, but ethical problems arise when the contract or agreement calls for the shipper to select the carrier and then bill the customer for the freight cost. In such a situation, the shipper may select a more expensive carrier that agrees to provide a larger discount or rebate. The hidden discount results in a higher price for the customer and additional profit for the shipper. While obtaining a discount may be sound business practice, hidden discounts can raise ethical questions.

Undercharges

With the passage of the Motor-Carrier Act of 1980 (MC-80), the ICC significantly relaxed tariff regulations and rate-filing requirements governing motor freight common carriers. As discussed previously, intensified pricing competition created by MC-80 during the 1980s created significant rate discounting and drove many motor carriers into bankruptcy. In an effort to recover their investment, many large unsecured creditors of the bankrupt carriers have pressed bankruptcy trustees to consider the possibility of undercharge actions against their former customers. Union pension funds, which are among the largest creditors of the insolvent carriers, view potential undercharge litigation as a source of cash recovery.

The basis of the undercharge issue is the ICC's "filed rate doctrine," which prior to deregulation held that the only legal rate for a transportation transaction was the filed rate. The foundation of the ruling goes back to 1887, when the passage of the Act to Regulate Commerce included a provision prohibiting railroads from charging rates other than the filed rate and from refusing service to any shipper at the published legal rate. Enforcement of this prohibition required creation of the legal precedent known as the "filed rate doctrine," which ensured that carriers would comply with the published rates and terms of service.[30]

While deregulation did away with the requirements to file rates, the filed rate doctrine itself was not eliminated because of the speed with which the legislation passed. ICC interpretation of the Interstate Commerce Act and any amendments to it (such as MC-80) has traditionally been upheld by the courts. In fact, throughout the 1980s, ICC interpretation of the filed rate doctrine as affected by MC-80 was upheld on several different occasions. However, in 1990 the United States Supreme

---

[30]Jeffery M. Sharp and Robert A. Novack, "Motor Carrier Deregulation and the Filed Rate Doctrine: Catalysts for Conflict," *Transportation Journal* 32:2, 1992, pp. 46–54.

Court ruled in *Maislin Industries v. Primary Steel, Inc.* that the ICC interpretation of MC-80 was inconsistent with the Interstate Commerce Act and that MC-80 did not give the ICC authority to alter the requirements of the filed rate doctrine.[31]

Following this ruling, a wave of undercharge litigation was unleashed. The litigation contends that the bankrupt carriers and, indirectly, their creditors are owed the difference between the "filed rate" and the discounted rate actually charged. The difference, which has been termed an "undercharge," is estimated to exceed $27 billion.[32]

The undercharge issue continues to work its way through the legal system as shippers and carriers attempt to minimize their liability while creditors such as the Teamsters attempt to maximize their claims. The Negotiated Rates Act (NRA) of 1993[33] and a recent ICC decision granted relief to defendants in pending undercharge suits by (1) permitting settlements of all cases in amounts ranging from 5 to 20 percent of the claimed amount, depending on the type of case and the defendant; (2) granting a *complete* exemption from liability for certain types of claims (such as small businesses as well as charitable and recycling organizations); (3) permitting the ICC to grant relief from claims by finding the carriers' higher tariff rate or practice of negotiating unfiled rates to be unreasonable and in violation of the Interstate Commerce Act; (4) reaffirming the ICC's power to determine the validity of contracts, rather than the courts; and (5) permitting carriers to seek a waiver of undercharges resulting from inadvertent tariff errors.

While the Negotiated Rates Act resolved many undercharge issues from the shipper's perspective, the trucking industry was able to impose some restrictions in exchange for its support of the bill. The changes include (1) reregulation of agreements with contract carriers and establishment of a fine for each day of violation; (2) prohibiting "off-bill discounting" and imposing stiff fines for receiving unlawful discounts; (3) requiring "loading and unloading allowances" on the basis of the carrier's cost of performing the service; (4) placing a two-year limit on the settlement options under the bill; (5) reaffirming Congress' intent that filed tariff rates be strictly enforced; and (6) reducing the statute of limitations for filing overcharge claims from thirty-six to eighteen months, thus severely reducing the time to have freight bills audited.

In response to these changes, transportation lawyers suggest that:[34]

1 Firms must examine their dealings with customers and vendors for possible violations of the new off-bill discounting prohibition. This provision will have far-reaching effects on firms that are retaining any portion of a discount based on their total freight volume with a carrier when they pass freight costs on to their customers. The new law prohibits carriers from granting a reduction in a rate in its tariff *or contract* to any person other than the person paying the carrier *directly,* or its agent.

---

[31]Ibid.
[32]Ibid.
[33]H.R. 2121, 103d Congress.
[34]W. J. Angello, "Are You Ready to Conduct Business under the New Transportation Law?" Northport, N.Y.: Law firm of Angello, Pezold & Hirschmann, January 1994.

2 Firms presently dealing with common carriers should reexamine their exposure to future undercharges because of the difficulty of verifying *on a daily basis* that *every* rate has been lawfully filed in their carriers' tariffs. Most firms will conclude that the most expedient way to avoid the consequences of the "filed rate doctrine" in the future is to convert to contract carriage. In that event, a carefully drawn contract can fully protect the parties from the "surprises" that have occurred in the distribution cycle.

3 Freight bills must now be audited much earlier than previously to allow the filing of overcharge claims before the new eighteen-month time limit outlaws such claims. This reduction in the deadline for filing suggests the implementation of a prepayment audit program for all freight bills.

To summarize the environment after NRA, shippers and receivers have new regulations to consider for distribution operations. The constraints introduced and reintroduced post-NRA may prove to be hazardous enough to cause the business community to again join forces to urge Congress to *complete* the deregulation of the motor carrier industry. The industry may even be interested in further reducing these restrictions because of stiff fines and possible criminal prosecution.

Hazardous Materials

An increasingly critical problem for material handling and transportation management is the treatment of hazardous commodities that are either radioactive, corrosive, poisonous, explosive, toxic, or flammable. Federal safety regulations currently specify proper procedures regarding strength and type of shipping container, load composition and acceptable combinations of various hazardous commodities, proper labeling for easy identification, warehouse storage, and loading in transportation vehicles. Carriers must use a placard that is color-coded to identify the general type of commodity in transit and mark it with a four-digit number to indicate the specific hazardous substance. The placards provide critical information to police, firefighters, and medical personnel at the scene of an accident. In certain geographic areas of the United States, vehicles transporting hazardous materials may also be required to follow special routes. In 1993, U.S. Hazardous Material Regulations were standardized with the international regulations to increase material-handling and transportation safety.[35]

The Hazardous Materials Transportation Uniform Safety Act of 1990 provides the federal government with control over equipment design, hazardous materials classification, packaging and handling, and precedence over state and local environmental regulations. DOT regulations that became effective in early 1993 require virtually all hazardous materials employers to train and test employees involved in hazardous materials operations at least once every two years.[36] The new regulations also require a systematic program that provides increased general awareness, safety, and function-specific training. The level, duration, and specific content of any

---

[35]Paul Bomgardner, "HazMat Haulers: The Rules Are Changing on October 1," *Transport Topics,* September 27, 1993, p. 6.

[36]Stanley Hoffman, "HAZMAT: The New Facts of Life," *Distribution* **92:**1, January 1993, pp. 40–44.

training program are at the discretion of each hazardous materials employer. The new regulations will certainly increase firms' operating costs and are likely to heighten their hazardous materials enforcement activity as well as their exposure to civil and criminal penalties.

SUMMARY

This chapter provided background on significant changes in transportation regulation during the past two decades. The basic belief is that a logistical manager needs to have some appreciation of where regulation has been to fully understand some key transitional problems and opportunities. The chapter provided a brief overview and history of regulation. Next, attention was directed to major changes in interstate and intrastate regulation. Finally, the chapter concluded with an examination of current regulatory issues that confront logistical operations.

The status of transportation regulation remains a fluid topic. After decades of constant expansion, the tide began to swing toward increased deregulation during the late 1970s. In 1980 the avalanche of deregulation began with the passage of landmark legislation covering both motor carriers and railroads. The tempo of change continued throughout the decade of the 1980s and into the 1990s as countless administrative rulings and judicial decisions reduced effective regulation. Perhaps the deregulation wave crested in 1994 with the passage of the Trucking Industry Regulatory Reform Act. One expert characterized the dynamics of deregulation by concluding that more change in regulatory structure took place in the last ninety days of 1994 than in all the years of the previous decade combined.[37] Given where we stand in 1995, one might logically conclude that in the years ahead the pendulum may begin to swing back toward selective reregulation.

QUESTIONS

1   What was the prime justification for regulation of transportation in the first place? Is that justification still valid?
2   Discuss the key differences between economic and social regulation.
3   In your opinion, why has intrastate deregulation lagged behind interstate deregulation? Is such delay in the public interest?
4   What role will the ICC have in the future given the passage of the Trucking Industry Regulatory Reform Act of 1994?
5   Given deregulation, is there any real difference between common, contract, and exempt carriers?
6   How can the federal government simply deregulate intrastate trucking, as it appeared it did in the Trucking Industry Regulatory Reform Act of 1994?
7   Describe the undercharge issue and its legal resolution.
8   What is a hidden discount? Does it have any justification?
9   In your opinion what is the justification, if any, for continued antitrust immunity.
10   What areas, if any, may be candidates for future reregulation?

---

[37]Comments by Daniel J. Sweeney, Esq., at Health and Personal Care Distribution Conference, Longboat Key Club, Longboat Key, Fla., October 24, 1994.

CHAPTER 12

TRANSPORTATION MANAGEMENT

BASIC TRANSPORT ECONOMICS AND PRICING
    Economic Factors
    Cost Structures
    Pricing Strategies
    Rating
TRANSPORT DECISION MAKING
    Transport Documentation
    Traffic Department Responsibilities
SUMMARY
QUESTIONS

This final chapter on transportation focuses on the economics and pricing of transport services. The discussion that follows reviews both the theoretical and the practical aspects. The theoretical discussion contrasts cost-of-service with value-of-service pricing methods. The practical discussion considers cost structures, rating practices, and special rates and services. Next, the chapter reviews responsibilities of effective transport management including department activities, carrier evaluation, and freight documentation. Together, the sections of Chapter 12 provide an overview of transportation management in today's industry structure.

BASIC TRANSPORT ECONOMICS AND PRICING

Transport economics and pricing are concerned with the factors and characteristics that determine transport costs and rates. To develop an effective logistics strategy and to successfully negotiate transport agreements, it is necessary to understand the economies of the industry. A discussion of transportation economics and pricing requires coverage of three topics. First are the factors that influence transport economics. Second are the cost structures that influence expense allocation. Finally there are the rate structures that form the foundation for actual customer charges. Each topic is discussed.

Economic Factors

Transport economics is influenced by seven factors. While not direct components of transport rate tables, each factor is considered when developing rates. The specific factors are distance, volume, density, stowability, handling, liability, and markets. In general, the above sequence reflects the relative importance of each factor. The specific characteristics are discussed below.

Distance   Distance is a major influence on transportation cost since it directly contributes to variable cost, such as labor, fuel, and maintenance. Figure 12-1 shows the general relationship and illustrates two important points. First, the cost curve does not begin at the origin because there are fixed costs associated with shipment pickup and delivery regardless of distance. Second, the cost curve increases at a decreasing rate as a function of distance. This characteristic is known as the *tapering principle,* which results from the fact that longer movements tend to have a higher percentage of intercity rather than urban miles. Intercity miles are less expensive since more distance is covered with the same fuel and labor expense as a result of higher speeds and also because frequent intermediate stops typical of urban miles add additional loading and unloading costs.

Volume   The second factor is load volume. Like many other logistics activities, transportation scale economies exist for most movements. This relationship, illustrated in Figure 12-2, indicates that transport cost per unit of weight decreases as load volume increases. This occurs because the fixed costs of pickup and delivery as well as administrative costs can be spread over additional volume. The relation-

FIGURE 12-1   Generalized relationship between distance and transportation cost.

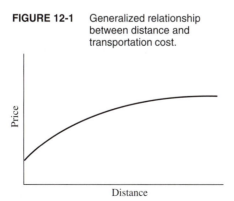

FIGURE 12-2   Generalized relationship between weight and transportation cost/pound.

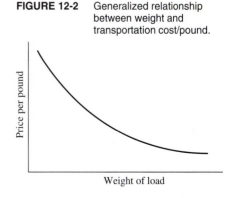

ship is limited to the maximum size of the vehicle (such as a trailer). Once the vehicle is full, the relationship repeats for the second vehicle. The management implication is that small loads should be consolidated into larger loads to take advantage of scale economies.

Density   The third economic factor is product density, which incorporates weight and space considerations. These are important since transportation cost is usually quoted in terms of dollars per unit of weight, such as amount per ton or amount per hundredweight (cwt). In terms of weight and space, an individual vehicle is constrained more by space than by weight. Once a vehicle is full, it is not possible to increase the amount carried even if the product is light. Since actual vehicle labor and fuel expenses are not dramatically influenced by weight, higher density products allow relatively fixed transport costs to be spread across additional weight. As a result, these products are assessed lower transport costs per unit of weight. Figure 12-3 illustrates the relationship of declining transportation cost per unit of weight as product density increases.

In general, logistics managers attempt to increase product density so that more can be loaded in a trailer to better utilize capacity. Increased packaging density allows more units of product to be loaded into the fixed cube of the vehicle. At a certain point, no additional benefits can be achieved through increased density because the vehicle is fully loaded. For example, from a capacity perspective, liquids such as beer or soda "weigh out" a highway trailer when it is about half full. As such, the weight limitation is reached before the volume restriction is met. Nevertheless, efforts to increase product density will generally result in decreased transportation cost.

Stowability   The stowability factor refers to product dimensions and how they affect vehicle (railcar, trailer, or container) space utilization. Odd sizes and shapes, as well as excessive weight or length, do not stow well and typically waste space. Although density and stowability are similar, it is possible to have products with the same density that stow very differently. Items with standard rectangular shapes are much easier to stow than odd-shaped items. For example, while steel blocks and rods have the same density, rods are more difficult to stow because of their length and shape. Stowability is also influenced by the shipment size; sometimes

FIGURE 12-3   Generalized relationship between density and transportation cost/pound.

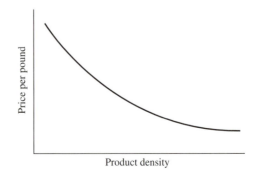

large numbers of items can be ''nested'' that might otherwise be difficult to stow in small quantities. For example, it is possible to accomplish significant nesting for a truckload of trash cans, while a single can is difficult to stow.

Handling   Special handling equipment may be required for loading or unloading trucks, railcars, or ships. Furthermore, the manner in which products are physically grouped together (e.g., taped, boxed, or palletized) for transport and storage also affects handling cost. Chapter 15 specifically addresses the economic issues of packaging and storage.

Liability   Liability includes six product characteristics that primarily affect risk of damage and the resulting incidence of claims. Specific product considerations are susceptibility to damage, property damage to freight, perishability, susceptibility to theft, susceptibility to spontaneous combustion or explosion, and value per pound.[1] Carriers must either have insurance to protect against possible claims or accept responsibility for any damage. Shippers can reduce their risk, and ultimately the transportation cost, by improved protective packaging or by reducing susceptibility to loss or damage.

Market Factors   Finally, market factors, such as lane volume and balance, influence transportation cost. A transport lane refers to movements between origin and destination points. Since transportation vehicles and drivers must return to their origin, either they must find a load to bring back (''back-haul'') or the vehicle is returned empty (''deadhead''). When deadhead movements occur, labor, fuel, and maintenance costs must be charged against the original ''front-haul'' move. Thus, the ideal situation is for ''balanced'' moves where volume is equal in both directions. However, this is rarely the case because of demand imbalances in manufacturing and consumption locations. For example, many goods are manufactured and processed on the east coast of the United States and then shipped to consumer markets in the western portion of the country, which result in more volume moving west than east. The imbalance causes rates to be generally lower for eastbound moves. This balance is also influenced by seasonality such as the movement of fruits and vegetables to coincide with the growing season. Demand directionality and seasonality result in transport rates that change with direction and season. Logistics system design must take this factor into account and add back-haul movement where possible.

Conclusion   The previous discussion identified major factors influencing transportation economics from a shipper's perspective. Although the relative influence on transportation cost is generally weighted in the sequence presented, the precise effect of each factor may vary because of specific product characteristics. Logistics managers have a responsibility to understand these influences and manage product and shipment characteristics to minimize transport expense.

---

[1]John E. Tyworth, Joseph L. Cavinato, and C. John Langley, Jr., *Traffic Management: Planning, Operations and Control,* Prospect Heights, Ill.: Waveland Press, Inc., 1991, p. 87.

Cost Structures

The second dimension of transport economics and pricing concerns the criteria used to allocate cost components. Cost allocation is primarily the carrier's concern, but since cost structure influences negotiating ability, the shipper's perspective is important as well. Transportation costs are classified into a combination of categories.

Variable Costs   Variable costs are those costs that change in a predictable, direct manner in relation to some level of activity during a time period. Variable costs can be avoided only by not operating the vehicle. Aside from exceptional circumstances, transport rates must at least cover variable costs. The variable category includes direct carrier costs associated with movement of each load. These expenses are generally measured as a cost per mile or per unit of weight. Typical cost components in this category include labor, fuel, and maintenance. On a per mile basis, TL carrier variable costs range from $0.75 to $1.50 per vehicle mile. As explained in any elementary economics text, it is not possible for any carrier to charge below its variable cost and expect to remain in business.

Fixed Costs   Fixed costs are those costs that do not change in the short run and must be covered even if the company is closed down (e.g., during a holiday or a strike). The fixed category includes carrier costs not directly influenced by shipment volume. For transportation firms, fixed components include terminals, rights-of-way, information systems, and vehicles. In the short term, expenses associated with fixed assets must be covered by contributions above variable cost on a per shipment basis. In the long term, the fixed cost burden can be reduced somewhat by the sale of fixed assets; however, it is often very difficult to sell rights-of-way or technologies.

Joint Costs   Joint costs are expenses unavoidably created by the decision to provide a particular service. For example, when a carrier elects to haul a truckload from point A to point B, there is an implicit decision to incur a "joint" cost for the back-haul from point B to point A. Either the joint cost must be covered by the original shipper from A to B, or a back-haul shipper must be found. Joint costs have significant impact on transportation charges because carrier quotations must include implied joint costs based on considerations regarding an appropriate back-haul shipper and/or back-haul charges against the original shipper.

Common Costs   This category includes carrier costs that are incurred on behalf of all shippers or a segment of shippers. Common costs, such as terminal or management expenses, are characterized as overhead. These are often allocated to a shipper according to a level of activity like the number of shipments handled (e.g., delivery appointments). However, allocating overhead in this manner may incorrectly assign costs. For example, a shipper may be charged for delivery appointments when it doesn't actually use the service (such as when the shipper's deliveries are unloaded on an "as available" basis). Chapter 21 discusses more appropriate contribution margin or activity-based costing approaches for analyzing transport economics.

Conclusion   The previous discussion identified major cost components that carriers must consider when quoting rates to shippers. The significance of joint and common transportation costs makes it difficult to maintain rates that are both profitable and competitive over time. While it is necessary for carriers to establish and negotiate rates with shippers, these rates must be assessed periodically to ensure that they are accurate and profitable. The following discussion reviews several rate strategies or philosophies used by carriers.

Pricing Strategies

When setting rates to charge shippers, carriers can adopt one or a combination of two strategies. Although it is possible to employ a single strategy, the combination approach considers trade-offs between the cost of service incurred by the carrier and the value of service to the shipper.

Cost-of-Service Strategy   The cost-of-service strategy is a "buildup" approach where the carrier establishes a rate based on the cost of providing the service plus a profit margin. For example, if the cost of providing a transportation service is $200 and the profit markup is 10 percent, the carrier would charge the shipper $220. The cost-of-service approach, which represents the base or minimum transportation charge, is a pricing approach for low-value goods or in highly competitive situations.

Value-of-Service Strategy   Value-of-service is an alternative strategy that charges a rate based on perceived shipper value rather than the cost of actually providing the service. For example, a shipper perceives transporting 1,000 pounds of electronic equipment as more critical or valuable than 1,000 pounds of coal since the equipment is worth substantially more than the coal. As such, a shipper is probably willing to pay more to transport it. Carriers tend to utilize value-of-service pricing for high-value goods or when limited competition exists.

Value-of-service pricing is illustrated in the premium overnight carrier market. When Federal Express first introduced overnight delivery, there were few competitors that could provide the service, so it was perceived by shippers as a high-value alternative. They were willing to pay $22.50 to obtain the value of an overnight shipment. Once competitors such as UPS and the United States Postal Service entered the market, rates dropped to current discounted levels of $5 to $10 per package. This rate decrease is more in line with the actual cost for the service.

Combination Strategy   The combination strategy establishes the transport price at some intermediate level between the cost-of-service minimum and the value-of-service maximum. In standard practice, most transportation firms use such a middle value. Logistics managers must understand the range of prices and the alternative strategies so that they can negotiate appropriately.

Net Rate Pricing   By taking advantage of regulatory freedom generated by the Trucking Industry Regulatory Reform Act (TIRRA) of 1994 and the reduced applicability of the filed rate doctrine, a number of common carriers are experimenting with a simplified pricing format called *net rate pricing.* Because TIRRA eliminated tariff filing requirements for motor carriers that set rates individually with customers, carriers are now, in effect, able to simplify pricing schedules that are designed for an individual customer's circumstances and needs. Specifically, carriers can replace individual discount sheets and class tariffs with a single price sheet—and thus make the customer's interpretation of the rate-making process much simpler. The net rate pricing approach, which is being applied to both interstate and intrastate carriers, will do away with the complex and administratively burdensome discount pricing structure that has been the common practice since deregulation.

Established discounts and accessorial charges are built into the net rates. In other words, the net rate represents a final price. The goal is to drastically reduce carriers' administrative costs and directly respond to customer demand to simplify the rate-making process. Carriers thus hope to win over new shippers and solidify current shipper accounts by taking much of the calculation out of finding a price. Shippers welcome pricing simplification because it promotes billing accuracy and provides a clear understanding of how to generate savings in transportation.

Rating

The previous discussion reviewed key strategies used by carriers to set prices. Building on this foundation, the following section will now present the actual pricing mechanics used by carriers. This discussion applies specifically to common carriers, although contract carriers utilize similar concepts.

Class Rates   In transportation terminology, the price in dollars and cents per hundredweight to move a specific product between two locations is referred to as the *rate.* The rate is listed on pricing sheets or computer files known as *tariffs.* The term *class rate* evolved from the fact that all products transported by common carriers are *class*ified for pricing purposes. All products legally transported in interstate commerce can be shipped via class rates.

Determination of common carrier class rates is a two-step process. The first step is the classification or grouping of the product being transported. The second step is the determination of the precise rate (i.e., price) based on the classification of the product and the origin-destination points of the shipment. Typically, this procedure is referred to as *rate administration.* Each step is discussed below.

Classification   All products transported together are typically grouped into uniform classifications. The *classification* takes into consideration the characteristics of a product or commodity that will influence the cost of handling or transport. Product with similar density, stowability, handling, liability, and value characteristics are grouped together into a class, thereby reducing the wide range of possible ratings to a manageable size. The particular class that a given product or commodity receives is its rating. The *rating* is the product's classification placement, which is used to determine the freight rate. It is important to understand that the classification does not define the price charged for movement of a product. It refers to a product's transportation characteristics in comparison to other commodities.

Motor carriers and rail carriers each have independent classification systems. The motor carrier system uses the *National Motor Freight Classification,* while rail classifications are published in the *Uniform Freight Classification.* The motor classification system has twenty-three classes of freight, and the rail system has thirty-one. In local or regional areas, individual groups of carriers may publish additional classification listings. Since deregulation, considerable attention has been directed to overall simplification of the classification scheme.

Classification of individual products is based on a relative percentage index of 100. Class 100 is considered the class for an average product, while other classes run as high as 500 and as low as 35 in the motor system. Each product is assigned an item number for listing purposes and then given a classification rating. As a general rule, the higher the class rating, the higher the transportation cost for the product. Historically, a product classified as 400 would be approximately four times more expensive to transport than a product rated 100. While the multiple is not four today, a class 400 rating is still substantially higher than a class 100 rating. Products are also assigned classifications on the basis of the quantity shipped. Less-than-truckload (LTL) shipments of identical products will have higher ratings than carload (CL) or truckload (TL) shipments.

Table 12-1 illustrates a page from the *National Motor Freight Classification.* It contains general product grouping 86750, which is "glass, leaded." Notice that the leaded glass category is further subdivided into specific types of glass such as "glass, microscopical slide or cover, in boxes," which is item 86770. For LTL shipments, item 86770 is assigned a 70 rating. TL shipments of leaded glass are assigned a class 40 rating provided that a minimum of 360 hundredweight is shipped.

Products are also assigned different ratings on the basis of packaging. Glass may have a different rating when shipped loose, in crates, or in boxes than when shipped in wrapped protective packing. It should be noted that packaging differences influence product density, stowability, and damage, illustrating how the cost factors discussed earlier enter into the rate determination process. Thus a number of different classifications may apply to the same product depending on where it is being shipped, shipment size, transport mode, and product packaging.

One of the major responsibilities of logistics managers is to obtain the best possible rating for all goods shipped by the enterprise. Although there are differences in rail and motor classifications, each system is guided by similar rules. However, rail rules are more comprehensive and detailed than those for motor freight. It is useful for members of a traffic department to have a thorough understanding of the classification systems.

It is possible to have a product reclassified by written application to the appropriate classification board, which reviews proposals for change or additions with respect to minimum weights, commodity descriptions, packaging requirements, and general rules and regulations. An alert traffic department must take an active role in classification. Significant savings may be realized by finding the correct classification for a product or by recommending a change in packaging or shipment quantity that will reduce a product's rating. For example, paper products such as

TABLE 12-1   NATIONAL MOTOR FREIGHT CLASSIFICATION 100-S

Item	Articles	Classes		MW
		LTL	TL	
86737	*Note:* TL provisions will also apply when glass is shipped on its flat surface in wooden boxes on pallets.			
86750 Sub 1 Sub 2	**Glass,** leaded, see Note, item 86752: With landscape, pictorial, or religious designs, packed in boxes. With curved, angled, or straight-line patterns, or with designs other than landscape, pictorial, or religious, in boxes.	 200. 100.	 70. 70.	 24. 24.
86752	*Note:* The term "leaded glass" means glass either colored or clear, set in lead or in other metal.			
86770	**Glass,** microscopical slide or cover, in boxes.	70.	40.	36.
86830	**Glass,** rolled, overlaid with aluminum strips with metal terminals attached, in boxes, crates, or Package 1339.	77.5	45.	30.
86840	**Glass,** rolled, overlaid with aluminum strips, NOI, in boxes, crates, or Package 1339.	70.	37.5	36.
86900 Sub 1 Sub 2 Sub 3 Sub 4 Sub 5 Sub 6 Sub 7 Sub 8 Sub 9	**Glass,** silvered for mirrors, not framed, backed, or equipped with hangers or fastening devices: Shock (window glass, silvered), in boxes, see Note, item 86902; also TL, in Packages 227 or 300. Other than shock glass; also TL, in Packages 227 or 300: Bent: Not exceeding 15 feet in length or 9 feet in breadth, in boxes. Exceeding 15 feet in length or 9 feet in breadth, in boxes. Not bent, see Package 785: 120 united inches or less, in boxes, crates, or Packages 198, 235, or 1339. Exceeding 120 united inches but not exceeding 15 feet in length or 9 feet in breadth, in boxes or crates. Exceeding 15 feet in length or 9 feet in breadth, in boxes or crates.	 85. 100. 250. 70. 100. 200.	 40. 70. 70. 40. 40. 45.	 30. 24. 24. 30. 40. 40.
86902	*Note:* Glass, silvered for mirrors, which has been framed or backed, or equipped with large hangers or fastening devices, is subject to the classes for mirrors, NOI.			
86940	**Glass,** window, other than plate, with metal edging other than sash or frames, in boxes.	77.5	45.	30.
86960	**Glazing units,** glass, not in sash, see Note, item 86966, in boxes, crates, or Packages 2133, 2149, or 2281.	70.	45.	30.
86966	*Note:* Applies on units consisting of sheets of glass separated by air or vacuum, sealed at all edges with same or other materials.			
87040	**Skylight, roofing, or sidewall construction material** consisting of rough rolled glass, wired or not wired, and installation accessories, see Note, item 87042, in boxes or crates.	65.	35.	40.

Source: National Motor Freight Classification, Alexandria, Va.: American Trucking Association, 1992.

tissue have a high rating of 125 since they are normally a low-density product. However, managers at firms such as Kimberly-Clark and Procter & Gamble have negotiated lower ratings of 77.5 as a result of changes in packaging that increased product density.

Rate Administration Once a classification rating is obtained for a product, the specific rate must be determined. The rate per hundredweight is usually based on the shipment origin and destination, although the actual price charged for a particular shipment is normally subject to a minimum charge and may also be subject to surcharges or ancillary assessments. Historically, the origin and destination rates were maintained in notebooks that had to be updated and revised regularly. Today, rates are provided in diskette form by carriers, and thus much of the process is computerized via either mainframe rating and audit systems or PC-based rate tables.

Origin and destination rates are organized by three- or five-digit ZIP codes. Table 12-2 illustrates rates for all freight classes from Atlanta, Georgia (ZIP 303), to Lansing, Michigan (ZIP 489). The table lists rates for all shipment sizes from the smallest LTL (less than 500 pounds, listed as L5C) to the largest TL (greater than 40,000 pounds, listed as M40M).

The rate is quoted in cents per hundredweight. Assuming a shipment of 12,000 pounds, the rate for class 85 between Lansing and Atlanta is $12.92 per hundredweight.

Historically, the published rate had to be charged for all shipments of a specific

TABLE 12-2   EXAMPLE OF RATES FROM ATLANTA, GEORGIA (ZIP 303), TO LANSING, MICHIGAN (ZIP 489)

Origin 303: Destination 489: MC: 81.00: RBNO 00775E									
Rate class	L5C	M5C	M1M	M2M	M5M	M10M	M20M	M30M	M40M
500	233.58	193.89	147.14	119.10	84.05	65.37	40.32	32.25	28.24
400	188.24	156.25	118.58	95.98	67.73	52.69	32.55	26.03	22.79
300	144.11	119.63	90.78	73.48	51.86	40.34	24.94	19.95	17.45
250	126.30	104.84	79.56	64.40	45.45	35.34	21.86	17.48	15.31
200	98.37	81.66	61.97	50.16	35.40	27.53	17.00	13.60	11.91
175	88.65	73.58	55.84	45.20	31.90	24.81	15.30	12.24	10.72
150	76.11	63.18	47.94	38.81	27.38	21.30	13.20	10.56	9.24
125	64.76	53.76	40.80	33.03	23.31	18.12	11.25	9.00	7.88
110	56.27	46.71	35.43	28.69	20.25	15.75	9.88	7.90	6.92
100	52.62	43.68	33.15	26.83	18.94	14.73	9.22	7.38	6.46
92	49.79	41.33	31.37	25.39	17.92	13.94	8.91	7.12	6.24
85	46.15	38.31	29.07	23.53	16.61	12.92	8.58	6.86	6.01
77	42.91	35.62	27.03	21.88	15.44	12.01	8.34	6.67	5.84
70	40.48	33.59	25.50	20.64	14.57	11.33	8.10	6.48	5.67
65	38.46	31.92	24.22	19.61	13.84	10.76	8.02	6.41	5.61
60	36.84	30.58	23.21	18.78	13.26	10.31	7.94	6.35	5.56
55	34.81	28.90	21.93	17.75	12.53	9.74	7.85	6.28	5.50
50	32.79	27.22	20.66	16.71	11.80	9.18	7.77	6.22	5.44
Weight limits (lb)	Under 500	500– 1,000	1,000– 2,000	2,000– 5,000	5,000– 10,000	10,000– 20,000	20,000– 30,000	30,000– 40,000	Over 40,000

Source: TNT Freightways Rate Diskette, February 1993.

class and origin-destination combination. This required frequent reviews and maintenance to keep rates current. Following deregulation, carriers offered more flexibility through rate discounts. Now instead of developing an individual rate table to meet the needs of customer segments, carriers apply a discount from class rates for specific customers. The discount, generally in the range of 30 to 50 percent, depends on the shipper's volume and market competition.

An alternative to the per hundredweight charge is the per mile charge commonly applied to TL shipments. As discussed previously, TL shipments are designed to reduce handling and transfer costs. Since the entire vehicle is used in a full TL delivery and there is no requirement to transfer the shipment at a terminal, the per mile charge is a more appropriate pricing approach. For a one-way move, charges range from $1.25 to $3.00 per mile depending on the market. Although it is negotiable, this charge includes typical LTL services such as loading, unloading, and liability.

In addition to the variable shipment charge on either a per hundredweight or a per mile basis, two additional charges are common for transportation: minimum charges and surcharges. The minimum charge represents the amount a shipper must pay to *make* a shipment regardless of weight. To illustrate, assume that the applicable class rate is $15/cwt, and the shipper wants to transport 100 pounds to a specific location. If no minimum charge exists, the shipper would pay $15. However, if the minimum charge is $150 per shipment, the shipper would pay the minimum. Minimum charges cover fixed costs associated with a shipment.

A surcharge is an additional fee designed to cover specific carrier costs. Surcharges are used to protect carriers from costs not included in published rates. The surcharge may be assessed as a flat charge, a percentage, or a sliding scale based on shipment size. A common use of surcharges is to compensate carriers for dramatic changes in fuel cost. For example, when fuel prices experience steep increases, it is common to see transportation rates with 10 to 20 percent surcharges. The surcharge approach provides immediate relief for the carrier for unexpected costs while not building a ''temporary'' cost into the long-term rate structure.

Class rates, minimum charges, arbitrary charges, and surcharges form a pricing structure that, in various combinations, is applicable within the continental United States. The tariff indicates the class rate for any rating group between specified origins and destinations. In combination, the classification scheme and class rate structure form a generalized pricing mechanism for rail and motor carriers. Each mode has specific characteristics applicable to its tariffs. In water, specific tariff provisions are made for cargo location within the ship or on the deck. In addition, provisions are made to charter entire vessels. Similar specialized provisions are found in air cargo and pipeline tariffs. Nonoperating intermediaries and package services also publish tariffs specialized to their service.

Commodity Rates   When a large quantity of a product moves between two locations on a regular basis, it is common practice for carriers to publish a commodity rate. *Commodity rates* are special or specific rates published without regard to classification. The terms and conditions of a commodity rate are usually indicated in a contract between the carrier and the shipper. Such contracts were legalized by the Staggers Rail Act. Commodity rates are usually published on a point-to-point basis and apply to specified products only. Today most rail freight moves under commodity rates. They are less prevalent in motor carriage. Whenever a commodity rate exists, it supersedes the corresponding class rate.

Exception Rates   *Exception rates,* or exceptions to the classification, are special rates published to provide shippers lower rates than the prevailing class rate. The original purpose of the exception rate was to provide a special rate for a specific area, origin-destination, or commodity when either competitive or high-volume movements justified it. Rather than publish a new tariff, an exception to the classification or class rate was established.

Just as the name implies, when an exception rate is published, the classification that normally applies to the product is changed. Such changes may involve assignment of a new class or may be based on a percentage of the original class. Technically, exceptions may be higher or lower, although most are less than the original class rates. Unless otherwise noted, all services provided under the class rate remain under an exception rate.

Since deregulation, several new types of exception rates have gained popularity. For example, an *aggregate tender* rate is utilized when a shipper agrees to provide multiple shipments to a carrier in exchange for a discount or exception from the prevailing class rate. The primary objective is to reduce carrier cost by permitting multiple shipment pickups during one stop at a shipper's facility or to reduce the rate for the shipper because of the carrier's decreased management and marketing expenses. To illustrate, UPS offers customers that require multiple small package shipments a discount based on aggregate weight and/or cubic volume. Since 1980 numerous pricing innovations have been introduced by common carriers on the basis of various aggregation principles.

A *limited service* rate is utilized when a shipper agrees to perform services typically performed by the carrier, such as trailer loading, in exchange for a discount. A common example is a *shipper load and count* rate, where the shipper takes responsibility for loading and counting the cases. Not only does this remove the responsibility for loading the shipment from the carrier, but it also implies that the carrier is not responsible for guaranteeing the number of cases transported. Another example of limited service is a *released value* rate, which limits carrier liability in case of loss or damage. Normally, the carrier is responsible for full product value if loss or damage occurs in transit. The quoted rate must include adequate *insurance* to cover the risk. Often it is more effective for manufacturers of high-value product to absorb the risk in return for lower transportation rates. Limited service is used when shippers have confidence in the carrier's capability, and cost can be reduced by eliminating duplication of effort or responsibility.

Under aggregate tender and limited service rates, as well as other innovative exception rates, the basic economic justification is the reduction of carrier cost and subsequent sharing of benefits based on shipper-carrier cooperation.

Special Rates and Services   A number of special rates and services provided by for-hire carriers are available for logistical operations. Several important examples are discussed.

Freight-All-Kinds Rates   As indicated earlier, *freight-all-kinds* (FAK) rates are important to logistics operations. Under FAK rates, a mixture of different products is transported under a generic rating. Rather than determine the classification and applicable rate of each product, an average rate is applied for the total shipment. In essence, FAK rates are line-haul rates since they replace class, exception, or commodity rates. Their purpose is to simplify the paperwork associated with the movement of mixed commodities and thus lower the costs. As such, they are of particular importance in physical distribution.

Local, Joint, Proportional, and Combination Rates   Numerous *special rates* exist that may offer transportation savings on specific freight movements. When a commodity moves under the tariff of a single carrier, it is referred to as a *local rate* or *single-line rate.* If more than one carrier is involved in the freight movement, a *joint rate* may be applicable even though multiple carriers are involved in the actual transportation process. Because some motor and rail carriers operate in restricted territory, it may be necessary to utilize the services of more than one to complete a shipment. Utilization of a joint rate can offer substantial savings over the use of two or more local rates.

Proportional rates offer special price incentives to utilize a published tariff that applies to only part of the desired route. Proportional provisions of a tariff are most often applicable to origin or destination points outside the normal geographical area of a single-line tariff. If a joint rate does not exist and proportional provisions do, the strategy of moving a shipment under proportional rates provides a discount on the single-line part of the movement, thereby resulting in a lower overall freight charge.

Combination rates are similar to proportional rates in that two or more rates may be combined when no published single-line or joint rate exists between two locations. The rates may be any combination of class, exception, and commodity rates. The utilization of combination rates often involves several technicalities that are beyond the scope of this discussion. Their use substantially reduces the cost of an individual shipment. In most cases that involve regular freight movements, the need to utilize combination rates is eliminated with publication of a through rate. A *through rate* is a rate that applies from origin to destination for a shipment.

Transit Services   *Transit services* permit a shipment to be stopped at an intermediate point between its initial origin and final destination for unloading, storage, and/or processing. The shipment is then reloaded for delivery to the final destination. Typical examples of transit services are milling for grain products and processing for sugar beets. When transit privileges exist, the shipment is charged a through rate from origin to destination plus a transit privilege charge. Transit services are typically performed by railroads. From the viewpoint of the shipper, the use of this specialized service is restricted to specific geographical areas once the product enters into transit service. Therefore, a degree of flexibility is lost when the product is placed in transit because the final destination can be altered only at significant added expense or, at the least, with loss of the through rate and assessment of the transit charge. Finally, the utilization of transit privileges increases the paperwork of shippers in terms of both meeting railroad record requirements and ultimately settling the freight bills. The added cost of administration must be carefully weighed in evaluating the true benefits gained. During the last decade railroads have generally discouraged use of transit services.

Diversion and Reconsignment   For a variety of reasons, a shipper or *consignee* may desire to change routing, destination, or even consignee once a shipment is in transit. This flexibility can be extremely important, particularly with regard to the transportation of food and other perishable products where markets quickly change. It is a normal practice among certain types of marketing intermediaries to purchase commodities with the full intention of selling them while they are in transit. *Diversion* consists of changing the destination of a shipment prior to its arrival at the original destination. *Reconsignment* is a change in consignee prior to delivery. Both services are provided by railroads and motor carriers for a specified charge.

Split Delivery   A split delivery is desired when portions of a shipment need to be delivered to different facilities. Under specified tariff conditions, pickup and delivery can be extended to points beyond the initial destination. The payment is typically structured to reflect a rate as if the shipment were going to the farthest destination. In addition, there is a charge for each delivery stop-off.

Demurrage and Detention   Demurrage and detention are charges assessed for retaining freight cars or truck trailers beyond specified loading or unloading time. The term *demurrage* is used by railroads for holding a railcar beyond forty-eight hours before unloading the shipment. Motor carriers use the term *detention* to cover similar delays. In the case of motor carriers, the permitted time is specified in the tariff and is normally limited to a few hours.

Accessorial Services   In addition to basic transportation, motor and rail carriers offer a wide variety of special or ancillary services that can aid in planning logistical operations. Table 12-3 provides a list.

Carriers may also offer environmental services and special equipment. *Environmental services* refer to special control of freight while in transit, such as refrigeration, ventilation, and heating. For example, in the summer, Hershey's typically transports its chocolate and confectionery products in refrigerated trailers to protect them from high temperature levels. *Special equipment charges* refer to the use of equipment that the carrier has purchased for the shipper's economy and convenience. For example, specialized sanitation equipment is necessary to clean and prepare trailers for food storage and transit when the trailer has been previously utilized for nonfood products or commodities.

TABLE 12-3   TYPICAL CARRIER ANCILLARY SERVICES

- *COD.* Collect payment on delivery.
- *Change COD.* Change COD recipient.
- *Inside delivery.* Deliver product inside the building.
- *Marking or tagging.* Mark or tag product as it is transported.
- *Notify before delivery.* Make appointment prior to delivery.
- *Reconsignment or delivery.* Redirect shipment to a new destination while in transit.
- *Redeliver.* Attempt second delivery.
- *Residential delivery.* Deliver at a residence without a truck dock.
- *Sorting and segregating.* Sort commodity prior to delivery.
- *Storage.* Store commodity prior to delivery.

Although this brief coverage of special services is not all-inclusive, it does offer several examples of the range and type of services available. Thus the carrier's role in a logistical system is often far greater than line-haul transportation.

TRANSPORT DECISION MAKING

Transport decision making requires the availability of information and the assignment of knowledgeable, trained individuals to process the information in order to serve the enterprise's functional and strategic transportation needs. Information is provided through a variety of transport documents. Utilization and analysis of the information are the responsibility of various members of the traffic department. Each aspect of transport decision making is discussed.

Transport Documentation

Several documents are required to perform each transport movement. The three primary types are bills of lading, freight bills, and shipping manifests.

Bill of Lading   The *bill of lading* is the basic document utilized in purchasing transport services. It serves as a receipt and documents commodities and quantities shipped. For this reason, accurate description and count are essential. In case of loss, damage, or delay, the bill of lading is the basis for damage claims. The designated individual or buyer on a bill of lading is the only bona fide recipient of goods. A carrier is responsible for proper delivery according to instructions contained in the document. In effect, title is transferred with completion of delivery.

The bill of lading specifies terms and conditions of carrier liability and documents responsibility for all possible causes of loss or damage except those defined as acts of God. It is important that terms and conditions be clearly understood so that appropriate actions can be taken in the event of substandard performance. Recent ICC rulings permit uniform bills of lading to be computerized and electronically transmitted between shippers and carriers.

In addition to the *uniform* bill of lading, other commonly used types are order-notified, export, and government. It is important to select the correct bill of lading for a specific shipment.

An *order-notified* or *negotiable* bill of lading is a credit instrument. It provides that delivery not be made unless the original bill of lading is surrendered to the carrier. The usual procedure is for the seller to send the order-notified bill of lading to a third party, usually a bank or credit institution. Upon customer payment for the product, the credit institution releases the bill of lading. The buyer then presents it to the common carrier, which in turn releases the goods. This facilitates international transport where payment for goods is a major consideration.

An *export* bill of lading permits domestic use of export rates, which are sometimes lower than domestic rates. Export rates may reduce total cost if applied to domestic origin or destination line-haul transport.

Government bills of lading may be used when the product is owned by the United States government. They allow the use of *Section 22 rates,* which are normally lower than regular rates.

Freight Bill   The *freight bill* represents a carrier's method of charging for transportation services performed. It is developed using information contained in the bill of lading. The freight bill may be either prepaid or collect. A *prepaid* bill means that transport cost must be paid prior to performance, whereas a *collect* shipment shifts payment responsibility to the consignee.

Considerable administration is involved in preparing bills of lading and freight bills. There has been considerable effort to automate freight bills and bills of lading through EDI transactions. Some firms now elect to pay their freight bills at the time the bill of lading is created, thereby combining the two documents. Such arrangements are based on relative financial benefits of reduced paperwork costs. Many attempts are also under way to produce all transport documents simultaneously. This has become more practical with the use of computers.

Shipping Manifest   The shipping manifest lists individual stops or consignees when multiple shipments are placed on a single vehicle. Each shipment requires a bill of lading. The manifest lists the stop, bill of lading, weight, and case count for each shipment. The objective of the manifest is to provide a single document that defines the contents of the total load without requiring a review of individual bills of lading. For single-stop shipments, the manifest is the same as the bill of lading.

Traffic Department Responsibilities

In most organizations, the traffic department has the responsibility for managing all freight-related transportation activities. While the historical view of the traffic department often depicted individuals with green eyeshades sitting amid bookcases filled with rate tables, the responsibilities of the modern traffic department go far beyond this scenario. In fact, the traffic department influences over 50 percent of the average firm's logistics cost, so the department can make a significant operational and strategic impact. In addition to rating freight, traffic department responsibilities include (1) auditing and claim administration, (2) equipment scheduling, (3) rate negotiation, (4) research, and (5) tracing and expediting. Each activity is described below.

Auditing and Claim Administration   When transportation services or charges do not meet predetermined standards, shippers can make claims for restitution. Claims are broken down into two categories: loss and damage, and overcharge-undercharge. Loss and damage claims occur when a shipper demands that the carrier pay for partial or total financial loss resulting from poor performance or when the shipper breaks a transportation agreement. As the name implies, loss and damage claims are usually incurred when product is lost or damaged in transit. Overcharge-undercharge claims result when charges are different from those published in tariffs. These claims are typically resolved through freight bill audit procedures described below.

Rules regulate the proper procedure for claim filing and define which of the involved parties are responsible. Two factors are of primary importance. First, detailed attention should be given to claim administration because recoveries are achieved only by aggressive audit programs. Second, a large volume of claims are indicative of carriers that are not performing their service obligations. Regardless of the dollars recovered by claim administration, the breakdown in customer service performance from loss and damage claims affects a shipper's reputation with its customers.

Auditing freight bills is an important function of the traffic department. The purpose of auditing is to ensure billing accuracy. Transport rate complexities result in higher error probabilities than in most other purchasing decisions. There are two types of freight audits. A *preaudit* determines proper charges prior to payment of a freight bill. A *postaudit* makes the same determination after payment. Auditing may be either external or internal. If external, specialized freight auditing companies are employed utilizing personnel who are experts in specific commodity groupings. This is generally more efficient than the use of internal personnel, who may not have the same level of expertise. Payment for an external audit is usually based on a percentage of the revenues reclaimed through overcharges. It is crucial that a highly ethical firm be employed for this purpose, because valuable marketing and customer information is contained in the freight bill and corporate activities may be adversely affected if confidentiality is not upheld.

A combination of internal and external auditing is frequently employed according to the value of the freight bill. For example, a bill of $600 with a 10 percent error results in a $60 recovery, but a $50 bill with a 10 percent error results in only a $5 recovery. As such, bills with larger recovery potential are typically audited internally.

External versus internal auditing may also be affected by the size of the firm and the degree of rate computerization. For instance, large traffic departments are in a position to have specialized clerks for auditing purposes. Also, firms utilizing computerized systems of freight payment can build in rates on a majority of origin-destination points and weights. Automatic checks on proper payment can then be made by specially designed computer programs.

Equipment Scheduling   One major responsibility of the traffic department is equipment scheduling regardless of whether common carriers or private transportation is used. A serious operational bottleneck can result from carrier equipment waiting to be loaded or unloaded at a shipper's dock. Proper scheduling requires careful load planning, equipment utilization, and driver scheduling. Additionally, necessary equipment maintenance must be planned, coordinated, and monitored. Finally, any specialized equipment requirements must be assessed and carried out.

Rate Negotiation   Earlier in the chapter, a description of basic transportation rates and rate regulation was presented. For any given shipment it is the responsibility of the traffic department to obtain the lowest possible rate consistent with the service requirements. The prevailing transport price for each method of movement—rail, air, motor, pipeline, parcel post, United Parcel, freight forwarders, and so on—is found by referring to the tariffs.

Since 1980 the prevailing tariff represents the point at which transportation negotiation is initiated. The key to effective negotiation is to seek ''win-win'' agreements wherein both carriers and shippers share productivity gains. As indicated several times throughout this text, the lowest possible cost for transportation may not be the lowest total cost of logistics. The traffic department must seek the lowest rate consistent with service standards. For example, if two-day delivery is required, the traffic department seeks to select the method of transport that will meet this standard at the lowest possible cost.

Research   Beyond administration, the traffic department maintains responsibility for research. Traffic managers should always be on the lookout for information that improves carrier service or obtains lower freight rates. This means that an aggressive performance measurement program should be a continuous activity for transportation research.

Unfortunately, carrier performance measurement is one of the least developed areas of traffic research. Information is normally accumulated from individual carrier claims. Shippers should also attempt to measure how well carriers meet stated service obligations. Such carrier obligations involve (1) carrier integration, (2) carrier evaluation, and (3) transport services integration. Each topic is discussed below.

Carrier Integration   Carrier integration refers to the practice of combining new carrier products and services into logistics operations. The two basic categories concern long-term trends and service capabilities. These trends and services may be used to enhance the shipper's performance in the marketplace.

For example, a manager might track the number of trailers or railcars that are necessary to meet industry shipping needs on a seasonal or yearly basis, or the manager might monitor equipment trends to predict whether containers or trailers are expected to be in greater demand over the next year or two. Such monitoring allows effective negotiation by the manager through awareness of supply and demand.

Monitoring the demand for particular types of carrier services is also an important obligation and strategic necessity for traffic research. The increased use of third-party service offerings such as warehousing, special packaging, and labeling is an example of a logistical trend that carriers and shippers must be aware of to remain competitive in the transportation marketplace.

Carrier Evaluation   Prior to deregulation, purchasers of transportation services had a relatively easy task. Shippers selected a carrier for a specific shipment from a long list of possible carriers knowing that each offered essentially standardized service for a set price. Because of federal economic regulation, there wasn't much room to negotiate price or service.

Since deregulation, however, carrier evaluation is more complex and important. It is complex because a number of factors must be compared to identify the appropriate carrier. To effectively complete the trade-off analysis, it is necessary to establish criteria to guide the selection choice. The following discussion suggests appropriate criteria and illustrates the analysis process. Analysis should focus on criteria judged important by the consignee rather than the shipper. Considerations should include cost, transit time, reliability, capability, accessibility, and security.

Transportation cost is an obvious consideration, but the freight rate is not the only cost component. A low freight rate is desirable. However, overall logistical system cost must consider equipment terms, responsibility for claims, and other related activities such as loading and counting.

Length of transit time is also an important carrier evaluation criterion since it directly influences inventory levels. Carriers or modes that can offer faster service should be rated more highly because of their ability to deliver goods rapidly. Transit time should also consider any delays for consolidation or clearance. Reliability is a criterion closely related to length of time and refers to the carrier's ability to achieve consistent delivery performance. Regardless of how fast a supplier is able to ship, if the transport carrier provides inconsistent delivery, inventory problems will result. Likewise, sales are lost and production lines shut down if carriers fail to meet their service obligation. Generally speaking, smaller shipments result in greater service variance between consecutive deliveries. Thus, while a truckload or carload shipment may regularly meet published schedules, the same efficiency may break down for LTL or package shipments. Some carriers are superior to others, and the task is to determine which carrier is the most consistent.

A typical assessment of transit reliability is based on order delivery performance. For example, once an order has been completed and the shipment delivered, the arrival time and date are recorded at the warehouse and transmitted to central purchasing. Both the release date and arrival date are retained in a computer on an individual carrier basis along with a statement of expected performance. The variation between actual and expected performance is calculated and updated on a regular basis. At specified times, the performance record of each carrier is reported for purchasing and traffic management review. This consistency report provides valuable data for carrier evaluation. Unless this information is collected on a routine basis, it is difficult to make specific evaluation about erratic carrier performance or to take corrective action.

The fourth criterion is carrier capability, which includes both hauling and service. Hauling capability refers to the ability to provide appropriate specialized vehicles for temperature control, bulk products, or side unloading. For services, capabilities include EDI scheduling and invoicing, on-line shipment tracking, and storage and consolidation.

The fifth criterion is carrier accessibility to shipper and consignee. While accessibility is generally not a problem for motor carriers, it can be a consideration for other modes. The specific concern is initial product movement to and from airport, railhead, port, or pipeline access point. While physical accessibility has become less of an issue as a result of extensive intermodal offerings, accessibility to carriers with "through" or "joint" operating agreements has increased in importance. These agreements reduce the necessity to negotiate multiple rates, prepare multiple copies of shipping documentation, or make multiple calls to trace shipments.

The final criterion is the carrier's security capability. Security refers to the carrier's ability to protect a load from loss, damage, and theft. A related criterion is the carrier's ability to quickly resolve a claim when a loss occurs. A security evaluation must consider both protection and claims resolution.

Carrier Evaluation Process   Using the above criteria, one suggested approach to perform a comparative evaluation of individual carriers is a two-step process. The first step determines the relative importance of each criterion from the shippers' perspective by assigning it a weight. For example, very important criteria should be rated a "1," while less important criteria are rated a "3." Table 12-4 illustrates this approach.

The second step involves rating carrier performance for each measure. Table 12-4 also illustrates a three-point rating scale ranging from "1" (good performance) to "3" (poor performance). The carrier performance evaluation should include both quantitative and qualitative elements as measured by the traffic department. A combined carrier rating is created by multiplying relative importance and carrier performance measures. The total carrier evaluation is the sum of individual factor ratings, which totals "23" for the example. Using this approach, the best carrier would be the one with the lowest point total. The totals for alternative carriers should be compared to assist in assigning future loads and establishing alliances.

In today's logistics environment, carrier selection and evaluation are more difficult because of increased offerings and capabilities. While prior evaluations might have focused on cost and service, today it is necessary to explicitly consider many additional factors when evaluating carriers. A similar evaluation is possible when comparing separate modes or intermodal alternatives.

Transport Services Integration For any given operating period, traffic management is expected to provide the required transportation services within the stated operating budget. It is also traffic management's responsibility to search for alternative ways in which transportation can be effectively utilized to reduce overall logistical system costs. For example, a slight change in packaging may create an opportunity for negotiation of a lower classification rating for a product. Although packaging costs may increase, this added expense can be offset by a substantial reduction in transportation cost. Unless such proposals originate from the traffic department, they will likely go undetected in the average firm. As indicated earlier, transportation is the highest single cost area in most logistical systems. Because of this cost and the dependence of the logistical system on an effective transport capability, the traffic department must play an active role in future planning.

Tracing and Expediting Two other important responsibilities of transportation management involve tracing and expediting. Tracing is a procedure to locate lost or late deliveries. Shipments committed to the vast transportation network of

TABLE 12-4 SAMPLE CARRIER EVALUATION

Evaluation factor	Relative importance	×	Carrier performance	=	Carrier rating
1 Cost	1	×	1	=	1
2 Transit time length	3	×	2	=	6
3 Transit time reliability	1	×	2	=	2
4 Capability	2	×	2	=	4
5 Accessibility	2	×	2	=	4
6 Security	2	×	3	=	6
		Total carrier rating			23

Relative importance measure: 1 = high importance; 2 = moderate importance; 3 = low importance.

Carrier performance measure: 1 = good performance; 2 = fair performance; 3 = poor performance.

the United States are bound to be misplaced or delayed from time to time. Most large carriers maintain a tracing department and computerized service to aid in locating a shipment. The tracing action must be initiated by the shipper's traffic department, but once initiated, it is the carrier's responsibility to provide the desired information. Expediting occurs when the shipper notifies a carrier that it needs to have a specific shipment move through the carrier's system as quickly as possible and with no delays.

Tracing and expediting are greatly facilitated through the use of information

---

THE GLASS PARTNERSHIP

Today's shipper considers more than cost and service when looking for a transportation supplier. Libbey-Owens-Ford (LOF), an architectural and automotive glass manufacturer, faces the challenge of handling and transporting a large and awkward product. LOF's customer service commitment demands that the firm utilize competitively priced carriers that can also provide superior logistics service. These service demands require LOF to seek innovative carriers and strong channel partnerships.

In the past, LOF utilized as many as 534 carriers for inbound and outbound transportation. Glass transport often requires specialized equipment to minimize damage. However, the specialized equipment means that if LOF could not offer a back-haul, either carriers back-hauled a competitive product or LOF was charged for the empty load. The number of shipments to and from LOF plants resulted in a large number of empty back-hauls.

LOF solved this problem through alliances with two carriers. All inbound and outbound LTL shipments were assigned to Roadway Logistics Services (ROLS). ROLS does not necessarily haul all shipments, although it is responsible for routing, tracing, and payment for all of them. This arrangement allows LOF to provide its suppliers with a toll-free telephone number to co-ordinate all inbound-shipments. The ''Rite Route'' system selects the lowest-cost mode and carrier for both internal and external transport. The system has reduced a $3 million freight budget by $500,000 and eliminated 70,000 pieces of paper. Cass Logistics, a third-party payment service, handles all billing information electronically.

While cost is one consideration in LOF alliances, there is also a strong quality concern for its TL archi-

tectural glass movements. Schneider National's specialty truckload operation required eighteen months to qualify as one of LOF's primary TL carriers. Don Schneider, president of Schneider National, claimed it was one of the toughest qualification processes that he had been through. Schneider National, in partnership with the trailer manufacturer Wabash National, patented a specialized trailer to haul LOF glass. The trailer is an A-frame design that converts to a standard flatbed truck. This design eliminates the problem of specialized equipment that is unsuitable for other back-hauls. Exclusive arrangements between LOF, Schneider National, and Wabash National ensure that all equipment is utilized for the three-way partnership and that one company does not bear an inordinate amount of development or financial risk. All three companies enjoy a competitive advantage in their respective industries as a result of this unique transportation partnership.

LOF establishes very high service expectations and requests other commitments in addition to technology. Rather than awarding business on the basis of price, LOF focuses on total-cost reduction potential. While LOF recognizes that its partners must have a sufficient return for their business, it believes that excessive profits damage partnerships. LOF maintains extensive communication between its partners at all organizational levels. This helps develop an understanding of partnership values and conditions. Throughout this partnership process, LOF believes that logistics creates significant value for its customers.

Based on information found in ''Libbey-Owens-Ford Company,'' *Transportation and Distribution,* September 1992, p. 54.

technologies such as bar coding, on-line freight information systems, and satellite communications. Bar coding provides quick and error-free transfer of information that facilitates shipment tracking at intermediate points. On-line freight information systems allow shippers or consignees to dial directly into the carrier's computer to determine the status of a particular delivery. Libbey-Owens-Ford traces glass shipments throughout the country via access to Roadway Logistics Services computers. In addition, satellite tracking systems provide carriers with the ability to monitor vehicle movement throughout the country. Schneider National utilizes satellite tracking for its truck fleet in order to identify potential problems and work with its customers in advance of problems to achieve acceptable solutions.

SUMMARY

Chapter 12 described basic transport economics and pricing. The primary factors influencing transportation costs were discussed and illustrated. These include distance, volume, density, stowability, handling, liability, and market factors. First, the chapter described transport cost elements that affect pricing and negotiating strategies, including variable, fixed, joint, and common elements. Next, the rating strategies of the cost-of-service and value-of-service pricing methods were discussed and contrasted. Once the theoretical foundation for transport economics was established, the chapter illustrated transportation pricing using class-based, commodity, and exception-based rates.

Attention was then directed to specialized rates and services including freight-all-kinds, local, joint, proportional, and combination rates. In addition, specialized transit services, diversion and reconsignment, split delivery, demurrage and detention, and accessorial services were presented.

Finally, the chapter reviewed transport management activities. First, attention was directed to major types of transport documentation including bills of lading, freight bills, and shipping manifests. Next, traffic department responsibilities of auditing, claim administration, equipment scheduling, rate negotiation, research, tracing, and expediting were described and illustrated. The carrier evaluation process was then discussed, including a description of the major evaluation criteria.

Transportation is usually *the* largest single cost expenditure in most logistics operations. Prior to deregulation, transportation services were standardized and inflexible, so there was limited ability to develop a competitive advantage. However, deregulation has both expanded service offerings and relaxed restrictions, allowing transportation resources to be effectively integrated into the overall value chain. While logistics managers must understand the history of transport economics and pricing, they must also push the envelope to take advantage of new services and capabilities while simultaneously achieving lower costs.

QUESTIONS

1 Seven economic factors influencing transportation cost were presented. Select a specific product, and profile the relative importance of each factor in the determination of a freight rate.

2   Compare and contrast variable, fixed, and joint costs.

3   What is the concept of net pricing? How does it fit into the cost-of-service and value-of-service classification?

4   Why do carriers offer class rates?

5   What is the purpose of freight classification?

6   How do carriers charge for special rates and services?

7   Why are freight-all-kinds (FAK) rates important to an enterprise engaged in the delivery of a broad product line to customers?

8   Provide an example of how diversion and reconsignment can be used to increase logistical efficiency and effectiveness.

9   What is the role of the freight bill and the bill of lading in a transportation transaction? Are they both essential to a successful transaction?

10 In today's environment, what (in your opinion) is the most important responsibility of a traffic manager? Support your selection.

PROBLEM SET C: TRANSPORTATION

1 The XYZ Chemical Company must ship 9,500 gallons of pesticides from its plant in Cincinnati, Ohio, to a customer in Columbia, Missouri. XYZ has a contract in place with Henderson Bulk Trucking Company as well as with the Central States Railroad. Both carriers are available for the move. Henderson will charge $600 per tank truck, and Central States' rate is $1,000 per tank car. Henderson tanks can hold a maximum quantity of 7,000 gallons. XYZ has a fleet of 23,500-gallon tank cars available in Cincinnati.

   a   Given the above information, evaluate the cost of each alternative.

   b   What other qualitative factors should be considered in this decision?

2 Shatter Industries, Inc., manufactures a variety of household and commercial glass products. The glass products serve a variety of purposes in homes and businesses.

   a   Refer to the National Motor Freight Classification 100-S, Table 12-1, to determine the less-than-truckload (LTL) and truckload (TL) product classifications for these Shatter items:
Item 86960, glazed glass, boxed
Glass slides for microscopes
Bent mirror glass, dimensions 7 feet by 5 feet

   b   Shatter ships many of its products from a warehouse in Atlanta, Georgia, to a distribution center in Lansing, Michigan. Refer to the rate tariff in Table 12-2 to find applicable charges for the following shipments over the route:
5,200 pounds of mirrored shock glass (item 86900, sub 1: class 85)
32,000 pounds of class 65 product
200 pounds of class 60 product
19,000 pounds of class 150 product
2,500 pounds of class 200 product with a 5 percent temporary fuel surcharge added to the line-haul charge

3 Gigoflop Electronics has three shipments of class 100 product to be transported from Atlanta, Georgia, to Lansing, Michigan. The shipments weigh 5,000 pounds, 10,000 pounds, and 7,000 pounds, respectively. Gigoflop can ship each quantity individually or consolidate them as a multiple-stop shipment. Each shipment is to be delivered to a different location in Lansing. The carrier, Eckgold Trucking, charges $50 for each stop-off (not including the final destination). Refer to Table 12-2, and evaluate the costs of shipping individually versus consolidation. Which option should be used by Gigoflop?

4 Stanley Harris, traffic manager of This 'n' That Manufacturers, is considering the negotiation of a freight-all-kinds (FAK) rate for shipments between Atlanta and Lansing. The company ships 200 (class 65) shipments of 5,000 pounds, 40 (class 400) shipments of 1,200 pounds, 30 (class 100) shipments of 10,000 pounds, and receives a 45 percent discount on published rates.

   a   Refer to Table 12-2 to determine the current freight bill for the above shipments. (*Note:* Take the discount from the published rate, and round *up* for the applicable hundredweight rate.)

   b   Should Mr. Harris accept an FAK rate of $10 per hundredweight?

   c   What factors aside from price should Mr. Harris consider with an FAK rate?

5 Carole Wilson, transportation manager of Applied Technologies, has a shipment of 150 computer monitors originating at the company's plant in Santa Fe Springs, California. The shipment, valued at $29,250, is destined for a distribution center in St. Louis, Missouri. John Miller, receiving manager at the St. Louis distribution center, has established a standardized transit time for the shipment to be 2.5 days. Mr. Miller assesses an opportunity

cost of $6.00 per monitor for each day beyond the standard. Ms. Wilson has three transportation options. Evaluate the cost of each transportation alternative.

a Cross Country Haulers, a long-haul trucking company, can ship the monitors at a contracted rate of $1.65/mile. The distance from Santa Fe Springs to St. Louis is 1,940 miles. Cross Country estimates that it can deliver the shipment in three days. A truck can carry 192 monitors.

b The Sea-to-Shining Sea (STSS) Railway can pick up the shipment at the plant's dock and deliver the monitors directly to the St. Louis distribution center. STSS can ship the railcar of monitors for a flat charge of $1,500. Ms. Wilson has recently experienced delays with the switching of railcars on STSS and expects delivery to take five days.

c Ms. Wilson has also negotiated an agreement with Lightning Quick Intermodal, Inc. (LQI), a third-party carrier that utilizes both motor and rail transportation. LQI can pick up the shipment by truck at the plant and deliver it to an intermodal railyard in Bakersfield, California, where the trailer is placed onto a flat railcar. The Rocky Mountain Railway (RMR) then delivers the trailer to another intermodal yard near St. Louis, where the trailer is unloaded and transported by truck to the distribution center. Lightning Quick offers the origin-to-destination transportation for $2,500. Transit time is anticipated at 2.5 days. From past experience, Mr. Miller has discovered that the additional handling inherent with Lightning Quick's service results in 3 percent product loss and damage. Recovery of these losses is difficult and typically yields only 33.3 percent immediate reimbursement.

6 Moving Hands, Inc., ships alarm clocks from Atlanta to Lansing. The company has begun packaging the clocks in a stronger corrugated box to reduce the likelihood of damage in storage and transit. As a result of the improved packaging, the clocks' product classification has dropped from 100 to 85 without significantly adding weight to the package.

a What effect does the new packaging have on the transportation cost of a single 1,000-pound shipment? Refer to Table 12-2.

b Suppose Moving Hands ships 300 loads of the 1,000-pound quantity each year and the new packaging costs $10,000 to develop and produce. Will Moving Hands realize a full payback of the packaging investment in its first year?

7 Bill Berry, transportation sales manager of Speedy Trucking Company, has considered serving a new customer, El Conquistador, Inc., an importer of Venezuelan goods, by hauling 12 truckloads of product each month from the receiving port in Bayonne, New Jersey, to a distributor in Pittsburgh, Pennsylvania, for $850 per truckload. Each serving truck must depart from the Speedy terminal in Secaucus, New Jersey, 12 miles from the seaport. The distance from Bayonne to Pittsburgh is 376 miles. Upon unloading at Pittsburgh, trucks return empty ("deadhead") to the Secaucus terminal 380 miles from the distributor.

a If it costs Speedy an average of $1.20 per mile to operate a truck, should Mr. Berry accept the business at the negotiated rate? Why or why not?

b Mr. Berry has coordinated back-haul moves for the El Conquistador shipments above with a new customer in Youngstown, Ohio. The new customer, Super Tread, Inc., ships tires from its plant in Youngstown to the port of Bayonne for exporting. Each Conquistador shipment will be accompanied by a return shipment from Super Tread (12 truckloads/month). Speedy will charge Super Tread $1.30 per mile. Bayonne is 430 miles from Youngstown. The distance from Pittsburgh to Youngstown is 65 miles. Trucks must return to the terminal in Secaucus upon delivering product from the back-haul (before picking up again at Bayonne). The terms of the El Conquistador agreement outlined in part (a) remain intact. How much can Mr. Berry expect Speedy to profit (lose) per trip from the new arrangement?

c How much can Mr. Berry expect Speedy to profit (lose) per month from the new arrangement should the company accept the business?

d It is worthwhile for Mr. Berry to arrange for the back-haul? Why or why not?

WAREHOUSE MANAGEMENT

STORAGE FUNCTIONALITY AND PRINCIPLES
    The Concept of Strategic Storage
    Warehouse Functionality
    Warehouse Operating Principles
DEVELOPING THE WAREHOUSE RESOURCE
    Warehousing Alternatives
    Warehousing Strategy
    Planning the Distribution Warehouse
    Initiating Warehouse Operations
SUMMARY
QUESTIONS

Because it involves many logistical components, warehousing does not fit the neat classification schemes typically utilized when discussing order processing, inventory, or transportation. A warehouse is typically viewed as a place to store inventory. However, in many logistical system designs, the role of the warehouse is more properly viewed as a switching facility as contrasted to a storage facility. This chapter offers a unified treatment of strategic warehousing throughout the logistical system. The discussion is relevant for all types of warehouses as well as distribution centers, consolidation terminals, and break bulk and cross-dock facilities.

A major problem in logistical operations during the past several decades has been the level of labor productivity. The basic nature of raw materials, parts, and finished goods flowing through and between a vast network of facilities makes logistics a labor-intensive process. Productivity is the ratio of physical output to physical input. To increase productivity, it is necessary either to obtain greater output with the same input or to maintain existing output with a reduction of input factors.

Labor productivity growth is influenced by the boom and recession pattern of business, which has been a traditional characteristic of American industry since the turn of the century. When business is extremely good and the economy approaches full employment, output per worker-hour falls as marginal productive workers are employed. Warehousing operations get more than their fair share of such new employees because few, if any, skills are required to perform many of the manual tasks. When business activity plummets, union labor contract provisions often prohibit a rapid reduction in payrolls. While not all distribution facilities are unionized, logistics activities have traditionally been a union strength. Although separate productivity figures for warehouse workers are not available, it may be assumed that warehouse labor productivity has lagged most other areas in the private sector.

Chapter 13 reviews warehousing from a number of different perspectives. First, the chapter focuses on storage functionality and principles. The discussion outlines the concept of strategic storage, describes warehouse functionality in terms of both economic and service benefits, and illustrates primary warehouse operating principles.

Next, the chapter reviews strategies for developing or retaining warehouse facilities. The alternatives include private ownership, public facilities, and third-party contract warehousing services.

STORAGE FUNCTIONALITY AND PRINCIPLES

This section describes the role of warehousing in a logistical system. First, the discussion focuses on the role and importance of strategic storage. While effective distribution systems should not be designed to hold inventory for an excessive length of time, there are occasions when inventory storage is justified. Second, economic and service benefits of warehousing are described. Finally, fundamental warehouse operating principles are reviewed.

The Concept of Strategic Storage

Storage has always been an important aspect of economic development. In the early stages of its expansion, the United States consisted of individual households that functioned as self-sufficient economic units. Consumers performed storage and accepted the attendant risks. Meats were kept in smokehouses, and perishable products were protected in underground food cellars.

As transportation capability developed, it became possible to engage in economic specialization. Product storage was shifted from households to retailers, wholesalers, and manufacturers. Early business literature indicates that the warehouse was initially viewed as a storage facility necessary to accomplish basic marketing processes. That is, the warehouse served as a static unit in the material and product pipeline, necessary to match products in a timing sense with consumers. This perspective of storage created a tendency to consider warehouses ''a necessary evil'' that added costs to the distribution process and that resulted in creation of operating expenses with little appreciation of the broader logistical spectrum in which warehousing played a vital role. Warehousing capability used to group products into assortments desired by customers was given little emphasis. Internal control and maximum inventory turnover received little managerial attention.

Literature of the early era correctly described the situation. Firms seeking to operate effectively between points of procurement, manufacturing, and consumption gave little attention to internal warehouse operations. The establishment of warehouses was essential for survival, but little emphasis was placed on improving storage and handling effectiveness. Engineering efforts were centered on manufacturing problems.

Operation of early warehouses illustrated the lack of concern with material-handling principles. The typical warehouse received merchandise by railcar or truck. The items were moved manually to a storage area within the warehouse and hand-piled in stacks on the floor. When different products were stored in the same warehouse, merchandise was continually lost. Stock rotation was handled poorly. When customer orders were received, products were handpicked for placement on wagons. The wagons or carts were then pushed to the shipping area where the merchandise was reassembled and hand-loaded onto delivery trucks.

Because labor was relatively inexpensive, human resources were used freely. Little consideration was given to efficiency in space utilization, work methods, or material handling. Despite their shortcomings, these early warehouses provided the necessary bridge between production and marketing.

Following World War II, managerial attention shifted toward increasing warehouse efficiency. Management began to question the need for so many warehouses. In the distributive industries such as wholesaling and retailing, it was not unusual for every sales territory to have a dedicated warehouse and inventory. As forecasting and production scheduling techniques improved, the need for extensive inventory buildup was reduced. Production became more coordinated as time delays during the manufacturing process decreased. Seasonal production still required warehousing, but the overall need for storage to support manufacturing was reduced.

However, changing requirements of the retail environment more than offset any reductions in warehousing gained through manufacturing improvements. The retail store, faced with the necessity of stocking an increasing variety of products, was unable to order in sufficient quantity from a single supplier to enjoy the benefits of consolidated shipment. The cost of transporting small shipments made direct ordering prohibitive. This resulted in a need to utilize warehouses to provide timely and economical inventory assortments to retailers. At the wholesale level of the channel of distribution, the warehouse became a support unit for retailing. Progressive wholesalers and integrated retailers developed state-of-the-art warehouse systems capable of providing necessary retail support.

Improvements in wholesale warehousing efficiency related to retailing soon were adopted in manufacturing. For manufacturers producing products at multiple locations, efficient warehousing offered a method of reducing material and parts storage and handling costs while optimizing production. Warehousing became an integral part of JIT and stockless production strategies. While the basic notion of JIT is to reduce work-in-process inventory, the concept of manufacturing must be supported by highly dependable delivery. Such logistical support, in a nation as geographically vast as the United States, may be possible only through the use of strategically located warehouses. A basic stock of parts can be staged at a central warehouse, thereby reducing the need to maintain inventory at each assembly plant. Using consolidated shipments, products are purchased and transported to the supply warehouse and then distributed to manufacturing plants as needed. When fully integrated, the warehouse is a vital extension of manufacturing.

On the outbound side of manufacturing, warehouses created the possibility of direct customer shipment of mixed products. The capability to provide factory-direct mixed product shipments appealed to marketers because it enhanced service capability. For the customer, direct mixed shipments have two specific advantages. First, logistical cost is reduced because full product assortment can be delivered while also taking advantage of the benefits of consolidated transportation. Second, inventory of slow-moving products can be reduced because they can be received in small quantities as part of consolidated shipments. As the level of competition in the marketplace increases, manufacturers capable of rapidly providing direct mixed shipments gain a competitive advantage. During the 1960s and 1970s emphasis in warehousing focused on the application of new technology. Technology-based improvements affected almost every area of warehouse operations and created new and better techniques and procedures to perform storage and handling activities. In the 1980s, central focus was on improved configuration of warehouse systems and handling technologies.

During the 1990s, the primary focus of warehousing is flexibility and effective use of information technology. Flexibility is necessary to respond to expanding customer demands in terms of product and shipment profiles. Advanced information technology offers some of this flexibility by allowing warehouse operators to quickly react to changes and measure performance under a wide range of conditions.[1]

Warehouse Functionality

Benefits realized from strategic warehousing are classified on the basis of economics and service. From a conceptual perspective, no warehouse should be included in a logistical system unless it is fully justified on a cost-benefit basis. While there is some overlap, the major warehouse benefits are reviewed individually.

Economic Benefits   Economic benefits of warehousing result when overall logistical costs are directly reduced by utilizing one or more facilities. It is not difficult to quantify the return on investment of an economic benefit because it is

[1]Kenneth B. Ackerman, ''The Changing Role of Warehousing,'' *Warehousing Forum*, **8**:12, November 1993, p. 1.

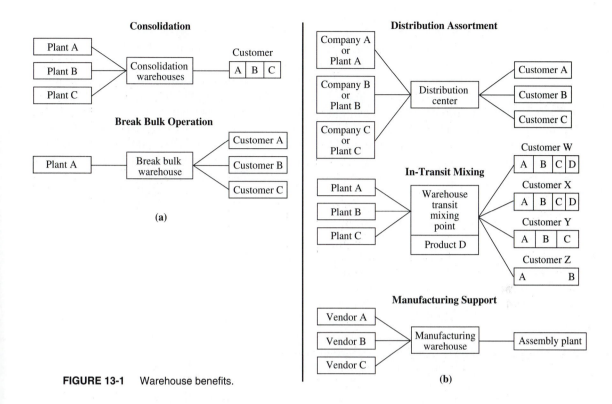

FIGURE 13-1   Warehouse benefits.

reflected in a direct cost-to-cost trade-off. For example, if adding a warehouse to a logistical system will reduce overall transportation cost by an amount greater than the fixed and variable cost of the warehouse, then total cost will be reduced. Whenever total-cost reductions are attainable, the warehouse is economically justified. Four basic economic benefits are consolidation, break bulk and cross dock, processing/postponement, and stockpiling. Each is discussed and illustrated.

Consolidation   Shipment consolidation is an economic benefit of warehousing. With this arrangement, the consolidating warehouse receives and consolidates materials from a number of manufacturing plants destined to a specific customer on a single transportation shipment. The benefits are the realization of the lowest possible transportation rate and reduced congestion at a customer's receiving dock. The warehouse allows both the inbound movement from the manufacturer to the warehouse and the outbound movement from the warehouse to the customer to be consolidated into larger shipments. Figure 13-1*a* illustrates the warehouse consolidation flow.

In order to provide effective consolidation, each manufacturing plant must use the warehouse as a forward stock location or as a sorting and assembly facility. The primary benefit of consolidation is that it combines the logistical flow of several small shipments to a specific market area. Consolidation warehousing may be used by a single firm, or a number of firms may join together and use a for-hire consolidation service. Through the use of such a program, each individual manufacturer or shipper can enjoy lower total distribution cost than could be realized on a direct shipment basis individually.

Break Bulk and Cross Dock Break bulk and cross-dock warehouse operations are similar to consolidation except that no storage is performed. A break bulk operation receives combined customer orders from manufacturers and ships them to individual customers. Figure 13-1*a* illustrates the break bulk flow. The break bulk warehouse or terminal sorts or splits individual orders and arranges for local delivery. Because the long-distance transportation movement is a large shipment, transport costs are lower and there is less difficulty in tracking.

A cross-dock facility is similar except that it involves multiple manufacturers. Retail chains make extensive use of cross-dock operations to replenish fast-moving store inventories. Figure 13-1*b* illustrates a retail cross-dock application. In this case, full trailerloads of product arrive from multiple manufacturers. As the product is received, it is either sorted by customer if it is labeled or allocated to customers if it has not been labeled. Product is then literally moved ''across the dock'' to be loaded into the trailer destined for the appropriate customer. The trailer is released for transport to the retail store once it has been filled with mixed product from multiple manufacturers. The economic benefits of cross docking include full trailer movements from manufacturers to the warehouse and from the warehouse to retailers, reduced handling cost at the cross-dock facility since product is not stored, and more effective use of dock facilities because all vehicles are fully loaded, thus maximizing loading dock utilization.

Processing/Postponement Warehouses can also be used to postpone, or delay, production by performing processing and light manufacturing activities. A warehouse with packaging or labeling capability allows postponement of final production until actual demand is known. For example, vegetables can be processed and canned in ''brights'' at the manufacturer. Brights are cans with no preattached labels. The use of brights for a private label product means that the item does not have to be committed to a specific customer or package configuration at the manufacturer's plant. Once a specific customer order is received, the warehouse can complete final processing by adding the label and finalizing the packaging.

Processing and postponement provide two economic benefits. First, risk is minimized because final packaging is not completed until an order for a specific label and package has been received. Second, the required level of total inventory can be reduced by using the basic product (brights) for a variety of labeling and packaging configurations. The combination of lower risk and inventory level often reduces total system cost even if the cost of packaging at the warehouse is more expensive than it would be at the manufacturer's facility.

Stockpiling The direct economic benefit of this warehousing service is secondary to the fact that seasonal storage is essential to select businesses. For example, lawn furniture and toys are produced year-round and primarily sold during a very short marketing period. In contrast, agricultural products are harvested at specific times with subsequent consumption occurring throughout the year. Both situations require warehouse stockpiling to support marketing efforts. Stockpiling provides an inventory buffer, which allows production efficiencies within the constraints imposed by material sources and the customer.

Service Benefits   Service benefits gained through warehouses in a logistical system may or may not reduce costs. When a warehouse is primarily justified on the basis of service, the supporting rationale is an improvement in the time and place capability of the overall logistical system. It is often difficult to quantify the return on investment of such a rationale because it involves cost-to-service trade-offs. For example, placing a warehouse in a logistical system to service a specific market segment may increase cost but might also increase market share, revenue, and gross margin. At a conceptual level, a service-justified warehouse would be added if the net effect was profit-justified. At an operational level, the problem is how to measure the direct revenue impact.

Five basic service benefits are achieved through warehousing: spot stock, assortment, mixing, product support, and market presence. Each is discussed and illustrated.

Spot Stock   Stock spotting is most often used in physical distribution. In particular, manufacturers with limited or highly seasonal product lines are partial to this service. Rather than placing inventories in warehouse facilities on a year-round basis or shipping directly from manufacturing plants, delivery time can be substantially reduced by advanced inventory commitment to strategic markets. Under this concept, a selected amount of a firm's product line is placed or ''spot stocked'' in a warehouse to fill customer orders during a critical marketing period. Utilizing warehouse facilities for stock spotting allows inventories to be placed in a variety of markets adjacent to key customers just prior to a maximum period of seasonal sales.

Suppliers of agricultural products to farmers often use spot stocking to position their products closer to a service-sensitive market during the growing season. Following the sales season, the remaining inventory is withdrawn to a central warehouse.

Assortment   An assortment warehouse—which may be utilized by a manufacturer, wholesaler, or retailer—stocks product combinations in anticipation of customer orders. The assortments may represent multiple products from different manufacturers or special assortments as specified by customers. In the first case, for example, an athletic wholesaler would stock products from a number of clothing suppliers so that customers can be offered assortments. In the second case, the wholesaler would create a specific team uniform including shirt, pants, and shoes.

The differential between stock spotting and complete line assortment is the degree and duration of warehouse utilization. A firm following a stock spotting strategy would typically warehouse a narrow product assortment and place stocks in a large number of small warehouses dedicated to specific markets for a limited time period. The distribution assortment warehouse usually has a broad product line, is limited to a few strategic locations, and is functional year-round.

Assortment warehouses improve service by reducing the number of suppliers that a customer must deal with. The combined assortments also allow larger shipment quantities, which in turn reduce transportation cost.

Mixing   Warehouse mixing is similar to the break bulk process except that several different manufacturer shipments may be involved. When plants are geographically separated, overall transportation charges and warehouse requirements can be reduced by in-transit mixing. In a typical mixing situation, carloads or truckloads of products are shipped from manufacturing plants to warehouses. Each large shipment enjoys the lowest possible transportation rate. Upon arrival at the mixing warehouse, factory shipments are unloaded and the desired combination of each product for each customer or market is selected.

The economies of in-transit mixing have been traditionally supported by special transportation tariffs that are variations of in-transit privileges. Under the mixing warehouse concept, inbound products may also be combined with products regularly stored in the warehouse. Warehouses that provide in-transit mixing have the net effect of reducing overall product storage in a logistical system. Mixing is classified as a service benefit because inventory is sorted to precise customer specifications.

Production Support   The economics of manufacturing may justify relatively long production runs of specific components. Production support warehousing provides a steady supply of components and materials to assembly plants. Safety stocks on items purchased from outside vendors may be justified because of long lead times or significant variations in usage. In these, as well as a variety of other situations, the most economical total-cost solution may be the operation of a production support warehouse to supply or ''feed'' processed materials, components, and subassemblies into the assembly plant in an economic and timely manner.

Market Presence   While a market presence benefit may not be as obvious as other service benefits, it is often cited by marketing managers as a major advantage of local warehouses. The market presence factor is based on the perception or belief that local warehouses (and presumably local inventory) can be more responsive to customer needs and offer quicker delivery than more distant warehouses. As a result, it is also thought that a local warehouse will enhance market share and potentially increase profitability. While the market presence factor is a frequently discussed strategy, little solid research exists to confirm its actual benefit impact.

Conclusion   Many possible warehouse services exist that involve more than inventory storage. In fact, many of the services reduce the basic need for storage. This adaptation of traditional warehouse capabilities to contemporary service requirements and cost reduction is an excellent example of modern logistical management. Figure 13-1 provides flow diagrams of five benefits available from warehousing. The benefits not illustrated (processing/postponement, stockpiling, and spot stock) are primarily time-related rather than material- or product-flow-related.

Warehouse Operating Principles

The previous discussion has provided the justification for using warehouses as intermediaries between manufacturers and customers. Once it has been determined to use a warehouse, the next step is designing it. The following discussion reviews basic warehouse design principles. Whether the warehouse is a small manual operation or a large automated facility, the following three principles are relevant: design criteria, handling technology, and storage plan. Each is discussed and illustrated.

Design Criteria   Warehouse design criteria address physical facility charac-teristics and product movement. Three factors to be considered in the design process are the number of stories in the facility, height utilization, and product flow.

The ideal warehouse design is limited to a single story so that product does not have to be moved up and down. The use of elevators to move product from one floor to the next requires time and energy. The elevator is also often a bottleneck in product flow since many material handlers are usually competing for a limited number of elevators. While it is not always possible, particularly in central business districts where land is restricted or expensive, warehouses should be limited to a single story.

Regardless of facility size, the design should maximize the usage of the available cubic space by allowing for the greatest use of height on each floor. Most ware-houses have 20- to 30-foot ceilings, although modern automated and high-rise facilities can effectively use ceiling heights up to 100 feet. Through the use of racking or other hardware, it should be possible to store products up to the buil-ding's ceiling. Maximum effective warehouse height is limited by the safe lifting capabilities of material-handling equipment, such as forklifts, and fire safety reg-ulations imposed by overhead sprinkler systems.

Warehouse design should also allow for straight product flow through the facility whether items are stored or not. In general, this means that product should be received at one end of the building, stored in the middle, and then shipped from the other end. Figure 13-2 illustrates this flow principle. Straight-line product flow minimizes congestion and confusion.

Handling Technology   The second principle focuses on the effectiveness and efficiency of material-handling technology. The elements of this principle concern movement continuity and movement scale economies.

Movement continuity means that it is better for a material handler or piece of handling equipment to make a longer move than to have a number of handlers make numerous, individual, short segments of the same move. Exchanging the product between handlers or moving it from one piece of equipment to another

FIGURE 13-2   Typical warehouse design.

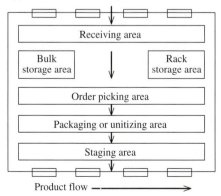

Product flow ————————————⟶

wastes time and increases the potential for damage. Thus, as a general rule, fewer longer movements in the warehouse are preferred.

Movement scale economies imply that all warehouse activities should handle or move the largest quantities possible. Instead of moving individual cases, warehouse activities should be designed to move groups of cases such as pallets or containers. This grouping or batching might mean that multiple products or orders must be moved or selected at the same time. While this might increase the complexity of an individual's activities since multiple products or orders must be considered, the principle reduces the number of activities and the resulting cost.

Storage Plan   According to the third principle, a warehouse design should consider product characteristics, particularly those pertaining to volume, weight, and storage.

Product volume is the major concern when defining a warehouse storage plan. High-volume sales or throughput product should be stored in a location that minimizes the distance it is moved, such as near primary aisles and in low storage racks. Such a location minimizes travel distance and the need for extended lifting. Conversely, low-volume product can be assigned locations that are distant from primary aisles or higher up in storage racks. Figure 13-3 illustrates a storage plan based on product movement.

Similarly, the plan should include a specific strategy for products dependent on weight and storage characteristics. Relatively heavy items should be assigned to locations low to the ground to minimize the effort and risk of heavy lifting. Bulky or low-density products require extensive storage volume, so open floor space or high-level racks can be used for them. On the other hand, smaller items may require storage shelves or drawers. The integrated storage plan must consider and address the specific characteristics of each product.

FIGURE 13-3   Storage plan based on product movement.

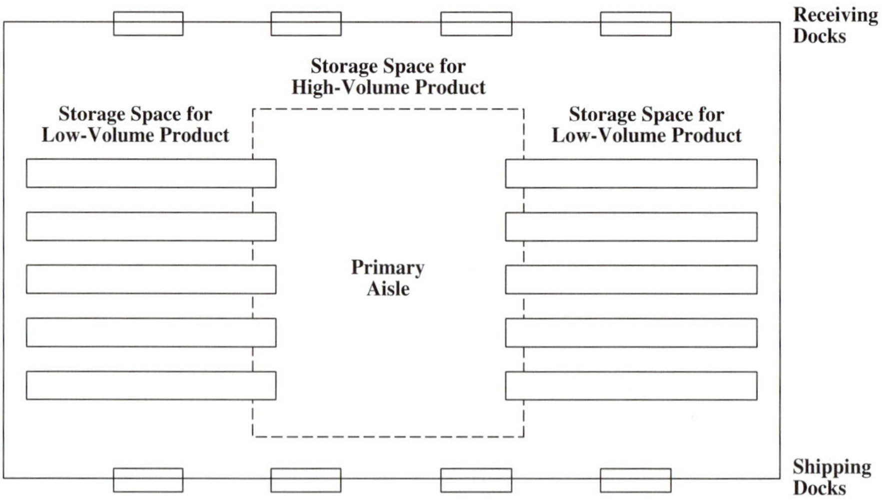

Conclusion The preceding principles suggest guidelines for designing and refining warehouse space when economic and service benefits are justified. However, there are situations when these principles may conflict. For example, the handling technology purpose is best served by using different equipment to pick orders and load trailers. Such a decision causes product to be exchanged between two handlers, resulting in increased time. However, specialized order picking and loading activities may be more cost-effective. As such, the principles should be considered as general guidelines.

DEVELOPING THE WAREHOUSE RESOURCE

This section discusses strategies and considerations for acquiring and developing warehouse space. First, alternative warehouse strategies are identified and compared. These include (1) private, (2) public, and (3) contract warehouses. Second, the major considerations for each type are presented and illustrated. Finally, a sample integrated warehousing strategy is described.

Warehousing Alternatives

This chapter focuses on the options of private, public, and contract warehousing. A private warehouse facility is owned and managed by the same enterprise that owns the merchandise handled and stored at the facility. A public warehouse, in contrast, is operated as an independent business offering a range of services—such as storage, handling, and transportation—on the basis of a fixed or variable fee. Public warehouse operators generally offer relatively standardized services to all clients. Contract warehousing, which is evolving from the public warehouse segment, provides benefits of both the private and public alternatives. Contract warehousing is "a long term, mutually beneficial arrangement which provides unique and specially tailored warehousing and logistics services exclusively to one client, where the vendor and client share the risks associated with the operation."[2] Important dimensions that differentiate contract warehousing operators from public warehouse operators are the extended time frame of the service relationship, tailored services, exclusivity, and shared risk. The benefits of private, public, and contract warehouse options are reviewed next.

Private Warehouses A private warehouse is operated by the firm owning the product. The actual facility, however, may be owned or leased. The decision as to which strategy best fits an individual firm is essentially financial. Often it is not possible to find a warehouse for lease that fits the exact requirements of a firm. For example, a warehouse requires substantial material-handling activities. Existing or leased facilities may not be adequately designed. As a general rule, an efficient warehouse should be planned around a material-handling system in order to encourage maximum efficiency of product flow.

---

[2]"Contract Warehousing: How It Works and How to Make It Work Effectively," Oak Brook, Ill.: Warehousing Education and Research Council, 1993, p. 7.

Real estate developers are increasingly willing to build distribution warehouses to a firm's specifications on a leased basis. Such custom construction is available in many markets on lease arrangements as short as five years.

The major benefits of private warehousing include control, flexibility, cost, and other intangible benefits. Private warehouses provide more control since the enterprise has absolute decision-making authority over all activities and priorities in the facility. This control facilitates the ability to integrate warehouse operations with the rest of the firm's internal logistics process.

Private warehouses generally offer more flexibility since operating policies and procedures can be adjusted to meet unique needs. Firms with very specialized customers or products are often motivated to develop their own warehouse facilities.

Private warehousing is usually considered less costly than public warehousing because private facility costs do not have a profit markup. As a result, both the fixed and variable cost components should be less. This perceived benefit, however, may be misleading since public warehouses often are more efficient or may operate at lower wage scales. It is important to develop an accurate assessment of total warehouse-related costs prior to making a decision regarding warehouse strategy.

Finally, private warehousing has some intangible benefits, particularly with respect to market presence. A private warehouse with a firm's name on it may produce customer perceptions of responsiveness and stability. This perception sometimes provides a firm with a marketing advantage over other enterprises.

Public Warehouses   Public warehouses are used extensively in logistical systems. Almost any combination of services can be arranged with the operator either for a short term or over a long duration. A classification of public warehouses has been developed. On the basis of the range of specialized operations performed, they are classified as (1) general merchandise, (2) refrigerated, (3) special commodity, (4) bonded, and (5) household goods and furniture. Each warehouse type differs in its material handling and storage technology as a result of the product and environmental characteristics.

General merchandise warehouses are designed to handle general package commodities such as paper, small appliances, and household supplies. Refrigerated warehouses (either frozen or chilled) handle and maintain food, medical items, and chemical products with special temperature requirements. Commodity warehouses are designed to handle bulk material or items with special handling considerations, such as tires or clothing.

Bonded warehouses are licensed by the government to store goods prior to payment of taxes or duties. They exert very tight control over all movements in and out of the facility since government documents must be filed with each move. For example, cigarettes are often stored in bonded warehouses prior to having the tax stamp applied. This tactic saves the firm money by delaying tax payments; it also reduces inventory value substantially. Finally, a household goods or furniture warehouse is designed to handle and store large, bulky items such as appliances and furniture. Of course, many public warehouses offer combinations of these operations.

Public warehouses provide financial flexibility and scale economy benefits as well. They frequently offer greater operating and management expertise since warehousing is their core business. This means that public warehouse operators understand the risks inherent in warehouse operations and are motivated to take advantage of market opportunities.

From a financial perspective, public warehousing may also have a lower variable cost than comparable privately operated facilities. The lower variable cost may be the result of lower pay scales, better productivity, or economy of scale. Public warehouses certainly result in lower capital costs. When management performance is judged according to return on investment (ROI), the use of public warehousing can substantially increase enterprise return.

Public warehousing offers another type of flexibility in that it is easy to change the location, size, and number of facilities, allowing a firm to quickly respond to supplier, customer, and seasonal demands. Private warehouses are relatively fixed and difficult to change because buildings have to be constructed or sold.

Public warehousing can also offer significant scale economies since the volume for each customer is leveraged with that of other users. This results in high-volume operations that can spread fixed costs and justify more efficient handling equipment. A public warehouse can also leverage transportation by providing delivery of loads that represent many public warehouse customers. For example, rather than have vendor A and vendor B each deliver to a retail store from their own warehouse, a public warehouse serving both vendors could deliver a single combined load more efficiently.

A great many firms utilize public warehouses for physical distribution because of the range of services and flexibility. Harley-Davidson (sidebar) illustrates a creative use of public warehousing for its presold products. In a variety of situations, public warehouse facilities and services can be arranged to meet exact operational requirements.

A public warehouse charges clients a basic fee for handling and storage. In the case of handling, the charge is based on the number of cases or pounds handled. For storage, the charge is assessed on the number of cases or weight in storage during the month. Such charges normally exceed the cost of private warehousing if adequate private facility volume exists. However, when economies of scale are not possible in a private facility, public warehousing may be a low-cost alternative.

Contract Warehouses   Contract warehousing combines the best characteristics of both private and public operations. The long-term relationship and shared risk will result in lower cost than typical public warehouse arrangements, although minimum fixed assets are still required for facilities. At the same time, contract warehouse operations can provide benefits of expertise, flexibility, and economies of scale by sharing management, labor, equipment, and information resources across a number of clients. Although it is common for contract warehouse operators to share resources across clients in the same industry such as grocery products, it is not common that direct competitors will want to share resources.

Contract warehouse operators are also expanding the scope of their services to include other logistics activities such as transportation, inventory control, order

---

HARLEY-DAVIDSON GOES PUBLIC

Planning, building, and operating a new distribution center represent a substantial investment for any organization. Many companies consider public warehousing as a viable option to obtain management expertise and increase operating efficiency. Public warehouses may offer a competitive edge by (1) reducing overhead and thus freeing up corporate capital for investment in other areas, (2) allowing companies to concentrate on their specific strengths, (3) allowing start-up companies and foreign manufacturers to enter the United States market effortlessly, and (4) enabling companies to strengthen their bottom lines and obtain optimum logistics efficiency.

For example, in the early 1980s, Harley-Davidson desired to increase the productivity of its existing facilities when it considered public warehousing as a logistical option.

Streamlined operations, reduced production times, and JIT inventory control have improved Harley-Davidson's competitive position. Today, the company controls 60 percent of the market for heavyweight (850 or more cubic centimeters) motorcycles—a significant increase from its 20 percent share in 1982. The increase in sales forced the company to consider alternative ways of moving presold inventory at its York, Pennsylvania, plant in order to increase its production capacity. In Harley-Davidson's case, presold inventory

(e.g., product that has been sold to consumers or dealers but not yet delivered or desired by the customer) may be in storage for up to several months. This inventory typically involves 500 to 1,000 motorcycles.

Each of the motorcycles is designated for a specific customer and requires a detailed identification tag defining customer and delivery requirements. The public warehouse has the responsibility to make sure the right motorcycle is shipped to the right customer. This means that each motorcycle must be stored so that it and the identification tag are easily accessible.

"By turning our presold inventory over to a public warehouse, we have the extra capacity we need and, most importantly, we have the specialized inventory management we require," says the general manager, Tom Sowarz. The move to public warehousing has also helped Harley-Davidson maintain tighter control over labor cost. Sowarz further commented that "even during a market slowdown, the staff of a private warehouse must be maintained to cover the workload when sales accelerate again. The advantages of public warehousing are inherent; you're only paying for the space you need, when your company needs it."

Source: M. L. Jenkins, "Utilizing Public Warehouses," *Plants, Sites & Parks,* **19**:7, November/December 1992.

---

processing, customer service, and returns processing. There are contract warehouses capable of assuming total logistics responsibility for enterprises that desire only to manufacture and market.[3]

For example, Rich Products, a frozen food manufacturer in Buffalo, New York, has increasingly utilized contract warehousing. Since 1992, Rich has had a long-term commitment with a refrigerated warehousing and distribution company, Christian Salvesen, for storage, handling, and distribution services at its facilities in New York. The nature of the arrangement benefits both parties and allows Rich to expand its distribution network without incurring any fixed facility cost. Rich is assured that there will always be storage space for its products. Christian Salvesen doesn't have to be concerned with filling space in its warehouses and can focus on providing service. Moreover, the longer Rich Products utilizes Christian Salvesen's services,

---

[3]For a more comprehensive discussion of contract warehouse services, see the Warehousing Research Council, "Contract Warehousing: How It Works and How to Make It Work Effectively," Oak Brook, Ill.: Warehousing Education and Research Council, 1993.

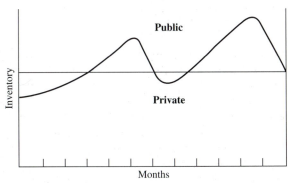

FIGURE 13-4 Combined private and public warehouse facilities.

the better the contract warehousing firm will be able to understand Rich's business needs and provide customized services.

Warehousing Strategy

As would be expected, many firms utilize a combination of private, public, and contract facilities.[4] A private or contract facility may be used to cover basic year-round requirements, while public facilities are used to handle peak seasons. In other situations, central warehouses may be private, while market area or field warehouses are public facilities. A contract facility could be used in either case. Each use of warehouse combinations is discussed and illustrated.

Full warehouse utilization throughout a year is a remote possibility. As a planning rule, a warehouse designed for full-capacity utilization will in fact be fully utilized between 75 and 85 percent of the time. Thus from 15 to 25 percent of the time, the space needed to meet peak requirements is not utilized. In such situations, it may be more efficient to build private facilities to cover the 75 percent requirement and use public facilities to accommodate peak demand. Figure 13-4 illustrates this concept.

The second form of combined public warehousing may result from market requirements. A firm may find that private warehousing is justified at specific locations on the basis of distribution volume. In other markets, public facilities may be the least-cost option. In logistical system design the objective is to determine whatever combination of warehouse strategies most economically meets customer service objectives.

An integrated warehouse strategy focuses on two questions. The first concerns how many warehouses should be employed. Chapter 17 discusses this in detail. The second question concerns which warehouse types should be used to meet market requirements. For many firms, the answer is a combination that can be differentiated by customer and product. Specifically, some customer groups may

---

[4]For a comprehensive discussion of the strategic use of warehousing, see Ken Ackerman, "Warehouse Profitability: A Manager's Guide," Columbus, Ohio: *Ackerman Publications*, 1994.

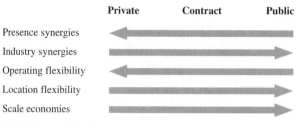

FIGURE 13-5   Qualitative decision factors.

be served best from a private warehouse, while a public warehouse may be appropriate for others.

Figure 13-5 illustrates other qualitative factors that should be considered and their likely influence. Across the top, the figure presents a strategy continuum ranging from private to contract to public. Qualitative considerations, listed on the vertical dimension, are (1) presence synergies, (2) industry synergies, (3) operating flexibility, (4) location flexibility, and (5) scale economies. Each consideration and its rationale are discussed.

Presence synergies refer to the marketing benefits of having inventory located nearby in a building that is clearly affiliated with the enterprise (e.g., the building has the firm's name on the door). It is widely thought that customers are more comfortable when suppliers maintain inventory in nearby locations. Products and customers that benefit from local presence should be served from private or contract facilities.

Industry synergies refer to the operating benefits of colocating with other firms serving the same industry. For example, firms in the grocery business often receive substantial benefits when they share public warehouse facilities with other suppliers serving the same industry. Reduced transportation cost is the major benefit since joint use of the same public warehouse allows frequent delivery of consolidated loads from multiple suppliers. Public and contract warehousing increases the potential for industry synergy.

Operating flexibility refers to the ability to adjust internal policies and procedures to meet product and customer needs. Since private warehouses operate under the complete control of the enterprise, they are usually perceived to demonstrate more operating flexibility. On the other hand, a public warehouse often employs policies and procedures that are consistent across its clients to minimize operating confusion. While conventional wisdom would suggest that private warehouses can offer more operating flexibility, there are many public and contract warehouse operations that have demonstrated substantial flexibility and responsiveness.

Location flexibility refers to the ability to quickly adjust warehouse location and number in accordance with seasonal or permanent demand changes. For example, in-season demand for agricultural chemicals requires that warehouses be located near markets that allow customer pickup. Outside the growing season, however, these local warehouses are unnecessary. Thus, the desirable strategy is to be able to open and close local facilities seasonally. Public and contract warehouses offer the location flexibility to accomplish such requirements.

VALUE-ADDED WAREHOUSING

In addition to traditional economic and service benefits, warehouse operators must offer other value-added services to remain competitive today. This is true for both public and contract warehouse operators as well as for private warehousing operations. Warehouse value-added services may focus on packaging and/or production.

The most common value-added services relate to packaging. Product is shipped to the warehouse in bulk or unlabeled form, so inventory is undifferentiated. Once a customer order is received, the warehouse operator customizes and releases the product. An example of this service is an automotive battery manufacturer that ships unmarked product to the warehouse. The warehouse is supplied with decals for the brand names the batteries are sold under. Once an order for a specific private label is received, the warehouse operator places the decals on the batteries and packages the product in a customized box. The customer receives customized product and packaging even though the product is not differentiated at the warehouse. The battery manufacturer reduces its inventory because less safety stock is required to support individual customer demand. A corresponding reduction in forecasting and production planning complexity is also achieved.

Warehousing can increase the value added by refining product packaging to better meet the needs of customers down the channel. For example, the warehouse may add value by stretch-wrapping or changing pallets. This allows the manufacturer to deal with only one type of unitization while postponing commitment to specialized packaging requirements. Another example of warehousing value added is the removal of protective packaging prior to product delivery to consumers. This is a valuable service offering in the case with large appliances, since it is sometimes difficult for consumers to dispose of large amounts of packaging. Therefore, a warehouse operator that removes or recycles packaging offers a value-added service.

Warehouse operators can also add value by changing packaging characteristics such as for an antifreeze supplier that ships in bulk quantities to the warehouse. The warehouse operator bottles the product to meet brand and package size requirements. This type of postponement minimizes inventory risk, reduces transportation cost, and can reduce damage (i.e., for product packaged in glass).

Warehousing can also complete production activities to postpone product specialization and refine product characteristics. At times, reassembly at a warehouse may be done to correct a production problem. For example, automobile engines might be shipped to the warehouse. If a quality problem arises with the carburetors, they might be changed at the warehouse without returning each unit to the engine plant. In this case, the warehouse is operating as the last stage of production.

Another value-added service is climatizing products such as fruits and vegetables. Warehouse operators can promote or delay the ripening process of bananas depending on storage temperature. The product can be ripened as required by market conditions.

Value-added warehousing services can also provide market confidentiality. One importer relabels a product for private brand customers. The relabeling is done after the product has entered the United States, to prevent the supplier from identifying the ultimate customers of the importer.

Providing value-added warehousing services places a special responsibility on the warehouse operator or the distribution center manager overseeing the contract operations. While outsourcing activities and operations may increase inventory effectiveness and operating efficiency, it also takes key responsibilities outside the control of the firm. For example, warehouse packaging requires that the warehouse operator conform to the exact quality standards applied internally by the firm. The warehouse must learn to operate to the same quality and service standards as the outsourcing firm.

In addition to the challenges of distribution within the United States, the global marketplace represents an added opportunity. As goods are shipped over longer supply lines, the importance of value-added services at the warehouse level increases. Deregulation has provided new opportunities for logistics suppliers to diversify as markets have presented such challenges. Logistics service suppliers have responded to this challenge, and it is likely they will continue to use their creativity to develop new ways to add value to the product at the warehouse level.

Source: Kenneth B. Ackerman, ''Value-Added Warehousing Cuts Inventory Costs,'' *Transportation and Distribution*, July 1989, pp. 32–35.

Scale economies refer to the ability to reduce material-handling and storage cost through application of advanced technologies. High-volume warehouses generally have a greater opportunity to achieve these benefits because they can spread technology's fixed cost over larger volumes. In addition, capital investment in mechanized or automated equipment and information technology can reduce direct variable cost. Public and contract warehouses are generally perceived to offer better scale economies since they are able to design operations and facilities to meet higher volumes of multiple clients.

In recent years, the traditional role of public warehouses as supplemental storage facilities has changed dramatically. The nature of modern business places considerable emphasis on inventory turnover and the ability to satisfy customer orders rapidly. To achieve these two requirements, flexibility must be maintained within the logistical structure. Many public warehouses have formed partnerships that allow a firm to purchase total order processing and local delivery systems in a number of cities across the United States. In addition to basic warehousing, these associations provide specialized services such as inventory control and billing.

Some larger public and contract warehouse firms are also expanding their operations to encompass a network of warehouses located in key markets. This trend has the potential to offer manufacturers a service that is effectively a logistical utility. Under this concept, all functions required to service a firm's customers are provided by the public warehouse logistics specialist. That is, transportation, order processing, inventory control, warehousing, and selected administrative matters are provided as an integrated service. Indications are that these multifacility, corporately managed public warehouse networks will increase substantially in number, geographic coverage, and capability in the future.

Warehouse operators are looking for other value-added services to differentiate their offerings. Traditionally, the decision to use public warehousing was based on relative storage economies and flexibility. In the future, the choice will be based increasingly on the public or contract warehouse organization's ability to perform necessary logistical tasks more effectively and efficiently than private systems.

From an analytical viewpoint, the private versus contract or public warehouse decision is analogous to the procurement decision of making or buying component parts or the transportation purchasing decision. Private warehouse facilities require substantial investment, and such commitments should provide the same rate of return as other capital investments.

A final consideration regarding the use of public warehouse associations and single-ownership networks is the natural reluctance of firms to turn over all managerial responsibility for an area as vital as logistics. The risks—potential loss of control, problems in customer goodwill, and the inability to rapidly replace or supplement a system that fails to perform—are the prime reasons given by logistical managers for not adopting single-management contract or public warehouse networks. Although many organizations use contract and public warehouses exclusively, the typical arrangement is for each facility to be under individual ownership, with logistical network control resting with the manufacturing, wholesaling, or retail enterprise. There has been a definite shift toward the use of contract and public warehouses because of their increased flexibility, economies, and synergies.

Planning the Distribution Warehouse

The initital decisions of warehousing are related to planning. The modern notion that warehouses provide an enclosure for material handling requires detailed analysis before the size, type, and shape of the facility can be determined. However, the buildings are often designed and under construction before the material-handling system is finalized. A master plan of the layout, space requirements, and material-handling design should be developed first and a specific site for the warehouse selected. These decisions establish the character of the warehouse, which, in turn, determines the degree of attainable handling efficiency.

Site Selection   Location analysis techniques are available to assist in selecting a general area for warehouse location. These are discussed in detail in Chapter 18. Once locational analysis is completed, a specific building site must be selected. Three areas in a community may be considered for location: commercial zones, outlying areas served by motor truck only, and central or downtown areas.

The primary factors in site selection are the availability of services and cost. The cost of procurement is the most important factor governing site selection. A warehouse need not be located in a major industrial area. In many cities, one observes warehouses among industrial plants and in areas zoned for light or heavy industry. Interestingly, this is not a legal necessity because most warehouses can operate under the restrictions placed on commercial property.

Beyond procurement cost, setup and operating expenses such as rail sidings, utility hookups, taxes, insurance rates, and highway access require evaluation. These expenses vary between sites. For example, a food distribution firm recently rejected what otherwise appeared to be a totally satisfactory site because of insurance rates. The site was located near the end of a water main. During most of the day, adequate water supplies were available to handle operational and emergency requirements. The only possible water problem occurred during two short periods each day. From 6:30 to 8:30 in the morning and from 5 to 7 in the evening, the demand for water along the line was so great that a sufficient supply was not available to handle emergencies. Because of this deficiency, abnormally high insurance rates were required and the site was rejected.

Several other requirements must be satisfied before a site is purchased. The location must offer adequate room for expansion. Necessary utilities must be available. The soil must be capable of supporting the structure, and the site must be sufficiently high to afford proper drainage. Additional requirements may be situationally necessary, depending on the structure to be constructed. In summary, the final selection of the site must be preceded by extensive analysis.[5]

Product-Mix Considerations   A second and independent area of quantitative analysis is a precise study of the products to be distributed through the proposed warehouse. The design and operation of a warehouse are related directly to the character of the product mix. Each product should be analyzed in terms of annual

[5]Steven Gold, "A New Approach to Site Selection," *Distribution* **90**:13, December 1991, pp. 29–33; and "A Guide to Site Selection in the '90s," *Traffic Management*, September 1991, pp. 205–235.

sales, stability of demand, weight, bulk, and packaging. It is also desirable to determine the total size, bulk, and weight of the average order processed through the warehouse. These data provide necessary information for determining requirements in warehouse space, design and layout, material-handling equipment, operating procedures, and controls.

Expansion   Future expansion is often neglected when an enterprise considers initial establishment of its warehouse facilities. Inclusion of a warehouse into the logistical system should be based partially on estimated requirements for future operations. Well-managed organizations often establish five- to ten-year expansion plans. Such expansion considerations may require purchase or option of a site three to five times the size of the initial structure.

Special construction is often considered to ease expansion without seriously affecting normal operations. Some walls may be constructed of semipermanent materials to allow easy removal. Floor areas, designed to support heavy movements, are extended to these walls in a manner that facilitates expansion.

Selection of Material-Handling System   A material-handling system is one of the initial considerations of warehouse planning. As noted previously, movement is the main function within a warehouse. Consequently, the warehouse is viewed as a structure designed to facilitate maximum product flow. It is important to stress that the material-handling system should be selected early in the warehouse design stage. Chapter 14 develops principles of material handling.

Warehouse Layout   Layout of a warehouse depends on the proposed material-handling system and requires development of a floor plan to facilitate product flow. It is difficult to generalize about warehouse layouts since they must be refined to fit specific needs. If pallets are to be utilized, the first step is to determine the pallet size. A pallet of nonstandard size may be desirable for specialized products, but whenever possible, standardized pallets should be used because of their lower cost. The most common sizes are 40 by 48 inches and 32 by 40 inches. In general, the larger the pallet load, the lower the cost of movement per pound or per package over a given distance. One forklift truck operator can move a large load in the same time and with the same effort required to move a smaller load. The packages to be placed on the pallet and the related patterns will determine, to a certain extent, the size of pallet best suited to the operation. Regardless of the size finally selected, management should adopt one size for the total operation.

The second step in planning a layout involves the pallet positioning. The basic method of positioning pallets in a mechanized warehouse is a ninety-degree, or square, placement. The square method is widely used because of layout ease. Square placement means that the pallet is positioned perpendicular to the aisle. Figure 13-6 shows this method of positioning.

Once all details have been isolated, the handling equipment selected must be integrated into a final layout. The path of product flow will depend on the material-handling system. To indicate the relationship between material handling and layout, two systems and their respective layouts are reviewed. These are only two of many possibilities.

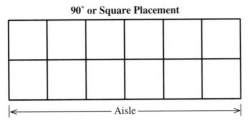

90° or Square Placement

|← ———————————— Aisle ———————————— →|

FIGURE 13-6   Basic method of pallet placement.

Layout A, illustrated in Figure 13-7, represents a material-handling system with related layout utilizing forklift trucks for inbound and transfer movements and tow tractors with trailers and rider pallet trucks for order selection. The products are assumed adaptable to a palletized operation. This layout is greatly simplified because offices, special areas, and other details are omitted.

The floor plan in layout A is approximately square. The advocates of this type of system feel that a square structure provides the best plan for operating efficiency. As indicated earlier in this chapter, products are typically clustered in a specific area of the warehouse for order selection. Such is the case in layout A. This area is labeled the ''selection area,'' and its primary purpose is to minimize the distance order pickers must cover when selecting an order.

The selection area is supported by a storage area. When products are received by rail or truck, they are palletized and placed in the storage area. The selection area is then replenished from storage as required. When a compact selection area is utilized, products are placed in this area according to weight, bulk, and replenishment velocity characteristics in an attempt to minimize outbound-movement problems. Special orders are then accumulated by an order selector moving a tow tractor with trailers or a rider pallet truck through the selection area. The arrows in layout A indicate the flow of product movements.

Layout B, illustrated in Figure 13-8, represents a material-handling system utilizing forklift trucks for inbound and transfer movements and a continuous-movement towline for order selection. As in layout A, palletized products are assumed, and the illustration is greatly simplified. The floor plan is rectangular. In a system with a continuous-movement towline, the special selection area is omitted and order selection occurs directly from storage. Products are moved from rail and truck receiving areas into storage areas adjacent to the towline. The orders are then selected from storage and loaded onto four-wheel carts or trailers, which are propelled by the towline. Merchandise is placed in the storage area to minimize inbound movement. The weakness of the fixed towline is that it moves by all products at an equal speed and frequency and, therefore, does not consider special needs of high-velocity products. The arrows in layout B indicate major product movements. The line in the center of the layout illustrates the path of the towline.

As indicated, both layouts A and B are greatly simplified; their purpose is to indicate the relationship of material-handling systems and warehouse layouts. Both represent mechanized warehouses and are not applicable to automated or information-directed handling.

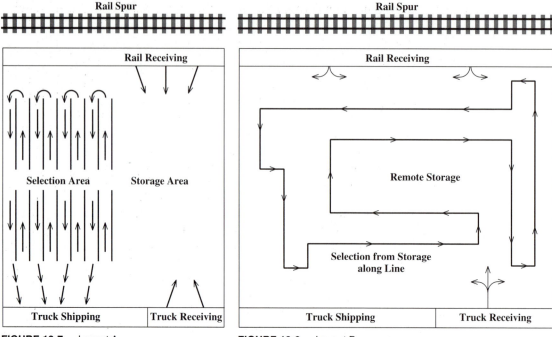

FIGURE 13-7   Layout A.   **FIGURE 13-8**   Layout B.

Precise Determination of Warehouse Space   Several methods are used to estimate the final size of the required warehouse. Each method begins with a sales forecast or some projection of the total tonnage expected during a given period. This tonnage estimate is then used to develop base and safety stocks. Some techniques consider both constant and peak utilization rates. Failure to consider utilization rates can result in overbuilding, with a corresponding increase in cost. It is important to note, however, that a major complaint of warehouse managers is management underestimation of warehouse size requirements. A good rule of thumb is to allow 20 percent additional space to account for increased volume, new products, and so on. Warehouse size determination techniques are discussed in Chapter 19.

Warehouse Design   Warehouse design is a special area of planning usually contracted to an architect. It is critical that design and construction characteristics do not hinder product flow. Consequently, management must communicate to the architect the need for unrestricted movement. In order to design a warehouse properly, the architect will require specifications for warehouse size, layout, and the predetermined path of material-handling equipment. The material-handling specialist must work closely with the design specialist to develop an integrated system.

Careful attention should be paid to placement of overhead obstructions such as lights, steam pipes, sprinkler systems, heating ducts, and communication antennae.

These items must be kept above the tier height to provide material-handling clearance. The placement of supporting columns is also an important design consideration. Generally, some latitude exists in positioning, depending on which way the columns run in relation to the supporting walls of the structure. Column placement is important to ensure a minimum of restricted storage bays. The floor areas, which must be specially treated for sufficient hardness, depend on the predetermined path of the material-handling equipment.

These items illustrate just a few reasons why the warehouse must be designed to facilitate product flow. The modern warehouse is founded on the efficient use of every cubic foot of space and available material-handling equipment, and the structure should be designed to stimulate this efficiency.

Initiating Warehouse Operations

To initiate operations, management must stock merchandise, hire personnel, develop work procedures, establish a method of billing and inventory control, and initiate a system of local delivery.

Stocking the Warehouse   The ideal procedure to follow when stocking a warehouse is to obtain the complete inventory prior to initiating operations. Individual products to be distributed through the warehouse and the quantities of each basic inventory SKU should be determined when the warehouse is planned. The problem in stocking is to schedule the arrival of this merchandise to achieve an orderly inbound flow. The time required to initially stock a warehouse depends on the number and quantity of products. In many situations, it may take over thirty days to complete initial stocking.

In a storage area, full pallet loads of product are assigned to a predetermined pallet position. Two common methods of slot assignment are variable and fixed. A variable-slot placement system, also called *dynamic slotting,* allows the product position to be changed each time a new shipment arrives in order to most efficiently utilize warehouse space. With a fixed-slot placement system, each product is assigned a permanent position in the selection area. The product retains this position as long as its volume of movement maintains the same level. If volume increases or decreases, the product may be reassigned. Fixed placement has an advantage over variable-slot placement because it provides a method of immediately locating a product. However, with computer-controlled warehouse locator systems, this is not a problem. Regardless of which slot system is employed, each inbound product should be assigned an initial location.

Personnel Training   Hiring and training qualified personnel to operate a warehouse can be a serious problem. Regardless of how efficient the proposed system is in theory, in practice it will be only as good as the operating personnel. Proper training is necessary to ensure desired system results.

Training is not a difficult task if executed properly. The full workforce should begin prior to the arrival of merchandise. Personnel hired for specific assignments should be fully indoctrinated in their job requirements and the role they play in the total system. Examination of the scale model and tours of the actual structure will familiarize personnel with the system.

After indoctrination, each group of employees should be given specific training. Personnel hired to operate a warehouse may be grouped in the following categories: administrators, supervisors, selectors, equipment operators, laborers, material handlers, and miscellaneous workers (maintenance, salvage, etc.).

Prior to actual operations it is desirable to simulate the various activities that each group of workers will perform. This type of training provides hands-on experience under near typical working conditions. When initial stocking begins, the workforce receives experience in merchandise handling under typical conditions. Normally, the manufacturer supplying the basic material-handling equipment sends an instructor to help train equipment operators under both simulation and initial stocking conditions. Once the basic inventory is in stock, it is a good practice to spend some time running sample orders through the warehouse. Simulated orders can be selected and loaded into delivery trucks, and the merchandise may then be treated as a new arrival and transferred back into stock.

Developing Work Procedures   The development of work procedures goes hand in hand with training warehouse personnel. Design of a material-handling system generally includes work procedures. It is management's responsibility to see that all personnel understand and use these procedures.

In the mechanized warehouse, approximately 65 percent of the floor personnel are employed in some phase of order selection. Modifications of two basic methods of order picking are employed in distribution warehouses: individual selection and area selection. Under the individual system, one selector completes a total order. This system is not widely used. Its primary application occurs when a large number of small orders are selected for repack or consolidated shipment on the same truck. Under the more commonly used area selection system, each selector is assigned a certain portion of the warehouse and many selectors handle portions of the same order. Because each selector has a thorough knowledge of the selection area, no time is lost in locating items. JC Penney (sidebar) illustrates the importance of developing sound work procedures to support quality and technology improvements.

Specific procedures must also be established for receiving and shipping. Merchandise received must be checked to ensure its entry into the inventory accounting system. If pallets are used, the merchandise must be stacked in patterns to ensure maximum load stability. Personnel working in shipping must have a knowledge of loading procedures. In specific types of operations, particularly when merchandise changes ownership, items must be checked during loading.

Work procedures are not restricted to floor personnel. A definite procedure must be established for proper handling of inventory control records. Most firms employ some type of automatic data processing equipment. The purchasing or reordering of merchandise for the warehouse can cause a serious operational problem if proper procedures are lacking. Normally, there is little cooperation between buyers and warehouse personnel if the facility is operating below capacity. The buyer tends to purchase in quantities that afford the best price, and little attention is given to problems of space utilization. Under such conditions, the danger of overstocking

WAREHOUSE QUEST FOR QUALITY

JC Penney's Columbus, Ohio, distribution center processes more than 9 million catalog orders annually, or 25,000 orders per day. The DC ships catalog orders for the 264-store midwest region with a service objective of reaching them all, retail outlet or consumer's home, within forty-eight hours. The 2 million-square-foot facility employs 1,300 full-timers and 500 part-timers in peak seasons. JC Penney feels that the real competitive edge of its Columbus facility is superior service. Management feels that the service edge is due to three initiatives taken during the mid-1980s: quality circles, focus on accuracy, and laser technology.

JC Penney initiated the quality circles in 1982 to maintain and even improve the service level. Management feared that the quality service idea would result in supervisors attempting to ''solve problems'' by simply throwing money at them. Instead, the solutions tended to be well thought out small improvements that removed major frustrations in the workplace. For example, the workers suggested the creation of a centralized tool bank to increase efficiency and tool availability.

The second initiative focused on improving service accuracy by eliminating defects in receiving, picking, and shipping activities. Providing accurate customer information and order fulfillment is the number one priority. This level of service accuracy means being able to tell the customer if an item is in stock and when it will be delivered as the order is phoned in. Another accuracy focus concerns product received from vendors. In order to ensure that vendor orders contain the correct product in terms of quality and quantity, JC Penney performs quality control and physical count inspections against one item in each shipment. If there is a variance, 100 percent of the vendor order is inspected. Similarly, 2.5 percent of customer shipments are audited. Order fulfillment required the most attention with the focus on improving accuracy. Roger Kerkman, the DC manager, said, ''We were making some errors, and we wanted to be able to make accuracy checks just

before merchandise went to the customer.'' The question is whether the solution should be found in quality circles or automating the process. Kerkman found that it ''was a people solution but automation sure makes it easier.'' A computer system was used to coordinate the movement of merchandise into a ''forward pick'' area to reduce order picker walk time.

The third initiative applied laser scanning technology to track the 230,000-SKU inventory at 99.9 percent accuracy. In the original JC Penney Milwaukee distribution center, items were sorted and tracked manually and then key-entered into the computer. This resulted in item accuracies of 80 percent or less. Scanning was seen as the means to improve both recording accuracy and speed. Initial scanning results were frustrating because of the number of scans required to accurately read each box. In some cases, four scans were required to obtain an acceptable read. JC Penney desired a system that could read various package sizes, from any angle, at the rate of three times per second. The company's internal systems support group refined the hardware and software technology to meet this objective. The four scanning stations in the DC cost $12,000 and reduced the need for sixteen key entry personnel each.

The application of ''job enrichment'' quality circles and ''job elimination'' technologies resulted in an interesting dilemma. JC Penney needed to maintain interest and involvement while introducing scanning. The timing was perfect since vast expansion plans would require additional employees. As a result, the company could tell employees that there would be no layoffs resulting from technological improvements. JC Penney has successfully implemented these quality initiatives in its other three DCs in Kansas City, Missouri; Reno, Nevada; and Manchester, Connecticut, allowing them to serve 90 percent of the nation in an average of twenty-four hours.

Source: E. J. Muller, ''Warehousing: JC Penney,'' *Distribution,* December 1986, p. 17.

the warehouse always exists. The problem can be avoided if the proper procedures are employed.

Buyers should be required to check with the warehouse manager before any abnormally large orders or new products are purchased. Some companies feel so strongly about this point that buyers are required to obtain a space allotment for all merchandise ordered. An equally serious problem is the quantity of cases ordered at a given time. The buyer should be required to order in pallet-multiple quantities. For example, if a product is placed on pallets in a pattern containing 50 cases, the buyer should order in multiples of 50. If an order is placed for 110 cases, upon arrival the cases will fill 2 pallets plus 10 on a third pallet. The extra 10 cases will require the same space as 50 and will need the same amount of movement effort. These illustrations indicate a few of the operational bottlenecks that can result from poor work procedures.

Security Systems In a broad sense, security in a warehouse involves protection against merchandise pilferage and deterioration. Each form of security is worthy of management attention.

Pilferage Protection Protection against theft of merchandise has become a major factor in warehouse operations. Such protection is required with respect to employees and as a result of the increased vulnerability of firms to riots and civil disturbances. All normal precautions employed throughout the enterprise should be strictly enforced at each warehouse. Security begins at the fence. As standard procedure, only authorized personnel should be permitted into the facility and surrounding grounds, and entry to the warehouse yard should be controlled through a single gate. Without exception, no private automobile—regardless of management rank or customer status—should be allowed to penetrate the yard adjacent to the warehouse.

To illustrate the importance of the stated guidelines, the following actual experience may be helpful. A particular firm enforced the rule that no private vehicles should be permitted in the warehouse yard. Exceptions were made for two handicapped office employees. One night after work, one of these employees accidentally discovered a bundle taped under one fender of his car. Subsequent checking revealed that the car was literally a delivery truck. The matter was promptly reported to security, which informed the employee not to alter any packages taped to the car and to continue parking inside the yard. Over the next several days, the situation was fully uncovered, with the ultimate arrest and conviction of several warehouse employees who confessed to stealing over $100,000 of company merchandise. The firm would have been better off purchasing a small vehicle to provide transportation for the handicapped employees from the regular parking lots to the office.

Shortages are always a major consideration in warehouse operations. Many are honest mistakes in order selection and shipment, but the purpose of security is to restrict theft from all angles. The majority of thefts occur during normal working hours.

Computerized inventory control and order processing systems help protect merchandise from being carried out of the warehouse doors. No items should be released from the warehouse unless accompanied by a computer release document. If samples are authorized for use by salespersons, the merchandise should be separate from other inventory. Not all pilferage occurs on an individual basis. Numerous instances have been discovered where organized efforts between warehouse personnel and truck drivers resulted in deliberate overpicking or high-for-low-value product substitution in order to move unauthorized merchandise out of the warehouse. Employee rotation, total case counts, and occasional complete line-item checks can reduce vulnerability to such collaboration.

A final comment is in order concerning the increased incidence of hijacking over-the-road trailer loads from yards or while in transit. Hijacking has become a major concern during the past decade. Over-the-road hijack prevention is primarily a law enforcement matter, but in-yard total trailer theft can be eliminated by tight security provisions.

Product Deterioration   Within the warehouse, a number of factors can reduce a product or material to a nonusable or nonmarketable state. The most obvious form of product deterioration is damage from careless transfer or storage. Another major form of deterioration is noncompatibility of products stored in the same facility.

The primary concern is deterioration that results from improper warehouse work procedures. For example, when pallets of merchandise are stacked in great heights, a marked change in humidity or temperature can cause packages supporting the stack to fall. The warehouse represents an environment that must be carefully controlled or measured to provide proper product protection.

A constant concern is the carelessness of warehouse employees. In this respect, the forklift truck may well be management's worst enemy. Regardless of how often operators are warned against carrying overloads, some still attempt such shortcuts when not properly supervised. In one situation, a stack of four pallets was dropped off a forklift truck at the receiving dock of a food warehouse. Standard procedure was to move two pallets per load. The value of the damaged merchandise exceeded the average daily profit of two supermarkets. Product deterioration from careless handling within the warehouse is a form of loss that cannot be insured against and constitutes a 100 percent cost with no compensating revenue.

Billing and Inventory Control   Most firms handling a large number of products with varied turnover characteristics find it economical to employ computers for billing and inventory control. Receipt tickets are prepared for each case of merchandise at the warehouse. When an order is received, products are listed according to warehouse placement. For example, if an area method of selection is employed, the order will be grouped by areas and listed in either numerical or slot order for the selector. It is possible to print an inventory of merchandise on hand at any given time. The computer inventory must be checked at times against a physical inventory in order to ensure accuracy in receiving and shipping records. On a periodic basis, all inventory should be cycle-counted to match physical inventory with the book inventory maintained by the computer.

Initiating and Programming Local Delivery   Most shipments from distribution warehouses to customers are made by truck. When private trucking is utilized, a problem is encountered in scheduling movements to ensure maximum utilization at minimum cost. Routing techniques discussed in Chapter 19 have been developed to assist management in solving this problem. In programming local deliveries, the objective is to minimize the cost of distribution, which may be expressed as a function of vehicle mileage, for example.

Safety and Maintenance   Accident prevention is a paramount concern within the warehouse. A well-balanced safety program should include constant examination of work procedures and equipment to locate and correct unsafe conditions before they result in accidents. Accidents occur when workers become careless or are exposed to mechanical and/or physical hazards. The floors of a warehouse may cause accidents if not properly cleaned. During normal operation, rubber and carbon deposits collect along aisles, and from time to time, broken cases will cause product seepage onto the floor. Proper cleaning procedures can reduce the risk of accidents from these hazards. Work environment safety has become a major concern of government under such programs as OSHA and cannot be neglected by management.

A preventive maintenance program is necessary for material-handling equipment. Unlike production machines, movement equipment is not stationary, and it is easy to neglect proper maintenance. A preventive maintenance program requiring a periodic check of all handling equipment should be installed in every warehouse.

SUMMARY

Chapter 13 discussed the principles, role, and activities of warehousing and materials management. First, the chapter reviewed the functionality and principles of strategic storage. It illustrated the development and role of storage for both manufacturing and retailing applications. While the traditional warehousing role has been to maintain a supply of goods to protect against uncertainty, contemporary warehousing offers many other value-added services. These services can be described in terms of economic and service benefits. Economic benefits include consolidation, break bulk and cross dock, processing/postponement, and stockpiling. Service benefits include spot stocking, assortment, mixing, product support, and market presence. The chapter also reviewed and illustrated warehouse operating principles in terms of design criteria, handling technology, and storage plans. Design criteria concern vertical and horizontal product movement within the warehouse facility. Handling technology refers to movement continuity and scale economies. The storage plan involves product storage locations within the warehouse.

Next, the chapter described approaches for developing and initiating a warehouse operation. It reviewed the characteristics and benefits of private, public, and contract warehousing. Private warehousing generally provides control, flexibility, low cost, and some intangible benefits. Public warehousing generally offers financial advantages, adjustment flexibility, and scale economy benefits. Depending on the agreement, contract warehousing may offer the best of both. The chapter then presented a discussion of an integrated warehousing strategy that incorporated a combination of private, public, and contract warehouses. The chapter concluded with a review of approaches for planning, equipping, and initiating warehouse operations.

QUESTIONS

1 Provide a definition and an example of strategic storage from a logistical system you are familiar with.

2 Under what conditions could it make sense to combine private and public warehouses in a logistical system?

3 Discuss and illustrate the economic justification for establishing a warehouse.

4 What is the logic for considering a warehouse a ''necessary evil''?

5 Why would a warehouse be used to perform cross-dock operations?

6 What is the concept of market presence, and how does it relate to the functionality of warehousing?

7 Discuss and illustrate the strategy of spot stocking.

8 What role can a warehouse play in postponement strategies?

9 Illustrate the relationship between the size and shape of a distribution warehouse and the material-handling system. Why do some warehouses have square design while others are rectangular?

10 Explain the following statement: ''A warehouse should merely consist of a set of walls enclosing an efficient handling system.''

MATERIAL HANDLING

MANAGING THE WAREHOUSE RESOURCE
    Handling Requirements
    Storage Requirements
MATERIAL HANDLING
    Basic Handling Considerations
    Mechanized Systems
    Semiautomated Handling
    Automated Handling
    Information-Directed Systems
    Special Handling Considerations
    Conclusion
SUMMARY
QUESTIONS

Chapter 14 develops greater understanding of the principles of material handling. The handling of products is a key to warehouse productivity for several important reasons.

First, the relative number of labor hours required to perform material handling creates a vulnerability to any reduction in the output rate per labor hour. Warehousing is typically more sensitive to labor productivity than manufacturing since material handling is highly labor-intensive. Second, the nature of warehouse material handling is limited in terms of direct benefits gained by improved information technology. While computerization has introduced new technologies and capabilities, the preponderance of material handling requires significant manual input.

Third, until recently warehouse material handling has not been managed on an integrated basis with other logistical activities, nor has it received a great deal of top management concern. Finally, automation technology capable of reducing material-handling labor is only now beginning to reach full potential.

Within the warehouse system, material handling is the prime consumer of labor. The application of labor to product selection and handling represents one of logistics highest personnel cost components. The opportunity to reduce this labor intensity and improve productivity lies with emerging handling technologies. In logistics, the primary emphasis is placed on material and product inbound and outbound flows rather than inventory storage. The warehouse represents the primary arena for material-handling operations. Therefore, warehouse design is an integral aspect of overall handling efficiency and is also of vital concern in obtaining increased labor productivity.

First, Chapter 14 introduces issues related to managing the warehouse in terms of handling and storage requirements. Handling requirements are discussed as they pertain to receiving, instorage handling, and shipping. Storage requirements are presented for both planned and extended storage. Next, the chapter provides an overview of material handling in terms of basic to special requirements. Degrees of automation are discussed along with levels of flexibility. Finally, the chapter describes how warehouse design and operations affect material handling. It focuses on considerations for receiving, storage, shipping, and order selection. The operations discussion emphasizes the activities and the options for material-handling automation.

MANAGING THE WAREHOUSE RESOURCE

The warehouse contains materials, parts, and finished goods on the move. Operating procedures consist of breaking bulk and regrouping merchandise in accordance with customer requirements. The objective is to efficiently move large quantities of inventory into, and specific customer orders out of, the warehouse. The ideal arrangement would be for products to arrive and depart the warehouse during a single working day.

This section describes basic handling and storage requirements, discusses alternative material-handling technologies, and presents the steps to plan a warehouse. The functions performed in a warehouse are classified as movement and storage. Movement is emphasized; storage is secondary. Within these two broad categories, movement is divided into three activities and storage into two activities.

Handling Requirements

The primary handling objective in a warehouse is to sort inbound shipments according to precise customer requirements. The three handling activities are receiving, instorage handling, and shipping. Each is discussed.

Receiving   Merchandise and materials typically arrive at the warehouse in larger quantities than when they depart. The first handling activity required is unloading the transportation vehicle. In most warehouses, unloading is manual. Limited automated and mechanized methods have been developed that are capable of adapting to varying product characteristics. Generally, one or two people unload a shipment. The product is hand-stacked on pallets or slip sheets to form a unit load for movement efficiency. In some cases, conveyors are employed to unload vehicles more rapidly. Larger types of merchandise may be unloaded directly from the car or truck to be moved into the warehouse. As discussed previously, container-erized or unit-load shipments dramatically reduce unloading time.

Instorage Handling Instorage handling consists of all movement within a warehouse facility. Following product receipt, it is necessary to transfer merchandise within the warehouse to position it for storage or order selection. Finally, when an order is received, it is necessary to accumulate the required products and to transport them to a shipping area. The two types of instorage handling are transfer and selection.

There are at least two and sometimes three *transfer* movements required within a typical warehouse. The merchandise is first moved into the building and placed at a designated storage location. The inbound movement is handled by forklift trucks when pallets or slip sheets are used or other mechanical traction for larger unit loads. A second internal movement may be required prior to order assembly depending on the operating procedures of the warehouse. When products are required for order selection, they are transferred to an order selection or picking area. When the merchandise is physically large or bulky, such as a stove or washing machine, this second movement may be omitted. In the final transfer, the assortment of products required for a customer shipment is moved from the warehouse to the shipping dock.

Selection is the primary function of the warehouse. The selection process groups materials, parts, and products into customer orders. It is typical for one section of the warehouse to be established as a selection area to minimize travel distance. The typical selection process is coordinated by a computerized control system. The primary focus for warehouse automation is the selection process. Various forms of automation are discussed later in this chapter.

Shipping Shipping consists of checking and loading orders onto transportation vehicles. As in receiving, shipping is manually performed in most systems. Shipping with unit loads is becoming increasingly popular because considerable time can be saved in vehicle loading. A unit load consists of grouped products, while a dead-stack or floor-stack load consists of boxes loaded directly from the floor. A checking operation is required when merchandise changes ownership as a result of shipment. Checking generally is limited to carton counts, but in some situations a piece-by-piece check for proper brand, size, and so on, is necessary to ensure that all items ordered by the customer are being shipped.

Storage Requirements

The warehouse performs two types of storage: planned and extended. Each is discussed.

Planned Storage   As previously noted, primary emphasis is placed on product flow in the warehouse. Regardless of inventory turnover velocity, all goods received must be stored for at least a short time. Storage for basic inventory replenishment is referred to as planned storage. Its duration varies in different logistical systems depending on performance cycles.[1] Planned storage must provide sufficient inventory to fulfill the warehouse's function within the logistical system.

Extended Storage   Extended storage, a somewhat misleading term, refers to inventory in excess of that planned for normal warehouse operation. In some special situations, storage may be required for several months prior to customer shipment. A warehouse may be used for extended storage for other reasons as well. In controlling and measuring warehouse performance, care should be taken to separate inventory turnover according to the type of storage used.

The basic nature of some products, such as seasonal items, requires that they be stored to await demand or to spread supply across time. When extensive storage is needed to match supply and demand, very little turnover results. One justification of warehousing is to accommodate seasonality in the logistical system. Other extended storage rationales include erratic demand items, product conditioning, speculative purchases, and discounts.

When a product has erratic demand fluctuations, it may be necessary to carry additional supplies or safety stocks to satisfy customer service standards. An example is air conditioners. Because air conditioners are expensive items, dealers prefer to carry small inventories. When a period of high temperature begins, manufacturers have limited time to distribute additional units.

Product conditioning is sometimes required (such as to ripen bananas), and this can be accomplished at the warehouse. Food distribution centers typically have ripening rooms to hold items until they reach peak quality.

The warehouse may also contain goods purchased for speculative purposes. The degree to which this activity takes place will depend on the specific materials and industries involved. For example, it is not unusual to store grain for this reason.

The warehouse often is used to realize special discounts. Early purchase discounts may justify extended storage. The purchasing manager may be able to realize a substantial reduction during a specific period of the year. Under such conditions the warehouse holds inventories in excess of planned storage. Manufacturers of fertilizer, toys, and lawn furniture often attempt to shift the warehousing burden to customers by offering off-season storage allowances.

MATERIAL HANDLING

One extremely encouraging aspect of contemporary logistics is the productivity potential that can be realized from capital investment in material-handling equipment. Material handling cannot be avoided in the performance of logistics. It should, however, be minimized. The technical aspects of material handling are extensive and beyond the scope of this text. However, the following section will

---

[1]See Chapter 8.

discuss handling methods and efficiency. Then the discussion will focus on recent developments in automated handling.

Basic Handling Considerations

Material handling in the logistics system is concentrated in and around the warehouse facility. A basic difference exists in the handling of bulk materials and master cartons. Bulk handling is a situation where protective packaging at the master carton level is unnecessary. Specialized handling equipment is required for bulk unloading, such as for solids, fluids, or gaseous materials. The following discussion focuses on master carton handling within the logistical system.

Over the years a variety of guidelines have been suggested to assist management in the design of material-handling systems. These are representative:

1   Equipment for handling and storage should be as standardized as possible.
2   When in motion, the system should be designed to provide maximum continuous product flow.
3   Investment should be in handling rather than stationary equipment.
4   Handling equipment should be utilized to the maximum extent possible.
5   In handling equipment selection, the ratio of deadweight to payload should be minimized.
6   Whenever practical, gravity flow should be incorporated in system design.

Handling systems are classified as mechanized, semiautomated, automated, and information-directed. A combination of labor and handling equipment is utilized in mechanized systems to facilitate receiving, processing, and/or shipping. Generally, labor constitutes a high percentage of overall cost in mechanized handling. Automated systems, in contrast, attempt to minimize labor as much as practical by substituting capital investment in equipment. An automated handling system may be applied to any of the basic handling requirements depending on the situation. When selected handling requirements are performed using automated equipment and the remainder of the handling is completed on a mechanized basis, the system is referred to as semiautomated. An information-directed system uses computers to maximize control over mechanized handling equipment. Mechanized handling systems are the most common. However, the use of semiautomated and automated systems is rapidly increasing. As noted earlier, one factor contributing to low logistical productivity is that information-directed handling has yet to achieve its full potential. This situation is predicted to dramatically change during the 1990s.

Mechanized Systems

Mechanized systems employ a wide range of handling equipment. The types of equipment most commonly used are forklift trucks, walkie-rider pallet trucks, towlines, tractor-trailer devices, conveyors, and carousels. Figure 14-1 provides examples of a variety of mechanized handling equipment.

Forklift Trucks   Forklift trucks can move loads of master cartons both horizontally and vertically. A pallet or slip sheet forms a platform upon which master

Two-wheeled hand trucks come in three constructions: hardwood/steel, all steel, or aluminum/magnesium. Load capacities range up to 2,000 lb. Special designs are available.

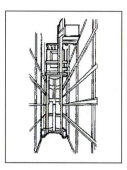

Outrigger rising-cab turret trucks lift the operator to the same height as the pallet. These trucks are for stacking pallets on both sides of very narrow aisles to 40-ft heights.

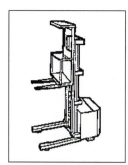

Orderpicker trucks place the operator on an elevating platform along with the forks. The operator picks items or cases from racks onto a pallet or shelf-type structure.

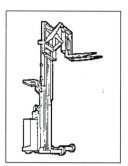

Reach trucks operate in narrow aisles, storing and retrieving pallets in racks. Some are equipped with a pantograph mechanism and can shelve pallets two-deep.

Balance-tilt floor trucks are highly maneuverable, even with long or bulky loads, because the truck balances on the center wheels and on one or two smaller swivel casters.

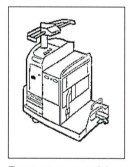

Tow tractors are straightforward, operator-aboard, self-powered tractors for towing wagons or carts over long distances. Some can operate outdoors.

Shelf-type truck superstructures customize a nontilt platform truck to carry loose items and packages, and make the truck useful for orderpicking.

Counterbalanced lift trucks can be battery-powered or powered by LP, gas, or diesel engines. Three- or four-wheel models are available, with pneumatic or cushion tires.

Walkie pallet trucks are highly versatile low-lift pallet and/or skid handlers with load capacities from 3,000 to 8,000 lb. These trucks are very popular in grocery warehouses.

Pallet trucks or "pallet jacks" remain one of the basic unit-load handlers. Load capacities now reach 10,000 lb. Trucks can be customized with options such as skid adapters.

Burden carriers have large heavy-duty cargo platforms and a driver's compartment. They are excellent for long hauls, and most can be used indoors or outdoors.

FIGURE 14-1 Mechanized handling equipment examples. (Modern Materials Handling, *September 1992.*)

cartons are stacked. A slip sheet consists of a thin sheet of material such as solid fiber or corrugated paper. Slip sheets are an inexpensive alternative to pallets and are ideal for situations when product is handled only a few times. A forklift truck normally transports a maximum of two unit loads (two pallets) at a time. However, forklifts are not limited to unit-load handling. Skids or boxes may also be transported depending on the nature of the product.

Many types of forklift trucks are available. High-stacking trucks capable of up to 40 feet of vertical movement, palletless side-clamp versions, and trucks capable of operating in aisles as narrow as 56 inches can be found in logistical warehouses.[2] Particular attention to narrow-aisle forklift trucks has increased in recent years, as warehouses seek to increase rack storage density and overall storage capacity. The forklift truck is not economical for long-distance horizontal movement because of the high ratio of labor per unit of transfer. Therefore, forklifts are most effectively utilized in shipping and receiving, and to place merchandise in high cube storage. The two most common power sources for forklifts are propane gas and electricity.

Many forklift operations are utilizing new forms of communication technology to increase their productivity. For example, radio frequency data communication (RFDC) discussed in Chapter 6 is utilized to speed load putaway and retrieval assignments for forklift truck operators in warehousing, manufacturing, and distribution operations. Instead of following handwritten or preprinted instructions, workers receive their assignments through either handheld or vehicle-mounted RF terminals. Use of RF technology provides real-time communication capability to central data processing systems, and when combined with bar code scanning of cartons and pallets, it allows forklift truck operators to receive and update item status inquiries, material orders and movements, and inventory adjustments. The Pioneer Hi-Bred International Company exhibits this application of technology to forklift operations (see sidebar).

Walkie-Rider Pallet Trucks Walkie-rider pallet trucks provide a low-cost, effective method of general material-handling utility. Typical applications include loading and unloading, order selection and accumulation, and shuttling loads over longer transportation distances throughout the warehouse. Electricity is the typical power source.

Towlines Towlines consist of either in-floor or overhead-mounted drag devices. They are utilized in combination with four-wheel trailers on a continuous-power basis. The main advantage of a towline is continuous movement. However, such handling devices do not have the flexibility of forklift trucks. The most common application of towlines is for order selection within the warehouse. Order selectors place merchandise on a four-wheel trailer, which is then towed to the shipping dock. A number of automated decoupling devices have been perfected that route trailers from the main line to selected shipping docks.

A point of debate involves the relative merits of in-floor and overhead towline installation. In-floor installation is costly to modify and difficult to maintain from

---

[2]Bernie Knill, ''Lift Trucks: New Development Boosts a Sagging Market,'' *Material Handling Engineering*, April 1981, pp. 62–69.

LOOK MOM, NO HANDS!

Pioneer Hi-Bred International, located in Durant, Iowa, is the world's largest seed company. It produces 600 genetic products that represent thousands of SKUs.

As well as being a leader in agricultural genetics and seed production, Pioneer has a reputation for experimenting with warehouse technologies to support its operations. In recent years, as the number of specialized products increased, the company decided to explore some of the newer warehouse technologies to increase efficiency. Several years ago, Pioneer replaced its manual inventory tracking methods with a customized warehouse management system that allowed personnel to collect data with handheld terminals. However, warehouse personnel were not comfortable with the need to key in data. Management initially considered bar codes and RF identification tags in order to eliminate the need for a keyboard, but ultimately it determined that either option would require too many major systems changes.

In late 1993, Pioneer began testing a ''hands-free'' mobile terminal-data collection system that utilized voice recognition technology at one of its seed production locations. ''We were looking for a system we could work into an existing warehouse, and we felt our way into keyless data collection might be with voice recognition systems,'' explains Mike Doty, Pioneer's information systems manager. How does the system work? It consists of a headset equipped with a microphone, speaker, and a miniature head-mounted display terminal that measures 1.2 by 1.3 inches. Although the display terminal is very tiny, to the mind it looks like a full-screen computer monitor—similar to the way a viewfinder operates. Voice is used to collect data and send the information via RF link to a host computer. The system directs a warehouse order selector to each picking location by displaying one line item at a time. As the order selector retrieves an item, he/she reads aloud the storage location. The system verifies that the right pallet of merchandise has been selected by repeating the information back to the operator and flashing it on the display terminal.

The rationale for the system was to give the warehouse forklift operators the ability to collect inventory data in real time while simultaneously providing the mobility to perform routine warehouse activities such as storing and selecting product, building mixed pallet loads for shipping, and processing returns. As these productivity objectives have been achieved while maintaining warehouse safety standards, the major savings have been derived from the improved inventory tracking capability. Specifically, the tracking allows random storage of pallets in bulk stacking areas, which translates into a better than 20 percent improvement in storage efficiency. ''We've streamlined shipping, and are moving a lot more material with a lot less people,'' says plant manager Joe Kaufman. Considering that part of the warehouse is refrigerated, the savings have produced an impressive 200 percent return on investment.

Pioneer is so satisfied with the experimental technology that it is preparing to test out the system at some of its more complex warehouses. As Mike Doty says, ''For a voice recognition system this is probably the best way to go to get the most productivity out of the people. You have a display that handles all the complex interaction with the data entry person, and let the voice simply be the keyboard.''

Source: ''Hands-Free Data Collection Blazes New Trail at Pioneer,'' *Modern Material Handling*, October 1993, pp. 46–48.

a housekeeping viewpoint. Overhead installation is more flexible, but unless the warehouse floor is absolutely level, the line may jerk the front wheels of the trailers off the ground and risk product damage.

Tow Tractor with Trailers   A tow tractor with trailer consists of a driver-guided power unit towing a number of individual four-wheel ''trailers'' that hold several palletized loads. The typical size of the trailers is 4 by 8 feet. The tow tractor with trailer, like the towline, is typically used to support order selection. The main advantage of tow tractor with trailers is flexibility. It is not as economical as the towline because it requires greater labor participation and is often idle.

Considerable advancements have been made in automated-guided vehicle systems (AGVS). These are discussed under semiautomated material handling.

Conveyors   Conveyors are used widely in shipping and receiving operations and form the basic handling device for a number of order selection systems. Conveyors are classified according to (1) power, (2) gravity, or (3) roller or belt movement. In power systems, the conveyor uses a drive chain from either above or below. Considerable conveyor flexibility is sacrificed in such power configuration installations. Gravity and roller or belt systems permit the basic installation to be modified with minimum difficulty. Portable gravity-style roller conveyors are often used at the warehouse for loading and unloading and, in some cases, are transported on over-the-road trailers to assist in unloading at the destination.

Carousels   A carousel operates on a different concept than most other mechanized handling equipment. It delivers the desired item to the order selector by using a series of bins mounted on an oval track. The entire carousel rotates and brings the desired bin to the operator. A wide variety of carousels are available. The typical application involves selection of individual packages in pack-and-repack and service parts operations. The rationale behind carousel systems is to shrink order selection labor requirements by reducing walking length/paths and time. Carousels, particularly modern stackable or multitiered systems, also significantly reduce storage floor requirements.

Pick-to-Light Systems   Technology has also been applied to carousel systems in an application known as ''pick to light.'' In these systems, order selectors pick designated items and put them directly into cartons from carousel bins or conveyors. A series of lights or a ''light tree'' in front of each pick location indicates the number of items to pick from each location. The light system may also be used to indicate when a carton is ready to move on. In systems where an item is picked to fill multiple orders, ''softbars'' show the order selector how many items are needed in a carton, since each carton typically represents a separate order. Some carousel systems also utilize computer-generated pick lists and computer-directed carousel rotation to further increase selection productivity. These systems are referred to as ''paperless picking'' because no paperwork exists to slow down employee efforts.

The types of mechanized material-handling equipment discussed are basic samples of the wide range available for use. Most systems combine different types of handling devices. For example, forklift trucks may be used for vertical movements while tow tractor with trailers and walkie-rider pallet trucks are used for horizontal transfers.

Semiautomated Handling

The semiautomated system supplements a mechanized system by automating specific handling requirements. Thus, the semiautomated warehouse is a mixture of mechanized and automated handling. Typical equipment utilized in semiautomated warehouses are automated-guided vehicle systems, computerized sortation, robotics, and various forms of live racks.

Automated-Guided Vehicle Systems   The automated-guided vehicle system (AGVS) performs the same type of handling function as a mechanized tow tractor with trailer or rider pallet truck. The essential difference is that an AGVS does not require an operator. It is automatically routed and positioned at the destination without operator intervention.

Typical AGVS equipment relies on an optical or magnetic guidance system. In the optical application, tape is placed on the warehouse floor, and the equipment is guided by a light beam that focuses on the guidepath. A magnetic AGVS follows an energized wire installed in the floor. The primary advantage is the elimination of a driver. Newer AGVs use video and information technology to follow paths without the need of fixed tracks. Contemporary AGVs are smaller, simpler, and more flexible than their predecessor systems of the 1980s. AGVs have declined in popularity in recent years industry orders have dropped by 40 percent (in dollar volume) since 1985.[3] It is possible that the new, more flexible systems may reverse this trend.

Sortations   Automated sortation devices are typically used in combination with conveyors. As products are selected in the warehouse and conveyorized out, they must be sorted to specific shipment docks. In order for automated sortation systems to operate, the master carton must have a distinguishing code. These codes are read by optical scanning devices and automatically routed to the desired location. Most controllers are able to be programmed to permit a customized rate of flow through the system to meet changing requirements.

Automated sortation provides two primary benefits. The first is the obvious reduction in labor. The second benefit is a significant increase in speed and accuracy. High-speed sortation systems can divert and align packages at rates exceeding one package per second. In these systems, packages are diverted to the desired destination and can be positioned to accommodate unit loading.

Robotics   The robot is a humanlike machine that can be programmed by microprocessors to perform one or a series of activities. The appeal of robotics lies in the ability to program the robot to function as an expert system capable of implementing decision logic in the handling process. The popularity of robotics resulted from their widespread adoption in the automotive industry during the early 1980s to replace selected manual tasks. However, a warehouse provides a different type of challenge than a typical manufacturing plant. In warehousing, the goal is to accommodate the exact merchandise requirements of a customer's order. Thus, warehouse specification can vary extensively from one customer order to the next and results in far less routine activities than typically found in manufacturing.

The primary use of robotics in warehousing is to break down and build unit loads. In the breakdown process, the robot is programmed to recognize stocking patterns and place products in the desired position on a conveyor belt. The use of robots to build unit loads is essentially the reverse operation.

Another prime potential use of robotics in warehousing occurs in environments

[3]"The Incredible Shrinking AGV System," *Modern Materials Handling*, November 1993, pp. 12, 19.

where humans find it difficult to function. Examples include high noise areas and extreme temperature environments like cold-storage freezers.

Significant potential exists to use robots in a mechanized warehouse to perform selected functions. The capability to incorporate artificial intelligence—in addition to their speed, dependability, and accuracy—makes robotics an attractive alternative to traditional manual handling methods.

Live Racks   Storage rack design, in which product flows forward to the desired selection position, is a commonly used device to reduce manual labor in warehouses. The typical live rack contains roller conveyors and is constructed for rear loading. To complete the installation, the rear of the rack is elevated higher than the front, causing a gravity flow forward. When unit loads are removed from the front, all other loads in that specific rack automatically move forward.

Live racks are a prime example of incorporating gravity flow into material-handling system design. The use of the live rack replaces the need to use fork trucks to reposition unit loads. A significant advantage of this form of storage is the automatic rotation of product that results from rear loading of a live rack. Rear loading facilitates "first-in, first-out" management of inventory. Applications of gravity flow racks are extremely diverse. For example, such racks are utilized to "stage," or store and position, fresh biscuits or bread for bakery manufacturers on individual pallet loads in preparation for shipping. Flow-rack staging is also typically utilized for automotive seats in JIT systems.

Automated Handling

For several decades the concept of automated handling has been long on potential and short on accomplishment. Initial efforts directed toward automated handling concentrated on order selection systems at the master carton level. Recently, emphasis has switched to automated high-rise storage and retrieval systems (ASRS). Each is discussed in turn after a brief review of automated handling concepts.

Potential of Automation   The appeal of automation is that it substitutes capital investment in equipment for labor required in mechanized handling systems. In addition to using less direct labor, an automated system operates faster and more accurately. Its shortcomings are the high degree of required capital investment and the complex nature of development and application.

To date, most automated systems have been custom designed and constructed for each application. The six guidelines previously noted for selection of mechanized handling systems are not applicable to automated systems. For example, storage equipment in an automated system is an integral part of the handling capability and can represent as much as 50 percent of the total investment. The ratio of deadweight to payload has little relevance in an automated handling application.

Although computers play an important part in all handling systems, they are essential to automated systems. The computer provides programming of the automated selection equipment and is used to interface the warehouse with the remainder of the logistical system. The warehouse control system is vastly different in automated handling. One factor that prohibited rapid development of automated systems was the high cost of minicomputers. Breakthroughs in microprocessors have eliminated this barrier.

Order Selection Systems   Initially, automation was applied to master carton selection or order assembly in the warehouse. Because of high labor intensity in order selection, the basic objective was to integrate mechanized and automated handling into a total system.

The initial concept was as follows. An automated selection device was preloaded. The device itself consisted of a series of racks stacked vertically. Merchandise was loaded from the rear and permitted to flow forward in the "live" rack on gravity conveyors until stopped by a rack door. Between or down the middle of the racks, power conveyors created a merchandise flow line, with several flow lines positioned above each other, one at each level of rack doors.

Upon receipt of an order, the information system that controlled distribution operations generated sequenced instructions to trip the rack doors, which allowed the desired merchandise to flow forward onto the powered conveyors. The conveyors, in turn, transported merchandise to an order-packing area for shipment. Product was often loaded sequentially so that it could be unloaded in the sequence in which it would be used.

When compared to modern applications, these initial attempts at automated package handling were highly inefficient. Considerable labor was required during the merchandise input and output phases, and the automated equipment was expensive. Applications were limited to merchandise of extremely high value or situations where working conditions justified such investment. For example, these initial systems were adopted widely for frozen food order selection.

Substantial advancements have been made recently in automated selection of case goods. The handling of fast-moving products in master cartons can be fully automated from the point of merchandise receipt to placement in over-the-road trailers. Such systems use an integrated network of power and gravity conveyors linking power-motivated live storage. The entire system is controlled by a computer coupled with the inventory and order processing control systems of the warehouse facility.

Upon arrival, merchandise is automatically routed to the live storage position, and inventory records are updated. Upon order receipt, merchandise is precubed to vehicle size and scheduled for selection. At the appropriate time, all merchandise is selected in loading sequence and automatically transported by conveyor to the loading dock. In most situations, the first manual handling of the merchandise within the warehouse occurs when it is stacked into the transport vehicle.

The solution of the input/output interface problem and the development of sophisticated control systems resulted in a highly effective and efficient package-handling system. Such systems are common today.

ASRS Systems   The concept of automated unit-load handling using high-rise storage has received considerable attention recently. The high-rise concept of handling is fully automated from receiving to shipping. Four main components constitute the basic system: storage racks, storage and retrieval equipment, input/output systems, and control systems.

The name *high-rise* derives from the physical appearance of the vertical storage rack. It is made of steel and can be up to 120 feet high. When one considers that the stacking height of palletized cartons in a mechanized handling system is normally 20 feet, the potential of high-rise storage is clear.

The typical high-rise facility consists of rows of storage racks, separated by aisles running from 120 to over 800 feet. Primary storage and retrieval is completed within these aisles. The storage and retrieval machine travels back and forth in an aisle. Its primary purpose is to move products in and out of storage. A variety of storage and retrieval equipment is available. Most machines require guidance at the top and bottom to provide the vertical stability necessary for high-speed horizontal movement and vertical hoisting. Horizontal speeds range from 300 to 400 feet per minute (fpm) with hoisting speeds of up to 100 fpm or more.

The initial function of the storage and retrieval equipment is to reach the desired storage position rapidly. A second function is to deposit or retract a load of merchandise. For the most part, load deposit and retraction are achieved by shuttle tables, which can enter and exit from the rack at speeds up to 100 fpm. Since the shuttle table moves only a few feet, it must be able to accelerate and stop rapidly.

In some installations, the storage and retrieval machine can be moved between aisles by transfer cars. Numerous transfer arrangements and layouts have been developed. Such transfer units may be dedicated or nondedicated. The dedicated transfer car is always stationed at the end of the aisle in which the storage and retrieval equipment is working. The nondedicated transfer car works a number of aisles and retrieves product on a scheduled basis to achieve maximum equipment utilization. The decision as to whether or not to include aisle-to-aisle transfer in a high-rise storage system rests with the economics of throughput rate and number of aisles included in the overall system.

The input/output system in high-rise storage is concerned with moving loads to and from the rack area. Two types of movement are involved. First, loads must be transported from receiving docks or production lines to the storage area. Second, within the immediate peripheral area of the racks, loads must be positioned for entry or exit. The greatest potential handling problem is in the peripheral area. A common practice is to assign pickup and discharge stations capable of staging an adequate supply of loads to each aisle, in order to fully utilize the storage and retrieval equipment. For maximum input/output performance, the normal procedure requires that different stations for transfer of inbound and outbound loads be assigned to the same aisle. The pickup and discharge stations are linked to the handling systems that transfer merchandise to and from the high-rise storage area.

The control system in high-rise storage is similar to the automated order selection systems described earlier. In the case of high-rise storage, considerable sophistication in programming and control measurement is required to achieve maximum equipment utilization and rapid command cycles. Recent advancements in the speed and cost of microprocessors have resulted in computers being fully dedicated to the ASRS.

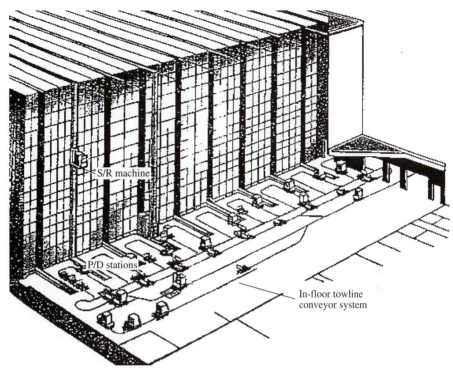

FIGURE 14-2   High-rise warehouse facility with ASRS. (Modern Materials Handling, *July 1992, p. 37.*)

Figure 14-2 illustrates the concept of a high-rise system. The center's enormous ASRS contains an estimated 3.3 million cubic feet of storage area and soars over 100 feet into the air. Merchandise flowing from production is automatically stacked to create a unit load. The unit load is then transported to the high-rise storage area by power conveyor. When the load arrives, it is assigned to a storage bin and transferred by power conveyor to the appropriate pickup (P/D) station. At this point the storage and retrieval equipment takes over and moves the unit load to its planned storage location.

In addition to scheduling arrivals and location assignments, the control system handles inventory and stock rotation. When orders are received, the command control system directs the retrieval of specified unit loads. From the outbound delivery stations, the unit load flows by power and gravity conveyor to the appropriate shipping dock. While retrieval and outbound delivery are being accomplished, all the paperwork necessary to initiate product shipment is completed.

An innovative application of ASRS technology is found in the United States automotive industry. In Toledo, Ohio, the Chrysler Corporation manufactures vehicle bodies for both pickup trucks and jeeps at one plant. As manufacturing is completed, two SR machines pick up each body in sequence and load it onto canvas-sided over-the-road trailers to transport the vehicle bodies to a second Chrysler plant four miles away, where final assembly is completed. At the second plant, two SR machines take over to coordinate the JIT staging and delivery of the vehicle bodies to the appropriate assembly lines for each model.

These examples are typical of ASRS currently operating in a variety of industries. They are designed to increase material-handling productivity by providing maximum storage density per square foot of floor space and to minimize the direct labor required in handling. The highly controlled nature of the system combines reliable pilferage-free and damage-free handling with extremely accurate control.

Information-Directed Systems

The concept of information-directed handling is relatively new and is still in the testing process. The idea is appealing because it combines the control of automated handling with the operational flexibility of mechanized systems.

The information-directed system uses mechanized handling equipment. The typical source of power is the forklift truck. In layout and design, the warehouse facility is essentially the same as any mechanized operation. The difference is that all fork-truck movements are directed and monitored by the command of a microprocessor.

In operation, all required handling movements are fed into the computer for analysis and equipment assignment. A computer is utilized to analyze handling requirements and to assign equipment in such a way that direct movement is maximized and deadhead movement is minimized. Work assignments are provided to individual forklift trucks by terminals located on the truck. Communication between the computer and the truck uses radio frequency (RF) waves with antennae located on the forklifts and high up in the warehouse. Less exotic applications use computer-generated movement printouts picked up at selected terminal locations throughout the warehouse. Information-directed handling has noteworthy potential in that selected benefits of automation can be achieved without substantial capital investment. Information-directed systems can also increase productivity by tracking material handler performance and allowing compensation to be based on activity level. The main drawback is the flexibility of work assignments. As a specific forklift truck proceeds during a work period, it may be involved in loading or unloading several vehicles, selecting many orders, and completing several handling assignments. The wide variety of work assignments increases the complexity of work direction and can decrease performance accountability.

Special Handling Considerations

As expected, the primary objective of material movement is for merchandise to flow in an orderly and efficient manner from manufacturer to point of sale. However, material-handling systems must also be capable of handling reverse merchandise flows within the logistical network.

For a variety of reasons, merchandise may be recalled by or returned to a manufacturer. Normally such return flows are not of sufficient quantity or regularity to justify mechanized movement. Therefore, the only convenient method for processing reverse flows of merchandise is manual handling. To the degree practical,

TABLE 14-1   STORAGE GUIDELINES FOR THE WAREHOUSE

Equipment	Type of materials	Benefits	Other considerations
		Manual	
Racking:			
Conventional pallet rack	Pallet loads	Good storage density, good product security	Storage density increased further by storing loads two deep
Drive-in racks	Pallet loads	Fork trucks can access loads, good storage density	Fork truck access is from one direction only
Drive-through racks	Pallet loads	Same as above	Fork truck access is from two directions
High-rise racks	Pallet loads	Very high storage density	Often used in ASRS and may offer tax advantages when used in rack-supported building
Cantilever racks	Long loads or rolls	Designed to store difficult shapes	Each different SKU can be stored on a separate shelf
Pallet stacking frames	Odd-shaped or crushable parts	Allow otherwise unstackable loads to be stacked, saving floor space	Can be disassembled when not in use
Stacking racks	Odd-shaped or crushable parts	Same as above	Can be stacked flat when not in use
Gravity-flow racks	Unit loads	High density storage, gravity moves loads	FIFO or LIFO flow of loads
Shelving	Small, loose loads and cases	Inexpensive	Can be combined with drawers for flexibility
Drawers	Small parts and tools	All parts are easily accessed, good security	Can be compartmentalized for many SKUs
Mobile racking or shelving	Pallet loads, loose materials, and cases	Can reduce required floor space by half	Come equipped with safety devices
		Automated	
Unit-load ASRS	Pallet loads, and a wide variety of sizes and shapes	Very high storage density, computer-controlled	May offer tax advantages when rack-supported
Car-in-lane	Pallet loads, other unit loads	High storage density	Best used where there are large quantities of only a few SKUs
Miniload ASRS	Small parts	High storage density, computer-controlled	For flexibility, can be installed in several different configurations
Horizontal carousels	Small parts	Easy access to parts, relatively inexpensive	Can be stacked on top of each other
Vertical carousels	Small parts and tools	High storage density	Can serve dual role as storage and delivery system in multi-floor facilities
Man-ride machines	Small parts	Very flexible	Can be used with high-rise shelving or modular drawers

Source: "Storage Equipment for the Warehouse," *Modern Materials Handling, 1985 Warehousing Guidebook 40,* vol. 4, Spring 1985, p. 53.

material-handling design should consider the cost and service impact of reverse logistics. Such flows often involve pallets, cartons, and packaging materials, as well as damaged, dated, or excess merchandise. In addition, ecological pressure to eliminate nondisposable containers will increase the quantity of returnable containers moving through the logistical system. Overall logistical systems design in many industries will require the ability to handle two-way movement efficiently.

Conclusion

The managerial question to consider is whether a specific handling system should be designed on a mechanized, semiautomated, or information-directed basis. Table 14-1 suggests guidelines and considerations for specific types of manual and automated warehouse storage systems. The initial cost of an automated system will be higher than for one that is mechanized. An automated system will require less building space, but the equipment investment will be greater. The key benefit from automation is reduced operating cost. An automated handling system, if properly designed and controlled, should outperform a mechanized system in terms of labor, damage, accuracy, product protection, and rotation. In the final analysis, the design to be used must be evaluated on the basis of return on investment.

SUMMARY

Chapter 14 presented a review of material-handling considerations in the day-to-day operations of a warehouse. Both handling and storage activities were discussed. Handling activities include receiving, instorage handling, and shipping. Storage activities were subdivided into planned and extended storage. Next, the discussion focused on basic material-handling considerations. Starting from mechanized systems, the discussion reviewed material-handling technologies ranging from semiautomated to automated and information-directed systems. The discussion concluded with treatment of specialized handling situations that must be accommodated in the material-handling effort.

QUESTIONS

1   Contrast planned and extended storage.
2   Why might it be economically justified to have multiple instorage handlings of a product in a warehouse?
3   In terms of basic material handling, what is the role of a unit load?
4   Until recently, why have automated handling systems failed to meet their expected potential? What changed to encourage automation in the 1980s?
5   To what extent has robotics been adapted in warehouse material handling? What are the causal factors behind your answer?
6   Compare and contrast order selection and unit-load automation.
7   What is the main limitation of information-directed handling?
8   What is the logic of a "live rack"?
9   What type of products and logistics applications are most suitable to ASRS handling?
10 Discuss the statement that "the best type of material handling is no handling at all!"

PACKAGING

PERSPECTIVES
    Consumer Packaging (Marketing Emphasis)
    Industrial Packaging (Logistics Emphasis)
DAMAGE PROTECTION
    Physical Environment
    Outside Elements
MATERIAL-HANDLING
    EFFICIENCY/UTILITY
    Product Characteristics
    Unitization
    Communication

CHANNEL INTEGRATION
ALTERNATIVE MATERIALS
    Traditional Materials
    Emerging Trends
SUMMARY
QUESTIONS

Chapter 15 discusses the role and importance of logistics packaging. The chapter first contrasts the marketing, logistics, and environmental perspectives of packaging and then reviews packaging's role in the logistics system with regard to damage protection, material handling, and information transfer. The packaging role in containerization and unitization is covered next. Finally, the discussion focuses on bar coding and symbology.

Packaging has a significant impact on the cost and productivity of the logistical system. The purchase of packaging materials, the institution of automated or manual packaging operations, and the subsequent need for material disposal are the most obvious costs. What is not readily apparent, however, is that purchase and disposal costs are borne by firms at opposite ends of a distribution channel, and that productivity gains generated by efficient packaging are spread throughout a logistical system. As a result, the impact of packaging is easily overlooked or, at minimum, underestimated.

An integrated logistics approach to packaging operations can yield dramatic savings. However, few firms manage their packaging with a systems approach. Any central planning logic designed to control total distribution costs must incorporate all relevant costs and trade-offs, including those related to packaging.

This chapter discusses (1) the packaging interface with the total logistical system and its role in both consumer and industrial markets; (2) the three primary functions of packaging performance (utility and handling efficiency, damage protection, and communication); and (3) traditional packaging materials, emerging technologies, and related environmental issues.

Packaging affects the cost of every logistical activity. Inventory control depends on the accuracy of manual or automatic identification systems that are keyed by product packaging. Order selection speed, accuracy, and efficiency are affected by package identification, configuration, and handling ease. Handling cost depends on unitization capability and techniques. Transportation and storage costs are influenced directly by package size and density. Customer service depends on packaging to achieve quality control during distribution, to provide customer education and convenience, and to comply with environmental regulations. The concept of packaging postponement to achieve strategic flexibility is particularly important given the increasing length and complexity of the global supply chain and the costs of locating new facilities.

PERSPECTIVES

Packaging can generally be categorized into two types: consumer packaging, which has a marketing emphasis, and industrial packaging, which has more of a logistics emphasis. The following discussion explores design issues for each packaging type.

Consumer Packaging (Marketing Emphasis)

Final package design is most often based on manufacturing and marketing considerations at the neglect of logistical requirements. For example, shipping such products as fully assembled motorcycles results in a substantial reduction in density. A low-density package means higher transportation rates and greater warehouse storage requirements. Consumer packaging design focuses on customer convenience, market appeal, retail shelf utilization, and product protection. In general, ideal consumer packaging (e.g., large containers and odd sizes that increase consumer visibility) makes very poor logistical packaging. The proper package design should be based on a comprehensive assessment of logistical packaging requirements. This assessment requires an evaluation of how the package is influenced by all components of the logistical system.

Industrial Packaging (Logistics Emphasis)

Individual products or parts are normally grouped into cartons, bags, bins, or barrels for handling efficiency. These containers are used to group individual products and are referred to as *master cartons*. When master cartons are grouped into larger units for handling, the combination is referred to as *containerization* or *unitization:* both concepts are discussed further in this chapter.

The master carton and the unitized load provide the basic handling unit in the logistics channel. The weight, cube, and fragility of the master carton in an overall product line determine transportation and material-handling requirements. If the package is not designed for efficient logistical processing, overall system performance will suffer.

Retail sale quantity should not be the prime determinant of master carton size. For example, beer typically sold in units of six individual containers is normally packed in master cartons (cases) in quantities of twenty-four units. The prime packaging objective is to design for operation with a limited assortment of standard master cartons. Standardization of master cartons facilitates material handling and transportation.

The importance of standardization can be illustrated by an example adapted from the shoe industry. The initial physical distribution system to ship shoes from the warehouse to retail shoe stores consisted of reusing vendor packaging. Individual pairs of shoes were grouped as best as possible into available repack cartons. The result was a variety of carton sizes going to each retail store.

The method of selection used to assemble a retail store's order was to work from warehouse-sequenced picking lists that grouped requirements by shoe style and quantity. Shoes were selected in the warehouse, packed into cartons, and then manually stacked on a four-wheel truck for transfer to the shipping dock. The cartons were then loaded into over-the-road trailers for transport to the retail store. While the order picking list provided a summary of all shoes in the total shipment, it was impossible for the retail store to determine the contents of any given carton.

Viewing material handling as an integrated system resulted in the economically justified decision to discontinue reusing vendor cartons. The new procedure required a standardized master shipping carton that was cost-justified by changes in the method of order picking and material handling. The revised system was designed around two concepts. First, standardized shipping cartons were adopted to permit continuous conveyor movement from point of warehouse order selection to the transportation trailer. Second, the integrated system used a computer process to ensure that each standardized master carton was packed to maximum practical cube utilization.

Under the new system, a picking list was generated for each carton. After the individual pairs of shoes were placed into the carton, the pick list was attached, providing a summary of contents for retail store personnel.

The advantages of a standardized carton extended even to the retail store's back room. Because the contents of each master carton were easily determined, it was not necessary to search through many cartons for a particular style or size of shoe. Standardization allowed master cartons to be more efficiently stocked, resulting in less backroom congestion. Finally, complete identification of master carton contents facilitated completion of retail inventory and merchandise reorder.

As expected, the new integrated system required the regular purchase of master cartons, since each could be reused only about three times. However, this added cost was more than justified by reduced order picking labor, continuous movement of cartons into over-the-road trailers, and more efficient utilization of transportation trailer capacity. Since each master carton was "cubed out," or utilized to near capacity, "dead" space was reduced substantially. The standardized carton size was selected for maximum conformity with a high-cube over-the-road trailer, thereby eliminating dead space in stacking. The end result of standardized master carton usage was a substantial reduction in total cost combined with a far more effective material-handling system at both the warehouse and the retail shoe store.

This example illustrates both the systems approach to logistical planning and the principle of total cost. However, the most important point to be derived is that master carton standardization facilitated total system integration.

Naturally, few organizations can reduce their master carton requirements to a single size. When master cartons of more than one size are required, extreme care should be taken to arrive at an assortment of compatible units. Figure 15-1 illustrates one such concept utilizing four standard sizes. The sizes of the four master cartons result in modular compatibility.

Of course, logistical considerations cannot fully dominate packaging design. The ideal package for material handling and transportation would be a perfect cube having equal length, depth, and width with maximum possible density. Seldom will such a package exist. The important point is that logistical requirements should be evaluated along with manufacturing, marketing, and product design considerations when standardizing master cartons.

A critical issue confronted in package design is to determine the degree of protection required to cope with the anticipated physical and element environments. The package design and material should combine to achieve the desired level of protection without incurring the expense of overprotection.

It is also possible to design a package that has the correct material content but

FIGURE 15-1 Example and benefits of the modular system of packing. *(Adapted from the work of Walter Frederick Friedman and Company.)*

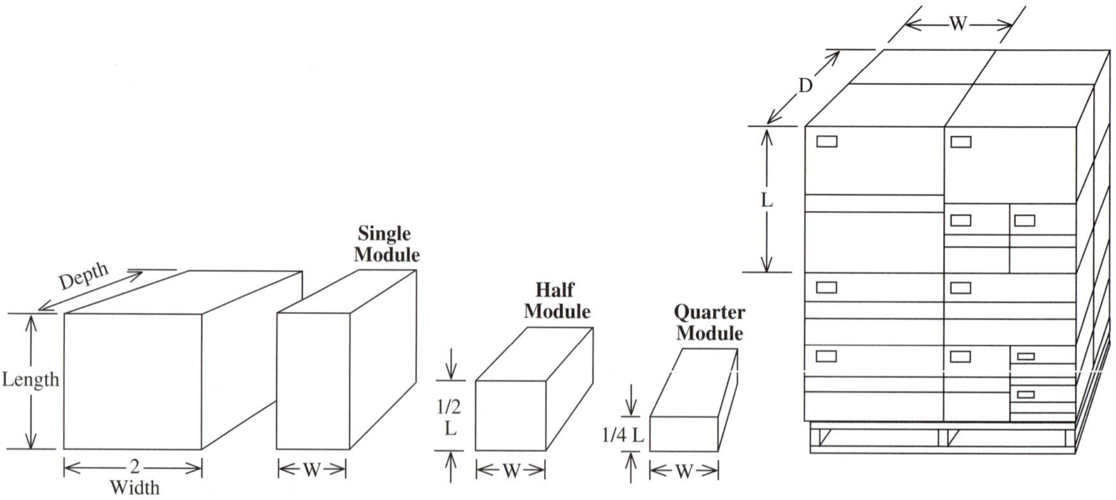

does not provide the necessary protection. Arriving at a satisfactory packaging solution involves defining the degree of allowable damage in terms of expected overall conditions and then isolating a combination of design and materials capable of meeting those specifications. The important points are (1) that in most cases the cost of absolute protection will be prohibitive, and (2) that package construction is properly a blend of design and material.

The determination of final package design requires considerable testing to ensure that specifications are satisfied at minimal cost. Such tests can be conducted in a laboratory or on an experimental shipment basis. During the past decade the process of package design and material selection has become far more scientific. Laboratory analysis has become the most reliable means of evaluation because of advancements in testing equipment and measurement techniques. To a large degree, care in design has been further encouraged by increased federal regulation of hazardous materials.

New instrumented recording equipment is available that measures severity and nature of shock while a package is in transit. Use of instrumented shipments on a selected sample of movements can reduce the bias inherent in trial-and-error test shipments. This form of testing is expensive and difficult to conduct on a scientific basis. To obtain increased accuracy, computerized environmental simulations can be used to replicate typical conditions that a package will experience in the logistical system. Laboratory test equipment is available to evaluate the impact of shock on the interaction of product fragility and packaging materials and design.

In general, the three broad functions of packaging can be described as damage protection, utility/efficiency, and communication. Each function is addressed in the following sections.

DAMAGE PROTECTION

A major function of the master carton is to protect products from damage while moving and being stored in the logistical system. Master cartons also serve as a deterrent to pilferage. Achieving the desired degree of protection involves tailoring the package to the product and selecting proper material for package construction. The crucial question is the desired degree of product protection.

As noted previously, the cost of absolute protection is prohibitive for most products. The determining factors are the value and fragility of the product: the higher the value, the greater the economic justification for nearly absolute protection. If a product is fragile and has high value, then the cost of absolute protection can be significant.

The susceptibility to damage of a given package is directly related to the environment in which it moves and is stored. Product fragility can be measured by product/package testing utilizing shock and vibration equipment. The test result allows a predetermined level of product cushion to be built into the package to provide protection while in the logistical system. If packaging requirements and cost are prohibitive, alternative product designs can be evaluated utilizing the same testing equipment. The end result is the determination of the exact packaging required to protect the product. The environment should be evaluated in terms of its physical and element characteristics. Each is briefly reviewed.

Physical Environment

The physical environment of a product is the logistical system. This environment both influences and is influenced by damage potential.

Package damage results from the transportation, storage, and handling systems utilized. If privately owned and operated transportation is used, the product will move to its destination in a relatively controlled environment. On the other hand, if common carriers are utilized, the product enters a noncontrolled environment. In the common carrier situation, the product may be handled by one or more break bulk terminals and transported on a variety of vehicles. The less control a firm has over the physical environment, the greater the packaging precautions required to prevent damage. The logistical environment thus influences the packaging design decision.

During the logistical process, the product can experience a number of situations that can cause damage. The four most common causes are vibration, impact, puncture, and compression. Within the logistical system, combinations of these forms of damage can be experienced whenever a package is in transit or being handled. In addition, stacking failure can result in damage while the product is in storage. The potential physical damage of poor stacking ranges from surface scuffing and marring to complete product crushing, buckling, and cracking.

Damage can be limited to a significant degree by securing the package while it is in transit. Typical methods are strapping, tie-downs, and various dunnage materials that prevent product shifting and limit vibration and shock. The best method of prevention is to load an over-the-road trailer or railcar in a tight pattern to reduce shifting. Proper securing and loading reduce the damage prevention burden that the product package must provide.

As noted earlier, package requirements also influence logistical system design. The standard distribution practice for mainframe computers provides an excellent example. Because the basic product is of high value and extreme fragility, a substantial investment in packaging would be required to perform physical distribution using normal carrier service. Consequently, computers are usually distributed by specialized household movers. The equipment and handling procedures employed by household moving specialists are highly oriented to damage prevention. Therefore, while the cost of transportation is higher, product packaging capable of providing absolute product protection is not required.

Outside Elements

The element environment of a package refers to potential damage from temperature, humidity, and foreign matter. For the most part, these environmental factors are beyond the control of logistical management. However, the protective package must be designed to cope with the range of possible adversity during transit.

To illustrate, it is not unusual for a package to be subjected to snow and below freezing temperatures during loading, to be exposed to rain at an intermediate transfer point, and to arrive at a hot and humid destination. The crucial problem in evaluating the element environment is determining in advance how the contents of the package will react with respect to these various elements in terms of instability and deterioration.

Temperature extremes naturally will affect package contents. At very high temperature levels, some products will melt, spoil, blister, peel, fuse together, and discolor. Exposed to cold, the contents may experience cracking, brittleness, or complete spoilage. The package can offer only minimal protection from extreme temperatures. For example, frozen foods in prolonged transit cannot be maintained by package construction alone. However, the package design should be capable of protecting against natural environmental elements for a reasonable period of time.

Another environmental impact involves water and vapor. The humidity problem is in many ways far more severe than the effect of temperature extremes on package contents. A typical product has very limited tolerance for water exposure without causing dissolution, separation, corrosion, or pitting. For the most part, water exposure occurs during transfer between transport carriers or distribution organizations. Therefore, the package may constitute the product's sole source of protection. Even if the product is protected, the package could very well lose its exterior identification if exposed to excessive moisture.

Foreign matter elements consist of any damage or loss of content stability caused by miscellaneous factors. For example, package contents can become contaminated or absorb tastes and odors if exposed for prolonged periods to chemical, noxious, or toxic elements. For certain kinds of products extreme care must be taken to protect against insects and rodents. Sometimes the package must protect against deterioration caused by prolonged exposure to air or light.

Many products—such as film, chocolate, confectionery, livestock, and produce—are so perishable that design of logistical systems must be geared to provide controlled environmental movement. Surprisingly, products clearly identified as perishable often do not create as severe an element problem as their more durable counterparts. It is the unexpected short-term excessive temperatures, high humidity, or foreign matter that cause most product damage.

MATERIAL-HANDLING EFFICIENCY/UTILITY

Utility is concerned with how packaging affects logistical productivity and efficiency. All logistical operations are affected by packaging utility—from truck loading and warehouse picking productivity to transportation and storage cube utilization.

Logistical productivity is the ratio of the output of a logistical activity (loading a truck) to the input (labor and forklift time required). Most logistical productivity studies center around making the input work harder. Packaging initiatives, however, increase the output. Almost all logistical activity outputs can be described in terms of packages, such as number of cartons loaded per hour into a trailer, number of cartons picked per hour in a warehouse or distribution center, etc. Material-handling efficiency is strongly influenced by the product, unitization, and communication characteristics. Each is discussed.

Product Characteristics

Packing products in certain configurations and standard order quantities assists in increasing logistical activity output. For example, reducing package size can improve cube utilization. This can be accomplished by concentrating products (e.g., orange juice and fabric softener) or eliminating air inside packages by shipping items unassembled, nested, and with minimal dunnage. In most cases, dunnage materials (like polystyrene foam peanuts) can be minimized simply by reducing box size. IKEA, the Swedish retailer of unassembled furniture, emphasizes cube minimization to the point that it ships pillows vacuum-packed. IKEA uses a cube minimization packaging strategy to successfully compete in the United States even though the company ships furniture all the way from Sweden. Some experts believe that improving cube utilization is packaging's greatest opportunity and predict that, in general, packaging cube can be reduced by 50 percent, which essentially doubles transportation efficiency.[1]

Cube minimization is most important for lightweight products (such as assembled lawn furniture) that ''cube out'' a transport vehicle far below its weight limit. On the other hand, heavy products (like liquid in glass bottles) ''weigh out'' a transport vehicle before it is filled. Weight can be reduced by changing the product or the package. For example, substituting plastic bottles for glass significantly increases the number of bottles that can be transported in a trailer.

Unitization

An important part of packaging as it relates to storage and material handling is the concept of unitization. Unitization describes the physical grouping of master cartons into one restrained load for material handling or transport.

The concept of containerization includes all forms of unitization, from taping two master cartons together to the use of specialized transportation equipment. All types of containerization have the basic objective of increasing material-handling efficiency. The present discussion is limited to methods of unitization that extend up to, but do not include, total vehicles. The first part concerns unit loads that utilize rigid enclosure. Next, the nonrigid-enclosure approach to unitization is discussed. Finally, the relative advantages and disadvantages of both are reviewed.

Rigid Containers   Rigid containers provide a device within which master cartons or loose products are placed during warehousing and transportation. The premise is that placing merchandise within a container will both protect it and make it easier to handle. The prospects for extensive domestic containerization have been the subject of considerable attention since the early 1950s. The potential for increased productivity by containerization is obvious. Approximately one-half the total cost of transporting domestic goods is spent shuffling between vehicles, transporting across docks and platforms, packaging, and filing loss and damage claims for pilferage and for insurance. Table 15-1 summarizes the potential benefits of increased containerization.

Nonrigid Containers   As the name implies, nonrigid containerization does not protect a product by complete enclosure. A common example is stacking master

---

[1]James Goff, ''Packaging-Distribution Relationships: A Look to the Future,'' *Logistical Packaging Innovation Proceedings,* Oakbrook, Ill.: Council of Logistics Management, 1991.

TABLE 15-1 POTENTIAL BENEFITS OF RIGID CONTAINERIZATION

• Improves overall material movement efficiency.	• Provides greater protection from element environment.
• Reduces damage in handling and transit.	• Provides a shipment unit that can be reused a substantial
• Reduces pilferage.	number of times, thereby reducing waste and the need to
• Reduces protective packaging requirements.	dispose of the container.

cartons on pallets or slip sheets. A hardwood pallet is illustrated in Figure 15-2. A slip sheet is similar to a pallet in size and purpose. Because the slip sheet lies flat on the floor, special forklift trucks are required to handle slip sheet unit loads. The primary advantages of slip sheets are their cost, which permits one-way utilization, and their insignificant weight.

There are also other methods of stacking master cartons on pallets. These are briefly reviewed in the following discussion. Finally, alternative ways to secure unit loads during transport and material handling are discussed.

Unit Loads Unit-load shipment has many benefits. First, unloading time and congestion at destination are minimized. Second, products shipped in unit-load quantities facilitate material handling. Inbound shipment checking is simplified, and the inventory can be positioned rapidly for order selection. Unit loads utilize only one-fifth the time required for manual unloading. Finally, damage in transit can be reduced by unit-load shipping and specialized transportation equipment. All these factors reduce logistical cost.

Industry organizations such as the Grocery Manufacturers of America have been active in encouraging unitized shipment programs. In many industries, pallet shipments are common in the manufacturing support phase of logistics, where shipments occur between company facilities. For interorganizational systems to function efficiently, a high degree of standardization and cooperation is required.

Load Securing A unit load can increase damage potential if it is not properly restrained during handling or transport. In most situations, the stability of stacking

FIGURE 15-2 Example of a hardwood pallet.

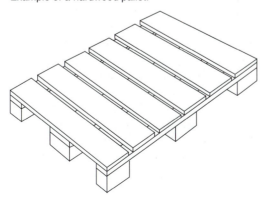

is insufficient to secure a unit load while it is being handled or in transit. Standard methods of additional stability include rope ties, corner posts, steel strapping, taping and antiskid treatment, breakaway adhesives, and wrapping. Shrink-wrap and stretch-wrap are also popular methods.

Unit-Load Platforms   Most industry associations recommend a standardized pallet or slip sheet size to be used as a unit-load platform. The Grocery Manufacturers of America have adopted the 40- by 48-inch pallet with four-way entry and similar size slip sheets for food distribution. Throughout industry, the sizes most frequently used are 40 by 48, 32 by 40, and 32 by 36 (all dimensions in inches). It is common practice to first identify the dimension of the most frequent entry used by the handling equipment.

Generally, the larger the platform, the more economical the resultant material handling. For instance, the 40- by 48-inch pallet provides 768 more square inches per stacking tier than the 32- by 36-inch size. Assuming that master cartons can be stacked as high as 10 tiers, the total added unitization space of the 40- by 48-inch pallet is 7,680 square inches. This is 60 percent larger than the 32- by 36-inch size. The final determination of size should be based on load, compatibility with the handling and transport equipment used throughout the logistical system, and standardized industry practice. With modern handling equipment, few restrictions are encountered in weight limitations.

Master Carton Stacking   While a variety of different approaches can be used to tier master cartons on slip sheets and pallets, four are the most common: block, brick, row, and pinwheel. The block method is used with cartons of equal width and length. With different widths and lengths, the brick, row, or pinwheel pattern is employed. These are illustrated in Figure 15-3. Except for the block method, cartons are arranged in an interlocking pattern with adjoining tiers placed at ninety-degree angles to each other. Load stability is increased by interlocking. The block pattern does not have this benefit.

Communication

The third important logistical packaging function is communication, or information transfer. This function is increasingly critical to content identification, tracking, and handling as they become more powerful and necessary to total channel success.

Content Identification   The most obvious communications role is identifying package contents for all channel members. Typical information includes manufacturer, product, type of container (can versus bottle), count, and universal product code (UPC) number. The carton information is used to identify product for receiving, order selection, and shipment verification. Visibility is the major consideration, and material handlers should be able to see the label from reasonable distances in all directions. The only exception is for high-value products, which often have small labels to minimize the temptation of theft.

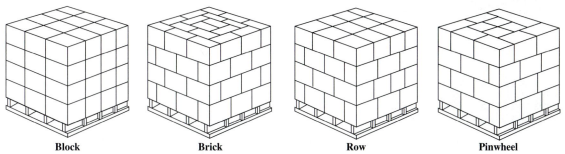

FIGURE 15-3 Basic pallet master carton stacking patterns. *(Adapted from palletization guides of the National Wooden Pallet Manufacturers Association.)*

Tracking   Tracking is another important aspect of logistics packaging. A well-controlled material-handling system tracks product as it is received, stored, retrieved, and shipped. This positive control of all movement reduces product loss and pilferage and is very useful for monitoring employee productivity. Such detailed tracking would be prohibitively expensive were it not for the extensive availability of portable bar code scanners and RF communication. Low-cost scanning equipment and coding standardization increase tracking capabilities and effectiveness.

Handling Instructions   The final role of logistics packaging is to provide handling and damage instruction. The information should note any special product handling considerations such as glass containers, temperature restrictions, stacking considerations, or potential environmental concerns. If the product is dangerous, such as the case with chemicals, the packaging or accompanying material should provide instructions for dealing with spills and container damage.

CHANNEL INTEGRATION

Although discussed separately, packaging, containerization, and material handling represent integral parts of the logistical operating system. All three areas influence each other. For example, automated handling cannot be efficiently designed without a high degree of master carton standardization, which in turn provides the opportunity to containerize individual products. This section illustrates some aspects of the interaction of packaging, material handling, and containerization in the context of a total movement system.

A number of integrated shipping programs between manufacturing firms and customers have been successfully implemented. The impetus for such programs is to integrate material-handling capability, transportation, warehousing, inventory policy, and communications into the customer's logistical system. The objective is to minimize handling during the exchange of merchandise. To the degree that duplication can be reduced, cost savings are possible for both the manufacturer and the customer. This type of integrated exchange is most common in physical distribution.

ALTERNATIVE MATERIALS

Numerous types of materials are used for logistics packaging, ranging from traditional fiberboard (cardboard) to more exotic plastics. First, the traditional alternatives are reviewed, followed by a discussion of emerging packaging alternatives.

Traditional Materials

Since the early 1900s, common carriers in the United States have attempted to ''regulate'' the nature of the packages they transport. The American Trucking Association and the American Association of Railroads publish packaging material ''requirements'' in their freight classification books. These standards, which have primarily been developed in conjunction with the Fiber Box Association (or its predecessors), generally require more corrugated fiberboard material than is often necessary to achieve adequate performance.

Historical justification for these standards has been carrier responsibility for payment of in-transit damage claims. Since one of the carrier's common law defenses is ''an act of the shipper'' (which includes insufficient packaging), carriers maintained that only packages in compliance with the cardboard classifications were sufficient to ensure safe transportation and handling.

Existence of the standards has caused many firms to ignore logistical packaging as an area of proactive management; in fact, packaging requirements have traditionally been a barrier to innovation. In recent years, however, these barriers have been greatly reduced for two reasons. First, large integrated channel members in today's competitive environment have a considerable stake in preventing damage and controlling packaging-related costs. Second, transportation deregulation has reduced the amount of freight subject to common carriers' packaging rules and has increased the amount of freight moving under negotiated contracts with released value rates. As a result, cardboard content rules today apply primarily to LTL common carrier freight. Many LTL carriers now accept packaging containers that differ from traditional standards provided the containers pass designated performance tests.

In addition to corrugated fiberboard boxes (commonly known as cardboard), other traditional packaging materials include burlap bags and blankets; steel cans, pails, drums, and straps; cages; and multiwall paper bags and drums.

Options to the more traditional logistical packaging forms include low-density plastic film shrink-wrap, stretch-wrap, bags and barriers, high-density plastic boxes and totes, plastic strapping, and plastic foam cushioning and dunnage for fragile and irregular shapes.

Shrink-wrapping consists of placing a prestretched plastic sheet or bag over the platform and master cartons. The material is then heat-shrunk to lock the cartons to the platform. Stretch-wrap consists of wrapping the unit load with a tightly drawn external plastic material. The unit load is rotated on a turntable to place the stack under tension. The platform is wrapped directly into the unit load. With shrink- and stretch-wrapping the unit load assumes many of the characteristics of a rigid container. However, the shrink- and stretch-wrap provide greater physical protection than a rigid container because of exact fit and weight support. Other benefits of wrapping are reduced exposure of master cartons to the logistical environment, low cost, adaptability to various shipment sizes, insignificant added weight, and the ability to identify contents and damage.[2] The major problem of shrink-wrap is waste material disposal.

Bags and barriers are paper or plastic containers that provide protection by wrapping bulk or loose product. They are flexible and relatively easy to dispose of. The weakness of such packaging is a failure to provide much product protection against damage and an inability to be used for a wide variety of products.

High-density plastic boxes or totes are lidded containers similar to those purchased for home storage applications. They are rigid and sturdy, offering substantial product protection. Totes work well for selecting and shipping combinations of small items to retail stores. The weakness of totes is that they are inflexible, are reasonably heavy, and must be returned for economic usage to be achieved.

Plastic strapping is used to contain or unitize a load so that multiple smaller containers can be handled as a single larger container. The strapping is usually about one-half to one inch wide and is banded tightly around the containers.

Plastic foam dunnage consists of the familiar ''peanuts'' used to pack irregular-shaped product into standard-shaped boxes. The peanuts are light and do not increase transportation cost while providing substantial protection. Environmental problems associated with disposal are the major issues here.

Emerging Trends

The loosening of traditional cardboard standards, competitive industry conditions encouraging an integrated systems approach, and technological innovation have triggered a renaissance in logistical packaging. Shippers are increasingly questioning traditional and alternative packaging materials and forms, and are encouraging experimentation with new, less costly, and creative packaging systems.

The following discussion explores recent trends in logistical packaging methods: film-based packaging, blanket wrapping, returnable containers, intermediate bulk containers, pallet pools, plastic pallets, and alternatives that require special material-handling equipment. Although several of these trends are adaptations of traditional packaging concepts, they are different in two critical respects. First, they are customized for specific logistical systems and products; and second, they are designed to minimize the costs of packaging and solid waste disposal.

Film-Based Packaging   Film-based packaging utilizes flexible materials rather than rigid packaging such as corrugated fiberboard boxes. Traditionally, film-based shrink-wrap and stretch-wrap systems have been used to stabilize unit loads. In today's emerging applications, they are used to form actual shipping ''packages'' for consumer goods such as cans and bottles, furniture, appliances, and small vehicles. The new packages generally are combined with rigid materials: cans are shrink-wrapped into a corrugated fiberboard tray, plastic bottle trays have corner

---

[2]''Unitization: Getting It All Together,'' *Handling and Shipping Management*, May 1981, pp. 83–90.

support for stacking, filing cabinets have corrugated corner protection from nicks, and appliances have panel protection on two sides to facilitate clamp handling.

Flexible packaging offers several advantages over traditional rigid packaging methods. Film-based systems operate automatically, reducing labor costs of manually boxing products. Packaging standardization is achieved since a roll of film fits most product configurations equally well and thus eliminates the need to maintain inventories of various sized boxes. A related benefit is that film-based systems minimize shipment weight and cube because the package is essentially the same size as its contents. Film-based systems provide reductions in inventory storage space because a roll of film is smaller than pallets of empty or flattened boxes; in addition, less trash remains after the product is unpacked. A final advantage, and the one that may seem contrary, is that damage is reduced compared with traditional rigid packaging methods. Research shows that freight is generally handled more carefully when it is clearly visible rather than concealed in a box. Besides the reduction in product damage, immediate identification of damage, when it does occur, reduces the complexity of freight claims and administrative haggling.

Film-based packaging applications work best for strong products that are able to bear a topload, since the package "walls" do not provide compression strength for stacking. Suitable product types include square products such as filing cabinets, loads of cans or bottles, appliances like furnaces, or round products like insulation rolls. In comparison, irregular-shaped products such as chairs do not lend themselves very well to film-based packaging.

Blanket Wrapping   Blanket wrapping is a traditional form of packaging provided by "moving van" carriers of household goods. Packaging of this nature is ideally suited for "nesting" irregular-shaped products like chairs that otherwise would have to be individually packed in corrugated fiberboard boxes. Support decking is erected with plywood and bars that lock into trailer walls; products are stacked into the decking, and the product surfaces are protected with blankets.

The blanket-wrap concept has been extended into premium commercial "uncartoned" transportation service offered by divisions of many household goods carriers. These carriers own, supply, and manage the package system materials; load and unload the trailers; and are directly accountable for any damage incurred in the process.

Uncartoned transportation service is best suited for truckload quantities of large rugged products like sofas, office furniture, laboratory equipment, restaurant furnishings, or store fixtures. Advantages include elimination of package material and waste, minimization of transportation cube, and easier unpacking of products.

Returnable Containers   Returnable containers have always been a part of logistical systems. Most reusable packages are steel or plastic, although some firms reuse corrugated fiberboard boxes. Automobile manufacturers use returnable racks for interplant shipment of body parts, and chemical companies reuse steel drums. There is an increasing trend, however, toward reusable packaging applications for many small items and parts, such as ingredients, and for interplant shipments as well as retail warehouse-to-store totes.

The growing number of returnable applications all have one common characteristic: an integrated marking system that enables control of the movement of containers. In a returnable package system, the parties must explicitly cooperate in order to maximize container usage; otherwise, containers may be lost, misplaced, or forgotten. Alternatively, deposit systems may be necessary in more free-flow marketing channels, where members are linked by occasional or nonrepetitive transactions. Deposit systems are frequently used for beverage bottles, pallets, and steel drums.

The decision to invest in a returnable package system involves explicit consideration of the number of shipment cycles and transportation costs versus the purchase and disposal cost of expendable containers. Benefits of improved housekeeping and reduced damage should be taken into account, as well as the future costs of sorting, tracking, and cleaning the reused containers. Financial analysis of returnable systems should be based on net present value calculations rather than the ''payback period'' method to accurately assess the operational and strategic potential of returnable packaging systems.

Intermediate Bulk Containers   IBCs are used for granular and liquid product shipment quantities that are smaller than tank cars but larger than bags or drums. Typical products include resin pellets, food ingredients, and adhesives. The most frequently used intermediate bulk containers are bulk bags and boxes. Bulk bags are made from woven plastic with a liner barrier and have a one- to two-ton capacity. Bulk boxes (sometimes called ''gaylords,'' after the major manufacturer) are usually pallet size and are lined with a plastic bag. IBCs for wet products require the use of a rigid box or cage.

Pallet Pools   Pallet pools have been developed to overcome traditional problems with the disposal and exchange of pallets. Palletization is arguably the most important contribution to logistical productivity. Pallets are, however, a costly investment and a significant disposal problem. Poorly constructed pallets fall apart easily and are more likely to cause product damage. Distribution centers and warehouses routinely exchange their worst pallets and keep the higher quality ones when pallet transfers occur.

Pallet pools are third-party suppliers that maintain and lease high-quality pallets throughout the country. They offer reduced damage, lower disposal costs, and improved utilization of pallet resources. Pallet pools are common in Europe and are making substantial inroads in the North American grocery industry.

Plastic Pallets   Plastic pallets have been an issue of research and examination for many years, particularly within the grocery industry. They attempt to address the shortcomings of wooden pallets and are sanitary, lightweight, and recyclable. Their life-cycle costs are comparable to traditional wooden pallets. However, they do require greater initial investment, and because of that expense, the only way they can be utilized on an industrywide basis is through tightly controlled networks of management.

Although no specific pallet material or design has been approved by the Grocery

TABLE 15-2   PALLET TYPE COMPARISON: How the Unit-Load Bases Stack Up

Unit-load base	Cost, $*	Base weight, lb†	Durability‡	Repair-ability	Typical applications
Wood pallet	3.50–25.00	55–112	Medium	High	Wide general use, including grocery, automotive, durable goods, hardware
Pressed wood fiber pallet	4.75–6.65	30–42	Medium	Low	Bulk bags, orderpicking, printing, building materials
Solid molded plastic pallet	30–80	35–75	High	Medium	Captive or closed loop systems, FDA and USDA applications, ASRS, automotive
Metal pallet	30–350	32–100	High	Medium	Captive or closed loop systems, FDA and USDA applications, ASRS, military, heavy equipment, aerospace
Corrugated fiberboard pallet	3.00–8.00	8–12	Low	Low	Export shipping, one-way shipping applications in grocery, lightweight paper products, industrial parts
Corrugated fiberboard slip sheet	1.00–4.00	2–6	Low	Low	One-way export shipping applications, slip sheet one-way shipping applications requiring a cushioned base, grocery, lightweight paper products

*Numbers in this table represent a range of values. Prices may be higher or lower, depending on the specific requirements of the application, dimensions, load capacity, quantity ordered, and manufacturer.

†Weight of the unit-load base may be higher or lower, depending on the specific requirements of the application. Check with individual manufacturer for load capacities.

‡Durability is defined as the expected number of trips to first repair.

Source: Modern Materials Handling, November 1993, p. 43.

Manufacturers Association, a set of specifications has been released. Pallet manufacturers can submit designs to independent laboratories for testing in order to assess whether or not specifications have been met. Table 15-2 compares the cost, durability, repairability, environmental impact, and typical applications of alternative pallet types.

One interesting design is the plastic pallet. The pallet is black, so that it resists the ultraviolet rays that weaken plastic. The posts in the pallet are white, which makes it easier for forklift drivers to handle them in poorly lit truck trailers and warehouses. Other logistical packaging methods have been developed for specific applications that require special material-handling equipment. These applications include clamp handling (for lightweight squeezable loads like tissue and breakfast cereal), slings (for bags), and toplift "baseload" boxes (for appliances). A significant issue with clamp handling and slip sheets concerns the potential damage caused by the special equipment when utilized by unskilled operators.

Refrigerated Pallets[3]   The refrigerated pallet illustrates a technology that integrates the environmental and unitization demands of specialty products. It is a self-contained refrigerated shipping unit (comparable in size to a loaded shipping pallet) that can be placed inside a regular dry van as an LTL shipment. It eliminates dependency on refrigerated trucks and makes just-in-time delivery of perishable

[3]Con-Way Transportation Services, Press Release, Menlo Park, Calif., May 17, 1994.

products possible. An integrated technology such as the refrigerated pallet can facilitate the efficient and effective flow of a full range of products that depend on controlled temperatures to extend shelf life and marketability, including fresh foods, flowers, chemicals, pharmaceuticals, confections, and frozen foods.

SUMMARY

Consumer and logistics packaging is a key component in developing an integrated logistics strategy. Packaging influences both the efficiency and the effectiveness of logistics operations. This chapter reviewed packaging from both consumer and logistics perspectives. Consumer packaging focuses on customer convenience, market appeal, retail shelf utilization, and product protection. Logistics packaging—including individual units, master cartons, and containers—focuses on handling, protection, and communication. While these objectives sometimes conflict, the importance and benefits of enhanced logistics packaging are significant.

Chapter 15 discussed the role of logistics packaging in terms of damage protection, material-handling efficiency/utility, communication, channel integration, and alternative packaging material. The presentation on damage protection stressed the importance of logistics packaging to protect products from the physical environment and to protect the environment from dangerous products. Material-handling efficiency/utility is influenced by packaging characteristics pertaining to the product, unitization, and unit load. The communication role of logistics packaging provides content identification, tracking, and handling instructions. Logistics packaging also contributes substantially to value chain integration by maximizing packing consistency and requirements throughout the channel. Packaging integration implies consistent labeling, handling, and unitization requirements. The discussion closed with a review of traditional and emerging packaging technologies.

QUESTIONS

1   What benefits can be gained by a modular system of packaging?
2   Provide an illustration that highlights the differences between consumer and industrial packaging.
3   In what ways do master carton stocking patterns influence package design?
4   What is the primary purpose of bar coding in packaging? Is the role of bar coding different in material handling?
5   Discuss the differences between rigid and nonrigid containers. Discuss the role of load securing in unitization.,
6   How do shrink- and stretch-wrap differ in terms of logistical benefits? Are there other differences?
7   What benefits do flexible unit-load materials have in contrast to rigid containers? How do return or reverse logistics considerations impact the two approaches?
8   What is the primary benefit of ''uncartoned'' logistical capability? For what type of industries and products does this approach have appeal?
9   What trade-offs are involved in the use of returnable racks?
10   Since plastic pallets appear to have many advantages over hardwood, why aren't they more widely adopted throughout the United States?

PROBLEM SET D: WAREHOUSING-HANDLING

1 Super Performance Parts (SPP) produces braking devices exclusively for the Ace Motor Company, an automotive manufacturer. SPP has been leasing warehouse space at a public facility twenty miles from the company's plant. SPP has been approached by a group of four other Ace suppliers with the idea of building a consolidated warehouse to gain transportation and material-handling economies. An investment of $200,000 would be required by each of the five companies to acquire the warehouse. Payment of the initial investment secures ten years of participation in the agreement. Annual operating expenses are anticipated to be $48,000 for each party. SPP is currently charged $6,000 per month for use of the public warehouse facilities.

SPP's outbound transportation from the public warehouse often consists of less-than-truckload (LTL) quantities. Its annual outbound transportation bill is currently $300,000. SPP expects consolidated warehousing to more fully utilize truckload quantities with transportation expenses shared among the supplier pool. SPP's annual outbound bill would be reduced by 25 percent in the consolidated plan. Differences in inbound transportation costs are assumed negligible in this case.

  a Compare the storage and shipping costs associated with consolidated warehousing as opposed to SPP's current, direct shipping plan. Are any efficiencies apparent through consolidation?

  b Aside from potentially reducing costs, how else might SPP benefit by participating in the consolidated warehouse?

  c What disadvantages might exist in a consolidated warehouse as opposed to a direct shipping situation?

2 Essen Beer Company has a brewery in Michigan's upper peninsula and is setting up distribution at Jackson, Michigan, in the state's lower peninsula.

Essen packages its beverages in barrels and in twenty-four-can cases. Barrels must be maintained at temperatures below sixty degrees Fahrenheit until retail delivery. The company's logistics department must determine whether to operate individual private warehouses for barrels and cases or to utilize a single warehouse with barrels placed in a carefully controlled environment separate from cases. Assume that cases are not to be stored or transported in refrigerated environments.

Essen experiences a weekly demand of 300 barrels and 5,000 cases. The company has arranged truckload transportation with Stipe Trucking Service. Stipe operates refrigerated and nonrefrigerated trailers, as well as multicompartmented trailers that are half refrigerated and half not. A refrigerated truckload can hold 72 barrels, while a nonrefrigerated truckload holds 400 cases. The multicompartmented trailer can hold 36 barrels and 200 cases. The costs for these services and other related expenses are detailed below:

Truckload costs	
Refrigerated	$550
Nonrefrigerated	$400
Multicompartmented	$500

Warehouse expenses	
Individual warehouses	
For case storage only:	
Capital	$1,250/week
Labor	$2,500/week
For barrel storage:	
Capital	$2,500/week
Labor	$1,600/week
Single, consolidated warehouse	
Capital	$3,500/week
Labor	$3,200/week

452

a Considering demand and all costs depicted above, does the single, consolidated warehouse or the two individual warehouses represent the least-total-cost alternative?

b Now assume that Stipe Trucking Service will provide *only* the multicompartmented trailers to serve the proposed consolidated warehouse. Which plan is the least-cost alternative in this scenario?

3 Comfy Mattresses, Inc., is opening a new plant in Orlando, Florida. Ron Lane, distribution manager, has been asked to find the lowest cost outbound logistics system. Given an annual sales volume of 24,000 mattresses, determine the costs associated with each option below:

a Build a private warehouse near the plant for $300,000. The variable cost, including warehouse maintenance and labor, is estimated at $5 per unit. Contract carrier transportation costs $12.50 per unit on average. No external transportation services are necessary for shipment of mattresses from the plant to the warehouse in this scenario. The fixed warehouse investment can be accrued evenly over ten years.

b Rent space in a public warehouse ten miles from the plant. The public warehouse requires no fixed investment but has variable costs of $8 per unit. Outbound contract carrier transportation would cost $12.50 per unit on average. The carrier also charges $5 per unit to deliver the mattresses to the warehouse from the plant.

c Contract the warehousing and transportation services to the Freeflow Logistics Company, an integrated logistics firm with a warehouse location twenty-five miles from the plant. Freeflow requires a fixed investment of $150,000 and charges $20 per unit for all services originating at the plant. The fixed investment covers a ten-year agreement with Freeflow.

d Name a few advantages aside from cost that the low-cost alternative above may have over the other alternatives.

4 Ms. Sara Ritter is the distribution manager for the Fiesta Soft Drink Company. She is considering full automation of the plant's warehouse. At present, the warehouse utilizes a mechanized system of material handling. The current system employs twenty laborers at an average wage rate of $13/hour. Laborers work an average of 2,000 hours per year. The mechanization costs $18,000 annually to main-

tain. The equipment was purchased two years ago with uniform payments of $25,000 made annually. In year nine the mechanical equipment will be replaced by new machinery with fixed annual costs of $35,000. In addition, it will cost Fiesta $12,000 per year to maintain the new equipment with the same twenty laborers.

The automated equipment would cost $1.2 million up front for implementation. Only eight laborers and an automation specialist would be required to maintain operations in the new system. The laborers would earn $16/hour over 2,000 hours each year. The automation specialist would earn a salary of $56,000 per year increasing 2 percent annually after the first year. Much of the old mechanized equipment could be sold immediately for a total of $125,000. Maintenance of the automated system is estimated at $60,000 each year with this cost growing by 3 percent annually after the first year. The automated system is expected to serve Fiesta for fifteen years.

a Examine the cash flow under each system. What is the payback period for automation?

b What advantages aside from long-term cost savings might an automated warehouse have over more labor-intensive systems?

5 Dandy Collectibles is opening a new warehouse. Bob Lee, the warehouse manager, is trying to determine the labor compensation package that most productively utilizes resources. The typical compensation plan offers an hourly wage rate of $13. Mr. Lee is also considering an incentive plan. The incentive plan rewards solely on performance with order pickers earning $0.40/unit prepared for shipping. A typical week shows the number of ordered units that must be prepared for shipping:

Monday	3,400	Thursday	3,380
Tuesday	3,625	Friday	3,670
Wednesday	3,205		

Errors sometimes happen in Dandy's order picking. Product mishandling occurs in 1 percent of the orders under the incentive plan and in 0.5 percent of the orders under the hourly wage plan. Errored orders are scrapped and result in lost revenue of $60 per occurrence. Hourly workers pick 20 units per hour. Incentive workers pick 28 units per hour. Regardless of the plan designation, employees work 40-hour weeks. Union restrictions prevent Dandy from operating on Saturday and Sunday. The labor union also restricts Dandy from hiring part-time workers. Orders need not be filled daily, but all orders must be shipped by week's end (Friday). Assume that hiring and training costs are negligible.

a How many workers are needed under each plan for the typical week's demand?

b Which plan meets the typical week's demand at the lowest cost, including lost sales resulting from errors?

6 Mitchell Beverage Company produces Cactus Juice, a popular alcoholic beverage. Recently the firm has experienced problems of product pilferage at the warehouse. In one month, 3,200 bottles of Cactus Juice, representing 0.4 percent of the month's volume, could not be located for shipping. Should the problem go unresolved, it is anticipated that it will continue at this rate. The forecasted annual sales volume for Cactus Juice is 9.6 million bottles. Each bottle sells for $4.50.

Steve Davis, vice president of distribution, has asked you to look into the following security options to reduce the pilferage problem.

a Hire four security guards to patrol the warehouse floor all hours of the day, seven days a week. The firm would offer a wage of $14.50/hour to the guards as well as a benefits package expected to be worth $2,000 per employee per year. The presence of security guards should lower pilferage to 0.2 percent of volume. Only one guard would be on duty at any one time.

b Implement an electronic detection system based on bar code technology. This would require purchasing bar code equipment for the packaging facility and warehouse. Electronic scanning devices must also be purchased and placed at warehouse entrances. Alarms sound whenever a bar-coded item passes through a warehouse entrance without clearance. The electronic detection package, including bar code printers and readers, will cost $120,000. In addition, employees at the plant and warehouse will be trained to use the new equipment at a one-time cost of $8,000. Monthly maintenance of the system is expected to cost $800. Also, a bar code specialist must be hired. The specialist would earn a salary of $49,000 per year. Product pilferage is expected to be lowered to 0.1 percent of volume with the electronic security system. The system has an estimated life of eight years.

Accrue all costs evenly over the life of the equipment.

c Install security cameras in key locations throughout the warehouse. It has been determined that six cameras could adequately record warehouse operations. Each camera costs $1,200. The support devices and installation will cost $36,000. Four security guards would be hired for the purpose of viewing the security monitors for suspicious activity. One guard would be on duty at all times. The guards each earn $12/hour, in a forty-two-hour workweek, and receive a benefits package worth $1,000 per year. Pilferage under this system would be 0.05 percent of volume. The monitoring equipment is expected to have a life of twelve years. Accrue all fixed costs evenly over the life of the equipment.

Should the firm implement any of the options above, or make no investment and allow the pilferage to continue at the rate of 0.4 percent of volume? Compare the costs and benefits of each option on an annual basis.

7 Chronotronics produces two models of clock radios, the X-100 and the X-250 deluxe. Both products are currently packaged in single-wall corrugation. Through close observation, the firm has discovered that 0.5 percent of both X-100s and X-250s are damaged between packaging and customer delivery. Chronotronics can package either model, or both, in double-wall corrugated fiberboard, which would reduce product damage by half. The current single-wall packaging costs $0.80 per unit. Double-wall packaging costs 20 percent more. The X-100 and X-250 have market values of $40 and $70, respectively. Damaged units are a total loss. Chronotronics sold 12,000 X-100s and 7,000 X-250s last year. Forecasts indicate consistent sales for the X-100 and a 5 percent increase in X-250 sales over the next year. *Note:* Round up for whole units lost.

a From a least-cost perspective, should Chronotronics utilize double-wall corrugation with the X-100 next year?

b From a least-cost perspective, should Chronotronics utilize double-wall corrugation with the X-250 next year?

c From discussion earlier in the text, how might packaging improvements affect transportation costs?

PART THREE

THREE

LOGISTICS SYSTEM DESIGN

Chapter 16   Logistics Positioning
Chapter 17   Integration Theory
Chapter 18   Planning and Design Methodology
Chapter 19   Planning and Design Techniques
   Case D   Westminster Company: A System Design
            Assessment
   Case E   Alternative Distribution Strategies
   Case F   Michigan Liquor Control Commission

LOGISTICS POSITIONING

LOGISTICS REENGINEERING
    Systems Integration
    Benchmarking
    Activity-Based Costing
    Quality Initiatives
REENGINEERING PROCEDURE
LOGISTICS ENVIRONMENTAL
    ASSESSMENT
    Industry-Competitive Assessment
    Geomarket Differentials
    Technology Assessment
    Material-Energy Assessment
    Channel Structure
    Economic-Social Projections
    Service Industry Trends
    Regulatory Posture
    Conclusion

TIME-BASED LOGISTICS
    Postponement
    Consolidation
    Operating Arrangements: Anticipatory
        versus Response-Based
    Conclusion
ALTERNATIVE LOGISTICS STRATEGIES
    Structural Separation
    Logistical Operating Arrangements
STRATEGIC INTEGRATION
LOGISTICS TIME-BASED CONTROL
    TECHNIQUES
    Supply-Driven Techniques
    Demand-Driven Techniques
SUMMARY
QUESTIONS

The key to world-class logistics is to achieve integration of both internal and external operations. Such integration requires clear identification concerning the role that logistical competency is expected to play in overall enterprise strategy. Previous chapters in Part Two developed specific functions that are integral to logistical operations. The focus of Chapter 16 is to position alternative ways that logistics can be deployed as a core competency.

First, the chapter focuses on the specifics of logistics reengineering. To be effective, such reengineering must include the development of a procedure that incorporates benchmarking, activity-based costing, and quality initiatives. Second, the chapter outlines environmental areas that a firm's management should consider when formulating a logistics strategy. Environment, as used in this chapter, includes all external factors important to a firm's management planning and implementation of a logistics strategy.

Technology has created the potential for time-based logistics, which is developed next in the chapter. Most aspects of time-based logistics shift managerial and operational emphasis from an anticipatory to response-based arrangements. Successful implementation requires development of postponement capabilities while maintaining the economics of shipment consolidation. Chapter 16 also presents the concept of structural separation as the foundation for mixing and matching echeloned and direct logistical deployment in a flexible format.

Next, the chapter combines varied aspects of previous discussions into a presentation of the constructs, descriptors, and conclusions of integrated logistics. Using a research-based model, logistics practices necessary to achieve internal and external integration are detailed. The basic conclusion is that formalization is a key to generating the flexibility needed for exploiting logistics as a core competency.

Finally, Chapter 16 develops time-based control techniques that can be mixed and matched to achieve logistical operating objectives. While specific techniques can be powerful attributes to achieving logistical excellence, the point to keep in mind is that they all represent alternative ways to enable managers to exploit logistical competency.

In total, the topics of this chapter transform the treatment of logistics from a functional to an integrated process. This chapter is the foundation for Chapters 17, 18, and 19, which represent the balance of logistical system design.

LOGISTICS REENGINEERING

The popular framework for implementing system integration principles is through a procedure referred to as process reengineering.[1] The basic idea is to identify and study the steps required to perform specific work in order to increase the likelihood of integrating performance. No rules or laws exist concerning what constitutes the ideal or even the minimal focus for a reengineering initiative. The appropriate scope is determined by management. Near identical procedures can be followed to redefine how a specific job, task, resource, functional area, or even the overall logistics competency is performed.

Four factors are common to all logistical reengineering initiatives. First, the objective is to increase integration of some or all aspects of the activities under review. The analytical foundations for integration draw on principles of systems

---

[1]For more information on process reengineering, see Michael Hammer and James Champy, *Reengineering the Corporation: A Manifesto for Business Revolution*, New York: Harper Business, 1993; and Thomas H. Davenport, *Process Innovation: Reengineering Work through Information Technology*, Boston, Mass.: Harvard Business School Press, 1993.

analysis. Second, benchmarking is a critical part of reengineering. Third, the activities under review need to be decomposed or de-averaged to achieve effective integration. Such decomposition can be achieved only by developing activity-based metrics. Finally, reengineering is continuous in the quest for quality. Each point will now be elaborated and cross-referenced.

Systems Integration

The foundation for logistics reengineering is based on the logic of systems analysis. The exact origin of systems analysis is difficult to trace since the concept is closely related to all forms of organized activity. Faced with unprecedented challenges, scientists during World War II developed an organized methodology to guide research and development of complex physical and organizational problems.[2] This approach is now commonly referred to as *system integration*. A basic understanding of the systems concept is desirable for a full appreciation of integrated logistics. Early articles describing the potential of integrated logistics relied heavily on systems analysis to overcome the shortfalls of treating logistical functions as isolated work.[3]

The systems concept stresses total integrated effort toward the accomplishment of predetermined objectives. Systems analysis is a proven methodology to view how specific functions can be combined to create a whole that is greater than the sum of the individual parts or functions. Such a ''holistic'' approach seeks to stimulate a *synergistic* relationship between the individual parts of a system for the good of the overall effort. In terms of systems methodology, functional excellence is defined as contribution to the process as contrasted to individual area performance. Until the last few decades such process thinking was foreign to managers, who had been trained to perform a specific function to the best of their ability.

When evaluated from a systems viewpoint, integrated logistics identifies a need for compromise between and among functional areas. For example, manufacturing economics is typically minimized by long production runs and low procurement costs. In contrast, logistics raises questions concerning the total cost and customer impact of such practices. The traditional financial orientation favors minimal inventories. While inventory should always be as low as practical, arbitrary reductions

---

[2]For an early discussion of the systems approach to problem solving, see Geoffrey Gordon, *System Simulation*, Englewood Cliffs, N.J.: Prentice-Hall, Inc., 1969, chap. 1 and 2; Jay W. Forrester, *Principles of Systems*, Cambridge, Mass.: Wright-Allen Press, 1969; Stanford L. Optner, *Systems Analysis*, Englewood Cliffs, N.J.: Prentice-Hall, Inc., 1960; Stanley F. Stasch, *Systems Analysis for Marketing Planning and Control*, Glenview, Ill.: Scott, Foresman and Company, 1972; Van Court Hare, Jr., *Systems Analysis: A Diagnostic Approach*, New York: Harcourt Brace Jovanovich, 1967; and Robert H. Kupperman and Harvey A. Smith, *Mathematical Foundations of Systems Analysis*, Reading, Mass.: Addison-Wesley Publishing Company, Inc., 1969.

[3]For example, see Harvey N. Shycon and Richard B. Maffei, ''Simulation: Tool for Better Distribution,'' *Harvard Business Review*, **38**:6, November–December 1960, pp. 65–75; Donald D. Parker, ''Improved Efficiency and Reduced Cost in Marketing,'' *Journal of Marketing*, **26**, April 1962, pp. 15–21; James L. Heskett, ''Ferment in Marketing's Oldest Area,'' *Journal of Maketing*, **26**, October 1962, pp. 40–45; and John F. Magee, ''The Logistics of Distribution,'' *Harvard Business Review*, **40**:4, July–August 1962, pp. 89–101.

below a level required to facilitate smooth operations will usually increase total cost. Marketing's traditional preference is to have finished goods inventory available in local markets. The fundamental paradigm of local presence is to stock inventory in anticipation of sales. Such anticipatory logistics is risky and may be in direct conflict with the most economical logistical arrangement. The basic point is that functional trade-offs must be evaluated when planning a strategic initiative. *Synergism*, wherein the interaction of functions creates superior performance, can result only from integration. Managers who are responsible for functional areas may not be properly trained to perform such integrated analysis.

When managers utilize a systems orientation, their attention is directed to the interaction of all parts of the system. These parts are referred to as *components*. Each component has a specific function to perform toward facilitating system objectives. To illustrate, consider a high-fidelity stereo system. Many components are integrated for the single purpose of sound reproduction. The speakers, transistors, amplifier, and other components exist only to assist in producing the desired sound quality. Yet, failure of any one component will cause the entire stereo system to fail.

Some principles can be stated concerning general systems architecture. First, the performance of the total system is of singular importance. Components exist and are justified only by the extent to which they enhance total system performance. For example, if the stereo system can achieve superior sound with two speakers, then it is unnecessary to include additional speakers. In other words, additional speakers are not justified because they will not enhance total system performance. Second, components do not individually require best or optimum design. Emphasis is based on the integrated relationship of all components that constitute the system. Transistors, as an example, are inside the stereo system. As such, they do not need to be aesthetically pleasing since they are hidden from view. To spend money and time designing a fashionable transistor is not necessary in terms of integration within the entire system. Third, a functional relationship, called a *trade-off*, exists between components that serve to stimulate or hinder combined performance. Suppose a trade-off exists such that a lower-quality amplifier can be used if an extra transistor is added to the system. The cost of the extra transistor must be justified in terms of savings in amplifier cost. Finally, components linked together as a combined system are expected to produce end results greater than possible through individual performance. In fact, the desired result may be unattainable without such synergy. For example, a stereo system will technically operate without speakers, but audible sound is impossible.

These principles are basic and logically consistent. It follows that a logistical system with cross-functional integration should achieve greater results than one deficient in coordinated performance. Although logical and indisputable in concept, effective application of systems integration in logistics is operationally difficult.

As noted earlier, the traditional practice of logistics has been to perform specific work on an independent basis. For example, transportation and inventory were managed by separate organizational units with little or no attention given to interrelationships. Individual goals for managing transportation and inventory can be contradictory. Transportation goals may result in larger average inventory to gain

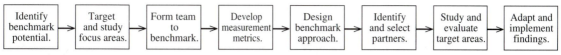

FIGURE 16-1   Common benchmarking steps.

the economic benefits of consolidated movement. On the other hand, financial goals may seek to reduce average inventory to achieve high-velocity asset turnover. Somewhere between these two dichotomous goals is the desired best practice to integrate overall performance. Isolated performance can create serious barriers to achieving operating goals of integrated logistics. In the final analysis, it matters little how much a firm spends to perform any individual activity, such as transportation, as long as overall logistical performance goals are realized at the lowest total-cost expenditure.

Improvement in information technology has increased the potential for integrated logistics performance, sparking renewed interest in process reengineering. Whereas traditional systems analysis tended to focus on broad functional integration, reengineering techniques are applicable to all aspects of logistics ranging from specific jobs to total system redesign.

Benchmarking

A critical step in process reengineering is benchmarking. The technique has gained popularity as a way to help managers gauge how well their organization performs a specific task or specialization. A formal definition of benchmarking is that it consists of a systematic procedure for identifying the best practice and modifying actual knowledge to achieve superior performance.[4]

Benchmarking is supported by two basic beliefs. First, progressive firms must seek to continuously improve all facets of their operations. Therefore, their attitude should be one of fixing or improving a work method before it breaks, as contrasted to the ''don't fix it if it ain't broke point of view.'' Second, best practice should be identified and studied, which typically means searching outside one's own enterprise. Commitment to avoiding a ''not invented here'' mentality means that a firm should unrestrictively seek to identify best overall practice wherever it may be. An industry executive recently spoke of the need to get outside the firm to avoid becoming the ''queen of the hogs.''[5]

Figure 16-1 illustrates the steps usually involved in benchmarking. It is important that managers who undertake reengineering develop approaches to incorporate benchmarking into their initiative. Specifics concerning how benchmarking fits into overall operational evaluation are discussed in Chapter 22.

---

[4]Robert C. Camp, *Benchmarking: The Search for Industry Best Practices That Lead to Superior Performance,* New York: Quality Resources, 1989.

[5]Based on a discussion with Richard L. Rankin of Ameritech Services, at the Health and Personal Care Distribution Conference on October 21, 1993, at Long Boat Key, Florida.

Activity-Based Costing

A critical aspect for improving a process is the development of meaningful metrics to measure existing practice and evaluate the relative attractiveness of alternatives. Most accounting practices generate averages that hide the true costs of performing specific activities or of providing a unique service to specified customers. The challenges of ''de-averaging'' and developing activity-based costs (ABC) that reflect true metrics are critical to reengineering. The specific challenges are detailed in Chapter 21. At this point the need to develop meaningful metrics is highlighted because of its importance to successful logistics reengineering.

Quality Initiatives

In Chapter 2, the commitment to operational quality was highlighted as a fundamental objective of integrated logistics. It is important to note that reengineering is the procedure that enables firms to improve quality on a continuous basis. Regardless of the scope of the reengineering effort, the idea of seeking continuous improvement is consistent with a total quality management philosophy.

REENGINEERING PROCEDURE

Figure 16-2 details a standard six-step procedure to guide a firm's reengineering initiative. Each step is briefly discussed.

Step 1 of reengineering is target identification. This initial step is the most important aspect of the overall reengineering procedure. It is essential to identify exactly which work is the candidate for potential change. It is equally important to identify the known range of potential improvements. While it is exciting to envision major breakthroughs in customer service or cost reduction, it must be kept in mind that quantum leaps are not necessary to justify reengineering. Small, continuous steps can aggregate to significantly improved performance.

The second step in reengineering is to fully understand the work sequence being evaluated. The traditional way to evaluate a work stream is to develop a detailed flowchart or process map of the steps required to complete the activity. This is the point in reengineering where it is essential to de-average and apply meaningful metrics. Regardless of the scope of the reengineering effort, potential improvements

FIGURE 16-2   Standard reengineering procedure. *(Adapted from Timothy R. Furey, "The Six Steps to Process Reengineering," Oxford Associates.)*

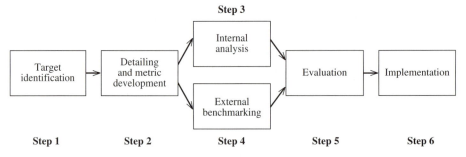

will be meaningless without the capability to ultimately measure and evaluate alternatives. In situations that require capital commitment, the metrics will need to incorporate alternative investment strategies and return-on-investment calculations.

Steps 3 and 4 of reengineering involve the creative aspect of the exercise. One approach to identifying improvement is to model the activity under consideration in an effort to identify the best possible design. Simultaneously, a firm should initiate external benchmarking to seek improved alternative approaches. The final result should be a combination of internal and external perspectives.

The fifth step of reengineering is to evaluate modifications to the activity being reviewed. Care should be taken to judge and creatively adapt ideas generated during the benchmarking exercise. The primary focus of an evaluation is the accurate assessment of expected benefits from implementation of a modified activity. While the activity under consideration may not be totally changed, it is likely that improvement will result from careful completion of the initial steps in the reengineering procedure. The key is to quantify and justify all potential changes on a cost-benefit basis.

The final step of reengineering involves implementation. Identification of a better way to perform a process falls short of having the improvement in place and working. Depending on the scope of the proposed change, it may be necessary to undertake significant testing and employee training. The appropriate rate and comprehensiveness of implementation will depend on the risk involved and the magnitude of the change that must be managed.

In conclusion, it is important to stress that reengineering in logistics is a technique that is equally applicable for all levels of potential change. The detail nature of logistical operations means that numerous opportunities exist for incremental improvement. Identifying and implementing incremental change is consistent with continuous quality improvement. The reengineering procedure is also applicable to evaluation of larger scale changes that may radically modify the traditional way that a major part or all logistics is integrated. Finally, careful reengineering can eliminate the need for performing some specific work tasks and can significantly reduce waste and duplication. The fundamental concept of process reengineering is not new and is well grounded in principles of systems analysis. The attractiveness of reengineering is its combined focus on improved information and external benchmarking, coupled with senior executive acceptance of the concept as a logical management procedure for change.

LOGISTICS ENVIRONMENTAL ASSESSMENT

An important responsibility of executives is to formulate a strategy to guide the logistics process. Just as the overall enterprise requires strategic positioning to place relative importance on various potential competencies, each area of operations requires an implementation vision. This vision is naturally referred to as the logistics strategy.

The strategy consists of a plan that details financial and human resource commitment across physical distribution, manufacturing support, and purchasing operations. The purpose of the strategic logistics plan is to provide policies and deploy facilities, equipment, and operating systems to achieve performance goals at the lowest total-cost expenditure. The plan provides guidelines concerning (1) how many, what type, and where distribution warehouses will be located; (2) what inventory assortment will be stocked at each facility; (3) the philosophy and practice of purchasing; (4) how transportation will be performed and integrated into other areas; (5) which methods of material handling will be utilized; and (6) the basic methods of order processing and so forth. The most important feature of the plan is that it specifies system design structure through which the varied aspects of logistical operations are coordinated.

A primary factor in developing a strategic logistics plan is to gain an understanding of internal and external forces that will influence performance. *The only constant in today's dynamic business environment is change.* An important input to logistical planning is to access, monitor, and evaluate environmental changes. Table 16-1 provides a summary of the types of environmental factors that should be considered and serves to illustrate their dynamic nature. The purpose of considering environmental impact when formulating logistical strategy is to assess the varied direction and rate of change in relation to planned logistical operations. External to the enterprise is a range of forces that may limit flexibility. The most common are (1) industry-competitive assessment, (2) geomarket differentials, (3) technology assessment, (4) material-energy assessment, (5) channel structure, (6) economic-social projections, (7) service industry trends, and (8) regulatory posture. These external forces combine to form the logistics strategic planning environment. For effective planning, logistical executives should be informed about trends related to these environmental factors and other industry-specific matters. This is accomplished by supporting an initiative to collect data, evaluate, and project probable direction and magnitude of change. Each force is briefly discussed to illustrate its potential impact on logistical operations.

TABLE 16-1   DYNAMICS OF ENVIRONMENTAL CHANGE

Selected environmental factor	Dominant view				
	1980	1985	1990	1995	2000
Inflation	High	Medium-low	Medium-low	Medium	Medium
Interest rates	High	Medium	Medium	Medium-low	Medium
Energy	Available at high cost	Available at medium cost	Available at medium cost	Available at medium cost	Varied projections
Population: U.S. millions	227.8	239.2	250.4	260.1	268.2
Household: U.S. millions	80.3	88.5	93	100	105.6
Transportation regulation	Deregulation: legislative	Administrative: judicial	Administrative: judicial	Antitrust: state deregulation	Varied projections
Productivity	Stabilized	Increasing	Increasing	Varied projections	Varied projections

Industry-Competitive Assessment

This assessment involves a systematic review of opportunities and potential limitations within a firm's specific industry based on such factors as market size and growth rate, profitability potential, critical success factors, off-shore competition, and labor issues. Analysis of competitive forces includes industry leadership influence and control, international competition, rivalry and confrontation, customer and supplier power, and core competencies of key competitors. A careful benchmarking study of competitors' logistical competency is important to understand the basic level of customer performance required to be an effective industry participant.

Geomarket Differentials

The logistics facility structure of an enterprise is directly related to customer and supplier location. Population density of geographical areas, traffic patterns, and projected demographic shifts all affect logistics facility location decisions. The U.S. Census Bureau indicates that six out of every ten Americans have lived in the southern or western sun belt since 1989, and while growth in these regions continues, it is estimated to be less pronounced in the 1990s than it was in the early 1980s.[6] The Census Bureau also predicts a transfer of employment and income from the industrialized North to the South and West. However, even within the sun belt, growth in specific areas is erratic and even split within specific states.

Companies ranging from Wal-Mart to McDonald's to Southland (7-Eleven Stores) must stay on top of these geomarket factors to determine which retail store locations offer the most favorable market potential. Demographic information such as age, income, and education is fundamental to identify and pinpoint specific market potential. Mapping and understanding industry demographics are essential to effective logistical planning.

Technology Assessment

Among the technology areas that influence logistical systems, the most prominent are information, transportation, material handling, and packaging. Many of these technological impacts were treated in the previous chapters when discussing how computers, satellites, scanning, bar coding, and relational databases have revolutionized logistical practice. The flow of timely and accurate information is critical to an enterprise. Integrated databases capable of tracking the movement of materials, work-in-process, and finished goods inventory are being used to improve real-time managerial control and decision support.

Soft-sided trucks, intermodal and double-stack containers, and new routing options are examples of changing transportation technologies. Robots, computer vision, mechanized storage, and an increased usage of automated-guided vehicle

---

[6]"State Population and Household Estimates: July 1, 1989," U.S. Department of Commerce, Bureau of the Census, Current Population Reports, Series P-25, No. 1058.

BAR CODES: AN INFORMATION ADVANCEMENT

Bar codes have increasingly become a part of everyday life. Not many products bought in a store or supermarket are without a bar code on the box or price tag. As such, technological advances for this popular tracking tool are continuously being tested. One of the latest advances is the two-dimensional code. A 2-D code (and possibly a 3-D code) provides the ability to capture and hold significantly more information.

The ordinary bar code holds only twenty to thirty characters per inch. The new 2-D bar codes may hold hundreds of words in an area smaller than a postage stamp. For example, a 2-D bar code could contain the information on an entire bill of lading (a document required to transport goods that lists the type and quantity of the products shipped). In essence, the bar code itself could be used as the bill of lading. Imagine being able to use a code rather than a stack of papers.

Two-dimensional bar codes can contain virtually any information and could be used in conjunction with other technologies to provide more than just paper reduction. Bar codes could be combined with EDI to provide faster, more accurate exchange of information. Suppose a company overseas is sending a shipment to the United States. The product cargo could be shipped and labeled with a 2-D bar code that held not only bill of lading information but also customs documentation and handling instructions. The 2-D bar code could simultaneously be transmitted through EDI to the customer in the United States in advance of the shipment. This advanced notification would allow the customer to prepare customs for the delivery and arrange for any special handling procedures to be in place on delivery. This provides a massive reduction in paperwork, advanced preparation for delivery, a cross-check to match the physical product as depicted by the bar code with the EDI system, and elimination of lost or damaged documentation that would cause the product to be held unnecessarily in customs.

Based on Joseph Bonney, ''Bills of Lading in Bar Code,'' *American Shipper*, August 1992, pp. 51–52.

---

systems (AGVS) are technological tools affecting material handling. Innovative developments in packaging include stronger materials, nesting returnable containers, improved pallets, and a host of key identification technologies. The need for assessment is highlighted by the fact that most of the innovations noted above were not commercially available as recently as a decade ago.

Material-Energy Assessment

The continued dependence of logistical operations on fossil-based fuels is predicted to last well into the twenty-first century. This dependency requires that management understand political dynamics and maintain a search for alternative fuels as substitutes in case of material and energy shortages. Firms must continuously assess their required resources and evaluate potential alternatives. As key resources become scarce and their prices rise or their usage is limited, owing to environmental impact, a transition to alternatives may be required. Trucking fleets are currently experimenting with alternative fuel conversions.[7] Experimentation is also occurring with battery-powered vehicles as evident by the Advanced Battery Consortium, a research endeavor started in 1991 by the United States government, General Mo-

[7]Mitchell E. MacDonald, ''What's New at the Pump?'' *Traffic Management*, **31**:2, February 1992, pp. 48–53.

tors, Ford, and Chrysler to develop technology necessary for electric vehicles. All three automakers are planning to develop and sell battery-powered vehicles by the end of the century. Further evidence of the transition to alternative fuels is found in the emergence of the Alternative Motor Fuels Act of 1988, an amendment to the Motor Vehicle Information and Cost Savings Act, which promotes research and development on methanol, ethanol, and natural gas as transportation fuels.[8] Awareness regarding the range of potential alternatives supplemented by an assessment of possible material-energy scenarios is essential for effective strategic planning. Such planning should position an enterprise to implement a transition rather than a panic reaction when change becomes economically feasible or mandated.

Channel Structure

Logistical strategies are, in part, determined by channel structure. All enterprises, regardless of size, must conduct immediate logistical operations within a defined set of business relationships. As noted in Chapter 4, supply chains consist of relationships that exist among businesses in buying and selling of products and services.[9] An enterprise must plan and accommodate changes in channel structure. In many situations managers should proactively stimulate change when logistical performance can be improved. For example, throughout industry the reduction in the number of material suppliers is a clear trend aimed at achieving improved product and delivery service.[10]

Enterprises regularly evaluate the relative advantage of distributing or buying products direct as contrasted to using the services of wholesalers. In some industries, the trend is away from wholesalers, while in others, wholesalers appear to be gaining in popularity. Pharmaceutical and health care products, for example, are increasingly handled through wholesalers, which permits faster delivery and lower inventories to be maintained by pharmacists and hospitals. The growth trend in mail order and telemarketing also has a potential major impact on traditional marketing channel structure for some retail industries. Changes in the composition of demand, structure of supply, number of channel participants, and traditional channel relationships need to be regularly monitored to maintain logistical relevancy.

Economic-Social Projections

The level of economic activity and the rate of change, as well as prevailing social attitudes and perceptions, are important to logistics. They are also difficult to predict. The slow recovery from economic decline in the early 1990s is a good

---

[8]Public Law 100–494.

[9]Donald J. Bowersox and M. Bixby Cooper, *Strategic Marketing Channel Management*, New York: McGraw-Hill, Inc., 1992.

[10]"Ford to Phase Out Almost 90 Percent of Its Suppliers," *Detroit Free Press,* October 22, 1994, p. 16a.

example of how experts can disagree concerning social-economic trends. The actual trends that materialize directly affect logistical requirements. The illustrations that follow present the interrelationship of such impacts. For example, aggregate demand for transportation is directly related to level of gross domestic product (GDP). This transportation demand is also dependent on labor cost and value of the dollar. When labor costs rise or the dollar becomes strong in relation to foreign currencies, imports increase. Interest rates, extremely volatile over the past few decades, dropped during the 1990s to the lowest level since World War II. Changes in interest rates directly influence inventory strategy. When interest rates increase, pressure to reduce inventory throughout the marketing channel increases. The desire to reduce inventory cost may, in turn, justify use of premium transportation to maintain service while enjoying an increase in inventory turn velocity.

Social trends, lifestyles, expectations, and attitudes all affect logistical requirements. Today, the potential spill of hazardous materials is a major social issue that influences public safety and jeopardizes quality of life. Monitoring public sentiment and leading economic indicators can help an enterprise avoid potentially disabling circumstances and regularly assess risk involved in existing logistical practices.

Service Industry Trends

Over the past several decades, growth in the service sector of the American economy has increasingly made it a greater part of GDP. Of particular interest to logistics are services related to transportation, warehousing, order assembly, and inventory fulfillment, plus a variety of computer-based information systems. These and other related services can be purchased from specialists when reengineering logistics system design. Logistics service providers range from relatively small local and regional firms to nationwide full-service enterprises. The option exists to outsource the performance of overall logistical requirements to a third party on a turnkey basis. The portion of the logistical dollar allocated to the acquisition of essential services from specialists continues to increase. The public warehouse industry in the United States is now twice the size of the railroad industry. From the viewpoint of logistical system design, such services have the potential to increase flexibility and reduce fixed cost. To be an astute buyer of services, it is essential that logistical managers maintain knowledge of prevailing practices and the rate of technology adoption throughout the service sector. Such a diverse supply structure places an extra burden on logistical managers to ensure that they receive competitive services and prices.

Regulatory Posture

Perhaps the most viable environmental change since the late 1970s has been in the regulatory structure of such industries as transportation, banking, and communication. Logistical managers have been confronted with a need to evaluate and predict the most likely national, state, and local government regulatory changes they will encounter. In retrospect, it is clear that some firms did a far better job than others and were better positioned to take advantage of the significant regulatory changes that occurred in transportation during the 1980s and early 1990s. The failure of other firms to plan for regulatory change was apparent on both the demand and the supply side of transportation. To illustrate, well over 100 common motor carriers have declared bankruptcy since passage of the Motor-Carrier Regulatory Reform and Modernization Act of 1980. During this same time period, other traditional carriers such as Roadway, Yellow, and UPS, as well as new firms founded during the 1980s, have enjoyed record growth and earnings.

Conclusion

In conclusion, logistics strategy is properly viewed as being developed and modified within environmental constraints. In a single planning horizon, environmental factors may be relatively constant. However, over a longer time period, economic and institutional change may render a once outstanding logistical competency inadequate. The competitive environment requires that firms modify strategy in an effort to maintain and improve performance. The enterprise that does a superior job in gaining and maintaining customer loyalty typically enjoys competitive advantage. This advantage may be rapidly eliminated if competitors gain superior insight into what is most relevant to customers.

To satisfy basic survival objectives, all parts of an enterprise must function as a total unit. This macroperception of overall integration is illustrated by Figure 16-3. Only to the extent that each part of an enterprise contributes to the total effort does that specific activity find economic justification.

Viewing an enterprise as an integrated system of goal-directed actions facilitates

FIGURE 16-3   The enterprise: a competitive environmental setting.

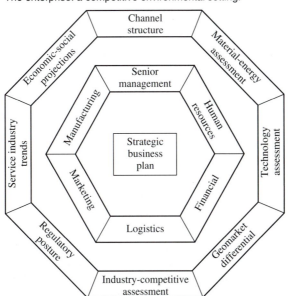

GRIDLOCK ON TOBACCO ROAD

Patrick Carrico has plenty of Marlboros, thank you. Carrico's Master Distributors Inc., a South Bend, Indiana, wholesaler, bought so many of the cigarettes at the end of last year that it didn't reorder until late February. Usually, the company restocks every 10 days. At the end of March, Master still had $1 million in excess inventory, enough to last through April.

By now, everyone knows how cheap cigarettes rode into town, took aim at the Marlboro Man, and caught him square between the eyes. Philip Morris Co. shook the consumer-brands universe when it shot back earlier this month, announcing that it would slash prices on its premium brand and boost promotional spending—forfeiting as much as $2 billion in profits. Rival RJR Nabisco Inc. reacted on April 13, eliminating the $.32 dividend it had planned to pay on new shares of its tobacco operation.

But there's more to this saga of a fallen cowboy. Some distributors and analysts contend Marlboro relied too heavily on a practice called trade loading to boost short-term revenues. The result: $200 million to $300 million in bloated inventories at many of the nation's cigarette distributors, estimates Gary Black, a tobacco analyst at Sanford C. Bernstein & Company. Some industry insiders say the figure is even higher. The sudden discounting, says Black, certainly represents the company's attempt to regain control of its market. But some observers suspect the costs also mask the losses Philip Morris would have had to take to correct a big supply miscalculation.

Philip Morris says there's no big problem. "We think our inventories are just about right," says a spokeswoman. "It's up to the wholesaler to manage their inventories. We would not encourage anybody to overstock." For years, though, tobacco companies have employed trade loading to push additional inventories into the distribution channel before a price increase. Sometimes, the strategy worked well: Distributors got a price break and manufacturers booked extra revenues at the end of a quarter. But back in 1989, R. J. Reynolds Tobacco Company took a $400 million charge when it announced it would stop the practice. And in January, Philip Morris executives admitted they had been burned, because a slowdown in consumer demand left too many cigarettes on warehouse shelves. At that point, William I. Campbell, president of its tobacco subsidiary, promised to kick the tradeloading habit for good.

But distributors say Campbell didn't quit. Of the 44 tobacco wholesalers surveyed recently by analyst Black, 58% said their Marlboro inventories were too high at the end of this year's first quarter. The same was true at the end of 1992. "People are saying they've got a ton of inventory they can't move," says Black.

How bad is the inventory backlog? Philip Morris says trade loading does happen, but the company doesn't know how much it has left in the channel. A lot, says its wholesalers. Valley Wholesalers in Winona, Minnesota, says it doesn't normally trade load much. But when Marlboro pushed cheap cigarettes this winter, it bought heavily. Multiply behavior like that by 1,000 distributors and the fallout could hit hard.

From Maria Mallory, "Gridlock on Tobacco Road," *Business Week,* April 26, 1993, pp. 36–38. Reprinted with permission.

---

maximum competitive impact. Those firms that develop superior logistical competency are strategically positioned to enjoy hard-to-duplicate competitive advantage in terms of cost and service performance.

TIME-BASED LOGISTICS

The availability of low-cost information has ushered in what is commonly referred to as the era of *time-based competition*. Managers are learning how to exploit information technology in an effort to improve both the speed and the accuracy of logistical performance. For example, logistics managers are learning to use information sharing to improve forecasting accuracy and reduce dependence on anticipatory deployment of inventory. This resource transformation is possible because managers can rapidly obtain accurate information concerning sales activity and can exercise improved operational control. The benefit of more timely and comprehensive information is the design of a logistics strategy that reduces traditional reliance on safety stock.

The time value proposition is relatively straightforward. Firms seek to perform logistics activities faster to reduce the level of financial assets required to support performance. The goal is to compress and control time from order receipt to order delivery in an effort to accelerate inventory turns. Inventory reduction is possible because the uncertainties of forecast error and delivery performance are reduced to an absolute minimum. Given discount terms and invoicing practices, it is possible for firms to sell merchandise before they legally take ownership and still qualify for prompt payment discounts. For example, terms of sale offering a discount of 2 percent net ten days mean that a 2 percent discount off the invoice total will be given to the buyer if payment is made within ten days. If the invoice is for $1,000, a payment made within ten days will result in a $20 discount, or a payment of $980 for the product. If the firm buying the product takes delivery on the first of the month and pays for the product prior to the tenth day of the month, a discount will be received. If the firm can sell the product for cash before the payment due date, it will, in effect, enjoy free inventory and may even earn interest on invested money for some number of days before payment is due. In inventory-intense situations with rapid turnover, such discounts and interest can be substantial. The sidebar illustrates how an enterprise, sensitive to time-managed performance, can significantly reduce inventory investment. Replenishment arrangements that are highly responsive to customer requirements add value and reduce cost.

Time-based logistics builds on two concepts to facilitate timely performance and reduce total cost: postponement and consolidation. Each of these concepts is discussed, followed by a contrast of anticipatory and response-based logistics arrangements. Successful time-based systems require that managers in both buying and selling organizations understand the potential of postponement and consolidation to improve logistical productivity.

Postponement

The concept of *postponement* has long been discussed in business literature.[11] However, practical examples in logistical arrangements have been publicized only

---

[11]For more information concerning postponement in logistics, see Donald J. Bowersox and M. Bixby Cooper, *Strategic Marketing Channel Management*, New York: McGraw-Hill, Inc., 1992; James H. Perry, "Emerging Economic and Technological Futures: Implications for Design and Management of Logistics Systems in the 1990's," *Journal of Business Logistics*, **12**:2, 1991, pp. 1–16; and Walter Zinn and Donald J. Bowersox, "Planning Physical Distribution with the Principle of Postponement," *Journal of Business Logistics*, **9**:2, 1988, pp. 117–136. For a historical perspective on postponement, see Wroe Alderson, "Marketing Efficiency and the Principle of Postponement," *Cost and Profit Outlook*, **3**, September 1950; Wroe Alderson, *Marketing Behavior and Executive Action*, Homewood, Ill.: Irwin, 1950; and Louis P. Bucklin, "Postponement, Speculation, and the Structure of Distribution Channels," *Journal of Marketing Research*, **2**, February 1965, pp. 26–32.

recently. Postponement offers a strategy to reduce the anticipatory risk of logistics. In traditional arrangements, most inventory movement and storage are performed in anticipation of future transactions. To the degree in which commitment to final manufacturing or distribution of a product can be postponed until receipt of a customer order, the risk associated with improper or wrong manufacturing or inventory deployment is automatically reduced or eliminated. Two types of postponement are critical to formulating a logistical strategy: manufacturing or *form* postponement, and logistical or *time* postponement.

Manufacturing Postponement   The global competitive climate of the 1990s is forcing the introduction of new manufacturing techniques designed to increase flexibility while maintaining unit cost and quality. The current challenge to long-run manufacturing logic is at least as far-reaching as Frederick Taylor's original concept of scientific management introduced in the early 1900s. However, the new flexible manufacturing logic is motivated by a desire to be much more responsive to customers.

A response-based manufacturing capability places primary emphasis on flexibility to accommodate customer requirements. The vision of manufacturing postponement is one of products being manufactured *an order at a time* with no preparatory work or component procurement until exact customer specifications are fully known and purchase commitment is received. The dream of building to order is not new. What is new is the expectation that flexible manufacturing can achieve such responsiveness without sacrificing efficiency. To the degree technology can support market-paced flexible manufacturing strategies, firms would be totally freed from depending on sales forecasts to guide anticipatory logistics.

In actual practice, manufacturing lot-size economics cannot be ignored. The challenge is to quantify cost trade-offs between procurement, manufacturing, and logistics. The nature of such analysis is developed in Chapter 17. At this point, it is sufficient to understand that the trade-off is between the cost and risk associated with anticipatory manufacturing and the loss of economy of scale resulting from the introduction of flexible procedures. Manufacturing lot sizing requires a streamlining of line setup or switchover and associated procurement expense, balanced against cost and risk associated with stockpiling finished inventory. In the traditional functional style of management, manufacturing schedules were established to realize the lowest unit cost of production. From an integrated perspective, the goal is to achieve desired customer satisfaction at the lowest total cost. This may require manufacturing postponement to facilitate overall enterprise efficiency.

The goal of manufacturing postponement is to maintain products in a neutral or noncommitted status as long as possible. The ideal application of postponement is to manufacture a standard or base product in sufficient quantities to realize economy of scale while deferring finalization of features, such as color, until customer commitments are received. Given a postponement-driven manufacturing scenario, economy of scope is introduced into the logistics equation by allowing a standard or base product to accommodate the unique needs of a wide range of different customers. One of the first commercially viable examples of manufacturing postponement was mixing paint color to individual customer request. Perfecting the in-store mixing process dramatically reduced the number of stockkeeping units required at retail paint stores. Rather than hold premixed colors, retail stores inventoried a base paint and customized the color to accommodate specific orders.

A similar manufacturing postponement application is Sunoco's system to mix gasoline octane grades at the retail pump. Under this scenario, Sunoco maintains one tank of low-octane gasoline. When a customer chooses a higher octane product, the gas is taken from the low-octane tank and additives are introduced as the gasoline is pumped to increase the octane to the level purchased. This allows Sunoco to hold one tank of inventory that can be used for all unleaded products rather than maintaining a unique tank for each product grade.

In other industries it has become common manufacturing practice to process and store product in bulk, postponing final packaging configuration until customer orders are received. In some situations products are processed and packed in ''bright cans,'' with brand labeling postponed until customer commitments are finalized. Other examples of manufacturing postponement include the increased practice of installing accessories at automobile, appliance, and motorcycle dealerships, thereby customizing products at time of purchase.

These manufacturing postponement examples have one thing in common. They reduce the number of stockkeeping units maintained in logistical inventory to support a broad-line marketing effort while helping preserve mass manufacturing economies of scale. Until the product is finalized, it has the potential to serve many different customers.

The impact of manufacturing postponement is twofold. First, the variety of differentiated products, moved in anticipation of sale, can be reduced. Therefore, the risk of logistical malfunction is lower. The second, and perhaps more important, impact is the increased use of logistical facilities and channel relationships to perform light manufacturing and final assembly. To the extent that a degree of specialized talent or highly restrictive economy of scale does not exist in manufacturing, product customization may be best delegated and performed near the customer destination market. The traditional mission of logistical warehouses in some industries has changed rapidly to accommodate manufacturing postponement. The sidebar on Calyx and Corolla provides an example.

Logistics Postponement   In many ways logistics or geographic postponement is the exact opposite of manufacturing postponement. The basic notion of *logistical postponement* is to maintain a full-line anticipatory inventory at one or a few strategic locations. Forward deployment of inventory is postponed until customer orders are received. Once the logistical process is initiated, every effort is made to move products direct to customers as rapidly as possible. Under this concept, the anticipatory nature of distribution is completely eliminated while manufacturing economy of scale is retained.

An example of logistical postponement is Sears store-direct delivery system. Utilizing rapid-order communications, the logistics for an appliance is not initiated until a customer order is received. An appliance purchased on Monday could be ready for in-home installation as early as Wednesday. The distinct possibility exists that the appliance sold on Monday was not manufactured until that night or early Tuesday.

Many applications of logistical postponement involve service supply parts. Crit-

A UNIQUE ARRANGEMENT

Imagine receiving a floral or plant arrangement from Federal Express that looks as if it was picked that morning and lasts for weeks. This situation is what Calyx and Corolla, a San Francisco–based catalog company, promises, and from the personal testimonies printed in its catalog, this is what it delivers. However, the most unique feature of the operation is that Calyx and Corolla never physically handles the flowers. Instead, Calyx and Corolla acts as the catalyst in a three-party arrangement. Catalog publishing, marketing, order entry, and administration operations are handled by Calyx and Corolla. Flower picking, arranging, and packing are primarily done by eight main growers, while delivery is performed by Federal Express. Supplemental business is handled at thirteen other growers, and United Parcel Service performs additional ground deliveries of dried flowers and bulb kits.

This three-leg arrangement, originated by Ruth M. Owades, president of Calyx and Corolla, is facilitated by information technology. It allows customer orders to be sent electronically to the growers. Pickup and delivery times are sent via fax to Federal Express. Customers place orders through an 800 number, by fax, or by mail.

Calyx and Corolla's arrangements are time-focused, allowing five to ten days to be taken out of the order cycle since inventory doesn't need to pass through its facilities. This enables flowers to be picked and arranged after a customer order is received. In this way, no anticipatory risk is taken by the grower or catalog operation. Furthermore, since the flowers are picked and shipped so soon after an order, they last days to weeks longer than arrangements delivered through traditional distribution channels. Special iced gel packs are inserted in the package by the grower to ensure freshness. Handwritten notes and cards with care instructions and information about the gift are also enclosed. A phone number for a plant doctor is available in case the recipient has any questions or concerns. Arrangements are guaranteed with replacements or monetary refunds.

The main competitors for Calyx and Corolla are wire services such as FTD, supermarkets like Kroger, as well as local or regional florists. Prices typically range from $30 to $100 for catalog arrangements, which is comparable to the competition.

Because of the uniqueness and freshness of the product, Calyx and Corolla estimates that its sales will top $13 million in 1992, which is more than three times the sales of its first full year in operation. Some of the more unique items available through the catalog are exotic flowers such as protea, various bonsai plants, European hand-cut leaded crystal vases, beautiful baskets, and wreaths. Calyx and Corolla also offers special programs including corporate gift planning and even a "year of flowers" that consists of twelve different bouquets delivered each month, ending with long-stemmed roses in December.

Delivery, limited to the United States, is available Monday through Saturday and usually has a one- to five-day window. However, delivery can be organized to occur on an exact date. Same-day delivery is even possible if orders are received by a specific time as well.

Based on Stephanie Strom, "In the Mailbox, Roses and Profits," *New York Times National Edition*, February 14, 1992, pp. C1–C4.

---

ical and high-cost parts are maintained in a central inventory to ensure availability to all potential users. When demand for a part occurs, orders are electronically transmitted to the central inventory area and shipments are made directly to the service facility using fast, reliable transportation. The end result is improved service with lower overall inventory investment.

The potential for logistical postponement has been facilitated by increased capability to process, transmit, and deliver orders with a high degree of accuracy and speed. Logistical postponement substitutes rapid order and delivery for the anticipatory deployment of inventory to local market warehouses. Unlike manufacturing postponement, systems utilizing logistical postponement maintain full manufacturing economies of scale while meeting customer service requirements using direct shipment capabilities.

In combination, manufacturing and logistics postponement offer alternative ways to refrain from anticipatory product/market commitment until customer orders are received. They both serve to reduce the anticipatory nature of business. However, the two types of postponement reduce risk in different ways. Manufacturing postponement focuses on product form by moving nondifferentiated items forward in the logistics system for modification to customer specification prior to delivery time. Logistics postponement focuses on time by stocking differentiated products at a central location and responding rapidly when a customer order is received. The centralization of inventory reduces the amount of stock required to offer high levels of availability to all market areas. The factors favoring one or the other form of postponement hinge on volume, value, competitive initiatives, economies of scale, and desired customer delivery speed and consistency. In some situations both types of postponement can be combined into a logistical strategy. Both forms represent powerful alternatives to the traditional practice of anticipatory logistics.

Consolidation

One of the major operational concerns in finalizing any logistical strategy is the retention of transportation economies associated with large-size shipments. Earlier discussion of transportation economics illustrated the importance of moving large shipments over distances that are as long as possible. Transportation, similar to manufacturing, has economy of scale that must be realized when designing operating arrangements. Freight rates typically are structured to reward shippers with discounts for large shipments. Generally speaking, the larger the shipment, the lower the freight rate per hundredweight mile.

Anticipatory logistics arrangements facilitate consolidation. In contrast, response-based arrangements, such as those created by postponement strategies, generate small shipments that move in erratic patterns. Time-based logistics tends to transpose the impact of unpredictable demand from inventory safety stock to generation of small shipment transportation requirements. To maintain transportation cost in a time-based strategy, considerable managerial attention has been directed to the development of ingenious ways to realize benefits of transportation consolidation. To plan consolidation, it is necessary to have reliable information concerning both current and planned inventory status. It is also desirable to be able to reserve or commit scheduled production for a future consolidation load. To the extent practical, consolidations should be planned prior to order processing and selection to avoid delays. All aspects of consolidation require timely and relevant information concerning planned activity.

From an operational viewpoint, there are three ways to achieve effective freight consolidation: market area, scheduled delivery, and pooled delivery. The extent to which each can be realized in day-to-day operations is critical to formulating logistical strategy.

Market Area   The most fundamental type of consolidation is to combine small shipments going to different customers in a market area. This procedure does not interrupt the natural freight flow by modifying when shipments are made. Rather, the quantity being shipped to customers in the overall market provides the consolidation basis.

The difficulty of developing either inbound or outbound market area consolidations is the availability of sufficient daily volume. To offset the volume deficiency, three consolidation arrangements are commonly used. First, consolidated shipments may be sent to an intermediate break bulk point for purposes of line-haul transportation savings. There, individual shipments are separated and forwarded to their destination. Second, firms may select to hold consolidated shipments for scheduled delivery on specific days to given destination markets. Third, firms may achieve consolidation of small shipments by utilizing the services of a third-party logistics firm to pool delivery. The last two methods require special arrangements, which are discussed in greater detail below.

Scheduled Delivery   Scheduled delivery consists of limiting shipments for specific markets to selected days each week. The scheduled delivery plan is normally communicated to customers in a way that highlights the mutual benefits of consolidation. The shipping firm commits to the customer that all orders received prior to a specified cutoff time will be guaranteed for delivery on the scheduled day.

Scheduled delivery may conflict with the trend toward customer-specified delivery appointments. Specified delivery time means that an order is expected to be delivered within a narrow time window. In today's world, a requirement to provide plus or minus one-hour delivery of a component or part may be written into the purchase contract. Carried to its ultimate, the use of rigid delivery appointments could require a logistical capability to arrange for any size shipment to be delivered at any specified time at the required customer facility. The logistical challenge is to satisfy such demanding customer service standards when they are justified while achieving, at the same time, the benefits of consolidation.

Pooled Delivery   Participation in a pooled delivery plan typically means that a freight forwarder, public warehouse, or transportation company arranges consolidation for multiple shippers serving the same market area. Firms that provide pooled consolidation services typically have standing delivery appointments with high-volume delivery destinations. It is common, under such arrangements, for the consolidation company to perform value-added services such as sorting, sequencing, or segregation of inbound freight to accommodate customer requirements.

Operating Arrangements: Anticipatory versus Response-Based

The fundamental difference in anticipatory and response-based logistical arrangements is timing. Anticipatory arrangements are traditional and reflect best practice developed during a period prior to widespread availability of information technology. In contrast, response-based arrangements reflect strategies to exploit the potential of time-based logistics.

TABLE 16-2   ANTICIPATORY AND RESPONSE-BASED VALUE CHAIN ARRANGEMENTS

Anticipatory-driven value chain	Response-driven value chain
At manufacturer	
Financial forecast	Customer-focused forecast
MRP/DRP: manufacturing-based	MRP/DRP: customer-based
Build to anticipatory inventory	Build to customer requirements
Mixed-product shipment capability from stock	Alternative shipment/special packaging
At wholesaler or chain distribution center	

Reorder point inventory strategy:
  Forecast
  Safety stock
	Requirements-based inventory strategy:
	  Shared requirements
	  Continuous replenishment

Inventory speculation:
  Stock
  Turn
  Promotional
	Inventory postponement:
	  Flow through
	  Turn
	  Promotional

Selection waves based on fixed replenishment schedule	Selection waves based on requirements
Profit center philosophy	Service center philosophy
At retailer	

Model stock:
  Reorder point
  Safety stock
	Model stock:
	  POS activity
	  Safety stock

Case lot–based	Case/inner-pack/repack-based
Scheduled replenishment	Demand–based replenishment

Financial measurement:
  Category sales
  Average turn
  Average profitability
	Performance–driven measurement:
	  Category coverage
	  Profiled turns
	  Direct product profitability performance

Table 16-2 illustrates contrasting priorities and practices that managers can be expected to employ with logistics-related activities at each stage of the supply chain. Even a casual review of the detailed paradigms illustrates the stark differences between the two operating arrangements.

Anticipatory practices were developed during a time period when business was primarily conducted on a transactional basis. Because information was not shared freely and technology was not available to facilitate such sharing, firms tended to operate on the basis of long-term forecasts. The operational goal was to build and push inventory to the next level in the channel. Because of high cost and risk associated with anticipatory practices, the prevailing relationship between trading partners was typically adversarial. Each party to the transaction needed to look out for its own self-interest.

Response-based arrangements stress cooperation and information sharing. Because of channelwide data concerning requirements, timely point-of-sale experience can now be substituted for total reliance on forecasts. When all members in a marketing channel synchronize their operations, opportunities exist to reduce total supply chain inventory and eliminate duplicate practices that increase cost without generating customer value.

The reality of today's best practice logistics is that it does not reflect the extreme of either an anticipatory or a response-based arrangement. Many well-established beliefs and practices tend to preserve conformance to anticipatory paradigms. Perhaps the greatest barrier to adopting response-based arrangements is the need for publicly held corporations to report and project quarterly earnings to financial observers and investors. This accountability factor means that financial goals must be reflected in operating plans and forecasts. Such goals often encourage promotional strategies to "load the channel" in order to create timely sales volume. The financial burden to "deload" the channel in order to create a response-based environment is never timely. This deloading occurs, for example, every year in many retail stores right after Christmas. Stores promote heavily to sell their remaining Christmas stock before the end-of-the-year inventory is counted to help reduce the expense of taking inventory and to lower inventory taxes.

A second barrier to implementing response-based operations is the fact that it is easier to manage on an adversarial, power-dominated basis than to develop and leverage cooperative relationships. Most business managers simply do not have training or experience for instituting cooperative arrangements designed to share both benefits and risks. While logistics managers report a high degree of belief in the long-term potential for response-based alliances, they report considerable frustration in how to get the job done.[12]

For the foreseeable future it appears that most firms will be simultaneously involved in various combinations of anticipatory and response-based logistical arrangements. The trend toward increased involvement in response-based relationships with specific customers and suppliers appears to be well established and will continue to expand. This need for firms to participate in a variety of different delivery arrangements has placed new performance demands on logistical strategy.

Conclusion

Few managers doubt the benefits that can result from applying time-based principles to logistical system design and operational strategy. However, a valid question is, How fast is fast enough? Speed simply for the sake of being fast has little, if any, enduring quality.[13] The fact of the matter is that time is a powerful metric that has introduced substantial innovation into best practice logistics. The answer to

---

[12]In a global logistics practice survey of the members of the Council of Logistics Management taken at Michigan State University in May 1993, it was shown that managers believed cooperative alliance relationships were an important business opportunity. However, these members also reported that their firms lacked clear guidelines and procedures to develop and maintain cooperative business arrangements. For more information on these survey findings, see Donald J. Bowersox, David J. Closs, M. Bixby Cooper, Lloyd M. Rinehart, and David J. Frayer, "Adapting to the Global Environment," *Annual Proceedings of the Council of Logistics Management,* Oak Brook, Ill., 1993, pp. 357–366.

[13]George Stalk, Jr., and Alan M. Webber, "Japan's Dark Side of Time," *Harvard Business Review,* **71**:4, July–August 1993, pp. 93–102.

how much speed is desirable must be found in the benefits that accrue to customers. The process of creating value dictates that faster, more flexible, and more precise ways of servicing customers are justified as long as they can be economically offered and result in increased customer loyalty.

ALTERNATIVE LOGISTICS STRATEGIES

The natural conclusion regarding time-based logistics is the operational realization that no single best way exists to service all customers. Individual customers require and expect suppliers to accommodate their unique requirements. Meeting and exceeding these service expectations are at the heart of creating customer success. The success equation is further complicated by the fact that performance demands of an individual customer constantly change. The specific service requirements surrounding any given shipment are subject to time, location, seasonal constraints, and a variety of other factors that constantly redefine what constitutes expected performance. Firms with world-class logistical competencies maintain flexibility to modify their performance to accommodate changing customer service requirements.

In the next section, the potential of time-based logistics is operationalized in the context of alternative logistics strategies. The capability to perform alternative logistics is rooted in structural separation. A firm must position its operating resources to structurally achieve economy of scale while maintaining flexibility. The following presentation discusses structural separation and flexible logistical operating arrangements.

Structural Separation

Logistical operations can be specialized by designing unique channel relationships and structures. The term *structure* is used to describe business relationships for performing work required to complete the logistical process. Careful analysis and classification of such work provide the basis for logistical specialization.

Over the years, several different authors have developed the idea of work separation within the overall structure of the distribution channel.[14] The most common approach to separation focuses on isolating efforts related to ownership transfer and logistical compliance. While these primary work flows must be coordinated, there is no reason why they need to be performed by the same channel specialists or at the same time.

The support for structural separation is that typical channel arrangements are not normally ideal to accomplish both marketing and logistics performance. One

---

[14]A number of authors have developed the flow concept. Contributions of noteworthy mention in the authors' opinion included Roland Vaile, E. T. Grether, and Reavis Cox, *Marketing in the American Economy*, New York: Ronald Press, 1952; Ralph F. Breyer, "Some Observations on Structural Formation and Growth of Marketing Channels," in *Theory in Marketing*, eds. Reavis Cox, Wroe Alderson, and Stanley J. Shapiro, Homewood, Ill.: Richard D. Irwin, Inc., 1964, pp. 163–175; George Fisk, *Marketing Systems,* New York: Harper & Row, 1967, pp. 214–279; Louis P. Bucklin, "Postponement, Speculation and the Structure of Distribution Channels," *Journal of Marketing Research*, **2**, February 1965, pp. 26–31; and Louis W. Stern and Adel I. El-Ansary, *Marketing Channels,* Englewood Cliffs, N.J.: Prentice-Hall, Inc., 1977, pp. 391–430.

channel arrangement may be more effective for generating marketing transactions, whereas another structure might be more efficient for logistics. Factors that tend to increase or decrease the total cost of logistics are often contradictory to those that improve or hinder marketing performance. Advertising, promotions, credit, personal selling, and other transaction-creating elements of marketing have a significant influence on logistical requirements and vice versa. The opportunity of marketing and logistics to both benefit from specialization can be facilitated by channel structural separation.

A marketing channel consists of firms engaged in the buying and selling of transactions. The goal of marketing is to negotiate, contract, and administer transactions on a continuing basis. The full force of creative promotion occurs within the marketing structure. Participants in the marketing channel are transaction specialists, such as manufacturing agents, salespeople, jobbers, wholesalers, and retailers.

The logistics channel represents a network of working relationships specializing in achieving inventory movement and positioning. The work of logistics involves transportation, inventory storage, material handling, and order processing, plus an increasing variety of value-added services. Those involved in the logistics process are concerned with resolving time and space requirements.

When one channel participant, such as a dealer, performs both marketing and logistics work, the arrangement is referred to as a single-structure system. The use of a single structure to perform the essential work of both marketing and logistics ignores the possibility that a very effective partner in one area of expertise may not be the best choice for or even be capable of performing other essential requirements. Successful marketing of a product assortment may require specialized channels to operate and complete transactions in unique market segments. For example, grocery products are marketed, in addition to supermarkets, through convenience stores, club stores, mass merchandisers, drugstores, and a variety of other outlets, all of which have unique requirements. It is also typical to sell industrial products and components through multiple channels. Using the same multiple or fragmented channels to perform logistics could result in inadequate performance. At the very least, forcing the marketing structure on logistical operations could result in small, uneconomical shipments that negate substantial economies of scale otherwise possible from specialization.

Separation in Practice   Figure 16-4 illustrates structural separation. In this situation, the marketing channel consists of five levels: general sales office, district sales office, distributor, retailer, and consumer. The logistical channel consists of seven levels: factory warehouse, company truck, regional warehouse, motor common carrier, public warehouse, local delivery, and customer. The two channels converge only at the customer level.

Figure 16-4 illustrates several important points. First, three levels of logistical work are performed by managerial units of the manufacturing enterprise. The logistical work begins when product is warehoused at the factory. Next, product is transported in company trucks to the point where it is finally stored in a regional warehouse. Second, once product is positioned at the regional warehouse, logistics

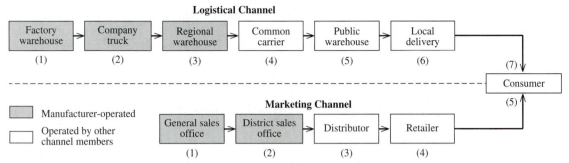

FIGURE 16-4   Distribution channel: logistical and marketing separation.

specialists perform the necessary work. In the logistical structure, three specialists exist: a common carrier trucking company, a public warehouse, and a specialized local delivery firm. How these specialists operate will be discussed in conjunction with the presentation on marketing structure.

In this example, the manufacturer operates the first two levels within the marketing channel. The operational objective of the manufacturer is to sell finished product to consumers. The general sales office works with district sales offices to facilitate the exchange of finished product. Each district sales office forecasts expected sales. Products that are forecasted to be sold are then shipped in advance of demand (anticipatory) to the regional warehouse that services the district.

Each district sales office attempts to sell product to distributors. They, in turn, seek commitments from retailers. The distributor takes legal title to the product from the manufacturer upon sale. In this marketing arrangement the distributor performs a unique role, because while it never physically has possession of the product, it has legal title until the product is delivered to the consumer. In this example, the distributor selected to use a public warehouse instead of establishing a private warehouse facility.

The retailer is another of the marketing specialists involved in selling the product. The retailer displays a limited number of products and offers next-day delivery to consumers. Stock is limited to display units and minimal backup inventory. Products on display at the retailer's store are often on consignment from the distributor. Consumer sales typically include a promise to deliver a specified model, color, or style of the product to a designated location at a particular time. Although the transaction is initiated at a retail store, logistical support is usually provided by direct shipment to a customer's residence from the public warehouse, which may be located a significant distance away. Typically, the delivery is made using the distributor's stock held in the public warehouse and the services of a specialized local delivery firm.

Structural separation, as illustrated, reflects common practice in a wide variety of industries such as furniture, appliances, and television sets. These businesses offer products with a variety of options, models, and colors. As such, it would be difficult for a retailer to stock the full range of products. Instead, as stated previously, the retailer limits inventory commitment to display items, keeping color swatches and option books on hand for customer demonstration. The benefits of logistical specialization result in low-cost delivery and effective marketing.

An additional example of separation is a factory branch sales office that carries no inventory. The office exists for the sole purpose of stimulating ownership transactions. The physical product exchange between seller and buyer may logistically move in a variety of combinations of transport and storage, depending on value, size, bulk, weight, and perishability of the shipment. Generally, no economic justification exists for locating warehouses and inventories at the same site as the branch offices. The network of branch sales offices is best designed to facilitate maximum marketing impact. The logistical structure should be designed to accomplish the required delivery performance and economies.

A final example of separation comes from the rapidly growing home shopping industry. An order placed by phone or at a local catalog desk is typically shipped from a factory or distribution warehouse directly to the buyer's home. All direct marketing systems exploit separation to realize specialization benefits.

Interdependence Marketing and Logistics   The separation of marketing and logistics in terms of how they contribute to the process of creating customer value should not be interpreted to mean that either can stand alone. Both are essential to create customer value. The major argument favoring operational separation is increased opportunity for specialization.

Structural separation does not necessarily require outsourcing work to specialized service firms. A single firm may be able to internally satisfy all marketing and logistical requirements. The desired degree of operational separation depends on available service providers, economies of scale, available resources, and managerial capabilities. The benefits of separation are independent of combining internal organization units with outside specialists. From an ownership transfer viewpoint, the customer value creation process is not complete until logistical promises are fully performed. Depending on the products involved, the logistical operations may start in anticipation of, be simultaneous with, or follow transactional negotiation. Logistical performance with respect to time, location, and terms of delivery must comply to specifications established during such negotiation.

Logistical Operating Arrangements

The potential for logistical services to favorably impact customers is directly related to operating system design. The many facets of logistical performance make channel design a complex task. The selection of a basic system design offering an acceptable balance of performance, cost, and flexibility should be the first priority. When one considers the variety of logistical systems used throughout the world to service widely diverse markets, it is astonishing that any structural similarity exists. However, all logistical arrangements have two common characteristics. First, they are designed to facilitate inventory management. The focal asset of logistics is inventory. The risks involved are directly related to inventory positioning and velocity. Second, alternative systems are designed around the prevailing level of technology adopted within logistical functional areas. These two determinants of logistical structure result in somewhat common operating arrangements. Three widely utilized structures are echelon, direct, and flexible.

Echelon Structure   Classification of a logistical system as having an echeloned structure means that the flow of products typically proceeds through a common arrangement of firms and facilities as it moves from origin to final destination. The use of echelons usually implies that total-cost analysis justifies stocking some amount of inventory at each consecutive level of the supply chain.

Typical echelon systems utilize break bulk and consolidation warehouses. A break bulk facility usually receives large-volume shipments from a variety of suppliers. The resultant inventory is sorted in anticipation of customer requirements. Food distribution centers operated by major grocery chains and wholesalers are examples of break bulk warehouses. Consolidation warehouses operate in a reverse manner. Consolidation is typically required by manufacturing firms that have plants at different geographical locations. Consolidation in a central warehouse facility of products manufactured at different plants permits shipment of assortments to customers. The inventory consolidation in a single warehouse allows firms to offer customers mixed shipments of all products in a single delivery with one invoice. Major consumer product firms are prime examples of enterprises using echeloned systems to consolidate items. Manufacturing operations often use warehouses or industrial suppliers to perform inbound consolidation of components and subassembly.

Echelon systems utilize warehouses to create inventory assortments and achieve consolidation economies associated with large-volume transportation shipments. Inventories positioned in warehouses are available for rapid deployment in accordance with customer requirements. Figure 16-5 illustrates the typical echeloned value chain.

Direct Systems   In contrast, direct systems are logistical arrangements designed to ship products direct to the customer's destination from one or a limited number of centrally located inventories. Direct systems typically do not enjoy the potential consolidated volume necessary to support an echeloned structure.

Direct distribution typically uses premium transport combined with information technology to rapidly process customer orders and achieve delivery performance. This combination of capabilities, designed into the order delivery cycle, reduces time delays and overcomes geographical separation from customers. Examples of direct shipments are plant to customer truckload deliveries, direct store deliveries, and various forms of direct deliveries to consumers who utilize catalog and in-home shopping. A direct logistical structure is commonly used for inbound com-

FIGURE 16-5   Echeloned structured logistics.

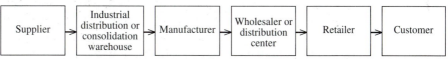

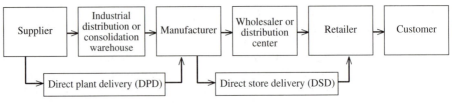

FIGURE 16-6   Echeloned and direct structured logistics.

ponents and materials at manufacturing plants because the average shipment size is large.

When the economics justify, logistics executives tend to desire direct alternatives because they reduce anticipatory inventories and intermediate product handling. The potential for direct systems is limited by high transportation cost and possible loss of control. However, the latter situation has dramatically improved as a result of advances in information technology. In general, most firms do not operate the number of warehouses today that were common a few years ago and have been able to modify echelon structures to include direct systems. Figure 16-6 illustrates direct logistics capability added to an echeloned logistics structure.

Flexible Systems   The ideal logistical arrangement is a situation wherein the inherent benefits of echeloned and direct structures are combined into a flexible logistics system. As noted earlier, anticipatory commitment of inventory should be postponed as long as possible. Inventory positioning strategies can place fast-moving products or materials in forward warehouses, while other more risky or costly items can be stocked at a central location for direct distribution to customers. The basic service commitment and the order size economics should determine the most desirable and economical structure to service a specific customer.

To illustrate, automobile manufacturers typically distribute replacement parts utilizing a flexible logistics strategy. Specific parts are inventoried in warehouses located at various distances from dealers and retail outlets in accordance with the pattern and intensity of demand. As a general rule, the slower the part turnover, the more erratic the demand and therefore the larger the incentive to use a centralized inventory. The slowest or least demanded parts are usually stocked at one location that services customers throughout the entire world. Fast-moving parts that have more predictable demand are stocked in forward warehouses close to dealers in order to facilitate fast delivery.

A contrasting example is an enterprise that sells machine parts to industrial firms. The nature of this business supports a completely opposite flexible distribution strategy. In order to offer superior service to customers that experience machine failure and unexpected downtime, the firm stocks slow movers in all local warehouses. In contrast to the automotive firm, high-demand, fast turnover parts in this industry can be accurately forecasted because of routine preventive maintenance. The least-cost logistical method for the fast movers is to ship direct from a warehouse located adjacent to the parts manufacturing plant.

These alternative logistics strategies, both of which use different flexible capabilities, are justified because of unique customer requirements and intensity of competition. The automotive manufacturer is the sole supplier of parts during the new-car warranty period and must provide dealers rapid delivery to promptly repair customer cars. Dealers require fast replenishment of parts inventory in order to satisfy customers while minimizing inventory investment. As cars grow older and the demand for replacement parts increases, alternative manufacturers enter the replacement parts market. During this highly competitive stage of the model's life cycle, rapid logistical response is required to be competitive. As a model ages, competition drops out of the shrinking market, leaving the original manufacturer as the sole supplier.

The industrial component supplier, in contrast to the automotive company, offers standard machine parts having a high degree of competitive substitutability. Whereas products used on a regular basis can be forecasted, this is not possible for those with slow or erratic demand. Such a situation forces customers to measure suppliers in terms of how fast unexpected machine breakdowns can be remedied. Failure to perform to the level of customer expectation can open the door for a competitor to prove its capability.

Each enterprise faces a unique customer situation and utilizes a different flexible logistics strategy to achieve competitive superiority. The channel strategy that satisfies customer expectations at the lowest attainable total cost typically utilizes a combination of echeloned and direct capabilities.

Beyond the basic channel structure, flexible capabilities can be designed into a logistical system by developing a program to service customers using alternative facilities. This aspect of flexibility can be justified on an emergency or routine basis.

Emergency Flexible Structure Emergency flexible operations represent contingencies to resolve failures in planned logistical performance. A typical emergency occurs when an assigned shipping facility is out of stock or for some other reason cannot ship a customer's order. For example, a warehouse may be out of an item with no replenishment inventory scheduled to arrive until after the customer's specified delivery date. To avoid the use of back-orders or item cancellation, an operating policy could specify that the total order, or at least those items not available, be shipped from an alternative warehouse. The use of emergency flexible operation procedures is usually based on the importance of the specific customer or the critical nature of the product being ordered.

Use of an alternative shipping location typically increases logistical expense. The customer will receive the previously promised service but at an increased cost to the supplier. This service commitment and increased expense must be justified by customer contribution margin. Conceptually, a firm can afford to perform emergency logistical solutions that involve excessive cost up to the last penny of gross margin contribution for each customer.

Routine Flexible Structure A flexible logistics capability gaining popularity involves backup procedures that are part of the basic logistical system design for serving specified customers. The flexible logistics rules and decision scenarios—concerning alternative ways to service the customer, which facility to ship from, and under what circumstances to follow which procedures—are preestablished. A strategy that exploits routine flexible operations is typically justified in at least four different situations.

First, the customer-specified delivery location may be near a point of equal cost or time for delivery from two different logistics service facilities. Customers located at such points of indifference offer the supplying firm an opportunity to fully utilize available logistical capacity. Orders can be serviced from whichever facility has the best inventory positioning to satisfy customer requirements and the available work capacity to achieve timely delivery. This form of flexible logistics offers a way to fully utilize system capacity by balancing workloads between facilities while protecting superior customer service commitments. The benefit is an operating efficiency that is transparent to the customer.

A second situation justifying routine flexible distribution is when the size of a customer's order creates an opportunity to improve logistical efficiency if serviced through an alternative channel arrangement. For example, the lowest-total-cost method to provide small shipment delivery may be through a distributor. In contrast, larger shipments may have the lowest total logistical cost when shipped factory direct to customers. Provided that alternative methods of shipment meet customer service expectations, total logistical cost may be reduced by implementing routine flexible policies.

A third type of situation often results from a selective inventory stocking strategy. The cost and risk associated with stocking inventory require careful analysis to determine which items to place in each warehouse. With replacement parts, a common strategy, as mentioned earlier, is to stock selected items in specific warehouses, with the total product line stocked only at a central facility. In general merchandise retailing, a store or distribution center located in a small community may stock only a limited or restricted version of a firm's total line. When customers desire nonstocked items, orders are accepted for promised delivery at a future time. Such customer shipments are often made from a larger store or a central warehouse. The term *mother facility* is often used to describe inventory strategies that designate larger warehouses for backup support of smaller restricted facilities. Selective inventory stocking by echelon level is a common practice used to reduce inventory risk. Systems that utilize multiecheloned inventory strategies normally cannot justify full-line stocking at all warehouses. The reasons for selective echelon stocking range from low product profit contribution to high per unit cost of inventory maintenance. One way to operationalize a fine-line inventory classification strategy is to differentiate stocking policy by system echelons. In situations following such classified stocking strategies, it may be necessary to obtain customer advanced approval for split order delivery. However, in some situations, firms that use differentiated inventory stocking strategies are able to reconfigure customer orders for same-time delivery, thereby making the arrangement transparent.

The fourth type of routine flexible operation results from agreements between firms to move selected shipments outside the established echeloned or direct logistics system. Two special arrangements gaining popularity are flow through cross docks and third-party consolidation. These procedures were previously discussed in the chapters on management and material handling, so they are only briefly referenced here.

The flow through cross-dock arrangement is typically deployed in situations where storage and material handling can be avoided. A cross-dock operation involves

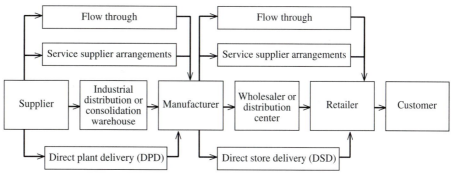

FIGURE 16-7   Complex alternative logistics structure.

multiple suppliers arriving at a designated time at the handling facility. Inventory receipts are sorted across the dock and consolidated into outbound trailers for direct destination delivery. Cross-dock operations are growing in popularity in the food industry for building store-specific assortments and are common methods of continuous inventory replenishment for mass merchandising and club stores.

Another form of specialized service is to use a third-party logistics company to assemble products for consolidated delivery. This is similar to consolidation for transportation purposes discussed earlier in the chapter. However, for this form of flexible logistics, specialists are used to avoid storage and handling of slow-moving products through the main stream of the echeloned logistics structure. Figure 16-7 adds the elements of flexibility to the logistical operating structures previously illustrated.

A prerequisite to effective flexible operations is the adoption of information technology to monitor inventory status throughout the network and to introduce the capability of rapidly switching customer orders within the logistical system. The use of flexible operations for emergency accommodation has a well-established track record. The development of routine flexible arrangements as an integral part of day-to-day logistical operations is relatively new and rapidly growing. To a significant degree, an effective, flexible logistics strategy can substitute for the safety stock maintained in a traditional anticipatory system.

The attractiveness of specialized service providers is directly related to the flexibility of a firm's logistics strategy. If a firm selects to offer direct distribution, the services of highly reliable, fast carriers are typically required. An echelon structure means that opportunities may exist for volume-oriented carriers and firms that specialize in operating cross-docking facilities. A strategy that seeks the combined benefits of echeloned and direct logistics may be an ideal candidate for the integrated services of a contract logistics specialist. It is important to keep in mind that the selected logistics strategy directly affects channel structure and relationships. To a significant degree, information technology is forcing firms to reconsider long-standing paradigms regarding rigid ways of conducting business. These developments can be illustrated by an examination of managerial practices required to achieve internal and external integration of logistical operations.

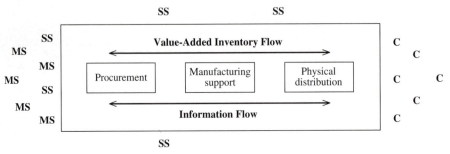

FIGURE 16-8   Basic value chain.

STRATEGIC INTEGRATION

For a firm to effectively exploit logistical competency, a wide variety of operational factors must be synchronized into an integrated strategy. At this point, these factors can be integrated using the supply chain structure originally discussed in Chapter 4. Figure 16-8 reproduces the basic value chain chart with the addition of a set of symbols representing customers (C), material suppliers (MS), and service suppliers (SS). These independent businesses represent the varied constituencies that a firm must accommodate in order to survive. To succeed in the long run, a firm must be able to achieve sufficient internal and external integration to satisfy fundamental business objectives.

As noted earlier in this chapter, the challenge to positioning logistics as a key competency is to develop programs with suppliers and customers that leverage internal integration of logistical resources. The combined effort of the firm and its preferred material and service suppliers must, in turn, be focused on creation of value for selected customers.

Developing logistics as a core competency can be operationalized for a value chain by incorporating flexible best practices. Figure 16-9 illustrates a value chain that has congealed into a formalized set of relationships that are orchestrated on an interorganizational basis. To fully leverage logistics, the power of external integration must be incorporated into a best practice model. In terms of overall performance, the boundary spanning an extended organization needs to incorporate and facilitate the core competencies of business partners. External integration is critical to enhance supply chain performance, because the activities of logistics

FIGURE 16-9   Integrated enterprise value chain.

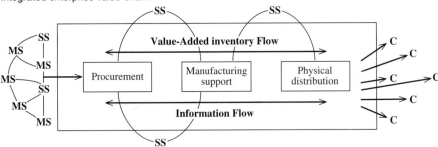

function not only within but also between firms. To truly embrace the full benefit of integration, firms must manage across traditional organizational and ownership boundaries to coordinate the entire supply chain as inventory moves through the value-added process. This integration is often facilitated by forging a combination of information linkages and by human resource sharing. Both are illustrated by the Bose Corporation sidebar.

Starting from the perspective of customer value creation, the chain is envisioned as a series of unique relationships that are integrated with specific customers and suppliers. Each vector constitutes a partnership that highlights those performance factors perceived as important. Naturally, a firm cannot focus operations to meet the unique needs of all customers, but it must accommodate the requirements of those targeted as high-value or high-potential relationships. Less attractive customers in terms of profit contribution can receive basic high-level service in a standardized format. The end result of integrated logistics is a series of synchronized capabilities that implement time-based principles in a resource efficient format based on customer-focused requirements.

Integration with material and service suppliers is important to gain the full leverage of an extended enterprise. Figure 16-9 illustrates the integration of suppliers into procurement and manufacturing performance cycles. The key objective of these relationships is to leverage the combined logistical resources of suppliers to achieve maximum synergy. Next, the chapter reviews time-based tools available to help managers orchestrate logistical operations.

LOGISTICS TIME-BASED CONTROL TECHNIQUES

To effectively implement time-based logistics in a flexible framework, a manager needs to draw on a variety of different control techniques. Each technique has unique characteristics and capabilities that render it the approach of choice, depending on the operational situation confronted. For purposes of discussion, the techniques are classified as either supply- or demand-driven. This classification does not limit or restrict the applicability of a specific control approach.

Supply-Driven Techniques

Two types of supply-driven control techniques are just-in-time (JIT) and requirements planning (RP). These techniques are designed to coordinate the arrival of exact inventory requirements to satisfy a planned event. The most common applications are to fulfill material and component requirements of production schedules. Therefore, most applications are dependent demand situations.[15] As will be noted later, a variation of requirements planning (DRP) is being successfully used to program inventory flow in integrated supply chain arrangements such as efficient consumer response.

---

[15]The term *dependent demand* is used to illustrate that demand for material and component requirements in a time-based environment is dependent on demand for finished goods. In other words, the amount of materials and components going into a production facility *depends* on the amount of finished products expected to come out of that facility.

PROCESS INTEGRATION AT BOSE

Bose Corporation, the largest manufacturer of hi-fi audio systems, has a unique way to ensure process integration between its inbound supply chain. This integration is accomplished by creating a new customer/supplier relationship that goes well beyond traditional adversarial arrangements.

At Bose, a representative from a supplier, such as G & F Industries, acts as an in-plant. Basically, this in-plant has an office at G & F Industries where official employment occurs, as well as an office at Bose. The in-plant visits both facilities daily to provide an integrative position to span both organizations. The in-plant works at Bose with manufacturing to perform proactive planning and production scheduling and places purchasing orders for G & F Industries in Bose's system. The in-plant knows both businesses intimately to perform the day-to-day necessary operations.

This arrangement allows the in-plant to view the entire supply process as a total system. This means that the in-plant has access to people, customer data, and other processes to effectively manage the relationship.

Here, no traditional buyer and sales representative exist. The in-plant acts as both. Also, the in-plant is involved early in the design process to suggest improvements or provide inside knowledge to decrease the time it takes to bring a new product to market. In a more traditional buyer/supplier role, the sales representative would worry about how to manufacture a single part or component, but in this arrangement, an in-plant worries with Bose about how to manufacture the entire hi-fi system.

The benefit to suppliers is a long-term contract with no yearly bidding on price. Also, because the in-plant places orders for the company, the supplier knows actual production requirements, so no forecast is generated. Both companies benefit from reduced cost by eliminating duplicate effort. The overall inbound system is more efficient as well since the entire process is managed by in-plants rather than managing separate activities without the necessary integration.

Based on a video produced by Bose Corporation entitled JIT-II®.

Just-in-Time Strategy   The initial popular approach to time-based logistics was established by the Japanese in the 1950s when the Toyota Motor Company introduced a system known as kanban.[16] The popular appeal of JIT was the potential elimination of work-in-process inventories by restricting procurement and component manufacturing to the exact quantities required to complete the assembly production schedule. The initial JIT applications focused on moving materials and components in the exact quantity, at the exact time, to where they were required. The key to JIT manufacturing operations is that demand for components and materials depends on the finalized production schedule. Requirements can be determined by focusing on the ''lead'' or primary product being manufactured. Once the production schedule is established, just-in-time arrival of components and materials can be planned to coincide with production requirements, resulting in reduced handling and minimal carryover inventory. To achieve this goal in the original JIT applications, a combination of requisition and production cards, called sign boards, was utilized to control material flow and authorize component manufacturing. From a logical viewpoint, JIT is very similar to a two-bin inventory control logic for production without any restriction regarding minimum lot size.

[16]See Richard J. Shonberger, *Japanese Manufacturing Techniques*, New York: Macmillan Free Press, 1982; George C. Jackson, ''Just in Time Production: Implications for Logistics Managers,'' *Journal of Business Logistics*, **4**:2, 1983; and Richard J. Ackonberger, *Japanese Manufacturing Techniques, Nine Hidden Lessons in Simplicity*, New York: The Free Press, 1982.

The implicit assumption is that everything manufactured is in direct and timely response to market need.

The natural expansion of the original JIT concept incorporated advanced production technology. Advanced JIT is a focused manufacturing logic that seeks to implement *zero inventory* or *stockless production*.[17] As noted earlier, manufacturing culture and technology are changing to accommodate maximum flexibility. As such, advanced JIT now embraces a variety of manufacturing concepts such as reduced lot sizes, quick switchover, load leveling, group technology, statistical process control, preventive maintenance, and quality circles. These techniques are applicable to both made-to-stock and the variety of assemble and made-to-order manufacturing processes.

A recently introduced extension of JIT is often referred to as JIT-II. The objective of JIT-II was to work out ways to incorporate human resource expertise into the planning and coordination process. The idea is that joint participation in planning and execution of material requirements can facilitate overall operations by giving early warning of potential disruptions. In part, enhancements to basic JIT concepts occurred because of a general disappointment among American firms in the results realized from attempting to duplicate Japanese successes. Significant United States companies—such as Federal-Mogul, General Motors, Whirlpool, General Electric, and Corning—have turned to other ways of efficiently meeting supply requirements. One such alternative involves more comprehensive planning techniques, which are discussed next.

Requirements Planning   The most popular comprehensive requirements planning techniques are materials/manufacturing requirements planning (MRP) and distribution requirements/resource planning (DRP). These were discussed and illustrated in Chapter 9, which dealt with managing inventory resources. Applications referred to as MRP are typically applied to inbound materials movements. DRP applications are used to plan forward allocation of finished inventory in the distribution channel. More advanced applications of DRP seek to link the process of planning finished goods allocation to warehouse network requirements, master manufacturing schedules, and point-of-sale inventory requirements. When DRP is applied to replenishment planning for the total channel, its application is very close to a demand-driven technique.[18] However, the distribution operating environment is different. The relationship between manufacturing and customers does not have the stability of a production schedule. Retailers and wholesalers order merchandise on the basis of customer purchases.

Demand-Driven Techniques

The application of demand-driven techniques is most appropriate in situations where requirements are independent. In other words, techniques that are positioned

---

[17]Yasukiro Monden, ''Adaptable Kanban Systems Help Toyota Maintain Just-in-Time Productions,'' *Industrial Engineering*, May 1981, pp. 29–45; and Kazuo Higashi, ''A Zero-Inventory Manufacturing Approach,'' Unpublished Paper, Michigan State University, 1980.

[18]Here, demand is independent in that it is guided by consumers. In other words, it is not dependent on factors within the firm's control.

to provide maximum response to whatever occurs in the marketplace are classified as demand-driven. Four such techniques are used for response-based logistics: rules-based reorder (ROP), quick response (QR), continuous replenishment (CR), and automatic replenishment (AR). Each is briefly described and illustrated.

Rules-Based Reorder (ROP)   Reorder point logic is among the oldest techniques for managing inventories using statistical probability. The ROP technique and its application to plan safety stocks to accommodate variability in demand and lead time were discussed in Chapter 8.

Original application of ROP techniques relied heavily on forecast accuracy. Because forecasting success was minimal, little confidence or enthusiasm developed around ROP as a way to manage inventory. Consequently, when the supply-driven techniques discussed earlier became available, ROP was widely discarded as an effective means of control. Its rebirth was stimulated by advancements in information technology that permitted accumulation of accurate point-of-sale (POS) information and elimination of substantial variability in the performance cycle. Whereas ROP was originally used primarily in anticipatory inventory applications, most response systems use a variation of reorder logic to guide inventory replenishment from forward stocking locations.

QR, CR, and AR   These response-based control techniques are all variations on a theme that concentrates on rapidly replenishing forward inventories according to sales experience. Because of their similarity, the techniques are discussed as a group, highlighting their differences.

To accommodate the ''independent'' nature of customer demand, world-class logistics organizations are perfecting time-based strategies. Major retailers such as Wal-Mart and Target have been leaders in the application of these systems. The objective of time-based strategies is to reduce inventory for the total supply chain. Each variation is discussed.

Quick response (QR) is a cooperative effort between retailers and suppliers to improve inventory velocity while providing merchandise supply closely matched to consumer buying patterns. QR is implemented by monitoring retail sales for specific products and sharing information across the supply chain to guarantee that the right product assortment will be available when and where it is required. Information sharing facilitates the QR process between retailers and manufacturers. For example, instead of operating on fifteen- to thirty-day order cycles, a QR arrangement can replenish retail inventories in six or fewer days. Continuous information exchange regarding availability and delivery reduces uncertainty for the total supply chain and creates the opportunity for maximum flexibility. With fast, dependable order response, inventory can be committed as required, resulting in increased turnover and improved availability.

The following example illustrates how a typical QR arrangement works. Orders from retailers are sent to manufacturers via EDI. The manufacturer then plans the most effective and efficient way to satisfy requirements. Specifics regarding the replenishment shipment are communicated to the retailer ahead of product arrival so that labor and deliveries can be scheduled. This closed loop or engineered performance arrangement reduces uncertainty, total cost, and inventory assets and typically improves service performance. Such response is as simple as using technology to perform age-old activities faster and more precisely.

A *continuous replenishment* (CR) strategy, sometimes called vendor managed inventory, is a modification of QR that eliminates the need for replenishment orders. The CR goal is to establish a supply chain arrangement so flexible and efficient that retail inventory is continuously replenished. By receiving daily transmission of retail sales or warehouse shipments, the supplier assumes responsibility for replenishing retail inventory in the required quantities, colors, sizes, and styles. In essence, the customer agrees to honor replenishment of retail sales or warehouse shipments as a purchase commitment. The supplier commits to keeping the retailer in stock and to maintaining inventory velocity. In some situations, replenishment involves cross docking or direct store delivery (DSD) designed to eliminate the need for warehousing between the factory and retail store. There are two basic requirements for CR to operate efficiently. First, there must be an effective means of communicating requirements and advanced ship notification between manufacturer and retailer. Second, sales volume must be sufficiently large to maintain transport scale economies.

Some manufacturers, wholesalers, and retailers are experimenting with an even more sophisticated sharing of replenishment responsibility known as automatic or profile replenishment (AR). The AR strategy extends QR and CR by giving suppliers the right to anticipate future requirements according to their overall knowledge of a merchandise category. A category profile details the combination of sizes, colors, and associated products that usually sell in a particular type of retail outlet. Given AR responsibility, the supplier can simplify retailer involvement by eliminating the need to track unit sales and inventory level for fast-moving products. Profile response offers suppliers increased flexibility and visibility since they can replenish in accordance with their understanding of the overall product category. The supplier manages retail inventory and accepts responsibility in return for better full-line positioning in stores. From the retailer's perspective, the output of a supplier's AR strategy is fail-safe replenishment designed to maximize category profitability. This strategy also reduces retailer cost by shifting inventory and replenishment responsibility to participating suppliers.

Since QR, CR, and AR increase supplier responsibility and accountability, a frequent question evolves concerning why manufacturers and wholesalers would want to get involved in such relationships. In addition to the tremendous volume that high-clout retailers command, there are two important additional reasons for such alliances. First, enhanced information flow through exchange of requirements, order adjustments, and shipment schedules offers the supplier better inventory visibility throughout the supply chain. Manufacturers and wholesalers can better plan requirements when they know the sales volume and finished inventory at retail, distribution center, and manufacturing sites. With improved visibility, a supplier can quickly determine whether an order surge is based on consumer purchases or channel inventory buildup. While the former requires quick response, the latter can be planned to maintain channel efficiency by scheduling releases within capacity limitations. Supply chain visibility also enables a supplier to establish production and distribution priorities between products and customers.

Second, time-based relationships and information sharing improve coordination between all members of the supply chain. Alliances based on sharing information and risk increase the opportunity for both parties to improve operational efficiency. The alliance creates a long-term relationship between supply chain participants. The retailer in such alliances can depend on wholesalers and manufacturers to perform required activities. Well-defined responsibility adds stability to the supply chain. When problems occur, they can be quickly resolved. This close working arrangement reduces the cost of doing business through resulting operating efficiencies.

SUMMARY

The strategic integration of logistics is fundamental to an enterprise's success. While a firm may not select to differentiate competitively on the basis of logistical competency, it must perform logistical responsibilities as part of the fundamental process of creating customer value. The relative importance that a firm places on logistical competency will determine the degree of emphasis on achieving internal and external integration.

Flexibility is a key to logistical competency. Logistical flexibility results from integration and from implementing time-based control techniques. To perform at the leading edge requires a shift in managerial emphasis from an anticipatory to a response-based operational philosophy. The achievement of leading-edge status typically means that a firm is capable of simultaneous use of alternative logistic strategies to satisfy specific key customer requirements.

QUESTIONS

1   Define benchmarking, and provide an example of how an enterprise would perform it internally and externally.
2   What environmental factors enable time-based competition in today's business arena? Discuss the impact of time-based competition on logistics operations.
3   Compare and contrast logistical environmental assessment with similar requirements for overall enterprise strategy planning. Discuss two ways that these assessments are similar and different.
4   Define manufacturing postponement. Provide two examples, not discussed in the chapter, of the concept applied in a business situation.
5   Why is structural separation an important concept? How is logistics affected by it?
6   What is the fundamental importance of achieving transportation consolidation? How does time-based competition affect consolidation?
7   How is flexibility accommodated in a logistics arrangement? How can operations increase their flexibility?
8   Compare and contrast internal and external integration attributes. Provide an example of how these attributes can be achieved.
9   How do supply- and demand-based logistical control techniques differ? What is the importance of independent demand?
10 What are the downsides of vendor managed inventory programs? Can whole categories be effectively managed by one supplier of products sold in that category?

CHAPTER 17

INTEGRATION THEORY

LOGISTICS LOCATION STRUCTURE
Spectrum of Location Decisions
Local Presence Paradigm
WAREHOUSE LOCATION PATTERNS
Market-Positioned Warehouses
Manufacturing-Positioned Warehouses
Intermediately Positioned Warehouses
TRANSPORTATION ECONOMIES
Cost-Based Warehouse Justification
Transportation Cost Minimization
INVENTORY ECONOMIES
Service-Based Warehouse Justification
Inventory Cost Minimization

LEAST-TOTAL-COST DESIGN
Trade-off Relationships
Critical Assumptions and Limitations
FORMULATING LOGISTICAL STRATEGY
The Least-Total-Cost System Design
Threshold Service
Service Sensitivity Analysis
Finalizing Logistical Strategy
SUMMARY
QUESTIONS

The challenge of this chapter is to present a theoretical framework to assist managers in the formation and implementation of a logistical strategy. For the most part, managers confront a new and challenging assignment when they are asked to participate in a logistical reengineering effort. Because of the rapid rate of change in almost every facet of operations, a manager can expect considerable discontinuity when previous experience is used to guide the creation and integration of new logistical competencies. Therefore, success or failure may depend on how well the planning team is able to conceptualize the forces at work and rationalize them into a logical and believable course of action. Having a comprehensive understanding of the theoretical constructs that serve as the foundations of integration is the first step toward conceptualizing a logistical system.

In Chapter 16, the essence of logistical strategy was identified as achieving and maintaining operational flexibility. Flexibility is the key to simultaneously providing a high level of basic customer service while retaining sufficient operating reserves to meet and exceed key customer expectations when extraordinary opportunities arise. To exploit flexibility, an enterprise needs to achieve high levels of overall value chain integration. Such integration is required at two levels. First, the operating areas of logistics must be integrated, consistent, and supportive of marketing, manufacturing, and financial initiatives of the enterprise. Such internal integration is essential if a firm seeks to make a logistical impact. Second, integration must transcend internal operating boundaries and seek to establish trading channel and procurement relationships that serve to leverage overall performance. This chapter addresses key concerns that managers must reconcile and strategically position if value chain integration is to become a reality.

Subject coverage initially focuses on the importance of location selection in logistical system reengineering. The location network provides the basic structure from which logistical operations are launched. Since the primary facilities are various forms of warehouses, the chapter reviews the alternative facility strategies. Next, Chapter 17 develops a conceptual framework to help identify and evaluate temporal and spatial trade-offs critical to logistical facility network design. The facility impact on transportation and inventory costs is reviewed. Then these two main cost factors are treated simultaneously to arrive at a least-total-cost logistical network design. Finally, the chapter introduces cost service trade-offs that lead to positioning logistics as an integral part of overall enterprise strategy.

The reader is cautioned that this chapter stresses fundamental constructs that underpin logistical system design. The material offers a theoretical structure to guide trade-off analysis. While theory tends to be somewhat abstract, the principles demonstrated are logically consistent regardless of the business or cultural setting within which logistical reengineering is performed.

LOGISTICS LOCATION STRUCTURE

Prior to the availability of low-cost dependable transportation, most of the world's commerce relied on movement by water. During this early era, commercial activity centered around port cities. Overland transport of goods was costly and slow. For example, the lead time for ordering a designer outfit from across the continental United States could exceed nine months. Although the need for fast and efficient transport existed, it was not until the invention of the steam locomotive in 1829 that the transportation technological revolution began in the United States. Today, the transportation system in this country is a highly developed network of rail, water, air, highway, and pipeline services. Each transport alternative provides a different type of service available for use within a logistical system. This availability of economical transportation requires managers to identify superior locations from which to conduct logistical operations.

The importance of location analysis has been recognized since at least the middle of the nineteenth century, when the German economist Joachim von Thünen developed *The Isolated State*.[1] To von Thünen, the primary determinants of economic development were the price of land and the cost to transport products from production to market. The value of land was viewed as being directly related to the cost of transportation and the ability of a product to command an adequate price to cover all costs and result in profitable operations. Von Thünen's basic principle was that the value of specific produce at the growing location decreases with distance from the primary selling market.

Following von Thünen, Alfred Weber generalized location theory from an agrarian to an industrial society.[2] Weber's theoretical system consisted of numerous consuming locations spread over an area and linked together by linear weight-distance transportation costs. Weber developed a scheme to classify major materials as either ubiquitous or localized. Ubiquitous materials were those available at all locations that could not in themselves serve to attract industrial facilities. Localized raw materials consisted of mineral deposits found only in selected areas. On the basis of his analysis, Weber developed a *material index*. This was the ratio of the localized raw materials in the weight of the finished product. Each type of industry could be assigned a *locational weight* according to the material index. Utilizing these two measures, Weber generalized that industries would locate facilities at the point of consumption when the manufacturing process was weight-gaining and near the point of raw material deposit when the manufacturing process was weight-losing. Finally, if the manufacturing process was neither weight-gaining nor weight-losing, firms would select plant locations at an intermediate point of convenience.

Several location theorists followed von Thünen and Weber. The most notable contributions were developed by August Lösch, Edgar Hoover, Melvin Greenhut, Walter Isard, and Michael Webber.[3] In their writings, these five authors highlighted the importance of geographical specialization in industrial location and included thorough development of the fundamental importance of transportation.

In the most basic sense, transport capacity makes available to local communities goods and commodities that are mined or manufactured elsewhere. Without transportation, a community would have to be economically self-sufficient. The consequence would be a limited variety of products, high prices, and inefficient utilization of natural resources. As such, transportation provides *spatial* closure and permits specialization. Transportation should be viewed as an overall cost-reducing

[1] Joachim von Thünen, *The Isolated State*, Rostock, 1842–1863; reprinted Jena, 1921.

[2] Alfred Weber, *Theory of the Location of Industries*, translated by Carl J. Friedrich, Chicago: University of Chicago Press, 1928.

[3] August Lösch, *Die Räumliche Ordnung der Wirtschaft*, Jena: Gustav Fischer Verlag, 1940; Edgar M. Hoover, *The Location of Economic Activity*, New York: McGraw-Hill Book Company, 1938; Melvin L. Greenhut, *Plant Location in Theory and Practice*, Chapel Hill, N.C.: University of North Carolina Press, 1956; Walter Isard et al., *Methods of Regional Analysis: An Introduction to Regional Science*, New York: John Wiley & Sons, Inc., 1960; Walter Isard, *Location and Space Economy,* Cambridge, Mass.: The MIT Press, 1968; and Michael J. Webber, *Impact of Uncertainty on Location,* Cambridge, Mass.: The MIT Press, 1972.

factor in the sense that the services provided permit economies in the process of manufacturing and marketing.

Spectrum of Location Decisions

From the vantage point of logistics planning, transportation offers the potential to link geographically dispersed manufacturing, warehousing, and marketing locations into an integrated system. In a broad sense, facilities included in the logistical system consist of all locations at which materials, work-in-process, or finished inventories are handled and stored. Thus, all retail stores, finished goods warehouses, manufacturing plants, and material storage warehouses constitute logistical locations. Among these many different types of facilities, the number and location of distribution and material warehouses are most often the focus of logistical system reengineering.

A manufacturing plant location decision may require several years to implement. In contrast, some warehouse arrangements are sufficiently flexible to be used only for spot stocking inventory at specified times during an operating year. The selection of retail locations represents a specialized type of analysis that is influenced by marketing and competitive conditions. The discussion that follows concentrates on warehouse location analysis. Among all the location decisions faced by logistical managers, those involving warehouses are the most frequently reviewed. When, from time to time, manufacturing plant location decisions are confronted, considerable attention should be directed to the impact on logistical operations when identifying the best overall location. A refined body of knowledge concerning the location of manufacturing facilities has emerged over the years. Today, management can draw on analytical sophistication tempered by sound theory to guide the selection of plant locations offering maximum economic and competitive benefits.

Local Presence Paradigm

A long-standing belief in business is that a firm must have local facilities in order to successfully conduct business. As noted previously, during the early economic development of North America, transportation services were sufficiently erratic to cause serious doubts about a firm's ability to promise merchandise delivery in a timely and consistent manner. In short, customers felt that unless a supplier maintained inventory in each local market area, it would be difficult, if not impossible, to provide desired service. This perception, commonly referred to as the *local presence paradigm*, resulted in logistical strategies that were highly committed to forward deployment of inventory. As recently as the early 1960s it was not uncommon for manufacturers to operate twenty or more distribution warehouses to service mainland United States. Some firms went so far as to have full-line inventories located at all major sales offices. There were instances where total warehouses exceeded fifty facilities.

When a tradition is part of a successful business strategy, it is difficult to change. However, for the past two decades the economics and risks associated with the local presence paradigm have been increasingly reexamined. Two technological developments have motivated this reexamination. First, transportation services have dramatically expanded, and reliability has increased to the point where arrival times are much more dependable and predictable. Second, the implementation of information technology has reduced the time needed to identify and communicate customer requirements. Technology has made it economical to constantly track transportation vehicles, thereby providing *accurate delivery information.*[4] Next-day delivery from a warehouse facility located as far away as 800 to 1,000 miles has become common practice. As a general rule, the fewer the distribution warehouses used to service a market area, the lower the total inventory required to provide a specified level of basic service.

Thus, transportation, information technology, and inventory economics all favor using fewer rather than greater numbers of distribution warehouses to service customers in a geographical area. The fact that these logistical designs challenge long-standing beliefs regarding local presence often serves to hinder implementation of the most economical logistics solutions. In many situations, customer perceptions concerning local presence continue to influence decentralization of inventory. The answer to how much local presence is required is best understood by carefully examining the relationships that affect distribution system design.

WAREHOUSE LOCATION PATTERNS

In logistical system design, a warehouse should be established if it can render service or cost advantages. The appropriate number and geographic sites of warehouses are determined by customer and manufacturing locations and product requirements. Warehouses represent one part of a firm's overall effort to gain time and place utility. From a policy viewpoint, warehouses should be established in a logistical system only when sales and marketing impact is increased or total cost is reduced. Using a traditional classification developed by Edgar Hoover, warehouse locations may be classified as market positioned, manufacturing positioned, or intermediately positioned.[5]

Market-Positioned Warehouses

The market-positioned warehouse is typically devoted to providing inventory replenishment to customers. A warehouse geographically positioned near key customer locations affords maximum long-haul inbound transport consolidation from manufacturing points with relatively short secondary movement to customers. The

---

[4]Transportation vehicles can be tracked via wireless data systems. The main form of tracking is through various mobile communication systems that are common among truckload carriers (for more information, see Jim Mele, ''Guide to Mobile Communications,'' *Fleet Owner*, December 1992, pp. 45–52). Another form of wireless data system is satellite-based tracking. These systems require a more significant investment but allow complete national tracking coverage. As such, satellite systems are more relevant for national truckload markets, not local LTL deliveries. Satellite systems may be increasing as a result of the Federal Communications Commission's plan to develop a national satellite system to reduce costs so that more operators could utilize satellite technology (for more information, see Jim Mele, ''Wireless Data Communications,'' *Fleet Owner*, February 1993, pp. 44–50).

[5]Edgar M. Hoover, *The Location of Economic Activity,* New York: McGraw-Hill Book Company, 1938.

geographic size of a market area served from a market-positioned warehouse will depend on the desired speed of delivery, size of average order, and cost per unit of local delivery. Market-positioned warehouses are operated by retailers, manufacturers, and wholesalers. They all exist to provide inventory replenishment to customers and are justified on the basis of service capability or as the lowest-cost way of providing logistical support.

Market-positioned warehouses usually serve as locations to assemble products from different origins and various suppliers. The assortment of product processed is typically broad. In contrast, the demand for any specific product is small in comparison to total warehouse throughput volume. A retail store usually does not have sufficient demand to order inventory in large quantities directly from wholesalers or manufacturers. The typical retail requirement is an assortment variety of products produced by many different and widely scattered manufacturers. In order to maintain rapid replenishment of such an inventory assortment at low logistical cost, a retailer may elect to establish a warehouse or use the services of a wholesaler.

Examples of market-positioned warehouses are found in the food and mass merchandise industries. The modern food distribution warehouse usually is located geographically near the center of the supermarkets it services. From this central warehouse location, economical shipments can be accomplished rapidly to retail stores because product does not have to be shipped long distances. Often the most distant retail outlet serviced will be about 350 miles from the warehouse. Other examples of market-positioned distribution warehouses are found in manufacturing logistical support, where components and parts are sequenced to enable just-in-time strategies.

Market-positioned warehouses are easily observable throughout industry. Location of a warehouse close to the market served is justified as the lowest-cost way to replenish inventory rapidly.

Manufacturing-Positioned Warehouses

A manufacturing-positioned warehouse is typically located close to production plants to serve as an assembly and consolidation point for items being produced. The fundamental reason for these warehouses is to facilitate the shipment of product assortments to customers. Items are transferred from specialized plants, where they are produced, to the warehouse, from which full-line assortments can be shipped to customers.

Location of warehouses to support manufacturing plants allows mixed product shipments to customers at consolidated transport rates. This consolidated shipment of product assortments facilitates quantity purchase. The advantage of a manufacturing-positioned warehouse is the ability to furnish superior service across a full product assortment. If a manufacturer can offer a combination of all products sold on a single invoice at consolidated transportation rates, a competitive differential advantage may result. In fact, the capability of a manufacturer to provide such service may be the reason for selection as a preferred supplier.

Several major firms currently operate manufacturing-positioned warehouses. Leading examples are General Mills, Johnson & Johnson, Kraft, General Foods, and Nabisco Foods. At Johnson & Johnson, warehouses that support hospital and consumer business sectors serve as consolidators for a variety of different business units. As such, customers are afforded full assortments of products across business units on a single invoice and in one transportation vehicle. At Nabisco Biscuit Division, shipping branch warehouses are located adjacent to each bakery. Inventories of all major products are maintained at each branch to offer customers full-service shipments.

Intermediately Positioned Warehouses

Warehouses located between customers and manufacturing plants are intermediately positioned. These are similar to manufacturing-positioned warehouses and provide single shipments of broad inventory assortments at a reduced logistics cost.

Industrial location theory illustrates that manufacturing plants producing a specific product line often must locate near sources of energy or required raw materials.[6] To realize competitive or cost-effective manufacturing, firms confront a need to geographically decentralize manufacturing. When products from two or more plants are sold to a single customer, an intermediate consolidation and assortment warehouse may be the least-total-cost logistics solution.

TRANSPORTATION ECONOMIES

From the preceding discussion, it is clear that warehouses enter a logistical system only when a differential advantage in service or cost results from their inclusion between manufacturing and customers. From the viewpoint of transportation economies, cost advantage is accomplished by using the warehouse to achieve maximum consolidation of freight. The next discussion illustrates the economics of transportation consolidation that justify establishment of a single warehouse. Then the chapter focuses on transportation cost minimization across a network of warehouses.

Cost-Based Warehouse Justification

The basic economic principle justifying establishment of a warehouse is transportation consolidation. A manufacturer typically sells products over a broad geographical market area. If customer orders tend to be small, then the potential to consolidate may provide economic justification for establishing a warehouse.

To illustrate, assume that a manufacturer's average shipment size is 500 pounds and the applicable freight rate to a customer is $7.28 per hundredweight. Each shipment made direct from the manufacturing location to the market would have a transportation cost of $36.40. The quantity or volume transportation rate for shipments 20,000 pounds or greater is $2.40 per hundredweight. Finally, local delivery within the market area is $1.35 per hundredweight. Under these conditions,

[6]Melvin L. Greenhut and Hiroshi Ohta, *Theory of Spatial Pricing and Market Areas*, Durham, N.C.: Duke University Press, 1975.

products shipped to the market via quantity rates and distributed locally would cost $3.75 per hundredweight, or $18.75 per 500-pound shipment. If a warehouse could be established, stocked, and operated for a total cost of less than $17.65 per 500-pound shipment ($36.40 − $18.75), or $3.53 per hundredweight, the overall cost of distributing to the market using a warehouse would be lower. Given these economic relationships, establishment of a warehouse might reduce total logistics cost.

Figure 17-1 illustrates the basic economic principle of warehouse justification. *PL* is identified as the manufacturing location, and *WL* is the warehouse location within a given market area. The vertical line at point *PL* labeled *Pc* reflects the handling and shipping cost associated with the preparation of a 500-pound LTL shipment (*C*) and a 20,000-pound truckload shipment (*A*). The slope of line *AB* reflects the truckload freight rate from the plant to *WL*, the warehouse, which is assumed for this example to be linear with distance. The vertical line labeled *WC* at point *WL* represents the cost of operating the warehouse and maintaining inventory. The lines labeled *D* reflect delivery cost from the warehouse to customers within the market area *Ma* to *Ma'*. The slope of line *CD* reflects the less-than-truckload rate from the plant to customers located between the plant and the boundary *Ma'*. The shaded area represents the locations to which the total cost of a 500-pound customer shipment using a consolidation warehouse would be lower than direct shipment from the manufacturing plant.

From the perspective of cost alone, it would make no difference whether customers located exactly at points *Ma* and *Ma'* were serviced from the manufacturing plant or the warehouse.

Transportation Cost Minimization

As a general rule, warehouses would be added to the logistical system in situations where

$$\sum \frac{P_{\bar{v}} + T_{\bar{v}}}{N_{\bar{x}}} + W_{\bar{x}} + L_{\bar{x}} \leq \sum P_{\bar{x}} + T_{\bar{x}}$$

where $P_{\bar{v}}$ = processing cost of volume shipment
$T_{\bar{v}}$ = transportation cost of volume shipment
$W_{\bar{x}}$ = warehousing cost of average shipment
$L_{\bar{x}}$ = local delivery of average shipment
$N_{\bar{x}}$ = number of average shipments per volume shipment
$P_{\bar{x}}$ = processing cost of average shipment
$T_{\bar{x}}$ = direct freight cost of average shipment

The only limitation to this generalization is that sufficient shipment volume must be available to cover the fixed cost of each warehouse facility. As long as the combined cost of warehousing and local delivery is equal to or less than the combined cost of shipping direct to customers, the establishment and operation of additional warehouse facilities would be economically justified.

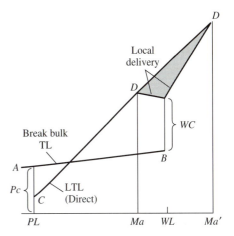

FIGURE 17-1 Economic justification of a warehouse facility based on transportation cost.

The generalized relationship of transportation cost and consolidation location is illustrated in Figure 17-2. Total transportation cost will decrease as consolidation locations are added to the logistical network. In actual operation, consolidation locations can be transportation break bulk or cross-dock facilities. It is not necessary to stock inventory to achieve the lowest transportation cost. The reduction in transport cost results from consolidated volume shipments to the break bulk location, coupled with short-haul small shipments to final destination. The cost of shipping small orders direct from manufacturing to customers is at the extreme upper left of the cost curve illustrated in Figure 17-2. At the low point near the middle of the transportation cost curve, the number of facilities required to achieve maximum consolidation is indicated; and thus, lowest transportation cost is identified.

If facilities are expanded beyond the maximum consolidation point, total cost will increase, because the inbound volume capable of being consolidated to each facility decreases. The increased frequency of smaller inbound shipments results in a higher rate per hundredweight shipped into the facility. In other words, the frequency of small inbound shipments increases, and total transportation cost begins to increase.

INVENTORY ECONOMIES

Inventory level and velocity are directly related to the location structure of a logistical system. The framework for planning inventory deployment is the performance cycle. Although one element of the performance cycle is transportation, which provides spatial closure, the key factor in inventory economics is time. The forward deployment of inventory in a logistical system improves service response time. Such deployment also increases the overall system inventory requirements, resulting in greater costs and risk. In the following discussion, the impact of inventory on service response capability is initially presented, followed by a review of the impact of increasing the number of warehouses on total system inventory requirements.

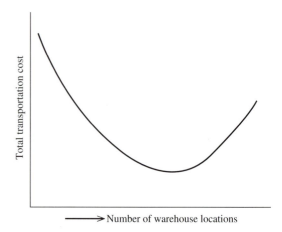

FIGURE 17-2   Transportation cost as a function of the number of warehouse locations.

Service-Based Warehouse Justification

The use of warehouses can be a vital part of the logistics strategy of a firm engaged in national distribution. To achieve essential economy of scale, firms are often required to sell over broad geographical areas. These manufacturing economies of scale often compel firms to locate plants where low production costs can be realized.

The dynamics of spatial competition enter an industry when products begin to gain customer acceptance in other than prime markets or near manufacturing locations. The enterprise may find it desirable to deploy inventory to support marketing. In highly competitive industries, the policy may be to locate a warehouse in a particular market area even if operation of the facility increases total cost. The availability of a local inventory offers the potential to provide high levels of customer service. For customers, this means faster replenishment and an overall reduction of inventory. Thus, the enterprise that commits to establishing a warehouse may be viewed as having a differential advantage.

The inventory required to support a warehouse consists of transit, base, and safety stock. Chapter 8 defines the various inventory components and describes how each relates to average inventory level.

Base Inventory   Adding warehouses to a logistical system increases the number of performance cycles. The impact on transit inventory and safety stock can be significant. In contrast, the impact on base stock by adding inventory is not significant. The base stock level within a logistical system is determined by manufacturing and transportation lot sizes, which do not change as a function of the number of warehouses. The combination of maintenance and ordering cost, adjusted to take into consideration volume transportation rates and purchase discounts, determines the replenishment EOQ and the resultant base stock. In just-in-time procurement situations, base stock is determined by the discrete order quantity required to support the planned manufacturing run or assembly. In either situation, the base stock determination is independent of the number of warehouses included in the logistical system.

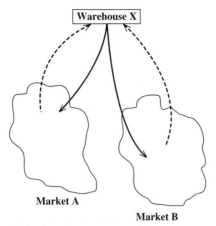

FIGURE 17-3 Logistical network: two markets, one warehouse.

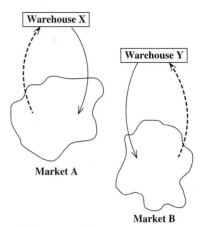

FIGURE 17-4 Logistical network: two markets, two warehouses.

Transit Inventory Transit inventory is important to logistical system design because it requires capital commitment. As more performance cycles are added to a logistical network, the expected result is that existing cycles will experience a reduction in transit inventory. This reduction occurs because the total transit days in the system are reduced. To illustrate, assume that a single product is being sold in markets A and B and is currently being supplied from warehouse X, as presented in Figure 17-3. Assume that the forecasted average daily sales are 6 units for market A and 7 for market B. The performance-cycle duration is six days to market A and ten days to market B.

With all things held constant, what will happen to transit inventory if a second warehouse is added, such as illustrated in Figure 17-4? Table 17-1 provides a summary of results. The main change is that the performance cycle to market B has been reduced from ten to four days. Thus, the second warehouse reduced average transit inventory for the network from 53 to 32 units. It should be noted that the second warehouse did not create additional performance cycles on the physical distribution side of the logistics flow. However, on the inbound side, each

TABLE 17-1 TRANSIT INVENTORY UNDER DIFFERENT LOGISTICAL NETWORKS

Forecasted average daily sales	Market area	Warehouse X only	Two-warehouse facilities		
			Warehouse X	Warehouse Y	Combined
6	A	36	36	—	36
7	B	70	—	28	28
	$\Sigma A + B$	106			64
	$\bar{i}_a$	18			18
	$\bar{i}_b$	35			14
	$\Sigma \bar{i}$	53			32

TABLE 17-2   LOGISTICAL STRUCTURE: ONE WAREHOUSE, FOUR PLANTS

Manufacturing plant	Warehouse X			
	Performance-cycle duration	Forecasted average sales	Transit inventory	$\bar{i}$
A	10	35	350	175
B	15	200	3,000	1,500
C	12	60	720	360
D	20	80	1,600	800
	57	375	5,670	2,835

product stocked in the new warehouse requires a replenishment source. Assuming a full product line at each warehouse, the number of performance cycles required to replenish the system will increase each time a new warehouse is added.

Despite the increased need for inventory replenishment, the average in-transit inventory for the total system will drop as new warehouses are added because of a reduction in days required to service customers. Assume that warehouse X is supplied by four manufacturing plants whose individual performance cycles and forecasted average usage are as illustrated in Table 17-2. For purposes of comparison, assume a unit value of $5 for all warehouse products. Utilizing only warehouse X, the average transit inventory would be 2,835 units at $5 each, or $14,175.

Table 17-3 illustrates the addition of warehouse Y. Average transit inventory under the two-warehouse logistical structure dropped to 2,248 units or, at $5 each, $11,240. Thus, even though four new plant to warehouse replenishment cycles were added to the logistical system, the average transit time was reduced because of the reduction in total replenishment days.

In summary, the addition of facilities will generally have the net effect of reducing total in-transit days and, thus, inventory level. This result will vary in accordance with the particulars of each situation. Each network of locations must be carefully analyzed to determine the exact impact on average transit inventory. The key to understanding the impact of increasing warehouses on transit inventory is to remember that total transit days are reduced even though the number of required performance cycles increases. A qualification is that while an increase in the number of performance cycles typically reduces transit days, it may also increase overall lead time uncertainty. As the number of performance cycles is increased, the possibility of breakdowns leading to potential service failures also increases. This potential impact is treated under safety stock.

Safety Stock Inventory   From the viewpoint of safety stock, the expected result of adding warehouses will be an increase in average system inventory. In Chapters 8 and 9, the impact of sales and performance-cycle uncertainty on inventory was evaluated using two independent frequency distributions. The purpose of safety stock is to protect against unplanned stockouts during inventory replenishment. Thus, if safety stock is predicted to increase as a function of adding warehouses, then *the overall system uncertainty must also be increasing.*

TABLE 17-3 LOGISTICAL STRUCTURE: TWO WAREHOUSES, FOUR PLANTS

Manufacturing plant	Performance-cycle duration	Forecasted average sales	Transit inventory	$\bar{i}$
		Warehouse X		
A	10	20	200	100
B	15	100	1,500	750
C	12	35	420	210
D	20	30	600	300
	57	185	2,720	1,360
		Warehouse Y		
A	5	15	75	38
B	8	100	800	400
C	6	25	150	75
D	15	50	750	375
	34	190	1,775	888
	$\Sigma xy = 91$	$\Sigma xy = 375$	$\Sigma xy = 4,495$	$\Sigma \bar{x}xy = 2,248$

The addition of warehouses to the logistical system impacts uncertainty in two ways. First, since performance-cycle days are reduced, the variability in sales during replenishment and the variability in the cycle are both reduced. Therefore, reducing the length of the performance cycle relieves, to some degree, the need for safety stock to protect against variability.

The second impact of adding locations has a direct and significant effect on average inventory. Each new performance cycle added to the system creates the need for additional safety stock. The introduction of an additional warehouse to service a specific market area reduces the applicable size of the demand database used to determine safety stock requirements. In effect, the size of the market area serviced by a given facility is reduced without a corresponding reduction in uncertainty. For example, when the demand of several markets is aggregated to a single warehouse, the variability of demand is averaged across markets. This allows peaks in demand in one market to be offset by low demand in another. In essence, the use of probability allows the idle stock of one market to be used to meet safety stock requirements of other markets.

To illustrate, Table 17-4 provides a summary of monthly sales in three markets on a combined and separate basis. Average sales for the three markets combined are 22 units per month, with the greatest variation above the average in month six, when sales reached 29 units, or 7 units over the average. If the goal is to provide 100 percent protection against stockout and total sales of 29 units have an equal probability of occurring in any month, a safety stock of 7 units would be required.

The average monthly sales for markets A, B, and C are 8, 4, and 10 units (rounded), respectively. The maximum demand in excess of forecast in market A is 4 units in month twelve; for market B, 3 units in month eight; and for market C, 4 units in month six. The total for each of these three extreme months equals

TABLE 17-4   SUMMARY OF SALES IN ONE COMBINED AND THREE SEPARATE MARKETS

| Month | Combined sales, all markets | Unit sales per market | | |
		A	B	C
1	18	9	0	9
2	22	6	3	13
3	24	7	5	12
4	20	8	4	8
5	17	2	4	11
6	29	10	5	14
7	21	7	6	8
8	26	7	7	12
9	18	5	6	7
10	24	9	5	10
11	23	8	4	11
12	23	12	2	9
Total sales	265	90	51	124
Average monthly sales	22.1	7.5	4.3	10.3
Value greater than average	7	4	3	4

11 units. If safety stocks were being planned for each market on a separate basis, 11 units would be required for the total system, in contrast to only 7 units required to service all markets from a single warehouse. An increase in total system safety stock of 4 units is required when three facilities are utilized.

This is a simplified example illustrating the impact of adding warehouses on system safety stock. The important point to understand is that the increase in safety stock results from an inability to aggregate the uncertainty across a large market area. As a consequence, separate safety stocks must accommodate all local demand variation.

Inventory Cost Minimization

The overall impact on average inventory of increasing the number of warehouses in a logistical system is generalized in Figure 17-5. A reduction in average transit inventory is assumed as illustrated by the line $\bar{I}_t$. The assumption is that a linear relationship exists between average transit inventory and the number of warehouses in the network.

The curve labeled $\bar{I}_{ss}$ (average safety stock) increases as warehouses are added. The actual inventory increases at a decreasing rate since the net increase for each facility is limited (the added safety stock required to accommodate uncertainty is related only to demand assigned to that warehouse less the reduction in safety stock required for less lead time uncertainty resulting from a shorter replenishment cycle). Thus, the incremental inventory required to maintain customer service performance diminishes for each new warehouse location added to the system. The average inventory curve $\bar{I}$ represents the combined impact of safety stock and transit

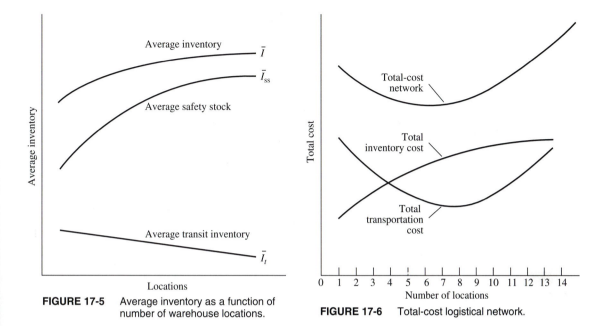

FIGURE 17-5 Average inventory as a function of number of warehouse locations.

FIGURE 17-6 Total-cost logistical network.

inventory. The significant observation is that the safety stock dominates the impact of transit inventory reduction. For the overall system, the average inventory is the safety stock plus half of the order quantity plus transit inventory. Thus, given the same demand and customer service goals, total inventory increases at a decreasing rate as the number of warehouses used in a logistical system increases.

LEAST-TOTAL-COST DESIGN

As noted earlier, the identification of the least-total-cost system design is the goal of logistical integration. The basic concept of total cost for the overall logistical system is illustrated in Figure 17-6. The low point on the total transportation cost curve is eight facilities. Total cost related to average inventory commitment increases with each additional warehouse. For the overall system, the lowest total-cost network is six locations. The point of lowest inventory cost is a single warehouse.

Trade-off Relationships

The identification of the least-total-cost design of six warehouses in Figure 17-6 illustrates the trade-offs between cost-generating activities. The minimal total-cost point for the system is not at the point of least cost for either transportation or inventory. This is the hallmark of integrated logistical analysis.

In actual practice, a great many problems must be overcome to effectively examine total cost. Foremost among them is that many assumptions must be made to operationalize the logistical system analysis. A second concern is the fact that a two-dimensional analysis, such as illustrated in Figure 17-6, does not encompass the complexity of total-cost integration. Each of the critical assumptions and associated implementational problems is discussed.

Critical Assumptions and Limitations

The two-dimensional display in Figure 17-6 represents a projected level of sales volume across a single planning period. Transportation requirements are represented by one average-size shipment. In actual operations, neither of these simplifying assumptions would be valid. First, the nature of logistical network design is not a short-term planning problem. When facility decisions are involved, the planning horizon extends across several years and must accommodate a range of different annual sales projections. Second, actual shipment and order sizes will vary substantially around an average. In fact, the assumption that shipments must be serviced through a warehouse must be relaxed to accommodate high-volume customer-direct truckload or container distribution. A realistic approach to planning must incorporate a range of shipment sizes supported by alternative logistical methods to satisfy customer service requirements. In actual operation, alternative modes of transportation are employed, as necessary, to upgrade the speed of delivery.

Significant cost trade-offs exist between inventory and transportation. Inventory cost as a function of the number of warehouses is directly related to the desired level of inventory availability. If no safety stock is maintained in the system, the total inventory requirement is limited to base and transit stock. Under a no-safety-stock situation, the total least cost for the system would be at or near the point of lowest transportation cost. Thus, assumptions made with respect to the desired inventory availability and fill rate are essential to trade-off analysis and have a significant impact on the least-total-cost design solution.

The locational selection aspect of logistical network planning is far more complex than simply deciding how many facilities to choose from a single array of locations such as illustrated in Figure 17-6. A firm engaged in nationwide logistics has a wide latitude in choice of where to locate warehouses. In the United States there are fifty states within which one or more distribution warehouses could be located. Assume that the total allowable warehouses for a logistical system cannot exceed fifty and that locations are limited to a maximum of one in each state. Given this range of options, there are 1.1259×10^{15} combinations of warehouses to be evaluated in the selection of a least-total-cost network.

To overcome some of the above noted simplifying assumptions, variations in shipment size and transportation alternatives need to be introduced to the two-dimensional illustration in Figure 17-6. Extending the analysis to a more complete treatment of variables typically demands the use of computer planning models and techniques. Such refinement requires linkage of a full range of variables. At least three critical ones to be considered are shipment size, transportation mode, and location alternatives. The constants are level of inventory availability, performance-cycle duration, and the specific warehouse locations being evaluated.

In constructing a more comprehensive analysis, shipment size can be grouped in terms of frequency of occurrence and transportation mode economically justified to handle each shipment size within the specified performance-cycle time constraints. For each shipment size, a total-cost relationship can be identified. The result is a two-dimensional analysis for each shipment size and appropriate transportation mode. Next, the individual two-dimensional profiles can be linked by joining the points of least cost to make a planning curve. In a technical sense, this is an envelope curve that joins the low total-cost points of individual shipment size–transport mode relationships. Figure 17-7 offers a three-dimensional pictorial of integrated shipment size, transportation mode, and location.

The planning curve joins the point of total least cost for each shipment size. It does not join locational points. For example, the number of locations to support least cost for one size of shipment may be more or less than for another. Further analysis is required to identify the specific locations that offer the least-cost alternative for each shipment size and transport combinations. Assume that the locations under consideration consist of a network ranging from one to twelve warehouses. Within this range, the planning curve will identify a smaller number of acceptable locations for detailed evaluation. In Figure 17-7, the points of least cost, shipment size, and transportation combinations fall within a range of four to eight locations. A compromise is required to select the final warehouse network. Initially, the time duration of the performance cycle and inventory availability assumptions should be held constant. The service availability and performance-cycle duration serve as parameters to help isolate an initial least-cost approximation. At a later point in strategy formulation, these parameters can be relaxed and subjected to sensitivity analysis. The fit of the least-cost planning curve requires marginal cost analysis for each shipment size–transportation mode combination for networks of four, five,

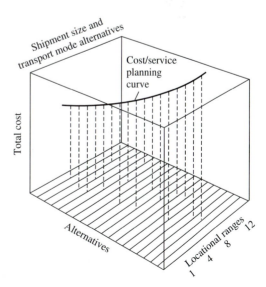

FIGURE 17-7   Three-dimensional total-cost curve.

six, seven, and eight warehouse locations. Provided that customer service requirements are achieved within the four-to-eight warehouse range, an initial least-total-
cost network of potential warehouses is identified.

A final refinement requires the evaluation of specific warehouse sites or facilities.
In the case of Figure 17-7, which is also the situation in most complex modeling
approaches, the best-fit location network is limited to the initial warehouses selected
for the analysis. The results may be managerially satisfactory but not cost superior
to a different group of locations. Each warehouse assortment selected for analysis
will have a least-cost combination. The final policy may require that the analysis
be completed with several different network combinations to identify those most
suitable for a given business situation. The final warehouse selection using such a
trial-and-error method will never identify the mathematically optimal solution to
minimize total logistical cost. It will, however, help management identify a network
superior to the existing operation that may better service customers at lower total
logistics cost.

In order to evaluate the wide range of variables in designing a logistical system,
complex models have been developed. Several are discussed in Chapter 18. The
assumptions required to support an integrated system are important from the viewpoint of their impact on strategy formulation. The integrated total-cost curve must
take into consideration all relevant variables that are critical to logistical system
design.

FORMULATING LOGISTICAL STRATEGY

To finalize logistical strategy, it is necessary to evaluate the relationships between
alternative customer service levels and associated cost. While substantial difficulties exist in the measurement of marginal revenue, the comparative evaluation of
marginal service performance and related marginal cost offers a way to approximate
an ideal logistical system design. The general approach consists of (1) determining
a least-total-cost system design, (2) measuring service availability and capability
associated with the least-total-cost system design, (3) conducting a sensitivity
analysis related to incremental service and cost directly associated with revenue
generation, and (4) finalizing the plan. Following is a discussion of the logic that
underlies the formulation of a service-oriented logistical strategy.

The Least-Total-Cost System Design

Just as a physical replication of a geographical area illustrates elevations, depres-
sions, and contours of land surface, an economic map can highlight logistical cost
differentials. Generally, peak costs for labor and essential services occur in large
metropolitan areas. However, because of demand concentration, least total logistics
costs resulting from transportation and inventory consolidation benefits are often
minimized in metropolitan areas.

A strategy of least total cost seeks a logistical system design with the lowest
fixed and variable expenses. Such a design is determined purely by cost-to-cost
trade-offs and was illustrated in Figure 17-6. The level of customer service that is
associated with a least-cost logistical design results from safety stock policies and

the locational proximity of warehouses to customers. The overall level of customer service associated with any least-total-cost system is referred to as the *threshold* service level.

Threshold Service

To establish a threshold service level it is necessary to initiate the system reengineering with policies regarding desired inventory *availability* and *capability* performance for the logistical system. It is common practice to have the customer service capability based on the existing order entry and processing system, warehouse operations based on standard order fulfillment time at existing facilities, and transportation delivery time based on capabilities of least-cost transport methods. Given these assumptions, existing cycle speed and consistency serve as the initial measure of customer service performance capability.

The typical starting point for customer service availability analysis is to assume performance at a fill rate level that is generally acceptable. Often the prevailing industry standard is used as a first approximation. For example, if the safety stock availability goal is established at 97.75 percent performance for combined probability of demand and lead time uncertainty, it would be anticipated that approximately 98 out of 100 items ordered would be delivered to specification.

Given the initial assumptions, each customer is assigned a shipment location on the basis of least total cost. In multiproduct situations, selection of service territories for each facility will depend on the products stocked at each warehouse and the degree of consolidation required by customers. Because costs have significant geographical differentials, the service area for any given facility will vary in size and configuration. Figure 17-8 provides an illustration of the assignment of warehouse service areas based on equalized total delivered cost. The irregularity of service territories results from outbound transportation cost differentials from the three warehouses.

In Figure 17-8 the warehouses are identified by the letters X, Y, and Z. The hypothetical cost associated with each facility represents all logistical cost for an average order except transportation. The differential of average order cost between facilities reflects local differentials.

Around each facility, total-cost lines are displayed at intervals of $1.50, $2.50, and $3.50. The cost represented by the line is the total cost of logistics, including transportation to points connected along the line. Customers located within a given area can be serviced at a cost less than displayed on the line. The overall service area of each warehouse is determined by lowest-total-cost assignment. The territory boundary line represents the point of equal total cost between two warehouses. Along this line of equal costs, an enterprise would be indifferent on a cost basis as to which warehouse would be assigned to service a specific customer. From the customer's viewpoint, a substantial difference could result in delivery time.

Two conditions are assumed in Figure 17-8. First, the illustration is based on distribution of an average order. Thus outbound logistics costs are equated on the average. To the degree that order size varies from the average, alternative boundaries based on shipment size might be required. Second, delivery time is estimated

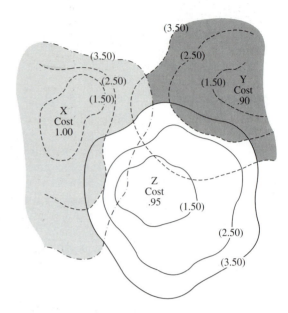

FIGURE 17-8   Determination of service territories: three-point, least-cost system.

on the basis of distance. Transit inventory also is calculated on the basis of estimated delivery time. In accordance with this initial analysis of threshold service, it cannot be concluded that delivery times will be consistent within territories or that equal total logistics cost will be experienced within a service area.

The fact that the initial network is designed to achieve logistical least cost does not mean that threshold customer service will be low. The elapsed time from the customer's order placement to product delivery in a least-cost system is expected to be longer on average than would be experienced in alternative networks that have been modified to improve overall service performance. However, customers located near a warehouse facility in all networks will experience rapid delivery. Because the least-cost location tends to favor areas of high demand concentration, a substantial number of customers will be positioned to experience rapid delivery.

Given an estimate of expected order cycle time, management is in a position to make basic customer delivery commitments. A service statement policy may be as follows: "Order performance for area A will be five days from receipt of orders at the warehouse facility. It is our policy to be able to fill 90 percent of all orders within the five-day period."

The actual performance of a logistical system is measured by the degree to which such service standards are consistently achieved. Given quantification of the variables involved, the threshold service related to the least-total-cost system offers the starting point of developing a firm's basic service platform. The next step in policy formulation is to test the customer suitability of the threshold service level.

Service Sensitivity Analysis

The threshold service resulting from the least-total-cost logistical design provides a basis for sensitivity analysis. The basic service capabilities of a system can be increased or decreased by a variety of methods such as (1) variation in number of warehouses in the system, (2) change in one or more performance cycles to increase speed or consistency of operations, and/or (3) change in safety stock policy. Each form of modifying threshold service as well as the expected impact on total cost is briefly discussed.

Locational Modification The warehouse structure of the logistical system establishes the service that can be realized without changing the performance cycle or safety stock policy. To illustrate the relationship between number of warehouses and resultant service time, assume that an important measure is the percentage of demand fulfilled within a specified time interval. The general impact of adding warehouses to the system is presented in Table 17-5. Several points of interest are illustrated.

First, incremental service is a diminishing function. For example, the first five warehouse locations provided 24-hour performance to 42 percent of all customers. In order to double the percentage from 42 to 84 percent, nine additional warehouses, or a total of fourteen, are required.

Second, high degrees of service are achieved much faster for longer performance intervals than for the shorter intervals. For example, four warehouse locations provide 85 percent performance within the 96-hour performance cycle. Increasing the total locations from four to fourteen improved the 96-hour performance by only 9 percent. In contrast, a total of fourteen warehouses cannot achieve 85 percent given a 24-hour performance cycle.

Finally, the total cost associated with each location added to the logistical network increases dramatically. Thus, while the incremental service resulting from additional locations diminishes, the cost associated with each new location is increasing. Thus, the service payoff for each new facility is incrementally less.

TABLE 17-5 SERVICE CAPABILITIES WITHIN TIME INTERVALS
AS A FUNCTION OF NUMBER OF LOCATIONS

Network locations	Percentage demand by performance-cycle duration (hours)			
	24	48	72	96
1	15	31	53	70
2	23	44	61	76
3	32	49	64	81
4	37	55	70	85
5	42	60	75	87
6	48	65	79	89
7	54	70	83	90
8	60	76	84	90
9	65	80	85	91
10	70	82	86	92
11	74	84	87	92
12	78	84	88	93
13	82	85	88	93
14	84	86	89	94

Performance-Cycle Modification   Speed and consistency of service can be varied to a specific market or customer by a modification of some aspect of the performance cycle. To improve service, computer-to-computer ordering and premium transportation can be adopted. Therefore, geographical proximity and the number of warehouses do not equate directly with fast or consistent delivery. The decision to increase service by adopting a faster performance-cycle arrangement will typically increase variable cost. In contrast, service improvement by virtue of added warehouses involves a high degree of fixed cost and could result in less overall system flexibility.

No generalizations can be offered regarding the cost/service improvement ratio attainable from performance-cycle modification. The typical relationship of premium to lowest-cost transportation results in a significant incentive in favor of large shipments. Thus, if order volume is substantial, the economics of logistics can be expected to favor use of a warehouse or consolidation point to service a market area.

The impact of using premium transportation on the least-total-cost system is twofold: the transportation cost curve will shift up to reflect higher per shipment expenditure, and the inventory cost curve will shift down to reflect any reductions in average inventory resulting from lower transit stocks. In almost all cases, the net of these cost modifications will be an increase in total expenses. Adjustments in the least-total-cost logistical system can typically be justified if the improved service results in increased revenue. The sidebar on Timberland Company illustrates how one firm adjusted its threshold service level after realizing that its customer profile was changing.

Safety Stock Modification   A direct way to change service is to increase or decrease the amount of safety stock held at one or more warehouses. Increasing the safety stock across a total system will shift the average inventory cost curve upward and increase customer service availability. As service is increased, the safety stocks required to achieve each equal increment of availability will increase.

Finalizing Logistical Strategy

Finalizing customer service standards is critical to logistical strategy. Management often falls into the trap of being overly optimistic in terms of service commitments to customers. The result may be excessively high customer expectations followed by erratic performance. In part, such overcommitment results from lack of understanding the total cost required to support high zero defect service.

The final step in establishing a strategy is to evaluate the cost of incremental service in terms of generating offsetting revenue. To illustrate, assume that the current system is geared to service at least 90 percent of all customers at a 95 percent inventory availability within 60 hours of order receipt. Furthermore, assume that the current logistical system is meeting these objectives at the lowest total cost by utilizing a network of five warehouses. Marketing management, however, is not satisfied and believes that service capability should be increased to the point where 90 percent of all customers receive 97 percent inventory availability delivered

PUTTING A SHINE ON SHOE OPERATIONS

At Timberland Co., reengineering has unraveled some old assumptions. The Hampton (N.H.) shoemaker had always measured productivity by the size of each delivery, so priority was given to department-store orders rather than those from small retailers. But managers of the $291 million company began to realize that small boutiques were a growing chink of their business. Two years ago, they set out to change their routine.

Timberland began by scheduling two or more shipments to each customer a week, instead of one big delivery. Scanners automatically track inventory and create shipping bills, so it's as efficient to handle small orders as big ones.

Reengineering is hitting other operations, too. In-

stead of having one department take orders and another verify credit, the two were merged. Now, orders are sent to manufacturing via a network, faster and with fewer errors.

Timberland is also taking to the electronic highway to reach customers. By letting stores transmit orders automatically to its computers, the company expects to double sales volume for every 25 percent increase in its sales force. At Timberland, staying a top shoemaker means not sticking to its last—or the past.

From Gary McWilliams, "The Technology Payoff: A Sweeping Reorganization of Work Itself Is Boosting Productivity," *Business Week*, June 14, 1993, p. 59.

---

within 24 hours. Logistical management is faced with a critical strategic consideration.

Figure 17-9 illustrates how the alternative strategies can be evaluated. Marketing is requesting a 2 percent improvement in inventory availability combined with a 36-hour improvement in delivery capability. Assume design analysis identifies that twelve warehouse facilities represent the lowest-cost network capable of achieving the new service standards. The total cost of this expanded service capability is measured on the vertical axis of Figure 17-9 by the distance between points *A* and *B*. The total cost of achieving marketing's requested service requires a $325,000 per year increase in logistical expenses. Assuming that the firm averaged a before-tax profit margin of 10 percent of sales, it would be necessary to generate $3.25 million in incremental sales to break even on the cost of providing the added service.[7]

Acceptance or rejection of marketing's proposal for increased service is a choice of strategic positioning. Logistics can provide whichever performance the firm's overall customer service strategy requires. Policy changes, once adopted, will influence the logistical system design. To finalize logistical policy management typically requires considering a range of strategic alternatives. In addition to lowest total cost, at least four other strategies are available: maximum service, profit maximization, maximum competitive advantage, and minimum asset deployment. Each strategy usually requires unique logistical system design.

Maximum Service   A maximum service strategy is rarely implemented. A system designed to provide maximum service attempts to consistently deliver products on a two- to four-hour basis. Such systems shift design emphasis from

---

[7]This relationship is based on the assumption that no change, favorable or unfavorable, would take place in existing fixed or variable cost per unit as a result of an increase in volume.

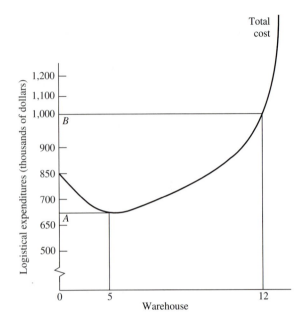

FIGURE 17-9   Comparative total cost for five-
and twelve-distribution point
systems.

cost to availability and delivery performance. For maximum service, areas can be
developed similar to the least-cost service areas illustrated in Figure 17-8. However,
the cost lines are replaced by service time boundaries. The limits of each facility
service area are determined by the capability to provide the required delivery. As
with cost-oriented service areas, time-oriented areas will be irregular because of
transport route configurations. Total-cost variation between a least-cost and maximum service system to service the same customers will be substantial. Servicing
the total United States market on an overnight basis may require thirty to forty
warehouses and the use of highly dependable transportation. The number of warehouses can be significantly reduced if the firm is in a position to utilize premium
overnight transportation.

   Profit Maximization   Most enterprises aspire to maximize profit in the design
of logistical systems. Theoretically, the service area of each warehouse is determined by establishing a minimum profit contribution for customers located at
varying distances from the facility. Because warehouses are normally located near
high-volume markets, the greater the distance a customer is located from the service
area center, generally the higher the cost of logistics. This cost increase occurs not
only because of distance but also because of lower customer density at the periphery
of the warehouse service area. At the point where the costs of serving peripheral
customers result in minimum allowable profit margins, further extensions of the
service territory become unprofitable on a total-cost basis.
   If the customer were provided improved service, it is possible that it would
purchase more of the overall product assortment sold by a firm. Conceptually,
additional service should be introduced to the point where marginally generated

revenue equals marginal costs. At this point of theoretical equilibrium, no additional service would be justified. Additional service may or may not result from increasing the number of warehouses. The desired service might be provided best by a supplemental delivery system using direct or dual distribution. The theoretical profit maximization position is easier to state than to actually measure. Referring back to Figure 17-6, the point of equalization would normally be found along the total-cost curve to the right of the least-cost point but considerably short of the point where total costs rise rapidly. For the situation illustrated in Figure 17-8, the profit maximization system as a first approximation could be expected to fall between six and ten warehouses.

Table 17-5 presented a quantification of the service capabilities of fourteen warehouses for a given customer configuration. The actual service gains that will result from adding warehouses can be expected to vary in each business situation. As a general rule, the service benefits of each additional facility become smaller. The dollar increase for adding each warehouse reflects the additional cost of achieving faster delivery. Such operating cost estimates allow an assessment of the value of increased service in terms of incremented cost. Given a range of cost/service relationships, management has considerable information to help in the establishment of a customer service strategy.

Maximum Competitive Advantage   Under special situations, the most desirable strategy to guide logistical system design may be to seek maximum competitive advantage. Although there are many ways in which systems can be modified to gain such an advantage, two are presented here to illustrate the strategic considerations.

Selective Service Programs   A common modification in least-cost design consists of improving service to protect major customers from competitive inroads. Management needs to be concerned with how expectations of key customers are being satisfied. If the existing service policy is capable of providing only 42 percent of the customers with 24-hour delivery at 95 percent inventory availability, care must be taken to be sure that the most profitable customers are getting the best service possible.

To illustrate, assume that a firm is a typical mass marketer and that 20 percent of its customers purchased 80 percent of its products. Furthermore, assume that this group of critical customers are located at 75 different delivery destinations. The key to strategic positioning is to determine if the 75 critical customer destinations are included in the 42 percent of all customers receiving 24-hour delivery. Under conditions of equal customer geographical dispersion, the probability is about 0.5 that an individual customer would be included in the 42 percent. In other words, the expectation would be that, on the average, approximately 40 to 45 of the core customers would receive 24-hour service.

Once core customer locations are isolated, it is a relatively easy process to identify the service that these customers will receive. Core customers are identified as critical delivery points. The standard service expectation can then be assessed. Table 17-6 presents the type of results generated from such an assessment process. The actual number of core customers receiving 24-hour delivery service in this

TABLE 17-6   CORE CUSTOMER INTERROGATIVE RESULTS

Total core customers	Number of core customers serviced by hour intervals			
	24	36	48	60
75	53	16	4	2

example is 53. Thus, although 42 percent of *all* customers receive 24-hour service, 76 percent of the *core* customers receive this service. In addition, the iterative process identifies core customers that receive less than superior service. In this analysis, two key customers are getting 60-hour delivery.

Provided that management is so inclined, this situation can be rectified by modifying capability to accommodate customers. The cost of a system providing 24-hour service to all core customers can be isolated, and management can equate the dollar-and-cents requirements of a segmental service policy. A logical alternative would be the use of premium transportation to service key customers that do not currently receive 24-hour delivery.

Several systems modifications may be evaluated similar to the core customer illustration. Management may wish to examine service provided to the most profitable customers. Evaluations can be made regarding customers or noncustomers with the greatest growth potential. In addition, an enterprise may wish to evaluate the incremental cost of providing superior service to the best customers of major competitors. Although all such modifications may increase total cost and decrease short-range profits, the long-term gain may be a substantial improvement in competitive position.

Justified High-Cost Location   An additional application of design modification to capitalize on competitive situations is an economically justified high-cost warehouse. This situation is pertinent especially to smaller or niche businesses. Because of the rigidities inherent in large firms, pricing policies are likely to be inflexible. Antitrust legislation reinforces such rigidities. The result is that large firms selling in broad geographical markets tend to disregard unique cost and demand situations in localized markets or find it nearly impossible to adjust marketing and logistical systems to accommodate such opportunities. The flexibility of smaller firms enables them to make significant investment in logistical capability to attract the localized market segment.

Location of a small-scale plant or warehouse facility in a minor market some distance from major competitors can establish a localized service capability more or less insulated from competition. The logic of this special situation was developed under the general discussion of factors influencing facility location. At this time, it is sufficient to highlight that major firms typically follow one or two policies concerning these unique opportunities.

First, a large enterprise can elect to avoid such localized situations. This policy of concentrating on primary markets can be an opportunity for higher-cost smaller competitors. Second, major producers may introduce smaller-scale facilities or institute direct logistical systems in an effort to service local demand. Following the first policy will result in a system approaching a least-cost configuration. The second policy will require substantial logistical system modification, with higher costs and lower short-range profits.

Minimal Asset Deployment   A final strategy may be motivated by a desire to minimize assets committed to the logistical system. A firm that desires to maintain maximum flexibility may use variable-cost logistical components such as public warehouses and for-hire transportation. Such a strategy might result in higher total logistical costs than could be realized by asset commitment to obtain economies of scale. However, risk would be less and the strategy would increase overall flexibility.

In conclusion, integration of logistical strategy to support overall enterprise operations requires precise customer service commitment. From the viewpoint of designing a logistical system, total least cost and associated threshold service offer an ideal platform for undertaking cost/service sensitivity analysis.

SUMMARY

The objective of this chapter was to develop a basic framework for formulating logistical strategy. Transportation and inventory were identified as critical design considerations. When firms are seeking least cost, transportation deals with the spatial aspects of logistics and provides the primary justification for including warehouses in a system design. Inventory deals with the temporal aspects of logistics. Average inventory is expected to increase as the number of warehouses in a system increases. Total-cost integration provides a way to simultaneously combine these two basic logistical activities. Thus, total-cost analysis is a methodology for integration within and between specific operations areas of logistics.

The formulation of a total-cost analysis is not without practical problems. Foremost is the fact that a great many important costs are not specifically measured or reported in standard accounting systems. Issues related to relevant cost identification are discussed in greater detail in Chapter 22. A second problem is the need to consider a wide variety of design alternatives. To develop complete analysis of a planning situation, alternative shipment sizes, modes of delivery, and range of available warehouse locations must be considered.

These problems can be overcome if care is taken in the reengineering study design. The format recommended for total-cost analysis is to group all functional costs associated with inventory and transportation. The significant contribution of total-cost integration is that it provides a simultaneous analysis of time- and space-related expenses in logistical system design.

The formulation of a logistical strategy requires that total-cost analysis be evaluated in terms of customer service performance as measured by *availability, capability,* and *quality.* The ultimate realization of each service attribute is directly related to logistical system design. To accomplish the final integration of logistical operations within overall enterprise planning, customer service should be provided to the point where marginal cost is equal to marginal revenue. Such balance is not practical to achieve. However, the relationship serves as a normative planning goal.

The formulation of a service policy starts from the identification and analysis of the least-total-cost system design. Given an assumed initial inventory availability level, the service capability associated with the least-cost design is referred to as the *threshold service level*. To evaluate potential modifications in the least-cost design, several forms of sensitivity analysis are possible. Three ways were identified to improve service levels: variation in the number of facilities, change in one or more activities of the performance cycle, and/or change in safety stock policy. The impact of each modification was explored in detail.

Next, attention was directed to finalizing a logistical policy. Beyond least cost, four additional strategies were identified: maximum service, profit maximization, maximum competitive advantage, and minimal asset deployment. Regardless of the final strategy selected, the desired level of customer service performance should be obtained at the associated lowest total cost.

QUESTIONS

1   Describe in your own words the meaning of spatial-temporal integration in logistical systems.
2   What justification of logic can be presented to support the placement of a warehouse in a logistical system?
3   Why do transportation costs decrease as the number of warehouses in a system increases? Why do inventory costs increase as the number of warehouses in a system increases?
4   In your own words, what is the locational impact of inventory? How does it differ for transit inventories and safety stocks?
5   What is meant by the level of threshold service of a least-cost system?
6   Why does customer service not increase proportionately to increases in total cost when a logistical system is being designed?
7   In Table 17-5, why does service speed of performance increase faster for customers located greater distances from a warehouse facility? What is the implication of this relationship for system design?
8   Discuss the differences between improving customer service through faster and more consistent transportation, with higher inventory levels, and/or by expanding the number of warehouses.
9   What is the difference between minimum total cost and short-range profit maximization policies in system design?
10   In what ways can customer service performance be improved by incorporating flexible distribution operations into a logistical system design?

PLANNING AND DESIGN METHODOLOGY

METHODOLOGY

PHASE I: PROBLEM DEFINITION
AND PLANNING
  Feasibility Assessment
  Project Planning

PHASE II: DATA COLLECTION
AND ANALYSIS
  Assumptions and Data Collection
  Analysis

PHASE III: RECOMMENDATIONS AND
IMPLEMENTATION
  Recommendations
  Implementation
  Conclusion

DECISION SUPPORT SYSTEMS
  Define Functional Requirements
  Define Relative Importance
  Identify Alternatives
  Rate Each Alternative
  Select Package and Negotiate with Supplier

SUMMARY

QUESTIONS

The logistics environment is constantly evolving as a result of changes in markets, competitors, suppliers, and technology. In order to develop or refine an enterprise strategy to match this changing environment, a systematic planning and design methodology is necessary to formally include the relevant considerations and effectively evaluate alternatives. Chapter 18 provides a generalized approach that includes an overview of the types of analysis tools used for logistics planning. Chapter 19 contains more specific information related to analysis and design techniques.

First, Chapter 18 provides an overview and then a detailed discussion of a three-phase logistics planning methodology. The first phase involves problem definition through a feasibility assessment and project planning, which includes identifying objectives, constraints, measurements, analysis techniques, and the anticipated workplan. The second phase concerns data collection and analysis. Included here are definitions of assumption, data collection, validation, baseline analysis, and alternative analyses. The final phase involves recommendations and development of an implementation plan. This typically includes cost-benefit evaluation and risk appraisal of the best alternative. The implementation discussion focuses on plan definition, scheduling, and defining acceptance criteria. Finally, the chapter discusses the evolution of decision support systems (DSS) and provides a guideline to help evaluate the applicability of specific DSS alternatives to logistic design requirements.

METHODOLOGY

The logistics relational and operating environment is constantly changing. Even for established industries, a firm's markets, demands, costs, and service requirements change rapidly in response to customer and competitive behavior. In response to these changes, firms often face questions such as, (1) How many distribution centers should be used, and where should they be located? (2) What are the inventory/service trade-offs for each distribution center? (3) What types of transportation equipment should be used, and how should vehicles be routed? and (4) Should a new material-handling technology be applied in our distribution centers?

The above questions are representative of the issues logistics managers regularly face. Such questions are usually characterized as complex and data-intensive. The complexity is due to the large number of factors influencing logistics total cost and the number of potential alternatives. The data-intensiveness is due to the large amount of information required to evaluate logistics alternatives. Typical information analyses must include possible service alternatives, cost characteristics, and operating technologies. These analyses require that a structured process and effective analytical tools be applied to solve logistics problems.

Just as no ideal logistical system is suitable for all enterprises, the method for identifying and evaluating alternative logistics strategies can vary extensively. However, there is a general process applicable to most logistics design and analysis situations. Figure 18-1 illustrates the generalized process flow.

The process can be segmented into three phases: problem definition and planning, data collection and analysis, and recommendations and implementation. The following discussion describes each phase and illustrates the types of issues encountered.

PHASE I: PROBLEM DEFINITION AND PLANNING

Phase I of logistics system design and planning provides the foundation for the entire project. A thorough and well-documented problem definition and plan are essential to all that follows.

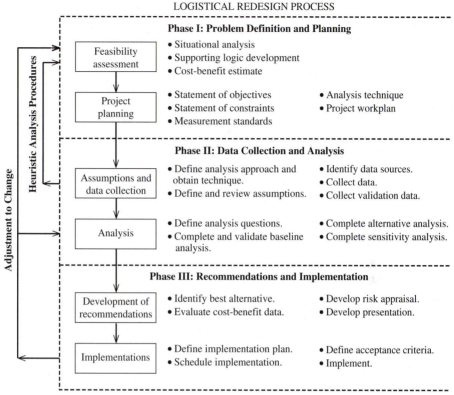

FIGURE 18-1 Research process.

Feasibility Assessment

Logistics design and planning must begin with a comprehensive evaluation of the current logistics situation. The objective is to understand the environment, process, and performance characteristics of the current system and to determine what, if any, modifications appear appropriate. The process of evaluating the need and desirability for change is referred to as feasibility assessment, and it includes the activities of situational analysis, supporting logic development, and cost-benefit estimation. Each is discussed.

Situational Analysis Situational analysis is the collection of performance measures and characteristics that describe the current logistics environment. A typical appraisal requires an internal review, a market assessment, a competitive evaluation, and a technology assessment to determine improvement potential.

The internal review is necessary to develop a clear understanding of existing logistics processes. It profiles historical performance, data availability, strategies, operations, and tactical policies and practices. The review usually covers the overall logistics process as well as each logistics function.

A complete self-appraisal for an internal review examines all major resources such as workforce, equipment, facilities, relationships, and information. In particular, the internal review should focus on a comprehensive evaluation of the existing system's capabilities and deficiencies. Each element of the logistics system should be carefully examined with respect to its stated objectives and its capabilities to meet those objectives. For example, is the logistics management information system consistently providing and measuring the customer service objectives desired by the marketing department? Likewise, does the material management process adequately support manufacturing requirements? Does the current network of distribution centers effectively support customer service objectives? Finally, how do logistics performance capabilities and measures compare across business units and locations? These and many similar questions form the basis of the self-appraisal required for the internal analysis. The comprehensive review attempts to identify the opportunities that might motivate or justify logistics system redesign or refinement.

Table 18-1 lists some of the topics frequently covered during an internal review. While the table is not all-inclusive, it does identify many key points. Although the suggested format is not the only approach, it does highlight the fact that the assessment must consider the processes, decisions, and key measures for each major logistics activity. Process considerations focus on physical and information flows through the value-added chain. Decision considerations focus on the logic and criteria currently used for value chain management. Measurement considerations focus on the key performance indicators and the firm's ability to measure them.

The specific review content depends on the scope of the analysis. It is unusual that the information desired is readily available. The purpose of the internal review is not detailed data collection but rather a diagnostic look at current logistics processes and procedures as well as a probe to determine data availability. Most significantly, the internal review is directed at the identification of areas where substantial opportunity for improvement exists. The external assessment is a review of the trends and service demands required by customers. The market assessment objective is to document and formalize customer perceptions and desires with regard to changes in the firm's logistics capabilities. The assessment might include interviews with selected customers or more substantive customer surveys.[1]

Table 18-2 illustrates typical market assessment topics. The assessment should focus on external relationships with suppliers, customers, and consumers. Customers are other institutions downstream in the distribution channel. In the case of manufacturers, for example, customers are wholesalers and retailers. Consumers are the ultimate users of a product. The assessment should consider trends in requirements and processes as well as enterprise and competitor capabilities. While Table 18-2 does not identify all topics required for the assessment, it does indicate the major items.

Technology assessment focuses on the application and capabilities of key logistics technologies, including transportation, storage, material handling, packaging,

---

[1] Francis J. Gonillart and Frederick D. Sturdivant, ''Spend a Day in the Life of Your Customers,'' *Harvard Business Review* **72**:1, January–February 1994, pp. 116–125.

TABLE 18-1   INTERNAL REVIEW TOPICS

Processes	Decisions	Measurements
Customer service		
What is the current information flow? What is the order profile, and how is it changing? How are orders received?	How are order sourcing decisions made? What happens when inventory is not available to fill an order?	What are the key measures of customer service? How are they measured? What is the current performance level?
Materials management		
What is the current material flow through plants and distribution centers? What processes are performed at each manufacturing site and distribution center?	How are manufacturing and distribution center capacity allocation decisions made? How are production planning and scheduling decisions made?	What are the key manufacturing and distribution center capacity limitations? What are the key measures of material management performance? How are they measured? What is the current performance level?
Transportation		
What modes are currently used? What is the weight profile of orders and shipments, and how are they different? What is the flow for requesting, paying, and exchanging information with carriers? What is the information flow for shipment documentation?	How is the mode and carrier choice decision made for each shipment? How are carriers evaluated?	What are the key transportation performance measures? How are they measured? What is the current performance level? What are the relative economic performance characteristics of each mode and carrier?
Warehousing		
What storage and handling facilities are currently used, and what functions do they perform? What product lines are maintained in each facility? What are the storage, handling, and other value-added functions that are or may be performed at each facility?	How are shipment consolidation decisions made at each facility? What decisions are made by material handlers, and how do they make those decisions? How is product stored in the facility, and how are product selection decisions made?	What is the throughput and storage volume of each facility? What are the key warehouse performance measures? How are they measured? What is the current performance level? What are the relative economic performance characteristics of each facility?
Inventory		
What value-added functions do current inventory stockpiles play?	How are inventory management decisions made? Who makes them, and what information is used to support their decisions?	What is the corporate inventory carrying cost? What are the key inventory performance measures? How are they measured? What is the current performance level?

TABLE 18-2   EXTERNAL ASSESSMENT TOPICS

Market trends	Enterprise capabilities	Competitive capabilities
Suppliers		
What value-added services are suppliers providing? What are the major bottlenecks with current suppliers?	What are the opportunities to internalize or outsource value-added services? How can processes be changed to reduce bottlenecks?	What actions are competitors taking to refine product and information flow with suppliers? What are competitive benchmarks in terms of number of suppliers, cost characteristics, and performance measures?
Customers		
What are the major constraints and bottlenecks when servicing key customers? What are the cost impacts of these constraints and bottlenecks? How are customer ordering patterns changing? What are the primary customers' criteria?	What functions or activities can be shifted to or from customers to enhance logistics system performance? How do customers evaluate our performance on their key measurement criteria?	What services are competitors providing our customers? How do competitors perform on key performance measures as identified by customers?
Consumers		
How are consumer purchasing patterns changing with respect to purchase locations, times, and selection criteria? What are the consumer trends with respect to logistics activities such as purchase quantities, packaging, home delivery, and product quality?	How are we able to respond to changes in consumer purchasing patterns and selection criteria?	How are our competitors responding to changes in consumer purchasing patterns and selection criteria?

and information processing. The assessment considers the firm's capabilities in terms of current technologies and the potential for applying new technologies. For example, can advanced material-handling capabilities offered through third-party suppliers enhance logistics performance? What is the role of decentralized computing architectures, such as personal computers and client/servers, in supplying responsive logistics information systems? Finally, what can satellite and scanning communications technologies contribute to logistics performance? The objective of the technology assessment is to identify advancements that can provide effective trade-offs with other logistics resources such as transportation or inventory. Table 18-3 illustrates typical technology assessment topics for a number of logistics functions. While the topics are not all-inclusive, the major issues are identified. Such an assessment should be completed with respect to each component of the logistics system as well as from the perspective of overall integration.

TABLE 18-3   TECHNOLOGY ASSESSMENT

Current technology	State-of-the-art technology
Forecasting	
What are the current technologies for collecting, maintaining, and developing forecasts?	How are the best firms developing forecasts?
Order entry	
What order entry technologies are used currently?	How are the best firms performing order entry?
What order entry technologies are customers requiring?	What new technologies are available to improve order entry effectiveness?
Order processing	
What is the process to allocate available inventory to customer orders?	How are the best firms performing order processing?
What are the limitations of the current approach?	What new technologies (hardware and software) are available to improve order processing effectiveness?
Requirements planning	
What decision processes are used to determine production and distribution inventory requirements?	How are the best firms making production and inventory planning decisions?
How are these processes supported with current information and decision aids?	What new technologies are available to improve requirements planning effectiveness?
Invoicing and EDI	
How are invoices, inquiries, advanced shipment notifications, and payments currently transmitted?	How are the best firms using EDI?
	What new communications and data exchange technologies are available to improve invoicing and other forms of customer communication?
Warehouse operations	
How are warehouse personnel and scheduling decisions made?	How are the best firms using information and material-handling technologies in the warehouse?
How are warehousing operating instructions provided to supervisors and material handlers?	What new information and material-handling technologies are available to improve warehouse operating effectiveness?
How do warehouse supervisors and material handlers track activities and performance?	
Transportation	
How are transportation consolidation, routing, and scheduling decisions made?	How are best firms using information, packaging, and loading technologies with carriers?
How is transportation documentation developed and communicated with carriers and customers?	What new information, packaging, loading, and communication technologies are available to improve transportation operating effectiveness?
How are transportation costs determined, assessed, and monitored?	
What packaging and loading technologies are used?	
Decision support	
How are logistics tactical and strategic planning decisions made?	How are the best companies making similar tactical or strategic decisions?
What information is used, and what analysis is completed?	What information and evaluation technologies are available to enhance decision effectiveness?

Supporting Logic Development   The second feasibility assessment task is development of a supporting logic to integrate the findings of the internal review, external assessment, and technology study. Supporting logic development often constitutes the most difficult part of the strategic planning process. The purpose of the situational analysis is to provide senior management with the best possible understanding of the strengths and weaknesses of existing logistics capabilities for both current and future environments. Supporting logic development builds on this comprehensive review in three ways.

First, it must determine if there are sufficient logistics improvement opportunities to justify detailed research and analysis. In a sense, supporting logic development forces a critical review of potential opportunities and a determination of whether additional investigation is justified. Supporting logic development uses the logistics principles (e.g., tapering principle, principle of inventory aggregation) discussed in previous chapters to determine the desirability and feasibility of conducting detailed analysis and the resulting benefits or costs. While completing the remaining tasks in the managerial process does not commit a firm to implementation or even guarantee a new logistics system design, the potential benefits of change should be clearly identified when developing the supporting logic.

Second, supporting logic development critically evaluates current procedures and practices using comprehensive, factual analysis and evaluation that is not influenced by opinion. Identification of areas with improvement potential, as well as those where operations are satisfactory, provides a foundation to determine the need for strategic adjustment. For example, it may be apparent that excess inventory is a serious problem and that significant potential exists to improve cost and service. While the appraisal process frequently confirms that many aspects of the existing system are more right than wrong, the focus should be on improvement. In other words, if supporting logic affirms the current number and location of distribution centers, subsequent analysis can focus on streamlining inventory levels without serious risk of suboptimization. The deliverables of this evaluation process include classification of planning and evaluation issues prioritized into primary and secondary categories across short- and long-range planning horizons.

Third, the process of developing supporting logic should include clear statements of potential redesign alternatives. The statement should include (1) definition of current procedures and systems, (2) identification of the most likely system design alternatives based on leading industry and competitive practices, and (3) suggestion of innovative approaches based on new theory and technologies. The alternatives should challenge existing practices, but they must also be practical. The less frequently a project is conducted to reevaluate current procedures and designs, the more important it is to identify a range of options for consideration. For example, evaluation of a total logistics management system or distribution network should include a wider range of options if done every five years than if completed every two years.

At this point in the planning and design process, it is well worth the effort to construct flow diagrams and/or outlines illustrating the basic concepts associated with each alternative. The illustrations frame opportunities for flexible logistics practices, clearly outline value-added and information flow requirements, and provide a comprehensive overview of the options. Some refined or segmented logistics practices are difficult to illustrate in a single flow diagram. For example, regional variations, product-mix variations, and differential shipment policies are difficult to depict, although they do form the basis of design alternatives. When segmental strategies are proposed, it is easier to portray each option independently.

A recommended procedure requires the manager responsible for evaluating the logistical strategy to develop a logical statement and justification of potential benefits. Using the customer service concept (Chapter 3) and logistics integration logic and methodology (Chapters 16 and 17), the manager should commit to paper the most attractive strategy alternatives.

Cost-Benefit Estimate   The final feasibility assessment is a preplanning estimate of the potential benefits of performing a logistics analysis and implementing the recommendations. Benefits should be categorized in terms of service improvements, cost reduction, and cost prevention. The categories are not mutually exclusive given that an ideal logistics strategy might recognize some degree of all three benefits simultaneously.

Service improvement includes results that enhance availability, quality, or capability. Improved service increases loyalty of existing customers and may also attract new business.

Cost reduction benefits may be observed in two forms. First, they may occur as a result of a one-time reduction in financial or managerial resources required to operate the existing system. For example, logistical redesign may allow the sale of distribution facilities, material-handling devices, or information technology equipment. Reductions in capital deployed for inventory and other distribution-related assets can significantly enhance a firm's performance if ongoing costs are eliminated and capital is free for alternative development. Second, cost reductions may be found in the form of out-of-pocket or variable expenses. For example, new technologies for material handling and information processing often reduce variable cost by allowing more efficient procedures and operations.

Cost prevention reduces involvement in programs and operations experiencing cost increases. For example, many material-handling and information technology upgrades are at least partially justified through financial analysis of the implications of future labor availability and wage levels. Naturally, any cost prevention justification is based on an estimate of future conditions and therefore is vulnerable to some error. While logistics system redesign may not be approved entirely on the basis of cost prevention because of such uncertainty, these preventive measures are still important to consider.

No rules exist to determine when a planning situation offers adequate cost-benefit potential to justify an in-depth effort. Ideally, the review should be a continuous process undertaken at regularly specified intervals to ensure the viability of current and future logistics operations. In the final analysis, the decision to undertake in-depth planning will depend on how convincing the supporting logic is, how believable estimated benefits are, and whether estimated benefits offer sufficient return on investment to justify organizational and operational change. These potential benefits must be balanced against the out-of-pocket cost required to complete the process.

Although they are not always a goal of the planning and design project, immediate improvement opportunities are a frequent feasibility assessment result. Enhanced logistics performance achieved through immediate improvements can often increase revenue or decrease cost sufficiently to justify the remainder of an analysis. As the project team identifies these opportunities, a steering committee should evaluate them to determine the return and implementation requirements.

Project Planning

Project planning is the second phase I activity. Logistics system complexity requires that any effort to identify and evaluate strategic or tactical alternatives must be planned thoroughly to provide a sound basis for change. Project planning involves five specific items: statement of objectives, statement of constraints, measurement standards, analysis procedures, and project workplan.

Statement of Objectives   The statement of objectives documents the cost and service expectations for the logistics system revisions. It is essential that they be stated specifically and in terms of measurable factors. The objectives define market or industry segments, the time frame for revisions, and specific performance requirements. These requirements typically define specific service levels. (Specific cost objectives are addressed later.) For example,

1   Inventory availability:
99 percent for category A products
95 percent for category B products
90 percent for category C products
2   Desired delivery of 98 percent of all orders within 48 hours after order is placed
3   Minimal customer shipments from secondary distribution centers
4   Mixed commodity orders filled without back-order on a minimum of 85 percent of all orders
5   Back-orders held for a maximum of five days
6   The fifty most profitable customers provided with minimum performance standards on 98 percent of all orders

Specific definitions of these objectives direct system design efforts to achieve explicit performance levels. Total system cost can then be determined. To the extent that logistics total cost does not fall within management expectations, alternative customer service performance levels can be evaluated using sensitivity analysis.

Alternatively, performance objectives can establish maximum total-cost constraints, and then a system that achieves maximum customer service level within an acceptable logistics budget may be designed. Such cost-oriented objectives are practical since recommendations are guaranteed to function within acceptable budget ranges. The deficiency of a maximum budget approach is a lack of sensitivity to service-oriented system design.

Statement of Constraints The second project planning consideration concerns design constraints. On the basis of the situational analysis, it is expected that senior management will place restrictions on the scope of permissible system modifications. The nature of such restrictions will depend on the specific circumstances of individual firms. However, two typical examples are provided to illustrate how constraints can affect the overall planning process.

One restriction common to distribution system design concerns the network of manufacturing facilities and their product-mix assortment. To simplify the study, management often holds existing manufacturing facilities and product mix constant for logistical system redesign. Such constraints may be justified on the basis of large financial investments in existing production facilities and the ability of the organization to absorb change.

A second example of constraints concerns marketing channels and physical distribution activities of separate divisions. In firms with a traditional pattern of decentralized profit responsibility, management may elect to include some divisions while omitting others from redesign consideration. Thus some divisions are managerially identified as candidates for change, while others are not.

All design constraints serve to limit the scope of the plan. However, as one executive stated, ''Why study things we don't plan to do anything about?'' Unless there is a reasonable chance that management will be inclined to accept recommendations to significantly change logistics strategy or operations, their limitations may best be treated as a study constraint.

The purpose of developing a statement of constraints is to have a well-defined starting point and overall perspective for the planning effort. If computerized analysis techniques are used, major constraints may be reconsidered later. In contrast to the situation assessment discussed earlier, the statement of constraints defines specific organizational elements, buildings, systems, procedures, and/or practices to be retained from the existing logistical system.

Measurement Standards The feasibility assessment often highlights the need for development of managerial performance standards. Such standards direct the project by identifying cost structures and performance penalties and by providing a means to assess success. Management must stipulate guidelines for each category as a prerequisite to formulation of a plan. It is important that the standards adequately reflect total system performance rather than a limited, suboptimal focus on logistics functions. Once formulated, such standards must be held constant throughout system development. Although considerable managerial discretion exists in the formulation of standards, care must be exercised not to dilute the validity of the analysis and subsequent results by setting impractical goals.

An important measurement requirement is to quantify a list of assumptions that underlie or provide the logic supporting the standards. These assumptions should receive top managerial approval because they can significantly shape the results of the strategic plan. For example, a relatively small variation in the standard cost and procedure for evaluating inventory can create major variations in the strategic plan.[2]

Measurement standards should include definitions of how cost components such as transportation, inventory, and order processing are calculated, including detailed financial account references. The standards must also include specification of relevant customer service measures and methods for calculation.

Analysis Procedures   Once the critical issues and alternatives are defined, the appropriate analysis technique should be determined. Analysis techniques range from simple manual methods to elaborate computerized decision support tools. For example, models incorporating optimization or simulation algorithms are common when evaluating and comparing alternative logistics warehouse networks. However, many planning and design projects can be effectively completed using only manual or spreadsheet-based analyses. Once the project objectives and constraints are defined, planning must identify alternative solution techniques and select the best approach. Andersen Consulting annually publishes information regarding software applications for logistics decision support.[3]

Selection of an analysis technique must consider the information necessary to evaluate the project issues and options. Specifically, critical performance measures and logistics system scope must be identified and evaluated. Technique selection must also consider the availability and format of required data.

Project Workplan   On the basis of feasibility assessment, objectives, constraints, and analysis technique, a project workplan must be determined and the resources and time required for completion identified. The alternatives and opportunities specified during the feasibility assessment provide the basis for determining the scope of the study. In turn, the scope determines the completion time.

Project management is responsible for the achievement of expected results within time and budget constraints. One of the most common errors in strategic planning is to underestimate the time required to complete a specific assignment. Overruns require greater financial expenditures and reduce project credibility. Fortunately, there are a number of PC-based software packages available to structure projects, guide resource allocation, and measure progress. Such methodologies identify deliverables and the interrelationship between tasks.[4]

PHASE II: DATA COLLECTION AND ANALYSIS

Once the feasibility assessment and project plan are completed, phase II focuses on data collection and analysis. This includes activities to (1) define assumptions and collect data, and (2) analyze alternatives. Each is discussed below.

---

[2]For a detailed measurement discussion, see Chapter 10 in Patrick M. Byrne and William J. Markham, *Improving Quality and Productivity in the Logistics Process,* Oak Brook, Ill.: Council of Logistics Management, 1991.

[3]Andersen Consulting, *Logistics Software,* Oak Brook, Ill.: Council of Logistics Management, 1994.

[4]An example of such planning software is *Harvard Project Manager,* Mountain View, Calif.: Software Publishing Company, 1992.

Assumptions and Data Collection

This activity builds on the feasibility assessment and project plan to develop detailed planning assumptions and identify data collection requirements. Specific tasks are as follows: (1) define analysis approach and technique, (2) define and review assumptions, (3) identify data sources, (4) collect data, and (5) collect validation data. Each task is discussed.

Define Analysis Approach and Technique   Although it is not necessarily first, an early task is the determination of the appropriate analysis approach and the acquisition of necessary analysis techniques. While a wide number of options are available, the most common techniques are analytical, simulation, and optimization. The analytical approach uses standard numerical methods, such as those available through spreadsheets, to evaluate each logistics alternative. A typical example is the determination of inventory service trade-offs using the formulas discussed in Chapter 19. Spreadsheet availability and capability have increased the use of analytical tools for distribution applications.

A simulation approach can be likened to a ''wind tunnel'' for testing logistics alternatives. Simulation is widely used, particularly when significant uncertainty is involved. The testing environment can be physical (for example, a ''model'' material-handling system that physically illustrates product flow in a scaled-down environment) or numerical (such as a computer model of a material-handling environment that illustrates product flow on a computer screen). Current software makes simulation one of the most cost-effective approaches for dynamically evaluating logistics alternatives.[5] For example, a PC-based simulation can model the flows, activity levels, and performance characteristics. Many simulations can also illustrate system characteristics graphically.

Optimization uses linear or mathematical programming to evaluate alternatives and select the best one. While it has the benefit of being able to select the best option, optimization applications are typically smaller in scope than simulation approaches. Because of its powerful capabilities, optimization is used extensively for evaluating logistics network alternatives such as the number and location of distribution centers.

Define and Review Assumptions   Assumption definition and review build on the situation analysis, project objectives, constraints, and measurement standards. For planning purposes, the assumptions define the key operating characteristics, variables, and economics of current and alternative systems. While the format will differ by project, assumptions generally fall into three classes: business assumptions, management assumptions, and analysis assumptions.

Business assumptions define the characteristics of the general business environment, including relevant market, consumer, and product trends and competitive actions. The assumptions define the broad environment within which an alternative logistics plan must operate. Business assumptions are generally outside the ability of the firm to change.

---

[5]For a comprehensive discussion of simulation alternatives, see James J. Swain, ''Flexible Tools for Modeling,'' *OR/MS Today,* December 1993, pp. 62–78.

Management assumptions define the physical and economic characteristics of the current or alternative logistics environment and are generally within the firm's ability to change or refine. Typical management assumptions include a definition of alternative distribution facilities, transport modes, logistics processes, and fixed and variable costs.

Analysis assumptions define the constraints and limitations that must be included to fit the problem to the analysis technique. These assumptions frequently concern problem size, degree of analysis detail, and solution methodology. Table 18-4 offers descriptions for each assumption category.

Identify Data Sources   In actual practice, the process of data collection begins with a feasibility assessment. In addition, a fairly detailed specification of data is required to formulate or fit the analytical technique. However, at this point in the planning procedure, detailed data must be collected and organized to support the analysis. For situations when data are extremely difficult to collect or when the necessary level of accuracy is unknown, sensitivity analysis can be used to identify data collection requirements. For example, an initial analysis may be completed using transportation costs estimated with distance-based regressions. If analysis indicates that the best answer is very sensitive to the actual freight rates, there should be additional effort to obtain more precise transport rates from carrier quotes. Once operational, sensitivity analysis can be used to determine the major factors involved. Once these factors, such as outbound transportation expense, are identified, more effort can be directed to increase transportation accuracy; and correspondingly less effort can be directed toward other data requirements.

TABLE 18-4   ELEMENTS OF ASSUMPTION CATEGORIES

Business assumptions
1 *Scope.* Definition of business units and product lines to be included
2 *Alternatives.* Range of options that can be considered
3 *Market trends.* Nature and magnitude of change in market preferences and buying patterns
4 *Product trends.* Nature and magnitude of change in product buying patterns, particularly with respect to package size and packaging
5 *Competitive actions.* Competitive logistics strengths, weaknesses, and strategies

Management assumptions
1 *Markets.* Demand patterns by market area, product, and shipment size
2 *Distribution facilities.* Locations, operating policies, economic characteristics, and performance history of current and potential distribution facilities
3 *Transportation.* Transportation rates for movement between potential and existing distribution facilities and customers
4 *Inventory.* Inventory levels and operating policies for each distribution facility

Analysis assumptions
1 *Product groups.* Detailed product information aggregated to fit within the scope of analysis technique
2 *Market areas.* Customer demand grouped to aggregate market areas to fit the scope of analysis technique

For purposes of discussion, the types of data required in a logistical design study can be divided into three classes: business assumptions, management assumptions, and analysis assumptions. Table 18-4 identifies each class and describes the data. The major data requirements, including those concerning sales and transportation, are also presented in the following discussion.

The majority of data required in a logistical study can be obtained from internal records. Although considerable searching may be needed, most information is generally available.

The first major data category is sales and customer orders. The annual sales forecast and percentage of sales by month, as well as seasonality patterns, are usually necessary to determine logistics volume and activity levels. Historical samples of customer order invoices are also needed to determine shipping patterns by market and shipment size. The combination of aggregate measures of demand and detailed order profiles projects the requirements that the logistics system must be capable of satisfying.

Specific customer data are also required to impart a spatial dimension to a logistics analysis. The spatial dimension reflects the fact that effective logistics must consider the cost and time associated with moving product across distance. Customers and markets are often aggregated by location, type, size, order frequency, growth rate, and special logistical services to reduce analysis complexity while not substantially reducing accuracy.

For integrated channel analysis, it is necessary to identify and track the costs associated with manufacturing and purchasing. This often requires further classification by raw materials and parts. While manufacturing plant locations may not be a variable component in a logistical system design, it is often necessary to consider the number and location of plants, product mix, production schedules, and seasonality. Policies and costs associated with inventory transfer, reordering, and warehouse processing must be identified. In particular, inventory control rules and product allocation procedures are often important elements. Finally, for each current and potential warehouse, it is necessary to establish operating costs, capacities, product mix, storage levels, and service capabilities.

Transportation data requirements include the number and type of modes utilized, modal selection criteria, rates and transit times, and shipping rules and policies. If private transportation is included in the analysis, then corresponding information is required for the private fleet.

The preceding discussion offers some perspective regarding the necessary data to evaluate logistics alternatives. The primary justification for placing the formal data collection process after the selection of analysis technique is to allow data collection to match specific analysis requirements. In other words, the design solution can be no better than the data it is based on.

For most logistics analysis applications, a select amount of future market data is useful for evaluating future scenarios. Management can normally provide an estimate of anticipated sales for future planning horizons. The difficulty lies in obtaining a market-by-market projection.

One solution to the problem is to use demographic projections that correlate highly with sales. For example, assume that sales or usage correlates highly with population. Using such a correlation and government population projections, it is possible to estimate future demand levels and thus determine future logistics requirements. A variety of projections concerning demographic factors are regularly published by various government agencies and universities. A number of ZIP code sources exist that provide useful data for logistics planning.[6] Thus a reasonable data bank of environmental information is readily available.

It is also useful to document competitive logistical system designs and flows to provide information regarding competitor strategies and capabilities. In most cases, this information is readily available from published material, annual reports, and general knowledge of company executives. The main purpose in collecting such data is to provide competitive benchmarks that compare customer service capabilities, distribution networks, and operating capabilities.

Collect Data Once alternative data sources have been identified, the data collection process can begin. The process includes assembly of required data and conversion to appropriate formats for the analysis tool. This is often a tedious and time-consuming task, so errors are likely. Potential errors include collecting data from a misrepresentative time period or overlooking data that do not reflect major components of logistics activity, such as customer pickup volume. For this reason, the data collection process should be carefully documented to assist in identifying errors that might reduce analysis accuracy and also to determine any necessary changes to achieve acceptable accuracy.

Collect Validation Data In addition to collecting data to support alternative analysis, base case or validation data must also be collected to verify that the results accurately reflect reality. The specific question concerns whether the chosen analytical approach accurately replicates historical results when distribution practices and operating environments are evaluated. Comparison should focus on historical activity (e.g., sales and volume) and expense levels both in total and by facility, if possible.

The objective of validation is to increase management credibility regarding the analysis process. If the process does not yield credible results, management will hold little confidence in the alternative analysis. It is critical that data collection efforts include investigations into why analytical results may not accurately reflect the past. For example, changes in distribution center operating practices or a one-time event such as a strike may make it impossible to exactly replicate the past. When such situations occur, the validation data collection process should include an assessment of the likely impact of such changes so that appropriate considerations can be made.

Analysis

The analysis uses the technique and data from the previous activity to evaluate logistics strategic and tactical alternatives. Specific tasks are as follows: (1) define

---

[6]American Map Corporation, *United States ZIP Code Atlas,* Maspeth, N.Y.: published annually.

analysis questions, (2) complete and validate baseline analysis, (3) complete alternative analysis, and (4) complete sensitivity analysis. Each task is briefly described.

Define Analysis Questions   The first task defines specific analysis questions concerning alternatives and the range of acceptable uncertainty. The questions build on research objectives and constraints by identifying specific operating policies and parameters. For example, the questions for a distribution center site analysis must identify the specific location combinations to be evaluated. In the case of an inventory analysis, questions might focus on alternative service and uncertainty levels.

Suppose that a strategic planning effort is focusing on the identification of an optimal network of distribution facilities to serve the United States domestic market. Assume that the current network uses four distribution centers located in Newark, New Jersey; Atlanta, Georgia; Chicago, Illinois; and Los Angeles, California. Table 18-5 summarizes the shipment volume, cost, and service characteristics of the existing system. Shipment volume is defined in terms of weight shipped. Cost is defined in terms of transportation and inventory carrying expenses. The service level is defined in terms of the percentage of sales volume within two days' transit of the distribution center. Likely questions for the sample analysis include, (1) What is the performance impact of removing the Chicago distribution center? (2) What is the performance impact of removing the Los Angeles distribution center? and (3) What is the performance impact of removing the Atlanta distribution center?

These questions represent a small subset of the potential alternatives for evaluation. Other alternatives could include fewer or more distribution centers or evaluation of different locations. It is important to recognize that care must be taken to define the questions so that a wide range of possible options can be evaluated without requiring time-consuming analysis of choices that have little likelihood of implementation.

Complete and Validate Baseline Analysis   The second task completes the baseline analysis of the current logistics environment using the appropriate method or tools. Results are compared with the validation data collected previously to determine the degree of fit between historical and analytical findings. The comparison should focus on identifying significant differences and determining sources of

TABLE 18-5   SUMMARY DISTRIBUTION PERFORMANCE

Distribution center	Shipment volume (000 lb)	Inbound transportation ($)	Outbound transportation ($)	Inventory carrying cost ($)	Total cost ($)
Newark	693,000	317,000	264,000	476,000	1,057,000
Atlanta	136,400	62,000	62,000	92,000	216,000
Chicago	455,540	208,000	284,000	303,000	795,000
Los Angeles	10,020	5,000	5,000	6,000	16,000
Total	1,294,960	592,000	615,000	877,000	2,084,000

possible error. Potential errors may result from incorrect or inaccurate input data, inappropriate or inaccurate analysis procedures, or unrepresentative validation data. As discrepancies are encountered, errors should be identified and corrected. In some cases the error cannot be corrected but can be explained and rationalized. Once discrepancies have been removed or explained (generally requiring a fit of plus or minus 5 percent), the approach can be accepted as valid and the analysis can continue.

Complete Alternative Analysis   Once the approach has been validated, the next step is to complete an evaluation of systems alternatives. The analysis must be accomplished either manually or electronically to determine the relevant performance characteristics of each alternative. The options should consider possible changes in management policies and practices involving such factors as the number of distribution centers, inventory target levels, or the transportation shipment size profile.

Complete Sensitivity Analysis   Once this analysis is completed, the best performing alternatives can be targeted for further sensitivity evaluation. Here uncontrollable factors such as demand, factor costs, or competitive actions are varied to assess the ability of potential alternatives to operate under a variety of conditions. For example, suppose the alternative analysis indicates that five distribution centers provide the ideal cost/service trade-off for the firm's market area regarding the base demand. Sensitivity analysis investigates the appropriateness of this ideal solution for different demand or cost levels. In other words, would five distribution centers still be the correct decision if demand increased or decreased by 10 percent? Sensitivity analysis in conjunction with an assessment of potential scenario probabilities is then used in a decision tree to select the best alternative.

PHASE III: RECOMMENDATIONS AND IMPLEMENTATION

Phase III operationalizes planning and design efforts by making specific management recommendations and developing implementation plans. Specific activities or tasks are discussed.

Recommendations

Alternative and sensitivity analysis results are reviewed to determine recommendations to management. Four tasks are included: identify the best alternative, evaluate costs and benefits, develop a risk appraisal, and develop a presentation. Each is discussed.

Identify the Best Alternative   The decision tree analysis should identify the best alternative for implementation. However, multiple alternatives often yield similar or comparable results. Performance characteristics and conditions for each alternative must be compared to identify the two or three best options. Although the concept of ''best'' may have different interpretations, it will generally be the alternative that meets desired service objectives at the minimum total cost.

Evaluate Costs and Benefits   In the earlier discussion of strategic planning, potential benefits were identified as service improvement, cost reduction, and cost prevention. It was noted that these benefits are not mutually exclusive and that a sound strategy might realize all of them simultaneously. When evaluating the potential of a particular logistical strategy, an analysis comparing present cost and service capabilities with projected conditions must be completed for each alternative. The ideal cost-benefit analysis compares the alternatives for a base period and then projects comparative operations across some planning horizon. Benefits can thus be projected on the basis of both one-time savings that result from system redesign as well as recurring operating economies. The importance of viewing cost-benefit results across the planning horizon is illustrated by the following examples.

For the first example, suppose a heuristic analysis established three design alternatives that management wished to evaluate in detail: (1) expand existing facilities, (2) expand existing facilities and add two more, and (3) expand existing facilities and add three more. The cost/service results of the detailed simulation runs are graphically illustrated in Figures 18-2 and 18-3.

These figures show dramatically different performance characteristics for each alternative. Alternative 1 offers low cost in the initial years, but the service level is low and declines further as demand grows in distant markets. Alternative 2 provides the lowest cost during years 5 through 8, and service level actually increases as the demand grows in distribution centers. Alternative 3 offers substantially better service, although there are significant cost penalties early in the planning horizon.

All three alternatives can achieve the management objective of 90 percent volume within five days in the early years. While the lowest-cost option is alternative 1 for the first year, alternative 2 is superior for years 2 through 8. From a strategic perspective, management has the option of enhancing the firm's competitive position by offering better than competitive service using alternative 3 (albeit at a higher cost). After year 8, management would select alternative 3 since it provides better service at relatively lower total cost.

Prior to the planning process, management believed that additional warehouses would be required to maintain desired service standards and that total system cost

FIGURE 18-2   Example 1: Total cost.

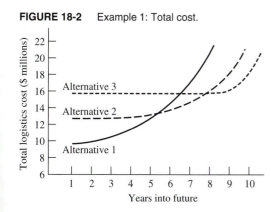

FIGURE 18-3   Performance-cycle characteristics.

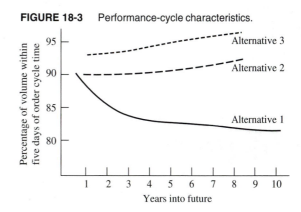

would increase substantially with increased distribution centers. The planning analysis identified the most effective long-term plan to maintain competitive or even enhanced service.

A second example concerns inventory planning for a market area of eight states. In this situation, the marketing organization desires the addition of a second warehouse to improve service capability and the average order cycle by reducing transit time. Expectations suggest that the total cost of servicing the overall market will increase by adding a second facility. Another alternative to improve customer service is to increase safety stock at the existing warehouse. This is expected to improve average order cycle time by reducing back-orders. The existing cycle time is 4.6 days with 75 percent of all orders filled within 5 days. The marketing department desires a 10 percent improvement at minimum total cost.

Addition of the warehouse (alternative 1) reduces the average order cycle time to 4.1 days while increasing orders filled within 5 days from 75 to 92 percent. Increasing safety stock at the existing warehouse (alternative 2) reduces the average order cycle time to 4.3 days. This is equivalent to improving the percentage of orders filled within 5 days from 75 to 87 percent. Over the ten-year planning horizon, the addition of a second warehouse provides the lowest-total-cost alternative.

The cost/service relationship of the two alternatives is illustrated in Figures 18-4 and 18-5. In this situation, the warehouse addition results in the lowest total cost and provides the highest average customer service. It is interesting to note that the addition of a warehouse is the more costly alternative for approximately the first three years of simulated operations; however, it is the least costly over the ten-year planning horizon. In other words, marketing could realize a 12 percent increase in service capability for the initial three years at the lowest total cost by increasing safety stock at the existing warehouse. Establishment of a second warehouse to be operational by the fourth year would realize an additional 5 percent improvement in service and a continuation of the least-cost arrangement. This relationship of

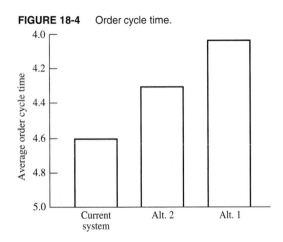

FIGURE 18-4 Order cycle time.

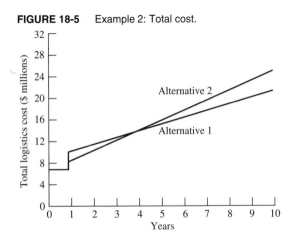

FIGURE 18-5 Example 2: Total cost.

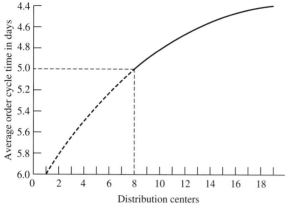

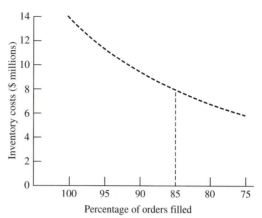

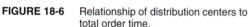

FIGURE 18-6 Relationship of distribution centers to total order time.

FIGURE 18-7 Percentage of orders filled in five average order cycle days (eight warehouses).

cost and service over the planning horizon is one of many applications that illustrate the importance of a dynamic planning structure.

The third example, in Figure 18-6, illustrates the management trade-offs associated with increasing the number of distribution centers. The specific issue concerns increasing the number from six to eight. An analysis is conducted to determine the relationship of inventory carrying cost to average performance delays for the eight-warehouse configuration. In effect, the original constraint of 90 percent of all orders satisfied within five average order cycle days is simulated to obtain the service improvement possible from increased levels of safety stock. Figure 18-7 shows that for the eight-distribution-center alternative, an increase from $10 million to $14 million of annual inventory cost would be required to increase service from 90 to 100 percent of all orders filled within five average order cycle days.

The illustrated examples demonstrate typical results and recommendations from cost-benefit evaluations. Each example was selected from an overall strategic planning situation to show the importance of a planning time horizon. The illustrations indicate the depth of cost-benefit justification necessary to support a suggested logistical strategy.

Develop a Risk Appraisal   A second type of justification necessary to support strategic planning recommendations is an appraisal of the risk involved. Risk appraisal considers the probability that the planning environment will match the assumptions. It also considers the potential hazards related to system changeover.

Risk related to adoption of a selected alternative can be quantified using sensitivity analyses. For example, assumptions can be varied, and the resulting influence on system performance for each alternative can be determined. To illustrate, sensitivity analysis can be used to identify the system performance for different demand and cost assumptions. If the selected alternative is still best even though demand increases or decreases by 20 percent, management can conclude that there is little risk associated with moderate errors in the demand environment. The end result of a risk appraisal provides a financial evaluation of the downside risk if planning assumptions fail to materialize.

Risk related to system changeover can also be quantified. Implementation of or change in a logistics strategic plan may require several years to execute. The typical procedure is to develop an implementation schedule to guide system changeover. To evaluate the risk associated with unanticipated delays, a series of contingency plans can be tested to determine their possible impact.

Typical sources of external risk include uncertainty associated with demand, performance cycle, and competitive actions. Typical sources of internal risk include labor and productivity considerations, changes in firm strategy, and changes in resource accessibility. These considerations must be assessed both quantitatively and qualitatively to provide management with direction and justification.

Develop a Presentation   The final task develops a presentation to management that identifies, rationalizes, and justifies suggested changes. The presentation and accompanying report must identify specific operating and strategic changes, provide a qualitative rationale as to why such change is appropriate, and then quantitatively justify the changes in terms of service, expense, asset utilization, or productivity improvements. The presentation should incorporate extensive use of graphs, maps, and flowcharts to illustrate changes in logistics operating practices, flows, and distribution network.

Implementation

The actual plan or design implementation is the final process activity. An adequate implementation procedure is critical since putting the plan or design into action is the only means to obtain a return on the planning process. While actual implementation may require a number of events, there are four broad tasks required: define implementation plan, schedule implementation, define acceptance criteria, and implement. Each task is discussed.

Define Implementation Plan   The first task defines the implementation plan in terms of the individual events, their sequence, and their dependencies. While the planning process may initially develop at a macrolevel, it must ultimately be refined to provide individual assignment responsibility and accountability. Plan dependencies identify the interrelationships between events and thus define the completion sequence.

Schedule Implementation   The second task schedules the implementation and builds on the assignments identified previously. The schedule must allow adequate time for acquiring facilities and equipment, negotiating agreements, developing procedures, and training. Implementation scheduling should employ one of the software aids discussed earlier.

Define Acceptance Criteria   The third task defines the acceptance criteria for evaluating the success of the plan. Acceptance criteria should focus on service improvements, cost reduction, improved asset utilization, and enhanced quality. If the primary focus is service, acceptance criteria must identify detailed components such as improved product availability or reduced performance-cycle time. If the primary focus is cost, the acceptance criteria must define the expected changes (both positive and negative) in all affected cost categories. It is important that the acceptance criteria take a broad perspective so that motivation focuses on total logistics system performance rather than performance of an individual function. It is also important that the acceptance criteria incorporate broad organizational input.

Implement   The final task is actual implementation of the plan or design. Implementation must include adequate controls to ensure that performance occurs on schedule and that acceptance criteria are carefully monitored.

Conclusion

While the preceding methodology supports logistics planning and design analysis, it can be adapted to guide logistics information system design. For a system design application, the situation analysis focuses on the characteristics and capabilities of the current system, while the data collection and analysis activities focus on new system design, development, and validation.

DECISION SUPPORT SYSTEMS

Significant advances in computer technology; increasing uncertainty regarding the economy, material resources, market competition, and government regulation; and increased decision complexity are stimulating interest in computer-aided tools to improve logistics decision effectiveness. These tools, referred to as decision support systems (DSS), have become more practical with advancements in distributed and personal computing. DSS are basically interactive, computer-based systems that integrate data, solution techniques, and reporting capability to help decision makers solve unstructured problems—that is, problems with many difficult-to-define variables.

Until the 1980s, computer modeling required substantial resources and expertise. Mainframe applications were slow, and standardized models existed for only a limited number of decision support situations. The models were complicated and required significant refinement to evaluate each alternative. For example, it was common for data collection, preparation, and validation to consume 75 to 90 percent of the project time and budget. Rapid development of logistics modeling and analysis applications has reduced the time and effort required to conduct logistics analysis. Technological development now offers significantly improved database management capabilities, faster processing, and enhanced solution approaches through microprocessors that are completely controlled by logistics management. In addition, a broad range of analysis applications is now available from sources such as software vendors, consulting organizations, and computer hardware manufacturers. A wide variety of logistics analyses can benefit from DSS application. The following discussion suggests guidelines for identifying, evaluating,

TABLE 18-6   DEFINITIONS OF DSS REQUIREMENTS

Functional requirements

1 *Data entry.* Can accept data from common spreadsheet packages including LOTUS and EXCEL.
2 *Data manipulation.* Facilitates data manipulation to complete "what if" analysis.
3 *Scope.* Considers relevant logistics costs including inbound transportation, distribution center operations, and customer freight.
4 *Search algorithms.* Includes algorithm or heuristic to search for and identify the optimum or best alternative.
5 *Reporting.* Includes graphical reporting and display capability.

Technical requirements

1 *Operating requirements.* Consideration of the compatibility of the package with existing hardware, planned hardware, and system software.
2 *Design quality.* Consider the overall software design and the resulting ease of software modification. Structure design techniques, modular program, and table-driven processing make installation easier.
3 *Documentation.* Includes current, complete, and cross-referenced technical documentation to expedite modification and installation effort.
4 *Technical sophistication.* Consideration that packages with a large amount of functionality, features, and processing flexibility require higher skill levels to install and maintain. Learning or providing these skills can be difficult or costly.

Vendor characteristics

1 *Vendor stability.* Consider the length of time the vendor has been in business.
2 *Vendor references.* Talk to other package users.
3 *Vendor responsiveness.* Consider how the vendor has historically responded to problem situations and development requests.

---

and selecting among alternative DSS techniques and software. The ideal evaluation process includes five steps: define functional requirements, define relative importance, identify alternatives, rate each alternative, and select package and negotiate with supplier. Each step is described.

Define Functional Requirements

The first step defines the desired functions and features for the decision support system. Functions include the analysis and evaluation capabilities. A desired feature list defines the data entry, manipulation, and reporting capabilities of the system. Table 18-6 provides an extensive, although not necessarily exhaustive, list of features that should be considered for logistics DSS. Input from functional managers, information systems personnel, and experienced users should be obtained when defining requirements.

Define Relative Importance

The second step determines the importance ranking for each function and feature. This should be determined by a combined group of logistics and information system managers. Each function and feature should be rated on an importance scale from "1" to "3," where a "3" implies that the function or feature is absolutely necessary and a "1" implies that it is nice to have but not essential.

Identify Alternatives

The third step identifies alternative packages for consideration. Alternatives can be found through vendor material as well as through comprehensive software guides. Once the possible vendors have been identified, they should be requested to provide detailed information that permits a critical review of the features and capabilities of each package.

Rate Each Alternative

The fourth step rates individual packages on the basis of demonstrated ability to provide the prescribed functions and features. For each requirement, the review should rate each alternative on a scale from "1" to "3." A value of "1" indicates that the software does not support a specific feature, while a "3" indicates that it performs exactly as required.

The overall score for each alternative is determined by multiplying the importance rating for a specific feature by the ranking for the specific supplier. For example, if the DSS user placed high importance on graphical reporting and the package does this well, the vendor score for that feature would be a "9" ("3" importance × "3" ranking). The overall vendor score is the sum of ratings on the individual features. Table 18-7 illustrates a sample evaluation of two vendors. In this case, vendor B obtains a higher overall score because it ranked higher for key requirements in terms of a search algorithm.

Select Package and Negotiate with Supplier

While the above analysis offers a quantitative evaluation of alternative packages, the final step requires a qualitative evaluation of the package and its supplier. The selection committee must consider the package features and characteristics that do not allow for quantitative evaluation and incorporate these into the analysis. Characteristics that might be included are software language, vendor track record,

TABLE 18-7   SAMPLE EVALUATION

Functional requirement	Importance	Vendor A		Vendor B	
		Rank	Score	Rank	Score
Data entry	1	3	3	1	1
Data manipulation	2	2	4	2	4
Scope	3	3	9	3	9
Search algorithm	3	1	3	2	6
Reporting	3	2	6	2	6
Total score			25		26

compatibility with current capabilities, and software flexibility. Once these qualitative considerations have been incorporated into the analysis, the selection committee must determine the best alternative and negotiate with the supplier.

SUMMARY

Chapter 18 provided a comprehensive review of the logistics planning process, decisions, and techniques. It was designed to guide the logistics manager through the overall process of situation analysis, alternative identification, data collection, quantitative evaluation, and development of a viable recommendation.

The chapter began with a detailed description of a methodology to guide evaluation of logistics design alternatives. The methodology, which is generic enough for most logistics problem solving, included three phases: problem definition and planning, data collection and analysis, and recommendations and implementation. The problem definition and planning phase was concerned with the feasibility assessment and project planning. The feasibility assessment included the situation analysis, development of supporting logic, and the cost-benefit estimate. Project planning involved statements of objectives and constraints, definition of measurement standards, identification of analysis technique, and development of the project workplan.

The data collection and analysis phase developed assumptions, collected data, and completed the analysis. Assumptions development and data collection included tasks to define the analysis approach, formalize assumptions, identify data sources, and collect data. The analysis step involved a definition of analysis questions, completion of validation and baseline analyses, and completion of alternative and sensitivity analysis.

The recommendations and implementation phase developed the final plan. The recommendation development step included identification and evaluation of the best alternatives. The implementation step provided definition of a plan, schedule development, definition of acceptance criteria, and final implementation. Each step was discussed and illustrated.

Finally, Chapter 18 described the process and criteria for identifying and selecting decision support software (DSS). The discussion included a listing of the major sources of information and the specific criteria, such as graphical and analytical capabilities, for comparing alternatives.

QUESTIONS

1   What is the basic objective in a logistics design and analysis study? Is it normally a one-time activity?
2   Both internal and external review assessments must consider a number of measures. What are they, and why are they important?
3   Discuss the role of identifying state-of-the-art performance while assessing such factors as technology.
4   What is sensitivity analysis, and what is its role in systems design and analysis?
5   Why is a cost-benefit evaluation important to logistical systems design efforts?

6 What is a segment profitability report, and what is its role in systems analysis?
7 Why is it important to develop supporting logic to guide the logistical planning process?
8 Illustrate how risk associated with a specific logistics alternative can be calibrated for managerial review.
9 What are decision support systems, and how have they evolved in the past several decades?
10 Why is it important to conduct both a quantitative and a qualitative evaluation of decision support system packages?

PLANNING AND DESIGN TECHNIQUES

LOGISTICS AD HOC ANALYSIS
    Freight Lane Analysis
    Inventory Analysis
    Segment Profitability
LOCATION APPLICATIONS
    Location Decisions
    Location Analysis Techniques
    Location Analysis Data Requirements
INVENTORY APPLICATIONS
    Inventory Analysis Decisions
    Inventory Analysis Techniques

TRANSPORTATION APPLICATIONS
    Transportation Analysis Decisions
    Transportation Analysis Techniques
    Transportation Analysis Data Requirements
    Conclusion
ENTERPRISE MODELING
SUMMARY
QUESTIONS

One of the fastest-growing aspects of logistics planning is the range of design techniques that are available to assist managers. These techniques are typically utilized during phase II of the planning and design methodology as discussed in Chapter 18.

Chapter 19 begins with an examination of common logistical ad hoc analyses used to manage transportation, inventory, and customer profitability. These analyses are often done to evaluate transportation, inventory, and segment effectiveness. Although there are formal techniques for completing the analyses, they are often accomplished using relatively simple database reports.

Next, the chapter describes more formal decision support techniques for use in location, inventory, transportation, and enterprise analysis. The discussion includes the types of decisions that must be made, alternative analytical techniques, and typical analysis data requirements. The specific presentations also review analysis decision support software capability and availability.

LOGISTICS AD HOC ANALYSIS

Logistical management requires a number of relatively standardized analyses to identify system characteristics and performance. While these analyses may be completed on a regular basis, they are often requested and refined on an ad hoc or on an as-needed basis to provide management information. Three of the most typical include freight lane analysis, inventory analysis, and segment profitability. Each is discussed and illustrated.

Freight Lane Analysis

One common logistics analysis concerns transportation movements on specific freight lanes. A freight lane refers to the shipment activity between a pair of origin and destination points. The analysis can be completed on a very specific basis between facilities or on a broader regional basis. Freight lane analysis focuses on the balance of volume between origin and destination points. To maximize vehicle utilization, movements should be balanced, or roughly equal, in both directions. Lanes may include two or more points, as Figure 19-1 illustrates. Triangular freight lanes attempt to coordinate movement between three points by transporting combinations of material and finished product between suppliers, manufacturers, and customers.

Freight lane analysis involves both movement volume and the number of shipments or trips between points. The objective is to identify imbalances that offer opportunities for enhanced logistics productivity. Once lane imbalances are identified, management attempts to identify volume that can be transported in the underutilized direction. This might be accomplished by switching carriers or modes, shifting volume to or from a private fleet, increasing back-haul of raw materials, or creating an alliance with another shipper. Conversely, volume in the overutilized direction might be diverted to other carriers or shippers.

Table 19-1 illustrates a lane analysis that clearly identifies shipment imbalances. The transportation manager should attempt to balance the triangular movement by

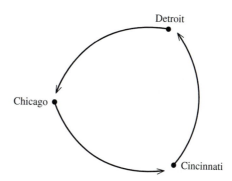

FIGURE 19-1   Example of triangular freight lane.

TABLE 19-1   FREIGHT LANE ANALYSIS MONTHLY MOVEMENTS

Origin	Destination	Weight (cwt)	Shipments
Detroit	Chicago	8,740	23
Chicago	Cincinnati	5,100	17
Cincinnati	Detroit	2,000	8

developing additional volume between Cincinnati and Detroit. The volume could be developed either by moving product sources to the Cincinnati area or by creating an alliance with a shipper that moves volume between Cincinnati and Detroit with no back-haul. The logistics manager should identify supplier, customer, or alliance partner product flows that can be used to balance under/over movements.

Inventory Analysis

The second common logistics ad hoc analysis focuses on inventory performance and productivity. Typically, the analysis considers relative product sales volume and inventory turnover and is performed on an ABC basis, as discussed in Chapter 9. For example, by listing the top ten sales and inventory groupings in decreasing sequence, a logistics manager can quickly determine product groups that have a major influence on volume and inventory levels. As indicated in Chapter 9, 80 percent of sales are usually accounted for by 20 percent of the items. It is also typical that 80 percent of the inventory account for only 20 percent of the volume. Knowledge of these characteristics and the items that make up each product group is useful in targeting inventory management efforts. Items that demonstrate a large inventory commitment relative to sales can be selected for intensive management efforts to reduce inventory level and improve performance.

Table 19-2 illustrates a typical inventory analysis report. This example is sorted by item sales, although there is some logic to sequencing the report by decreasing inventory level or inventory turns. Items with relatively high inventories or low turns should be targeted for management attention.

Segment Profitability

The third logistics ad hoc analysis focuses on market, customer, or item profitability—particularly from the perspective of logistics expenses. Table 19-3 illustrates a segment profitability report by customer. A typical report assigns direct logistics expenses, including transportation, warehousing, order administration, inventory, and accounts receivable.

The result of a segment profitability report is a profit and loss statement that includes the costs of serving and satisfying the customer. Although marketing managers often develop brand-level profit and loss statements, it is uncommon to complete an analysis at the customer segment level and to include distribution-related expenses. A segment profit and loss statement identifies the logistics cost

TABLE 19-2 TYPICAL INVENTORY ANALYSIS REPORT

Date 7/01/91
Total sales: $74,282

Product Rank Analysis Report
Total inventory: $22,470

Inrank list
Total items: 53

Part number	Loc	Item count	Pct items	Unit cost	Sales at cost	Cum sales at cost	Cum pct sales	Dollar inventory	Cum dollars inventory	Cum pct inventory	Inv turns	Unit sales	Class
SQDFAL36100 3P-600V 100A CDR BREAKER	1	1	1.9	141.780 E	14,462	14,462	19.5	2,836	2,836	12.6	5.1	102	A
SQDFAL36040 3P-600V 40A CDR BREAKER	1	2	3.8	115.420 E	14,428	28,890	38.9	4,040	6,876	30.6	3.6	125	A
SQDFAL36015 3P-600V 15A CDR BREAKER	1	3	5.7	115.420 E	11,311	40,201	54.1	2,539	9,415	41.9	4.5	98	A
SQDFAL36030 3P-600V 30A CDR BREAKER	1	4	7.5	115.420 E	7,156	47,357	63.8	2,424	11,839	52.7	2.9	62	A
SQDFAL36050 3P-600V 50A CDR BREAKER	1	5	9.4	.000 E	5,194	52,551	70.7	0	11,839	52.7	0.0	45	A
SQDFAL36060 3P-600V 60A CDR BREAKER	1	6	11.3	115.420 E	4,501	57,052	76.8	693	12,532	55.8	6.5	39	A
SQDFAL36020 3P-600V 20A CDR BREAKER	1	7	13.2	115.420 E	2,308	59,360	79.9	1,385	13,917	61.9	1.7	20	A
SQDQ0215 2P-120/240V 15A CDR BREAKER	1	8	15.1	9.500 E	1,796	61,156	82.3	437	14,354	63.9	4.1	189	B
SQDQ0220 2P-120/240V 20A CDR BREAKER	1	9	17.0	9.500 E	1,748	62,094	84.7	760	15,114	67.3	2.3	184	B
SQDQ0230 2P-120/240V 30A CDR BREAKER	1	10	18.9	9.500 E	1,748	64,652	87.0	817	15,931	70.9	2.1	184	B
SQDQ0120 3P-120/240V 20A CDR BREAKER	1	11	20.8	4.180 E	1,739	66,391	89.4	67	15,998	71.2	25.9	416	B
SQDQ0130 3P-120/240V 30A CDR BREAKER	1	12	22.6	4.180 E	1,267	67,658	91.1	109	16,107	71.7	11.6	303	C
SQDQ0240 3P-120/240V 30A CDR BREAKER	1	13	24.5	9.500 E	1,235	68,893	92.7	627	16,734	74.5	1.9	130	C
SQDQ0115 2P-120/240V 40A CDR BREAKER	1	14	26.4	4.180 E	1,124	70,017	94.3	422	17,156	76.4	2.7	269	C
SQDQ0140 3P-120/240V 20A CDR BREAKER 3P-120/240V 40A CDR BREAKER	1	15	28.3	4.180 E	1,066	71,083	95.7	435	17,591	78.3	2.4	255	D

Source: Adapted from Eugene R. Roman, Inventory Management Seminar, Systems Design, Inc., South Holland, Ill., 1993.

TABLE 19-3   CUSTOMER PROFITABILITY ANALYSIS

	Customer A ($)	Customer B ($)	Customer C ($)
Revenue	3,105	335	605
Variable manufacturing	1,446	161	283
Manufacturing contribution	1,659	174	322
Variable selling	289	34	54
Transport	45	4	31
Warehousing	17	3	4
Order administration	19	1	69
Total marketing distribution cost	370	42	158
Net segment contribution	1,289	132	164
Asset charges			
Inventory	21	6	4
Account received	121	10	19
	142	16	23
Net customer	1,147	116	141

Source: Thomas C. Harrington, Douglas M. Lambert, and Jay U. Sterling, "Simulating the Financial Impact of Marketing and Logistics Decisions," *International Journal of Physical Distribution and Logistics Management,* **22**:7, 1992, p. 8.

differential associated with serving different customers. Select customers may be relatively more expensive to serve because of smaller shipment sizes (requiring higher transportation costs), more diverse inventory (which requires inventory carrying cost), or special packaging requirements (which increase handling expense). Logistics segment profitability information can be used to focus cost reduction efforts or to refine pricing strategies. While these analyses can be grouped by solution technology, another orientation is by functional area. The most common applications include location, inventory, and transportation analysis. Each application is discussed in terms of decision requirements, analysis techniques, and data requirements.

LOCATION APPLICATIONS

Plant and distribution center location is a common problem faced by logistics managers. Increased production economies of scale and reduced transportation cost have focused attention on distribution centers.[1] In recent years, location analysis has been further extended to include logistics channel design as a result of global

---

[1] A number of authors have discussed the issues and process used to locate distribution centers. A representative sample includes A. M. Geoffrion and G. W. Graves, "Multicommodity Distribution System Design by Bender's Decomposition," *Management Science*, **20**:5, January 1974, pp. 822–844; P. Bender, W. Northrup, and J. Shapiro, "Practical Modeling for Resource Management," *Harvard Business Review*, **59**:2, March–April 1981, pp. 163–173; and Jeffrey J. Karrenbauer and Glenn W. Graves, "Integrated Logistics Systems Design," in James M. Masters and Cynthia L. Coykendale, Eds., "Logistics Education and Research: A Global Perspective," *Proceedings of the Eighteenth Annual Transportation and Logistics Educators Conference*, St. Louis, Mo., October 22, 1989, pp. 142–171.

sourcing and marketing considerations. Global operations increase logistics channel decision complexity, design alternatives, and related logistics cost. As a result, the importance of location analysis has increased substantially. The specific decisions, techniques, and data requirements are discussed.

Location Decisions

As the name implies, location decisions focus on selecting the number and location of distribution centers. Typical management questions included, (1) How many distribution centers should the firm use, and where should they be located? (2) What customers or market areas should be serviced from each distribution center? (3) Which product lines should be produced or stocked at each plant or distribution center? (4) What logistics channels should be used to source material and serve international markets? and (5) What combination of public and private distribution facilities should be used? More refined logistics network problems increase issue complexity and require combinatorial analysis to integrate the above questions.

Location Analysis Techniques

Typical location analysis problems can be characterized as very complex and data-intense. Complexity is created because of the number of locations multiplied by the alternative location sites multiplied by the stocking strategies for each location. Data intensity is created because the analysis requires detailed demand and transportation information. Sophisticated modeling and analysis techniques must be employed to effectively deal with such complexity and data intensity in order to identify the best alternatives. The tools used to support location analysis generally fall into the categories of analytic techniques, optimization or linear programming techniques, and simulation. Each is described and illustrated.

Analytic Techniques Analytic techniques generally describe methods that identify the center of gravity of a logistics geography. A center of gravity method is appropriate for locating a single distribution center or plant. A number of methods, both mathematical and nonmathematical, can be applied to the problem of a single location. The cost and complexity of the technique should be matched to the difficulty of the problem.

In the following example, an analytical technique for solving a location problem is presented. Through the use of this technique, it is possible to locate a facility at the ton center, mile center, ton-mile center, or time-ton-mile center within a service territory—whichever results in the lowest total cost. When it is necessary to locate multiple distribution warehouses in a total system network, techniques similar to those discussed in the following section should be used.

The technique employed in this example evolved from analytic geometry. The model is based on cartesian coordinates, where the horizontal or east-west axis is labeled the x axis and the vertical or north-south axis is labeled the y axis. Figure 19-2 illustrates such a coordinate system. The coordinates are overlaid on the relevant geography as illustrated in Figure 19-3.

SITE SELECTION: MORE THAN JUST A LOCATION

As software and program capability make the logistical modeling process faster, more flexible, and more realistic, a manager or firm could easily—and, as it turns out, incorrectly—make the assumption that modeling logistics is becoming a more simple and straightforward task. However, in certain situations, the result has been just the opposite.

In particular, the facility site selection process has been considerably complicated by the impact of environmental legislation and related political issues. For example, in 1993 the department store chain Target was in the process of establishing a site for a new 1-million-plus-square-foot distribution center to serve its developing Chicago regional market. Target used in-house modeling software to analyze the cost and tax incentives offered by fifty-five communities, which involved factors such as proximity to market, transportation costs, and labor cost and availability. Initial analysis narrowed the site selection to three prospects, and from that group, an industrial park in Oconomowoc, Wisconsin, was chosen.

Target had completed all the necessary legal procedures to break ground for the Oconomowoc site and believed that the site selection process had been completed. At this point, however, a not-for-profit environmental group known as the Silver Lake Environmental Association filed a number of court cases in the state of Wisconsin to require further hearings. The group's concerns focused on issues of storm water runoff and its impact on the groundwater table, air pollution created by employee traffic, and whether conformance with current zoning regulations would harm the environment in any way. Opponents to the Target project believed that everything about it was rushed for political expediency. "They ramrodded this thing through," says Stan Riffle, lawyer for the Silver Lake Environmental Association. "We're involved in a number of different court cases at a variety of levels. The bottom line is, this will be tied up for a couple of years. We understand Target wants to move very quickly, so I think they'll come to their senses and move closer to where the jobs are and in an area more suitable to this facility."

From the perspective of the state of Wisconsin, it is important to portray an aggressive probusiness attitude rather than an antidevelopment stance. Tony Honzeny, public information officer for the Wisconsin Department of Development, says, "The people in the community knew about this project before it was announced. There are fifty-eight separate conditions you have to meet to protect a site. So it's not as if you can walk in one day and have a permit the next day. In this state, we try not to be bureaucratic, so if you can get a permit processed in ninety days, which is what we did here, that's good news."

From Target's point of view, the company has determined that in future situations it must allow sufficient time to prepare for both the permit process (which it did in this case) and any potential political unrest. In the not too distant past, communities were more receptive to big projects like Target's. But as environmental, social, and infrastructure problems take their toll, advocacy groups are placing themselves squarely in the site selection process. Given these conditions, it would appear that the best strategy for companies is to directly confront the environmental process because it is more likely to confer legitimacy on the result. In other words, this strategy might mean a lengthier, slower process, but the end result will likely provide a resolution that all involved parties can more easily accept and be satisfied with.

Source: Tom Andel, "Site Selection: How to Avoid Rough Landings," *Transportation & Distribution*, August 1993, pp. 30–35.

Any given point in a quadrant can be identified with reference to the x and y coordinates. Taken together, these coordinates define unique points. Figure 19-3 illustrates the x and y coordinates of Detroit, Michigan, and Columbus, Ohio. The coordinates for Detroit are 3.5 and 3. The coordinates for Columbus are 3.8 and 2. The x and y coordinate system can be used to calculate the distance between any two points on the plane using the pythagorean theorem. The form for calculating

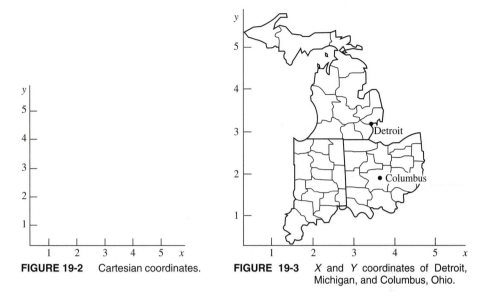

FIGURE 19-2 Cartesian coordinates.

FIGURE 19-3 X and Y coordinates of Detroit, Michigan, and Columbus, Ohio.

distance using these coordinates is discussed later in this chapter. The use of uniform mileage scales along the axes permits all points in the quadrant to be located relative to each other.

By use of this basic system of orientation, it is possible to replicate the geographic market area in which the distribution center is to be located. All markets are plotted on the cartesian plane. Similarly, each market and distribution center is established relative to all others using unique x and y coordinates.

The analytic method to solve the location problem determines the ideal coordinate position of the distribution warehouse on the basis of distance, weight, or a combination of both. The computation is essentially a weighted average of the distance, weight, or combined factors, with the warehouse location as the dependent variable. The algebraic process is solved for the warehouse coordinates. For simplicity, it is convenient to independently solve for the x- and y-coordinate locations.

The algebraic solution may use either the weighted average x and y coordinates or the median location. The median location, which has become accepted as more efficient by geographers, uses the coordinate location with half the demand on each side. The formula for this calculation depends on the independent variables expressed in the location measure. The problem is structured so that identical service standards exist for all potential distribution warehouse locations. Given this service standard, the objective is to minimize transportation costs.

Generally, transportation costs are a function of time, weight, and distance. Historically, however, when mathematical techniques were employed, it was not always possible to consider all the factors together. The four solution methods that consider combinations of factors include the ton-center solution, the mile-center solution, the ton-mile-center solution, and the time-ton-mile-center solution. As the titles suggest, the first three are limited to variables related to weight and distance. The fourth includes both weight and distance plus time as cost determinants.

In the ton-center solution, the location point represents the center of gravity or movement in the market area. The assumption is that the center of movement represents the least-cost location. However, accepting cost as a function of time, weight and distance reveal the basic limitation of the ton-center solution: only weight is given consideration.

All demand locations are plotted on the coordinate plane and identified by subscripts. To express tonnage requirements to each demand center, annual tonnage is reduced to standard units, such as trailers. One such unit is a standard forty-eight-foot trailer with a capacity of 40,000 pounds. Once each demand location is defined and the total unit loads to each demand center are known, the best warehouse location can be determined.

The location solution is found by adding the products of location and delivery frequency to each demand center from the x coordinate and dividing by the total number of units, such as trailers. The process is repeated from the y coordinate. The result is a location in terms of x and y for the distribution warehouse. The final location solution indicates the point that provides the balance of weight between destinations over a specific period. This basic algebraic procedure is followed for all mathematically derived location solutions, with appropriate modifications necessary to handle the inclusion of different variables. The algebraic formula for the ton-center computation is

$$x = \frac{\sum_{i=1}^{n} x_i F_i}{\sum_{i=1}^{n} F_i} \qquad y = \frac{\sum_{i=1}^{n} y_i F_i}{\sum_{i=1}^{n} F_i}$$

where x, y = unknown coordinate values of the warehouse
x_n, y_n = delivery locations, designated by the appropriate subscript
F_n = annual tonnage to each destination, expressed as standard trailers, identified by the appropriate subscript

The mile-center solution determines the geographical point that minimizes the combined distance to all demand centers. The assumption underlying the solution is that delivery costs are solely a function of distance. Therefore, if distance is minimized, a least-cost location is determined. The basic deficiency in the mile-center solution is the omission of weight and time considerations.

Unlike the ton-center solution, the mile-center solution cannot be determined simply by solving for the weighted average coordinate location along each dimension. The mile-center solution requires an iterative process to determine an increasingly improved warehouse location. This optimum location is determined by utilizing the general formula for the length of a straight line between two points. The exact procedure is developed below.

The solution uses initial x and y coordinates to initiate an iterative process that refines the previous mile-center warehouse x, y location coordinates. The location problem is solved when the incremental changes to the coordinates are within an acceptable tolerance of the initial or previous values. For example, if the initial values of x and y are 30 and 40, respectively, the location solution is obtained by utilizing these values to determine the new warehouse coordinates. Assuming that the new values are $x = 36$ and $y = 43$, the new coordinates indicate a substantial shift, so the procedure is not completed. Thus, additional iterations are required. For the next iteration, the most recent values ($x = 36$ and $y = 43$) are used. If this iteration results in the values $x = 36$ and $y = 43$, the suggested adjustment is minimal or zero, so the problem is optimized. An acceptable tolerance of ± 1 mile is usually established for the x and y warehouse coordinates. This means that solutions are correct within a 4-square-mile area.

The algebraic formula for determining the mile-center solution is

$$x_k = \frac{\sum_{i=1}^{n} \dfrac{x_i}{d_i}}{\sum_{i=1}^{n} \dfrac{l}{d_i}} \qquad y_k = \frac{\sum_{i=1}^{n} \dfrac{y_i}{d_i}}{\sum_{i=1}^{n} \dfrac{l}{d_i}}$$

where x_k, y_k = coordinate values of the warehouse for iteration k

$\qquad x_i, y_i$ = demand point, designated by the appropriate subscript

$\qquad\quad d_i$ = distance between each demand point (x_i, y_i) and warehouse location for iteration k

The value for the distance "d_i" from a warehouse can be determined from direct measurement on the coordinate plane or by utilizing the following straight-line formula:

$$d_i = \sqrt{(x_i - x_k)^2 + (y_i - y_k)^2}$$

where d_i = distance between destination and warehouse, designated by the appropriate subscript

x_k, y_k = given coordinates of the warehouse

x_i, y_i = delivery location, designated by the appropriate subscript

Since the distance for all destinations changes each time a new set of warehouse coordinates is determined, the distance formula is utilized in each step of the process.

The ton-mile-center solution combines the variables of weight and distance in selecting warehouse locations. The assumption is that costs are a function of ton-miles. The ton-mile solution is superior to the mile-center solution because it considers the frequency of delivery to each destination when selecting a warehouse location. It is superior to the simple ton-center solution because the impact of distance is considered. The ton-mile-center solution also requires an iterative process since the distance between the demand point and warehouse is included.

The ton-mile-center formulation is

$$x_k = \frac{\displaystyle\sum_{i=1}^{n} \frac{x_i F_i}{d_i}}{\displaystyle\sum_{i=1}^{n} \frac{F_i}{d_i}} \qquad y_k = \frac{\displaystyle\sum_{i=1}^{n} \frac{y_i F_i}{d_i}}{\displaystyle\sum_{i=1}^{n} \frac{F_i}{d_i}}$$

where x_k, y_k = coordinate values of the warehouse for iteration k

$\quad x_i, y_i$ = demand point designated by the appropriate subscript

$\qquad F_i$ = annual tonnage to each demand point, expressed as standard units (e.g., trailers) identified by the appropriate subscript

$\qquad d_i$ = distance between each demand point (x_i, y_i) and warehouse location for iteration k

The fourth location measurement device includes all factors influenced by cost. Because costs are a function of time, weight, and distance, the warehouse site derived as a product of this device should represent a superior least-cost location. The procedure for selecting the time-ton-mile-center solution is also iterative, because both time and distance factors are differentiated from a given warehouse location. The formulation is

$$x_k = \frac{\displaystyle\sum_{i=1}^{n} \frac{x_i F_i}{M_i}}{\displaystyle\sum_{i=1}^{n} \frac{F_i}{M_i}} \qquad y_k = \frac{\displaystyle\sum_{i=1}^{n} \frac{y_i F_i}{M_i}}{\displaystyle\sum_{i=1}^{n} \frac{F_i}{M_i}}$$

where x_k, y_k = unknown coordinate value of a warehouse

$\quad x_i, y_i$ = delivery locations, designated by the appropriate subscript

$\qquad F_i$ = annual tonnage to each location expressed as standard trailers, identified by the appropriate subscript

$\qquad M_i$ = delivery location differentiated in terms of miles per minute from the initial warehouse location and sequentially from each new location until the iterative process is complete

The value of M_i considers both distance and time to all demand points from the warehouse location for each iteration. The distance value is determined by a basic distance formula. The time in minutes to each demand point is determined by calculating a time value from the coordinate plane. Estimation of delivery time must include number of miles, type of highway, and traffic. A general rule is that time per mile decreases as the number of miles per stop increases. To account for the basic factors that influence driving time, zones representing attainable movement rates should be established for the market area. These zones consist of two basic types: rural and urban. Such estimates must be developed from engineering time studies for each warehouse location alternative. Given the values of distance and time through rural and urban zones, M_i is calculated in the following manner:

$$M_i = \frac{d_n}{t_n}$$

The location of a single facility is a common logistics planning problem. Since it is not always necessary to complete a total logistics system evaluation, a simple approach for a single-facility location is useful. In cases where inbound transportation is an important cost, the model can be modified to include both inbound and outbound transportation cost. More comprehensive analytical techniques are discussed next.

Linear Programming   Linear programming methods, which are classified as an optimization technique, are one of the most widely used strategic and tactical logistics planning tools. Linear programming selects the optimal course of action from a number of available options while considering specific constraints. Robert House and Jeffrey Karrenbauer provided an early definition of optimization regarding logistics.[2]

> An optimization model considers the aggregate set of requirements from the customers, the aggregate set of production possibilities for the producers, the potential intermediary points, the transportation alternatives and develops the optimal system. The model determines an aggregate flow basis where the warehouses should be, where the stocking points should be, how big the warehouses should be and what kinds of transportation options should be implemented.

In order to solve a problem using linear programming, several conditions must be satisfied. First, two or more activities or locations must be competing for limited resources. For example, shipments must be capable of being made to a customer from at least two locations. Second, all pertinent relationships in the problem structure must be deterministic and capable of linear approximation. Unless these enabling conditions are satisfied, a solution derived from linear programming, while mathematically optimal, may not be valid for logistical planning.

While linear programming is frequently used for strategic planning, it is also applied to operating problems such as production assignment and inventory allocation. Within optimization, distribution analysts have used two different solution methodologies for logistics analysis.

One of the most widely used forms of linear programming for logistics problems is network optimization. Network optimization treats the distribution channel as a network consisting of nodes (distribution centers) and arcs (transportation links). Costs are incurred for handling goods at nodes and for moving goods between nodes. The network model objective is to minimize the variable production, in-

---

[2]Robert G. House and Jeffrey J. Karrenbauer, ''Logistics System Modeling,'' *International Journal of Physical Distribution and Materials Management,* **8:**4, May 1978, pp. 189–199.

bound, and outbound transportation costs subject to supply, demand, and capacity constraints.

One of the more straightforward approaches to network optimization is the transportation method. This method derived its name from early applications directed at the minimization of transportation costs. In part, the popularity of the transportation method is due to its relatively simple specification and quick solution time. The general formulation of the transportation method is set up in terms of a matrix that relates demand and supply locations.

Table 19-4 illustrates an example matrix formulation of a transportation problem. In the matrix, a_i represents the demand quantity for each market area, b_j represents the supply quantity for each distribution center, and c_{ij} represents the cost of transportation from distribution center b_j to demand location a_i. The matrix represents a network of geographical points connected by links over which the transportation flow can be routed. The matrix illustrated in Table 19-4 represents the classical transportation problem structure. Given the limited supply at source locations and specific demand requirements, the analysis objective is to satisfy all needs at the lowest possible transportation cost.

The general procedure for the transportation method is to identify the optimum combination of distribution centers from the list of possible choices. For example, if the objective is to identify the best combination of warehouse locations that will result in the lowest total system cost, the analysis procedure would consist of a series of evaluations considering the existing system and variations with other combinations of facilities. The final solution would be the combination of existing warehouses plus additional facilities that results in the desired service level and the lowest total cost compared with all the alternatives tested. Because the solution is constrained by the preselected list of locations, optimality is limited to the specific alternatives being evaluated.

Beyond the basic considerations for all analytical techniques, network optimization has specific advantages and disadvantages that both enhance and reduce its application for logistics analyses. Rapid solution times and ease of communication between specialists and nonspecialists are the primary advantages of network models. They may also be applied in monthly, rather than annual, time increments, which allows for longitudinal (e.g., across time) analysis of macro-inventory-level changes. Network formulations may also incorporate fixed costs to replicate facility ownership. The results of a network model identify the optimum set of distribution facilities and material flows for the logistics design problem, as it was specified for the analysis.[3]

The traditional disadvantages of network optimization have been the size of the problem that can be solved and the inclusion of fixed-cost components. The problem size issue was of particular concern for multiple stage distribution systems such as those including suppliers, production locations, distribution centers, whole-

---

[3]Examples of time-based linear programming applications are discussed in S. Kumer and S. Arora, "Customer Service Effect in Parts Distribution Design," *International Journal of Physical Distribution and Logistics Management,* **20**:2, 1990, pp. 31–39; and M. Cohen, P. Kamesan, P. Kleindorfer, H. Lee, and A. Tekerian, "Optimizer: IBM's Multi-Echelon Inventory System for Managing Service Logistics," *Interfaces* **20**:1, January–February 1990, pp. 65–82.

TABLE 19-4   BASIC TRANSPORTATION METHOD MATRIX

Source locations	Demand locations			
	a_1	a_2	a_3	a_i
b_1	c_{11}	c_{21}	c_{31}	c_{i1}
b_2	c_{12}	c_{22}	c_{32}	c_{i2}
b_3	c_{13}	c_{23}	c_{33}	c_{i3}
b_j	c_{1j}	c_{2j}	c_{3j}	c_{ij}

salers, and customers. While problem size is still a concern, advancements in solution algorithms and hardware speed have significantly improved network optimization capabilities. The fixed-cost limitation concerns the capability to optimize both fixed and variable costs for production and distribution facilities. There have been significant advancements in overcoming this problem through the use of a combination of network organization and mixed-integer programming, which is presented next.

Mixed-integer programming is the other optimization solution technique that has been successfully applied to logistics problems. The formulation offers considerable flexibility, which enables it to incorporate many of the complexities and idiosyncrasies found in logistical applications. The primary advantage of the mixed-integer format is that fixed as well as different levels of variable cost can be included in the analysis. For example, demand can be treated on a noninteger basis, thus allowing increments to system capacity in specific step increases. In other words, mixed-integer programming allows solutions to accurately reflect increased fixed costs and economies of scale as larger distribution centers are employed. The mixed-integer approach permits a high degree of practicality in order to accommodate restrictions found in day-to-day logistics operations.

Historically, the major limitation of optimization has been constraints on problem sizes that could be solved. Along with other advances in mixed-integer programming, problem size constraints have been overcome, for a considerable period of time, through the application of *decomposition* to the solution techniques.[4] Decomposition permits multiple commodities to be incorporated into logistical system design. Most firms have a variety of products or commodities that are purchased by customers in varied assortments and quantities. While such products may be shipped and stored together, they are not interchangeable from the viewpoint of servicing customers.

The decomposition technique provides a procedure for dividing the multicommodity situation into a series of single-commodity problems. The procedure for arriving at commodity assignment follows an iterative process wherein costs associated with each commodity are tested for convergence until a minimum cost or optimal solution is isolated.

---

[4]For a discussion of the application of decomposition to logistical system design, see A. M. Geoffrion and G. W. Graves, ''Multicommodity Distribution System Design by Bender's Decomposition,'' *Management Science,* **20:**1, January 1974, pp. 822–844; and Arthur M. Geoffrion, ''Better Distribution Planning with Computer Models,'' *Harvard Business Review,* **54:**4, July–August 1976, pp. 92–99.

This decomposition procedure has been incorporated in a *multicommodity distribution system design program* that includes a mixed-integer algorithm for evaluating the configuration of warehouse location. The procedure for arriving at a system design follows a two-stage iterative process. First, given the combination of possible distribution centers, individual commodities are optimally assigned to the center that minimizes cost in a manner similar to basic transportation solutions. However, the procedure is formatted on a multiproduct basis using the decomposition technique. Second, a mixed-integer algorithm is utilized to enumerate the facility structure in terms of individual commodity customer's assignments. The combined solution is tested for optimality, and the two-step procedure is repeated until convergence is within accepted tolerance. Figure 19-4 illustrates the combined linear programming procedure.

The network optimization and mixed-integer approaches provide effective tools for analysis of location-related issues such as facility location, optimum product flow, and capacity allocation. Mixed-integer approaches are typically more flexible in terms of capacity to accommodate operational nuances, while network approaches are more computationally efficient. Both types are effective techniques for evaluating situations where significant facility capacity limitations exist.

Notwithstanding the value of optimization, linear programming confronts some major problems when dealing with complex logistical system designs. First, to format a comprehensive design, it is necessary to develop explicit functional relationships for the full range of design options. The functional relationship must consider all possible combinations for suppliers, production locations, distribution locations, wholesalers, markets, and products. The sheer number of alternatives and the associated constraints result in a very large problem. Second, the optimality feature of the technique is relative; that is, it is only as valid as the design problem definition. Too many simplifying assumptions can render a solution mathematically optimal but useless in terms of business practice. Third, the capability of existing linear programming procedures is typically limited by the number of echelons or

FIGURE 19-4   Mixed-integer solution flow with decomposition feature.

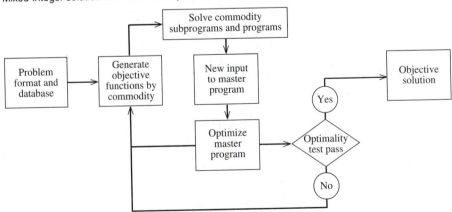

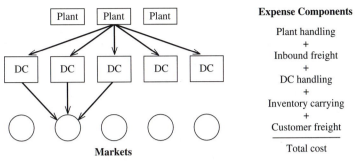

FIGURE 19-5   Total-cost analysis approach.

stages in the distribution system and by the problem size. For example, problems requiring the analysis of flows from production locations to distribution centers and then to markets have three echelons, which can be solved easily by most optimizers. However, the size limitations may make it difficult to perform a complete channel analysis.

Significant advancements have been made in both the speed and the capability of optimization algorithms and software. While there are still some scope and complexity limitations, new capabilities are continuously reported in the literature.[5]

Simulation Techniques   A third location analysis method is static simulation. The term *simulation* can be applied to almost any attempt to replicate a situation. Robert Shannon originally defined simulation as "the process of designing a model of a real system and conducting experiments with this model for the purpose of either understanding system behavior or of evaluating various strategies within the limits imposed by a criterion or set of criteria for the operation of the system."[6]

Static simulation replicates the product flows and related expenses of existing or potential logistics channel networks. Figure 19-5 illustrates a typical network and the major cost components. The network includes plants, distribution centers, and markets. The major expense components are inbound freight (plant to distribution center), fixed and variable distribution center cost, customer freight (distribution center to customer), and inventory carrying cost.

Static simulation evaluates product flow as if it all occurred at a single point during the year. In this sense, the primary difference between static and dynamic simulation is the manner in which time-related events are treated. Whereas dynamic simulation evaluates system performance across time, static simulation makes no attempt to consider the dynamics between time periods. Static simulation treats

[5]For an overview of facility location models including optimization, see T. Miller, "Learning about Facility Location Models," *Distribution,* May 1993, pp. 47–50. For a discussion of the current capabilities of logistics optimization, see J. Karrenbauer and G. Graves, "Integrated Logistics Systems Design," in J. Masters and C. Coykendale, Eds., "Logistics Education and Research: A Global Perspective," *Proceedings of the Eighteenth Annual Transportation and Logistics Educators Conference,* St. Louis, Mo., October 22, 1989, pp. 142–171.

[6]Robert E. Shannon, *Systems Simulation: The Art and Science,* Englewood Cliffs, N.J.: Prentice-Hall, Inc., 1975, p. 1.

each operating period within the overall planning horizon as a finite interval. Final results represent an assumption of operating performance for each period in the planning horizon. For example, in the formulation of a five-year plan, each year is simulated as an independent event.

Static simulation seeks to project the outcome of a specified plan or course of future action. If the potential system design is identified, simulation can be used to quantify customer service levels and total-cost characteristics. Used in this sense, a static simulator provides a tool to rapidly measure the capabilities and costs related to system design and sensitivity analyses.[7]

An expanded use of static simulation involves a heuristic computation procedure to assist in the selection of warehouses. In this capacity, the static simulator can be programmed to evaluate and quantify various combinations of warehouses from a potential list of locations provided during problem specification.

When utilized to help identify the best logistics network, the typical heuristic procedure includes all possible warehouse locations in the initial simulation. Customer destinations are assigned to the best warehouse on the basis of lowest total logistics cost. A major benefit of simulation is the flexibility in the distribution channel alternatives that can be evaluated. Static simulation heuristics can be designed to consider lowest total cost, maximum service, or a combination of the two in the algorithm that assigns markets to distribution centers.

Given the design objective, the simulation deletes warehouse locations one at a time from the maximum number of potential sites until it arrives at a managerially specified minimum, or until only one facility remains in the system. The typical deletion procedure eliminates the most costly warehouse from the remaining ''in-system'' facilities on a marginal cost basis. The demand previously serviced by the ''eliminated'' warehouse is then reassigned to the next-lowest-cost supply point, and the quantification procedure is repeated. If a full system deletion process is desired, the static simulation will require as many iterations as there are potential warehouse locations under consideration.

For example, as Figure 19-6 illustrates, the first simulation might consider a logistics network with ten warehouses. The simulation heuristic would then evaluate the relative value of the tenth facility by weighing the fixed-cost reductions and variable cost increments that would occur if the tenth facility were closed. If the heuristic determines that the total cost would decline (as illustrated in Figure 19-6), the simulator would ''close'' the tenth facility and recompute the cost and service characteristics of a nine-warehouse network. The iterative process continues until the minimal cost distribution network is identified. For this example, the minimum cost network is six warehouse locations.

Static simulation identifies the ''best'' solution by comparing the total cost and threshold service capabilities of the distribution facility combinations resulting from the deletion procedure. This analysis is performed by direct comparison of cost and service characteristics of the alternative networks. There is no guarantee that

---

[7]Examples of software to complete static simulation analyses can be found in R. Ballou and J. Masters, ''Commercial Software for Locating Warehouses and Other Facilities,''*Journal of Business Logistics,* **14:**2, 1993, pp. 71–107.

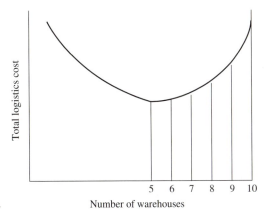

FIGURE 19-6   Heuristic simulation methodology.

the combination of facilities selected as a result of the deletion procedure will be the optimum or even the near optimum facility configuration. The fact that a warehouse location, once it is deleted, is no longer available for consideration in subsequent replications is one of the major shortcomings of static simulation procedures. Figure 19-7 illustrates the solution flow for a typical static simulation model. The system design algorithm represents the facility deletion procedure discussed above.

The main advantage of static simulation is that it is simpler, less expensive to operate, and more flexible than most optimization techniques. The replication capabilities of a multicheloned static simulator create almost unlimited design possibilities. Unlike mathematical programming approaches, simulation does not guarantee an optimum solution. However, static simulation offers a very flexible tool that may be used to evaluate a wide range of complex channel structures. As a result of the process of numerical computation, static simulation does not require explicit functional relationships. The capabilities and operating range of a comprehensive static simulator can often incorporate significantly more detail in terms of markets, products, distribution facilities, and shipment sizes than optimization techniques.

Conclusion   While site analysis, particularly for a single location, can be done manually or with a spreadsheet, more complex problems often require the use of specialized computer applications.[8] A number of commercial software products exist that are specifically designed to address the location analysis problem. Ronald Ballou and James Masters have (1) identified available software; (2) specified characteristics such as price, nature of the problem that can be handled, solution methodology, and distinguishing features; (3) assessed the state of the art in program development; and (4) asked users about their satisfaction with location pro-

---

[8]For small-scale logistics optimization problems, spreadsheets such as EXCEL and LOTUS 1-2-3 can be used. The specific solution approach is discussed in the ''Solver'' documentation of the appropriate user manual.

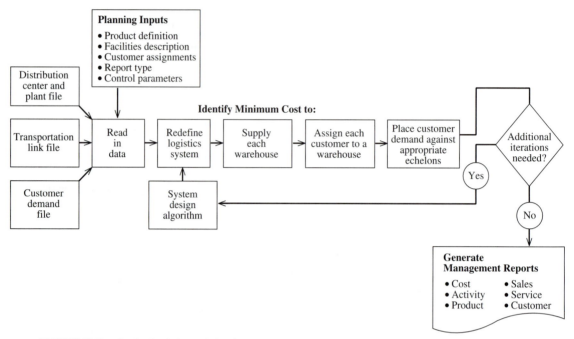

FIGURE 19-7 Static simulation solution flow.

grams and the factors they consider important in selecting such programs.[9] Their article, along with the Arthur Andersen Logistics Software Guide, offers the most current information for logistics network analysis software.

Location Analysis Data Requirements

The primary location analysis data requirements are definitions of markets, products, network, customer demand, transportation rates, and variable and fixed costs. Each element is discussed briefly.

Market Definition Location analysis requires that demand be classified or assigned to a geographic area. The combination of geographic areas constitutes a logistics service area. Such an area may be a country or a global region. The demand for each customer is assigned to one of the market areas. The selection of a market definition method is an extremely important element of the system design procedure.

A number of market definition structures have been developed. The most useful for logistics modeling are (1) county, (2) standard metropolitan statistical area (SMSA), and (3) ZIP or postal codes (postal codes are the international equivalent

---

[9]Ronald H. Ballou and James M. Masters, ''Commercial Software for Locating Warehouses and Other Facilities,'' *Journal of Business Logistics,* **14:**2, 1993, pp. 71–107.

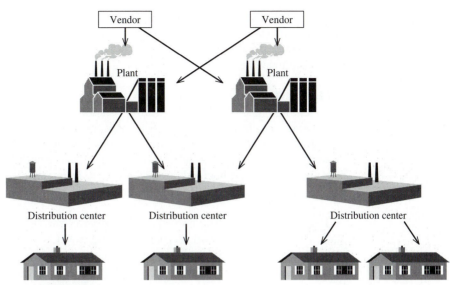

FIGURE 19-8   Channel network example.

of ZIP codes). The most common structure uses ZIP or postal codes since company records usually include such information. In addition, extensive government and transportation data are available by ZIP codes. The major issues for selecting a market definition approach concern the number of areas required to provide accurate results. While more market detail increases accuracy, it also increases analysis efforts. Research indicates that approximately 200 markets offer an effective trade-off between accuracy and analysis effort.[10]

Product Definition   Although individual product flows can be considered when performing a location analysis, it is usually not necessary to use such detail. Individual items—especially those with similar distribution characteristics, production sites, and channel arrangements—are grouped or aggregated to simplify the analysis.

Network Definition   The network definition specifies the channel members, institutions, and possible locations to be included in the analysis. Specific issues concern the combinations of suppliers, production locations, distribution centers, wholesalers, and retailers that are to be included. Network definition also includes consideration of new distribution centers or channel member alternatives. Figure 19-8 illustrates a channel network. While using a more comprehensive definition

[10]For original research regarding the number of market areas, see Robert G. House and Kenneth D. Jaime, ''Measuring the Impact of Alternative Classification Methods in Distribution Planning,'' *Journal of Business Logistics,* **2:**2, 1981, pp. 1–31; and Ronald H. Ballou, ''Information Considerations for Logistics Network Planning,'' *International Journal of Physical Distribution and Materials Management,* **17:**7, 1987, pp. 3–14.

reduces the chance of suboptimizing logistics system performance, total channel location analysis increases complexity. Location analysts must evaluate the trade-offs between increasing analysis complexity and improved potential for total supply chain optimization.

Market Demand   Market demand defines shipment volume to each geographic area identified as a market. Specifically, location analysis is based on the relative product volume shipped to each market area. While the volume may pertain to the number of units or cases shipped to each market, most location analyses are based on weight, since transportation cost is strongly influenced by the amount of weight being moved. Market demand utilized in the analysis may also be based on historical shipments or anticipated volume if substantial changes are expected.

Transportation Rates   Inbound and outbound transportation rates are a major data requirement for location analysis. Rates must be provided for shipments between existing and potential distribution channel members and markets. In addition, rates must be developed for each shipment size and for each transportation link between distribution centers and markets. It is common for location analysis to require in excess of a million individual rates. Because of the large number, rates are commonly developed using regressions or are retrieved from diskettes provided by most carriers.

Variable and Fixed Costs   The final location analysis data requirements are the variable and fixed costs associated with operating distribution facilities. Variable costs include expenses related to labor, energy, utilities, and materials. In general, variable expenses are a function of throughput. Fixed costs include expenses related to facilities, equipment, and supervisory management. Within a relevant distribution facility operating range, fixed costs remain relatively constant. While variable and fixed cost differences by geography are typically not substantial, there are minor locational considerations that should be included to ensure analysis accuracy. The major differences result from locational peculiarities in wage rates, energy cost, land values, and taxes.

Conclusion   Substantial logistics planning emphasis is placed on location analysis. In the past, distribution networks were relatively stable, so it was unnecessary for firms to complete logistics system analyses regularly. However, the dynamics of alternative distribution channel options, changing logistics cost structures, and availability of third-party services require that logistics networks be evaluated and refined more frequently today. It is common for firms to perform evaluations annually or monthly.

INVENTORY APPLICATIONS

The second class of logistics decision support applications focuses on enhancing inventory performance. Inventory analysis decisions, techniques, and data requirements are reviewed.

Inventory Analysis Decisions

Inventory analysis decisions focus on determining the optimum inventory management parameters that meet desired service levels with minimum investment. This analysis can be designed to refine parameters on a periodic or daily basis. Daily refinements make parameters more sensitive to environmental changes such as demand levels or performance-cycle length; however, they may also result in ''nervous'' inventory management systems. System nervousness causes frequent expediting and deexpediting of numerous small shipments.

Inventory analysis focuses on the decisions discussed in Chapter 8. Specific questions include, (1) How much product should be produced during the next production cycle? (2) Which distribution centers should maintain inventories of each item (e.g., should slow-moving items be centralized)? (3) What is the optimum size of replenishment orders (the order quantity decision)? and (4) What is the necessary reorder point for replenishment orders (the safety stock decision)?

Inventory Analysis Techniques

There are two methods to evaluate and select from inventory management options: analytic and simulation. The characteristics of each method are discussed.

Analytic Inventory Techniques Analytic inventory methods utilize functional relationships such as those discussed in Chapter 8 to determine ideal inventory stocking parameters and the desired service level. Figure 19-9 illustrates the analytic inventory concept. The technique uses service objectives, demand characteristics, performance-cycle characteristics, and logistics system characteristics as input to calculate optimum inventory parameters. From an inventory management perspective, service objectives are typically defined in terms of case or order fill rates. Demand characteristics depict the periodic average and standard deviation

FIGURE 19-9   Analytic inventory overview.

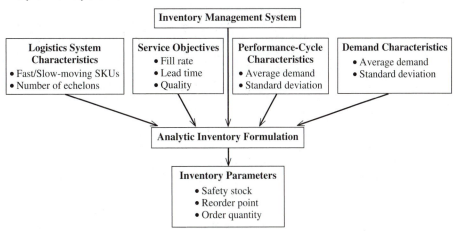

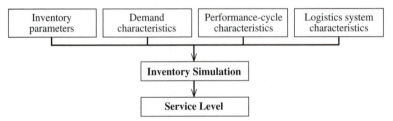

FIGURE 19-10   Inventory simulation overview.

of customer demand. Performance-cycle characteristics describe the average and standard deviations for replenishment performance cycles. Logistics system characteristics define the number of distribution stages or echelons requiring inventory management decisions. The analytic inventory technique is based on the assumptions describing the logistics system characteristics (stocking echelons) and the probabilities relating demand and performance-cycle characteristics. The probability relationships, along with the service level objectives, determine the optimal inventory management parameters in terms of replenishment order quantities and reorder points. Numerous examples of software applications exist that utilize analytic techniques to determine optimum inventory management parameters.[11]

The advantage of analytic inventory techniques is their ability to directly determine optimum inventory parameters given certain assumptions regarding operating environment. On the other hand, analytic techniques are limited in terms of accuracy when assumptions are not met. For example, since most of them assume normally distributed demand and performance cycles, the techniques lose accuracy when the shape of actual demand or performance cycles deviates from the normality assumption.[12] Nevertheless, analytic inventory techniques are often a good place to start when attempting to determine optimum inventory parameters.

Simulation Inventory Techniques   The inventory simulation approach creates a mathematical and probabilistic model of the logistics operating environment as it actually exists. As illustrated in Figure 19-10, the approach is similar to creating a "wind tunnel" testing environment for the logistics network and operating policies. Simulation is similar to the analytic approach except that the roles of the inventory parameters and service levels are reversed.

In simulation, inventory parameters, such as the order quantities and the reorder points that are to be tested, become the simulation inputs. These inputs define the

[11]Examples of such inventory management systems include Linx from Numetrix Software, Toronto, Ontario, Canada; Optimal Planner from Cleveland Consulting Associates, Cleveland, Ohio; and Inventory Analyst from Intex Solutions, Inc., Needham, Mass. The first two contain inventory management applications within a much larger enterprise modeling system. The final application is an example of a spreadsheet-based model that primarily computes the inventory parameters.

[12]These assumptions regarding normal demand and lead times can be overcome with numerical methods such as discussed in J. Masters, "Determination of Near Optimal Stock Levels for Multi-Echelon Distribution Inventories," *Journal of Business Logistics,* **14:**2, 1993, pp. 165–196.

environment to be tested. The major simulation outputs are the service level and inventory performance characteristics of the testing environment. The simulation, in effect, evaluates the performance of a specific situation. If the reported performance does not achieve desired objectives (e.g., simulated service level is below desired levels), the inventory parameters must be changed and a new environment is simulated. It is sometimes necessary to complete a number of simulations to identify the combination of inventory parameters that yields optimum performance.

The major benefit of inventory simulation techniques is the ability to model a wide range of logistics environments without requiring simplifying assumptions. It is possible to accurately simulate variability in the logistics environment by incorporating characteristics and operating policies. The major shortfall of simulation techniques is their limited ability to search for and identify optimum solutions. While there are inventory simulation examples that incorporate search algorithms, they are limited in capability and scope. There are indications that simulation is becoming more popular as firms attempt to understand inventory dynamics in the logistics channel.[13]

Conclusion   Inventory decision support applications are increasing in importance because of the emphasis on streamlining inventory levels to reduce the logistics asset base. The demand for more refined inventory parameters has increased the need for more sophisticated inventory analysis techniques. Software firms have responded by developing both stand-alone and integrated applications.[14]

TRANSPORTATION APPLICATIONS

The third class of logistics decision support applications focuses on enhancing transportation resource performance. Transportation analysis decisions, techniques, and data requirements are reviewed.

Transportation Analysis Decisions

Transportation analyses focus on routing and scheduling of transportation equipment to optimize vehicle and driver utilization while meeting customer service requirements. Transportation decisions can be characterized as strategic or tactical. Strategic transportation decisions concern long-term resource allocation, such as for extended time periods. Thus, strategic routing decisions identify fixed transport routes that may be used for months or years. Tactical transportation decisions involve short-term resource allocations such as daily or weekly routes. The objective of transportation analysis is to minimize the combination of vehicles, hours, or miles required to deliver product. Typical transportation analysis questions

---

[13]Process simulation is broadly discussed in K. Mabrouk, "Mentorship: A Stepping Stone to Simulation Success," *Industrial Engineering,* February 1994, pp. 41–43. Simulation package capabilities are described in J. Swain, "Flexible Tools for Modeling," *OR/MS Today,* December 1993, pp. 62–78.

[14]Examples include L. Buclos, "Hospital Inventory Management for Emergency Demand," *International Journal of Purchasing & Materials,* **29:**4, Fall 1993, pp. 30–37; and J. Santa-Clara, "Logistics Simulation in Multi-Supplier Operations," *Human Systems Management,* **12:**1, 1993, pp. 41–48.

SIMULATION AND SERVICE

Fisher Controls International, Inc., is the largest manufacturer of automatic control valves and related equipment in the world. Yearly sales in the early 1990s exceeded $1 billion. The company has 50 manufacturing and service centers in 22 countries and 200 sales offices in 75 countries.

Product differentiation achieved through a "strategic pyramid" of high quality, leading engineering design, and superior customer service had clearly established Fisher as the value leader for all markets within the valve industry. In the late 1980s, however, some competitors began to shift their focus from a low-cost strategy to strategies similar to Fisher's. As the competitive gap closed, a serious problem became apparent. Indications from Fisher's representatives and customers showed that the customer service side of Fisher's replacement parts business, particularly its distribution capability, lacked the basic foundation to support a superior customer service strategy. In emergency situations, Fisher representatives and service companies were able to respond through innovation and strong commitment to customers; however, this method was not efficient, nor did it allow Fisher to further differentiate its products through consistent customer service.

A multifunctional task force supported by an outside consulting firm generated three specific recommendations to improve Fisher's position in the valve aftermarket. The first recommendation involved creating an internal focus on the replacement parts business by dedicating resources and management talent to this area to meet customer expectations. The second recommendation suggested developing a logistics strategy to improve Fisher's quality image and reduce costs associated with non-value-added activities. The final recommendation involved meeting other marketing issues by developing focused parts sales efforts in the field and corporate promotion of the replacement parts business. In order to address these recommendations, Fisher had two options: develop the strategy internally, or select a third-party partner. After further research, Fisher chose to achieve its goals through a third-party logistics provider, Caterpillar Logistics Services, Inc. (CLS).

CLS performs all warehousing, transportation management, inventory management, and some consulting support for Fisher. A particular concern of the CLS package is the portion that deals with forecasting and the inventory management of slow-moving items. In fact, 88 percent of items stocked in parts warehouses sell less than twelve times per year. Although the items do not contribute substantially to total parts sales, they do contribute to total inventory investment.

In order to define each client's customer service program, a mission must be established. CLS accomplishes this task through the use of a computer simulation model that allows the client to evaluate the cost and impact of many different potential stocking, inventory, customer service, and warehousing policies. The simulation model contains several key features: (1) a Poisson probability distribution for customer arrivals;

include, (1) How should deliveries be grouped to form routes? (2) What is the best delivery sequence for servicing customers? (3) Which routes should be assigned to which vehicle types? (4) What is the best type of vehicle for servicing different customer types? and (5) How will delivery time restrictions be imposed by customers? Figure 19-11 illustrates a typical routing or delivery problem. The distribution center represents the central departure site for all delivery vehicles, and each stop indicates a customer location such as a retailer.

Transportation Analysis Techniques

Routing and scheduling analysis has been well researched for logistics design and planning. It is particularly important for firms completing partial load delivery

(2) a desired SKU service level formula (which is a function of overall customer service regarding all items, the item forecast, unit cost, economic order quantity, and several other variables); (3) an assessment of EOQ costs with customer service, inventory, and safety stock; and (4) actual client sales history. After several different strategies have been tested using the model, further options are usually identified and evaluated, and the best option is jointly selected between Fisher and CLS.

Inventory management software specifically assesses three issues in support of the simulation model analysis: item forecasting, item replenishment, and system reporting performance. In terms of item forecasting, Fisher's demand history is analyzed at the SKU level, and different forecasts are used for SKUs depending on their individual characteristics. At minimum, twenty-four months of item history are required to produce the analysis. On the basis of tests of statistical significance, the analysis then places each SKU into one of several classes: (1) very slow moving items, (2) demand pattern shifts, (3) override based on outside knowledge, (4) periodic forecast adjustments based on overall business conditions, (5) older products with declining sales that are being phased out, and (6) mechanical (rather than manual) add-to-stock/remove-from-stock calculation capability. These techniques provide a monthly mean sales estimate by SKU and are combined with the appropriate probability distribution formulas and control parameters from the simulation process to calculate the replenishment point. Item replenishment is carried out through a DRP model that creates firm purchase orders and a purchase order forecast over a twelve-month planning horizon. Special expedite order policies also exist for generating emergency purchase orders. Report performance covers a variety of subjects. The most critical is the customer service management report because a customer service guarantee exists in the Fisher/CLS contract agreement. Service losses are separately tracked on a weekly basis in three major categories: vendor delay (which causes back-orders), inventory management (actual service loss versus simulation predicted loss), and warehouse management. All categories and their subcategories may be tracked at the individual SKU level.

The Fisher/CLS agreement has enabled Fisher to regain most of its lost market share and meet or exceed customer parts delivery expectations. In addition, Fisher has achieved a position of industry leadership in parts availability and delivery while reducing the price or order nonconformance and improving the overall profitability of its parts replacement business. Specifically, replacement parts availability increased from 63 percent in 1987 to over 94 percent in the early 1990s. Customer satisfaction with Fisher increased over a variety of service measures. Sales dollars increased 70 percent, while volume of lines shipped from the warehouse increased 44 percent. Inventory turns increased nearly 25 percent from 2.1 to 2.6. Effective inventory management, due in large part to simulation modeling and support software, has dramatically improved Fisher company performance on a global basis.

Source: Michele Rhilinger and David Giffin, "Forecasting and Inventory Management for Slow-Moving Parts," *Proceedings of the Council of Logistics Management,* vol. **2**, 1991.

activities, such as package or beverage distribution. The techniques can generally be classified as heuristic approaches, exact approaches, interactive approaches, and combination approaches.[15] Heuristic approaches utilize rule-of-thumb clustering or savings techniques to develop routes by sequentially adding and deleting stops. Exact, or optimal, approaches use mathematical (linear) programming to identify the best routes. Historically, optimization solution methods have been too computationally complex for even the fastest computers. However, recent mathematical programming advances have enhanced their capabilities. The main difficulties with most exact procedures are (1) the large number of constraints

[15]For a discussion of each of these approaches, see Kevin Bott and Ronald H. Ballou, "Research Perspectives in Vehicle Routing and Scheduling," *Transportation Research,* **20A**:3, 1986, pp. 239–243.

SKATING INTO THE FUTURE

Rollerblade, Inc., of Minnetonka, Minnesota, is a skate manufacturer that had a very big problem with regard to its distribution activities: its warehouse workers were unable to find product to ship because of poor storage facilities. Worse yet, when the products were eventually located, overcrowded aisles and other space constraints made any efficient product movement highly unlikely. Specifically, usable warehouse space was nonexistent, there was a significant backlog of customer orders, and the error level in the order selection process was clearly unacceptable.

The solution to Rollerblade's problem was achieved through the use of a simulation software program. The simulation program enables users to generate both simple and complex layout alternatives on a PC-based system and to actually see how the prospective changes will affect product flows in terms of storage and distribution. Effective layout designs are able to analyze service issues such as customer demand, product mix, and throughput volume. Design solutions include consideration of cross-docking, just-in-time, and flexibility requirements.

Rollerblade's implementation of the best design solution achieved a 32 percent improvement in cubic space utilization, increased the number of daily customer orders processed from 140 to 410, reduced order selection errors, and eliminated order backlog. Ian Ellis, director of facilities and safety, says, ''Now we have a different business. The new layout has taken us from being in a crunch, to being able to plan.''

Applying simulation to warehouse layout and design can be a powerful logistical tool because it enables a warehouse manager to see his/her ideas in a simple yet clear and dramatic manner. Several simulation packages now go as far as to provide layout animation. They provide the user with a three-dimensional vision in which trucks move through aisles, conveyor speeds can be rated, and shipping and receiving operations can be timed. In effect, the warehouse is . . . a virtual reality.

Source: Cindy Muroff, ''Warehouse Layouts: A Virtual Reality,'' *Distribution*, March 1993, pp. 84–85.

---

and variables needed to represent even the most basic routing and scheduling problem, and (2) the impact of this size on computation time and computer storage space.

Interactive approaches utilize a combination of simulation, cost calculator, or graphics capability to support a decision process. The decision maker identifies the alternatives for evaluation. The interactive decision support system then determines and plots the routes and calculates the performance characteristics in terms of time and cost. The decision maker then interactively evaluates the performance characteristics of each alternative and refines the strategy until no additional improvement is likely. The obvious drawback of interactive approaches is the dependence on the skill and ability of the decision maker, particularly as the problem size and complexity increase.

Combinations of the three approaches have proved very effective. Two criteria are important when evaluating alternative solutions: generalizability and accuracy. Generalizability is the ability to efficiently incorporate extensions for special situations such as pickups and deliveries, multiple depots, time windows, vehicle capacities, and legal driving times. It concerns the ability to implement a particular solution when applied in an actual setting. Accuracy refers to the ability to closely approximate performance characteristics and the results' proximity to an optimal solution. Accuracy determines the level and credibility of possible savings as a

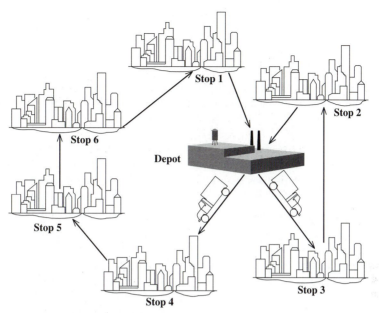

FIGURE 19-11   Typical routing or delivery problem.

result of decreased vehicle operating expense, better customer service, and improved fleet productivity.[16]

Transportation Analysis Data Requirements

Transportation analysis requires three types of data: network, pickup or delivery demand, and operating characteristics. The network defines all possible routes and is the backbone of any transportation system analysis. In some cases, a network is defined using street maps of the delivery area. Each intersection is a node, and the streets become links. The network contains the links between each node, the road distance, the transit time, and any special constraints such as weight limits or tolls. A street-level network is very accurate and precise particularly when there are constraints such as rivers and mountains. The deficiency of a street-level network is the high cost of development and maintenance. The other approach involves plotting customers on a grid and then computing the possible links between them using the straight-line distance. Latitude and longitude coordinates are often used. While a grid system is less costly to develop and maintain than a street-level network, it is less accurate and does not consider constraints as well.

---

[16]For an expanded discussion of alternative analysis approaches, see Kevin Bott and Ronald Ballou, "Research Perspectives in Vehicle Routing and Scheduling," *Transportation Research*, **20A**:3, 1986, pp. 239–243; Ronald H. Ballou and Yogesh K. Agerwal, "A Performance Comparison of Several Popular Algorithms for Vehicle Routing and Scheduling," *Journal of Business Logistics* **9**:1, 1988, pp. 51–64; and Ronald H. Ballou, "A Continued Comparison of Several Popular Algorithms for Vehicle Routing and Scheduling," *Journal of Business Logistics* **11**:2, 1990, pp. 111–126.

Demand data define periodic customer pickup and delivery requirements. For strategic or long-term analysis, demand is specified in terms of average periodic pickups or deliveries per customer. Routes are then created on the basis of average demand with a capacity allowance for extremely high demand periods. For tactical routing analysis, demand typically represents customer orders scheduled for delivery during the period being planned, such as daily. Tactical analysis allows the routes to be precisely designed for delivery requirements with no allowance for uncertainty.

Operating characteristics define the number of vehicles, vehicle limitations, driver constraints, and operating costs. Vehicle limitations include capacity and weight restrictions as well as unloading constraints such as dock requirements. Driver constraints involve driving time and unloading restrictions. Operating costs include fixed and variable expenses associated with vehicles and drivers.

Conclusion

Transportation analysis for vehicle routing and scheduling is receiving increased interest because of the effectiveness and availability of low-cost software. Many firms involved in day-to-day transportation operations have reduced expenses by 10 to 15 percent through the use of tactical or strategic analysis. As customers continue to demand smaller orders, transportation analysis will become increasingly important to make effective routing, scheduling, and consolidation decisions.

ENTERPRISE MODELING

Demands for increased return on investment, along with a more complex logistics environment, have caused many firms to seek out sophisticated decision support applications that can quantitatively identify the impact of complex logistics strategies. These DSS applications have been described as ''enterprise models,'' since their scope includes the entire enterprise and they incorporate both spatial and temporal dimensions of logistics. Specifically, enterprise models consider the activity-based costs such as transportation and handling and the time-based costs associated with inventory, storage, and production capacities. While the location and inventory applications discussed earlier specifically focus on either location or inventory, more or less assuming the other dimension away, enterprise models consider both spatial and temporal elements.

The typical enterprise model considers the facility locations of major suppliers, production sites, distribution centers, and even major customers. The fixed and variable cost differentials associated with sourcing, processing, and moving product between locations are incorporated. In addition, enterprise modeling considers the temporal dimension by including the cost and service impact of production and distribution facility capacity constraints. For example, while the production/logistics system may be able to accommodate customer demands if they were spread evenly across the year, seasonal production or sales may inhibit effective supply chain performance. For such seasonal supply-and-demand situations, enterprise modeling can identify major bottlenecks, their cost implications, and the possible resolutions. Enterprise models generally operate on a monthly or weekly time frame.

HAVING TROUBLE SLEEPING? TRY SITE DECISION AND TRANSPORTATION SOFTWARE

In the mid-1980s, the mattress and box spring manufacturer Simmons Company maintained forty warehouses and eight large plants throughout the United States. Unfortunately, the distribution network that Simmons utilized led to excessive inventory and poor customer service. The problem was that most mattress showrooms face a difficult marketing and logistical problem: limited space. Sleep shops in strip malls do not typically have much storage area, and so they are forced to rely on suppliers to replenish inventory on scheduled or committed days. As the level of competition increased from rival mattress makers, Simmons decided to radically redesign and streamline its manufacturing and logistical strategy. Today, the company supplies U.S. department stores, furniture stores, and sleep shops directly from a given plant under its just-in-time make-to-order program.

Under Simmons' new plan, inventories were sharply reduced and many warehouses closed. Today, the company has fifteen manufacturing plants with minimal inventory at each, and no separate warehouses. Production is keyed directly to retail orders. Order cycle time from order entry to production to delivery is typically four to five days, and oftentimes much quicker. Most mattresses come off the production line ready for immediate customer shipment. A plant has about 1,200 finished units in storage at any given point in time: under the old setup, the level of finished inventory was usually 50,000 or more units.

A crucial factor that has allowed Simmons to adopt a highly flexible manufacturing and logistical strategy is computer modeling. The company utilized site selection software to manage the enormous complexity involved in building multi-million-dollar production plants, and also uses transportation software to provide efficient, timely customer service without a warehouse network and support inventory.

Simmons uses a site selection optimization program for a variety of purposes. First, the program assigns each customer to one of its strategically located production plants. This capability has allowed the company to move to smaller and less expensive facilities. Second, the optimization program determines specific locations by examining the company's current account base from a geographical perspective and identifies small, medium, and large customers. It compares factors of labor rates, carrier availability, and inbound movement of raw materials. The program also establishes optimum production volumes for each plant and can determine whether a particular geographic region can support an additional facility.

To support the site selection process, Simmons examines overall transportation impact through the use of route optimization software. The model studies how a shift in customer assignment affects the size of Simmons' fleet, its drivers, transit time, and trailer utilization. The best routes for delivery from plant to customer are also calculated, along with carrier, equipment, and optimum load plan.

The use of site selection and transportation route modeling now allows Simmons to operate without the buffer of large inventories. The company is able to combine modern modeling characteristics of capacity, speed, and sensitivity analysis with intuitive human decision making to reduce warehouse and transportation costs and, most important, product cycle time. That translates into improved customer service and increased market share, which helps Simmons Company and its customers to sleep a little easier at night.

Source: "Keying into Versatility," *Distribution*, May 1993, pp. 54–61.

Enterprise modeling is receiving increased interest because of the demand for better logistics system capacity utilization. While there is limited literature describing its use, there are a growing number of software applications.[17] Enterprise

---

[17]One article describing enterprise modeling is J. F. Shapiro, V. Singhal, and S. N. Wagner, "Optimizing the Value Chain," *Interfaces*, **23**:2, March–April 1993, p. 102. Firms providing enterprise modeling software and consulting include CSC Consulting, Austin, Tex.; Insight Inc., Alexandria, Va.; and Numetrix Inc., Toronto, Ontario, Canada.

models are utilized for decisions that include both strategic and tactical considerations. Typical questions that enterprise modeling can evaluate include, (1) What product lines should be assigned to each manufacturing site given seasonality in raw material availability or consumption? (2) How should distribution network locations and capacity change in response to product buildups and market seasonality? and (3) How should weekly or monthly production be scheduled to optimize the trade-off between production costs and finished goods inventory carrying cost? Enterprise modeling will be the decision support solution for managers who recognize that high-level logistics and supply chain performance can be achieved only when both spatial and temporal logistics elements are considered.

SUMMARY

Chapter 19 described the problem analysis approaches commonly used in logistics. The first group of decisions focused on less formal ad hoc issues that are encountered on a regular basis. Typical analyses requirements concern freight lane balancing, ABC inventory analysis, and product and customer profitability from a logistics perspective. Each analysis was described and illustrated.

The chapter then discussed more formal decision support applications for location, inventory, transportation, and enterprise decisions. Location decisions concern the identification of sites and service areas for manufacturing and distribution centers. Inventory decisions consider stocking policies and levels. Stocking policies determine *where* inventory should be maintained, while levels indicate *how much* inventory should be maintained. Enterprise modeling seeks to fully integrate the spatial and temporal aspects of logistical planning. Transportation decisions consider transport consolidation and vehicle routing. The chapter discussed each application in terms of the specific questions, applicable analytical techniques, and major data requirement.

QUESTIONS

1 Compare and contrast the center of gravity models with linear programming models.
2 Compare and contrast strategic and tactical transportation decisions.
3 What is the advantage of ad hoc analysis? How does it fit into a more comprehensive analysis?
4 What is the key objective in freight lane analysis?
5 Compare and contrast inventory classification with segment profitability. What do the two concepts have in common, and how do they differ?
6 In a general sense, what are the essential differences between analytic and simulation techniques?
7 What is the main advantage of simulation compared to the typical optimization technique?
8 What is the main advantage of the typical optimization technique in comparison to simulation?
9 Since enterprise modeling is by far the most comprehensive planning and analysis approach, why do managers focus on less encompassing analysis techniques?
10 At what point in the typical analysis does the technique give way to the managerial review and evaluation process?

CASES

CASE D: Westminster Company: A System Design Assessment

COMPANY PROFILE

Westminster Company is one of the world's largest manufacturers of consumer health products; its distinctive name and company logo are recognized throughout the world. Originally founded as a family-owned pharmaceutical supply business in 1923, the company's corporate headquarters is still located in a scenic town of 60,000 people in the northeast United States. Westminster also maintains regional offices in Europe, Latin America, and the Pacific Rim to support overseas manufacturing and distribution.

Westminster's domestic operations consist of three separate sales divisions, each of which manufactures and distributes its own product line. Decentralized divisional management is a proud historical tradition at Westminster. According to President Jonathan Beamer, it is a process that requires and encourages responsibility, enhances self-ownership of the work process, and provides the key component of corporate success. Westminster's products are marketed through a network of diverse retailers and wholesalers. Trade class as a percentage of sales is 37 percent grocery, 31 percent drug, 21 percent mass merchandise, and 11 percent miscellaneous.

WESTMINSTER TODAY

Pressure from domestic and global competitors, as well as from domestic Westminster customers, has recently forced the company to reevaluate its current distribution practices. In particular, attention has focused on the changes that will be required to effectively compete in the marketplace of the 1990s.

Robb Frankel prepared this case for class discussion. Actual facts have been altered to maintain confidentiality and to provide an enhanced business situation.

Westminster just concluded several months of extensive research that focused on customers' primary logistics concerns for the future. The research findings addressed a variety of issues, but two key topics were identified: customer composition and customer service requirements.

The most significant trend with regard to customer composition over the past decade has been the evolution of the company customer base into either very large or very small accounts. This development is expected to continue at a comparable pace in the foreseeable future. The major shift in the mix of accounts is not expected, however, to dramatically alter the historical composition of product sales. Approximately 50 percent of domestic consumer sales volume is concentrated within 10 percent of Westminster's customers. What may affect the composition of product sales to large retail accounts, however, is the rapid growth of private-label nonprescription drugs and consumer health products. Cost-efficient private-label manufacturers offer large retail accounts higher profit margins, willingness to quickly change or customize products, and the ability to appeal to increasingly price-conscious consumers. Specifically, sales volume of private-label health and beauty aids businesses totaled $3 billion in 1992.

Research findings have confirmed top management's belief that these large accounts require an intense commitment by Westminster to increase the firm's logistics efficiency. To maintain and increase the percentage of sales volume Westminster derives from these important customer accounts, the company has identified several key customer service concerns. These concerns specifically address the second issue of customer service requirements. Company research has also concluded that the formulation of supply chain partnerships between Westminster and its large customers has now become a competitive necessity. In many instances, powerful retailers now demand such arrangements and oftentimes have the leverage to dictate the conditions of the arrangements. Westminster will have to maintain considerable flexibility in order to accommodate different solutions for a variety of large, powerful customers. Ideally, Westminster would like to establish a position of leadership within these partnership arrangements where practical.

Westminster is well aware that successful retailers and wholesalers are focusing strategic effort on more timely, efficient, and accurate inventory positioning. Many large firms have identified supply chain management techniques as a primary tool in achieving successful inventory management and improving overall financial performance. "I visualize three important changes for our operations with regard to large accounts," says Alex Coldfield, Westminster's vice president of logistics. "First, traditional inventory replenishment procedures will be replaced by POS-driven information systems. Customers will transmit daily or biweekly product sales movement to us in order to ensure timely inventory replenishment and allow production to be scheduled according to sales-driven forecast rather than marketing forecasts. We will also establish and utilize customer support 'work teams' that operate on-site with key customer accounts to better manage ordering and distribution. Second, order cycle times will have to be reduced from current levels. Large accounts will increasingly demand two rather than one delivery per week. In addition, many large accounts want to simplify their manufacturing contacts and are questioning why we cannot provide consolidated order shipment from our three consumer product divisions when cost reductions are achievable. The demand for direct store delivery (DSD) may also significantly increase. Third, products will increasingly have to meet specific customer requirements, such as assembly of individual store shipments and customized inner packs and display units. Bar codes will have to utilize industry standards such as UCC 128. Invoicing and payment, particularly with regard to promotional allowances and discounts, will become paperless transactions conducted via EDI. Our pricing will evolve to reflect services provided, rather than purely traditional logistical order fulfillment, transportation and handling."

For the balance of Westminster's customers, distribution service will be provided much as it is today. Although other customers may not be willing or able to initiate such close working relationships, they will be entitled to a high standard of basic service that provides timely and consistent performance. For these ac-

counts, purchase price will remain the priority, although there will be some increased pressure for improved order fill rates and decreased cycle times. Traditional purchase order invoicing and payment will also remain the rule.

In response to the issues raised by company research, CEO Wilson McKee directed the company's executive management committee to organize a logistics task force. The task force, which includes top-level managers from each division's functional departments, has been directed to identify potential changes within the three domestic sales division networks that will achieve improved distribution performance and responsiveness.

WESTMINSTER'S DISTRIBUTION NETWORK

Table 1 outlines Westminster's existing distribution network for the three domestic consumer sales divisions. Each division consists of a number of company-owned and operated manufacturing plants and distribution facilities. Table 2 presents a number of key demand and inventory statistics for the facilities.

Each manufacturing plant produces stockkeeping units (SKUs) unique to that particular facility. All SKUs are distributed on a national basis. Because of significant capital outlays and fixed costs associated with each manufacturing plant, the logistics task force has already eliminated the possibility of relocating any manufacturing facilities from their present locations.

Manufacturing plants must route products through a distribution center before final delivery to a retail or wholesale customer. Any distribution center may be utilized within its own division. Distribution centers may ship product to any region of the country; however, customers are typically serviced by the closest distribution center according to Westminster's regional boundaries. Transfer shipments between distribution centers are also permissible.

Most shipments from manufacturing plants to distribution centers are delivered via motor carrier on a truckload basis. Air freight may be utilized for emergency shipments but also must pass through a distribution center before delivery to a final destination. Most shipments between distribution centers and retail or wholesale customers are delivered by motor carrier on a less-than-truckload basis and vary in size from a few pounds to nearly truckload quantities. Table 3 illustrates the three domestic sales divisions' shipments by typical weight brackets and the number of bills of lading issued

TABLE 1 WESTMINSTER COMPANY
FACILITY LOCATIONS

Division "A"

Manufacturing plants	Percentage of total pounds produced
1 Los Angeles, Calif.	53
2 Atlanta, Ga.	24
3 Jacksonville, Fla.	23

Distribution centers	Percentage of total pounds shipped
1 Newark, N.J.	28
2 Atlanta, Ga.	31
3 Dallas, Tex.	41

Division "B"

Manufacturing plants	Percentage of total pounds produced
1 Philadelphia, Pa.	39
2 Newark, N.J.	37
3 Atlanta, Ga.	24

Distribution centers	Percentage of total pounds shipped
1 Philadelphia, Pa.	78
2 Los Angeles, Calif.	22

Division "C"

Manufacturing plants	Percentage of total pounds produced
1 Chicago, Ill.	75
2 Houston, Tex.	10
3 Trenton, N.J.	15

Distribution centers	Percentage of total pounds shipped
1 Newark, N.J.	38
2 Chicago, Ill.	54
3 Los Angeles, Calif.	8

TABLE 2 WESTMINSTER CUSTOMER DEMAND
(1992)

Characteristics	Division "A"	Division "B"	Division "C"
Total demand			
(000,000 lb)	150	72	60
Sales ($000,000)	475	920	271
Cases (000,000)	13.2	8.5	9.8
Shipments (000)	80	88	73
Lines ordered (000)	1,060	683	340
Inventory turns			
per year	6.5	10.8	7.2
Total SKUs	1,260	430	220

Distribution center locations are based on both market and production factors. The majority of distribution centers are strategically located throughout the country to service geographic territories that contain the strongest demand for Westminster products. Demand patterns for consumer products follow major population centers and are generally consistent across the country for all three divisions. Several distribution centers are located near manufacturing plants to reduce transportation costs. The customer demand profile follows the state-by-state population profile.

Table 4 lists the current system's transportation and warehousing costs for each of the three divisions. Freight rate classification for product shipments is different for each of the three divisions. Division "A" freight has a rating of class 60, division "B" freight has a rating of class 70, and division "C" freight has a rating of 200. Transfer freight costs are based on truckload rates from the manufacturing plants to the distribution centers. Customer freight costs are based on less-than-truckload shipments from distribution centers to retail and wholesale customers. Average number of days transit time from the distribution centers to the

TABLE 3 SHIPMENT PROFILES

Shipment size	Percent of weight	Percent of shipments
Package delivery	6	25
< 500 lb	8	22
500 < size ≤ 2,000 lb	13	20
2,000 < size ≤ 5,000 lb	18	15
5,000 < size ≤ 10,000 lb	22	10
> 10,000 lb	32	8

within each bracket. The first weight bracket (0 to 70 pounds) represents shipments typically delivered by small parcel carriers; the majority of these shipments represent order fulfillment of back-ordered SKUs. Approximately 67 percent of all shipments are 500 pounds or less.

TABLE 4 WESTMINSTER 1992 DISTRIBUTION COSTS ($000,000)

	Division "A"	Division "B"	Division "C"
Transportation			
Transfer freight	4.2	3.2	2.8
Customer freight	9.9	8.3	8.5
Total transportation costs	14.1	11.5	11.3
Warehousing			
Storage and handling	6.2	4.4	3.2
Fixed	2.3	1.6	4.2
Total warehousing costs	8.5	6.0	7.4
Total distribution costs	22.6	17.5	18.7
Average number of days transit time (distribution center to customer)	2.8	2.9	2.3

TABLE 5 HOURLY WAGE RATE FOR U.S. CITIES

City	Wage rate ($)
Chicago, Ill.	16.20
Seattle, Wash.	17.87
Buffalo, N.Y.	15.59
Syracuse, N.Y.	15.59
Pittsburgh, Pa.	16.96
Atlanta, Ga.	12.72
Houston, Tex.	15.14
Phoenix, Ariz.	12.87
Kansas City, Mo.	15.90
Philadelphia, Pa.	15.75
Laredo, Tex.	13.63
El Paso, Tex.	13.63
Dallas, Tex.	13.78
Detroit, Mich.	19.38
Los Angeles, Calif.	16.96
Minneapolis, Minn.	16.96
Denver, Colo.	16.96
Memphis, Tenn.	12.57
New York, N.Y.	15.14
San Francisco, Calif.	17.87

customer is the shipment time from the point an order leaves the distribution center's loading dock until it reaches a customer. Any potential system redesign must consider the effect of labor costs. Table 5 lists average hourly wage compensation for a number of major United States cities.

The logistics task force is considering these three options or alternatives:

1 Consolidate the current three distribution systems into a single system serving all three divisions using fewer warehouses than at present.

2 Use public or third-party warehousing and third-party transportation rather than the current system network.

3 Continue with the current arrangement as is.

QUESTIONS

1 What effects would the two new alternatives have on transfer and customer freight costs? Why?

2 What effects would warehouse consolidation have on inventory carrying costs, customer service levels, and order fill rate?

3 How are warehousing costs affected by the decision to use public or private warehouse facilities? What effect would this have on handling, storage, and fixed facility costs?

4 What effect would transporting mixed shipments from consolidated distribution centers have on shipment profiles?

5 What factors should be taken into consideration when determining the appropriate number of warehouses?

6 What selection criteria should be used when evaluating a service provider's (public or third-party warehouse, or third-party transportation provider) ability to meet critical logistical concerns?

CASE E: Alternative Distribution Strategies

Sugar Sweets, Inc. (SSI) was considering ways to increase market coverage and sales volume on its candy and snack products. Historically, the majority of SSI products were sold to consumers through various grocery and convenience stores. Vending machines and institutional sales, such as airports, represent the remaining consumer market segments. The selling environment for candy and snack foods was becoming increasingly competitive, and traditional channels of distribution were being distorted, especially in the grocery and convenience trade.

Grocery and convenience stores were traditionally serviced through distributors known as candy and tobacco jobbers. These distributors purchased SSI products in large quantities and then sold them to the retail stores for sale to consumers. The number of candy and tobacco jobbers was decreasing, which was distorting the traditional distribution channel. Two factors were causing this distortion. First, the wholesaler and distributor industry in general was going through consolidation as large distributors continued to get larger and more profitable, while smaller and less profitable distributors either were bought up or closed. Second, the popularity of warehouse club stores threatened candy and tobacco jobbers. Small mom-and-pop grocery or convenience stores were able to purchase many products they needed at these warehouse clubs at the same price or less than what the distributors offered. Furthermore, the warehouse clubs provided a one-stop shopping experience, so that the grocery stores could purchase a wider range of products at the club store than was sold by any one candy and tobacco distributor. For example, a club store may offer a narrow selection of the most popular SSI products as well as its competitors' products, while an individual distributor may handle SSI products exclusively. While SSI encouraged grocery and convenience stores to carry its products, regardless of whether these stores purchase from distributors or club stores, there was a concern about how the products were serviced. Distributors provide a significant benefit in that they carry a broader line of SSI products than most club stores. Also, some candy and tobacco jobbers visit their retail customers regularly to ensure that the stores remain stocked with a large variety of fresh product. In this sense, candy and tobacco

jobbers provided a marketing service for SSI that is not achieved with club stores.

As such, SSI began looking for an alternative channel system that would not only increase market coverage in light of the new competitive environment but also provide the important marketing service to ensure a large variety of fresh product available for consumers. In order to accomplish this, SSI questioned the reliance on its traditional marketing channel, as well as the typical outlets its products were sold through. Andy Joslin, the vice president of integrated logistics, had an idea. Andy began to focus on new retail outlets where SSI products could be sold and how these sales could be uniquely managed via a new channel arrangement. It was determined that direct store delivery of SSI products could be handled using telemarketing for order processing and small package delivery. The notion was that any retail outlet that had sufficient counter space and high customer traffic was likely to sell high-impulse snack items such as SSI products. Examples of potential retail outlets that traditionally did not carry snack items included dry cleaners, barbers and beauty shops, hardware stores, and drinking establishments. The concept is summarized in Table 1.

The alternative distribution plan offers various ben-

TABLE 1   ALTERNATIVE DISTRIBUTION CONCEPT

- *What is it?*
  A unique new concept for distributing and selling SSI snack foods through new retail outlets to broaden market coverage.

- *How does it work?*
  Display units of popular snack foods are provided to retail outlets for direct purchase by consumers.

  Fast-selling items are easily restocked by telephone order with an 800 number and rapid small-package delivery service.

- *What are the special features?*
  Minimal effort is required on the retailers' part since the popularity of well-known SSI brands makes selling easy.

  Freshness is guaranteed by direct shipment from SSI's warehouses through rapid delivery service.

  Incremental money is made by selling high-profit "impulse" snack foods to customers at *no risk*, since SSI will remove slow-moving products at no cost to the retail outlet.

Judith M. Schmitz prepared this case for class discussion. Actual facts have been altered to maintain confidentiality and to provide an enhanced business situation.

efits. First, it is a unique selling concept in that it provides retailers with a way to increase their business through incremental sales of snack products with little risk of cannibalization by other retail outlets because of the impulse nature of the product. Furthermore, retailers are not required to make a significant capital investment to try the concept, and there is little risk to the retailer if the plan fails. SSI will provide countertop units or shelving to display the products and will suggest pricing for maximum sales volume and profit. The alternative distribution concept benefits SSI as well by providing market growth and exposing its products to a wider range of customers. Also, SSI will have direct contact with retailers, providing a great opportunity for testing and tracking new products while ensuring timely delivery.

One potential drawback is that the retailers may feel the incremental revenue received is insufficient, which will dissuade product reordering. Also, retailers may have pilferage problems that would discourage their participation. Finally, the arrangements could threaten candy and tobacco jobbers that rely on similar retail accounts. Resentment from candy and tobacco jobbers could potentially result in decreased service to grocery and convenience stores.

From initial interviews with target retailers, SSI became convinced that the alternative distribution concept had merit. The next step was to evaluate whether the idea was viable in terms of retail interest versus actual participation. An internal operating plan for managing the alternative distribution program would also need to be devised to identify and determine the internal costs and potential profit.

RETAIL INTEREST

Research, summarized in Table 2, illustrates important considerations for retail sales. Fifteen types of retail stores were targeted for participation, and thirty product lines were considered for distribution. Estimates concerning expected retail participation and sales were a critical part of business viability. To start, SSI estimated that it could contact only 20 percent of all target retailers. The remaining retailers would be approached after a one-year test period if the program was successful.

Two types of display units were designed as well as two reorder packages. An initial order would include two boxes shrink-wrapped together. One box would hold the product, and the other would hold the display unit. Table 3 provides display and product package

TABLE 2   RETAIL CHARACTERISTICS

Sales regions	Total number of target retailers
Eastern	320,000
Midwestern	290,000
Western	210,000

Percent of retailers for initial contact: 20 percent

Projected retailers that will participate after initial contact: 30 percent

Retailers that will continue after six-month trial period: 55 percent

Expected average retail sales transaction: $1.40 per customer purchase

Expected average unit sale: 1.12 units per customer purchase

Expected average customer traffic in retail store: 100/day

Expected average number of customers who will purchase product: 10 percent

characteristics. Reorder packs would contain the same product weight and units as shown for the initial order.

OPERATING PROCEDURES

Two logistics networks are under consideration for the new channel. Both networks facilitate direct retail customer contact: no distributors are included in the channel. One network uses three distribution centers, while the other uses four. Service for the first network is estimated at two to four days, with some outlying areas serviced in five days. Service through the second network is estimated at one to three days and to outlying areas in four days. The number of outlying areas is reduced under the second network. Table 4 compares the costs of both networks.

TABLE 3   INITIAL DISPLAY AND PRODUCT PACKAGE CHARACTERISTICS

	Large	Small
Weight	25 lb	14 lb
Cubic feet	2.75 ft^3	2.00 ft^3
Product included	24 lb	12 lb
Cost of display unit	$35	$18
Units of product	180 units	92 units
Production costs	$190	$98

TABLE 4 OPERATING COSTS PER ORDER

Costs	Three dist. centers	Four dist. centers
Handling	$3.00	$3.00
Storage	.11	.21
Transportation of average package	6.25	5.90
Ordering costs per order	.75	.75
Total logistics costs per order	10.11	9.86

The information flow would start with order entry at the telemarketing department. Retail orders would be transmitted to the appropriate distribution center and compiled each night. Orders would be picked and packed; then delivery would be arranged according to the aforementioned service levels.

SUMMARY

Before SSI can determine whether the alternative distribution concept should be initiated, it must analyze the information gathered and the project potential sales and profits. Profits must be determined for SSI as well as the retail customers. If retailers do not make sufficient incremental profit, it is unlikely that they will continue participating in the plan. A team has been assigned to perform the data analysis. Andy Joslin has identified five questions that he feels are critical for the team to analyze. These questions are provided below.

QUESTIONS

1 Determine the total number of retailers in the program initially as well as after the trial period.

2 Determine what the average retailer will sell on a daily basis as well as annually. Provide sales in terms of unit and dollar amounts. (Assume 260 business days per year, with 5 business days each week.)

3 Translate the annual sales for an average retailer into the number of large packs this retailer will order per year. Repeat for the small pack order. (Round off if necessary.) Include the initial order in the calculation.

4 SSI would like to determine its potential sales for the first year on the basis of information in question 3. However, there is some concern that the estimate of average retail sales is too high. SSI assumes only 40 percent of the participating retailers will actually achieve the average sales and reorders (this group is designated as high performers). Twenty percent of the retailers are expected to have medium performance success and will only sell/reorder 75 percent of the average suggested order. Low-performing retailers represent the remaining 40 percent and will achieve half the sales/reorder expected on average. Calculate the orders (separate initial and reorder quantities) for the six-month trial period if 45 percent of retailers exclusively order/reorder large packs and the remaining retailers exclusively order/reorder small packs. Calculate the second six months accounting for the dropout. (Round off if necessary.) Assume that the ''performer'' ratios remain the same after the trial period (i.e., 40 percent are average performers, 20 percent sell 75 percent of average, and 40 percent sell 50 percent of the average).

5 Assume retailers pay $205 for a large pack (initial or reorder) and $115 for a small pack. On the basis of the first year's sales calculated in question 4, determine the profit to SSI if three distribution centers are used. Repeat for the four-distribution-center network. Which network, if either, should be used? What factor(s) aside from cost/profit might influence the network decision?

CASE F: Michigan Liquor Control Commission

On a Friday afternoon in October 1994, Joseph Duncan, a third-year distribution systems analyst for the Michi-

Robb Frankel prepared this case for class discussion. Actual facts have been altered to maintain confidentiality and to provide an enhanced business situation.

gan Department of Commerce, was sitting at his office desk reading through some background material on distilled liquor distribution in Michigan. Prior to his current position, Joseph had worked as a distribution analyst in private industry for several years after graduating from a large midwestern university with a degree in materials and logistics management. His direct supervisor, Donna Mills, had given Joseph his next assignment earlier that day. "Be prepared to head up a project team and prepare a proposal on distilled liquor distribution," Donna said. "We'll meet Wednesday afternoon at 2 p.m. to lay out an initial plan." This was Joseph's first "lead" project assignment, and although he was unfamiliar with the topic, he was excited about the opportunity to demonstrate his ability. He placed the background material in his briefcase and decided to reexamine it at home over the upcoming weekend.

HISTORY OF MICHIGAN
LIQUOR DISTRIBUTION SYSTEM

In the early 1900s, brewers in Detroit were the dominant force in the state because of efficiencies of size, new bottling technology, and local "option laws" that restricted or outlawed in-county production. This created a sharp division between outstate and Detroit brewers and prevented the formation of a strong state liquor association. Prohibition forces also benefited from this divisiveness; by the year 1917, Michigan had forty-five dry counties. Michigan enacted a statewide prohibition on liquor in May 1918, approximately eighteen months prior to passage of federal prohibition (the Eighteenth Amendment). By the late 1920s and early 1930s, significant pressure existed throughout the country to repeal prohibition. In early 1933, Congress passed a bill authorizing 3.2 percent beer. In the same year, a similar bill was considered in Michigan, and along with it, a state board was introduced that came to be known as the Michigan Liquor Control Commission (MLCC). In April 1933, Michigan became the first state to ratify the repeal of federal prohibition, and the present-day liquor distribution system was designed and put into place.

A bill for beer and wine (defined legally as under 21 percent alcohol by volume) was passed that allowed distribution from brewers and wineries to private wholesalers, which then resell to retailers. However, all distilled "spirits" (defined legally as over 21 percent alcohol by volume) were to be purchased by the state of Michigan. Michigan's "come-to-rest" laws required that any distilled liquor moving through or stored in state bailment warehouses must be handled by state employees. Package liquor sales were allowed through any hotel or established merchant. Many of the merchants were druggists who also had the right to dispense "medicinal" liquors as well as valid medical prescrip-

tions. A local option was also set up to provide for on-premise consumption.

The state of Michigan's decision in 1933 to exercise public, rather than private, control over distilled liquor distribution was due to a variety of reasons. First, Michigan's geographical proximity to Canada made politicians familiar with Ontario's system of monopoly control. Second, there was a strong influence of "dry" sentiment and a fear of bootlegging, which was common during the prohibition years. Third, druggists exerted considerable political influence at the time and were positioned to benefit from state control. Finally, the state believed that government control would protect the public from middleman profiteering and excessively high private enterprise pricing.

Currently, Michigan is one of eighteen states in the United States that completely control the wholesale distribution of liquor between distillers and retail licensees. The remaining thirty-two states utilize an "open" private license system in which the state government is not involved in wholesale distribution.

In 1993, Michigan and many other states throughout the country faced the problem of rapidly increasing costs of government services and strong citizen resistance to any tax increases to provide those services. Unlike nearly all other Michigan government functions, the control and distribution of liquor generate a considerable revenue contribution for the state.

Public sensitivity toward liquor as a social issue and its ability to provide the state with significant revenue make liquor control a high-profit government activity. Under a recent directive from the governor, all state functions must be examined to determine how government efficiency could be improved. Despite the contribution of current operations, considerable room for improvement appears to exist. For example, despite technological improvements and the addition of more modern facilities, the cost of liquor distribution has continued to increase. Specifically, administrative cost as a percentage of sales has risen 121 percent over the past eleven years, while the number of inventory turns has decreased from 6.7 to 5.5.

THE LIQUOR DISTRIBUTION PROCESS

Distilled liquor distribution in the state of Michigan during the fiscal year 1992–1993 involved the shipment of 6.97 million cases of liquor to retail markets and generated $515 million in revenue for the state. After purchase costs and operating expenses, the net contribution to the state came to $61.5 million. The state also realizes roughly $50 million per year from taxes on distilled liquor plus excise taxes of over $70,000.

Contributions from the sale of distilled liquor are generated in the following manner: the state buys liquor directly from a distiller at a delivered price of, for example, $10.00 per bottle. Then, the state factors in transportation and other costs, and marks up the $10.00 bottle a state-mandated 65 percent to $16.50. Retailers buy liquor from the state at a 17 percent discount off the ''markup'' price, and in this example, they would pay a wholesale price of $13.70. The net result is that consumers pay the same retail price for distilled liquor everywhere throughout the state. The state-imposed taxes of 9.85 percent are assessed on the $16.50 price and are collected by the retailer upon sale to consumers.

Any alteration of Michigan liquor distribution must consider potential effects on liquor prices at the retail level. In terms of consumer purchase behavior, liquor quantity is generally price inelastic. The price elasticity of liquor sales with respect to total expenditures is, however, fairly elastic. These conditions imply that as prices are raised, consumers will generally purchase the same quantity of liquor but will shift their consumption to cheaper brands. This shift reduces projected consumer expenditures and tax revenues. If system changes require that prices be raised, the effect on tax revenues could be detrimental.

Currently, distilled liquor is distributed through a two-tier network consisting of 3 state-operated warehouses; 75 smaller second-tier state warehouses (known as *state stores*), which function as wholesale outlets; and 12,000 retail licensees serving the consuming public throughout the state (see Figure 1). Licensees are divided into two categories of approximately 6,000 members each: on-premise bars, restaurants, and hotels that serve liquor by the ''glass''; and off-premise ''package'' liquor dealers/stores. The package liquor dealers represent a wide variety of businesses, ranging from ''traditional'' liquor or party stores to large retail grocery superstores like Meijer, Inc. The first 600 retail licensee outlets were authorized in 1934 and have steadily increased to their current level. State store locations originally served as retail outlets. The number of state stores has declined in recent years, though most of the original seventy-five stores remain in their original cities.

The cost to operate the current distribution network is approximately $20 million per year. Average distilled

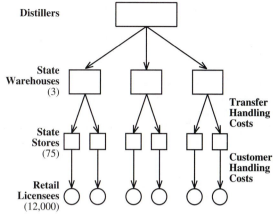

FIGURE 1   MLCC distribution network.

Distillers

State Warehouses (3)

Transfer Handling Costs

State Stores (75)

Customer Handling Costs

Retail Licensees (12,000)

- Off-premise (packaged)
- On-premise (by glass)

liquor inventory within the seventy-five second-tier warehouses is $25 million. Inventory carrying cost is assumed to be 15 percent and is considered a conservative estimate compared with figures used in private industry liquor analysis.

Distillers ship their products to the three state-operated warehouses according to state-suggested shipping quantities. The distillers are charged a handling fee for storage of their product because the state of Michigan does not take title to the liquor until it has been shipped from the three warehouses to one of the state stores. The process of title transfer in the system is essentially a consignment arrangement. A product is sent to a sales agent (in this case, the state of Michigan) for sale or safekeeping. From the state of Michigan's perspective, the consignment arrangement reduces inventory ownership risk and inventory carrying costs because the state does not take title until retail licensee demand is established. This operational arrangement was implemented several years ago; however, distillers circumvented the state's fiscal efforts by sufficiently raising prices to cover their increased storage costs.

No direct shipments are made from the three state-owned and operated warehouses to retail licensees. Transshipment among the three state-operated warehouses and the state stores is minimal. Licensees place their orders weekly through a centralized order processing system and may either pick up an order in person or have it delivered by common carrier. The

TABLE 1   MLCC DISTRICT OPERATING
CHARACTERISTICS

	District 1	District 2	District 3
Population (% of state)	4,363,850 (48.7%)	4,267,531 (47.6%)	334,518 (3.7%)
Cases sold of distilled liquor (% of state)	3,945,441 (56.6%)	2,749,611 (39.9%)	286,013 (4.1%)
Fixed cost of district warehouse	$924,542	$576,294	$93,825
Variable cost per case at warehouse	$0.41	$0.35	$1.48
Warehousing cost per case	$2.20	$3.91	$13.13
Average fixed cost per state store	$163,810	$65,274	$54,341
Variable cost per case per state store	$1.37	$1.43	$3.64
Number of state stores	12	46	17

only exception to this delivery system occurs in the Detroit metropolitan area, where state delivery service is mandated from the largest state store to all its retail licensees. A private transportation company provides the service at the licensees' expense.

Geographically, Michigan's liquor distribution network is broken down into three operating districts. Each

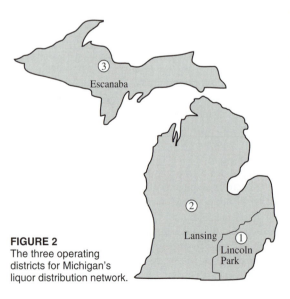

FIGURE 2
The three operating districts for Michigan's liquor distribution network.

district contains one of the major state-operated warehouses. The Lincoln Park warehouse serves the Detroit area (district 1); the Lansing warehouse serves the western and central portion of the state (district 2); and the Escanaba warehouse serves the northern portion, or Upper Peninsula, of the state (district 3). District population, case liquor sales, and facility costs are shown in Table 1 and Figure 2.

While the state does not directly pay the cost of inbound freight from distillers, research indicates that the cost is approximately $1 per case. Transfer freight is defined as movements from and between the three state-operated warehouses to the seventy-five state stores. Customer freight is defined as movements between state stores and a retail licensee. Transfer and customer freight charges are listed in Table 2.

CURRENT ISSUES

Redesigning the liquor control system in Michigan is not a new idea. Lawrence Desmond, business manager for the MLCC, says, "When you talk about the liquor commission you're really talking about two distinct aspects. One is a regulatory agency that enforces the state's liquor laws. The other is the fact that we're the state's sole wholesaler of spirits, and along with our licensing process, we directly contribute to the state's general fund." The subject of system redesign has been raised numerous times for a variety of reasons, and many powerful economic and political special interest groups have strong opinions on the two issues of liquor enforcement and sales and licensing.

Liquor enforcement is a highly sensitive social issue. From 1982 to 1992, nationwide per capita consumption of distilled liquor declined about 3 percent per year. Michigan sales figures mirror the national trend (see Figure 3). Increased public awareness of alcohol abuse

TABLE 2   MLCC TRANSFER AND CUSTOMER
FREIGHT CHARGES

	District 1	District 2	District 3
Transfer freight (per case)	$0.35	$0.28	$0.60
Customer freight (per case)	$1.00	$0.40–0.70 (south) $1.10–1.30 (north)	No service available; "pickup" only

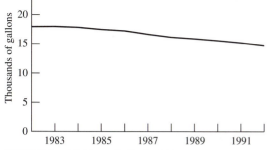

FIGURE 3   Michigan distilled spirits consumption (1982–1992).

has been heightened through the efforts of distillers and brewers, government agencies, and groups such as Mothers against Drunk Driving (MADD). Antialcohol groups such as MADD argue that the state's highly controlled system contributes to strong enforcement of liquor violations and thereby acts as a deterrent to alcohol abuse. "Alcohol is a problem-causing narcotic drug, and we need to retain as much control as possible," says the Reverend Allen West of the Michigan Council on Alcohol Abuse and Problems.

The chairperson and the five commissioners of the MLCC are appointed by the governor of Michigan. Given the nature of the political process, the MLCC and its licensing procedures have historically been subject to frequent charges of political patronage, graft, and corruption by whichever political party is out of power in the state legislature. The MLCC employs approximately 620 people, and a considerable number of the positions are well-paying, low-skill jobs. Although the population of Michigan is concentrated in the lower third of the state, many of the MLCC positions are located in geographically remote areas where it is unlikely that employees would be able to secure similar private sector jobs if system redesign eliminated their positions. Also, approximately 500 MLCC employees are represented by United Auto Workers (UAW) local unions. Teamsters Union delivery firms with long-term contracts for hauling liquor also exist, especially in the Detroit metropolitan area.

A number of state budget analysts and legislators, as well as academic and professional consultants, believe that the state liquor distribution system is considerably less efficient than private industry. They argue that, for example, mandated state delivery contracts and state employees with little job performance incentive hinder productivity improvement.

Lower-volume retail licensees fear that redesigning the current system may hinder their ability to purchase small quantities of liquor, particularly if minimum order sizes or delivery freight breaks are instituted. They believe that changing the current setup will severely disadvantage them relative to larger high-volume chains and retailers. Jerry Faust, spokesperson for a state organization representing retailers, says, "If the system ain't broke, don't fix it." Many consumer advocates argue that the current distribution system of state-set single pricing at all retail outlets provides consumers with an economically equitable system.

CHALLENGES OF SYSTEM REDESIGN

Before leaving the office, Joseph Duncan outlined two general objectives of distribution network redesign: increase the state's return from liquor distribution by reducing costs and inefficiencies, and improve inventory management by utilizing management information systems (MIS) to further increase efficiency. He identified four specific objectives: maintain the current service level, increase inventory turns, decrease administrative costs, and maintain the current level of control over a highly sensitive social-economic policy area.

Joseph realized that he would need to contact a variety of people on his return to work on Monday in preparation for Wednesday's meeting. He sketched out plans to meet with representative MLCC staff and operations personnel, MIS staff, external industry experts in liquor and custom delivery operations, and academics in marketing and logistics at the nearby state university.

Joseph decided that any changes in distilled liquor distribution would have to reflect key operational issues of pricing, service level, projected retail sales and tax impact, direct delivery from distillers to major chain warehouses, and delivery cost considerations—not to mention a host of economic and political special interest group concerns. He began to realize that the topic of liquor distribution in Michigan was a much more complex issue than it had seemed a few hours earlier.

QUESTIONS

1 What alternative designs for distilled liquor distribution in Michigan might be considered? Explain the rationale for your suggestions.

2 Discuss the benefits and risks of alternative designs for distilled liquor distribution. Which political,

economic, geographic, or special interest group considerations would exert the strongest influence on system redesign?

3   Are the historical conditions that the current liquor distribution system is based on still important to-day? What, if any, other factors exist that require consideration?

4   Does an inherent social conflict exist when state governments rely on tax contributions from liquor sales to fund educational programs.

5   How would you organize the final report on distilled liquor distribution in Michigan if you were Joseph Duncan?

PART FOUR

FOUR

LOGISTICS ADMINISTRATION

Chapter 20   Organization
Chapter 21   Planning, Costing, and Pricing
Chapter 22   Performance Measurement and Reporting
Chapter 23   Dimensions of Change: A Seminar Focus
Case G   Woodson Chemical Company
Case H   Performance Control
Case I   Managing Change in Wholesaling: The Case of Wilmont Drug Company

ORGANIZATION

LOGISTICAL ORGANIZATIONAL
  DEVELOPMENT
STAGES OF FUNCTIONAL AGGREGATION
  Stage 1 Organization
  Stage 2 Organization
  Stage 3 Organization
  Empirical Confirmation: Stages 1 to 3
STAGE 4: A SHIFT IN EMPHASIS FROM
  FUNCTION TO PROCESS
STAGE 5: BEYOND STRUCTURE:
  VIRTUALITY AND ORGANIZATIONAL
  TRANSPARENCY

ISSUES AND CHALLENGES
  Concepts Having Logistical Significance
  Careers and Loyalty
  Managing Change
THE MANAGEMENT OF ALLIANCES
  Initiating an Alliance
  Implementing an Alliance
  Maintaining Alliance Vitality
SUMMARY
QUESTIONS

Among the topics of logistics, few hold more managerial interest than organization. The vast change taking place in logistical organization practice makes it one of the most difficult topics to accurately describe. The information revolution is forcing logistics managers to rethink nearly every aspect of traditional organization logic. For example, a few years ago it was a sacred principle that a manager should not supervise more than eight employees. In contrast, today's flat organization structures often feature individual managers with spans of control containing sixteen or more direct reports. The traditional idea that middle managers serve as information gatekeepers and bastions of control is being replaced by a highly empowered frontline workforce having access to virtually all information. Guided by continuous redesign and reengineering of basic work, hierarchical organizations are being modified to accommodate information networking and self-directed work teams.

The vertical bureaucratic structure that has prevailed for centuries is giving way to horizontal approaches that focus on managing key processes.

Because of the geographically dispersed nature of logistics work and the fact that operations typically span more than one business, no absolutely right or wrong organization structure exists. Two firms that compete for the same customers may choose to organize their affairs in substantially different ways. Each will seek to match its unique capabilities to satisfy what is perceived as critical customer requirements. Each will seek to create differential competitive advantage. One conclusion is certain: organization practice is undergoing unprecedented change to accommodate business requirements. The old-fashioned notion of stamping out organization charts using ''cookie cutter''principles of management doesn't work in today's dynamic world and is not likely to work in the future.

Chapter 20 will trace the evolution of logistics organization to what is generally accepted as today's best practice model. Given an understanding of past and present organizational structure, it is possible to single out forces most likely to shape the enterprise of the future. The chapter uses a model with stages to track the evolution of organizational development, presenting the proposition that firms initially move toward functional aggregation as they seek to integrate logistical performance. As integrated logistics becomes a reality, pressure to continue to aggregate functions into a single organizational structure is reduced. The need for formal grouping becomes increasingly less important as information networking emerges.

Next, the chapter details three stages of observable organization development focused on functional aggregation. Then, Chapter 20 addresses new paradigms that are emerging to stimulate horizontal as contrasted to vertical approaches to organization. A unified organization model is presented that seeks to reconcile the combined attributes of vertical bureaucracy and its horizontal alternatives. The chapter reviews the growing impact of information technology on organization structure. One challenge of the future is to develop ways to facilitate, coordinate, and control the work of logistics throughout the overall organization using information networking. The text presents selected contemporary issues and challenges that firms and their employees face. Of particular interest is an organization's tolerance for accommodating change and its impact on managers and workers. Finally, the chapter deals with the special challenges of managing alliances and partnerships. The specific focus is on how to best integrate and manage logistical relationships in day-to-day operations.

Two comments are in order concerning chapter coverage. First, recognizing that organization structure is a highly customized activity, no attempt is made to illustrate how any specific firm organizes logistics. In today's competitive environment, organizations change rapidly to accommodate new opportunity.

A second qualification is that logistical organization trends and practices are not unique. Observable changes in organization structure are a microcosm of widespread changes in business structure reflecting an overall shift in organization philosophy. One should not lose sight of this broader revolution in overall organization structural thinking that is destined to redefine the way people work in the future.

LOGISTICAL ORGANIZATIONAL DEVELOPMENT

Prior to the 1950s, functions now accepted as logistics were generally viewed as facilitating or support work. Organizational responsibility for logistics was dispersed throughout the firm. This fragmentation often meant that aspects of logistical work were performed without cross-functional coordination, often resulting in duplication and waste. Information was frequently distorted or delayed, and lines of authority and responsibility were typically blurred. Managers recognizing the need for total-cost control began to reorganize and combine logistics functions into a single managerial group. Structuring logistics as an integrated organization first appeared in the 1950s.[1]

The motivation behind functional aggregation was the belief that grouping logistics functions into a single organization would increase the likelihood of integration. The paradigm was that functional proximity would facilitate improved understanding of how decisions and procedures in one area affect performance in other areas. The belief was that eventually all functions would begin to work as a single group focused on total system performance. This integration paradigm, based on organizational proximity, prevailed throughout a thirty-five-year period. However, by the mid-1980s, it was becoming increasingly clear that the paradigm of functional aggregation might not, in final analysis, offer the best approach to achieve integrated logistics. For many firms, the ink had barely dried on what appeared to be the perfect logistics organization when new and far more pervasive rethinking of what constituted the ideal structure emerged.

Almost overnight, the emphasis shifted from function to process. Firms began to examine the role logistical competency could play in the overall process of creating customer value. This ushered in new thinking regarding how to best achieve integrated logistical performance. To a significant degree, the focus on process reduced the pressure to aggregate functions into all-encompassing organization units. The critical question became not how to organize individual functions but rather how to best manage the overall logistical process. The challenges and opportunities of functional disaggregation and information-driven integration began to emerge.

The mission of logistics is to position inventory when and where it is required to facilitate profitable sales. This supportive work must be performed around the clock and typically throughout the world, which means that logistics needs to be an integral part of all processes. The ideal structure for logistics would be an organization that performs essential work as part of the processes it supports while achieving the synergism of cross-functional integration.

Information technology introduced the potential of electronic integration as contrasted to physically combining logistics functions. Using information technology to coordinate or orchestrate integrated performance allows the responsibility

---

[1]For early articles discussing this initial integration of logistics activities, see Donald J. Bowersox, ''Emerging Patterns of Physical Distribution Organization,'' *Transportation and Distribution Management,* May 1968, pp. 53–59; John F. Stolle, ''How to Manage Physical Distribution,'' *Harvard Business Review,* July–August 1967, pp. 93–100; and Robert E. Weigand, ''The Management of Physical Distribution: A Dilemma,'' *Michigan State University Business Topics,* Summer 1962, pp. 67–72.

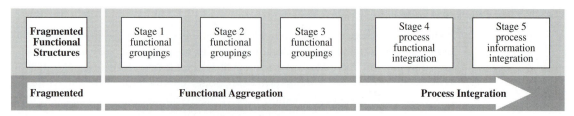

PREVAILING PARADIGM

FIGURE 20-1   Logistical organization development cycle.

for work itself to be distributed throughout the overall organization. Integration requires that logistics combine with other areas such as marketing and manufacturing. For example, rather than focusing on how to relate transportation and inventory, the real challenge is to integrate transportation, inventory, new-product development, flexible manufacturing, and customer service. In order to achieve overall organizational integration, a firm must combine a wide variety of capabilities into new organizational units. This means that the traditional single-function department must be assimilated into a process. Such assimilation often requires that traditional organization structures be disaggregated and then recombined in new and unique ways. In one sense, such functional disaggregation may appear to come full circle back to the early days of fragmented single-function departments. However, the critical difference in the emerging organizational model is the widespread availability of unbridled information. The new organization format is characterized by an extremely different culture concerning how information is managed and shared.

Logistics managers can benefit from understanding the organization development process. Such understanding permits them to evaluate their firm's current state of organization and plan changes that can be accommodated. To fully understand structural positioning and change management, it is useful to have an application concerning how traditional bureaucratic organizations evolved. Research suggests that managers initially stabilized logistics through functional aggregation. Such aggregation was essential prior to embarking on the use of information networking to facilitate process integration. Figure 20-1 illustrates five stages of organizational development based on the relative balance of functional aggregation and information integration.

At any given time, the array of observable logistics organizations runs the full gamut of the development stages. Some firms are just embracing the challenge of stage 1, while others are pushing the frontiers of stage 5. While the organizational evolution can be accelerated, it appears doubtful that it can be jump-started. The challenge for managers is to be able to assess how their particular organization should be structured given current competency to best exploit logistics.

The chapter next discusses specifics of the five stages of organization development. The three stages of functional aggregation are combined in a single presentation, and this is followed by a discussion of process focus and information-based integration.

STAGES OF FUNCTIONAL AGGREGATION

Figure 20-2 illustrates a traditional organizational structure with dispersed logistical functions. *Only those functions typically involved in logistical operations are highlighted in this hypothetical chart.* The initial belief was that integrated performance would be facilitated by grouping logistical functions normally spread throughout the traditional organization into a single command and control structure. It was felt that these functions would be better managed, trade-offs better analyzed, and least-total-cost solutions better identified if all logistics work was integrated into one organization. In order for operational integration to occur, managers had to believe that performance could be improved. Without this belief, they would continue to emphasize structure as opposed to management practice.

While the idea of functional integration is logical and appeals to common sense, it is not always supported by other unit managers. It is natural that any attempt to reposition management authority and responsibility will meet resistance. Many logistics executives can provide examples of how attempts to reorganize were met with rivalry and mistrust—not to mention accusations of empire building. Traditionally, in organizational structures, financial budgets follow operational responsibility. Likewise, power, visibility, and compensation result from managing large head counts and substantial budgets. Logistial reorganization, therefore, was typically seen as a way for logistical managers to gain power, visibility, and compensation at the expense of other managers. This also was ample reason for other managers to protect their power by resisting logistics functional integration. As a result, unified logistical organizations faced considerable resistance. But in an

FIGURE 20-2   Traditional organization of logistically related functions.

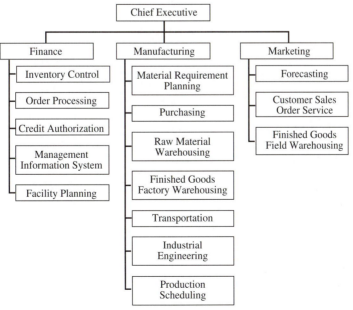

increasing number of firms, benefits were sufficient to empower reorganization. The resulting evolution typically involved three stages of functional aggregation.

Stage 1 Organization

The initial attempt at grouping logistical activities emerged during the late 1950s and early 1960s. Organizations with even a minimal degree of formal unification emerged only after senior management became committed to the belief that improved performance would result. The typical evolutionary pattern was for two or more logistics functions to be operationally grouped without significant change in the overall organization hierarchy. Such initial aggregation occurred at both the staff and line levels of organization. Seldom were organization units engaged in purchasing and physical distribution integrated during this initial development stage.

Figure 20-3 illustrates a typical stage 1 organization. Although completely separate, physical distribution and material management units serve to aggregate related functions. As the potential of integrated logistics developed recognition within an enterprise, one or two clusters of unified operations emerged. In the marketing area, the cluster typically centered around customer service. In the manufacturing area, concentration was usually on inbound materials or parts procurement. However, with few exceptions, most traditional departments were not changed and the organization hierarchy was not altered significantly. For the most part, stage 1 organizational change involved grouping functions within the traditional domains

FIGURE 20-3   Stage 1 logistical organization.

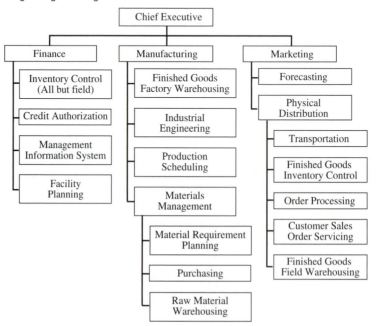

of marketing and manufacturing. The notable deficiency of a stage 1 organization was a failure to focus direct responsibility for inventory. For example, initial physical distribution organizations typically controlled warehousing, transportation, and order processing. Few stage 1 organizations had direct responsibility to manage trade-offs between transportation and finished inventory deployment.

Stage 2 Organization

As the overall enterprise gained operational experience with unified logistics and cost benefits, a second stage of organization began to evolve. Figure 20-4 illustrates stage 2, which began to emerge in the late 1960s and early 1970s.

The significant feature of stage 2 was that logistics was singled out and elevated to a position of higher organizational authority and responsibility. The motivation was simple: positioning logistics at a higher organization level increased the likelihood of strategic impact. Independent status allowed logistics to be managed as a core competency. A likely candidate for elevated status was physical distribution in firms where customer service performance was critical to overall success. The grocery manufacturing business was an example where materials management often increased in operational authority and responsibility because inbound materials and production were a major portion of product costs. Thus, the focal group that was elevated to higher organizational prominence in stage 2 organizations typically depended on the nature of the enterprise's primary business. The example in Figure

FIGURE 20-4   Stage 2 logistical organization.

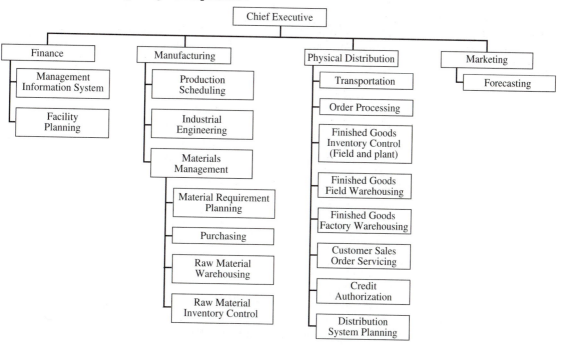

20-4 illustrates a situation wherein physical distribution was restructured and elevated.

In order to establish a stage 2 organization, it was necessary to reassign functions and position the newly created organization at a higher level within the overall enterprise structure. In the stage 2 organization, the concept of a fully integrated logistics unit was not achieved. Rather, integration was focused on either physical distribution or materials management. This failure to synthesize logistical management into an integrated system was due in part to a preoccupation with the performance of specific functions, such as order processing or purchasing, which were perceived as essential to traditional operations. A second limiting factor to total integration was the lack of cross-functional logistical information systems. As a general rule, organizational integration reflected the information systems capability of the firm.

A significant point about the stage 2 organization is that integrated physical distribution and/or materials management began to gain acceptance among financial, manufacturing, and marketing counterparts. The other corporate officers viewed these integrated organizations as something more than purely reactive efforts aimed at cost reduction or containment. In the stage 2 organization, it was common for the integrated unit to become a primary contributor to business strategy. The stage 2 organization is readily observable in industry today and may well remain the most adopted approach to logistical facilitation.

Stage 3 Organization

Stage 3 organizations emerged in the 1980s as the logistical renaissance began. This organizational structure sought to unify all logistical functions and operations under a single senior manager. Stage 3 organizations, having the comprehensive nature illustrated in Figure 20-5, were and continue to be rare. However, the trend at the stage 3 level of organization structuring is clearly to group as many logistical planning and operational functions as practical under single authority and responsibility. The goal is the strategic management of all materials and finished product movement and storage to the maximum benefit of the enterprise.

The rapid development of logistical information systems provided an impetus for stage 3 organizations. Information technology became available to plan and operate systems that fully integrated logistical operations. Several aspects of the stage 3 organization justify further discussion.

First, each area of logistics—purchasing, manufacturing support, and physical distribution—is structured as a separate line operation. The lines of authority and responsibility directly enabled each bundle of supportive services to be performed within the overall integrated logistical effort. Since areas of operational responsibility are well defined, it is possible to establish manufacturing support as an operational unit similar to purchasing and physical distribution. Each of the units is operationally self-sufficient. Therefore, each can maintain the flexibility to accommodate critical services required by its respective operational area. In addition, since overall logistical activities can be planned and coordinated on an integrated basis, operational synergies between areas can be exploited.

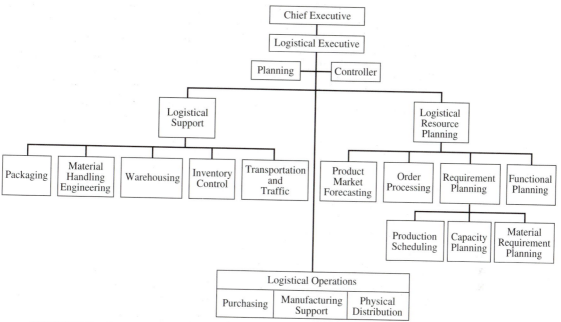

FIGURE 20-5   Stage 3 logistical organization.

Second, five capabilities grouped under logistical support are positioned as operational services. This common service orientation is the mechanism to integrate overall logistical operations. It is important to stress that logistical support *is not* a staff organization. Rather, the group manages day-to-day logistics work, which is structured with matrix accountability for direct liaison between physical distribution, manufacturing support, and purchasing operations.

Third, logistical resource planning embraces the full potential of management information to plan and coordinate operations. Order processing triggers the logistical system into operation and generates the integrated database required for control. Logistical resource planning facilitates integration. The plans are based on product/market forecasting, order processing, inventory status, and capacity strategy to determine overall requirements for any planning period. On the basis of identified requirements, the planning unit operationalizes manufacturing by coordinating production scheduling, capacity planning, and materials requirement planning.

Finally, overall planning and controllership exist at the highest level of the stage 3 organization. These two efforts serve to facilitate integration. The planning group is concerned with long-range strategic positioning and is responsible for logistical system quality improvement and reengineering. The logistical controller is concerned with measurement of cost and customer service performance and with provision of information for managerial decision making. The development of procedures for logistical controllership is one of the most critical areas of integrated logistical administration. The need for careful measurement is a direct result of the increased emphasis placed on customer service performance. The measurement task is extremely important because of the large operating and capital dollar expenditures involved in logistics.

The stage 3 logistical organization approach offers a single logic to guide the efficient application of financial and human resources from material sourcing to customer delivery. As such, a stage 3 logistical organization positions a firm to manage trade-offs between purchasing, manufacturing support, and physical distribution.

Empirical Confirmation: Stages 1 to 3

The evolutionary stages of integrated logistical organizations have been documented by empirical research. The initial study of organizational trends was completed by Kearney Management Consultants in 1978, updated in 1984, and again revised in 1991 and 1993.[2] The Kearney research team was among the first to confirm massive realignment of organizational responsibilities in logistics. The research concluded that firms implementing integrated logistics management achieved superior financial results. Those that integrated logistical management to the level of stage 1 realized an additional contribution to pretax profits of 2.6 points in comparison with firms that had managed on a fragmented basis. Those that expanded integration to include the entire logistics process achieved a total additional contribution to profits of 3.4 points in comparison with those less integrated. The stage 3 firms also reported (1) increased sales due to improved customer service; (2) improved productivity of the resources devoted to logistics; (3) improved operating results from manufacturing and marketing; and (4) improved balance sheet strength as a result of reduced inventories, reduced accounts receivables, and increased cash flow.

At regular intervals over the past twenty-two years, research completed at the Ohio State University calibrated career patterns among United States logistics executives.[3] This research has identified trends related to background, training, work experience, and demographic characteristics. In addition, the research has quantified attitudes and opinions on critical issues related to organizational development.

A composite of results over the study period identifies and reconfirms several prominent trends: (1) a shift from staff to line organization or a combination of staff and line; (2) an upward repositioning of the chief logistical executive with

---

[2]For original information, see A. T. Kearney, *Measuring Productivity in Physical Distribution: The $40 Billion Gold Mine,* Oak Brook, Ill.: Council of Logistics Management, 1978; A. T. Kearney, "Organizing Physical Distribution to Improve Bottom Line Results," *Annual Proceedings of the Council of Logistics Management,* 1981, pp. 1–4; A. T. Kearney, *Measuring and Improving Productivity in Physical Distribution: The Successful Companies,* Oak Brook, Ill.: Council of Logistics Management, 1984; and A. T. Kearney, *Improving Quality and Productivity in the Logistics Process: Achieving Customer Satisfaction Breakthroughs,* Oak Brook, Ill.: Council of Logistics Management, 1991. A. T. Kearney completed and published studies in Europe, Asia, and North America in 1993. These studies were distributed by Kearney in captive interest publications.

[3]See the *Annual Proceedings of the Council of Logistics Management* for yearly updates. For the latest research, see Bernard J. LaLonde and James M. Masters, "The 1994 Ohio State University Survey of Career Patterns in Logistics," *Annual Proceedings of the Council of Logistics Management,* 1994, pp. 87–106.

more vice presidents and directors; (3) broadened responsibility to include more functions; (4) a shift in "outer directed" focus, with a significantly larger share of time interacting with marketing, production, finance, and data processing; (5) emphasis shifting from activity-based issues to broader economic and technological concerns; and (6) steadily increasing recognition of a more "scientific" approach to logistics. The importance of basic analytical tools to assist in solving logistical problems has been increasingly recognized.

In 1989, the book *Leading Edge Logistics: Competitive Positioning for the 1990s* reported research completed at Michigan State University that examined leading companies in logistics and identified their managerial and operational commonalities.[4] This research provided additional evidence that logistical organizations were following the functional aggregation paradigm. Firms that were classified as leading-edge using a multifaceted index were organizationally responsible for an average of 12.19 traditional logistics functions, and many of the organizations studied typically had responsibility for activities not directly related to logistical performance. Analysis of functional responsibility indicated that firms with leading-edge status were generally supportive of the evolutionary stages theory and the functional aggregation paradigm.

In the early 1990s, Michigan State University's basic research was extended to examine external integration. On the basis of interviews with executives who were early adopters of logistics alliances, it became increasingly clear that achieving excellence required extending organizational considerations to include key service suppliers, material and component suppliers, and, most important, customers. The book *Logistical Excellence: It's Not Business as Usual* extended understanding of where organizational integration imperatives were heading.[5]

The overall conclusion of the Michigan State University research was that leading-edge logistical performance resulted from a composite of factors, of which organizational structure was important but not necessarily an overriding consideration. Managerial emphasis was moving from structural concerns to focus on best practice. It was clear that the best practice era was coming of age.

A composite of research has developed empirical support that logistics organizations, over the past decade, have become increasingly functionally integrated as they evolved from fragmented to stage 3 status. Until the mid-1990s, it appeared safe to conclude that the stage 3 logistical organization structure had expanded to encompass alliance relationships and would remain at the leading edge for the foreseeable future. However, it also became clear that best logistics practice requires a commitment to performance excellence that extends far beyond organization structure. Today, there remains some validation of the stage 2 model. However, evidence is accumulating that information technology is affecting best logistics practice and that the preferred organization structure of the future might once again undergo radical change.

[4]Donald J. Bowersox, Patricia J. Daugherty, Cornelia L. Dröge, Dale S. Rogers, and Daniel L. Wardlow, *Leading Edge Logistics: Competitive Positioning for the 1990s,* Oak Brook, Ill.: Council of Logistics Management, 1989.

[5]Donald J. Bowersox, Patricia J. Daugherty, Cornelia L. Dröge, Richard N. Germain, and Dale S. Rogers, *Logistical Excellence: It's Not Business as Usual,* Burlington, Mass.: Digital Press, 1992.

STAGE 4: A SHIFT IN EMPHASIS FROM FUNCTION TO PROCESS

Independent of functional aggregation or disaggregation, it is clear that organizations are struggling to position their operating capabilities to better support process-oriented management. As one observer concluded, "The search for the organization perfectly designed for the 21st century is going ahead with the urgency of a scavenger hunt."[6] McKinsey consultants Frank Ostroff and Doug Smith proposed an architecture to illustrate how the functional hierarchical vertical organization could transition to become a process-oriented horizontal organization. The Ostroff/Smith model is presented in Figure 20-6.

The concept of the twenty-first-century organization is envisioned as the result of three factors: first, the development of a highly involved work environment with self-directed work teams (SDWT) as a vehicle to empower employees to generate maximum performance; second, improved productivity that results from managing processes rather than functions (this notion has always rested at the core of integrated logistics); and third, the rapid sharing of accurate information that allows all facets of the organization to be integrated. Information technology is viewed as the load-bearing structure of the new enterprise, replacing organizational hierarchy.

The essence of the argument for radical restructuring is that the traditional evolutionary concept of organization change is not sufficient to stimulate major breakthroughs in service or productivity. Rather, traditional organization change shifts the balance of centralization and decentralization or realigns operating structure between customers, territories, or products without any serious redesign of the basic work process. Because such restructuring typically assumes that functional organizations will continue to perform basic work, little or no difference in actual practice results. In essence, companies are refocusing old business practices rather than designing new, more efficient processes.

The challenges of managing logistics as a process are threefold. First, all effort must be focused on value added to the customer. An activity exists and is justified only to the extent that it contributes to customer value. Therefore, a logistical commitment must be motivated by a belief that customers desire a specific activity to be performed. Logistical managers must develop the capacity to think externally. Second, organizing logistics as part of a process requires that all skills necessary to complete the work be available regardless of their functional organization. Organizational grouping on the basis of selected functions can artificially separate natural work flows and create bottlenecks. When horizontal structures are put in place, critical skills need to be positioned to ensure that required work is accomplished. Finally, work performed in a process context should stimulate synergism. With systems integration, the design of work as a process means that overall organizational trade-offs are structured to achieve maximum output for minimum input investment.

The radical changes proposed by a shift from functional to process orientation have mixed messages for managers involved in logistics. On the positive side, general adoption of a process orientation builds on the basic principles of systems

---

[6]Thomas A. Stewart, "The Search for the Organization of Tomorrow," *Fortune,* May 18, 1992, pp. 91–98. The following discussion draws heavily on Stewart's article.

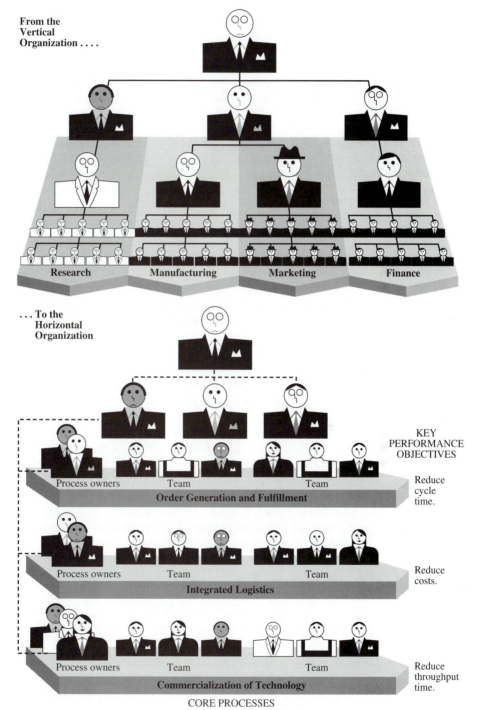

From the Vertical Organization . . . .

Research   Manufacturing   Marketing   Finance

. . . To the Horizontal Organization

KEY PERFORMANCE OBJECTIVES

Process owners   Team   Team
Order Generation and Fulfillment
Reduce cycle time.

Process owners   Team   Team
Integrated Logistics
Reduce costs.

Process owners   Team   Team
Commercialization of Technology
Reduce throughput time.

CORE PROCESSES

FIGURE 20-6   From vertical to horizontal organizations. *(Thomas A. Stewart, "The Search for the Organization of Tomorrow,"* Fortune, *May 18, 1992, p. 94.)*

integration. At the core of integrated logistics is a commitment to functional excellence in the context of contribution to process performance. A general shift in managing logistics as a process means that it will be positioned as a central contributor to all initiatives that focus on new-product development, customer order generation, fulfillment, and delivery. The overall trend of process integration expands the operational potential and impact of logistics.

Less clear is a full understanding of how processes themselves will be performed and managed. The most advanced logistical solutions observed during the past decade have combined organization form and best practice performance to manage the overall logistics process using a modified hierarchical structure. The concept of matrix organization has emerged as the most acceptable structure to facilitate horizontal management.[7] The availability of superior information to operationalize a matrix approach relaxes dependence on a rigid formal organization structure. In terms of architecture for a logistical organization, the critical questions are, (1) How much formal hierarchical structure can and should be retained while stimulating a process orientation? and (2) How can an organization be structured so that it can manage a process as complex as global logistics without becoming overly bureaucratic? To address these questions, managers need to fully understand the potential of stage 5, which advocates information-driven logistical networks that integrate across organizational boundaries.

STAGE 5: BEYOND STRUCTURE: VIRTUALITY AND ORGANIZATIONAL TRANSPARENCY

It is highly unlikely that the attention being given to process will end management's quest for the ideal logistical organization. While several different scenarios concerning the organization of the future are technologically feasible, one of the most intriguing is speculation that formal hierarchical command and control organization structure will be replaced with an informal electronic network often referred to as a virtual organization.[8] The word *virtual* implies an underlying existence without formal recognition.[9] In other words, a virtual organization, whether it is a total enterprise or a specific core competency, would exist as a provider of integrated performance but not as an identifiable unit of formal organization structure.[10] In the case of logistics, key work teams may be electronically linked to perform critical activities in an integrated fashion. These work teams could be transparent

---

[7] The relevancy of the matrix organization structure is developed in greater detail in the Issues and Challenges section of this chapter.

[8] For more detail concerning network organizations, see Thomas W. Malone and John F. Rockart, "Computers, Networks and the Corporation," *Scientific American,* **265:**3, September 1991, pp. 128–135; Charles C. Snow, Raymond E. Miles, and Henry J. Coleman, Jr., "Managing 21st Century Network Organizations," *Organizational Dynamics,* **20:**3, Winter 1992, pp. 5–20; Walter Kiechel III, "How We Will Work in the Year 2000," *Fortune,* **127:**10, May 17, 1993, pp. 38–52; and Jerald Hage, *Theories of Organizations: Form, Process, and Transformation,* New York: Wiley, 1980.

[9] Webster's Dictionary defines *virtual* as "being such in essence or effect though not formally recognized or admitted."

[10] For more detail concerning virtual organizations, see William H. Davidow and Michael S. Malone, *The Virtual Corporation: Structuring and Revitalizing the Corporation for the 21st Century,* New York: Harper Business, 1992; and John A. Byrne, "The Virtual Corporation: The Company of the Future Will Be the Ultimate in Adaptability," *Business Week,* February 8, 1993, pp. 98–102.

in terms of the formal organization structure of their membership. In other words, formal organization charts may not be related to actual work flow. In fact, logistics organizations of the future could be characterized by functional disaggregation throughout the organization in an attempt to focus on work flow rather than structure.

In the concluding chapter of *Logistical Excellence,* eight propositions were hypothesized concerning emerging trends in how individual firms define the magnitude and direction of leading-edge practice.[11] Proposition eight, which focused on how logistical organizations were adapting to constantly changing customer requirements, captured the essence of functional disaggregation:

> To meet customer requirements for speed and response, authority will be pushed down the organization. Strategic direction can be expected to originate at headquarters. Operational adaptations will increasingly be made on the front lines. Frontline managers will be expected to define strategy and apply it directly to operations. Centralization and decentralization will increasingly become meaningless terms. Organizations of the future will seek to capture the best of centralization and decentralization without commitment to either concept.
>
> Organizations will increasingly discover they can capture the benefits of integrated logistics without command and control organization structures.

In order to fully exploit the benefits of information technology, a major structural and philosophical shift must take place. Command and control structures have a significant historical precedence in business that is difficult to change. In fact, some believe that such radical change can be accomplished only if the original organization solutions are completely abolished or disintegrated. In other words, the change cannot be made by simply modifying the existing organization. The belief that disintegration of traditional organization structure is required before the benefits of information technology can be embraced is a documented proposition.[12] What is proposed by the disaggregation of logistics is consistent with disintegration theories.

The idea behind disaggregation is that the power of information technology will allow integrated management and performance of logistics work without grouping or aggregating functions into a formal organization unit. The responsibility for performing logistics work will be organizationally positioned by users. The *user,* in this sense, is the organization that requires transportation, warehousing, inventory, or any other logistics service to complete its mission. Making those who perform the logistical services an integral part of the user organization has the potential to increase relevancy and flexibility. In essence, ultimate empowerment would result. Each organization throughout an enterprise would perform its required logistical services. The disintegration paradigm is based on the belief that logistical functionality need not be organizationally assigned to a special command and control structure to efficiently and effectively coordinate performance.

---

[11]Donald J. Bowersox, Patricia J. Daugherty, Cornelia L. Dröge, Richard N. Germain, and Dale S. Rogers, *Logistical Excellence, It's Not Business as Usual,* Burlington, Mass.: Digital Press, 1992, pp. 173–174.

[12]Christopher Meyer and David Power, "Enterprise Disintegration: The Storm before the Calm," *Commentary,* Lexington, Mass.: Temple, Barker and Sloane, 1989.

There are many arguments counter to functional disaggregation. First and foremost is the fear that disaggregation will create a danger of reverting to a functional fixation or myopia characteristic of fragmented logistics (prestage 1 organization). A second concern is that critical scale and scope in logistical operations will be lost and result in diseconomies. Finally, standardization and simplification of work may decrease if similar types of work are spread throughout user organizations without formal feedback mechanisms.

While the above arguments are not exhaustive, they are characteristic of the concerns managers have about abandoning formal integrated organizations. The key to improved performance is the realization that relevancy and flexibility may be increased by creating an electronic network to facilitate logistical coordination as contrasted to reliance on formal organizational structuring. Actually, the information technology did not exist when the paradigm of functional organizational grouping was launched in an effort to achieve integration requirements. Because of the newness of the ideas, it is difficult to perceive how a stage 5 organization could be managed.

From a technological perspective, it is reasonable to assume that the formal logistics organizations we know today may not continue to exist in terms of current command and control arrangements. Integration will increasingly be achieved via electronic imaging and networking of logistics work on an informal basis. Under such coordination, the essential aspects of integrated performance can be retained and scarce knowledge and expertise shared to achieve maximum standardization and simplification. *All* logistics work, regardless of when and where it is performed, can be captured as part of the informal logistics network.[13] Sharing common information regarding requirements and performance metrics while retaining local control offers the potential to facilitate a logistical core competency that far exceeds today's best practice model.

The logistics organization of the future, as described above, is essentially what amounts to an *electronic keritsu.* Adopted from Eastern culture, the keritsu is a loosely affiliated group of business firms that share commonalities and are committed to cooperative behavior. The transparent logistical network organization is properly viewed as a composite of affiliated business functions that are motivated and directed by common interest and goals. The informal network is facilitated by information sharing.

The jury is out concerning if and when the functionally disaggregated information coordinated network will become a realistic logistics organization solution. As noted repeatedly, the information technology exists today to make electronic imaging for organization structure and coordinated behavior a reality. Research on best practice indicates that some firms are at the initial stages of linking disparate work electronically rather than physically or organizationally.

The idea of a virtual organization is broader than simply creating structural transparency. The notion that entities can join forces to achieve common goals and

---

[13]For a complete discussion of informal networks, see David Krackhardt and Jeffrey R. Hanson, "Informal Networks: The Company behind the Chart," *Harvard Business Review,* **71:**4, July–August 1993, pp. 104–111.

McKINSEY'S PLAN

It's hot stuff at McKinsey & Co. these days—a ten-point blueprint for a horizontal company prepared by Frank Ostroff and Doug Smith, consultants in the firm's organization-performance group. The blueprint is shown as follows:

1 *Organize primarily around process, not task.* Base performance objectives on customer needs, such as low cost or fast service. Identify the processes that meet (or don't meet) those needs—order generation and fulfillment, say, or new-product development. These processes—not departments, such as sales or manufacturing—become the company's main components.

2 *Flatten the hierarchy by minimizing subdivision of processes.* It's better to arrange teams in parallel, with each doing lots of steps in a process, than to have a series of teams, each doing fewer steps.

3 *Give senior leaders charge of processes and process performance.*

4 *Link performance objectives and evaluation of all activities to customer satisfaction.*

5 *Make teams, not individuals, the focus of organization performance and design.* Individuals acting

alone don't have the capacity to continuously improve work flows.

6 *Combine managerial and non-managerial activities as often as possible.* Let workers' teams take on hiring, evaluating and scheduling.

7 *Emphasize that each employee should develop several competencies.* You need only a few specialists.

8 *Inform and train people on a just-in-time, need-to-perform basis.* Raw numbers go straight to those who need them in their jobs, with no managerial spin, because you have trained front-line workers—salesmen, machinists—how to use them.

9 *Maximize supplier and customer contact with everyone in the organization.* That means field trips and slots on joint problem-solving teams for all employees all the time.

10 *Reward individual skill development and team performance instead of individual performance alone.*

From Thomas A. Stewart, ''The Search for the Organization of Tomorrow,'' *Fortune,* May 18, 1992, p. 96. Reproduced with permission.

then disband has significance for the challenges of managing alliances, as discussed later in this chapter. The aspects of virtuality that deal with a fluid and flexible group of firms working together to combine their individual core competencies will have a major impact on the future of logistical service suppliers. It gives substance to the idea of a disposable logistics competency that users can acquire when needed and then abandon when no longer required. The idea of disposable logistics has application in such areas as special promotion, seasonality, and new-product development and introduction. The fact that firms today constantly form and then dismantle alliances gives credibility to the notions of both transparency and virtuality.

ISSUES AND CHALLENGES

The popular management literature is filled with a litany of ever-emerging buzz-words and organizational concepts that are touted as paths to instant success. Given this continuous bombardment of new ideas, it becomes confusing for executives who are responsible for managing logistics to sort out and implement the proper balance of proven traditional organizational concepts and a mix of new, innovative ways to improve logistical productivity and operational flexibility. The challenge is to differentiate concepts that satisfy the unique requirements of each particular organization from those that are simply fads, offering limited or no relevancy. This challenge is amplified by the discrepancies that exist between words and realities.

This section addresses three important considerations that a manager concerned with logistical organization architecture should carefully review. First, new organization concepts that appear to have particular logistics relevancy are examined. Second, attention is directed to the impact that an overall business environment characterized by rampant change has on the logistics workplace. It is clear that both traditional career paths and loyalty relationships are undergoing significant change. Finally, the challenges of managing organizational change and transformation are discussed. The overall objective of this section is to increase managerial awareness of the challenges involved in logistical organization restructuring.

Concepts Having Logistical Significance

The observable evolution of logistical structures over the past few decades was discussed earlier. At the present time, organization restructuring is focused on facilitating process goal attainment. For logistics, this means that operational competencies need to achieve maximum customer value. Information technology is creating the potential for logistical networks that transcend traditional lines of authority and responsibility. The potential exists to create transparent organizations that coordinate logistical work everywhere a firm does business. Instead of logistics being managed by a department at headquarters or at some plant, logistics organizations may extend throughout and permeate all user locations.

In light of where organization structure has been and where it might go, logistical managers need to assess those ideas that have the greatest applicability and are most likely to be implemented. Four general concepts appear to be particularly relevant for logistics managers: structural compression, empowerment, teaming, and learning. Each is briefly discussed.

Structural Compression   Many different terms and concepts have been used to capture highly visible aspects of organizational change. Terms such as *downsizing, flattening, networking, clustering, right-sizing, delayering, reengineering,* and *nonhierarchical* are abundant in the popular managerial press. All these ideas have one thing in common—the desire to structure organizations so that they can perform required work better while using fewer human resources. However, what is at stake is broader than simply trying to do more with less. The nature of logistical work is changing, and it is only logical that organization structures will change to facilitate lean execution.

The motivation for logistical structural compression starts with the changing role of the chief logistics executive. In an environment characterized by restricted head count and intensive asset control, the senior logistics manager is emerging as an integral part of a firm's continued struggle to gain and maintain customer loyalty. In today's competitive environment, senior logistics executives may spend more than 50 percent of their time working directly with customers. This frontline commitment typically means performing as a member of a cross-functional or category team. While logistics officers may have traditionally visited with customers at the request of sales executives to explain performance failures, their current role is less that of a sacrificial lamb and more as a planner of upcoming events or a provider of strategic vision. To achieve effective customer participation, logistics executives need to have direct access to all types and levels of information.

Change at the top typically results in change throughout an organization. For the most part, such change in logistics organizations has focused on restructuring and downsizing middle management. A great deal has been written about the changing needs of business in terms of white-collar information workers and their traditional contribution to data flow and control. The knowledge revolution may have its greatest impact on middle management. The availability of transaction-based data warehouses means that time and personnel, previously used to analyze and format information, are no longer required. In fact, the delays encountered by such analysis cannot be tolerated in a time-based competitive environment. Rather, managers and workers must be capable of performing their own analysis. Organization arrangements must facilitate sharing of operational and strategic information when and as needed. Elaborate internal clearance procedures to obtain operational information can no longer support the quick analytical trade-offs required today. Rather, information sharing needs to transcend all layers of the organization and be easy for appropriate personnel to access. It follows that the fewer the organization layers, the less chance of information delay, distortion, amplification, or omission.

Therefore, while restructuring typically means fewer people, the desire to change is also related to improved response speed and flexibility. The bureaucratic command and control organization structure that effectively served the needs of yesterday simply does not satisfy the requirements of the information age. Beyond determining the layers of management that offer the correct balance between effective supervision and desired agility, the changing of basic structure requires careful review of long-standing beliefs. Of particular interest to logistical management are traditional relationships regarding centralization/decentralization, line and staff distinction, and matrix structuring.

Centralization/Decentralization The distinction between centralized and decentralized organization has traditionally been based on the degree of authority and profit responsibility delegated to specific operating units. Within an enterprise, units or divisions are considered highly decentralized if they function on an autonomous basis. In a fully decentralized structure, each organizational unit would have responsibility for providing its own logistical planning and execution. For example, in a decentralized environment, individual plants may control and coordinate their own transportation and procurement needs. The opposite would be the case in a centralized organization. Logistical planning and execution would be directed from a central headquarters group, such as corporate traffic or procurement, that dictates which carriers and suppliers each plant will use. In today's information-intense world, such clear-cut centralization/decentralization demarcations are becoming blurred.

Over the past several decades logistical management trends have been toward more centralized organizations. However, recent developments in distributed information processing no longer require a centralized logistics organization to provide efficient data processing. The result is a trend toward pushing logistical responsibility down the organization. One factor that has encouraged centralization is the high cost of logistical facilities and equipment. To the extent that centralized operations exist, high-cost resources and specialized talent can be shared among users. A direct relationship exists between the desired degree of centralization and the overall nature of business operations. A popular form of logistical centralization is a division or service company that operates as a combined support group for a variety of different business units. Examples of what appear to be highly centralized organizations are Johnson & Johnson's Hospital and Consumer Support Distribution Companies, American Stores Logistics Service Company, Kraft/General Foods Customer Service, Inc., and Kodak's Global Logistics Group. Many cross-divisional or strategic business unit logistical consolidations have been encouraged by customers that desire a variety of all products sold by different business units of a conglomerate on a single invoice delivered in a single truck or container.

While the above forces support highly centralized organization, the availability of information technology also results in attributes of local accommodation that are typically considered to be the major benefits of decentralization. For example, American Stores continues to perform most of its day-to-day logistics work in its operating subsidiaries, such as Jewel, Osco, and Lucky. Johnson & Johnson Consumer is similarly decentralized in that specific operating groups are dedicated to Wal-Mart, Kmart, and a conglomerate of Los Angeles and New York customers.

The inescapable conclusion is that the traditional notion of centralization and decentralization has lost its relevancy. It simply does not fit contemporary practice. Latitude in organizational philosophy and operating practice is possible as a result of the current state-of-the-art capability in logistical information systems. Managers concerned with restructuring logistics organizations need to reconcile the discrepancies that executives have concerning these long-standing beliefs. In today's world, agile organizations can simultaneously enjoy the best that both centralization and decentralization have to offer.

Line and Staff Distinction Another concept requiring reconsideration is the distinction between line and staff in a logistical organization. The traditional distinction was that line performed or executed day-to-day operations, while staff engaged in planning. This distinction has lost its relevancy.

To a significant degree, contemporary logistics managers, at all levels, are involved in both planning and operations. As will be discussed under empowerment, the need to become directly involved and to assume some responsibility for both why and how work should be performed is critical to leading-edge logistical practice. Logistics managers are well aware that frontline employees, such as delivery drivers, interface more with customers than employees at any other level of their organization. A driver's understanding of customer requirements and what works best is critical to planning and achieving high-level performance.

Depending on the nature and urgency of the task, what could be defined as a line function one day may very well be a staff function the next. Once again, the impact of management information systems has all but eliminated the traditional staff/line distinction. With fewer middle managers, more analysis must be performed and implemented in frontline jobs. Executives need to establish and communicate the desired and delicate balance of the staff and line nature of all jobs.

The result is an organization that reflects total employee resources dedicated to servicing customers through maximum integration.

Matrix to Horizontal Structure   As indicated earlier, the dominant organizational structure in logistics for the past three decades has been based on aggregating functional groupings. Under a functional structure, logistical activities such as transportation and warehousing are grouped into clusters and related by direct lines of authority and responsibility. Such functional groupings typically utilize line command and control to allocate resources to operations.

As an enterprise begins to confront the challenge of process management, it becomes difficult and even undesirable to maintain the crystal-clear lines of authority and responsibility representative of functional organization structures. In a command and control structure, it is difficult to achieve the cross-functional flexibility required to satisfy unique customer requirements. One solution that managers developed to resolve cross-functional operations was initially referred to as a matrix organization.[14]

In the original matrix organization, two senior managers shared overall responsibility for the enterprise. The first senior manager focused on financial aspects and was responsible for the profitability of specific organizational units that were often structured around product categories, geographical proximity, or class of business. The second senior manager focused on resources and was responsible for the deployment of human and physical assets across organizational units.

The matrix model of structuring authority and responsibility gained popularity in service organizations such as consulting and public accounting. Business managers were given full accountability for specific clients or projects and were assigned skilled personnel from resource pools on the basis of project requirements. While the skilled personnel were directly responsible to the resource manager, they were temporarily assigned to the business manager. The business manager had direct authority for work design, temporary assignment of functional staff, and project control. The business manager typically shared recommendations concerning promotion, salary increase, and other benefits for the skilled personnel with the resource manager. On completion of the project, skilled personnel would return to the functional pools for reassignment.

The potential of a matrix organization structure has gained renewed interest as managers struggle with the challenges of process management. The matrix approach requires a technical resource group that can be geographically deployed as necessary to satisfy line-unit requirements. The approach offers a way to share scarce assets and technical resources on a flexible basis. As such, it reduces the potential duplication of highly skilled personnel across business units. An offsetting factor is that temporary personnel may not feel the same commitment that is characteristic of a traditional functional organizational arrangement.

The modern extension of the matrix approach to business structure is increas-

---

[14]For more information, see John Peters, "On Structures," *Management Decision,* **31**:6, 1993, pp. 60–62; Robert C. Ford and Alan W. Randolph, "Cross-Functional Structures: A Review and Integration of Matrix Organization and Project Management," *Journal of Management,* **18**:2, June 1992, pp. 267–294; and Richard F. Benedetto, *Matrix Management: Theory in Practice,* Dubuque, Iowa: Kendall/Hunt Publishing Company, 1985.

SEVEN KEY ELEMENTS OF THE HORIZONTAL CORPORATION

Simple downsizing didn't produce the dramatic rises in productivity many companies hoped for. Gaining quantum leaps in performance requires rethinking the way work gets done. To do that, some companies are adopting a new organization model. Here's how it might work:

1 *Organize around process, not task.* Instead of creating a structure around functions or departments, build the company around its three to five "core processes" and establish specific performance goals. Assign an "owner" to each process.

2 *Flatten hierarchy.* To reduce supervision, combine fragmented tasks, eliminate work that fails to add value, and cut the activities within each process to a minimum. Use as few teams as possible to perform an entire process.

3 *Use teams to manage everything.* Make teams the main building blocks of the organization. Limit supervisory roles by making the team manage itself. Give the team a common purpose. Hold it accountable for measurable performance goals.

4 *Let customers drive performance.* Make customer satisfaction—not stock appreciation or profit-

ability—the primary driver and measure of performance. The profits will come and the stock will rise if the customers are satisfied.

5 *Reward team performance.* Change the appraisal and pay systems to reward team results, not just individual performance. Encourage staff to develop multiple skills rather than specialized know-how. Reward them for it.

6 *Maximize supplier and customer contact.* Bring employees into direct, regular contact with suppliers and customers. Add supplier or customer representatives as full working members of in-house teams when they can be of service.

7 *Inform and train all employees.* Don't just spoon-feed sanitized information on a "need to know" basis. Trust staff with raw data, but train them in how to use it to perform their own analyses and make their own decisions.

Source: John A. Byrne, "The Horizontal Corporation: It's about Managing Across, Not Up and Down," *Business Week,* December 20, 1993, pp. 76–79.

---

ingly referred to as a horizontal organization. Similar to the McKinsey model discussed earlier, the horizontal organization is designed to facilitate process, not to perform tasks.[15] Figure 20-7 illustrates a horizontal organization. The associated sidebar details the seven key elements of the horizontal corporation.

While the matrix organization of the 1980s is not identical with the horizontal corporation of the 1990s, several key concepts are similar. In subsequent parts of this chapter, other developments critical to horizontal management, such as teaming and learning, are discussed.

When restructuring an organization, the key question for the logistics manager concerns how innovative to make the new structure. Issues related to organization capacity, resource availability, critical knowledge and skill-set requirements, economy of scale, and economies of scope serve to mediate the degree of desirable transition from vertical to horizontal management. The judgment of how horizontal to become will vary with each enterprise and will directly relate to the extent of information technology adoption.

[15]See Thomas A. Stewart, "The Search for the Organization of Tomorrow," *Fortune,* **125:**10, May 18, 1992, pp. 92–98; and John A. Byrne, "The Horizontal Corporation: It's about Managing Across, Not Up and Down," *Business Week,* December 20, 1993, pp. 76–81.

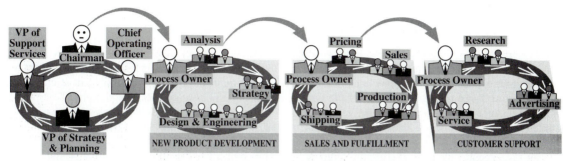

FIGURE 20-7 The horizontal corporation: it's about managing across, not up and down. *(Adapted from John Byrne, "The Horizontal Corporation: It's about Managing Across, Not Up and Down,"* Business Week, *December 20, 1993.)*

Empowerment   To empower means to delegate. The delegation of authority is not a new management concept. What is new about contemporary empowerment is the extent to which employees are permitted and *expected* to make decisions related to performance of their assigned work. Empowerment starts with availability and willingness of senior management to freely share relevant information.

The motivation behind empowerment is a belief that the overall effort to satisfy customers will be enhanced if frontline employees are permitted to take, what in their judgment is, appropriate action. Such on-the-spot decision making can greatly speed up a firm's response to customer requests.

In logistics, empowerment could range from accommodating all order requirements on a one-call basis to on-the-spot resolution of delivery discrepancies. What it all boils down to is trusting frontline employees to use sound judgment in dealing with day-to-day situations. Likewise, an empowered organization permits midlevel management to resolve problems and use proactive judgment. The extent to which an organization is empowered is reflected in response speed. A wide range of decisions do not need to transcend a business hierarchy for approval in an empowered organization. Employees are afforded maximum opportunity to perform their assigned work.

Empowerment in logistics takes on a special meaning. The multitude of details required to support the work of logistics makes it essential that frontline managers be positioned to complete all aspects of their respective work. If the essence of leadership is flexibility, then details of how work is ideally performed must be formalized through standardized methods and maximum simplification. By achieving such formalization, the foundation is established to capitalize on flexible operations to satisfy important customer requirements. Empowerment can be effective only in an organization that has fully established ways and means for gaining differential advantage. For an example on empowerment of frontline employees, see the sidebar on Saturn.

Teaming   The concept of a self-directed work team (SDWT) has its origins in the cross-functional committee. The idea that multiple viewpoints are often better than one has long standing in administrative practice. The development of SDWTs, however, extended the power of group behavior in two important ways.

COMMITMENT EQUALS EMPOWERMENT AT SATURN

Saturn Corp. employee Annette Ellerby has a startling admission: Her workload is too light. But she and her fifteen-member work team, which checks electrical systems on Saturn subcompacts as they roll off the assembly line, are about to change that. "We're trying to figure out how to use one less person," she says.

That's not the sort of thing you hear a production worker say, except at the Saturn factory in Spring Hill, Tennessee. The General Motors Corp. subsidiary was designed as a laboratory for innovative ideas, and one of the most revolutionary is its approach to employee empowerment. Saturn is organized as a collection of small, self-directed business units such as Ellerby's. Each team manages everything from its own budget and inventory control to hiring, without direct oversight from top management.

PRESENTEEISM

While the system doesn't work perfectly, many experts believe that workers can be the most effective managers of complex manufacturing operations. Their experience helps them make better, faster decisions than office-bound managers, says Eugene E. Jennings, professor emeritus of business management at Michigan State University. For instance, Mel Prevost and the other fourteen members of a Saturn machine maintenance team can order many of the tools and parts they need on their own. That speeds repairs and gets rid of time-consuming, bureaucratic purchase orders. Prevost's team also recently decided that an outside supplier was the cheapest place to sharpen cutting tools for transmission components, a task once done in-house. Saturn's no-layoff policy means that such decisions won't cost jobs.

At Saturn, added responsibility appears to have made workers more accountable. Absenteeism averages just 2.5 percent, versus 10 to 14 percent at other GM plants. The reason is partly peer pressure. Team members must take up the slack when coworkers don't show up. Another example is that each team regulates personal calls on its phones. Some use an honor system, while others make team members use a personal credit card.

Saturn workers show a remarkable commitment to their company. When a malfunction in the plant's powerhouse recently interrupted the flow of crucial cooling water to the paint shop, a maintenance team worked thirty-six straight hours to fix the problem. Says Michael Bennett, president of Saturn's United Auto Workers local, "You couldn't get people to do that in General Motors."

ENHANCED TRAINING

To help its employee teams function effectively, Saturn has set up a comprehensive training program. Before production began two years ago, workers got 300 to 400 hours of schooling, covering basic skills such as conflict management and problem solving. That has been followed by ongoing training in specific areas, such as interviewing techniques. The company's goal this year is for workers to spend at least 5 percent of their working time, or ninety-two hours a year, in further training.

Source: David Woodruff, "Where Employees Are Management," *Business Week,* Special Bonus Issue, 1992, p. 66.

First, the SDWT is not typically structured for special assignment or problem solving. The original concept was that a committee would convene to review or evaluate a special situation, make recommendations, and then be dismantled. A similar expectation is common in special-purpose work groups. In logistics, such special committees or work groups might be formulated to facilitate development of a new software application or to handle a unique requirement, such as selecting a new distribution warehouse location. In other situations, standing committees are structured to meet on a regular basis to perform some specified duties. For example, a standing committee might be assigned to perform audit and compensation reviews. In contrast, the SDWT is positioned as a permanent way to organize the

TABLE 20-1   NOT ALL GROUPS ARE TEAMS: HOW TO TELL THE DIFFERENCE

Working group	Team
Strong, clearly focused.	Shared leadership roles.
Individual accountability.	Individual and mutual accountability.
The group's purpose is the same as the broader organizational mission.	Specific team purpose that the team itself delivers.
Individual work products.	Collective work products.
Runs efficient meetings.	Encourages open-ended discussion and active problem-solving meetings.
Measures its effectiveness indirectly by its influence on others (e.g., financial performance of the business).	Measures performance directly by assessing collective work products.
Discusses, decides, and delegates.	Discusses, decides, and does real work together.

Source: Jon R. Katzenbach and Douglas K. Smith, "The Discipline of Teams," *Harvard Business Review*, **71**:2, March–April 1993, p. 113.

performance of basic work. The team is an alternative to the more traditional departmental organization structure.

A second unique characteristic of an SDWT is the way its performance is planned and executed. The label *self-directed* means that the team membership is empowered to do whatever it takes to most effectively and efficiently perform designated work. A characteristic of a disciplined work team is that the members develop individual and mutual accountability.[16] The idea is to focus the team on performance of cross-functional work. A group of highly motivated people selected to represent different skills and knowledge would, on the surface, appear to have greater synergistic potential than a traditional vertical organization consisting of workers with a permanent supervisor. Part of the appeal of the team is its focus on process as contrasted to functional parochialism. Finally, a team approach provides the opportunity for the tasks involved to be guided by workers, as opposed to managers. Table 20-1 presents a summary of key differentials between working groups, such as committees and teams.

Adopted from popular sports, the notion of a team is appealing because it implies that working together will create an end result greater than the sum of the skills of individual members.[17] As one might expect, managers encounter problems in structuring effective SDWTs. One observer has gone so far as to conclude that ''when managers try to form teams, they usually fail.''[18] A summary of reasons for this follows:

---

[16]Jon R. Katzenbach and Douglas K. Smith, "The Discipline of Teams," *Harvard Business Review,* **71**:2, March–April 1993, pp. 111–120.

[17]Peter F. Drucker, "The New Society of Organizations," *Harvard Business Review,* **70**:5, September–October 1992, pp. 95–104; and Jon Katzenbach, "The Right Kind of Teamwork," *Wall Street Journal,* November 9, 1992, p. 10, Section A, col. 2.

[18]Jon Katzenbach, "The Right Kind of Teamwork," *Wall Street Journal,* November 9, 1992, p. 10, Section A, col. 2.

• Failure to establish specific performance goals or challenges related to expected results. Teams need clear goals to establish directions, momentum, and dedication.

• Failure to clearly establish the role of individual accountability in the context of team performance. While the focus is on the team, the individual participant is the building block to synergistic performance.

• Formation of teams often creates rivalries founded in turfism. All work is typically viewed as the ''rightful'' domain of some existing group or department. These traditional departments have an approach to doing work that each participant carries like baggage to the team. How the team will work can become a matter of considerable debate. A lack of clear consensus or commitment to the team approach can result in such debate becoming dysfunctional, even to the extent that team members begin to work independently.

• Supervisors and managers often have problems letting teams perform without restriction. Letting go isn't easy for managers who are used to operating under traditional supervisor-subordinate relationships. Problems related to managerial involvement can be magnified when team members are assigned from vastly different organizational units within an enterprise. The danger is that the agendas of the different employee parent units often hinder team performance. The inability of management to relinquish control is a real threat to the SDWT.

• Finally, teams confront the need to reconcile the members' various backgrounds, different skill sets, educational preparation, titles, and compensation levels. Perhaps the most difficult problem to resolve is compensation discrepancy. An individual team member may resent being expected to provide the same level of commitment or responsibility as another teammate who is receiving significantly higher compensation. While employees are motivated by a variety of factors, the need for comparative compensation levels is significant among peers performing at a similar level of empowerment.

The fact that significant changes are required in how work is structured to achieve major performance breakthroughs is acceptable to most managers and workers. To date, it appears that teams have greater success when given special achievement assignments as contrasted to the performance of continuous work. One reason for this may be the fact that permanent teams are not typically supported by development of performance measurement systems to gauge their progress toward goal achievement.[19] To the extent that it requires a ''skunkworks'' environment for a team to excel, the potential range of SDWTs is limited.[20] The nature of work performed in logistics offers ample opportunity to apply team concepts. Selection and assembly of warehouse orders, receipt and processing of customer orders, and resolution of shipment quantity discrepancies are all areas where teams can provide productivity improvements. In contrast, the effective structure from a trucking viewpoint may be limited to a single driver or at best a two-person team.

The insights and potential achievements of SDWTs, as opposed to traditional

---

[19]Christopher Meyer, ''How the Right Measures Help Teams Excel,'' *Harvard Business Review*, **72**:3, May–June 1994, pp. 95–103.

[20]Jon Katzenbach, ''The Right Kind of Teamwork,'' *Wall Street Journal*, November 9, 1992, p. 10, Section A, col. 2.

committees, have appeal. The unleashing of creativity and the benefit of synergistic results are powerful motivators to encourage consideration of team structures. However, questions remain concerning the long-team viability of the "group" versus the "individual" in Western culture.[21] Robert Bresticker warns that motivational concepts that work well in one society, such as Japan, may not be fully transferable to another part of the world, as shown below:

> We should consider the possibility that the veneration of "The Team" denigrates the American strengths of individuality and creativity. When we blindly copy the organization methods of our Asian competitors, we are playing on their home field and doom ourselves to second class status. By all means, we should take the best of their methods and join that to our strengths, as a multicultural work force.[22]

Learning   *Organizational learning* is a relatively new term in management. While learning has always been a recognized attribute for individual workers and managers, its extension to the overall organization introduces some significantly different challenges and potential benefits. Some say that the primary challenge for senior management is to promote and nurture the organization's capacity to improve and innovate. In this sense, learning becomes the unifying force for the organization, replacing control as the fundamental responsibility of management.[23]

There can be little debate that today's logistical executives and workers need to become better educated to cope with challenges embodied in the widespread change discussed throughout this text. The ability to manage processes and avoid pitfalls of steep organizational hierarchies means that all employees at all levels need to enhance their capacity to learn. This capacity for rapid learning may be the essential difference between future winners and losers.[24]

However, learning involves more than developing new individual skills and knowledge to achieve superior results. An organization needs to develop the capacity to retain experience and pass it along through generations of workers and managers. Far too often critical knowledge based on invaluable experience is lost to an organization when an employee retires or otherwise departs. Thus, learning in the broadest sense involves programs and devices to retain and share knowledge. Once again, the power of information technology seems to be the saving grace.

On-line transaction systems can be designed to "window" or display critical "data-banked" experience to assist workers who are empowered to make decisions. The key to effective flexible logistics rests with a capability to hypothesize and evaluate alternative operating scenarios. The point is that learning must transcend technique to encompass use of information. In order to benefit from experience, an organization must learn how to retain it and make it available to others. Finally,

[21]Peter F. Drucker, "The New Society of Organizations," *Harvard Business Review*, **70**:5, September–October 1992, pp. 95–104.

[22]Robert B. Bresticker, *American Manufacturing and Logistics in the Year 2001*, Hoffman Estates, Ill.: Brigadoon Bay Books, 1992.

[23]Peter F. Drucker, "The New Society of Organizations," *Harvard Business Review*, **70**:5, September–October 1992, pp. 95–104.

[24]David A. Garvin, "Building a Learning Organization," *Harvard Business Review*, **71**:4, July–August 1993, pp. 78–91.

WHEN INFORMATION TECHNOLOGY ALTERS THE WORKPLACE . . .

MANAGERS MUST . . .

1 *Instill commitment in subordinates, rather than rule by command and control*

2 *Become coaches, training workers in necessary job skills, making sure they have resources to accomplish goals, and explaining links between a job and what happens elsewhere in the company*

3 *Give greater authority to workers over scheduling, priority setting, and even compensation*

4 *Use new information technologies to measure workers' performance, possibly on the basis of customer satisfaction with the accomplishment of specific goals*

WORKERS MUST . . .

1 *Become initiators, able to act without management direction*

2 *Become financially literate, so that they can understand the business implications of what they do and the changes they suggest*

3 *Learn group interaction skills, including how to resolve disputes within their work group and how to work with other functions across the company*

4 *Develop new math, technical, and analytical skills to use newly available information on their jobs*

Source: James B. Treece, ''Breaking the Chains of Command,'' *Business Week,* Special Edition on the Information Revolution, 1994, pp. 112–114.

---

learning has a direct relationship to individual careers and the more general topic of loyalty, which is developed in more detail in the next part of this chapter. The sidebar on how information technology is altering the workplace sums up many of the issues discussed.

Careers and Loyalty

One author has referred to the state of affairs in industry as the ''new Darwinian workplace.''[25] The challenge for both workers and managers is a growing belief that old and well-established career paths no longer exist. The most highly publicized impact of change is the decline of middle management as a result of the evolving flat nature of the enterprise. However, less publicized change and career modifications are also taking place at top management and frontline work levels.

In previous times, new employees could be given a fairly detailed map illustrating how their career path would develop if they performed to expectation. From entry level to at least upper middle management, the assumption was that as employees demonstrated an ability to learn prerequisite skills and demonstrated dedication to the enterprise, they would be rewarded with promotions to positions leading to increased compensation and added responsibility. However, the security that was once an integral part of career development no longer exists in most corporations, particularly those that have been shattered by repeated efforts to reconfigure organization structures.

In today's enterprise, employees at all organization levels must assume full

---

[25]Stratford Sherman, ''A Brave New Darwinian Workplace,'' *Fortune,* **127:**2, January 25, 1993, pp. 50–56.

TABLE 20-2   COMPARATIVE LOYALTY PERCEPTIONS AMONG LOGISTICS EXECUTIVES
IN ELEVEN COUNTRIES*

Country	Employees are more loyal to their firms today than five years ago.			Firms are more loyal to their employees today than five years ago.		
	Mean	Standard deviation	Respondents	Mean	Standard deviation	Respondents
Australia	3.25	0.94	280	3.42	0.94	280
Canada	3.62	0.90	103	3.70	0.88	103
France	2.94	0.85	34	3.29	0.84	34
Germany	3.29	0.74	318	3.44	0.72	317
Japan	3.15	0.78	323	2.90	0.78	324
Korea	3.85	0.98	124	2.95	0.94	124
Norway	2.63	0.93	27	3.25	0.84	28
Netherlands	3.34	0.65	32	3.16	0.68	32
Sweden	2.51	0.82	167	3.19	0.80	167
United Kingdom	3.46	0.93	1,010	3.75	0.86	1,013
United States	3.81	0.83	1,221	3.93	0.89	1,221
Overall average	3.48	0.92	3,639	3.62	0.92	3,643

*Scale: 1 = strongly agree; 3 = neutral; 5 = strongly disagree
Source: Global Logistics Research, Michigan State University, 1993.

responsibility for their individual careers. This means continuous learning to develop skills that fit ever changing job requirements. Skills for the future will be based much less on specialized knowledge and focused far more on capabilities related to analysis, integration, motivation, and creativity. The capability to think critically and innovatively will be considered a more attractive attribute than the ability to perform a specific task. The reason is obvious: the task may become obsolete overnight.

It is a fact that loyalty of both employees to organizations and organizations to employees is at an all-time low.[26] A survey conducted at Michigan State University in 1993 among logistics executives in eleven countries highlights that the decline of loyalty is not geographically localized. Table 20-2 reports responses to loyalty perceptions of logistics managers. To a significant degree, decline in loyalty is directly related to massive change in organizational structure throughout industry.

Each new wave of organizational delayering is typically concluded with management assurance that necessary restructuring is now completed and no further layoffs or cutbacks are "anticipated or planned." Such statements are translated by those who have jobs at the fringe of the cutback to mean that they have survived another wave of layoffs and are safe until the next round hits. No one, senior managers or otherwise, really knows what the ultimate organization structure will be or what this structure will require in terms of human resources. As a result, it can be expected that employees at all levels will be quick to change jobs and employers will not hesitate to improve their status if they see an opportunity. Thus,

[26]Sue Shellenbarger, "Work Place: Work-Force Study Finds Loyalty Is Weak, Divisions of Race and Gender Are Deep," *The Wall Street Journal*, September 3, 1993, p. 1, Section B.

the future is likely to see fewer managers who spend their careers in one or even a few firms. Unless management can rekindle loyalty throughout the organization, external mobility will increasingly become the career path of the future.

Enter, the challenges of learning! A solution for dealing with rapidly changing career requirements is to regenerate loyalty through continuous learning. One way for a logistics organization to keep its outstanding employees is to demonstrate a willingness to invest in their education. As an employee, if your learning is expanding in terms of depth and scope of knowledge, then the dangers of personal obsolescence decline. A person's career has always been a race between obsolescence and retirement. The essence of the problem is that the speed of the race has accelerated to the point where learning cannot be left to chance. Employees who are motivated and supported in continuous education are both more valuable and more marketable. The key to rebuilding loyalty is expanding commitment to individual worth. Such commitment demonstrates loyalty to the employee and encourages reciprocal loyalty for the enterprise. The sidebar on staying power illustrates this commitment.

Managing Change

A final topic of concern to logistics managers is how to deal with change. It is one thing to decide what should be done. It is an entirely different thing to get it done. Once again, logistics managers cannot expect to find a blueprint to guide them. As a general rule, they are involved in three primary types of change.

First, there are issues related to strategic change. This involves the implementation of new and improved ways to service customers. The topic of strategic change management has been dealt with at several different places throughout the text.

The second type of change concerns modifications in a firm's operational structure. On the basis of strategic considerations, logistics executives are constantly engaged in modifying where products are positioned, how customer requirements are handled, and so forth. Such operational reengineering represents a great deal of the change that must be managed to keep a firm's capabilities in line with its strategic requirements.

The third type of change concerns human resource structure. As the mission and scope of logistics change, managers have traditionally found it difficult to alter organization structures in a timely manner. Research clearly illustrates that organizational change is frequent. In responses of 820 logistics managers throughout the United States, 77 percent reported that their logistics organization had undergone major restructuring in the past five years.[27] The really startling fact is that despite frequent articles suggesting what should be done, few provide any meaningful dialogue concerning how to get it done!

One of the first steps in bringing about organization structure modification is to create a positive attitude among managers and workers. This requires understanding

[27]Global Logistics Research, Michigan State University, 1993.

STAYING POWER HAS REWARDS—AND A PRICE TAG

Nancy P. Karen, forty-six, is pretty sure her job won't be destroyed. In her twenty-four years with the company, she has been an energetic workaholic in the critical area of information systems. As director of the company's personal computer network, Karen is facing new and tougher demands as a result of management's efforts.

She joined New York Telephone in 1969 during the company's big bulge in hiring, often referred to as "the service glut." To meet explosive growth, the company hired tens of thousands of people in the late 1960s and early 1970s. Karen, a Vassar college graduate with a degree in math, was one of 103,000 employees at New York Telephone in 1971. Today, NYT has about 40,220 people. Working in a regulated monopoly, she felt a sense of comfort and security that now seems a distant memory. "Downsizing was totally unheard of," she says. "Just about everybody here started with the company at a young age and retired off the payroll."

WORKING SMARTER AND HARDER

Management's plan—and Nynex's earlier efforts to slash the payroll—have changed all that. Of the seventy-nine people who report directly to Karen, fifty-nine have already seen colleagues forced off the payroll in previous rounds of cutbacks. Her department is likely to suffer a 30 percent reduction in staffing. "When they started talking about another round of downsizing, people were a little more anxious because they feel they're already stretched thin. Now we'll have to learn to work smarter and completely change the way we do things."

Working smarter also means working harder—much harder. She once directly supervised twenty-six people, instead of seventy-nine, and she used to work more normal hours as well. No longer. Karen now puts in fifty to sixty hours a week, from 8 a.m. to 7 p.m. every weekday, at Nynex's White Plains, New York, office. Wherever she goes these days, she carries a beeper and a cellular phone and checks her voice mail every hour. "It's a different mentality," she says. "My weekends and holidays are not reserved." On a recent biking vacation through California's wine country, she called the office at least once a day from "every little town." Since Karen is single, "nobody complains about my work hours," she says.

Nynex didn't push Karen into her new and grueling pace completely unprepared. The company dispatched her to the local Holiday Inn in early 1993 for a workshop on culture change put together by Senn-Delaney Leadership, a Long Beach, California, consulting firm. She was skeptical at first. "To me, it was yet another program," she says.

Surprisingly, Karen left a believer. The sessions—dubbed Winning Ways—are an effort to inculcate the new values and skills that Nynex believes it needs to make management's reengineering changes take hold. It's a quick-and-dirty roundup of today's managerial commandments, stressing teamwork, accountability, open communications, respect for diversity, and coaching over managing.

Although impressed by how the sessions encouraged employees to speak more freely to each other, Karen saw her share of nonconverts at the initial two-and-one-half-day meeting. "Some people come back to work unchanged," she says. "But there's a big middle section that seems willing to change, and then there's a small percentage at the top that's very enthusiastic about it."

BRAIN DRAIN?

Not that Karen, who earned an MBA from Columbia University on the company's tab in 1981, doesn't have some big worries about the change effort. One of them is that the downsizing will get ahead of the company's ability to figure out ways to get the work done more efficiently. She's also worried that the company will lose expertise and talent. That would mean that she and other managers won't have enough of the right people to accomplish the tasks placed before them. "It's not going to work perfectly," she says. "There will be cases when the downsizing occurs before the reengineering."

Despite the increased workload and her concern over employee morale, Karen considers herself lucky. "This is a wonderful challenge," she says. "I'm looking at a task of building a new organization in the next six months to a year. I have the chance to test myself as I've never been tested before."

Source: John A. Byrne, "The Pain of Downsizing," *Business Week*, May 9, 1994, p. 67.

the need for change. Hopefully a commitment to learning and development of mutual loyalty initiatives will go a long way toward establishing a positive change culture. All those involved must accept the fact that organization change is inevitable if a firm is to remain competitive.

A second important consideration is to avoid a quick-fix mentality. The prevailing command and control structure has survived for centuries: it need not all be dismantled overnight. The key is development of a change model that charts a meaningful and believable course of transition. As noted earlier, managers should use caution in trying to accelerate the transition of logistical organization structures through the five evolutionary stages discussed earlier in this chapter. While it may be possible to accelerate change, it appears that trying to skip, what research indicates is, the natural evolution of organizations can be highly dangerous and may result in aborted restructuring attempts. The level of contemporary competition affords little or no latitude for error. Therefore, despite the appeal of changing quickly, real success may be enhanced by proceeding with care.

A final consideration concerning change is an organization's capacity to absorb new and challenging ways to improve performance. While all of the desired change is taking place, the day-to-day business still needs to be run. Though some advocate radical change, it does not appear to fit logistical organizations very well.

The notion of radical change is not new or unique. Despite the fact that knowledge expands rapidly, associated skills and accepted practices change at a much slower pace. Joseph Schumpeter envisioned a need for what he labeled "creative destruction."[28] Peter Drucker has warned that firms must develop skills for systematic abandonment and build into its fundamental structure a mechanism for managing change.[29] The problem in part is magnified by the fact that most significant changes do not result from self-improvement initiatives. Rather, radical improvements are typically generated by external creativity. This prompts the belief among some experts that massive change can be achieved only by total destruction of existing structural arrangements.[30] In the final analysis, the tempo of change that a firm can accommodate remains unique to each organization. How much change a firm can absorb requires precise calibration. Typically it is less than most change managers gauge it to be, and actual change takes longer than anticipated.

THE MANAGEMENT OF ALLIANCES

The growing popularity of alliances has been covered at various points throughout the text. In Chapter 4, the overall nature of logistical relationships was developed. Attention also focused on factors that stimulate alliances with logistics service providers. At this point, it is appropriate to discuss special considerations related to managing across organization boundaries. The critical question is, How should

---

[28]Joseph A. Schumpeter, *Capitalism, Socialism and Democracy*, 6th ed., London: Urwin Paperbacks, 1987.

[29]Peter F. Drucker, "The New Society of Organizations," *Harvard Business Review*, **70**:5, September–October 1992, pp. 95–104.

[30]Christopher Meyer and David Power, "Enterprise Disintegration: The Storm before the Calm," *Commentary*, Lexington, Mass.: Temple, Barker and Sloane, 1989.

internal and external efforts be organized to achieve desired performance objectives?

Despite the large number of firms seeking to create alliances, the majority of managers report that their organizations do not have clear policies or guidelines for implementing or measuring performance of such arrangements.[31] While trade and academic literature offers some guidelines concerning what alliances should seek to achieve, most are very general. However, six concerns have been identified as critical to the development of successful alliances: channelwide perspective, selective matching, information sharing, role specification, ground rules, and exit provisions.

Several reasons why alliances fail have also been identified: (1) fuzzy goals, (2) inadequate trust, (3) lip-service commitment, (4) human incompatibility, (5) inadequate operating framework, and (6) inadequate measurement. While the list is interesting, it fails to go beyond description and does not specify underlying reasons for alliance failure.

In an effort to better understand the anatomy of what makes for a successful alliance, in-depth case studies were completed with grocery manufacturing firms that are generally recognized as leaders in interorganizational arrangements.[32] Guidelines were developed concerning (1) initiating an alliance, (2) implementing an alliance, and (3) maintaining alliance vitality.

Initiating an Alliance

The alliances studied were typically initiated by the dyad partner that was the "customer" in the relationship. This was true in all the manufacturer–material supplier and manufacturer–service supplier relationships. Interestingly, a number of the material suppliers said that they had tried to establish alliances with other manufacturer customers but to no avail. As such, the material suppliers began to initiate alliances with their inbound material suppliers, where they are the customer, as opposed to alliances across their customer base.

One potential explanation for the initiating pattern is the exercise of buying power. In a buyer-seller relationship, the seller will often implement reasonable changes at the request of its customer in order to facilitate interorganizational exchange. Also, the manufacturers' personnel, who initially approached the suppliers regarding an alliance, were sold on the alliance philosophy by their top managers. When a selling firm approaches a potential customer about forming an alliance, the suggestion does not carry the same weight and impact as when the suggestion is generated within the buying firm's organization.

The manufacturer-merchandiser alliances showed some anomalies to this initiation pattern. Although all alliances studied at this channel level were officially

---

[31]In a 1993 survey of logistics executives conducted by Michigan State University, only 22 percent of United States executives agreed that their firm had clear policies and procedures for creating alliances (N = 820) and maintaining alliances (N = 819).

[32]This section was adapted from Judith M. Schmitz, Robert Frankel, and David J. Frayer, "ECR Alliances: A Best Practices Model," Joint Industry Project on Efficient Consumer Response, Grocery Manufacturers Association, Washington, D.C., 1995.

initiated by the merchandiser, it was apparent in some cases that the manufacturer had actually sparked the initial idea. In other words, the manufacturer had planted the seed as far as conceptualizing the viability of the alliance. When the merchandiser was ready to form the alliance, it initiated more detailed discussion.

Another critical consideration during the development of an alliance is the need for the initiating firm to perform an in-depth assessment of its internal practices, policies, and culture. The initiating firm should evaluate its ability to make any necessary internal changes in order to implement and support a successful alliance. For example, in the manufacturer–material supplier alliances, the manufacturers had to examine their ability to redefine the importance of piece price. Buyers needed a method to incorporate the intangible benefits of an alliance in competitive evaluations. The key for the buyer was the evaluation of total market value, not strictly market price.

Another internal assessment includes the ability to truly empower the key alliance contacts to manage the relationship. For example, manufacturers needed to honestly assess the level of operational and strategic integration they could foster with service suppliers. Integration that generated the type of competitive advantage envisioned at the alliance's initial design, such as increased productivity or rapid response to customer orders, could be achieved only through extensive information sharing. The questions to be addressed concerned the level of systems capability, data collection, analysis, performance measurement, and training that was necessary to enable the information to be shared in a timely and accurate manner.

Integration capability also needs to be evaluated if the alliance involves a number of partner plants, warehouses, and/or stores that operate under different conditions, capabilities, or competitive requirements. This was especially important for merchandisers with multiple distribution centers and/or store locations. A key concern in this situation is the ability for internal units to utilize common operating practices and compatible information systems. The flexibility to adapt to meet specific market-based requirements is important for long-term viability.

Implementing an Alliance

The key to successful implementation is choosing a partner wisely. The partners should have compatible cultures, a common strategic vision, and supportive operating philosophies. It is not necessary that organizational cultures be identical. Rather, the strategic intentions and philosophies must be *compatible* to ensure that core competencies and strengths are *complementary*.

For example, manufacturers initiated alliances with service suppliers in part to achieve improved warehousing operations, transportation reliability, and/or increased consolidation programs that supported their particular strategic competitive advantage in the marketplace. Although the service suppliers were the leaders, manufacturers typically had a more sophisticated conceptualization and operationalization of quality, performance measurement standards, and expertise. The attraction between the partners was based, to a considerable degree, on the service suppliers' ability and willingness to provide creative, innovative operational and information-based solutions to the manufacturers' problems and on the service suppliers' desire to internalize the quality and performance measurement expertise that is the hallmark of the manufacturers. In this sense, the alliance partners' operating philosophies supported and complemented each other, in particular by enhancing their common strategic vision of improving systemwide logistics processes.

The alliance should start on a small scale to foster easily achievable successes or early wins. It is important that such early wins be acknowledged in order to motivate key contacts and build confidence concerning alliance performance. In the manufacturer–material supplier alliances, starting small meant that investments were not initially made in information technology. Manual communication systems were sufficient and provided the opportunity for key contact. A critical issue is to implement the alliance in its simplest form and then fine-tune the arrangement with technological sophistication when improvements will add substantial value.

Maintaining Alliance Vitality

Long-term continuity is dependent on three key activities: mutual strategic and operational goals, two-way performance measurements, and formal and informal feedback mechanisms. Each activity is described.

Strategic and operational goals must be mutually determined when the alliance is implemented. This proposition has been discussed extensively in the academic and business press and appeals to common sense. It is perhaps less well understood that these goals must be tracked, reviewed, and updated frequently to gain improvements over the long term. For example, if a manufacturer develops a new product, a mutual goal must be set concerning that product's position, especially its market launch. This goal must include consideration of the merchandiser's critical role in new-product introduction and acceptance.

Goals should be translated into specific performance measures that can be continually tracked. The performance measurements used and the measurement frequency should be jointly determined. Also, the measures should be two-way. Oftentimes, performance measures between manufacturers and material suppliers focus specifically on the suppliers' performance attributes, such as on-time delivery and quality. One of the alliances studied developed a joint measure of success— total system inventory. The manufacturer acknowledged that it was important for both partners to reduce inventory, not just the manufacturer. Manufacturers have historically accomplished reductions by pushing inventory back upstream on material suppliers. The measure of total system inventory includes consideration of both partners to ensure that reductions are real and benefit both parties.

Feedback on performance can be provided through formal and informal methods. Annual reviews are formal assessments of alliance performance. These reviews typically involve top managers and are focused primarily on examining and updating strategic goals.

Quarterly or monthly reviews were used in only a portion of the alliances studied. These reviews were not as formal as the annual assessments and usually did not include top managers. They focused on tracking and reviewing strategic goals and operational performance. When used, the reviews enabled changes in operating practice to achieve strategic goals and created an avenue for continuous improvement to be identified.

Weekly or daily reviews occurred on an informal basis in all the alliances. These reviews were managed by the key contacts and were initiated to solve problems and identify potential opportunities for improvement. They were critical for resolving or avoiding conflicts and allowed key contacts to develop close working relationships. Although the process was typically informal in nature, the resolution mechanisms were often quite detailed. For example, in two manufacturer–service supplier alliances that did not operate on the same physical site, the involved partners had specific lists of contact personnel between each plant and the service supplier's customer center or warehouse facility.

SUMMARY

Logistics is undergoing massive change. New concepts and ideas concerning the best organization to achieve logistical goals appear daily. The challenge is to sort through the best of time-proven practices and merge them with the most applicable new ideas and concepts.

A careful review of logistics organization development suggests that most advanced firms have evolved through three stages of functional aggregation. The evolution started from a highly fragmented structure in which logistical functions were assigned to a wide variety of different departments. For over four decades firms have been grouping an increasing number of logistical functional responsibilities into single organizational units. The typical format for aggregation was the traditional bureaucratic organization structure. The objective was to aggregate functions in an effort to improve operational integration.

The advent of management focusing on critical processes began to usher in what is referred to as the horizontal organization. Today, leading-edge firms are beginning to experiment with stage 4 organizations as they shift from functional to process management.

There is increasing evidence that a fifth stage of organization may emerge. Stage 5 adopts the use of information technology to implement and manage logistics as a transparent organizational structure. While stage 5 structural arrangement remains more conceptual than real, the required information technology is available today. The concept has particular appeal to the management of logistics, which involves substantial challenge in terms of time and geographical scope of operations.

Chapter 20 focused on a range of issues and challenges confronting logistics managers. Attention was directed to key concepts, careers and loyalty, and challenges of managing change. The chapter concluded with an overview of issues related to managing beyond boundaries.

QUESTIONS

1   Describe why teams are being formed more frequently in business today. What are some of the special considerations required for a team to be successful?
2   Compare and contrast the five stages of functional aggregation.

3 What is the functional aggregation paradigm, and why is it important?

4 Discuss the three challenges that logistics faces as it manages on a process, rather than a functional, basis. Describe each challenge, and give an example of how it may be overcome.

5 Defend a position on the following question: Does radical organizational change require disintegration of existing structures?

6 What is a horizontal company, and how would this type of company be organized? What are the strengths to this type of organizational structure?

7 Describe a situation where empowerment has been used. What are the benefits and drawbacks to empowerment in this situation?

8 What is meant by the term *structure compression?* How does this term affect logistics?

9 Describe four reasons why alliances fail. How can these failures be avoided?

10 What is the distinction between centralization and decentralization? How do these concepts relate to logistics with the advent of information technology?

CHAPTER 21

PLANNING, COSTING, AND PRICING

OPERATIONS PLANNING
  The Nature of Logistical Plans
  The Final Operating Plan
  Operating Plan Modification
LOGISTICAL DESIGN METRICS
  Total-Cost Analysis
  Outsource Considerations
  Cost-Revenue Analysis

PRICING
  Price Fundamentals
  Various Pricing Issues
SUMMARY
QUESTIONS

Logistical administration deploys and monitors the resources necessary to achieve the logistics mission. Logistics administration is challenging because the activities occur across a wide geography, involve multiple time zones, and encompass many firm functions.

The task begins with the establishment of clearly defined strategic goals and acknowledged commitment to continuous improvement. A primary requirement for an organization is to continuously improve a comprehensive performance measurement system. Chapter 21 focuses on operational direction and control of logistical activities and processes. First, the chapter presents a general framework to guide operational planning. Effective planning provides a foundation to measure actual logistics operations. A special concern is the need to simultaneously control day-to-day operations while implementing system modifications. In other words, since corporate cash flow and operations depend on customer orders, it is not possible to ''shut down'' the logistics system for any extended period to modify or reengineer the process. All logistics reengineering must be done ''on the fly'' while the system is actively processing customer orders.

Next, the chapter discusses the measurement issues related to logistics system design. The presentation compares and contrasts the role of financial accounting practice and activity-based costing. Typical financial measures are used in a standard format to provide consistent performance measurements across organizations for financial markets. In contrast, activity-based costing is more relevant for logistics decision making. The development and implementation of total-cost analysis are also discussed. As activity-based cost provides more refined performance measures, firms may elect to outsource specific logistics activities to achieve either an economic or a strategic advantage. Chapter 21 reviews some of these outsourcing considerations and discusses how logistical cost components can be related to the associated revenue.

Finally, the chapter discusses pricing. While pricing is not typically a direct administrative responsibility of logistics managers, a significant interrelationship does exist between pricing and logistical operations. First, logistical operations are directly affected by the timing and magnitude of price changes, discounts, and promotions. Second, price administration is required when a firm assumes or assigns responsibility for logistics-related activities in a business agreement. For example, logistics must be capable of delivering product to a customer within the contracted delivery time frame once a purchase order has been assigned.

OPERATIONS PLANNING

Achievement of logistical goals is highly dependent on the development of a sound operating plan. The operating plan is ideally a short-term action aimed at making incremental progress toward long-term strategic objectives. Such integration requires reconciliation of information that is typically unavailable from standard costing or accounting systems. In this section attention is initially directed to the nature of logistics operating budgets and planning. System change management and achievement of operating goals are discussed and illustrated next. The budgeting process is presented as the primary device for implementing and controlling such logistics operating plans. Finally, plan modifications that accommodate unexpected opportunities and capitalize on operational flexibility are discussed.

The Nature of Logistical Plans

Operational planning is crucial because talented human resources are always in short supply. This shortage is expected to become even more acute in the future. Therefore, senior management cannot afford the luxury of allowing their organization to become ''firefighters'' bogged down in day-to-day operational problem solving.

The device that coordinates logistical efforts within an organization is the operating plan. A logistics operating plan is typically short-range; that is, detailed operations are normally not planned for longer than one fiscal year. Given a strategic plan (generally extending over multiple years), operating plans (generally by month, over a period of a year) are typically used to direct day-to-day efforts. Long-range strategies represent dynamic goals within which short-range operating plans detail objectives for each specified time period. Such goals typically concern system modifications, performance, and budgeting. Each goal reflects a set of short-term logistical management objectives.

The overall importance of logistics operating plans made it a topic for some consideration in many of the preceding chapters. For example, the topic of planning was initially discussed in Chapter 2, where the importance of coordinating cross-functional activities was introduced in the context of internal value chain integration. In Chapter 7, the foundation for planning was developed in greater depth with regard to information system architecture. At that time, forecasting was introduced as an integral component of overall logistics planning and coordination. Chapter 7 focused on the generation of accurate and timely information to guide the formulation of strategic and operating plans. In Chapters 8 through 15, planning was also identified as a critical activity for functional logistics performance. The subject of longer-term strategic planning was also highlighted in Chapters 16 (''Logistics Positioning'') and 17 (''Integration Theory''). Chapter 16 discussed the role of a strategic plan in positioning the long-term deployment of logistics resources. The critical dimension of the discussion was identification of the logistical resources required to meet marketing and financial objectives. The strategic plan defines a firm's relative positioning of logistics among its alternative core competencies. Chapter 17 expanded the strategic plan to include logistical system design elements. Customer service requirements and corresponding cost structure characteristics influence geographic inventory positioning and transportation practices (i.e., the logistics network), which, in turn, form a major element of the strategic plan. The fundamental point was made that the logistics network can be designed to achieve nearly any service and performance level that is strategically justified. From a logistics network design perspective, it is critical to fully understand the relationship of service performance and total cost.

In this chapter, discussion focuses on the extension and combination of all previous aspects of strategic planning to develop guidelines to control day-to-day logistical work. As such, the logistics operating plan becomes the mechanism to achieve the organization's strategic goals.

Logistical System Modification   During any operating period, several adjustments in logistics system design may be planned. A comprehensive logistical system reengineering effort typically spans a number of consecutive operating plans and requires specific implementation of selected parts of the overall long-range strategic plan. For example, an enterprise may have a long-range strategic plan calling for the consolidation of twenty-five local warehouses into ten regional distribution centers. Full implementation of the network consolidation effort may require several years and embrace parts of multiple operating plans. The initial operating plan may call for the construction of one or two regional facilities and the closing of several local warehouses. Future operating plans may schedule initial occupancy of the two regional facilities, the actual closing of specified local ware-

PLANNING IS PLANNING

Planning logistics processes is a critical component of any business. Ignore the drab green uniforms, and the officers at the United States Transportation Command (USTranscom) sound very similar to corporate logistics planners. Of course, there are differences between the commercial and military worlds: companies can predict their logistics needs more accurately, their contracting requirements are more flexible, and they don't have to deal with the surprise and uncertainty of war. Still, there are many similarities for military and commercial applications. The most obvious cross-fertilization between the military and commercial sectors is evident today in USTranscom's Global Transportation Network (GTN), a multi-million-dollar database system that collects, integrates, and distributes military logistics data.

GTN is an ambitious project that potentially has far-reaching effects on both commercial and military logistics business. Although several commercial vendors are in the process of developing automated systems for cargo tracking and logistics planning, no commercial shipper or carrier has the size or the complexity that approaches USTranscom, which oversees Army, Navy, and Air Force logistics from its headquarters at Scott Air Force Base in Illinois. For example, military transportation volume exceeds that of General Motors or General Electric. Military logistics is doing its best to adapt successful techniques and technologies from the private sector. "We're trying to take advantage of the best things that we have viewed in the commercial systems," says Col. Victor Wald, chief of the logistics management division at USTranscom.

Although GTN has been under development for several years, it was given additional impetus by the 1991 Persian Gulf War. Operation Desert Shield/Desert Storm was widely hailed as a logistical triumph, but it also pointed out the shortcomings of military cargo identification and tracking systems as they dealt with intermodalism. Of the 35,000 containers with material to support the Gulf War, 27,000 had to be opened on Saudi Arabian docks in order to determine their contents. Container identification problems caused tremendous dock congestion and were one of the critical constraints in the Gulf War supply chain. The problem of container identification led USTranscom to focus its efforts in 1994 on improving in-transit visibility, which it defined as the ability to identify and track the movement of defense cargo and personnel from origin to destination during peace and war. In-transit visibility is only one element of GTN. Military officials envision it as a tool that will provide officers and staff with information to develop plans for moving cargo and personnel. Officials are counting on the data to provide an overview of capacity, bookings, and shipment contents and to reduce order cycle times by shortening the lag between requisition and delivery. This could prove to be vital in a short-term conflict.

USTranscom is still in the initial stages of testing GTN in a limited scope. A prototype went into operation in March 1993 for air transportation, which includes integrated passenger reservation, airport, and logistics decision support data. Numerous technical enhancements have been added to the prototype, and early in 1994 it was extended to include ocean shipments. USTranscom is in the process of seeking bids from contractors for full implementation and expects to award contracts by the end of 1994.

GTN planners have focused on connecting existing systems to standardize and understand how the data are utilized within military information systems. This is a necessity to identify how technology can assist the military in doing its job better, more efficiently, and faster. Most military cargo moves via commercial transportation carriers, so that the more compatible the system is with commercial applications, the better. Given this situation, USTranscom is attempting to incorporate as much commercially available "off-the-shelf" technology as possible into GTN.

USTranscom was able to recently test commercial optical laser card and radio frequency tag technologies for cargo tracking and identification during Operation Restore Hope in Somalia. The country proved to be a good test of the military's ability to plan, develop, and test movement of a long supply line of material and personnel on very short notice—and on both an inbound and outbound nature in a place where infrastructure ranged from inadequate to nonexistent. USTranscom is currently evaluating how these and other new technologies might be coordinated with the GTN database.

In the past, the military was able to cover up for logistical planning inefficiencies through its immense resources. But today, in an era of shorter wars and Defense Department downsizing, logistics officers must work smarter. The Department of Defense report concerning Desert Storm found the distribution process "complex, segmented and unfocused . . . a patchwork quilt of functions and responsibilities that optimizes component parts at the expense of system efficiency." In response to that critique, USTranscom is looking to GTN to standardize, collect, and make information available when and where it is needed to better support logistical planning and decision making.

Based on Joseph Bonney, "U.S. Military Transportation Network," *American Shipper*, **36**:5, May 1994, pp. 54–56.

houses, commitment to establish additional regional facilities, and the closing of additional local warehouses.

When system adjustments are planned within a specific operating period, special capital budgets may be required. As is the case when managing one-time operating costs, unique capital expenditures need to be isolated for control purposes. For example, shifting to a new distribution center implies additional one-time operating costs since both the old and the new center may be operating simultaneously for a period of time. Two factors must be clearly understood when system adjustments are included in specific operating plans. First, budget allocations should identify both one-time costs associated with establishing new operations and the potential savings. The impact of these unique costs should be anticipated and separated from day-to-day operational expenditures so that they are not included in future budgets. Second, special efforts and associated costs necessary to safeguard against customer service disruptions during system readjustment should be identified and managed. For example, provisions to service a major customer from an alternative or secondary warehouse may be required during the period that facilities are being relocated. Because such provisions are the result of a one-time system modification, the associated expense will not occur in future planning periods. Unless the one-time costs associated with changes are isolated and reported separately, comparative performance measurement from one planning period to the next will be seriously flawed. Transitional planning must also anticipate the potential impact of special provisions on period-to-period operating comparisons such as sales, expenses, and production. For example, shipment history to support forecasting may need to be modified to reflect temporary servicing of a customer from a secondary warehouse.

Performance Goals   The development of target performance goals is typically based on a combination of strategic plans, forecasts, and managerial input regarding future business activities. To develop goals and realistic performance plans, considerable cross-functional coordination is required. For logistical goals to be realistic and relevant, they must integrate marketing plans with manufacturing capabilities. Without effective coordination, the potential benefits of integrated logistical performance will not be achieved.

As noted previously, operating plan activities usually span a one-year horizon. The typical plan is divided into increments or intervals consistent with the firm's accounting and financial reporting system. Many enterprises plan and report performance in intervals based on twelve calendar months. Others plan and operate on the basis of 13 four-week operating periods. Planned activities may extend across all or parts of consecutive periods or months. For example, new-product introduction rollouts extend as long as 90 to 120 days, while individual promotions may be initiated and completed in 10 to 21 days.

The detailed activities and logistical performance required to support new-product introduction and promotions are typically contained in the logistics operating plan. For example, during a specific operating period, such as the month of May, a grocery manufacturer may have plans to market two new products and conduct promotions of three existing products in a selected geographic area. The planning of logistical activities for the periods prior to May should include required inventory buildup and a deployment plan to complete product allocation and positioning to support new-product and promotional requirements. Performance goals may seek to achieve 100 percent product availability during initial distribution. For example, Microsoft's performance goal is to be able to deliver new software releases simultaneously around the world. This requires that all software, packaging, and manuals be assembled and shipped in time to support such a goal. It may also be necessary to provide promotional items with special support, such as two-day reorder availability, during the first two weeks of the promotion. In order to avoid building up excess inventories that must be carried over and redistributed following the promotion, performance goals may be less stringent during the final two weeks of the marketing effort.

In combination, target performance goals and associated activity schedules create the structure for achieving specific logistical objectives. The operating plan serves as the short-range tactical guide to allocate resources and prioritize day-to-day actions in a manner consistent with the strategic plan. Since most firms seeking to implement logistics best practice place a premium on flexibility, it is common for operating plans to be frequently revised or updated to reflect changing competitive situations. The financial budget is the yardstick to control such refinements.

Budgeting   Once the operations planning process has identified system modifications, performance goals, and scheduled activities, the next step is to budget anticipated expenditures. Typically, firms have unique methodologies that reflect their corporate culture for generating and approving budgets. Budgeting is considered a rationalization process in the sense that management authorizes resource expenditures that support desired performance. However, as will be illustrated throughout the following discussion, the task of arriving at a fair and equitable budget can, at times, be a highly controversial and circulatory exercise.

The budgeting process is typically initiated by requesting managers to identify the resources required to achieve operating plan goals. Thus, line management first details the work to be performed and then formulates a desired funding request. Budgets thus constitute a manager's estimate of the resources necessary to achieve specified goals. To a significant degree, budgeting is a management process in which senior and operating or line managers negotiate the level and timing of expenditures. Naturally, senior executives desire lower budgets, whereas operating managers may attempt to build as much slack as possible. To overcome potential bias in the "budget game," many firms structure expenses on a line-item basis. A *line item* defines a budget allocation for a specific activity. For example, the transportation budget might include line items for parcel, less-than-truckload, and truckload shipments. If budgeted amounts are "line-itemed," it is not possible to shift "overbudget" parcel accounts to "underbudget" truckload accounts. When budgets are constructed on a line-item basis, transfer of expenditures between specific accounts is restricted to authorized changes in the operating plan.

A budget supports two types of analyses. The simple budget establishes a resource allocation for a specific function or process. For example, a simple transportation budget of 4 percent of revenue defines the anticipated level of transportation expense. However, the simple budget figure does not indicate a need for, or suggest a direction for, change. A comparative budget provides direction by suggesting time-based, locational, or competitive benchmarks. Time-based benchmarks compare current performance levels with previous performance results within the same activity. The likely assumption is that performance should improve over time. Locational benchmarks can be used to compare divisions or operating units within an organization. Locational budget comparisons serve to highlight best practices that can be transferred to other organizational units. Competitive benchmarks compare budgets or performance measures with external organizations and are useful to evaluate relative performance and to identify improvement opportunities from other industries.

A finalized budget becomes the foundation for implementing a logistics cost control program. Four basic types of budgets are used in logistical controllership: fixed-dollar, flexible, zero-level, and capital. The first three types are used to control direct expenditures. The last type is used to fund major adjustments in logistical system design such as facilities, equipment, or information technology applications.

Fixed-Dollar Budgeting   A fixed-dollar budget is an estimate of functional cost accounts for an anticipated logistical activity. Examples of functional accounts include transportation, warehouse labor, and customer service. Given a sales volume projection, the budgeting process seeks to identify a realistic expenditure level to achieve performance goals. The purpose of a finalized budget is to provide a basis for comparison and control. For example, budgeted costs for a specific month or year-to-date operating plan can be evaluated in terms of planned to actual expenditure. The fixed budget is not used often because it does not consider the influence of environmental changes.

Flexible Budgeting   A flexible budget offers a way to accommodate unexpected increases or decreases in volume during an operating period. Normally, a flexible budget is structured on a standard cost basis. A *standard cost* is typically defined as an expected norm. Standard costs can be developed to measure a variety of logistical activities such as receiving and put away, order selection, packing, and transportation. As such, typical logistics standard cost measures include cases per hour, lines per order, cost per mile traveled, and so forth. The process of developing standard costs should be a coordinated, interdepartmental effort that involves logistics, accounting, and industrial engineering personnel. The authorized expenditure level is then computed on the basis of the standard cost measure multiplied by the anticipated activity level. Thus, authorized expenditures automatically adjust to the anticipated activity level. Although flexible budgeting is preferable to rigid or fixed budgeting, it is necessary to have a high degree of sophistication to implement the process. Flexible budgeting requires disciplined cost tracking and complex information systems to monitor activity levels and costs. Most flexible budgets are constructed on a line-item basis.

Table 21-1 illustrates a flexible budget with variances for major logistics activities. The initial budget for both line items and categories is illustrated in columns A_1 and A_2. The budget is developed using forecasted operating levels and standard costs. Forecasted operating levels are specified in terms of anticipated unit weight or order volume. Table 21-2 illustrates the calculation of the flexible budget figure for the transportation line item.

TABLE 21-1   EXAMPLE OF FLEXIBLE BUDGET

	(A₁)	(A₂)	(B)	(C)	(D)	(E)
				Variation from budget		
	Line-item budget	Category budget	Actual sales and expense level achieved	Variance due to ineffectiveness/ activity level above (below) budget	Variance due to inefficiency/ performance above (below) standard	Actual results
Net sales		$ 126,000	$112,000	$ 14,000	—	$112,000
Cost of goods sold						
Raw materials	$22,050		$19,600	$ 2,450		
Variable manufacturing costs	40,950		36,400	4,550		
Total cost of goods sold		$ 63,000	$ 56,000	$ 7,000	—	$ 56,000
Manufacturing contribution		$ 63,000	$ 56,000	$ 7,000	—	$ 56,000
Variable marketing and logistics costs						
Order processing	4,050		3,200	(450)	(400)	
Sales commissions	6,750		6,000	(750)		
Transportation	12,150		9,800	(1,350)	(1,000)	
Warehouse handling	4,050		4,600	(450)	1,000	
Total variable marketing/logistics costs		$ 27,000	$ 23,600	($ 3,000)	$ (400)	$ 23,600
Customer segment contribution margin		$ 36,000	$ 32,400	($ 4,000)	$ 400	$ 32,400
Assignable fixed costs						
Inventory carrying	2,500		2,500			2,500
Product advertising	5,500		5,500			5,500
Salaries	2,000		2,000			2,000
Total assignable fixed costs		$ 10,000	$ 10,000			$ 10,000
Customer controllable margin		$ 26,000	$ 22,000	($ 4,000)	$ 400	$ 22,000

Column B is the allowable budget amount based on the actual activity level. Since actual net sales were only $112,000, the transportation standard allowed is 0.89 ($112,000/$126,000) of the original budgeted amount, or $10,800.

Column E is the actual amount expensed in each category for the budget period. The difference between the original budget amount (column A₂) and the actual amount (column E) is known as the budget variance. Variances may be attributed to a combination of ineffectiveness and inefficiency. Variances due to ineffective-

TABLE 21-2   FLEXIBLE BUDGET COMPUTATION
FOR TRANSPORTATION

Sales level	$126,000
Based on average of ($) per pound	$10.00
Sales level (pounds)	12,600
Standard cost for transportation per pound	$0.96
Transportation flexible budget	$12,150

ness may result from the fact that net sales are less than anticipated. Since the activity level was 89 percent of anticipated sales, the amount budgeted for the variable cost categories is 89 percent of the original budget. Note that the allocations for the assignable fixed costs do not change.

Variances due to inefficiency may be attributed to performance of required activities at a level above or below standard cost. A positive variance occurs when an activity has been completed at less than standard cost; a negative variance occurs when an activity has been completed at greater than standard cost. In Table 21-1, the transportation category illustrates a positive efficiency variance, while the warehouse handling category illustrates a negative efficiency variance.

As discussed in Chapter 16, management's attention concerning cost and systems analysis should be directed to identify variations or exceptions from performance standards. In essence, the utilization of standard costing techniques establishes what costs should actually be rather than creating and predicting future performance levels based on historical cost behavior.

The concept of flexible budgeting allows management to examine a range of activity levels. Depending on the particular activity levels that actually occur, managers are able to utilize predetermined standard cost measures to decide what the relevant costs should have been and to understand the reasons for differences.

Zero-Level Budgeting Zero-level or target budgeting is usually used to facilitate operational control in two forms. At a line management level, a typical zero budgeting process starts without any authorized funds at the inception of budget planning. Funding is developed in a *zero up* manner; that is, funds are justified on the basis of planned activity levels and associated or standard cost performance. The expenditure of each dollar must be judged in accordance with the anticipated benefits. A second zero-level budgeting form is used to identify and commit staff activities. Zero-level staff budgeting assigns or allocates all costs necessary to perform a range of support services for functional units. Each functional unit must then justify the utilization of the support staff. Both types of zero-level budgeting seek to tie operational expenditures to specific tasks and to improve the basis for managerial review and control.

Capital Budgeting Capital budgeting specifies the amount and timing of significant financial investments for logistics resources. As noted earlier, numerous major logistical system changes may be initiated, continued, or completed during a specified operating period. These changes might require expenditure authorization for construction of a new facility, installation of a new order processing system, purchase or lease of transportation equipment, or institution of other nonrepetitive large expenditures. When major system changes are planned, the capital budget formulation process is straightforward. The expenditure is researched and, if justified, the necessary funding is approved.

A more difficult situation occurs when capital investment is required for research and development. At inception, such expenditures are nearly impossible to justify on a cost-benefit basis and thus are typically allocated over a number of future time periods.

A "creeping" capital commitment can occur when day-to-day operations result in unplanned expenditures. For example, logistical operations may experience unplanned inventory buildups. While annual inventory increases may not be significant, inventory turnover may decline substantially over a number of years. This leads to a creeping increase in the capital committed to inventory. If such trends in capital investment are not rigorously monitored, a substantial unplanned capital commitment may result.

A final note on capital budgeting concerns identification of which costs are tied to specific capital investment decisions. The typical capital budgeting process considers only those investments that require new capital. If planned system modifications can be achieved that result in operational savings without new capital commitment, they are not typically subjected to the rigid controls of the capital budgeting process.

Conclusion   The budget development and approval process is critical to logistical administration. In particular, senior executives must be concerned with total system performance rather than individual budgets of specific functions. Development of an integrated budget that assesses total system performance provides senior management with an estimate of expenditures required to achieve operating objectives. The budget also provides the basis for financial performance measurement. The essence of operational planning and control is reconciling individual budgets with total system performance.

As mentioned previously, budget requests by line managers typically exceed the level of funding senior management desires to authorize. This is understandable because no individual manager is positioned to envision the total system. A tendency also exists to view requirements in any area on a unit-cost basis. A bias toward unit costs often encourages actions resulting in efficiency in one area without full appreciation of the impact on other areas. For example, a traffic manager held responsible for achieving lowest possible transportation unit cost could be motivated to select low-cost transport without necessary consideration of on-time performance.

Why are individual managers asked to formulate budget requests if such deficiencies and misallocations can result? The answer is twofold. First, it is essential that the individual manager participate in budget formulation to gain a complete understanding of and assume ownership for the integrated nature of total system performance. Budget formation is one of the most potent training and control tools available to senior management. Second, individual unit managers are often aware of items that must be considered in a specific operating plan but do not come to the attention of senior management. The greatest danger in total system planning is overall complacency with regard to the impact on the firm's long-range strategy. Logistics management interaction is essential to the development and implementation of realistic but demanding operating plans.

The Final Operating Plan

The final plan becomes the blueprint to guide short-range operations and measure performance. It typically states goals, details authorized budgets for all organization units or teams participating in logistical operations, and links individual work to total system performance. The final plan is designed to integrate relevant cost centers into a single unified effort. Each operating manager is committed to coordinated performance since cost increases or decreases in specific functions will be treated secondary to achieving overall goals. The concept of total cost accountability is an essential aspect of logistical management.

Operating Plan Modification

Once the final operating plan is developed, some aspects of anticipated performance will likely require modification. Tactical adjustments may be necessary at different times during an operating period. Such modification may result from planning errors or adjustments to accommodate and take advantage of unanticipated events. For example, a transportation strike may require use of alternative modes that might significantly affect transport expenses. The transportation budget would thereby require modification to maintain its effectiveness as a tool.

Because individual managers have participated in the development of operational plans and have ownership in them, they should be sensitive to the impact of day-to-day decisions on performance in other functional areas. As managers become aware of the need to accommodate unanticipated events, collaboration is necessary to be able to significantly modify operational plans and exploit timely opportunities. Two rules must be followed when implementing operating plan modifications. First, modifications must be formally documented and approved prior to any deviation from the plan. Second, all modifications must be positioned and evaluated in terms of total system performance. Once modifications are adopted, formal written amendments should be shared with all the managers involved. Attention is now directed to design metrics to support identification and evaluation of alternative strategies.

LOGISTICAL DESIGN METRICS

The achievement of logistical integration requires the establishment of a cost-revenue analysis framework. Total cost provides the logic for integrating logistical operations across the value chain. The basic idea is that all firms participating in a value chain need to cooperate to achieve superior performance. Such integration boils down to each participant being responsible for the logistics activities that maximize overall performance in terms of market position or profit. While simple to describe, such cross-functional, multiple enterprise trade-offs are quite difficult to identify and manage in day-to-day operations.

This section examines issues and barriers concerning the establishment of cost and customer performance metrics. Problems related to using traditional accounting reports to perform logistical costing are identified. The use of activity-based costing (ABC) is developed as the most promising way to identify and control logistics expenses. Attention is also directed to analysis of circumstances that may justify outsourcing of some or all of a firm's logistical work. The discussion of total-cost analysis then proceeds to service performance integration.

Total-Cost Analysis

The basic integrative concept in logistical network design is total cost. The original application of total cost was presented by Howard Lewis, James Culleton, and Jack Steel in *The Role of Air Freight in Physical Distribution.*[1] Their example illustrated a total-cost justification for using high-cost air freight. The basic thesis was that in situations where the speed and dependability of air delivery would permit other costs (such as warehousing and inventory) to be reduced or eliminated, high-cost premium transportation would be justified by achievement of lower total cost. The Lewis, Culleton, and Steel framework demonstrated cost-to-cost trade-off analysis and illustrated how total cost could be reduced by careful integration of logistical activities.

The basic concept of total cost is simple and complements the notion of designing logistics as an integrated performance system. The main problem in operationalizing total cost is that traditional accounting practice for classifying and reporting critical expenses does not typically provide adequate logistical metrics. To understand the demand of measuring logistics, it is necessary to review traditional accounting methods in terms of analysis requirements and to identify costs relevant to integrated logistical systems.

Public Accounting Practice   The two main financial reports of a business enterprise are the balance sheet and the profit and loss statement (P&L). The balance sheet reflects the financial position of a firm at a specific point in time. The purpose of a balance sheet is to summarize assets and liabilities and to indicate the net worth of ownership. The P&L statement reflects the revenues and costs associated with specific operations over a specified period of time. As the name *profit and loss* implies, its purpose is to determine the financial success of operations. Logistical functions are an integral part of both statements. However, the primary deficiency in determining logistical costing and analysis is the method by which standardized accounting costs are identified, classified, and reported.

Accountants are responsible for the preparation of financial statements that follow general accepted accounting practices. It is a legal requirement that organizations with public investors be audited regularly to ensure that accounting practices are standardized and sound. What has resulted over the years is a reporting methodology designed to meet the requirements of investors and the taxation agencies of federal, state, and local governments. Unfortunately, these conventional methods of accounting do not fully satisfy logistical costing requirements.

The first problem results from the fact that accounting practice aggregates costs on a standard or natural account basis rather than on an activity basis. The practice of grouping expenses into natural accounts such as salaries, rent, utilities, and depreciation fails to identify or assign operations responsibility. To help overcome the natural account aggregation, it is common for statements to be subdivided by managerial or organizational areas of responsibility within an enterprise. This

---

[1]Howard T. Lewis, James W. Culleton, and Jack D. Steel, *The Role of Air Freight in Physical Distribution,* Boston: Division of Research, Graduate School of Business Administration, Harvard University, 1965.

results in financial information related to each unit of an organization. The process of classification and assignment helps but does not satisfy the requirements for total-cost analysis. Internal P&L statements generally classify and group expenses along organization budgetary lines. Thus, costs are detailed by managerial responsibility. In reality, many expenses associated with logistical performance cut across organizational units. For example, efforts to reduce inventory will reduce inventory carrying cost, but they may also lead to more back-orders, which would increase total transportation cost. The result is deficient data for integrated performance measurement.

The practice of classifying costs on a natural basis also creates a problem in activity-based cost analysis. In order to design and evaluate logistical operations, it is necessary to identify costs associated with performing specific activities or tasks, such as the warehousing expenses for a specific SKU. This means that the individual logistical activities must be identified and that costs must be allocated or assigned. While the data to classify costs by logistical function are available in most accounting systems, the accepted procedures for allocation of logistical costs do not break them down by individual activities. As early as 1972, Michael Schiff highlighted the allocation problem and discussed traditional practice.[2]

> What is of primary concern . . . is the suitability of (logistics) cost reporting for internal use, and failure to identify these costs and classify them as operating expenses can only suggest that management and accountants do not think these costs are important enough to warrant the attention and concern of the receiver of the report or that they can be influenced by the manager to whom the report is addressed. It is difficult to find a logical basis for this position. The costs are identified and assembled in accounts and in all cases they are of significant dollar value to warrant identification. It would take a minimum of effort and re-education to alter the classification wherein freight and other distribution costs would be identified as operating expenses and thus more closely relate responsibility with reported results.

Considerably more logistical activity-based costing is taking place now than ever before. Increased awareness of the need for improvement in this area has resulted in a great deal of research and development during the past decade.[3] While progress is being made, significantly more managerial attention is needed before logistical activity-based costing will become a universal practice.

A somewhat overlapping deficiency of accounting involves the traditional methods of reporting transportation expenditures. It remains standard practice in retail accounting to deduct freight from gross sales as part of the cost of goods to arrive at a gross margin figure. This is similar to the way promotional and cash discounts as well as merchandise returns are handled. The practice has evolved over the years as a firmly entrenched accounting procedure. In part, it seems to be based on the

[2]Michael Schiff, *Accounting and Control in Physical Distribution Management,* Chicago: National Council of Physical Distribution Management, 1972, pp. 1–10.

[3]For information, see Ronald L. Lewis, *Activity-Based Costing for Marketing and Manufacturing,* Westport, Conn.: Quorum Books, 1993; John K. Shank and Vijay Govindarajan, *Strategic Cost Management: The New Tool for Competitive Advantage,* New York: Maxwell Macmillan International, 1993; Michael C. O'Guin, *The Complete Guide to Activity-Based Costing,* Englewood Cliffs, N.J.: Prentice-Hall, 1991; and Robert S. Kaplan and H. Thomas Johnson, *Relevance Lost: The Rise and Fall of Management Accounting,* Boston: Harvard Business School Press, 1987.

belief that managers can do little about inbound freight. However, the problem extends beyond *where* freight is accounted for and reported. In many purchasing situations, freight is not reported at all as a specific cost. Many products are purchased on a delivered price basis, which includes transportation cost. This practice, however, has changed radically since the passage of the transportation acts of 1980 and also because of the increasing availability of customer pickup allowances. Most progressive procurement procedures require that expenses for all services, including transportation, be debundled from the total purchase cost for evaluative purposes.

A final deficiency in traditional accounting practice is the failure to specify and assign inventory cost. This deficiency has two aspects. First, full costs associated with the maintenance of inventory, such as insurance and taxes, are not identified and assigned, thereby resulting in an understatement or obscurity in reporting inventory cost. For example, if a brand manager is not held responsible for his brand's inventory carrying cost, he is not motivated to reduce inventory levels. Second, the financial burden for assets committed to material, work-in-process, and finished goods inventory is not identified, measured, and separated from other forms of capital expense incurred by the enterprise. In fact, if a firm deploys internal funds to support inventory requirements, it is likely that no capital expenses will be reflected by the profit and loss statement.

In summary, several modifications to traditional accounting are required to track logistical activity-based costs. In particular, the two largest individual expenses in logistics, transportation and inventory, have traditionally been reported in a manner that creates obscurity. Although the situation is improving, routine isolation and reporting of logistical activity-based costs still remain far from standard practice.

Logistics Activity-Based Costing   Activity-based costing seeks to relate all relevant expenses to the value adding activities performed. For example, costs are assigned to a customer or product to reflect all relevant activity costs independent of when and where they occur. The fundamental concept of activity-based costing is that expenses need to be assigned to the activity that consumes a resource rather than to an organizational or budget unit. For example, two products, produced in the same manufacturing facility, may require different assembly and handling procedures. One product may need an assembly or packaging operation that requires additional equipment or labor. If total labor and equipment costs are allocated to the products on the basis of sales or units produced, then both items will be charged for the additional assembly and packaging operations required by only one of them. This unjustly reduces the profitability of the simplified product by forcing that product to pay for operations it does not need. In a manufacturing sense, identifying and assigning cost factors means that a specific product will be fully assigned its fair share of all overhead and operating costs.

While somewhat different when applied to logistics, the objectives of activity-based costing are appealing. In the case of logistics, the key event is a customer order and the related activities and relevant costs that reflect the work required to fulfill the order. In other words, logistical activity-based costing must provide managers the insights needed to determine if a specific customer, order, product, or service is profitable. This requires matching specific revenue with specific costs. Revenue considerations will be discussed later in this section. For now, a closer look at logistical activity-based costing is in order.

Effective costing requires identification of the specific expenses to include in an analysis framework. A second concern is to specify the relevant cost time frame. Finally, costs must be allocated or assigned to specific factors that are relevant to assessing alternative actions. To accomplish such effective grouping, the focus of decision making must be specified.

Each of the above areas of activity-based costing is judgmental. The rules and procedures used to identify, group, and assign costs can have substantial influence in both logistical system design and operational decision making. The guiding criteria for effective logistical activity-based costing are relevancy and consistency. Relevancy is important in the sense that the cost assignments help managers to better understand the major factors affecting logistics expenses. Consistency is important in terms of comparing related activities over time.

In the final analysis, a logistical costing system has to make sense only to the managers who are using it as a guide to decision making. No rules or laws require that activity-based cost allocations be comprehensive or even representative of the general financial reports of an enterprise.

Cost Identification   To have a representative presentation, all costs associated with the performance of a logistics function should be included in the activity-based cost classification. The total costs associated with forecasting and order management, transportation, inventory, warehousing, and packaging must be isolated. Typical logistics costs can be categorized under three headings: direct costs, indirect costs, and overhead.

Direct or *operational* costs are those expenses specifically caused by the performance of logistics work. Such costs are not difficult to identify. The direct cost of transportation, warehousing, material handling, and some aspects of order processing and inventory can be extracted from traditional cost accounts. For example, the transportation costs for an individual truckload order can be directly attributed to a specific order. Likewise, only minor difficulty is experienced in isolating the direct administration cost of logistical operations.

Indirect expenses are more difficult to isolate. Costs associated with indirect factors are experienced on a more or less fixed basis as a result of allocation of resources to logistical operations. For example, the cost of capital invested in real estate, transportation equipment, and inventory—just a few of the areas within the capital structure of logistics—must be identified to arrive at a comprehensive total cost. The manner by which indirect costs are attributed to logistics activities is determined by managerial judgment. For example, how should the indirect costs, such as equipment, associated with a warehouse be allocated to the customer order shipped from that warehouse? One approach is to allocate the overhead cost on the basis of the average cost per unit. Alternatively, a good case can be made that such indirect factors are important to issues relating to system design but offer little insight into effective operational decision making.

All capital allocated to the logistical system represents a scarce commodity. Therefore, all expenses paid to support capital investment in logistical operations are relevant to logistical activity-based costs. If capital requirements are sourced from the asset base of an enterprise, a charge based on a hurdle rate for capital utilization is typically credited for inclusion into total cost. The amount of such indirect cost may range from the prime interest rate to a figure based on alternative uses of capital and expected rate of return. The judgment applied in arriving at cost of capital will greatly influence logistical system design. Thus, procedures and standards used to calculate indirect logistical costs are critical. They are also essential for potential outsourcing, which is discussed later in this section.

A final costing allocation concern is *overhead.* An enterprise incurs considerable expense on behalf of all organizational units, such as for lighting and heat in various facilities. Judgment is required to determine how and to what extent various types of overhead should be allocated to specific activities. One method is to directly assign total corporate overhead on a uniform basis to all operational units. A traditional and increasingly controversial method of assigning general overhead is on the basis of direct labor expense. At the other extreme, some firms withhold all overhead allocations to avoid distorting the ability to measure direct and indirect logistical activity-based costs. Given these variations, it is difficult to generalize best practice. From the viewpoint of effective logistical activity-based costing, it is sound practice not to allocate any overhead cost that cannot be directly assigned to a logistical activity.

The above discussion should serve to illustrate the judgmental nature of logistical activity-based costs. Which costs are included and how they are assigned are of fundamental importance. A general rule to follow is that a specific cost should not be assigned to logistical factors unless it is under the managerial control of the logistical organization. Because of subjective cost allocation, enterprises in the same industry will report vastly different logistical expenses. It is important to realize that such cost differentials may have no direct relationship to the actual efficiency of logistical operations.

Cost Time Frame A basic concern in logistical activity-based costing is to identify the period of time over which costs are accumulated for measurement. Generally accepted accounting principles call for accrual methods to relate revenues and expenditures to the actual time period during which services are performed. However, unique timing problems can be associated with establishing logistical activity-based costs. Expenses associated with raw material procurement through finished product distribution and almost all other logistical operating costs are incurred in anticipation of future transactions, making accrual methods difficult to administer.

To overcome the time problem, accountants attempt to break costs into two groups: costs assigned to a specific product and costs associated with the passage of time. Using this classification, an attempt is made to match appropriate product and time period costs to specific periods of revenue generation.

From a logistical perspective, a great many of the expenses associated with procurement and manufacturing support can be assigned and absorbed into direct product cost. Thus, because they can be assigned to a specific product, inventories are valued on the basis of fully allocated cost. Such practices can significantly influence logistical system design, depending on the characteristics of a business.

In situations where a considerable period of time elapses between production and sales, such as in highly seasonal businesses, significant costs of maintaining inventory and performing logistical operations may not be associated with revenue generation. Unless this potential mismatch is clearly understood and accommodated in the assignment process, logistics can be significantly mismeasured.

Cost Formatting   The typical way to format activity-based costs is to assign expenses to the event being managed. For example, if the object of analysis is a customer order, then all costs that result from the associated performance cycle contribute to the total activity cost. Typical units of analysis in logistical activity-based costing are customer orders, channels, products, and value-added services. The cost allocations will vary depending on which analysis unit is selected for observation.

In addition to activity-based costing, management may wish to format financial reports regarding operational measurement and control. Logistical expenses can be presented in a number of ways for managerial use. Three common ways are functional grouping, allocated grouping, and fixed-variance grouping. Each method is discussed.

To format costs by *functional grouping* requires that all expenditures for direct and indirect logistical services performed for a specified operating time be formatted and reported by master and subaccount classifications. Thus, a total-cost statement can be constructed for comparison of one or more operating periods. No standard format of activity costs or functional groupings is available that fits the needs of all enterprises. Logistical functional cost statements must be designed to facilitate control within each unique environment. It is important to identify as many cost accounting categories as practical and to develop a coding system that will facilitate assignment to these cost accounts. Effective total-cost groupings can be maintained over time only if appropriate coding to reclassify natural accounts into functional groups is incorporated in the basic logistics information system.

Allocated cost formatting or grouping consists of assigning overall logistical expenditures to a measure of physical performance. For example, total logistical cost can be generated on a per ton, per hundredweight, per product, per order, or per line-item basis, or on some other physical measure that is useful for comparative analysis of operating results. While important for assigning overall expenses to physical performance measures, this grouping typically has limited use outside logistics management.

Fixed-variance grouping is the most useful for identifying the logistics cost implications of current or alternative operating practices. This method of formatting consists of assigning costs as either fixed or variable to approximate the magnitude of change in operating expenditure that will result from different volumes of logistical throughput. Costs that do not directly vary with volume are classified as fixed. In the short run, these expenses would remain if volume were reduced to zero. Costs influenced by volume are classified as variable. For example, the cost of a delivery truck is fixed: if the truck costs $40,000 to purchase, the firm is charged $40,000 whether the truck is used for 1 or 1,000 deliveries. However, gasoline to operate the truck is variable: total gasoline costs depend on how frequently the truck is driven. The use of fixed and variable cost formatting offers a convenient way to handle expenses in logistical system design models.

Total-Cost Presentation   For purposes of implementing and presenting logistical total-cost analysis, it is common practice to focus on inventory and transportation as the two main network design factors. Both inventory and transportation expenses can be defined in a format sufficiently broad to include activity and functional cost relationships for related logistical components. For example, communication costs that are associated with order processing and with expenditures required for warehouse storage and material handling can be classified under the inventory umbrella.

In terms of inventory, total cost includes all expenses related to inventory carrying cost and customer ordering. Inventory carrying cost, as discussed in Chapter 8, includes taxes, storage, capital, insurance, and obsolescence. The cost of ordering includes the full expense of inventory control, order preparation, communications, update activities, and managerial supervision.

The total cost of transportation includes for-hire transport expenses and accessorial charges plus costs related to the hazards incurred with the various modes, legal forms of transport, and associated administrative expenses. If private transportation is used, accounts can be structured to identify the associated direct, indirect, and overhead costs.

A brief summary of the total cost of logistical activities is presented in Table 21-3. Classification of costs in terms of inventory or transportation highlights the basic trade-offs that determine the cost justification for logistical network design. The basic logic for focusing on transportation and inventory as key factors is that they represent the spatial and temporal dimensions of logistical operations. Transportation deals with the geographic (spatial) dimensions of logistical operations by positioning product where the customer wants to purchase. Inventory involves the rate at which capital assets are used (temporal) to meet customer requirements by having product available when the customer wants to purchase. A second justification for focusing on transportation and inventory is that these two factors include 80 to 90 percent of overall logistics expenses for the typical firm. In subsequent sections of this chapter, the nature of trade-offs between the cost of transportation and inventory will be illustrated.

The columns on the right side of Table 21-3 reflect potential activities that may be used to segment costs for managerial review. For example, an ordering cost can be assigned to a specific order, or it may be grouped by customer. If the objective is to determine the expenses associated with any specific level of de-aggregated activity, it is essential to assign specific costs to the actual targets or events. For example, if the de-aggregated activity is the ordering cost for one specific product, the actual expenses for that product alone must be identified. As noted earlier, the extension of total costs to an activity-based format need not meet public accounting precision. The purpose of activity-based extension is to give managers a better perspective of the total cost associated with performance of a specific activity.

Outsource Considerations

When an enterprise identifies a need for a specific product or service, the first step in fulfilling the need is to determine if the requirement will be produced or performed. The enterprise must decide whether to make the product or perform the

TABLE 21-3   TOTAL COSTS CLASSIFIED BY INVENTORY AND TRANSPORTATION

	Activity-based assignments			
	Customer	Order	Product	Value-added service
Inventory-related costs				
Inventory carrying cost:				
Tax				
Storage				
Capital				
Insurance				
Obsolescence				
Ordering:				
Communication				
Processing, including material handling and packaging				
Update activities, including receiving and data processing				
Inventory control				
Management				
Transportation-related costs				
Direct:				
Rates				
Accessorial charges				
Indirect, liability not protected by carrier				
Managerial				

service internally (make) or to purchase the requirement from an external source (buy). This decision requires evaluation of two options.

The classic make-versus-buy decision has been a historical debate centered around the *economic* trade-offs associated with each option.[4] Recently, attention has expanded to the analysis of the *strategic* trade-offs, with the result that the desired course of action no longer focuses strictly on economic cost. Rather, a broad-based evaluation includes an assessment of strategic core competency. This more recent focus requires that make-versus-buy decisions examine not only which firm has the lowest total cost but also which one can produce or market the product or perform superior service. Both questions must be answered from a long-term perspective. For example, when an enterprise evaluates the alternatives of establishing a private trucking fleet or outsourcing to for-hire carriers, current rates and costs are not the only factors to consider. Long-term cost trends and strategic vision should also be included.

[4]For information on the classic economic perspective, see George J. Stigler, ''The Division of Labor Is Limited by the Extent of the Market,'' *The Journal of Political Economy,* **LIX:**3, June 1951; Oliver E. Williamson, *Markets and Hierarchies,* New York: The Free Press, 1975; and Oliver E. Williamson, ''Transaction-Cost Economics: The Governance of Contractual Relations,'' *Journal of Law and Economics,* **XXII:**22, October 1979, pp. 233–261.

One critical aspect of the make-versus-buy decision is the idea of specialization, which has both economic and strategic elements. Every enterprise has specific skills that differentiate it from its competitors. For example, Schneider National Inc. was one of the first motor carriers to implement a satellite tracking service capable of quickly pinpointing the location of a truck so that it can provide customers with accurate delivery status information. This technology provided Schneider a unique competitive advantage in the eyes of customers that valued the availability of instantaneous information tracking. An enterprise could outsource transportation and thereby obtain these specialized skills from Schneider rather than develop the same capability internally. Specialization typically provides cost advantages through economies of scale. Schneider operates nationwide, allowing the investment in satellite technology to be allocated over its national customer base. It is less likely that an individual shipper would have the scope of operation necessary to justify such investment based solely on operation of a private fleet.

Specialization also can provide strategic benefits. Schneider's specialized technology involves difficult-to-duplicate expertise. Not only does Schneider have leading-edge technology, but it has also developed methods for using that technology to create customer value. For example, the satellite system allows performance standards to be tracked to better evaluate achievement related to objectives such as perfect order performance. Satellites allow Schneider to provide critical pickup and delivery information for customers. Such capabilities also allow Schneider to reroute or reconsign material to an alternative destination while enroute to its original destination.

When a service firm has achieved a competitive advantage through specialization, it makes little sense for a customer to perform that activity internally. If another enterprise can do the job better, even if the cost is higher than internal performance, specialization often mandates outsourcing. This allows a firm to concentrate on its own specialized skills. The following sections discuss the economic and strategic factors that influence the make-versus-buy decision and focus specifically on the consideration of outsourcing logistical activities such as transportation and warehousing.

Economic Factors   Oliver Williamson examined economic factors in terms of transaction costs. From his perspective, transaction costs are those expenses associated with performing a specific activity.[5] The fundamental Williamson proposition was that free market allocation would result in a balance of internal sourcing and outsourcing that would minimize transaction cost. However, loss of internal control creates less than ideal conditions and encourages firms to perform activities internally. For example, outsourcing creates a situation where external firms can behave opportunistically at the expense of their customer. An example would be a service provider withholding poor performance information to ensure its operational success. Such information withholding could result in a major problem for the service provider's customers.

Another issue of control involves the number of alternative sources. If only a

---

[5] Williamson, *Markets and Hierarchies;* and Williamson, ''Transaction-Cost Economics.''

few companies exist with capability to perform the required logistics services, the ideal free or competitive market is replaced by one that approximates monopoly power. This situation is further complicated if the requested logistics services require transaction-specific assets such as dedicated trucks, buildings, or workforces. Such assets are typically tailored to accommodate specific service requirements. In the event of cancellation, such customized assets may not be easily transferred to other customers. For instance, Coors Brewing Company stipulates that its products be distributed in refrigerated carriers. Most of Coors' competitors do not have the same requirements. In order to outsource transportation services, Coors must find distributors willing to invest in refrigerated warehouses. This warehouse capacity cannot be easily transferred to other brewing companies. Because of these transaction-specific assets, Coors may have to internally perform the distribution activities because many distributors do not have, or are unwilling to invest in, refrigerated warehouse capability.

Transaction cost analysis suggests that logistics activities be performed internally if the transaction costs are lower than expenses associated with outsourcing. Internal costs are usually lower when (1) only a few potential third-party suppliers are available for outsourcing, (2) transaction-specific assets are required, or (3) various suppliers of such services are in a position to take advantage of the transactional setting.

Major cost elements to consider when evaluating logistics activities that are performed internally or outsourced are shown in Table 21-4. Typically the trade-offs depend on which party is best positioned to achieve the best economies of scale. For example, when considering outsourcing or owning a warehouse, volume is a critical factor. Suppose the product requiring storage follows an erratic demand pattern. On average, 25,000 units need to be stored to meet monthly requirements. However, peak storage demand requires 50,000 units, while the lowest point of seasonality requires only 5,000. If a privately owned warehouse is used, it must have the capacity to hold 50,000 units. When demand justifies only 5,000 units in storage, the warehouse would be operating at approximately 10 percent of capacity (5,000/50,000 = 10 percent capacity). Under such utilization, fixed, overhead, labor, and managerial expenses would be spread over so few units that the cost per unit would be very high.

On the other hand, outsourcing to a public warehouse could result in standard per unit cost that is independent of month to month storage requirements. When

TABLE 21-4   COST ELEMENTS IN THE OUTSOURCING DECISION

Internal performance	
Fixed capital costs (e.g., warehouse facility)	Managerial costs
Variable costs (volume-based)	Direct labor costs (e.g., drivers)
Equipment costs	Overhead costs (e.g., warehouse lighting)

Outsourcing performance
Transportation costs (e.g., carrier rates)
Warehouse charges (e.g., cost per square foot)

warehousing is outsourced, the customer typically negotiates a rate that requires it to pay only for space used. Therefore, the price is the same per unit whether the firm stores 5,000 or 50,000 units. If the price per square foot is $1.50 and a unit takes up 2 square feet, the total charge per unit is $3.00, regardless of the total number of units stored. The warehouse specialist is capable of absorbing seasonality as a result of the total business pattern of all customers utilizing the facility. The level of rate typically charged would reflect average utilization as contrasted to either a minimum or maximum.

Other cost factors involved in outsourcing are not as visible as those listed in Table 21-4 and may not be easily calculated. One such expense is the alternative opportunity cost of capital. A private trucking fleet requires substantial equipment investment. To fully evaluate outsourcing, an enterprise should consider alternative uses of the capital that would be invested in a private fleet of trucks. For example, the same amount of money could be used to increase manufacturing capacity, improve logistics facilities, or expand other aspects of the business. The enterprise must determine which types of investment offer the best long-term advantage.

Another consideration is cost associated with obsolescence. The internal performance of logistics activities typically requires a firm to invest in technologies that may become obsolete before the enterprise can fully amortize cost. When such is the case, the technology may not have paid for itself in productivity and efficiency before it must be replaced. Outsourcing logistics activities means that the third-party service provider is responsible for technology investments, and this reduces the risk of obsolescence by spreading replacement cost across a large customer base. Because of high-volume usage, it is likely that service providers will amortize the cost of technology investments before they become obsolete. Furthermore, if their equipment is outdated, service providers will be forced to update their technology to maintain attractiveness to their customer base.

A final important cost consideration in outsourcing is related to labor. When moving from internal to external performance of logistics, the labor requirements and management responsibilities of the customer will be reduced or shifted to the service supplier. This shift affects cost in numerous ways. Early retirement, layoffs, reassignment morale, productivity unionization, and retraining are among the issues an enterprise must evaluate when initially switching from internal to external logistics performance. When deciding to move a logistical service in-house from a third-party provider, hiring, training, internal labor shifts, and implementation time are key considerations that may serve to limit flexibility.

Strategic Factors The key strategic factor to consider during the make-versus-buy decision is performance capability. The decision to outsource involves evaluating which supplier is the most capable of performing the service at a best practice level. This requires an evaluation of potential outsource services in terms of their contribution to a firm's core and noncore activities. Typically a firm will not want to run the risk of diluting core competencies by having external firms perform isolated, highly sensitive activities. Once a firm has isolated those activities that are ''core supportive,'' the balance of required activities or the noncore requirements become outsource candidates.

The most difficult step for most firms is to identify which activities are critical core capabilities.[6] Many companies focus on current organizational assets, not the skills and resource capabilities that enable best practice performance and achieve desired results.[7] The outsourcing decision should not be limited to asset investment. Instead, it must center around capabilities provided or achieved *through* the asset investment. If the capabilities achieved by performing activities internally do not extend an enterprise's core competencies, then such activities should be outsourced.

The desirability of outsourcing is based in part on the benefits of specialization. Typically this means better utilization of facilities, equipment, or labor—in other words, doing more with less. If required service can be improved or an enterprise can reduce its overall investment or operating requirements, then outsourcing is an attractive alternative. The sidebar discusses a comparison of private and public warehousing. It provides an example of the typical range of economic and strategic trade-offs required to make an evaluation.

In summary, make-versus-buy decisions involve trade-off analysis among economic and strategic factors. A large portion of such analysis examines cost-to-service elements. Outsourcing is easily justified if visible costs decrease and service improves, as long as other economic and strategic requirements are satisfied. Specialization can result in economies of scale enabling simultaneous achievement of reduced cost and improved service. While such results are highly desirable, other economic and strategic requirements that introduce risk or reduce flexibility must be carefully considered in arriving at a final policy.

Cost-Revenue Analysis

In Chapter 3, the nature of logistical performance was discussed in detail. The point was made that almost any level of logistical service is achievable if an enterprise is willing to pay the required cost. A firm's broad strategic objective is to achieve high-level basic service without full dependence on inventory stockpiling as the sole means of meeting requirements.

In customer service performance, *availability* means providing a product or material on a predictable basis. Availability results from safety stock policy and is based on a combination of stockout fill rate frequency and orders shipped complete. *Performance* is the ability to achieve a predetermined speed, consistency, and flexibility in delivery. A system's capability results from the design and dependability of activities that make up the performance-cycle structure. *Reliability* is the overall quality of service performance. The development and maintenance of quality performance are based on continuous measurement of logistical operations. To be effective, a logistical system must achieve a level of each attribute of customer service performance. It is also necessary to develop and implement performance measures concerning each aspect of the logistical service mix.

---

[6]Ravi Venkatesan, "Strategic Sourcing: To Make or Not to Make," *Harvard Business Review,* **70:**6, November–December 1992, pp. 98–107.

[7]Robert H. Hayes and Gary P. Pisano, "Beyond World-Class: The New Manufacturing Strategy," *Harvard Business Review,* **72:**1, January–February 1994, pp. 77–86.

MAKE VERSUS BUY: THE WAREHOUSE DECISION

A manufacturer, who currently outsources the warehousing of finished goods, is considering performing the warehouse function internally. Under the current arrangement, after final assembly, the product is transported by truck two miles to a public warehouse. The warehouse personnel unload the trucks and place the product in storage. The manufacturer's sales representatives contact the public warehouse when customer orders are received. Orders are forwarded to the warehouse electronically. The warehouse personnel pick and pack the order and arrange customer shipment. When the order is shipped, the warehouse electronically transmits the information to the manufacturer so that inventory status can be updated.

The manufacturer has been looking for ways to reduce costs. Many cost reductions have occurred in the manufacturing facility, which has reduced its workforce. At the production facility, jobs have been eliminated or combined. In total, thirty full-time hourly employees and three managers have been laid off. Other employees are afraid their jobs will be cut next, so morale is low. In response to this problem and as an additional cost-cutting measure, the manufacturer is considering performing the warehouse function in-house instead of using a public warehouse.

The initial benefit to having an in-house warehouse is direct cost savings in per unit warehouse charges. Assuming that the warehouse operates for ten years with no unforeseen major investments, per unit storage costs will decrease from $2.90, which is the current price at the public warehouse, to $2.36 at the private warehouse.

An additional benefit to the private warehouse deals with the reduced labor force. The employees that were laid off could perform the warehousing functions with extensive training (training courses are included in the cost estimate). This would help employee morale.

Another benefit is that the sales personnel could have their offices in the private warehouse. This would eliminate the necessary outside contact with the public warehouse personnel.

Management could have greater control over the warehouse operations, including inventory management. Furthermore, the site for the proposed in-house warehouse is located outside a large metropolitan area. This would allow the manufacturer to have a visible market presence by having the company logo on the warehouse facility. This site would not change the transportation charges currently incurred by using the public warehouse. The distance and route to the proposed site are similar to the public warehouse.

The costs to the private warehouse are as follows:

Annual charges	
Building and equipment (depreciation of initial investment)	$ 25,000
Employee training	10,000
Overhead expenses	50,000
Management expenses	70,000
	$155,000
Annual capacity	180,000 units
Cost per unit	
Annual charges ($155,000/180,000 units)	$ .86
Variable costs	1.00
Direct labor costs	.50
	$2.36/unit

A cost savings of $.54 per unit allows an annual savings of ($.54/unit for 180,000 units) $97,200.

Strategic drawbacks to the in-house warehouse surround the issue of specialization. The manufacturer has no expertise in operating a finished goods warehouse. Training will be extensive for management and hourly employees. The implementation time will also disrupt business flow. It is likely that facility construction and training will take sixteen months to complete.

The sales representatives will also face job structure changes that may have negative consequences to productivity. The sales representatives will be assigned the additional task of tracking customer orders to ensure they are shipped on time. This task is currently performed by the public warehouse.

Finally, the largest concern about internal performance of warehousing is the capital outlay required to invest in the warehouse facility. The initial investment is $250,000 (shown in the costs as an annual fee of $25,000 for estimation). The capital outlay will mean that other investments, such as an additional production lien to increase production capacity, cannot be made this year. This investment and the delay in other investments create a risk that may affect the strategic focus of the manufacturer. Another risk is the loss of performance expertise at the public warehouse.

While the obvious decision based on costs alone is to build the private warehouse, other factors must be carefully considered and evaluated to determine if the strategic benefits and cost savings cover the strategic loss of specialization and expertise at the public warehouse as well as the other strategic disadvantages of the private warehouse.

Achieving and maintaining superior service typically require information systems that have the capacity to orchestrate the implementation of flexible distribution strategies. From the viewpoint of logistical system design, it is essential to determine a balance between the level of basic service that a firm desires to offer customers and the operating cost required to consistently achieve the targeted performance.

From the viewpoint of theoretical economics, the issue of how much service to offer a customer is a relatively straightforward calculation. A typical goal of most commercial enterprises is to maximize profits. The assumption is that, all other things being equal, service generates revenue. In other words, customer demand will increase if service meets or exceeds expectations. Given a positive service elasticity of demand, it follows that higher service will increase the quantity purchased. Under these conditions, a supplier would rationally increase expenditures for improved logistical performance to the point where the marginal cost (MC) of providing the last unit of service would be equal to the marginal revenue (MR) generated by the last unit sold. At this point, the firm would have achieved the classical profit maximization equilibrium, wherein MC = MR and short-run profit would be maximized.

Although easily stated, marginal equality is difficult if not impossible to accomplish in actual practice. Some of the major problems are (1) measurement of incremental cost, (2) isolation of logistical impact from the remainder of an enterprise's performance, (3) inability to make incremental or minor changes in logistical system performance, (4) inability to quickly modify commitments such as leases and contracts related to the logistical system, and, perhaps most significant, (5) inability to measure revenue elasticity as a direct function of logistical performance.

Various attempts have been made to approach the marginality solution by identifying revenue lost when expected sales are not realized. In other words, when sales are lost because of poor logistical services, costs associated with required activities such as ordering and performing a credit check are incurred but no revenue is generated. Thus logistical services are critical to customer service.[8] Approaching the analysis from the perspective of lost sales provides assistance in arriving at a justified level of inventory availability. It does not answer the question of what might have been sold if a firm had offered customers competitively superior logistical performance. Even though measurement and the real potential of flexibility make it difficult to arrive at exact solutions to the marginality problem, one objective of logistical policy formulation is to approximate the ideal solution. The most common procedure is to undertake sensitivity analysis initiated with the least-total-cost logistical design.

The determination of how much basic customer service to offer must be justified in terms of relative cost and benefit. The analysis begins by quantifying the cost of providing a specific level of overall service and then estimating the expected benefits in terms of revenue and long-term customer loyalty. The cost side of the

---

[8]For more information on the importance of logistics to customer service, see Karl B. Manrodt and Frank W. Davis, Jr., ''The Evolution of Service Response Logistics,'' *International Journal of Physical Distribution and Logistics Management,* **22**:9, 1992, pp. 3–10.

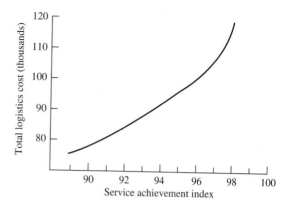

FIGURE 21-1   Estimating the cost/service relationship.

equation is substantially easier to quantify than expected revenue. The following illustrates cost-benefit analysis.

One approach to determining target customer service levels is to estimate the relationship between the cost of a firm's basic service platform and revenue generation. Figure 21-1 illustrates the generalized relationship expected between revenue and cost. The vertical axis represents logistical cost to provide service availability, performance, and reliance. The horizontal axis represents service achievement in the form of a percentage of customer desires. In terms of revenue generation, it is assumed that the higher the level of service, the greater the revenue generated. The general relationship is that the cost of upgrading basic service increases at an increasing rate as overall commitment moves toward zero defects (100 percent). In other words, incremental service improvements cost more to achieve as overall service improves, such that a 2 percent service improvement costs substantially more to achieve when service is already at 98 percent than when service is at 88 percent.

The impact on cost of a change in basic service can be estimated if a firm is able to quantify the relationship described in Figure 21-1. For illustrative purposes, assume that a firm is currently performing at a 91 percent service achievement level. Table 21-5 summarizes the cost impact of changing basic service achievement from 91 percent. As shown, reducing the service level to 89 percent reduces logistics cost by $10,000. In contrast, increasing the service level to 98 percent raises cost by $40 million. While it is relatively easy to quantify the cost impact, benefits are more difficult to isolate.

Table 21-5 illustrates one approach to estimating revenue required to justify increased service. Assuming that net profits are 2 percent of sales and that service

TABLE 21-5   TOTAL-COST IMPACT SERVICE MODIFICATION BASED ON 91 PERCENT ACHIEVEMENT*

Cost saving for service reduction to 89 percent	$10
Cost increase for service improvement to 95 percent	$15
Cost increase for service improvement to 98 percent	$40

*In thousands.

level is decreased from the current 91 to 89 percent, the break-even point is $500,000 in sales. In other words, any loss of business up to $500,000 could be offset by savings resulting from reduced service. While such sales reduction may not be tolerable for a variety of reasons, it does quantify the impact of logistical service in isolation. Conversely, if the basic service is increased from 91 to 98 percent, the required revenue increase, assuming that net profit remains at 2 percent of sales, is $2 million to break even. While one can debate the assumptions of direct cause and effect that are implied by such break-even analysis, the direction, not the magnitude of change, is fundamental. Unless management feels that the basic sales response will equal or exceed the imagined break-even point, increased commitment to inventory availability is not sound business. Table 21-6 summarizes the break-even points for other service and net profit levels.

The use of break-even analysis helps frame the cost associated with providing customers a given level of basic service. This type of quantitative information provides managerial guidance but does not give a complete answer to formulating a basic customer service platform. In the final analysis, determination of an appropriate service level depends on a host of factors such as the competitive situation, the extent to which logistics is positioned as a core competency, customer sensitivity to logistical performance of suppliers, and a firm's capability to perform as promised. Whatever the basic customer service platform is, it must be positioned in terms of a firm's overall marketing mix strategy and be administered to all customers without discrimination. These decisions cannot be determined without a careful review of a firm's manufacturing strategy and current capabilities.

PRICING

Various aspects of pricing directly affect logistical operations. The terms and conditions of pricing determine which party has responsibility for performing logistics activities. A major trend in purchasing has been to debundle the price of products and materials so that services such as transportation, which were traditionally included in price, are now identified as separate items. Beyond issues of control, pricing practices have a direct impact on the timing and stability of logistical operations. In this section, several basic pricing structures are reviewed followed by a discussion of pricing impact areas. No attempt is made to review the broad range of economic and psychological issues related to pricing decisions. The focus is on the relationship between pricing and logistical operations.

Price Fundamentals

Pricing decisions directly determine which party in the transaction is responsible for performance of logistics activities, passage of title, and liability. F.O.B. origin and delivered pricing are the two most common methods.

F.O.B. Pricing   The term *F.O.B.* technically means "free on board" or "freight on board." A number of variations of F.O.B. pricing are used in practice.

TABLE 21-6   INCREMENTAL SALES FOR BREAK-EVEN PROFITS*

Net profit as a percentage of sales	89% alternative	91% existing	95% alternative	98% alternative
At 2% net of sales	(500)	0	750	2,000
At 4% net of sales	(250)	0	375	1,000
At 6% net of sales	(167)	0	250	667
At 8% net of sales	(125)	0	188	500
At 10% net of sales	(100)	0	150	400

*In thousands.

F.O.B. origin is the simplest way to quote pricing. Here the seller indicates the price at point of origin and agrees to tender a shipment for transportation loading, but assumes no further responsibility. The buyer selects the mode of transportation, chooses a carrier, and pays transportation charges, in addition to taking responsibility for in-transit loss and/or damage. In contrast, under F.O.B. destination pricing, title does not pass to the buyer until delivery is completed. Under such circumstances, the seller arranges for transportation and the charges are added to the sales invoice.

The range of terms and corresponding responsibilities for pricing are illustrated in Figure 21-2. Review of the various sales terms makes it clear that the firm paying the freight bill does not necessarily assume responsibility for ownership of goods in transit, for the freight burden, or for the filing of freight claims.

Delivered Pricing   The primary difference between F.O.B. and delivered pricing is that with a delivered pricing arrangement the seller offers a price that includes transportation of the product to the buyer. In other words, the transportation cost is not "debundled" and highlighted as a separate item. The following describes varied delivered pricing practices.

Single Zone Pricing   Under a single zone delivered pricing system, buyers pay a single price regardless of where they are located. Since the seller arranges transport, delivered prices typically reflect average transportation cost. In actual practice, some customers will pay more than their fair share for transportation while others are subsidized. The United States Postal Service uses a single zone pricing policy throughout the United States for first-class letters and parcel post. The same fee or postage rate is charged for a given size and weight regardless of distance traveled to the destination.

Single zone delivered pricing is typically used when transportation costs are a relatively small percentage of selling price. It is a common method of pricing when sellers use national advertising for promotion. The main advantage to a seller is the high degree of control over logistics. For the buyer, despite being based on averages, such pricing systems have the advantage of simplicity. This is particularly appealing to small retailers.

Multiple Zone Pricing   The practice of multiple zone pricing establishes different prices for specific geographic areas. The underlying idea is that logistics

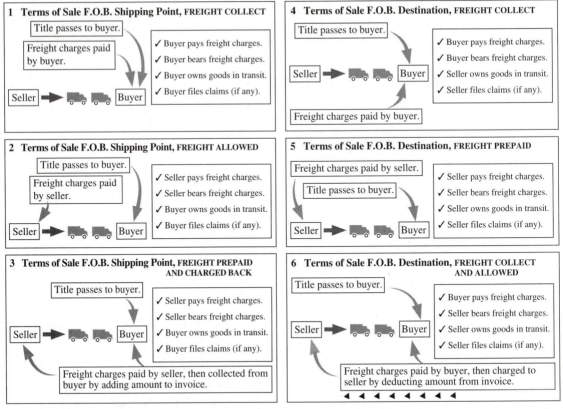

FIGURE 21-2   Terms of sale and corresponding responsibilities. *(Reprinted with permission from* The Purchasing Handbook, *National Association of Purchasing Management.)*

cost differentials can be more fairly assigned if two or more zones are used to quote delivered prices. Most direct marketers or mail-order catalogs use multiple pricing zones, which are typically based on distance.

Basing Point Pricing   The most complicated and controversial form of delivered pricing is the use of a base point system in which the final delivered price is determined by the product's list price plus transportation cost from a designated basing point, usually the manufacturing location. This designated point is used for computing the delivered price regardless of whether or not the shipment actually originates from that base location.

Figure 21-3 illustrates how a basing point pricing system typically generates different net returns to a seller. The customer has been quoted a delivered price of $100 per unit. Plant A is the basing point. Actual transportation cost from plant A to the customer is $25 per unit. Plant A's base product price is $85 per unit. Transportation costs from plants B and C are $20 and $35 per unit, respectively.

When the customer's shipments are made from plant A, the company's net return, less transportation, is $75 per unit (the $100 delivered price minus the $25 transportation cost). The net return to the company varies if shipments are made

MANAGING YOUR INBOUND

Country General Stores, Inc., a retailer based in Grand Island, Nebraska, provides customers in the Western and Plains states with farm, home, and ranch products. Several years ago, Country General began requesting its suppliers to furnish two price quotes for each order, one quote for merchandise plus freight transportation and a second quote that included prepaid freight. Companies want to separate the product or commodity purchase price from the cost of transporting it. Within this scenario, companies are able to determine whether it is cheaper to source the product without paying freight charges or obtain the product from another supplier for a lower price. While the request appeared simple enough, many of the retailer's suppliers were less than enthusiastic about providing such information. "Our suppliers weren't always willing to tell us what they're paying for freight," says Jim Fairfield, vice president of distribution at Country General Stores.

Once Country General had accumulated a representative sample of quotes, the new process resulted in approximately 35 percent of the company's 1,500 to 2,000 suppliers providing products on an F.O.B. origin basis. Purchasing products under F.O.B. origin required Country General to arrange for transportation of merchandise from the seller's dock. Country General's approach to exert control over its inbound freight is not an unusual strategy. The practice is used increasingly in business today, particularly by retailers to obtain control of their freight dollar. By controlling their inbound shipments through close attention to freight economics and pricing, companies believe that they can save on transportation costs and avoid paying inflated freight charges.

Buying merchandise F.O.B. origin isn't the best strategy for every company. In some situations, the seller can obtain lower freight costs because it can use its leverage to achieve volume contracts with carriers. It takes considerable extra work and frequent hassles to manage inbound transportation, particularly if specific pieces of equipment, such as refrigerated trailers, are

necessary to transport merchandise. Also, many consignees do not want to deal with the hassle of loss and damage claims or arrangements for special equipment or storage. There are, however, significant benefits to be gained by careful analysis of a company's transportation costs. For example, Fairfield estimates that purchasing a third of the company's merchandise F.O.B. origin has saved Country General between $350,000 and $400,000 per year in transportation costs. "Nine times out of ten there's a savings in buying F.O.B. origin," says Fairfield, who notes that his company plans to convert most of its suppliers to those sales terms over the next five years.

Many companies, including Country General, are concerned that suppliers are profiting from standard transportation arrangements. As a result, many companies request comparative price quotations from suppliers. Fairfield believes that many suppliers make money on freight, and that companies must remain vigilant regarding supplier pricing practices. This is particularly true when suppliers utilize the common industry practice of "off-bill discounting." In these situations, a supplier cuts a deal with a carrier for a certain discount, perhaps 50 percent off the standard freight charge for an outbound shipment. But the supplier has the carrier prepare a freight bill that shows only a 25 percent discount, and the supplier receives the other 25 percent discount off the freight bill. Thus, the buyer believes the supplier is receiving only a 25 percent discount. Such practices make it difficult to measure actual freight expense.

In any event, the key issue for buyers like Country General is to gain an understanding of the transport economics of their inbound transportation, and utilize that knowledge to improve their pricing structure and strategy—and ultimately, their company's bottom line.

Based on James Aaron Cooke, "Should You Control Your Inbound?" *Traffic Management*, **32**:2, February 1993, pp. 30–33.

---

from plant B or plant C. With a delivered price of $100, plant B collects $5 in "phantom freight" on shipments to a customer. Phantom freight occurs when a buyer pays transportation costs greater than those actually incurred to move the shipment. For all effective purposes, phantom freight represents a charge over and

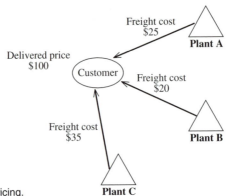

FIGURE 21-3   Basing point pricing.

above actual cost recovery. If plant C is the shipment origin, the company must absorb $10 of the transportation costs. Freight absorption occurs when a seller pays all or a portion of the actual transportation cost and does not recover the full expenditure from the buyer. In other words, the seller decides to absorb transportation cost to be competitive. Freight absorption amounts to reducing list price.

Basic point pricing simplifies price quotations but can have a negative impact on customers. For example, dissatisfaction may result if customers discover they are being charged more for transportation than actual freight costs. Such pricing practices may also result in a large amount of freight absorption for sellers.

Various Pricing Issues

Beyond control, pricing practices are integral to logistics operations in at least four ways: potential discrimination, quantity discounts, pickup allowances, and promotional pricing. Each is discussed.

Potential Discrimination   The legality of basing point pricing is an important consideration and must be carefully reviewed and administered to protect against potential discrimination. The Clayton Act of 1914 as amended by the Robinson-Patman Act of 1936 prohibits price discrimination among buyers when the practices "substantially lessen competition."

Zone pricing has the potential to be discriminatory because some buyers pay more than actual transportation cost while others pay less. Zone pricing systems are illegal when the net result is to charge different delivered prices for identical products to direct competitors. In recent years, determination of the legality of delivered zone pricing systems has centered around the issue of whether or not a "seller acts independently and not in collusion with competitors." The Federal Trade Commission is unlikely to take action unless there is clear-cut evidence of such conspiracy.

In the past, selected base point pricing has been found illegal under both the Robinson-Patman Act and the Federal Trade Commission Act. The concern is whether it results in direct competitors having differential margins.

To avoid potential legal problems, the majority of firms use either basic F.O.B. or uniform delivered pricing policies. This strategy is generally preferable compared to defending average costing practice required in zone pricing or contending with the potential legal difficulties associated with basing point pricing. The following guidelines should be considered when establishing geographic pricing.[9]

> Some of the geographic pricing strategies . . . may be illegal in certain circumstances. Three general principles can be used to guide policy in this respect. First, a firm should not discriminate between competing buyers in the same region (especially in zone pricing for buyers on either side of a zonal boundary) because such action may violate the Robinson-Patman Act of 1936. Second, the firm's strategy should not appear to be predatory, especially in freight absorption pricing, because such a strategy would violate Section 2 of the Sherman Act of 1890. Third, in choosing the basing point or zone pricing, the firm should not attempt to fix prices among competitors because such action would violate Section 1 of the Sherman Act.

Quantity Discounts   Quantity discounts are generally offered by a firm as an inducement to increase order size or overall volume of business. To be nondiscriminatory, an identical discount structure must be available to all buyers. Under the Robinson-Patman Act, it is the responsibility of the seller to prove that the identical, noncumulative discounts are available to all qualified buyers. The quantity discount offered must be justifiable on the basis of direct cost saving.

The exact provision of the law regarding quantity discounts is as follows:[10]

> . . . to discriminate in price between different purchasers for commodities of like grade and quality . . . where the effect of such discrimination may be to substantially lessen competition or tend to create a monopoly in any line of commerce or to injure, destroy, or prevent competition with any person who either grants or knowingly received the benefit of such discrimination, or with customers of either of them . . . provided that nothing . . . shall prevent differentials which make only due allowance for difference in the cost of manufacture, sale, or delivery.

The Robinson-Patman Act states that cost differences can be justified on the basis of savings in the manufacturing, delivery, or selling of goods. Quantity-related discounts based on reductions in manufacturing or selling cost are difficult to prove. Logistics-related savings are relatively easier to document since many are shipment-specific. Transportation and handling savings are often used to justify quantity discounts; thus lower transportation rates for volume shipments are common.

In contrast to noncumulative discounts, cumulative discounts—based on consecutive purchases over some specified time period—are more difficult to justify. Cumulative discounts, by the very nature of their calculation base, favor large-volume purchases while discriminating against smaller buyers. However, price

---

[9]Gerard J. Tellis, ''Beyond the Many Facets of Price: An Integration of Pricing Strategies,'' *Journal of Marketing,* **50,** October 1986, pp. 146–160.

[10]The Robinson-Patman Act of 1936 specified price discrimination initially established in the Clayton Act of 1914.

discrimination can be proved only when potential or real injury to competition is determined.

Pickup Allowances   Pickup allowances are equivalent to purchasing merchandise on an F.O.B. origin basis. Buyers are given a reduction from the standard delivered price if they or their representatives pick up shipments at the seller's location and assume responsibility for transportation. It is also legal for a buyer to use a for-hire carrier to perform merchandise pickup. Such discounts were legal prior to transportation deregulation; however, the incidence of pickup has increased dramatically in recent years. The provisions of Section Eight of the Motor Carrier Regulatory Reform and Modernization Act of 1980 encouraged pickup and backhaul allowances in the food and grocery industry, which had traditionally followed delivered pricing practices for many years.[11] Firms have realized significant savings by using private and for-hire carriers to pick up rather than purchasing merchandise on a delivered basis.

While some confusion exists concerning how to best establish a pickup allowance, a safe rule is that a seller should provide the same allowance to all directly competitive buyers. A uniform pickup allowance is often the price incentive offered to the customer closest to the shipping point. Other common policies offer pickup allowances equivalent to the applicable common carrier rate for the shipment.

The use of pickup allowances offers potential benefits for both the seller and the buyer. Shippers are required to deal with fewer small shipments, thereby reducing the need for extensive outbound consolidation. Buyers gain control over the merchandise earlier and are in a position to achieve greater utilization of captive transportation equipment and drivers.

Promotional Pricing   A final aspect of pricing that impacts logistical operations is the use of short-term promotions to provide incentives for purchases. Firms that pursue aggressive promotional strategies have a choice of designing their budgets to encourage consumers (via coupons) or wholesalers and retailers (via trade allowances) to purchase their products. For example, Procter & Gamble has an annual advertising and promotional budget that exceeds $1.5 billion. Marketing management must allocate these funds between media advertising focused on consumers and a combination of coupons and trade promotion. Budget dollars allocated to trade promotion "push" the purchase of P&G products and cause two results. First, the logistics systems of Procter & Gamble and its customers must handle increased product volume just before, during, and oftentimes immediately after a promotional period. Second, trade promotion spending lowers the effective price at which product is being sold. From a logistical perspective, the short-term interval increase in volume is of primary concern. Thus, while ultimate consumption may not demonstrate seasonal characteristics, logistical operations may have to deal with "seasonal surges" caused by promotional pushes.

The widespread practice of promotional pricing has traditionally been the way to provide incentives for trade purchasing. The current intensity of the practice can

---

[11]See Public Law 96-296 signed by President Carter on July 1, 1980.

be traced to price controls that were instituted during the Nixon administration to curb inflation. Many firms that marketed consumer products found themselves locked into prices that allowed little or no room to engage in promotions. Following release of price control restrictions, a new pricing practice emerged. Manufacturers began to establish list or sheet prices at an artificially high level with the expectation of reducing the effective price by trade promotion, consumer coupons, and new-product slotting allowances. The timing and intensity of trade incentives are critical to logistical operations. The trade incentives combine with the timing of list price changes to create large swings in specific product volume at any one point in time in the value chain. Administration of regular price changes usually involves advanced notification to customers, creating the opportunity for them to "forward buy." This practice stimulates volume surges, which add excessive costs and create practices that do not add value. Forward buying involves purchasing merchandise beyond a customer's current needs. Reselling the extra product to other channel participants through the use of agents is known as diverting. In effect, a firm is profiting by taking advantage of purchase incentives available to some channel participants and not others.

In an effort to stabilize promotional pricing, firms have begun to develop co-ordinated value chain programs. Manufacturers and retailers working together can negotiate "net prices" that are administered over a specific time horizon. The manufacturer and retailer jointly plan the promotion and advertising strategy for a product or merchandising category. On the basis of the promotional strategy, a "dead net price" is determined that takes into account quantity purchase discounts, prompt payment discounts, and any other applicable price incentives. For example, agreements may be reached concerning such events as over/short reconciliation, damaged product disposition, and invoice discrepancies. Finally, an agreement is reached concerning the duration during which the negotiated price will be in effect. These agreements also specify how performance will be measured during the operating period as a basis for future agreements.

The price negotiation framework described above has resulted in what is known as *everyday low pricing* (EDLP). Wal-Mart is generally credited with having created EDLP, which is the strategy around which it seeks to build consumer loyalty. Other firms have developed EDLP purchase strategies with suppliers while following a promotional pricing format for consumer merchandising.

Few firms operate at the extremes of either EDLP or promotional pricing. However, most creative merchandisers develop a combination approach to stimulate consumer purchasing. While price or "loss leaders" are used to generate consumer traffic and encourage in-store impulse buying, few items are consistently sold as loss leaders, thereby reducing the risk of predatory pricing allegations.[12]

Because the cost reduction benefits of stable or level volume are so significant, strategies are developing to managerially restrict promotional pricing. The most highly publicized industry initiative is effective consumer response (ECR). This food industry initiative is a senior management effort that seeks to stabilize product

---

[12]*Efficient Consumer Response: Enhancing Value in the Grocery Industry,* Kurt Salmon Associates, Inc., January 1993.

flow and achieve the dual objectives of increasing inventory velocity and reducing waste. While the ECR initiative does not eliminate promotional efforts, it does develop a framework to more effectively administer their impact on efficient logistics processes.

In a more general sense, business in a free market society will and should engage in a wide variety of promotional and advertising activities. The challenge is to rationalize how such promotional efforts affect logistics. The timing and magnitude of promotional pricing need to be evaluated in terms of ability to consume and the capacity to efficiently handle volume surges. To a significant degree, ''trade loading'' practices result from end of period or end of year earnings pressures. This so-called Wall Street effect goes hand in hand with the use of promotional pricing to stimulate product flow so that sales can be ''booked'' during a specific time period. Such practices may offer short-term earnings relief but do little, if anything, to stimulate consumption. They are, however, guaranteed to increase logistics cost.

Conclusion   The setting of prices typically does not fall within the administrative domain of logistics. However, logistics is directly involved in pricing in two significant ways. First, the form of pricing that a firm elects to follow defines who controls logistics and how the process of ownership transfer will be administered. Second, how a firm elects to position prices in terms of discounts, timing of changes, and magnitude of promotion will have a profound impact on logistical operating efficiency. For these reasons, logistics executives need to understand the many challenges and nuances involved in pricing and should seek to become persuasive members of the pricing team.

SUMMARY

Chapter 21 discussed the role and methods of logistics performance measurement and controllership. Research indicates that sophisticated planning and performance measurement systems are a common practice among leading logistics organizations. Since pricing is a key element of the marketing mix, state-of-the-art performance measurement and controllership capabilities must allow revenues to be matched with appropriate expenses. Thus, the chapter included a discussion of the influence of pricing on logistics administration.

First, Chapter 21 described the role and process of operations planning. Operating plans are the guideposts for logistics activities. They provide the basis for measuring logistics performance by monitoring current practices and facilitating comparison with historical and budgeted revenues and expense levels. Operating plans direct logistics operations by identifying performance variances and suggesting the need for logistics strategy modifications. These might include distribution network changes, new technology applications, organizational changes, or operating practice changes.

Next, Chapter 21 discussed logistical design metrics. Attention was initially directed to total costing requirements to support logistics decision making. The issues of public accounting adequacy for logistical costing were reconciled in terms of activity-based costing and total-cost presentation. The chapter also examined how economic and strategic factors influence logistical cost-revenue analysis.

Finally, Chapter 21 reviewed the interaction of pricing and logistics administration. The fundamentals of the continuum between F.O.B. and delivered pricing were illustrated and described. Delivered pricing typically includes product transportation. F.O.B. pricing charges the customer for some portion of the transportation expense. While delivered pricing is much less complex administratively, many customers prefer F.O.B. pricing because they are better able to control their inbound logistics expenses. The pricing discussion concluded by reviewing various issues that are affected by logistics, such as price discrimination, discounts, pickup allowances, and promotional pricing. These issues influence many customer decisions, which in turn determine logistics operating requirements.

QUESTIONS

1 Define short-range and long-range strategies. How do they affect logistics management objectives?

2 What is meant by structuring budgets on a ''line-item basis''? How does this approach affect the budget process?

3 Why is flexible budgeting a valuable tool for logistics managers?

4 ''Logistics management is concerned with management by exception.'' What does this mean?

5 Why do logistical system modifications need to be accomplished ''on the fly''?

6 What is the primary purpose of activity-based costing?

7 Compare and contrast activity-based costing with total-cost analysis.

8 How does cost-revenue analysis facilitate logistical planning?

9 What is a shipper's responsibility concerning transportation charges when the terms of purchase are F.O.B. origin? Why would a shipper want this responsibility? How does F.O.B. origin contrast with F.O.B. destination?

10 When can quantity discounts be perceived as discriminatory? What legislative acts have had a major impact on justifying quantity discounts?

CHAPTER 22

PERFORMANCE MEASUREMENT AND REPORTING

LOGISTICAL MEASUREMENT
    Dimensions of Performance
       Measurement
    Internal Performance Measurement
    External Performance Measurement
    Comprehensive Supply Chain
       Measurement
CHARACTERISTICS OF AN IDEAL
    MEASUREMENT SYSTEM
    Cost/Service Reconciliation
    Dynamic Knowledge-Based Reporting
    Exception-Based Reporting

LEVELS OF MEASUREMENT
    AND INFORMATION FLOW
    Direction
    Variation
    Decision
    Policy
REPORT STRUCTURES
    Status Reports
    Trend Reports
    Ad Hoc Reports
SUMMARY
QUESTIONS

Effective logistics performance measurement and controllership are necessary to allocate and monitor resources. As logistics competency becomes a more critical factor in creating and maintaining competitive advantage, accurate logistics measurement and controllership increase in importance because the difference between profitable and unprofitable operations becomes increasingly narrow.

Chapter 22 discusses the important topic of performance measurement and reporting. The objectives of logistical controllership are to track performance against operating plans and to identify opportunities for enhanced efficiency and effectiveness. Although historical logistical measurement has maintained a functional perspective, a process orientation is more appropriate in today's competitive environment. Such an orientation considers the total cost associated with fulfilling customer orders and allows more effective identification and evaluation of trade-offs. Following the discussion of performance measurement, key internal measures are reviewed. Internal measures are generally collected and analyzed by the firm. While many of them are functionally based, quality measures such as "the perfect order" evaluate overall customer satisfaction. Next, external performance measurement is illustrated through customer perception measures and "best practice" benchmarking. The perception measures focus on service from the customer's, rather than the firm's, perspective. Benchmarking compares practices, processes, and performance with comparable firms. Finally, attention is directed to issues and challenges related to comprehensive supply chain performance measurement.

Finally, Chapter 22 examines logistical measurement and reporting in greater detail. It delineates the characteristics of an ideal measurement system, focuses on levels of measurement to support managerial control and related information requirements, and illustrates how logistical data can be formatted to facilitate dissemination of critical control information.

LOGISTICAL MEASUREMENT

The combination of slower economic growth and increased competition has forced firms in every industry to concentrate on efficient and effective deployment of logistical resources. One result of these efforts has been the emergence of a new corporate position devoted to logistical controllership. The logistics controller is concerned with continuous measurement of a firm's performance. In order to carry out the measurement process, controllership focuses on the assessment of resource deployment and goal attainment.

Numerous research initiatives have identified the high correlation between superior performance and the development and use of sophisticated assessment or measurement capabilities. As early as 1985, A. T. Kearney Consultants noted that firms engaging in comprehensive performance measurement realized improvements in overall productivity in the range of 14 to 22 percent.[1] Research continues to support the proposition that leading-edge firms exhibit an almost compulsive commitment toward performance measurement. Table 22-1 reports how executives at Michigan State University Global Research ranked their desire for information regarding performance. Overall, performance measurement ranked second across the combined regions, and in almost all cases, it was identified as one of the top three areas of research needs.

Dimensions of Performance Measurement

Substantial effort has been expended to improve the quality of information that logistics managers have at their disposal to measure, compare, and guide logistical performance. In most firms, old reporting formats need to be redesigned to take advantage of new computer-based control systems. In place of traditional status and trend reports, today's managers require flexible and on-demand ad hoc report-

---

[1] A. T. Kearney, *Emerging Top Management Focus for the 1980's*, Chicago: Kearney Management Consultants, 1985.

TABLE 22-1 RESEARCH INTEREST RANKING REGIONAL ANALYSIS

Topic	Rank by region		
	Europe	N. Am.	Pac. Rim
Alliances-relationship management	4	3	7
Environmental issues	9	10	9
Globalization	10	8	10
Information technology	1	1	1
Inventory deployment	5	5	4
Logistics network reengineering	6	6	2
Organization structure	8	9	8
Performance measurement	2	2	3
Time-based logistics strategies	7	7	5
Unique distribution strategies tailored to specific customers	3	4	6

Source: World Class Logistics: The Challenge of Managing Continuous Change, Oak Brook, Ill.: Council of Logistics Management, 1995.

ing methods to facilitate problem prevention and rapid response to market opportunities.

Objectives The three objectives for developing and implementing performance measurement systems include monitoring, controlling, and directing logistics operations. *Monitoring* measures track historical logistics system performance for reporting to management and customers. Typical monitoring measures include service level and logistics cost components.

Controlling measures track ongoing performance and are used to refine a logistics process in order to bring it into compliance when it exceeds control standards. An example of a control application is transportation damage tracking. If a system is in place to periodically report product damage, logistics management can identify the cause and adjust the packaging or loading process as needed.

Directing measures are designed to motivate personnel. Typical examples include "pay for performance" practices used to encourage warehouse or transportation personnel to achieve higher levels of productivity. Specifically, consider warehouse material handlers or delivery drivers who are paid for eight hours of work based on standard production rates. If the material handlers can complete the assigned tasks in less than the allotted time, they are allowed personal or unassigned time. On the other hand, if they require more than the allotted time, the disincentive is that they are not compensated for the additional time. In some cases, employees are actually given a bonus when the task is completed in less than the allotted time. When such directed measures are used, it is important that both positive and negative performance be measured. For example, the completion of an assigned task, such as order selection, in less than the standard time must be traded off against increased errors or damage.[2]

[2]For a document recommending a common set of supply chain performance measures, see PRTM Consulting, "Integrated-Supply-Chain Performance Measurement: A Multi-Industry Consortium Recommendation," Weston, Mass.: PRTM, October 1994.

TABLE 22-2   TYPICAL LOGISTICS ACTIVITY-BASED MEASURES

1 Order entry time per order	6 Order selection time per customer
2 Delivery time per order	7 Delivery time per customer
3 Order selection time per order	8 Order selection time per product
4 Inquiry time per order	9 Delivery time per product
5 Order entry time per customer	

Perspective   The appropriate measurement perspective must also be evaluated and determined. The continuum of possibilities ranges from all activity-based measures to entirely process-based measures.

Activity-based measures focus on individual tasks required to process and ship orders. Examples include customer orders entered, cases received from suppliers, and cases shipped to customers. These measures record the level of activity (i.e., number of cases) and, in some instances, the level of productivity (i.e., cases per labor hour). Table 22-2 lists typical activity-based measures for logistics applications.

While activity-based measures focus on the efficiency and effectiveness of primary work efforts, they do not usually measure the performance of the overall process of satisfying customers. For example, order takers who are judged on the number of calls per hour may be rated high with respect to activity-based measurement but may do poorly in the overall satisfaction process because they fail to take the time to listen carefully to customers. For this reason, it is important that some performance measures take an overall process perspective.

Process measures consider the customer satisfaction delivered by the entire supply chain. They examine total performance-cycle time or total service quality, both of which measure the collective effectiveness of all activities required to satisfy customers. Today's firms are placing more attention on process measures while trying not to suboptimize individual activities. An increasingly common process measure, ''the perfect order,'' is discussed later in this chapter.

Internal Performance Measurement

Internal performance measures focus on comparing activities and processes to previous operations and/or goals. For example, customer service might be compared to last period's actual performance as well as to this period's goal. Internal measures are commonly utilized because management understands the sources of information and it is relatively easy to collect. Research suggests that logistics performance measures can generally be classified into these categories: (1) cost, (2) customer service, (3) productivity, (4) asset management, and (5) quality.[3] Each is discussed and illustrated.

Cost   The most direct reflection of logistics performance is the actual cost incurred to accomplish specific operating objectives. Cost expectations are the

[3]Donald J. Bowersox et al., *Leading Edge Logistics: Competitive Positioning for the 1990's*, Oak Brook, Ill.: Council of Logistics Management, 1989.

TABLE 22-3 LOGISTICS COST PERFORMANCE MEASURES

Performance measure	Percentage by business type		
	Manufacturer	Wholesaler	Retailer
Total-cost analysis	87.6	74.8	82.1
Cost per unit	79.7	63.8	78.6
Cost as a percentage of sales	83.3	81.2	79.5
Inbound freight	86.0	80.0	87.5
Outbound freight	94.4	88.3	90.6
Warehouse costs	89.0	85.7	89.9
Administrative costs	80.0	79.1	76.7
Order processing	52.0	45.8	45.7
Direct labor	78.6	71.4	86.2
Comparison of actual vs. budget	96.6	86.6	86.5
Cost trend analysis	76.9	59.1	61.4
Direct product profitability	59.2	46.8	27.8

essence of the budgeting process discussed earlier. Logistics cost performance is typically measured in terms of total dollars, as a percentage of sales, or as a cost per unit of volume. Table 22-3 lists typical logistics cost performance measures and reports the percentage of manufacturers, wholesalers, and retailers that use each measure.

Customer Service The second common set of logistics performance measures focuses on customer service. These measures, some of which were discussed in Chapter 3, examine a firm's relative ability to satisfy customers. Table 22-4 lists common customer service measures and reports the percentage of manufacturers, wholesalers, and retailers that use each measure.

Productivity Measures Productivity is another measure of organizational performance. It is unclear whether it is the most important, or even necessarily a critical, measure of performance for all systems.

TABLE 22-4 LOGISTICS CUSTOMER SERVICE PERFORMANCE MEASURES

Performance measure	Percentage by business type		
	Manufacturer	Wholesaler	Retailer
Fill rate	78.2	71.0	66.2
Stockouts	80.6	72.9	71.6
Shipping errors	83.0	78.9	81.9
On-time delivery	82.7	70.5	76.9
Back-orders	77.1	69.2	58.7
Cycle time	69.9	34.7	56.4
Customer feedback	90.3	85.6	84.1
Sales force feedback	87.9	85.0	51.5
Customer surveys	68.8	51.6	58.9

TABLE 22-5 LOGISTICS PRODUCTIVITY PERFORMANCE MEASURES

Performance measure	Percentage by business type		
	Manufacturer	Wholesaler	Retailer
Units shipped per employee	54.8	53.1	61.4
Units per labor dollar	51.9	43.7	63.9
Orders per sales representative	38.7	51.7	15.5
Comparison to historical standards	76.3	74.6	86.4
Goal programs	76.2	69.2	82.1
Productivity index	55.8	44.9	56.3

Productivity is a relationship (usually a ratio or an index) between output (goods and/or services) produced and quantities of inputs (resources) utilized by the system to produce that output. Productivity is thus a very simple concept. If a system has clearly measurable outputs and identifiable, measurable inputs that can be matched to the appropriate outputs, productivity measurement is quite routine. However, it can be difficult and frustrating if (1) outputs are hard to measure and input utilization is difficult to match up for a given period of time, (2) input and output mix or type constantly changes, or (3) data are difficult to obtain or unavailable.

Conceptually, there are three basic types of productivity measures: static, dynamic, and surrogate. If all the output and input in a given system are included in the productivity equation, it would be a total factor static productivity ratio. The ratio is considered static because it is based on only one measurement.

A dynamic measure, on the other hand, is completed across time. If outputs and inputs in a system compare static productivity ratios from one period to another, the result is a dynamic productivity index, for example:

$$\frac{\text{Outputs 1994/inputs 1994}}{\text{Outputs 1990/inputs 1990}}$$

The third type is called a surrogate productivity measure. This represents factors that are not typically included in the concept of productivity but are highly correlated with it (customer satisfaction, profits, effectiveness, quality, efficiency, etc.). Most managers operationalize productivity in this manner.

Table 22-5 lists typical logistics productivity measures and reports the percentage of manufacturers, wholesalers, and retailers that use each measure.

Asset Measurement   Asset measurement focuses on the utilization of capital investments in facilities and equipment as well as working capital application to inventory to achieve logistics goals. Logistics facilities, equipment, and inventory can represent a substantial segment of a firm's assets. In the case of wholesalers, the amount exceeds 90 percent. Asset management measures focus on how fast liquid assets such as inventory "turn over" as well as how well fixed assets generate return on investment. Table 22-6 lists typical logistics asset management measures and reports the percentage of manufacturers, wholesalers, and retailers that use each measure.

TABLE 22-6   LOGISTICS ASSET MANAGEMENT PERFORMANCE MEASURES

Performance measure	Percentage by business type		
	Manufacturer	Wholesaler	Retailer
Inventory turns	81.9	85.2	82.6
Inventory carrying costs	68.6	68.3	55.6
Inventory levels, number of days' supply	86.9	80.7	74.1
Obsolete inventory	85.7	79.7	73.1
Return on net assets	66.9	65.9	55.0
Return on investment	74.6	74.8	67.9

Quality   Quality measures, which are the most process-oriented evaluations, are designed to determine the effectiveness of a series of activities rather than an individual activity. However, quality is usually difficult to measure because of its broad scope. Table 22-7 lists typical logistics quality measures and reports the percentage of manufacturers, wholesalers, and retailers that use each measure. It is clear from Table 22-7 that fewer firms measure quality than any other logistics performance characteristic.

A contemporary measurement concept that is increasing in interest is "the perfect order." Delivery of the perfect order is the ultimate measure of quality in logistics operations; that is, the perfect order concerns the effectiveness of the overall integrated logistical firm performance rather than individual functions. It measures whether an order proceeds smoothly through every step—order entry, credit clearance, inventory availability, accurate picking, on-time delivery, correct invoicing, and payment without deductions—of the order management process without fault, be it expediting, exception processing, or manual intervention.[4]

The perfect order represents ideal performance. From an operational perspective, a multi-industry consortium defines the perfect order as one that meets all the following standards:[5] (1) complete delivery of all items requested; (2) delivery to customer's request date with one-day tolerance; (3) complete and accurate docu-

[4]William C. Copacino, "Creating the Perfect Order," *Traffic Management*, February 1993, p. 27.
[5]PRTM Consulting, "Integrated-Supply-Chain Performance Measurement: A Multi-Industry Consortium Recommendation," Weston, Mass.: PRTM, October 1994.

TABLE 22-7   LOGISTICS QUALITY PERFORMANCE MEASURES

Performance measure	Percentage by business type		
	Manufacturer	Wholesaler	Retailer
Frequency of damage	67.4	44.7	60.8
Dollar amount of damage	74.6	55.6	67.1
Number of credit claims	75.7	68.9	67.5
Number of customer returns	77.1	69.0	63.9
Cost of returned goods	68.0	57.7	54.2

TABLE 22-8 PERFECT ORDER "BUSTERS"*

Order-entry error	Picking error	Damaged shipment
Missing information (e.g., product code)	Inaccurate picking paperwork	Invoice error
	Late shipment	Overcharge error
Unavailability of ordered item	Late arrival	Customer deduction
Credit hold	Incomplete paperwork	Error in payment processing
Inability to meet shipment date	Early arrival	

*At least nine out of ten orders in a typical company get "busted" for reasons such as these.
Source: William C. Copacino, "Creating the Perfect Order," *Traffic Management*, February 1993, p. 27.

mentation supporting the order, including packing slips, bills of lading, and invoices; and (4) perfect condition, that is, faultlessly installed, correct configuration, customer-ready with no damage. However, there are many roadblocks to achieving such a level of success. Table 22-8 provides a sample list of perfect order "busters," or common causes of failure. Today, the best logistics organizations report achieving a 55 to 60 percent perfect order performance, while most organizations report less than 20 percent.

Conclusion Internal performance measures focus on the activities required to serve customers. Measurement of these activities, as well as comparison with goals and standards, is necessary to improve performance and motivate and reward employees. Cost measurement is the minimum component of any performance measurement system. More sophisticated firms incorporate customer service, asset management, and productivity measurement. While such measures generally monitor internal process efficiency, they do not examine external process effectiveness very well, particularly from the customer's viewpoint. The quality measures applied today by the most sophisticated logistics organizations offer such an external perspective. While the individual internal measures discussed above offer a broad performance evaluation, they do not provide an integrated point of view. For example, many customers desire high performance regarding both service and quality.

External Performance Measurement

While internal measures are important for detailed organizational monitoring, external performance measures are also necessary to monitor, understand, and maintain a focused customer perspective and to gain innovative insights from other industries. The topics of customer perception measurement and best practice benchmarking, which address these requirements, are discussed and illustrated below.

Customer Perception Measurement An important component of leading-edge logistical performance is the regular measurement of customer perceptions. Such measures can be obtained through company- or industry-sponsored surveys or by systematic order follow-up. Such surveys ask questions regarding the firm's

THE EVOLUTION OF BENCHMARKING AT XEROX

In North America, the term *benchmarking* is synonymous with the Xerox Corporation. More than 100 companies have come to Xerox over the past fifteen years to study its expertise in this area. Xerox's recognition of benchmarking's value began in 1979 when Japanese rivals in the photocopy business that were focused on high-quality, lower-priced units had reduced Xerox's market share from 49 to 22 percent within a matter of a few years. In response to this challenge, top Xerox managers initiated several quality and productivity programs, one of which was competitive benchmarking.

Robert C. Camp, manager of benchmarking quality and customer satisfaction at Xerox Corporation in Rochester, New York, formally defines benchmarking as "the continuous process of measuring our products, services, and practices against those of our toughest competitors or companies renowned as leaders." Camp notes, however, that a more concise operational definition of benchmarking is "finding and implementing the best business practices—it needn't be any more complicated than that." At Xerox, the operational definition goes further than best practice and includes consideration of customer satisfaction. One way to please customers is to display how easy it is to do business with the company. The primary conduit to achieve that objective is the contact point between the company (Xerox) and the client. For example, the processes of taking and filling orders, repair, invoicing, and collection must incorporate the best practices available to ensure customer satisfaction. This is Xerox's priority.

At Xerox, benchmarking is a four-stage, ten-step process:

Stage 1

1 Identify what is to be benchmarked.
2 Identify comparative companies.
3 Determine data collection method and collect data.

Stage 2

4 Determine current performance levels.
5 Project future performance levels.
6 Communicate benchmark findings and gain acceptance.

Stage 3

7 Establish functional goals.
8 Develop action plans.

Stage 4

9 Implement specific actions and monitor progress.
10 Recalibrate benchmarks.

A typical benchmarking operation takes from six to nine months until the point of implementation is reached. From that point in time, the length of the implementation/action stage is dependent on what the team discovers. In general, a good benchmarking study requires three to six people working 25 to 33 percent of their time for as long as one year; in other words, the cost will be between one and two worker-years.

Benchmarking includes both strategic and operational components. Strategic benchmarking is concerned with basic company direction such as level of international involvement, centralization, and core competencies. This type of benchmarking requires a highly structured, focused approach to make on-site visits productive. That is, a company must have the necessary understanding and perspective of its internal operations in order to make such visits valuable as external comparisons.

Operational benchmarking focuses on the activities and processes that perform the basic business functions. Darel R. Hull, manager, reengineering and benchmarking for AT&T in Morristown, New Jersey, believes that operational benchmarking can be divided into four types. The first type is *working-task benchmarking*, which covers singular logistics activities such as loading trucks, palletizing shipments, scheduling pickups, etc. The second type is *functionwide benchmarking*, which involves simultaneously assessing all the tasks in a logistics function. For example, benchmarking warehousing to improve performance would include every operation from storage, put away, order selection, and shipping. The third type is *management-process benchmarking*, in which managers from different functions jointly look at broad issues such as quality, employee motivation, and reward systems. "This type of benchmarking is more complex because it crosses functional lines and examines processes," says Hull. It also provides tremendous payback potential. The fourth type is known as *total-operation benchmarking*, in which management examines the entire logistics operation: distribution centers, transportation, inventory management systems, and customer service.

According to Xerox's Camp, one of the most significant reasons to conduct benchmarking is that it is a proactive way to "break down ingrained reluctance to change operations." Additionally, the benchmarking process validates or legitimizes a company's goals by linking them with external markets. For example, it establishes standards for customer requirements, encourages employees to think competitively, and oftentimes increases employee awareness of company costs and product/service performance. Camp also believes that the biggest reason for benchmarking failure is lack of preparation. Site visits to other companies first require that a manager thoroughly understand the process within the firm. That understanding identifies what they want to accomplish and what information to seek from a benchmarking partner.

Over the past fifteen years, the mix of Xerox's benchmarking activities has radically changed. In the early years, the company spent 80 percent of its benchmarking time looking at the competition. Today, Xerox spends 80 percent of its time focusing on performance outside the industry. This shift in focus directly reflects the innovative ideas Xerox has discussed and utilized from other industries. Today, Xerox competes on qual-

ity more so than on price. The company's extraordinary devotion to its suppliers helps them meet its own strict requirements. The company has reduced manufacturing costs by 50 percent and product development cycles by 25 percent, and increased revenue per employee by 20 percent. Xerox suppliers went from a 92 percent defect-free rate to 99.5 percent. Component lead time is down from thirty-nine weeks in 1980 to eight weeks in 1992. The cost of purchased parts has been reduced by 45 percent. Best of all, the company's market share is now growing instead of shrinking; in fact, in the United States its share has increased each of the past seven years and now stands at 18 percent.

Based on Y. K. Shetty, "Aiming High: Competitive Benchmarking for Superior Performance," *Long Range Planning*, **26**:1, February 1993, pp. 39–44; Robert C. Camp, "A Bible for Benchmarking, By Xerox," *Financial Executive*, **9**:4, July/August 1993, pp. 23–27; "Supplier Management—Xerox," *Financial World*, **162**:19, September 28, 1993, p. 62; Helen L. Richardson, "Improve Quality through Benchmarking," *Transportation & Distribution*, **33**:10, October 1992, pp. 32–37; and Thomas A. Foster, "Logistics Benchmarking: Searching for the Best," *Distribution*, **91**:3, March 1992, pp. 30–36.

and competitors' performance in general or for a specific order in particular. The typical survey incorporates measurement of customer perceptions regarding availability, performance-cycle time, information availability, problem resolution, and product support. The survey may be developed and administered by the firm itself or by consultants, delivery agents, or industry organizations.

Best Practice Benchmarking   The discussions of benchmarking were first introduced in Chapter 16 in relation to logistical system reengineering. Benchmarking is also a critical aspect of comprehensive performance measurement. More and more firms have adopted benchmarking as a technique to compare their operations to those of both competitors and leading firms in related and nonrelated industries. Manufacturers in particular are using benchmarking in important strategic areas as a tool to calibrate logistics operations. Table 22-9 indicates the key areas and the proportion of firms benchmarking in each area.

A best practice benchmarking review focuses on the measures, practices, and processes of a comparable organization. The review identifies key performance measures and, if possible, tracks historical and current performance levels. For example, the benchmarking organization might determine that certain customer service levels and "the perfect order" are key factors of customer satisfaction; and

TABLE 22-9   BENCHMARKING PRACTICES BY AREA AND BUSINESS TYPE*

Benchmarking area	Manufacturer	Wholesaler	Retailer
Asset management	36.6	30.3	24.3
Cost	78.1	59.7	56.4
Customer service	84.8	53.7	40.3
Productivity	57.5	41.5	46.8
Quality	79.1	46.2	38.2
Strategy	53.0	27.8	39.2
Technology	47.2	36.4	34.8
Transportation	56.3	44.4	60.5
Warehousing	51.1	51.5	57.9
Order processing	51.9	39.5	28.8
Overall	59.6	43.1	43.4

*Percentage by business type.
Source: D. J. Bowersox, P. J. Daugherty, C. L. Dröge, D. S. Rogers, and D. L. Wardlow, *Leading Edge Logistics: Competitive Positioning for the 1990's*, Oakbrook, Ill.: Council of Logistics Management, 1989, p. 149.

therefore, it desires to match those performance standards. The benchmarking organization would also need to review the practices and processes used to plan, execute, and measure those logistics activities that constitute the foundation for such customer satisfaction and ''the perfect order.'' The practices and processes would likely focus on organizational structure, information systems, facilities and equipment, and interorganizational relationships.

Firms are employing combinations of three benchmarking methods. The first uses published logistics data available from consultants, periodicals, and university researchers. Table 22-10 lists several such sources. While published data are easily obtained, their public nature hardly provides a competitive advantage. The second method is to benchmark privately against noncompetitive firms in one's own or a related industry. Here each organization reviews the others' measures, practices, and processes to develop insights that will improve performance. While a bilateral approach provides in-depth and proprietary knowledge, it does not offer a particularly broad perspective. The third method consists of an alliance of organizations that systematically share benchmark data on a regular basis. These alliances require more effort to maintain but usually provide substantially better information than the preceding methods.

TABLE 22-10   SOURCES OF BENCHMARK INFORMATION

Information type	Source
Davis Data Base	Herb Davis & Associates
Logistical Excellence: It's Not Business as Usual	Michigan State University
Traffic Management Quarterly Updates	*Traffic Management*
World Class Logistics: The Challenge of Managing Continuous Change	Council of Logistics Management

TABLE 22-11   INTEGRATED SUPPLY CHAIN METRIC FRAMEWORK

Outcomes	Diagnostics
Customer satisfaction/quality	
Perfect order fulfillment	Delivery-to-commit date
Customer satisfaction	Warranty costs, returns, and allowances
Product quality	Customer inquiry response time
Time	
Order fulfillment lead time	Source/make cycle time
	Supply chain response time
	Production plan achievement
Costs	
Total supply chain costs	Value-added productivity
Assets	
Cash-to-cash cycle time	Forecast accuracy
Inventory days of supply	Inventory obsolescence
Asset performance	Capacity utilization

Source: PRTM Consulting, "Integrated-Supply-Chain Performance Measurement: A Multi-Industry Consortium Recommendation," Weston, Mass.: PRTM, October 1994.

Comprehensive Supply Chain Measurement

Increased focus on overall supply chain performance and effectiveness demands measures that offer an integrated perspective. This perspective must be comparable and consistent across both firm functions and channel institutions. Without integrated performance measures, the manufacturer's definition and perspective of adequate customer service may be quite different from that of the wholesaler. For example, the manufacturer may measure service availability as the ability to ship when ordered, while the wholesaler may measure service as the ability to ship when promised. In the first case, the manufacturer is graded on its ability to ship to customer demands, while in the second case, a lower standard is allowed since the wholesaler can extend a promise date if stock is not available.

In order to develop integrated measures that can be used throughout the supply chain, a consortium of firms, universities, and consultants proposed a common framework.[6] The integrated framework incorporates four types of metrics and monitors both outcomes and diagnostics. Table 22-11 illustrates the framework. The metric types reflect the performance dimensions that must be monitored for effective supply chain management. The specific types are customer satisfaction/quality, time, costs, and assets. Each metric is monitored on both an outcome and

[6]This section's discussion and definitions draw substantially from PRTM Consulting, "Integrated-Supply-Chain Performance Measurement: A Multi-Industry Consortium Recommendation," Weston, Mass.: PRTM, October 1994.

TABLE 22-12   KEY CUSTOMER SATISFACTION DIAGNOSTICS

- *Delivery to original committed date.* The percentage of orders fulfilled on or before the original committed date.
- *Warranty costs.* The average of actually incurred warranty costs expressed as a percentage of revenue.
- *Customer inquiry response and resolution time.* The inquiry response time is the average elapsed time between receipt of a customer call and connection with the proper company representative. Inquiry resolution time is the average elapsed time required to completely resolve a customer inquiry.

---

a diagnostic basis. The outcome measures focus on overall process results such as the process of satisfying customers and the process of managing time. The diagnostic measures focus on specific activities within the process. The metric types and specific measures are discussed below.

Customer Satisfaction/Quality   Customer satisfaction/quality metrics measure the firm's ability to provide overall customer satisfaction. The outcome-based measures of customer satisfaction/quality include perfect order fulfillment, customer satisfaction, and product quality. A *perfect order* was defined earlier as one that is delivered complete on the requested date, with accurate documentation, and in perfect condition. Customer satisfaction is measured by perceptions regarding performance-cycle time, perfect order fulfillment components, and the ability to respond to order status and inquiry requests.

While the outcome metrics measure the effectiveness of the entire process, it is often useful to measure individual activities as well. Table 22-12 lists and defines the key customer satisfaction diagnostics.

Time   Time metrics measure the firm's ability to respond to customer demands. In other words, how long does it take from the customer's authorization of a purchase until the product is available for customer use? The specific lead time elements include order entry to release for schedule time, release to shippable time, shipment time to customer, and acceptance by the customer. Effective monitoring of time performance requires measurement of the overall process from the customer's perspective and the segmentation into the individual elements. Table 22-13 lists and defines the key time diagnostics.

TABLE 22-13   KEY TIME DIAGNOSTICS

- *Source/make cycle time.* The cumulative external and internal lead time to build a shippable product if you start with no inventory on hand or parts on order
- *Supply chain response time.* The theoretical time to recognize a major shift in marketplace demand, internalize that finding, replan demand, and increase production by 20 percent
- *Production plan achievement.* The average actual frequency of production schedule achievement ($\pm 5\%$)

TABLE 22-14   SUPPLY CHAIN COST COMPONENTS

A Order fulfillment costs	**D** Logistics-related finance and management information
1 New-product release and maintenance	systems costs
2 Customer order creation	**1** Finance
3 Order entry and maintenance	**2** MIS/systems
4 Contract/program management	**3** Supply chain support costs
5 Installation planning	**E** Manufacturing labor and inventory overhead costs
6 Order fulfillment	**1** Direct labor
7 Distribution	**2** Indirect labor
8 Installation	**3** Manufacturing and quality engineering
9 Customer accounting	**4** Information systems
B Material acquisition costs (production materials only)	**5** Scrap and rework
1 Commodity management and planning	**6** Depreciation
2 Supplier quality engineering	**7** Lease expense
3 Inbound freight and duties	**8** Plant occupancy
4 Receiving	**9** Equipment maintenance
5 Incoming inspection	**10** External support
6 Component engineering	**11** Environmental
7 Tooling	
C Total inventory carrying costs	
1 Cost of capital/opportunity	
2 Shrinkage	
3 Insurance and taxes	
4 Obsolescence	

Source: PRTM Consulting, "Integrated-Supply-Chain Performance Measurement: A Multi-Industry Consortium Recommendation," Weston, Mass.: PRTM, October 1994.

Costs   Supply chain costs are the third metric type. The single cost element includes total supply chain expenses. Table 22-14 lists the major supply chain components used to track overall outcome cost. The diagnostic cost metric focuses on human resource productivity by tracking the value added per employee. Value-added productivity is defined as the total company value-added revenues less the value of externally sourced materials expressed as a ratio of total company head count or payroll.

Assets   The final metric focuses on asset utilization. Since logistical management is responsible for substantial assets including inventory, facilities, and equipment, integrated performance measurement must incorporate an asset dimension. Asset metrics basically focus on the sales level that can be supported with a specified asset level. The outcome-based asset metrics are the cash-to-cash cycle time, inventory days of supply, and asset performance. The cash-to-cash cycle time, which measures the effectiveness of cash utilization, is the theoretical time, on average, to convert a dollar spent to acquire raw materials into a dollar collected for finished product. The cash-to-cash cycle time is enhanced by acquisition or payment for raw material or by quick delivery to and payment collection from the customer.

Inventory days of supply measure inventory velocity or turnover. Days of supply are defined as the plant-finished goods and all field-finished inventories converted

TABLE 22-15   KEY ASSET DIAGNOSTICS

- *Forecast accuracy.* The historical measure using the most recent three-month period of average absolute accuracy of product forecasting
- *Inventory obsolescence.* The expenses incurred due to inventory writedowns expressed as a percentage of average gross inventory value
- *Capacity utilization.* The percentage of total available capacity currently utilized calculated as the current actual output divided by output achievable in a twenty-four-hour, seven-day operation

to calendar days of sales based on recent activity levels. Increased sales without a comparable inventory increase results in higher inventory velocity or turnover, implying that additional profit can be achieved without additional inventory carrying cost expense.

The final metric focuses on total asset utilization. Asset performance is defined as the ratio of sales to total assets. It is influenced by both the utilization and the ownership of current assets. Table 22-15 lists and defines key asset diagnostics.

Conclusion   While some of these metrics were discussed earlier in this chapter, this section offered a common framework for measuring integrated performance across a supply chain and for benchmarking across organizations. While this is certainly not the only framework, it is being promoted by a number of large organizations and has achieved wide acceptance. These metrics illustrate characteristics important to any integrated performance measurement scheme: clear definition and consistency.

CHARACTERISTICS OF AN IDEAL MEASUREMENT SYSTEM

The ideal performance measurement system incorporates three characteristics that provide accurate and timely direction for management: cost/service reconciliation, dynamic knowledge-based reporting, and exception-based reporting. Each is described and illustrated.

Cost/Service Reconciliation

Because of the difficulty in collecting certain types of data and in coordinating cause and effect relationships, a majority of reports show logistics expenditures only during a specific period of time. For example, freight bills may not be received until some time after a shipment is made. This practice often causes a problem matching the freight bill with the invoice. Similarly, it is not easy to assign the extra costs related to customer service to those orders that require additional customer service effort. Typical reports fail to reflect cost/service trade-offs critical to generating revenue. It is important to identify and coordinate relevant costs and revenues in order for managers to make meaningful logistics decisions. For example, in the toy industry, products are typically manufactured in the spring and sold with early order discounts to encourage purchase commitment by retailers for the holiday season. Unless costs are appropriately sequenced with revenues, management may obtain a distorted view of the performance effectiveness of its logistics system. An important benefit provided by an operational plan is that activity levels are matched to projected cost levels. When planned activities generate costs that are related to future sales, it is possible to reconcile the cost with the corresponding revenues.

Dynamic Knowledge-Based Reporting

The biggest challenge in logistical reporting is to present a dynamic, rather than static, picture of operational performance over an extended time period. In general, most logistics operational reports provide the status of important activities such as current inventory position, transportation cost, warehouse cost, and other measures of expenditures or activity level for a single reporting period. Such reports provide vital statistics that can be compared with previous operational periods to determine if performance is tracking as planned. The deficiency of static status reports is a failure to provide a picture over extended past periods and an inability to project critical trends in the future. Logistics managers require a reporting system that can project adverse trends before they surge out of control. Ideally, the reporting system can also query available logistics data and extract relevant information that will guide corrective management action. Thus, reporting systems should ideally possess diagnostic capacity to project where operational trends are heading and to suggest appropriate corrective actions.

Exception-Based Reporting

Logistical measurement should be exception-based. The comprehensive and detailed nature of logistics requires that managerial attention be directed to exceptions from anticipated results. The existence of an exception to planned results is proof that unanticipated activity is occurring. Therefore, an ideal reporting system will assist managers in isolating activities and processes requiring attention. Such attention may identify areas requiring problem-solving efforts or facilitate taking a more in-depth assessment of a specific process or function.

LEVELS OF MEASUREMENT AND INFORMATION FLOW

From a management perspective, a mechanism for system monitoring is essential. An assessment and control system exists to reassure management that the total operation is within stated parameters. If and when a significant exception appears, a major deviation was obviously overlooked during its formative stages. However, few managers are willing to sit back and wait for an exception to appear.

The following example from inventory management illustrates the relationship between system monitoring and exceptions. Suppose that the dollars allocated to an open-to-buy program at a given point in a planning period are nearly depleted. At the same time, a critical item may be approaching its reorder point. Placing the suggested order as indicated by economic order quantity formulations could result in a commitment beyond the authorized expenditure level. One might assume that the individual merchandise controller would bring this situation to management's attention so that appropriate adjustments could be made.

However, if the original open-to-buy program was sufficient to cover customer needs, the current deficiency resulted from improperly allocated dollars regarding a past purchase decision of the item in question. In such a situation, the controller needs assistance to rectify the error. Unfortunately, few individuals feel free to expose themselves to such management scrutiny. This reticence may cause the controller to gamble that existing stock of the item in question will last until new funds are authorized. A rush order is then planned when the new funds are available. In reality, the gamble involves customer service policy since a stockout on a critical item is involved. Given the opportunity for review, management might choose to add dollars to the open-to-buy program to reduce or eliminate the risk of an out-of-stock situation. Unless the firm has a comprehensive monitoring system, management may never get the opportunity to express its choice until the out-of-stock situation becomes an exception to stated policy.

In inventory management, the assessment and control system can signal that a critical item has passed the point of normal reorder without issuance of a purchase order. The inventory control manager would be expected to take appropriate action and request assistance from upper-level management if necessary. These procedures prevent the monitored trend from becoming a full-scale exception.

The discussion makes it clear that management would rather prevent, not correct, exceptions. The purpose of the assessment and control system is to signal a breakdown that requires corrective action to prevent recurring problems.

The nature of measurement requires that several levels of information be developed within the enterprise. As a general rule, the higher the level of management review, the more selective the data and reporting should be. The following four levels of information are applicable to logistical measurement: direction, variation, decision, and policy. At each level, information may be related to trend monitoring or exception correction.

Direction

At the direction level, information flow and measurement are concerned with execution of the operational plan. A stream of transaction documents signals a need, and the action document identifies appropriate steps necessary to meet objectives. For example, an order is received, credit is checked, and the order is assigned to a warehouse where it is picked, packed, and shipped. Upon shipment, the customer is billed in accordance with the agreed upon terms of sale. The order receipt is a transaction document; the remainder of the activities are generated by action documents.

At specified time intervals, all transaction and action documents are combined in a series of status reports. The status reports summarize individual activities and their ability to meet expected transaction requirements. For example, total inventory usage may be summarized by each item in the product line and a comparison made to current inventories. Prompted by status reports, additional action documents may be issued to replenish stock of specific items.

Two important features should be kept in mind concerning information flow and measurement at the direction level. First, information focuses on day-to-day business transaction activities and is selectively limited to status review in accordance with predetermined decision rules. In other words, information flow at the direction level is concerned with execution of predetermined programs.

The second feature is accumulation of records to formulate a database for all other levels of control. The database generates reports concerning effectiveness and efficiency, monitoring of trends, and detection of exceptions. Although managerial discretion at the direction level is limited, all subsequent measurement activity is based on the accuracy of information generated and processed from transaction and action documents.

Variation

As suggested by its title, variation measurement is concerned with accumulated deviations from plan. As indicated earlier, variation measurement ideally results in identification of trends that could develop into problems. However, the variation may first appear as an exception to the desired level of performance at the direction level.

Managerial discretion concerning resource allocation initially occurs at the variation level. First, the manager must ascertain if the situation in question is an isolated event or symptomatic of a more serious problem. Second, the manager must determine if a solution to the problem is within his/her scope of authority or whether it requires additional resource allocations. Depending on the manager's interpretation of these two questions, either corrective instructions will be issued to direct operations or assistance will be requested from the decision level.

It is important to realize that the scope of information reviewed to identify variations is considerably narrower than that required to set direction. In the case of variance identification, management is concerned with the specific efficiency of individual transactions.

Decision

Decision measurement is concerned with modifications to the operation plan. Exceptions or problems that have materialized at the direction and variation levels require a reappraisal of the original operational plan. As one would expect, the assortment of information presented at the decision level will be very selective. It is important to note that the decision level is the initial measurement level at which a formal change in the operational plan may be considered.

Modifications normally require allocation of additional resources. The range of decisions should not involve a change of system objectives. In other words, at the decision level, customer service standards will not be modified if performance has been deficient. Rather, additional expenditures will be authorized to meet system objectives. Managerial activities at the decision level must be evaluated in terms of total system consequences. As noted earlier, decisions that modify the plan must be relayed to all managers involved in total system performance.

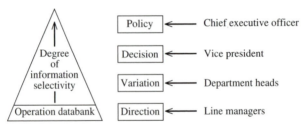

FIGURE 22-1   Information flow and levels of measurement.

Policy

Policy measurement involves a change in objectives. Once again, the areas of system design and administration merge when questions of policy are confronted. The arena of concern becomes enterprisewide in scope and includes all management levels. Formulation of new policies requires an evaluation of the planned system design as well as the total cost of achievement. Requests for policy revisions may originate from any point within the enterprise. Thus far, discussion has centered around information generated from the logistical database and from variations in either logistical performance or expenditure plans. However, policy changes may initiate from other areas of management. For instance, the marketing department may desire an overall upgrade of customer service standards.

Figure 22-1 clarifies the four levels of measurement involved in logistical administration. Adjacent to each level, reference is made to the approximate corresponding organizational rank within an enterprise. On the left side of the chart, a data pyramid is developed to reflect the selectivity of information considered at each measurement level. As noted earlier, each level is concerned with system monitoring as well as exception reporting. However, as information flows from the direction level to the policy level, the subject matter decreases in quantity and increases in importance to the welfare of the enterprise.

REPORT STRUCTURES

An essential feature of all measurement systems concerns the quality of reports generated from the management information system. Unless available information can be presented rapidly and accurately with respect to relevant subject matter, only a minimum level of control can transpire. In general, three types of reports are used in a logistical control system: status, trend, and ad hoc. Each is illustrated using inventory control. Similar types of reports are required for all functional areas of a logistical system to ensure compliance with operational plan objectives.

Status Reports

As the name implies, a status report provides detailed information about some aspect of the logistical operation. One of the most common is the stock status report, which tracks multiple-item inventories at more than one stocking location. The amount of information contained in an individual report will depend on the firm, its degree of inventory management sophistication, and the extent to which

TABLE 22-16   EXAMPLE OF A STOCK STATUS REPORT

			ABC Company Distribution Warehouse Stock Status Report								Date 3/10/95 Controller A	
A	B	C	D E Unit inventory		F	G	H	I	J	K L M Open purchase order detail		
			On hand	On order	Forecasted average weekly use	Back- order	Suggested order quantity	Dollars on hand	Inventory on order	Date placed	Date due	Quantity
Item	Location	Status	On hand	On order	Forecasted average weekly use	Back-order	Suggested order quantity	Dollars on hand	Inventory on order	Date placed	Date due	Quantity
10-326-01	Detroit	Normal	183		25			457.50				
	Chicago	Out of stock	0	365	40	45		0	912.50	2/15/95	2/26/95	365
	Atlanta	Expedite	29	145	15			72.50	462.50	3/01/95	3/12/95	145
	Newark	Overstock	293		30			732.50				
	Los Angeles	Order	55		10		75	137.50				
	Dallas	Normal	103		23			257.50				
Total			663	510	143	45	75	1,657.50	1,375.00			510

the system is computerized. Table 22-16 provides an example of an inventory stock status report.

In Table 22-16, inventory items are controlled from one central management location for distribution warehouses located in Detroit, Chicago, Atlanta, Newark, Los Angeles, and Dallas. The unit inventory is maintained on a central computer linked to the warehouses on a real-time basis. Individual items have been assigned to stock controllers responsible for inventory status at all six distribution warehouses. This particular report is for controller A (noted in the upper-right portion of the output). The individual item or unit number is printed in column (A). The item numbers do not appear in numerical sequence, since only items requiring attention are printed. However, if an item requires action at a specific distribution warehouse, item status for all other warehouses is also printed on the report. Thus, when an inventory controller plans action concerning an item, its status at all stocking locations can be reviewed. The location is displayed in column (B), and its inventory status is reflected in column (D). Of particular interest is the required action printed in column (C). On the basis of inventory control system rules, the controller is informed why a particular item appears on the stock status report. The remainder of the columns are self-explanatory and provide the necessary information for the controller to direct inventory replenishment.

Status reports can be developed for all logistical activity centers. Some relate to individual unit or transaction control; others are financial in nature. The purpose of the status report is to provide line managers with relevant information to fulfill their responsibility in the overall logistical system.

Trend Reports

Trend reports are used by administrators at levels of control higher than the line manager. In keeping with the flow of data outlined in Figure 22-1, trend reports are more selective in content than status reports. To illustrate, Tables 22-17 and 22-18 provide examples of trend reports that might be based on the inventory stock status report.

Table 22-17 provides an inventory recap for all items, controllers, and stock

TABLE 22-17   DAILY INVENTORY SUMMARY

	A	B	C	D	E
				Dollar values inventory	
Location	Total items stocked	Percentage in stock	In stock	On order	Forecasted
Detroit	1,075	92	17,385	3,231	7,115
Chicago	1,093	91	20,265	3,695	5,940
Atlanta	1,041	88	15,197	3,780	8,201
Newark	1,073	75	18,243	9,361	11,116
Los Angeles	1,075	89	23,116	5,143	4,307
Dallas	1,026	90	19,450	2,184	1,993
Total system	6,383	87.5	$113,656	$27,394	$38,672

	F	G	H	I		
				Out of stock by class		
Controller	Total items	Percentage in stock	Percentage expedite	A	B	C
A	1,250	91	10	30	40	50
B	1,300	89	9	36	71	38
C	1,100	82	15	65	47	91
D	1,275	85	9	15	81	95
E	1,458	95	8	20	70	40
Total	6.383	87.5	10	166	309	314

	J	K	L
Location	Items out of stock + 5 days	Items overstocked	Percentage of orders shipped on schedule
Detroit	12	31	96
Chicago	16	11	97
Atlanta	11	38	99
Newark	21	5	92
Los Angeles	14	17	87
Dallas	19	0	94
Total	93	102	96

locations. A report of this type is used by department heads to review the overall inventory situation. The data contained in a daily inventory summary are developed as a by-product of the stock status report printed for inventory controllers. Thus management possesses a quick recap of the total system and can evaluate overall performance.

Table 22-17 provides a variety of information. General performance is available on all locations as well as individual controllers. For example, the Newark warehouse is 75 percent in stock [column (B)], 21 percent of the items have been out of stock longer than five days [column (J)], and 92 percent of the orders scheduled for shipment were sent as planned [column (L)]. The report also indicates that controller C is having problems. This person is in stock on only 82 percent of the items [column (G)], 15 percent of the assigned items in stock currently require expedite efforts to prevent future stockouts [column (H)], and the out-of-stock items fall heavily into the critical area of classified merchandise as identified by the ABC system [column (I)].

Armed with this information, the department head is in a position to review the current situation and take corrective action. If desired, ad hoc reports can be requested that will provide further detail to analyze a possible trend. For example, the department head in this case would probably desire detailed facts concerning the Newark facility and the activities of controller C. There is no end to the selective information that can be generated from a database of the type maintained to develop Tables 22-16 and 22-17.

Table 22-18 provides an executive summary of selected critical facts regarding inventory performance. Condensed information of this type would most often be used at the vice presidential or decision level of an operation. As noted earlier, an executive who is content to wait for exceptions to appear is rare. Most would prefer to see performance trends in their areas of responsibility.

Table 22-18 covers a four-week period. The first three weeks are presented in aggregate, and the fourth week is developed on a daily basis. Reports of this nature provide the basis for trend evaluation and are useful in selecting areas for diagnostic analysis. For example, the data in Table 22-18 point out that although inventory performance over the past three weeks has deteriorated, performance on the most recent days indicates that corrective action has been taken. Of particular interest in Table 22-18 is line 2, weighted performance. This is a measure of stock availability in the quantities desired by customers. A system may enjoy a very high level of in-stock items but be out of stock on those most desired by customers. Measures of weighted performance generally run lower than measures of system in stock.

The data presented in Table 22-18 contain inventory trend information generated from the inventory stock status report (Table 22-16) and the daily inventory summary (Table 22-17). In all probability the executive receiving the performance recap would be responsible for additional logistical system activity centers. The report could be expanded to include data on transportation, warehouse performance, order processing, material movement, or other desired areas. In addition, similar reports can be generated in materials management and inventory transfer operations. Because the information is selective and highly condensed, these reports can often be confined to a single page.

TABLE 22-18   LOGISTICAL PERFORMANCE RECAP
Date of report 12/5

Performance area	Week 11/7	Week 11/14	Week 11/21	Week of 11/28				
				Mon.	Tues.	Wed.	Thurs.	Fri.
1 System in stock (%)	88.0	86.0	81.0	82.0	85.0	86.2	87.3	87.5
2 Weighted performance (%)	83.8	84.2	90.0	79.8	83.2	84.0	86.3	87.0
3 Inventory ($)	121,614	119,381	111,843	95,417	98,106	96,412	110,807	113,706
4 Shipments on schedule (%)	99	97	98	99	96	97	98	96
5 Back-orders	365	691	780	193	217	238	165	101

Ad Hoc Reports

Ad hoc reports may be created at any level of logistical administration and for a variety of reasons. Most often, they are developed to provide detail on specific areas of performance. Three types of ad hoc reports are common in administration.

The first type is a diagnostic report, which provides detail on a specific phase of operations. For example, a report might be requested to obtain greater detail on current back-orders and subsequent corrective action. If the firm operates a real-time order processing system, special diagnostic reports may be provided from either hard copy or direct inquiry.

The second type of ad hoc report is a position paper. Given a current or anticipated problem, a report outlining alternative courses of action and probable consequences is often desirable. In terms of control levels (see Table 22-16), position papers are usually developed by line managers and department heads for use by executives at the decision level of the organization. These position papers will often request additional resources. If the request is approved, the operational plan will have to be modified. In accordance with the levels of administrative control, position papers and related actions may involve a greater allocation of resources, but they will not require changes in performance objectives.

The final ad hoc report is concerned with policy modification. Earlier in this chapter an example of a policy report was discussed in which the marketing department requested that customer service objectives be substantially upgraded. Policy reports are always directed to or initiated from the chief executive officer of a firm. Their content almost always involves areas of activity beyond logistics.

The content of control reports is highly customized to the individual enterprise, its organization, and management information system sophistication. The content should be geared to levels of administrative control: the higher the level of control, the more selective the nature of information contained in the report.

For the most part, status reports are used by line managers to direct logistical activities in accordance with predetermined operational plans. Trend reports to monitor progress are highly condensed and are used by executives at the variation and decision levels. The higher the control level, the more condensed and selective the trend report. Trend reports prepared at the decision level should contain information related to all aspects of an integrated logistical system. Ad hoc reports contain selected information on certain units of the system. Performance with respect to the operating plan can be evaluated to permit rapid and efficient management response to any externally or internally generated change.

SUMMARY

Chapter 22 focused on the specifics of performance measurement and reporting. Initially the chapter outlined the dimensions of performance measurement that are critical to effective logistical management. Attention was then directed to three aspects. First, internal measures typically used to monitor logistical performance were reviewed. Next, external measures of customers' service perceptions and best practice benchmarking were presented. The final perspective on performance measurement focused on issues related to comprehensive supply chain measures. One easy-to-spot practice of logistically superior firms is their almost compulsive commitment to all aspects of performance measurement.

Finally, Chapter 22 dealt with various facets of sophisticated measurement and reporting. It profiled characteristics of an ideal performance measurement system; identified levels of information requirements and flows to support effective controllership; and illustrated status, trend, and ad hoc reporting formats.

QUESTIONS

1   Briefly discuss the three objectives for developing and implementing performance measurement systems.

2   Compare and contrast the focus of internal and external performance measures.

3   Why is it critical that logistics reporting systems reflect dynamic rather than static performance?

4   How does benchmarking related to performance measurement differ from benchmarking related to logistical reengineering?

5   Why is it important that a firm measure customer perception as a regular part of performance measurement?

6   Is the ideal of a perfect order a realistic operational goal?

7   Describe and illustrate dynamic knowledge-based reporting.

8   Why are comprehensive measures of supply chain operations difficult to develop on a regular basis?

9   What managers in a logistical organization are most apt to be concerned with direction-focused information? How does direction information relate to variation and decision information.

10   What is the purpose of a trend report? How does it utilize status report information?

CHAPTER 23

DIMENSIONS OF CHANGE:
A SEMINAR FOCUS

A VIEW TOWARD THE NEW MILLENNIUM

A SEMINAR FOCUS

SEMINAR TOPIC 1: HOW ADEQUATE IS
THE GLOBAL LOGISTICS
INFRASTRUCTURE?
   Issues and Questions

SEMINAR TOPIC 2: ASSESSMENT AND
CONTROL TO IMPROVE LOGISTICS
PERFORMANCE
   Issues and Questions

SEMINAR TOPIC 3: ORGANIZATIONAL
EVALUATION
   The Case for Functional Specialization
   The Case for Functional Decentralization
   The Case for Horizontal Expansion
   Issues and Questions

SEMINAR TOPIC 4: FULL-SERVICE
DISTRIBUTION COMPANIES
   Forces Stimulating FSDC Development
   Service Risk
   Issues and Questions

SEMINAR TOPIC 5: INFORMATION
TECHNOLOGY
   The Evolution of Application Development
   End-User Computing
   Who Should Do What?
   Issues and Questions

SEMINAR TOPIC 6: GLOBAL LOGISTICS
   The Prerequisites for Global Success
   Issues and Questions

EPILOGUE

This concluding chapter offers a perspective on the future of logistics. Chapter 23 commences with a brief look at what might constitute the setting for logistical operations in the new millennium. The remaining sections introduce specific seminar topics for critical review. The essence of management is to think critically in a constructive and innovative manner. Successful change management requires such vision.

692

A VIEW TOWARD THE NEW MILLENNIUM

Given the extreme changes that have occurred in logistical management concepts and practices during the past several decades, an appropriate question is, What can we expect to happen as the world moves toward and into a new millennium? The primary determinant of the shape and form of future logistical requirements will be the nature of demand that will need to be serviced.

The logistical renaissance developed a sound foundation to guide logistics managers as they move toward the new millennium. While significant lessons have been learned over the past decades, the process of change is far from finished. The globalization of business promises to offer new and unique challenges for the logistical competencies of most firms. Few will be able to escape the impact of a global economy. Challenges will also increase in the environmental aspects of logistics, often referred to as *green* issues. The full ramification of long-term cradle-to-cradle responsibility for the environmental impact of all products and services is just emerging. Finally, firms can fully expect that customers making major business commitments to alliance partners will expect near perfect logistical performance. Even in today's operational environment, firms that build strong customer and supplier relationships must be committed to operational excellence. Tolerance for logistical error will be even less in the future.

Current projections are that the gross domestic product of the United States will exceed $7 trillion by the year 2000. Significant growth is projected in both goods and services. However, most futurists predict that the United States and most of the industrialized world will increasingly become service-oriented economies. In comparison to today, a significantly larger share of the world's total population will seek participation in the good life possible in the new millennium. Logistical systems of the future will face complex and challenging performance requirements. Even more so than today, logistics will be required to support multiple-product distribution to globally dispersed heterogeneous markets through a variety of channels.

Barring a catastrophic event, it is difficult not to expect a world population exceeding 6.5 billion people by the year 2000. To put this population growth into perspective, at a bare minimum it will be necessary to provide logistical support for one additional person for every 5.5 in the world today. People in general will increasingly have resources to participate in economic growth. However, significant differences are expected in lifestyle and related social priorities. Evidence suggests that consumers of the future will demand services and conveniences contained in the products they purchase. For instance, such items as frozen meat might well be precooked and ready for consumption when bought. To the extent that this service/convenience pattern accelerates, more value will be added to the typical product before it begins the logistical process. To support this trend, the complexity of the total manufacturing/marketing system will increase.

The most serious challenge facing managers will be the continued need to shift fundamental practice from a functional to a process orientation. Despite the fact that this challenge has existed for the last half of the twentieth century, real change has been almost nonexistent in some firms. Process integration requires a cultural shift in the basic work practices of logistics. Such change does not come easy.

Managers have been trained to supervise functions. Organizations are structured to control assets assigned to functional units. Accounting serves to measure functional performance. Perhaps the most serious barrier to achieving true process management is that information systems and databases have been designed to help managers direct and control functions. To overcome these obstacles, managers who desire to exploit superior logistical performance need to develop new paradigms related to process management.

A new definition of what constitutes functional excellence is being forged. While high-level performance is important, it must be subordinate to the achievement of overall logistical integration. Simply stated, a function is excellent only when it makes maximum contribution to the attainment of overall operational goals. Functions are means to the end goal of process integration. Functional excellence in isolation is obsolete and dysfunctional.

The priority placed on development of integrated management skills rests on the contribution that superior logistics performance can make to strategic success. A firm can achieve sustainable competitive advantage when important customers perceive that it has the capabilities to logistically outperform competitors. A prerequisite to strategic logistics is the development and implementation of supply chain integration. Managing logistics on an integrated basis is becoming increasingly relevant for the following reasons.

First, there is considerable interdependence between areas of logistical requirements that can be exploited to the advantage of an enterprise. The idea of a *total* movement/storage system offers efficiency and synergistic potential. Throughout the logistical system, management is faced with ever increasing labor costs. Since logistical work is among the most labor-intensive performed within an enterprise, logistics managers must develop methods to substitute capital for labor-intensive processes. Complete integration increases the economic justification for substituting capital for labor.

A second reason for approaching logistics on an integrated basis is that a narrow or restricted functional approach may create dysfunctional behavior. The potential exists that concepts relevant solely to physical distribution, manufacturing support, or procurement can create diametrically opposite operational priorities and goals. The failure to develop integrated logistical management creates the potential for suboptimization.

A third reason to integrate logistics is that the control requirements for each individual aspect of operations are similar. The primary objective of logistical control is to reconcile operational demands in a cross-functional manner in order to focus on overall goals.

A fourth reason for the integration of logistical operations is an increasing awareness that significant trade-offs exist between manufacturing economies and marketing requirements and that these can be reconciled only by a soundly designed logistical capability. The traditional practice of manufacturing is to produce products in various sizes, colors, and quantities in *anticipation* of future sale. The *postponement* of final assembly and initial distribution of products to a later time when customer preferences are more fully identified can greatly reduce risk and increase overall enterprise flexibility. Innovative new systems are emerging to make use of logistical competency to increase responsiveness and reduce the traditional anticipatory commitment and risk of business.

A final, and perhaps the most significant, reason for integration is that the complexity of future logistics will require innovative arrangements. The challenge for the new millennium is to develop *new ways* of satisfying logistical requirements, not simply using technology to perform *old ways more efficiently*. While this is similar to the challenge faced in the 1990s, the stakes are getting higher. In the world of the future, leading firms can be expected to increasingly use integrated logistical competency to gain differential advantage. The broad-based achievement of integrated logistical management will remain a prerequisite for such innovative breakthrough.

The combined impact of these factors is that logistics will increasingly be managed on an integrated basis. However, the job of reengineering logistics as an integrated process is far from completed. Research continues to point out that a significant number of firms worldwide have not made much progress toward logistical integration. Approximately 10 percent of North American firms have achieved a level of integration that facilitates their use of logistical competency to gain and maintain customer loyalty. Events of historical significance—like the radical restructuring of Eastern Europe; the decomposition of communism in the Soviet Union; and even the combined campaigns of Desert Shield, Desert Storm, and Desert Farewell—serve to underline the increasing importance of logistics to all aspects of society. In many ways, these events highlight just how demanding logistical requirements are and how challenging they are capable of becoming. The reality is that a great deal of work remains to make the full potential of the logistics renaissance an everyday reality.

Ever present in future society will be the continued problems and pressures of energy and ecology. The dependence of the logistical system on a ready supply of energy is and will continue to be a critical concern. The cost of energy remains significant in the logistical sector and will continue to be so for the foreseeable future. From an ecological viewpoint, continued pressures will exist to reduce the negative impact of logistics on the environment. These pressures reflect socially worthwhile goals, although compliance will be costly. It can be anticipated that ecological considerations will eliminate some current logistical practices such as specific types of packaging material. Finally, the remainder of the twentieth century is projected to be a period during which selected raw materials will from time to time be in relatively short supply.

A SEMINAR FOCUS

The remainder of Chapter 23 presents six seminar topics suitable for small group discussion. The topics are not presented in priority sequence. They range from computers to managerial issues to multinational logistics. Each topic is introduced by a brief presentation designed to highlight some issues related to the subject under consideration. The background discussion is positioned to suggest a way to improve logistical productivity or presents a problem or concern that managers can expect to confront in the future. The topics are not comprehensive and in no way attempt to give all sides of an issue or situation. At the conclusion of each seminar topic, issues and questions are presented to stimulate student discussion. It is expected that supplemental reading and research on the subject will result in lively discussion.

SEMINAR TOPIC 1: HOW ADEQUATE IS THE GLOBAL LOGISTICS INFRASTRUCTURE?

Assuming full maturity of integrated logistics, are the present and planned global infrastructure and capability adequate to meet future logistical demands? With a continued 5 percent level of unemployment, the logistical infrastructure and managerial practices of today will be hard-pressed if not unable to support future market demand. In our society, logistics is second only to personal services as a consumer of labor. Logistics is a labor-intensive process. The situation becomes even more critical when marginal workers are employed, which occurs when more qualified labor is fully employed. Logistical systems employ more than their rightful share of marginal workers because of the manual nature of the tasks. Physical handling of goods around a twenty-four-hour clock does not rank as choice employment when alternative jobs are available. Thus, employees with marginal skills and motivation may be the prime source of labor available to perform the work of logistics. The result has been, and will continue for the foreseeable future to be, a problem of maintaining, let alone trying to improve, labor productivity.

One substitute for labor is the invention and implementation of new technology. For the past decades, logistical systems have kept pace with growth by applying new technology to the performance of traditional logistical work. For example, load capacity of transportation vehicles has been expanded in water, rail, truck, and air operations. Today, each mode can carry larger payloads faster and cheaper than a few years ago. Similarly, computing and data transmission have increased the capacity to receive and process customer orders faster and more accurately while simultaneously capturing critical information. During the past decades, significant advancements have also been made in automation of material handling.

Throughout the world, technological developments have been applied to keep pace with increased demand for logistical capacity. Considering the track record, even the most severe critic would have to acknowledge outstanding performance. However, after all is said and done, logistical systems in the new millennium will continue to require massive amounts of physical labor. Despite the historical track record of having adequate logistics capability, the existing system is now strained to keep up with growth. The capacity situation will become increasingly critical in the decades ahead.

From the viewpoint of technological assessment, the prospects for continued development to satisfy future logistical demands are not encouraging. For example, load capabilities and transportation speeds have reached near maximum for highway, rail, harbor, and airport infrastructures. Future technology will emerge at a significantly slower rate. It appears safe to conclude that new technology will not provide all the capacity needed to satisfy tomorrow's logistical requirements.

The capacity problems anticipated in the future can be resolved. However, performing more of the same activities in logistics in the manner they have been performed during the past decades is not the answer. The historical practice of overpowering logistical requirements by application of new technology will no longer be viable. The challenge for the future is to develop *new* ways to satisfy logistical requirements, instead of attempting to perform *old* ways more efficiently. The solution rests with innovative reengineering of logistics arrangements to fully exploit technological resources. Many traditions that characterize today's logistics practices are both archaic and symbolic of a bygone era.

In summary, the critical issue is demand versus system adequacy. The remaining years of the twentieth century as well as the new millennium are projected to be periods of continued affluence. The sheer numbers of people and their creative requirements will produce unprecedented demands for logistical services. Complexity of the logistical process will increase as a result of changing lifestyles, continued high cost of energy, and increased ecological and environmental compliance requirements. Unlike the past, the era of global logistics cannot look forward to a steady stream of new technology to plug into existing practices as the solution to meeting logistical requirements. Almost all real improvements in operating capability over the past several decades have resulted from technology. Throughout the world, managers have overpowered problems of logistical growth by depending on technology deployment. Now, for the first time since World War II, the continued potential of using technology to satisfy increased demand is not encouraging.

A variety of approaches to help meet future logistical requirements do exist within the philosophy of integrated logistics. Each represents a new or different way of formulating and conducting logistical operations using currently available technology. To be fully implemented, each concept requires a major change in current logistical operating practices. The significant point is that the application of *today's technology* to cope with tomorrow's logistical needs requires innovative management. While many legal and/or regulatory barriers exist to hinder such innovation, the most serious limitation is management attitude and inflexibility.

Issues and Questions

1   What major changes can be forecasted for the logistical infrastructure?

2   Is the marginal labor claim presented in the seminar a justified position? How about the statement that management attitude and inflexibility represent the greatest barriers to innovative change? Does labor deficiency apply to all areas of the world, or is it limited to selected highly industrialized regions?

3   The discussion makes the point that future advancements cannot depend on technological developments to solve problems associated with growth.

    a   Does this position present a fair assessment of future technology?

    b   If the position of the seminar is correct, why is there so much attention to "high-tech" development?

    c   Is capital availability a greater issue than technology?

4   What is a traditional logistical task?

5   Present an example of a new or innovative way to perform an old logistical task.

6   If the world cannot depend on technological development to assist in satisfying future growth-related logistical requirements, what is the solution? Do you agree with this doomsday assessment?

SEMINAR TOPIC 2: ASSESSMENT AND CONTROL TO IMPROVE LOGISTICS PERFORMANCE

Control systems are the key to ensuring that logistical operations achieve managerial plans for profitability and performance. By improving operational efficiency and tracking progress toward goal achievement, assessment and control systems support managerial efforts to achieve customer service objectives, reach planned business and profit levels, and control deployment of assets such as inventory.

Logistics assessment and control serve three primary functions. First, they measure performance through reports, audits, and observations. Second, they make comparison of measured performance against standards or goals. Third, they identify areas requiring action. A diagram of a typical logistical control system is presented in Figure 23-1. The objective of the system is to measure and report information that will assist management to achieve organizational objectives.

In general, methods to help measure, compare, and guide logistics performance have not received adequate attention in information system development. Increased competition and erratic marketplace growth have forced industry to concentrate on tighter control to improve productivity. Productivity improvements can be achieved only with formal and comprehensive measurement systems. Successful companies have standards of performance for each logistical activity within the overall logistics process. These firms also require readily available information for all managers who are involved in maintaining control. Progressive firms are making substantial

FIGURE 23-1   Logistics control system.

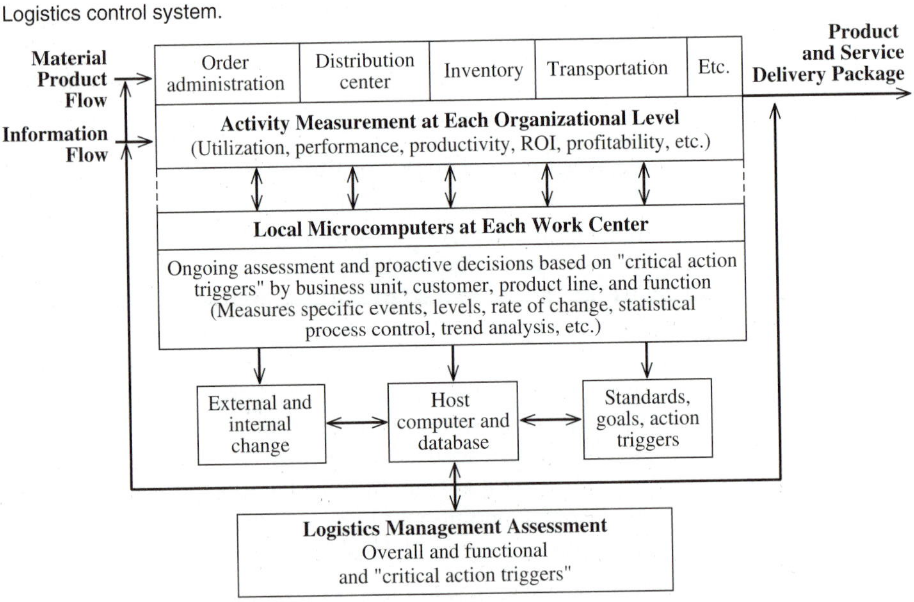

investments in the establishment of *data warehouses* that are integral to their information system architecture. The primary purpose of the data warehouse is to facilitate information accessibility for all managers and even customers and suppliers. At the Whirlpool North American Appliance Group, for instance, the information initiative is known as LIFE—logistics information for everyone. To provide maximum value to managers, these assessment and control systems should be integrated with transaction and planning systems such as order entry and processing, logistics requirement planning, inventory management, master production scheduling, warehousing, and transportation.

Most logistics information systems provide ample data to measure past performance. The problem with the performance report card approach is that far too little emphasis is given to measurement that permits managers to proactively identify and prevent problems. Action triggers or other early warning devices are necessary parts of proactive assessment and control. Action triggers are information messages and measures suggesting that management take initiative to prevent future performance problems. A trigger can identify problems developing from resource constraints such as lack of equipment. An example might be a key customer's order that is not proceeding toward fulfillment in accordance with service expectations. The distribution control system should isolate priority orders for special managerial action to prevent a critical customer service breakdown. Another example of an action trigger could be notification that overall order processing activity is tracking in excess of the planned level. Such tracking could be an early warning of future inadequate capacity to keep up with promised deliveries.

The development of an early warning capability requires that information systems be focused on creating a knowledge database. This database could contain a series of dynamic and static measures to facilitate assessment and control. Examples of dynamic measures would be ratios for current compared to previous periods. Dynamic measures would compare ratios for all periods to the expected level or base and formulate how to respond by recommending corrective action before the actual problem materializes.

The implementation of proactive assessment and control has the potential to significantly improve logistical performance. The benefits may be far greater than most managers realize.

Issues and Questions

1   What are the possible measures of logistical effectiveness? Is it possible to define the most important measure for a company?

2   Define three action triggers and three dynamic measures that would be important to a vice president of logistics in (a) a consumer packaged goods company and (b) an industrial products company with equipment and parts.

3   How are utilization, performance, and productivity related.

4   How are logistics assessment and control similar to the environment in an automated production control process? What are some of the differences?

5   Do MRP (or DRP) systems eliminate the need for a separate logistics assessment and control system?

6 Should productivity measurement improve managers' diagnostic capabilities and, therefore, their effectiveness?

SEMINAR TOPIC 3: ORGANIZATIONAL EVALUATION

Chapter 20 was devoted to the subject of organization. The general case was presented that the effectiveness and efficiency of overall logistical operations have traditionally been improved by grouping authority and responsibility for individual work into a single organizational unit.

The development of an integrated logistical operation typically takes place over time. The pattern presented in Chapter 20 identified three stages of organization functional integration. Stage 1 is characterized by the formal recognition of a limited functional group concerned with physical distribution and/or materials management. The focal characteristic of stage 2 development is the establishment of an officer-level executive responsible for a significant part of logistics such as transportation. In addition to positioning logistics at the officer level, stage 2 organization typically assembles more functions within the integrated structure.

The most comprehensive model of traditional command and control is the stage 3 organization. In terms of functional grouping, a stage 3 structure represents the ultimate; that is, all functions involved in physical distribution, manufacturing support, and purchasing are grouped under a single managerial responsibility. In this most comprehensive concept of formal logistical organization, all planning and operational activities are combined within a single structure.

Various research has been cited to support the conclusion that firms typically evolve through these three stages as they seek to improve control over integrated logistics. In part, the organizational solution to control has been facilitated by rapid advancement in information system capabilities. The combination of advanced transaction process systems, decision support systems, and assessment and control capabilities provides the information necessary to manage a comprehensive logistics organization on a national or global basis. However, gaining and exercising control may be different challenges.

Three arguments support the alternative structures beyond stage 3 organizations: the case for functional specialization, the case for functional decentralization, and the case for horizontal expansion.

The Case for Functional Specialization

Whereas the stage 3 organization structure favors integration of the three logistical operation areas of physical distribution, manufacturing support, and procurement, a counter viewpoint is to place a premium on deep specialization in an area that can serve as a core competency. The issue goes beyond efficiency to embrace an expertise that will attract customer loyalty. The position contrary to the stage 3 organization logic is that each area requires sufficient asset deployment and operating expenditures in a large corporation to justify specialization.

Those who favor such specialization present the argument that cross-area trade-offs are really limited to transportation efficiency and that such benefits can be realized without organization integration. The position in defense of functional specialization is that economy of scale can be realized while improving control as a result of detailed knowledge regarding physical distribution, manufacturing support, or purchasing. Such specialization could be lost or restricted in a stage 3 organization. As one executive put it, ''It's the old case of the cavalry versus the infantry.''

The Case for Functional Decentralization

The position in favor of functional decentralization is also supported by the drive to gain specialization benefits. Those favoring decentralization argue that the functions of physical distribution, manufacturing support, and purchasing should be integrated but not at a global or headquarters level. The decentralization advocate favors pushing logistical operating responsibility to lower levels of the business such as a plant, distribution warehouse, or regional sales office. There logistics can be integrated in the day-to-day operations of the enterprise. Advocates of functional decentralization contend that headquarters' activities should be restricted to strategic coordination and technical support.

The Case for Horizontal Expansion

The horizontal organization perspective is becoming increasingly popular among large companies. The horizontal organization focuses on process and was described earlier as a stage 4 of structural evolution.

An example of integration in a horizontal structure would be the performance of physical distribution operations for a number of business units by one service organization. Provided that several different business units sell to the same class of trade or to different customers located within a given geographical concentration, the most significant productivity gains could well be realized by concentration of all physical distribution operations into a single organization. A similar grouping in purchasing would be a concentrated maintenance, repair, and operating organization (MRO).

The question of how big is too big to control economy of scale may be the critical organization issue. In theory, a single logistical organization could have the depth and breadth to operate both as a stage 3 vertical extension and as a stage 4 horizontal structure.

Issues and Questions

1 Support or reject the assumption that formal organization structures are essential for gaining control but may not be effective in exercising control.

2 ''It's the old case of the cavalry versus the infantry.'' What does this statement mean?

3 Is the position that functional specialization results in increased productivity justified?

4 Why would an organization be more effective if control was decentralized? Does this run contrary to the concept of integration, which is at the very heart of logistical management?

5 Is horizontal expansion really different from vertical expansion? Is the logical extension a matrix structure?

6 Does the concept of a super organization exist that can satisfy all requirements? Is the notion of a virtual organization acceptable in terms of the human need to be a part of organized behavior? How would a manager view career tracking in a virtual organization?

SEMINAR TOPIC 4: FULL-SERVICE DISTRIBUTION COMPANIES

Changes in the distribution environment have given rise to the formation of full-service distribution companies (FSDC). These firms provide a comprehensive range of distribution services for their customers. To qualify as full service, a company would need to have the capabilities to perform two or more operational areas of logistical services on an integrated basis. However, to be a serious comprehensive service supplier, a firm should be positioned to perform all of a customer's logistics requirements. The range of services could include inventory management, transportation, warehouse operations, information processing, order processing, consolidation, and whatever else was needed to fully satisfy logistical requirements.

The growth of the logistics service industry was extensively discussed throughout this text, particularly the role of service providers in contemporary logistics. This seminar topic focuses on the forces that have stimulated this development and then discusses issues related to using full-service distribution companies.

Forces Stimulating FSDC Development

Three basic forces have stimulated the mushrooming growth of FSDCs: deregulation, focus on asset productivity, and core competency attractiveness. Each is briefly discussed.

The impact of deregulation on logistics in general and on transportation in particular has been discussed in detail. One result has been a refocus on the process of negotiating rates and services. Such negotiations have resulted in interorganizational arrangements that have benefits for both shippers and service suppliers. For example, the development of consistent high-volume transportation movement to a specific market area offers significantly greater transportation efficiencies. As a result, a market opportunity has emerged for service business specialists to perform consolidation and cross docking in an effort to achieve maximum operational impact. Consolidation potential is greater when a large number of businesses combine their goods for transport. The use of an FSDC can stimulate consolidation.

The second force creating the potential for FSDCs is the widespread attention to improvement in asset productivity. This need to improve return on assets has resulted in many firms seeking to reduce capital committed to logistical operations. The development of FSDCs offers a way to jointly share in asset productivity. First, the assets deployed to perform logistics such as warehouse facilities and transportation equipment belong to the FSDC. For the customer, assets are freed when operations are contracted to a distribution company. Expenses for the customer become a variable rather than a fixed cost, and the customer's assets are reduced, resulting in decreased ROI pressures.

A third change that has stimulated development of FSDCs is the increased benefit of specialization that results when a business focuses on a core competency. In essence such specialization is occurring for both the shipper that is outsourcing and the service specialists. Each has the opportunity to benefit from economy of scope and scale. For example, benefits in the form of cost reductions may result from the use of automated or specialized equipment. If a distribution service firm can increase overall transaction volume, it may be able to justify the acquisition of more sophisticated handling, storage, or transportation equipment.

Service Risk

The FSDC typically provides a combination of services such as (1) inventory management, (2) warehouse operations, (3) information processing, (4) order processing, (5) transportation, and (6) value-added services. Each of these activities is critical to the successful operation of a business. Many critics feel that outsourcing firms confront substantial risk. If the FSDC fails to serve key customers as promised, the outsourcing firm may be devastated. Whereas failure to perform may be disastrous for the service firm, it could be catastrophic for the organization that outsourced its complete logistical requirements to the distribution company.

Another issue relates to the real benefits of specialization. While an FSDC may have expertise in performing required services, it may not fully understand the business application it is logistically supporting. In other words, the FSDC may be a functional specialist but have serious deficiencies concerning the business proposition involved.

Issues and Questions

1 What, if any, potential antitrust problems are created by development of FSDC organizations?

2 Do you buy the catastrophe theory related to outsourcing? Are the potential rewards offset by the risks? What could a firm do to reduce the risk?

3 What are the potential conflicts that may develop as an essential distribution service is contracted to an outside vendor? What precautions should be taken?

4 Should special laws or government action be taken to control FSDC organization?

5 What criteria should a company use to determine whether it should enter the FSDC business?

6 What criteria should a company use to determine whether it should utilize an outside service specialist?

SEMINAR TOPIC 5: INFORMATION TECHNOLOGY

Historians are already describing the current stage of civilization as the information age. Developments in terms of computer and communications hardware and their associated software have advanced far faster than management's ability to apply the technology. At the same time, these advances are viewed as the primary source of increased logistical productivity. The wave of the future envisions moving information as a substitute for moving goods and services. This seminar topic reviews some of these technological advances in terms of implications for logistical management.

The Evolution of Application Development

One of the most dramatic advances in information technology involves new programming languages. Initially, when information resources were expensive and human resources were less costly, application programming was labor-intensive. The goal was to create programs to minimize computer requirements. Table 23-1 provides a brief overview of first-, second-, and third-generation programming language capabilities. All three of these languages required programmers to instruct computers on what to do and how to do it. To achieve an effective application, it was necessary for a programmer to instruct the computer on where to find data and exactly how to process the information.

Fourth- and fifth-generation languages facilitated the process of application development by permitting a program to be structured in more "English-like" language. Furthermore, the programming process required the person developing the application to instruct the computer only on what to do but *not* how to do it. For example, instead of the application developer providing instructions on how to access and process a file to generate a summary of data, fourth-generation languages only require the developer to instruct the computer to summarize the information and indicate how to present it. Driven by advanced languages, the computer generates its own program instructions and then completes the computations necessary to produce the required information. These new languages can generate report formats, develop summary statistics, and provide report headings. The event that made advanced languages possible was the development of faster and cheaper computing. The cost of computing has become significantly less than the cost of most programming.

TABLE 23-1 PROGRAMMING LANGUAGE CHARACTERISTICS

- *First generation (e.g., machine code).* Requires that the programmer enter machine instructions and specific variable addresses. Requires that the programmer communicate with the computer in the computer's internal language.

- *Second generation (e.g., assembly language).* Instead of instruction codes and specific addresses, assembly languages allow the programmer to use mnemonic instruction codes and labels for variables. This allows programs to be more intelligible to programmers but requires the computer to perform some translation, which makes it a little less efficient.

- *Third generation (e.g., compiled languages such as* FORTRAN *or* COBOL*).* The third-generation languages use English instructions that tell the computer to perform a number of internal operations. While third-generation languages are more understandable, they need a significant amount of structure and specificity. These languages require that the computer perform considerable translation, resulting in less efficient operation.

The development of advanced languages means that far less technical background is now necessary to effectively program computers. Where it once required a significant amount of formal education and training for an individual to develop computer applications, advanced programming languages have reduced, although not eliminated, such requirements. This advance has allowed people with minimal computer expertise and possibly strong background in a functional area to be able to address development of computer programs to satisfy information requirements. The overall process of developing effective applications has been facilitated by such breakthroughs as object-oriented programming and graphical user interfaces (GUI).

End-User Computing

Partly as a result of the development of high-powered desktop computers and user-friendly languages, there is a trend to assign both program development and actual computing to users. Instead of a centralized group completing development of appropriate applications, the burden for developing programs increasingly rests with the user. The role of the expert is to provide users with the tools that enable them to develop their own reports and applications and also to serve as a technical consultant. The birth of software products such as spreadsheets, database packages, report generators, and decision support systems has made it feasible for a moderately trained individual to develop and use complex applications. These applications range from spreadsheet analysis of logistical alternatives to the development of a freight history system to aid in the negotiation of rates. Not only does end-user computing decrease the time required for application development, but it also brings the development effort closer to the end user.

Who Should Do What?

The basic question is, How far should this trend toward end-user application development and computing be allowed to progress? For example, should end users be authorized to develop and implement transaction processing applications such as order processing and invoicing? Furthermore, who in an organization should be responsible for database management? In fact, where should the database be located, and to what degree should it be centralized, distributed, or shared? Is application standardization important? The potential to push responsibility for selected applications and computing to end users has appeal, but it also involves substantial risk.

Issues and Questions

1 The development of end-user computing and advanced program generations implies shifting some information processing roles. What changes are required in the logistical management organization to accommodate these new responsibilities? Discuss whether these changes will have positive or negative impacts on logistical productivity.

2 What changes will these advances in information technology bring about in the training requirements of entry-level logistical positions?

3 Given that there will be trained information technology people in the logistical function, should these individuals receive their primary education in logistics or in information technology? What are the arguments for each position?

4 Do fourth- and fifth-generation languages really provide the productivity improvements that they have promised, or is this merely a shift in work? In what types of logistical applications are the benefits real?

5 The development of new languages and end-user computing significantly increases the potential for duplication as multiple users develop their own applications that may contain significant overlap with other areas. What procedures should be put into place to minimize this, and what controls should be established to maintain information and decision-making integrity?

6 Should there be changes in the education and training process for logistical managers in order for them to support end-user computing? What should these changes be?

SEMINAR TOPIC 6: GLOBAL LOGISTICS

Prior to the last few decades, global business for many firms was more or less an afterthought—the opportunity to generate some incremental volume. As developed in Chapter 5, there is substantial evidence to suggest that future business will involve global competitiveness of vast and complex multinational institutions. In today's business environment the only relevant focus for logistical planning and operations for many firms is a global perspective.

Progressive firms recognize that they must produce and distribute products worldwide to achieve substantial long-term success. To gain and maintain competitive superiority and achieve maximum manufacturing economies of scale, it is necessary to capitalize on the inherent advantages available from all nations within which a firm operates.

Such a global perspective has created a need for development of a logic to guide worldwide logistical management. This logistical logic must be capable of controlling the complex process of asset deployment within and between large numbers of countries that have different laws, cultures, levels of economic development, and national aspiration. There are only limited examples where firms have become stateless enterprises on a truly global scale. There is a general consensus that planning and operating practices of many businesses that conduct international activity leave a great deal to be desired. Typically, operations are tactically, as opposed to strategically, oriented.

Development of a coordinated international logistics logic is essential for two reasons. First, the potential of a global movement/storage system provides an opportunity for a higher order of trade-off and synergistic benefits than is attainable from logistical operations on a nation-by-nation basis. Second, the more limited concepts of internal or national logistical integration face a danger of becoming dysfunctional when a firm tries to transplant systems and working arrangements to multinational situations. Only a truly global system has the potential to guide the orderly, efficient flow of assets from worldwide material sourcing into a multinational manufacturing and assembly complex through a variety of domestic distribution systems to customers located throughout the world. Multinational logistics offers the potential for such an integrated logic. The problem is that such a logic does not currently exist.

What exists is a series of individual national logistics systems, each with its own legal and operating infrastructure and management style. From the variety of national applications, each multinational concern is faced with the challenge of developing a unique and coordinated logistical capability.

The Prerequisites for Global Success

What logistical prerequisites or qualifications must a firm possess to compete on a multinational basis? Beyond the fundamental economic and technological resource base, several managerial attributes appear desirable.

First, it is mandatory that the participating firm have an integrated logic of logistics that is commonly accepted by its corporate managers. Specifically, the organizational structure must have the capability to transfer knowledge and skills required to succeed on a global basis to all national operations. It must also be organized to provide both visibility and accountability to strategic movement and storage. Global operations require a substantial degree of central control if they are to be effective.

Second, multinational logistics requires a unique set of performance measurement standards. Primary concerns are the substantial fluctuations in national currencies, the varying inflation rates among both industrialized and developing countries, and the necessity to manufacture or assemble locally, which less developed countries frequently impose on foreign ownership. It is necessary for firms to develop procedures and methods to trade and barter products and commodities to realize units of payment having marketable worth.

Third, firms engaged in multinational manufacturing and distribution need to plan for greater inventory holdings than typically required to support national operations. The average United States manufacturing firm has between 25 and 30 percent of its assets committed to inventory. Retailing counterparts characteristically approach or exceed 50 percent. As a result of the simple realities of geography, lead times are longer in international logistics and variations in transit times are more frequent and greater in magnitude. As a result, multinational inventories are typically larger than required for domestic operations. Likewise, the range of potential uncertainties inherent in multinational arrangements requires increased safety stock to avoid supply discontinuities and demand variations.

Fourth, beyond inventory, it appears reasonable to estimate that the overall costs of logistics, as a percentage of revenue, will be greater for multinationals than for their domestic counterparts. This increase in logistical cost per unit results in part from the geographic realities of international operations, as well as from the substitution of logistical services for other activities. Longer transit times between continents and sometimes across continents can result in more storage. However, international sourcing provides an opportunity to postpone final assembly of finished products by performing this activity at strategic locations throughout the global operational arena. Thus, the key to efficient global operations is to make sourcing decisions based on the combined least cost of procurement, conversion, and distribution.

Fifth, the methods by which such logistical costs are accounted for may also be unique to multinational business arrangements. The typical practice in domestic logistics is to evaluate the burden of capital and direct expenditure to arrive at the lowest possible total cost of operation. In multinational situations, the desirability of investing capital in distribution-related assets other than inventories may be substantially reduced by economic and political uncertainties. In fact, the typical global enterprise may not seek an overall capital allocation process that supports profitable operations independent of national border lines. The risk of host countries seeking to control the enterprise's local operations in such a way as to serve their own national interests is always present. The logical conclusion is that global firms may place a much greater emphasis on expending rather than capitalizing the costs of logistical operations.

A sixth, and final, requirement of international logistics is the need to master a complex set of business relationships. This managerial concern is not unique to logistical operations, but it is pertinent. Without a doubt, the details involved in international movement are among the most extensive of any operational area. To the extent that an enterprise shifts from a primarily domestic to a multinational base, managerial control must be directed to a mass of documentation and detail that expands geometrically with the number of involved nations.

Issues and Questions

1 Some logistical managers are of the opinion that global logistics is only the collection of a group of national logistics requirements. Therefore, in reality international logistics as a separate discipline does not exist. Do you support or reject this position and why?

2 Why are larger inventories required to support global operations?

3 Why would a firm seek to expand the cost of logistical operations? Discuss the full ramifications of this concept.

4 What dangers exist in trading or bartering as a form of payment?

5 Discuss and illustrate the notion of higher level synergism that is possible when business is conducted on a global basis.

6 How could national operations cause a dysfunctional interface when extended to global business situations?

EPILOGUE

In the final analysis, the logistical management challenge is to rise above traditional incremental thinking in an effort to help capture and promulgate the need for businesses to reinvent what they are all about. What they should be about is very simple—servicing customers. While it is sometimes hard to comprehend why, the fact is that most business firms are in need of significant reengineering to reposition resources to most effectively and efficiently accomplish this basic goal. For a host of reasons, complexity dominates the modern enterprise. Reinvention of a business is all about simplification and standardization. It is all about getting back to basics. Logistics is basic.

The logistics manager of the future will be much more of a change agent and much less a technician. The challenge of change will be motivated by the need to synchronize the speed and flexibility of logistical competency into the process of creating customer value. Technology and technique will not be limiting factors. If no new technology is invented for a decade or more, we will still not have fully exploited what is currently available. The techniques being promoted as new ways to improve productivity are for the most part old and quite adequate to perform the work at hand. In fact, the latest concepts and buzzwords such as activity-based costing, time-based competition, ABC inventory analysis, continuous replenishment, quick response, segmentation, and so forth, are all relatively old ideas. What is new is that today's manager is using information technology to make them work.

Of course, the challenge to reinvent the enterprise is not the sole responsibility of logistics. But it *is* a responsibility of logistical managers to participate in the process, especially those who direct global operations, have stewardship for extensive capital and human resources, and facilitate the actual delivery of products and services to customers. The logistical executive of the future will not be able to neglect responsibility for contributing to and participating in the change management required to reinvent the enterprise.

To this end, all authors collect quotations and statements that they feel capture the meaning and intensity of their message. To the logistics manager of today and tomorrow who will face the challenges of change, we offer the following quotes as a source of compassion and inspiration:

Concerning Change: Logistics Is Not an Ordinary Occupation

Experience teaches that men are so much governed by what they are accustomed to see and practice, that the simplest and most obvious improvements in the most ordinary occupations are adapted with hesitation, reluctance and by slow graduations.

Alexander Hamilton, 1791

Concerning Organization: It Is a Matter of Perspective

We trained hard . . . but it seemed that every time we were beginning to form up into teams we would be reorganized. I was to learn later in life that we tend to meet any new situation by reorganizing; and a wonderful method it can be for creating the illusion of progress while producing confusion, inefficiency and demoralization.

Petronius, 200 B.C.

Concerning New Ideas: Every Dog Has Its Day

One may even dream of production so organized that no business concern or other economic unit would be obligated to carry stocks of raw materials or of finished goods . . . picture supplies of every sort flowing into factories just as machines are ready to use them; goods flowing out to freight cars and trucks just pulling up to shipping platforms; merchandise arriving at the dealer's shelves just when space was made available . . . under such conditions the burden of expense and risk borne by society because of the stocks necessary to the production process would be at a minimum.

Leverett S. Lyon, 1929

Concerning Appreciation: What Have You Done for Me Lately?

The Logistician

Logisticians are a sad and embittered race of men who are very much in demand in war, and who sink resentfully into obscurity in peace. They deal only in facts, but must work for men who merchant in theories. They emerge during war because war is very much a fact. They disappear in peace because peace is mostly theory. The people who merchant in theories, and who employ logisticians in war and ignore them in peace, are generals.

Generals are a happily blessed race who radiate confidence and power. They feed only on ambrosia and drink only nectar. In peace, they stride confidently and can invade a world simply by sweeping their hands grandly over a map, pointing their fingers decisively up terrain corridors, and blocking defiles and obstacles with the sides of their hands. In war, they must stride more slowly because each general has a logistician riding on his back and he knows that, at any moment, the logistician may lean forward and whisper: ''No, you can't do that.'' Generals fear logisticians in war and, in peace, generals try to forget logisticians.

Romping along beside generals are strategists and tacticians. Logisticians despise strategists and tacticians. Strategists and tacticians do not know about logisticians until they grow up to be generals—which they usually do.

Sometimes a logistician becomes a general. If he does, he must associate with generals whom he hates; he has a retinue of strategists and tacticians whom he despises; and, on his back, is a logistician whom he fears. This is why logisticians who become generals always have ulcers and cannot eat their ambrosia.   *Author and date unknown*

CASES

CASE G: Woodson Chemical Company

From the perspective of Melinda Sanders, the problems of Woodson Chemical Company (WCC) were straightforward and easily identifiable. Solutions, however, appeared to be far more difficult and complex. Sanders had just turned twenty-nine years old and was in her sixth year of employment with WCC. After graduating from a top university in the western United States with an M.B.A. degree in marketing, she had steadily progressed through a series of positions in marketing, sales, and distribution operations. Her current title is lead distribution planner in the chemical and performance products division of WCC's North American operations.

The most recent WCC North American customer service report revealed that "our customers continually give the company average to poor marks in customer service performance. In particular, they express extreme dissatisfaction with the order information process." Sanders was of the opinion that the more WCC sales and distribution systems were expanded, the more management and communication bottlenecks seemed to be created. She was also well aware that the issue of order information status was problematic throughout all of WCC's North American operations. Each division had been hard at work over the past eighteen months developing and instituting a variety of software packages aimed at improving their service performance. During a recent meeting with Barry McDonald, director of customer service at the chemical and performance products division, Sanders had been given a copy of a report regarding projected directions and importance ratings of customer service requirements in the chemical industry. The report stated:

> . . . customers specifically desire instantaneous access to real-time order information status. This information accessibility is necessary throughout the supply chain—from

Robb Frankel prepared this case for class discussion. Actual facts have been altered to maintain confidentiality and to provide an enhanced business situation.

the customer's initial inquiry to production status, shipment loading, and arrival at the final destination. A critical goal is to be able to both commit and monitor inventory from the point in time an order is placed. While integrated logistics is a major goal for many chemical companies, efforts are frequently being hindered by inadequate information systems and organizational structure design.

COMPANY BACKGROUND

WCC was founded in 1899 by Alexander Woodson. The company originally was located in southeast Texas; in the early 1960s the corporate headquarters was moved to St. Louis to capitalize on the city's central geographic location. Approximately one-third of WCC's business is conducted overseas. Most arrangements are wholly owned subsidiaries; there are few industrialized countries in the world where WCC does not have some manufacturing or sales presence. WCC North America, a wholly owned subsidiary of Woodson Chemical Company, is the sixth largest chemical firm in North America and produces a diversified range of products used as raw materials for manufacturing in the food, personal care, pharmaceuticals, pulp and paper, and utility industries.

The company operates four product groups that are broken down into three divisions (see Table 1). Division 1 is composed of chemical and performance products, which are mainly used as raw materials in the manufacture and/or processing of consumer products. Division 2 contains two product groups: plastic products, and hydrocarbons and energy. Plastic products are utilized in numerous markets such as packaging, automotive, electrical appliances, building and construction, housewares, recreation, furniture, flooring, and health care. Hydrocarbons and energy are concerned with the purchase of fuels and petroleum-based materials as well as the production of power and steam used to manufacture WCC's plastics, chemicals, and metals. Division 3

TABLE 1   WCC SALES 1988–1992 ($000,000)

Division	1988	1989	1990	1991	1992
1 Chemical and performance products	3,630	3,785	3,562	3,165	3,130
2 Plastic products	4,857	4,896	5,174	4,775	4,701
Hydrocarbons and energy	1,051	1,243	1,547	1,353	1,214
3 Consumer specialties: medical/ health, agricultural, consumer products	2,120	2,387	3,537	3,838	4,184
Total	11,658	12,311	13,820	13,131	13,229

consists of consumer specialties, which serve the food care, home care, and personal products markets.

In terms of functional support, each division maintains its own marketing, manufacturing, logistics, and administrative departments. Currently, divisional information processing responsibilities for customer service, transportation, and warehousing are provided by the logistics group. Information processing responsibility for finance and accounting is provided by the administration group. Figure 1 presents the organizational structure for WCC's North American operations.

Across the four product groups, performance has varied considerably over recent years. Although chemical and performance products sales have been declin-

ing or flat, increased volume and profit improvement are projected as a result of growth opportunities. In division 2, plastic products has exhibited reduced sales; although moderate growth is attainable, prices are projected to remain under pressure because of a weak global economy and considerable industry oversupply. Hydrocarbons and energy sales have declined significantly in the past three years; although feedstock and energy purchase costs have been reduced, lower sales have more than offset procurement savings. Industry overcapacity remains a severe problem; additional development in the industries of Korea and China will only exacerbate the situation. Consumer specialties continues to exhibit very strong sales gains, particularly in medical and health and consumer product categories. Agricultural sales are relatively unchanged. Steady growth for consumer specialties is projected to continue, although perhaps not at the rapid rate of the past five years.

The major cost and expense areas of distribution and marketing (see Table 2) are significant concerns of WCC management. The company has made considerable progress in reducing the cost of purchased raw material inputs, but other category expenses are increasing at a rate in excess of sales.

INDUSTRY BACKGROUND

Chemical manufacturing has historically been a very cyclic industry; recessions and periods of slow economic growth typically depress sales for several years at a time. As economies begin to rebound, manufacturing picks up and chemical production often leads the United States economy into a recovery period.

The chemical industry's attempts to alter its strategic

FIGURE 1   Woodson Chemical Company, North American operations organizational structure.

TABLE 2 SELECTED WCC OPERATING COSTS AND EXPENSES 1988–1992 ($000,000)

Division	1988	1989	1990	1991	1992
1 Costs of goods sold	6,864	7,335	9,125	8,863	8,893
2 Research and development	540	611	795	811	902
3 Promotion and advertising	291	346	447	505	557
4 Selling and administrative	1,138	1,231	1,459	1,527	1,630
Total	8,833	9,523	11,826	11,706	11,982

planning with regard to markets and strategy are changing. The expansion of a global economy and leading-edge chemical technology have dramatically altered the manner in which the chemical industry operates today. In the past, a large, fully integrated chemical company with control of raw materials, economies of scale, and modern plants possessed significant cost advantages that could eliminate marginally efficient chemical producers throughout the world. Today, such a strategy is easily negated. The availability of cutting-edge chemical technology that goes into building premier chemical plants can make a low-cost producer out of most any company that can structure an arrangement for a constant supply of chemical feedstock from an oil-producing country. Contemporary competitive advantage is typically derived from a focused market position, good raw materials supply without the heavy investment required in a completely vertically integrated structure, and a lean and efficient organization. Industry leaders must maintain efficient resource and organizational structure while they leverage their technological expertise across as many chemical applications as possible. In addition, many chemical manufacturers are diversifying into specialty chemicals in an attempt to balance the cyclic nature of their earnings.

Faced with mounting pressure to become increasingly globalized, especially during difficult economic conditions, chemical industry information systems leaders are scrambling to implement more cost-efficient and effective strategies to track and share business information. Angela Lowrey, director of WCC's North American information resources planning, says that "better logistics information across business divisions is integral to instituting a strategic business plan. With current spending on computer information systems accounting for approximately 2 percent of corporate revenues, [business] information is a premium commodity and a potential strategic asset that many firms in our industry are just beginning to recognize."

The determination of where to focus chemical operations is also becoming increasingly complex as the geographic nature of the industry changes economically. Uncertainty in Eastern Europe, rapid growth in the Pacific Rim, and potential markets in Latin America and the Caribbean have upset the traditional patterns of global chemical manufacturing. Very high research and development costs are necessary in order to maintain a steady stream of new high-margin products. Environmental problems and liability issues are a significant concern for the chemical manufacturing industry. Although compliance with increasingly stringent emission controls has improved the relationships between chemical manufacturers, government, and public interest groups, the transportation and handling of hazardous materials remains a high-profile issue, particularly in North America and Western Europe.

WCC's NORTH AMERICAN DISTRIBUTION NETWORK

WCC North America produces and sells more than 1,500 products in many different formulations, packaging containers, and labeling arrangements. The products are manufactured at one or more of the 22 plants located in the United States; they are distributed through 5 WCC distribution centers to field warehouses and then to 325 stocking points (cooperatives and dealers). Table 3 lists the WCC manufacturing plants and distribution centers located in North America.

Chemical manufacturing does not contain significant levels of WIP (work-in-process) inventories, and managing them is typically not difficult. However, managing finished goods inventories is a considerable problem. Short customer lead times, high customer service levels, large manufacturing and distribution replenishment quantities, and long manufacturing and distribution lead times require that many products be in inventory when customer orders are received. The size and complexity of the WCC distribution network make distribution management complicated and difficult.

According to Melinda Sanders, WCC's organizational structure does not match up well to the compa-

TABLE 3 WCC NORTH AMERICA DISTRIBUTION NETWORK

Manufacturing plants	
Schaumburg, Ill.	Gary, Ind.
Los Angeles, Calif.	Omaha, Nebr.
Harrisburg, Pa.	Spokane, Wash.
Memphis, Tenn.	Denver, Colo.
New Orleans, La.	Little Rock, Ark.
Shreveport, La.	Raleigh-Durham, N.C.
St. Louis, Mo.	Morristown, N.J.
Houston, Tex.	Toledo, Ohio
Lubbock, Tex.	Wilmington, Del.
Tulsa, Okla.	Jacksonville, Fla.
Montgomery, Ala.	Billings, Mont.

Field warehouses (as necessary). Primarily public facilities

Distribution centers	
Reno, Nev.	Charlotte, N.C.
Louisville, Ky.	Omaha, Nebr.
Shreveport, La.	

Dealers and cooperatives. Contractual throughout North America

ny's need for supply chain management. Recently, however, WCC has begun to implement an integrated logistics system to coordinate planning, purchasing, manufacturing, marketing, and distribution functions. Increased attention has been directed to the problems of providing manufacturing with the necessary information to determine the level of individual SKU production (via MRP) as well as how much and where to deploy products (via DRP). Improved communication between marketing, manufacturing, and distribution has led to better forecasts of customer demand.

However, although each division of WCC is beginning to operate in a more integrated manner, each continues to maintain separate responsibility for customer orders and information status. Each division also designs, plans, and executes its manufacturing, warehousing, picking, and loading activities. The majority of warehouses utilized are public facilities. Transportation is provided by common and contract carriage and railroad. A significant portion of WCC's product moves by rail; in fact, WCC owns and operates a sizable private railcar fleet because of the specialized nature of its products. The link between transportation and customer service is vital. "Logistics at WCC's North American

chemical and performance products division is a competitive tool," says Michael Davidson, logistics manager. "I make sure that we always have more than enough carriers on our inbound and outbound traffic lanes to keep product moving throughout our system."

Traditionally, a general level of attention to customer service was acceptable; but as WCC restructured its divisional operations by product grouping and, in particular, diversified into specialty chemicals, the requirements across divisions became very differentiated. The complexity of customer service is additionally complicated because each division serves a considerable number of common customers, many of whom are high-volume, key accounts. WCC North America's decentralized divisional structure has historically allowed each division to provide tailored, high-quality customer service to meet the differentiated and demanding requirements of WCC customers. The ability to tailor such services is considered a competitive strength at WCC. Sales, marketing, and cost control efforts are becoming increasingly customer-responsive: the level of focus is now not only division-specific but individual customer account–specific. In particular, the consumer specialties division serves a highly time sensitive market that includes many powerful, large retailers and mass merchandisers.

Melinda Sanders and her staff have a meeting scheduled tomorrow morning with Douglas Liddell, vice president of WCC's corporate information systems group, to discuss the direction of WCC North American's chemical and performance products division. Sanders strongly believes that any investment in information systems should directly support a specific business strategy. The question is, What investments should be made, and what exactly should WCC's strategy be?

QUESTIONS

1 What is (are) the critical issue(s) confronting WCC North America?

2 What changes, if any, should be initiated to address the critical issue(s)?

3 Identify the risks and benefits of your proposed changes from the perspective of WCC North America corporate management, WCC North America line distribution management, and WCC North America customers.

4 What would be the impact on WCC North America operations if the proposed changes were successfully implemented?

5 What changes, if any, would you recommend in WCC North America's information processing arrangements?

6 Is Melinda Sanders in a position to properly understand North America's problems? Why or why not?

7 Do you think WCC North America's current situation is applicable across its global operations? How, if at all, does it change the nature of the problem?

CASE H: Performance Control

Wendell Worthmann, manager of logistics cost analysis for Happy Chips, Inc., was faced with a difficult task. Harold L. Carter, the new director of logistics, had circulated a letter from Happy Chips' only mass merchandise customer, Buy 4 Less, complaining of poor operating performance. Among the problems cited by Buy 4 Less were (1) frequent stockouts, (2) poor customer service responsiveness, and (3) high prices for Happy Chips' products. The letter suggested that if Happy Chips was to remain a supplier to Buy 4 Less, it would need to eliminate stockouts by (1) providing direct store delivery four times a week (instead of three), (2) installing an automated order inquiry system to increase customer service responsiveness (at a cost of $10,000), and (3) decreasing product prices by 5 percent. While the previous director of logistics would most certainly have begun implementing the suggested changes, Harold Carter was different. He requested that Wendell prepare a detailed analysis of Happy Chips' profitability by segment. He also asked that it be prepared on a spreadsheet to permit some basic analysis. This was something that Wendell had never previously attempted, and it was needed first thing in the morning.

COMPANY BACKGROUND

Happy Chips, Inc., is the fifth largest potato chip manufacturer in the metropolitan Detroit market. The company was founded in 1922 and, following an unsuccessful attempt at national expansion, has remained primarily a local operation. The firm currently manufactures and distributes one variety of potato chips to three different types of retail accounts: grocery, drug, and mass merchandise. The largest percentage of business is concentrated in the grocery segment, with 36 retail customer locations accounting for 40,000 annual unit sales and more than 50 percent of annual revenue.

David J. Frayer prepared this case for class discussion. Actual facts have been altered to maintain confidentiality and to provide an enhanced business situation.

The drug segment consists of 39 customer locations accounting for 18,000 annual unit sales and more than 27 percent of annual revenue. In the mass merchandise segment, Happy Chips has one customer with 3 locations, which accounts for 22,000 annual unit sales and almost 22 percent of annual revenue. All distribution is store-direct, with delivery drivers handling returns of outdated material and all shelf placement and merchandising.

Recently, Happy Chips has actively sought growth in the mass merchandise segment because of the perceived profit potential. However, while the company is acutely aware of overall business profitability, there has never been an analysis on a customer segment basis.

PERFORMANCE STATISTICS

Wendell recently attended a seminar at a major midwestern university concerning activity-based costing. He was anxious to apply the techniques he had learned at the seminar to the current situation, but was unsure exactly how to proceed. He did not understand the relationship between activity-based costing and segment profitability analysis, but he knew that the first step in both is to identify relevant costs. Wendell obtained a copy of Happy Chips' most recent income statement (Table 1). He also knew specific information concerning logistics costs by segment (Table 2).

All deliveries were store-direct with two per week to grocery stores, one per week to drugstores, and three per week to mass merchandisers. In order to obtain feedback concerning store sales, Happy Chips purchased scanner data from grocery and mass merchandise stores at an aggregate annual cost of $1,000 per segment. The drugstore segment required use of handheld scanners by delivery personnel to track sales. The cost of delivery to each store was dependent on the type of vehicle used. Standard route trucks were used for drugstores and grocery stores, while extended vehicles were used to accommodate the volume of mass merchandisers.

TABLE 1   INCOME STATEMENT

Income	
Net sales	$150,400.00
Interest and other income	3,215.00
	$153,615.00
Costs and expenses	
Cost of goods sold	84,000.00
Other manufacturing expense	5,660.00
Marketing, sales, and other expenses	52,151.20
Interest expense	2,473.00
	$144,284.20
Earnings before income taxes	9,330.80
Income taxes	4,198.86
Net earnings	$5,131.94

Trade prices for each unit were different for grocery ($1.90), drug ($2.30), and mass merchandise ($1.50) customers. Wendell was also aware that Buy 4 Less required Happy Chips to cover the suggested retail price with a sticker bearing its reduced price. The machinery required to apply these labels had an annual rental cost of $5,000. Labor and materials cost an additional $0.03 per unit.

CONCLUSION

As Wendell sat in his office compiling information to complete the segment profitability analysis, he received several unsolicited offers for assistance. Bill Smith, manager of marketing, urged him not to bother with the analysis: "Buy 4 Less is clearly our most important customer. We should immediately implement the suggested changes."

Steve Brown, director of manufacturing, disagreed. He felt that the additional cost required to meet Buy 4 Less' requirements was too high: "We should let Buy 4 Less know what we really think about its special requirements. Stickers, of all things! What business do they think we are in?"

The sales force had a different opinion. Jake Williams felt that the grocery segment was the most

TABLE 2   ANNUAL LOGISTICS COSTS BY SEGMENT

Cost category/ segment	Grocery	Drug	Mass merchandise
Stocking cost ($/delivery)	$1.80	$1.20	$2.80
Information cost (annual)	$1,000.00	$8,000.00	$1,000.00
Delivery cost ($/delivery)	$5.00	$5.00	$6.00

important: "Just look at that volume! How could they be anything but our best customers."

The broad interest generated by this assignment worried Wendell. Would he have to justify his recommendations to everyone in the company? Wendell quietly closed his office door.

On the basis of the available information and his own knowledge of activity-based costing systems, Wendell Worthmann needed to complete a segment profitability analysis and associated spreadsheet before his meeting with Harold in the morning. With all these interruptions, it was going to be a long night.

QUESTIONS

1 What is the difference between activity-based costing and segment profitability analysis? How would you counter the arguments by other managers concerning the most attractive segments? Using the relevant costs provided above, determine the profitability for each of Happy Chips' business segments.

2 On the basis of your analysis, should Happy Chips consider the changes desired by Buy 4 Less? Why or why not?

3 Should Happy Chips eliminate any business segments? Why or why not?

4 If the price to mass merchandise stores were to increase by 20 percent, would that change your answer to the previous question?

5 Are there factors other than segment profitability that should be considered? If so, what are they?

CASE I: Managing Change in Wholesaling: The Case of Wilmont Drug Company

As Charlie Smith, vice president of logistics at Wilmont Drug Company, headed down the corridor toward the conference room, he once again reviewed events of the past several months. After a decade of unprecedented sales growth, Wilmont Drug, a wholesaler, had experienced its fifth consecutive quarterly loss in March 1995. While revenue continued to grow, albeit at a much slower rate than the previous decade, expenses had outpaced sales. The company's approach to high-service wholesaling, which had been the cornerstone of its national growth strategy, had fallen into disfavor with some outspoken shareholders.

Founder and former president Robert H. Wilmont, Sr., advocated a strategy of low-price, no-frills service supported by a drastic cost reduction initiative. As the company's primary shareholder, he was an influential individual whose support would be critical to any revitalization plan. John W. Brown, the current president of Wilmont Drug Company, had successfully established leadership at his previous employer in the computer industry by implementing a high-service strategy similar to the one in place at Wilmont Drug. He recommended that the company "stay the course," because revenue growth would eventually return to previous levels and eliminate the current losses.

Charlie Smith was a realist. He knew that strategic change was necessary but disagreed with the drastic shift advocated by the company's founder. A high-service wholesaling strategy had served the company well during its growth period, but ever increasing customer demands made high service on a universal basis very costly. While studying for his M.B.A. degree in logistics at a major midwestern university, Charlie was introduced to the concepts of segmentation and selective determination of service levels. Over the summer, he had developed a four-stage plan for reorienting the company on the basis of these concepts. He now had to convince Bob Wilmont, John Brown, and the senior management team assembled in the conference room that his plan could work if given the chance.

COMPANY BACKGROUND

Wilmont Drug Company, the second largest wholesaler of drugs and ethical pharmaceuticals in the United

David J. Frayer prepared this case for class discussion. Actual facts have been altered to maintain confidentiality and to provide an enhanced business situation.

States, was founded by Robert H. Wilmont, Sr., in 1948. At first, the company prospered as a small regional wholesaler serving drugstores and hospitals in the northeastern United States. In the ensuing decades, Wilmont Drug grew primarily by acquisition. By 1970, the company had acquired three additional warehouses and reached $10 million in sales. By 1978, sales exceeded $250 million and coverage extended as far west as Ohio. In spite of a general decline in wholesaling across the United States, Wilmont Drug continued to expand. The company achieved national distribution in 1985 with the purchase of Jones Drug Company, then the seventh largest drug wholesaler in the United States.

Wilmont Drug was able to offer consistent and dependable overnight delivery service, despite significant operational differences between the networks of the acquired companies. As the firm grew, the development of customer-specific service offerings by geographic market was viewed as a unique strength. Creative solutions to customer requirements rapidly expanded the service base and made Wilmont Drug the preferred supplier for many national chains. However, with this uniqueness came difficulties. When revenue growth began to decline in the mid-1990s, the inefficiency of the extensive service offerings combined with the lack of operational consistency led to consecutive quarterly losses.

WHOLESALING

The problems experienced by Wilmont Drug Company were not unique to the drug industry. Because of changes brought about by transportation deregulation and improved technology, wholesalers across the United States were forced to reexamine traditional supply chain roles. The basic cost/service relationship changed in favor of companies with both efficient and effective customer service strategies. The notion of high-performance wholesaling, which focuses on clear delineation of customer needs and provision of differentiated service, emerged as a logical strategic alternative.

Charlie Smith recognized this shift in wholesaling and chose to make it the focus of his revitalization plan. He believed that by developing and implementing a high-performance wholesaling strategy before the competition, Wilmont Drug would be able to (1) define the competitive structure of the drug industry and (2) lock in the most attractive customers.

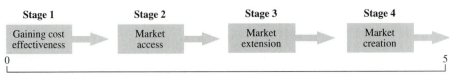

Change management model.

REVITALIZATION PLAN/CHANGE MANAGEMENT MODEL

With these goals in mind, Charlie drafted the following memorandum to John W. Brown, president of Wilmont Drug Company, detailing his proposed revitalization plan and associated change management model:

MEMORANDUM

Date: September 1, 1995

To: John Brown

From: Charlie Smith

Re: Change Management Model to Revitalize Wilmont Drug Company

The following model and discussion detail a plan to propel Wilmont Drug Company to the forefront of the wholesale drug industry. I hope you will give this plan your most serious consideration and let me know when you would like to discuss its potential implementation.

The plan has an expected time span of five years. While some aspects of implementation can be completed simultaneously, the first two stages must be completed prior to launching the market extension and creation phases of development. See the accompanying diagram.

Cost-Effectiveness

During the cost-effectiveness stage, the objective is to achieve operational control necessary to support segmentation strategies. It is essential that basic services be provided at a consistently high level of performance and in a cost-effective manner. To gain cost-effectiveness requires that supplier, product, and facility rationalization be completed. Typical key services used by all areas are centralized to achieve economies of scale and standardization of business processes. Such standardization is necessary to gain the operational competence and credibility required to move forward.

Market Access

This aspect of implementation consists primarily of customer segmentation. Selected customers are identified and operations are focused to position Wilmont Drug as the preferred supplier to those customers targeted as high-potential buyers. Emphasis in this stage of implementation is on high-quality basic service to selected customers. The segmentation plan should be as simple as possible.

Market Extension

Market extension involves programs to increase business penetration to selected customers. It consists of continuous improvement of basic service toward zero defect performance and the introduction of value-added services to solidify and expand business relationships with top customers. Value-added innovations include extensive use of bar coding, computer linkages, vendor managed inventories, business consulting, and other programs designed to improve customer operating efficiency and increase their overall market presence. Such value-added services can be offered only to customers that are willing to commit to extended business arrangements.

Market Creation

The final stage of strategic implementation consists of carrying out programs to expand the profitability and competitiveness of top customers and to assist them in developing business growth strategies. To gain share in a low-growth market, a wholesaler must facilitate growth in customer market share. Implementation of joint systems that leverage the combined resources of the wholesaler and selected customers is a key consideration.

The foundation of the strategic change management model proposed by Charlie Smith depends on full implementation of stage 1 (gaining cost-effectiveness) and stage 2 (market access). For the most part, these stages require managerial brute force implementation and continuous reinforcement of initiatives designed to standardize operating processes and service offerings. By achieving the first two stages of the model, a business is prepared to exploit a leadership position. Success is highly unlikely in stage 3 unless the foundation of the first two stages is in place. Stage 3 (market extension) and stage 4 (market creation) represent increased penetration of target customer relationships. Unlike the first two stages, these stages are customer-specific. Therefore, associated initiatives can be implemented simultaneously, rather than sequentially. Once a customer is firmly established in the stage 3/4 category, significant improvements can be projected in sales penetration, quality of transactions, and deployment of assets.

After reviewing the memorandum, John Brown was skeptical of the plan. He had never personally been involved in such an initiative. Nevertheless, he recommended that Charlie present the revitalization plan and associated change management model to the entire senior management team.

CONCLUSION

Charlie sincerely believed that improving the firm's performance would take considerable time and effort on the part of both senior and middle management. He also believed that the vast majority of managers had neither the training nor the work experience to implement such initiatives. He expected strong resistance from the senior management team. While he had prepared responses to all anticipated questions, an implementation plan detailing specific actions remained to be developed.

Charlie Smith paused outside the conference room. He recognized that the revitalization plan and change management model he was about to propose would significantly alter the destiny of Wilmont Drug Company. If senior management agrees with his plan, the question remains whether middle management will accept the challenge of implementing change of this magnitude. Charlie took a deep breath and entered the conference room.

QUESTIONS

1 Discuss internal and external influences that affected Wilmont Drug's need to reorient the company.
2 Critically evaluate the revitalization plan and change management model proposed by Charlie Smith. Can you suggest any changes?
3 Would your evaluation change if Wilmont Drug Company had significant international business operations? Why or why not?
4 Using the model provided or your own change management model, develop a detailed implementation plan for reorienting the company.

AUTHOR INDEX

Ackerman, Kenneth, B., 392, 403, 405
Acdonberger, Richard J., 490
Agerwal, Yogesh K., 577
Alderson, Wroe, 97, 471, 479
Allen, Mary K., 208, 305, 306
Andel, Thomas, 72, 556
Anderson, James C., 100
Angello, W. J., 361
Armstrong, J. Scott, 232
Arora, S., 562
Austin, Nancy, 83

Bacon, Kenneth H., 150
Baker, Michael J., 90
Baker, Stephen, 131
Ballou, Ronald H., 14, 566, 568, 575, 577
Bardi, Edward J., 316
Barks, Joseph, V., 157
Beatenbough, W. Doyle, 348
Beckman, Theodore N., 13
Bender, Paul S., 554
Benedetto, Richard F., 615
Bergoffen, Gene S., 321
Blattberg, R. C., 61
Bomgardner, Paul, 362
Bonney, Joseph, 635
Borsodi, Ralph, 13,
Bott, Kevin, 575, 577

Bowersox, Donald J., 13, 17, 19, 71, 79, 92, 139, 467, 471, 478, 597, 605, 609, 671, 678
Bresticker, Robert B., 621
Brookman, Faye, 215
Brown, Drusilla K., 137
Bryer, Ralph F., 479
Bryne, John A., 608, 616
Bucklin, Louis P., 100, 471, 479
Buclos, L., 573
Burt, David N., 100
Byrne, John A., 625
Byrne, Patrick, 112, 534

Cabocel, Eric, 152, 153
Camp, Robert C., 461
Campbell, Bernard, 321
Carter, Jimmy, 350, 354
Carey, John, 39
Cavinato, Joseph L., 62, 316, 328, 367
Cawthorne, David M., 357
Champy, James, 458
Cizneros, Lee, 348
Clark, Fred E., 13, 95
Clark, Eugene, 95
Clinton, Steve, 169, 177
Clinton, William J., 18
Closs, David J., 131, 149, 282, 478
Cohen, M., 562

Cohodes, Marilyn, J., 143
Coleman, Henry J., 608
Coleman, James E., 100
Conway, Betty, 84
Cooke, James Aaron, 155, 352, 661
Cooper, James, 152, 153
Cooper, Martha C., 67, 100
Cooper, M. Bixby, 92, 467, 471, 478
Cooper, Robin, 12
Copacino, William C., 102, 674, 675
Cornelius, Tom, 348
Cornwell, David A., 344
Cox, Reavis, 479
Coykendall, Deborah S., 100
Coyle, John J., 316
Culliton, James W., 10, 643

Daugherty, Patricia J., 71, 79, 605, 609, 678
Davidow, William H., 608
Davis, Frank W., 656
Davis, Mackenzie L., 344
Davenport, Thomas H., 458
Dawson, Leslie M., 13
Delany, Robert V., 4, 5, 112, 245
Demming, W. Edwards, 17
Dixon, Jim, 348
Doyle, Michael F., 100

Droge, Cornelia L., 71, 79, 605, 609, 678
Drucker, Peter, 104, 619, 621, 626
Drury, D. H., 131
Duncan, Robert M., 131

El-Ansary, Adel I., 479
Ellram, Lisa M., 100
Emmelhainz, Margaret A., 205
Evans, Phillip, 14, 210

Farris, Martin T., 316
Feigenbaum, Armand V., 319
Fisk, George, 479
Ford, Robert C., 615
Forrester, Jay W., 230, 459
Foster, Thomas A., 344
Frankel, Robb, 106, 581, 587, 627
Franzblau, B. A., 348
Frayer, David J., 106, 478, 627
Fuller, Joseph B., 79
Furey, Timothy R., 462

Garvin, David A., 621
Gelderman, Carol, 88, 89
Geoffrion, Arthur M., 554, 563
Germain, Richard N., 605, 609
Giffin, David, 575

Gilroy, Roger, 357
Goff, James W., 442
Gold, Steven, 407
Gonillart, Francis J., 526
Gordon, Geoffrey, 459
Govindarajan, Vijay, 644
Graff, Stan, 207
Graves, G. W., 554, 563, 565
Greenhut, Melvin L., 497, 501
Grether, E. T., 479
Groff, James E., 150
Grosse, Robert, 148
Guigley, Hugh, 156

Hage, Jerald, 608
Hall, Robert W., 42
Hamel, Gary, 108
Hammer, Michael, 458
Hanley, L. H., 346
Hanson, Jeffrey R., 610
Hardin, Joe, 62
Harrington, Lisa H., 111
Hart, Christopher W. L., 68
Harter, Gregory, B., 218
Hayes, Robert H., 654
Heckert, J. Brooks, 11
Heide, Jan B., 100
Helferich, Omar K., 208, 305, 306
Hendrick, Thomas, 100
Herndon, Booton, 89
Heskett, James L., 11, 14, 68, 459
Hines, Peter, 100
Hof, Robert D., 21
Hoffman, Stanley, 344, 362
Hoffman, Wayne M., 348
Hoover, Edgar M., 497, 499
House, Robert G., 561, 569
Huey, John, 62
Hunt, Shelby D., 100

Idelson, Holly, 313
Introna, Lucas D., 40
Isard, Walter, 497

Jackson, George C., 490
Jaime, Kenneth D., 569
Jedd, Marcia, 155
Jenkins, M. L., 402
John, George, 100
Johnson, James, 323
Johnson, Thomas, 644
Johnston, Russell, 17
Juran, Joseph M., 17

Kamesan, 562
Kaminski, Peter F., 62
Kanter, Rosabeth Moss, 17, 107

Kaplan, Robert S., 12, 644
Karrenbauer, Jeffrey J., 554, 561, 565
Katzenbach, Jon, 619, 620
Kenderdine, James M., 100
Kerr, Andrew, 16
Kiechel, Walter III, 608
Kleindorfer, P., 562
Kleit, Andrew N., 354
Knill, Bernie, 424
Krackhardt, David, 610
Kujawa, Duane, 148
Kumer, S., 562
Kupperman, Robert H., 459

LaLonde, Bernard J., 13, 66, 67, 220, 604
Lambert, Douglas M., 247, 255
Langley, C. John, 328, 367
Lapin, Lawrence L., 226
Larson, Andren, 100
Lee, H., 562
Lele, Milind, 62
Levitt, Theodore, 61, 62, 355
Lewis, Howard T., 10, 643
Lewis, Peter, 207
Lewis, Ronald L., 644
Longman, Donald R., 11
Losch, August, 497
Lusch, Robert D., 100, 102

Mabrouk, K., 573
McCray, John P., 150
Machalba, Daniel, 319
MacDonald, Mitchell E., 358, 466
McWilliams, Gary, 517
Maffei, Richard, B., 459
Magee, John F., 459
Makridakis, Spyros, 232
Mallen, Bruce, 106
Mallory, Maria, 470
Malone, Michael S., 608
Malone, Thomas W., 608
Manrodt, Karl B., 656
Markham, William J., 534
Martin, Andre J., 102
Masters, James M., 566, 568, 572, 604
Melamed, Leo, 133
Mele, Jim, 499
Meyer, Christopher, 609, 620, 626
Miles, Raymond E., 608
Miller, Karen L., 59
Miller, T., 565
Milner, Robert B., 11
Molpus, C. Manly, 108

Moore, Cassandra C., 356, 357
Moore, Thomas, 44, 352
Monden, Yasukiro, 491
Morgan, Robert M., 100
Muller, E. J., 112, 413
Muroff, Cindy, 576
Murphy, Rupert L., 348

Narus, James A., 100
Newman, Harry J., 348
Noordewier, Thomas G., 67
Norman, James R., 206
Norman, Richard, 84
Northrup, William D., 554
Novack, Robert A., 360

Oaks, Susan L., 131
O'Conor, James, 79
O'Guin, Michael C., 644
Ohmae, Kenichi, 17, 130, 132, 133, 140
Ohta, Hiroshi, 501
O'Laughlin, Kevin A., 152, 153
Optner, Stanford L., 459
Ostroff, Frank, 606

Parker, Donald D., 459
Parker, John G., 135
Perry, James H., 471
Peters, John, 615
Peters, Thomas J., 89
Peterson, Rein, 273
Pierson, Thomas R., 91
Pisano, Gary P., 654
Plowman, E. Grosvenor, 348
Power, Christopher, 64
Power, David, 609, 626
Prahalad, C. K., 100

Quigley, Hugh, 315

Ramirez, Rafael, 84
Randolph, Alan W., 615
Rankin, Richard L., 461
Rawlinson, Richard, 79
Ray, Garry, 207
Reagan, Ronald, 18
Rhilinger, Michele, 575
Richardson, Helen L., 72, 154
Richmond, Bruce, 210
Rinehart, Lloyd M., 478
Rink, David R., 62
Robicheaux, Robert A., 100
Robins, Gary, 205
Rockart, John F., 608
Rogers, Dale S., 71, 79, 605, 609, 678
Romeo, Jean B., 44

Root, Ed, 82, 113
Ruriani, Deborah, 53

Sampson, Roy J., 316
Santa-Clara, J., 573
Saplukus, Agis, 77
Sasser, W. Earl, Jr., 68
Sawhney, Kirti, 100
Schaaf, Dick, 83
Schiff, Michael, 11, 644
Schiller, Bacharg, 121
Schlesinger, Leonard A., 83
Schmitz, Judith M., 106, 172, 585, 627
Schumpeter, Joseph A., 626
Sen, S. K., 61
Sengupta, Sanjit, 100
Shank, John K., 644
Shannon, Robert E., 565
Shapiro, Jeremy F., 554, 579
Shapiro, Roy D., 14
Shapiro, Stanley J., 479
Sharlach, Jeffrey, R., 157
Sharman, Graham, 14
Sharp, Jeffrey M., 360
Shaw, Arch W., 43
Shellenberger, Sue, 623
Sherman, Stratford, 622
Shonberger, Richard J., 490
Shrock, David L., 316
Shulman, Lawrence E., 14, 210
Shycon, Harvey N., 459
Silver, Edward A., 273
Singhal, V., 579
Smale, John, 62
Smith, Bernard T., 232
Smith, Douglas K., 606, 619
Smith, Harvey A., 459
Smith, Wendell R., 61
Snow, Charles C., 608
Sonnenberg, Frank K., 100
Spekman, Robert E., 100
Speed, J. B., 348
Stalk, George, 14, 210, 478
Stasch, Stanley F., 459
Steele, Jack D., 10, 643
Stenger, Alan J., 16
Stern, Gabriella, 99
Stern, Louis W., 479
Stern, Robert M., 137
Stevens, Larry, 27
Stewart, Thomas A., 606, 607, 616
Stigler, George E., 96, 650
Stock, James R., 19, 40, 43
Stolle, John F., 597
Strah, Thomas A., 356, 357
Strom, Stephanie, 474
Sturdivant, Frederick D., 526

Swain, James J., 535, 573
Sweeney, Daniel J., 363

Taff, Charles A., 316
Taylor, John C., 149
Tekerian, A., 562
Tellis, Gerald J., 663
Therrien, Lois, 131
Thuermer, Karen E., 135
Tinghitella, Stephen, 348
Tousley, Rayburn D., 95
Treece, James B., 19, 622
Trezise, Philip H., 137

Trunick, Perry A., 72
Tyworth, John E., 328, 367

Vail, Bruce, 135
Vaile, Roland, 479
Van Der Hoop, Hans, 152
Venkatesan, Ravi, 654
von Thünen, Joachim, 497
Voorhees, Mark, 112

Wagner, S. N., 579
Walton, Mary, 17
Walton, Sam, 62

Wantuck, K. A., 42
Wardlow, Daniel L., 71, 79,
    605, 678
Waterman, Robert H., Jr., 89
Webber, Alan M., 478
Weber, Alfred, 497
Webber, Michael J., 497
Weber, Joseph, 319
Webster, Richard, 13
Weigard, Robert E., 597
Weinberger, Marc G., 44
Whalley, John, 137
Wheelwright, Steven C., 232

Wight, Oliver W., 232
Williamson, Oliver E., 12,
    650, 651
Wisdo, Joseph P., 131
Wood, Donald F., 323
Woodruff, David, 618

Youngblood, Clay, 205

Zemke, Ron, 83
Zinn, Walter, 471
Zinszer, Paul H., 66

SUBJECT INDEX

A. T. Kearney Consultants, 112, 604, 669
ABC inventory classification, 298, 300
Ace Hardware, 103, 244
Activity-based costing, 12, 462, 642, 645
Adidas, 132, 137
AFTA (ASEAN Free Trade Area), 154
Air France, 134
Airbus Industries, 138
Alliances:
    cooperation emphasis in, 110
    and core specialization, 109
    defined, 108
    emergence of, 17
    global, 166
    implementing of, 628
    initiating, 627
    maintaining vitality of, 629
    management of, 626
    mutual dependency in, 109
    and power clarity, 110
American Marketing Association, 90
American Stores, 614
AmeriCares, 206
AMR Distribution Services, 124
AMTRAK (National Railroad Passenger Corporation), 347
Andersen Consulting, 43, 109
Anticipatory arrangements, 476
Antitrust immunity, 358
Artificial intelligence, 207
Asea Brown Boveri, 142, 177

ASEAN Free Trade Area (AFTA), 154
Asia-Pacific Region, 154
Assembly wholesalers, 116
Associated Warehouse, Inc., 112
AT&T (American Telephone and Telegraph), 142, 143
Auditing, 380
Automatic replenishment (AR), 16, 493
Avon Products, 118

Bar coding, 211, 466
Basic service capability:
    availability of, 67
    fill rate of, 69
    and orders shipped complete, 69
    and stockout frequency, 68
Baxter Healthcare Corporation, 84
Benchmarking, 461, 677
Bergen Brunswig, 84, 103, 244
Black & Decker, 102
BMW (Bavarian Motor Works), 43
Boeing, 138
Bose Corporation, 490
Brooklyn Brewery, 11
Budgeting:
    capital, 640
    fixed-dollar, 638
    flexible, 638
    zero-level, 640
Buffer stock, 248
Buick Motor Division, 18
Burlington Northern, 111, 150
Business Week, 142

Cabotage, 134, 135, 152
Calyx and Corolla, 474
Canada Pacific Ltd., 150
Canadian National Railway, 149
Cash-and-carry wholesalers, 116
Carolina Freight, 135
Cass Logistics, 82, 112
Caterpillar Logistics Services, 124, 574
Central America, 157
Central Freight Lines, 111
Channel, defined, 90
Channel arrangements:
    conventional, 119
    global, 138
    single-transaction, 119
    voluntary, 120
Channel functions:
    assortment of, 94, 97
    customization of, 98
    exchange of, 95
    facilitating, 95
    physical distribution of, 95
    specialization of, 95
Channel members:
    characteristics of, 114
    defined, 114
    descriptive institutional approach to, 115
    and functional middlemen, 117
    graphic approach to, 118
    and merchant middlemen, 115
    power of, 103, 104
    relative risks of, 103, 104

Channel participants, 93
Channel relationships:
  arm's-length, 144
  described, 100
Channel separation, 479
Channel structure:
  commodity grouping in, 119
  defined, 90, 467
  descriptive institutional, 115
  direct, 483
  echelon in, 483
  and emergency flexibility, 485
  as factor in logistical development, 467
  flexible, 484
  and functional approach, 119
  and graphic approach, 118
  and routine flexibility, 485
  and separation, 479
China, 142
Christian Salvesen, 402
Chrysler, 467
Claim administration, 379
CNN (Cable News Network), 132
Coca-Cola, 103
Collective rate making, 358
Colonial Hospital Supply, 78, 103
Common Market, 148
Communication:
  standards for, 218
  as a system component, 209
CONRAIL (Consolidated Rail Corporation), 348
Consolidated Freightways, 111, 321, 352
Consolidation, 475–476
Continuous replenishment, 16, 493
Contract definition, 359
Contract logistics, 112
Coors Brewing Company, 652
Core competency, 8, 61
Cost formatting, 648
Cost-revenue analysis, 654
Council of Logistics Management (CLM), 4, 139, 152, 153, 186
Cradle-to-cradle support, 43
CSX Corporation, 355
Customer-focused marketing, 58
Customer satisfaction, 83
Customer service:
  availability of, 654
  defined, 66
  expectations of, 75
  measurement of, 73
  performance of, 654
  as philosophy of management, 66
  reliability of, 654
  sensitivity analysis of, 514
  threshold potential of, 513
  trade-offs in, 509
  value-added, 67

Customer value as universal process, 8
Customs union, 148

Dean Foods, 130, 131
Decision support system (DSS):
  development of, 545
  and enterprise modeling, 578
  functional requirements of, 546
  inventory applications of, 570
  location applications of, 554
  transportation applications of, 573
Demand:
  dependent, 223
  independent, 224, 491
  uncertainty of, 267
Demand-driven control techniques, 491
Demurrage and detention, 377
Deregulation:
  of air transport, 353
  financial, 133
  of interstate transportation, 350
  of intrastate transportation, 356
  of motor carriers, 350
  of rail transport, 350
  of transportation, 133
DHL, 333
Dillards, 244
Discrete lot sizing:
  and least-total-cost, 266
  lot-for-lot, 264
  and part-period balancing, 266
  and period order quantity, 264
  time-series, 265
Discrete order quantity, 264
Distribution channel (see Channel)
Distribution requirements planning (DRP):
  benefits and constraints of, 293
  description of, 197, 291, 491
  example of, 295, 304
Dow Chemical, 43, 142, 143, 244
Dupont, 102

Eastern Europe, 156, 157
EC (see European Community)
Economic order quantity:
  characteristics of, 260
  defined, 260
  in discrete lot sizing, 264
  formula for, 260
  least-total-cost approach in, 266
  least-unit-cost approach in, 265
  in lot-for-lot sizing, 264
  and part-period balancing, 266
  and period order quantity, 264
  and quantity discounts, 263
  and time-series lot sizing, 265
  and volume transportation rates, 261
Economic-social projections, 467
Economic union, 148

Effective consumer response (ECR), 103
Electronic data interchange (EDI), 204, 215
Electronic keritsu, 610
Emery Worldwide, 333
Enterprise modeling, 578
Equipment scheduling, 380
European Community (EC), 43, 92, 130, 134, 138, 151, 152, 157
European Free Trade Act (EFTA), 151
Everyday low pricing (EDLP), 665
Excel Logistics, 82
Expediting, 383
Expert systems, 207
Exporting restrictions, 140
External performance measurement:
  and benchmarking, 677
  and customer perception, 675

Fed Ex (Federal Express), 321, 333
Fill rate, 69, 275
Fine-line inventory classification, 31,
Fisher Controls International, 574
Fleming Companies, 103, 244
Flexible budgeting, 638
Food Marketing Institute, 103
Ford, Henry, 88
Ford Motor Company, 467
Forecasting:
  base demand for, 225
  causal techniques of, 236
  components of, 224
  cyclic factors in, 225, 226
  irregular, 226
  measurement level in, 238
  promotional component of, 226
  qualitative techniques in, 233
  seasonality of, 225
  trend in, 225
Forecast approaches:
  top-down, 227
  bottom-up, 227
Forecast error:
  and mean absolute deviation (MAD), 237
  measurement of, 237
Forecast process:
  administration of, 229
  support system for, 229
  techniques of, 228
Forecast techniques:
  adaptive smoothing, 235
  exponential smoothing, 234
  extended smoothing, 235
  moving averages, 233
  time-series methods, 233
FoxMeyer, 103
Frank's Nursery & Crafts, 216
Free trade agreement, 147
Freight bill, 379

Fuller, 118
Functional middlemen:
    auction companies, 117
    brokers, 117
    commission merchants, 117
    manufacturers' agents, 117
    petroleum bulk stations, 117
    selling agents, 117

G & F Industries, 490
Gap, 105
GATT (General Agreement on Tariffs
    and Trade), 137, 138
GDP (gross domestic product), 31, 127,
    128
General Foods, 500
General Mills, 500
General Motors, 18, 47, 466
Global logistics:
    and barriers, 135
    and borderless operations, 129
    and deregulation, 133
    and distribution channels, 138
    discussion of, 706
    and documentation, 160
    and economic growth, 129
    and exporting, 140
    and importing, 140
    and national economies, 127
    and regionalization, 130, 147
    and supply chains, 130
    and systems integration, 165
    and technology, 131
Global operating levels, 144
GNP (gross national product), 31, 127,
    128
Grace Logistics Services, 124
Grocery Manufacturers of America,
    103, 108

Harley-Davidson, 402
Hazardous materials, 362
Hertz Truck Leasing, 123
Hidden discounts, 359
Hoechst, 142
Honda, 82, 132
Hong Kong, 154

IBM (International Business Machines),
    143
ICI, 142
IKEA, 84, 442
Immaculate recovery, 68
Importing restrictions, 140
Inbound logistics, 52
Independence marketing and logistics,
    482
Inference engine, 208
Information flow:
    defined, 36
    described, 202

Information flow (*Cont.*)
    forecasting of, 39
    and inventory deployments, 38
    and logistics requirements, 38
    and manufacturing, 38
    and operational requirements, 39
    and procurement requirements, 38
Information technology, 46, 204
Information systems (*see* Logistical in-
    formation systems)
Integrated logistics:
    defined, 33
    goal of, 509
    global, 165
    integral parts of, 34
    overview of, 33
    service providers of, 112
    spatial, 8
    strategy of, 488, 496
    temporal, 8
Integrated wholesaling, 118
Intermodal transportation:
    and container on flatcar (COFC), 334
    coordinated air and truck, 336
    European, 153
    piggyback, 334
    Roadrailer, 334
    swap bodies, 153
    trailer-on-flatcar (TOFC), 334
Internal integration barriers:
    and information technology, 46
    and inventory ownership, 45
    and knowledge transfer capability, 46
    and measurement systems, 45
    and organization structure, 45
Internal operations:
    and insider business practices, 145
    and internal export, 145
    and local market presence, 145
Internal performance measurement:
    of assets, 673
    cost of, 671
    and customer service, 672
    of productivity, 672
International logistics:
    characteristics of, 159
    documentation of, 160
    and economic growth, 129
    and forces driving, 129
    and supply chain perspectives, 130
    and regionalization, 130
    and technology, 131
International Monetary Fund (IMF),
    128, 133
Inventory:
    and ABC classification, 298, 300
    average, 251, 252
    balancing, 248
    base stock, 251, 504
    and combined uncertainty, 273
    control of, 282

Inventory (*Cont.*)
    cost of, 254
    cost minimization of, 508
    cycle of, 251
    and decoupling, 248
    and economic order quantity (EOQ),
      260
    and economies and facility location,
      503
    and fill rate, 257
    and fine-line classification, 298, 300
    and functionality, 34, 244, 247
    and geographical specialization, 247
    and information systems, 201
    in-transit, 251
    and lot-size stock, 251, 259
    and numerical compounding of un-
      certainty, 274
    and order quantity, 251
    and pipeline, 251
    policy on, 250, 282
    and reorder point, 258
    and replenishment ordering, 278
    and safety stock, 249, 277, 506
    and sawtooth diagram, 252
    and service level, 250
    transit of, 251, 505
    types of, 245
Inventory analysis:
    decisions in, 571
    and simulation, 572
    techniques of, 571
Inventory carrying costs:
    and capital cost, 255
    determination of, 254
    financial impact of, 256
    and insurance, 255
    and obsolescence, 255
    and storage, 256
    strategic impact of, 256
    and taxes, 255
Inventory control systems:
    modified, 285
    and optional replenishment, 286
    and periodic review, 284
    and perpetual review, 282
    and reactive methods, 287
    and reorder point, 492
    and target-level replenishment, 285
Inventory management strategy alterna-
    tives:
    adaptive logic, 294
    distribution requirements planning
      (DRP), 197, 291
    fair share allocation, 289
    integrated, 301
    planning logic, 289
    reactive logic, 287
Inventory management systems:
    information, 201
    strategic, 298

Inventory types:
  manufacturing, 246
  retail, 246
  wholesale, 246
Ito-Yokado Company (7-Eleven), 59

J. B. Hunt Transport Services, Inc., 111
Japan, 141
JC Penney, 102, 244, 413
Jewel, 614
Johnson & Johnson, 43, 67, 77, 244,
    500, 614
Just-in-time (JIT) strategy, 16, 489, 490
  JIT-II, 491

Kellogg Company, 38
KLS Logistics Services, 124
Kmart, 102, 244, 614
Kodak, 614
Kraft/General Foods, 500, 614
Kuczmarski & Associates, 64
Kurt Salmon Associates, Inc., 102

Lands' End, 53
Large Retail Stores Law (1974), 141
Latin America, 156, 157
Laura Ashley, 27
Leading-edge firms, 12, 17
Least-total-cost design (see Logistical
    integration)
Levi Strauss & Co., 43, 102
Libbey-Owens-Ford, 82, 384
Life-cycle planning, 43, 62
Linear programming:
  defined, 561
  and network optimization, 562
  and transportation method, 562
Local market presence, 145
Local presence paradigm, 498
Location analysis:
  analytic techniques of, 555
  data requirements of, 568
  fixed-cost, 570
  and linear programming, 561
  and market definition, 568
  and market demand, 570
  and network definition, 569
  and product definition, 569
  and simulation, 565
  and transportation rates, 570
  and variable costs, 570
Locational weight, 497
Logic Corporation, 124
Logistical activities:
  basic work of, 7
  competencies in, 8
  functions of, 7
  and performance cycle, 8
  strategic positioning and universal
    process of, 8

Logistical design, and metrics, 642
Logistical environmental assessment:
  described, 463
  and geomarket differentials, 465
  and industry competitiveness, 465
  and material energy, 466
  and technology, 465
Logistical expenditure in economy, 5
Logistical information systems:
  architecture of, 194
  in distribution operations and inven-
    tory control, 200
  exception-based, 191
  flow in, 202
  functionality of, 187
  and future, 218
  and inventory management, 197
  and networks, 207
  and order processing, 199
  principles of, 190
  and technologies, 204
  and transportation and shipping, 200
Logistical integration:
  and barriers, 158
  and least-total-cost design, 509, 512
  and location structure, 496
  and manufacturing support, 35
  and physical distribution, 35
  and procurement, 35
  strategy of, 488, 512
  and trade-off relationships, 509
Logistical mission, 8
Logistical objectives:
  minimum inventory, 41
  movement consolidation, 42
  quality, 42
  rapid response, 41
  variance, 41
Logistical performance cycles:
  defined, 46
  effectiveness of, 47
  efficiency of, 47
  global, 158
  input-output, 47
  level of, 46
  links in, 46
  and manufacturing support, 50
  nodes in, 46
  and physical distribution, 48
  and procurement, 51
  under uncertainty, 54
Logistical planning:
  ad hoc analysis of, 551
  in freight lane analysis, 551
  in inventory analysis, 552
  and location applications, 554
  and outsourcing, 649
  and segment profitability, 552
Logistical policy:
  and justified high-cost location, 520
  and least-total-cost design, 509, 512

Logistical policy (Cont.)
  and maximum competitive advantage,
    519
  and maximum services, 517
  and minimal asset deployment, 521
  and profit maximization, 518
  and selective service programs, 519
  and threshold services, 513
  and trade-off relationships, 509
Logistical processes:
  and information flow, 34, 38, 194
  and value-added inventory flow, 34,
    38, 194
Logistical redesign procedures:
  analysis of, 534, 538
  assumptions of, 535
  and cost-benefit estimates, 531
  and feasibility assessment, 525
  implementation of, 525, 540, 544
  planning of, 524
  and problem definition, 524
  and project planning, 532
  and project workplan, 534
  and recommendations, 525, 540
  and situational analysis, 525
  supporting logic of, 530
Logistical renaissance, 13
Logistical services:
  availability of, 9
  flexibility of, 10
  operational performance of, 9
  providers of, 112
Logistical work:
  and information, 4, 28
  and inventory, 4, 30
  and material handling, 4, 32
  and network design, 4, 25
  and packaging, 4, 32
  and transportation, 4
  and warehousing, 4, 32
Logistics as a core competency, 6, 61
Lucky stores, 614

Maastricht Treaty, 151, 153
McKesson, 103
McKinsey & Company, 606, 611
Manufacturing requirements plan
    (MRP), 198
Manufacturing support, 35, 50
Maquiladora, 150
Marketing concept defined, 59
Marketing functions:
  exchange, 95
  facilitating, 95
  physical distribution, 95
Master carton, 33
Master production scheduling (MPS),
    198
Material handling:
  automated, 428
  basic considerations in, 422

Material handling *(Cont.)*
  efficiency and utility of, 441
  information-directed, 432
  mechanized, 422
  and radio frequency data communication (RFDC), 424
  semiautomated, 426
  special considerations in, 432
Material-handling equipment:
  automated-guided vehicle systems (AGVSs), 427
  automated high-rise storage and retrieval systems (ASRSs), 428, 429
  carousels, 426
  conveyors, 426
  live racks, 428
  and order selection systems, 429
  and pick-to-light systems, 426
  robotics, 427
  sortation, 427
  towline, 424
  walkie-rider pallet trucks, 424
Material index, 497
Materials requirement planning, 198, 491
Mercer Management Consulting, 103
Merchant middlemen:
  assembly wholesalers, 116
  cash-and-carry wholesalers, 116
  drop shippers, 116
  industrial distributors, 116
  regular wholesalers, 115
  semijobbers, 117
  wagon distributors, 116
Mexico, 131
Microprocessor technology, 15
Mother facility, 486
Motorola, 79

Nabisco Foods, 67, 501
NAFTA (North American Free Trade Agreement), 130, 135, 138, 146, 148, 151, 323
National Cooperative Research Act (1984), 18
National Cooperative Production Amendments (1993), 18
National Council of Physical Distribution Management *(see* Council of Logistics Management)
National Motor Freight Classification, 371
Nestle, 142
Norfolk Southern Railroads, 150
NYNEX, 625

OECD (Organization for Economic Co-operation and Development), 132
Operating arrangements, 476
Operational performance:
  consistency of, 9, 71

Operational performance *(Cont.)*
  flexibility in, 9, 71
  malfunction of, 71
  recovery time in, 10, 71
  speed of, 9, 70
Operational planning:
  denationalized, 147
  internal operations, 145
Operational requirements:
  and distribution, 40
  and inventory management, 40
  and order management, 39
  and order processing, 40
  and procurement, 40
  and transportation and shipping, 40
Operations planning:
  and budgeting, 637
  logistical, 633
  and logistical system modification, 634
  and outsourcing, 649
  and performance goals, 636
Order-processing information systems, 199
Organizational development:
  and functional aggregation, 598
  history of, 597
  stage 1, 600
  stage 2, 601
  stage 3, 602
  stage 4, 606
  stage 5, 608
Organizational issues:
  careers and loyalty, 622
  centralization vs. decentralization, 613
  change, 624
  empowerment, 617
  and horizontal structure, 614
  and learning, 621
  line and staff distinction, 614
  matrix structure, 614
  structural compression, 612
  teaming, 617
Organizational transparency, 608
Osco Stores, 614
Outsourcing:
  and economic trade-offs, 650
  as logistical consideration, 649
  and strategic trade-offs, 650
Overnite Transportation Company, 110
Owens-Corning Fiberglass, 102

Pacific Rim, 130, 154
Packaging:
  blanket wrapping, 448
  as a means of communication, 444
  consumer, 436
  and content identification, 444
  for damage protection, 439
  film-based, 447

Packaging *(Cont.)*
  and handling instructions, 445
  industrial, 436
  in intermediate bulk containers, 449
  and load securing, 443
  and material selection, 446
  in nonrigid containers, 442
  and physical environment, 440
  and product characteristics, 441
  and outside elements, 440
  and returnable containers, 446
  in rigid containers, 442
  and tracking, 445
  and unit loads, 443
Pallet:
  and master carton stacking, 444
  plastic, 449
  and pools, 449
  refrigerated, 450
  and unit-load platform, 444
Pareto principle, 31
Perfect order, 76
Performance cycle uncertainty, 271
Performance reporting and measurement:
  ad hoc, 690
  control of, 670
  decisions on, 685
  and dimensions, 669
  and direction, 684
  direction of, 670
  dynamic knowledge-based, 683
  exception-based, 683
  external, 675
  internal, 671
  objectives of, 670
  perspective on, 671
  policy on, 686
  and reports, 686
  status of, 686
  in supply chain, 679
  trend in, 687
  variations in, 685
Personal computers, 205
Philip Morris Company, 470
Philips Electronics, 142
Pioneer Hi-Bred International, 425
Planning and coordination flows:
  and capacity constraints, 37
  forecasting and, 39
  and inventory deployment, 38
  and logistics requirements, 37
  and manufacturing requirements, 38
  and procurement requirements, 38
  and strategic objectives, 37
Postponement:
  form of, 472
  logistics of, 473
  in manufacturing, 472
  time of, 472
  as warehousing benefit, 394

Pricing:
  base point, 660
  delivered, 659
  F.O.B., 658
  issues in, 662
  multiple-zone, 659
  and pickup allowances, 664
  potential discrimination in, 662
  promotional, 664
  quantity discounts in, 663
  single-zone, 659
Process-oriented management, 606
Procter & Gamble Company, 99, 142, 247, 664
Procurement, 35, 51
Product, defined, 36
Product life-cycle stages, 63
Product recall, 43
Profile replenishment, 493

Quality initiatives, 16, 42, 462
Quick response, 16, 492

Ralston Purina, 111
Rate negotiation, 380
Reengineering, defined, 458
Reengineering procedure, 462
Regulatory posture, 468
Relationship management, 93
Reliability:
  defined, 71
  and measurement base, 72
  and measurement units, 72
  and measurement variables, 72
Replenishment cycle, uncertainty, 271
Replenishment ordering, 278
Requirements planning (RP), 489
Resource Net International, 103
Response-based arrangements, 476
Rich Products, 402
RJR-Nabisco, 244
Roadway Systems, Inc., 111, 333, 352
Roadway Logistics Services, 82, 384
Roadway Package System, 150, 331
Rollerblade, 576

Santa Fe Railway, 111
Saturn Corporation, 618
Schneider National, Inc., 77, 210, 651
Scrambled merchandising, 65, 118
Sears Logistics, 124
Segment profitability, 552
Self-directed work teams (SDWT), 606, 617
Sensitivity analysis, 514
Shaw's Markets, 82
Shipment consolidation:
  and market area grouping, 476
  and pooled distribution, 476

Shipment consolidation (*Cont.*)
  and scheduled distribution, 476
Shipping manifest, 379
Shrinking service window, 75
Siemens, 177
Simmons Company, 579
Simplot, J. R., 91, 92
Simulation:
  and heuristic computation decision, 566
  static, 565
Singapore, 154
Single administrative document (SAD), 151
Situational analysis:
  in external assessment, 528
  in internal assessment, 527
  in technology assessment, 529
South America, 157
South Korea, 154
Southeastern Freight, 111
Southern Pacific Railroad, 111
Spartan Stores, 103
Spatial closure, 497
Standard Oil Company, 347
Stateless enterprise, 142
Stockkeeping units (SKUs), 281
Stockless production, 491
Sun Microsystems, 21
Super Valu, 103
Supply chain management, 34, 101
  comprehensive measurement of, 679
  global, 158
Supply chain measurement:
  of assets, 681
  of costs, 681
  and customer satisfaction, 680
  described, 679
  and quality, 680
  and time, 680
Supply-driven control techniques, 489
Sysco, 103
Systems integration, 459

Taiwan, 154
Tariff, 136
Target Stores, Inc., 47, 102, 556
Third-party logistics, 112
3-M Company, 76, 112, 146
Threshold service, 513
Timberland Company, 517
Time-based competition, 470
Time-based logistics:
  and control techniques, 489
  described, 29, 470
TNT Freightways, 164, 321, 352
Total cost:
  air freight example of, 10, 643
  and cost-to-cost trade-off, 509
  and functional analysis, 12
  inventory economics, 503

Total cost (*Cont.*)
  least total cost design, 10, 642
  in logistical development, 6
Total quality management (TQM), 16, 42
Tower Group International, 124
Toyota Motor Company, 79
Toys ''R'' Us, 141
Tracing, 383
Traffic department responsibilities, 379
Traffic research, 381
Trailer on flatcar (TOFC):
  defined, 334
  plans for, 335
Transport documentation:
  bill of lading, 378
  freight bill, 379
  shipping manifest, 379
Transport economics and pricing:
  and common costs, 368
  and density, 366
  and distance, 365
  and fixed costs, 368
  handling of, 367
  and joint costs, 368
  and liability, 367
  and market factors, 367
  and stowability, 366
  and tapering principle, 365
  and variable costs, 368
  and volume, 365
  and warehouse justification, 501
Transport functionality:
  and product movement, 312
  and product storage, 313
Transport modes:
  air, 324
  motor carrier, 319
  pipeline, 324
  railroad, 317
  water, 321
Transport pricing and rates:
  administration of, 373
  and aggregate tender, 375
  and class, 370
  and classification, 370
  combination, 369, 376
  and commodity, 374
  contract for, 328
  and cost-of-service strategy, 369
  and count, 375
  and exceptions, 375
  and freight-all-kinds (FAK), 376
  joint, 376
  and limited service, 375
  local, 376
  National Motor Freight Classification, 371
  and net pricing, 370
  proportional, 376
  and shipper load, 375

Transport pricing and rates *(Cont.)*
  special, and services, 375
  and through rate, 376
  and transit services, 376
  Uniform Freight Classification, 371
  value-of-service strategy, 369
Transportation:
  and accessorial charges, 377
  and bill of lading, 378
  and carriers, 315
  and common carriage, 29, 327
  and consignees, 315
  consistency of, 30
  and contract carriage, 29, 328
  cost of, 29
  and cost minimization, 502
  and demurrage and detention, 377
  and diversion, 377
  and economy of distance, 314
  and economy of scale, 314
  and exempt carriers, 329
  formats of, 326
  and government, 315
  and infrastructure, 316
  intermodal, 334
  of less-than-truckload (LTL) ship-
    ments, 314, 321
  and modal characteristics, 316, 327
  and modal classification, 325
  and nonoperating intermediaries, 336
  and operating authority, 326
  and performance factors, 29
  and private carriage, 29, 328
  and public convenience and necessity,
    316
  rates for, 342, 358
  and reconsignment, 377
  and regulation, 341
  and shippers, 315
  speed of, 30
  in trailer on flatcar (TOFC), 334
  and transit services, 376
  of truckload (TL) shipments, 314,
    321
Transportation analysis:
  data requirements for, 577
  and decisions, 573
  techniques of, 574
Transportation regulatory acts:
  Act to Regulate Commerce, 341, 345
  Airline Deregulation Act, 349
  Airport and Airway Improvement
    Act, 15
  Bus Regulatory Act (1982), 355
  Civil Aeronautics Act, 346
  Custom Brokers Act (1984), 356
  Elkins Act, 345
  Emergency Transportation Act, 346
  Hazardous Materials Transportation
    Uniform Safety Act (1990), 362
  Hepburn Act, 347

Transportation regulating acts *(Cont.)*
  history of, 343
  Interstate Commerce Act, 345, 351
  Motor Carrier Act, 15, 346
  Motor Carrier Regulatory Reform and
    Modernization Act (MCA-1980),
    14, 327, 350, 358, 664
  Negotiated Rates Act, 15, 361
  Railroad Revitalization and Regula-
    tory Reform Act (1976), 348, 349
  Rail Transportation Improvement Act
    (1976), 348
  Regional Rail Reorganization (3-R)
    Act (1973), 347, 354
  Robinson-Patman Act, 663
  Staggers Rail Act, 15, 318, 354
  Surface Freight Forwarder Deregula-
    tion Act (1984 and 1985), 355
  Transportation Act (1920), 345;
    (1940), 345
  Trucking Industry Regulatory Reform
    Act (TIRRA), 15, 353, 356, 370
Transportation regulatory agencies:
  Civil Aeronautics Authority (CAA),
    346
  Civil Aeronautics Board (CAB), 347
  Department of Commerce, 348
  Department of Transportation (DOT),
    348, 350, 359
  Federal Aeronautics Administration
    (FAA), 347
  Interstate Commerce Commission
    (ICC), 326, 327, 346, 349, 353,
    357, 359
  National Aeronautics and Space Ad-
    ministration (NASA), 347
Transportation regulatory history:
  current issues in, 358
  entry, 341
  and environmental laws, 344
  and future, 356
  and interstate deregulation, 350
  and intrastate deregulation, 356
  from pre-1920 to present, 345–347
  and rates, 342
  and safety and social regulation, 343
  and services, 343
  and zone of rate flexibility (ZORF),
    349, 351
Transportation services:
  basic package of, 331
  brokers of, 338
  and containerships, 335
  and cooperatives, 337
  cost of, 502
  and freight forwarders, 337
  intermodal, 334
  and nonoperating intermediaries, 336
  premium package of, 333
  and shippers' associations, 337
  and single-mode carriers, 331

Transportation services *(Cont.)*
  and specialized carriers, 331
  and suppliers, 330

Uncertainty:
  and demand, 267
  and numerical compounding, 274
  and performance cycle, 271
  and replenishment, 274
Undercharges, 360
Uniform Code Council (UCC), 219
Uniform Freight Classification, 371
Union Pacific, 110, 319
Unisource, 103
Unisys Corporation, 154, 155
United Kingdom, 134
Unit-load platforms, 443
United States, 134
U.S. Air Force, 306
United States–Canada Free Trade
  Agreement, 137, 146, 148, 151
U.S. Customs Service, 137
U.S. Department of Commerce, 4, 26,
  96
U.S. Department of Transportation
  (DOT), 343
U.S. Postal Service, 331, 333, 369
U.S. Supreme Court, 357, 360
U.S. Transportation Command (US-
  Transcom), 635
UPC (Universal Product Code), 444
UPS (United Parcel Service), 93, 109,
  111, 134, 150, 164, 210, 217, 318,
  321, 331, 333, 369
USA Today, 132
Utility, 60

Value-added services:
  basic, 82
  defined, 67, 78
  customer-focused, 80
  promotion-focused, 80
  manufacturing-focused, 80
  time-focused, 81
Viking Freight, 111
Virtual organization, 608
Voluntary arrangements:
  administered systems, 122
  alliances, 122
  contractual systems, 123
  joint ventures, 124
  partnerships, 122

W. W. Grainger, 103
Walgreen, 102
Wal-Mart, 47, 62, 102, 614, 665
Warehouse benefits:
  assortment, 395
  break bulk operations, 394
  consolidation, 393
  cross-dock operations, 394
  economic, 392

Warehouse benefits *(Cont.)*
  and market presence, 396
  mixing, 395
  processing/postponement, 394
  production support, 396
  service, 395
  spot stock, 395
  stockpiling, 394
Warehouse handling requirements:
  for instorage handling, 420
  for receiving, 419
  for shipping, 420
Warehouse location patterns:
  intermediately positioned, 501
  manufacturing-positioned, 500
  market-positioned, 499
Warehouse operations:
  design criteria for, 397
  handling technology in, 397

Warehouse operations *(Cont.)*
  initiation of, 411
  personnel training for, 411
  principles of, 396
  and stocking, 411
  storage plan for, 398
  work procedures in, 412
Warehouse options:
  contract, 401
  private, 399
  public, 400
Warehouse storage requirements, 421
Warehousing:
  alternatives in, 399
  billing and inventory control in, 415
  cost-based justification for, 501
  design of, 410
  expansion of, 408
  initiating operations in, 411

Warehousing *(Cont.)*
  and layout, 408
  and local delivery, 415
  material-handling system in, 408
  and pilferage, 414
  and product deterioration, 415
  product-mix considerations in, 407
  security systems in, 414
  service-based justification for, 504
  and site selection, 407
  strategic storage in, 390
  space determination in, 410
  strategy in, 403

Xerox, 677

Yellow Transport, 111, 135, 321, 352

Zellerbach, 103
Zero inventory, 41, 491